It's new! It's free! It's the first online price guide!

S0-AJZ-386

Register for your free subscription to Antique Trader's Online Price Guide through December 1999. This online guide will include all the information from the 1995-1999 annuals, giving you access to five years of history in a searchable database.

1. Register online at http://www.collect.com/priceguide/register.html

2. Fill in the information below:

Name _____

Phone # _____

Address _____

City _____ State _____ Zip + 4 _____

E-mail address(required) _____

3. Return this card to have your online subscription activated!

TWO WEEKS FREE TO *Antique Trader*

❏ **YES!** Send me two **FREE** issues of *Antique Trader*.

Each week *Antique Trader* delivers thousands of Antique & Collectible items to your door. Use the classified listings to add to your collection, sell off duplicate pieces, or monitor prices in the marketplace. Also use the auction and show listings to plan your travels.

Each issue also provides you with in-depth editorial coverage on the Antique & Collectible hobby you need to make informed decisions about your collecting.

Send in the card today to receive your two **FREE** issues.

Name _____

Address _____

City _____ State _____

| Source |
| BPG99 |

Zip + 4 _____ Phone _____

ANTIQUE TRADER WEEKLY

NO POSTAGE
NECESSARY
IF MAILED
IN THE
UNITED STATES

BUSINESS REPLY MAIL
FIRST CLASS MAIL PERMIT NO. 50 DUBUQUE, IA

POSTAGE WILL BE PAID BY ADDRESSEE

ANTIQUE TRADER WEEKLY
PO BOX 1050
DUBUQUE IA 52004-9969

ANTIQUE TRADER WEEKLY

NO POSTAGE
NECESSARY
IF MAILED
IN THE
UNITED STATES

BUSINESS REPLY MAIL
FIRST CLASS MAIL PERMIT NO. 50 DUBUQUE, IA

POSTAGE WILL BE PAID BY ADDRESSEE

ANTIQUE TRADER WEEKLY
PO BOX 1050
DUBUQUE IA 52004-9969

1999 ANNUAL EDITION

ANTIQUE TRADER BOOKS

Antiques & Collectibles Price Guide

Edited by
Kyle Husfloen

An illustrated comprehensive price guide to the entire field of antiques
and collectibles for the 1999 market

ISBN: 0-930625-14-5
ISSN: 1083-8430

Editor: *Kyle Husfloen*
Editorial Assistants: *Ruth Willis, Pat B. Scott, Barbara Reed*
Book Designer: *Virginia Hill*
Design Assistants: *Janell Edwards, Barb Brown, Donna Bruun, Lynn Bradshaw,*
　　　　　　　　　Aaron Wilbers, Jill Hohmann,
Cover Design: *Chris Decker*

Cover photo credits:
Front cover: clockwise from top: 1913 Coca-Cola serving tray, $950, photo courtesy
of Allan Petretti; turn-of-the-century carved oak dining table, 60" diameter, part
of a 14-piece set, $4,250, photo courtesy of Gene Harris Antique Auction Center;
Chinese porcelain vase, Guangxu mark and period, 16" h., $4,000, photo courtesy
of Sandra Andacht; Beatles and Yellow Submarine alarm clock, by Sheffield
Watch, Inc., $600, photo courtesy of Marty Eck; "Twigs" the Giraffe Beanie
Baby, by Ty, Inc., $22, photo courtesy of Shawn Brecka.

Back cover: Top: Heintz Art Metal table lamp with helmet-shaped shade, silver Arts
& Crafts geometric design, 9½" h., $880, photo courtesy of David Surgan.
Center: Bret Maverick figure on horse, Hartland, 1958, $150-$200, photo
courtesy of Toy Scouts, Akron, Ohio. Bottom: American Classical carved and
stenciled recamier, ca. 1826-30, $18,400, photo courtesy of Sotheby's, New York,
New York.

Printed in the United States of America

For information about *Antique Trader Weekly* subscriptions or
Antique Trader Online Price Guides contact:

Antique Trader Publications
P.O. Box 1050
Dubuque, Iowa 52004
1-800-334-7165

 **Antique Trader Books**
A division of Landmark Specialty Publications

A WORD TO THE READER

Welcome to the newest edition of *Antique Trader's Antiques & Collectibles Price Guide*. As many of you may know, the Antique Trader has been producing regular pricing guides to the collecting market for nearly 30 years. To offer an even handier and more compact pricing reference, we introduced in 1984 our annual edition. Here we're proud to present our newest edition, over 900 pages of detailed descriptions and photographs of all types of antiques and collectibles.

With each of our annual editions we present fresh data on a myriad of categories, from traditional antiques to "hot" new fields of collecting. This year we've continued this trend with a new section on Beanie Babies as well as expanded coverage in the areas of Kitchen Collectibles, Compacts & Vanity Cases, Sporting Collectibles, Postcards and Radios, to name a few. We are especially grateful to our growing list of "Special Contributors," whose expertise and input has helped us expand our coverage of many collecting specialties. Many dealers, collectors and auction firms around the country have been most generous in the sharing of market information which will help you gain a broader understanding of the fascinating world of collecting. You'll find our "Special Contributors" listed according to their specialty on the following pages. They would be happy to hear from our readers. Keep in mind, however, that they are very busy individuals, so please be courteous should you write, phone or e-mail them.

In addition to our growing network of outside experts, our in-house staff continues to work diligently to compile and enter material in our data base and integrate the listings and photographs supplied by our contributors. It is a year-round, never-ending process, for as soon as one annual edition is completed we must begin rebuilding our files for the next one.

As with any pricing reference, we ask that you remember that this book should be used only as a guide to evaluating and pricing items you may own. Factors such as condition, rarity and even regional demand can have a major impact on what a piece is truly worth. Keep in mind also that most values listed here represent retail prices, in other words, what you might likely have to pay for a similar example.

Our Antiques & Collectibles Price Guide follows a basically alphabetical format for most categories. However, we have arranged the larger categories of Ceramics, Furniture and Glassware into their own sections where each specific type or maker will be listed alphabetically within that section. We begin nearly every category with a brief introduction. In the Ceramics and Glass sections we also often include a sketch of a mark or markings which will help you identify examples you may encounter. We often cross-reference to other categories in our category introductions, and our comprehensive Index at the conclusion of the price listings will also help you locate specific items you may be interested in.

Please keep in mind that although our descriptions, prices and illustrations have been double-checked and every effort has been made to ensure accuracy, neither the editor nor publisher can assume responsibility for any losses that might be incurred as a result of consulting this guide, or of typographical or other errors.

Photographers who have contributed to this issue include: Adele Armbruster, Dearborn, Michigan; E. A. Babka, East Dubuque, Illinois; Stanley L. Baker, Minneapolis, Minnesota; Donna Bruun, Galena, Illinois; Herman C. Carter, Tulsa, Oklahoma; Robert Cohen, Albertson, New York; Susan N. Cox, El Cajon, California; J. D. Dalessandro, Cincinnati, Ohio; Ruth Eaves, Marmora, New Jersey; Susan Eberman, Bedford, Indiana; Scott Green, Manchester, New Hampshire; Jeff Grunewald, Chicago, Illinois; Robert G. Jason-Ickes, Olympia, Washington; Louise Paradis, Sparta, Wisconsin; Joyce Roerig, Waltersboro, South Carolina; Molly Schroeder, Danville, Illinois; David H. Surgan, Brooklyn, New York; and Tom Wallace, Chicago, Illinois.

For other photographs, artwork, data or permission to photograph in their shops, we sincerely express appreciation to the following auctioneers, galleries, museums, individuals and shops: American Social History and Social Movements, Pittsburgh,

Pennsylvania; American West Archives, Cedar City, Utah; Andre Ammelounx, Palatine, Illinois; Aston Americana Auctions, Endwell, New York; Bell Tower Antique Mall, Covington, Kentucky; Bertoia Sales, Vineland, New Jersey; Brown Auctions, Mullinville, Kansas; The Burmese Cruet, Montgomeryville, Pennsylvania; Burns Auction Service, Bath, New York; Busby Land & Auction Company, Ridge Farm, Illinois; Butterfield & Butterfield, San Francisco, California; Charles Casad, Champaign, Illinois; The Cedars - Antiques, Aurelia, Iowa; Norm & Diana Charles, Hagerstown, Indiana; Frank Chiarenza, Newington, Connecticut; Christie's, New York, New York; Cincinnati Art Galleries, Cincinnati, Ohio; Cohasco, Inc., Yonkers, New York; Collector's Auction Services, Oil City, Pennsylvania; Collector's Sales & Services, Middletown, Rhode Island; Copake Auction, Copake, New York; Bill Correll, Bedford, Indiana; S. Davis, Williamsburg, Ohio; DeFina Auctions, Austenburg, Ohio; William Doyle Galleries, New York, New York; Dunbar's Gallery, Milford, Massachusetts; Dunnings Auction Service, Elgin, Illinois; Early American History Auctions, Inc., La Jolla, California; Early's Auction Company, Milford, Ohio; Robert Edward Auctions, Hoboken, New Jersey; T. Ermert, Cincinnati, Ohio; John Fontaine Auction, Pittsfield, Massachusetts; Garth's Auctions, Inc., Delaware, Ohio; Glass-Works Auctions, East Greenville, Pennsylvania; the former Morton M. Goldberg Auction Galleries, New Orleans, Louisiana; Robert Gordon, San Antonio, Texas; Green Valley Auctions, Mt. Crawford, Virginia; Grunewald Antiques, Hillsborough, North Carolina; and Guyette and Schmidt, West Farmington, Maine.

Also to Vicki Harmon, San Marcos, California; the Gene Harris Antique Auction Center, Marshalltown, Iowa; Kenneth S. Hays & Associates, Louisville, Kentucky; the late William Heacock, Marietta, Ohio; Historical Collectible Auctions, Burlington, North Carolina; International Carnival Glass Association, Mentone, Indiana; Jackson's Auctions, Cedar Falls, Iowa; Jewel Johnson, Tulsa, Oklahoma; James Julia, Fairfield, Maine; Agnes Koehn Antiques, Cedar Rapids, Iowa; Peter Kroll, Sun Prairie, Wisconsin; Bev Kubesheski, Dubuque, Iowa; Lang's Sporting Collectables,

Raymond, Maine; Billy Long Auctioneers, Inc., Springfield, Missouri; Jim Ludescher, Dubuque, Iowa; Joy Luke Gallery, Bloomington, Illinois; J. Martin, Mt. Orab, Ohio; Mastro & Steinbach Fine Sports Auctions, Oakbrook, Illinois; Randall McKee, Kenosha, Wisconsin; McMasters Doll Auctions, Cambridge, Ohio; Dr. James Measell, Marietta, Ohio; Norton's Auctioneers, Coldwater, Michigan; O'Gallerie, Inc., Portland, Oregon; Pacific Glass Auctions, Sacramento, California; Past Tyme Pleasures, Los Altos, California; Pettigrew Auctions, Colorado Springs, Colorado; R.A.M. Quality Auctions, Joliet, Illinois; Dave Rago Arts & Crafts, Lambertville, New Jersey; Jane Rosenow, Galva, Illinois; Sandy Rosnick Auctions, Manchester, Massachusetts; Royal Bayreuth Collectors Club, Kalamazoo, Michigan; Skinner, Inc., Bolton, Massachusetts; Slawinski Auction Company, Felton, California; Sotheby's, New York, New York; Doris Spahn, East Dubuque, Illinois; Stanton's Auctions, Vermontville, Michigan; Rose Mary Taylor, Pecatonica, Illinois; Temples Antiques, Eden Prairie, Minnesota; Theriault's, Annapolis, Maryland; Dennis M. Thompson, Fairview Park, Ohio; Town Crier Auction Service, Burlington, Wisconsin; Trader Lukes, Wilmington, California; Mrs. James Trautman, Orton, Ontario, Canada; Treadway Gallery, Cincinnati, Ohio; Victorian Images, Marlton, New Jersey; Lee Vines, Hewlett, New York; Doris Virtue, Galena, Illinois; Web Wilson's Antique Hardware Auctions, Portsmouth, Rhode Island; Whalen Auction Company, Neapolis, Ohio; Wolf's Auctioneers and Appraisers, Cleveland, Ohio; Woody Auctions, Douglass, Kansas; and Yesterday's Treasures, Galena, Illinois.

We hope that everyone who consults our *Antiques & Collectibles Price Guide* will find it the most thorough, accurate and informative guide on the ever-changing world of collecting.

The staff of *Antique Trader's Antiques & Collectibles Price Guide* welcomes all letters from readers, especially those of constructive critique, and we make every effort to respond personally.

—Kyle Husfloen, Editor

SPECIAL CATEGORY CONTRIBUTORS

GENERAL CATEGORIES

Autographs
Bill Butts
Main Street Fine Books &
 Manuscripts
206 N. Main
Galena, IL 61036

Beanie Babies
Shawn Brecka
3571 Page Dr.
Plover, WI 54467
sbrecka@coredcs.com
Author: *The Bean Family
 Album and Collector's
 Guide*

Big Little Books
Ken Mitchell
710 Conacher Dr.
Willowdale, Ontario
 Canada M2M 3N6
(416) 222-5808

Cat Collectibles
Marilyn Dipboye
33161 Wendy Dr.
Sterling Heights, MI 48310

Coca-Cola Items
Allan Petretti
21 S. Lake Dr.
Hackensack, NJ 07601

Compacts & Vanity Cases
Roselyn Gerson
P.O. Box 40
Lynbrook, NY 11563
Author: *Ladies' Compacts
 of the Nineteenth &
 Twentieth Centuries* and
 *Vintage & Contemporary
 Purse Accessories
 (Lipsticks, Mirrors and
 Solid Perfumes)*

Disney Collectibles
Robert G. Jason-Ickes
3600 Elizabeth Ave. S.E.
#19-203
Olympia, WA 98501

Golf Clubs—Wooden Shafted
Peter Georgiady
6101 O'Bryant Ct.
Greensboro, NC 27410
Fax: (336) 668-7260
ahp@greensboro.com
Author: *Wood Shafted
 Golf Clubs* (Airlie Hall
 Press)

Graniteware
Jo Allers
Cedar Rapids, IA

Heintz Art Metal Shop Wares
David Surgan
328 Flatbush Ave.
Suite 123
Brooklyn, NY 11238
(718) 638-3768

Jewelry (Costume)
Marion Cohen
P.O. Box 39
Albertson, NY 11507

Kitchenwares

General
Carol Bohn
KOOKS
501 Mark St.
Mifflinburg, PA 17844
(717) 966-1198

Egg Timers, Pie Birds & String Holders
Ellen Bercovici
5118 Hampden La.
Bethesda, MD 20814
(301) 652-1140

Juice Reamers & Napkin Dolls
Bobbie Zucker Bryson
1 St. Eleanoras La.
Tuckahoe, NY 10707
Napkindoll@aol.com

Kitchen Glassware
Kate Trabue
1603 Pine St., #1
Eureka, CA 95501-2280
(707) 444-3326

Whistle Cups
Deborah Gillham
47 Midline Ct.
Gaithersburg, MD 20878
dgillham@erols.com

Laundry Room Items

Irons
David Irons
223 Covered Bridge Rd.
Northampton, PA 18607
Fax: (610) 262-2853
Author: *Irons by Irons,
 More Irons by Irons*
 and *Pressing Iron
 Patents*

Sprinkling Bottles
Ellen Bercovici
5118 Hampden La.
Bethesda, MD 20814
(301) 652-1140

Militaria & Wartime Memorabilia
Jim Trautman
R.R. 1
Orton, Ontario
Canada L0N 1N0
(519) 855-6077

Nutting (Wallace) Collectibles
Michael Ivankovich
P.O. Box 2458
Doylestown, PA 18901
(215) 345-6094
Fax: (215) 345-6692
wnutting@comcat.com

Parrish (Maxfield)
Denis C. Jackson
P. O. Box 1958
Sequim, WA 98382
(360) 683-2559
ticn@olypen.com

Phonographs
Mike Ellingson
1412 Second Ave. S.
Fargo, ND 58103
(701) 280-1413

Postcards
Susan Brown Nicholson
P.O. Box 595
Lisle, IL 60532
(630) 964-5240
Author: *Encyclopedia of Antique Post Cards*

Radios
Harry Poster
P.O. Box 1883
S. Hackensack, NJ 07606
(201) 794-9606
Fax: (201) 794-9553
hposter@worldnet.att.net

Railroadiana
Jon Prideaux Auctions
940 S. 250th St.
Pittsburg, KS 66762

Razor Blade Banks
Deborah Gillham
47 Midline Ct.
Gaithersburg, MD 10878
dgillham@erols.com

Salt & Pepper Shakers (Novelty)
Sylvia Tompkins & Larry Carrey
c/o Novelty Salt & Pepper Shakers Club
Lula Fuller
P.O. Box 3617
Lantana, FL 33462
(561) 588-5368

Sewing Adjuncts
Beth Pulsipher
Prairie Home Antiques
240 N. Grand
Schoolcraft, MI 49087
(616) 679-2062

Stocks & Bonds
Sam Withers
P.O. Box 6706
St. Louis, MO 63144
(314) 968-1647

Tarzan Items
Glen Erardi
122 Union St.
N. Andover, MA 01845
(978) 685-6142
Fax: (978) 794-9407

Gerardi01@aol.com

Tiffany Lamps
Carl Heck
P.O. Box 8416
Aspen, CO 81612

Tobacciana
Tony Hyman
Treasure Hunt Publications
P.O. Box 3028
Pismo Beach, CA 93448

Tools
Philip Whitby Antique & Used Tools
P.O. Box 1003
Kingston, NH 03848
(603) 642-4054

Toys, Character Collectibles
Bill Bruegman
Toy Scouts
137 Casterton Ave.
Akron, OH 44303
(330) 836-0668
Fax: (330) 869-8668
toyscout@newreach.net

Tramp Art
Clifford Wallach & Michael Cornish
277 W. 10th St.
New York, NY 10014
Authors: *Tramp Art: One Notch At a Time*

Vending & Gambling Devices
Jack Kelly
Michigan
(616) 983-0311

CERAMICS

Flow Blue & Mulberry
Ellen Hill
Mulberry Hill South
655 - 10th Ave. N.E.
Apt. 5
St. Petersburg, FL 33701

Lefton China
Loretta DeLozier
1101 Polk St.
Bedford, IA 50833
(712) 523-2289
LeftonLady@aol.com
Author: *Collector's Encyclopedia of Lefton China (Books I & II)*

Weller Pottery
Al Wunsch
625 - 30th Ave. W., #409G
Bradenton, FL 34205

GLASS

Imperial 'Candlewick'
Mary M. Wetzel-Tomalka
P.O. Box 594
Notre Dame, IN 46556
(219) 254-9817
Author: *Candlewick—The Jewel of Imperial*

Milk Glass
Frank Chiarenza
National Milk Glass Collectors Society
80 Crestview
Newington, CT 06111-2405
(860) 666-5576

Tiffany Glass
Carl Heck
P.O. Box 8416
Aspen, CO 81612

Audubon "Great American Hen & Young"   Courtesy of Sotheby's

ADVERTISING ITEMS

Thousands of objects made in various materials, some intended as gifts with purchases, others used for display or given away for publicity are now being collected. Also see various other categories.

Ashtray, "Gallagher & Burton, Fine Whiskies, Philadelphia," round, contor depicts bottle of Black Label Whiskey, marked "Made by the Chas. W. Shonk Co. Litho Chicago," ca. 1910-1925, 4½" d . . . **$66.00**

Ashtray, "Lemp Beer," metal, round, dark maroon w/gold lettering, reads "Extra Pale Famous Old Lemp Beer," 5½" d. (minor ding under "M" on right side) **44.00**

Tucker Ashtray

Ashtray, "Tucker," metal, gold colored car on rectangular green base marked "Tucker," brick design under car, cigarette compartment under car, 9" w., 3½" h (ILLUS.). . **1,540.00**

Badge, "Gilmore Lionhead," embossed tin in scroll shape, reads "Gilmore (motif of lion head) Lionhead" above, "Pennsylvania Oil" emblem & "Purest Pennsylvania Motor Oil" w/signature slot below, 2¾" w., 1¼" h **385.00**

Badge, "Shell Oil," metal cloisonné design, seashell-shaped w/"Shell" in red lettering on gold background, 1½" w., 1½" h **110.00**

Bank, "Big Boy," rubber, ca. 1977, 4 x 5¼", 9⅜" h **17.00**

Bank, "Boscul Coffee," tin, round, orangish red, reads "Boscul Coffee" in gold & black lettering on cream background label, depicts waiter serving coffee in diamond label, marked "Wm. S. Scull Co. N.J., N.Y., Ohio," 2½" d., 2¼" h. **44.00**

Bank, "Esso," glass w/embossed lettering, reads "Watch Your Savings Grow With Esso," 4¾" w., 3¼" d., 4¾" h. **105.00**

Esso Bank

Bank, "Esso," molded plastic, service attendant in blue uniform w/Esso logo on shirt, missing trap on back, crackling to logo, 3¼" w., 2½" d., 5" h (ILLUS).................. **105.00**

Bank, "Mobilgas," baseball shape w/red Pegasus horse on one side & Indian head on reverse, metal screw cap on bottom w/coin slot, 3" d., 3" h. **77.00**

Bank, "Phillips 66 Trop-Arctic Motor Oil," tin, oil can-shaped **24.00**

Bank, "Sinclair," figural dinosaur, metal w/painted green head, 9¼" l., 5¼" h.................. **198.00**

Bank, "Mission Orange Drink," cylindrical tin, dated 1954, 12 oz. **35.00**

Atlantic Motor Oil Banner

Banner, "Atlantic (motif of plane) Motor Oil (motif of car) Aviation Tested," cloth, red, navy blue, gold & white, marked "Sweeny Litho Co. Inc. Belleville, N.J. Litho in U.S.A.," some minor fading, 53½" w., 28⅝" h (ILLUS.).............. **550.00**

Banner, "New 1956 Chevrolet Task Force Trucks On Display!," cloth, red & black lettering on yellow background, right side depicts black truck on white background, 91" w., 33¼" h. (soiling & white paint spots) **77.00**

Banner, "Remington," cloth, depicts vintage Flintlock w/powder horn hanging from firearm, "Remington Since 1816 America's Oldest

Gunmakers Sporting Firearms Ammunition," fringed bottom, 29" l., 20" h.................. **29.00**

Barometer & thermometer "Gillette," blue porcelain, reads "Blue Gillette Blades" beneath picture of razor blade at top, thermometer in center & barometer at bottom, reads "Blue Gillette Blades" 6¼" w., 27½" h... **1,925.00**

Blotter, "Socony," cold test motor oil & winter gear oil, 1920s.......... **28.00**

Book, "Post Cereal," titled "A Trip Through Postumville," hard cover, colorful, 1920 .... **45.00**

Booklet, "Hercules Powder," 1927 ... **40.00**

Booklet, "Pabst Beer, Milwaukee," fine color lithography, ca. 1893 .... **30.00**

Bottle carrying case, "Watkins," wooden, stenciled "Watkins Products" one side, "Quality for over 70 years" other, "Watkins Gold Medal Vanilla" one end w/"Watkins Coconut Oil Shampoo" on other, includes six Watkins products, five w/Watkins likeness on label, high middle handle, 24" l., 8" deep, 10" h................ **127.00**

Bowl, "Mobil," china, red & navy blue Mobil emblem on cream background w/navy blue stripes around upper & lower parts of bowl, marked "Shenango China, U.S.A.," 5¾" d., 2¼" h. (scratches, chips on lower rim) **55.00**

Box, "Mrs. S. A. Allen's World Hair Restorer," cardboard, depicts bust of lady w/full head of hair, 9" l., 4½" deep, 7½" h. (minor soiling & scratching).................... **316.00**

Box, "Williams' Root Beer Extract," wooden, paper label depicts comical scene of family in background w/boy spraying baby from bottle w/root beer, foreground depicts couple toasting, "No Other Root Beer Extract Equals Williams' in Strength and Purity" on paper fan, end labels read "The Kind That Suits," 10" l., 5" deep, 7½" h **230.00**

Box opener, "Wrigley's," wood, paddle-style w/string hanger at end, "Wrigley's Spearmint, Doublemint and Juicy Fruit," 14" l. ... **52.00**

Brochure, "J.I. Case Threshing Machine Company," depicts Case car on front w/red lettering & black background, 36 pages, 5¾" w., 8½" h. **33.00**

Broiler, "Quaker Oats," graniteware, speckled black & light greenish aqua, 8" d., 8¼" h............... **121.00**

Bubble gum wrapper, "Mickey Mouse," depicts large Mickey w/smaller images of Mickey, Minnie, Pluto, Clarabelle & Horace, matted & framed, 10 x 11"......... **86.00**

Calendar, 1890, "Feldstein's Restaurant, New York City," in fancy embossed slip-cover **30.00**

Calendar, 1893, "Hires Root Beer," color lithographed cardboard in pastel tones showing two young children w/a black & white cat, complete w/full pad, 7 x 9" **700.00**

Calendar, 1895, "American Railway Supply Co.," pocket-style, metal case w/calendar sheets, marked "Compliments of American Railway Supply Co. 24 Park Place New York" on front, calendar sheets on reverse, 2⅛" w., 2¾" h. (some soiling) **22.00**

Calendar, 1898, "Hood's Sarsaparilla," rectangular color printed cardboard, round central reserve showing a pretty blond-headed baby, flowers around the border, printed at bottom "Hood's Coupon Calendar - 1898," 4½ x 7".. **150.00**

Calendar, 1898, "National Life Insurance" **25.00**

Calendar, 1898, "The Union Metallic Cartridge Co.," paper, depicts Molly Pitcher priming cannon during Revolutionary War, entitled "Molly Pitcher at Monmouth June 28 - 1778" by "The Knapp Co. Litho.," original metal bands on top & bottom, 22" w., 34" h. (minor creasing & chipping to outer edges) **2,875.00**

Calendar, 1900, "Larkin Soap Company," colored lithograph, oval, a scene of a seated woman in a white & blue dress below an American flag, wording across top "Rah, Rah, Rah - Columbia," attached football-form calendar to side w/full pad, signed by Ellen Clapsaddle, 19 x 24"............ **176.00**

Calendar, 1903, "Snag-Proof Shoes," colorfully lithographed scene of Old Woman who lived in a Snag-Proof shoe, pad incomplete, 7 x 10" **110.00**

Calendar, 1906, "Berger & Wirth," color lighographed paper, a scene of a native woman, reads "Berger & Wirth Manufacturers of Fine Dry Colors. Lithographs and Printing Inks, Office and Factory Centre & Broome Sts. New York," 14¾ x 29¾" (edge tears, hole in shoulder of woman) **55.00**

1909 Bennett & Hall Calendar

Calendar, 1909, "Bennet & Hall, Commission Merchants," color lithographed paper, a rectangular sheet w/advertising at top on a dark blue ground above a keyhole reserve w/th the bust portrait of a smiling dark-haired young girl below an arch of large pink & red roses, small pad at the bottom, January-May sheets missing, soiling, 12 x 18¼" (ILLUS.) **100.00**

Calendar, 1909, "New England Confectionery (Necco)," three-section die-cut cardboard fold-out, chromolithographed scene of children in Colonial costume **85.00**

Calendar, 1909, "Pabst Extract," paper, depicts "Rose Girl" in garden scene, original cardboard roll at bottom 7½" w., 36½" h...... **460.00**

Calendar, 1910, "First American Life Insurance Company," paper, round, depicts bust of American Indian on front, calendar on reverse, signed by artist H. Vos, 13" d. (some overall staining & chipping) **288.00**

Calendar, 1912, "Cherry Smash," color lithographed cardboard w/a tall scene of a young lady seated in a large swing holding a glass of the product, small monthly calendar scattered around the bottom section, 7½ x 15" **600.00**

Calendar, 1912, "Cunard Line Dock," lithographed ceramic tile, black & white scene of steamers on front, calendar on the back, printed "Cunard Line Dock New Boston," 4⅝" w., 3¼" h, (minor edge chips) **11.00**

Calendar, 1914, "Clay, Robinson & Co.," paper, depicts lady by sea, signed by artist R. Gord Harper, 17½" w., 44" h. (slight creasing & spotting)..................... **230.00**

Calendar, 1915, "Winchester," paper, depicts eagle attacking mountain goats, "Forbes Litho. Mfg. Co.," by artist Lynn Bogue Hunt, original metal bands at top & bottom, 21" w., 36" h. **2,103.00**

1916 DeLaval Calendar

Calendar, 1916, "DeLaval Cream Separators," color lithographed paper, a long rectangular scene w/advertising across the top above an indoor view of a young girl seated on a crate w/a young boy holding a bouquet of wild flowers, calendar at the bottom, full pad, edge tear at top & bottom, wrinkles, 12 x 24½" (ILLUS.) **303.00**

Calendar, 1918, "Bristol Fishing Rods," paper, depicts fishing scene w/lady catching fish, signed by artist Philip R. Goodwin, lithographer "Horton Mfg. Co.," original metal rims at top & bottom, 22" w., 37½" h. **3,450.00**

Calendar, 1920, "Glenshaw Glass Co.," scene of woman sitting by water w/note in her lap, reads "Glenshaw Glass Co., Inc., Glenshaw, Pennsylvania Manufacturers of Flint, Green and Amber Bottles," picture titled "From Over There,", 17" w., 32" h. (minor deterioration) **83.00**

Calendar, 1926, "Chero-Cola," color printed long scene of a young woman seated in a wicker armchair in a garden holding a book in her lap & a bottle of the product in one hand, complete w/pad **500.00**

Calendar, 1927, "Nehi Beverages," color-printed paper, a scene of a young flapper wearing an orange dress seated on the edge of a rowboat on a beach & drinking a bottle of soda, marked "Copyright Chero-Cola Co.," framed, 11 x 21" **231.00**

1936 Nehi Soda Calendar

Calendar, 1936, "Nehi," color printed paper, a long bust portrait of a pretty dark-haired lady wearing a bright red wide-collared blouse & red kerchief, calendar at bottom (ILLUS.) **250.00**

Calendar, 1936, "Westinghouse," Christmas, colorful **30.00**

Calendar, 1937, "Dr. Pepper," long color scene of a young woman seated on a round hassock & wearing an elegant gown, holding a bottle of Dr. Pepper in one hand, complete w/full pad **800.00**

Calendar, 1941, "DeLaval Cream Separators," four-section, color scene of Native American in a canoe by R. Ewell **165.00**

Calendar, 1942, "Pepsi-Cola," color-printed paper, large winter landscape scene of snow-covered hills w/a road in the foreground, calendar at the bottom, 17 x 23" . . . **60.00**

1944 John Deere Calendar

Calendar, 1944, "John Deere," color-printed paper, a rectangular scene at the top of a young boy & girl standing in front of a John Deere dealer's storefront, name & locale of business below picture w/calendar pad at bottom, soiling, bent corners, 10¾ x 16" (ILLUS.) . . . **66.00**

1946 Atlantic Petroleum Calendar

Calendar, 1946, "Atlantic Petroleum Products, The Atlantic Refining Company," color-printed paper, "Atlantic" in large white letters on red across the top, long calendar pad below, creases, edge tears & soiling, 16 x 28½" (ILLUS.) **50.00**
Calendar, 1947, "Hercules Powder" . . **75.00**

1949 Kelly Tires Calendar

Calendar, 1949, "Kelly Tires," color-printed paper, a long rectangular form w/a pale green background w/a sketched-in front end of a car w/a full-length color portrait of a pin-up girl seated on the front bumper wearing a short white tennis outfit & holding a racket, dealer advertising below picture & above calendar pad, full pad, picture signed "Medcalf," wrinkles, 16 x 34" (ILLUS.) **176.00**

1951 Goodyear Tire Calendar

Calendar, 1951, "Goodyear Tires," color-printed heavy paper, a large rectangular color picture at the top of a giant Uncle Sam launching bomber airplanes w/a pilot & Boy Scout in the foreground, signed "Dean Cornwell," full pad, minor creases, minor edge tears, 20½ x 28" (ILLUS.) **66.00**
Calendar, 1956, "Grogan Robinson Lumber Company," paper depicts autumn scene of man hunting pheasant, entitled "Up & Ready," original metal rims at top & bottom, 18" w., 30" h. **86.00**
Charcoal briquets picnic kit, "Ford," metal box w/bail handle, marked "Ford Charcoal Briquets" **193.00**
Clock, "Atlas Tires," metal & glass, octagonal, reads "Atlas Tires Batteries Accessories" in white lettering on blue, 18¼" x 18¼" (restored glass on front) **880.00**
Clock, "Duffy's Pure Malt Whiskey," wall-type, wording around clock face, pendulum door w/reverse-painted glass decoration depicting an alchemist & the words "Absolutely Pure & Unadulterated Trade Mark," clock works made by "The New Haven Clock Co., New Haven, CT," 32¼" h. (reverse-paint shows some separation & loss, repainted face lettering) **1,348.00**
Clock, "Enjoy Canada Dry," electric, wall-type w/light, glass & metal, Canada Dry logo on white clock face, marked "Copyright 1962 Pam Clock Co. Inc. New Rochelle NY," 15" d. (minor scratches) **000.00**
Clock, "Green River The Whiskey Without a Headache, J.W. McCulloch Distiller Owensboro Kentucky," table model, cast brass, depicts two men shaking hands

over a bottle, stamped "Pat. Sep.
22 85 Other Pat. Apld. For" on
back, ca. 1885-1900, 13" w.,
15¾" h. **770.00**

Clock, "Gulf," electric, plastic,
triangular, orange, blue & white
Gulf colors, 22" w., 22" h. (small
hand broken) **187.00**

Clock, "John Deere (motif of deer)
Quality Farm Equipment," electric,
wall-type w/light, glass & metal,
round w/yellow & green John
Deere emblem on white
background, marked "John Deere-
2 Telechron Inc. Ashland, Mass,
U.S.A. Ng. Co.," 14¾" d. (wear to
cord & casing, soiling) **660.00**

Clock, "Lewis 66 Rye, The Strauss,
Pritz Co. Cincinnati, O," wall-type,
white, silver & black reverse-
painted decoration, ca. 1890-1920,
12" d. (some separation &
discoloration of paint, minor
chipping along edge) **176.00**

Clock, "Lewis Red Jacket Bitters,"
wall-type, white, black & red face
w/lithograph on paper of Indian
chief in center, ca. 1890-1910, 14¼
x 21¼," clock face 9¼" d., (some
chipping of paint on clock face) **743.00**

Clock, "Mishler's Herb Bitters Purifies
The Blood Improves The Appetite
Sold Here," wall-type, wood
w/raised plaster embossing,
marked "Made by Baird Clock Co.
Plattsburgh, N. Y. U.S.A.," ca.
1880-1900, 18½" x 31" (letter "T" in
Appetite is missing) **3,300.00**

Clock, "Mopar," neon, metal & glass,
octagonal, reads "Mopar Parts &
Accessories Use Chrysler
Corporation Parts Division
Products," red, yellow & white
lettering on clock face, neon trim,
18½" w., 18½" h. (soiling & fading) . . **605.00**

Clock, "Oldsmobile," electric, wall-
type w/light, glass front w/heavy
metal body, white background,
15¼" w., 17¾" h. (scratches,
soiling) **303.00**

Clock, "Oldsmobile," mantel-type,
wind-up, metal & wood w/beveled
glass front, marked "The Ansonia
Clock Co. Manufacturers U.S.A.,"
4" w., 6" l., 7" h. (soiling &
scratches) **165.00**

Clock, "Pepsi-Cola" beneath "Say
Pepsi Please," electric, wall-type
w/light, glass & metal, 4" w.,
14¾" l., 15⅝" h. **121.00**

Clock, "Pepsi-Cola," electric, wall-
type, round, metal & glass, ca.
1944, 15" d. (scratches, denting &
paint loss to hands) **358.00**

Clock, "Pontiac Service," electric,
wall-type, round molded plastic,
outer rim w/white lettering on blue
background, blue lettering on blue
background, blue letttering on
yellow clock in center, metal hands,
15" d. (fading & paint chipping to
lettering & numbers) **275.00**

Clock, "Quaker State, Oils &
Greases," neon, wall-type w/glass
& metal, white background & green
trim & lettering, new chrome ring
holding glass face, 19" w., 16" h.
(scratches, new neon) **605.00**

Clock, "Veedol Motor Oil," square,
metal, wind-up, Veedol logo
w/black lettering on pale yellow
background, signed "Japy," 9⅛" x
9⅛" **154.00**

Coat, "Quaker State," beige leather
w/sheepskin lining, Quaker State
logo on vinyl breast patch, never
worn (some fading to sleeves) **61.00**

Cork screw, "Champion,"
mechanical, cast iron, "Harter's
Wild Cherry Bitters" plate attached
to wooden bill, ca. 1900-1910,
8¾" h. **242.00**

Cork screw, "Sample Dr. Harter's
Wild Cherry Bitters The Best on
Earth Pat. Apld.," mechanical
counter top-style, iron, ca. 1900-
1910, 8⅝" l. **358.00**

Bosch Battery Counter Display

Counter display, "Bosch Battery,"
chalkware, figural gas station
attendant holding battery, 7 x 7½",
25" h. (ILLUS.) **660.00**

Counter display, "Buss Auto Fuses,"
metal, depicts motorist in front of
stationary vehicle & package of
Buss Auto Fuses, yellow lettering &
decoration on black background,
8½" w., 3" deep. 7½" h.......... **154.00**

Counter display, "Clayton's Dog
Remedies," figural bulldog,
embossed "Clayton's Dog
Remedies" on both sides, includes
"Dr. Clayton's Treatise on all
Breeds of Dogs" booklet, 27" l.,
19½" h.................... **1,725.00**

Counter display, "Curry & Metzgar,
Pittsburgh, Pa. Gunpowder," tin,
roll-top style, black background
paint w/gold, white & red lettering &
decoration, ca. 1870-1880, minor
denting & chipping, 13¼" w., 15½"
deep, 19½" h. **253.00**

Counter display, "Dr. Morse's Indian
Root Pills," multicolored lithographs
on a board, includes tri-fold display,
paper banner & four individual
countertop displays contained in
original cardboard folder, all depict
various scenes of Native
Americans, ca. 1915-1925 ...... **358.00**

Counter display, "Gainsborough
HairNet," wood, lower front &
marquee depict lady w/mirror
admiring hair w/hair net, contains
18 original Gainsborough Hair Net
envelopes, 15" w., 17½" deep,
17½" h. **230.00**

Counter display, "Trico Wiper
Blades & Rods," tin lithograph
w/paper lithograph label on back,
depicts woman at top, orange,
black & cream, 2½ x 9½ x 14"..... **242.00**

Counter display, "West Electric Hair
Curler Company," tin, triangular
w/"West Hair Nets," "West Electric
Hair Curlers," & "Softex Shampoo"
on different sides, round rotating
pedestal, ca. 1922, 10 x 8½ x 18".. **460.00**

Counter display box, "Gowan's
Preparation For Pneumonia For
Croup," cardboard w/hanging
string, white & black depicting a
box of the product, printing on all
four sides, ca. 1900-1910, 6 x 9½".. **99.00**

Counter display cabinet, "Belding
Brothers & Company," oak, 13
spool drawers on each side,
bottom marked "Spool" on one side
? "Silk" on other, 04" w., 14½"
deep, 35½" h................ **1,438.00**

Counter display cabinet, "Brighton
Silk Garters," wood & glass,
rectangular, 8-drawer w/simulated
stained glass front, stenciled wood

on other three sides & marked
"Brighton Silk Garters for 25 cents,"
14" w., 10½" deep, 19" h. **575.00**

Counter display cabinet, "Diamond
Dye," oak w/tin front, depicts
children skipping rope in front of
mansion, includes numerous
pieces of product, 16" w., 8½"
deep, 25" h.................. **345.00**

Counter display cabinet, "Dy-O-La
Dye," oak w/tin facing on front
door, full insert & instructions on
inside front door, wood facing on
back, 13¾" w., 8½" deep, 17" h.... **202.00**

Counter display cabinet, "Hohner
Harmonica," wood, tiered tri-fold
design w/paper marquee depicting
people from around the world
playing Hohner harmonicas,
includes 9 lithographed harmonica
tin boxes, 18 cardboard boxes
w/graphics including 13 original
harmonicas, 5½" w., 10½" h...... **920.00**

Counter display cabinet,
"Humphrey's Specifics," wood, blue
background w/two-sided two-faced
listings of 35 veterinary products,
22" w., 9" deep, 28" h. (minor
soiling) **1,265.00**

Counter display cabinet, "Munyon's
Homopathic Remedies," wood w/tin
facing, lists products & prices on
front, 17" w., 8¼" deep, 24" h...... **920.00**

Counter display case, "Arrow
Collars," wood w/glass front,
includes 12 original Arrow collars,
8½" deep, 25½" h.............. **472.00**

Counter display jar, "Lance," clear
glass w/blue & white decals,
marked "Lance" in red decals on
two sides, lid & base etched
"Lance," 7" w., 8½" deep, 12½" h.
(soiling) **77.00**

Counter display jar, "Planters
Peanuts," embossed glass
w/oversized peanut on each
corner, "Planters" vertically
embossed between peanuts,
peanut finial on lid, 14" h. **345.00**

Counter display jar, "Planters
Peanuts," glass, octagonal, highly
embossed on all eight sides w/"Mr.
Peanut" on four panels, peanut
finial on lid, 13" to top of finial ... **230.00**

Counter display jar, "Planters
Peanuts," glass, oval w/rectangular
base, embossed "Planters Salted
Peanuts" on front & back, peanut
finial on lid, 9" h. (very small chip in
lid) **288.00**

Counter display rack, "Beech-Nut Gum," metal w/double tier, 15" w., 9½" h. **21.00**

Counter display rack, "Simple Simon Nuts," metal, dark green w/gold lettering, reads "Simple Simon Salted Nuts 5¢," upright stand w/round black base, holds individual sacks of nuts, made by "American Nut Co. Indianapolis Ind." (scratches & some paint loss) . . **121.00**

Crate, "Dr. Harter's Wild Cherry Bitters Dayton, Ohio, U.S.A. Dr. Harter The Dr. Harter Medicine Co. Dayton, O.," wood w/black stenciling on all four sides, 13¼" w., 9" h. **209.00**

Mobiloil Crate

Crate, "Mobiloil," wood, contains three glass quart oil bottles w/metal tops, all w/minor wear (ILLUS.) **193.00**

Cuff links, "Sunoco," metal, blue lettering on yellow triangles, original box, 1" w., ½" h, pr **176.00**

Cups, "Dickinson's Ace Clover & Pine Tree Timothy Seed," porcelain over metal, blue & black lettering over creamy white background, 2⅝" d., 2⅝" h. (some chipping to porcelain) . . **35.00**

Desk accessory, "Texaco," wooden base, two metal Scottie dogs on one end, recessed cup holder on other, 6⅝" w., 2½" h. **242.00**

Dice shaker, "Dr. Daniel's Remedies," glass, dome paperweight-shaped, depicts Dr. Daniel's on bottom & reads "Don't Gamble - Use Dr. Daniel's Remedies, Patd. Aug. 18, 1903," five dice, 3" d. **403.00**

Dispenser, "Pulver Chewing Gum," porcelain, three-column tab vendor w/beveled mirror on front & "Pulver Chewing Gum" below, 31" h. (some slight chipping) **202.00**

Michelin Doll

Doll, "Michelin," plastic, counter top model, marked "1966 Michelin ETCIE-Made in France" on back, 19" h. (ILLUS.). **231.00**

Door pane, "Lucky Strike It's Toasted Cigarettes," glass in red, white & black, depicts pack of cigarettes, reverse marked "Thank You - Call Again!," ca. 20th c., 10¼" x 14¼" . . **187.00**

Door push, "Crescent Flour," rectangular, embossed tin, – "Push-And Try A Sack Of (flour bag w/Crescent Flour logo) Crescent Flour Sold Here" in white lettering on black background, 33¾" w. **182.00**

Door push, "Hart Batteries," porcelain, white lettering on black background, 32" w., 3¼" h (scratches). **110.00**

Door push, "Savage Stevens Fox," wood, painted "Savage. Stevens . Fox" above w/American Indian logo & "World Famous Rifles & Shotguns" below, 3" w., 20" l. **288.00**

Door push, "Texas Punch," tin, 4 x 10". . **140.00**

Door push, "Five Roses Flour," porcelain **125.00**

Doorway arch, "Buster Brown," wood, two-panel die-cut, depicts "Buster Brown" & "Tige" playing in trees, each panel 42" w., 36" h. **58.00**

Envelope, "Winchester Store," 1925 . . **40.00**

Fan, "Bordens Condensed Milk Company," cardboard, color illustration of a young girl on ice skates, ca. 1910 . . . . **48.00**

Fan, "Sinclair," cardboard, funnel shape, depicts mechanic & old car w/young girl sitting in front seat & sign reading "Garage Storage Parking Car Oil Service Accessories," 7½" w., 10½" h. (one ragged edge) **94.00**

Kasco Feed Scale

Feed scale, "Kasco Feeds," metal w/debossed lettering, marked "Milk at Low Cost (numbered dial) Use the Scales, Weigh the Milk, Weigh the Feeds," some tarnish, 4½" w., 16" h. (ILLUS.) **143.00**

Flag, "Mobilgas," linen cloth w/wooden pole, black & white checkered flag w/red Pegasus horse, 35" w., 36" h. **176.00**

Floor display rack, "Blackman's Medicated Salt Brick," wood w/tin marquee, top marquee depicts horse licking "Salt Brick" w/"Blackman's Medicated" above & "Every Animal Its Own Doctor" below, manufactured by "Blackman Stock Remedy Co. of Chattanooga, Tenn.," 16½" w., 31½" h. **288.00**

Floor display rack, "Blu-J Brooms," embossed tin, depicts a Blue Jay sitting atop a broom, advertising front & back, includes four brooms, 23½" w., 35" h. **518.00**

Floor display rack, "Pennzoil, Outboard Motor Oil, 100# Pure Pennsylvania, Safe Lubrication," two-sided sign above two-tier metal rack, marked "A-4-60," 39" h. (scratches & dents on sign, slight rusting on rack) **154.00**

Flour barrel, "Portland Milling Company," wood, end paper label depicts trademark picture of girl wearing large hat, 28" h. **58.00**

Funnel, "Dr. Van Dyke's Holland Bitters Van Dyke Bitters Co St. Louis," copper w/soldered spout & riveted handle, ca. 1890-1910, 7⅜" h. **50.00**

Glass, "Ritschler and Tiesse Malting Co., Clinton, Iowa," clear w/heavy gilt decoration depicting a lion & shield, ca. 1910-1920, 4¾" h. **61.00**

Glasses w/carrier, "Mobil Pegasus," metal carrier w/six glasses, white glasses w/red Pegasus horse designs, 6" h., the set **226.00**

Globe, "Red Goose Shoes," milk white globe w/debossed red goose on one side & "Friedman-Shelby All Leather Shoes" on reverse, milk white pedestal base, 10" w., 12" h. (repaired & repainted globe) **288.00**

Hat, "Harley-Davidson," black cloth & vinyl, Harley-Davidson logo on front, white rope trim, log stamped in fabric inside hat, size 7¼" **160.00**

Hat, "Kool-Aid," red cloth soda jerk-style, promotes "Junior Aviation Corps" **60.00**

Hat, "Sunoco Laceby Dealer," beige & brown, gasoline station attendant -style, vinyl bill, cloth top w/metal enameled badge, size 7¼" **237.00**

Fina Hat Badge

Hat badge, "Fina," triangular, metal w/porcelain inlay in red, yellow & blue, 1½" w., 1¾" h. (ILLUS.) **165.00**

Jar, "Edison," ceramic, white figural battery w/"Edison-Lalande Battery March 20, 1888" on lid, 14" h. **115.00**

Jar, "Horlick's Malted Milk, Racine," clear glass, ½ pint **20.00**

Key holder, "Texaco, Registered Rest Rooms," plastic, rectangular, white & black w/red "Rest Rooms" seal on front, black & white background & printing on reverse . . **132.00**

Key ring, "Texaco, Registered Rest Rooms," plastic, rectangular, white & black w/red "Rest Rooms" seal on front, black & white background & printing on reverse **132.00**

Lamp, "Bosch," figural spark plug w/glass globe, plastic, reads "Bosch Germany," 10" d., 21½" h. . . . **231.00**

Lamp, "Mobiloil Special," figural oil
can in gold, blue & red w/Mobiloil
logo, celluloid, metal & cardboard,
7" d., 9½" h. (soiling, cardboard
peeling on top). **275.00**

License Plate Attachment

License plate attachment,
"Pembroke Air Park," painted metal
w/reflective lettering, reads "Fly
(motif of airplane) At Pembroke Air
Park, Inc. On Route Five," 11" w.,
6" h. (ILLUS.). **66.00**

Tracy's Coffee Light Globe

Light globe, "Tracy's Coffee," glass,
top light fixture, round, white globe
w/gold lettering, reads "Tracy's
Fresh Roasted Coffee," soiling,
minor chipping on base edges,
7" h. (ILLUS.). **281.00**

Lighter, "Wayne Gas," metal, figural
gas pump w/"Wayne" in gold oval
on front, top lifts to expose lighter,
2" w., 1¼" deep, 3⅝" h. **121.00**

Lighter fluid dispenser, "Shell
Gasoline," metal w/glass cylinder,
figural gas pump, clear upper
w/white lettering, red bottom on
cylindrical footed base, side penny
slot, 19" h. **198.00**

Map rack, "Conoco," painted black
metal w/decal at bottom, marked
"M2-33-Made in U.S.A.," includes
thirteen newer brochures, 11⅛" w.,
26⅜" h. (scratches, nail holes) **187.00**

Match holder, "Purol Tiolene," metal,
red & yellow w/black lettering,
reads "Purol Tiolene (motif of arrow
& circle target) Gasoline Motor Oil,"
standard size (paint chips) **94.00**

Menu board, "Pepsi-Cola," tin,
original chain, 19½ x 30" (some
scratches) **140.00**

Mirror, "Player's Navy Cut Tobacco,"
depicts Player's logo of sailor &
vintage ships framed by life
preserver, "Tobacco and
Cigarettes" below, wooden frame,
18" w., 22" h. **202.00**

Mug, "Dr. Swett's," china, highly
embossed, depicts bust of Dr.
Swett on front & floral decoration
on reverse, 6" h. **202.00**

Mug, "Drink Hires Rootbeer," china,
depicts trademark boy holding
Hires Rootbeer mug, Mettlach,
Germany, 4½" h. **403.00**

Needle case, A&P stores, mint
w/contents **8.00**

Ointment tin, "Petrolina," depicts oil
derricks in black & red graphics, 3"
w., 3" deep, 4" h. **33.00**

Paperweight, "Kellogg Toasted Corn
Flakes," milk white glass, flat,
depicts trademark image of little girl
in wicker basket, 3¼" w., 5" l. **109.00**

Paperweight, "Nassau Bank," figural
turtle, brass w/metal oval button
reading "The Nassau Bank Safe
Solid Sound Safe Deposit Vaults,"
marked "Whitehead & Hoag Co.
Newark, Pat. May 3, 1904," 2½" w.,
4¼" l., 1" h. (some scratches &
soiling) **88.00**

Pennant, "Marble's," depicts gun &
hatchet w/"Game Getting Gun and
Specialties for Sportsman," 10½"
w., 33" l. **219.00**

Perfume sample dispenser,
"Continental Novelty Company of
Buffalo, NY.," painted bull's head
w/directions in glass circle above,
pull horns to spray perfume, ca.
1908, 14" h. **2,900.00**

Phonograph record, "Pepsi-Cola,"
1943, complete w/mailing folder **55.00**

Photograph, "Kodak" on metal plate,
black & white in original frame,
depicts woman taking photograph
of four children & an older woman
looking at a book, original label on
back marked "This advertisement
is the property of the Eastman
Kodak Company.," ca. 1935-1945,
27¾" x 34¼" **231.00**

Pin, "Carl's Toyland," celluloid over
metal, round, depicts Santa Claus
w/"Carl's Toyland" in gold lettering
above, all on dark bluish purple
background. 1¼" d **34.00**

Pin, "Lion Motor Oil," metal, cloisonné design of man in black barrel, brown base, marked "The Oil With the Right Body In It," ⅝" w., 1" h. . . . **28.00**

Pin, "Mobiloil," metal w/cloisonné design, stick pin-type, oval head w/gargoyle & "Mobiloil," ⅝" w., 2⅛" h. **66.00**

Shell Oil Pin

Pin, "Shell Oil," plastic, round w/fluted edging, yellow & gold Shell logo in center, black outer trim reading "Tractor Lubrication" in yellow lettering, 1¼" d. (ILLUS.) **17.00**

Pin, "Standard Oil," Standard Oil emblem in cloisonné design w/diamond at bottom, ⅝" w., ½" h. . . **138.00**

Pitcher, "Dr. Harter's Wild Cherry Bitters" & motif of bottle w/"Relieves All Distress of the Stomach," thermos-type, silver w/intricate raised design, stamped "E. Jaccard Jewelry Co. St. Louis, Mo Quadruple Plate" on base, ca. 1890-1910, 13" h **330.00**

Pitcher, "Dr. Van Dyke's Holland Bitters Van Dyke Bitters Co. St. Louis," thermos-type, silver plate w/intricate design, stamped "Pelton Bros & Co St. Louis Quadruple Plate" on base, ca. 1880-1910, 13⅜" h. **242.00**

Pitcher, "Tho's. Maddock's Son's Co.," tankard-style, ceramic, depicts two portly gentlemen bowling on one side w/rack of pool balls on other, silver handle, 12½" h. (slight chipping & silver loss to handle) **98.00**

Plate, "Hood & Sons Milk," metal w/porcelain center, round, silver w/outer black lettering reading "Sales Achievement 1983 Home Service Division," depicts cow in center w/"H.P. Hood & Sons Milk" in white lettering on red background, 11" d. **66.00**

Playing cards, "Dr. Harter's The Only True Iron Tonic For The Bold," & "Dr. Harter's Little Liver Pills Cures Sick Headache Do Not Gripe or

Sicken," complete set w/extra card advertising Dr. Harter's compnay, ca. 1892 . . . . **148.00**

Playing cards, "Dr. Van Dykes' Holland Bitters," complete set in original box w/tax stamp (some deterioration to box) **154.00**

Gulf Oil Disney Magazine

Poster, "Gulf Exclusive Wonderful World of Disney Magazine, 25¢," paper, depicts Donald Duck in lower left corner, 44" w., 33¾" h. (ILLUS.) **77.00**

Poster, "Gulfpride," paper w/linen backing, depicts squirrel on nut & reading "Winter's Ahead, Change to Gulfpride Now!," gold background, marked "Form SS-78 For Posting October 16-31, 1940 All Divisions," ca. 1940, 28" w., 42" h. **143.00**

Poster, "Sterling Motor Oil," paper, depicts baseball umpire, catcher & man at bat & reading "Play Safe! Change to Sterling Motor Oil For Summer Driving," Sterling Motor Oil logo on mid-right side, 22" w., 31¾" h. (some creases & soiling) . . **187.00**

Punch board, "Camel Cigarettes," 1¢ play, 1940s, unused **55.00**

Puzzle, jigsaw-type, "Chase & Sanborn Coffee," their famous New England country grocery store scene, colorful, complete in original box **68.00**

Radio, "Prestolite," counter top-style, black & orange hard rubber, white dials on front, "Prestolite Hi-level Needs Water Only 3 Times a Year" on reverse, 6¾ x 10⅛", 8" h. **226.00**

Columbus Flour Rolling Pin

Rolling pin, "Columbus Flour," milk white glass w/wooden handles, reads "Use Columbus Flour, Always Satisfactory and Uniform, There's No Better Flour" in blue lettering & flour sack logo, 17⅝" l., 2½" d. (ILLUS.) 88.00

Salt & pepper shakers, Ball Mason Jar, glass w/aluminum caps, blue, w/box, pr. 160.00

Salt & pepper shakers, Bert & Harry Pell, mascots of Pell's Beer, dressed in black, both bald, Bert in a yellow & red vest, Harry tall figure w/bow-tie, 1970s, pr. 270.00

Salt & pepper shakers, Blue Nun Wine, cobalt blue robe w/white headdress & collar, holding a basket filled w/green grapes, white base inscribed "BLUE NUN. Correct with any dish.," U.S.A., 1980s, pr. 195.00

Salt & pepper shakers, Bob's Big Boy, Japan, 4¼" h., pr. 350.00

Salt & pepper shakers, Coca Cola Bottle, brown w/silver top, 3¾" h., unmarked, pr. 59.00

Salt & pepper shakers, Dairy Queen cones, vanilla (salt) & chocolate (pepper) ice cream w/distinctive Dairy Queen curl atop yellow "Safe-T-Cups," 3¾" h. pr. 29.00

Salt & pepper shakers, Elsie & Elmer, impressed mark "The Borden Co.," 4¼" h., pr. 100.00

Salt & pepper shakers, Esso gas pump, plastic, 2¾" h., unmarked, pr. . . . 37.00

Salt & pepper shakers, Firestone tires w/"Firestone" on one, "U.S. Rubber" on other, pr. 57.00

Salt & pepper shakers, Handy Flame, blue gas flame, tear-drop shaped, w/triangular black eyes, round cheeks & nose & smiling red lips, 1940s, impressed "Handy Flame," pr. 39.00

Salt & pepper shakers, Harvestore silo, cobalt blue, marked "A O Smith Harvestore System," 4¾" h., pr. 45.00

Salt & pepper shakers, Ken-L Ration dog & cat, Fido & Fifi, plastic, yellow dog & white cat, sitting up, begging, F&F, pr. 22.00

Salt & pepper shakers, Nikolai Vodka Man, pr. 195.00

Salt & pepper shakers, "RCA Victor," figural porcelain Nipper the dog w/"His Master's Voice" inscription, Lenox China, ca. 1930s, pr. 85.00

Salt & pepper shakers, Richfield gas pump, plastic, yellow, 2⅝" h., pr. . . . . 50.00 to 60.00

Salt & pepper shakers, "Richfield," plastic, figural gas pump w/Richfield decals, one w/orange lettering & one w/black lettering, marked "Eagle Oil Co, Fort Plain, N.Y.," 1" w., 2⅝" h., pr. 132.00

Salt & pepper shakers, Sandeman Brandy, figure of man w/black cape & hat, probably by Wedgwood, 5½" h., pr. 120.00

Salt & pepper shakers, Schlitz bottle, plastic w/metal cap, 4" h., pr.. . . . 15.00

Salt & pepper shakers, Seagram's 7, plastic, red crown atop numeral seven, white base marked in red "Seagram's," unmarked, 3½" h., pr. 35.00

Standard Crown Gas Pumps

Salt & pepper shakers, Standard Crown gas pump, plastic w/decals, marked "T.E. Gessele Your Standard Oil Agent Phone GI 7-4140 Mercer N.D.," 3¼" h., 1" w., soiling & small pieces missing to decals on both, pr. (ILLUS.) 171.00

Salt & pepper shakers, Sunshine Baker, rotund figure in white apron, yellow bow tie, w/mustache, gold detailing, inscribed "Sunshine," pr. . . . 15.00

Salt & pepper shakers, Tappan Chef, soft (squeezable) plastic, bell-shaped stylized figure w/goatee, flattened toque, white w/black trim, 1950s, 4⅞" h., pr. 29.00

Texaco Gas Pumps

Salt & pepper shakers, Texaco Sky Chief & Fire Chief gas pump, plastic, silver & red, 2¾" h. pr. (ILLUS.) **50.00**

Salt & Pepper Shakers, Westinghouse washing machine & dryer, plastic, white w/turquoise controls & transparent plastic ports .pr. **16.00**

Sheet music, "Moxie One Step," 1921 . . . . **45.00**

Sign, "Austin Powder Company," paper w/wooden frame, depicts two pointers in field above "Austin Powder Company," 23" w., 19" h. . . **518.00**

Sign, "Dad's Root Beer," die-cut tin, depicts large bright orange, red & yellow bottle cap at top, "The Old Fashioned Root Beer" in rectangle below, 20" w., 28" h. **196.00**

Sign, "Fairbank's Gold Dust Washing Powder," die-cut cardboard, two-sided, depicts black children at each end holding box of Fairbank's Gold Dust Washing Powder, a box under each "Gold Dust" letter, each pc., 7½ x 15½" **7,475.00**

Sign, "Kickapoo Indian Remedies," paper, depicts Chief Red Spear dressed in full regalia, by lithographer J. Ottmann, 18" w., 24" h. **432.00**

Sign, "Kow-Kare," tin, two-sided flange depicting tin packaging of Kow-Kare, Bag Balm Dilators & Bag Balm, cow logo, 12½" w., 9½" h. **288.00**

Sign, "Gillette," die-cut porcelain, depicts package of "Blue Gillette Blades" & razor, reads "Gillette" across front in bright red letters, yellow background, 22" w., 19½" h. **4,950.00**

Sprayer, "White Rose Sprayer, For White Rose Insecticide Spray," pump-style, tin w/glass bottle & wooden handle, 12½" l. (paint chips). **33.00**

Stationery, "Standard Oil Company," linen paper, letterhead reads "Panama Pacific International Exposition San Francisco, California, 1915," includes envelope (yellowing) **66.00**

String holder, "Red Seal White Lead," die-cut tin, depicts Dutch Boy painting from scaffolding, 3-dimensional pail holds string, two-sided, 14½" w., 7" h. to bottom of bucket. **2,875.00**

String holder, "Swift's Syphilitic Specific," cast-iron pot w/bale handle, embossed "S.S.S. For The Blood," ca. 1870-1890, 4⅜" h. (some rust & scratching) **77.00**

String holder, "U.S. Hame Company," hanging two-sided tin, depicts trademark buffalo standing atop company logo framed by two horses, "U.S. Hame Company" above logo, "USH Co Hames Sold Here" below w/string at bottom, by lithographer Chas. W. Shonk Co.,11½" w.,26" h. **3,450.00**

Mobilgas Telephone

Telephone, "Mobilgas," plastic, figural gas pump, cream color w/red emblems, black lettering on dial, marked "Copyrighted 1984 Synanon Made in Taiwan," 3" d., 9½" h. (ILLUS.) **94.00**

Theater slide, "Hamlin's Wizard Oil Liniment, For All Painful Ailments, The Pattern Drug Store, 48 Genessee St.," glass in blue, yellow, red & pink hand coloring, ca. 1900-1925, 3¼" h. **55.00**

Thermometer, "Abbott's Angostura, Abbott's Angostura Bitters Aid Digestion," wood, oblong, black lettering & decoration, 8¾" w., 47¾" h. **468.00**

Thermometer, "Atlas Perma-Guard,"
metal tapering oblong, marked
"Atlas Perma-Guard Anti-Freeze
Coolant" above in white lettering on
red, "Year-round Protection" in blue
lettering below, red, white & blue
sun w/ray design, 8" w., 24" h.
(scratches, soiling, paint chips) **83.00**

Thermometer, "Eyouem," porcelain,
rectangular, marked "Eyouem" in
white lettering on black background
above, depicts spark plug on
yellow background below, 12¼" w.,
38¾" h. (chips on edge, scratches) . . **50.00**

Hires Root Beer Thermometer

Thermometer, "Hires," painted tin in
soda bottle shape, "Hires Since
1876 Root Beer With Roots Barks
Herbs," 7¾" w., 28½" h. (ILLUS.) . . **171.00**

Thermometer, "Kendall Motor Oil,"
porcelain, rectangular, orange logo,
black lettering on white
background, marked "Kendall
Refining Company Bradford, PA.,"
9" w., 27" h. (soiling) **550.00**

Thermometer, "Motley's Big Roller
Flour," wood w/rounded top,
painted "Motley's Big Roller Flour,
Rochester, N.Y., Moseley & Motley
Milling Co." in circle above, "High
Quality Bread Flour, Buy It Here"
on side below, 9" w., 20½" h. **58.00**

Thermometer, "Prestone Anti-
Freeze" (black background above),
"You're Safe…And You Know It"
(red background below), porcelain,
oblong, 9¼" w., 36" l. (waterstained
& some chipping). **99.00**

Thermometer, "Valentine's Valspar,"
rectangular, porcelain w/wooden
frame, depicts man & woman
above "Valentine's Valspar The

Weatherproof Varnish," shows can
of varnish below, marked "Beach
Coshocton, Pat. Mar. 16, 1915,"
black, white & mauve, 21½" w., 96"
h. (chips overall) **715.00**

Thermometer, Frostie Root Beer, tin,
3 x 11⅝" **350.00**

Toy car, "Mobil," fiberglass, metal
steering mechanism & rubber tires,
Mobil logos & number "1" on front,
back & sides, white w/red & blue
striping, 53" l., 19" h. (some
scratches & soiling) **143.00**

Toy Tractor, "Farmall," cast metal
painted red, marked "Farmall"
w/logo on sides, 21" h.
(paint chips) **1,320.00**

Texaco Toy Truck

Toy truck, "Texaco," metal, red
w/"Texaco" decals on tank sides,
Texaco logo on doors (ILLUS.) **183.00**

Trophy, "Stanocola Polarine," metal,
engraved "Awarded To State Of
Tennessee Memphis Agency as
Winners Third Year 1922" on one
side, "Awarded to State Of
Arkansas Memphis Agency As
Winners Second Year Stanocola
Polarine Contest Year 1921" on
reverse, 10" d., 10½" h. **187.00**

Umbrella, "Patton's Sun-Proof Paint
Umbrella" & "The Iola Hdwe. Co."
on alternating panels, wooden
handle, 27" h. (some staining &
holes). **41.00**

Umbrella stand, "M. J. Ades &
Company," ornate nickel-plated
cast iron, half-moon shape
advertising medallion in center &
seven umbrella tip holes across
top, embossed "M. J. Ades & Co.
The Winner Umbrella," includes
seven umbrellas w/simulated gold
or mother of pearl & simulated gold
handles, 16½" l., 4½" h. without
umbrellas **1,275.00**

Water bag, "Pep Boys," metal & cloth
w/plastic cap, marked "The Pep
Boys" above three men in vehicle,
"Drinking Water Bag Keeps Water
Cool Fresh Palatable" below, all on
cream cloth background, metal top
closure & hanging holes, 10½" w.,
16½" h. **44.00**

ALMANACS

Almanacs have been published for decades. Commonplace ones are available at $4.00 to $12.00; those representing early printings or scarce ones are higher.

Lady's Almanac, 1854 . . . . **$45.00**
Mobil, 1945, Flying Red Horse on
   cover **38.00**
Shaker Almanac, 1884, colorful
   covers, 32 pp. **48.00**
Velvet Joe's, 1922 . . . . **10.00**

ARCHITECTURAL ITEMS

In recent years the growing interest in and support for historic preservation has spawned a greater appreciation of the fine architectural elements which were an integral part of early building, both public and private. Where, in decades past, structures might be razed and doors, fireplace mantels, windows, etc., hauled to the dump, today all interior and exterior details from unrestorable buildings are salvaged to be offered to home restorers, museums and even builders who want to include a bit of history in a new construction project.

Barn shutter, painted wood,
   rectangular frame w/arched top
   above vertical louvers & two hinged
   horizontal louvered blinds below,
   Massachusetts, mid-19th c.,
   painted green, 34" w., 54½" h **$575.00**
Building finials, molded zinc,
   stepped shaped square plinth
   supporting a pointed beehive finial,
   American, 19th c., 24" h. (dents,
   minor losses) **259.00**
Building ornament, cast iron,
   gargoyle head w/old bluish grey
   paint, on custom-made stand, 19th
   c., 7⅝" h. **288.00**

Copper Lion's Head Ornament

Building ornament, molded copper
   figural head of a growling lion
   flanked by scrolls, late 19th c.,
   verdigris surface, minor
   imperfections, 78" w., 33" h.
   (ILLUS.) **2,645.00**

Corbel, molded copper, wide
   acanthus leaf motif against a
   curved bracket w/roundel ends & a
   molded flat back, fine verdigris,
   19th c., 30¼" h. (dents, minor
   losses) **575.00**

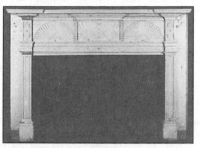

Federal Carved Fireplace Mantel

Fireplace mantel, carved & painted
   wood, Federal style, a raised panel
   of two carved fans flanked by
   recessed fans & carved & molded
   pilasters, ca. 1790, Hudson, New
   York, imperfections, 87" w.,
   62¾" h. (ILLUS.). **2,760.00**
Fireplace mantel, striped pine &
   composition, a long narrow flat
   shelf w/blocked corners over a
   stepped cornice above three
   panels, two w/spread-winged
   eagles & floral swags flanking a
   central one w/a classical scene
   depicting the flight of Athena, the
   side pilasters w/raised decoration
   of anchors & leafy scrolls over
   acanthus leaf capitals above bands
   of grapevines down the sides,
   England, late 18th c., 74½" w.,
   58¾" h. **2,990.00**
Gate, painted wood, mortise & tenon
   constructed frame w/a lattice
   design, New England, early 19th c.,
   32¼" w., 24" h. **173.00**
Gate post finial, cast iron, in the form
   of a stylized pineapple w/foliate
   designs, late 19th - early 20th c.,
   20½" h. **546.00**

Carved Wood Overdoor Ornament

Overdoor ornament, carved wood,
   carved floral design border
   centered w/ornately carved bust of

woman carrying a sheaf of wheat,
attributed to Herter Bros., 77" l.,
27" h. (ILLUS.) **2,300.00**

Roof vent, sheet metal, three-tiered
pagoda-form, signed "Joseph
Leeds, patent August 1852,"
43½" h. (corrosion, minor dents) . . **403.00**

Urns, molded copper, 19th c.,
15½" h., pr. (dents) **489.00**

ART NOUVEAU

*Art Nouveau's primary thrust was between
1890 and 1905 but commercial Art Nouveau
productions continued until about World War I.
This style was a rebellion against historic
tradition in art. Using natural forms as
inspiration, it is primarily characterized by
undulating or wave-like lines and whiplashes.
Many objects were made in materials ranging
from glass to metals. Figural pieces with
seductive maidens with long, flowing hair are
especially popular in this style. Interest in Art
Nouveau remains high with the best pieces by
well known designers bring strong prices. Also
see JEWELRY, ANTIQUE and FURNITURE.*

Bowl, silver, a round silver framework
of pierced undulating ribbed leaf-
like design w/rows of small upright
discs applied around the rim, on a
low foot & w/upright rounded
triangular end handles, Germany,
impressed marks, ca. 1900, 9" d.,
3¼" h. **$460.00**

Candelabrum, bronze, an oblong
undulating base cast w/wave-like
undulations continuing up to a
slender branch shaft flaring into
four upright stems each supporting
a tall trumpet flower candle socket,
marked "J. Preston - Chicago,"
early 20th c., 13½" l., 17¼" h. **3,850.00**

Glazed Stoneware Fireplace Surround

Fireplace surround, glazed
stoneware, three-part, w/central
section cast w/female masque

w/Medusa-like hair, flanked on
either side w/flowing stylized
leafage, glazed in shades of white,
orange, green & yellow, ca. 1902,
probably by Zavier Schoelkopf,
restorations, 52 x 9½", 46" h.
(ILLUS.) **5,750.00**

Plaque, pierced to hang, ceramic,
rectangular w/uneven tapering
knobby border, the flat center
decorated in polychrome w/an Art
Nouveau lady standing in a
landscape & holding one bunch of
flowers while sniffing another
unpicked cluster, wearing a pale
yellow gown, pale blue & moss
green background, B. Bloch & Co.,
impressed "BB" on the back &
incised "CG," 20" w., 30" h. **880.00**

Diot Mahogany & Gilt-Bronze Sideboard

Sideboard, mahogany & gilt-bronze,
the mirrored arched backsplash
above a shaped counter centering
a door opening to a shelved
interior, flanked by two short
drawers w/foliate cast gilt-bronze
pulls above open shelves, the
whole carved w/raspberries &
leafage, Diot, France, ca. 1900,
51 x 18", 39" h. (ILLUS.). **3,450.00**

Majorelle Mahogany Table

Table, mahogany, the top w/molded
edges above a long drawer, raised
on twist-carved legs, Louis
Majorelle, France, ca. 1900,
35½ x 24", 30" h. (ILLUS.) **3,737.00**

AUDUBON PRINTS

John James Audubon, American ornithologist and artist, is considered the finest nature artist in history. About 1820 he conceived the idea of having a full color book published portraying every known species of American bird in its natural habitat. He spent years in the wilderness capturing their beauty in vivid color only to have great difficulty finding a publisher. In 1826 he visited England, received immediate acclaim, and selected Robert Havell as his engraver. "Birds of America," when completed, consisted of four volumes of 435 individual plates, double-elephant folio size, which are a combination of aquatint, etching and line engraving. W. H. Lizars of Edinburgh engraved the first ten plates of this four volume series. These were later retouched by Havell who produced the complete set between 1827 and early 1839. In the 1840s, another definitive work, "Viviparous Quadrupeds of North America," containing 150 plates, was published in America. Prices for Audubon's original double-elephant folio size prints are very high and beyond the means of the average collector. Subsequent editions of "Birds of America," especially the chromolithographs done by Julius Bien in New York (1859-60) and the smaller octavo (7 x 10½") edition of prints done by J. T. Bowen of Philadelphia in the 1840s, are those that are most frequently offered for sale.

Anyone interested in Audubon prints needs to be aware that many photographically-produced copies of the prints have been issued during this century for use on calendars or as decorative accessories so it is best to check with a print expert before spending a large sum on an Audubon purported to be from an early edition.

American Beaver - Plate XLVI, hand-colored lithograph by J.T. Bowen, Philadelphia, ca. 1844, framed, 21⅞ x 28" (two short tears at right sheet edge, mat stain, faint foxing throughout) $2,070.00

American Magpie - Plate CCCLVII, hand-colored etching, engraving & aquatint by Robert Havell, Jr., London, 1827-38, framed, 25½ x 33⅝" (mat stain & a few isolated specks of foxing) 5,462.00

American Robin - Plate CXXXI, hand-colored etching, engraving & aquatint by Robert Havell, Jr., London, 1827-38, framed, 25¾ x 39⅛" (faint traces of foxing, repaired 4" tear in lower margin) . . 8,050.00

Arctic Fox - Plate CXXI, hand-colored lithograph by J.T. Bowen, Philadelphia, ca. 1847, framed, 21⅞ x 27⅞" (a few specks of foxing, tiny losses at sheet edges) . . 2,300.00

Arctic Tern - Plate CCL, hand-colored etching, engraving & aquatint by Robert Havell, Jr., London, 1823-38, 12⅜ x 19⅝" . . . **3,737.00**

Baltimore Oriole - Plate 217, hand-colored lithograph by J. Bien, New York, ca. 1859-60, framed, 22 x 31¾" (some surface soiling, occasional foxing, a few handling creases) 1,150.00

Barn Owl

Barn Owl - Plate CLXXI, hand-colored etching, engraving & aquatint by Robert Havell, Jr., London, 1823-38, framed, traces of staining in outer margins, two repaired tears at sheet edges, 25⅜ x 37½" (ILLUS.) 18,400.00

Barn Swallow - Plate CLXXIII, hand-colored etching, engraving & aquatint by Robert Havell, Jr., London, 1823-38, 26¾ x 39⅜" (few spots of foxing, outer margins w/some losses, soiling, discoloration & tears) 4,887.00

Belted Kingfisher - Plate 77, hand-colored etching, engraving & aquatint by Robert Havell, Jr., London, 1827-38, 25¼ x 38¼" (isolated specks of foxing & faint staining on verso) 11,500.00

Bemaculated Duck - Plate CCCXXXVIII, hand-colored etching, engraving & aquatint by Robert Havell, Jr., London, 1827-38, 26⅝ x 39¾" (isolated specks of foxing, minor soiling) 7,175.00

Black Vulture or Carrion Crow - Plate CVI, hand-colored etching, engraving & aquatint by Robert Havell, Jr., London, 1827-38, 26⅛" x 38¾" (light foxing, small abrasion

& pin hole to right of outstretched wing, water stains & short tears in sheet edges). **4,887.00**

Black-throated Green Warbler, Blackburnian Warbler, Mourning Warbler - Plate CCCXCIX, hand-colored engraving by Robert Havell, Jr., London, 1827-38, framed, 11⅞ x 19" (foxing) **489.00**

Blue Jay - Plate CII, hand-colored etching, engraving & aquatint by Robert Havell, Jr., London, 1827-38, 26⅜ x 39½" (minor soiling & foxing, several tears backed w/tape & losses). **10,925.00**

Blue Winged Yellow Warbler - Plate 20, hand-colored etching, engraving & aquatint by Robert Havell, Jr., London, 1827-38, 26¼ x 39⅛" (minor soiling & discoloration in margins, minor tears & nicks in extreme sheet edges) **2,587.00**

Blue-Winged Teal - Plate CCCXIII, hand-colored etching, engraving & aquatint by Robert Havell, Jr., London, 1827-38, 25⅝ x 38⅛" (short tears & 1" loss on sheet edges, minor soiling & discoloration in outer margins, stitch holes along disbound sheet edge). **11,500.00**

Boat-Tailed Grackle - Plate XCVI, hand-colored etching, engraving & aquatint by Robert Havell, Jr., London, 1827-38, 24⅞ x 38" (slightly discolored sheet w/remains of hinges on upper edge, specks of foxing) **8,625.00**

Bonaparte's Fly Catcher - Plate V, hand-colored etching, engraving & aquatint by W. H. Lizars, 26 x 39¼" (minor soiling & foxing, tears & losses in extreme edges) **1,610.00**

Brown Pelican - Plate CCCCXXI, hand-colored etching, engraving & aquatint by Robert Havell, Jr., London, 1827-38, 25½ x 38⅝" . . . **16,100.00**

Brown Titlark - Plate X, hand-colored etching, engraving & aquatint by Robert Havell, Jr., London, 1827-38, 24 x 38⅛" (offprint on verso, spot of foxing in lower margin). **690.00**

Canadian Titmouse - Plate CXCIV, hand-colored engraving by Robert Havell, Jr., London, 1827-38, full margins, framed, overall 25⅝ x 38⅞" **1,725.00**

Carolina Parrot - Plate 26, hand-colored etching, engraving & aquatint by Robert Havell, Jr.,

London , 1827-38, repaired tear on left sheet edge, minor soiling, foxing in margins, 26¼ x 39⅛" . . **51,750.00**

Carolina Pigeon - Plate 17, hand-colored etching, engraving & aquatint by Robert Havell, Jr., London, 1827-38, framed, 26⅜ x 36⅝" (short tear right sheet edge, tiny scrapes in lower margin, minor soiling in outer margins) **14,950.00**

Cedar Bird - Plate 43, hand-colored etching, engraving & aquatint by Robert Havell, Jr., London, 1827-38, framed, 25⅜ x 38⅜" (isolated specks of foxing, slightly rippled & discolored in outer sheet margins). . **4,887.00**

Children's Warbler - Plate 35, hand-colored etching, engraving & aquatint by Robert Havell, Jr., London, 1827-38, 26⅜" x 39⅜" (minor soiling & discoloration to outer margins, repaired tears, nicks & losses in extreme edges) **1,150.00**

Common Mouse - Plate XC, hand-colored lithograph by J.T. Bowen, Philadelphia, ca. 1846, framed, 18¾ x 23¼" (four tiny surface abrasions, slight discoloration at sheet edges, faint foxing) **3,450.00**

Florida Jay - Plate 87, hand-colored etching, engraving & aquatint by Robert Havell, Jr., London, 1827-38, 25¾ x 37" (spots of foxing in margins) **9,200.00**

Frigate Pelican - Plate CCLXXI, hand-colored etching, engraving & aquatint by Robert Havell, Jr., London, 1823-38, framed, 25¼ x 38⅜" (specks of foxing & tiny rubbed spot in upper blank area). . **8,050.00**

Great American Cock Male - Plate 1, hand-colored etching, engraving & aquatint by Robert Havell, Jr., London, 1827-38, 25¼ x 37½" (short tears & tape stains on verso, soft rippling) **23,000.00**

Great American Hen & Young - Plate VI, hand-colored etching & aquatint by W.H. Lizars, minor soiling, tiny tears in extreme shoulder, 25⅛ x 37⅞" (ILLUS. pg. 1). **13,225.00**

Great Blue Heron - Plate CCXI, hand-colored etching, engraving & aquatint by Robert Havell, Jr., London, 1823-38, trace of staining in lower margin, foxing & tiny loss at upper sheet edge, 25¼ x 38" . . **93,250.00**

Great Footed Hawk - Plate 16, hand-colored etching, engraving & aquatint w/touches of gum arabic by Robert Havell, Jr., London, 1827-38, 26¼" x 39⅛" (minor soiling & faint fox marks) **10,925.00**

Great White Heron - View Key-West - Plate CCLXXXI, hand-colored etching, engraving & aquatint by Robert Havell, Jr., London, 1823-38, framed, 25⅝ x 38" (foxing & bottom sheet edge w/minor water stains & soiling, stitch holes along disbound sheet edge) **46,000.00**

Green Black-Capt Flycatcher - Plate CXXIV, hand-colored etching, engraving & aquatint by Robert Havell, Jr., London, 1827-38, 25⅝ x 38" (faint stains, repaired tear left sheet edge, short tears at sheet edges, minor soiling in margins) **1,150.00**

Hawk Owl - Plate CCCLXXVIII, hand-colored etching, engraving & aquatint by Robert Havell, Jr., London, 1827-38, 26 x 39¼" (crease in lower right margin, small stain upper margin, foxing, tiny losses & slight discoloration to sheet edges) **4,600.00**

Hooping Crane - Plate CCXXVI, hand-colored etching, engraving & aquatint by Robert Havell, Jr., London, 1823-38, 25⅞ x 38¾" (foxing in margins & on verso, sheet rippling in margins, stitch holes along disbound edge) **57,500.00**

Key West Pigeon - Plate CLXVII, hand-colored etching, engraving & aquatint by Robert Havell, Jr., London, 1823-38, 25¾ x 37¾" (slight discoloration at sheet edges & outer side margins) **6,900.00**

Long-Legged Avocet - Plate CCCXXVIII, hand-colored etching, engraving & aquatint by Robert Havell, Jr., London, 1827-38, 25½ x 38⅛" (tiny spots of foxing, right sheet edge w/short tears & minor losses) **2,875.00**

Louisiana Water Thrush - Plate 19, hand-colored etching, engraving & aquatint by Robert Havell, Jr., London, 1827-38, 26⅛ x 38⅞" (minor soiling & discoloration in margins, short repaired tear & two small losses at bottom of sheet edge) **997.00**

Mangrove Humming Bird - Plate CLXXXIV, hand-colored etching, engraving & aquatint by Robert Havell, Jr., London, 1823-38, 26⅜ x 39¼" (soiling & discoloration to

outer edges, small tears, creases & losses, 55 mm. tear backed w/tape in left margin) **4,887.00**

Meadow Lark - Plate CXXXVI, hand-colored etching, engraving & aquatint by Robert Havell, Jr., London, 1823-38, 26" x 38¾" (specks of foxing & minor soiling at sheet edges, stitch holes along disbound edge) **27,600.00**

Night Hawk - Plate CXLVII, hand-colored etching, engraving & aquatint by Robert Havell, Jr., London, 1823-38, 26⅝ x 39⅝" (faint foxing, soft crease to lower margin, short tears to sheet edges, minor losses, soiling & minor staining) **9,775.00**

Passenger Pigeon - Plate 62, hand-colored etching, engraving & aquatint by Robert Havell, Jr., London, 1827-38, framed, 25½ x 37" (repaired tear in upper left & right margin corners, small stain in upper right margin, specks of faint foxing, stitch holes along disbound edge) **18,400.00**

Pectorial Sandpiper - Plate CCXIV, hand-colored etching, engraving & aquatint by Robert Havell, Jr., London, 1823-38, 26⅛ x 39⅜" (spots of foxing & discoloration to outer margins, stitch holes & glue remains along disbound edge) **920.00**

Pigeon Hawk - Plate 92, hand-colored etching, engraving & aquatint by Robert Havell, Jr., London, 1827-38, 26⅜ x 39¼" (a few isolated specks of foxing) . . . **3,737.00**

Purple Martin - Plate 22, hand-colored, engraving & aquatint by Robert Havell, Jr., London, 1827-38, 26⅛ x 39⅛" (slight abrasion below eye of bird at lower left, creases, minor soiling & foxing in margins, w/touches of gum arabic) **4,025.00**

Red Headed Woodpecker - Plate 27, hand-colored etching, engraving & aquatint by Robert Havell, Jr., London, 1827-38, 26⅜ x 39" (fox marks, minor soiling in margins, crease in upper right margin, tiny tears in extreme sheet edges) **5,175.00**

Ruddy Duck - Plate CCCXLIII, hand-colored engraving by Robert Havell, Jr., London, 1827-38, framed, 24⅝ x 36⅞" (scattered foxing & staining) **4,887.00**

Sea-Side Finch - Plate 93, hand-colored etching, engraving & aquatint by Robert Havell, Jr., London, 1827-38, framed, 25⅝ x 38" (colors slightly faded, surface scrapes & spots of foxing, discoloration at sheet edges) **1,725.00**

Snow Bird - Plate 13, hand-colored etching, engraving & aquatint by Robert Havell, Jr., London, 1827-38, 26⅛ x 39¼" (minor soiling, short red mark in lower right margin, several small tears in extreme sheet edges) **747.00**

Summer or Wood Duck - Plate 391 hand-colored etching, engraving & aquatint by Robert Havell, Jr., London, 1827-38, 26⅜ x 39¾" (framed, minor soiling, tape stains to edges) **3,450.00**

Summer Red Bird - Plate 44, hand-colored etching, engraving & aquatint by Robert Havell, Jr., London, 1827-38 25¾ x 37" (faint foxing & creasing, minor soiling & foxing in margins). **5,175.00**

The Bird of Washington - Plate 11, hand-colored etching, engraving & aquatint by Robert Havell, Jr., London, 1827-38, 26⅛ x 39¼" (fox marks, minor soiling, a few tiny tears & losses in extreme sheet edges) **8,050.00**

The Cougar. Male. - Plate XCVI, hand-colored lithograph by J.T. Bowen, Philadelphia, 1846, 21¼ x 27½" (short tears & minor losses at sheet edges). **2,587.00**

The Jaguar. Female. - Plate CI, hand-colored lithograph by J.T. Bowen, Philadelphia, ca. 1846, 21⅜ x 27" (repaired tear in upper margin, soft diagonal crease, stitch holes along disbound sheet edge). . **7,475.00**

Towee Bunting - Plate 29, hand-colored etching, engraving & aquatint by Robert Havell, Jr., London , 1827-38, 26¼ x 39" (tiny abrasion on right of "No. 6," minor soiling in margins, repaired tear to lower sheet, other minor tears). . . **2,587.00**

Trumpeter Swan

Trumpeter Swan - Plate CCCLXXVI, hand-colored etching, engraving & aquatint by Robert Havell, Jr., London, 1827-38, 25⅝ x 38¼", faint mottled discoloration in the sky, stitch holes along disbound sheet edge (ILLUS.) **23,000.00**

Turn-Stone - Plate CCCIV, hand-colored etching, engraving & aquatint by Robert Havell, Jr., London, 1827-38, 25 x 38" (short tear at upper sheet edge). **1,380.00**

Vigors Vireo - Plate 30, hand-colored etching, engraving & aquatint by Robert Havell, Jr., London, 1827-38, 26¼ x 38¾" (soft horizontal creasing center of sheet, minor soiling, discoloration & nicks on extreme edges) **920.00**

White Heron - Plate CCCLXXXVI, hand-colored etching, engraving & aquatint by Robert Havell, Jr., London, 1827-38, 25⅜ x 38⅛" (staining in margins, stitch holes w/associated losses along upper sheet edge) **46,000.00**

White-Breasted Black-Capped Nuthatch - Plate CLII, hand-colored etching, engraving & aquatint by Robert Havell, Jr., London, 1823-38, 26⅝ x 39½" (outer margins w/soiling & staining, creases, losses & tears). **3,737.00**

Wood Thrush - Plate 73, hand-colored engraving by Robert Havell, Jr., London, 1827-38, framed, 19⅞ x 27⅞" (backed w/paper, toning & staining to margins) **431.00**

Wood Thrush - Plate 73, hand-colored etching, engraving & aquatint by Robert Havell, Jr., London, 1827-38, 25¼ x 37½" (short tears & losses at sheet edges) **1,465.00**

Wren House - Plate LXXXIII hand-colored etching, engraving & aquatint by Robert Havell, Jr., London, 1827-38, 25½ x 38" (small stains & fox marks in outer margins, faint offprint, short tear at bottom sheet edge) **5,462.00**

Yellow Billed Cuckoo - Plate II, hand-colored etching, engraving & aquatint by W. H. Lizars, 26¾ x 39" (minor soiling, reworked title, several tears w/some repairs) . . . **4,887.00**

Yellow-Crowned Heron - Plate CCCXXXVI, hand-colored etching, engraving & aquatint by Robert Havell, Jr., London, 1827-38, framed, 26 x 38⅝", foxing, short

Yellow-Crowned Heron

tear in lower margin, slight
discoloration at sheet edges, stitch
holes along disbound sheet edge,
(ILLUS.) **17,250.00**

**Yellow-Winged Sparrow - Plate
CXXX,** hand-colored etching,
engraving & aquatint by Robert
Havell, Jr., London, 1827-38, 24⅞
x 37¾" (minor stains in margins,
remains of hinge along left sheet
edge of verso) **2,185.00**

AUTOGRAPHS

*The importance of excellent content and
superb condition cannot be stressed enough
when it comes to autograph material. Remember,
too, that it is not how famous a person is, but
rather the relative supply and demand for that
person's autograph that helps determine price
level. Values for autograph material of the major
players in all area of human endeavor continue
to rise.*

*ALS means "Autograph Letter Signed," TLS
means "Typed Letter Signed," LS means "Letter
Signed," DS means "Document Signed" and PS
means "Photograph Signed."*

Addams, Jane (1860-1935), Social
worker, founder of Chicago's Hull
House, TLS, 1 page, dated
January 19, 1909, arranges a
speaking engagement, 5 x 8" **$150.00**

Anthony, Susan B. (1820-1906),
women's suffrage reformer &
temperance advocate, LS, 1 page,
regards women's suffrage,
w/handwritten postscript, dated
November 28, 1902, 8 x 10" **675.00**

**Armstrong, Louis "Satchmo"
(1900-71),** jazz trumpeter & band
leader, signed concert program, 4
pp., November 1965, 5 x 8" **425.00**

**Astaire, Fred (1899-1987) & Rogers,
Ginger (1911-95),** Hollywood
dancing & acting duo, PS, color
reproduction of "Gay Divorcee"
poster, no date, 5 x 7" **195.00**

Barrymore, John (1882-1942), "The
Great Profile," star of film & stage,
ALS, transmits a play, ca. 1919,
1 page, 5 x 8" **235.00**

Barton, Clara (1821-1912), founder
of The American Red Cross, ALS,
discusses the Red Cross, dated
February 7, 1910, 4 pages, 8 x 10" .. **800.00**

**Bell, Alexander Graham (1847-
1922),** teacher of the deaf, inventor
of the telephone, PS, ca. 1905,
choice & rare, 108 x 166 mm. **3,200.00**

Berlin, Irving (1888-1989), composer
of "White Christmas" & "God Bless
America," signed sheet music of
"Oh! How I Hate to Get Up in the
Morning," undated, 11 x 14" **600.00**

Bonaparte, Napoleon (1769-1821),
French emperor & military
conqueror, DS, dated March 4,
1813, on vellum, grants freedom to
political prisoners, 14 x 18" **1,600.00**

**Burroughs, Edgar Rice (1875-
1950),** adventure novelist known
for Tarzan series, LS, #l page,
dated March 6, 1939, concerns a
Tarzanclub, 8 x 10" **280.00**

Carnegie, Andrew (1835-1919),
American steel magnate &
philanthropist, PS, inscribed bust
pose, dated Jan. 8, 1919, 7 x 9" ... **700.00**

Cather, Willa (1873-1947), American
novelist, author of "O Pioneers!,"
LS, dated December 4, 1943,
concerning "Death comes for the
Archbishop," 8 x 10" **850.00**

Chaplin, Charles (1889-1977), silent
film comedian, PS, half-length
pose, dated 1941, 8 x 10" **650.00**

Churchill, Winston (1874-1965),
British Prime Minister during World
War II, LS, thanks for election help,
dated June 18, 1955, 1 page,
8 x 10" **1,300.00**

Clinton, William Jefferson (1946-),
Forty-second President of the
United States, TLS, dated January

20, 1994, thanks to a
Congressman for condolences on
the death of Clinton's mother,
1 page, 8 x 10" **750.00**

Curie, Marie (1867-1934), Nobel
Prize-winning chemist who
discovered radium, LS, dated
November 5, 1922, discusses her
biography of husband Pierre, w/a
copy of the book, 1 page, 8 x 10". . **1,500.00**

Custer, George A. (1839-76),
flamboyant cavalry commander,
died at the Battle of the Little
Bighorn, ALS, dated March 31,
1875, orders a soldier's arrest,
1 page, 8 x 10" **3,750.00**

Davis, Jefferson (1808-89),
President of the Confederacy, LS,
dated March 16, 1863, to a
Confederate governor mentioning
slaves working on fortifications,
1 page, 8 x 10" **3,800.00**

Dempsey, Jack (1895-1983),
heavyweight boxing champion
known as "The Manassa Mauler,"
PS, inscribed vintage boxing pose,
undated, 5 x 7" **175.00**

Dickens, Charles (1812-70), British
novelist, DS, check made out for
five pounds, dated August 1, 1859,
1 page, 3 x 7" **600.00**

Douglass, Frederick (1817-95),
escaped slave turned writer &
Abolitionist, DS, dated April 19,
1886, 2 pages, land document
signed as recorder of deeds,
framed, 8 x 10" **550.00**

Doyle, Arthur Conan (1859-1930),
British author of the Sherlock
Holmes stories, ALS, thank you
letter, undated, 1 page, 5 x 8" **500.00**

Earhart, Amelia (1897-1937),
American aviator whose
disappearance still causes
controversy, PS, inscribed portrait,
undated, framed, 6 x 8" **1,400.00**

Edison, Thomas (1847-1931),
prolific inventor of incandescent
lighting, phonograph, talking
motion pictures, etc., DS, minutes
from a meeting of the Edison
Storage Battery Co. board of
directors, also signed by his son
Charles, dated June 30, 1926,
4 pages, 8 x 10" **700.00**

Einstein, Albert (1879-1955),
physicist who developed the
Theory of Relativity, PS, signed
twice, undated, 8 x 10" (some
damage) **1,700.00**

Eisenhower, Dwight D. (1890-1969),
Army general & thirty-fourth
President of the United States, PS,
profile pose, undated, 8 x 10" **500.00**

Emerson, Ralph Waldo (1803-82),
American essayist &
transcendental philosopher, ALS,
arranges a lecture, dated January
31, 1853, 3 pages, 5 x 8" **250.00**

Fitzgerald, F. Scott (1896-1940),
Jazz age chronicler in novels such
as "The Great Gatsby," ALS, to his
publisher w/interesting literary
comments, 1 page, ca. 1923,
8 x 10" **2,100.00**

Ford, Henry (1863-1947), pioneering
automobile manufacturer, PS, half-
length pose, undated, 8 x 10". . . . **1,300.00**

Franco, Francisco (1892-1975),
Spanish military hero & dictator,
PS, portrait in uniform, undated,
3 x 5" **500.00**

Franklin, Benjamin (1706-90),
Colonial statesman, inventor &
scientist, DS, land grant dated
June 13, 1787, 8 x 14" **6,000.00**

Freud, Sigmund (1856-1939),
Austrian father of psychoanalysis,
printed greeting w/signature, a form
note giving thanks for 80th birthday
greetings, dated May 1936, 1 page,
5 x 6" **975.00**

Frost, Robert (1874-1963), American
poet famed for rural New England
imagery, signed book "New
Hampshire," first edition, 1923,
w/dust jacket, signed & inscribed . . **450.00**

Gable, Clark (1901-60), Hollywood
leading man, DS, check made out
to Pacific Telephone and
Telegraph, dated April 20, 1950,
1 page, 3 x 8" **325.00**

Gandhi, Mahatma (1869-1948),
father of modern India, ALS,
requests an inverview, dated April
10, 1931, 2 pages, 5 x 8" (some
defects) **800.00**

Garbo, Greta (1906-90), silent &
talking film beauty, DS, grants
power of attorney regarding a
safety deposit box, dated
December 5, 1928, 1 page,
8 x 13" **3,000.00**

Gehrig, Lou (1903-41), New York
Yankees baseball star, signature &
inscription on hotel letterhead, ca.
1935, 5 x 8" **475.00**

Geronimo (1829-1909), Apache
warrior & leader, PS, half-length
portrait, signed horizontally in
pencil, ca. 1905, 5 x 7" **6,950.00**

Gershwin, George (1898-1937),
American composer of works such
as "Rhapsody in Blue" & "Porgy
and Bess," PS, inscribed w/first bar
from "Rhapsody in Blue" added,
undated, 11 x 15" **2,700.00**

Grant, Ulysses S. (1822-85), Union
general, eighteenth President of
the United States, DS, appointment
of a U.S. marshal, dated April 9,
1869, 1 page, 8 x 14" **1,100.00**

Greeley, Horace (1811-72), "New
York Tribune" journalist
remembered for writing "Go West,
young man," ALS, fine content
concerning writing for the
"Tribune," dated September 12,
1858, 2 pages, 5 x 8" **500.00**

Griffith, D.W. (1875-1948), silent film
director for "Birth of a Nation," etc.,
PS, shows him w/Douglas
Fairbanks & others on a film set,
signed by Fairbanks also, dated
1927 . . . . **500.00**

Hancock, John (1737-93), American
Revolutionary patriot & first signer
of the Declaration of
Independence, DS, appointing a
coroner for Essex, Massachusetts,
undated, 1 page, 9 x 14" **2,200.00**

Hemingway, Ernest (1899-1961),
American novelist famed for "The
Sun Also Rises" & "A Farewell to
Arms," PS, portrait w/journalist
Martha Gellhorn, inscribed,
ca. 1941, 10 x 13" **3,500.00**

Hitler, Adolf (1889-1945), notorious
German Third Reich leader, DS,
promotion of an SS officer, dated
January 30, 1936, 1 page,
8 x 10" **1,700.00**

Holiday, Billie (1915-50), jazz
vocalist virtuoso, PS, inscribed
close-up portrait, undated,
archivally framed, 8 x 10" **1,500.00**

**Holmes, Oliver Wendell, Jr. (1842-
1935),** U.S. Supreme Court
associate justice, brief ALS, thank
you note for a gift of apples, dated
December 25, 1926 . . . . **750.00**

Houston, Sam (1793-1863), Texas
patriot, military commander,
president of Republic of Texas,
U.S. Senator, ALS, recommends
an envoy from Republic of Texas to
U.S., dated December 10, 1836,
1 page, 8 x 14" **2,600.00**

Hugo, Victor (1802-85), French
novelist, ALS, explains that he
cannot read English, 1 page, 5 x 8"
(some defects) **450.00**

Jefferson, Thomas (1743-1826),
third President of the United
States, author of The Declaration
of Independence, scientist,
statesman, inventor, DS, land grant
for tract in New York state, co-
signed by James Madison, on
vellum, dated January 20, 1809,
1 page, 9 x 14" **1,900.00**

Kennedy, Jacqueline (1929-94),
First Lady, ALS, thanking a
journalist for a book sent to her
ailing husband, dated December
1954, 2 pages, 5 x 8" **800.00**

Kennedy, John F. (1917-63), thirty-
fifth President of the United States,
TLS, thanks a campaign volunteer
for help in recent election, dated
November 30, 1956, 1 page,
8 x 10" **650.00**

King, Martin Luther, Jr. (1929-68),
assassinated Civil Rights crusader,
TLS, agreeing to appear on "Meet
The Press," dated March 29, 1957,
1 page, 8 x 10" **1,600.00**

Kipling, Rudyard (1865-1936),
English author of "The Jungle
Book", "Captains Courageous",
etc., ALS, discusses a visit to a
spa, dated March 11, 1910,
2 pages **500.00**

**Laurel, Stan (1890-1965) & Hardy,
Oliver (1892-1957),** famous
American comedy film duo, PS,
inscribed by both, undated, 5 x 7" . . **600.00**

Lee, Robert E. (1807-70), leading
military commander of the
Confederacy, PS, carte-de-visite
portrait by Matthew Brady, signed
& inscribed, dated September
1866, 3 x 4" (some damage) **4,500.00**

Lincoln, Abraham (1809-65),
sixteenth President of the United
States, LS, responds to an
autograph request, dated
September 17, 1860, 1 page,
5 x 8" **5,000.00**

Lincoln, Mary Todd (1818-82), First
Lady, ALS, recommends someone
for a job, undated, 2 pages,
6 x 8" **3,250.00**

Lindbergh, Charles A. (1902-74),
American aviator, made first solo
transatlantic flight in 1927, PS,
shown standing beside the "Spirit
of St. Louis," dated December 9,
1927, 7 x 9" **1,700.00**

Liszt, Franz (1811-86), Hungarian
composer & pianist, ALS, nice
music content, undated, 1 page,
5 x 7" **1,125.00**

Louis, Joe (1914-81), heavyweight boxing champion known as "The Brown Bomber," PS, signed front cover of "Boxing" magazine, November 1971, 8 x 10" **120.00**

Marx Brothers: Groucho (1890-1977), Chico (1891-1961), Harpo (1893-1964), zany film comedy team, PS, signed by all three & inscribed by Groucho, ca. 1939, 5 x 7" **550.00**

Masterson, Bat (1853-1921), American frontier lawman, legal document for sale of lot in Dodge City, Kansas **11,110.00**

Melville, Herman (1819-91), American novelist, author of "Moby Dick," ALS, discusses sales of his early book "Omoo" in England, dated March 31, 1847, 3 pages, 8 x 10" **11,000.00**

Miller, Glenn (1904-44), Big Band leader & trombonist, PS, undated, 8 x 10" **575.00**

Mitchell, Margaret (1900-49), author of "Gone With the Wind," TLS, nice personal content, dated June 30, 1942, 1 page, 8 x 10" **1,250.00**

Monet, Claude (1840-1926), French Impressionist painter, ALS, regrets he has too much work to do, dated October 25, 1916, 3 pages, 5 x 8" **1,500.00**

Monroe, Marilyn (1926-62), American actress & sex symbol, signature on an album page in red pencil, undated, 4 x 5" **900.00**

Morgan, John Pierpont (1837-1913), American banker & financial giant, ALS, consents to serve on a committee, dated November 22, 1882, 1 page, 8 x 10" **1,300.00**

Morse, Samuel F.B. (1791-1872), American painter & inventor of the telegraph, ALS, angry about demands to lower telegraph rates, dated June 6, 1860, 4 pp, 5 x 8" . . **3,250.00**

Nightengale, Florence (1820-1910), English nursing pioneer & hospital reformer, ALS, congratulates a friend on a new hospital job, dated November 19, 1884, 2 pp, 5 x 7". . . **525.00**

Nixon, Richard M. (1913-95), thirty-seventh President of the United States, PS, undated, 8 x 10" **140.00**

Pasteur, Louis (1822-95), French chemist, ALS, mentions rabies, w/envelope, dated February 7, 1884, 2 pages, 5 x 8" **3,750.00**

Patton, George S. (1885-1945), famed World War II American general, TLS, discusses the war in China & his inaction in Europe w/another general, dated July 3, 1944, 1 page, 8 x 10" **3,000.00**

Picasso, Pablo (1881-1973), noted Spanish painter & sculptor, PS, shows him w/one of his sculptures, undated, 8 x 10" **1,100.00**

Presley, Elvis (1935-77), Rock & Roll king, signed program, Las Vegas Hilton Showroom, w/his portrait, 1971 . . . . **450.00**

Rochne, Knute (1888-1931), Notre Dame football coach, PS, group portrait of a Notre Dame football team, signed by them all, 1924, 5 x 7" **1,700.00**

Rockefeller, John D. (1839-1947), American industrialist, president of Standard Oil, DS, Standard Oil Trust stock certificate, dated February 24, 1883, 8 x 12" **1,300.00**

Rockwell, Norman (1894-1978), noted American artist & illustrator, PS, color reproduction of the painting "Three Umpires," undated, 4 x 6" **270.00**

Rogers, Will (1879-1935), American actor, humorist & homespun philosopher, PS, undated, 6 x 8" . . **700.00**

Rommel, Erwin (1891-1944), German World War II tank commander known as "The Desert Fox," DS, recommends a military decoration for three soldiers, dated September 9, 1941, 2 pages, 8 x 10" **900.00**

Roosevelt, Eleanor (1884-1962), First Lady, diplomat & humanitarian, TLS, thanks for condolences on the death of a relative, dated October 4, 1941, 1 page, 5 x 8" **140.00**

Roosevelt, Franklin D. (1882-1945), thirty-second President of the United States, PS, undated, 9 x 11" **800.00**

Roosevelt, Theodore (1858-1919), twenty-sixth President of the United States, PS, dated 1902, 8 x 12" **950.00**

Ruth, George H. "Babe" (1895-1948), New York Yankees baseball home run king, PS, undated, 7 x 9" **1,700.00**

Sandburg, Carl (1878-1967), American poet & Lincoln biographer, brief TLS, friendly note to a Lincoln scholar, dated December 28, 1939, 1 page, 3 x 5" **95.00**

Schweitzer, Albert (1875-1965), French physician, philosopher & humanitarian, PS, inscribed in French, undated, 5 x 8" **225.00**

Sheridan, Philip H. (1831-88), famed Union cavalry commander, LS, declines to attend a G.A.R. reunion, dated January 11, 1883, 2 pages, 8 x 10" **300.00**

Sherman, William T. (1820-91), Union Civil War general famous for his "March to the Sea," PS, undated, 4 x 8" **1,100.00**

Sousa, John Philip (1854-1932), band leader & composer of famous marches, PS, inscribed to composer Carrie Jacobs Bond, dated 1928, 8 x 10" **650.00**

Steinbeck, John (1902-68), Nobel Prize-winning American novelist, ALS, concerns "The Grapes of Wrath" being banned in one California county, dated August 28, 1939, 1 page, 9 x 11" **1,900.00**

Thoreau, Henry David (1817-62), author of "Walden," a record of his life at Walden Pond, ALS, asks publisher to send a copy of "Walden" to a friend, dated August 11, 1854, 1 page, 5 x 8" **7,500.00**

Tolstoy, Leo (1828-1910), Russian novelist & philospher, PS, dated September 28, 1904, 8 x 10" (some defects) **800.00**

Twain, Mark (1835-1910), American humorist & novelist, signature, dated July 1883, matted & framed, 9 x 13" . . **600.00**

Victoria, Alexandrina (1819-1901), long-reigning British monarch, DS, grants a pardon to a thief, dated May 5, 1863, 2 pages, 9 x 14" **400.00**

Washington, George (1732-99), first President of the United States, DS, Revolutionary War discharge paper, dated June 9, 1783, 8 x 11" (some defects) **6,500.00**

Wayne, John (1907-79), film star cowboy & war films, PS, inscribed portrait, dated 1970, 8 x 10" **550.00**

Webster, Daniel (1782-1852), versatile American statesman, DS, check payable for $50, dated December 15, 1832, 1 page **85.00**

Wilson, Ellen (1860-1914), first wife of President Woodrow Wilson, A.L.S., letter expressing her consideration of the President's feelings, dated 1913 . . . . **900.00**

Wright, Frank Lloyd (1867-1959), architect who championed the "Prairie School" style, PS, nicely inscribed, dated August 24, 1950, 11 x 14" . . **1,200.00**

Wright, Wilbur (1867-1912) & Orville (1871-1948), bicycle manufacturing brothers credited w/first motor-powered airplane flight, PS, group portrait & inscribed by Wilbur only, rare, ca. 1910 . . . **6,000.00**

Wright, Wilbur (1867-1912) & Orville (1871-1948), bicycle manufacturing brothers credited w/first motor-powered airplane flight, PS, shows the first flight at Kitty Hawk, signed by Orville only, undated, 4 x 5" **2,000.00**

Young, Brigham (1801-77), Joseph Smith's successor as head of the Morman Church, DS, promissory note for $1, dated January 20, 1849, 2 x 3" **475.00**

AUTOMOTIVE COLLECTIBLES

Also see ADVERTISING ITEMS and CANS & CONTAINERS

Ashtray, "Allstate," tire-form, glass & rubber balloon-style, outside rubber tire w/glass center, 5⅜" w., 2¼" h. . . **$11.00**

Attendant's shirt, "Phillips 66," white w/emblem above left pocket, red trim above both pockets, size 14, 14½" (some soiling). **22.00**

Banner, "Esso," cloth, depicts red-gloved hands holding can marked "Esso Motor Oil Unexcelled," reads "Change Now!" in white lettering, all on navy blue background, 64" w., 33" h. (soiling & wrinkles) **127.00**

Banner, "Winter Richlube," cloth, reads "Safety, Instant Lubrication at Zero and Below, Winter Richlube 100% Pure Pennsylvannia Motor Oil," marked "Sweeney Litho Co. Belleville N.J.," white & yellow lettering on navy blue background, 70" w., 36" h. **198.00**

Blotter, "Texaco," heavy paper, depicts race car driver, older model race car & two attendants & reads "Under The Rack And Strain Of Racing Wise Drivers Use Texaco Motor Oil, Protect Your Car The Same Way, Brennen & Canney, 124 Market Street Lowell, Mass.," 6" w., 3" h. **187.00**

Cigarette lighter, "Husky," pocket-size, metal w/emblem, lettering & dog above "Husky," 1½" w., 2¼" h... **83.00**

Cigarette lighter, "Mobil Oil," desk-top style, clear plastic panels w/red Pegasus horse, brass component, 2" w., 3½" h. **93.00**

Cigarette lighter, "Buick," metal, car-form desk-top model, pull hood ornament to open, made in Occupied Japan, loose headlight & grill, 5" l., 1¾" h. **165.00**

Crown Gas Pump

Gas pump, "Crown," Model No. 117, Pump No. 20-5531, original round white glass globe marked "Crown" in red letters, white body marked w/"Fry" decal, red base, completely restored (ILLUS.) **1,650.00**

Gas pump, "Essolene," No. 711, red metal body, round globe, all original parts (holes in globe, paint loss & wear). **770.00**

Gasoline pump globe, "Clark," round white milk glass w/painted orange, black & white "Clark" emblem, 13½" d. **270.00**

Gasoline pump globe, "Esso," round, milk glass lens w/"Esso, Extra (logo emblem) Extra," red low profile body, marked "Made in Canada," 16" d. (some fading to lens). **385.00**

Figural Crown Pump Globe

Gasoline pump globe, figural crown-shaped, milk glass crown painted in gold design, metal base, minor paint loss at top, 16" w., 16½" h. (ILLUS.). **413.00**

Ford Pump Globe

Gasoline pump globe, "Ford," round milk glass, marked "Ford (winged-logo) Service" in black, metal base, repainted, 16" w., 16½" h. (ILLUS.) **4,950.00**

Gasoline pump globe, "Frontier," round three-piece milk glass, black horse & rider on white background above, "Frontier, Rarin' - To - Go" in white lettering on red background below, 14" d. (soiling) .. **990.00**

Gasoline pump globe, "Gulf," round one-piece milk glass w/"Gulf" in navy lettering on orange backgound w/navy trim, metal base, 16" w., 18" h. (fading to lens) .. **495.00**

Guyler Pump Globe

Gasoline pump globe, "Guyler" round glass, marked "High-Tech Guyler Brand Gasoline" in white lettering on red background, red ripple body, 13½" d. (ILLUS.).... **2,178.00**

Gasoline pump globe, "Indian Gas," round, three-piece white glass, "Indian" above & "Gas" below in blue lettering, red center circle, metal base, 13½" d. **770.00**

Gasoline pump globe, "Loreco," round, marked "Loreco Gas" in red lettering around "Ethyl" emblem, low profile light yellow metal body, 15" d. **495.00**

Gasoline pump globe, "Mobil," round, milk glass lens w/"Mobil Kerosene" below Pegasus, high profile white metal body, 16½" d. (paint loss & wear to body, slight rust to base) **770.00**

Gasoline pump globe, "Red Star," round, milk glass lens painted "Red Star Valvoline Gasoline" in black lettering, high profile black base (base repainted) **1,430.00**

Gasoline pump globe, "Richfield," round, milk glass lens painted "Richfield, Hi-Octane" in black lettering below, bird logo above, black painted low profile metal body, 15" d. (paint chipping & rust to body) **770.00**

Gasoline pump globe, "Shell," milk glass in figural shell shape, "Shell" w/red decal lettering, marked "Property of Shell Mex & BP

Limited/2-4-53" inside base, 19½ " w., 20" h. (dime-size chip on reverse side base). **770.00**

Gasoline pump globe, "Sinclair," round, milk glass w/wide body, marked "Sinclair, Marine, Gasoline" in orange & green lettering, scratches, 13½" d. **523.00**

Gasoline pump globe, "Sinclair," round one-piece milk glass w/black striped center, outer rim marked "Sinclair Gasoline" in white lettering on painted black background, 16" w., 16" h. (fading & paint loss to sides). **847.00**

Gasoline pump globe, "Spur Gas," round milk glass, navy train gas tank marked "Spur Gas" w/"Spur" above & "Gasoline" below in painted red lettering, 13½" d. (some paint chipping) **1,485.00**

Gasoline pump globe, "Sterling," round, wide white globe w/"Sterling Gasoline" in black lettering on gold background, "A Quaker State Product" on affixed porcelain sign above, lens 13½" d., sign 16½" w., 5" h. **825.00**

Gasoline pump globe, "Stoll's," round, marked "Stoll's" above & "Gasoline" below arrow marked "Golden Tip," painted canary yellow high profile body, 15½" d. (repainted body, reverse lens cracked). **550.00**

Gasoline pump globe, "Texaco," round milk glass, "Texaco" above Texaco star w/black circle trim, wide body, marked "B-57", 14" d. ... **715.00**

Gasoline pump globe, "Vickers," round, lens w/"Vickers" & "V" logo, red plastic body, 13½" h. **468.00**

Grease can, "Sambo Axle Grease" above face of black man & "Nourse Oil Co., Kansas City, Mo., Business Is Good," black lettering on white label w/checkerboard wrap, tin w/contents, 3½" d., 4½" h. (dents, fading, paint chipping, rust & soiling) **198.00**

Hand cleaner tin, "Cleanzum," painted orangish yellow tin, depicts "Bucky" character w/mask & red attendant hat on lid & round, White & Bagley Co., 3" d., 2½" h. **1,540.00**

Hood ornament, "Mustang," metal, painted dark red Mustang on primitive cylindrical capped base, 7½" h. (denting & rust at bottom) ... **55.00**

License plate, 1915, California, porcelain **50.00**

License plate attachment, "Boston Police," porcelain, one-sided cylindrical form, outer circle marked "Police" above & "Boston" below in red lettering on white background, black center marked "CD" in white diamond w/"Mass." below, 4" w., 5¼" h. (small chips to edge) **50.00**

License plate attachment, "Chamber of Commerce" above & "Pittsburgh" below in black lettering on gold background in oval, "Safety League" in white lettering on black background below oval, one-sided porcelain, 4" w., 5½" h. (chips to edge & mounting hole) **66.00**

License plate attachment, "Jaguar," embossed metal, oval-shaped w/crown on top & jaguar cat in center, marked "Jaguar Clubs" above & "Of North America, Inc." below, 4" w., 5½" h. **28.00**

License plate attachment, "Mobil," embossed tin, red Pegasus above, "Drive Safely" on band below, 6½" w., 5⅜" h. (some scratches & soiling) **143.00**

License plate attachment, "Harold's Club," one-sided die-cut metal, depicts man walking in front of oxen pulling covered wagon reading "Harold's Club or bust! Reno, Nevada," scratches & minor denting, 13¾" w., 8" h. **61.00**

Lubricant dispenser, "Socony," metal & glass top dispencer, red base w/Socony logo & "SAE 50" decals, 9½" w., 16" deep, 47" h. . . . **495.00**

Lubricant oil can, "Texaco," tin, "Texaco Home Lubricant (Texaco star logo) The Texaco Company" in label on green background, long pointed nozzle, 2½" d., 6⅛" h. (denting, scratches & soiling) **479.00**

Lubricant oil can, "Shell," cone-shaped tin, "Golden Shell" logo above "Shell Oil," yellow background, 6½" w. base, 11" h., qt. (scratches overall, missing top) . . **176.00**

Map, "Michelin" map of Ireland, tin, reproduction Michelin Map No. 986, 25" w., 34½" h. (scratches) **55.00**

Mechanical pencil, "Mopar," metal & plastic, includes parts & accessories, "Allied Motors, Inc. 7500 Kansas City, Mo," piston floats in oil, 5½" l. **55.00**

Monogram Car Kit

Monogram kit, paper decals in wooden box, ornamental borders, includes lodge emblems & letters, soiling & water stain, 12⅜" w., 10" deep, 1⅝" h. (ILLUS.) **154.00**

Motor oil can, "Ace High," tin, orange wrap w/navy, orange & white label depicting a motor car & airplane in clouds, minor denting & soiling, qt., 4" d., 5½" h. **523.00**

Motor oil can, "Black Bear," tin, depicts black bear beside "Black Bear Motor Oil, SHDX 10W-30," black lettering on deep orange background, dents & scratches, five gal., 11" d., 16" h. **72.00**

Motor oil can, "Husky," tin, depicts jumping Husky on yellow background below "Husky Heavy Duty Motor Oil," marked "Western Oil & Fuel Company Minneapolis, Minnesota," qt., 4" d., 5½" h. (denting, scratches & rust spotting at top & bottom) **413.00**

Motor oil can, "Mobiloil," white label w/"Gargoyle"(motif of gargoyle) above "Mobiloil 'B' Extra Heavy," made by Vacuum Oil Company, New York, U.S.A., qt., 3½" d., 7½" h. (scratches, soiling & denting) . . . **154.00**

Motor oil can, "Pennzoil," yellow tin, "Pennzoil Lubricates All Transcontinental Streamliners," depicts transcontinental streamline w/three owls on back w/largest owl wearing conductor's hat, qt., 4" d., 5½" h. (denting & scratches) **360.00**

Motor oil can, "Red Indian," tin, red American Indian in full headdress on white background above, "Red Indian Motor Oil" in white lettering on red band below, five qt., 6½" d., 9½" h. (scratches) **193.00**

Motor oil can, "Texaco," tin, gold wrap w/ "Texaco, Synthetic Aircraft, Turbine Oil, 35" & orange & black logo, qt., 4" d., 5½" h. (denting & scratches) **220.00**

Motor oil can, "Texaco," tin, green w/"Texaco 574 Oil" above Texaco star logo, made by The Texas Company, Port Arthur, Texas, minor scratches & denting, qt., 3¾" d., 6¼" h. **121.00**

Motor oil can, "Workingman's Friend," green tin, depicts worker w/hard hat & tool box on white background, 4" d., 5½" h., qt. (denting, scratches & soiling) **204.00**

Motor oil rack, "Imperial," eight clear quart bottles marked "Hep" above decaled logo, each w/metal screw-on nozzles, wire-rack carrier w/handle, 17½" w., 9" d., 15½" h., the set (soiling, wear tops) **303.00**

Navigator tin, "Michelin," cylindrical, depicts Michelin man smoking, white design on red background, 1¼" d., 5½" h. **105.00**

Padlock, "Socony Mobil Oil Co. Inc. Padlock," metal w/debossed lettering, marked "WB 620," 1½" w., 2½" h, (no key) **39.00**

Padlock, "Sinclair," metal, embossed lettering, marked "WB 622," 2" w., 3" h. (some scratches, no key) **11.00**

Pennant, "Gilmore (head of lion) Lion Head Motor Oil," paper, red background w/printing on both sides, marked "Permit No. 232," 10" w., 21" h. **468.00**

Pin, "Mobiloil," metal, Pegasus horse design w/clear coating, 1⅛" w., 7⅛" h. **176.00**

Pin, "Shell Oil," metal, seashell-shaped, silver, 1" w., 1" h. **11.00**

Pin, "Sunoco," celluloid over metal, round, depicts lamb jumping over fence, reads "Change Over Now!" above & "to summer Oil and Grease Sunoco" below **132.00**

Pin, "Texaco," metal cloisonné design in Texaco Oil Company star logo, round, ⅞" h. **176.00**

Poster, "Quaker State," paper, depicts police officer w/whistle directing traffic & reads "Keep 'Em Rolling..., Change Now To Quaker State Motor Oil For Summer Driving," some soiling **66.00**

Program, "Indianapolis Speedway," 1926, front reads "Official Program Indianapolis Motor Speedway Company" below picture of driver, car & tower, includes advertisements from Coca-Cola, Richfied, Lockhead, Delco,

Polarine, Sinclair, Auburn, Olzum, Chrysler & others, black, white & orange pages (tears & soiling) **176.00**

Radiator cap, "Chevrolet," cast metal, oblong, bust of woman holding figural plane & medallion w/Chevrolet insignia & "Quota Trophy" on front, marked "October 1927" on side, wooden base, 6" w., 4" h. (repainted, some minor cracking) **330.00**

Salesman sample kit, "Gulf," metal box containing lighter fluid, household lubricant, rejuvenator, preservers, electric motor oil, penetrating oil & insect killer samples, all w/Gulf colors & logo (missing one can, some scratching). . **275.00**

Salt & pepper shakers, "Conoco", plastic, gas pump shape w/orange Conoco logo on white background, black base, marked "Primary Oil Company New London Iowa" on back, 1" w., ¾" d., 2¾" h. pr. **50.00**

Salt & pepper shakers, "Mobilgas," plastic, gas pump shape w/Mobiloil logo, one w/red background & one w/red & white background, marked "Basha's Service Station Main St. Westminister, Mass. Tel Tr. 4-9977," 1" d., 2¾" h., pr. (overall soiling) **99.00**

Salt & pepper shakers, "Phillips 66," plastic, gas pump shape, orange w/black base & Phillips 66 logo, marked "Compliments of Key City Oil Co. Mankato, Minn." on back, in original box, 1" w., 1"d., 2¾" h., pr. (wear to box) **61.00**

Aeroshell Sign

Sign, "Aeroshell," one-sided die-cut porcelain, reads "Aeroshell Lubricating Oil Stocked Here" below seashell w/wings, minor chipping to edges, 38" w., 10¾" h. (ILLUS.) **3,850.00**

Sign, "Boyce Moto Meter," painted metal cut-out depicts woman in red dress & hat pointing to emblem, reads "Boyce Moto Meter

Authorized Service Station" in white & red lettering on black background, rare, 21" w., 18¾" h. (some fading & paint chipping). . . **1,980.00**

Sign, "Esso," circular metal sign w/cast-iron base, curb-side style, "Aviation Products" in white lettering on black background below "Esso" logo on obverse, "Stand Clear" in white lettering on red backgound above "Esso" logo on reverse, black base, marked "A22124-38," scratching & soiling, 24" w., 62" h. **1,100.00**

Sign, "Indian Gasoline," one-sided porcelain painted in green, orange, navy blue, yellow & white Indian design, 10¼" w., 18" h. **303.00**

Sign, "Michelin," one-sided porcelain, rectangle tapering to point at bottom, green center circle depicts "Michelin Man" on tractor, reads "Michelin" in black lettering at top, yellow background, marked "Email, Koek, TP 8141.99.65," 18¼" w., 24¼" h. **330.00**

Sign, "Mobil," one-sided die-cut porcelain, painted red Pegasus horse, 54" hoof to wing. **1,100.00**

Sign, "Mobiloil," porcelain, marked "Gargoyle (motif of gargoyle), Mobiloil, A,' Vacuum Oil Company Ltd" in orange & navy blue on white background, 11¼" w., 9" h. **403.00**

Mother Penn Motor Oil Sign

Sign, "Mother Penn," two-sided porcelain painted in red, white & blue, depicts elderly woman in circle above, "1879 Mother Penn 1979, All Pennsylvania, Motor Oil, Dryer Clark & Dryer Oil Co." in rectangle below, scratches, 8½" w., 5¾" h. (ILLUS.) **523.00**

Sign, "Pennzoil," curb-side style, "Supreme Pennsylvania Quality Pennzoil (brown bell) Safe Lubrication" on two-sided porcelain, cast-iron base & lollipop, 20" w., 5" h. **935.00**

Sign, "Pure-Pep," one-sided porcelain, reads "Pure-Pep, (logo), Be sure with Pure" in navy blue & orange on white background, orange trim, marked "I.R., 46-712," 10" w., 12" h. (scratches) **60.00**

Sign, "Sunoco Motor Oil," one-sided porcelain, marked "Mercury Made, Sunoco, Motor Oil" in black lettering on painted yellow background, 10" w., 12" h. **495.00**

Sign, "Texaco," porcelain, cylindrical, reads "Texaco" above star logo on white background, marked "Made in U.S.A./3-5-61," (scratches & small chips to edges). **825.00**

Thermometer, "Champion Dependable Spark Plugs," wooden, oblong w/upper half spark plug shape, black lettering, 5⅛" w., 11½" h. **121.00**

Thermometer, "Shell Gasoline, Shell Motor Oil," porcelain, oblong, yellow background w/red trim & lettering, marked "Pat. Mar. 16, 1915.," 7" w., 77" h. **3,750.00**

Thermometer, "Shellzone Anti-Freeze," metal & wood, oblong, marked "Shellzone Anti-Freeze Permanent Type" above w/Shell logo below, yellow lettering on orange background, 3" w., 17" h. (scratches & soiling, minor rust on back) **176.00**

Thermometer, "Veedo Motor Oil," porcelain, rectangular, marked "le film de protection" in white lettering above, Veedo logo below, all on red background, (fading, chipping, soiling & loss of luster) **176.00**

Tire inflator, "Eco," red metal casing, chrome-trimmed glass on front, reads "Air (meter numbers) Eco Tireflator," restored, 9" w., 10" deep, 16½" h. **468.00**

Tire inflator island, "Eco," service-station type, white over-head lamp w/upright red cast-iron body, glassed-front meter reads "AIR," 98" h. (restored) **2,420.00**

Watch, "Shell," Swiss pocket-style, metal & plastic, promotional prize, ca. 1940, 1¼" d. (missing original fob & chain) **330.00**

Water can, "Mobilgas," metal, red w/Mobilgas logo in circle, 23" w., 17" h. (professionally restored) **110.00**

BABY MEMENTOES

Everyone dotes on the new baby and through many generations some exquisite and unique gifts have been carefully selected with a special infant in mind. Collectors now seek items from a varied assortment of baby mementoes, once tokens of affection to the newborn babe.

Carriage, w/three glazed windows & fold down landau top, black w/yellow trim, piping, raised on curvi-linear springs w/delicate spoked wheels, ca. 1870, S.H. Kimball, Boston, MA., 40" l. (some cracking to leather top) **$460.00**

Early Baby Carriage

Carriage, three wheels, wicker sides, wooden tongue-type handles, wooden wheels on wood & iron base, 30 x 62" (ILLUS.) **173.00**

Convertible Highchair

Highchair, convertible up & down-type, Eastlake style rattan seat in back, iron wheels (ILLUS.) **288.00**
Rattle, celluloid, round, painted face w/moving eyes, atop handle w/ring, original case **81.00**

Child's Wicker Stroller

Stroller, three wheels, wicker w/canvas top, iron handles, 32 x 39" (ILLUS.) **69.00**

BANKS

Original early mechanical and cast-iron still banks are in great demand with collectors and their scarcity has caused numerous reproductions of both types and the novice collector is urged to exercise caution. The early mechanical banks are especially scarce and some versions are seldom offered for sale but, rather, are traded with fellow collectors attempting to upgrade an existing collection. Numbers before mechanical banks refer to those in John Meyer's Handbook of Old Mechanical Banks. *However, another book* Penny Lane—A History of Antique Mechanical Toy Banks, *by Al Davidson, provides updated information and the number from this new volume is indicated in parenthesis at the end of each mechanical bank listing.*

In past years, our standard reference for cast-iron still banks was Hubert B. Whiting's book Old Iron Still Banks, *but because this work is out of print and a beautiful new book,* The Penny Lane Bank Book—Collecting Still Banks *by Andy and Susan Moore pictures and describes numerous additional banks, we will use the Moore numbers as a reference preceding each listing and indicate the Whiting reference in parenthesis at the end. The still banks listed are old and in good original condition with good paint and no repair unless otherwise noted. An asterisk (*) indicates this bank has been reproduced at some time.*

MECHANICAL

2 **Afghanistan,** cast iron
   (PL 3) **$2,587.00**

4 **(I) Always Did 'Spise a Mule,**
   cast iron, on bench (PL 250). . **2,070.00**

5 **(I) Always Did 'Spise a Mule,**
   cast iron, riding mule,
   (PL 251) **1,495.00**

217 **American Bank,** cast iron,
   semi-mechanical, model of a
   sewing machine (PL 9) **5,175.00**

6 **Artillery - Square Block**
   House, cast iron, some wear to
   cannon & soldier (PL 11) **690.00**

12 **Bear - Paws Around Tree**
   Stump cast iron (PL 30) **575.00**

Boy and Bulldog Bank

64 **Boy and Bulldog,** cast iron,
   PL 49 (ILLUS.) **1,725.00**

Boy Robbing Bird's Nest Bank

20 **Boy Robbing Bird's Nest,** cast
   iron, replaced trap, PL 51
   (ILLUS.). **8,050.00**

21 **Boy Scout Camp,** cast iron,
   replaced arms & flag detached
   (PL 52) **4,600.00**

22 **Boys Stealing Watermelons,**
   cast iron (PL 53) **3,306.00**

Rare Bread Winners Bank

24 **Bread Winners,** cast iron, one
   small casting flaw, PL 54
   (ILLUS.). **28,750.00**

33 **Cabin,** cast iron, trap missing,
   small crack on side (PL 93) **632.00**

35 **Called Out Bank,** cast iron,
   soldier standing on top of
   pyramid, J. & E. Stevens Co.,
   Connecticut,ca. 1900
   (PL 95) **11,500.00**

42 **Chief Big Moon,** cast iron,
   repair on Indian (PL 108) **1,150.00**

47 **Circus,** cast iron, paint worn,
   trap & crank replaced (PL 114). . **5,980.00**

119 **Clown,** Harlequin and
   Columbine, cast iron, recast
   (PL 121) **6,325.00**

Coin Registering Bank, cast iron,
   dome-topped building, replaced
   rear door (PL 129). **2,300.00**

53 **Creedmore - Soldier Aims**
   Rifle at Target in Tree Trunk,
   cast iron, crack on leg
   (PL 137). **805.00**

57 **Dentist,** cast iron, some
   restoration (PL 152) **4,600.00**

63 **Dog - Bulldog Bank - Coin on**
   Nose, cast iron (PL 64) **8,625.00**

70 **"Dog Tray Bank,"** cast iron,
   some touch-up, tray & twist pin
   replaced (PL 130) **3,220.00**

71 **Dog - Trick,** cast iron
   (PL 481) **2,587.00**

75 **Eagle & Eaglets,** cast iron,
   green grass version (PL 165). . **2,185.00**

88 **Elephant & Three Clowns on**
   Tub, cast iron, some paint loss,
   top of clown rider possibly
   replaced (PL 170) **862.00**

"Gem" Bank, Registering, cast iron,
   ca. 1895, paper label
   w/operating instructions, base
   plate replaced, 5" l. (PL 207) . . **690.00**

Rare Giant Bank

10 Giant, cast iron, PL 212
(ILLUS.)................. **23,000.00**
117 Guessing Bank, cast iron, thin
crack on chair & base
(PL 224) **2,990.00**

Hold the Fort Bank

123 Hold the Fort, cast iron, repaint
& repair PL 240 (ILLUS.)..... **3,220.00**
129 Indian Shooting Bear, cast
iron (PL 257) **2,415.00**
138 Jonah and the Whale, cast
iron (PL 282)............. **5,175.00**
147 Lion and Monkeys, cast iron,
Kyser & Rex, ca. 1885, 9½" h.,
small monkey & trap replaced
(PL 300).................. **920.00**
66 Lost Dog, cast iron, lever-
operated (PL 308) **345.00**
153 Magic, cast iron, slight retouch
on framing trim & button, coated
w/protective sealant (PL 311) .. **805.00**
140 Mama Katzenjammer, cast
iron, paintworn, trap replaced
(PL 317) **5,750.00**

Mammy and Child Bank

155 Mammy and Child, cast iron,
some corrosion, repaint on
head & kerchief, spoon
replaced, (PL 318) (ILLUS.) **5,463.00**

Mason Bank

156 Mason & Hod Carrier, cast
iron, break on trap plate,
(PL 321) (ILLUS.) **6,469.00**
52 Milking Cow, cast iron, thick
base & reddish brown cow
version, replaced base leg,
(PL 327) **6,900.00**
52 Milking Cow, cast iron, thin
base version w/chocolate brown
cow (PL 327) **39,100.00**
163 Monkey and Cocoanut, cast
iron (PL 332)............. **1,035.00**
166 Moody and Sanky, cast iron,
model of a house featuring the
portraits of revivalist preacher
Dwight Moody & his musical
director Ira Sanky, ca. 1870,
5"h., cornice replaced
(PL 338) **1,840.00**

168 **Mosque,** cast iron, replaced
finial & trap, professionally
repaired steps (PL 340) **690.00**

228 **Motor Bank,** cast iron,
w/keywind mechanism, some
touch-up & repairs, replaced
top trap (PL 341) **11,500.00**

169 **Mule Entering Barn,** cast iron,
trap replaced (PL 342) **920.00**

178 **Organ Bank - with Boy & Girl,**
cast iron (PL 368) **3,450.00**

177 **Organ Bank - with Monkey,
Cat and Dog,** cast iron, some
wear, crank possibly repaired
(PL 369) **690.00**

181 **Organ Grinder and Dancing
Bear,** cast iron, trap broken
(PL 372) **4,025.00**

185 **Paddy & His Pig,** cast iron
brown coat, some wear
(PL 376) **1,840.00**

186 **Panorama Bank,** cast iron,
house-shaped, some repair &
repaint to roof (PL 377) **4,600.00**

191 **Piano,** nickel-plated cast iron,
musical, clockwork, E. M.
Roche Novelty Co., Newark,
N.J., ca. 1910, 7¾" l., 5¾" h.
(PL 383) **575.00**

196 **Pony - Trick,** cast iron, some
chipping, trap missing
(PL 484) **3,162.00**

"Punch and Judy," cast iron & tin,
slight retouch on green
background, England, 7" h.
(PL 402) **5,175.00**

Queen Victoria, cast iron, w/"Jubilee
1887 God Save The Queen" on
front of the bust, "Patent No.
14197" on the right side & on
the back "Born May 24th 1819
Crowned June 20th 1837
Married Fby 10th 1840," ca.
1887, England, repaint, 9" h.
(ILLUS.). **5,750.00**

45 **Reclining Chinaman,** cast iron,
repaint, recast hands, replaced
tray (PL 410) **1,610.00**

212 **Rooster,** cast iron (PL 419) **748.00**

89 **"Royal 'Trick' Elephant
Bank,"** cast iron w/verse on
each side of base, "Put a coin in
the slot then you'll see
something funny. Press my tail
hard and I'll swallow the money"
& just beneath coin holder
"Place Coin Here," original tail,
some scuffs & minor
retouching, ca. 1910, Germany
(PL 420) **2,587.00**

214 **Santa Claus at Chimney,** cast
iron, some wear (PL 428) **1,610.00**

218 **Shoot the Chute,** cast iron
w/nickel plated boat version,
some paint loss, possible repair
on underplate (PL 441) **24,150.00**

The Smyth X-Ray Bank

Smyth X-Ray (The), nickel-plated
cast iron, PL 443 (ILLUS.). . . . **1,840.00**

Queen Victoria Bank

Speaking Dog Bank

69 Speaking Dog, cast iron,
rectangular coin trap & maroon
base variation, some paint wear
on top of base, 7" h., PL 447
(ILLUS.). **2,185.00**

Springing Cat Bank

41 Springing Cat, cast lead
w/wooden baseplate, designed
by Charles A. Bailey, patented
July 18, 1882, stress cracks
towards bottom of base, some
repair to top plate, 9" l., PL 450
(ILLUS.). **9,775.00**
222 Stump Speaker, cast iron,
replaced top plate (PL 453). . . **2,300.00**
226 Teddy and the Bear in Tree,
cast iron (PL 459) **2,300.00**

"Tommy" Bank

"Tommy" Bank, cast iron, patent
issued October 14, 1914,
registered trademark "Beatrice"
on bottom, John Harper & Co.,
Ltd., Willenhall, England,
11½" l., PL 477 (ILLUS.) **2,530.00**
230 Uncle Remus, cast iron,
replaced fence, minor touch-up
(PL 492) **4,025.00**
**231 Uncle Sam with Satchel &
Umbrella,** cast iron, 11" h.
(PL 493) **2,070.00**
235 "Uncle Tom," w/star & lapels,
cast iron, trap replaced (PL 496) . . **862.00**
233 U.S. Bank, cast iron, building
w/policeman on inside,
professionally restored, some
cracks on one side (PL 501) . . **4,025.00**
61 Watch Dog Safe, cast iron
(PL 560) **1,265.00**
237 William Tell, cast iron,
(PL 565). **862.00**
245 Zoo, cast iron (PL 576). **2,185.00**

STILL

Baby in Egg Bank

261 Baby in Egg, lead, featuring
japanned egg w/green
highlights, key locked trap,
American-made, possible
retouch on yolk,replaced trap,
7¼" h. (ILLUS.) **460.00**
717 Bear, Bear with Honey Pot,
cast iron, Hubley Mfg. Co., ca.
1936,6Z\x" h., W. 327* (minor
wear) **94.00**
74 "Billiken," on base, cast iron,
A.C. Williams Co., 1909-12,
2½" w., 4¼" h. (W. 50) **58.00**
1079 Building, Bank, "State Bank,"
roof w/arched dormers, arched
door & windows, cast iron,
Kenton Hardware, ca. 1900 &
Grey Iron Casting Co., ca.
1899, 4¼ x 5½", 6¾" h. **475.00**
1217 Building, High Rise, cast iron,
Kenton Hardware, 2⅞ x 2⅞",
5½" h. **245.00**
1179 Building (House) - Villa, two-
story building w/ornamental top
& four corner towers, cast iron,
Kyser & Rex, ca. 1894, 3 x 4⅞",
5½" h. (W. 376) **374.00**
1241 Building, Skyscraper (six
posts) w/turrets on roof, cast
iron, silver repaint, A.C.
Williams, 1900-09, 3 x 4", 6½"
h., W.411* (silver repaint, trap
missing) **138.00**
1080 Building - State Bank, cast
iron, Kenton Hardware,
ca. 1900s, 3½ x 4⅝", 5⅞" h.
(W.445) **288.00**

1049 Building, "Washington"
Monument, cast iron, A.C.
Williams, 1910-12, 2½ x 2½",
7½" h. **350.00**

5 Capitalist (The), cast iron,
American-made, ca. 1890, paint
worn, 5" h. **575.00**

1545 Clock, Gold Dollar (Eagle
Clock), tall-case style, cast iron
& steel, Arcade Mfg. Co.,
1910-13, 2¹⁵⁄₁₆ x 3½" **145.00**

615 Duck, cast iron, traces of old
gold paint, A.C. Williams,
1909-35, 4⅞" h. (W. 211) **83.00**

Eiffel Tower Bank

1074 Eiffel Tower, cast iron,
Sydenham & McOustra,
England, 1908, 8¾" h.
(ILLUS.). **1,035.00**

Electric Railroad Bank

1470 Electric Railroad, cast iron,
trolley car featuring five
windows on each side, raised
on four wheels, some
restoration, replaced figure, 8" l.
(ILLUS.) **977.00**

Fish, cast iron, marked "IFC" in
raised letters on side, gold
w/red highlights, old repaint
over green, 7" h. **575.00**

Gas Pump Bank

1485 Gas Pump, cast iron, red
w/gold globe & original Arcade
decal, missing hose, American-
made, 2⅛" sq., 5¹¹⁄₁₆" h.
(ILLUS.) **805.00**

Gingerbread House

1029 Gingerbread House, cast iron,
France (ILLUS.) **1,725.00**

508 Horse, Good Luck Horseshoe
(Buster Brown & Tige), cast
iron, Arcade, 1908-32, 4¼" h.
(W. 83) **149.00**

70 "I Luv a Copper," brass, two-
sided, featuring a smiling
woman w/pie in hand & "I Luv a
Copper" on one side, the other
features an English Bobby
(Copper) & "Every Copper
Helps," japanned finish,
England, 6" h. (PL 410). **1,323.00**

13 "King Midas," cast iron,
holding bag of "Gold," Hubley,
ca. 1930, 4½" h. (W. 47) **920.00**

234 **Laughing Clown,** lead, h.p.
clown w/oversized ears,
exaggerated nose, ruffled collar
& black fitted cap w/askew
cone-shaped hat, key-locked
trap, Germany, 3⅞" h. (some
chips, light corrosion on edge of
collar) **402.00**

754 **Lion -Tail Right,** cast iron,
worn gold paint, A.C. Williams,
1905-31, 6¼" l., 5¼" h. **72.00**

164 **Mary & Little Lamb,** cast iron,
American-made, 1902, paint
worn, screw replaced, 4⅜" h.
(W.1) **402.00**

1184 **Multiplying Bank,** cast iron, in
the form of a Gothic Revival
house w/steps leading to a
glass paneled archway
revealing an interior fitted w/two
mirrors which create the illusion
of multiplying coins, ca. 1883,
5⅛ x 5¹/₁₆", 6½" h. **5,175.00**

157 **Mutt & Jeff,** cast iron, A.C.
Williams, 1912-31, 4¼" h. (W. 13). . **135.00**

990 **Old South Church,** cast iron,
modeled after the Old South
Church in Boston,
Massachusetts, ca. 1900, 9¼" h.,
American-made (paint worn,
sealed w/protective coating,
broken window). **3,450.00**

Rocking Chair Bank

1375 **Rocking Chair,** cast iron,
American-made, ca. 1898,
6¾" h., W. 277 (ILLUS.). **805.00**

548 **Rooster,** silver, gold paint
w/red comb & wattles, cast iron,
Hubley Mfg. Co. (no date) &
A.C. Williams Co., 1910-34,
4¾" h. (W. 187)* **173.00**

890 **Safe,** "Security Safe," cast iron,
American-made, ca. 1894, 2¾ x
4⅛", 6" h. **150.00**

891 **Safe,** "Security Safe Deposit,"
cast iron, Kyser & Rex (?), ca.
1881, 2⅜ x 2 13/16", 3⅞" h. **95.00**

651 **Stork Safe,** cast iron, (thin
crack on top corner). **977.00**

109 **Taft & Sherman** cast iron,
("Smiling Jim" and "Peaceful
Bill"), mask of each back to
back, American-made, 2¾" w.,
4" h. (W. 314) **2,760.00**

"Time is Money" Clock Bank

1555 **"Time is Money" Clock,** cast
iron & tin, a tinplate clock
w/moveable hands & paper
label face marked "Time is
Money," some wear, H. C. Hart
Co., patented 1885, 5" h.
(ILLUS.) **460.00**

154 **Trust Bank (The),** figure of old
banker w/lettering on vest, cast
iron, J. & E. Stevens Co., late
19th c., 7¼" h. (W. 317) **1,610.00**

POTTERY

Model of a cat head, realistically
incised w/wide, flaring ears, white
clay w/a dark green glaze, 3" h. **275.00**

Model of a dog's head, realistically
modeled Spaniel's head, white clay
w/a dark green glaze, 2½" h. (small
flake at coin slot) **110.00**

TIN

Darky Bust, ca. 1915,
Germany (PL 148) **1,495.00**

Early Tin House Bank

Model of a house, a square two-
story home w/front portico &
steeply pitched roof centered by
a chimney, a side wing w/round
chimney to one side w/covered
porch, brick decoration, mid-
19th c., minor losses, minor
paint wear, 7" l., 7⅞" h.
(ILLUS.)................ **4,025.00**
Saluting Sailor, Germany, ca. 1910
(PL 425) **1,380.00**
**236 Weeden's Plantation Darky
Saving Bank,** Japanned
tinplate, finish loss, roof loose
(PL 562) **1,035.00**

WOODEN

Bank, carved & painted wood,
pierced cornices, egg & dart
moulding, front featuring applied
pierced oval panel incorporating
shamrock & "War Savings Bank,"
sides adorned w/figures of soldiers,
ca. 1918, 10" h. **11,500.00**
Box-form, rectangular overhanging
black-painted top w/two coin slots
& h.p. w/two coins above the
rectangular case polychrome
decorated w/a continuous
landscape depiction of Noah's Ark
& animals, conforming rectangular
black-painted base, early 20th c.,
4¹¹⁄₁₆ x 5⅝", 3⅞" h. **431.00**

BARBERIANA

*A wide variety of antiques related to the
tonsorial arts have been highly collectible for
many years, especially 19th and early 20th
century shaving mugs and barber bottles and,
more recently, razors. We are now combining
these closely related categories under one
heading for easier reference. A selection of other
varied pieces relating to barbering will also be
found below.*

BARBER BOTTLES

Amber, ovoid base w/two-ringed
neck, multicolored label-underglass
w/roses & wording "Witch-Hazel,"
tooled lip, smooth base, ca. 1885-
1925, 7⅛" h. **$187.00**
Apple green, ovoid base tapering to
a lady's leg neck, white enameled
Mary Gregory-style decoration
depicting a woman & the word
"Vegederma," rolled lip, pontil-
scarred base, ca. 1885-1925,
7⅛" h. **551.00**
Blue opaque, footed tapering
cylindrical base w/scrolling around
a plain oval slugplate, rolled lip,
smooth base, 10¼" h. **105.00**
Clear, bell-form base tapering to a
cylindrical neck, rolled lip, smooth
base, copper wheel-engraved
lettering "Checkerberry," late
19th c., 6⅝" h. **77.00**
Clear, cylindrical base w/bottom & top
rings on swollen neck, red, black &
white label-under-glass reading
"Pompeian Hair Massaage Does
Remove Dandruff," tooled lip,
smooth base, original high-top
metal stopper, ca. 1920-30, 8⅛" h. ... **231.00**

Rare Tree Bark Barber Bottle

Clear encased w/bark, tree-trunk
form, multicolored label-under-
glass depicting a pretty girl & the
word "Cologne," smooth base, late
19th c., 7¾" h. (ILLUS.).......... **770.00**

Clear shading to cobalt blue,
tapering oval base w/long neck,
raised-rib patt., cobalt coloration
near base, ground lip, smooth
base, late 19th c., 7½" h. **330.00**

Clear w/applied ruby threading,
ovoid base w/exaggerated lady's-
leg neck, ground & polished lip,
smooth lip, ca. 1920-30, 7¾" h. . . . **495.00**

Clear w/cranberry & white spatter,
square base w/long cylindrical
neck, cranberry red upper half &
white lower half, tooled mouth,
smooth base, late 19th c., 9" h. . . . **770.00**

Clear w/red, white & yellow spatter,
square base w/long cylindrical
neck, tooled lip, smooth base,
9¼" h. **605.00**

Silver Overlay Barber Bottle

Clear w/silver overlay, squatty
bulbous base w/long cylindrical
neck, tooled lip, polished pontil,
original pewter figural rabbit
stopper w/"Al" monogram on side
of neck, late 19th - early 20th c.,
6¼" h. (ILLUS.) **440.00**

Cobalt blue, bell-form base, bulbous
lower neck ring tapering to wide
upper neck, Rib patt., multicolored
enameled floral decoration, rolled
lip, pontil-scarred base, ca. 1900,
7⅝" h. **198.00**

Cobalt blue, flared bell-form w/long
cylindrical neck, Optic Rib patt.
w/yellow & gold enameled Art

Nouveau floral decoration, rolled
lip, pontil-scarred base, ca. 1900,
7⅝" h. **440.00**

Cobalt blue, ovoid base, curved neck
w/finger grooves, embossed
"Cremex Shampooing Vase
Registered Design," tooled lip,
smooth base, late 19th - early
20th c., 7⅞" h. **110.00**

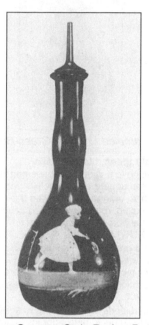

Mary Gregory-Style Barber Bottle

Cobalt blue, ovoid base tapering to a
lady's-leg neck, white enameled
Mary Gregory-style decoration of a
young girl playing tennis, rolled lip,
pontil-scarred base, ca. 1900,
8⅛" h. (ILLUS.) **350.00**

Cobalt blue cut to clear, tapering
cylindrical body w/diamond-cut
design, tooled lip, smooth base, ca.
1900, 9⅝" h. **578.00**

Cranberry, bulbous base w/long
neck, Broken Rib patt. swirled to
the right, sheared lip, smooth base,
ca. 1900, 6¾" h. **715.00**

Cranberry, bulbous base w/four-
ringed neck, Hobnail patt., rolled
lip, polished pontil, ca. 1900,
7⅛" h. **176.00**

Cranberry, ovoid base tapering to a
bulbous lower neck ring, cylindrical
neck, Optic Rib patt. w/white & blue
enameled decoration, sheared lip,
pontil-scarred base, ca. 1900,
7⅜" h. **715.00**

Enameled Emerald Green Bottle

Emerald green, bulbous base tapering to a wide neck base ring & swollen upper neck, Optic Rib patt. w/white, orange, green & red dot enameling, rolled lip, pontiled base, original porcelain stopper, ca. 1900, 7¾" h. (ILLUS.) **275.00**

Emerald green, squatty bulbous base w/bottom exaggerated ring & lady's-leg neck, silver overlay floral decoration, rolled lip, pontiled base, ca. 1900, 7⅞" h. **99.00**

Green, bulbous base tapering to a lady's-leg neck, pale color in Inverted Thumbprint patt., white enameled Art Nouveau cameo-style decoration, ground lip, smooth base, ca. 1900, 7⅜" h. **440.00**

Milk white opalescent, bell-form w/long cylindrical neck, multicolored enameled decoration of a cherub, sheared lip, pontiled base, original porcelain stopper, ca. 1900, 7½" h. **385.00**

Milk white opalescent, slightly tapering body w/a long cylindrical neck, decorated w/multicolored enameled floral decoration & the word "Shampoo," rolled lip, base marked "EW - INC.," ca. 1900, 9⅛" h. **240.00**

Milk white opalescent, slightly tapering cylindrical body w/center neck band, flesh-colored ground enameled w/a colorful winter scene w/cottage & the wording "C.F. Hawman Bay Rum," base marked "W.T. & Co.," original pewter screw cap, ca. 1900, 9½" h. **468.00**

Milk white opalescent, slightly tapering cylindrical base w/a center neck band, decorated w/colorful enameled florals & a bird w/"Jos. Doan. Tonic" on a banner, ground lip, smooth base marked "W.T. & Co.," original pewter screw stopper, ca. 1900, 9½" h. **550.00**

Milk white porcelain, squatty bulbous base w/tapering collar below a bell-form body, neck base ring on cylindrical neck, decorated w/multicolored enameled florals & gold trim, late 19th c., 7⅛" h. **1,045.00**

Opalescent clambroth, bulbous base w/three-ringed neck, Hobnail patt., hint of pink coloring, tooled mouth, polished pontil, ca. 1900, 6⅝" h. **413.00**

Opalescent clear & white, bulbous base tapering to tall neck, Stars & Stripes patt., tooled mouth, polished pontil, late 19th c., 7⅛" h. . . **176.00**

Opalescent clear & white, cylindrical w/long neck, Swirled Stripe patt., rolled lip, smooth base, late 19th - early 20th c., 9" h. **138.00**

Cranberry Opalescent Stripe Bottle

Opalescent cranberry, bulbous melon-lobed shouldered base tapering to a tall cylindrical neck w/rolled rim, Stripe patt., satin finish, smooth base, late 19th c., 6⅞" h. (ILLUS.) **187.00**

Opalescent cranberry, bulbous base w/four-ringed cylindrical neck w/rolled lip, Hobnail patt., late 19th c., 7" h. **209.00**

Opalescent cranberry, square base w/cylindrical neck, rolled lip, Swirled Stripe patt., smooth base, 8⅛" h. **688.00**

Opalescent cranberry cased,
bulbous base tapering to a long
cylindrical neck, Hobnail patt.
cased in clear, ground pontil, late
19th c., 8¼" h. **303.00**

Opalescent lime green, bulbous
base w/long cylindrical neck, Stripe
patt., rolled lip, smooth base, 7" h. . . **440.00**

Opalescent turquoise blue, bulbous
base w/four-ringed cylindrical neck
tapering to a white mouth, Hobnail
patt., polished pontil, late 19th c.,
7¼" h. **204.00**

Seaweed Opalescent Barber Bottle

Opalescent turquoise blue, square
base tapering to a long cylindrical
neck w/rolled lip, Seaweed patt.,
polished pontil, late 19th c., 8⅛" h.
(ILLUS.) **523.00**

Opalescent turquoise blue, square
base tapering to a cylindrical neck
w/rolled lip, Daisy & Fern patt.,
smooth base, late 19th c., 8½" h. . . . **165.00**

Pink amethyst, bulbous base
tapering to a lady's-leg neck, white
enameled Mary Gregory-style
decoration of a woman & the word
"Vegederma," rolled lip, pontiled
base, ca. 1900, 8⅛" h. **330.00**

Purple, bulbous base tapering to a
cylindrical neck, Optic Rib patt.,
white, orange & gilt floral
decoration, rolled lip, pontiled base,
ca. 1900, 6⅞" h. **72.00**

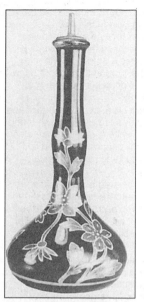

Art Nouveau Decorated Bottle

Purple, squatty bulbous base
tapering to a lady's-leg neck
w/rolled rim, yellow & gold
enameled Art Nouveau florals
around the base & up the neck,
pontiled base, ca. 1900, 7¾" h.
(ILLUS.) **605.00**

Purple, ovoid base tapering to a
lady's-leg neck, white enameled
Mary Gregory-style decoration of a
figural nude woman on rockwork
base forming a fountain in a
garden, rolled lip, pontiled base,
ca. 1900, 8" h. **2,585.00**

Purple, ovoid base tapering to a
lady's-leg neck, white enameled
Mary Gregory-style decoration of a
young boy facing right among
flowers, rolled lip, pontiled base,
ca. 1900, 8⅛" h. (small flake off
base edge) **209.00**

Purple, ovoid base tapering to a
lady's-leg neck, white enamel
decoration of a grist mill & wording
"Bay Rum," rolled lip, pontiled
base, ca. 1900, 8½" h. **237.00**

Ruby red cut to clear, bulbous base
w/long cylindrical neck & lower
neck ring, wording "Toilet Water"
engraved, rolled lip, polished pontil,
ca. 1900, 7" h. (tiny base flake) . . . **176.00**

Ruby red cut to clear, ovoid base
w/long cylindrical neck, Bohemian-
style decoration of a running stag
in forest, ground lip, smooth base,
ca. 1900, 8½" h. **798.00**

Ruby red cut to clear, ovoid base w/long cylindrical neck, cut in the Bohemian style w/a windowed tower flanked by leafy plants & branches & scrolled cartouche panels, ground lip, smooth base, original porcelain stopper, ca. 1900, 8½" h. **275.00**

Sapphire blue, ovoid base tapering to a lady's-leg neck, melon-lobed sides, white & orange enameled butterfly decoration, rolled lip, pontiled base, original metal stopper, 8¼" h. **94.00**

Topaz, corseted bulbous base centered by a tall cylindrical neck, Optic Rib patt., red, white & yellow enamel decoration, sheared lip, pontil-scarred base, ca. 1900, 7⅞" h. **523.00**

Turquoise blue, squatty bulbous body w/a long cylindrical neck, exaggerated Optic Rib patt., sheared lip, smooth base, ca. 1900, 6¾" h. **72.00**

Turquoise blue, bell-form base tapering to a long cylindrical neck, Optic Rib patt., white enameled Mary Gregory-style decoration of a young boy among flowers, sheared lip, pontiled base, ca. 1900, 7½" h. . . **578.00**

Turquoise blue, bulbous corseted body centered by a tall cylindrical neck, sheared lip, pontiled base, ca. 1900, 7¾" h. **143.00**

Turquoise blue, bell-form base tapering to a long cylindrical neck, Optic Rib patt., white, red & gold enameled decoration, sheared lip, pontiled base, ca. 1900, 8" h. **187.00**

Yellow w/amber tone, bulbous base tapering to a cylindrical four-ringed neck, Hobnail patt., rolled lip, smooth base, ca. 1900, 7⅛" h. **77.00**

Decorated Yellowish Amber Bottle

Yellowish amber, ringed, tapering "lighthouse" form w/a short cylindrical neck, Optic Rib patt., decorated w/yellow & gold beaded enamel florals, sheared lip, smooth base, original porcelain stopper, ca. 1900, 7" h. (ILLUS.). **303.00**

Yellowish green, bell-form base w/bottom neck ring, long cylindrical neck, Optic Rib patt., decorated w/colored enameled florals, sheared lip, pontiled base, ca. 1900, 7⅞" h. **523.00**

Yellowish green, ovoid base tapering to a lady's-leg neck, white enameled Mary Gregory-style decoration of a young girl facing left & standing among flowers, rolled lip, pontiled base, ca. 1900, 7⅞" h. **253.00**

Yellowish green, ovoid base tapering to a bulbous, flared neck, white enameled Mary Gregory-style decoration of a young girl facing left & standing among flowering vines, rolled lip, pontil-scarred base, ca. 1900, 8" h. **285.00**

Yellowish topaz, wide tapering 'lighthouse' form w/a short cylindrical neck, Optic Rib patt., white, green & orange enameled floral decoration, ca. 1900, 7" h. **330.00**

MUGS

FRATERNAL

Elks Shaving Mug

Benevolent and Protective Order of Elks, decorated w/their emblem & initials of owner, base marked "T & V Limoges - France," ca. 1900, 3⅞" h. (ILLUS.) **77.00**

Benevolent Order of Railroad Trainmen, decorated w/their emblem & sprigs of flowers on each side, owner's name above, base stamped "P. Germany," ca. 1900, 3¾" h. **187.00**

Brotherhood of Locomotive Firemen, depicts a locomotive & initials "B. of L.F. 48," base marked "T & V Limoges - France," ca. 1900, 3⅝" h. **275.00**

Catholic Order of Foresters, decorated w/emblem & "FHC" on cross & deer jumping in front, signed w/owner's name, base marked "T & V Limoges," ca. 1900, 3½" h. **743.00**

Fraternal Order of Eagles, decorated w/emblem w/eagle & "F.O.E.," owner's name above, full black wrap, ca. 1900, 3⅝" h. **361.00**

Improved Order of Redmen, decorated w/a colorful bust portrait of a Native American chief flanked by the letters "I.O.R.M.," base stamped "Ph. Eiselman," ca. 1900, 3⅝" h. **660.00**

Independent Order of Odd Fellows & Knights of Pythias, decorated w/the Odd Fellow emblem above the Knights of Pythias emblem & the owner's name, base stamped "T & V Limoges - France," ca. 1900, 3⅝" h. **495.00**

Junior Order of United Auto Mechanics, depicts a man in uniform holding a baton below the owner's name flanking their emblem, ca. 1900, 3¾" h. **2,465.00**

Knights of Columbus, decorated w/their emblem & the owners name above, base stamped "V+D Austria," ca. 1900, 3⅝" h. **131.00**

Knights Templer & Masonic Mug

Knights Templar & 32nd Degree Mason, decorated w/a double fraternal emblem & the owner's name, base stamped "T & V Limoges," ca. 1900, 3½" h. (ILLUS.). **633.00**

Order of Owls Hoo Hoo, order emblem w/three owls, owner's name above "Frankfort Nest No. 112," base marked in gold "G.B.S. Co.," full maroon wrap, ca. 1900, 3⅝" h. (crack on the back) **1,021.00**

Patriotic Order of Sons of America, decorated w/their emblem & full black wrap w/owner's name below, ca. 1900, 3¾" h. **149.00**

OCCUPATIONAL

Auctioneer Occupational Mug

Auctioneer, scene of a comical-looking auctioneer wearing a top hat, name in gold above, base stamped "T & V France," ca. 1900, 3⅞" h. (ILLUS.) **911.00**

Baker, scene of a baker putting bread into an oven, name in gold above, ca. 1900, 3⅝" h. (worn gilt) **303.00**

Bartender, decorated w/a keg marked "Whiskey" on one end, name in gold, ca. 1900, 3⅝" h. (some gilt wear) **303.00**

Rare Baseball Player Mug

Baseball player, depicts a uniformed player leaning on a bat, crossed bats to one side, name in gold above, base stamped "Germany," early 20th c., 3¾" h. (ILLUS.) **2,530.00**

Blacksmith, scene of a man shoeing a horse, name in gold above, base stamped "Koken Barber's Supply Co. St. Louis U.S.A.," ca. 1900, 3⅝" h. **330.00**

Boiler tender, scene of a man standing next to a large boiler, full wrap & gilt trim, name in gold above, base stamped "D & Co.," ca. 1900, 3½" h. **1,320.00**

Boiler tender, scene of a man shoveling coal into a large boiler, name in gold above, base stamped "T & V Limoges France," 3¾" h. (small base rim chip) **1,045.00**

Bookkeeper, scene of a bookkeeper at a desk writing in a ledger, full purple wrap, name in gold above, gilt trim, ca. 1900, 3⅝" h. **851.00**

Unusual Boxer Shaving Mug

Boxer, decorated w/a pair of hanging boxing gloves, full flesh-tone wrap, name in gold below, base stamped "Germany," good gilt trim, ca. 1900, 3¾" h. (ILLUS.). **2,200.00**

Boxer, shows scene of two boxers in a ring, name in gold above, gilt trim, base impressed "Germany," ca. 1900, 3¾" h. **5,280.00**

Brick layer, depicts various mason's tools, owner's name in gold above, base stamped "Leonard Vienna Austria," ca. 1900, 3½" h. **303.00**

Brick mason, depicts brick mason building a wall w/window frame at right & "O.M.K." monogram above left, base stamped "T & V Limoges - France," ca. 1900, 3½" h. **743.00**

Butcher, scene of a butcher shop w/a woman customer, full dark wrap, owner's name in gold, base stamped "Royal China International," ca. 1900, 3½" h. . . . **385.00**

Butcher, depicts steer's head & crossed butcher's tools, name in gold, base stamped "J & C Bavaria," ca. 1900, 3⅞" h. **154.00**

Cabinetmaker, depicts a chisel, block plane & saw above owner's name in gold, ca. 1900, 3⅜" h. (worn gold) **143.00**

Coal delivery man, scene of a man driving a wagon marked "Coal" being pulled by a team of mules, base stamped "T & V Limoges," ca. 1900, 3⅝" h. **963.00**

Conductor, depicts a railroad passenger car, owner's name in gold, base impressed "Germany," ca. 1900, 3¾" h. **413.00**

Dairy wagon driver, scene of a horse-drawn wagon marked "Milk & Cream" on the side, owner's name in gold above, base stamped "T & V Limoges - France," ca. 1900, 3⅝" h. **668.00**

Doctor, scene of a doctor jumping from his buggy w/bag in hand, name in gold above, base stamped "John Hudson Moore Co. Sportsman Div. The Lambert Company", gilt trim, 20th c., 3⅞" h. . **99.00**

Druggist, scene in an apothecary shop w/a druggist waiting on a woman, name in gold above, base stamped "Germany," ca. 1900. . . . . **715.00**

Electric trolley driver, scene of an electric trolley, name in gold above, base stamped "T & V Limoges France," ca. 1900, 3⅝" h. **468.00**

Grocery clerk, scene of a grocery store interior w/a male clerk tying a bag of flour for a lady customer, sprigs of flowers on both sides, owner's name above in gold, base stamped "Decorated by Koken Brothers Supply Co. St. Louis, Mo. Congress Chairs Best in World," gilt trim, ca. 1900, 3⅞" h. **523.00**

Hotel clerk, scene of a clerk waiting on a man wearing a trench coat & hat, owner's name in gold above, base stamped "T & V France," ca. 1900, 3⅝" h. **1,210.00**

House painter, scene of a man on scaffold painting a house, owner's name in gold above, ca. 1900, 3⅝" h. **570.00**

House painter, depicts a can of paint & brush, owner's name in gold above, base stamped "Haviland & Co. Limoges," ca. 1900, 3⅞" h. . . . **131.00**

Hunter, depicts a hunting dog w/a bird in its mouth, owner's name in gold above, ca. 1900, 3¾" h. **209.00**

Hunter, scene of a hunter in a field of snow walking towards town w/two rabbits watching, owner's name in gold above, ca. 1900, 3⅞" h. **385.00**

Ice Delivery Man Mug

Ice delivery man, scene of a horse-drawn wagon marked "Ice" on side & man standing at left, owner's name in gold above, base stamped "T & V," ca. 1900, 3½" h. (ILLUS.) . . . **768.00**

Jeweler, depicts a pocket watch w/flower sprays on each side, owner's name in gold above, base stamped "J.P.L. France," ca. 1900, 3⅝" h. **330.00**

Jockey, a scene of a jockey racing a horse, full black wrap, owner's name in gold above, gilt trim, ca. 1900, 3⅝" h. (minor surface crack on outside rim edge) **330.00**

Jockey, depicts a horse's head framed by a scrolled design, owner's name in gold below, base stamped "T & V Limoges - France," ca. 1900, 3⅝" h. **94.00**

Lamp lighter, scene of a man lighting early street lamp, marked above "Lamp Lighter," base marked in gold "Sportsman," 20th c., 3⅞" h. **88.00**

Livery stable owner, scene of a livery stable w/sprigs of flowers on each side, owner's name in gold above, base stamped "M. Riethueler, Steam Grinding, Barbers Furniture, Mug Decoration, St. Louis, Mo.," gilt trim, ca. 1900, 3⅞" h. (missing most of gilt trim) . . **798.00**

Musician, depicts a lyre w/owner's name in gold above & below, full purple wrap, base stamped "T & V Limoges," ca. 1900, 3⅝" h. **440.00**

Oilman, scene of a worker at a derrick inside a building, full pink wrap, owner's name in gold, ca. 1900, 3⅝" h. **6,600.00**

Oilman, scene of three men in an oil field, black wrap, marked "The Oilman" above, base stamped "John Hudson Moore Co. Sportsman Div. The Lampbert Company 1953 Edition," ca. 1953, 3⅞" h. **172.00**

Photographer, scene of man w/camera photographing a lady, owner's name in gold, base stamped "T & V Limoges France," ca. 1900, 3⅝" h. **1,073.00**

Policeman, shows a policeman on a street corner w/night stick in hand, marked above "The Policeman," base impressed "Sportsman," 20th c., 3¾" h. **83.00**

Railroad ticket master, scene of a man at a railroad ticket booth w/door on one side & clock above bench on other, booth marked

"N.Y.C. & H.R.R.R. Ticket Office," owner's name in gold, full green wrap, ca. 1900, 3⅞" h. **5,830.00**

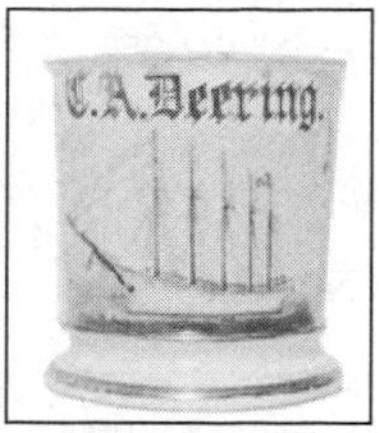

Rare Seaman's Shaving Mug

Seaman, depicts a large five-masted schooner, owner's name in gold above, base stamped "T & V Limoges - France," ca. 1900, 3⅞" h. (ILLUS.). **3,630.00**

Steamboat captain, depicts a steamboat below "The Captain," full pink wrap, ca. 1900, 3⅞" h. . . . **132.00**

Tailor, scene of a tailor shop w/the tailor measuring a customer, name in gold above, base stamped "Made in Germany," ca. 1920s, 3¼" h. **763.00**

Telegrapher, shows a man at a telegraph table w/sprigs of flowers on each side, full lavender wrap, owner's name in gold above, ca. 1900, 3½" h. **1,210.00**

Train engineer, shows a locomotive & tender, owner's name in gold above, base marked "T & V Limoges - France," ca. 1900, 3⅝" h. **232.00**

Trainman's Shaving Mug

Trainman, shows a caboose marked "NYP & NRP," owner's name in gold, base stamped "Lang & Co. Balto MD," gilt trim, ca. 1900, 3⅝" h. (ILLUS.) **990.00**

Undertaker, shows a horse-drawn funeral hearse, full black wrap, name in gold above, base stamped "Leonard Vienna Austria," ca. 1900, 4⅛" h. (chip at top of base below decoration) **1,155.00**

PATRIOTIC

American & British flags, depicts an eagle in shield w/American flag on right & British flag on left, owner's name in gold above, base stamped "T & V Limoges - France," ca. 1900-20, 3⅝" h. **495.00**

American flag, flag shown w/owner's name below, base impressed "Germany," ca. 1900, 3¾" h. **131.00**

Mug with American & Irish Flags

American & Irish flags, shows an eagle atop a globe w/crossed flags, owner's name in gold below, base stamped "T & V Limoges - France," ca.1900, 3⅝" h.(ILLUS.) **231.00**

American shield, depicts the shield surrounded by olive branches, owner's name in gold across shield, ca. 1900, 3⅝" h. **131.00**

Eagle, scene of eagle flying among clouds, owner's name in gold banner, base impressed "Germany," ca. 1900, 3¾" h. **165.00**

Eagle on globe, American eagle on a globe w/the American flag, olive branch & arrows in talons, owner's name in gold below, white & red bands around base, stamped "Vienna Austria," ca. 1900, 3⅝" h. . . **154.00**

Eagle w/banner, American eagle w/a banner for owner's name in gold, arrows, olive branch & shield, background of clouds wraps around sides, ca. 1900, 3⅝" h. **240.00**

Green flag, plain green flag w/sprigs of flowers on each side, owner's name in gold, ca. 1900, 3⅞" h. **209.00**

GENERAL

China, cameo-style bust portrait of a woman, owner's name in gold above, ca. 1900, 3½" h. **358.00**

Skull & Crossbones Mug

China, decorated w/a large skull & crossbones w/the owner's name in gold above, base stamped "T & V Limoges," gilt trim, ca. 1900, 3⅝" h. (ILLUS.) **1,210.00**

China, decorated w/a scene of a man bent over preparing to bounce a ball, owner's name in gold above, 3⅝" h., (worn gold, repairs) **2,145.00**

China, scene of a large Victorian house w/a man on the front porch, full pink wrap, owner's name in gold above, base stamped "KPM Germany - Andrew Faglestad 32 Reed Av Evertt," ca. 1900, 3⅝" h. . **2,200.00**

China, scene of a man driving a motorcar, full blue wrap, owner's name in gold above, base stamped "T & V Limoges - France" on base, ca. 1900, 3⅝" h. (worn gilt) **1,155.00**

China, cameo-style bust portrait of a man, base stamped "W.G. & Co.," ca. 1900, 3¾" h. **495.00**

Figural Face Scuttle Mug

China, figural face, scuttle-style, a colorfully painted unshaven man's face on one side, shaven face on other, marked "Before and After" on base, England, 20th c., 3¾" h. (ILLUS.) **209.00**

China, tropical sunset scene w/sprigs of flowers on each side, owner's name in gold above, base stamped "J & C Bavaria," ca. 1900, 3⅞" h. . . . **231.00**

RAZOR BLADE BANKS

Occupied Japan Razor Blade Bank

Barber, holding pole, Occupied
Japan, 4" h. (ILLUS.). **50.00-60.00**

Barber Stroking Chin Razor Blade Bank

Barber, "Tony," standing wearing
blue coat & stroking chin, 5¾" h.
(ILLUS.). **60.00-80.00**

"Looie" Razor Bank

Barber, "Looie," found in right handed
& left handed versions, 7" h.
(ILLUS.). **85.00-100.00**

Wooden Barber Razor Blade Bank

Barber, wooden, "The Old Blade,"
bottom unscrews, Woodcroft,1950,
6" h. (ILLUS.) **65.00-75.00**
Barber, wooden, w/key & metal
holders for razor & brush,
9" h. **85.00-95.00**
Barber chair, small, 4¾" h. . . **100.00-125.00**

"Tony" Razor Blade Bank

Barber, "Tony," Ceramic Arts Studio,
4¾" h. (ILLUS.) **90.00-100.00**

Barber Chair Razor Blade Bank

Barber chair, large, 5¾" h.
(ILLUS.). **125.00-150.00**

Cleminson Barber Head Blade Bank

Barber head, Cleminson, different
colors on collar, 4" h. (ILLUS.) . . **30.00-35.00**
Barber pole, ceramic, half-round
hanging-type, "Razor Blades," by
Kreiss, 5" h. **40.00-60.00**

Barber Pole Razor Blade Bank

Barber poles, red & white (various
designs), 6" h. (ILLUS. of one). . **25.00-35.00**

Barbershop Quartet Razor Blade Bank

Barbershop quartet, "The Gay
Blades," 5¼" x 4¼" (ILLUS.) . . **75.00-100.00**

Bell-Shaped Cleminson Blade Bank

Bell-shaped, man shaving,
Cleminson, 3¼" h. (ILLUS.) . . **25.00-35.00**

Wooden Razor Blade Bank

Box, wooden, souvenir, "Old Razor
Blades - For Gay Old Blades By
Cracky," w/hillbilly, side w/names of
city & state, 5½" h. (ILLUS.) . . **35.00-45.00**

Donkey Razor Blade Bank

Donkey, ceramic, Listerine, 2¼" h.
(ILLUS.). **20.00-30.00**

Elephant Razor Blade Bank

Elephant, ceramic, Listerine, 2½" h.
(ILLUS.). **25.00-35.00**

Plastic Dandy Dan Razor Blade Bank

Figure of Dandy Dan, plastic, 6¾" h.
(ILLUS.). **25.00-35.00**

Frog Razor Blade Bank

Frog, ceramic, Listerine, 3" h.
   (ILLUS) **15.00-25.00**

Green & Yellow Frog Razor Blade Bank

Frog, "For Used Blades," found in
   green & yellow, 3" h. (ILLUS.). . **60.00-70.00**
Metal box, policeman holding up one
   hand, reads "Old Razor Blades,"
   4" h. **75.00-100.00**
Safe, green, says "Blade Safe" on the
   front, 2½" h. **45.00-55.00**
Shaving Brush, ceramic, wide at top
   w/decal, 4½" h. **50.00-60.00**
Shaving cup, half-round hanging-
   type, "Gay Old Blade," w/quartet,
   4" h. **65.00-75.00**

Villain Razor Blade Bank

Villain, or Matador, "Gay Blades,"
   6" h. (ILLUS.) **55.00-65.00**

GENERAL ITEMS

Barber bowl, stamped & soldered
   metal, round w/oval chin cut-out,
   late 19th c., 10⅞" d, 4¾" h **358.00**

Early Decorated Barber Bowl

Barber bowl, ceramic, oblong w/wide
   flattened flanged rim w/soap
   indentation & notched-out side, h.p.
   w/leafy floral vines in red, blue &
   green, some minor glaze crazing,
   19th c., 8 x 10½", 3" h. (ILLUS.) . . . **303.00**

Barber Pole

Barber pole, porcelain, building
   mount, reads "Barber Shop" on
   one-piece top globe, red, white &
   blue striping, some fading in globe
   (ILLUS.) **3,025.00**

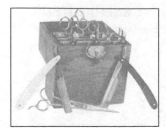

Traveling Barber's Kit

Barber's kit, traveling-type, a hardwood case w/metal hardware opens to slots for three pairs of scissors & fifteen straight razors, contains three scissors & thirteen straight razors w/celluloid handles, late 19th - early 20th c., case 3½ x 6¼", 8¼" h., the set (ILLUS.). **187.00**

Razor, straight razor, black plastic handle w/applied photos of nude women on both sides, made by "Clause Tremont O., U.S.A.," late 19th c. (slight surface rust on blade) **110.00**

Razors, straight razors, celluloid handles marked "Gondola," each stamped w/a different German town & coat of arms, marked "Gondola Made in Germany," includes hard blue case lined w/pink felt, tag in box reads "Souvenir of Solingen," ca. 1920s, set of 7 . . . . **358.00**

Safety razor, "Schick Eversharp," Bakelite handle, 1937 . . . . **65.00**

Safety razor display, "Ever-Ready," counter-top style, simulated wood-grained tin w/"Ever-Ready" trademark die-cut marquis of man shaving face, includes original razor & razor blade packaging, 12½" w., 9" deep, 11" h. (overall chipping, scratching & minor creasing) **935.00**

Salesman Sample Barber Chair

Salesman sample barber chair, Koken's exact working replica, leather upholstery, porcelain construction, original headrest & child's booster seat, embossed "Koken Companies, St. Louis" on foot rest, minor cracking & crazing to base of chair, spot on leather seat, 15" high to top of headrest (ILLUS.) **51,750.00**

Scalp treatment display, tapered-wood countertop style, stenciled "Pinol Scalp Treatment" above & "For Dandruff and Falling Hair" below in gold lettering on front & back, ends marked "A Complete and Effective Treatment," includes two original bottles w/celluloid labels, 11" w., 11½" h. (some loss to lettering) **303.00**

Shaving paper vase, light apple green glass, Inverted Thumbprint patt., white, yellow & orange enameled decoration, polished rim, smooth base, late 19th c., 7¼" h. . . **330.00**

Shaving paper vase, deep cobalt blue glass, Optic Rib patt., white & gold enameled decoration, polished rim, smooth base, ca. 1900, 7½" h. **1,430.00**

Shaving paper vase, purple glass, white enameled Mary Gregory-style decorated w/a scene of a man & woman playing tennis, ground & polished rim, ca. 1900, 8" h. **798.00**

Straight razor display case, countertop style, oak casing w/routered top & bottom edging, holds fifteen razors in individual felt-lined front sections, nicely restored, 24½" l., 7" deep, 6½" h. . . **220.00**

Straight Razor Display Case

Straight razor display case, wall-type, oak w/columns on either side of beveled glass door, individual display compartments inside, marked "Fine Razors" across top, 36" w., 8" deep, 41" h. (ILLUS.) . . **1,760.00**

BASEBALL MEMORABILIA

Baseball was named by Abner Doubleday as he laid out a diamond-shaped field with four bases at Cooperstown, New York. A popular game from its inception, by 1869 it was able to support its first all-professional team, the Cincinnati Red Stockings. The National League was organized in 1876 and though the American League was first formed in 1900, it was not officially recognized until 1903. Today, the "national pastime" has millions of fans and collecting baseball memorabilia has become a major hobby with enthusiastic collectors seeking out items associated with players such as Babe Ruth, Lou Gehrig, and others who became legends in their own lifetimes. Though baseball cards, issued as advertising premiums for bubble gum and other products, seem to dominate the field there are numerous other items available.

Mickey Mantle Day Baseball

Baseball, August 25, 1996 Mickey Mantle Day Yankee autographed baseball, includes Mantle's No. 7 & his facsimile autograph in the design, signed by 24 members of the 1996 Championship Yankees, Joe Torre signature on the sweet spot (ILLUS.) **$905.00**

Baseball, autographed by 1950 New York Yankees, 23 signatures include Joe DiMaggio on sweet spot, Official American League (Harridge) baseball **1,347.00**

Baseball, autographed by 1955 Brooklyn Dodgers, 22 signatures include Alston on the sweet spot, Robinson, Campy, Hodges, Snider & Reese, 1955 was championship year, Official National League (giles) baseball **1,081.00**

Baseball, autographed by Babe Ruth & Lou Gehrig, signed by Ruth on sweet spot & Gehrig on adjacent panel, red & blue stitching, Official American league "Johnson," 1927 model **7,310.00**

Baseball, autographed by Cy Young, signed "Saturday June 6th 1931 - Cy Young" to the right of the sweet spot in blue ink, red & blue stitched D&M "Official League Ball" **5,019.00**

Baseball, Babe Ruth game-used ball, w/elaborate designed period notations covering two panels, one reads "Babe Ruth Home run Baseball hit Off Pitcher Hill, October 9, 1927," opposite panel reads "1927 World Series 4th Game," signed by Babe Ruth on sweet spot, red & blue stitched, Official American League (signature & stamped markings have faded, covered w/shellac which has browned w/age) **13,890.00**

Baseball, girls model, marked "All-American Girls Professional Base Ball," MacGregor Goldsmith, ca. 1940s (a few minor scuffs) **837.00**

Baseball bat, autographed by Hank Aaron, H&B Louisville Slugger Pro Model 125, ca. 1964½- 1972 . . . . . **926.00**

Baseball bat, autographed by Mickey Mantle, signed "My Best Wishes Mickey Mantle 9/18/65," this was "Mickey Mantle Day" at Yankee Stadium, H&B Louisville Slugger. . **5,421.00**

Baseball bat, Jackie Robinson, game-used, H&B Louisville Slugger, Pro Model 125 "rookie-era," ca. 1947-48, uncracked, shows some game wear **6,722.00**

Baseball bat, Joe DiMaggio, game-used, H&B Louisville Slugger, Pro Model 125, from DiMaggio's rookie days w/the San Francisco Seals in the Pacific Coast League, ca. 1932-36 . . . . **5,964.00**

Baseball bat, Joe Jackson, game-used, H&B Louisville Slugger, Pro-Model 125, used after Jackson's banishment from baseball, ca. 1922-26, w/letter of authenticity (uncracked, heavy use, some dry rot on reverse of barrel) **6,722.00**

Baseball bat, Lou Gehrig, game-used, Pro Spalding, "rookie-era," pre-1925, 37" l. (uncracked) **12,323.00**

Baseball card, 1914, Cracker Jack, Honus Wagner, No. E145 (cut slightly askew) **1,231.00**

Baseball card, 1933, Goudey, Lou Gehrig, R319 . . . . **3,834.00**

Baseball card, 1948, Leaf, Joe DiMaggio, No. 1 . . . . **2,309.00**

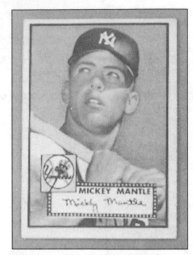

Mickey Mantle Baseball Card

Baseball card, 1952, Topps, Mickey Mantle, No. 311 (ILLUS.) **7,087.00**

Baseball card, 1952, Topps, Mickey Mantle, No. 311 (slight corner wear & minor surface crease) **5,598.00**

Baseball card, 1952, Topps, Willie Mays, No. 261 . . . . **3,606.00**

Baseball cards, 1928, W502, complete set of 60, the set (some browning to some cards) **2,215.00**

Baseball cards, 1951, Bowman, complete set of 324, the set . . . **11,929.00**

Baseball cards, 1956, Topps, complete set of 340, the set (good to excellent condition) **7,215.00**

Baseball cards, 1962, Topps, complete set of 598, the set **1,480.00**

Baseball cards, 1970, Topps, complete set of 720, the set **557.00**

Baseball cards, 1973, Topps, unopened box of 24 10-cent packs . . **811.00**

Batting helmet, autographed, signed by over 60 former Mets from the late 1960s through the 1990s **337.00**

Bobbing head doll, bobbing-head type, Giants team, gold base **90.00**

Bobbing head doll, Mickey Mantle, shows Mantle in Yankees uniform holding baseball bat at his side, on round base w/facsimile signature . . **1,308.00**

Bobbing head doll, Roberto Clemente, shows Clemente in Pirates uniform holding baseball bat at his side, on round white base w/facsimile signature, w/original box **2,463.00**

Bobbing head doll, Roger Maris, shows Maris in Yankees uniform holding baseball bat at his side, on round base w/facsimile signature . . **739.00**

Cereal box, "Wheaties," features eight baseball cards including Ted Williams & George Mikan, complete box including flaps, has been unassembled & folded flat, 1952 . . . **614.00**

Display box, "New York Champions Chocolates," wood, top paper label in red, white & green reads "N.Y. Champions Penny Sweet Chocolates Can't Be Knocked Out" surrounding batter & catcher, front label reads "The New York Champions Chocolates," 1890s . . . **696.00**

Figure, cast metal, figure of a pitcher wearing a blue & red cap, on red base, marked "N. Muller. N.Y.," patent 1868 . . . . **6,270.00**

Figure, cast metal, figure of a player at bat wearing a blue & red cap, on red base marked "N. Muller. N.Y.," patent 1868 . . . . **6,600.00**

Guide, "Dewitt Baseball Guide," cover reads "Hand Books" below "De Witts" above an image of a pitcher surrounded by "The - Base Ball - Guide - 1868," first edition, 1868 (some paper loss near spine) **798.00**

Magazine, "Baseball" Magazine, December 1927 . . . . **100.00**

Magazine, "Life," 1941, Ted Williams cover & feature article **45.00**

Magazine, "Life," April 13, 1962, complete w/Maris & Mantle baseball cards **95.00**

Magazine, "Look," 1951, Joe DiMaggio cover & six-page feature **45.00**

Magazine, "Sport Magazine," March, 1957, Mickey Mantle on cover **50.00**

Photograph, New York Giants, team picture of 1912 Giants team, includes Hall of Famers John McGraw, Christy Mathewson & Rube Marquard, framed, 15 x 28½" in frame **1,852.00**

Picture book, souvenir-type, New York Mets, shows players w/signatures, Dairylea advertising on back, 1977. . . . **10.00**

Pinback button, Phillies, w/red & white ribbon, metal glove & ball hanging charms **15.00**

Program, 1933 All-Star Game, unofficial program to the first All-Star game issued by John J. Hayes Men's Stores of Chicago, pictures all 36 all-stars around perimeter (neatly scored, minor horizontal crease) **696.00**

Program, 1962 "Nassau County Adopts the "Mets" Dinner," signed, dinner held in honor of the New York Mets at The Garden City Hotel on Monday, April 16, 1962, autographed by 23 of the original Mets including Hodges, Stengel, Ashburn & Coach Ruffing, 4 pp. **652.00**

Program, "1964 World's Series" **60.00**

Program, 1978 World Series Official Program, 75th Anniversary Edition . . **100.00**

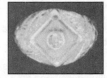

First World Series Ring

Ring, 1922 World Series, New York Giants, "Ralph Shinners" engraved inside band, designed w/crossed bats, a glove, a ball & diamond set in the center of the baseball diamond design, reads "Giants World's" on one side & "Champions 1922" on the other, diamond is chipped, extremely rare example of the very first World Series ring (ILLUS.) . . . **6,441.00**

Ticket, 1903 World Series at Boston, game three, the first World Series, mounted on Japanese rice paper, unused, rare (minor restoration). . **4,480.00**

Ticket, 1910 World Series at Philadelphia, game one, unused . . **1,740.00**

Ticket, 1919 World Series at Cincinnati, game one, unused . . . **1,636.00**

Tour program, Chicago White Sox, string bound, from their 1912 tour of Texas, in the shape of a glove w/picture of Charles Comiskey in the center, includes yearbook-style photos & biographies of team officials & prominent team members, mounted, two pages separated, 32 pp. **980.00**

World Series Trophy

Trophy, 1978 Yankees World Series, features 26 team flags surrounding enamel Yankee & Dodger logos., 12" h. (ILLUS.) **6,218.00**

Ted Williams Uniform

Uniform, 1969, Ted Williams Washington Senators road flannel manager's uniform, "Senators" in red w/blue trim across front, No. 9 on reverse also in red w/blue trim, baseball's "100th Anniversary" patch on left sleeve, "1969" in black on outside left tail & autographed by Williams in the collar & the waistband w/blue marker, labels & tags complete & intact, the set (ILLUS.). . **5,819.00**

Wallet, leather, w/image of Stan Musial w/facsimile signature, ca. 1950s . . **336.00**

Watch, Babe Ruth, face has image of Ruth's head above a baseball bat above a baseball diamond, Arabic numerals, in original baseball-shaped case, case reads "Official - Babe Ruth - Wrist Watch - Sports Watch - Of Champions," ca. 1948 . . **904.00**

Yearbook, 1959 New York Yankees World's Series edition, shows the winning 1958 team **200.00**

BASKETS

The American Indians were the first basket weavers on this continent and, of necessity, the early Colonial settlers and their descendants pursued this artistic handicraft to provide essential containers for berries, eggs and endless other items to be carried or stored. Rye straw, split willow and reeds are but a few of the wide variety of materials used. The Nantucket baskets, plainly and sturdily constructed, along with those made by specialized groups, would seem to draw the greatest attention to this area of collecting.

Painted "Buttocks" Basket

"Buttocks" basket, tightly-woven splint, fine-ribbed construction w/wrapped rim & bentwood handle, painted black, America, 19th c., 9" d., 9 ½" h. plus handle, minor breaks & paint loss (ILLUS.) **$805.00**

"Buttocks" basket, miniature, woven splint, dark brown patina, good age & form, 3½ x 4" (old damage) **165.00**

"Buttocks" basket, woven splint, wrapped rim, 5½ x 6¼", 3½" h. plus bentwood handle **105.00**

Small "Buttocks" Basket

"Buttocks" basket, eighteen-rib construction, woven splint w/wrapped rim & short bentwood handle, good patina, 5¾ x 7⅞", 3½" h. plus handle (ILLUS.) **248.00**

"Buttocks" basket, thirty-eight rib construction, woven splint, bentwood handle, natural patina, 7 x 7½", 4" h. plus handle **138.00**

"Buttocks" basket, twenty-six rib construction, woven splint, natural patina w/faded red & green, bentwood handle, 7¼ x 7½", 4¼" h. plus handle **220.00**

"Buttocks" basket, woven splint w/bentwood handle, good detail, 9½" d., 5" h. plus handle **248.00**

"Buttocks" basket, forty-rib construction, woven splint, narrow bentwood handle, old greyish paint, 13½ x 14", 7" h. plus handle **660.00**

"Buttocks" basket, twenty-two rib construction, woven splint, natural w/bluish black stripe around the rim & down around the center, bentwood handle, some age, 13½ x 16 ½", 8½" h. plus handle . . **138.00**

"Buttocks" basket, forty-two rib construction, woven splint, deep half-round form w/upcurved rims & central low bentwood handle, sprayed w/brown stain, minor damage, 14 x 21", 13" h. **149.00**

"Buttocks" baskets, finely woven splint, light natural finish, smallest w/28-rib construction, largest w/52-rib construction, 2" to 5¼" d., graduated set of 5 . . . . **1,100.00**

Gathering basket, woven splint, round wrapped base band below the deep rounded sides w/wrapped rim & high bentwood handle, good patina, 10½" d., 5½" h. plus handle **275.00**

Gathering basket, woven splint, round w/wrapped rim & swivel handle, good brown patina, 11½" d., 7" h. (some damage & bottom is missing two rows of splints). **275.00**

Knife basket, woven splint, long low oval form w/wrapped rim, two-section, good color, 9 x 13½" **50.00**

Laundry basket, woven splint, oblong w/bentwood rim handles, good brown patina, 25 x 26½", 10½" h. (minor damage) **358.00**

Laundry basket, woven splint, deep rectangular sides w/ rounded corners & wrapped bentwood rim, good age & color, 20 x 27", 14" h. (some wear & damage) **138.00**

Market basket, woven splint, deep round sides w/wrapped rim, raised rim loops supporting the bentwood swing handle, good color, 9½" h. (some damage) **66.00**

Market basket, woven splint, flat-bottomed round form w/deep sides & wrapped rim, bentwood handle, old green paint, 13¼" d., 7" h. plus handle **440.00**

"Melon" basket, eight-rib construction, woven splint w/ wrapped rim, end-to-end bentwood handle, 11½ x 1 ½", 4 ½" h. plus handle (minor damage) **94.00**

"Melon" basket, woven splint, ten-rib construction, half-round woven splint w/wrapped rim & "eye of God'"design at end of bentwood handle, old varnish, 11¼ x 12½", 5½" h. plus handle **61.00**

Nantucket basket, finely woven splint, by R. Folger, stenciled on interior "R. Folger maker Nantucket Mass.," 20th c., 6" d., 4" h. (minute splits & losses) **748.00**

Nantucket basket, finely woven splint, round, w/paper label on base reading "Lightship Basket made by Fred S. Chadwick Nantucket Mass. 4 Pine St.," early 20th c., 7¾" d., 4⅞" h. **920.00**

Nantucket basket, finely woven splint, by Mitchell Ray, paper label on base, 20th c., 8¼" d., 5¼" h. (minor splits) **633.00**

Nantucket basket, finely woven splint, round, early 20th c., 11" d., 7" h. (scattered minor breaks & losses) **575.00**

Nantucket basket, woven splint, rounded wide tightly woven form w/rounded lip w/two carved wood heart-form rim handles, solid base, late 19th - early 20th c., 14 3/8" d., 6¾" h. (one handle repaired) **546.00**

Nantucket basket pocketbook, finely woven splint, a carved ivory unicorn-form jagging wheel applied to the wooden lid, Jose Formoso Reyes, dated 1978, 11" l., 8" h. (break to catch) **748.00**

Fine Nantucket Basket

Nantucket "Lightship" basket, finely woven splint, round w/wrapped rim & bentwood swing handle, paper label on base reads "made on board South Shoal Lightship by William Sandsbury

sold...George R. Folger Main Street, Nantucket Mass.," illegible ink inscription, dated 1891, losses to label & lashing, very minor losses to basket, 8¾" h., 4" h. plus handle (ILLUS.) **1,495.00**

Storage basket, woven splint, deep rectangular sides w/wrapped rim & center swing bentwood handle, yellow bands w/blue potato print designs, 15½ x 23", 10¾" h. (minor damage) **275.00**

Utility basket, woven splint, square base w/deep rounded sides & wrapped round rim w/long bentwood handle, painted red, 6¼ x 6¾", 4" h. plus handle **468.00**

Paint Decorated Utility Basket

Utility basket, woven splint, rectangular woven bottom w/rounded wrapped rim & small bentwood handles, painted pink & black, America, 19th c., 10 x 15", 5" h., minor losses & wear (ILLUS.) **489.00**

Utility basket, woven splint, round w/wrapped rim & bentwood handle, good old brown patina, 12" d., 8" h plus handle **193.00**

Utility basket, woven splint, round w/wrapped rim & small bentwood rim handles, good detail, traces of old yellow varnish, 14½" d., 4½" h. plus handles (minor damage) **385.00**

Utility basket, woven splint, oblong w/bentwood rim handles, brown varnish over old white paint, 20½ x 35", 9¾" h. plus handles **413.00**

BEANIE BABIES

Beanie Babies are manufactured by Ty Inc. They first appeared in the marketplace in 1994 and quickly became one of the hottest collectibles of the 1990's. The secondary market exploded with retired and hard-to-find variations of the Beanie Babies. Many things affect the value of a particular Beanie Baby. The tags, in particular, are of great importance. The red heart tag that is usually attached to the front or "top" of the beanie is referred to as the "hang tag." The sewn-in tag at the bottom or "rear" of the beanie is typically referred to as the "tush tag." If there is a dent, crease, fold or other marking on the hang tag, the value of the Beanie Baby can be reduced by up to 50%, depending on the severity of the damage. A missing hang tag may diminish the value by as much as 75%. All prices listed here are for mint Beanie Babies with mint tags. For more details and an in-depth look into the world of bean bag plush, see The Bean Family Album *by Shawn Brecka (Antique Trader Publications, 1998.)*

Ally the alligator, retired 1997 . . . . . **$50.00**
Bessie the cow, retired 1997 . . . . **60.00**
Bongo the monkey, "Nana" tag,
    retired 1995 . . . . **4,000.00**
Bronty the brontosaurus, retired
    1996 . . . . **1,400.00**

Bubbles the fish

Bubbles the fish, retired 1997
    (ILLUS.) **175.00**
Bucky the beaver, retired 1997 . . . . . . **30.00**
Bumble the bee, retired 1996 . . . . . . **675.00**
Caw the crow, retired 1996 . . . . **800.00**
Chilly the polar bear, retired 1995. . **2,400.00**
Chops the lamb, retired 1997 . . . . . . **225.00**
Coral the fish, retired 1997 . . . . **130.00**
Cubbie the bear, "Brownie" tag,
    retired 1994 . . . . **4,200.00**
Cubbie the bear, retired 1997 . . . . . . **25.00**
Derby the horse, fine mane,
    retired 1995 . . . . **4,000.00**
Digger the crab, orange,
    retired 1995 . . . . **800.00**
Digger the crab, red, retired 1997 . . . **125.00**

Doodle the rooster

Doodle the rooster, discontinued
    1997 (ILLUS.) **45.00**
Flash the dolphin, retired 1997 . . . . . **130.00**
Flip the cat, retired 1997 . . . . **30.00**

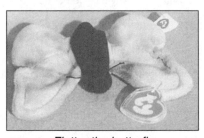

Flutter the butterfly

Flutter the butterfly, retired 1996
    (ILLUS.) **1,200.00**
Garcia the teddy bear, retired 1997. . **175.00**
Goldie the fish, retired 1997 . . . . **50.00**

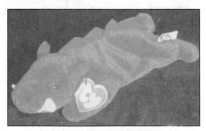

Grunt the razorback

Grunt the razorback, retired 1997
    (ILLUS.). **180.00**
Hoot the owl, retired 1997 . . . . **40.00**
Humphrey the camel, retired 1995 . . **2,800.00**

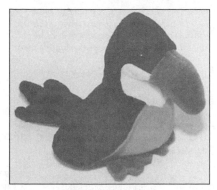

Kiwi the toucan

Kiwi the toucan, retired 1997
   (ILLUS.) **225.00**

Lefty the donkey

Lefty the donkey, retired 1997
   (ILLUS.) **350.00**
Legs the frog, retired 1997 . . . . **18.00**
Libearty the bear, retired 1997 . . . . . **400.00**
Lizzy the lizard, blue, retired 1997 . . . . **18.00**
Lizzy the lizard, tie-dyed,
   retired 1996 . . . . **1,300.00**
Magic the dragon, hot pink thread,
   retired 1995 . . . . **75.00**
Magic the dragon, light pink thread,
   retired 1997 . . . . **45.00**
Mystic the unicorn, coarse mane,
   brown horn, discontinued 1997 . . . . . **22.00**
Mystic the unicorn, fine mane,
   discontinued 1994 . . . . **600.00**
Nip the cat, all gold, retired 1996 . . . . **900.00**
Nip the cat, gold face w/white paws,
   retired 1997 . . . . **25.00**
Nip the cat, white face and belly,
   retired 1996 . . . . **450.00**
Patti the platypus, deep magenta,
   retired 1995 . . . . **800.00**
Peanut the elephant, dark blue,
   retired 1995 . . . . **5,000.00**
Peking the panda bear,
   retired 1996 . . . . **2,400.00**
Pinchers the lobster, "Punchers"
   tag, retired 1994 . . . . **3,100.00**

Quackers the duck, without wings,
   retired 1995 . . . . **2,800.00**
Radar the bat, retired 1997 . . . . **200.00**
Rex the tyrannosaurus,
   retired 1996 . . . . **750.00**
Righty the elephant,
   retired 1997 . . . . **300.00**
Seamore the seal, retired 1997 . . . . . **175.00**
Slither the snake, retired 1995 . . . . **1,800.00**
Snowball the snowman,
   retired 1997 . . . . **35.00**
Sparky the dalmation,
   retired 1997 . . . . **150.00**

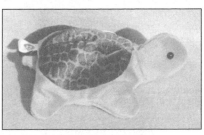

Speedy the turtle

Speedy the turtle, retired 1997
   (ILLUS.) **25.00**
Splash the whale, retired 1997 . . . . . **100.00**
Spooky the ghost, "Spooky" tag,
   retired 1997 . . . . **35.00**
Spooky the ghost, "Spook" tag,
   retired 1995 . . . . **650.00**
Spot the dog, with spot,
   retired 1997 . . . . **50.00**
Spot the dog, without spot,
   retired 1994 . . . . **2,200.00**
Steg the stegosaurus,
   retired 1996 . . . . **1,000.00**

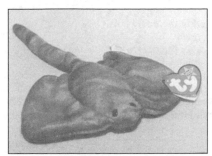

Sting the manta ray

Sting the manta ray, retired 1997
   (ILLUS.) **200.00**

Tabasco the bull

Tabasco the bull, retired 1997
(ILLUS.) **175.00**
Tank the armadillo, 7 lines and no
shell, retired 1996 . . . . **200.00**
Tank the armadillo, 9 lines and no
shell, retired 1996 . . . . **400.00**
Tank the armadillo, with shell,
retired 1997 . . . . **80.00**
Teddy the 1997 Holiday Bear,
brown, retired 1997 . . . . **40.00**
Teddy the bear, brown, new face,
retired 1997 . . . . **85.00**
Teddy the bear, brown, old face,
retired 1995 . . . . **2,400.00**
Teddy the bear, cranberry, new face,
retired 1996 . . . . **2,000.00**
Teddy the bear, cranberry, old face,
retired 1995 . . . . **2,500.00**
Teddy the bear, jade, new face,
retired 1996 . . . . **2,000.00**
Teddy the bear, jade, old face,
retired 1995 . . . . **1,600.00**
Teddy the bear, magenta, new face,
retired 1996 . . . . **1,700.00**
Teddy the bear, magenta, old face,
retired 1995 . . . . **2,000.00**
Teddy the bear, teal, new face,
retired 1996 . . . . **2,400.00**
Teddy the bear, teal, old face,
retired 1995 . . . . **2,000.00**
Teddy the bear, violet, new face,
retired 1996 . . . . **2,200.00**
Teddy the bear, violet, old face,
retired 1995 . . . . **1,800.00**
Trap the mouse, retired 1995 . . . . . **1,800.00**
Tusk the walrus, retired 1997 . . . . . . **200.00**
Velvet the panther, retired 1997 . . . . . **20.00**
Web the spider, retired 1996 . . . . . **1,400.00**

BIG LITTLE BOOKS

*The original "Big Little Books" and "Bettery
Little Books" small format series were originated
in the mid-30s by Whitman Publishing Co.,
Racine, Wisconsin, and covered a variety of
subjects from adventure stories to tales based on*
comic strip characters and movie and radio stars.
The publisher originally assigned each book a
serial number. Most prices are now in the $25.00
- $50.00 range with scarce ones bringing more.*

Air Fighters of America, No. 1448,
1941 (N. Mint-) **$50.00**
Andy Panda & Tiny Tom, No. 1425,
1944 (VF-) **40.00**
Aquaman, Scouge of the Sea,
No. 2017, 1968 (FN/VF) **10.00**
Barney Baxter, In the Air With the
Eagle Squadron, No. 1459, 1938
(VF+) **45.00**
Batman, Cheetah, No. 2031 (NM) **15.00**
Big Chief Wahoo, Lost Pioneers,
No. 1432, 1942 (VF+) **45.00**
Billy the Kid, No. 773, 1935 (VG) **18.00**
Blaze Brandon, No. 1447, 1938 (Fine) . . **25.00**
Blondie, Count Cookie in Too!
No. 1430, 1947 (VG/FN) **30.00**
Blondie, Everybody's Happy, 1948,
No. 1438 (VF++) **50.00**
Blondie, In Hot Water, No. 1410 (Fine) . . **38.00**
Blondie, The Bumsteads Carry On,
No. 1419, 1941 (VF+++) **60.00**
Blondie, Who's Boss? No. 1423,
1942 (VG) **28.00**
Bobby Benson, H-Bar-O Ranch,
No. 1108, 1934 (VF) **45.00**
Brad Turner In Transatlantic Flight,
No. 1425, 1939 (NVF) **45.00**

Brick Bradford - City Beneath the Sea

Brick Bradford, City Beneath The
Sea, No. 1309, 1934, VG (ILLUS.) . . **10.00**
Bronc Peeler, The Lonely Cowboy,
No. 1417, 1937 (VG) **25.00**
Buccaneers (The), No. 1646, 1958
TV (VF-) **25.00**
Buck Jones, Killers Crooked Butte,
No. 1451 (VF) **55.00**
Buck Jones, Rough Riders in
Forbidden Trails, No. 1486, 1943
(N.Mint) **80.00**
Buck Jones, Two-Gun Kid, No.
1404, 1937 (VG/FN) **33.00**

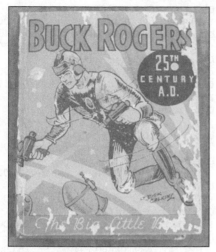

Buck Rogers 25th Century A.D.

Buck Rogers, 25th Century A.D., No.
  742, 1933, Fine (ILLUS.) **20.00**
Buck Rogers, Depth Men of Jupiter,
  No. 1169, 1935 (VF) **75.00**
Buck Rogers, Doom Comet, No.
  1178 (VG+) **45.00**
Buck Rogers, Fiend of Space, No.
  1409 (Fine) **65.00**
Buck Rogers, Overturned World, No.
  1474, 1941 (FN+) **65.00**
Buck Rogers, Planetoid Plot, No.
  1197, 1936 (VG+) **40.00**
Buck Rogers, Super-Dwarf Space,
  No. 1490, 1943, all pictures, VG/FN (4 pgs.
  half off) **25.00**
Buck Rogers, War With the Planet
  Venus, No. 1437, 1938 (VF+) **85.00**
Buffalo Bill, Plays A Lone Hand, No.
  1194, 1936 (VG+) **30.00**
Bugs Bunny, No. 1435, 1944, all
  pictures (FN+/FN) **35.00**
Bugs Bunny, Pirate Loot, 1947, all
  pictures (VF) **40.00**
Bullet Benton, No. 1169, 1939
  boxing strip (VF+) **35.00**
Buz Sawyer and Bomber 13, No.
  1415, 1946 (FN/VF). **35.00**
Calling W-I-X-Y-Z, Jimmy Kean &
  Radios Spies, No. 1412, 1939 (VG) . . **20.00**
Captain Easy, Behind Enemy Lines,
  No. 1474, 1943 (VF/NM) **50.00**
Captain Easy, Soldier of Fortune,
  No. 1128, 1934 (VG+) **30.00**
Captain Midnight, Moon Woman,
  No. 1452, 1943 (N.Mint) **100.00**
Captain Midnight, Secret Squadron
  vs Terror of the Orient, No. 1488,
  1942 (VF+) **75.00**

Charlie Chan, Honolulu Police, No.
  1478 (N.Mint-) **80.00**
Chester Gump, City of Gold, No.
  1146, 1935 (FN+) **40.00**

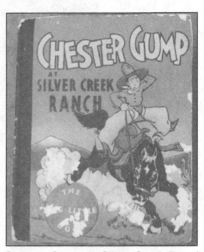

Chester Gump At Silver Creek Ranch

Chester Gump, Silver Creek Ranch,
  No. 734, 1933, FN (ILLUS.). **35.00**
Chuck Malloy, Railroad Detective on
  the Streamliner, No. 1453, 1938
  (FN). **35.00**
Cinderella, Magic Wand, No. 711-10
  (FN+). **35.00**
Coach Bernie Bierman, No. 1480
  (VF/NM). **45.00**
Convoy Patrol, No. 1469, 1942 (VG). . **60.00**
Cowboy Lingo, No.1457, 1938
  (VG/FN). **25.00**
Cowboy Millionaire, No. 1106, 1935
  (N.MInt) **70.00**
Cowboy Stories, No. 724, 1933
  (VG/FN). **30.00**
Crimson Cloak, No. 1161, 1939
  (VF/NM). **45.00**
Dan Dunn, Trail Counterfeiters, No.
  1125, 1936 (NFN) **35.00**
Dan Dunn, Trail of Wu Fang, No.
  1454, 1938 (VG) **25.00**
Danger Trails in Africa No. 1151,
  1935 (FN+) **35.00**
Detective Higgins, Racket Squad,
  No. 1484, 1938 (VG) **15.00**
Dick Tracy, Bicycle Gang, No. 1445,
  1948 (VF) **55.00**
Dick Tracy, Boris Arson Gang, No.
  1163, 1935 (Fine) **45.00**
Dick Tracy, Chains of Crime, No.
  1185, 1936 (VG) **35.00**
Dick Tracy, Crooks in Disguise, No.
  1479, 1939 (NM) **125.00**

Dick Tracy & Dick Tracy Junior

Dick Tracy, Dick Tracy Junior, No.
710, 1933, VF (ILLUS.) **24.00**
Dick Tracy, FBI Operative, No. 1449,
1943 (N.Mint). **120.00**
Dick Tracy, G-Men, No. 1439, 1941
(VF/NM). **95.00**

Dick Tracy - Larceny Lu

Dick Tracy, Larceny Lu, No. 1170,
1935, VF (ILLUS.) **35.00**
Dick Tracy, Mad Killer, No. 1435,
1947 (VF+) **65.00**
Dick Tracy, On High Seas, No. 1454,
1938 (VF) **75.00**

Dick Tracy Out West

Dick Tracy, Out West, No. 723,
1933, VG (ILLUS.). **35.00**
Dick Tracy, Phantom Ship, No. 1434,
1940 (N.Mint). **125.00**
Dick Tracy, Racketeer Gang,
No. 1112, 1936 (VG+) **35.00**
Dick Tracy, Returns, No. 1195, 1939
based serial (VF/NM) **95.00**
Dick Tracy, Super Detective,
No. 1488, 1939 (VG) **38.00**
Dick Tracy, Tiger Lilly Gang,
No. 1460, 1949 (VG+) **35.00**
Dick Tracy, Wreath Kidnapping,
No. 1482, 1946 (N.Mint) **130.00**
Don O'Dare, Finds War, No. 1438,
1938 (VG) **17.00**
Don Winslow, Giant Girl Spy,
No. 1408, 1946 (N. Mint). **80.00**
Don Winslow, Navy & Great War
Plot, No. 1489, 1940 (VF+) **65.00**
Don Winslow, Navy Intelligence Ace,
No. 1418, 1942 (NM-N. Mint) **80.00**
Don Winslow, Scorpion Gang,
No. 1419 (VG+). **30.00**
Don Winslow, USN, No. 1407, #1
(FN) **35.00**
Donald Duck, Ghost Morgan's
Treasure, No. 1411, 1946 (VG+). . . . **38.00**
Donald Duck, Headed for Trouble,
No. 1430 (VG) **35.00**
Donald Duck, Lays Down the Law,
No. 1449 ,1948 (FN/VF-). **45.00**
Donald Duck, Off the Beam,
No. 1438, 1943 (VG/FN) **35.00**
Donald Duck, Says Such A Life,
No. 1404, 1939 (VG) **20.00**
Donald Duck, Up In Air, No. 1486
(FN/VF) **60.00**
Eddy Cantor, An Hour With You,
No. 774, 1934 (VG+) **65.00**

Ella Cinders - Mysterious House

Ella Cinders, Mysterious House,
No. 1106, 1934, FN++ (ILLUS.) **45.00**
Ellery Queen, Last Man Club,
No. 1406, 1940 (VG). **30.00**

Erik Noble and the Forty-Niners,
No. 772, 1934 . . . . **25.00**

Flame Boy & Indian Secret,
No. 1464, 1938 (VF/NM) **40.00**

Flash Gordon, Forest Kingdom,
No. 1492 (VF-VF) **75.00**

Flash Gordon, Jungles Mongo,
No. 1424, 1947 (VF/NM+) **95.00**

Flash Gordon, Perils Mongo,
No. 1423, 1940 (VF+) **80.00**

Flash Gordon, Red Sword Invader,
No. 1479, 1945 (VF++) **80.00**

Flash Gordon, Tyrant Mongo,
No. 1484, 1942 (VF++) **95.00**

Flash Gordon, Water World,
No. 1407, 1937 (VF/NM) **100.00**

Flying the Sky Clipper, No. 1108,
1936 (VG) **15.00**

Foreign Spies, Dr. Doom, No. 1460,
1939 (Fine) **25.00**

Frank Buck Presents Ted Towers,
Animal Master, No. 1175, 1935 (VG) . . **18.00**

Frank Merriwell At Yale, No. 1121,
1935 (NFN) **20.00**

G-Man, And the Gun Runners,
No. 1469, 1940 (N.Mint-) **60.00**

G-Man, Breaking Gambling Ring,
No. 1493, 1938 (VG/FN) **25.00**

G-Man, In Action, No.1173, 1940
(VG/FN) **30.00**

G-Man, On Lightning Island, 1936,
Dell (VG) **40.00**

G-Man, Radio Bank Robberies,
No. 1434, 1937 (FN) **30.00**

G-Man, Vs Red X, No. 1147, 1936
(VF+) **40.00**

G-Man, Vs The Fifth Column,
No. 1470, 1941 (NM) **60.00**

G-Men, On the Job, No. 1168, 1935
(VF) **35.00**

G-Men, On the Trail, No. 1157, 1938
(VF) **40.00**

Gang Busters In Action!, No. 1451,
1938 (FN/VF) **35.00**

Gene Autry, Bandits of Silver Tip,
No. 700-10, 1949 (VF) **35.00**

Gene Autry, Cowboy Detective,
No. 1494, 1940 (VF++) **75.00**

Gene Autry, Gun-Smoke Reckoning,
No. 1434, 1943 (VG) **25.00**

Gene Autry, Hawk of Hills, No. 1493,
1942 (N.Mint) **95.00**

Gene Autry, Law of the Range,
No. 1483, 1939 (Fine+) **45.00**

Gene Autry, Public Cowboy No. 1, #
1 (FN+) **35.00**

Gene Autry, Range War, No. 714-10,
1950 (NM) **50.00**

Gene Autry, Special Ranger,
No. 1428, 1941 (NM- N.Mint) **90.00**

Gene Autry, Special Ranger Rule,
No. 1456, 1945 (VG+) **35.00**

George O'Brien, Gun Law, No. 1418,
1938 (FN) **35.00**

George O'Brien, Hooded Riders,
No. 1457, 1940 (VF/NM) **75.00**

Ghost Avengers, No. 1462, 1943
(VF+) **50.00**

Green Hornet Returns, No. 1496,
1941 (VF/NM) **145.00**

Green Hornet Strikes, No. 1453,
1940 (Fine+) **95.00**

Harold Teen, Swinging at the Sugar
Bowl, No. 1418, 1939 (VF/NM) **55.00**

Huckleberry Finn, No. 1422, 1939
(Near Mint) **60.00**

Inspector Wade, Red Aces,
No. 1148, 1937 (FN/VF) **35.00**

Jack Armstrong, Iron Key, No. 1432,
1939 (VF) **45.00**

Jack Armstrong, Ivory Treas.,
No. 1435, 1937 (FN) **30.00**

Jackie Cooper, Gangster's Boy,
No. 1402, 1938 (Fine+) **35.00**

Jerry Parker, Police Reporter,
No. 1147, 1941 (VG) **22.00**

Jim Craig, Kidnapped Governor,
No. 1466, 1938 (Fine+) **30.00**

Jim Hardy, Ace Reporter, No. 1180,
1940 (Near Mint) **100.00**

Joe Louis, Brown Bomber, No. 1105,
1936 (NVF) **65.00**

John Carter of Mars, No. 1402, 1940
(VF/N.Mint) **175.00**

Jungle Jim, No. 1138, 1936, #1
(VF/NMint) **75.00**

Junior Nebb, Joins the Circus,
No. 1470, 1939 (N.Mint) **60.00**

**Katzenjammer Kids in the
Mountains,** No. 1305, 1934
(VF/N.Mint) **140.00**

Kay Darcy & Mystery Hideout,
No. 1411, 1937 (FN+) **25.00**

Kazan, King of the Pack, No. 1471,
1940 (VF+) **35.00**

Keep 'Em Flying, U.S.A. for
America's Defense, No. 1420,
1943 (N. Mint) **80.00**

Ken Maynard, Western Justice,
No. 1430, 1938 (N. Mint) **75.00**

King of Royal Mounted, Gets His
Man, No. 1452, 1938 (NM) **75.00**

King of Royal Mounted, Great Jewel
Mystery, No. 1486, 1939 (VF+) **50.00**

King of Royal Mounted, Northern
Treasure, No. 1179, 1937 (VF+) **50.00**

Lightning Jim, US Marshall,
No. 1441, 1940 (FN/VF) **35.00**

Lil' Abner, Among the Millionaires,
No. 1401, 1939 (VF+) **70.00**
Lil' Abner, In New York, No. 1198,
1936 (VG) **35.00**
Little Annie Rooney, Highway to
Adventure, No. 1406, 1938 . . . . **45.00**
Little Annie Rooney, Orphan House,
No. 1117, 1936 (VF+) **40.00**
Little Orphan Annie, Chizzler,
No. 748, 1938 (Fine+) **55.00**
Little Orphan Annie, Junior
Commandos, No. 1457, 1943 (VG). . **30.00**
Little Orphan Annie, Million Dollar
Formula, No. 1186, 1936 (VG) **30.00**
Little Orphan Annie, Mysterious
Shoemaker, No. 1149, 1938 (VG). . . **35.00**
Little Orphan Annie, No. 708, 1933,
VG (missing pg. 304) **35.00**
Little Orphan Annie, Underground
Hide-out, No. 1461, 1945 (VF++) . . . **45.00**
Lone Ranger, Barbary Coast,
No. 1421, 1944 (VG) **30.00**
Lone Ranger, Black Shirt
Highwayman, No. 1450, 1939 (FN). . **40.00**
Lone Ranger, Follows Through,
No. 1468, 1941 (VF/NM) **80.00**
Lone Ranger, Great Western Span,
No. 1477, 1942 (N.Mint) **95.00**
Lone Ranger, His Horse Silver,
No. 1181, #1, 1935 (VG+) **38.00**
Lone Ranger, Menace Murder
Valley, No. 1465, 1937 (VF) **65.00**
Lone Ranger, Outwits Crazy Cougar,
No. 5774 (NM) **15.00**
Lone Ranger, Secret of Sombre
Canyon, No. 712-10, 1950 (NM) **55.00**
Lone Ranger, Silver Bullets,
No. 1498 (N.Mint-) **75.00**
Lone Ranger, The Red Renegades,
No. 1489, 1939 (Fine+) **48.00**
Lone Star Martin of Texas Rangers,
No. 1405, 1939 (NM) **40.00**
Lone Star Martin of Texas Rangers,
No. 1405, 1939 (VG/FN) **20.00**
Mary Lee, Mystery Indian Beads,
No. 1438, 1937 (NM-NM) **45.00**
Masked Man of the Mesa, No. 1165,
1939 (Fine+) **30.00**
Maximo, Amazing Superman-
Crystals Doom, No. 1444, 1941
(N.Mint) **60.00**
Mickey Mouse, 7 Ghosts, No. 1475,
1940 (FN/VF). **65.00**
Mickey Mouse, Foreign Legion,
No. 1428, 1940 (VF-VF) **65.00**
Mickey Mouse, Haunted Island,
No. 708-10 (NM) **50.00**
Mickey Mouse, 'Lectro Box,
No. 1413, 1946 (VF++) **65.00**

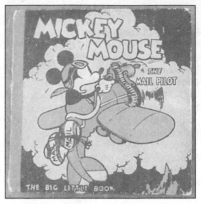

Mickey Mouse The Mail Pilot

Mickey Mouse, Mail Pilot, No. 731,
1933, Fine (ILLUS.) **25.00**
Mickey Mouse, Sky Island, No. 1417,
1941 (VF/NM) **75.00**
Mickey Rooney Himself, No. 1427,
1939 (VF/N Mint+) **55.00**
**Moon Mullins & Plushbottom
Twins,** No. 1134, 1935 (VG) **35.00**

OG Son Of Fire

OG, Son Of Fire, No. 1115, 1936,
Fine (ILLUS.) **10.00**
Our Gang, On the March, No. 1451,
1942 (NM-NM) **75.00**
Our Gang Adventures, No. 1456
(N.Mint) **75.00**
Pat Nelson, Ace of Test Pilots,
No. 1145, 1937 (VG) **15.00**
Phantom (The), Desert Justice,
No. 1421, 1941 (VF/NM) **75.00**
Phantom (The), Girl of Mystery,
No. 1416, 1947 (NM-N.Mint) **80.00**

Phantom (The), Sky Pirates,
No. 1468, 1945 (VF) 50.00

Pilot Pete, Dive Bomber, No. 1466,
1941 (VF++) 40.00

Popeye, Adventures of, No. 1051,
1934 (FN/VF). 150.00

Popeye, Deep Sea Mystery,
No. 1499 (VF+) 50.00

Popeye, Jeep, No. 1405, 1937
(Fine+). 39.00

Prairie Bill, Covered Wagon,
No. 758, 1934 (FN+) 35.00

Punch Davis Of Aircraft Carrier,
No. 1440, 1945 (G/VG) 22.00

Radio Patrol, Big Dan's Mobsters,
No. 1498, 1940 (VF+) 45.00

Radio Patrol, Outwitting Gang Chief,
No. 1496, 1939 (VF-). 34.00

Radio Patrol, Trailing Safeblowers,
No. 1173, 1937 (VF) 38.00

Range Busters, Saddle Mountain
Roundup, No. 1141, 1942 (VF-VF) . . 37.00

Ray Land of Tank Corps U.S.A.,
No. 1147, 1942 (N.Mint) 60.00

Red Barry, Hero of the Hour,
No. 1157, 1935 (FN) 30.00

Red Barry, Undercover Man,
No. 1426, 1939 (VF/N Mint+) 55.00

Red Death on the Range, No. 1149,
1940 (NM-NM). 50.00

Red Ryder, Code of the West,
No. 1427, 1941 (VF/NM) 75.00

Red Ryder, Fighting Westerner,
No. 1440, 1940 (NM-NM) 85.00

Red Ryder, Squaw-Tooth, No. 1414,
1946 (VF-VF). 45.00

Rider of Lone Trails, No. 1425, 1937
(VG). 15.00

Roy Rogers, Crossed Feathers
Ranch, No. 1494 (VG+). 30.00

Roy Rogers, Dwarf-Cattle, No. 1421,
1949 (VF-) 45.00

Roy Rogers, King of the Cowboys,
No. 1476, 1943 (N.Mint-) 70.00

Roy Rogers, Robinhood of Range,
No. 1460, 1942 (N.Mint) 80.00

Roy Rogers, Snowbound Outlaws,
No. 701-10 (VF+) 35.00

Secret Agent X-9, No. 1144, 1936
(VF) 45.00

Shadow (The), Ghost Makers,
No. 1495, 1942 (VG+) 75.00

Shadow (The), Masters of Evil,
No. 1443, 1941 (VF+) 165.00

Shirley Temple, Littlest Rebel,
No. 1115 (VG-) 35.00

Shooting Sheriffs of Wild West,
No. 1195, 1936 (VG+) 25.00

Silver Streak, No. 1155, 1935 (VF) . . . 40.00

Skeezix, Goes to War, No. 1414,
1944 (N. Mint) 60.00

Skeezix, Military Academy, No. 1408,
1938 (VG+) 30.00

Skyroads, Hurricane Hank,
No. 1127, 1936 (VG) 25.00

Smilin' Jack, Flying High With
Downwind, No. 1412, 1942
(FN+/FN) 45.00

Smilin' Jack, Jungle Pipeline,
No. 1419, 1947 (VF) 65.00

Smilin' Jack, Stratosphere,
No. 1152, 1937 (VF+) 70.00

Snow White & 7 Dwarfs, No. 1460,
1938 (FN/VF-) 60.00

Son of Mystery, No. 1152, 1939
(VF/NM). 40.00

SOS Coast Guard, No. 1191, 1936
(FN+). 25.00

Speed Douglas & Mole Gang,
No. 1455 (NM-) 45.00

Spider-man, Zaps Zodiac (1st)
No. 5779 (NM). 9.00

Spike Kelly of the Commandos,
No. 1467, 1943 (NM-N.Mint) 50.00

Steve Hunter, U.S. Coast Guard
Under Secret Orders, No. 1426,
1942 (NM) 50.00

Tailspin Tommy, Air Racer,
No. 1183, 1940 (FN/VF) 48.00

Tailspin Tommy, Dirigible to Flight
N. Pole, No. 1124, 1934 (VF+) 55.00

Tailspin Tommy, Famous Payroll
Mystery, No. 747, 1933 (VG+) 35.00

Tailspin Tommy, Hooded Flyer,
No. 1423, 1937 (VF/NM) 50.00

Tailspin Tommy, Lost Transport,
No. 1413 , 1939 (NM-). 55.00

Tarzan, Beasts of Tarzan, No. 1410,
1937 (VG/FN) 37.00

Tarzan, Golden Lion, No. 1148 (NM). . . 110.00

Tarzan, Jewels of Opar, No. 1495,
1940 (VF/NM 80.00

Tarzan, Journey of Terror,
No. 700-10 (Mint) 50.00

Tarzan, Of The Apes, No. 744, 1933
(VG+). 60.00

Tarzan, Of The Screen, No. 778,
1934, MS (VG-) 35.00

Tarzan, Return of Tarzan, No. 1102,
1936 (VF++) 75.00

Tarzan, Revenge, No. 1488, 1938
(VF/NM). 80.00

Tarzan, Son of Tarzan, No. 1477,
1939 (VF/NM) 80.00

Tarzan, Terrible, No. 1453, 1942
(NM-N.Mint). 95.00

Tarzan, Untamed, No. 1452, 1941
(NM-) 95.00

Terry and the Pirates, Giants
Vengeance, No. 1446, 1939 (VG)... **30.00**
Terry and the Pirates, Mountain
Stronghold, No. 1499, 1941
(NM-NM) **85.00**
Terry and the Pirates, No. 1156, #1,
1935 (VF) **65.00**
Terry and the Pirates, Shipwrecked
On Desert Island, No. 1412, 1938
(FN+)........................ **50.00**
Terry and the Pirates, War in the
Jungle, No. 1420, 1946 (VG/FN).... **35.00**
Texas Kid, No. 1429, 1937 (VF/NM) .. **39.00**
Texas Ranger, Trail of the Dog Town
Rustlers, No. 1135, 1936 .... **35.00**
Texas Ranger (The), No. 1135, 1936
(VG)......................... **25.00**
Tim McCoy, Sandy Gulch Stampede,
No. 1490, 1939 (NM-) **60.00**
Tim McCoy, Tomahawk Trail,
No. 1436, 1937 (VG) **25.00**
Tim McCoy, Westerner, No. 1193,
1936 (VG) **25.00**
Tim Tyler, Plot Exiled King,
No. 1479, 1939 (VF/NM)......... **65.00**
Tim Tyler's Luck, Adventures in the
Ivory Patrol, No. 1140, 1937 ...... **35.00**
Tiny Tim, Adventures Of, No. 767,
1935 (G/VG) **25.00**
Tiny Tim, Big, Big World, No. 1472,
1945 (NM-) **65.00**
Tiny Tim, Mechanical Men, No. 1172,
1937 (NFN) **39.00**
Tom Beatty, Ace of Service, No. 723,
1934 (FN+) **35.00**
Tom Beatty, Scores Again, No. 1165,
1937 (NVF) **30.00**
Tom Mix, Circus on the Barbary
Coast, No. 1482, 1940 (VG+) **33.00**
Tom Mix, Fighting Cowboy,
No. 1144, 1935 (VG)............ **25.00**
Tom Mix, Hoard Montezuma,
No. 1462, 1937 (VG)............ **30.00**
Tom Mix, Plays Lone Hand,
No. 1173, 1935 (NVF)........... **45.00**
Tom Mix, Stranger From the South,
No. 1183, 1936 (VG)............ **25.00**
Tom Mix, Terror Trail, No. 762, 1934
(VG)......................... **35.00**
Tom Swift, Giant Telescope,
No. 1485, 1939 (FN+)........... **45.00**
Tom Swift, Magnetic Silencer,
No. 1437, 1941 (VF) **55.00**
Tracked by a G-Man No. 1158,
1939, VF/NM.................. **40.00**
Treasure Island, No. 720, 1933
(FN+)........................ **45.00**
Two-Gun Montana, No. 1104, 1936 .. **40.00**

Uncle Ray's Story Of The United States

Uncle Ray's Story Of The United
States, No. 722, 1934 (ILLUS.)..... **10.00**
Vic Sands of US Flying Fortress,
No. 1455, 1943 (VG)............ **25.00**
Wash Tubs in Pandemonia,
No. 751, 1934 .... **35.00**
Will Rogers, No. 1576, 1935 (Fine) ... **25.00**
Wimpy the Hamburger Eater,
No. 1458, 1938 (FN)............ **45.00**
Windy Wayne & Flying Wing,
No. 1433, 1942 (Near Mint)....... **50.00**
Wings of the USA, No. 1407, 1940
(NM) **60.00**

BLACK AMERICANA

*Over the past decade or so, this field of
collecting has rapidly grown and today almost
anything that relates to Black culture or
illustrates Black Americana is considered a
desirable collectible. Although many
representations of Blacks, especially on 19th and
early 20th century advertising pieces and
housewares, were cruel stereotypes, even these
are collected as poignant reminders of how far
American society has come since the dawning of
the Civil Rights movement, and how far we still
have to go. Other pieces related to this category
will be found from time to time in such
categories as Advertising Items, Banks,
Character Collectibles, Kitchenwares, Cookie
Jars, Signs and Signboards, Toys and several
others. For a complete overview of this subject
see Antique Trader Books' Black Americana
Price Guide with a special introduction by
Julian Bond.*

Advertisement, paper, printed w/ad
for the book "History of Slavery," a
subscriber-funded volume of 800-
900 pp., reverse w/pencilled receipt
for 25 cent deposit, dated
November 3, 1859, 4 x 8½"
(folds) **$30.00**

Autograph, "Frederick Douglass," document signed, a four-page deed executed by hand with Douglass serving as recorder for the District of Columbia, dated "July 2, 1881," lightly ruled paper (some toning at folds) **219.00**

Autograph, James Meredith, typed letter signed, dated August 29, 1966, on his stationery, writing to Lawrence Spivak giving the expenses for appearance on "Meet The Press" on August 21, 1966 & asking for reimbursement, written only days after Meredith's enrollment at the University of Alabama (folds) **101.00**

Book, "Jack Johnson: In the Ring & Out," autobiography, 1927, first edition, National Sports Publishing Company, Chicago, introductory articles by Damon Runyon & "Mrs. Jack Johnson," 259 pp. (slightly scuffed cover, interior cover address label) **179.00**

Book, "Memoirs of Elleanor Eldridge," cloth covers, published by B.T. Albro, Providence, Rhode Island at author's expense, 1838, various endorsements, autobiographical accounts, 128 pp. (some pages slightly stained) **182.00**

Book, "The Work of Colored Women," published by Colored Work Committee of the Y.W.C.A., 1919, urges "racial harmony" during time of "racial disturbances," w/photos, paper wraps, 136 pp., 5½ x 8½ " (cover soiled, tear in upper rear, back cover spine tears) . . **145.00**

Booklet, "Entertainment & Minstrel Album," by Joe Davis, 1936 . . . . **70.00**

"Southern Types" Booklet

Booklet, "Southern Types," bound w/ribbon, cover bust portrait of smiling black boy, contents include 17 photogravures, published by Wittemann Souvenir Books & Postcards, The Albertype Co., Brooklyn, various views of rural Southern blacks in poverty & rags, various stereotypical images & names, ca. 1910, 16 pp., cover slightly soiled, tiny rear edge tear, 5¼ x 8¼ " (ILLUS.) **97.00**

World War II "Jim Crow" Booklet

Booklet, "The Story of Jim Crow in Uniform," by Nancy & Dwight McDonald, published by The March on Washington Movement, 1943, full title "The war's greatest Scandal! - The Story of Jim Crow in Uniform," cover art of a large fist marked "U.S." crushing down a black soldier, soiling on lower cover & following pages, water-stained, small bottom spine tear, 15 pp., 6 x 9" (ILLUS.) **52.00**

Booklet, "Pictures and Stories - Uncle Tom's Cabin," published by John Jewett & Co., Boston, 1853, adapted work for children told in poetry & prose w/engravings of scenes from the original book, yellow wraps, 32 pp., 7 x 9" (wraps moderately soiled, cover w/stain, interior w/some minor staining) **138.00**

Broadside, printed paper from slavery era, title reads "Administrator's Sale of SLAVE and PERSONAL PROPERTY...," further text describes offerings including a slave, sale for

Early Slavery Broadside

settlement of owner's debts, dated "November 16, 1859," Liberty, Missouri, 8¾ x 9½ " (ILLUS.) **1,898.00**

Cap badge, curved brass w/screw-back, an American eagle on shield above logo "Tuskegee Normal & Industrial Institute - Alabama - Labor & Humility - 1881," ca. 1890-1910, 1 x 2" (worn, bit rough at edges) **59.00**

Blanche K. Bruce Carte de Visite

Carte de visite photo, bust portrait of Blanche K. Bruce, elected to the United States Senate from Mississippi in 1874, photo by Matthew Brady, former slave & only black to serve full term in Senate until the 1960s, back printed "Brady's Nat'l. Portrait Gallery, Wash., D.C." (ILLUS.) **586.00**

Carte de visite photo, standing portrait of branded slave Wilson Chinn, age 60, shown wearing bizarre torture instruments & leg-hobbling rod used on slaves, forehead branded w/initials "VBM,"

initials for slave owner Volsey B. Marmillion of Louisiana who branded his slaves on arms, breasts & foreheads, Chinn & 104 others escaped to Union lines & photo proceeds went to educate blacks in the Department of Gulf under Maj. Gen. Banks, 1863 (very slight soiling) **363.00**

Cookie jar, cov., plastic, figural Aunt Jemima, F. & F. Mold & Die Works **795.00**

Doll, "Baby Grumpy" by Effanbee, composition head & cloth body, 1930s, 12" h. **138.00**

Cloth "Knock-Down" Game Figure

Games, carnival-type, "knock-down" game, a wooden board mounted w/five stylized "Mammy" figures w/painted cloth faces & stereotypical cloth clothing & bonnet, each figure evenly spaced along the board & attached by a hinge, each board w/five 10-12" h. figures, each board 4½ ' l., early 20th c., pr. (ILLUS. of one figure) . . **660.00**

Rare Blackamoor Inkwell

Inkwell, figural, ebonized wood, carved as the head of a Blackamoor w/realistic inset glass eyes, hinged head opens to brass inkwell, round base, Europe, probably Italy, 19th c., minute losses, 6¼ " h. (ILLUS.) **805.00**

Invitation, SNCC fundraising dinner, printed light board w/cover drawing by Ben Shahn of a black & white handshake, held at the New York City Hilton, April 25, 1965, many notables attending, 4 pp., 7 x 10" . . . **28.00**

Louis - Schmeling Fight Matchbook

Matchbook, multicolored paper, cover features sketched fight scene, copy reads "Tune in on the BIGGEST MATCH YET! - Joe Louis vs. Max Schmeling," further text on back cover & interior includes a Buick ad & composite drawing on matches of man looking through fence knothole & "It's a Knock...," also two men at mike w/"Hear Clem McCarthy & Edwin C. Hill describe this great battle. NBC stations, Red & Blue Network," fight on June 18, 1936, five matches remain, slight wear at top fold, 3¼ x 4¼" (ILLUS.) **36.00**

Menu, child's, "Coon Chicken Inn" **45.00**

Newspaper, "Herald of Freedom," June 11, 1836, Concord, New Hampshire, two woodcuts of contrast between lives of free blacks & slaves, 4 pp. (slight edge wear) **44.00**

Photograph, carte-de-visite, "Old Aunt Coly," reverse w/pencil inscription "For all my children. Old Aunt Coly," w/worn cardboard frame cut from album, inscribed "Old Aunt Coly, slave of the Jamison family who stayed on after liberation" (slight photo soiling, slight foxing) **300.00**

Photo of Black Maid & White Child

Photograph, cabinet-size, half-length portrait of an attractive young black maid holding a wiggling (slightly blurred) white toddler, marked "Douglass, Columbia, Missouri," ca.1890s, small oval print 2 x 2¾" (ILLUS.) **100.00**

Pinback button, brown & green on white, "American Negro Labor Congress - 1925" showing black hands shaking, for a movement that lasted only a few months, ¾" d. (slight top wear) **11.00**

Pinback button, political, 1940 campaign, celluloid in blue on white, "Joe & Me for Willkie," highlights Joe Louis' support for Wendell Wilkie in 1940 presidential race,.80" d. **72.00**

Pinback button, "Save the Scottsboro Boys," celluloid in red & white w/black prisoners behind bars held by large white arms, 7/8" d. **274.00**

Pinback button, "Black & Proud," celluloid in blue on yellow, manufactured by Magnificent Books & Mdse., Oakland, California, ca. 1960s, 1½" d. **13.00**

Pinback button, "Hands Off Huey," celluloid in blue & orange, appeal for Huey Newton, jailed Black Panther leader, 1960s, 1¾" d. **18.00**

Place mat, "Coon Chicken Inn" **45.00**

Poster, multicolor printed paper, "Remember ...Uncle Tom Says Only YOU Can Prevent Ghetto Fires," artwork by R. Cobb features caricature of a white-haired black field hand standing & pointing

1960s "Uncle Tom" Poster

w/one hand, a hoe in the other hand, published by Sawyer Press, Los Angeles, 1967, stains along upper edge, 22¼ x 33¼ " (ILLUS.).. **121.00**

Poster stamp, "Abolish Poll Taxes - Free America First," white lettering on blue w/Liberty Bell background, printed by the Southern Conference for Human Welfare, Birmingham, Alabama, probably World War II era, 1 x 1¼ " **12.00**

Record catalog, "Race Records by Columbia - Race Stars," photo portraits of various black recording artists on the cover, stamp of a Johnson City, Tennessee record store, ca. 1926, 44 pp., 5 x 7" (very worn, spine torn, covers almost detached, badly stained) **112.00**

Ribbon, anti-lynching, blue silk, produced by the American Liberty Defense League, reads "1st Anti-Lynching Demonstration - Providence, RI - October 30, 1894 - For Our Outraged Brethren We Plead," 2¼ x 6¼ " (slight stain in upper right, slight soiling) **825.00**

Ribbon, white silk w/gold lettering, "Official" for the Sleeping Car Porters-Ladies Auxilliary,1956, second tri-ennial convention, St. Louis, 1956, 1½ x 5" **22.00**

Salt & pepper shakers, figural "A Nod to Abe," bust of Abraham Lincoln w/removable top hat flanked by seated boy & girl, she wears a pink ribbon in her hair, pink dress & holds a yellow flower, the boy dressed in dark blue jumper w/light blue shirt, designed by Betty Harrington, for the 1991 S&P Club Convention, limited edition of 400 by Regal China, the set .... **300.00 to 350.00**

Salt & pepper shakers, figural, African face teapots, Japan, 1960s, 4"h., pr. **60.00**

Salt & pepper shakers, figural Aunt Jemima & Uncle Mose, plastic, made for Quaker Oats by Fiedler & Fiedler Mold & Die Works, Dayton, Ohio, small, pr. **55.00**

Salt & pepper shakers, figural Aunt Jemima & Uncle Mose, plastic, made for Quaker Oats by Fiedler & Fiedler Mold & Die Works, Dayton, Ohio, 5" h., pr. **62.00**

Salt & pepper shakers, figural Boy & Girl with ear of corn, he is wearing red & white checkered trousers over a blue shirt, she is wearing a short red dress & red hairbows, Japan, pr. **225.00**

Salt & pepper shakers, figural boy in alligator's mouth, pr. **125.00**

Salt & pepper shakers, figural boys playing leap frog, Japan, pre-1950, 3¾" h., pr. **95.00**

Salt & pepper shakers, figural Butler & Maid, 1950s, Brayton Laguna, 5½ ", pr. **150.00**

Salt & pepper shakers, figural Butler & Maid, 1950s, plaid apron, dress w/flowers, Japan, pr. **120.00**

Salt & pepper shakers, figural Chef & Maid, blue & white w/yellow trim, Brayton Laguna, 1950s, 5¾" h., pr. ... **105.00**

Salt & pepper shakers, figural Chef & Maid, red, Brayton Laguna, 1950s, 5½ " h., pr. **125.00**

Salt & pepper shakers, figural Chef & Maid w/stove grease jar, green w/gold trim, 5¼ " h., stove 4¾" h., U.S.A., 1960s, the set **190.00**

Salt & pepper shakers, figural Chef & Maid, yellow trim, U.S.A., 1950s, 5¾" h., pr. **95.00**

Salt & pepper shakers, figural Chef with knife, yellow coat, black tie, white cap, pre-1950s, Japan, pr..... **50.00**

Salt & pepper shakers, figural children in basket, Japan, 1950s-1960s, 3½ " h., the set **80.00**

Salt & pepper shakers, figural children shooting dice w/tray, one boy kneeling, one standing, dice attached to tray, pre-1950, Japan, 3" h., the set **145.00**

Salt & pepper shakers, figural clown face teapots, Japan, 1960s, 4" h., pr. **45.00**

Salt & pepper shakers, figural cute
children, bust of bald boy & girl
wearing straw hat, 1960s, G.
Novelty Co., Japan, 3" h. pr. **225.00**

Salt & pepper shakers, figural head
& watermelon slice, 2¼ " h., pr. **60.00**

Salt & pepper shakers, figural Jonah
& the whale, boy sits on knob on
whale's back, Japan, 1960s,
3½" h., pr. **85.00**

Salt & pepper shakers, figural
Luzianne Coffee Mammy,
green skirt, plastic, F & F,
5" h., pr. . . . . **200.00 to 225.00**

Salt & pepper shakers, figural
Mammy & Chef, small, Pearl
China, pr. **75.00**

Salt & pepper shakers, figural man
on toilet, Japan, pre-1950, pr. **64.00**

Salt & pepper shakers, figural
Matador & Bull, black matador in
white suit w/yellow trim, red belt &
black necktie, holding red cape,
brown bull w/white horns, Japan,
1970s, 4" h., pr. **54.00**

Salt & pepper shakers, figural
Native eating watermelon, Japan,
1960s, 3½ " h., pr. . . . . . . **100.00 to 120.00**

Salt & pepper shakers, figural
Native mother holding baby,
nesting-type, Japan, 1950s,
4¾" h.,pr. **40.00**

Salt & pepper shakers, figural
Native riding cucumber, Japan,
2¼ " h., pr. **75.00**

Salt & pepper shakers, figural
Native riding hippo, Japan, 1950s,
3¾" h., pr. **225.00**

Salt & pepper shakers, figural
Native with pot & hut, 1960s,
probably U.S.A., 2¼ " h., pr. **80.00**

Salt & pepper shakers, figural porter
carrying suitcases, figure wearing
white shirt, blue coat, red cap &
pants, carries suitcase shakers
(sometimes marked "S" & "P"),
Japan, pre-1950, 4½ " h., the
set . . . . **190.00 to 200.00**

Salt & pepper shakers, figural
Provincial couple, brown, tan &
white, Brayton Laguna, 1950s,
5½ " h., pr. **85.00**

Salt & pepper shakers, figural
"Salty" & "Peppy," Mammy & Chef,
Pearl China, U.S.A., 7¾" h., pr. **150.00**

Salt & pepper shakers, figural seal
trainer & seal, grey seal on yellow
& black drum, holding red ball,
trainer w/blue pants & tie, yellow
vest, red & white coat & green top
hat, Japan, 1960s, 3½ " h., pr. **85.00**

Salt & pepper shakers, figural tap
dancers, Japan, 1960s, 5" h., pr. . . . **95.00**

Valentine Couple

Salt & pepper shakers, figural
Valentine couple, man & woman
w/grey hair, Japan, 5" h., pr.
(ILLUS.) **185.00**

Salt & pepper shakers, figural
Valentine couple, young girl in red
dress w/red bow in hair, white
pinafore, boy in white shirt & pants
holding valentine, Japan, 1950s,
4¾" h., pr. . . . . **195.00 to 200.00**

Sheet music, "Eliza's Flight," black &
white cover art scene from "Uncle
Tom's Cabin," 1852, published in
Boston, sold in Pittsburgh by Miss
Collier & E. J. Loder, lithographed
by Bufford, 5 pp., 10¼ x 13"
(nearly disbound, soiling
throughout) **61.00**

Sheet music, "Christy's Melodies -
Snow Drop Ann," by Edwin P.
Christy of Christy Minstrels, 1847,
cover art w/bust portrait of Mr.
Christy as well as black cherubs &
minstrels, 4 pp., 10 x 13½ "
(disbound, slight soiling) **112.00**

Sheet music, "Blackamoors" Barn
Dance," by Fabian Rose, 1899,
multicolored lithographed cover art
of elegant black couple dancing, 8
pp., 10 x 14" (front & back nearly
separated, crimp & slight tear in
lower right) **30.00**

Sheet music, "The Jolly Coon," by
M.B. Lawry, 1899, red, blue &
white cover w/a stereotyped scene
of a wildly dancing long-legged
black banjo player in foreground
w/other dancing blacks in

Early Black-related Sheet Music

background, slight tears at top & bottom of spine, slight bottom wear, 6 pp., 10¾ x 14¼ " (ILLUS.) . . **53.00**

Slave bill of sale, paper, dated "1803," notes James King of Sullivan County, Tennessee buys slave "Andy" from Rob. Campbell of Virginia for $410, 7½ x 12¾" (folds, slight worming, reverse soiled) **200.00**

Stereo Card of Black Cotton Pickers

Stereo view card, black cotton pickers, shows women & children in fields, by J.A. Palmer, Aiken, South Carolina, No. 175 of "Characteristic Southern Scenes," children moved during photo shoot, foxing in sky (ILLUS.) **65.00**

"Cake Walk" Stereo View Card

Stereo view card, "Cake Walk in the Old Plantation," stereotypical view of a group of blacks dancing in front of a log cabin, caption indicates this was from a series by B.W. Kilburn, Littleton, New

Hampshire sold at the 1904 Louisiana Purchase Exposition, St. Louis (ILLUS.) **86.00**

Stereo view card, seated portrait of Booker T. Washington, inscribed "Pres. of the Negro Industrial School," Underwood & Underwood, 1906 (a bit light, minor wear) **101.00**

Stereo view card, "Toby's Cabin," photograph of a black family outside a dilapidated cabin, J. N. Wilson, Savannah, Georgia, marked "No. 103, Toby's Cabin, Sandfly Station. Just outside of city." (one image slightly lighter, slight soiling, black strip down one edge) **91.00**

Tintype, three-quarters length studio portrait of a young black woman wearing a bustle-style long dress, one arm resting on a square pedestal, darkening along top & left edge, ca. 1870s, 2½ x 3¼ " **57.00**

Tintype of Young Black Man

Tintype, bust portrait of a handsome young black man in a studio setting, center-parted hair, wearing a dark jacket & ruffled white shirt, ca. 1870-90, corners cropped, 2½ x 3½ " (ILLUS.) **63.00**

Black Dancers Jig Toy

Toy, jig-type, carved & painted wood, two stylized black male dancers w/hinged arms & legs raised atop a rectangular box platform w/twist handles at each end to control movement, American, late 19th c., paint wear, 8 x 17½ ", 14½ " h. (ILLUS.)................... **748.00**

Papier-Maché Clockwork Nodder

Toy, clockwork-type, papier-maché & cloth, figure of a standing black boy wearing a felt & cotton outfit, on a small wooden platform base, painted facial features, ca. 1900, some damage & fading, paper collar damage, face paint cracked, some flaking on hands, 24" h. (ILLUS.) **1,265.00**

Trade card, "Arm & Hammer Baking Soda," three-panel folder, shows a comical black woman baking a cake, black dialect **80.00**

Trade card, "Ayer's Cathartic Pills - The Country Doctor," kindly elderly black doctor holds crying black baby girl w/small boy kneeling beside him, advertising at bottom, olive green coat & background (ILLUS.)...................... **35.00**

Black "Country Doctor" Trade Card

Trade card, "Champion Fly Trap," black & white scene of stereotyped black man standing behind a table holding the tall wire mesh fly trap, flies swarming around, table apron printed "The Champion Fly Trap," stamped store advertising at bottom (light wear) **40.00**

Trade card, "Chase & Sanborn Coffee," three-panel folder, opens & a short black man becomes tall, holding a can of the coffee **75.00**

Trade card, "Czar Baking Powder," a comical scene of a large black Mammy & black boy amazed by the size of a baked loaf of bread ... **35.00**

Dixon's Stove Polish Trade Card

Trade card, "Dixon's Stove Polish," interior scene of 12 black men in the 'Lime Kiln Club,' one standing elderly man addressing the others, meant to be a folder but never folded (ILLUS.) **60.00**

Gold Dust Twins Trade Card

Trade card, "Fairbanks Gold Dust Washing Powder," color die-cut of Gold Dust Twins seated in tub of water, crease on one head (ILLUS.). . **50.00**

Trade card, "Fleischmann's Compressed Yeast - Aunty's Breakfast Cakes," attractive scene of a smiling black woman cooking pancakes w/a smiling curly-headed blonde girl standing beside her, packet in upper left background, further advertising across bottom **60.00**

"Jolly Nigger" Bank Trade Card

Trade card, mechanical bank-type, "'Jolly Nigger' - Toy Savings Bank - Patented...," further information at the bottom below the color image of the bank, very faint corner creases (ILLUS.) **400.00**

St. Louis Beef Canning Co. Card

Trade card, "St. Louis Beef Canning Co.," stereotyped comical black man seated smiling & waving, holding a packet of the product while sitting on another, dialect across the bottom, album page remnants (ILLUS.) **50.00**

BOTTLES

BITTERS

(Numbers with some listings below refer to those used in Carlyn Ring's For Bitters Only.)

African Stomach Bitters, cylindrical w/applied top, ca. 1872-1906, light golden amber, 9⅝" h. **$130.00**

Ayalla Mexican Bitters - M. Rothenberg & Co. San Francisco, Cal., square w/tooled lip, smooth base, ca. 1910-1911, amber w/reddish hue, 9½" h. **253.00**

Baker's Orange Grove - Bitters, square w/ribbed edges, applied sloping collar mouth, smooth base, ca. 1865-1870, medium copper w/subtle wisps of puce, 9⅜" h. (ILLUS.). **303.00**

Bodeker's Constitution Bitters Richmond, Va. - (motif of anchor), flask-shaped w/tooled mouth, smooth base, ca. 1880-1900, amber, 6⅜" h. (ILLUS) **303.00**

Bourbon Whiskey Bitters, barrel-shaped w/horizontal ribbing, applied mouth, smooth base, ca. 1860-1870, medium pinkish strawberry puce, 9¼" h. **440.00**

From left: Baker's Orange Grove Bitters,
Bodeker's Constitution Bitters,
Smith Druid Bitters

Brown's Celebrated Indian Herb Bitters - Patented 1867, figural Indian Queen, rolled lip, smooth base, medium golden amber, 12⅛" h. **633.00**

B.T. 1856 S.C. Smith Druid Bitters, barrel shape w/applied mouth, smooth base, ca. 1865-1875, yellow w/olive tone, 9⅜" h. (ILLUS.) **2,970.00**

Celebrated Crown Bitters - F. Chevalier & Co. Sole Agents, square w/large applied mouth, smooth base, ca. 1880-1885, amber, 9" h................... **165.00**

Cognac Bitters S. Steinfeld Sole Agents For The U.S., round w/applied double collar mouth, smooth base, ca. 1865-1875, olive green, 11⅛" h................. **440.00**

Drakes (S.T.) 1860 Plantation X Bitters - Patented 1862, square cabin-shaped, four-log panel, applied sloping collar mouth, smooth base, ca. 1862-1870, light to medium honey peach, 10" h., D-105 (ILLUS.) **600.00**

Electric Bitters - H.E. Bucklen & Co. Chicago, Ill., square w/tooled top. 90% original label, amber **40.00**

Fisch's (Doctor) Bitters - W.H. Ware Patented 1866, figural w/applied mouth, smooth base, ca. 1866-1870, yellow amber, 11⅝" h. (ILLUS.)..................... **688.00**

Fish (The) Bitters - W.H. Ware Patented 1866, figural w/applied mouth, smooth base, ca. 1866-1870, deep root beer amber, 11⅝" h. **231.00**

From left: Drakes Plantation Bitters
Doctor Fisch's Bitters
Henley's Wild Grape Root Bitters

Gates (C.) & Co. - Life Of Man - Bitters, rectangular w/applied mouth, smooth base, 90% original label, ca. 1890-1910, smoky sapphire blue, 8¼" h. **209.00**

German Balsam Bitters, W.M. Watson & Co. Sole Agents For U.S., square w/applied mouth, smooth base, ca. 1900-1904, milk glass, 9¼" h.................. **688.00**

Hall's Bitters - E.E. Hall New Haven Established 1842, barrel-shaped w/applied top, light to medium amber **200.00**

Henley's (Dr.) Wild Grape Root IXL (in oval) Bitters, square w/tooled mouth, smooth base, ca. 1880-1881, olive amber, 9⅜" h. (¼" chip on reverse) **300.00**

Henley's (Dr.) Wild Grape Root IXL (in oval) Bitters, cylindrical w/ringed tooled mouth, ca. 1885-1886, medium to deep green, 12" h. (ILLUS.) **1,500.00**

Hostetter's (Dr. J.) Stomach Bitters, square w/applied mouth, smooth base marked "L & W" w/backward "21," ca. early 1870s, golden amber w/green top, 9" h. **210.00**

Johnson's - Indian - Dyspeptic - Bitters, rectangular w/wide beveled edges, applied sloping collar mouth, pontil-scarred base, ca. 1840-1855, aqua, 6⅝" h....... **413.00**

Kelly's Old Cabin Bitters - Patented 1863, cabin shape w/applied sloping collar mouth, smooth base, ca. 1863-1870, medium amber, 9¼" h. **358.00**

From left: Lacours Sarapariphere Bitters, National Bitters, Old Dr. Townsend Celebrated Stomach Bitters

Knapps' - Health Restorative - Bitters, N.Y., rectangular w/applied sloping collar mouth, pontil-scarred base, ca. 1845-1855, aqua, 8⅛" h... **578.00**

Lacours Sarapariphere Bitters, cylindrical w/sunken side panel, tooled double rounded collar mouth, single shoulder ring, three-ringed base, ca. 1866-1869, medium amber, 9" h. (ILLUS.)..... **900.00**

Langley's (Dr.) Root & Herb Bitters, applied mouth, smooth base, ca. 1860-1870, orange amber, 5¾" h. .. **88.00**

Morning Inceptum (motif of five-point star) Bitters, round bell-shaped, applied sloping collar mouth, iron pontil, ca. 1865-1875, amber, 12¾" h. **231.00**

Morning Inceptum (motif of five-point star) Bitters, round bell-shaped, tooled lip, smooth base, ca. 1880-1890, yellow olive body shading to light yellow green in neck, 12¾" h. **1,980.00**

National Bitters, figural ear of corn, applied mouth, smooth base marked "Patented 1867," ca. 1867-1875, amber, 12⅝" h. (ILLUS.) **303.00**

Old Homestead Wild Cherry Bitters - Patent, square cabin-shaped w/applied sloping collar mouth, smooth base, ca. 1865-1875, amber, 9¾" h. **275.00**

Old Sachem Bitters And Wigwam Tonic, cylindrical barrel-shape form w/applied mouth, smooth base, ca. 1860-1870, reddish amber puce, 9⅜" h. **633.00**

Old Dr. Townsend Celebrated Stomach Bitters, chestnut shape, applied mouth & right-hand handle, pontil-scarred base, ca. 1860-1870, yellowish amber, 8⅝" h. (ILLUS.). . **11,550.00**

Panknin's - Hepatic Bitters New York, square w/beveled edges, applied mouth, smooth base, ca. 1875-1885, amber, 9" h. **72.00**

Peruvian Bitters - Chas. Noelle & Co., square w/applied double collar mouth, smooth base, ca. 1870-1880, amber w/hint of red, 9½" h... **150.00**

Red Jacket Bitters - Bennett Pieters & Co, square w/tooled mouth, smooth base, ca. 1875-1885, medium amber, 9⅝" h. **83.00**

Reed's Bitters, round w/lady's leg neck, applied double collar mouth, smooth base, ca. 1870-1880, medium amber, 12⅜" h. **275.00**

Renz (Dr.) Herb Bitters, square w/broad sloping collar mouth above beveled ring, ca. 1874-1878, amber, 9⅞" h. **350.00**

Royal Pepsin Stomach Bitters One Fifth Gallon (below motif of rampant lion & unicorn), rectangular, w/tooled mouth, smooth base, original glass stopper, red amber shading to yellow amber, 9" h. (ILLUS.) **83.00**

Schroeder's Bitter Louisville, KY., round w/lady's leg neck, applied mouth, smooth base, ca. 1880-1890, amber 11½" h............ **143.00**

Schroeder's Bitter Louisville, KY., round w/lady's leg neck, tooled mouth, smooth base, ca. 1875-1885, amber, 9" h............ **165.00**

Simon's - Prussian - Vegetable Bitters, square w/applied sloping collar mouth, smooth base, ca. 1875-1885, medium amber, 10¼" h. **165.00**

From left: Royal Pepsin Stomach Bitters Young America Stomach Bitters

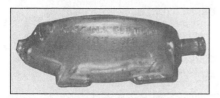

Suffolk Bitters

Suffolk Bitters - Philbrook & Tucker
Boston, figural pig, applied double
collar mouth, smooth base, ca.
1865-1875, yellow w/olive tone,
"rainbow" bruise on edge of a foot,
10⅛" l. (ILLUS.) **798.00**

Tyler's Standard American Bitters,
square w/applied sloping collar
mouth, smooth base, ca. 1870-
1880, root beer amber, 9⅜" h. **187.00**

Ulmer's Mountain Ash Bitters -
New German - Remedy,
rectangular w/applied sloping collar
mouth, pontil-scarred base,
ca. 1840-1855, aqua, 7" h. **990.00**

Young America - Stomach Bitters -
P. Rindskopf & Bro, square
w/applied mouth, smooth base, ca.
1870-1880, medium, amber,
9¼" h. (ILLUS.) **440.00**

FLASKS

*Flasks are listed according to the numbers
provided in* American Bottles & Flasks and
Their Ancestry *by Helen McKearin and Kenneth
M. Wilson.*

GI-21 - Washington bust (facing right)
below "Fells," "Point" below bust -
Baltimore Monument w/"Balto"
below, plain lip, vertical medical rib,
pontil- scarred base, aqua, qt. **172.00**

GI-54 - Washington bust without
queue - Taylor bust in uniform,
open pontil, bold impression,
pinkish amethyst, 8¾" h., qt. **2,695.00**

GI-71 - Taylor bust, facing left,
w/"Rough and Ready" below -
Ringgold bust, facing left, w/"Major"
in semicircle beneath bust, heavy
vertical ribbing, sheared lip, pontil-
scarred base, aqua, pt. **121.00**

GI-80 - "Lafayette" above & "T.S." &
bar below - "DeWitt Clinton" above
bust & "Coventry C-T" below,
sheared lip, pontil-scarred base,
ca. 1825 & 1827, yellow w/olive
overtone, pt. **853.00**

Franklin – Dyott Flask

GI-96 - Franklin bust below "Benjamin
Franklin" - Dyott bust below "T.W.
Dyott, M.D.," edges embossed
"Eropuit Coelo Fulmen.
Sceptrumque Tyrannis" and
"Kensington Glass Works,
Philadelphia," sheared lip, pontil-
scarred base, ca. 1825-1835,
overall stain inside, pale aqua, qt.
(ILLUS.) **264.00**

GI-99 - "Jenny Lind" above bust -
View of Glasshouse w/"Glass
Works" above & "Huffsey" below,
calabash, applied sloping collar
mouth, smooth sides, large open
pontil, ca. 1855-1860, deep
emerald green, qt. **1,650.00**

GI-117 - Columbia bust
w/"Kensington" inscribed below -
American Eagle w/"Union Co."
inscribed below, sheared lip, single
broad vertical rib, pontil-scarred
base, ca. 1820-1830, bluish
aqua, pt. **743.00**

GII-24 - American Eagle above
obverse & reverse, ribbon & two
semicircular rows of stars above &
elongated eight-point star in oval
below, edges corrugated
horizontally w/vertical medical rib,
sheared lip, pontil-scarred base,
ca. 1835-1845, medium sapphire
blue, pt.. . . . . **2,695.00**

GVIII-1 - Sunburst w/twenty-four
triangular sectioned rays obverse &
reverse, two concentric rings w/dot
at center, sheared mouth, pontil-
scarred base, ca. 1815-1825, light
clear green, pt. **523.00**

GIX-13 - Scroll w/two seven-point
stars above "Louisville" in straight
line near base obverse & reverse,
vertical medial rib, sheared lip, iron
pontil, ca. 1845-1855, deep olive
amber, pt. **440.00**

GIX-20 - Scroll w/large oval ornament
above large eight-point star above
large six-petaled flower obverse &

reverse, vertical medial rib,
sheared lip, pontil-scarred base,
ca. 1845-1855, medium yellow
green, pt. **1,430.00**

GXII-31 - Clasped hands above oval, all
inside shield - American Eagle above
oval, applied mouth, smooth base, ca.
1860-1870, yellow olive, ½ pt. **330.00**

Chestnut, 10-diamond patt., aqua,
sheared lip, 5" h. (scratched "M" in
one diamond, pot stones). **1,045.00**

Chestnut, 12-diamond patt., medium
purple amethyst, sheared & tooled
lip, pontil-scarred base, ca. 1820-
1850, 5⅛" h. **105.00**

Pitkin, 20 broken ribs swirled to right,
sheared lip, 4⅝" h. **495.00**

Pitkin, 30 broken ribs swirled to right,
yellow amber w/slight olive tone,
sheared lip, open pontil, ca. 1815-
1825, 6¾" h. **1,595.00**

Pumpkinseed, light yellow at edges to
deep orange amber, tooled lip, embossed "The Arlington M.A. Lindberg
Prop. Bakersfield, Cal. PCGW" on
base, ca. early 1900s, pt. **1,200.00**

MEDICINE

*From left: Apache Indian Herbiline
Clarke's World Famed Blood Mixture*

**Allen's (Martha J.) Female
Restorative,** rectangular w/tooled
lip, smooth base, ca. 1890-1910,
10⅝" h **88.00**

Apache Indian Herbiline, cylindrical
w/applied sloping collar mouth,
pontil-scarred base, printed label
states "Positively Cures Syphilis
And All Female Complaints, Will
Positively Cure Asthma,
Manufactured and For Sale Only
By Montana Harry, Sweet Water
Reservation, Big Timber,
Montana," ca. 1855-1865, olive
amber, 7⅜" h. (ILLUS.) **3,410.00**

Bigger's (Dr.) Huckleberry Cordial
Atlanta, Ga, rectangular w/tooled
mouth, smooth base, ca. 1890-
1905, clear, 5⅛" h. **39.00**

**Clarke's World Famed Blood
Mixture** Lincoln-England,
cylindrical w/applied mouth,
embossed "B.B. & Co. LD." on
smooth base, ca. 1880-1890,
cobalt blue, 11½" h. (ILLUS.) **149.00**

**Compound Fluid Extract Of
Manzanita** Drs. McDonald & Levy
Sacramento City, California, flask
shape w/rolled lip, open pontil, ca.
mid-1800s, light bluish aqua
(some light scratching) **850.00**

Dodge (L.P.) - Rheumatic Liniment-
Newburg, rectangular w/rolled lip,
open pontil, ca. 1845-1855,
medium blue green, 5⅛" h. **275.00**

Dudley's Emulsion - Pure Cod Liver
Oil - Pancreatine & Lime,
rectangular w/applied mouth,
smooth base, ca. 1880-1890,
cobalt blue, some light outside
haze spots, 10¼" h. (ILLUS.) **159.00**

Gun Wa's Chinese Remedy -
Warranted Entirely Vegetable and
Harmless, rectangular w/tooled
mouth, amber, 7¾" h. **450.00**

**Hampton's V Tincture Mortimer &
Mowbray Balto,** rectangular flask-
shaped w/applied mouth, open
pontil, ca. 1845-1855, yellowish
olive amber, 6¼" h. **1,210.00**

Indian Wigwam Remedies
Compounded Mineral Spring's M & I
Co. Denver, Colo., square w/applied
double collar mouth, smooth base,
ca. 1880-1890, yellow shading to
yellow amber near base, 7⅞" h. **715.00**

**Leving's - Hoarhound and
Alecampnae Syrup,** rectangular
w/beveled edges, applied top,
ca. 1892-1894, medium bluish
aqua, 7" h. **170.00**

*From left: Dudley's Emulsion
Jr. Nichols & Co.*

McBurney's Kidney & Bladder Cure
Los Angeles, Cal., rectangular
w/tooled lip & neck ring, light
amethyst, 5" h. 60.00

Nichols (Jr.) & Co. - Chemists -
Boston, rectangular w/tooled
mouth, smooth base, ca. 1885-
1900, deep cobalt blue, 9¼" h.
(ILLUS.) 198.00

**Oldridge's - Balm Of Columbia For
Restoring Hair** - Philadelphia,
rectangular w/beveled edges,
flared lip, pontil-scarred base,
ca. 1835-1850, aqua, 6½" h. 330.00

**Perry's (Dr.) Last Chance -
Liniment,** rectangular w/applied
top, ca. 1870s, aqua, 5¾" h. (tiny
radiating potstones) 100.00

Phillips (Dr. G.W.) - Cough Syrup -
Cincinnati,. O, rectangular
w/applied sloping collar mouth,
pontil-scarred base, ca. 1845-
1855, ice blue aqua, 7½" h. 176.00

**Rohrer's - Expectorol Wild Cherry
Tonic -** Lancaster, Pa., tapered
square w/roped corners, applied
sloping collar mouth, smooth base,
ca. 1855-1865, medium amber,
10⅝" h. 350.00

Rowler's Rheumatism Medicine
Prepared By Dr. J.R. Boyce
Sacramento, cylindrical w/tooled
lip, open pontil, ca. 1858, bluish
aqua, 7½" h. 3,800.00

Swaim's- Panacea

Swaim's- Panacea - Philada,
cylindrical w/series of small vertical
panels, applied sloping collar
mouth, pontil-scarred base, ca.
1835-1855, deep olive amber,
7⅝" h. (ILLUS.) 468.00

Tippecanoe - H.H. Warner & Co.,
log-shaped cylindrical w/ringed
neck & short sloping shoulder,
applied mouth, marked "Pat. Nov.
20 83 Rochester N.Y." on smooth
base, ca. 1875-1895, amber,
9" h. 440.00

True Daffy's Elixir

True Daffy's Elixir (obverse &
reverse), rectangular w/wide
beveled edges, tooled mouth,
pontil-scarred base, ca. 1850-1860,
light ice blue, 4⅝" h. (ILLUS.) 99.00

U.S.A. Hosp. Dept., cylindrical
w/applied double collar mouth,
smooth base, ca. 1860-1870, straw
yellow w/olive tone, 9½" h. 1,256.00

U.S.A. Hosp. Dept. (in oval),
cylindrical w/applied square mouth,
smooth base, ca. 1860-1870,
medium emerald green, 6" h. 660.00

Warner's Safe Cure (motif of safe)
Trade Mark Frankfurt A M,
rectangular w/rounded edges,
ABM, smooth base, Germany, ca.
1900-1910, medium amber,
9¼" h. 193.00

Wishart's Pine Tree Tar Cordial

**Wishart's (L.Q.C.) - Pine Tree Tar
Cordial** Phila - Patent (motif of
pine tree) 1859, square w/beveled
edges, applied sloping collar
mouth, smooth base, ca. 1860-
1870, yellow olive, 2" crack top of
mouth to shoulder, 9⅜" h.
(ILLUS.) 220.00

Wood's Great Peppermint Cure For
Cough & Colds, rectangular
w/tooled lip, smooth base, ca.
1885-1895, medium cobalt blue
w/subtle wisps of olive & darker
cobalt, 5½" h. **495.00**

Worm - Mixture - Stabler, six-sided,
sheared & tooled lip, pontil-scarred
base, ca. 1835-1845,
aqua, 3⅝" h. **143.00**

MINERAL WATER, SODAS & SARSAPARILLAS

Acme Soda Works Ventura Cal.,
cylindrical Hutchinson stopper-
form, w/tooled top, light blue **220.00**

Alpena Magnetic Spring Co,
cylindrical w/applied double collar
mouth, smooth base, ca. 1875-
1885, reddish amber, 8¾" h., qt.. . . **578.00**

Anker, (motif of anchor) Anchor
Sarsaparillian - F.AD. Richter & Co
Rotterdam "New York - F.AD.
Richter & Co Rudolstadt" Olten,
rectangular w/tooled mouth,
smooth base, Dutch & American,
ca. 1880-1900, greenish aqua,
9" h. **171.00**

Billings, (E.L.) Sac City Geyser
Soda, cylindrical w/blob top,
medium to light green **90.00**

From left: Blue Lick Water Bottle
Early Coca Cola Bottle

Blue Lick Water Co KY, cylindrical
w/applied top, twelve-sided petal-
type base, iron pontil, ca. 1850-
1865, deep emerald green, 8" h.,
pt. (ILLUS. above left) **2,200.00**

Boston & Co. From London, ten
pin-shaped w/applied mouth,
pontil-scarred base, ca. 1820-1830,
deep olive amber, 6⅝" h. **633.00**

**Coca Cola Bottling Co
Chattanooga,** Tenn, cylindrical
w/tooled lip, smooth base, ca.
1885-1895, greenish aqua, 7⅛" h.
(ILLUS. prev. column right) **1,155.00**

Condict (H.F.) Bakersfield, cylindrical
w/applied top, aqua **130.00**

From left: Crystal Soda Water Bottle
James Mineral Waters Bottle

Crystal Soda Water Co., Patented
November 12, 1872 USPI,
cylindrical w/applied top, footed
base, ca. 1873-1886, light to
medium green (ILLUS. above left) . . **180.00**

**Edic (A.L.) Utica Bottling.
Establishment,** - Superior Water
Mineral, cylindrical w/applied
mouth, iron pontil, ca. 1840-1855,
medium cobalt blue, 7½" h. **1,155.00**

**Empire Soda Works D & M San
Francisco,** round w/blob top, ca.
1864-1865, greenish aqua **275.00**

**Frost's Magnetic Spring Eaton
Rapids Mich,** cylindrical w/applied
double collar mouth, smooth base,
ca. 1875-1885, bluish aqua,
9½" h., qt. **413.00**

G.B. Co., soda, cylindrical w/tooled
crown top, ca. 1906-1916,
amethyst **80.00**

Gemenden (Geo.) Savannah Geo.,
soda, cylindrical w/applied sloping
collar mouth, iron pontil, ca. 1845-
1855, emerald green, 7⅛" h. **303.00**

**Hennessey & Nolan Albany. NY -
Hoxsie,** cylindrical w/applied
mouth, smooth base, ca. 1855-
1870, deep reddish amber,
6¾" h., pt. **83.00**

James (J.W.) Pure Mineral Waters, cylindrical w/wide, crude neck, embossed "Patent Safe Growth Sole Maker Dan Rylands Barnsley" on reverse, applied top, monogrammed base, copper stopper, greenish aqua (ILLUS. prev. page right) **250.00**

Kaier C.D. Mahanoy City, PA - This Bottle Not To Be Sold, cylindrical, applied mouth, smooth base, ca. 1875-1885, yellow green, 11¼" h. . . **187.00**

Torpedo-shaped Soda Bottle

Keach – Balt, torpedo shape w/applied sloping collar mouth, smooth base, ca. 1850-1860, deep green, 8½" h. (ILLUS.) **853.00**

Log Cabin – Sarsaparilla – Rochester, NY, eight-paneled neck & body w/applied top, marked "Pat. Sept. 6, '87" on base, original glass stopper, amber w/warm olive hue **190.00**

Lomax (C.) Chicago - Congress Water (inside shield), cylindrical w/applied blob top, iron pontil, ca. 1845-1855, medium cobalt blue, 7¼" h. **204.00**

Macer (V.) - Improved Mineral Water, cylindrical w/applied blob top mouth, iron pontil, ca. 1845-1855, sapphire blue, 7⅛" h. **154.00**

Owen Casey Eagle Soda Works Sac City, cylindrical w/blob top, ca. 1867-1871, deep cobalt blue **110.00**

Pacific Congress Water P. Caduc (vertically embossed), cylindrical w/blob top, light aqua **30.00**

Parker (J.C.) & Son New York, cylindrical w/blob top, iron pontil, sapphire blue. **80.00**

Sacrimento (M R), - Union Glass Works Phila. (in slugplate on reverse), cylindrical w/blob top, iron pontil, ca. 1851-1863, teal, 7" h.. . **1,900.00**

Sutton (I.) Cincinnati, cylindrical w/applied mouth, iron pontil, ca. 1845-1855, medium cobalt blue, 7½" h. **523.00**

Taylor & Co. Valparaiso Chili Soda Water, cylindrical w/applied top, iron pontil, medium aqua. **160.00**

From left: Dr. Townsend's Sarsaparilla W.S Wright Bottle

Townsend's (Dr.) Sarsaparilla, – Albany N.Y., square w/applied sloping collar mouth, iron pontil, ca. 1840-1855, light to medium blue green, 9½" h., pinhead flake of edge of lip (ILLUS. above left). **440.00**

Winkle (Henry) Sac City – XX (on reverse), cylindrical w/blob top, iron pontil, ca. 1852-1854, light aqua. . . **150.00**

Wright (W. S.), cylindrical, blob top, original wire bell, extremely whittled w/many air bubbles, ca. early 1860s, deep Cudworth green (ILLUS. above right). **1,200.00**

WHISKEY & OTHERS SPIRITS

Beer, "Henry Braun Beer Bottling Oakland, Cal.," cylindrical w/tooled mouth, smooth base, amber, 7¾" h. (shallow chip on base edge) . . **55.00**

Beer, "Cal Bottling Co. Export Beer S.F.," cylindrical w/applied top, dark amber **30.00**

Beer, "Jamaica Champagne Beer S.F. D.L. Fonseca & Co.," cylindrical w/blob top, ca. 1885-1886, cobalt **325.00**

Beer, "John Rapp & Son S.F. Cal." w/two "S" embossed backward, cylindrical w/tooled top, pt. **50.00**

Bourbon, "Newmark, Gruenberg & Co. Old Judge Bourbon, X S. F. X," cylindrical w/applied mouth, smooth base, ca. 1879-1884, bright medium amber, 11⅝" h. **633.00**

Bourbon, "Tea Cup Extra Trade (motif of tea cup) Mark Old Bourbon," cylindrical w/tooled lip, ca. 1891-1895, medium amber . . **2,200.00**

Gin, "Old London Dock – Gin – A.M. Bininger & Co No. 19 Broad St N.Y.," yellow w/strong olive tone, applied slopping collar mouth, smooth base, ca. 1860-1870, 9⅞" h. **193.00**

Schnapps, "Udolpho Wolke's - Aromatic Schnapps," applied top, sticky-ball pontil, medium to deep green **70.00**

Spirits, mold-blown, globular, 12 vertical ribs, folded lip, pontil-scarred base, ca. 1820-1830, clear, 8⅜" h. **330.00**

Spirits, mold-blown, globular, 24 ribs swirled to right, deep bluish aqua, rolled lip, pontil-scarred base, ca. 1820-1830, deep bluish aqua, 7⅝" h. **413.00**

Whiskey, "A A A Old Valley Whiskey," strap-side flask, applied rolled collar mouth, ca. 1870-1880, olive amber. **1,500.00**

Whiskey, "Bininger (A.M.) & Co. No 19 Broad St New York," jug-shaped w/applied double collar mouth & handle, smooth base, ca. 1860-1870, medium amber, 8" h. **231.00**

Whiskey, "Durham Whiskey" (motif of bull), cylindrical w/applied top, round foot on back, ca. 1876-1882, medium amber orange (some light scratches) **750.00**

Whiskey, "M Geary Liquor Dealer Woodstock, Va.," strap-side flask, applied mouth, smooth base, ca. 1875-1885, medium amber, 8" h. . . . **578.00**

From left: King Edward Reserve Whiskey
Markstein Whiskey

Whiskey, "King Edward Reserve," barrel-shaped w/applied double collar mouth, smooth base, ca. 1875-1890, amber, missing stopper, ⅛" shallow chip inside of mouth, ⅛" iridescent bruise on letter "N", 8½" h. (ILLUS.) **440.00**

Whiskey, "M. Markstein Corner 10th & Noble Anniston, Ala" below "Full Quart," square w/tooled mouth, smooth base, ca. 1880-1890, 80%

original label marked "Old Poplar Log Corn Whiskey M. Markstein," aqua, 9½" h. (ILLUS.) **94.00**

Whiskey, "The Old Mill Whitlock & Co." on applied neck medal, tapering ovoid w/applied mouth, pontil-scarred base, ca. 1860-1870, medium amber, 8⅛" h. **354.00**

Whiskey, "Wharton's Whiskey 1850 Chestnut Grove," teardrop flask, applied mouth, smooth base, ca. 1855-1870, cobalt blue, 5½" h. (⅛" flake of side of lip) **358.00**

BREWERIANA

Beer is still popular in this country but the number of breweries has greatly diminished. More than 1,900 breweries were in operation in the 1870s but we find fewer than 40 major breweries supply the demands of the country a century later, although micro-breweries have recently sprung up across the country.

Advertising items used to promote various breweries, especially those issued prior to prohibition, now attract an ever growing number of collectors. The breweriana items listed are a sampling of the many items available.

Bar light, "Peerless Amber," glass panel fitted into a metal base, features an elf w/white beard, dressed in red w/a green cap & shoes & holding a glass & a bottle of Peerless Amber Beer, large white letters read "Peerless Amber" & in red lettering below "The Beer of Good Cheer," new old stock, 12" w., 11" h. **$149.00**

Various Beer Glasses

Beer glass,
"Atlas Prager" & image of bottle in red, Chicago, Illinois (ILLUS. far left) **31.00**
"Bonn Pilsner" & logo in red & black, Random Lake, Wisconsin (ILLUS. 2nd from right) **57.00**
"Calumet Beer" in red, cylindrical form, Calumet, Wisconsin,

(ILLUS. far right prev. page) **99.00**
"Bevo The Beverage" in red, ovoid
shaped, St. Louis, Missouri
(ILLUS. 2nd from left prev. page) ... **40.00**

Etched Beer Glasses

Beer glass,
"Terre Haute Brewing Co." &
etched logo flanked by "Trade" &
"Mark," Terre Haute, Indiana,
cylindrical (ILLUS. right) **54.00**
"The Moerschel Spring Brewing
Company - Brewers and Bottlers of
Fine Beers.," & logo, St. Charles,
Missouri ovoid shaped (ILLUS. center). **66.00**
"Elgin Eagle Brewing Co. - Elgin,
Ill." & logo, yellow etching
(ILLUS. left)................. **440.00**
Beer glass, "Famous Old Lamp
Beer" within scrolled border, red
enamel, East St. Louis, Missouri.... **33.00**
Beer glass, "Grain Belt Beer" on red
enamel bottle cap logo above red
enamel "the friendly beer," Grain
Belt Brewing Co., Minneapolis,
Minnesota **193.00**
Beer glass, "Lubeck Royal Beer" on
black enamel w/logo, wide red
band flanked by narrow black band
around glass, South Bend, Indiana
& Chicago, Illinois **242.00**

Four Collectible Beer Glasses

Beer glass.
"Goebel's," Detroit, Michigan
(ILLUS. far right) **99.00**
"Esslinger's Premium Beer" & logo
in red, Philadelphia,
Pennsylvania (ILLUS. far left) **35.00**

"Falstaff" logo in yellow, red &
black, St. Louis, Missouri
(ILLUS. 2nd from left prev. column) .. **198.00**
"Fox Brew" on red w/head of fox,
Waukesha, Wisconsin (ILLUS. 2nd
from right) **55.00**
Beer glass, "P.O.N. Porter" printed in
blue enamel on opaque white,
Newark, New Jersey **33.00**

Pilsner Beer Glasses

Beer Glass,
"Old Milwaukee Light,", frosted
w/logo & circle, red enamel, reads
Milwaukee, Wisconsin
(ILLUS. far right)............... **33.00**
"Drewry's," South Bend, Indiana &
Chicago, Illinois. Drewry's logo in
black & red above red enamel
lettering (ILLUS. 2nd from
left) **61.00**
"Edelweiss" on black enamel,
Chicago, Illinois (ILLUS.
2nd from right)................. **88.00**
"Spuds" decoration, tapering footed
form w/colorful, Budweiser, Bud
Light (ILLUS. far left)............ **33.00**
Clock, "Southern Select Beer,"
electric, red, blue & white
w/chrome bezel, ca. 1940s-early
1950s, Pam Clock Company,
Brooklyn, New York for Galveston-
Houston Brewery, 14½" d. (some
rusting to chrome, minor paint drips
on back). **303.00**
Display mug, "Consumer Brewing
Company," w/reverse on glass
trademark of man holding
American flag amidst a variety of
Consumer Brewing products, 10" h.
(some paint loss & cracking in
label, rim chips) **690.00**
Figure, "Blatz" painted aluminum
figure of man w/keg torso w/logo,
holding mug of beer & standing
next to sign w/"Milwaukee's Finest
Beer," & "Blatz on draft" on base,
some minor paint loss, 15½" h...... **35.00**

Bud Light Spuds McKensie

Model of a dog, molded plastic, Bud Light "Spuds McKensie," March 10, 1988 stamped on bottom, 1986 Anheuser Busch Inc. embossed on back leg, white paint on feet, soiling, 15⅜" h. (ILLUS.) **165.00**

Pre-prohibition Mugs

Mug,
"Stroh's Beer" above logo, bulbous barrel-shaped , Detroit, Michigan (ILLUS. far right) **152.00**
"Kuebeler-Stang Brewing Co., Sandusky, O" pottery, footed cylindrical shape w/shield decoration above & "We use crystal rock spring water," Sandusky, Ohio (ILLUS. 2nd from left) **220.00**
"Original Fabacher's" pottery, barrel-shaped w/grain sheaf, New Orleans, Louisiana (ILLUS. far left) **110.00**
Pottery, barrel-shaped, w/narrow blue bands above & below "Rochester Brew. Co." & "Rochester, N. Y." at base, Rochester, New York (ILLUS. 2nd from right) **87.00**
Mug,
"Grant's Cabin" pottery, Budweiser, slightly tapering cylindrical shape w/molded narrow bands around the

Budweiser Mugs & Stein

top & base in tan & brown, w/horses in foreground, CS83 (ILLUS. 2nd from right) **65.00**
"Oktoberfest" pottery, Budweiser, tapering cylindrical shape w/colorful castle scene & "The Old Country" in red, CS42-variation (ILLUS. far left) **330.00**
"Busch Bavarian Beer" pottery, Budweiser, & eagle logo in blue, CS44-variation (ILLUS. 2nd from left) **295.00**

Schlitz Globe Radio

Radio, modeled as a globe, plastic & metal, w/"Schlitz" on circular band, switch is dirty, battery compartment at mounting hole is broken, not working, 5½" d., 8" h. (ILLUS.) **44.00**
Sign, "Drewry's," self-framed tin over cardboard, entitled "The Thrill of a Lifetime," depicting frontiersman & Mountie shooting the rapids w/beer laden canoe while trying to avoid a cougar readying to attack a porcupine, Drewry's logo on sides of canoe, artist-signed, American Art Works lithography, 17 x 23" (some minor inpainting, overall spotting & soiling) **460.00**
Sign, "Iroquois," porcelain, self-framed, curved corner depicts trademark Iroquois Indian, some chipping in frame around border & where bracket is attached to sign, 16¼ x 24" (ILLUS.) **2,300.00**

Iroquois Beer Sign

Sign, "Grain Belt," center of cardboard sign depicts dog having just retrieved a duck, border of various firearms & game, artist-signed, ca. 1947, Inland Lithography Company, 23½ x 27" (overall soiling, scratching w/chipping & tearing around border) **230.00**

Sign, "Kamm & Schellinger Brewing Company," paper, depicts company logo of lion climbing atop the world, wood frame, 29" w., 38½" h. to outside of frame (some staining, tearing & paper loss around edges, minor crease near lion's mane) **403.00**

Stein,
    pottery, blue & white relief-molded Balmoral Castle, Busch Gardens (ILLUS. far left) **176.00**
    pottery, cylindrical w/slightly domed hinged metal lid, "Bald Eagle," CS106 (ILLUS. far right w/mugs on prev. page) **375.00**

Various Busch Gardens Steins

    pottery w/colorful scene of wild animals & reads "Busch Gardens, 1st Extinction is Forever" (ILLUS far right)...................... **85.00**
    pottery, white & blue, reads "Busch Gardens, Tampa/Williamsburg/Los Angeles" & decoration of amusement park ride

(ILLUS. 2nd from right) **55.00**
pottery, white w/blue geometric design border & blue wording "Busch Gardens, Los Angeles, Tampa" (ILLUS. 2nd from left)..... **134.00**

Old Ranger Thermometer

Thermometer, metal w/glass front, "Old Ranger Beer and Ale - Hornell Brewing Co., Inc., Hornell N.Y.," center w/man hunter holding rifle, soiling & minor rust spotting, 10" d. (ILLUS.)...................... **55.00**

BUTTER MOLDS & STAMPS

While they are sometimes found made of other materials, it is primarily the two-piece wooden butter mold and one-piece butter stamps that attract collectors. The molds are found in two basic styles, rounded cup-form and rectangular box-form. Butter stamps are usually round with a protruding knob handle on the back. Many were factory-made items with the print design made by forcing a metal die into the wood under great pressure, while others had the design chiseled out by hand. An important reference book in this field is Butter Prints and Molds, *by Paul E. Kindig (Schiffer Publishing, 1986).*

Compass starflower, round, carved wood w/center starflower design & carved scalloped border design, scrubbed finish, smooth back, 5" d......................... **$110.00**

Cow stamp, wood, rectangular w/rounded sides & flat end handle, carved design of a cow & trees, worm holes, edge damage from use & old natural patina, 13¼ " l. **149.00**

Crown stamp, wood, round, crown-like design w/notched border design, one piece turned handle, scrubbed finish, 4¼" d.......... **110.00**

Flowers & initials "lollipop" stamp, round w/primitively carved sprig of round serrated blossoms & leaves, flattened oblong side handle, 6⅝" l....................... **248.00**

Heart-shaped stamp, wood w/deep geometric carved designs, very worn scrubbed finish, no handle, 5½" h. **220.00**

Pineapple & foliage stamp, round, carved wood w/central pineapple design, small hole in center, foliage around border, one piece w/turned handle, old finish, 4¼" d. **187.00**

"Lollipop" Stamps

Starflower "lollipop" stamp, round, wood, carved center starflower design surrounded by carved swags & zig-zag border, tapering square-shaped handle, 7" l. (ILLUS. right)................ **138.00**

Starflower "lollipop" stamp, round w/offset flat tapering handle, starflower carved on both sides, worn patina, 8½" l.............. **193.00**

Starflower stamp, round, carved geometric starflowers on both sides, no handle, chips, 3" d........................ **110.00**

Tulip lollipop stamp, "lollipop" stamp, arrowhead-shaped carved walnut w/large tulip design, 6¾" l. (ILLUS. left)................. **330.00**

Carved Floral Butter Stamps

Tulip one side, reverse w/starflower stamp, round, carved wood, no handle, scrubbed finish w/age cracks, 4½" d. (ILLUS. center)..................... **385.00**

Tulip stamp, round, carved center tulip design surrounded by leaves, stars & hearts, old dark varnish on sides, inserted handle missing, 4" d........................ **110.00**

Tulip stamp, round, large stylized blossom, scrubbed finish w/star, age crack, small knob handle, 4" d. (ILLUS. bottom)............... **110.00**

Tulip stamp, round, carved walnut, very stylized tulip center design flanked by carved hearts & leaves, scrubbed finish, inserted handle missing, 4½" d................ **138.00**

Tulip & star stamp, round, carved wood, center tulip design w/star beneath & other floral sprays on each side, scrubbed finish, one piece, turned handle 4⅜" d. (ILLUS. top).................. **275.00**

Tulip & stars stamp, round, carved wood, center w/carved stylized tulip & border w/carved flowers & stars, old dark finish, one piece turned handle, 4⅞" d................ **220.00**

CANDLESTICKS & CANDLEHOLDERS

Also see METALS, ROYCROFT ITEMS and SANDWICH under Glass.

Candelabra, silver plate, open wire lyre-form column, two-branch, three-light, removable bobeches, fluted base, 7⅝" h., pr. (rosing) . . . **$374.00**

Candelabra, reticulated rococo design, two-branch, Reed & Barton, late 19th c., 15⅞" h., pr. **575.00**

Fine Classical Candelabrum

Candelabra, gilt & patinated bronze, two-light, Classical style w/a stepped square base w/a cast fruit band & reeded & scrolled shaft supporting the model of a spread-winged eagle w/a tall standard on its back supporting a pierced-top ring above a band of drooping stems w/leaves & facet-cut prisms, the wings continuing to form long scrolled arms ending in urn-form candle sockets above further leafy stems suspending prisms, early 19th c., 18" h., pr. (ILLUS. of one) **4,312.00**

Candelabra, silver plate, three-light, two branches, convertible base, gadroon detail, 19th century, 18" h., pr. (rosing) **345.00**

Candelabra, silver on copper, three-light, Sheffield, 19" h., pr. (minor wear w/copper showing on edges, minor repair) **385.00**

Candelabra, silver plate, three-light, two branches w/gadroon borders & flame finial, convertible base, removable bobeches, Birks, 20⅝" h., pr. **288.00**

Candleholder, brass, Arts & Crafts style, the base composed of three oblong hinged brass sheets w/circular cut-out below a flat brass hinged shaft supporting a dished drip pan centered by a pricket spike, stamped mark of Samuel Yellin **358.00**

Candleholder, metal, loop w/star pendant & gilt fan-form holder, designed to hang & balance on a chair's crestrail, New England, 19th c., 10¼" h. **690.00**

Candleholder, black painted tin, double-light, adjustable, reticulated shades above candle sockets & cups over scrolling arms on a circular weighted base, possibly American, 19th c., electrified, 18¾" h. (imperfections) **489.00**

Candleholder, hanging-type, wrought iron, long slender twisted side bars tapering to a top hanging loop, joined at the bottom by a narrow bar centered by a small conical candle socket, early, 19" h. **385.00**

Candlestick, brass, Queen Anne-style, petal base, England, mid-18th c., 7⅛" h. **288.00**

Candlestick, brass, Queen Anne-style, scrolled base 7⅜" h. (stem soldered & epoxied to base) **193.00**

Candlestick, brass, square base w/feet & baluster stem, early, 7½" h. (stem refastened to base w/solder, pitted) **220.00**

Candlestick, brass, Queen Anne-style, scrolled & beaded base, 8⅛" h. (stem soldered to base w/pushup rod sticking out of solder) **165.00**

Candlestick, brass, Queen Anne-style, scalloped foot, 8¼" h. (small hole drilled in rim of socket & stem refastened to base w/solder) **165.00**

Candlestick, bronze, Queen Anne-style, scalloped detail, 8¼" h. **110.00**

Candlestick, pressed flint glass, a tall lavender petal-form socket attached w/a wafer to the tall ribbed columnar clambroth pedestal on a square stepped base, probably Boston & Sandwich Glass Co., mid-19th c., overall crizzled finish, 9¼" h. **605.00**

Candlestick, clear, pressed foot, blown baluster stem & hollow socket w/pewter insert, 10¼" h. (base has damage) **121.00**

Candlestick, pressed flint glass, crucifix-form, paneled tulip-form socket attached w/a wafer, hexagonal domed & stepped base, attributed to New England Glass Co., ca. 1860-80, deep violet, 11⅝" h. (minute bruise on cross) . . **275.00**

Brass Capstan Candlestick

Candlestick, brass, capstan style, candle socket on baluster-form standard over a flared drip tray & short pedestal above the bell-shaped circular base w/drip tray, Europe, 17th c., 13" h., together w/reproduction of candlestick & letters re. geneological descent & reproduction, 2 pcs. (ILLUS. of original). **16,100.00**

Candlestick, bronze, Arts & Crafts style, flat disc foot under a round tapering base w/a very tall, slender ribbed shaft w/spade-shaped leaves ending at the compressed conical candle socket w/a flattened, flared rim, original patina, unmarked Jarvie, early 20th c., 13¾" h. **1,320.00**

Candlestick, wrought iron, Arts & Crafts style, three small angled square legs ending in triangular flat feet supporting a wide dished blossom-form base centered by a tall slender squared shaft w/a center square block, a wide blossom-form bobeche centered by a pricket spike, original dark patina, impressed "YELLIN," Samuel Yellin, early 20th c., 7" d., 15" h. **3,960.00**

Candlesticks, silver, miniature, spiral column w/scalloped detail, separate bobeche, 2⅜" h., pr. **201.00**

Candlesticks, pressed glass, petal-shaped socket in opaque blue attached to fiery opalescent dolphin-shaped stem on domed base, pontil mark on base, Pittsburgh, mid-19th c., 5¾" h., pr. **7,810.00**

Candlesticks, carved whalebone, vasiform candle socket w/scribe line decoration above turned shaft on a square molded base, 20th c., 6¾" h., pr. (minor cracks, old repair) **546.00**

Candlesticks, polished pink brass or bronze, Neo-classical, 7" h., pr. (minor dents) **138.00**

Candlesticks, silver, hexagonal w/bobeche, weighted base, English, Sheffield marks for 1920, 7"h., pr. (dents) **110.00**

Candlesticks, brass w/push-ups, 19th c., 8" h., pr. **127.00**

Candlesticks, brass, scalloped bases, 8¼" h., pr. (minor damage, one is soldered). **880.00**

Candlesticks, brass w/double extracting holes, Europe, late 17th/early 18th c., 9" h., pr. (very minor dents) **1,380.00**

Clear Pressed Glass Candlestick

Candlesticks, clear pressed glass, stepped base w/reeded column attached w/wafers to double reeded knop stem & reeded socket w/lacy details, some chips, 9½" h., pr. (ILLUS. of one) **1,155.00**

Candlesticks, pressed glass, swirl molded body hung w/slender faceted prisms, 20th c., 9½" h., pr. **201.00**

Candlesticks, brass w/traces of silver plating, early, 9⅞" h., pr. **605.00**

Candlesticks, sterling silver, swelled baluster-form ribbed standard w/a matching candle socket w/flattened rim, on a domed & ribbed weighted base w/beaded edge band, probably the La Salle patt., Dominick & Haff, New York, 1929, 10¼" h., pr. **604.00**

Candlesticks, silver, matching bobeches, weighted base, English, Sheffield hallmarks for 1910, 11¼" h., pr. **990.00**

Candlesticks, brass, faceted & turned stem on a canted square foot, Europe, 19th c., 12" h., pr. . . . **115.00**

Candlesticks, bronze & glass, slit bronze bulbous candlecups w/blown-out green glass inserts raised on slender elegant tall bronze stems w/original dark patina, beaded bobeche, Tiffany Studios, impressed mark "S 1457," 20½" h., pr.. . . . . **2,300.00**

Early Wood Figural Candlesticks

Candlesticks, pricket-type, carved wood & polychrome, depicting a standing winged angel w/long flowing robes, holding a torch, on a rectangular base w/scrolling supports centering a winged putto head, Europe, 18th c., 31¼" h., facing pr. (ILLUS.) **6,900.00**

Chamberstick, copper, a primitive hand-made design w/a squared dished base centering a cylindrical socket stem w/a replaced hook push-up & a long strap handle extending from the rim, handle stamped "6," 6" h. (somewhat battered) **94.00**

Chamberstick, hand-hammered copper, Arts & Crafts style, round deep dished base centered by a tall slender cylindrical shaft w/a flattened flaring socket rim, a spade-tipped loop strap handle down the side of the shaft, original patina & bobeche, Gustav Stickley "Als Ik Kan" mark, 7" d., 9" h. **605.00**

Chambersticks, traveling-type, sterling silver, a round deeply dished base w/an overall foliate engraved design, w/a detachable chased cylindrical candle socket & ring loop handle, Dominick & Haff, late 19th c., pr.. . . **489.00**

CANDY CONTAINERS

* Indicates the container might not have held candy originally. +Indicates this container might also be found as a reproduction. ‡Indicates this container was also made as a bank. All containers are clear glass unless otherwise indicated. Any candy container that retains the original paint is very desirable and readers should follow descriptions carefully realizing that an identical candy container that lacks the original paint will be less valuable.

Airplane - "Liberty Motor," original propeller & nose, (replaced tin wings, wheels & undercarriage) . . **$1,430.00**

Airplane - "P-38 Lightning," contains original candy, original closure. **303.00**

Airplane - "Spirit of Goodwill," original propeller & original closure, 99% paint **165.00**

Airplane - "Spirit of St. Louis," blue glass, all original tin, top wing painted.. . . . . **358.00**

Airplane - "Spirit of St. Louis," green glass, all original tin. **605.00**

Airplane - "Spirit of St. Louis," pink glass, all original tin. **495.00**

Airplane - "U.S. Army," original wing, closure & propeller. **220.00**

"Amos and Andy," original closure, 99% original paint **660.00**

Automobile - "Coupe w/long hood," original wheels (repainted, reproduction closure). **132.00**

Automobile - "Large Flat Top w/Tassels," original closure, 90% black paint. **853.00**

Automobile - "V.G. Co. Airflow," original wheels, candy label, & closure, 90% silver paint **413.00**

Baby Chick Standing, original closure, 85% paint (tiny base chip). **220.00**

Baseball player on base, original closure, 80% paint. **605.00**

Bear on Circus Tub, original wheels, reproduction closure **523.00**

Bell "Liberty Bell Candy Container," original closure, 50% original label **121.00**

Bird Cage, reproduction closure. **220.00**

Boat - "Submarine F 6," all original.. **715.00**

Boat - "Submarine F 6," original superstructure, flag & closure (replaced periscope,). **440.00**

Bureau, original mirror & closure, 70% paint **209.00**

Bus - "Greyhound," original wheels,
70% paint (replaced closure)...... 303.00
Bus - "Jitney," original wheels &
closure (small chip under front grill). . 286.00
Camera on Tripod, donkey picture,
all original, 95% paint 495.00
Cannon - "Cobalt," all original...... 688.00
Carpet Sweeper - "Baby Sweeper,"
all original 385.00
Cash Register, reproduction closure. . 297.00
Cat - "Black Cat For Luck," original
closure, 40% paint............. 880.00
Charlie Chaplin, original closure,
95% paint, Borgfeldt & Co. 204.00
Chicken - "Crowing Rooster,"
original closure, 90% paint 523.00
Clock, octagonal shape, original
paper dial & closure, 90% paint,
(chip on rear base corner)....... 275.00
Coach - "Interurban-Angeline,"
original wheels & closure (chips
between wheel openings) 440.00
"Crouching Rabbit," original
closure, 80% paint............. 154.00
Dirigible - "Los Angeles," original
closure, 95% paint............. 193.00
Elephant - "G.O.P.," original closure. . 253.00
Fearless Frankie Candy Fireman,
all original, w/box.............. 358.00
Flossie Fisher's Sideboard, original
closure (some silhouette fading) . . . 880.00
Iron - "Flat Iron," original closure
(chips under closure, cracked at
back corner) 275.00
Jack O'Lantern, blue glass, original
bail & rim, 95% paint 330.00
Kewpie by Barrel original closure,
90% paint 110.00
"Lawn Swing," all original tin &
closure...................... 550.00
Mail Box, milk glass, original closure . . 215.00
Man on motorcycle w/sidecars,
original closure (some repaint) 633.00
Phonograph - "Glass Record
Type," original horn & closure 308.00
"Soldier By Tent," original closure,
90% paint (two small chips under
the closure).................. 2,310.00
Train - "J.J. Brainands 1923," all
original closures (some minor chips
on couplers).................. 908.00
Uncle Sam by Barrel, original
closure, traces of paint (some nicks
on barrel base) 319.00
Windmill - "Teddy Wind Mill," all tin
& closure original (tiny bottom
corner chip).................. 578.00
World Globe on Stand, original
stand & closure 330.00

CANES & WALKING STICKS

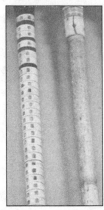

Baleen & Whalebone Walking Sticks

**Baleen & shark vertebrae walking
stick,** tapering baleen knob above
alternating vertebrae & baleen
spacers, continuing to a tapering
vertebrae shaft, cracks, 19th c.,
33⅞" l. (ILLUS. left)........... $374.00
**Ivory, whalebone & inlaid ebony
walking stick,** the ivory-inlaid
polyhedron knob above a shaped
ivory-inlaid neck continuing to a
rounded tapering whalebone shaft
ending in a brass tip, inlay loss,
minor cracks, 19th c., 36" l.
(ILLUS. right)................. 345.00

Ivory Canes & Walking Sticks

**Carved whale ivory & whalebone
cane,** angled whale's tooth handle
above a baleen spacer continuing
to a carved ivory panel of a horse's
head w/ropes, above a turned ivory
neck w/scribe line decoration &

silver spacer, continuing to a
tapering paneled whalebone shaft,
minor cracks, loss of inlay, 19th c.,
34" l. (ILLUS. left) **633.00**

**Carved & inlaid whale ivory &
whalebone walking stick,** an ivory
sailor's knot knob inlaid
w/tortoiseshell & silver above a
tapering neck w/spacer & carved
sailor's knot continuing to spiral
twist, tapering whalebone shaft,
brass tip, minor cracks, 19th c.,
33⅜" l. (ILLUS. center) **2,300.00**

**Carved whale ivory & whalebone
walking stick,** carved ivory "Turk's
turban" knob above alternating
carved & paneled baleen spacers
& intricately carved geometric &
spiral carved panels continuing to a
reeded, spiral twist then tapering
shaft, ivory tip, 19th c., minor
cracks, 34" l. (ILLUS. right) **8,050.00**

Three Ivory Walking Sticks

**Carved whale Ivory and whalebone
walking stick,** 19th century, ivory
hound's head form knob with blue
glass eyes continuing to tapering
whalebone shaft, (minor cracks,
loss to snout),
lg. 35¾" (ILLUS. left) **518.00**

**Carved whale ivory & whalebone
walking stick,** the ivory handle
carved in the form of a clenched
first holding a rod above a leaf-form
neck continuing to a tapering
spiral-carved whalebone shaft
w/polyhedron-form & tapering
paneled tip, 19th c., 35⅛" l.
(ILLUS. center) **2,760.00**

**Ivory and exotic wood walking
stick,** 19th century, tapering ivory
knob above a silver spacer
continuing to a tapering exotic
wood shaft, brass tip, (minor
cracks), lg. 35½" (ILLUS. right) **288.00**

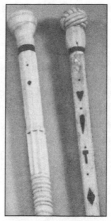

Two Inlaid Ivory Walking Sticks

**Inlaid ivory & whalebone walking
stick,** rounded knob w/scribe line
decoration above a paneled
whalebone shaft w/ivory inlay
continuing to a concave paneled
section, continuing to spiral carving
down the shaft, minor cracks, inlay
loss, 19th c., 35¼" l. (ILLUS. left) . . **1,150.00**

**Carved & inlaid ivory & whalebone
walking stick,** ivory sailor's knot
knob above a paneled octagonal
neck w/baleen spacers, continuing to
a paneled whalebone shaft inlaid
w/figural & geometric designs done in
tortoiseshell, mother-of-pearl, baleen
& exotic woods, continuing to a spiral-
turned lower shaft, minor inlay loss &
replacement, minor cracks, 19th c.,
37" l. (ILLUS. right) **2,185.00**

Carved hardwood cane, curved
roothead handle w/some burl
above the shaft carved w/two
snakes grabbing each end of a
small quadruped, very worn black
& yellow paint, 32½" l. **440.00**

Carved roothead walking stick, two
long snakes carved entwining up
the shaft, old black & brown paint,
brass knob top, 35¼" l. **110.00**

Carved softwood walking stick,
carved fist handle, low-relief carved
snake wrapping around up the shaft,
carved name "J.F. Williams," 36" l. . . . **165.00**

**Carved whale ivory & whalebone
cane,** angled carved ivory hoof-
form handle above baleen spacers
continuing to a tapering whalebone
shaft, 19th c., 34½" l. (minor cracks) . **748.00**

Hardwood & white metal walking stick, the cast white metal handle in the form of a man's head, the wooden shaft turned to resemble bamboo, 36" l. **165.00**

Inlaid ivory & ebony walking stick, rounded knob handle w/wax-inlaid scribe line decoration & mother-of-pearl inlay above alternating bands of ivory & ebony continuing to a tapering ebony shaft, ivory tip, 19th c., 40⅜" l. (minor cracks). **288.00**

Inlaid ivory & whalebone walking stick, ball-form ivory knob handle w/a wax-inlaid scribe line decoration & baleen inlay above the stepped neck w/wax-inlaid scribe line decorated loose ring above baleen spacer continuing to tapering whalebone shaft, 19th c., 35⅞" l. (minor cracks) **1,150.00**

Inlaid whale ivory walking stick, the rounded knob handle centering an 1856 seated Liberty silver quarter above a turned neck w/scribe line decoration continuing to alternating baleen spacers & tapering ivory panels, 19th c., 31⅝" l. (minor cracks). **1,955.00**

Ivory-handled walking stick, the cylindrical top in ivory carved w/a hand & sleeve cuff, metal ferrule above the ebony shaft, 36" l. **472.00**

Wooden & metal walking stick, political-type, the handle cast in metal as the full-figural head of William Jennings Bryant, 1896 Democratic presidential candidate, below the head is a spread-winged American eagle w/a banner reading "Free Coinage, Prosperity and 16 to One," attached to simple hardwood shaft **173.00**

Wooden 'pipe' walking stick, cylindrical wooden top turned to form a pipe bowl, top unscrews from shaft w/top continuing to form the metal & wood pipe shaft, simple hardwood stick shaft, 19th c. **230.00**

Wooden 'sword' cane, the wooden hook-shaped handle carved at one side w/a stylized human face, a metal ferrule joining a sword blade which slides into the wooden shaft, 19th c. **173.00**

Wooden walking stick, the carved baboon head knob enclosing a sundial - compass above a shaft carved w/various human & animal designs, one particular head enclosing three die, 19th c., 38½" l. (minor losses, cracks) **2,990.00**

CANS & CONTAINERS

The collecting of tin containers has become quite popular within the past several years. Airtight tins were first produced by hand to keep food fresh and, after the invention of the tin-printing machine in the 1870s, containers were manufactured in a wide variety of shapes and sizes with colorful designs. Also see: ADVERTISING, COCA-COLA COLLECTIBLES and TOBACCIANA.

Auto body polish, Royal Saxon tin, front & back scene of man polishing antique car, small screw-on top, 2 x 3 x 7" **$81.00**

Axle grease, Sambo (Nourse Oil Co.) 1 lb. can. **100.00**

Axle oil, Mather "Thousand Mile Axle Oil" 1 pt. can, image of buggies on both sides, ca. late 1800s **80.00**

Baking soda, Calumet sample tin . . . **125.00**

Baking soda, Calumet 1 lb. tin. **32.00**

Baking soda, Gold Label 6 oz. tin **45.00**

Baking soda, Snow King 5 oz. tin **45.00**

Baking soda, Staley's 6 oz. tin. **50.00**

Biscuit, Huntley & Palmer tin w/fire scenes. **235.00**

Biscuit, Huntley & Palmer tin, top w/hunting scene w/numerous dogs & riders, all sides decorated w/rabbits & very nice lithographed lid overhangs the body by ½", England, 2 x 8½ x 13¼" **230.00**

New Life Car Polish Tin

Car polish, New Life tin, 2½ x 4", 5¾" h. (ILLUS.) **149.00**

Cigars, Buster Brown tin, depicting Buster Brown & Tige & signature of R. F. Outcault (missing lid). **1,799.00**

Cigars, Buster Brown round tin, R. T. Outcault images on both sides of Buster Brown, Tige & master, including image on cans on table & in Buster's hands, slip lid, small blemishes, rust spots & uniform wear, 5 x 5" (ILLUS. right w/Yellow Cab Tin) **1,725.00**

Cigars, Green Turtle lunch box tin, green & white w/turtle decoration on front, bail handle & latch (ILLUS. bottom right w/Tobacco tins) **287.00**

Cigars, Happy round tin, front, back & top decorated w/devious bald man winking & smoking cigar, slip lid, 4 x 5¼". **397.00**

Cigars, Home-Run Stogie round tin, front & back w/batter & catcher on light blue ground, slip lid, National Can Co., 4¼ x 6" **4,600.00**

Cigars, Mohawk Chief tin, bust of Indian chief front & back, 4 x 5½ x 6" (severe fade to front). **173.00**

Cigars, Orioles round tin. **375.00**

Cigars, Sunset Trail tin, decorated w/scene of riders on horses, blue ground, 4 x 6". **345.00**

Cigars, Sunset Trail tin, scene of riders on horseback on white ground, hinged cover, 4 x 5½ x 6". . **230.00**

Cigars, War Eagle round tin, brown w/eagle on front & back, slip lid, 4¾ x 5" **138.00**

Cigars Yellow Cab, cylindrical tin w/taxi cab decoration **1,422.00**

Yellow Cab Cigar Tin

Cigars, Yellow Cab tin, round lid, orange, both sides w/lithographed cigar-smoking passenger driven by cab driver, some non-detracting small dents & light surface scratches, the word dark scratched into lid, 5¼ x 5¾" (ILLUS. left) . . . **2,875.00**

Cocoa, Hearthstone round tin, paper label showing scene of roaring fire on front, slip top, J.M. McCracken Co., Boston, 6 x 10" **29.00**

Coffee, Eagle Brand, 1 lb. tin, eagle decoration on front & back, screw-on lid, 4¼ x 6" **115.00**

Coffee, Franklin 3 lb. tin, red & gold w/lithograph of Ben Franklin (ILLUS. right, next page) **1,379.00**

Coffee, Franklin 3 lb. tin, image of Franklin on front & "Sugar" on back, small top, 6 x 9½", some staining **1,898.00**

Coffee, Jam-Boy 1 lb. can, boy w/toast & jam front & back, screw-on lid, 4 x 6½" (denting) **173.00**

Coffee, Hoosier Boy 1 lb. round, tin, boy w/pail of paint by fence on front & back, paper label, 4¼ x 6" **431.00**

Lily of the Valley Coffee Can

Coffee, Lily of the Valley 1 lb. tin, shows Lily of the Valley flowers on front & back, screw-on top, Continental Can Co., 4 x 6" (ILLUS.). **75.00**

Coffee, Mammy's Favorite 4 lb. pail, black woman w/tray w/steaming coffee in cup, 6 x 11". **288.00**

Massasoit Paper Label Coffee Can

Coffee, Massasoit round tin, paper label shows Indian on front & back, slip lid, paper loss to back, 4¼ x 5½" (ILLUS.). **150.00**

Coffee, Mohican, tin, cylindrical, black, orange & white, marked "The Mohican Company Distributors, New York," 4¼" w., 5¾" h. **121.00**

Coffee, Swansdown 1 lb. tin, swan pictured on front, snap-on top, Enterprise Stamping Co., 4¼ x 6¼" (some blemishes) **173.00**

Turkey Brand & Franklin Coffee Tins

Coffee, Turkey Brand 3 lb. tin
(ILLUS. left) 825.00
Coffee, Turkey 1 lb. tin, trademark
turkey on both sides, screw-on lid,
4 x 6" (dents) 460.00
Coffee, Turkey 3 lb. tin, depicts
trademark turkey on both sides,
small top, 5½ x 10½" 1,035.00
Engine degreaser, Triumph cycle
bath tin, 3" d., 4⅜" h. (minor
denting, fading & scratches) 248.00
Honey, Pride of Ontario pail w/bail
handle, shades of red & pink,
overall decoration of bees,
4¾ x 5" 92.00

Large Waldock Lard Can

Lard, Waldock 50 lb. tin, colorful
scene w/geese, slip lid, Heekin
Can Co., scattered surface rust
specks, 12 x 15" (ILLUS.) 173.00
Machine oil, Pfaff sewing machine oil
can, metal, Germany, 3 x 4", 7" h.
(scratches & soiling) 105.00
Malted milk, Carnation 25 lb. tin. 115.00
Marshmallows, Blue Bird triangular
tin showing winter scene on top,
Harry Horne Co., Canada, slight
fade to top, 7" l, 3¾" h. (ILLUS.) 98.00
Motor oil, Ace Wil-Flo 1 qt. can 130.00
Motor oil, Deep Rock "Prize" 1 qt.
can. 55.00

Blue Bird Marshmallow Tin

Motor oil, Exceloyl Oils 1 qt. can 130.00
Motor oil, Hancock ATF Type A 1 qt.
can, one side lists 1948-51 car
models & fill table 350.00
Motor oil, Hudson 1 qt. can, features
numerous images of cars,
airplanes & a tanker 525.00
Motor oil, Husky Hi-Lub 1 qt. can. . . . 235.00
Motor oil, Indian two cycle tin, red &
white, 2½" d., 3½" h.,1/2 pt. (minor
denting & spotting to lid) 220.00
Motor oil, Oneida 1 qt. can, outboard
grade, decorated w/Indian graphics. . 300.00
Motor oil, Premier Ranger 1 qt. can . . 120.00
Motor oil, Sunoco Outboard cone-
top, 1 qt. can 65.00
Motor oil, Vulcan 1 qt. can 65.00
Motor oil, Wolf's Head Lube 1 lb.
keywind can, full 50.00
Peanut butter, Kamo 25 lb. store bin,
tin, back & front depicts a duck,
¾ x 10½" (professionally restored). . . 288.00
Peanut butter, Mosemann's 1 lb. tin. . 115.00
Peanut butter, Ontario Brand Peanut
Butter pail, tin, blue design on light
greenish blue background, marked
"Oswego Candy Works Inc.
Oswego, New York," 3½" d., 3¾" h. . . 55.00
Peanut butter, Planters 25 lb. pail
w/Mr. Peanut decoration 874.00

Red Seal Peanut Butter Pail

Peanut butter, Red Seal 10 oz. tin
pail w/bail handle, decorated
w/nursery rhyme scenes around
sides, "The Newton Tea & Spice
Co. Cincinnati, Ohio" at bottom, slip
lid, rust to lid & handle, scratches &
paint chips, 3 x 3½" (ILLUS.). 121.00

Peanut butter, Sultana 1 lb. pail. **85.00**
Peanut butter, Toyland 1 lb. pail,
    parade scene, 3½ x 4" (dent & litho
    chips). **127.00**
Peanuts, Cream Dove 10 lb. store tin,
    round, dove on front, 8¼ x 9¾" **115.00**

Peanut Tins

Peanuts, Giant 10 lb. tin, red, white &
    blue (ILLUS. right). **236.00**
Peanuts, Robinson Crusoe 10 lb. tin,
    red, yellow & black (ILLUS. left) . . . **345.00**
Peanuts, Society Brand 10 lb. tin,
    man wooing woman w/peanuts. . . . **230.00**
Peanuts, Superior Peanut Company
    10 lb. tin. **236.00**
Soap, Lindbergh tin, fine graphics,
    1920s. **95.00**
Syrup, Dixie Maid 9 lb. pail, paper
    label w/child pouring syrup on
    waffle on front & back, 6 x 7" (dent
    & minor paper loss) **63.00**
Syrup, Tole's Wigwam 1 gal. tin,
    hotel size, wigwam on front, key-
    wind, copyright 1921, 6 x 8½
    (no lid) **431.00**
Tobacco, Boar's Head store bin. **210.00**
Tobacco, Buckingham pocket tin **95.00**

Burley Boy Tobacco Tin

Tobacco, Burley Boy (Bagley's) tin,
    little boxer boy on each side, ring
    latch & bail handle, paint chips &
    scratches, 5 x 6½", 4" h.
    (ILLUS.) **1,650.00**
Tobacco, Dixie Queen canister,
    Southern belle decoration on front
    & back, knobbed lid, 4 x 6½". **201.00**
Tobacco, Dixie Queen lunch box **127.00**

Various Lunch Box Tins

Tobacco, Fashion Cut Plug 1 lb.
    lunch box, scene of fasionably
    dressed couple on side, bail handle
    (ILLUS. top left) **258.00**
Tobacco, Fashion lunch box (few
    litho chips & crease to front) **178.00**
Tobacco, Fast Mail tin w/colorful train
    illustration **646.00**
Tobacco, Fountain round canister,
    slip lid, image of fountain on both
    sides, 5¼ x 6¼". **115.00**

Game Fine Cut Store Bin

Tobacco, Game Fine Cut store bin
    w/wild game (ILLUS.) **676.00**
Tobacco, Hi-Plane Smooth Cut tin. . . **609.00**
Tobacco, Hindoo tin w/colorful
    graphic of a snake charmer **1,100.00**
Tobacco, Honeymoon tin, depicting a
    couple cuddling on a crescent moon. . **852.00**
Tobacco, Honest Scrap shop counter
    tin, slant-top hinged lid, arm
    gripping hammer shown on each
    side, front lithograph of outdoor
    scene w/dog & cat fighting over box
    marked "Honest Scrap," some paint
    chips & crazing, hinge separated
    from lid, 14¼ x 18", 12" h. **2,310.00**
Tobacco, Ojibwa store bin, cardboard
    w/tin top & bottom, front & back
    decorated w/scene of Indian on
    shore beckoning to Indians in
    canoe, contains three packs of
    tobacco, 6½ x 8 x 11" (section of
    paper missing bottom rear) **173.00**
Tobacco, Old Colony (Bagley's)
    sample tin w/original tax stamp **686.00**

Tobacco, Pastime store bin,
lithographed scene of man on
horse inside lid, 4 x 9¼ x 12½"
(litho flaking, fading & litho chips
to sides)......................**115.00**
Tobacco, Peachey vertical pocket tin . . **115.00**
Tobacco, Pennsylvania Ensign
Perfection Cut tin..............**687.00**

Plow Boy Store Bin

Tobacco, Plow Boy slant-top store
bin, sides & front decorated
w/scene of man sitting on a plow
& smoking (ILLUS.)...........**1,694.00**
Tobacco, Poker Club Mixture square-
corner tin, showing a straight flush,
S. F. Hess & Co., 1½ x 3 x 4½"
(some fading)................**138.00**
Tobacco, Polar Bear store tin
(damage to one side & back).....**455.00**

Various Roly Poly Tobacco Tins

Tobacco, Roly Poly,
Dixie Queen Satisfied Customer tin
(ILLUS. top center).............**975.00**
Mayo's Dutchman tin
(ILLUS. bottom right)............**333.00**
Mayo's Inspector tin
(ILLUS. bottom left)............**711.00**
Mayo's Mammy tin
(ILLUS. top right)...............**532.00**
Mayo's Singing Waiter tin
(ILLUS. bottom center)..........**336.00**
Mayo's Store Keeper tin
(ILLUS. top left)...............**445.00**

Tobacco, Staple Grain Plug Cut
pocket tin....................**431.00**
Tobacco, Sterling Light store bin,
round, logo on front, pack on back,
silver & green, 8 x 12" (dents).....**230.00**
Tobacco, Sweet Burley Dark store
bin, round w/square top, pack on
back, red, 8½ x 11½" **230.00**
Tobacco, Sweet Cuba slant-front
store bin, green w/bust of woman . . **155.00**
Tobacco, Sweet Mist store bin......**333.00**

Tiger "Blue" Store Bin

Tobacco, Tiger "Blue" round store
bin, tiger on front & pack on back,
8½ x 11½" (ILLUS.)...........**1,610.00**
Tobacco, Trout-Line tin, scene of
fisherman....................**707.00**
Tobacco, Union Leader Cut Plug, 1
lb. lunch box, basketweave w/eagle
decoration on top (ILLUS. top
right w/Fashion tin) **34.00**
Tobacco, Von Eicken's Alright tin . . **2,498.00**
Tobacco, Whip vertical pocket tin,
3½" (litho chips)................**345.00**
Tobacco, Winner Cut Plug 1 lb. lunch
box, racing car scene on side, bail
handle (ILLUS. bottom left
w/Fashion tin) **317.00**
Tooth powder, Dr. Lyon's tin,
cylindrical w/small screw-on top **52.00**
Transmission oil, Iso-Vis 5 gal.
square tin w/bail handle, 50 lb., 12"
w., 11½" h. (rust spotting, fading
& scratches) **77.00**

CAROUSEL FIGURES

*The ever popular amusement park merry-go-
round or carousel has ancient antecedents but
evolved into its most colorful and complex form
in the decades from 1880 to 1930. In America a
number of pioneering firms, begun by men such
as Gustav Dentzel, Charles Looff and Allan
Herschell, produced these wonderful rides with
beautifully hand-carved animals, the horse*

being the most popular. Some of the noted carvers included M. C. Illusions, Charles Carmel, Solomon Stein and Harry Goldstein.

Today many of the grand old carousels are gone and remaining ones are often broken up and the animals sold separately as collectors search for choice examples. A fine reference to this field is Painted Ponies, American Carousel Art, *by* William Mannas, Peggy Shank and Marianne Stevens *(Zon International Publishing Company, Millwood, New York, 1986).*

Horse, galloping position, carved & painted wood, painted designs overall, ca. 1900, J.R. Anderson, Bristol, England, 47" h., 65" l. (minor imperfections) **$3,335.00**

Carousel Horse

Horse, jumping position, carved & painted wood, w/raised legs & head, open mouth, restored, cracks, very minor paint loss, ca. 1910-15, Stein & Goldstein, Brooklyn, New York, 38" h., 43½" l. (ILLUS.) **1,955.00**

Carousel Horse

Horse, jumping position, carved & painted wood, imperfections, late 19th c., Charles W.F. Dare, New York Carousel Manufacturing Co., Brooklyn, New York, 39" h., 56" l. (ILLUS.). **9,775.00**

Horse, prancing position, carved & painted wood, good detail w/carved mane, saddle over American flag, bridle & glass eyes, old polychrome

repaint, base & brass post added, tail & stirrups replaced, old sheet metal repairs over seams & breaks in legs, attributed to C.W. Park, 56" h. **1,760.00**

Horse, running position, carved & painted wood w/harness & animal skin, repaint in brown, black & yellow, attributed to Dentzel, 60" l. (wear & replaced rope tail) **2,750.00**

Horse, carved & painted wood w/swirled marble eyes, last quarter 19th c., probably from a two-row portable track machine, Charles Dare, New York Carousel Mfg. Co., 35¾" h., 51" l. (imperfections) . . . **1,265.00**

Horse, carved & painted wood, mouth in open position showing teeth & tongue, detailed carving of mane, black, white, red & blue, w/stand, Stern & Goldstein 51 x 58 (left ear chipped off, scratches overall) **3,450.00**

Rare Dentzel Lion

Lion, fierce standing animal w/head raised & mouth open, heavily carved mane & fine body detail, painted greenish yellow w/brown trim & red, pink, silver & white saddle & trappings, by Gustav Dentzel, ca. 1890 (ILLUS.) **35,200.00**

CASH REGISTERS

James Ritty of Dayton, Ohio, is credited with inventing the first cash register. In 1882, he sold the business to a Cincinnati salesman, Jacob H. Eckert, who subsequently invited others into the business by selling stock. One of the purchasers of an early cash register, John J. Patterson, was so impressed with the savings his model brought to his company, he bought 25 shares of stock and became a director of the company in 1884, eventually buying a controlling interest in the National Manufacturing Company. Patterson thoroughly organized the company, conducted sales classes, prepared sales manuals, and established salesman's territories. The success of the National Cash Register Company is due as much to these well organized origins as to the efficiency of its machines. Early "National" cash registers, as well as other models, are deemed highly collectible today.

Brass, "American Cash Register Manufacturing Company," highly embossed w/marble ledge, 24" to top of marquis (professionally restored, missing front lock) **$1,265.00**

Brass, "National," Model 5, scroll case design, narrow end caps, metal base, glass key checks. . . . **2,000.00**

Brass, "National," w/"W.A. Bevis" on front, marble ledge on three sides, last patent date listed is June 15, 1897, 22" to top of marquis **690.00**

National Model 6 1/2

Brass & copper, "National," Model 6½, mounted on oak base, ornate clock on side, 16 x 17", 21½" h. (ILLUS.) **805.00**

Brass & oak, floor model, "National," Model 542-EL-4F, original light-up top sign, large tape reel, front-facing time recorder clock, oak base, ca. 1912 . . . . **5,000.00**

Brass & oak, floor model, "National," Model 79, original top sign, name plate on back, glass key checks, narrow oak base, ca. 1904 . . . . . . **3,500.00**

Copper, "National," Model 245, oxidized finish, fleur-de-lis design case w/split counter & red, white & blue flag indication, original top sign **1,750.00**

Nickel-plate, "National," Model 130, original nickel-plate finish on Bohemian-style case w/glass key checks & custom name lid plate. . **1,000.00**

Nickel-plate, "National," Model 138, Art Nouveau design case w/original top sign, custom name lid plate, nickel-plated key stems, professionally restored **1,750.00**

CASTORS & CASTOR SETS

Castor bottles were made to hold condiments for table use. Some were produced in sets of several bottles housed in silver plated frames. The word also is sometimes spelled "Caster."

Castor set, five tall clear glass bottles w/cut thumbprints & engraved floral designs & pointed stoppers fitted in a round silver plate stand w/a tall bell-form base & a forked tall center handle, late 19th c., 16" h. . . . **$110.00**

Pickle castor, blue paneled glass cylindrical insert decorated w/polychrome enameled flowers, in a silver plate stand w/a high arched handle topped by a pierced scrolling crest & suspending the tongs, silver plate cover, late 19th c., 11¼" h. **248.00**

Pickle castor, clear pressed glass cylindrical insert w/reflective bull's-eye, icicle trim & hobnail borders, fitted in an ornate silver plate frame w/floral-embossed base & cover, w/tongs, insert 4" h. **303.00**

Pickle castor, clear pressed glass Diamond & Fan patt. insert, ornate silver plate holder w/high arched handle & tongs, holder marked by Aurora Silver Co., 11½" h. **275.00**

Pickle castor, cobalt blue blown glass insert w/gold enameled decoration, ornate silver plate frame, cover & tongs **450.00**

Pickle castor, cranberry glass bulbous ovoid insert tapering toward the top, enameled floral decoration, in a marked Webster silver plate frame w/a high arched handle w/scroll trim & a flaring round foot . . . **715.00**

Pickle castor, cranberry glass Inverted Thumbprint patt. insert w/enameled yellow roses, ornate silver plate frame **859.00**

Pickle castor, cranberry mold-blown glass Inverted Thumbprint patt. insert enameled w/white flowers & green leaves, ornate silver plate frame, cover & tongs **450.00**

Pickle castor, cranberry mold-blown insert w/a squatty bulbous bottom below cylindrical sides, Inverted Thumbprint patt., in a simple silver plate frame signed Forbes, w/tongs. . **358.00**

Pickle castor, cranberry mold-blown ovoid melon-lobed glass insert in the Inverted Thumbprint patt., decorated w/polychrome enameled

flowers, in an ornate silver plate
stand w/high arched & pierced
handle, late 19th c., 9" h.......... **330.00**
Pickle castor, cranberry mold-blown
Paneled Sprig patt. insert
decorated w/enameled flowers &
gold trim, silver plate frame marked
by the Colonial Silver Co., 11" h.... **851.00**
Pickle castor, ruby bulbous acorn-
form Inverted Thumbprint patt.
insert, set in a silver plate frame
w/a wide embossed base ring on a
wide domed base, high arched &
pointed handle w/pierced lattice
trim, w/tongs, insert 4¼" h. **660.00**
Pickle castor, shaded pink satin
ovoid deep insert fitted in an ornate
silver plate frame w/a flared ribbed
foot & scroll-pierced upright arched
handle & tongs, stepped, domed
cover w/finial, insert 4¼" h.,
overall 9¾" h. **963.00**
Pickle castor, cov., shaded pink
satin mother-of-pearl Diamond
Quilted cylindrical insert, ornate
silver plate frame w/leafy branches
around the sides, ringed base on
tiny ball feet, domed floral-
embossed cover w/pierced urn-
form finial, arched fixed chain link
handle, marked "Hartford Silver
Co.," insert 4¼" h., overall 9¾" h.
(sliver chip on bottom of insert) **468.00**

CAT COLLECTIBLES

BOOKS & MAGAZINES

"A Dog and His Cats," by Kurt
Unkelbach, New Jersey, 1969,
excellent condition w/dust jacket,
148 pp. **$20.00**
"Holiday Fun Book," booklet-size,
Walt Disney Christmas story plus
holiday activities & games,
produced in cooperation w/"Look"
magazine, copyright 1965, 24 pp.,
mint condition **5.00**
"National Geographic," November
1938, two cat-related articles, very
good condition................ **10.00**

BOTTLES

Avon, "Blue Eyes," white cat, 1½ oz.,
1975 .... **10.00**
Avon, "Cat-Napper," ceramic
pomander, white kitten in blue
blanket in brown basket, ca. 1983... **28.00**

Avon, "Purrfect Cat," cat lying down,
black w/gold collar, 1987......... **15.00**
Perfume flask, metal painted blue
w/embossed white kitten,
w/perfume dauber, made in China .. **60.00**

CHESSIE (Chesapeake & Ohio RR Mascot)

Playing cards, double-deck, mint in
cellophane-wrapped box.......... **30.00**
Prints, from original artwork by Guido
Gruenwald, 1970s, in original
mailing envelope, 10 x 11½",
set of 3..................... **65.00**
Scarf, silk, sleeping Chessie design,
1949-50.................... **50.00**

FIGURAL ITEMS

Mother Cat & Kittens Group

Earthenware, mother cat & two
kittens connected by chains, grey-
striped & white, stamped "Japan,"
mother cat 6½" h., the group
(ILLUS.)..................... **25.00**
Glass, clear cat sitting upright, inside
the stomach is a hungry bird
w/open mouth, 5½" h. **22.00**
Glass, clear crystal 'doughnut-
shaped' cat w/tail up in the air,
label marked "ACC Handmade
Crystal Taiwan," overall 5¼" h. **30.00**
Glass, milk glass covered animal
dish, reclining cat on the cover
w/blue eyes, Westmoreland Glass
Co., mark & paper label, 8" l. **140.00**
Porcelain, black & white cat lying
down, Royal Worcester, England,
1978, 5½" l................... **225.00**
Porcelain, brown & white tabby kitten
sleeping, Model 2579, Royal
Doulton, England, retired 1986,
3" l. **105.00**
Porcelain, Siamese cat standing
w/mouth open in a meow, by the
artist Granget, Hutschenreuther,
Germany, discontinued, 5¼ x 7" ... **425.00**

Porcelain, Toby jug in the shape of Alice (Alice in Wonderland), w/a tree trunk behind her, a grey Cheshire cat perched on her shoulder, marked "Tony Wood Studio Staffordshire England for Perennis," copyright 1982, 3½" h. . . . **85.00**

Pottery, Art Deco stylized cat, gold-painted textured body, one eye open, one eye closed, incised "Royal Haeger," ca. 1938, 15½" h. . **140.00**

Pottery, black cat w/glossy glaze, hollow slits for eyes, 1920-40, paper label, Cliftwood, Illinois, 11½" l. **125.00**

Pottery, black & grey-striped tabby, incised "Made in Portugal," 12½" l., 7½" h. **75.00**

Wood, hand-carved from solid piece, Egyptian-style cat, 17½" h. **195.00**

GARFIELD

Garfield Alarm Clock

Alarm clock, digital, plastic, head of Garfield, mint working order, overall 7" h. (ILLUS.) **55.00**

Creamer, ceramic, figural Garfield, stamped on the bottom "I love moo juice," Enesco, early 1980s **30.00**

MISCELLANEOUS

Ashtray with Figural Kitten

Ashtray, porcelain w/a lustre glaze, oblong scalloped dish w/six holes around the center to hold

cigarettes, small figure of a seated black & white kitten atop one edge, incised "Made in Japan," 3¾" l., 3¼" h. (ILLUS.) **25.00**

Cat on Basket

Basket, woven wicker, stylized cat lid, brown & tan w/red button eyes, wooden ears, 7¼" h. (ILLUS.) **23.00**

Book stand, "Cat in the Hat," red plastic **15.00**

Bottle cork, transfer-print of a ginger tabby on the top, 1⅝" d. **7.00**

Bubble pipe, child's, plastic w/embossed cat's face **5.00**

Dish towels, each representing a different day of the week w/cats doing different household chores, colorful stitchery, mint condition, 1940s, set of 7 . . . . **75.00**

Matchbox holder, cream background covered w/a playful cat in petitpoint design **85.00**

Matchbox holder, metal, decorated w/a frightened cat on the top, 1½ x 2¼", 3" h. **50.00**

Planter, ceramic, a pink & white striped box w/a brown & white kitten wearing green overalls & brown shoes in front, cat 4¼" h. **9.00**

Playing cards, double deck, Canasta rules brochure included, design of a white Angora on a blue background, near mint, 1950s **13.00**

Spoon & fork set, child's, metal w/embossed "Puss 'n Boots," the set **45.00**

Viennese bronze, figure group of cats playing tennis, marked "Austria," base 2¼ x 4" **295.00**

1   2 3   4 5   6   7   8

Courtesy of David Rago

Various Fulper Pieces

CERAMICS

ABINGDON

From about 1934 until 1950, Abingdon Pottery Company, Abingdon, Illinois, manufactured decorative pottery, mainly cookie jars, flowerpots and vases. Decorated with various glazes, these items are becoming popular with collectors who are especially attracted to Abingdon's novelty cookie jars.

Abingdon Mark

Book ends, figural horse head, black
    glaze, pr. **$50.00**
Cookie jar, "Humpty Dumpty,"
    yellow **160.00**
Cookie jar, "Jack-in-the-Box" **325.00**
Vase, double cornucopia-form, cream
    & gold w/florals **75.00**
Window box, No.476, blue glaze **20.00**

AREQUIPA

Dr. Philip King Brown established The Arequipa Sanitorium in Fairfax, California, in the early years of the 20th century. In 1911 he set up a pottery at the facility as therapy for his female tuberculosis patients since he had been impressed with the success of the similar Marblehead pottery in Massachusetts.

The first art director was the noted ceramics designer Frederick H. Rhead who had earlier been art director at the Roseville Pottery.

In 1913 the pottery was separated from the medical facility and incorporated as The Arequipa Potteries. Later that year Rhead and his wife, Agnes, one of the pottery instructors, left Arequipa and Albert L. Solon took over as the pottery director. The corporation was dissolved in 1915 and the pottery closed in 1918 although the sanitorium remained in operation until 1957.

Arequipa Marks

Vase, 3¼" h., 3" d., simple wide ovoid
    form w/closed rim, decorated in
    squeeze-bag w/stylized leaves in a
    fine organic matte green w/small
    red circles, against a matte yellow

1   2   3
Early Arequipa Vases

ground, incised mark "?27 -
Arequipa - California - 1912"
(ILLUS. No. 2) **$6,325.00**

Vase, 4¾" h., 3¼" d., swelled
cylindrical body w/a narrow
rounded shoulder to the short, wide
neck, smooth matte leathery dark
green glaze, incised "3 - Arequipa -
Cal." (ILLUS. No. 6) **358.00**

Vase, 6" h., 3¼" d., simple ovoid
body w/wide incurved rim,
decorated w/incised abstract
leaves in a flowing, glossy dark
blue against a turquoise ground,
restoration to small inner rim chip,
Frederick Rhead period, signed in
ink "Arequipa California - 1912 -
463 - 4" (ILLUS. No. 5) **2,420.00**

Vase, 6¼" h., 5" d., bulbous
shouldered ovoid body w/a wide
flat rim, decorated in squeeze-bag
w/stylized yellow flowers over
large, bright green leaves w/blue
veins, from the Frederick Rhead
period, blue ink mark "Arequipa -
California," ca. 1911-12, minute
glaze nick on raised point
(ILLUS. No. 1) **9,350.00**

4   5   6
Variety of Arequipa Vases

Vase, 7" h., 4" d., simple ovoid body
decorated in squeeze-bag
w/stylized leaves in brown on a
matte feathered green ground, a
dark green drip down from each

leaf, fine glaze nicks on rim, Rhead
period, ca. 1912, blue enamel mark
(ILLUS. No. 4) **3,740.00**

Vase, 7½" h., 4" d., bulbous base
below tapering cylindrical sides,
decorated in squeeze-bag w/a
wreath of heart-shaped leaves
under a fine leathery pea green
matte glaze, Frederick Rhead
period, marked in ink "Arequipa
California 1913 - 2123 - 123"
(ILLUS. No. 3) **1,980.00**

Vase, 11" h., 6¼" d., baluster-form
w/a short flaring neck, hand-cut
w/large upright bell-shaped flowers
around the sides & small daisy-like
blossomheads around the neck,
clear brown glossy glaze, die-
stamped mark & "403-22 -WI" **770.00**

AUSTRIAN

Numerous potteries in Austria produced
good-quality ceramic wares over many years.
Some factories were established by American
entrepreneurs, particularly in the Carlsbad area,
and other factories made china under special
brand names for American importers. Marks on
various pieces are indicated in many listings.

Austrian Marks

Dresser tray, squared form w/deeply
scalloped & scrolled dished rim
w/wide green border band trimmed
w/heavy gilt scrolls, the round
center reserve w/a gilt tracery band
framing a polychrome transfer-
printed scene of Romeo & Juliet,
marked "Victoria - Carlsbad -
Austria," 9" l. **$61.00**

Humidor, cov., cylindrical barrel-
shaped body w/a shaded dark
green ground decorated w/a
colored scene of Grecian figures
inspecting a wall, the round fitted
silver plate cover w/a rounded rim
band & concave top mounted w/a
large figural pipe, marked "Victoria
- Austria," late 19th - early 20th c.,
7¾" h. **303.00**

Mug, squatty bulbous base band
below slightly tapering wide
cylindrical sides, gilt rim & ornate
S-scroll gold handle, decorated w/a
h.p. scene of two women tending

sheep in a pasture, marked
w/retailer's mark in Des Moines,
Iowa, 5" h.................... **138.00**

Pitcher, tankard, 12" h., tall slightly
tapering cylindrical body w/a rim
spout & double loop gilt handle, the
side decorated w/a large lacy gilt
oval reserve framing the bust
portrait of a pretty young blonde
lady in a lavender dress, olive
green ground shading to gilt scroll
bands around the base, marked
"Imperial China - Austria" **138.00**

Smoker's set, figural, majolica, a
figure of a standing peasant
woman w/hands on her hips w/a
large rectangular basket holder
behind her & a smaller one beside
her, on a rectangular base
w/notched corners, polychrome
glazes, by Block, marked "Austria -
B.B.," 8" h.................... **138.00**

BAUER

The Bauer Pottery was moved to Los Angeles, California, from Paducah, Kentucky, in 1909, in the hope that the climate would prove beneficial to the principal organizer, John Andrew Bauer, who suffered from severe asthma. Flowerpots, made of California adobe clay, were the first production at the new location, but soon they were able to resume production of stoneware crocks and jugs, the mainstay of the Kentucky operation. In the early 1930s, Bauer's colorfully glazed earthen dinnerwares, especially the popular Ring-Ware pattern, became an immediate success. Sometimes confused with its imitator, Fiesta Ware (first registered by Homer Laughlin in 1937), Bauer pottery is collectible in its own right and is especially popular with West Coast collectors. Bauer Pottery ceased operation in 1962.

Bauer Mark

Batter bowl, Ring-Ware patt., large .. **$85.00**
Bean pot, cov., Plainware patt.,
black, 1 qt.................... **225.00**
Bean pot, cov., Plainware, yellow,
2 qt......................... **120.00**
Beer stein, Ring-Ware patt., light
rose........................ **400.00**

Bowl, Ring-Ware patt., No. 30,
black...................... **65.00**
Bowl, fruit, 7¾" d., three-footed,
Ring-Ware patt., white........... **75.00**
Butter dish, cov., round, Ring-Ware
patt., light blue................ **125.00**
Candleholder, spool-shaped, Ring-
Ware patt., yellow **95.00**
Casserole, cov., Ring-Ware patt.,
cobalt blue, medium size.......... **75.00**
Casserole, cov., Ring-Ware patt.,
yellow, in stand, medium size **125.00**
Casserole, cov., individual size, in
holder, red, 5½" d............... **85.00**
Casserole, cov., individual size,
Ring-Ware patt., cobalt blue,
5½" d....................... **95.00**
Casserole, cov., individual size,
Ring-Ware patt., green, 5½" d. **75.00**
Casserole, cov., individual size,
Ring-Ware patt., orange/red,
5½" d....................... **95.00**

Bauer Ring-Ware Casserole

Casserole, cov., Ring-Ware patt.,
orange/red, 9¾" d. (ILLUS.) **235.00**
Coffee carafe, cov., orange/red **60.00**
Cup & saucer, demitasse, Ring-
Ware patt., green.............. **225.00**
Cup & saucer, Ring-Ware patt.,
black...................... **160.00**
Flower bowl, deep, fluted, yellow.... **250.00**
Mug, handled, Ring-Ware patt.,
orange/red................... **125.00**
Pitcher, beater-type, Ring-Ware patt.,
cobalt blue................... **185.00**
Pitcher, water, Plainware patt.,
green....................... **95.00**
Pitcher, Ring-Ware patt., orange/red,
2 qt......................... **85.00**
Planter, model of a swan, turquoise,
medium...................... **95.00**
Plate, 7" d., Ring-Ware patt., black.... **85.00**
Plate, dinner, 10½" d., Ring-Ware
patt., red.................... **75.00**
Plate, chop, 12" d., Ring-Ware patt.,
orange...................... **58.00**
Plate, chop, 17" d., Ring-Ware patt.,
orange/red................... **275.00**

Punch bowl, pedestal base,
white **2,000.00**
Punch bowl, footed, Ring-Ware patt.,
green, 11" d. **445.00**
Punch cup, Ring-Ware patt., black . . . **85.00**
Salt & pepper shakers, beehive-
shaped, Ring-Ware patt., cobalt
blue, pr. **65.00**
Salt & pepper shakers, Ring-Ware
patt., beehive-shaped, jade green,
pr. **50.00**
Salt shaker, Ring-Ware patt.,
beehive-shaped, black **45.00**
Sugar shaker, Ring-Ware patt.,
orange/red **375.00**
Syrup pitcher, Ring-Ware patt.,
chartreuse (spout wear) **120.00**
Teapot, cov., Aladdin Lamp-shape,
yellow, large **250.00**
Teapot, cov., Ring-Ware patt.,
orange/red **150.00**
Teapot, cov., Ring-Ware patt.,
yellow **135.00**
Teapot, cov., Ring-Ware patt.,
orange/red, 2-cup size (inside
flake) **125.00**
Vase, 3½" h., Matt Carlton's Artware
line, ruffled, jade green **188.00**
Vase, 5" h., fan-shaped, Cal -Art line,
light blue **35.00**
Vase, 7½" h., Fred Johnson Artware
line, rust. **90.00**
Vase, 8" h., No. 151, ivory. **163.00**
Vase, 8¼" h., Ring-Ware patt.,
black **225.00**
Vase, 18" h., Rebekah shape, jade
green **1,650.00**

BAVARIAN

Ceramics have been produced by various potteries in Bavaria, Germany, for may years. Those appearing for sale in greatest frequency today were produced in the 19th and early 20th centuries. Various company marks are indicated with some listings here.

Cake plate, slightly scalloped round
form w/slender slightly arched
pierced gold rim handles, wide light
blue border band decorated
w/dainty clusters of violets, pink-
tinted center, 11" d. **$72.00**
Model of a bird, a long-tailed exotic
bird in shades of blue, grey-blue &
green perched atop a tall forked
shaded green upright branch,
marked "Bochmann, Alboth &

Kaiser, W. Germany," & gold overglaze "Alka-Kunst - Bavaria,"
No. 318, mid-20th c., 8" h. **94.00**
Plate, 8½" d., gently scalloped rim
w/a curved narrow pale yellow side
panel w/gilt trim beside an oblong
reserve w/a bust portrait of a young
blonde lady wearing a lavender
dress, shaded ground, marked
"Louise Bavaria" **61.00**
Plate, 9½" d., decorated w/a portrait
of a lady, maroon body w/gold trim,
marked underglaze "Bayreuth -
Crown - Bavaria" **50.00**
Plate, 9½" d., gently scalloped rim,
border band of lacy gilt scallops on
white, central bust color portrait of
Queen Louise **61.00**

Ornate Bavarian Plate

Plate, 11" d., scalloped rim w/wide gilt
band & three fan-shaped pierced
panels, decorated w/a large cluster
of red & pink roses w/yellow &
green leaves & small yellow
blossoms against a ground shading
from rust red to pale yellow, signed
(ILLUS.). **75.00**
Relish dish, h.p. yellow & red
flowers, 11" l. **23.00**

BELLEEK

Belleek china has been made in Ireland's County Fermanagh for many years. It is exceedingly thin porcelain. Several marks were used, including a hound and harp (1865-1880), and a hound, harp and castle (1863-1891). A printed hound, harp and castle with the words "Co. Fermanagh Ireland" constitutes the mark from 1891. Belleek-type china also was made in the United States last century by several firms, including Ceramic Art Company, Columbian Art Pottery, Lenox Inc., Ott & Brewer and Willets Manufacturing Co.

AMERICAN BELLEEK

Rose-decorated Ceramic Art Vase

Cup & saucer, beaded w/blue &
gold spirals (Willets) **$125.00**

Vase, 10½" h., footed bulbous ovoid
body tapering sharply to a tiny
short neck w/a widely flaring &
flattened rim, the sides h.p.
w/clusters of large purplish red
roses & green leaves on a dark
green shaded to white ground,
narrow gilt rim & base bands,
purple palette mark, Ceramic Art
Co. (ILLUS.) **385.00**

Vase, 18½" h., tall slender classical
form w/a slender pedestal & flaring
round foot supporting the tapering
shouldered body w/a slender neck
w/a widely flaring mouth, ornate gilt
scroll shoulder handles extending
down each side, enamel- and gilt-
decorated w/a center scene of a
classical maiden in a landscape on
one side & a floral bouquet on the
other, artist-signed, printed mark,
restoration, ca. 1900 (Ceramic
Art Co.) **316.00**

IRISH BELLEEK

Irish Belleek Mark

Basket, four-strand, shamrock-
shaped w/applied roses & leaves,
6½" w., 3rd black mark **375.00**

Bread tray, round w/pierced double-
loop rim handles, Neptune patt.,
1st green mark, 11¼" d. **99.00**

Cake plate, round w/loop side
handles, Shamrock-Basketweave
patt., 3rd black mark, 10¼" d. **110.00**

Cup & saucer, Limpet patt., 3rd black
mark **85.00**

Cup & saucer, Shamrock-
Basketweave patt., harp-shaped
handle, 3rd black mark **108.00**

Irish Belleek Pig

Model of a pig, seated animal,
undecorated, 4½" l., 2¾" h., 2nd
black mark (ILLUS.). **300.00**

Plate, tea, 6" d., Tridacna patt., 1st
black mark. **75.00**

Plate, 7" d., New Shell patt., pink trim,
1st green mark **59.00**

Early Hexagon Pattern Teapot

Teapot, cov., Hexagon patt.,
colortrim, 2nd black mark (ILLUS.). . . **635.00**

Early Limpet Tea Set

Tea set: cov. teapot, open sugar
bowl, creamer, four cups & saucers
& scalloped undertray; Limpet patt.,
color trim, 1st black mark, the set
(ILLUS.) **3,850.00**

BENNINGTON

Bennington wares, which ranged from stoneware to parian and porcelain, were made in Bennington, Vermont, primarily in two potteries, one in which Captain John Norton and his descendants were principals, and the other in which Christopher Webber Fenton (also once associated with the Nortons) was a principal. Various marks are found on the wares made in the two major potteries, including J. & E. Norton, E. & L. P. Norton, L. Norton & Co., Norton & Fenton, Edward Norton, Lyman Fenton & Co., Fenton's Works, United States Pottery Co., U.S.P. and others.

The popular pottery with the mottled brown on yellowware glaze was also produced in Bennington, but such wares should be referred to as "Rockingham" or "Bennington-type" unless they can be specifically attributed to a Bennington, Vermont, factory.

Bennington Marks

Book flask, Scroddle ware, light overall marbleized effect, 5½" h. (two small chips on mouth & spine, professional corner restorations). . **$880.00**

Book flask, binding impressed "Parted Spirits," overall Flint Enamel glaze in brown, green & orange, 8" h. (touched-up glaze rub in one corner) **1,760.00**

Rare Toby Barrel Bottle

Bottle, figural Toby barrel-type, overall brown, light orangish brown & blue Flint Enamel glaze, "1849" mark, some light restoration to mouth, small chip on base, 10½" h. (ILLUS.) **3,630.00**

Flint Enamel Candlesticks

Candlesticks, ringed columnar form w/heavy socket ring & flaring round base, overall brown, blue & green Flint Enamel glaze, 8" h., pr. (ILLUS.) **1,760.00**

Rare Bennington Doe Figure

Model of a doe, the recumbent animal on a deep oblong rockwork base w/applied "coleslaw" trim & a tree stump spill vase behind, an overall mottled green & orange Flint Enamel glaze w/a speckled effect, impressed patent mark, both ears professionally restored, 11" l., 9" h. (ILLUS.) **8,525.00**

Paperweight, Graniteware, rectangular base w/a model of a spread-winged American eagle w/shield on the top, trimmed in gold, 4" l., 3" h. **798.00**

Pitcher, 6" h., tapering cylindrical body w/a molded base & upper molded ring below the long pointed

spout & flat rim, C-form handle,
mottled brown Rockingham glaze
(very small spout chip) **132.00**

Fine Bennington Parian Pitcher

Pitcher, 9" h., Parian, Cherub &
Grapes patt., bulbous ovoid body
tapering to a shaped rim w/a wide
rim spout & vine handle, molded in
white high-relief w/cherubs among
grapevines against a blue ground
(ILLUS.) **308.00**

Bennington Graniteware Pitcher

Pitcher, 12¾" h., graniteware,
shallow footring supporting the
squatty bulbous base w/slightly
waisted cylindrical sides below the
undulating rim & high, wide arched
spout & vine handle, the upper side
panels w/relief-molded grapevines
above a band of molded acanthus
leaves around the base, heavy
bluish grey glaze, several 'In-the-
making' lines, area of stain on
spout w/hairline, small chip on
footring (ILLUS.) **303.00**
Toby jug, Scroddled Ware, the
seated Mr. Toby w/an overall
swirled light & dark clay design & a
grapevine handle, impressed
"U.S.P." mark, 6¼" h. (old base

restoration, hairline near base of
handle, a line & restored chip on
bottom of handles, few flakes at
rim) **1,430.00**

BERLIN (KPM)

The mark KPM was used at Meissen from 1724 to 1725, and was later adopted by the Royal Factory, Konigliche Porzellan Manufaktur, in Berlin. At various periods it has been incorporated with the Brandenburg sceptre, the Prussian eagle or the crowned globe. The same letters were also adopted by other factories in Germany in the late 19th and early 20th centuries. With the end of the German monarchy in 1918, the name of the firm was changed to Staatliche Porzellan Manufaktur and though production was halted during World War II, the factory was rebuilt and is still in business. The exquisite paintings on porcelain were produced at the close of the 19th century and are eagerly sought by collectors today.

Cup & saucer, ornately decorated &
heavy gold trim, marked w/KPM
scepter & blue underglaze, also
stamped w/cross & orb in red
overglaze "Berlinerware,"
mid-19th c.. . . . . **$120.00**

Lovely Marked K.P.M. Figurines

Figurines, a standing young couple
in late 18th c. costume, he w/a
cocked hat, long coat & trousers
above boots, she wearing an
Empire gown, fancy hat & holding a
fan, both in white w/ornate scrolling
black & brown decoration w/gilt
trim, underglaze-blue "K.P.M."
mark, on round gilt-lined bases,
3½" d., 8½" h., pr. (ILLUS.) **350.00**
Plaque, round, scene of the Madonna
& Child w/John the Baptist, after
Raphael, ca. 1920, impressed
"K.P.M." marks, 4½" d. **690.00**

Peasant Boy Berlin Plaque

Plaque, oval, depicting a peasant boy seated on a grassy mound w/his recorder, impressed mark on reverse, mounted in an ornate pierced scrolling vine & floral oval metal frame, early 20th c., 8½" h. (ILLUS.).................... **978.00**

Plaque, oval, a scene of a young girl wearing a simple late 18th c. costume & mob cap standing & holding a chamberstick shielded w/one hand, light falls on her face & upper body w/a dark background, artist-signed, impressed K.P.M. marks, in an ornate rectangular gilt plaster frame w/an oval opening, 6½ x 8½" **2,530.00**

Plaque, rectangular, a polychrome enamel scene of St. Anthony holding a child, in a rectangular giltwood frame, impressed "KPM" mark, late 19th c., 8⅞ x 11" **1,380.00**

Berlin Plaque of Marguerite

Plaque, rectangular, a scene of Marguerite in her long gown, holding a large bouquet of flowers

as she stands before a small niche w/a statue of the Virgin Mary & Christ Child, after Berraud, impressed mark, in a velvet frame, 7¾ x 12⅞ " (ILLUS.).......... **3,105.00**

Plaque, round, depicting a half-length portrait of the Madonna kneeling & cradling the Christ Child, both delicately lit against a dark background, artist-signed, Dresden, factory marks, early 20th c., matted in an ornate floral & scroll-embossed gilt plaster frame, plaque 13½" d............... **3,738.00**

Plaque, rectangular, polychrome decoration of a figural landscape scene showing "Parting Lovers," rectangular giltwood frame, impressed "KPM" mark, late 19th c., 12½ x 16½" **5,750.00**

Plaque, rectangular, scene w/a three-quarters portrait of the biblical Ruth holding a sheaf of wheat, wide rust velvet mat & giltwood rope-molded frame, marked "K.P.M.," 15 x 18½"................. **3,025.00**

Plaque, rectangular, colorful outdoor scene of a man & two ladies in long gowns surrounded by Viking warriors, artist-signed, paper labels on back w/longhand names of characters in an opera, ornate pierced gilt acanthus leaf frame, marked "K.P.M.," plaque 10¼ x 12½", overall 16½ x 18½" **4,950.00**

Plaque, rectangular, painted w/a scene of a young peasant woman standing upon a balcony beside a stone wall & gazing across a mystic mountainscape, she holds a tambourine w/a floor harp beside her, wide ornately carved acanthus leaf frame, marked "K.P.M.," 14¼ x 19¼" **6,325.00**

Plate, 8½" d., h.p. center vignette depicting couple in garden setting, ornate gold borders, signed w/underglazed scepter & crown w/red "KPM" mark, cross w/orb, late 19th c.................... **500.00**

BISQUE

Bisque is biscuit china, fired a single time but not glazed. Some bisque is decorated with colors. Most abundant from the Victorian era are figures and groups, but other pieces from busts to vases were made by numerous potteries in the U.S. and abroad. Reproductions have been produced for many years so care must be taken when seeking antique originals.

Victorian Children's Busts

Bust of a Classical maiden,
modeled w/one breast exposed,
within a border of scrolled leaftips,
Europe, 19th c., 7¾" w., 9" h. **$201.00**

Busts, girl & boy, blue intaglio eyes
w/molded lids, single-stroke brows,
open-closed mouths w/teeth,
molded & painted hair, molded
clothing on shoulders, molded hats,
blue pedestals w/gold bases,
unmarked, girl 8" h., boy 9" h., pr.
(ILLUS.). **120.00**

Candy container, figural clown
drummer character head w/intaglio
eyes, open-closed smiling mouth,
wire & wood body & limbs, wood &
paper drum, metal cymbals, cloth
outfit w/original price tag, early
20th c., Germany, 8¼" h. **345.00**

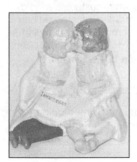

Bisque Figure Group of Girls

Figure group, two young girls
kissing, seated together holding a
large book in their laps, one
w/brown hair, one w/blonde, one
green dress, the other in pale
lavender & blue, open book printed
"I Am Not Angry," Germany, late
19th c., 4½" d., 4½" h. (ILLUS.). . . . **118.00**

Figure group, a young girl standing
& pushing a large rectangular
wheelbarrow planter w/the figure of
a young boy sitting on one corner
facing the girl, on a thin oval base,

all-white, Germany, marked on the
back "3116 LEA," late 19th c., 9" l.,
6" h. **55.00**

Bisque Boy by Ornate Fence

Figure of a boy, standing wearing an
ornate 18th c. costume in pale
pink, white & gold, holding a
shallow round basket w/applied
flowers, standing in front of a
fanned fence-form background
trimmed in gold & raised on a
molded scroll, gilt-trimmed base,
France, late 19th c., 5½" d., 7¼" h.
(ILLUS.). **125.00**

Bisque Figure of Boy in Early Costume

Figure of a boy, standing boy
wearing a 17th c. costume w/lacy
collar & ribbon belt, brown curly
hair & tinted face, blue & pink
costume w/gilt trim, on a rounded
rockwork base, 3⅜" d., 12" h.
(ILLUS.). **145.00**

Bisque Boy in Victorian Costume

Figure of a boy, standing figure of a
young boy wearing a lavender long
jacket w/pleated hem above blue-
striped pantelettes, brown hair &
tinted face, white tam w/pink
ribbons & yellow feather, holding a
basket, standing on a tan & grey
rockwork base, France, late
19th c., 4¾" d., 13½" h. (ILLUS.). . . **195.00**

Heubach Dutch Girl Figure

Figure of a Dutch girl, seated pose
w/her hands around her knees,
wearing a white bonnet over her
blonde hair, tinted face & arms,
pale green scarf & dark green
blouse w/rust red skirt & brown
clogs, marked "Heubach,"
Germany, late 19th c., 2⅝ x 5",
4¾" h. (ILLUS.) **165.00**
Figure of a girl, dancing pose w/her
arms holding out her pale green
pleated skirt, blonde hair & pink
tinted features, on a floral-colored

Bisque Dancing Girl Figure

molded base, marked "Heubach,"
Germany, late 19th c., 4¼" d.,
8¼" h. (ILLUS.) **175.00**
Figure of a Turk w/sword, nodder-
type, Germany. **95.00**

Bisque Boy & Girl in Armchairs

Figures of a boy & girl, each seated
in a large armchair, wearing ornate
green & white costumes w/gold
bead trim & large feathered hats,
chairs in brown & green, facing
pair, 2¾" d., 6¼" h., pr. (ILLUS.) . . . **135.00**
Figures of a boy & girl, each
supporting a basket on their
shoulder, polychrome decoration,
Germany, late 19th c., 16" h., pr. . . **288.00**
**Figures of a costumed man playing
a mandolin & a matching
dancing girl,** Europe, late 19th c.,
15¼" h., pr. **489.00**

French Figures in 18th Century Dress

Figures of a lady & man, each standing wearing ornate 18th c. costume in shades of blue, maroon, pink, white & yellow, on round socle bases w/green-tinted top over thin yellow beaded bands & a blue ribbon band, France, late 19th c., 11" h., pr. (ILLUS.) **395.00**

Ornate French Bisque Couple

Figures of a lady & man, each standing in 18th c. peasant costume, she pulling her cloak across her dress w/other hand holding a small mask, he w/one hand to his face, the other holding a mask, each on a shaped platform base, France, late 19th c., facing pair, minor chips, 22" h., pr. (ILLUS.) **1,093.00**

Figures of a young peasant boy & girl, he standing wearing a hat, loose shirt & floral-trimmed kneebreeches, she standing wearing a scarf & holding up the front edge of her flower-trimmed skirt, each on a flower-applied round base, delicate coloring, marked "P. Frank. Germany," each 12¾" h., pr. **231.00**

Figures of children, a boy & a girl each supporting a basket on their shoulder, polychrome decoration, Germany, late 19th c., 16" h., pr. . . **288.00**

Match holder, figural, model of a large colorful rooster walking beside a deep oval basket trimmed in brown, on a brown & green mound base w/pink base band, late 19th c., 3⅝" d., 4" h. (ILLUS. top next column) **110.00**

Piano baby, unjointed bisque figure, painted blue eyes w/single-stroke brows, open-closed mouth, molded & painted blonde hair, molded white bonnet w/blue bows, molded

Rooster & Basket Match Holder

white baby dress w/blue ribbon, Heubach (Gebruder), marked "89, (sunburst), GH (superimposed), Dep," 4¼" h. **105.00**

BLUE RIDGE DINNERWARES

The small town of Erwin, Tennessee, was the home of the Southern Potteries, Inc., originally founded by E.J. Owen in 1917 and first called the Clinchfield Pottery.

In the early 1920s Charles W. Foreman purchased the plant and he revolutionized the company's output, developing the popular line of hand-painted wares sold as "Blue Ridge" dinnerwares. Free-hand painted by women from the surrounding hills, these colorful dishes in many patterns continued in production until the plant's closing in 1957.

Blue Ridge Dinnerwares Mark

Bowl, 9½" d., Crab Apple patt. **$30.00**
Cake plate, round, Nocturne patt., 10½" d. **30.00**
Celery dish, leaf-shaped, floral decoration **85.00**
Celery dish leaf-shaped, French Peasant patt. **95.00**
Celery dish, leaf-shaped, Fruit Basket patt. **65.00**
Celery dish, Summertime patt. **59.00**
Character jug, "Pioneer Woman," 6½" h. **750.00**
Chocolate pot, cov., Rose Marie patt. **225.00**
Creamer & cov. sugar bowl, pedestal base, Easter Parade patt., pr. **100.00**
Cup & saucer, Christmas Tree patt. . . . **75.00**

Cup & saucer, demitasse, French
  Peasant patt.................. **50.00**
Cup & saucer, French Peasant patt... **75.00**
Plate, 10" d., Christmas Tree patt..... **75.00**
Salt & pepper shakers, Blossom
  Top patt., pr. **100.00**

Blue Ridge Boot Vase

Vase, boot-shaped, any floral
  decoration, 8" h. (ILLUS.) .. **80.00 to 90.00**

BLUE & WHITE POTTERY

The category of blue and white or blue and grey pottery includes a wide variety of pottery, earthenware and stoneware items widely produced in this country in the late 19th century right through the 1930s. Originally marketed as inexpensive wares, most pieces featured a white or grey body molded with a fruit, flower or geometric design and then trimmed with bands or splashes of blue to highlight the molded pattern. Pitchers, butter crocks and salt boxes are among the numerous items produced but other kitchenwares and chamber sets are also found. Values vary depending on the rarity of the embossed pattern and the depth of color of the blue trim; the darker the blue, the better. Some entries refer to several different books on Blue and White Pottery. These books are: Blue & White Stoneware, Pottery & Crockery by Edith Harbin (1977, Collector Books, Paducah, KY); Stoneware in the Blue and White by M.H. Alexander (1993 reprint, Image Graphics, Inc., Paducah, KY); and Blue & White Stoneware by Kathryn McNerney (1995, Collector Books, Paducah, KY).

Bean pot, cov., nearly spherical body
  w/small loop shoulder handle, inset
  flat cover w/knob finial, relief-
  molded label "Boston Baked
  Beans," blue Swirl patt., 6¾" h.
  (short base hairline)........... **$275.00**

Swirl Pattern Coffeepot

Coffeepot, cov., tapering ovoid body
  w/a pointed rim spout, heavy C-
  form handle w/thumbrest, inset lid
  w/acorn finial, tin base, blue Swirl
  patt., 9¾" h. (ILLUS.)........... **682.00**
Coffeepot, cov., flaring footring below
  the wide cylindrical body w/a
  narrow shoulder to the inset cover
  w/knob finial, squared loop handle,
  shaped short spout near rim, tin
  bottom, Diffused Blues patt.,
  10½" h...................... **1,320.00**
Crock, cov., deep, wide cylindrical
  body w/molded rim & inset flat
  cover, Diffused Blues bands
  around rim & base, side stenciled
  in dark blue "Bread or Cake,"
  12¼" d., 8" h. (minor lid rim
  chips) **1,018.00**
Jardiniere, wide bulbous body
  tapering toward the base & w/a
  wide slightly rolled flat rim,
  embossed scrolled flower sprig
  design against a swirled finely
  ridged ground, simple paneled rim
  band, 7⅞ " d., 6⅜" h. (rim
  hairline) **248.00**
Pitcher, 5½" h., wide conical body
  w/a pointed rim spout & C-form
  handle, embossed Grape Cluster
  on Trellis patt. **275.00**

Cattails Pitcher

Pitcher, 7" h., embossed Cattails
patt. (ILLUS.). **193.00**
Pitcher, 7¼" h., embossed Windmill
patt. (shallow table ring flake &
spout flake in-the-making). **193.00**

Avenue of Trees Pitcher

Pitcher, 8" h., embossed Avenue of
Trees patt., rim chips (ILLUS.) **193.00**
Pitcher, 8" h., embossed Doe &
Fawn patt. (minor chips &
hairlines) **165.00**

Flying Bird Pattern Pitcher

Pitcher, 8" h., embossed Flying Bird
patt., small edge flakes (ILLUS.). . . **572.00**
Pitcher, 8" h., embossed Scroll &
Leaf patt., printed Iowa advertising . . **423.00**

Swan & Leaping Deer Pitcher

Pitcher, 8" h., embossed Swan patt.
on one side, Leaping Deer on
reverse (ILLUS.) **550.00**
Pitcher, 8½" h., embossed Shield
patt. (hairline in handle,
professional repair) **226.00**
Pitcher, 8¾" h., printed blue Dutch
Landscape patt. w/two Dutch
children (small edge chips) **165.00**

Pitcher, 9" h., embossed Columns &
Arches patt. **440.00**
Pitcher, 9" h., embossed Indian Good
Luck Sign (Swastika) patt., minor
chips & hairlines **193.00**
Teapot, cov., spherical body w/row of
relief-molded knobs around the
shoulder, inset cover w/knob finial,
swan's-neck spout, shoulder loop
brackets for wire bail handle
w/turned wood grip, blue Swirl
patt., 6½" h. **704.00**
Water cooler, cov., tall columnar-
form w/paneled central section
w/cobalt blue bands, a bulbous
section at the top & bottom, the
lower section molded w/ornate
scrolls highlighted in cobalt blue &
the metal spigot, the upper section
w/a band of overlapping leaves
highlighted in cobalt blue around
the shoulder above the stamped
mark "The Allen Germ Proof Filter,
Toledo, O.," flat metal lid w/angled
filler tube to side & interior valve
w/glass float, late 19th - early
20th c., 14" h. (minor chips &
hairlines) **495.00**

BOCH FRERES

The Belgian firm, founded in 1841 and still in production, first produced stoneware art pottery of mediocre quality, attempting to upgrade their wares through the years. In 1907, Charles Catteau became the art director of the pottery and slowly the influence of his work was absorbed by the artisans surrounding him. All through the 1920s wares were decorated in distinctive Art Deco designs and are now eagerly sought along with the hand-thrown gourd-form vessels coated with earthtone glazes that were produced during the same time. Almost all Boch Freres pottery is marked, but the finest wares also carry the signature of Charles Catteau in addition to the pottery mark.

Boch Freres Mark

Inkstand, stoneware, white w/h.p.
blue floral sprigs & bands,
rectangular dished base w/rounded
corners & serpentine sides
centering a rectangular upright
block fitted in the top w/an open
inkwell & covered sander, 19th c.,
8¾" l. **$110.00**

Two Boch Freres Vases

Vase, 8" h., spherical body w/a short cylindrical ringed neck, decorated w/a strong geometric Art Deco design in green, brown & black against a white crackled glaze ground, signed (ILLUS. right) **825.00**

Vase, 9½" h., 4¼" d., bulbous body w/a cylindrical neck, decorated w/four rows of stylized flowers in turquoise, blue & yellow on a crackled white ground, circular stamp mark **173.00**

Vase, 11" h., tall ovoid body tapering to a short slightly flaring neck, decorated w/stylized swirling designs in yellow & black against turquoise blue vertical bands w/a black border, on a white crackled glaze ground, blurred mark (ILLUS. left) **770.00**

BOEHM PORCELAINS

Although not antique, Boehm porcelain sculptures have attracted much interest as Edward Marshall Boehm excelled in hard porcelain sculptures. His finest creations, inspired by the beauties of nature, are in the forms of birds and flowers. Since his death in 1969, his work has been carried on by his wife at the Boehm Studios in Trenton, New Jersey. In 1971, an additional studio was opened in Malvern, England, where bone porcelain sculptures are produced. We list both limited and non-limited editions of Boehm.

BIRDS

'Symbol of Freedom' Boehm Eagles

American Bald Eagle & Chicks, "Symbol of Freedom," perched above its nest w/curling branches & leaves, factory mark title & edition number '3' printed in black, heavily restored, ca. 1982, 29¾" h. (ILLUS.) **$4,887.00**

Baby Blue Jay, No. 436, introduced in 1957, 4½" h. **165.00**

Baby Bluebird, perched on leafy twigs, wings folded, head turned one-quarter left, No. 442, introduced in 1958, 4½" h. **175.00**

Baby Chickadee, No. 461, 1962-1972, 3" h. **165.00**

Baby Crested Flycatcher, standing on a twisted branch, screeching for food, No. 458, 1962-1972, 5 or 7". . **190.00**

Baby Goldfinch, perched on a log w/violets w/its beak open, No. 448, 1959-1972, 4½" h. **165.00**

Baby Robin, w/wings slightly spread, No. 437, introduced in 1957, 3½" h. **165.00**

Baby Wood Thrush, No. 444, introduced in 1958, 4½" h. **220.00**

Fledgling Blackburnian Warbler, sitting on a rock, No. 478, 2½" x 4 .... **245.00**

Fledgling Kingfisher, sitting on a log, No. 449, introduced in 1960, 6" h. **250.00**

Tree Sparrow, No. 468, 1963-1975, 8" h. **325.00**

BUFFALO POTTERY

Buffalo Pottery was established in 1902 in Buffalo, New York, to supply pottery for the Larkin Company. Most desirable today is Deldare Ware, introduced in 1908 in two patterns, "The Fallowfield Hunt" and "Ye Olden Days," which featured central English scenes and a continuous border. Emerald Deldare, introduced in 1911, was banded with stylized flowers and geometric designs and had varied central scenes, the most popular being from "The Tours of Dr. Syntax." Reorganized in 1940, the company now specializes in hotel china.

Buffalo Pottery Mark

DELDARE

Deldare "Fallowfield Hunt" Plates

Plates, 9½" d., "The Fallowfield Hunt
- The Start," artist-signed, set
of 4 (ILLUS. of part) **$902.00**
Vase, 8½" h., 6" d., footed tapering
ovoid body w/a flaring rim, "Ye
Village Schoolmaster," black ink
mark **413.00**

EMERALD DELDARE

Charger, round, central color scene
of "Dr. Syntax Sketching the Lake,"
stylized geometric border, 1911,
green ink stamp mark, 12¼" d. **935.00**
Plate, 8¼" d., "Dr. Syntax -
Misfortune at Tulip Hall" scene **485.00**

MISCELLANEOUS

Blue Willow Pitcher

Pitcher, wash, Blue Willow patt.
(ILLUS.) **220.00**
Pitcher, 6¼" h., transfer-printed w/the
inscription "Souvenir of New
Bedford Mass the Whaling City"
w/borders of coral & seashells
enclosing reserves of sperm
whaling & the Niger under full sail,
the interior rim decorated w/a
panoramic view of New Bedford
harbor, early 20th c. (minor
staining) **633.00**
Pitcher, jug-type, 7½" h., portrait of
George Washington, blue & white. . **485.00**

Pitcher, 8" h., Roosevelt Bears
patt. **2,500.00**
Platter, 11 x 13", oval, Blue Willow
patt., dated 1909 . . . . **100.00**

CAMARK

*The name "Camark" originated from its
location. The first three letters of two words,
"Camden" and "Arkansas" produced the name
Camark. The pottery was founded in late 1926
by Samuel (Jack) Carnes who had married
Gressie Umpstead whose wealthy family helped
Carnes in founding the Camark Art and Tile
Pottery. About 1927 John and Jeanne Lessell,
along with Jeanne's daughter, Billie, came to
work at Camark. John Lessell, as Art Director
for Camark, has been credited with creating
iridescent and lustre ware using Arkansas clays.
Even with Jack's pottery talents, being an astute
businessman, and the hiring of well-known
ceramic artists, art pottery was produced only a
few years. There were too many economic
hardships associated with the late 1920s. The
business was sold but Carnes stayed on to help
with the transition. As Camark moved into the
1930s, drip glazes became popular and creation
of simple commercial cast ware and utilitarian
items were manufactured. At that time, the
pottery began producing assorted novelty pieces,
some decorated art ware and a variety of bowls,
vases and planters. In 1962, the pottery was
purchased by the Daniels family. After Mr.
Daniels died in 1965, his wife, Mary, struggled
to keep the pottery open. Mostly, the merchandise
already produced was sold and not much new
production occurred. In 1982 the pottery closed.
However, in 1986, it was revived when the
Ashcraft brothers, Mark and Gary, purchased
the land, buildings, machinery, molds and
inventory. As of this date, they have not
produced any pieces and have stated that the old
Camark molds will not be used.*

CAMARK

CAMARK
HAND PAINTED
MADE IN USA

Camark Marks

Ashtray/cigarette holder, No. 196,
blue **$45.00**
Drip bowl, No. 315, green **55.00**

Camark Miniature Ewer

Ewer, miniature, four horizontal rings from base to shoulder, pink glaze, 4¾" h. (ILLUS.) **20.00**

Flower frog, figural fish, No. 413 ..... **85.00**

Model of a swan, gold trim, No. 521 .... **50.00**

Pitcher, pelican decoration, maroon... **75.00**

Planter, model of a deer, brown **45.00**

Planter, model of a rolling pin, green,w/original label, 14½" l. **22.00**

Vase, fan-shaped, No. 811, rust **55.00**

Vase, Lily patt., h.p., No. 806 .... **60.00**

Vase, ram's horn shape, gold trim, No. 810 .... **45.00**

Vase, ram's horn shape, h.p. Rose Garland patt., No. 810 .... **85.00**

Vase, 3" h., orange & green drip glaze **50.00**

Vase, 5" h., No. N3, purple gloss finish **35.00**

Vase, 5" h., pink & green drip glaze ... **75.00**

Vase, 6" h., fan-shaped, No. 811-6", brown & mustard yellow matte glaze **65.00**

Vase, 6" h., flared, metallic green glaze **60.00**

Vase, 8" h., Morning Glory patt., yellow & purple glaze **95.00**

Vase, 10" h., No. 640-10", royal blue matte glaze **50.00**

Vase, 11" h., Iris patt. **95.00**

Wall pocket, gull-shaped, green...... **95.00**

CANTON

This ware has been decorated for nearly two centuries in factories near Canton, China. Intended for export sale, much of it was originally inexpensive blue-and-white hand-decorated ware. Late 18th and early 19th century pieces are superior to later ones and fetch higher prices.

Basket & undertray, oval basket w/flaring reticulated sides on a matching undertray, 19th c., basket 11" l., 2 pcs. (minor chips)...... **$633.00**

Bowl, 9¼" w., 4¾" h., rounded w/cut corners, blue on white landscape w/gilt highlights, 19th c.......... **920.00**

Bowl, 9⅝" d., 4½" h., round w/squared flaring rim w/cut-corners, 19th c., (very minor rim chips, hairline) **546.00**

Canton Candlestick

Candlesticks, tall slender tapering cylindrical shaft flaring at the base, w/a flat rim, 11" h., pr. (ILLUS. of one) **1,955.00**

Plates, 7½" d., 19th c., set of 14 (minor chips, cracks)........... **403.00**

Plates, dinner, 8⅞ " d., 19th c., set of 15 (minor chips, cracks) **489.00**

Platter, 13¾" l., oblong w/chamfered corners, deep dished sides,19th c., (minor glaze chips) **374.00**

Platter, 13⅞ " l., oval w/cut corners, 19th c. (minor chips) **230.00**

Platter, 16⅛" l., well-and-tree-type, oblong w/cut corners, gilt rim, 19th c. (minor chips, gilt wear) **575.00**

Platter, 16¼" l., oval, typical landscape center scene **550.00**

Platter, 18¾" l., oval w/cut corners, 19th c. (rim chip) **633.00**

Soup tureen, cov., a flaring oval footring below the flaring oval body w/boar's head end handles, low domed cover w/fruit finial, 19th c., 12¼" l. (minor rim chips, minute hairline) **690.00**

Tea canisters, cov., square upright form w/round fitted cover, 19th c., 11½" h., pr. (damage to one, restoration to covers) **3,335.00**

Vegetable dish, cov., rectangular w/cut corners, 19th c., 9¾" l. (minute chips) **403.00**

CAPO-DI-MONTE

Production of porcelain and faience began in 1736 at the Capo-di-Monte factory in Naples. In 1743 King Charles of Naples established a factory there that made wares with relief decoration. In 1759 the factory was moved to Buen Retiro near Madrid, operating until 1808. Another Naples pottery was opened in 1771 and operated until 1806 when its molds were acquired by the Doccia factory of Florence, which has since made reproductions of original Capo-di-Monte pieces with the "N" mark beneath a crown. Some very early pieces are valued in the thousands of dollars but the subsequent productions are considerably lower.

Box, cov., rectangular, molded in relief w/polychromed classical figure & a battle scene, brass framed hinged cover, 19th c., 3" l. **$431.00**

Pitcher, 9" h., cylindrical w/enameled relief-molded figural w/a gilt background, scrolled handles, underglaze-blue mark, 19th c. **288.00**

Capo-di-Monte Stein

Stein, cov., cylindrical body decorated in relief w/a classical scene, a figural cherub finial on the domed cover, applied elephant head handle, trimmed overall in color, 14" h. (ILLUS.) **605.00**

Triptych, the three sections w/a continuous scene of a coach & figurines surmounted by a crest, 9¾" l., 9⅞ " h. **316.00**

Wall plaque, teardrop shield-form, a large central scroll-framed landscape scene of warriors w/horses, border cartouches w/military trophies & a grotesque

Capo-di-Monte Wall Plaque

head at the top, in a tooled leather frame, wear, late 19th c., 27" h. (ILLUS.) **863.00**

CARLTON WARE

The Staffordshire firm of Wiltshaw & Robinson, Stoke-on-Trent, operated the Carlton Works from about 1890 until 1958, producing both earthenwares and porcelain. Specializing in decorative items like vases and teapots, they became well known for their lustre-finished wares, often decorated in the Oriental taste. The trademark Carlton Ware was incorporated into their printed mark. Since 1958, a new company, Carlton Ware Ltd., has operated the Carlton Works at Stoke.

Large Carlton Ware Bowl

Bowl, 12⅜" d., 3¼" h., small shallow center w/a wide flattened rim, on a low pedestal foot, large brightly colored blossoms & green leaves against a pale green ground, gold trim, marked (ILLUS.) **$350.00**

Oriental-style Carlton Ware Jar

Jar, cov., footed hexagonal ovoid form w/a domed cover w/a gold Foo dog finial, deep blue ground decorated in gold w/Oriental landscapes including temples, trees & boats, highlighted in pink, aqua & grey, marked "Kang-Hsi 1662-1722" & company mark on base, 4¼" w., 9" h. (ILLUS.) **395.00**

Decorated Carlton Ware Tazza

Tazza, round dished top on a short pedestal foot, top & undersides in creamy yellow mottled in green & maroon & decorated w/h.p. orange gum tree blossoms & nuts & green leaves, marked, 7" d., 2½" h. (ILLUS. of top) **195.00**

Carlton "Rouge Royale" Tray

Tray, "Rouge Royale," oblong w/scrolled edges trimmed in heavy gold, deep red lustre w/a delicately

colored design of a kingfisher perched on a grapevine above water w/lily pads & flowers, 6¾ x 10¼" (ILLUS.) **175.00**

Carlton "Fantasia" Pattern Vase

Vase, 7" h., 4¼" d., wide ovoid body w/flaring rim, "Fantasia" patt., deep blue exterior ground decorated in gold & delicate colors w/an Art Deco style exotic landscape w/large flying bird & trees in the background, marked (ILLUS.) **450.00**

Vase, cov., 7⅜" h., 3" d., footed slender ovoid body w/a flared rim fitted w/a low pagoda-style cover, dark blue lustre ground decorated in gold, red & pale green w/an Oriental temple & a man & woman in a boat, marked **250.00**

Carlton Vase with Oriental Landscape

Vase, cov., 9½" h., 3¾" d., tall baluster-form w/a low domed cover w/button finial, dark blue lustre ground decorated w/an Oriental landscape including temples, houses, mountains, trees & people in a boat, decorated in gold trimmed w/delicate colors, marked (ILLUS.) **325.00**

Vase, 10½" h., 4¾" d., wide baluster-form w/angled shoulder to the short flaring neck, "Persian Scene" patt.,

"Persian Scene" Carlton Ware Vase

a dark blue ground decorated
lavishly in gold & delicate colors
w/a Persian ruler under a canopy
being waited on by servants in a
garden setting, base marked
"Persian" (ILLUS.) 350.00

CELADON

This ware is a highly-fired Oriental porcelain which features a glaze ranging in color from olive through tones of green, bluish green and grey. Such wares have been produced for centuries in China, Korea and Japan. Fine early celadon wares are costly while later examples can be found at more reasonable prices. Japanese celadon is called "Seiji."

Bowl, 4¼" d., 3⅛" h., three-footed,
green glazed on fitted wooden
stand, reticulated silver cover,
incised underglazed mark of
Zoroku, a Kioto potter, Japan,
1849-1878 . . . . $460.00
Bowl, 8¾" d., incised designs &
overglaze enamel decorations
w/bird & floral motifs & Famille
Rose color, green glaze, early
19th c., unmarked, China 150.00
Charger, incised floral design,
19th c., China, 16" d 130.00
Model of a Fu Dog, the celadon
animal lying on his back,
supporting a bowl & gourd on his
hind legs, fitted w/an ormolu collar
cast w/lambrequins, an ormolu
leafy branch & raised on an
asymmetrical molded base, based

Ormolu-mounted Celadon Fu Dog

inscribed "Escalier de Cristal,
Paris," 9" l., 7¼" h.
(ILLUS.). . . . . 7,000.00 to 9,000.00
Vase, 5¼" h., bulbous body w/straight
neck & flaring rim, incised floral
design obverse & reverse,
uncrackled glaze, narrow unglazed
footrim, early 19th c., China 100.00

CERAMIC ARTS STUDIO
OF MADISON

Founded in Madison, Wisconsin, in 1941 by two young men, Lawrence Rabbitt and Reuben Sand, this company began as a "studio" pottery. In early 1942 they met an amateur clay sculptor, Betty Harrington and, recognizing her talent for modeling in clay, they eventually hired her as their chief designer. Over the next few years Betty designed over 460 different pieces for their production. Charming figurines of children and animals were a main focus of their output in addition to models of adults in varied costumes and poses, wall plaques, vases and figural salt and pepper shakers.

Business boomed during the years of World War II when foreign imports were cut off and, at its peak, the company employed some 100 people to produce the carefully hand-decorated pieces.

After World War II many poor-quality copies of Ceramic Arts Studio figurines appeared and when, in the early 1950s, foreign imported figurines began flooding the market, the company found they could no longer compete. They finally closed their doors in 1955.

Since not all Ceramic Arts Studio pieces are marked, it takes careful study to determine which items are from their production.

Ceramic Arts Studio Marks

Ashtray, figural Hippo. $200.00
Bank, figural bust of "Tony the
Barber," 4⅞ " h. 125.00
Bell, figural, Lillibelle, 6½" h. 42.00

Farmer Girl Shelf-sitter

Figurine, shelf-sitter, Farmer Girl
(ILLUS.)..................... 50.00
Figurine, Winter Willie, 4" h.......... 80.00
Figurine, Autumn Andy, 5⅛" h. 135.00
Figurine, Gypsy Man, w/violin,
6⅝" h. 70.00
Figurine, Tragedy, dark green,
10" h........................ 80.00
Figurines, Colonial Boy & Girl, pr. ... 110.00
Figurines, Dutch kids dancing, Hans
& Katrinka, 5⅜" & 6⅛", pr......... 89.00
Figurines, Swedish Couple, 6½ &
7" h., pr...................... 275.00
Figurines, shelf-sitters, Maurice &
Michelle, 7⅛" & 8¼", pr. 125.00
Figurines, Fire Man & Fire Woman,
dark red, 11¼ & 11½" h., pr....... 895.00
Figurines, Water Man & Water
Woman, chartreuse, 11¼ &
11½" h., pr. 495.00
Model of a bunny, 1⅞ " h. 43.00
Model of a cat, Tomcat, standing,
4¾" h. 125.00
Model of a cat, Persian, shelf-sitter,
w/paw up, 5" h. 95.00

Persian Cat Shelf-sitter

Model of a cat, Persian, shelf-sitter,
5½" h. (ILLUS.) 85.00

Model of a dog, shelf-sitter, Cocker
Spaniel, paws over the edge,
original paper label, 4¾" l.,
1¼" h. 195.00
Model of a horse, Palomino Colt,
5⅜" h. 228.00
Models of seahorse & coral, pr...... 65.00
Salt & pepper shakers, figural Boy &
Chair, 2¼" h. & 2" h., pr. 95.00
Salt & pepper shakers, figural
Crocodile & Boy, 4⅝" l. & 2½" h.,
pr. 145.00
Salt & pepper shakers, figural Dutch
Love Boy and Dutch Love Girl,
4⅞ " h., pr.................... 75.00
Salt & pepper shakers, figural
Elephant & Boy, 5" h. & 2¾" h., pr. . 145.00
Salt & pepper shakers, figural
Elephant, pink, pr............... 70.00
Salt & pepper shakers, figural
Fighting Cocks, 3¼" h. & 3⅞ " h.,
pr. .... 60.00 to 80.00
Salt & pepper shakers, figural
Gingham Dog & Calico Cat, pr...... 61.00
Salt & pepper shakers, figural Girl in
Chair, 2¼" h. & 2" h., pr. 80.00
Salt & pepper shakers, figural Horse
head, 3⅜" h., pr. 65.00
Salt & pepper shakers, figural
Mother & Baby Bear, brown,
nesting-type, 4½" h. & 2¼" h., pr. ... 58.00
Salt & pepper shakers, figural
Mother & Baby Cow, nesting-type,
5¼" h. & 2¼" h., pr.............. 165.00
Salt & pepper shakers, figural
Mother & Baby Gorilla, nesting-
type, 4" h. & 2½" h., pr........... 75.00
Salt & pepper shakers, figural
Mother & Baby Kangaroo,
nesting-type, 4¾" h. & 2⅜" h.,
pr. .... 90.00 to 125.00
Salt & pepper shakers, figural
Mother & Baby Polar Bear, pr. 65.00
Salt & pepper shakers, figural
Mouse & Cheese, 2" h. & 1½ x
2¾", pr. 25.00
Salt & pepper shakers, figural Mr. &
Mrs. Penguin, pr.......... 50.00 to 60.00
Salt & pepper shakers, figural Oakie
on Spring Leaf, 2¼" h., 3¾" l., pr. 85.00
Salt & pepper shakers, figural Pete
& Polly Parrot, red 7⅞ " h. &
8⅛" h., pr. (small chip one wing)... 100.00
Salt & pepper shakers, figural
Realistic Bears, pr. 850.00
Salt & pepper shakers, figural
Running Bunny, pr.............. 550.00
Salt & pepper shakers, figural Sea
horse & Coral, 3½" h. & 3⅛" h., pr... 85.00

Salt & pepper shakers, figural
Siamese Cat & Kitten, sitting,
4¼" h. & 3¼" h., pr.............. 90.00

Salt & pepper shakers, figural
Siamese Cat, reclining, Thai &
Thai-Thai, 2⅛ x 4⅜" l. & 2 x 5¼" l.,
pr. 87.00

Salt & pepper shakers, figural Sitting
Girl w/Kitten & Sitting Boy w/Dog
on bench, 3⅝" h. & 4" h., pr. 95.00

Salt & pepper shakers, figural
Straight Tail Fish, pr............. 65.00

Salt & pepper shakers, figural
Toadstool & Frog, 2⅜" h. & 2" h.,
pr. 68.00

Salt & pepper shakers, figural Twist
Tail Fish, pr.................... 65.00

Salt & pepper shakers, figural Wee
Chinese Boy & Girl, pr. 36.00

Wee Dutch Boy & Girl

Salt & pepper shakers, figural Wee
Dutch Boy & Girl, 3" h. & 2¾" h.,
pr. (ILLUS.) 35.00

Salt & pepper shakers, figural Wee
Elephant Boy & Girl, bisque, pink,
3¾" h. & 3¼" h., pr.............. 65.00

Wee Scotch Boy & Girl

Salt & pepper shakers, figural Wee
Scotch Boy & Girl, 3½" h., pr.
(ILLUS.)...................... 69.00

Salt & pepper shakers, figural Wee
Swedish Man & Lady, 3" h., pr...... 67.00

Salt & pepper shakers, figural Dem
(donkey) & Rep (elephant), 4" h.,
pr. .... 150.00 to 280.00

Wall plaques, pierced to hang, figural
Zor & Zorina, pr. 125.00

Wall plaques, pierced to hang,
Chinese Lantern Man & Woman,
8" h., pr...................... 190.00

Wall plaques, pierced to hang, figural
Arabesque & Attitude, 9½" h., pr. ... 85.00

CHINESE EXPORT

Large quantities of porcelain have been made in China for export to America from the 1780s, much of it shipped from the ports of Canton and Nanking. A major source of this porcelain was Ching-te-Chen in the Kiangsi province but the wares were also made elsewhere. The largest quantities were blue and white. Prices fluctuate considerably depending on age, condition, decoration, etc.

CANTON and ROSE MEDALLION export wares are listed separately.

Bowl, 10" sq., blue "Nanking" patt.,
decorated w/pavilions, willow &
pine tree, etc., lattice & spearhead
borders, early 19th c. **$1,955.00**

Cider jug, cov., blue "Nanking" patt.,
barrel-shaped body painted
w/pavilions in a watery landscape,
interlaced handles molded
w/leaves & flowers, slightly domed
cover w/fu lion knop, mid-19th c.,
9¾" h. **977.00**

Plates, 9" d., "Famille Rose" palette,
decorated w/birds amid foliage,
19th c., pr. (very minor rim chips,
hairline, enamel wear).......... **316.00**

Platter, 16" l., oblong, blue "Fitzhugh"
patt., 19th c. (minor chips, knife
marks) **575.00**

Tea service: one 'lighthouse' cov.
teapot, two cov. teapots, one cov.
tea caddy, two sugar bowls & one
cover, two helmet creamers, one
waste bowl, seven tea bowls,
seven cups, four plates & 26
saucers; gilt & blue enamel border
& a monogram in an oval reserve,
early 19th c., chips & hairline, the
set. **2,070.00**

Chinese Export Covered Tureen

Tureen, cov., blue "Nanking" patt.,
bulbous oval body raised on a low
pedestal w/entwined strap end

handles, the stepped domed cover w/floral knop, painted w/pavilions in a watery landscape within diaper & spearhead borders, 12½" l. (ILLUS.) 805.00

Ornate Chinese Export Urn

Urns, classical ovoid body w/an angled shoulder & tapering cylindrical neck, ornate gilt floral sprig shoulder handles, raised on a short cylindrical pedestal above a small stepped, square base, the body decorated w/central oval small landscape reserves w/raised gilt borders framed by narrow floral bands, scattered butterflies & blossoms on the white ground, continuous landscape scenes around the neck, marbleized base, missing covers, chips & repairs to handles, 15¼" h., pr. (ILLUS. of one) 1,035.00

CHINTZ CHINA

There are over fifty flower patterns and myriad colors from which Chintz collectors can choose. That is not surprising considering companies in England began producing these showy, yet sometimes muted, patterns in the early part of this century. Public reception was so great that this production trend continued until the 1960s.

Basket, Rose du Barry patt., Rowsley shape, Royal Winton $350.00
Bowl, cereal, Majestic patt., Royal Winton 125.00
Bowl, fruit, Eleanor patt., Royal Winton 50.00

Bowl, Sweet Pea patt., Fife shape, Royal Winton 500.00
Bowl, 9" d., Eleanor patt., Royal Winton 225.00
Butter dish, cov., Evesham patt., Royal Winton 300.00
Butter dish, cov., Julia patt., Royal Winton 475.00
Cake plate w/metal handle, Como patt., Royal Winton 165.00
Candy dish, Fireglow patt., Olympic shape, Royal Winton 600.00
Celery dish, Tiger Lily patt., Royal Winton, large 75.00
Creamer, Clyde patt., Royal Winton . . . 45.00
Creamer, Old Cottage patt., Royal Winton 75.00
Creamer & cov. sugar, Chintz patt., Old Cottage shape, Royal Winton, pr. 295.00
Creamer & open sugar, Estelle patt., Royal Winton, pr. 135.00
Creamer & open sugar bowl, Silverdale patt., Royal Winton, 2 pcs. 95.00
Creamer & open sugar bowl, Welbeck patt., Royal Winton 275.00
Cup & saucer, Julia patt., Royal Winton 157.00
Cup & saucer, Poppy patt., Royal Winton 85.00
Cup & saucer, Rose Bud patt., Royal Winton 50.00
Cup & saucer, Spring patt., Royal Winton 135.00

Summertime Cup & Saucer

Cup & saucer, Summertime patt., Royal Winton (ILLUS.). 65.00
Cup & saucer, unnamed floral, Barker Bros. 25.00
Dish, shell-shaped, Julia patt., Royal Winton, 4½" w. 225.00
Gravy boat, Marguerite patt., Royal Winton 145.00
Hot water pot, cov., Sweet Pea patt., Royal Winton, six-cup 450.00
Pitcher, unnamed floral, Barker Bros. 120.00
Pitcher, jug-type, 3" h., Sweet Pea patt., Fife shape, Royal Winton 250.00

Pitcher, jug-type, 5" h., Hazel patt.,
Royal Winton **575.00**

Pitcher, jug-form, 7" h., Pansy patt.,
Lord Nelson, Elijah Cotton, Ltd.. . . . **160.00**

Pitcher, jug-type, 8" h., Black Pekin
patt., Royal Winton **150.00**

Plate, 5" d., Marion patt., Royal
Winton **65.00**

Plate, 5" square, English Rose patt.,
Royal Winton **95.00**

Plate, 6" d., Beeston patt., Royal
Winton **95.00**

Plate, 6" d., Rutland patt., Royal
Winton **110.00**

Plate, 6" d., Sweet Pea patt., Royal
Winton **100.00**

Plate, 6½" d., DuBarry patt., James
Kent. **95.00**

Plate, 7" d., Marion patt., Royal
Winton **100.00**

Plate, 7" d., Summertime patt., Royal
Winton **95.00**

Plate, 8" d., Ascot patt., Crown
Ducal **110.00**

Plate, 8" d., Marguerite patt., Royal
Winton **70.00**

Sauce dish, Marguerite patt., Royal
Winton **30.00**

Sauce dish, Summertime patt., Royal
Winton **50.00**

Sauce dish, square, Old Cottage
patt., Royal Winton, 4¾" w. **20.00**

Sweetmeat dish, Chintz patt., pink &
white, Royal Winton, 11" l. **275.00**

Tea set, individual size: cov. teapot,
creamer & sugar; Countess patt.,
Royal Winton, the set **359.00**

Teapot, cov., Blue Anemone patt.,
Royal Winton, four-cup **600.00**

Teapot, cov., Hazel patt., Royal
Winton, four-cup **650.00**

Teapot, cov., June Festival patt.,
Royal Winton, four-cup **475.00**

Teapot, cov., Marguerite patt.,
Norman shape, Royal Winton **475.00**

Teapot, cov., Summertime patt.,
Norman shape, Royal Winton **475.00**

Teapot, cov., unnamed floral, Barker
Bros. **195.00**

Tennis tray, Petunia patt., Royal
Winton **95.00**

Toast rack, three-bar, Tiger Lily patt.,
Royal Winton **100.00**

Tray, breakfast, Balmoral patt., Royal
Winton **150.00**

Tray, for breakfast set, Julia patt.,
Royal Winton **400.00**

Tray, English Rose patt., Royal
Winton, 9" l. **275.00**

Tray, Julia patt., Royal Winton,
10" l. **350.00**

Tray, sandwich, Blue Anemone patt.,
Royal Winton, 10" d. **175.00**

Vase, bud, Sweet Pea patt., Royal
Winton **200.00**

CLARICE CLIFF DESIGNS

Clarice Cliff was a designer for A. J. Wilkinson, Ltd., Royal Staffordshire Pottery, Burslem, England, when they acquired the adjoining Newport Pottery Company whose warehouses were filled with undecorated bowls and vases. About 1925 her flair with the Art Deco style was incorporated into designs appropriately named "Bizarre" and "Fantasque" and the warehouse stockpile was decorated in vivid colors. These hand-painted earthenwares, all bearing the printed signature of designer Clarice Cliff, were produced until World War II and are now finding enormous favor with collectors.

Note: Reproductions of the Clarice Cliff "Bizarre" marking have been appearing on the market recently.

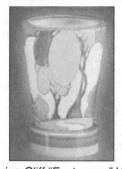

Clarice Cliff "Fantasque" Vase

Clarice Cliff Designs Mark

Bowl, 6½" d., 3" h., "Bizarre" ware,
footed deep slightly flaring sides,
Crocus patt., the sides divided into
two horizontal bands of color w/a
band of small crocus blossoms
along the upper half, in orange,
blue, purple & green, stamped
mark **$374.00**

Charger, "Bizarre," round w/dished center & wide flanged rim, "Rhodanthe" patt., large stylized blossoms & wavy stems in orange, yellow & browns, stamped mark, 13" d. **863.00**

Pitcher, 7" h., 7" d., "Bizarre" ware, tapering cylindrical body w/flat rim & wide pointed spout, flattened angled handle from rim to base, Slice Fruit patt., wide band of abstract fruit in yellow, orange & red, stamped mark **1,380.00**

Pitcher, 10" h., 7½" d., "Bizarre" ware, ringed ovoid body tapering to a flat, round mouth, rounded C-form loop handle, Secrets patt., stylized landscape scene in yellow, green & blue, stamped mark **1,035.00**

Pitcher, 10" h., 7½" d., "Bizarre" ware, Viscaria patt., ringed ovoid body tapering to a flat rim w/pinched spout, heavy rounded C-form handle, large stylized blossoms in blue, yellow & brown, stamped mark **690.00**

Pitcher, 11½" h., 8¾" d., "Bizarre" ware, wide ringed ovoid body tapering to a wide flat round mouth, rounded C-form handle, Area patt., wide central band of stylized florals in blue, red, yellow, purple, green & black, stamped mark **748.00**

Plate, 8¾" d., "Bizarre" ware, Secrets patt., stylized central landscape scene w/banded border in greens, yellow & orange, stamped mark (minor paint wear) **173.00**

Sugar shaker, "Bizarre" ware, small footring under slender tapering ovoid body w/rounded top, Viscaria patt., stylized blossom decoration in yellow, green & brown, stamped mark, 2¾" d., 4¾" h. **575.00**

Sugar shaker, "Bizarre" ware, flattened egg-shaped body set on two tiny log-form feet, Crocus patt., banded body w/a central row of stylized crocus blossoms, in yellow, blue, orange & purple, stamped mark, 2½" w., 5" h. **518.00**

Vase, 7" h., 4½" h., "Fantasque" ware, slightly tapering cylindrical body w/a closed rim & thick footring, decorated w/a stylized landscape in shades of blue, green, yellow & rose on an ivory ground, marked (ILLUS.) **770.00**

Vase, 7½" h., 5½" d., "Bizarre" ware, Inspiration patt., decorated in mottled blues, greens & purples, stamped mark **748.00**

COPELAND & SPODE

W. T. Copeland & Sons, Ltd., have operated the Spode Works at Stoke, England, from 1847 to the present. The name Spode was used on some of its productions. Its predecessor, Spode, was founded by Josiah Spode about 1784 and became Copeland & Garrett in 1843, continuing under that name until 1847. Listings dated prior to 1843 should be attributed to Spode.

Copeland & Spode Mark

Compote, open, green floral decoration, ca. 1860, 9⅜" d., 4¾" h. **$66.00**

Dessert plates, decorated w/raised floral border against lapis blue & overglazed floral enamel centers against white ground, ca. 1891-1915, No. 2694S, England, set of 12 . . . . **180.00**

Dinner service: 14 soup plates, 23 luncheon plates, a large 15" l. cov. tureen & undertray, a small tureen w/mismatched cover, two small trays, four graduated oval platters, largest 21" l., & ten 10¼" d. dinner plates; all in an Imari-style colorful transfer-printed decoration of black florals in center & around borders decorated w/underglaze-blue & red enamels, the set (chips, stains) **990.00**

Dinner service: eleven dinner plates, eight each luncheon plates, salad/dessert plates, bread & butter plates, cream soup bowls, saucers & teacups, sauce dishes, cereal bowls, six coffee cups & saucers, seven square dessert plates, two graduated platters, one each oval open vegetable dish, relish dish, butter cover, cov. teapot, milk pitcher, cov. sugar bowl, creamer & gravy boat w/undertray; Tower patt., pink, early 20th c., England, 112 pcs. (one dinner plate chipped, gravy boat stained). **1,100.00**

Dinner service: nine each dinner plates, salad/dessert plates, bread & butter plates, saucers & teacups, demitasse cups & saucers;

Maritime Rose patt., R4118, late
19th-early 20th c., England,
63 pcs............................ **950.00**

Dinner service: thirteen 9¾" d.
dinner plates, three rimmed soup
plates, six dessert plates; each
round w/a central botanical
specimen on a white ground,
continuing to a wide rim w/molded
scrolling leafage & dolphin
decoration ending in a gilt edge,
Spode, ca. 1813-15, some w/iron-
red factory mark, the set **920.00**

Dinner service: twelve each dinner
plates, luncheon plates, teacups &
saucers, fourteen square dessert
plates, ten each bread & butter
plates, soup/cereal bowls, sauce
dishes, cream soup bowls &
saucers, six egg cups, two each
round meat platters & square open
vegetable dishes, one each teapot,
cov. sugar bowl, creamer, gravy
boat w/undertray, round cov.
vegetable bowl, cov. soup tureen
w/ladle, scalloped round vegetable
bowl, rectangular cov. vegetable
dish, triple divided relish server &
relish dish; Tower patt., blue, early
20th c., England, 134 pcs. **1,900.00**

Plate, 8¼" d.,Caramanian patt.,
medium blue, Spode, first half
9th c. **220.00**

Plate, 10" d., Caramanian patt., light
to medium blue, Spode, first half
19th c. **176.00**

Plates, dinner, 10½" d., powder blue
banded border w/gilt floral & foliate
decorations, impressed & printed
marks, 20th c., set of 12 .... **374.00**

Platter, 18⅞ " l., oval, ironstone,
bluish black transfer-printed design
of delicate leaf swags & blossoms
around the wide flanged rim,
stylized leafy scrolls & stems of
stylized flowers around the inner
border, impressed "Copeland,"
19th c. **105.00**

Soup plate, Caramanian patt.,
medium blue, Spode, first half
19th c., 10" d. **220.00**

Teapot, cov., pate-sur-pate, nearly
spherical body w/an inset domed
cover, swan's-neck spout & C-
scroll handle, dark cobalt blue
ground w/bluish white-relief band of
classical figures below a leaf sprig
shoulder band, the cover w/white
radiating pointed leaves around the
white knop, marked, ca. 1894-
1910, 5" h.................... **165.00**

Vegetable set: 13" l. oval cov.
vegetable bowl & seven matching
bowls; blue & white transfer-printed
foliate design, factory marks, ca.
1880, the set (wear) **201.00**

COWAN

*R. Guy Cowan first opened a studio pottery
in 1913 in Cleveland, Ohio. The pottery
continued to operate almost continuously, at
various locations in the Cleveland area, until it
was forced to close in 1931 due to financial
problems. This fine art pottery, which was
gradually expanded into a full line of
commercial productions, is now sought out by
collectors.*

Cowan Mark

Book end, figural, a little girl standing
wearing a sunbonnet & full ruffled
dress, on a thick rectangular base,
overall matte green crystalline
glaze, impressed mark, 4" w.,
7¼" h. **$110.00**

Bust of a man, "Antinea," stylized
head covered in a smooth black
glaze, by Drexel Jacobson, 1928,
impressed "Jacobson," 14" h.... **4,950.00**

Candlestick, figural, a model of a
seated beaver beside a slender
tree trunk candle shaft & holding
upright a tall open book reading
"Light See High Light Doth Light of
Light Beguile," overall matte green
& gun-metal glaze, base inscribed
"ROWFANT CLUB 1925 - number
152 of 156 copies R.G. COWAN,"
5" w., 9" h. **1,210.00**

Charger, round w/wide flanged rim,
overall embossed undersea
designs of fish & plants in light
green on a bluish green ground,
impressed mark, 11¼" d. **550.00**

Figurines, Art Deco style Russian
dancer & three musicians, a lady
dancing wearing a kerchief &
flaring skirt & blouse, one arm
arched over her head, a male
accordian player crouching w/one
leg extended, a seated male
musician playing a hand drum &
the third male musician playing a
balalaika, all w/overall glossy beige

glaze, stamped mark & numbered, the set (restoration to boot of accordian player) **5,775.00**

Flower figure, "Swirl Dancer," a tall slender stylized lady standing & holding out her spiraling gown, original ivory glaze, No. 720, designed by R. G. Cowan, 1926, round die-stamped mark, 3½" d., 10½" h. **1,430.00**

Cowan Figural Flower Frog

Flower frog, figural, modeled as a small seated satyr on a wide flattened disc-form mushroom head w/holes around the rim, raised on a thick stem flanked by smaller mushrooms. designed by Waylande Gregory, smooth line to base, possibly from firing, smooth ivory glaze, impressed mark, 5" d., 9½" h. (ILLUS.) **550.00**

Jar, cov., tapering bulbous cylindrical multi-lobed base w/a matching stepped & domed cover w/button finial, overall bluish green crystalline glaze, impressed mark, 5" d., 5¾" h. **220.00**

Model of a horse, standing animal on an oblong base, mahogany & gold flambé glaze, impressed mark, 9" l., 9½" h. **1,870.00**

Vase, 5½" h., 5¼" d., footed wide bulbous slightly tapering body w/a wide short rolled neck, overall cinnabar red glaze, impressed mark (some glaze crackling at foot joint). **165.00**

Vase, 7¼" h., 5" d., bulbous baluster-form w/a short cylindrical neck & widely rolled rim, dripping brown crystalline glaze over a mirrored orange ground, ink mark **330.00**

Vase, 12" h., 6¼" d., swelled cylindrical body w/a narrow angled shoulder to the short cylindrical

wide neck w/rolled rim, overall glossy mahogany glaze, die-stamped mark **330.00**

CUP PLATES (EARTHENWARE)

Like their glass counterparts, these small plates were designed to hold a cup while the tea or coffee was allowed to cool in a saucer before it was sipped from the saucer, a practice that would now be considered in poor taste. The forerunner of the glass cup plates, those listed below are produced in various Staffordshire potteries in England. Their popularity waned after the introduction of the glass cup plate in the 1820s.

Staffordshire, Grecian Temple patt., medium blue, probably by Wood, 3⅞ " d. (heavy overall mellowing) . . **$66.00**

Staffordshire, Neptune patt., light blue, Alcock, 3⅞ " d. (tiny hairline off rim) **121.00**

Staffordshire pottery, Columbus patt., ship scene in center, vignettes in border, brown, Adams, 3¾" d. (minute rim glaze flake, small unseen table ring chip). **77.00**

Wood, Hunter - Dog - Pheasant patt., dark blue, ca. 1830, 3⅝" d. **187.00**

DEDHAM & CHELSEA KERAMIC ART WORKS

This pottery was organized in 1866 by Alexander W. Robertson in Chelsea, Massachusetts, and became A. W. & H. Robertson in 1868. In 1872, the name was changed to Chelsea Keramic Art Works and in 1891 to Chelsea Pottery, U.S.A. About 1895, the pottery was moved to Dedham, Massachusetts, and was renamed Dedham Pottery. Production ceased in 1943. High-fired colored wares and crackle ware were specialties. The rabbit is said to have been the most popular decoration on crackle ware in blue.

Since 1977, the Potting Shed, Concord, Massachusetts, has produced quality reproductions of early Dedham wares. These pieces are carefully marked to avoid confusion with original examples.

CHELSEA KERAMIC
ART WORKS
ROBERTSON & SONS.

*Dedham & Chelsea Keramic
Art Works Marks*

Dedham Scottie Dogs Plates

Bowl, three-sided, 4½" w., 2½" h., pinched-in sides, Rabbit patt., factory marks & initials of Hugh Robertson **$489.00**

Candle snuffer, decorated w/a dark blue rabbit outline, 1¼" d., 2" h. . . . **518.00**

Charger, round slightly dished form, applied decoration of two birds together on a long curving flowering bough, overall olive green glaze, titled "Love," by C.A. Walker, 1880, fully marked, 11" d. (some broken petals) **825.00**

Cup & saucer, Polar Bear patt., marked, 6" d., 3" h. **345.00**

Dish, figural, figure of a reclining lady, decorated in light blue, unmarked, 2½" w., 4½" l. **546.00**

Flower holder, figural, model of a standing rabbit, marked, 4¼" d., 6½" h. (small glaze pop) **748.00**

Paperweight, figural, model of a turtle, blue & white, faintly marked, 2¼" l., 3¼" h. **575.00**

Paperweight, figural, model of a squatting rabbit, blue & white, marked, 1½" w., 3½" l. **288.00**

Pitcher, 5" h., 5¼" d., "Night and Day" patt., bulbous ovoid body relief-molded on one side w/a rooster crowing & on the opposite side w/an owl, blue on white crackle ground, marked. **497.00**

Pitcher, 6" h., 5" w., the body decorated w/applied leaves in relief under a sea green glaze, impressed "C.K.A.W." & artist's initials for Hugh C. Robertson **575.00**

Plate, 6" d., Snow Tree patt. **95.00**

Plate, 8¼" d., Owl w/spaced wings patt., marked (rim nicks). **1,380.00**

Plate, 8½" d., Scottie Dog patt., deep blue decoration on very fine crackle glaze, stamped "Dedham Pottery Registered" in blue, impressed "Double Rabbit" mark **1,725.00**

Plate, 8½" d., Scottie Dog with Toad patt., impressed marks (ILLUS. bottom) **1,495.00**

Plate, 8½" d., Scottie Dogs patt., ca. 1931 (ILLUS. top) **1,955.00**

Plate, 10" d., Butterfly patt., marked **690.00**

Plate, 10" d., Crab patt., deep blue decoration on fine crackle glaze, crisp painting finished in a high glaze, stamped "Dedham Pottery" in blue, impressed "Rabbit" mark . . **546.00**

Plate, 10" d., Polar Bear patt., marked (rim nicks). **403.00**

Plate, 10" d., Turkey patt., marked . . . **259.00**

Plate, 10" d., Turtle patt., impressed mark **1,610.00**

Platter, 11½" d., round, Rabbit patt. . . . **289.00**

Group of Dedham & Chelsea Vases

Vase, 4" h., 2¼" d., small baluster-form body covered in a volcanic oxblood glaze, die-stamped "CKAW" (ILLUS. left) **660.00**

Vase, 5" h., 4½" d., bulbous ovoid body tapering to a short cylindrical neck, Crackleware painted around the sides w/large repeating curled blue plumes, marked "Dedham 38" (ILLUS. right) **1,760.00**

Vase, bud, 6" h., 3¼" d., slender baluster-form w/a widely flaring flattened rim, the shoulders applied w/ribbed acanthus leaf upright handles, shaded dark green to brown glossy glaze, die-stamped Chelsea Keramic mark & retailer's paper label. **385.00**

Vase, 6½" h., 5" d., cylindrical body w/a wide rounded shoulder tapering slightly to a wide flat mouth, covered in a rich garnet to green lustered flambé glaze, by Hugh Robertson, incised "Dedham Pottery - HCR" **1,320.00**

Vase, 6¾" h., 3½" d., tapering cylindrical form, dripping sea green glaze on a white crackle body, Chelsea Keramic Art Works, impressed mark **1,725.00**

Vase, 8½" h., 5¼" d., slightly flaring cylindrical body w/a rounded shoulder to the short wide cylindrical neck, experimental thick curdled dripping volcanic brown & green glaze, by Hugh Robertson, incised "DEDHAM POTTERY - HR" **1,210.00**

Vase, 9" h., 5" d., ovoid body tapering to a wide cylindrical neck, experimental dripping green over red flambé glaze, by Hugh Robertson, incised "DEDHAM" **880.00**

Vase, 9" h., 5½" d., ovoid body tapering to a wide cylindrical neck, experimental dripping light & dark green glossy glaze, by Hugh Robertson, incised "Dedham Pottery - BW - HCR" (small chip repair at base probably over firing flaw) **1,540.00**

Vase, 11" h., 7½" d., bulbous flat-bottomed base tapering to a wide, tall cylindrical neck, covered in a thick curdled volcanic moss & brown glaze, by Hugh Robertson, incised mark (ILLUS. center) **2,530.00**

DELFT

In the early 17th century Italian potters settled in Holland and began producing tin-glazed earthenwares, often decorated with pseudo-Oriental designs based on Chinese porcelain wares. The city of Delft became the center of this pottery production and several firms produced the wares throughout the 17th and early 18th century. A majority of the pieces featured blue on white designs, but polychrome wares were also made. The Dutch Delftwares were also shipped to England and eventually the English copied them at potteries in such cities as Bristol, Lambeth and Liverpool. Although still produced today, Delft peaked in popularity by the mid-18th century.

Polychromed Dutch Delft Charger

Charger, round w/dished center & wide flanged rim, polychrome stylized floral designs radiating around the central blossomhead w/geometric panels around the rim, Holland, late 18th - early 19th c., 13¾" d. (ILLUS.) **$546.00**

Charger, round, decorated in blue on white w/a farmhouse in a landscape, England, 19th c., 14¾" d. **460.00**

Charger, round w/wide flanged rim, polychrome floral decoration w/a flowering tree & exotic bird in the center, monogram mark on back, Holland, 18th c., 16½" d. (small edge chips) **715.00**

Charger, round w/wide flanged rim, central polychrome design of a large stylized urn filled w/flowers & leaf sprigs, oblong rim panels of leaf sprigs & fruit alternating w/panels of delicate checkered lattice & dots, Holland, 18th c., 16⅝" d. (small edge chips, plate ring drilled for hanging) **770.00**

Model of a sleigh, blue & white, a covered seat compartment w/pierced scroll sides at the back of the box raised on long runners w/curled tips, decorated w/blue scrolls & overall scattered delicate blue floral clusters, mark of Hendrich Van Hoorne, Delft, Holland, late 18th - early 19th c., 7" w., 11" l. (early visible repairs) . . **550.00**

Vases, cov., flattened tapering ovoid form w/a flared neck & base, domed cover w/scrolling leafage finial, overall polychrome decoration of leafy florals centered by a chinoiserie scene w/gilt highlights, marked "BP" in underglaze-blue on the base w/a faux Chinese iron-red mark, Holland, 18th c., 13" h., pr....... **1,725.00**

DERBY & ROYAL CROWN DERBY

William Duesbury, in partnership with John and Christopher Heath, established the Derby Porcelain Works in Derby, England, about 1750. Duesbury soon bought out his partners and in 1770 purchased the Chelsea factory and six years later, the Bow works. Duesbury was succeeded by his son and grandson. Robert Bloor purchased the business about 1814 and managed successfully until illness in 1828 left him unable to exercise control. The "Bloor" Period, however, extends from 1814 until 1848, when the factory closed. Former Derby workmen then resumed porcelain manufacture in another factory and this nucleus eventually united with a new and distinct venture in 1878 which, after 1890, was known as Royal Crown Derby.

A variety of anchor and crown marks have been used since the 18th century.

Derby & Royal Crown Derby Marks

Crown Derby Dessert Set

Dessert set: 12 plates, small cov. tureen, cov. vegetable dish, open dish, cov. teapot, cov. sugar bowl & three miscellaneous pieces; each in mostly cream ground w/red, green & gilt scrolls in the borders, Crown Derby, early 19th c., the set (ILLUS. of part) **$518.00**

Royal Crown Derby Tea Set

Tea set: cov. teapot, cov. sugar bowl & creamer; oval cylindrical bodies, each decorated in an Imari style design w/stylized Oriental blossoms in rust red w/green leaves against an oval black-ground center reserve w/gilt trim & rust red-outlined blossoms, a black-ground rim band w/gilt leafy bands & rust blossoms, Royal Crown Derby, ca.1850, teapot 5¾" h., the set (ILLUS.).......... **523.00**

Handsome Royal Crown Derby Tray

Tray, rectangular w/cut corners & rounded tab end handles, an ornate Imari-style design w/large stylized rust red Oriental blossoms w/scrolls over black & gold leaves on two sides & fan-shaped black-ground reserves at the ends, one w/birds in a tree, the other w/flowers, overall white ground w/outlined blossoms & leaves, black-ground border band w/gold & rust red leaves & blossoms, Royal Crown Derby, ca. 1850, 12½ x 19" (ILLUS.) **1,320.00**

Vase, 10" h., bulbous body, a beige ground decorated w/multicolored rocaille designs w/gilt trim, factory marks, late 19th c.............. **173.00**

Vase, 12" h., tall baluster-form body on a bell-form flaring foot & w/a tall tapering slender neck w/a flaring blossom-form cupped rim, teal blue ground decorated w/ornate raised

Ornate Royal Crown Derby Vase

gold scrolls, brackets & long swags
of blossoms around the sides w/gilt
striping down the neck, gilt
scalloped trim on the rim & base,
Royal Crown Derby, 1896
(ILLUS.)...................... **288.00**

DOULTON & ROYAL DOULTON

*Doulton & Co., Ltd., was founded in
Lambeth, London, about 1858. It was operated
there until 1956 and often incorporated the
words "Doulton" and "Lambeth" in its marks.
Pinder Bourne & Co., Burslem, was purchased
by the Doultons in 1878 and in 1882 became
Doulton & Co., Ltd. It added porcelain to its
earthenware production in 1884. The "Royal
Doulton" mark has been used since 1902 by this
factory, which is still in production. Character
jugs and figurines are commanding great
attention from collectors at the present time.*

Royal Doulton Mark

ANIMALS & BIRDS

Bird, Bullfinch, blue & pale blue
feathers, red breast, HN 2551,
1941-46, 5½" h................ **$180.00**
Cat, Siamese Cat, standing,
HN 2660, 5"................... **95.00**
Cat, seated animal, red "Flambé"
glaze, 5¼" h.................. **165.00**
Cat, seated animal, red "Flambé"
glaze, 11" h. **248.00**

Dog, Alsatian, "Benign of Picardy,"
HN 1117, 4½" **163.00**
Dog, American Great Dane, light
brown, HN 2602, 1941-60, 6½" h... **450.00**
Dog, Airedale Terrier, Ch. 'Cotsford
Topsail,' standing, dark brown &
black, light brown underbody,
HN 1024, 1931-68, 4" h. **275.00**
Dog, Airedale Terrier, K 5,
1¼" x 2¼" **250.00**
Dog, Boxer, Ch. "Warlord of
Mazelaine," HN 2543, 6½" **110.00**
Dog, Boxer, Champion "Warlord of
Mazelaine," golden brown coat
w/white bib, HN 2643, 1952-85,
6½" h. **125.00**
Dog, Bulldog, HN 1047, standing,
3¼" **213.00**
Dog, Bulldog, HN 1074, standing,
small size, 3¼" **182.00**
Dog, Bulldog, K 1, seated, 2½"...... **115.00**
Dog, Bulldog Puppy, K 2, 2" **95.00**
Dog, Bull Terrier, K 14,
1¼" x 2¾" **325.00**
Dog, Chow (Shibu Ino), K 15, 2½" ... **130.00**
Dog, Cocker Spaniel, Ch. 'Lucky Star
of Ware,' black coat w/grey
markings, HN 1021, 1931-68,
3½" h. **80.00**
Dog, Cocker Spaniel, golden brown
w/black highlights, K 9B, 1931-77,
2½" h. **50.00**
Dog, Cocker Spaniel,
HN 1037, 3½".................. **125.00**
Dog, Cocker Spaniel,
HN 1109, 5"................... **150.00**
Dog, Cocker Spaniel,
HN 1187, 5"................... **150.00**
Dog, Cocker Spaniel, K 9,
seated, 2½".................... **95.00**
Dog, Cocker Spaniel, "Lucky Star of
Ware," HN 1021, 3½" **125.00**
Dog, Cocker Spaniel, "Lucky Star of
Ware," HN 1020, 5".............. **110.00**
Dog, Cocker Spaniel w/pheasant,
seated, white coat w/dark brown
markings, red, brown & green
pheasant, HN 1029, 1931-68,
3½" h. **143.00**
Dog, Cocker Spaniel w/ Pheasant,
HN 1062, 3½" **195.00**
Dog, Cocker Spaniel w/ Pheasant,
HN 1137, 6½" x 7¾" **375.00**
Dog, Cocker Spaniel, white w/black
markings, HN 1078, 1932-68,
3" h. **125.00**
Dog, Collie, Ch. 'Ashstead Applause,'
dark & light brown coat, white
chest, shoulder & feet, HN 1057,
1931-60, 7½" h................. **675.00**

Dog, Collie, dark & light brown coat, white chest, shoulders & feet, medium, HN 1058, 1931-85, 5" h. **160.00**

Dog, Collie, HN 1059, small size, 3½" **95.00**

Dog, Dalmatian, "Goworth Victor," HN 1114, 4¼" **225.00**

Dog, Dalmatian, "Goworth Victor," HN 1113, 5½" **165.00**

Dog, Doberman, "Rancho Dobe's Storm," HN 2645, 6¼" **110.00**

Dog, English Bulldog, K 1, seated, 2½" **150.00**

Dog, English Setter, Ch. "Maesydd Mustard," off-white coat w/black highlights, HN 1051, 1931-68, 4" h. **140.00**

Dog, English Setter, "Maesydd Mustard," HN 1050, medium size, 5¼" **150.00**

Dog, English Setter w/pheasant, grey w/black markings, reddish brown bird, yellowish brown leaves on base, HN 2529, 1939-85, 8" h. **400.00**

Dog, Foxhound, K 7, seated, 2½". **95.00**

Dog, Fox Terrier, K 8, seated, 2½" **85.00**

Dog, Great Dane, HN 2602, medium size, 6½" **700.00**

Dog, Great Dane, "Rebeller of Ouborough," HN 2562, 4½". **699.00**

Dog, Greyhound, HN 1077, small size, 4½" **450.00**

Dog, Greyhound, standing, golden brown w/dark brown markings, cream chest & feet, HN 1065, 1931-55, 8½" h. **1,400.00**

Dog, Irish Setter, miniature, HN 1056, 6" l., 3¾" h. **83.00**

Dog, Irish Setter, Ch. "Pat O'Moy," reddish brown, HN 1056, 1931-68, 4" h. **137.00**

Dog, Irish Setter, Ch. "Pat O'Moy," reddish brown, HN 1054, 1931-60, 7½" h. **650.00**

Dog, Irish Setter, "Pat O'Moy," HN 1055, medium size, 5". **152.00**

Dog, Labrador, "Bumblikite of Mansergh," HN 2667, 5¼". **175.00**

Dog, Pekinese, "Biddee of Ifield," HN 1012, small size, 3" **100.00**

Dog, Poodle, HN 2631, 5¼" **155.00**

Dog, Rough-haired Terrier, Ch. "Crackley Startler," white w/black & brown markings, HN 1014, 1931-85, 3¾" h. **140.00**

Dog, St. Bernard, K 19, lying, 1½" x 2½" **95.00**

Dog, Sealyham, K 3, begging, 2¾". . . **125.00**

Dog, Springer Spaniel, HN 1078, 3" . . . **90.00**

Dog, Springer Spaniel, "Dry Toast," HN 2517, 3¾" **143.00**

Dog, Sealyham, "Scotia Stylist," HN 1031, 4". **295.00**

Dog, Scottish Terrier, "Albourne Arthur," HN 1016, 3½". **121.00**

Dog, Scottish Terrier, "Albourne Arthur," HN 1015, 5" **275.00**

Dog, Scottish Terrier, K 18, seated, 2¼" x 2¾" **113.00**

Dog, Wire Fox Terrier, K 8, seated, 2½" **75.00**

Dog, character dog yawning, white w/brown patches over ears & eyes, black patches on back, HN 1099, 1934-85, 4" h. **55.00**

Dogs, Cocker Spaniels sleeping, white dog w/brown markings & golden brown dog, HN 2590, 1941-69, 1¾" h. **55.00**

Duck, Drake, green, brown & white, HN 807, 1923-77, 2½" h. **70.00**

Duck, Drake, standing, green, 2½". . . . **50.00**

Duck, standing, white, HN 806, 1923-68, 2½" h. **70.00**

Elephant, trunk in salute, HN 2644, 4¼" **150.00**

Horse, Punch Peon, Chestnut Shire, brown w/black mane & black & white markings on legs, HN 2623, 1950-60, 7½" h. **650.00**

Horses, chestnut mare & foal, chestnut w/white stockings, fawn-colored foal w/white stockings, HN 2522, 1938-60, 6½" h. **575.00**

Kitten, sleeping, HN 2581, 1½" **70.00**

Kitten, looking up, HN 2584, 2" **25.00**

Kitten, licking hind paw, HN 2580, 2¼" **50.00**

Kitten, on hind legs, HN 2582, 2¾" . . . **70.00**

Monkey, Langur Monkey, long-haired brown & white coat, HN 2657, 1960-69, 4½" h. **175.00**

Penguin, K 22, 1¾". **200.00**

Leaping Salmon with Flambé Glaze

Salmon, Flambé glaze, curved
  leaping pose, early 20th c., printed
  mark, 12" h. (ILLUS. prev. page). . . **431.00**
Tiger, on a rock, style 4, HN 2639,
  10¼ x 12" **1,650.00**
Tiger, crouching, Flambé glaze,
  Model No. 111, HN 225, ca. 1912-
  68, 9½" l., 2" h. **525.00**

CHARACTER JUGS

Anne Boleyn, large, D 6644, 7¼" h.. . . **81.00**
Anne of Cleves, large, D 6653, 7¼" h.. . **100.00**
Antony & Cleopatra, large, D 6728,
  7¼" h. **138.00**
Apothecary, small, D 6574, 4" h. **47.00**
Aramis, miniature, D 6508, 2½" h. **45.00**
Aramis, small, D 6454, 3½" h. **50.00**
Aramis, large, D 6441, 7¼" h. **69.00**
'Arriet, tiny, D 6256, 1¼" h. **190.00**
'Arriet, miniature, D 6250, 2¼" h. **60.00**
'Arriet, small, D 6236, 3¼" h. **90.00**
'Arry, tiny, D 6255, 1½" h.. . . . . **140.00**
'Arry, miniature, D 6249, 2½" h. **65.00**
'Arry, small, D 6235, 3½" h. **90.00**

'Arry Jug

'Arry, large, D 6207, 6½" h. (ILLUS.) . **165.00**
Athos, small, D 6452, 3¾" h. **50.00**
Auld Mac, miniature, D 6253, 2¼" h. . . **40.00**
Auld Mac, small, D 5824, 3¼" h. **60.00**
Auld Mac, large, D 5823, 6¼" h. **70.00**
Auld Mac "A," large, D 5823, 6¼" h.. . **90.00**
Bacchus, miniature, D 6521, 2½" h.. . . **48.00**
Bacchus, small, D 6505, 4" h. **58.00**
Bacchus, large, D 6499, 7" h.. . . . . . . **59.00**
Baseball Player, small, D 6878,
  4¼" h. **60.00**
Beefeater, miniature, D 6251, 2½" h. . . **45.00**
Beefeater, small, D 6233, 3¼" h. **50.00**
Beefeater, large, D 6206, 6½" h. **66.00**
Beefeaters GR, large, D 6206,
  6½" h. **110.00**
Ben Franklin, small, D 6695, 4" h. . . . **60.00**
Blacksmith, miniature, D 6585,
  2½" h. **38.00**
Blacksmith, small, D 6578, 4" h. **60.00**
Bootmaker, small, D 6579, 4" h. **54.00**
Buzfuz, small, D 5838, 4" h. **95.00**

Cap'n Cuttle, small, D 5842, 4" h. **65.00**
Cap'n Cuttle, mid, D 5842, 5½" h. . . . **125.00**
Cap'n Cuttle "A,", small, D 5842,
  4" h. **150.00**
Captain Ahab, miniature, D 6522,
  2½" h. **48.00**
Captain Ahab, large, D 6500, 7" h. . . . **95.00**
Captain Henry Morgan, small, D
  6469, 3½" h. **75.00**
Captain Hook, small, D 660, 4" h. . . . **340.00**
Captain Hook, large, D 6597, 7¼" h. . . **513.00**
Cardinal, tiny, D 6258, 1½" h.. . . . . . . **160.00**
Cardinal, miniature, D 6129, 2¼" h. . . . **53.00**
Cardinal, large, D 5614, 6½" h. **150.00**
Cardinal "A," miniature, D 6129,
  2¼" h. **65.00**
Catherine Howard, large, D 6645,
  7" h. **130.00**
Catherine of Aragon, large, D 6643,
  7" h. **90.00**
Catherine Parr, large, D 6664,
  6¾" h. **130.00**
Cavalier "A" (The), large, D 6114,
  7" h. **115.00**
Cavalier (The), small, D 6173, 3¼" h. . . . **75.00**

Large Cavalier

Cavalier (The) large, D 6114, 7" h.
  (ILLUS.). **123.00**
City Gent, large, D 6815, 7" h. **89.00**
Cliff Cornell, large, 9" h. **300.00**
Cliff Cornell, large, var. 2, 9" h. **200.00**
Clown w/brown hair, large, D 5610,
  7½" h. **3,200.00**

Clown with White Hair

Clown w/red hair, large, D 5610,
7½" h. **2,695.00**
Clown w/white hair, large, D 6322,
7½" h. (ILLUS. previous page) . . . **1,200.00**
Collector, large, D 6796, 7" h. 150.00
Davy Crockett & Santa Anna, large,
D 6729, 7" h. 95.00
Dick Turpin, miniature, D 6128,
2¼" h. 55.00
Dick Turpin, pistol handle, small,
D 5618, 3½" h. 50.00
Dick Turpin, horse handle, small,
D 6535, 3¾" h. 43.00
Dick Turpin, pistol handle, large,
D 5485, 6½" h. 113.00
Dick Turpin, horse handle, large,
D 6528, 7" h. 100.00
Dick Turpin "A", pistol handle,
D 5485, 6½" h. 110.00
Don Quixote, miniature, D 6511,
2½" h. 48.00
Don Quixote, small, D 6460, 3¼" h. . . 50.00
Drake, small, D 6174, 3¼" h. 75.00
Falconer, miniature, D 6547, 2¾" h. . . . 54.00
Falconer, small, D 6540, 3¾" h. 59.00
Falstaff, miniature, D 6519, 2½" h. 50.00
Falstaff, small, D 6385, 3½" h. 45.00
Falstaff, large, D 6287, 6" h. 85.00
Farmer John, small, D 5789, 3¼" h. . . 75.00
Farmer John, large, D 5788, 6½" h. . . . 160.00
Fat Boy, tiny, D 6142, 1½" h. 150.00
Fat Boy, miniature, D 6139, 2½" h. 50.00
Fat Boy, small, D 5840, 4" h. 125.00
Fat Boy, mid, D 5840, 5" h. 160.00
Fortune Teller, small, D 6503, 3¾" h. . . 282.00
Friar Tuck, large, D 6321, 7" h. 365.00
Gaoler, small, D 6577, 3¾" h. 50.00
Gardener (The), miniature, D 6638,
2¾" h. 99.00
Gardener (The), second version,
small, D 6634, 4" h. 55.00
Gardener (The), large, D 6630,
7¾" h. 158.00
General Gordon, large, D 6869,
7¼" h. 175.00
Genie, large, D 6892, 7" h. 207.00
George Washington, large, D 6669,
7½" h. 98.00
Gladiator, small, D 6553, 4¼" h. 393.00
Gondolier, miniature, D 6595, 2½" h. . . 375.00
Gondolier, small, D 6592, 4" h. 365.00
Gone Away, miniature, D 6545, 2½" h. . . 55.00
Gone Away, small, D 6538, 3¾" h. 49.00
Gone Away, large, D 6531, 7¼" h. 93.00
Granny, miniature, D 6520, 2¼" h. 35.00
Granny, small, D 6384, 3¼" h. 50.00
Granny, large, D 5521, 6¼" h. 93.00
Guardsman, small, D 6575, 4¼" h. 50.00
Guardsman, large, D 6568, 6¾" h. 69.00
Gulliver, miniature, D 6566, 2½" h. . . 425.00
Gunsmith, miniature, D 6587, 2½" h. . . 38.00

Gunsmith, small, D 6580, 3½" h. **47.00**
Hamlet, large, D 6672, 7¼" h.. . . . . **79.00**
Happy John "A", large, D 6031,
8½" h. 150.00
Henry V, raised flag, large, D 6671,
7¼" h. 165.00
Henry VIII, large, D 6642, 6½" h. 78.00
Izaac Walton, large, D 6404, 7" h. . . . 100.00
Jane Seymour, large, D 6646, 7¼" h. . . 105.00
Jarge, small, D 6295, 3½" h.. . . . . 165.00

Jarge

Jarge, large, D 6288, 6½" h. (ILLUS.). . **300.00**
Jester, small, D 5556, 3⅛" h. **98.00**
Jester, seated, medium, D 6910,
5" h. 101.00
Jockey, second version, small,
D 6877, 4" h. 50.00
Jockey, large, D 6625, 7¾" h. 298.00
John Barleycorn, miniature, D 6041,
2½" h. 85.00
John Barleycorn, small, D 5735,
3½" h. 70.00
John Doulton, small, two o'clock,
D 6656, 4¼" h. 60.00
John Peel, tiny, D 6259, 1¼" h. 165.00
John Peel, miniature, D 6130, 2¼" h. . . 73.00
John Peel, small, D 5731, 3½" h. 80.00
John Shorter, small, D 6880, 4¼" h. . . 99.00
Johnny Appleseed, large, D 6372,
6" h. 247.00
Juggler, large, D 6835, 6½" h. 99.00
King Charles I, large, D 6917, 7" h. . . 239.00
Lawyer, miniature, D 6524, 2½" h. 50.00
Leprechaun, large, D 6847, 7½" h. . . . 99.00
Little Mester Museum Piece, large,
D 6819, 6¾" h. 149.00
Lobsterman, miniature, D 6652,
2¾" h. 50.00
Lobsterman, small, D 6620, 3¾" h. 60.00
London Bobby, miniature, D 6763,
2½" h. 45.00
Long John Silver, miniature, D 6512,
2½" h. 50.00
Lord Nelson, large, D 6336, 7" h. . . . 400.00
Lumberjack, small, D 6613, 3½" h. 55.00
Macbeth, large, D 6667, 7¼" h. 90.00
Mark Twain, small, D 6694, 4" h. 75.00

Large Mephistopheles

Mephistopheles, large, w/verse,
D 5757, 7" h. (ILLUS.) **2,750.00**
Mephistopheles "A", small, two-
faced, w/verse, D 5758, 3¾" h. . . **1,200.00**
Merlin, miniature, D 6543, 2¾" h. **48.00**
Merlin, large, D 6529, 7¼" h. **76.00**

The Mikado

Mikado (The), large, D 6501, 6½" h.
(ILLUS.) **600.00**
Mine Host, miniature, D 6513, 2½" h.. . . **40.00**
Mine Host, large, D 6468, 7" h. **80.00**
Monty, large, D 6202, 5¾" h. **77.00**
Mr. Micawber, tiny, D 6143, 1¼" h. . . . **150.00**
Mr. Micawber, miniature, D 6138,
2¼" h. **52.00**
Mr. Micawber, mid, D 5843, 5½" h. . . . **135.00**
Mr. Pickwick, tiny, D 6260, 1¼" h. . . . **168.00**
Mr. Pickwick, miniature, D 6254,
2¼" h. **75.00**
Mr. Pickwick, small, D 5839, 3½" h.. . . **70.00**
Mr. Pickwick, mid, D 5839, 4½" h.. . . . **190.00**
Mr. Quaker, large, D 6738, 7½" h. . . . **650.00**
Neptune, miniature, D 6555, 2½" h. . . . **45.00**
Neptune, small, D 6552, 3¾" h. **50.00**
Neptune, large, D 6548, 6½" h. **69.00**
Night Watchman, miniature, D 6583,
2½" h. **38.00**
North American Indian, miniature,
D 6665, 2¾" h. **50.00**
North American Indian, small,
D 6614, 4¼" h. **55.00**
North American Indian , large,
Canadian Centennial 1867-1967,
D 6611, 7¾" h. **143.00**
Old Charley, tiny, D 6144, 1¼" h.. . . . . **82.00**
Old Charley, miniature, D 6046,
2¼" h. **45.00**
Old Charley, small, D 5527, 3¼" h. . . . **70.00**

Old King Cole, small, D 6037,
3½" h. **90.00**
Old King Cole, large, D 6036,
5¾" h. **280.00**
Old Salt, miniature, D 6557, 2½" h. . . . **50.00**
Old Salt, large, D 6551, 7½" h. **85.00**
Oliver Twist, tiny, D 6677, 1½" h.. . . . **120.00**
Paddy, tiny, D 6145, 1¼" h. **88.00**
Paddy, miniature, D 6042, 2¼" h. **55.00**
Paddy, small, D 5768, 3¼" h. **58.00**
Paddy, large, D 5753, 6" h. **115.00**
Parson Brown, miniature, D 5529,
3¼" h. **45.00**
Parson Brown "A", small, D 5529,
3¼" h. **50.00**
Parson Brown "A", large, D 5486,
6½" h. **125.00**
Pearly King, small, D 6844, 3½" h. . . . **65.00**
Pearly King, large, D 6760, 6¾" h.. . . . **85.00**
Pearly Queen, small, D 6843, 3½" h.. . . **65.00**
Pearly Queen, large, D 6759, 7" h.. . . **79.00**
Pied Piper, small, D 6462, 3¾" h. **60.00**
Pied Piper, large, D 6403, 7" h. **250.00**
Poacher (The), miniature, D 6515,
2½" h. **45.00**
Poacher (The), small, D 6464, 4" h.. . . **50.00**
Poacher (The), variation 1, large,
D 6429, 7" h. **176.00**
Poacher (The), variation 2, large,
D 6429, 7" h. **90.00**
Punch & Judy Man, small, D 6593,
3½" h. **350.00**

Punch & Judy Man

Punch & Judy Man, large, D 6590,
7" h. (ILLUS.) **325.00**
Queen Victoria, small, D 6913, 3½" h. . . **85.00**
Red Queen (The), large, D 6777,
7¼" h. **90.00**
Regency Beau, small, D 6562, 4¼" h. . . **450.00**

Regency Beau

Regency Beau, large, D 6559, 7¼" h.
(ILLUS.). **950.00**
Ringmaster, large, D 6863, 7½" h.. . . **140.00**
Rip Van Winkle, miniature, D 6517,
2½" h. **45.00**
Rip Van Winkle, small, D 6463, 4" h. . . **50.00**
Rip Van Winkle, large, D 6438, 6½" h. . . **90.00**
Robin Hood, 1st version, miniature,
D 6252, 2¼" h. **65.00**
Robin Hood, 2nd version, miniature,
D 6252, 2¼" h. **43.00**
Robin Hood, 2nd version, small,
D 6234, 3¼" h. **44.00**
Robin Hood, large, D 6205, 6¼" h. . . **115.00**
Robinson Crusoe, small, D 6539,
4" h. **65.00**
Robinson Crusoe, large, D 6532,
7½" h. **90.00**
Romeo, large, D 6670, 7½" h. **85.00**
Ronald Regan, large, D 6718, 7¾" h. . . **475.00**
Sairey Gamp, tiny, D 6146, 1¼" h.. . . . **90.00**

Sairey Gamp

Sairey Gamp, miniature, D 6045,
2⅛" h. (ILLUS.) **50.00**
Sairey Gamp, small, D 5528, 3⅛" h. . . **35.00**
Sam Johnson, large, D 6289, 6¼" h. . . **290.00**
Sam Weller, tiny, D 6147, 1¼" h.. . . . . **87.00**
Sam Weller, miniature, D 6140,
2¼" h. **50.00**
Sam Weller, mid, D 5841, 4½" h.. . . . . **110.00**
Sancho Panza, miniature, D 6518,
2½" h. **56.00**
Sancho Panza, small, D 6461,
3¼" h. **50.00**
Sancho Panza, large, D 6456, 6½" h. . . **138.00**
Santa Claus, reindeer handle, large,
D 6675, 7¼" h. **160.00**
Santa Claus, doll & drum handle,
large, D 6668, 7½" h. **100.00**
Santa Claus, plain handle, large,
D 6704, 7½" h. **78.00**
Scaramouche, small, D 6561,
3¼" h. **375.00**
Scaramouche, second version,
large, D 6814, 6¾" h. **125.00**
Simon the Cellarer, small, D 5616,
3½" h. **53.00**
Simon the Cellarer, large, D 5504,
6½" h. **120.00**
Simple Simon, large, D 6374, 7" h. . . **465.00**

Sir Francis Drake, large, D 6805,
7" h. **108.00**
Sir Thomas More, large, D 6792,
6¾" h. **130.00**
Sleuth (The), miniature, D 6639,
2¾" h. **55.00**
Sleuth (The), small, D 6635, 3¼" h. . . **50.00**
Sleuth (The), large, D 6631, 7" h.. . . . **80.00**
Smuggler, small, D 6619, 3¼" h. **60.00**
Smuggler, large, D 6616, 7¼" h. **85.00**
Snooker Player, small, D 6879, 4" h.. . . **50.00**
Tam O'Shanter, small, D 6636,
3¼" h. **75.00**
Tam O'Shanter, large, D 6632, 7" h.. . . **100.00**
Toby Philpots, miniature, D 6043,
2¼" h. **45.00**
Toby Philpots, small, D 5737, 3¼" h. . . **60.00**
Toby Philpots, large, D 5736, 6¼" h. . . **96.00**
Tony Weller, miniature, D 6044,
2¼" h. **60.00**
Tony Weller, small, D 5530, 3¼" h. . . . **60.00**
Tony Weller, large, D 5531, 6½" h. . . **110.00**
Touchstone, large, D 5613, 7" h.. . . . . **275.00**
Town Crier, miniature, D 6544,
2½" h. **90.00**
Town Crier, small, style one, D 6537,
3¼" h. **120.00**
Trapper (The), small, D 6612, 3¾" h.. . . **55.00**
Trapper (The), large, D 6609,
7¼" h. **100.00**
Trapper (The), large, D 6609, 7¼" h. . . **102.00**
Ugly Duchess, small, D 6603, 3½" h. . . **265.00**
Ugly Duchess, large, D 6599,
6¾" h. **550.00**
Veteran Motorist, miniature, D 6641,
2½" h. **47.00**
Veteran Motorist, large, D 6633,
7½" h. **100.00**

The Vicar of Bray

Vicar of Bray (The), large, D 5615,
6¾" h. (ILLUS.) **200.00**
Viking, miniature, D 6526, 2½" h.. . . . . **95.00**
Viking, small, D 6502, 4" h. **80.00**
Viking, large, D 6496, 7¼" h. **180.00**
Walrus & Carpenter (The),
miniature, D 6608, 2½" h. **136.00**
Walrus & Carpenter (The), small,
D 6604, 3¼" h. **75.00**

Winston Churchill, large, D 6171,
9" h. **95.00**
Winston Churchill pitcher, large,
D 6907, 7" h. **135.00**
Yachtsman, large, D 6626, 8" h. **90.00**

DICKENSWARE

Bill Sikes plate, square, 8" d. **110.00**
Fat Boy plate, 10" d. **120.00**
Pitcher, scene from Oliver Twist. **195.00**
Platter, 17½" l., rectangular, Mr.
Micawber scene **140.00**

FIGURINES

Affection, HN 2236, purple, 1962 - . . . **90.00**
Afternoon Tea, HN 1747, pink &
blue, 1935-82 . . . . **400.00**
As Good As New, HN 2971, blue,
green and tan, 1982-85 . . . . **140.00**
Autumn Breezes, HN 1934, red,
1940- **156.00**
Babie, HN 1679, green dress, 1935-92 . . . **75.00**
Ballad Seller, HN 2266, pink, 1968-73 . . **255.00**
Ballerina, HN 2116, lavender,
1953-73 . . . . **225.00**
Beachcomber, HN 2487, matte,
purple & grey, 1973-76 . . . . **225.00**
Beat You To It, HN 2871, pink, gold
& blue, 1980-87 . . . . **350.00**
Bedtime Story, HN 2059, pink, white,
yellow & blue, 1950- **200.00**
Belle, HN 2340, green dress, 1968-88 . . **80.00**
Bernice, HN 2071, pink & red,
1951-53 . . . . **800.00**
Biddy Penny Farthing, HN 1843,
1938- **149.00**
Bluebeard, HN 2105, purple, green &
brown, 1953-92 . . . . **425.00**
Boatman (The), HN 2417, yellow,
1971-87 . . . . **180.00**

The Bride

Bride (The), HN 2873, white w/ gold
trim, 1980-89 (ILLUS.) **95.00**
Bride (The), HN 3284, style 4, white, . **170.00**
Captain Cook, HN 2889, black &
cream, 1980-84 . . . . **280.00**

Captain (The), HN 2260, black &
white, 1965-82 . . . . **195.00**
Carpet Seller (The) red "Flambé"
glaze, HN 2776, 9¼" h. **132.00**
Centurian, HN 2726, grey & purple,
1982-84 . . . . **195.00**
Chief (The), HN 2892, 1979-88 . . . . . **130.00**
Chief (The), HN 2892, gold, 1979-88 . . **180.00**
China Repairer, HN 2943, blue,
white & tan, 1983-88 . . . . **200.00**

Christmas Morn

Christmas Morn, HN 1992, red &
white, 1947- (ILLUS.) **135.00**
Christmas Parcels, HN 2851, black,
1978-82 . . . . **175.00**
Christmas Time, HN 2110, red
w/white frills, 1953-67 . . . . **360.00**

Cissie

Cissie, HN 1809, pink dress, 1937-
(ILLUS.). **95.00**
Clarinda, HN 2724, blue & white
dress, 1975-81 . . . . **150.00**
Clarissa, HN 2345, green dress,
1968-81 . . . . **150.00**
Coachman, HN 2282, purple, grey &
blue, 1963-71 . . . . **450.00**
Coralie, HN 2307, yellow dress,
1964-88 . . . . **155.00**
Cup O' Tea, HN 2322, dark blue &
grey, 1964-83 . . . . **133.00**
Daffy Down Dilly, HN 1712, green
dress, 1935-75 . . . . **325.00**
David Copperfield, M 88, black &
tan, 1949-83 . . . . **85.00**
Debbie, HN 2385, blue & white dress,
1969-82 . . . . **80.00**

Doctor, HN 2858, black & grey,
1979-92 . . . . **185.00**
Easter Day, HN 2039, multi-coloured,
1949-69 . . . . **375.00**
Elegance, HN 2264, green dress,
1961-85 . . . . **200.00**
Embroidering, HN 2855, grey dress,
1980-90 . . . . **195.00**
Emily, HN 3204, style 2, white &
blue, 1989- **145.00**
Eventide, HN 2814, blue, white, red,
yellow & green, 1977-91 . . . . **180.00**
Farmer's Wife, HN 2069, red, green
& brown, 1951-55 . . . . **370.00**
Favourite (The), HN 2249, blue &
white, 1960-90 . . . . **195.00**
Fiona, HN 2694, red & white,
1974-81 . . . . **198.00**
First Dance, HN 2803, pale blue
dress, 1977-92 . . . . **225.00**
First Waltz, HN 2862, red dress,
1979-83 . . . . **225.00**
Flower Seller's Children, HN 1342,
purple, red & yellow, 1929- **475.00**
Francine, HN 2422, green & white
dress, 1972-81 . . . . **80.00**
French Peasant, HN 2075, brown &
green, 1951-55 . . . . **420.00**
Gandalf, HN 2911, 1980-84 . . . . **165.00**
Genie (The), HN 2989, 1983-90 . . . . **138.00**
Genie (The), HN 2999, Flambé
glaze, 1989-present. **165.00**
George Washington at Prayer, HN
2861, blue & tan, 1977, LE of
750 . . . . **2,250.00**
Gillian, HN 3042, green, 1984-? **140.00**

Giselle, The Forest Glade

Giselle, The Forest Glade, HN 2140,
white & blue, 1954-65 (ILLUS.) **320.00**
Good King Wenceslas, HN 2118,
brown & purple, 1953-76 . . . . **335.00**
Gypsy Dance, HN 2230, lavender
dress, 1959-71 . . . . **175.00**
Happy Anniversary, HN 3097, style
1, purple & white, 1987- **160.00**

Hilary, HN 2335, blue dress, 1967-81 . . **180.00**
Honey, HN 1909, pink, 1939-49 . . . . . **450.00**
**HRH Prince Phillip, Duke of
Edinburgh,** HN 2386, black &
gold, 1981, limited edition of 1,500 . . **425.00**
Isadora, HN 2938, lavender, 1986-92 . . **220.00**
Jacqueline, HN 2001, pink dress,
1947-51 . . . . **495.00**
Janet, HN 1916, 5½" h. **154.00**
Jennifer, HN 2392, blue dress,
1981-92 . . . . **180.00**
Joan, HN 2023, blue, 1949-59 . . . . . . **260.00**
Joker (The), HN 2252, 1990-92 . . . . . **138.00**
Judge (The), HN 2443, 1972-76 . . . . **121.00**
Julia, HN 2705, gold, 1975-90 . . . . . . **120.00**
June, HN 2991, lavender & red,
1988- **175.00**
Kelly, HN 2478, white w/blue flowers,
1985-92 . . . . **160.00**
L'Ambitieuse, HN 3359, rose & pale
blue, 1991, limited edition of
5,000 . . . . **240.00**

La Sylphide

La Sylphide, HN 2138, white dress,
1954-65 (ILLUS.) **225.00**
Lady Betty, HN 1967, red, 1941-51 . . **355.00**
Lavinia, HN 1955, red dress, 1940-79 . . **140.00**
Lily, HN 1798, pink dress,1936-71 . . . **500.00**
Little Nell, HN 540, pink dress,
1922-32 . . . . **115.00**
Marie, HN 1370, style 2, purple
dress, 1930-88 . . . . **125.00**
Mary Had a Little Lamb, HN 2048,
lavender, 1949-88 . . . . **113.00**
Master (The), HN 2325, green &
brown, 1967-92 . . . . **195.00**
Maxine, HN 3199, pink & purple,
1989-90 . . . . **175.00**
Maytime, HN 2113, pink dress w/blue
scarf, 1953-67 . . . . **350.00**
Mendicant (The), HN 1365, brown,
1929-69 . . . . **219.00**

Miss Demure

Miss Demure, HN 1402, lavender &
pink dress, 1930-75 (ILLUS.) **175.00**
Ninette, HN 2379, yellow & cream,
1971- **285.00**
Oliver Twist, M 89, black & tan,
1949-83 .... **85.00**

The Orange Lady

Orange Lady (The), HN 1759,
1936-75 (ILLUS.) **207.00**
Pamela, HN 3223, style 2, white &
blue, 1989-89 .... **190.00**
Pantalettes, HN 1362, green & blue,
1929-38 .... **350.00**
Parisian , HN 2445, blue & grey,
matte glaze,1972-75 .... **180.00**
Paula, HN 3234, white & blue, 1990- .. **120.00**
Penelope, HN 1901, red dress,
1939-75 .... **260.00**
Piper (The), HN 2907, green,
1980-92 .... **225.00**
Premiere, HN 2343, green dress,
hand holds cloak, 1969-? **150.00**
Pride & Joy, HN 2945, brown, gold &
green, 1984-84 .... **295.00**
Promenade, HN 2076, blue &
orange, 1951-53 .... **1,250.00**
Punch & Judy Man, HN 2765, green
& yellow, 1981-90 .... **225.00**
Puppetmaker, HN 2253, green,
brown & red, 1962-73 .... **450.00**
Puppetmaker, HN 2253, green,
brown & red, 1962-73 .... **495.00**

Rachel, HN 2919, gold & green,
1981-84 .... **165.00**
Romance, HN 2430, gold & green
dress, 1972-81 .... **180.00**
Royal Governor's Cook, HN 2233,
1960-83 .... **275.00**

Sabbath Morn

Sabbath Morn, HN 1982, red,
1945-1959 (ILLUS.) **300.00**
Secret Thoughts, HN 2382, green
1971-88 .... **180.00**
Shepherd, HN 1975, light brown,
1945-75 .... **180.00**
Shore Leave, HN 2254, 1965-79 .... **176.00**
Simone, HN 2378, green dress,
1971-81 .... **138.00**
Southern Belle, HN 2229, red &
cream, 1958- **240.00**
Spring, HN 2085, 1952-59 .... **303.00**
Spring Morning, HN 1922, pink &
blue, 1940-73 .... **120.00**
Stop Press, HN 2683, brown, blue &
white, 1977-81 .... **150.00**
Sunday Morning, HN 2184, red &
brown, 1963-69 .... **375.00**
Susan, HN 2952, blue, black & pink,
1982- **225.00**
Sweet Dreams, HN 2380,
multicolored, 1971-90 .... **150.00**
Sweet Lavender, HN 1373, green,
red & black, 1930-49 .... **800.00**
Taking Things Easy, HN 2677, blue,
white & brown, 1975-87 .... **180.00**
Teresa, HN 1682, red and brown,
1935-49 .... **1,100.00**
Thanks Doc, HN 2731, white &
brown, 1975-90 .... **180.00**
This Little Pig, HN 1793, 4" h. **138.00**
Tiny Tim, HN 539, black, brown &
blue, 1922-32 .... **115.00**
Top O' The Hill, HN 1833, green &
blue dress, 1937-71 .... **225.00 to 300.00**
Top O' the Hill, HN 1834, red, 1937- .. **290.00**
Vanity, HN 2475, red dress, 1973-92.. **150.00**
Veneta, HN 2722, green & white,
1974-81 .... **140.00**

Veronica, HN 3205, style 3, white &
  pink, 1989-92. . . . . **160.00**
Wigmaker of Williamsburg, HN
  2239, white & brown, 1960-83. . . . . **165.00**
Willy-Won't-He, HN 2150, red,
  green, blue & white, 1955-59 . . . . . **235.00**
Young Dreams, HN 3176, pink,
  1988- **175.00**
Young Master, HN 2872, purple,
  grey & brown, 1980-89 . . . . **225.00**
Yvonne, HN 3038, turquoise, 1987- . . **160.00**

MISCELLANEOUS

Royal Doulton Charger

Charger, central scene of a lady
  riding horse side-saddle w/hound
  racing alongside, in yellow, brown,
  green, black & white, border band
  of dark green stylized grapevine,
  marked "George Morland #1784,"
  14" d. (ILLUS.). **125.00**
Dish, round w/flattened fluted rim
  w/gold edging around a floral band,
  center scene of romantic couples in
  a landscape, transfer-printed blue
  on white, late 19th c., 5½" d. **39.00**
Ewers, Carrara ware, bulbous body
  w/a tan ground decorated
  w/lifesized pink wild roses
  w/enameled white highlights, gold
  molded leaf & florals, grey rim &
  ornate handle, marked "Doulton
  Carrara Lambeth," 11½" h., pr. . . . **358.00**
Fish plates, 10" d., each transfer-
  printed in blue & white w/a different
  fish, late 19th c., set of 12 . . . . **288.00**
Jar, cov., Rouge Flambé, footed
  squatty bulbous body w/a wide low-
  domed cover, scattered black

splotches on crimson red ground,
  by Noke, fully stamped, 3¼" d.,
  2¾" h. **358.00**
Pitcher, Juliet, scene from
  Shakespeare's Romeo & Juliet **165.00**
Pitcher, 5½" h., Jackdaw of Rheims
  scene. **210.00**
Pitcher, 9¼" h., Shakespeare
  character series, standing portrait
  of Sir John Falstaff, tall waisted
  cylindrical form w/high arched
  spout, printed around the bottom
  border "A Tapster is a Good
  Trade," early 20th c. **165.00**
Pitcher, 11" h., Poplars at Sunset
  patt. **225.00**
Plate, 9⅛" d., Peony patt., dark blue
  floral center w/rectangular panels
  around the border, trimmed
  w/reddish rust & beige, ca. 1900 . . . **50.00**
Plate, 10" d., rack-type, Mr. Micawber . . **115.00**
Plate, 10" d., rack-type, Old Jarvey . . . **75.00**
Plate, 10" d., rack-type, The Mayor. . . . **90.00**
Plate, 10" d., rack-type, The Parson . . . **60.00**
Plate, 10" d., rack-type, The Squire . . . **65.00**
Plates, 7⅝" sq., creamware, transfer-
  decorated scenes, ca.1900,
  set of 6. . . . . **77.00**
Plates, 8" d., Coaching Days series,
  includes three scenes, "Boarding
  the Coach," "The Journey" &
  "Farewell," polychrome transfer
  decoration, early 20th c., set of 12 . . **413.00**

Shakespearean Sites Doulton Plates

Plates, 9" d., slightly dished
  w/scalloped rim, gilt-trimmed rim
  w/polychrome leafy vines bordering
  brown enameled Shakespearean
  sites, retailed by Theodore B. Starr,
  New York City, Doulton, Burslem,
  late 19th c., set of 12
  (ILLUS. of part) **460.00**
Platter, 17½" l., oval, Imari patt.,
  ca. 1860s **1,175.00**

Doulton Stoneware Soap Dish

Soap dish, stoneware, oblong w/large brown & lavender flying insect molded along one side of the dark blue glazed dish, impressed markings on base for Wright's Coal Tar Soap, 4¼ x 5¾", 1½" h. (ILLUS.) **135.00**

Teapot, cov., Nightwatchman scene . . **295.00**

Lovely Royal Doulton Covered Urn

Urn, cov., tall slender ovoid body raised on a ribbed & gadrooned gold & Kelly green pedestal base w/square foot & flanked by long gold full-length handles, tapering to a ringed & ribbed cylindrical neck w/flaring rim fitted w/a high Gothic spire-form cover, finely h.p. w/a colorful scene of highland cattle against a purplish mountain backdrop, glossy glaze, artist-signed by S. Kelsall, small professional repair to handle & pedestal, ca. 1910, 32" h. (ILLUS.) **3,025.00**

Vase, 5¼" h., 3⅛" d., stoneware, footed ovoid body w/short tapering neck, grey ground w/an incised design of pointed panels framing

Doulton Lambeth Stoneware Vase

stylized leafy scrolls in brown, green & light blue, artist-signed by Arthur Beeve, Doulton, Lambeth (ILLUS.) **195.00**

Doulton Rouge Flambé Vase

Vase, 7" h., 4¼" d., Rouge Flambé, footed ovoid body w/the wide shoulder tapering to a small, short rolled neck, black silhouetted desert landscape against the crimson red ground, shallow scratch, stamped "ROYAL DOULTON - FLAMBÉ - MADE IN ENGLAND" (ILLUS.) **248.00**

Doulton "Slater's Patent" Vase

Vase, 8" h., baluster-form w/a flaring domed foot tapering to a slender ovoid body w/a slender cylindrical neck w/a widely flaring rolled rim, dark green neck & foot, the body decorated overall w/a molded floral design on beige w/green, gold & turquoise blue highlights, "Slater's Patent" mark, ca. 1883 (ILLUS. prev. page) **94.00**

Vase, 9½" h., handled, flow blue, Babes in the Woods series **1,285.00**

Vase, 9⅝" h., Rouge Flambé, small footring under a spherical body tapering to a short 'stick' neck, red "flambe" glaze w/veined design ... **176.00**

Vase, 10¾" h., King's Ware, cylindrical w/raised scene of Dr. Johnson in a tavern scene, verse on the back **325.00**

Vase, 11¼" h., tall slender baluster-form w/flaring domed foot & waisted short widely flaring neck, the neck & foot in cobalt w/lacy gilt decoration, the body w/a creamy ground decorated w/scattered clusters of colorful flowers, Doulton-Burslem mark & incised "Lambeth - Doulton - Faience L6339," ca. 1882 .... **165.00**

DRESDEN

Dresden-type porcelain evolved from wares made at the nearby Meissen Porcelain Works early in the 18th century. "Dresden" and "Meissen" are often used interchangeably for later wares. "Dresden" has become a generic name for the kind of porcelains produced in Dresden and certain other areas of Germany but perhaps should be confined to the wares made in the city of Dresden.

Dresden Figure Group

Compotes, open, 14¼" h., figural, each shaped pierced oval bowl w/applied florettes & raised on

pedestals composed of two children on a base, printed marks, late 19th - early 20th c., pr....... **$345.00**

Figure group, a young boy in 18th c. costume standing & feeding geese, on a round base w/molded scrolls, polychrome decoration, gilt trim on base, 2⅞" d., 5⅛" h. (ILLUS.) **145.00**

Figure group, two young ladies in 18th c. attire, seated in billowing lacy dresses w/ornate folds, crimps & delicate applied blossoms, naturalistic coloring, one holding an open book, the other a basket of flowers, on a flower-strewn green grass ground raised on an oval scroll-molded & gilt-trimmed base, marked "VEB Porcelain Factory Unterweissbach," 12" l., 10" h. **413.00**

Figure of a girl w/basket of flowers, late 19th-early 20th c., Germany, 9¼" h. **180.00**

Figure of a man in 18th c. costume, late 19th-early 20th c., Germany, 6¾" h. **120.00**

Figure of a woman in 18th c. costume, holding fan, late 19th-early 20th c. Germany, 6¼" h...... **140.00**

Figures, Monkey Band, comprising a conductor & five various musicians wearing 18th c. costumes, late 19th c., 4 to 5¾" h., the set **173.00**

Dresden Potpourri Jar

Potpourri jars, cov., bulbous baluster-form encrusted overall w/colorful floral sprays & cherub faces, tall floral bouquet cover finial, 19th c., 9" h., pr. (ILLUS. of one)....................... **550.00**

Soup plates, flanged rim, each w/colored foliate sprays & gilt trim, 19th c., 9½" d., set of 7 .... **173.00**

FIESTA

Fiesta dinnerware was made by the Homer Laughlin China Company of Newell, West Virginia, from the 1930s until the early 1970s. The brilliant colors of this inexpensive pottery have attracted numerous collectors. On February 28, 1986, Laughlin reintroduced the popular Fiesta line with minor changes in the shapes of a few pieces and a contemporary color range. The effect of this new production on the Fiesta collecting market is yet to be determined.

Fiesta Mark

Ashtray
cobalt blue **$58.00**
grey 89.00
ivory 48.00
light green 45.00
medium green 228.00
rose 81.00

Bowl, cream soup
chartreuse 84.00
ivory 60.00
light green 43.00
turquoise 44.00

Bowl, dessert, 6" d.
light green 35.00
medium green 678.00
rose 49.00
turquoise 38.00
yellow 29.00

Bowl, fruit, 11¾" d.
ivory 294.00
light green 322.00
turquoise 340.00
yellow 306.00

Bowl, individual fruit, 4¾" d.
chartreuse 26.00
grey 27.00
ivory 26.00
light green 20.00
medium green 581.00
red 28.00
rose 29.00
turquoise 21.00

Bowl, individual fruit, 5½" d.
cobalt blue 30.00
grey 37.00
ivory 27.00
rose 34.00

Bowl, individual salad, 7½" d.
medium green 115.00
red 73.00

Bowl, nappy, 8½" d. chartreuse 48.00
cobalt blue 40.00
ivory 37.00
light green 35.00
rose 47.00

Bowl, nappy, 9½" d.
rose 57.00
turquoise 52.00

Bowl, salad, 9½" d.
cobalt blue 50.00
light green 32.00
yellow 28.00

Bowl, salad, large, footed
cobalt blue 378.00
ivory 375.00
light green 411.00
red 470.00
turquoise 455.00

Candleholders, bulb-type, pr.
cobalt blue 120.00
ivory 103.00
red 126.00
turquoise 99.00
yellow 90.00

Candleholders, tripod-type, pr.
ivory 742.00
red 749.00
turquoise 802.00
yellow 700.00

Carafe, cov.
ivory 283.00
light green 261.00
red 323.00

Casserole, cov., two-handled, 10" d.
cobalt blue 220.00
grey 337.00
ivory 208.00
light green 138.00
rose 265.00
yellow 139.00

Fiesta Tall Coffeepot

Coffeepot, cov.
    chartreuse **472.00**
    light green **233.00**
    red **254.00**
    rose **492.00**
    turquoise (ILLUS.) **237.00**
Coffeepot, cov., demitasse, stick handle
    red **520.00**
    turquoise **392.00**
    yellow **402.00**
Compote, 12" d., low, footed
    ivory **195.00**
    light green **118.00**
    yellow **125.00**
Compote, sweetmeat, high stand
    cobalt blue **79.00**
    ivory **106.00**
    turquoise **79.00**
Creamer chartreuse **31.00**
    light green **29.00**
    medium green **95.00**
    red **33.00**
    yellow **29.00**
Creamer & cov. sugar bowl,
    individual size, yellow on cobalt
    tray **275.00**
Creamer, stick handle
    cobalt blue **51.00**
    ivory **55.00**
    light green **36.00**
    red **57.00**
Cup & saucer, demitasse, stick handle
    chartreuse **537.00**
    forest green **508.00**
    grey **522.00**
    ivory **100.00**
    red **82.00**
    rose **513.00**
Cup & saucer, ring handle
    forest green **40.00**
    grey **40.00**
    ivory **34.00**
    light green **28.00**
    turquoise **26.00**
Egg cup
    chartreuse **137.00**
    forest green **150.00**
    red **75.00**
Fork (Kitchen Kraft)
    yellow **206.00**
Gravy boat
    cobalt blue **58.00**
    grey **59.00**
    light green **64.00**
    rose **68.00**
    yellow **30.00**
Lid for mixing bowl, size No. 1
    light green **862.00**
    red **950.00**
    yellow **759.00**

Lid for mixing bowl, size No. 2
    yellow **875.00**
Lid for mixing bowl, size No. 3
    yellow **777.00**
Lid for mixing bowl, size No. 4
    light green **1,106.00**
    yellow **938.00**
Marmalade jar, cov.
    light green **258.00**
    yellow **347.00**
Mixing bowl, nest-type, size No. 1, 5" d.
    cobalt blue **275.00**
    ivory **294.00**
    light green **204.00**
    red **225.00**
    yellow **239.00**
Mixing bowl, nest-type, size No. 2, 6" d.
    light green **124.00**
    turquoise **145.00**
Mixing bowl, nest-type, size No. 3, 7" d.
    ivory **213.00**
    red **172.00**
    turquoise **148.00**
    yellow **135.00**
Mixing bowl, nest-type, size No. 4, 8" d.
    turquoise **220.00**
    ivory **189.00**
    red **168.00**
    yellow **129.00**
Mixing bowl, nest-type, size No. 5, 9" d.
    cobalt blue **200.00**
    ivory **218.00**
    turquoise **195.00**
Mixing bowl, nest-type, size No. 6, 10" d.
    ivory **312.00**
    turquoise **317.00**
    yellow **218.00**
Mixing bowl, nest-type, size No. 7,11½" d.
    cobalt blue **443.00**
    ivory **437.00**
    yellow **275.00**
Mug,
    chartreuse **85.00**
    cobalt blue **68.00**
    grey **84.00**
    medium green **118.00**
    turquoise **47.00**
Mug, Tom & Jerry style cobalt blue . . **69.00**
    medium green **97.00**
    rose **78.00**
Mustard jar, cov.
    cobalt blue **290.00**
    light green **242.00**
    turquoise **242.00**
    yellow **176.00**
Onion soup bowl, cov.
    ivory . . . . **800.00 to 900.00**
    light green **603.00**
Pie server (Kitchen Kraft)
    cobalt blue . . . . **200.00 to 225.00**

Two-pint Jug Pitcher

Pitcher, jug-type, 2 pt.
   chartreuse **123.00**
   forest green **162.00**
   grey **160.00**
   rose **156.00**
   yellow (ILLUS.) **92.00**

Pitcher, juice, disc-type, 30 oz.
   forest green **314.00**
   ivory **120.00**
   light green **134.00**
   red **594.00**

Pitcher, w/ice lip, globular, 2 qt.
   cobalt blue **168.00**
   light green **122.00**
   turquoise **138.00**
   yellow **118.00**

Pitcher, water, disc-type
   cobalt blue **151.00**
   ivory **153.00**
   rose **275.00**
   turquoise **94.00**

Plate, 10" d.
   chartreuse **48.00**
   forest green . . . . **50.00 to 60.00**
   ivory **38.00**
   red **38.00**
   yellow **28.00**

Plate, 10" d., calender,
   ivory, 1954 . . . . **44.00**

Plate, 6" d.
   chartreuse **8.00**
   grey **9.00**
   medium green **25.00**

Plate, 7" d.
   chartreuse **14.00**
   grey **11.00**
   medium green **36.00**
   rose **14.00**

Plate, 9" d.
   forest green **19.00**
   light green **11.00**
   medium green **52.00**
   turquoise **15.00**

Plate, chop, 13" d.
   chartreuse **65.00**
   forest green **85.00**
   grey **80.00**
   light green **28.00**

   red **64.00**
   rose **82.00**

Plate, chop, 15" d.
   chartreuse **128.00**
   ivory **46.00**
   red **70.00**
   turquoise **41.00**

Plate, grill, 10½" d.
   cobalt blue **42.00**
   forest green . . . . **70.00 to 80.00**
   grey **93.00**
   turquoise **44.00**

Plate, grill, 11½" d.
   cobalt blue **69.00**
   light green **41.00**

Platter, 12" oval
   chartreuse **55.00**
   forest green **43.00**
   medium green **211.00**
   yellow **33.00**

Relish tray w/five inserts
   ivory . . . . **250.00 to 300.00**
   light green **190.00**
   multicolored **336.00**

Salt & pepper shakers, pr.
   cobalt blue **22.00**
   forest green **39.00**
   ivory **22.00**

Soup plate w/flanged rim, 8" d.
   chartreuse **46.00**
   forest green **52.00**
   light green **43.00**
   medium green **126.00**
   turquoise **39.00**
   yellow **39.00**

Spoon (Kitchen Kraft)
   cobalt blue . . . . **165.00 to 175.00**

Kitchen Kraft Spoon

   red (ILLUS.) **164.00**
   yellow **75.00**

Sugar bowl, cov.
   chartreuse **67.00**
   cobalt blue **60.00**
   forest green **71.00**
   light green **47.00**
   rose **68.00**

Syrup pitcher w/original lid
   cobalt blue **334.00**
   ivory . . . . **600.00 to 650.00**
   light green **359.00**
   yellow **295.00**

Teapot, cov., large size (8 cup)
   cobalt blue................... 290.00
   light green.................. 207.00
   red......................... 265.00
   turquoise................... 243.00
Teapot, cov., medium size (6 cup)
   chartreuse.................. 293.00
   forest green................ 358.00

Medium Six-cup Teapot

   grey (ILLUS.)................. 383.00
   light green.................. 157.00
   red......................... 213.00
Tom & Jerry set: footed salad &
   12 mugs; ivory & gold,
   13 pcs. .... **1,000.00 to 1,200.00**
Tray, Figure 8 turquoise........... 425.00
Tumbler, juice, 5 oz.
   cobalt blue................... 38.00
   grey........................ 415.00
   ivory....................... 40.00
   red......................... 45.00
   rose........................ 57.00
Tumbler, water, 10 oz.
   ivory....................... 65.00
   light green.................. 59.00
   yellow 61.00
Utility tray,
   ivory....................... 45.00
   light green.................. 37.00
   red......................... 42.00
   yellow 38.00
Vase, bud, 6½" h.
   cobalt blue................... 95.00
   red......................... 92.00
   yellow 81.00
Vase, 8" h.
   light green.................. 512.00
   turquoise............ **800.00 to 900.00**
Vase, 10" h.
   ivory....................... 810.00
   light green.................. 798.00
   red......................... 830.00
   yellow 828.00
Vase, 12" h.
   cobalt blue........ **1,400.00 to 1,500.00**
   ivory....................... 1,355.00

FLORENCE CERAMICS

Florence Ward began her successful enterprise in 1939. By 1946 she had moved her home workshop into a small plant in Pasadena, California. About three years later it was again necessary to move to larger facilities in the area. Semi-porcelain figurines, some with actual lace dipped in slip, were made. Figurines, such as fictional characters and historical couples, were the backbone of her business. To date, almost two hundred figurines have been documented. For about two years, in the mid-1950s, Betty D. Ford created what the company called "stylized sculptures from the Florence wonderland of birds and animals." Included were about a half dozen assorted doves, several cats, foxes, dogs and rabbits. Several marks were used over the years with the most common being the circle with 'semi-porcelain' outside the circle. The name of the figurine was almost always included with a mark. A "Floraline" mark was used on floral containers and related items. There was also a script mark and a block lettered mark as well as paper labels. The company was sold to Scripto Corporation in 1964 but only advertising pieces were made such as mugs for the Tournament of Roses in Pasadena, California. The company ceased all operations in 1977.

Florence Ceramic Marks

Figure of a boy, "Jim," 5½" h. **$88.00**
Figure of a boy, "Wynkin," standing
   wearing pajamas, 5½" h. 250.00
Figure of a boy, "Choir Boy," 6" h. ... 90.00
Figure of a boy, "David," 7½" h. 225.00
Figure of a girl, "Birthday Girl,"
   rare 500.00

Figure of a girl, "Joy," 6" h. **125.00**
Figure of a girl, "Summer," 6¼" h. . . **300.00**
Figure of a girl, "Pamela," 7¼" h. . . . **195.00**
Figure of a girl, "Linda Lou,"
7¾" h. **425.00**
Figure of a Madonna, "Our Lady of
Grace," 9¾" h. **225.00**
Figure of a man, "Edward," seated in
Victorian chair, 7" h. **450.00**
Figure of a man, "Douglas," 8½" h. . . **200.00**
Figure of a man, "Gary," 8½" h. **250.00**
Figure of a man, "Victor," 9¼" h. **325.00**
Figure of a man, "Leading Man,"
10¼" h. **395.00**
Figure of a woman, "Ava," tan
& rust **200.00**
Figure of a woman, "Charmaine,"
white w/gold trim **155.00**
Figure of a woman, "Jennifer,"
lavender dress **165.00**
Figure of a woman, "Rebecca," light
teal blue & ivory w/gold trim **200.00**
Figure of a woman, "Ann," 6" h. **85.00**

Elaine

Figure of a woman, "Elaine," Godey
series, 6" h. (ILLUS.). **78.00**
Figure of a woman, "Irene," Godey
series, 6" h. **95.00**
Figure of a woman, "Sue," Godey
series, 6" h. **100.00**
Figure of a woman, "Her Majesty,"
7" h. **200.00**
Figure of a woman, "Kay," Godey
series, 7" h. **125.00**
Figure of a woman, "Delia," Godey
series, 7¼" h. **150.00**
Figure of a woman, "Lillian," Godey
series, 7¼" h. **135.00**
Figure of a woman, "Louise,"
7¼"h. **145.00**
Figure of a woman, "Priscilla," grey,
7¼" h. **170.00**

Figure of a woman, "Grace," light
green, 7½" h. **220.00**
Figure of a woman, "Laura," fancy,
7½" h. **225.00**
Figure of a woman, "Laura," plain,
7½" h. **163.00**
Figure of a woman, "Mary," seated
in an armchair, 7½" h. **475.00**
Figure of a woman, "Melanie,"
Godey series, beige w/green,
7½" h. **143.00**
Figure of a woman, "Sarah,"
7½" h. **130.00**

Clarissa

Figure of a woman, "Clarissa,"
7¾" h. (ILLUS.) **275.00**
Figure of a woman, "Jenette,"
7¾" h. **225.00**
Figure of a woman, "Catherine,"
seated on an open-backed settee,
7¾" l., 6¾" h. **800.00**
Figure of a woman, "Abigail," Godey
series, 8" h. **185.00**
Figure of a woman, "Annabel,"
Godey series, 8" h. **495.00**
Figure of a woman, "Colleen,"
8" h. **250.00**
Figure of a woman, "Genevieve,"
plain, 8" h. **250.00**
Figure of a woman, "Shirley,"
8" h. **225.00**
Figure of a woman, "Amelia," Godey
series, 8¼" h. **425.00**
Figure of a woman, "Lisa," 8¼" h. . . **550.00**
Figure of a woman, "Masquerade,"
8¼" h. **650.00**
Figure of a woman, "Sue Ellen,"
Godey series, green & burgundy,
8¼" h. **125.00**
Figure of a woman, "Sue Ellen,"
Godey series, grey & maroon,
8¼" h. **160.00**

Figure of a woman, "Camille,"
8½" h. **325.00**

Figure of a woman, "Charmaine,"
colorful decoration, 8½" h. **450.00**

Figure of a woman, "Claudia," grey
over pink, 8½" h. **250.00**

Matilda

Figure of a woman, "Matilda,"
8½" h. (ILLUS.) **175.00**

Figure of a woman, "Roberta,"
8½" h. **295.00**

Figure of a woman, "Spring
Reverie," standing w/bird on hand,
8½" h. **850.00**

Figure of a woman, "Elizabeth,"
seated on settee, 7" w., 8½" h. **600.00**

Figure of a woman, "Victoria,"
seated on Victorian settee, 8½" l.,
7" h. **725.00**

Figure of a woman, "Musette,"
Godey series, 8¾" h. **495.00**

Figure of a woman, "Scarlett,"
Godey design, 8¾" h. **300.00**

Figure of a woman, "Scarlett,"
Godey series, hands free, 8¾" h. . . **850.00**

Figure of a woman, "Amber,"
9¼" h. **625.00**

Figure of a woman, "Vivian,"
w/parasol, 10" h. **385.00**

Figure of a woman, "Georgette,"
Godey series, 10¼" h. **650.00**

Figures, Chinese boy & girl, blue &
chartreuse, pr. **110.00**

Figures, "Scarlett" & "Rhett," 8¾" &
9" h., pr. **650.00**

Figures, Marie Antoinette & Louis
XVI, 10" h., pr. **1,295.00**

Figures, "Prima Donna" & "Leading
Man," 10¼" h., pr. **1,600.00**

Figures, "Blue Boy" & "Pinkie,"
12" h., pr. **1,500.00**

Figures, Madame Pompadour &
Louis XV, 12½" h., pr. **1,495.00**

Figure group, "Story Hour," mother
w/girl, 8" l., 6¼" h. **1,350.00**

Figure group, "Story Hour," mother
w/girl & boy, 8" l., 6¼" h. **1,750.00**

Flower holder, figural, "Lyn," a
standing Victorian lady wearing a
long flaring pleated dress, brunette
hair, cream dress & bonnet
w/emerald green trim, signed,
5¾" h. **50.00**

Flower holder, figural girl, "Wendy,"
6¼" h. **85.00**

Flower holder, figural girl, "Kay,"
7" h. **85.00**

Flower holder, figural lady, "Emily,"
8" h. **85.00**

Models of Pouter Pigeons, white, pr. . . **795.00**

Powder box, cov., figural "Diana" **325.00**

FLOW BLUE

Flow Blue ironstone and semi-porcelain was manufactured mainly in England during the second half of the 19th century. The early ironstone was produced by many of the well known English potters and was either transfer-printed or hand-painted (Brush stroke). The bulk of the ware was exported to the United States or Canada.

The "flow" or running quality of the cobalt blue designs was the result of introducing certain chemicals into the kiln during the final firing. Some patterns are so "flown" that it is difficult to ascertain the design. The transfers were of several types: Asian, Scenic, Marble or Floral.

The earliest Flow Blue ironstone patterns were produced during the period between about 1840 and 1860. After the Civil War Flow Blue went out of style for some years but was again manufactured and exported to the United States beginning about the 1880s and continuing through the turn-of-the-century. These later Flow Blue designs are on a semi-porcelain body rather than heavier ironstone and the designs are mainly florals.

ADAMS (Wood & Son, New Wharf Pottery, late)

Vegetable dish, open, oval, 7 x 12" . . **$55.00**

AMERILLIA (Podmore, Walker & Co., ca. 1840s-50s)

Plate, 8½" d. **75.00**

Plate, 10½" d. **160.00**

Amerillia Teapot

Teapot, cov., oval body style
(ILLUS.)..................... 800.00

AMOY (Davenport, dated 1844)

Creamer, 6"..................... 295.00
Cup & saucer, handleless 125.00
Gravy boat 395.00
Plate, 7½" d..................... 70.00
Plate, 8½" d..................... 80.00
Plate, 9" w..................... 175.00
Plate, 9½" d..................... 110.00
Plate, 10½" d.................... 150.00

Amoy Potato Bowl

Potato bowl, 12¼" d. (ILLUS.) 350.00
Soup plate w/flanged rim 150.00
Sugar, cov...................... 400.00
Teapot, cov..................... 650.00
Vegetable bowl, open, 8" l. 595.00
Vegetable bowl, open, 10" l. 795.00

Amoy Waste Bowl

Waste bowl, "double bulge" (ILLUS.) . 300.00

ARABESQUE (T.J. & J. Mayer, ca. 1845)

Creamer 495.00

ARGYLE (W.H. Grindley , ca. 1896)

Butter, cover & drainer 595.00
Cup & saucer, handled 95.00
Gravy boat 195.00
Ladle, sauce.................... 700.00
Pitcher, 1 pt.................... 375.00
Plate, 7" d..................... 65.00
Plate, 8" d..................... 75.00
Plate, 9" d..................... 85.00
Plate, 10" d.................... 95.00
Sauce dish 50.00
Sauce tureen, 3 pcs. 495.00
Soup plate w/flanged rim, 9" d...... 90.00
Vegetable bowl, open, small 165.00

ASHBURTON (Norwich, W.H. Grindley, ca.1890s)

Butter pat 50.00

BEAUTIES OF CHINA (Mellor, Venables, ca.1845)

Plate, 7½" w. 75.00

CAMBRIDGE (Alfred Meakin, ca. 1891)

Pitcher, milk 325.00
Soup plate 92.00

CANTON (John Maddock, ca. 1850)

Cup & saucer, handleless 175.00

CASHMERE (Francis Morley, until 1858)

Creamer, 5".................... 950.00
Creamer, 6", Primary shape 495.00
Pitcher, 2 qt. 1,500.00
Pitcher & bowl 4,000.00
Sauce tureen, 3 pcs. 995.00
Soup plate w/flanged rim, 10½" d. ... 200.00
Sugar, cov..................... 550.00
Teapot, cov., straightline, Primary
shape 1,200.00

CHAPOO (John Wedge Wood, ca. 1850)

Creamer, 6", Primary shape 500.00
Cup & saucer, handled 150.00
Gravy boat 250.00
Plate, 7⅜" d.................... 100.00
Platter, 16" l................... 550.00
Soup plate w/flanged rim, 10" d..... 135.00

Teapot, cov., Primary shape. **700.00**
Waste bowl, sixteen-panelled **175.00**

CHUSAN (Podmore,Walker & Co., ca. 1845)

Vegetable dish, cov. **995.00**

COBURG (John Edwards, ca. 1860)

Teapot, cov. **1,025.00**

CONWAY (New Wharf Pottery, ca. 1891)

Plate, 10½" l. oval **85.00**

DOROTHY (Johnson Bros., ca. 1900)

Bone dish **60.00**

DUNDEE (Ridgways, ca. 1910)

Bone dish **45.00**

FESTOON (W.H. Grindley, ca. 1891)

Washbowl & pitcher, the set **1,395.00**

FLORIDA (W. H. Grindley or Johnson Brothers, ca. 1895)

Cup & saucer, handled **100.00**
Plate, 8½" d. **100.00**
Plate, 10" d. **135.00**
Soup plate w/flanged rim, 8" d.. . . . . **130.00**
Vegetable bowl, open, small **125.00**

GOTHIC (Jacob Furnival, ca. 1850)

Platter, 18" l. **895.00**

GRAPE & BLUEBELL W/CHERRY BORDER (brush-stroke painted, m.u., ca. 1850)

Grape & Bluebell Plate

Plate, 8" d. (ILLUS.) **150.00**
Platter, 16" l. **500.00**

HONG KONG (Charles Meigh, ca. 1845)

Hong Kong Cup & Saucer

Cup & saucer, handled, farmer size,
  cup 4¼" d., 3½" h. (ILLUS.). **295.00**
Cuspidor, lady's **850.00**
Gravy boat **300.00**
Plate, 10½" d. **100.00**
Sugar bowl, cov. **595.00**
Teapot, cov. **1,095.00**
Waste bowl **175.00**

JAPAN (Thos. Fell & Co., ca. 1860)

Cup & saucer, handleless **130.00**
Pitcher, hexagonal, 8" h. **475.00**
Plate, 8½" d. **125.00**
Plate, 9½" d. **130.00**
Plate, 10½" d. **150.00**
Platter, 18" l. **350.00**

LA BELLE (Wheeling Pottery, ca. 1900)

Bowl, handled. **150.00**
Bowl, large, helmet-shaped **400.00**
Cake plate **175.00**
Celery dish. **225.00**
Charger, 13" d. **325.00**

La Belle Charger

Charger, 12" d. (ILLUS. prev. page). . **225.00**
Chocolate pot, cov. **875.00**
Cracker jar, cov., 7½" h. **575.00**
Creamer, 4" h. **350.00**
Cup & saucer, handled **175.00**

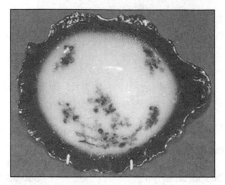

La Belle Dessert Dish

Dessert dish, fancy (ILLUS.) **125.00**
Mug, chocolate **600.00**

La Belle Pitcher

Pitcher, portrait-type, lip repair
    (ILLUS.) **770.00**
Pitcher, 6½" h. **375.00**
Pitcher, 7½" h. **400.00**
Plate, 8" d. **100.00**
Plate, 10" d. **135.00**
Soup plate, 8" d. **125.00**
Teapot set: cov. teapot, cov. sugar,
    creamer, 3 pcs. **4,000.00**

La Belle Vegetable Bowl

Vegetable bowl, cov., round
    (ILLUS.) **300.00**
Vegetable bowl, open, 7½" d. **175.00**

LA FRANCAIS (French China Co., ca. 1890)

Butter dish, cov. **95.00**
Butter pat **15.00**
Butter pat, scenic decoration **22.00**

LEAF & FLOWER (unknown maker, brush-stroke painted, ca. 1860)

Leaf & Flower Ale Mug

Ale mug, (ILLUS.). **195.00**
Platter, 16" l. **395.00**

LORNE (W.H. Grindley, ca. 1900)

Butter pat **60.00**
Platter, 14" l. **225.00**
Vegetable bowl, cov. **265.00**

LUCERNE (New Wharf Pottery, ca. 1891)

Vegetable dish, cov. **140.00**

MANHATTAN (Johnson Bros., ca. 1895)

Creamer **200.00**
Sugar, cov. **250.00**

Manhattan Teapot

Teapot, cov., (ILLUS.). 595.00
Wash basin 150.00

MANILLA (Podmore, Walker & Co., ca. 1845)

Creamer, 6", Primary shape 300.00
Dish, dessert, 6" d. 125.00
Gravy boat 225.00
Pitcher, milk, 7" h.. . . . . 350.00
Plate, 7" d.. . . . . 140.00
Plate, 8" d.. . . . . 125.00
Plate, 9" d.. . . . . 135.00
Plate, 10½" d. 150.00

Manilla Platter

Platter, 16" l. (ILLUS.). 450.00
Punch cup 200.00
Sauce dish 125.00
Sauce tureen, 3 pcs. 950.00
Sugar bowl, cov., full panel Gothic. . . 550.00
Vegetable bowl, cov., long octagon. . 600.00

MARECHAL NIEL (W. H. Grindley ca. 1891)

Vegetable dish, cov. 275.00

MARGUERITE (W.H. Grindley, ca. 1891)

Bone dish. 55.00

MELBOURNE (W.H. Grindley, ca. 1900)

Platter, 16" l. 275.00

NANKIN (Davenport, ca. 1850)

Vegetable bowl, cov. 850.00

NON PAREIL (Burgess & Leigh, ca. 1891)

Bone dish. 80.00
Cake plate, handled, 11" d. 395.00
Cup & saucer, handled 165.00
Plate, 8" d.. . . . . 90.00
Plate, 9" d.. . . . . 100.00
Plate, 10" d.. . . . . 120.00
Platter, 15½" l. 395.00
Sauce tureen, 4 pcs. 900.00
Soup plate, 8" d.. . . . . 120.00

Non Pareil Soup Tureen

Soup tureen, 2 pcs. (ILLUS.) 650.00
Soup tureen undertray 700.00

Non Pareil Teapot

Teapot, cov. (ILLUS.) 800.00

NORMANDY (Johnson Bros., ca. 1900)

Plate, 9" d. 90.00

OREGON (T. J. and J. Mayer, ca. 1845)

Creamer, classic Gothic, 5" h. 600.00
Plate, 7½" d.. . . . . 70.00
Plate, 9½" d.. . . . . 100.00

Plate, 10½" d. 150.00
Platter, 16" d. 475.00
Platter, 18" d. 550.00
Sugar bowl, cov., Primary shape 350.00
Teapot, cov. 650.00
Waste bowl. 250.00

OSBORNE (Ridgways, ca.1905)

Egg cup, large 125.00

PELEW (E. Challinor, ca. 1850)

Pelew Water Pitcher

Pitcher, water, 9" h. (ILLUS.) 900.00
Relish dish 275.00
Soup plate, 10½" d. 175.00
Teapot, classic Gothic style 650.00
Vegetable dish, open, rectangular
    w/cut-corners, 7⅝" l. 165.00

ROSE (W.H. Grindley, ca. 1893)

Bone dish 60.00

ROXBURY (Ridgway, ca. 1910)

Platter, 14 x 17½", oval w/serpentine
    beaded rim 165.00

SCINDE (J.&G. Alcock, ca.1840 & Thomas Walker, ca. 1847)

Casserole dish, cov., fourteen
    sided. 1,000.00
Chamber pot 425.00
Creamer, primary shape 350.00
Cup & saucer, handled 150.00
Cup & saucer, handleless 125.00
Gravy boat 250.00
Hot water plate 2,000.00
Pitcher, six-sided 475.00
Plate, 7½" d. 75.00
Plate, 8½" d. 85.00
Plate, 9½" d. 110.00

Plate, 10½" d. 150.00
Platter, 11" l. 250.00
Platter, 20" l. 1,895.00
Sauce tureen, long octagon, 2 pcs. . . 425.00
Soup plate, 10½" d. 150.00
Sugar, cov., primary shape 425.00
Sugar bowl, cov. 550.00
Sugar bowl, cov. 595.00
Teapot, cov., full panel, Gothic
    shape 1,000.00
Teapot, cov., Gothic shape, large (no
    harm interior spider) 950.00
Teapot, cov., pumpkin-shaped 650.00
Vegetable bowl, cov., figural rosebud
    finial. 950.00
Waste bowl 413.00
Waste jar, cov. 7,500.00

SHANGHAI (W.H. Grindley, ca. 1891)

Butter pat 55.00

SHELL (Wood & Challinor, ca. 1840; E. Challinor, ca. 1860)

Butter dish, cov. 895.00

SOBRAON (Unknown, probably English, ca.1850)

Platter, 15" l. 475.00
Platter, 20" l. 1,895.00
Waste bowl. 325.00

TEMPLE (Podmore, Walker & Co., ca. 1850)

Cup & saucer, handled 225.00
Cup & saucer, handleless 185.00
Pitcher, 8" h. 700.00
Pitcher, 10½" h. 150.00
Relish dish, mitten-shaped 325.00
Soup plate, 10½" d. 150.00
Vegetable bowl, cov. 500.00

TOURAINE (Henry Alcock, ca. 1898 & Stanley Pottery, ca. 1898)

Bone dish. 60.00
Bowl, cereal 60.00
Cake plate 175.00
Creamer 238.00
Creamer & cov. sugar bowl, pr. 495.00

Touraine Cup & Saucer

Cup & saucer, handled (ILLUS.) 93.00
Gravy boat 200.00
Milk jug, 6" h. 375.00
Pitcher, milk, large 1,095.00
Plate, 7" d. 65.00
Plate, 8" d. 70.00
Plate, 8¾" d. 68.00
Plate, 9" d. 80.00
Plate, 10" d. 135.00
Platter, 15" oval 235.00
Salt dip 100.00
Sauce dish 50.00
Soup plate, 7½" d. 80.00
Sugar bowl, cov. 350.00
Teapot, cov. 650.00
Vegetable bowl, cov. 363.00
Vegetable bowl, open, 9" l., oval 108.00
Waste bowl 163.00

TRILBY (Wood & Sons, ca. 1891)
Pitcher, hot water 150.00
Shaving mug, cov. 140.00

TROY (Charles Meigh, ca. 1840)
Soup plate, flanged rim, 10½" d. 150.00

VERMONT (Burgess & Leigh, ca. 1896)
Butter pat 50.00

WARWICK PANSY (Warwick China Co., ca.1900)
Creamer, embossed design 225.00
Dresser tray 225.00

WAVERLY (John Maddock & Son, ca. 1891)
Butter pat 50.00

WHAMPOA (Mellor and Venables, ca. 1840)
Gravy boat 175.00
Plate, 7½" d. 75.00
Plate, 8½" d. 85.00
Plate, 9½" d. 115.00
Plate, 10½" d. 160.00
Platter, 16" l. 450.00
Platter, 18" l. 500.00

Whampoa Sugar Bowl

Sugar bowl, cov., Primary shape
    (ILLUS.) 395.00

FRANCISCAN WARE

A product of Gladding, McBean & Company of Glendale and Los Angeles, California, Franciscan Ware was one of a number of lines produced by that firm over its long history. Introduced in 1934 as a pottery dinnerware, Franciscan Ware was produced in many patterns including "Desert Rose," introduced in 1941 and reportedly the most popular dinnerware pattern ever made in this country. Beginning in 1942 some vitrified china patterns were produced under the Franciscan name also.

After a merger in 1963 the company name was changed to Interpace Corporation and in 1979 Josiah Wedgwood & Sons purchased the Gladding, McBean & Co. plant from Interpace. American production ceased in 1984.

Franciscan Mark

Ashtray, Apple patt. $75.00
Ashtray, individual, Desert Rose patt. . . 25.00
Ashtray, Poppy patt. 35.00
Ashtray, individual, mariposa lily
    shape, Wildflower patt., 3½" d. 95.00
Baking dish, Cafe Royal patt., 8¾ x
    9½", 1 qt. 160.00
Bell, Cafe Royal patt., 3¾" d., 6" h. . . . 95.00
Bowl, berry, California Poppy patt. 25.00
Bowl, fruit, 5¼" d., Apple patt.,
    ca.1940 . . . . 12.00

Bowl, fruit, 5¼" d., Desert Rose patt.,
ca. 1941. . . . . **10.00**
Bowl, fruit, 5½" d., Desert Rose patt. . . . **8.00**
Bowl, cereal or soup, 6" d., Apple
patt., ca. 1940 . . . . **15.00**
Bowl, cereal or soup, 6" d., Desert
Rose patt., ca. 1941 . . . . **10.00**
Bowl, salad, 10" d., 3¼" h., Apple
patt. **25.00**
Bowl, salad, 10½" d., Desert Rose
patt. **110.00**
Bowl, salad, 11¼" d., 3¼" h., Ivy
patt., green rim band **125.00**
Box, cov., heart-shaped, Cafe Royal
patt., 5 x 5", 2¼" h. **115.00**
Butter dish, cov., Apple patt. **40.00**

Desert Rose Butter Dish

Butter dish, cov., Desert Rose patt.
(ILLUS.). **38.00**
Candleholders, Apple patt., pr. **65.00**
Casserole, cov., individual size,
handled, Apple patt., 4" **75.00**
Casserole, cov., Desert Rose patt.,
ca. 1941, 1½ qt., 4¾" h. **85.00**
Celery dish, Apple patt. **25.00**
Child's plate, divided, oval, Desert
Rose patt., 7 X 9" **188.00**
Cigarette box, cov., Apple patt. **145.00**
Coffeepot, cov., Desert Rose patt.,
7½" h. **90.00**
Coffeepot, cov., Ivy patt., green rim
band, 7½" h. **225.00**
Compote, open, Apple patt., 8" d.,
4" h. **55.00**
Cookie jar, cov., Apple patt. **275.00**
Cookie jar, cov., Desert Rose patt.,
9¼" h. **365.00**
Creamer, Desert Rose patt. **24.00**
Creamer, large, Apple patt., ca. 1940. . **20.00**
Creamer, Bountiful patt., 4¼" h. **35.00**
Creamer & cov. sugar bowl, Apple
patt., pr. **40.00**
Creamer & cov. sugar bowl,
demitasse, Apple patt., ca. 1940, pr. **65.00**
Creamer & cov. sugar bowl, Desert
Rose patt., pr. **30.00**
Creamer & cov. sugar bowl,
October patt., pr. **38.00**
Cup & saucer, Apple patt. **10.00**

Cup & saucer, California Poppy patt. . . **35.00**
Cup & saucer, demitasse, Desert
Rose patt. **53.00**
Cup & saucer, Desert Rose patt. **8.00**
Dish, heart-shaped, Desert Rose
patt. **115.00**
Egg cup, Desert Rose patt. **35.00**
Ginger jar, cov., Apple patt. **150.00**
Gravy boat w/attached undertray,
Apple patt. **48.00**
Jam jar, cov., Desert Rose patt. **70.00**
Jam jar, cov., re-designed style,
Apple patt. **450.00**
Mixing bowl, Apple patt., 7½" d. **125.00**
Mixing bowl set, Apple patt., 3 pcs. . . **350.00**
Mixing bowl set, Desert Rose patt.,
3 pcs. **500.00**
Mug, Apple patt. **25.00**
Mug, Desert Rose patt., 10 oz. **30.00**
Mug, bulbous shape, Desert Rose
patt., 7 oz. **20.00**
Mug, Cafe Royal patt., 2¾" h., 7 oz. . . . **40.00**
Mug, cocoa, Apple patt., 10 oz. **125.00**
Mug, Desert Rose patt., 12 oz. **40.00**
Napkin ring, Desert Rose patt. **35.00**
Pitcher, milk, 6¼" h., Apple patt.,
ca. 1940, 1 qt. **95.00**
Pitcher, water, 8¾" h., Apple patt.,
2 qt. **80.00**
Pitcher, water, 8¾" h., Desert Rose
patt., 2½ qt. **91.00**
Plate, 6" d., California Poppy patt. **10.00**
Plate, bread & butter, 6½" d., Apple
patt., ca. 1940 . . . . **6.00**
Plate, bread & butter, 6½" d., Desert
Rose patt. **6.00**
Plate, coupe desert, 7½" d., Desert
Rose patt. **115.00**
Plate, salad, 8" d., California Poppy
patt. **55.00**
Plate, snack, 8" sq., Desert Rose
patt. **233.00**
Plate, side salad, 4½ x 8", crescent-
shaped, Desert Rose patt. **38.00**
Plate, salad, 8½" d., Apple patt., ca.
1940 . . . . **18.00**
Plate, salad, 8½" d., Desert Rose
patt. **10.00**
Plate, dinner, 10½" d., Apple patt..
ca. 1940. . . . . **22.00**
Plate, dinner, 10½" d.,California
Poppy patt. **35.00**
Plate, dinner, 10½" d., Coronado
Table Ware, ivory matt **18.00**
Plate, dinner, 10½" d., Desert Rose
patt. **16.00**
Plate, grill, 11" d., Apple patt. **100.00**
Plate, chop, 12" d., California Poppy
patt. **120.00**
Platter, 8½ x 12" oval, Cafe Royal
patt. **32.00**

Platter, 12¾"l., Desert Rose patt. 30.00
Platter, 13" l. oval, Ivy patt., ca. 1948 . . 60.00
Platter, 14" l., Apple patt. 57.00
Platter, 14" l., Desert Rose patt. 46.00
Platter, 19" l., oval, Ivy patt., green
    rim band 275.00
Platter, 19" oval, turkey-size, Desert
    Rose patt., ... 195.00
Relish dish, Apple patt., 10" oval 12.00
Relish dish, three-part, Apple
    patt.,11¾" l. 68.00
Relish dish, three-part, oval, Desert
    Rose patt., 12" l. 40.00
Salt & pepper shakers, Desert Rose
    patt., pr. 18.00
Salt & pepper shakers, Apple patt.,
    tall, 6¼" h., pr. 125.00
Salt & pepper shakers, Desert Rose
    patt., tall, 6¼" h., pr. 48.00
Salt shaker & pepper mill, Desert
    Rose patt., pr. 195.00
Serving bowl, Cafe Royal patt., 7¾ x
    15½", 2¼" h. 400.00
Serving bowl, Desert Rose patt., 7¾
    x 15½", 2¼" h. 500.00
Sherbet, footed, Apple patt., 2½" h. . . . 19.00
Soup plate w/flanged rim, Apple
    patt., 8½" d. 19.00
Soup plate w/flanged rim, Desert
    Rose patt., 8½" d. 20.00
Sugar bowl, cov., Bountiful patt. 45.00
Sugar bowl, open, individual size,
    Desert Rose patt. 145.00
Syrup pitcher, Starburst patt.,
    5¾" h. 65.00
Syrup pitcher, Apple patt., 1 pt.,
    6¼" h. 80.00
Syrup pitcher, Desert Rose patt.,
    1 qt., 6½" h. 95.00
Tea tile, Apple patt., 6" w. 45.00
Teapot, cov., flask spout-style, Apple
    patt. 50.00
Teapot, cov., Ivy patt., green rim
    band, 4¾" h. 275.00
Trivet, round, Apple patt., 6" d. 225.00
Tumbler, juice, Apple patt., 6 oz.,
    3¼" h. 35.00
Tumbler, juice, Desert Rose patt.,
    6 oz., 3¼" h. 55.00
Tumbler, Apple patt., 10 oz., 5¼" h. . . . 40.00
Tumbler, Desert Rose patt., 10 oz.,
    5¼" h. 28.00
Tureen, cov., flat-bottomed, Desert
    Rose patt., 8" d., 5" h. 425.00
Tureen, cov., footed, Apple patt.,
    small, 8¾" d., 5¾" h. 395.00
TV tray, w/cup well, oval, Desert
    Rose patt., 14" l. 175.00
Vase, bud, 6" h., Desert Rose
    patt. . . . . 100.00 to 120.00

Vegetable bowl, 8" d., round, Desert
    Rose patt. 25.00
Vegetable bowl, 9" d., round, Desert
    Rose patt. 35.00
Vegetable bowl, divided, Desert
    Rose patt., 7 x 10¾" 45.00
Vegetable dish, divided, Apple patt.,
    7 x 10¾" 35.00

FRANKOMA

John Frank began producing and selling pottery on a part-time basis during the summer of 1933 while he was still teaching art and pottery classes at the University of Oklahoma. In 1934, Frankoma Pottery became an incorporated business that was successful enough to allow him to leave his teaching position in 1936 to devote full time to its growth. The pottery was moved to Sapulpa, Oklahoma in 1938 and a full range of art pottery and dinnerwares were eventually offered. In 1953 Frankoma switched from Ada clay to clay found in Sapulpa. Since John Franks' death in 1973, the pottery has been directed by his daughter, Janiece. In early 1991 Richard Bernstein became owner and president of Frankoma Pottery which was renamed Frankoma Industries. Janiece Frank serves as vice president and general manager. The early wares and limited editions are becoming increasingly popular with collectors today.

Frankoma Mark

Bucking Bronco Book Ends

Book ends, model of a bucking
    bronco, green glaze, Ada clay,
    Model No. 420, 6" h. pr.
    (ILLUS.) $175.00
**Figures of Gardener & Gardener
    Boy,** blue glaze, pr. 210.00

Figures of Gardener & Gardener
Boy, boy w/suspenders, Desert
Gold glaze, pr. **228.00**

1969 Elephant Mug

Mug, 1969 (Republican) elephant,
flame-red glaze (ILLUS.) **79.00**
Plate, 8½" d., Christmas, 1968,
"Flight Into Egypt" **28.00**

FULPER

The Fulper Pottery was founded in Flemington, New Jersey, in 1805 and operated until 1935, although operations were curtailed in 1929 when its main plant was destroyed by fire. The name was changed in 1929 to Stangl Pottery, which continued in operation until July of 1978, when Pfaltzgraff, a division of Susquehanna Broadcasting Company of York, Pennsylvania, purchased the assets of the Stangl Pottery, including the name.

Fulper Marks

Various Fulper Pieces

Bowl, 13½" d., 4½" h., the interior w/a striated blue & white glossy glaze, the rim w/a dark green striated glossy glaze shading to a satin matte glaze, vertical ink stamp mark **$460.00**
Candlesticks, creamy white glossy glaze on a tobacco brown ground, vertical ink stamp mark, 4½" d., 9½" h., pr. **173.00**
Candlesticks, flaring socket on a simple four-sided columnar standard above the flaring, stepped round foot, top w/a glossy ivory shading down to a streaked French blue glaze, rectangular ink mark, 4" d., 10½" h., pr. (ILLUS. of one, No.8, pg. 99) **770.00**
Center bowl, deep wide rounded ribbed bowl raised on a short tapering pedestal w/a flaring round foot, the rim w/a wide, flattened edge, blue crystalline glaze, vertical ink racetrack mark, 11" d., 6½" h. (ILLUS. No. 6, pg. 99) **385.00**
Center bowl, Effigy-type, a wide flat-bottomed shallow bowl w/incurved sides raised on three crouching figures resting on a molded thick disc base, peacock feather-effect cat's eye glaze, the exterior in a matte mustard yellow & cafe-au-lait brown, rectangular ink mark, 10½" d., 7½" h. **825.00**
Humidor, cov.,"Keramidor," wide gently tapering cylindrical body w/a low sloping fitted cover w/a large knob finial, overall dark gunmetal glaze, incised racetrack mark & paper labels, 7" d., 6¼" h. **330.00**
Lamp, table-model, molded in high-relief w/four stylized fish under a dramatic blue crystalline glaze, 7" d., 20" h. **920.00**
Urn, Classical-style, slender shoulder baluster-form w/trumpet neck flanked by incurved scroll handles from rim to shoulder, cobalt & periwinkle blue glaze, ink racetrack mark **220.00**
Urn, tall footed tapering ovoid body w/an angled shoulder mounted w/inward-scrolling upright handles flanking the cylindrical waisted neck, periwinkle blue & green flambé glaze, ink racetrack mark, 7½" d., 15" h. **660.00**
Vase, miniature, 3" h., 2½" d., footed squatty bulbous baluster form w/short flaring neck, overall gunmetal flambé glaze, rectangular ink mark (ILLUS. No. 4, pg. 99) **165.00**

Vase, miniature, 3¾" h., 3¾" d., small ovoid body w/a wide flat mouth, raised on a thin footring, sheer blue & ivory flambé glaze dripping over a matte mustard yellow ground, rectangular ink mark **193.00**

Vase, 4½" h., 4½" d., lobed bell pepper-shaped on a thin footring, small closed mouth, mottled matte green & purple microcrystalline glaze, rectangular ink mark **605.00**

Vase, 4½" h., 4½" d., spherical lobed bell pepper-form, dark blue flambé over mustard yellow speckled matte glaze, rectangular ink mark **990.00**

Vase, 4¾" h., 3¾" d., swelled cylindrical body w/an angled shoulder to the short cylindrical neck, cat's-eye over mustard yellow flambé glaze, rectangular ink mark **330.00**

Vase, 5" h., 3½" d., narrow footring on a swelled cylindrical body w/a rounded shoulder to the short rounded cylindrical neck, rich silvery Flemington Green glaze, early ink mark **413.00**

Vase, 5" h., 6" d., squatty bulbous bottom w/a wide angled shoulder at the center below the wide, tapering upper half, square curled handles from rim to shoulders, frothy Copperdust Crystalline glaze, incised racetrack mark (ILLUS. No. 2, pg. 99). **468.00**

Vase, 5½" h., 7" d., narrow footring on a bulbous nearly spherical body w/a small closed rim, mottled matte green, blue & Rose Famille glaze, rectangular ink mark (small grinding chips on base) **440.00**

Vase, 5½" h., 8" d., wide squatty bulbous body on a thin footring, the upper sides tapering to a small, short rolled neck, frothy green matte glaze, ink racetrack mark . . . **550.00**

Vase, 6½" h., 5" d., swelled cylindrical body w/a narrow angled shoulder to the wide short waisted cylindrical neck w/a widely flaring rim, three flat strap handles from rim to edge of shoulder, mahogany & elephant's breath flambé glaze, ink racetrack mark **495.00**

Vase, 6½" h., 7½" d., bulbous nearly spherical body w/a short cylindrical wide neck flanked by three small loop shoulder handles, leopard skin crystalline glaze, incised racetrack mark **715.00**

Vase, 7" h., 4" d., simple ovoid body tapering to a short cylindrical rim, copperdust crystalline & gunmetal flambé glaze, raised vertical mark . . **440.00**

Vase, 7½" h., 5" d., shouldered ovoid body w/a short cylindrical neck w/a widely flaring rim, mirrored black over Rose Famille glaze, incised racetrack mark **495.00**

Vase, 7½" h., 5½" d., bulbous ovoid body w/a short waisted cylindrical neck w/a widely flaring rim, lustrous green flambé glaze, ink racetrack mark **385.00**

Vase, 7¾" h., 5" d., baluster-form body w/bulbous upper section below the short flaring neck flanked by squared handles, frothy mirrored blue crystalline flambé glaze, incised racetrack mark (ILLUS. No. 5, pg. 99) **303.00**

Vase, 7¾" h., 6" d., footed squatty bulbous bottle-form body w/a tall neck & flared rim, overall Mirrored Black crystalline glaze, incised racetrack mark (ILLUS. No. 7 , pg. 99) **660.00**

Vase. 8" h., 4" d., bottle-form, ovoid body tapering to a tall slender cylindrical 'stick' neck, base of neck wrapped w/the model of a salamander, blue & dark green flambé glaze, rectangular ink mark **715.00**

Vase, 8" h., 5½" d., 'flag-type,' a bulbous baluster-form w/a nearly spherical body raised on a small flaring pedestal base & tapering to a small flaring cylindrical neck, the shoulder w/three slightly smaller flaring cylindrical necks, mahogany, ivory & green flambé glaze, rectangular ink mark **605.00**

Vase, 8" h., 6¾" d., small cylindrical foot supporting the bulbous ovoid body tapering to a wide cylindrical neck w/a flared rim, angled loop shoulder handles, mirrored green over mahogany flambé glaze, rectangular ink mark (scratch & minor roughness on rim) **330.00**

Vase, 8" h., 8" d., wide bulbous ovoid body w/the wide rounded shoulder centering a short cylindrical neck, gunmetal, blue & Rose Famille flambé glaze, raised vertical racetrack mark **660.00**

Vase, 8½" h., 5½" d., 'flag-type,' bulbous baluster-form body w/a small pedestal base short trumpet neck centering three other small trumpet necks around the wide shoulder, textured bluish green microcrystalline glaze, impressed vertical racetrack mark **880.00**

Vase, 9½" h., 7" d., bulbous body w/two handles, crystalline dust glaze striated over a green glossy ground, raised vertical mark **431.00**

Vase, 9½" h., 8" d., a half-round base w/an angled shoulder band below the tall tapering sides flanked by angled, pierced long buttress handles, bluish green & blush flambé glaze, raised racetrack mark **468.00**

Vase, 10" h., 5½" d., seven-sided gently tapering ovoid body, fine frothy mirror blue, brown & ivory flambé glaze, bruise & short line at rim, incised racetrack mark (ILLUS. No. 1, pg. 99) **440.00**

Vase, 10¾" h., 4½" d., slender baluster-form body, leopard skin crystalline glaze, incised vertical racetrack mark **495.00**

Vase, 11" h., 4½" d., tall slender slightly waisted cylindrical form w/pierced angular buttress handles from the rim down the sides, celadon green microcrystalline flambé glaze, incised racetrack mark **495.00**

Vase, 11" h., 5½" d., hexagonal baluster-form, turquoise crystalline & moss green flambé glaze, incised racetrack mark **330.00**

Vase, 11" h., 5½" w., hexagonal baluster-form, streaky dark green & blue flambé glaze below the streaky creamy neck, impressed vertical racetrack mark **523.00**

Vase, 12" h., 4½" d., slender baluster-form body w/a short trumpet neck, leopard skin crystalline glaze in shades of light & dark green, incised vertical racetrack mark, remnant of paper label **440.00**

Vase, 12" h., 9½" d., wide gently tapering cylindrical body w/a rounded bottom edge & closed flat rim, cat's-eye flambé glaze, incised racetrack mark **1,100.00**

Vase, 12½" h., 8" d., bulbous ovoid ring-molded body tapering to a waisted cylindrical neck, small scrolled loop shoulder handles, ivory, gunmetal & mahogany flambé glaze, incised racetrack mark **715.00**

Vase, 13" h., 11" d., wide bulbous ovoid body w/a broad shoulder below the rounded short cylindrical neck, frothy gunmetal & hare's fur glaze dripping over a textured microcrystalline sky blue glaze, raised racetrack mark **4,125.00**

Vase, 13" h., 11½" d., urn-form, wide ovoid body tapering to a wide short cylindrical neck w/a molded rim, four small C-form loop handles around the shoulder, fine blue crystalline glaze, incised vertical racetrack mark **1,430.00**

Vase, 13¼" h., 6" d., tall baluster-form body w/short flaring neck, vibrant Cat's Eye flambé glaze, stilt pull on base, incised racetrack mark (ILLUS. No. 3, pg. 99) **660.00**

Vases, bud, 5½" h., 3¾" d., footed wide very squatty body centered by a tall cylindrical 'stick' neck, Flemington Green glaze, rectangular ink mark, pr. **275.00**

GALLÉ POTTERY

Fine pottery was made by Emile Gallé, the multi-talented French designer and artisan, who is also famous for his glass and furniture. The pottery is relatively scarce.

Gallé Pottery Mark

Gallé Pottery Pieces

Pitcher, 9" h., figural, a footed bulbous squatty body w/swirled rib surface centered by a tall cylindrical neck w/rim spout & looped branch handle opposite a swan's-neck spout w/a duck head finial, underglaze decorated on pansies trimmed w/gold, impressed "E (cross) G" & marked in red "E. Gallé Nancy deposé," glaze chip on top rim (ILLUS. center) **$1,265.00**

Plaque, pierced to hang, round, decorated in the Limoges style w/a bucolic landscape featuring four cows, marked in black underglaze "E. Gallé - E (cross) G," 12½" d. (ILLUS. left) **748.00**

Plaque, pierced to hang, oblong cartouche from w/a large shell at the top center & small shells at the center of each side, decorative border bands & the center w/a large stylized birds on a scrolling branch in grey, amber & Delft blue in a tin glaze, inscribed "Gallé – Nancy," 12½ x 14" (ILLUS. right) . . **575.00**

Plates, 9" d., each enamel-decorated w/a variety of insects, fruits & vegetation, printed marks, late 19th c., set of 11 . . . . **1,495.00**

Tray, oval, painted underglaze w/a genre scene of a child at play w/a ram pull-toy & winged insect at each side, molded mark in lower left "E (cross) G," 19th c., 8¾ x 15¼" **633.00**

GAUDY DUTCH

This name is applied to English earthenware with designs copied from Oriental patterns. Production began in the 18th century. These copies flooded into this country in the early 19th century. The incorporation of the word "Dutch" derives from the fact that it was the Dutch who first brought the Oriental wares into Europe. The ware was not, as often erroneously reported, made specifically for the Pennsylvania Dutch.

Cup & saucer, handleless, Butterfly patt. (minor enamel flaking & small table ring chips) **$660.00**

Gaudy Dutch Plates

Plate, 8¼" d., Carnation patt., wear & repair (ILLUS. left) **220.00**

Plate, 8¼" d., Grape patt., wear, stains, faded enamel (ILLUS. center) **297.00**

Plate, 8⅜" d., Butterfly patt., chip on back rim, wear, repair, retouched colors (ILLUS. right) **385.00**

Waste bowl, footed deep flaring sides, Dove patt., 6⅜" d. (wear, stains, hairline) **660.00**

GOUDA

While tin-enameled earthenware has been made in Gouda, Holland since the early 1600s, the productions of modern factories are attracting increasing collector attention. The art pottery of Gouda is easily recognized by its brightly colored peasant-style decoration with some types having achieved a "cloisonné" effect. Pottery workshops located in, or near, Gouda include Regina, Zenith, Plazuid, Schoonhoven, Arnhem and others. Their wide range of production included utilitarian wares, as well as vases, miniatures and large outdoor garden ornaments.

Gouda Marks

Bowl, 8½" l., oval, squatty bulbous form w/rolled rim & loop end handles, black interior & handles, the sides w/a tannish orange ground decorated w/large lobed black leaves & burnt orange scrolls, "Regina" crown mark, glossy glaze, ca. 1900 . . . . **$83.00**

Bowl, 10" d., colorful peacock feather design, ca. 1920s **650.00**

Bowl, 13" d., pierced to hang, shallow w/widely flaring flattened rim, a cream ground decorated w/large multicolored flowers & green leaves in the center w/blossomheads around the rim, orchid banding, house mark & "2610 - 36 - Panow Co 4820 W. Gouda Holland," early 20th c. **66.00**

Butter pat, polychrome Art Nouveau design, marked "Regina 155 - (crown) - Lydia - WB - Gouda Holland," 3½" d. **50.00**

Candy dish, squared flaring sides w/a loop end handle, raised on three feet, dark matte green ground decorated w/bands of multicolored leaves & flowers around the exterior & interior, marked "Regina - Gouda - Holland - Luxor - 505H". . . **61.00**

Ewer, bulbous ovoid body tapering to a short rim spout & high arched strap handle, interior & handle in black, exterior in tannish orange ground w/overall large lobed black leaves, burnt orange scrolls & cream highlights, marked "Regina - Robur -Gouda - Holland," glossy glaze, early 20th c., 4½" h. **72.00**

Early Gouda Jug

Jug, bulbous ovoid body tapering to a short cylindrical neck w/a rolled incurved rim w/long spout & integral loop handle extending from rim to shoulder, the top in orchid, the sides decorated w/full-length tapering stripes of white stylized leaves alternating w/green bands w/white dots, scalloped orchid base band, "Zuid Holland" mark & "No. 2140," 20th c., 10½" h. (ILLUS.).................... **385.00**

Vase, 8¼" h., 4½" d., a squared foot issuing four curved buttress handles flanking the cylindrical central body w/a cylindrical neck, decorated w/stylized flowers in deep green & purple, marked w/factory symbol & "A to H" & "Zuid, Holland" **345.00**

GRUEBY

Some fine art pottery was produced by the Grueby Faience and Tile Company, established in Boston in 1891. Choice pieces were created with molded designs on a semi-porcelain body. The ware is marked and often bears the initials of the decorators. The pottery closed in 1907.

GRUEBY

Grueby Mark

Grueby Vase with Daffodils

Bowl-vase, wide squatty bulbous form w/incurved wide mouth, w/inscribed lines, light green high glaze, impressed "Grueby, Boston, Mass." **$316.00**

Jardiniere, tapering circular form under a deep green matte glaze, impressed mark (small tight hairline) **690.00**

Paperweight, figural, model of a scarab beetle, covered in a good matte green enamel, impressed pottery mark & paper label, 2 x 3" **770.00**

Paperweight, figural, model of a scarab beetle, fine overall matte green enamel, impressed Faience mark, 2½ x 3¾" (minor bottom flake) **715.00**

Paperweight, figural, model of a scarab beetle, matte blue glaze, impressed mark, 4" w., 2¾" h...... **374.00**

Tile, square, decorated in 'cuerda seca' technique w/a landscape w/trees & a river in blues, greens & yellow, impressed mark, 4" sq. (minute nicks on one edge) **935.00**

Vase, 2½" h., 3¾" d., wide squatty bulbous body tapering to a short, wide rolled neck, deep green matte glaze, impressed mark **460.00**

Vase, 5" h., 3" d., wide cylindrical body w/flaring rim, decorated w/impressed leaf-form, deep blue glaze, kiln pops, impressed marks (minor glaze nick & skip) **575.00**

Vase, 5¼" h., 3" d., footed swelled cylindrical body tapering at the base & shoulder, short rolled wide neck, tooled w/wide leaves up the sides, matte green glaze, by Ruth Erikson, impressed mark **1,320.00**

Vase, 5¾" h., 4" d., wide baluster body w/wide shoulder tapering to short flaring rim, bold incised leaf-forms under a rich, deep green matte glaze, impressed mark, partial initial "S, IV"............ **1,265.00**

Vase, 6" h., 4¾" d., bulbous ovoid body w/wide rolled rim, decorated w/five broad tooled leaves under a rich feathered matte green glaze, impressed mark, by Anne Lingley, artist's initials (interior glaze loss) **2,070.00**

Vase, 6" h., 9" d., wide squatty bulbous form w/a rounded shoulder to the wide, low rolled neck, embossed around the shoulder w/five-petal blossoms on thin stems alternating w/broad slightly pointed flat leaves, rich dark green matte glaze w/bluish green blossoms, impressed mark & artist's initials (restoration to small rim chip) **4,510.00**

Vase, 6¾" h., 3" d., bulbous cylindrical form on a thin footring & a small rolled rim, decorated w/nine vertical relief-molded stalks terminating in buds, thick warty blue/green matte glaze, impressed mark, artist's initials "E.R." **5,750.00**

Vase, 7" h., 4½" d., squatty bulbous base, the shoulder tapering to a wide flaring neck, five long stems & buds above five relief-molded leaves at base under a rich matte, feathered green glaze, by Ruth Erickson, impressed mark & artist's initials (minor glaze nick) **1,495.00**

Vase, 7¼" h., 4¾" d., squatty bulbous base, the shoulder tapering to a wide flaring neck, mottled light green matte glaze thinning to reveal five long stems & buds above five tooled leaves, unmarked **1,840.00**

Vase, 7¾" h., 4¾" d., swelled cylindrical body w/a flaring pinched three-lobed mouth, applied wide full-length leaves alternating w/buds, frothy matte green glaze w/white clay showing through leaf edges, impressed "GRUEBY FAIENCE" **2,090.00**

Vase, 9½" h., 7¾" d., bulbous body tapering to a wide cylindrical neck molded overall w/thin rings, rich deep green matte glaze w/white highlighting, three long handles applied near center of body & curled under at rim, remnant of paper label, oil font (nicks, minor glaze imperfections) **2,415.00**

Vase, 11¼" h., 5¼" d., slender swelled cylindrical body w/a six-sided gently flared rim, decorated w/tooled & applied yellow daffodils on a rich organic matte green ground, short, tight rim line, circular stamp mark & "ER" (ILLUS.) **8,250.00**

HALL CHINA

Founded in 1903 in East Liverpool, Ohio, this still-operating company at first produced mostly utilitarian wares. It was in 1911 that Robert T. Hall, son of the company founder, developed a special single-fire, lead-free glaze which proved to be strong, hard and non-porous. In the 1920s the firm became well known for their extensive line of teapots (still a major

product) and in 1932 they introduced kitchenwares followed by dinnerwares in 1936 and refrigerator wares in 1938.

The imaginative designs and wide range of glaze colors and decal decorations have led to the growing appeal of Hall wares with collectors, especially people who like Art Deco and Art Moderne design. One of the firm's most famous patterns was the "Autumn Leaf" line, produced as premiums for the Jewel Tea Company. For listings of this ware see "Jewel Tea Autumn Leaf."

Helpful books on Hall include, The Collector's Guide to Hall China *by Margaret & Kenn Whitmyer, and* Superior Quality Hall China - A Guide for Collectors *by Harvey Duke (An ELO Book, 1977).*

HALL CHINA

Hall Marks

Baker, fluted, French shape, Blue Bouquet patt. **$25.00**
Baker, fluted, French shape, Silhouette patt. **30.00**
Beanpot, one-handle, orange **100.00**
Bowl, fruit, 5¼" d., Mt. Vernon patt. **8.00**
Bowl, 6" d., Medallion shape, Silhouette patt. **23.00**
Bowl, 7" d., Medallion shape, Silhouette patt. **25.00**
Bowl, 7" d., Radiance shape, Crocus patt. **30.00**
Bowl, 9" d., Radiance shape, Crocus patt. **45.00**
Bowl, salad, 9" d., Silhouette patt. **25.00**
Casserole, cov., Medallion shape, Silhouette patt. **75.00**

Royal Rose Casserole

Casserole, cov., Royal Rose patt., thick rim (ILLUS.) **42.00**
Casserole, cov., tab-handled, Rose Parade patt. **34.00**

Casserole, cov., tab-handled, Rose
  White patt. 35.00
Casserole, cov., Yellow Rose patt.. . . . 30.00
Coffee server, cov., individual,
  Sundial shape, blue 95.00
Coffeepot, cov., Cathedral shape,
  ivory. 45.00
Coffeepot, cov., drip-type, Kadota
  shape, Springtime patt., all-china . . . 65.00
Coffeepot, cov., dripolator-type
  w/basket, Crocus patt., all-china . . . 50.00
Coffeepot, cov., Great American
  shape, Orange Poppy patt. 50.00
Coffeepot, cov., Meltdown shape,
  red band, large size. 45.00
Coffeepot, cov., Mt. Vernon patt.,
  all-china. 125.00
Coffeepot, cov., Orb shape, Bird of
  Paradise patt. 45.00
Coffeepot, cov., Russell shape w/Fuji
  decal 40.00
Coffeepot, cov., S-lid, Orange Poppy
  patt. 55.00
Coffeepot, cov., Sash shape, blue
  band w/white stars. 65.00
Coffeepot, cov., w/basket, Trellis
  shape, ivory. 45.00
Coffpot, cov., electric, Game Bird
  Pheasant patt. 75.00
Creamer, Boston shape, Blue
  Bouquet patt. 20.00
Creamer & cov. sugar bowl, Pert
  shape, Wildfire patt., pr. 50.00
Custard cup, Orange Poppy patt. 10.00
Drip jar, cov., Silhouette patt. 32.00
Gravy boat w/underplate, Mt.
  Vernon patt. 20.00
Jug, batter, Sundial shape, red. 120.00
Leftover, cov., oval, Westinghouse,
  red. 30.00
Mug, Irish coffee, black. 15.00

Irish Coffee Mug

Mug, Irish coffee, glossy yellow
  exterior, white interior (ILLUS.) 15.00
Pitcher, ball-type, Sundial shape, red. . 40.00
Pitcher, Radiance shape, # 5 . . . . 18.00
Pitcher, Simplicity shape, Silhouette
  patt. 165.00

Plate, 10" d., Mt. Vernon patt. 14.00
Pretzel jar, cov., Orange Poppy
  patt. 150.00
Punch set: bowl w/10 cups & ladle;
  Old Crow patt., 12 pcs. 200.00
Salt & pepper shakers, handled,
  Red Poppy patt., pr. 32.00
Salt & pepper shakers, handled,
  Royal Rose patt., pr. 32.00
Salt & pepper shakers, handled,
  Silhouette patt., pr. 85.00
Salt & pepper shakers, handled,
  Wildfire patt., pr. 35.00
Salt & pepper shakers, Medallion
  shape, Silhouette patt., pr. 57.00

Rose White Pert Shape Shaker

Salt & pepper shakers, Pert shape,
  Rose White patt., pr. (ILLUS. of
  one). 30.00
Salt & pepper shakers, teardrop-
  shaped, Wildfire patt., pr. 25.00
Spoon, Orange Poppy patt. 125.00
Teapot, cov., Airflow shape, emerald
  green. 55.00
Teapot, cov., Aladdin shape, black . . . 55.00
Teapot, cov, Aladdin shape, black
  w/gold 89.00
Teapot, cov., Aladdin shape, Blue
  Bouquet patt. 110.00
Teapot, cov., Aladdin shape, yellow
  w/gold trim, w/infuser. 58.00
Teapot, cov., Automobile shape,
  turquoise w/pink 600.00
Teapot, cov., Basket shape, lemon
  yellow 150.00
Teapot, cov., Birdcage shape,
  burgundy 400.00
Teapot, cov., Boston shape, canary
  yellow, two-cup size 45.00
Teapot, cov., Boston shape, maroon . . 35.00
Teapot, cov., Boston shape, red. 195.00
Teapot, cov., Cleveland shape, warm
  yellow 60.00
Teapot, cov., Cube shape, emerald
  green 100.00
Teapot, cov., Cube shape, turquoise,
  two-cup size 140.00
Teapot, cov., Doughnut shape,
  Chinese Red 400.00

Teapot, cov., Flareware line, Gold
  Lace design. 60.00
Teapot, cov., Globe shape, emerald
  green. 90.00
Teapot, cov., Gold Label line,
  Windshield shape, white w/gold
  dots 35.00
Teapot, cov., Hook Cover shape,
  cadet blue 30.00
Teapot, cov., Lipton shape, maroon . . 45.00
Teapot, cov., Medallion shape,
  Crocus patt. 70.00
Teapot, cov., Medallion shape,
  Silhouette patt. 70.00
Teapot, cov., New York shape,
  Dresden yellow 30.00

Red Poppy New York Shape Teapot

Teapot, cov., New York shape, Red
  Poppy patt. (ILLUS.) 75.00
Teapot, cov., Plume shape, pink,
  plain. 40.00
Teapot, cov., Rhythm patt., red 350.00
Teapot, cov., Star shape, cobalt
  blue 125.00
Teapot, cov., Streamline shape,
  Chinese Red 175.00
Teapot, cov., Sundial shape, ivory
  w/gold 140.00
Teapot, cov., Surfside shape, cadet
  blue 250.00
Teapot, cov., Surfside shape,
  emerald green w/gold, six-cup size. 120.00
Teapot, cov., Windshield patt.,
  turquoise w/gold 55.00
Tom & Jerry set: footed 4-qt. bowl
  w/6 cups; ivory, 7 pcs. 100.00
Tom & Jerry set: 5-qt. cov. bowl
  w/8 cups; black, 10 pcs. 200.00
Tom & Jerry set: footed 4-qt. bowl
  w/18 5-oz. cups; black, 19 pcs. . . . 250.00
Warmer, electric, holds three
  marmites 60.00
Watering can, orchid color 750.00

HAMPSHIRE POTTERY

Hampshire Pottery was made in Keene, New Hampshire, where several potteries operated as far back as the late 18th century. The pottery now known as Hampshire Pottery was established by J. S. Taft shortly after 1870. Various types of wares, including Art Pottery, were produced through the years. Taft's brother-in-law, Cadmon Robertson, joined the firm in 1904 and was responsible for developing over 900 glaze formulas while in charge of all manufacturing. His death in 1914 created problems for the firm and Taft sold out to George Morton in 1916. Closed during part of World War I, the pottery was later reopened by Morton for a short time and manufactured white hotel china. From 1919 to 1921, mosaic floor tiles became the main production. All production ceased in 1923.

          HAMPSHIRE

Hampshire Marks

Fine Hampshire Pottery Vases

Vase, 5" h., 4" d., squatty bulbous
  body w/a tall cylindrical neck
  w/flaring rim, matte green glaze
  w/silver overlay in an overall leafy
  scrolling design, incised "H"
  (ILLUS. left) $825.00
Vase, 6½" h., 3¾" d., slender ovoid
  body w/a closed rim, embossed up
  the sides w/long leaves & buds
  under a dark brown bronze-like
  glaze, impressed mark 468.00
Vase, 7" h., 4" d., two-handled
  cylindrical body flaring to base,
  feathered green matte glaze,
  impressed marks & artist's initials
  "T.O.". 431.00

Vase, 7½" h., 4" d., cylindrical body, feathered matte blue glaze, impressed mark, artist's initials "A.O.".........................**518.00**

Vase, 8" h., 6" d., gently flaring cylindrical body w/a wide scalloped & incurved rim, embossed w/flowers around the rim, dripping pink & blue matte glaze, hairline under base in-the-making, impressed mark (ILLUS. right) **880.00**

Vase, 9½" h., 6½" d., bulbous squatty footed base tapering to a tall cylindrical neck w/a flaring rim, unusual overall ochre-brown matte glaze, impressed mark (ILLUS. center).......................**495.00**

HARLEQUIN

The Homer Laughlin China Company, makers of the popular "Fiesta" pottery line, also introduced in 1938 a less expensive and thinner ware which was sold under the "Harlequin" name. It did not carry the maker's trade-mark and was marketed exclusively through F.W. Woolworth Company. It was produced in a wide range of dinnerwares in assorted colors until 1964. Out of production for a number of years, in 1979 Woolworth requested the line be reintroduced using an ironstone body and with a limited range of pieces and colors offered. Collectors also seek out a series of miniature animal figures produced in the Harlequin line in the 1930s and 1940s.

Ashtray, basketweave, rose........**$65.00**
Ashtray, saucer, red...............**90.00**
Bowl, 36s oatmeal, 6½" d., medium green........................**45.00**
Bowl, cereal, 6½" d., rose **20.00**
Bowl, individual salad, 7" d., chartreuse...................**25.00**
Casserole, cov., chartreuse.........**240.00**
Casserole, cov., maroon **215.00**
Casserole, cov., spruce green......**215.00**
Creamer, high-lip, blue............**375.00**
Creamer, high-lip, mauve **180.00**
Creamer, individual size, green.....**125.00**
Creamer, novelty, blue.............**45.00**
Creamer, novelty, grey.............**95.00**
Cup & saucer, demitasse, maroon...**195.00**
Cup & saucer, demitasse, red......**130.00**
Cup & saucer, demitasse, spruce green.......................**195.00**
Egg cup, double, rose **19.00**
Gravy boat, turquoise **20.00**
Nappy, medium green, 9" d.........**195.00**
Nut dish, individual size, rose........**11.00**
Nut dish, individual size, yellow **10.00**
Nut dish, maroon **11.00**
Nut dish, red.....................**12.00**

Pitcher, 9" h., ball-shaped w/ice lip, blue **75.00**
Pitcher, 9" h., ball-shaped w/ice lip, red **90.00**
Pitcher, 9" h., ball-shaped w/ice lip, rose.....................**95.00**
Pitcher, 9" h., ball-shaped w/ice lip, spruce green.................**95.00**
Pitcher, 9" h., ball-shaped w/ice lip, yellow **75.00**
Pitcher, jug-type, grey, 22 oz..".....**95.00**
Plate, 9" d., medium green **20.00**
Plate, 10 "d., medium green........**135.00**
Soup plate, w/flanged rim, maroon, 8" d............................**35.00**
Soup plate, w/flanged rim, medium green, 8" d. **125.00**
Sugar bowl, cov., blue **25.00**
Sugar bowl, cov., grey **45.00**
Sugar bowl, cov., maroon **45.00**
Teapot, cov., blue................**115.00**
Teapot, cov., forest green **225.00**
Teapot, cov., grey................**185.00**
Teapot, cov., maroon **195.00**
Tumbler, rose, 4½ " h. **75.00**

Harlequin Animals

Model of a cat, blue **250.00**
Model of a cat, maroon **275.00**
Model of a cat, spruce green **175.00**
Model of a cat, yellow **195.00**
Model of a donkey, spruce green ...**175.00**
Model of a donkey, yellow.........**250.00**
Model of a duck, blue **250.00**
Model of a duck, maroon..........**275.00**
Model of a duck, spruce green **275.00**
Model of a duck, yellow...........**195.00**
Model of a fish, blue **275.00**
Model of a fish, spruce green **250.00**
Model of a lamb, spruce green **175.00**
Model of a penguin, maroon **175.00**
Model of a penguin, maroon **285.00**

HAVILAND

Haviland porcelain was originated by Americans in Limoges, France, shortly before the mid-19th century and continues in production. Some Haviland was made by Theodore Haviland in the United States during the last World War. Numerous other factories also made china in Limoges. Also see LIMOGES.

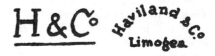

Haviland Marks

Haviland Game Set

Game set: twelve 8¼" d. plates, 18" l. oblong platter & 7½" l. leaf-shaped cream dish; each piece h.p. in the center w/a different game bird or birds in color w/floral trim & raised gilt designs, ca. 1880, printed marks (ILLUS.) **$1,495.00**

Plates, dinner, 8½" d., Marlborough patt., set of 8 . . . . **150.00**

Platter, 8½ x 11¾", oval, Yale patt. . . . **36.00**

Haviland Vase with Ladies

Vase, 5½" h., 3⅝" d., footring supports a wide gently swelled cylindrical body w/a wide shoulder gently sloping to the wide short neck, decorated at the top & base w/tan & pink bands, the sides w/two oval reserves w/portraits of standing ladies in early 20th c. deep red dresses, tan & pink berry & leaf bands at the top & bottom, Charles Field Haviland & "GDA Limoges" marks (ILLUS.) **245.00**

Haviland Vases with Boucher Nudes

Vases, 11" h., moon flask-shaped, footed w/round flat sides topped by a short flaring neck, each w/a impressionistic full-length portrait of a nude woman after Francois Boucher, mottled background, green, blue & brown ground, impressed "Haviland Limoges," pr. (ILLUS.) **3,500.00**

Haviland Vase with Rooster

Vases, 14" h., 13" w., moon flask-shaped, flaring foot below the flattened round sides w/a molded oval mouth, one decorated w/a colorful scene of a rooster, the other w/a hen & chicks, each on a mottled green & brown ground, impressed "Haviland Limoges," late 19th c., pr. (ILLUS. of one) **1,725.00**

HISTORICAL & COMMEMORATIVE WARES

Numerous potteries, especially in England and the United States, made various porcelain and earthenware pieces to commemorate people, places and events. Scarce English historical wares with American views command highest prices. Objects are listed here alphabetically by title of view.

Most pieces listed here will date between about 1820 and 1850. The maker's name is noted in parentheses at the end of each entry.

Albany, New York washbowl, floral border & embossed beaded rim, brown, 12" d., 2½" h. (Jackson) . . **$248.00**

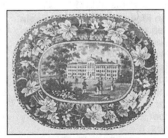

Almshouse, Boston Platter

Almshouse, Boston platter, vine border, dark blue, few minor rim glaze rubs,14½" l., Stevenson (ILLUS.) **1,430.00**

Arms of New York Punch Bowl

Arms of New York punch bowl, flowers & vines border, spoked wheels equidistant around border, footed, scalloped rim, dark blue, 10¾" d., 4½" h., professional restorations to hairlines reattached piece, Mayer (ILLUS.) **3,630.00**

Battery, New York (Flagstaff Pavilion) plate, vine leaf border, dark blue, 6⅞" d. (R. Stevenson) . . . **220.00**

Boreham House - Essex (England) cup plate, floral border, dark blue, 4½" d., Stevenson (unseen back rim chip) **143.00**

Boston Mails...Gentleman's Cabin open vegetable dish, vignette border, rectangular w/cut-corners, light blue, 10" l., J. & T. Edwards (small spots of wear) **358.00**

Boston Mails...Gentleman's Cabin plate, vignette border, paneled rim, brown, 7¾" w. (J. & T. Edwards) . . **165.00**

Boston Mails Plate

Boston Mails...Gentleman's Cabin plate, ship vignette border, brown, 8" d., Edwards (ILLUS.). **275.00**

Boston Mails...Gentleman's Cabin relish dish, central vignette, leaf-shaped, black, 9" l., J. & T. Edwards (hairline off the rim) **209.00**

Bunker Hill Monument plate, floral border, purple, 6⅛" d., Jackson (light mellowing) **215.00**

Bunker Hill Monument plate, floral border, purple, American Scenery series, 6¼" d. (Jackson) **204.00**

Cadmus (so-called) plate, irregular shells border, dark blue, 10" d. (Wood) **523.00**

Canterbury (England) plate, foliage & scroll border, dark blue, 10" d. (Clews) **248.00**

Castle Garden, Battery, New York cup plate, trefoil separated by knobs border, dark blue, 3¾" d. (E. Wood) **209.00**

Church in the City of New York plate, spread eagle border, dark blue, 6⅛" d., Stubbs (some minute pinpoints) **413.00**

City Hall New York cup & saucer, handleless, rose border, medium dark blue, Stubbs (minor chipping) . . **121.00**

City Hall, New York plate, spread eagle border, dark blue, 6¾" d. (Stubbs) **149.00**

City Hall, New York plate, flowers within medallions border, dark blue, 9⅞" d. (Ridgway) **148.00**

City Hotel, New York plate, oak leaf border, dark blue, 8½" d., R. Stevenson (faint scratching) . . . **110.00**

Columbia Bridge on the Susquehanna platter, lace band & small florals border, light blue, 13" l. (Ridgway). **204.00**

Columbus, Georgia cup plate, floral border, light blue, Celtic China series, 3⅞" d., Wood (two cracks) **198.00**

Court House, Baltimore soup plate, fruit & flowers border, dark blue, 8" d., Henshall (painted-over "Y" hairline in back) **385.00**

Dam & Water Works (The), Philadelphia plate, fruit & flowers border, dark blue, 9¾" d., Henshall (few face scratches) **440.00**

Dam & Water Works (The), Philadelphia (Sidewheel Steamboat) plate, fruit & flowers border, dark blue, 9⅞" d. (Henshall) **495.00**

Dam & Water Works (The), Philadelphia (Sidewheel Steamboat) pitcher, jug-form, fruit & flowers border, dark blue, 6½" h. (Henshall, Williamson & Co.) **2,640.00**

Deaf & Dumb Asylum, Hartford platter, flowers within medallions border, dark blue, 14⅞" l., Ridgway (several scratches) **358.00**

Episcopal Theological Seminary, Lexington, Kentucky plate, stylized floral bouquet border, purple, ca. 1840, 10⅝" d. (light overall crazing) **413.00**

Exchange, Charleston (base) & Esplanate & Castle Garden, New York (cover) cov. vegetable dish, vine leaf border, squared deep base w/rounded corners & a flaring

Exchange, Charleston Vegetable

rim w/embossed rim & rim handle,
tall domed & pointed cover w/large
blossom finial, dark blue, 10¾" w.,
8" h., tiny blued flake on finial,
Stevenson (ILLUS.) **1,540.00**

**Exchange Hotel, New Orleans
plate,** center vignette of hotel
w/name framed by a ring of small
stars, light blue w/rope-edged wide
border band & lightly scalloped rim,
importer's mark on reverse,
10⅛" d. (Davenport) **440.00**

Fair Mount Near Philadelphia plate,
spread-eagle border, dark blue,
10" d., Stubbs (light overall wear) . . . **154.00**

**Fair Mount Near Philadelphia soup
plate,** spread-eagle border, dark
blue, 10" d., Stubbs (light wear &
scratch on face) **110.00**

Unique Naval Heroes Cider Mug

Famous Naval Heroes cider mug,
floral border, cylindrical w/S-scroll
handle, dark blue, unknown maker,
two very shallow nearly unseen
table rim chips, 6¼" d., 5½" h.
(ILLUS.) **3,960.00**

**Fort Montgomery, Hudson River
plate,** flowers & birds border, light
blue, 5¾" d., Clews (two glaze rubs
on rim) **55.00**

**Fort Ticonderoga (Left Portion) cup
plate,** floral border, brown,
American Scenery series, 4" d.,
Jackson (heavy overall mellowing) . . **66.00**

**Gilpin's Mills on the Brandywine
Creek plate,** shell border, circular
center, dark blue, 9" d., E. Wood
(few light face scratches) **440.00**

**Harper's Ferry from the Potomac
Side plate,** no border, black,
8½" d. (Ridgway) **66.00**

**Holiday Street Theatre, Baltimore
cup plate,** fruit & flowers border,
dark blue, 3⅝"d., Henshall
(meandering crack off rim) **132.00**

Hudson River View plate, shell
border, circular center, dark blue,
5⅝" d., E. Wood (overall
mellowing) **880.00**

**Junction of the Sacandaga and
Hudson Rivers plate,** flowers &
birds border, pink, 6¾" d.(Clews) . . . **116.00**

**La Grange, The Residence of the
Marquis Lafayette plate,** flower &
leaf border, dark blue, 10" d.
(E. Wood) **248.00**

**Lafayette at Franklin's Tomb
creamer & cov. sugar bowl,** floral
border, dark blue, each w/a deep
footed bulbous body & collared
neck, creamer 6" h., sugar bowl 7"
h., E. Wood, pr. (creamer w/handle
restoration, sugar w/handle
restoration & few small rim chips) . . . **880.00**

**Landing of General Lafayette at
Castle Garden, New York, 16
August ,1824 gravy tureen, cover
& undertray,** floral & vine border,
dark blue, 8¼" d., 5½" h., Clews,
the set (shallow chip on handle,
minor glaze roughness) **1,210.00**

**Landing of General Lafayette at
Castle Garden, New York, 16
August 1824 plate,** primrose &
dogwood border, dark blue, 8¾" d.
(Clews) **303.00**

Log Cabin cup, handleless, exterior
w/views of log cabin, cider barrel &
American flag, interior w/two
medallions w/bust portrait of
William Henry Harrison, 1840
presidential campaign item, pink,
Adams, cup only (hairline off rim) . . **248.00**

**Lovejoy Inscription - Constitution
of The United States Amendment
cup plate,** vignette border, light
blue, 4" w. (hairline off rim) **413.00**

Near Fishkill, Hudson River plate,
flowers & birds border, black, 10¼"
d. (Clews) **110.00**

Near Hudson Vegetable Dish

Near Hudson, Hudson River vegetable dish, oval w/scalloped rim, floral border, black, 9¾" l., Clews (ILLUS.) 330.00

Rare New Orleans Coffeepot

New Orleans coffeepot, cov., lace border, purple, tall baluster-form w/pedestal base, angled shoulder to molded neck rim & high domed cover w/acorn finial, swan's-neck spout & C-scroll handle, some good spout & base restoration, 10¾" h., Jackson (ILLUS.) 770.00

Large Newburgh Platter

Newburgh, Hudson River platter, flower & bird border, brown, 20" l., Clews (ILLUS.) 605.00

Octagon Church, Boston soup plate, flowers within medallions border, dark blue, 9¾" d., Ridgway (trace of mellowing, small rim chip) . . 132.00

Park Theatre, New York plate, oak leaf border, dark blue, 10⅛" d. (R. Stevenson) 291.00

Pass in the Catskill Mountains plate, shell border, circular center, dark blue, 7½" d. (E. Wood) 605.00

Passaic Falls, State of New Jersey - Pass in the Catskill Mountains sauce tureen, cover & undertray, shell border, circular center, dark blue, squatty bulbous footed body w/scroll shoulder handles & stepped, domed cover w/berry

finial, conforming scalloped oval undertray, E. Wood, the set (restoration to handles) 2,090.00

Sancho Panza's Debate with Teresa plate, floral border, dark blue, 9" d. (Davenport) 281.00

Sancho Panza's Debate with Teresa plate, floral border, Don Quixote series, dark blue, 9" d., Clews (few light scratches) 275.00

Seal of the United States pitcher, flowers & scrolls border, footed bulbous ovoid body w/a short neck & wide spout, C-scroll handle, dark blue, Adams (overall glaze wear, hairline across base) 990.00

Shirely House, Surrey (England) plate, grapevine border, dark blue, 6⅜" d. (Wood) 94.00

State House, Boston 1818 tile, unbordered, square, dark medium blue, 6" w. (Mintons) 121.00

States series plate, two-story building w/curved drive, border w/names of fifteen states in festoons separated by five-point stars border, dark blue, 7¾" d., Clews (minor wear, small glaze flakes) 358.00

States series plate, building & fishermen w/net, names of states in festoons separated by five-point stars border, dark blue, 10½" d., Clews (minor wear & scratches) . . . 303.00

Steam Dredge plate, flowers border, Diorama series, dark blue, 8" d., unknown maker 358.00

Texian Campaigne cup plate, border only variation, pink, 3¾" d., Shaw (tight hairline off rim) 275.00

The Valley of the Shenandoah from Jefferson's Rock plate, narrow border, light blue, American Scenery series, 7" d., Ridgway (in-the-making rim chip) 121.00

The Waterworks, Philadelphia plate, floral border, purple, 9" d. (Jackson) 220.00

Thorton Castle, Staffordshire (England) soup plate, grapevine border, dark blue, 10" d. (Wood) . . 275.00

Union Line plate, shells border, dark blue, 10" d. (Wood) 495.00

Upper Ferry Bridge over the River Schuylkill plate, spread-eagle border, dark blue, 8¾" d., Stubbs (light facial wear) 227.00

Utica plate, tiny florals & floral swags border, light blue, American Cities and Scenery series, 6¼" d. (Meigh) 55.00

Utica soup ladle, light blue, American Cities and Scenery series, 11½" l. (C. Meigh) **165.00**

View of Liverpool (England) plate, irregular shells border, dark blue, 10" d. (Wood) **990.00**

View of the Catskill Mountain House, N.Y. plate, floral border, purple, 10½" d. (Jackson) **248.00**

View of the Catskill Mountain House, N.Y. plate, floral border, purple, 10½" d., Jackson (small unseen back rim chip) **248.00**

View of Trenton Falls - Three People on Rock plate, shell border, circular center, dark blue, 7½" d. (E. Wood) **440.00**

View of Trenton Falls - Three People on Rock plate, shell border, circular center, dark blue, 7⅝" d. (E. Wood) **275.00**

View on the St. Lawrence - Indian Encampment pitcher, ferns & moss border, light blue, footed octagonal form w/angled handle, 6" h. (Morely) **198.00**

Rare Village Near Catskill Dish

Village Near Catskill on the River Hudson vegetable dish, oval, flanged rim, floral & scroll border, dark blue, professional restoration on internal line, 8¾ x 11¾", A. Stevenson (ILLUS.) **3,090.00**

W. Penn's Treaty plate, latticework border, red, 9¼" d., Thomas Green (overall mellowing) **99.00**

Water Works (The) Philadelphia plate, floral cluster border, purple, 9" d. (Jackson) **143.00**

William Penn's Treaty plate, latticework border, red, 8½" d. (Thomas Green) **132.00**

Windsor Castle platter, foliate & scroll border, dark blue, 15¼" l. (Clews) **605.00**

Winter View of Pittsfield, Mass. (A) platter, vignette views & flowers border, dark blue, 14¾" l., Clews (shallow flaking on extreme rim) . . **1,375.00**

Winter View of Pittsfield, Mass. (Double Transfer) cup plate, dark blue, 3½" d., Clews (minute nicks on rim) **275.00**

Yale College, New Haven CT cup & saucer, handleless, vignette border w/three American eagles alternating w/three oval scenic reserves possibly showing the Wadsworth Tower, brown, unknown maker, ca. 1840 . . . . **330.00**

HULL

This pottery was made by the Hull Pottery Company, Crooksville, Ohio, beginning in 1905. Art Pottery was made until 1950 when the company was converted to utilitarian wares. All production ceased in 1986.

Reference books for collectors include Roberts' Ultimate Encyclopedia of Hull Pottery by Brenda Roberts (Walsworth Publishing Company, 1992), and Collector's Guide to Hull Pottery – The Dinnerware Lines by Barbara Loveless Gick-Burke (Collector Books, 1993).

Little Red Riding Hood Pieces

Bank, Little Red Riding Hood patt., standing-type (ILLUS. bottom left) . . **$588.00**

Basket, Bow-Knot patt., No. B25-6½", 6½" h. **225.00**

Basket, hanging-type, Open Rose patt., No. 102-7" **180.00**

Basket, Iris patt., No. 408-7", 7" h. . . **275.00**

Basket, Morning Glory patt., No. 62-8", 8" h. **200.00**

Basket, Bow-Knot patt., B12-10½", 10½" h. **700.00**

Basket, Open Rose patt., No.140-10½", 10½" h. **1,200.00**

Basket, Water Lily patt., tan & brown, No. L-14-10½" **245.00**

Basket, Woodland Gloss patt., pink to chartreuse, No. W22-10½" 10½" h. **175.00**

Batter pitcher, Little Red Riding Hood patt. **435.00**

Bowl, 14" d., Woodland Gloss patt.,
yellow & green, No. W29-14" **110.00**

Butter dish, cov., Little Red Riding
Hood patt. **343.00**

Candleholders, Calla Lily patt., pr. . . **125.00**

Candleholders, Wildflower patt., pink
& blue, pr. **95.00**

Canister, cov., Little Red Riding
Hood patt., "Coffee" **625.00**

Canister, cov., Little Red Riding
Hood patt., "Flour" **625.00**

Canister, cov., Little Red Riding
Hood patt., "Sugar" **625.00**

Canister, cov., Little Red Riding
Hood patt., "Tea". **625.00**

Console bowl, Bow-Knot patt., pink
& blue, No. B-16-13½", 13½" l. . . . **300.00**

Cookie jar, cov., Little Red Riding
Hood patt., closed-basket style . . . **275.00**

Cookie jar, cov., Little Red Riding
Hood patt., closed-basket style,
band of orange blossoms around
skirt (ILLUS. top) **500.00**

Cookie jar, cov., Little Red Riding
Hood patt., open basket style **307.00**

Cracker jar, cov., Little Red Riding
Hood patt., poinsettia decoration. . . **707.00**

Creamer, Little Red Riding Hood
patt., pour-through-head style **378.00**

Creamer, Little Red Riding Hood
patt., side-pour **132.00**

Creamer, Little Red Riding Hood
patt., top-pour, tab handle **438.00**

Dresser jar, cov., Little Red Riding
Hood patt., cold-painted **595.00**

Ewer, Serenade patt., blue, No. S2,
6½" h. **60.00**

Ewer, Wildflower patt., pink & blue,
No. W-11-8½,", 8½" h. **160.00**

Ewer, Magnolia patt., No. 18-13½",
13½" h. **300.00**

Flowerpot & saucer, Bow-Knot
patt., 2 pcs. **150.00**

Jardiniere, Bow-Knot patt., blue, No.
B-18-5¾", 5¾" h. **200.00**

Lamp, table model, electric, Little
Red Riding Hood patt. **2,200.00**

Mustard spoon, Little Red Riding
Hood patt. **395.00**

Pitcher, Butterfly patt., No.B11, gold
trim **75.00**

Pitcher, milk, Little Red Riding Hood
patt. **285.00**

Planter, model of a flower cart, No.
B14 . . . . **25.00**

Planter, Open Rose patt., pink &
blue, No. 118-6½" **130.00**

Salt & pepper shakers, Little Red
Riding Hood patt., large, pr. **140.00**

Salt & pepper shakers, Little Red
Riding Hood patt., small, pr. **65.00**

Spice jar, cov., Little Red Riding
Hood patt. **350.00**

String holder, Little Red Riding Hood
patt. (ILLUS. bottom right
w/Bank) **1,600.00**

Sugar bowl, cov., Little Red Riding
Hood patt., regular **450.00**

Crawling-style Red Riding Hood Sugar

Sugar bowl, open, Little Red Riding
Hood patt., crawling-style (ILLUS.). . **258.00**

Sugar bowl, open, Little Red Riding
Hood patt., side-pour **475.00**

Teapot, cov., Little Red Riding Hood
patt. **305.00**

Teapot, cov., Water Lily patt., No.
L18-6" **225.00**

Teapot, cov., Bow-Knot patt.,
turquoise & blue, B-20-6", 6" h. **495.00**

Vase, 4¾" h., Dogwood patt.,
turquoise & peach, No. 520-4¾" . . **100.00**

Vase, 5" h., Iris patt., No. 411-5" **75.00**

Bow-Knot Pattern Vase

Vase, 6½" h., Bow-Knot patt., blue &
cream, No. B-3-6½" (ILLUS.) **185.00**

Vase, 6½" h., Poppy patt., No. 606-
6½" **175.00**

Vase, 7" h., Iris patt., No. 402-7" **120.00**

Vase, 7½" h., Wildflower patt., tan &
brown, No. W8-7½" **80.00**

Vase, 8" h., Orchid patt., No. 303-8" . . **125.00**
Vase, 8" h., Sueno Tulip patt., blue &
pink, No. 105-33-8" **225.00**
Vase, 8½" h., Woodland Matte patt.,
No. W-10-8½" **170.00**

Large Hull Water Lily Vase

Vase, 10½" h., Water Lily patt., pink
& green, No. L-12-10½" (ILLUS.) . . **160.00**
Vase, 10½" h., Wildflower patt., tan &
brown, No. W-15-10½" **150.00**
Vase, 11" h., Ebb Tide patt., pink
ground **125.00**
Vase, 12" h., Serenade patt., pink
ground **275.00**
Vase, 12½" h., Magnolia patt., tassel-
type w/open handle,
No. 21-12½" **300.00**
Vase, 12½" h., Water Lily patt., pink
& green, No. L-15-12½" **360.00**
Vase, floor-type, 15" h., Wildflower
patt., tan & brown, No. W-20-15" . . **400.00**
Vase, 16" h., Iris patt., handled,
matte pink glaze **350.00**
Wall pocket, Bow-Knot patt., model
of a sad iron **300.00**
Wall pocket, Little Red Riding Hood
patt. **450.00**
Wall pocket, Woodland patt., rose &
chartreuse **25.00**
Wall pocket, Bow-Knot patt., model
of a bulbous pitcher, B-26-6" **265.00**
Wall pocket, Royal Woodland patt.,
grey & white, W13-7½", 7½" h. **75.00**

HUMMEL FIGURINES & COLLECTIBLES

*The Goebel Company of Oeslau, Germany,
first produced these porcelain figurines in 1934
having obtained the rights to adapt the beautiful
pastel sketches of children by Sister Maria
Innocentia (Berta) Hummel. Every design by the
Goebel artisans was approved by the nun until
her death in 1946. Though not antique, these
figurines with the "M.I. Hummel" signature,*

*especially those bearing the Goebel Company
factory mark used from 1934 and into the early
1940s, are being sought by collectors though
interest may have peaked some years ago.*

Hummel Figurine Marks

Adventure Bound

A Fair Measure, 1972-79, 4¾" h. . . . **$140.00**
Adventure Bound, 1972-79, 7¼ x 8"
(ILLUS.) **2,500.00**
Angel Duet font, 1956-68, 2 x 4¾" . . . **45.00**
Angel Serenade, (angel standing),
1940-57, 3" h. **83.00**
Angelic Song, 1972-79, 4" h. **90.00**
Apple Tree Boy, 1956-68, 4" h. **96.00**
Apple Tree Boy table lamp,
1956-68, 7½" h. **250.00**
Apple Tree Girl, 1934-49, 6" h. **358.00**
Apple Tree Girl, 1940-57, 6" h. **235.00**
Apple Tree Girl, 1956-68, 6" h. **170.00**
Auf Wiedersehen w/Tyrolean cap,
1940-57, 5¼" h. **1,800.00**
Ba-Bee Rings plaques, boy & girl,
1940-57, 5" h., pr. **175.00**
Ba-Bee-Ring plaque, boy, 1972-79,
5" d. **60.00**
Baker, 1956-68, 4¾" h. **140.00**
Band Leader, 1940-57, 5¼" h. **200.00**
Blessed Event, 1963-71, 5¼" h. **215.00**
Book Worm, 1972-79, 4" h. **140.00**
Boots, 1956-68, 6½" h. **213.00**
Boy w/ Horse candleholder, (Advent
group), 1956-68, 3½" h. **30.00**
Boy with Toothache, 1940-57,
5½" h. **195.00**
Brother, 1972-79, 5½" h. **100.00**
Builder, 1956-68, 5½" h. **165.00**
Busy Student, 1963-71, 4¼" h. **125.00**
Carnival, 1963-71, 6" h. **160.00**
Chick Girl, 1972-79, 3½" h. **104.00**
Chick Girl, music box, 4½ x 6¼" **300.00**
Chicken Licken, 1972-79, 4¾" h. **162.00**

Chimney Sweep, 1956-68, 4" h. **78.00**
Close Harmony, 1972-79, 5½" h.. . . . **165.00**
Congratulations, 1956-68, 6" h. **132.00**
Congratulations, 1934-49,
    8¼" h.. . . . . **3,900.00**
Crossroads, original edition,
    1972-79, 6¾" h.. . . . . **245.00**
Culprits, 1940-57, 6¼" h. **381.00**
Culprits table lamp, 1973-79,
    4 x 5½" **150.00**
Doll Mother, 1956-68, 4¾" h.. . . . . . **155.00**
Duet, 1940-57, 5¼" h. **263.00**
Duet, 1956-68, 5¼" h.. . . . . **225.00**
Duet, 1972-79, 5¼" h.. . . . . **150.00**
Eventide, 1956-68, 4¾" h. **238.00**
Farewell, 1934-49, 4¾" h.. . . . . **420.00**
Farm Boy, 1956-68, 5¼" h. **165.00**
Feeding Time, 1934-49, 4¼" h. **450.00**
Festival Harmony w/mandolin,
    1963-71, 8" h. **193.00**
Flower Madonna, white, open halo,
    1940-57, 9½" h.. . . . . **150.00**
For Father, 1940-57, 5½" h.. . . . . . . **230.00**
For Father, orange radishes,
    1956-68, 5½" h. **1,750.00**
Going to Grandma's, 1956-68,
    4¾" h. **180.00**
Going to Grandma's, 1940-57, 6" h. . . **425.00**
Good Friends, 1934-49, 4" h.. . . . . . . **325.00**
Good Friends book ends, 1972-79,
    5¼" h., pr. **240.00**
Good Night, (angel standing),
    1940-57, 3½" h.. . . . . **93.00**
Goose Girl, 1934-49, 4" h. **275.00**
Goose Girl, 1934-49, 4¾" h.. . . . . . . **325.00**
Goose Girl, 1934-49, 7½" h.. . . . . . . **600.00**
Guiding Angel, 1972-79, 2¾" h. **48.00**
Happy Days, 1934-49, 5¼" h. **725.00**
Happy Pastime, 1940-57, 3¼" h.. . . . **165.00**
Happy Traveler, 1956-68, 5" h. **225.00**
Hear Ye, Hear Ye, 1940-57, 7½" h. . . **650.00**
Heavenly Angel, 1972-79, 6" h.. . . . . **123.00**
Heavenly Protection, 1940-57,
    9¼" h. **900.00**
Heavenly Protection, 1972-79,
    9¼" h. **425.00**
Joseph, 1940-57, 7½" h. **145.00**
Just Resting, 1940-57, 3¾" h. **145.00**
Latest News, "US Zone," "Daily Mail,"
    1934-49, 5¼" h.. . . . . **550.00**
Letter to Santa, 1972-79, 7" h.. . . . . **216.00**
Little Bookkeeper, 1972-79, 4¾" h.. . **158.00**
Little Cellist, 1956-68, 8" h. **300.00**
Little Fiddler, 1934-49, 4¾" h.. . . . . . **330.00**
Little Gardener, 1972-79, 4¼" h.. . . . **125.00**
Little Goat Herder, 1934-49, 4¾" h.. . **375.00**
Little Guardian, 1934-49, 3¾" h. **250.00**
Little Guardian, 1972-79, 3¾" h.. . . . . **90.00**
Little Helper, 1940-57, 4¼" h. **193.00**
Little Hiker, 1934-49, 5½" h. **380.00**
Little Hiker, 1972-79, 5½" h. **120.00**

Little Sweeper, 1956-68, 4½" h.. . . . . **100.00**
Little Tailor, 1972-79, 5½" h. **140.00**
Little Tailor, old style, 1972-79,
    5½" h. **420.00**
Lost Sheep, 1940-57, 6¼" h. **325.00**
Lost Stocking, 1963-71, 4⅜" h.. . . . . **600.00**
M.I. Hummel Bust, color **300.00**
Madonna and Child font, 1963-71,
    3¼ x 4" **45.00**
Madonna praying, standing, no halo,
    white, 1940-57, 10¼" h. **250.00**
Madonna praying, standing, no halo,
    white, 1940-57, 11¼" h. **120.00**
Mail Is Here, 1972-79, 4½ x 6" **298.00**
March Winds, 1956-68, 5" h. **117.00**
March Winds, 1934-49, 6¼" h.. . . . . . **250.00**
Max & Moritz, 1934-49, 5¼" h.. . . . . . **262.00**
Merry Wanderer, 1940-57, 4¼" h.. . . . **185.00**
Merry Wanderer, 1956-68, 4¼" h.. . . . . **80.00**
Merry Wanderer, 1956-68, 9½" h.. . . . **850.00**
Merry Wanderer, 1940-57, 11¼" h. . . **1,650.00**
Merry Wanderer plaque, 1963-71,
    4¾ x 5⅛" **65.00**
Mother's Helper, 1972-79, 5" h.. . . . . **120.00**
Not For You, 1956-68, 6" h. **425.00**
Photographer, 1940-57, 4¾" h. **250.00**
Postman, 1940-57, 5¼" h. **205.00**
Postman, 1956-68, 5¼" h. **155.00**
Prayer Before Battle, 1940-57,
    4¼" h. **190.00**
School Boy, 1972-79, 7½" h.. . . . . . . **230.00**
School Boys, 1972-79, 7½" h.. . . . . . **850.00**
School Boys, 1940-57, 10¼" h. . . . **2,250.00**

School Girl

School Girl, 1972-79, 4¼" h.
    (ILLUS.). **80.00**
Serenade, 1972-79, 7½" h.. . . . . **250.00**
She Loves Me, She Loves Me Not
    book ends, 1972-79, 5" h., pr. **240.00**
Singing Lesson ashtray, 1940-57,
    3½ x 6" **154.00**
Singing Lesson candy box, 1972-
    79, 5¼" d. **108.00**
Smart Little Sister, 1963-71, 4¾" h.. . . **165.00**

Spring Dance

Spring Dance, 1972-79, 6½" h.
(ILLUS.) 275.00
Sweet Music, 1940-57, 5¼" h 225.00
To Market, 1940-57, 5½" h 345.00
Volunteers, 1956-68, 5½" h 300.00
Watchful Angel, 1963-71, 6¾" h 160.00
Worship, 1940-57, 5" h 155.00

IRONSTONE

The first successful ironstone was patented in 1813 by C. J. Mason in England. The body contains iron slag incorporated with the clay. Other potters imitated Mason's ware and today much hard, thick ware is lumped under the term ironstone. Earlier it was called by various names, including graniteware. Both plain white and decorated wares were made throughout the 19th century. Tea Leaf Lustre ironstone was made by several firms.

GENERAL

Jeddo Dinner Service

Dinner service: four graduated oval platters 10¼ - 13½", four 9½" d. plates, eight 8½" d. plates, four 10½" d. soup plates, 10½" h. cov. soup tureen, 6¾" h. sauce tureen, cover, undertray & ladle, 11¾" d. tazza, 9½" d. footed bowl, 4¾" h. creamer, three 10½" d. vegetable dishes w/two covers; Jeddo patt., Beech & Hancock, England, ca. 1870, hairlines, repairs, the set (ILLUS. of part) **$748.00**
Dinner service: twelve each service plates, dinner plates, luncheon plates, cream soup cups &

saucers, rimmed soup plates, bread & butter plates & eleven small bowls, 21 cups & 17 saucers, two open vegetable bowls & one platter; Windsor patt., Mason's Patent mark, the set (wear, lines) . . **1,495.00**

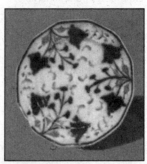

"Gaudy" Ironstone Plate

Plate, 10⅝" w., paneled rim, "gaudy" brush-stroke decoration of florals & strawberries, minor wear (ILLUS.) . . **385.00**
Platter, 15⅞" x 19⅝" oval, Japan patt., Edward F. Bodley & Son., ca. 1885 . . . . **173.00**
Platter, 20¼" l., oval, decorated in the Imari palette, illegible impressed mark on base, 19th c. (very minor chips, knife marks, enamel wear) **316.00**
Platter, 20½" l., oval well-and-tree type, Blue Pheasants patt., medium blue, marked "Masons Patent Ironstone China," mid-19th c. (small flake on extreme rim) . **440.00**
Platter, 21½" l., wide oblong form w/angled corners, well-and-tree-type, "gaudy" style, transfer-printed dark blue Oriental-style urn & flowers in center w/stylized floral border decorated in polychrome enamel & gilt trim, impress "Improved Stone" & marked "Granite China", WR. S. & Co., mid-19th c. (minor wear) **550.00**
Punch bowl, deep circular sides decorated in the Oriental style w/peonies & cloud bands centering phoenix birds, in cobalt blue & iron-red, raised on a round foot, England, late 19th c., 18" d. **1,150.00**
Soup plate w/flanged rim, Blue Pheasant patt., central design of large blossoms w/an exotic bird, blue & white w/polychrome highlights, Mason's Patent Ironstone mark, early 19th c. 9½" d. **83.00**

Soup tureen, cov., bulbous squatty deep body raised on four high scroll feet, angled loop side handles, high domed cover w/loop handle, decorated w/a black transfer-printed floral design trimmed w/polychrome enamels, impressed registry mark, ca. 1847, handle to handle 13½" l. **1,265.00**

Tureen, cover & matching undertray, hexagonal, blue & white underglaze & enamel overglaze decorations, ca. 1830s, John & William Ridgway Cauldon Place & Bell Works Staffordshire Potteries, the set (restoration & age crack, finial restored) **290.00**

Ironstone Wash Set

Wash set: wash pitcher, cov. chamber pot & cov. master waste jar; each decorated w/a transfer-printed design of birds & their nests, highlighted w/amber, red & blue polychrome lustre, late 19th c., 9", 13" & 17" h., 3 pcs. (ILLUS.) .. **110.00**

TEA LEAF IRONSTONE

Baker, plain oblong, Alfred Meakin, 7¾" l. **35.00**

Baker, rectangular, Peerless patt., Edwards, 7¾" l. **125.00**

Baker, oval, Chinese patt., Anthony Shaw, 9½" l. **100.00**

Boston egg cup, Alfred Meakin **425.00**

Bouillon cup, two-handled, Empress patt., Micratex by Adams, ca. 1960s **70.00**

Bowl, fruit, 11¾" d., 3" h., Niagara Fan patt., Anthony Shaw **350.00**

Bowl, oval, 10" l., Lily of the Valley patt., Anthony Shaw **120.00**

Brush box, cov., Cable patt., Burgess **325.00**

Brush box, cov., Lily of the Valley patt., Anthony Shaw (tiny glaze flake, underglaze chip on base) ... **775.00**

Brush box, cov., rectangular, Square Ridged patt., Red Cliff, ca. 1960s **160.00**

Butter dish, cov., Little Cable patt., Furnival **200.00**

Butter dish, cover & liner, Cable patt., Anthony Shaw, 3 pcs. .... **250.00 to 290.00**

Butter dish, cover & liner, Iona patt., gold Tea Leaf, Powell & Bishop, the set **40.00**

Butter dish, cover & liner, Lily of the Valley patt., Anthony Shaw (small base chip, plain liner) **280.00**

Cake plate, Empress patt., Micratex by Adams, ca. 1960s **175.00**

Cake plate, Iona patt., gold Tea Leaf, Powell & Bishop **50.00**

Cake plate, Red Cliff, ca. 1960s **45.00**

Cake plate, squared w/rounded corners & molded handles, Polonaise patt., Edge, Malkin **185.00**

Chamberpot, cov., Bamboo patt., Alfred Meakin **285.00**

Chamberpot, cov., Scroll patt., Alfred Meakin **220.00**

Chamberpot, cov., Square Ridged patt., Mellor, Taylor (minor chip & hairline in cover) **230.00**

Chamberpot, open, Lily of the Valley patt., Anthony Shaw **350.00**

Child's set, gold Tea Leaf, Mellor, Taylor, 16 pcs. **650.00**

Coffeepot, cov., Fig Cousin patt., pink lustre, Davenport **350.00**

Coffeepot, cov., Cable patt., H. Burgess, 10" h. **175.00**

Compote, open, 9" d., 4" h., fluted rim, Anthony Shaw **400.00**

Compote, open, 9" d., 5" h., footed, Wilkinson **225.00**

Compote, open, 8¾" d., 5¼" h., shallow round bowl on ringed pedestal w/flaring round foot, Anthony Shaw **175.00**

Compote, open, 9¼" sq., Square Ridged patt., Mellor, Taylor **400.00**

Compote, open, 5¼" d., 9¼" h., round w/ringed pedestal & domed foot, Davenport **425.00**

Creamer, Bamboo patt., Alfred Meakin **110.00**

Creamer, Cable patt., Anthony Shaw .. **200.00**

Creamer, Cable patt., Furnival **240.00**

Creamer, Chinese patt., Anthony Shaw **625.00**

Creamer, Daisy 'n Chain patt., Wilkinson **140.00**

Creamer, Fish Hook patt., Alfred Meakin **170.00**

Creamer, high-lipped, Chinese patt.,
Red Cliff, ca. 1960s 80.00
Creamer, Lily of the Valley patt.,
Anthony Shaw 380.00
Creamer, Little Cable patt., Furnival . . . 170.00
Creamer, ovoid, W. & E. Corn 150.00
Creamer, Square Ridged patt.,
Mellor, Taylor 210.00
Creamer & cov. sugar bowl, Iona
patt., gold Tea Leaf, Powell &
Bishop, pr. 55.00
Cup, child's, unmarked 130.00
Cup plate, Rondeau patt., Davenport,
3⅞" d. 75.00
Cup & saucer, handled, Lily of the
Valley patt., Anthony Shaw 80.00
Cup & saucer, handled, Polonaise
patt., Edge, Malkin 90.00
Cup & saucer, handleless, Chinese
patt., Anthony Shaw 80.00
Cup & saucer, Square Ridged patt.,
Red Cliff, ca. 1960s 18.00
Demitasse cup & saucer, Empress
patt., Micratex by Adams, ca.
1960s 65.00
Dish, cov., low rounded base w/side
tab handles, wide low domed
cover, Empress patt., Micratex by
Adams, ca.1960s, 9⅞" w., 2¼" h. . . 325.00
Dish, square, Square Ridged patt.,
Wedgwood, 6¼" w. 35.00
Dish, square, Victory patt., Edwards,
8½" w. 30.00
Dish, square w/scalloped rim,
Anthony Shaw, 8⅞" w. 45.00
Doughnut stand, Square Ridged
(Hearts) patt., Mellor, Taylor 325.00
Egg cup, Empress patt., Micratex by
Adams, ca. 1960s 115.00
Egg cup, unmarked 225.00
Fruit dish, Empress patt., Micratex
by Adams, ca. 1960s, 5¼" w. 15.00
Gravy boat, Bamboo patt., Alfred
Meakin 55.00
Gravy boat, Basketweave patt.,
Anthony Shaw (potting flaw in foot) . . 120.00

Fish Hook Tea Leaf Gravy Boat

Gravy boat, Fish Hook patt., Alfred
Meakin (ILLUS.) 45.00
Gravy boat, Gentle Square patt.,
Furnival 90.00

Gravy boat, Square Ridged patt.,
Red Cliff, ca. 1960s 50.00
Gravy boat & undertray, Square
Ridged patt., gold Tea Leaf,
Burgess, 2 pcs. 40.00
Lamp, table model, Kitchen Kraft line
by Homer Laughlin, gold Tea
Leaves, ca. 1930s 145.00
Measuring cup, cylindrical
w/flattened rim stick handle, Ruth
Sayres, ca. 1980s 40.00
Mixing bowl, Kitchen Kraft line, gold
Tea Leaf, Homer Laughlin,
ca. 1930s 45.00
Pitcher, 6" h., Empress patt.,
Micratex by Adams, ca. 1960s 75.00
Pitcher, 7" h., Peerless patt., Edwards . . 275.00
Pitcher, hot water, 7" h., Charles II
style, J. & E. Mayer 250.00
Pitcher, 7½" h., Chinese patt.,
Anthony Shaw 500.00
Pitcher, 7½" h., Fig Cousin patt., pink
lustre, Davenport 600.00
Pitcher, 8" h., Bordered Fuchsia
patt., Anthony Shaw 775.00
Pitcher, 8" h., Empress patt.,
Micratex by Adams 90.00
Pitcher, 8" h., Fish Hook patt., Alfred
Meakin 220.00
Plate, child's, Hughes 55.00
Platter, 6½" l., rectangular, Anthony
Shaw 65.00
Platter, 13" l., oval, Lily of the Valley
patt., Anthony Shaw 180.00
Platter, 10¼ x 14", rectangular,
Square Ridged patt., Mellor, Taylor . . 45.00
Platter, oval, 15" l., Brocade patt.,
Alfred Meakin 70.00
Platter, 12½ x 17" oval, Thomas
Elsmore 35.00
Platter, 14 x 17" oval, Polonaise patt.,
Edge Malkin 125.00
Posset cup, footed, unmarked 425.00
Punch bowl, footed, Cable patt.,
Anthony Shaw 375.00
Punch bowl, footed, Plain Round
patt., Anthony Shaw, 9" d., 6" h. . . . 525.00
Rasher, rectangular, Alfred Meakin,
4 x 5⅞" 50.00
Relish dish, Lily of the Valley patt.,
Anthony Shaw 250.00
Relish dish, mitten-shaped, DeSoto
patt., Anthony Shaw, rare
(numerous chips, 1" hairline) 250.00
Sauce ladle, attributed to Alfred
Meakin (spot in glaze on handle) . . 315.00
**Sauce tureen, cover, ladle &
undertray,** Bamboo patt., Alfred
Meakin, the set (rim roughness &
glaze chip on cover) 370.00

Sauce tureen, cover, ladle & undertray, Bullet patt., Anthony Shaw, the set (chip under cover & on ladle) 400.00

Sauce tureen, cover, ladle & undertray, Daisy patt., Anthony Shaw, the set (flake on tureen handle) 370.00

Sauce tureen, cover, ladle & undertray, Square Ridged patt., Red Cliff, ca. 1960s, the set 145.00

Sauce tureen, cover & undertray, Simple Square patt., Wedgwood, the set 160.00

Serving bowl, round, scalloped rim, Furnival, 7½" d. 120.00

Shaving mug, Chinese patt., Anthony Shaw 110.00

Shaving mug, Fish Hook patt., large, Alfred Meakin 215.00

Shaving mug, Lily of the Valley patt., Anthony Shaw 270.00

Shaving mug, Scroll patt., Alfred Meakin (worn lustre) 100.00

Soap dish, cov., Chelsea patt., Alfred Meakin (no liner, rim chip) 200.00

Soap dish, cover & liner, Heavy Square patt., Clementson, the set . . . 525.00

Soap dish, cover & liner, Lily of the Valley patt., Anthony Shaw, the set . . 725.00

Soap dish w/liner, Cable patt., Anthony Shaw 275.00

Soup tureen, cov., Cable patt., Anthony Shaw, 12" d. 420.00

Sugar bowl, cov., Bamboo patt., Alfred Meakin 90.00

Sugar bowl, cov., Chinese patt., Anthony Shaw 225.00

Sugar bowl, cov., Hanging Leaves patt., Anthony Shaw (repaired top rim chip) 210.00

Sugar bowl, cov., Square Ridged patt., Wedgwood 40.00

Teapot, cov., Chelsea patt., Alfred Meakin 290.00

Teapot, cov., Gentle Square patt., Furnival 275.00

Teapot, cov., Jumbo patt., Alcock (base glaze spider) 375.00

Toothbrush vase, Bamboo patt., Alfred Meakin 155.00

Toothbrush vase, cylindrical, side drain, Wedgwood 180.00

Toothbrush vase, cylindrical w/scalloped rim, Alfred Meakin 140.00

Toothbrush vase, footed tapering square form, H. Burgess 170.00

Toothbrush vase, Square Ridged patt., Mellor, Taylor 300.00

Toothbrush vase, square tapering shape, side drain hole, Anthony Shaw (small base rim chip) 190.00

Toothbrush vase & underplate, Fig Cousin patt., pink lustre, Davenport, the set (small rim chip on underplate) 875.00

Undertray, oval, Cable patt., Anthony Shaw, large 225.00

Vegetable dish, cov., rectangular, Bullet patt., Anthony Shaw, large . . 175.00

Vegetable dish, cov., square, Simple Square patt., Wedgwood 55.00

Vegetable dish, cov., Gentle Square patt., Furnival, 7" w. 125.00

Vegetable dish, cov., oval, Chinese patt., Anthony Shaw, 12" l. 340.00

Washbowl, Alfred Meakin, 15" d. . . . 180.00

Lily of the Valley Bowl & Pitcher Set

Washbowl & pitcher, Lily of the Valley patt., Anthony Shaw, the set (ILLUS.) 575.00

Waste bowl, round, large, Niagara Fan patt., Anthony Shaw 120.00

Water pitcher, Simple Square patt., gold Tea Leaf, Powell & Bishop 65.00

TEA LEAF VARIANTS

Bowl, open, 10" oval, Teaberry patt., Clementson 150.00

Coffeepot, cov., Morning Glory patt., Portland shape, Elsmore & Forster . . 380.00

Compote, open, Grape Octagon patt., lustre band trim, Livesley & Powell, large 375.00

Creamer, Gold Cloverleaf patt., bulbous body w/square foot & flaring square neck, loop scroll handle, S.B. & Son, England, ca. 1885 . . . . 80.00

Creamer, green Teaberry patt., round, unmarked 200.00

Creamer, Morning Glory patt., Portland shape, Elsmore & Forster (rim roughness) 220.00

Creamer, Teaberry patt., Prairie
shape, Clementson **625.00**
Creamer, Chelsea Grape patt.,
Primary shape, unmarked, 4½" h. . . . **360.00**
Cup & saucer, handled, child's,
Teaberry patt., Plain Round shape,
Clementson (small chip on bottom) . . **245.00**
Cup & saucer, handled, Teaberry
patt., Prairie shape, Clementson
(nick on cup) **50.00**
Cup & saucer, handled, Tulip patt.,
Micratex by Adams, ca. 1960s **55.00**
Cup & saucer, handleless, Laurel
Wreath patt., lustre trim, Elsmore &
Forster. **185.00**
Cup & saucer, Lustre Scallops patt.,
Wrapped Sydenham shape,
Edward Walley **150.00**
Cup & saucer, Pomegranate patt.,
Prairie Flowers shape, Powell &
Bishop **130.00**
Cup & saucer, Teaberry patt.,
Clementson. **130.00**
Dish, Teaberry patt., Heavy Square
shape, Clementson Bros., 10" w.,
4" h. **310.00**
Egg cup, Teaberry patt., unmarked
(flakes & chips, both rims, small
base hairline) **390.00**
Gravy boat, Laurel Wreath patt.,
lustre trim, Elsmore & Forster **650.00**
Nappy, round, Laurel Wreath patt.,
lustre trim, Elsmore & Forster,
5½" d. **180.00**
Pitcher, 8" h., Gothic patt., lustre
band trim, Red Cliff, ca. 1960s **50.00**
Pitcher, 8½" h., Teaberry patt., New
York shape, Clementson Bros. **500.00**
Pitcher, 9" h., hotel-type, Teaberry
patt., simple round shape,
Clementson **350.00**
Plate, child's, 5¼" d., Teaberry patt.,
Clementson **160.00**
Plates, 9" d., Pepperleaf patt., Crystal
shape, unmarked Elsmore &
Forster, the set **75.00**
Sauce dish, round, Teaberry patt.,
Clementson, 5" d. (slight under-rim
wear) **90.00**
Sugar bowl, cov., Morning Glory
patt., Portland shape, Elsmore &
Forster **475.00**
Teapot, cov., Teaberry patt., Prairie
Shape, Clementson **425.00**
Vegetable dish, cov., footed, oval,
New York patt., lustre band trim,
Clementson **200.00**
Wash pitcher, Pinwheel patt., Gothic
shape, unmarked, 13" h. **310.00**

Waste bowl, Morning Glory patt.,
Portland shape, Elsmore & Forster . . **250.00**
Waste bowl, Niagara patt., lustre
band trim, unmarked Walley **145.00**
Waste bowl, Teaberry patt., New
York shape, Clementson **325.00**

JASPER WARE (NON-WEDGWOOD)

Jasper ware is fine-grained exceedingly hard stoneware made by including barium sulphate in the clay and was first devised by Josiah Wedgwood, who utilized it for the body of many of his fine cameo blue-and-white and green-and-white pieces. It was subsequently produced by other potters in England and Germany, notably William Adams & Sons, and is in production at the present. Also see WEDGWOOD - JASPER.

Box, cov., miniature, round w/ringed
foot, fitted flat cover w/slightly
flared rim, the top w/a white relief
bust of an Art Nouveau lady
w/flowing hair, blue glossy ground,
2½" d. **$33.00**
Box, cov., deep round blue jasper
base raised on four small tab feet,
the sides decorated in white relief
w/leafy swags & ribbons, the
slightly domed cover w/four small
rim tabs decorated w/a blue border
band w/white relief blossom & leaf
band around a central medallion
w/a brown ground & a white relief
group of musicians, Germany, ca.
1910, 2¾" d., 3¾" h. **193.00**
Pitcher, wine, 13" h., King Gambrinus
astride a barrel w/incised "Das
Jahrist Butbraun Bierist Deralben,"
also featuring gnomes & leafy
vines, blue glazed & white matte
finish, late 19th c., Germany **110.00**
Plaque, oblong, white relief Native
American chief w/full headdress,
titled "Painted Horse," w/border of
owls, green ground, small **125.00**

Fisherman Jasper Ware Plaque

Plaque, round, pierced to hang, green ground w/a white relief central scene of a standing fisherman smoking & holding the end of a long coil of rope in his hand, a crate & post behind him, a white relief wide border band of wrapped cattails, Germany, early 20th c., 6¼" d. (ILLUS.) ... **50.00 to 75.00**

Vase, 6" h., white relief scene of ladies, royal blue ground, Schafer & Vater, Germany **165.00**

JEWEL TEA AUTUMN LEAF

Though not antique this ware has a devoted following. The Hall China Company of East Liverpool, Ohio, made the first pieces of Autumn Leaf pattern ware to be given as premiums by the Jewel Tea Company in 1933. The premiums were an immediate success and thousands of new customers, all eager to acquire a piece of the durable Autumn Leaf pattern ware, began purchasing Jewel Tea products. Though the pattern was eventually used to decorate linens, glasswares and tinware, we include only the Hall China Company items in our listing.

Jewel Tea Autumn Leaf Mark

Autumn Leaf Cereal Bowl

Baker, individual, oval **$90.00**
Bowl, cream soup **40.00**
Bowl, fruit, 5½" d. **5.00**
Bowl, cereal, 6½" d. (ILLUS.) **11.00**
Bowl, flat soup, 8½" **19.00**
Butter dish, cov., No. 1 .... **500.00**
Butter dish, cov.,¼ lb. **195.00**
Butter dish, cov.,¼ lb., regular **265.00**
Cup & saucer **10.00**

Cup & saucer, St. Denis-style **34.00**
Gravy boat **26.00**
Teapot, cov., long-spout type **45.00**

JUGTOWN

This pottery was established by Jacques and Juliana Busbee in Jugtown, North Carolina, in the early 1920s in an attempt to revive the skills of the diminishing North Carolina potter's art as Prohibition ended the need for locally crafted stoneware whiskey jugs. During the early years, Juliana Busbee opened a shop in Greenwich Village in New York City to promote the North Carolina wares that her husband, Jacques, was designing and a local youth, Ben Owen, was producing under his direction. Owen continued to work with Busbee from 1922 until Busbee's death in 1947 at which time Juliana took over management of the pottery for the next decade until her illness (or mental fatigue) caused the pottery to be closed in 1958. At that time, Owen opened his own pottery a few miles away, marking his wares "Ben Owen - Master Potter." The pottery begun by the Busbees was reopened in 1960, under new management, and still operates today using the identical impressed mark of the early Jugtown pottery the Busbees managed from 1922 until 1958.

Jugtown Mark

Bowls, 4¼" d., 2" h., a small raised footring supporting a deep wide rounded bowl w/a flat rim, Chinese blue glaze, impressed mark, pr. ... **$468.00**

Vase, 4" h., simple ovoid body tapering to a small flat mouth, vivid Chinese blue glossy glaze, impressed mark................ **242.00**

Large and Small Jugtown Vases

Vase, 4" h., 2¾" d., simple ovoid body w/a small closed rim, overall Chinese blue glaze, impressed mark (ILLUS. right) **303.00**

Vase, 5" h., bulbous ovoid body w/a wide shoulder tapering to a short rolled neck, mottled Chinese blue glaze over dark red clay body, impressed mark. **413.00**

Vase, 6" h., bulbous ovoid body tapering to a short molded flat mouth, unusual Chinese blue glaze in pale shades of aqua, lavender, blue & grey, impressed mark. **286.00**

Vase, 6¾" h., 5" d., bulbous ovoid body tapering to a closed rim, thick white semi-matte glaze dripping over a brown clay body, impressed mark **495.00**

Vase, 7¼" h., 5" d., simple ovoid body tapering to a closed rim, white satin glaze, stamped "Jugtown Ware", rim hairline (ILLUS. left). . . . **330.00**

Vase, 7½" h., 4½" d., footed simple ovoid body tapering to a small closed mouth, overall fine Chinese blue glaze, impressed mark (very tight rim line) **935.00**

Vase, 7¾" h., 5¼" d., bulbous ovoid body tapering to a short flared & pinched neck w/two nubby handles, the shoulder incised w/a wide band of thin vertical lines, glossy oatmeal glaze, impressed circular mark **303.00**

Vase, 8¾" h., 6½" d., stoneware, ovoid body w/a short cylindrical neck flanked by small eared handles, top half w/a matte mustard yellow glaze, bottom half w/a clear coating, impressed mark . . **935.00**

Vase, 9" h., 6¼" d., flat-bottomed ovoid form tapering to a rolled & flattened rim band, four small loop handles around the shoulder, nearly covered in a brown speckled lustre glaze over red clay, impressed mark (in-the-making glaze flakes) **715.00**

Vase, 11" h., 8½" d., footed wide ovoid body tapering to a wide cylindrical neck w/a slightly rolled rim, small angled loop shoulder handles, fine Chinese blue mottled glaze, impressed mark **3,520.00**

KAY FINCH CERAMICS

Kay Finch along with her husband, Braden, opened Kay Finch Ceramics in 1939 in Corona del Mar, California. An extremely talented and dedicated artist, Finch is more well known for her animals than any of her other creations. Dogs were a favorite of hers and can be found as figurines, decorating trays, trinket boxes, ashtrays, planters, plates and others. Ideas

seemed endless for Finch's creativity. Even in the early days, Kay's ceramics were expensive and have continued to be so today. During a period of production, Kay personally trained twenty-five decorators who assisted her. Braden died in 1963 and the business ceased. Kay used her energies for the good of dog breeding shows. In the mid-1970s, Freeman-McFarlin, another California company, hired Kay to create a set of dog figurines which was later followed with other Finch animal designs. These were done in a gold-leaf treatment and marked in block letters with the Kay Finch name and model numbers in the 800s. However, not all Freeman-McFarlin 800 numbers indicate a Finch creation. Freeman-McFarlin had previously purchased Kay's molds and the working relationship lasted until about 1980. Kay Finch died on June 21, 1993 at the age of eighty-nine.

K Finch   Kay Finch
Calif.   CALIFORNIA

Kay Finch Marks

Kay Finch Peasant Boy Figure

Figure of a Chinese man, "Court Prince," No. 451, 11¼" h. **$225.00**

Figure of a choir boy, standing, unusual pearlized gold trim, 7½" h. . . . **128.00**

Figure of a peasant boy, lavender vest, 6¾" h. (ILLUS.). **65.00**

Figures of Godey man & woman, No. 160, pr. **120.00**

Model of a cat, "Jezebel," recumbent position, 6" h. **425.00**

Model of a dog, "Yorkie Pup," No. 171, 6" h. **350.00**

Model of a kitten, "Muff" **65.00**

Model of a pig, "Grumpy," w/strawberries **350.00**

Model of a rooster, "Chanticleer," 10¾" h. **600.00**

Model of an elephant, flowered ears . . **225.00**

Model of an owl, "Tootsie," gray w/brown, No. 189 . . . . **40.00**

LEEDS

The Leeds Pottery in Yorkshire, England, began production about 1758. It made, among other things, creamware that was highly competitive with Wedgwood's. In the 1780s it began production of reticulated and punched wares. Little of its production was marked. Most readily available Leeds ware is that of the 19th century during which time the pottery was operated by several firms.

Charger, pearlware, blue feather-edge design w/h.p. center floral design of blue flowers within a circle surrounded by floral sprigs, 14¼" d. (blue bled in firing, professional repair) **$72.00**

Creamer, free-hand peafowl in yellow, blue & orange perched on a brown branch w/green leafage & overall pale blue overglaze, early 19th c., 4¼" h. (small chips) **863.00**

Plate, 8¼" d., pearlware, blue-feather edge design w/h.p. center floral decoration in dark brown, blue & ochre (small edge flakes) **193.00**

Plate, 8½" d., pearlware, large center "gaudy" floral decoration in black, blue, yellow, green & ochre, line & flower sprig design on border (hairlines). **72.00**

Teapot, cov., creamware, cylindrical w/incurved neck, C-form double-entwined handle & leaf-molded spout, low-domed cover w/daisy-type flower finial, decoration w/vertical bands of brown dots flanked by yellow striping on translucent green ground, chip repairs to tip of spout, 5¾" h. . . . **2,645.00**

LEFTON

What is Lefton China? The brain child of Mr. George Zoltan Lefton who had migrated to the United States from Hungary in 1939. In 1941 he embarked on a new career and starting shaping a business from his passion for collecting fine china and porcelains. He began with a small cash stake and a vision to develop a porcelain source by reviving postwar Japanese ceramic skills dating back to antiquity. As a trailblazer, George Zoltan Lefton soon earned the reputation as "The China King."

As one of the most desirable and sought-after collectibles of today, items such as the Bluebirds, Miss Priss, Angels, all types of dinnerware and any of the tea related items are eagerly acquired by collectors. As with any antique or collectible, prices vary depending on location, condition and availability. For additional information on the history of Lefton China, its factories, marks, products, and values, readers should consult the Collectors Encyclopedia of Lefton China Books I and II, and the 1998 Lefton Price Guide by Loretta DeLozier.

Ashtray, yellow w/butterfly, No. 1237 . . **$28.00**

Ashtrays, stacking-type in holder, Rose Chintz patt., the set **25.00**

Box, cov., candy, Berry Harvest patt., No. 297 . . . . **65.00**

Box, cov., footed, Eastern Elegance patt., No. 9. . . . . **55.00**

Box, hinged cover, Spring Bouquet, No. 8134, 4" h. **28.00**

Candleholders, Noel, No. 674, 4 pcs.. . . . . **60.00**

Candleholders, rose-shaped, Americana, No. 949, pr. **75.00**

Canister set, Rustic Daisy patt., No. 4115, 4 pcs.. . . . . **135.00**

Cigarette set: box w/two swans; No. 324, 4" l. **38.00**

Coffeepot, cov., Blue Paisley patt., No. 1972 . . . . **135.00**

Coffeepot, cov., Brown Heritage Fruit patt., No. 20591. . . . . **175.00**

Heirloom Elegant Coffeepot

Coffeepot, cov., tall gently waisted cylindrical body w/scalloped rim w/inset conical cover w/pointed gold finial, long gold spout & ornate gold handle, large pink blossoms & green leaves on a shaded blue & yellow ground w/gold trim, Heirloom Elegant patt., No. 5394 (ILLUS.). . . . . **110.00 to 150.00**

Compote, open, Victorian Ladies patt., No. 2765. . . . . **42.00**

Cookie Jar, cov., Dainty Miss patt., No. 040 . . . . **200.00**

Cookie Jar, cov., Honey Bee patt., No. 1279 . . . . **110.00**

Cookie jar, cov., Miss Priss patt. **85.00**

Cookie jar, cov., Old Lady **110.00**

Cookie jar, cov., Pixie Baby **125.00**

Cookie jar, cov., Scottish Miss **195.00**

Cookie jar, cov., Young Lady **95.00**
Cookie jar, cov. **110.00**
Cookie jar, cov. **125.00**
Cookie jar, cov. **195.00**
Cookie jar, cov. **95.00**

Lefton "Violets" Pieces

Cup & saucer, Violets patt., funnel-
shaped cup, No. 2300 (ILLUS.
front) . . . . **35.00 to 40.00**
Decanter set, dark green glassware,
No. 4107, the set **120.00**
Dish, bowl-form, green bisque
w/cherub, No. 837 . . . . **190.00**
Dish, three-compartment, Americana,
No. 971 . . . . **75.00**

Rose-decorated Lefton Ewers

Ewers, baluster-form body w/scrolled
& cupped rim, S-scroll handle & tall
ringed pedestal base, white ground
w/overall gilt scroll decoration &
eleven applied pink rose blossoms
& green leaves around the body,
No. 7074, 7" h., each
(ILLUS.) . . . . **95.00 to 115.00**
Figure group, guardian angel w/boy
& girl, No. 6493, 5½" h. **70.00**
Figure group, bobcat & raccoon, No.
351, 8¼" **129.00**
Figure group, fox & hare, No. 352,
9½" h. **100.00**
Figure group, drummer on horse,
No. 4989, 11" h. **195.00**
Figure of a boy, "Off to School,"
Hummel-style **25.00**

Figure of a lady, No. 615B, 8" h. **35.00**
Figurine group, Don Qioxote &
Sancho Panza, No. 4721, 8" h. **110.00**
Figurines, Spirit of 1976, No. 2041,
3 pcs. **145.00**
Figurines, angels, tumbling, No.
80159, 2¾" h., 4 pcs. **140.00**
Figurines, Chinese w/lantern, No.
10268, 8" h., pr. **165.00**
Figurines, provincial boy & girl
w/dog, No. 5642, 8½" h., pr. **200.00**
Jam jar, cov., figural Dutch girl,
No. 2697 . . . . **95.00**
Jam jar, cov., grape line, No. 3023,
4" h. **35.00**
Lady head vase, No. 2251, 6" h. **88.00**
Model of a Bird of Paradise, No.
140, 6¾" h. **80.00**
Model of a fawn, Bambi, white luster
w/stones, No. 871, 7" h., ... **30.00**

Lefton Decorated Lady's shoe

Model of a lady's high-heeled shoe,
white w/ornate applied lacy ruffles
around the opening w/large applied
pink rose blossoms & small blue
blossoms, gilt trim on the lace,
No. 459 (ILLUS.) . . . . **75.00 to 100.00**
Model of an owl, No. 7556, 12" h. **75.00**
Mug, bluebirds, No. 435 . . . . **75.00**
Mug, Robert E. Lee bust, No. 2365,
5½" h. **48.00**
Paperweight, glass, green apple,
No. 2390 . . . . **38.00**
Pitcher & bowl set, miniature,
Heritage Fruit patt., brown, pr. **35.00**
Planter, bucket, Mardi Gras
Collection, No. 50442, 5". **45.00**
Planter, figural Kewpie lying on
stomach, No.3823, 7" l. **35.00**
Plate, 8" d., Moss Rose patt.,
No. 3169 . . . . **16.00**
Plate, 9" d., Berry Harvest patt.,
No. 303 . . . . **28.00**
Plate, 9" d., Rose Heirloom patt.,
No. 1822 . . . . **32.00**
Plate, 9" d., Violets patt., No. 2910
(ILLUS. back) . . . . **30.00 to 35.00**

Salt & pepper shakers, Blue Paisley
   patt., No. 2346, pr.. . . . . **22.00**
Salt & pepper shakers, Daisytime
   patt., No. 3362, pr. **18.00**
Salt & pepper shakers, Fruit Basket
   patt., No. 1657, pr.. . . . . **22.00**
Salt & pepper shakers, Thumbelina,
   No. 1711, pr. **22.00**
Snack set, Blue Paisley patt., No.
   2340 . . . . **18.00**
Snack set: cup & matching indented
   plate; Rose Chintz patt., the set **25.00**
Snack set, Summertime patt.,
   No. 261 . . . . **25.00**
Snack set, To A Wild Rose patt.,
   No. 2580, 8" **23.00**
Tea set: cov. teapot, creamer &
   sugar bowl; Grape patt., the set . . . **150.00**
Tea set, stack-type, cov. teapot,
   sugar & creamer, Elegant Rose
   patt., No. 885, the set **185.00**
Teapot, cov., Blue Paisley pattern,
   No. 2373 . . . . **165.00**
Teapot, cov., Brown Heritage Floral,
   No. 3112 . . . . **200.00**
Teapot, cov., Heritage patt., green . . **125.00**
Teapot, cov., short, round w/swirled
   rib design, Violets patt., No. 20610
   (ILLUS. left). . . . . **65.00 to 85.00**
Teapot, cov., tall w/gently lobed pear-
   shaped body w/scroll handle,
   Violets patt., No. 092
   (ILLUS. right). . . . . **65.00 to 85.00**

Lefton Tidbit Server

Tidbit server, two-tier, graduated
   plates connected by gilt-metal
   stems w/a shield-form top handle,
   purple grapes & green leaves,
   Berry Harvest patt., No. WK911PL
   (ILLUS.). . . . . **75.00 to 100.00**

Tidbit tray, Heritage patt., No. 1153,
   green **60.00**

Lefton Vase with Roses

Vase, baluster-form w/the fanned
   neck flanked by incurved scrolling
   gold handles, large shaded pink
   roses & green stems on a shaded
   green to white ground, No. 4072
   (ILLUS.). . . . . **55.00 to 65.00**
Vase, 3¼" h., w/Lily Of The Valley,
   No. 198 . . . . **32.00**
Vase, 4" h., beige Italian Romance,
   No. 781 . . . . **18.00**
Vase, bud, 6" h., Eastern Elegance
   patt., No. 8. . . . . **22.00**
Vase, 7" h., stein-shaped w/raised
   roses, No. 7074 . . . . **95.00**
Vase, 8½" h., Heritage patt., green . . . **50.00**
Wall plaques, Four Seasons,
   No. 4927, each 8½", the set **120.00**
Wall pocket, figural, Miss Priss,
   No. 1509 . . . . **125.00**

Lefton Bluebird Wall Pockets

Wall pockets, models of bluebirds, a
   male w/a black top hat & gold bow
   tie, a female w/a large pink & red
   flower-trimmed bonnet, blue &
   yellow bodies, No. 283, pr.
   (ILLUS.). . . . . **275.00 to 350.00**

LIMOGES

Numerous factories produced china in Limoges, France, with major production in the 19th century. Some pieces listed below are identified by the name of the maker or the mark of the factory. Although the famed Haviland Company was located in Limoges, wares bearing their marks are not included in this listing. Also see HAVILAND.

An excellent reference is The Collector's Encyclopedia of Limoges Porcelain, Second Edition, *by Mary Frank Gaston (Collector Books, 1992).*

Candlesticks, a round flaring base raised on four tiny gold tab feet, the columnar shaft below a cupped socket rim, h.p. by an amateur decorator w/vining bands of blue forget-me-nots & blue bands against a creamy ground, gilt trim, blank marked "B & Co. - France" (Bernardaud & Co.), 7" h., pr. **$358.00**

Chocolate set: cov. pot & eight cups & saucers; cobalt blue ground decorated w/gilt trim, ca. 1900, pot 11" h., the set, Tresseman & Vogt mark (losses to pot, wear) **230.00**

Dessert set: 12" d. cake plate w/fourteen matching dessert plates; floral decoration, early 20th c., Wm. Guerin & Co., Limoges, France, the set **110.00**

Limoges Game Plate

Game plate, center h.p. decoration of two colorful pheasants in an autumn landscape, scalloped rim w/gilt band, 10⅝" d. (ILLUS.) **125.00**

Mug, tall cylindrical form, cherries on branches against a light green shaded to dark green ground, 8" h. (Guerin) **85.00**

Pitcher, 5½" h., narrow flaring base below the conical body tapering to a shaped rim w/pinched spout, gold rim band & scrolled handle, decorated around the top & center body w/bands of colorful leaves &

acorns w/gold trim, made specifically for Marshall Fields (Coiffe) **61.00**

Platinum-decorated Limoges Pitcher

Pitcher, 6" h., 5⅛" d., bulbous ovoid body w/a wide rim & pinched spout, loop handle, greyish white ground w/a platinum Art Deco design of stylized mistletoe w/pale pink behind the upper design, platinum handle, Jean Pouyat (J.P.) - Limoges mark (ILLUS.) **145.00**

Pitcher, 7¾" h., squatty bulbous wide body tapering to a short neck w/a wide, arched spout & high ornate C-scroll gilt handle, the neck & shoulder h.p. w/colorful roses, "T. & V. - Limoges" (Tresseman & Vogt) . . **193.00**

Plaque, pierced for hanging, round slightly dished shape, an ornate wide border design of facing pairs of long-tailed purple & green peacocks w/golden orange & green fruit clusters below the birds' bodies & above their tails, lacy gold border ground, signed & dated "1911," 14" d. (Chas. Martin) **138.00**

Plaques, rectangular, pate-sur-pate, each w/a Wedgwood blue ground decorated w/white relief classical figures, one w/a young lady dancing w/a veil, a putti nearby, the second w/a dancing lady holding a spear & a cluster of grapes w/a putti nearby, ca. 1890, matted & framed, 5½ x 7½", pr. (small flake at bottom of one) **715.00**

Limoges Plate with Seascape

Plate, 10¼" d., pierced to hang,
gently scalloped & scroll-molded
gold-trimmed rim, large seascape
scene w/a tower & buildings on the
shore, artist-signed, marked
(ILLUS.). **118.00**

Fruit-decorated Limoges Wall Plate

Plate, 12⅜" d., pierced to hang,
ornate scalloped & beaded gold
rim, h.p. colorful fruits among grass
& greenery, green, yellow orangish
red, marked (ILLUS.). **195.00**
Plates, 9¾" d., round w/a gold
beaded rim band, cobalt blue wide
border band w/stenciled lacy gold
trim & a large lacy gold medallion
in the center, J. Pouyat mark, pr. . . . **72.00**

Fine Limoges Punch Bowl & Base

Punch bowl & base, deep footed &
flaring bowl w/scroll-molded gold
rim above exterior sides decorated
w/grapevines in autumnal colors &
purple grapes, scroll-embossed
gold-trimmed separate pedestal
base, signed "T & V Limoges,"
Tresseman & Vogt, late 19th c., 14"
d., 2 pcs. (ILLUS.) **990.00**
Tray, dresser, rectangular
w/serpentine edges, pale blue &
peach ground h.p. w/violets,
8 x 12" (Elite) **135.00**
Tray, dresser, oval, white shaded to
green ground decorated w/yellow
roses w/green leaves, 9 x 12½"
(Coronet) **135.00**

LIVERPOOL

*Liverpool is most often used as a generic term
for fine earthenware products, usually of
creamware or pearlware, produced at numerous
potteries in this English city during the late 18th
and early 19th centuries. Many examples,
especially pitchers, were decorated with transfer-
printed patriotic designs aimed specifically at
the American buying public.*

Bowl, 8⅞" d., the interior transfer-
printed w/a scene of a three-
masted ship under sail surrounded
by reserves of armaments, the
exterior w/a portrait of George
Washington flanked by reserves of
mermaids & a portrait of Benjamin
Franklin, early 19th c. (repairs,
chips) **$403.00**

Rare Washington Liverpool Mug

Mug, tankard-type, tall cylindrical
creamware body, the front
decorated w/a black transfer-
printed oval medallion w/a profile
bust portrait of George
Washington, a banner below
reading "Long Live the President of
the United States," flanked on the
left by a female figure representing
Liberty & on the right by a figure
representing Justice, Liberty
w/dialog banner reading "My
Favorite Son," Justice w/a larger
inscribed dialog banner, ca. 1790s,
6¼" h. (ILLUS.). **5,060.00**
Pitcher, jug-type, 6" h., black
transfer-printed design of a three-
masted ship under sail & a figure of
"Hope," name under spout "Jennett
Lawson," early 19th c. (hairline in
base) **748.00**
Pitcher, jug-type, 7¾" h., front w/a
black transfer-printed reserve of
the ships, L'Insurgent &
Constellation, & reverse reserve of
a shipyard, early 19th c. (cracks,
chips, minor losses, staining,
transfer imperfections) **1,265.00**

Pitcher, jug-type, 8" h., creamware, one side transfer-printed in black w/a two-masted brig flying the American flag, the other side w/an American Eagle, an American Eagle also under the spout, early 19th c. (spout repaired) **920.00**

Pitcher, jug-type, 8¼" h., black transfer-printed decoration, one side w/the spread-winged American eagle Seal of the United States within a chain ring naming sixteen states, the reverse w/an oval wreath enclosing three classical ladies & the inscription "United We Stand - Divided We Fall," under the spout a wheat & grape wreath enclosing the initials "GHH," early 19th c. **2,090.00**

Pitcher, jug-type, 8½" h., black transfer-printed design w/one side showing a small oval medallion around the bust of George Washington in profile below the words "He in Glory - America in Tears," reverse w/a memorial urn w/ lengthy tribute inscription to Washington, under spout an oval medallion reading "A Man without example A Patriot without reproach," early 19th c. (hairlines) **2,420.00**

Pitcher, jug-type, 9¼" h., creamware, one side transfer-printed in black w/a large spread-winged eagle resting on a cannon & flags above a round reserve printed w/"Peace - Plenty - and Independence," classical allegorical figures on each side representing Peace and Plenty, the reverse w/a black transfer-printed three-masted sailing ship w/the American flag, under the spout is the American eagle w/shield & banner, traces of gilding around the rim & spout, early 19th c. (small reglued chip on the base rim) **1,210.00**

Very Rare Liverpool Pitcher

Pitcher, jug-type, 9½" h., creamware, black transfer-printed decoration, one side w/a large round medallion enclosing a grouping of three seated classical maidens surrounding a medallion bust portrait of John Adams, his name below, the reverse w/a scene of a ship under full sail flying the American flag, titled "The Constant," under the spout a wreath of leaves enclosing the initials "T W M" above a standing classical lady leaning on a large anchor symbolizing Hope, highlighted in yellow, green, red, white & blue, under handle a small American eagle, vines around rim, early 19th c. (ILLUS.) **15,400.00**

Extremely Rare Liverpool Pitcher

Pitcher, jug-type, 9¾" h., one side decorated w/a black transfer-printed oval portrait reserve of Thomas Jefferson, the other side w/a portrait of James Monroe misidentified as "Hancock," oval reserve w/initials under the spout, h.p. foliate gilt highlights, repairs, hairlines, minor chip, gilt & enamel wear (ILLUS.) **20,700.00**

Pitcher, jug-type, 10⅜" h., creamware, one side transfer-printed in black w/a "Plan of the City of Washington," the opposite side w/a scene of "Commodore Prebles Squadron Attacking the City of Tripoli, Aug. 3, 1804...," the Seal of the United States under the spout, a thorny rose printed below the Tripoli scene (excellent restoration to portion of the spout, handle & side of base) **2,475.00**

Pitcher, jug-type, 10¾" h., black transfer-printed oval reserve on one side features a memorial obelisk w/a profile portrait of George Washington flanked by willow trees & a weeping figure, inscribed "Washington in Glory - America in Tears," the reverse w/a

Washington Memorial Pitcher

scene of a three-masted American frigate titled "South Carolina," under the spout the initials "JG" inside a wreath w/a small Seal of the United States, vines & flowers around the rim & a small oval transfer below the handle inscribed "A MAN without example - A PATRIOT without reproach," early 19th c. (ILLUS.) **2,310.00**

Pitcher, jug-type, 12¼" h., creamware, one side transfer-printed in black w/a comical scene making fun of Thomas Jefferson, the other side w/a printed scene of the apotheosis of George Washington, the American Eagle & a quote by Jefferson under the spout, scattered floral sprigs around the scenes, gilt trim, early 19th c. (hairline along spout, minor darkening) **3,738.00**

Plate, 9¾" d., creamware, flanged rim, the center transfer-printed in black w/a large three-masted sailing ship, three long leafy sprigs around the rim, early 19th c. (knife scratches, rim chips) **230.00**

Plate, 10" d., lightly scalloped flanged rim, center w/a black transfer-printed three-masted ship under full sail flying the American flag, the rim w/a series of floral sprigs, back w/impressed mark "Herculaneum," late 18th - early 19th c. (two front rim chips, small flake on table ring) . . **523.00**

LOTUS WARE

Avidly sought by many collectors are these exquisite china wares made by Knowles, Taylor & Knowles of East Liverpool, Ohio, in the last decade of the 19th century. The firm also produced ironstone and hotel china.

Pitcher, 3½" h., squatty bulbous body, all-white w/raised netted pattern & tied bamboo handle, marked **$171.00**

Pitcher, 4½" h., squatty bulbous body decorated w/pink floral branches, green bamboo-form handle tied w/gold, gilt floral rim, marked **248.00**

Potpourri jar, cov., footed spherical body in pale green trimmed w/domed reticulated round side handles & a band of large white balls flanked by tiny beaded bands around the rim, an ornate domed & reticulated white cover w/an urn-form finial, marked, 4" h. **715.00**

Potpourri jar, cov., Persian-style, all-white, flaring foot w/a large band of beads flanked by two tiny bead bands below the large spherical body flanked by S-form domed & ornately reticulated handles, beaded bands repeated around the rim, ornate domed reticulated & bead-trimmed cover, marked, 7" h. **1,485.00**

Potpourri jar, cov., all-white, four curved tab feet supporting the large spherical body decorated w/ornate beaded swags around the rim & down the sides joining four domed ornately reticulated medallions around the sides, domed reticulated cover w/matching swags & an urn-form finial, marked, 7½" h. **1,870.00**

Rose bowl, spherical body raised on three knob feet, the sides applied w/leaves & berries trimmed in blue & gold against the white ground, marked "Lotusware KTK," 1890s, 3¾" h. **440.00**

Rose bowl, footed spherical body w/a wide flaring ruffled rim, white ground decorated overall w/raised lavender flowers & leaves & beaded rim, marked, 4" h. **303.00**

Tray, shell-shaped, white ground decorated w/raised gold floral & leafy branch & ornate fluted gilt-trimmed rim & scroll handle, marked on bottom "Compliments Knowles, Taylor and Knowles, E. Liverpool, Ohio, May 10th, 1905, on to Cairo Nine foot stage," w/company mark, 5½" w. **165.00**

LUSTRE WARES

Lustred wares in imitation of copper, gold, silver and other colors were produced in England in the early 19th century and onward. Gold, copper or platinum oxides were painted on glazed objects which were then fired, giving them a lustred effect. Various forms of lustre wares include plain lustre with the entire object coated to obtain a metallic effect, bands of lustre decoration and painted lustre designs. Particularly appealing is the pink or purple "splash lustre" sometimes referred to as "Sunderland" lustre in the mistaken belief it was confined to the production of Sunderland area potteries. Objects decorated in silver lustre by the "resist" process, wherein parts of the objects to be left free from lustre decoration were treated with wax, are referred to as "silver resist."

Wares formerly called "Canary Yellow Lustre" are now referred to as "Yellow-Glazed Earthenwares."

Silver & Silver Resist

Redware Circus Wagon Finial

Circus wagon finial, Redware, spherical w/molded recumbent lion finial & acanthus leaves, "Bailey & Batkin Sole Patentees" on center band, flat circular base, minor chip to base, lustre wear, 7⅛" h. (ILLUS.) $1,265.00

Sunderland Pink & Others

Pitcher, 4" h., footed wide bulbous squatty body tapering slightly to a short waisted neck w/wide arched spout & scalloped rim, ropetwist arched handle, black transfer-printed village scene w/florals around the neck, overall pink lustre glaze, first half 19th c. 110.00

Pitcher, 5¼" h., footed wide shell-ribbed lower body below a wide shoulder to the tall waisted neck w/a high, wide arched spout, S-scroll handle, black fruit & floral transfer-printed design around neck, overall pink lustre glaze, early 19th c. (minor surface edge wear) 176.00

Rare Lustre Decorated Watch Hutch

Watch hutch, figural, a tall central grandfather clock w/the top open to accept the watch, case flanked by a small figure of a boy & a girl, fine underglaze decoration in yellow, black, blue, green, grey, red, brown, flesh & pink lustre trim, impressed on top of the base "Dixon Austin & Co.," Sunderland, England, ca. 1820-26, professional restoration to top of clock & hairline across base, 11¼" h. (ILLUS.) . . **1,430.00**

MAJOLICA

Majolica, a tin-enameled glazed pottery, has been produced for centuries. It originally took its name from the island of Majorca, a source of figuline (potter's clay). Subsequently it was widely produced in England, Europe and the United States. Etruscan majolica, now avidly sought, was made by Griffen, Smith & Hill, Phoenixville, Pa., in the last quarter of the 19th century. Most majolica advertised today is 19th or 20th century. Once scorned by most collectors, interest in this colorful ware so popular during the Victorian era has now revived and prices have risen dramatically in the past few years. Also see WEDGWOOD.

GENERAL

Beer mugs, each modeled as a miniature barrel encircled by hop branches, painted design numbers, George Jones, England, ca. 1875, 4¼" h., pr. **$258.00**

Bowl, 4¼" d., modeled as a mushroom growing from a rockwork base supporting three naturalistically modeled frogs, impressed Minton marks & date code for 1870, England **2,300.00**

Bowl, 11¼" d., round w/flattened flanked rim molded w/blossomheads & leaf sprigs, brown edges flowing into pale blue streaked down to the brown center, base incised "Germany - 903" **66.00**

Bread tray, oval, molded w/blossoming branches on a basketweave ground, England, ca. 1875, 15" l. **402.00**

Bulb pot, demilune-form, modeled as a cluster of bamboo tied w/pink ribbons, England, ca. 1875, 6½" h. **575.00**

Cake stand, figural, a round dish top w/reticulated Greek Key border raised on a pedestal composed of three entwined dolphins on a shaped plinth, impressed Wedgwood mark & date code for 1864, England, 7" d. **862.00**

Candelabrum, three-light, figural, Neo-classical fluted column base molded w/swagged drapes & oval medallions supports three standing putti each holding a hunting horn aloft terminating in a molded cylindrical candle socket, modeled in the style of Hugues Protat, impressed Minton marks & dated 1864, England, 16" h. **3,220.00**

Candelabrum, three-light, figural, a Neo-classical pedestal supporting a top crossbar w/three candle sockets formed as Roman oil lamps, the pedestal flanked by two full-figure putti, cobalt blue ground, impressed Minton marks, date code for 1869, England, 16½" h. . . **4,887.00**

Candlestick, modeled in the style of Pierre-Emile Jeannest, w/elaborate Italian Renaissance ornament, impressed Minton marks, England, date code 1863, 15" h. **1,150.00**

Candlesticks, molded w/green leafage on a cobalt blue ground, England, ca. 1865, 8" h., pr. **575.00**

Majolica Baroque-style Candlestick

Candlesticks, Baroque-style w/ornately embossed design, wide domed foot w/scrolled feet, tall standard w/two graduated balls alternating w/rings below a drip pan & leaf embossed cylindrical socket, glazed in turquoise & cobalt blue, impressed marks & date code, 16¼" h., pr. (ILLUS. of one) **3,450.00**

Ornate Majolica Centerpiece

Centerpiece, central egg-form, shell-molded bowl, raised on the tails of three dolphins resting on three cockle shell-form bowls & three shell feet, painted design number, ca. 1875, George Jones, 9½" h. (ILLUS.). **3,680.00**

Centerpiece, figural, modeled as a putto riding a dolphin on a wave-molded oval plinth supporting an oval shell-form bowl, England, ca. 1875, 12" h. **1,092.00**

Centerpiece, figural, modeled as a trefoil openwork basket w/twig & ribbon handle supported by three putti standing on a shaped plinth, impressed Minton marks, date code for 1865, England, 13" h. . . **5,750.00**

Centerpiece, figural, modeled as a putto holding aloft a bowl formed from broad leaves & grapevines, standing on a square plinth w/molded masks at each corner, impressed Sarreguemines mark, France, ca. 1885, overall 15½" h. . . **2,070.00**

Majolica Minton Centerpiece

Centerpiece, modeled as two naiads on an oval base supporting a naturalistic shell w/laurel cables, ca. 1871, impressed marks & date code, Minton, 18" l. (ILLUS.) **7,475.00**

Cheese stand, cov., a simple form molded w/naturalistically colored bamboo, leafage & borders on a white ground, impressed Minton marks & date code for 1876, 11" h. **747.00**

Cheese stand, cov., modeled w/acanthus leaves within rope borders on a salmon pink ground, England, ca. 1875, 12" h. **805.00**

Cheese stand, cov., molded in the Apple Blossom patt., the high domed cover molded on the lower half w/a basketweave design & the upper half w/blossoming apple branches w/a twig handle on a pale blue ground, basketweave base, George Jones, England, ca. 1875, 12½" h. **2,760.00**

Majolica Covered Cheese Stand

Cheese stand, cov., the base modeled as reeds & the cover patterned w/waterlilies & insects on a cobalt blue ground, impressed monogram & registry mark of 1874, George Jones, 12½" h. overall (ILLUS.) **4,600.00**

Cheese stand, cov., the cover molded w/waterlilies & insects on a cobalt blue ground, the base modeled as green reeds, impressed monogram of George Jones & registry mark for 1874, England, overall 12½" h. **4,600.00**

Cheese stand, cov., figural, naturalistically modeled as a large thatched-top beehive on a square, rustic base, painted George Jones marks on stand, ca. 1872, overall 13¼" h. **11,500.00**

Cigar holder, figural, a model of a monkey wearing a smoking jacket & seated playing an upright piano w/the piano case forming cigar holder, impressed Sarreguemines marks, France, ca. 1890, 8" h. .. **2,070.00**

Creamer, figural, naturalistically modeled as a bulbous blow fish, England, ca. 1875, 5½" l. **287.00**

Cuspidor, molded w/blossoming branches on brown, rustic ground, England, ca. 1875, 7" h. **143.00**

Dish, oval, Dogwood Blossoms & Leaves patt., cobalt blue ground w/bird perched on edge, English registry mark, 7" l. **525.00**

Majolica Shell & Naiad Ewer

Ewer, Renaissance-style, heart-shaped shell molded body w/flaring pedestal foot w/scroll decoration & cylindrical scale molded neck, two naiads resting on the shoulders, long scrolling handle & rim, impressed marks, date code for 1868, modeled by Hugues Protat, Minton, 14" h. (ILLUS.) **6,325.00**

Ewer & undertray, in the Renaissance taste, the tall ovoid ewer on a knopped pedestal base & w/a tall slender neck w/arched spout, molded overall w/putti & scrolling foliage, modeled by Pierre-Emile Jeannest, impressed Minton marks & date marks, England, ca. 1876, undertray 11" d., ewer 13½" h., 2 pcs. **1,840.00**

Figures of fairground characters, a boy w/a gaming wheel & a girl w/an empty purse, Europe, 19th c., 8½" h., pr. **287.00**

Figures of vintagers, a young woman & young man wearing 18th c. costume & holding a grape basket aloft on one shoulder, on molded round bases, Europe, 19th c., 13" h., pr. **546.00**

Fish server, cov., formed as an oval twig basket holding a naturalistically modeled salmon on a bed of leafage, George Jones, England, impressed registry mark, ca. 1871, 19½" l. **2,875.00**

Flower basket, molded w/waterlilies on a cobalt blue ground w/a curved handle formed as reeds, George Jones, England, ca. 1875, 8" l. **690.00**

Flowerpot & undertray, modeled as a tree stump overgrown w/oak leaves & ivy, matching undertray, each w/impressed Minton marks & date code for 1879, overall 6" h., 2 pcs. **805.00**

Majolica Covered Game Dish

Game dish, cov., modeled as a basket supported by three fantail doves perched on leafy oak branches, the domed basketweave cover w/knop modeled as a fantail dove, ca. 1865, Minton (ILLUS.).. **8,050.00**

Game dish, cov., oval, modeled as a basket overgrown w/oak leaves, the cover modeled as dead game on a bed of leafage w/oak branch handle, Minton, England, impressed mark & dated 1876, 12¾" l. **1,725.00**

Majolica Garden Seat

Garden seat, Neo-classical style squatty bulbous top section w/pierced holes in flat top, raised on wide tapering scrolled legs w/fanned design, ca. 1880, George Jones, 17" h. (ILLUS.) **2,760.00**

Garden seat, footed baluster shape, molded overall w/scrollwork & masks in the Renaissance taste, glazed in brown & yellow on a green ground, England, ca. 1870, 18" h. **1,092.00**

Herb pot, modeled as an openwork basket, raised on three pine cone feet, probably Joseph Holdcroft, England, ca. 1875, 3¼" h. **143.00**

Humidor, cov., light blue ground, decorated on one side w/a bust portrait of a Native American chief in full headdress, flowers on two sides, the cover w/a full-figure Native American in war bonnet, sponge holder inside cover **650.00**

Humidor, cov., model of a cat's head wearing a large yellow straw hat, base marked "J.S." in shield & "Made in Austria," fine detail, 6" h. .. **450.00**

Jardiniere, footed, molded w/water lily plants on a brown ground, England, ca. 1875, 7¼" h. **488.00**

Jardiniere, figural, a model of a circus elephant w/howdah, designed by James Handley, impressed marks for Royal Worcester, printed retailer's mark of Richard Briggs, Boston, dated 1869, England, 9" l. **1,495.00**

Majolica Sphinx Jardiniere

Jardiniere, lozenge-form bowl supported by a pair of winged sphinxes on an oval pedestal, ca. 1875, George Jones, 9" l. (ILLUS.) **3,565.00**

Jardiniere, footed, bulbous cylindrical body w/rolled rim, decorated w/birds, insects & waterlilies on

Fine George Jones Jardiniere

cobalt blue ground, ca. 1875,
George Jones, 11¾" h.
(ILLUS.) **6,900.00**

Majolica "Continents" Jardiniere

Jardiniere, "Continents," footed wide
tapering ovoid body, decorated
w/profiles representing America &
Africa in oval cartouches, ring
handles, short cylindrical rim
w/geometric band design,
impressed marks, 1869, Minton,
13¼" h. (ILLUS.). **2,300.00**
Jardiniere, oval, molded w/floral
garlands & Minerva-head handles
in the Neo-classical taste, on a
cobalt blue ground, Joseph
Holdcroft, England, ca. 1875,
17½" l. **1,380.00**

Majolica Lozenge-form Jardiniere

Jardiniere, lozenge-form, molded
after Clodion, w/a continuous frieze
of mythical sea figures & cherubim,
including Triton blowing a conch
shell, ca. 1875, George Jones,
24" l. (ILLUS.). **5,980.00**
Jardiniere & stand, each
w/polychrome-glazed relief foliate
designs, late 19th c., jardiniere
13⅛" h., stand 36½" h., 2 pcs. . . **1,265.00**
Jardiniere underplate, the border
molded w/naturalistic foxgloves,
ferns & wildflowers on a brown &
rustic ground, impressed Minton
marks & date code for 1868,
22" d. **1,265.00**
Jardiniere & undertray, tapering
ovoid body w/rolled molded rim
above wide gently swirled molded
ribs molded w/two large fruit &
floral garlands joined by ram's
head terminals, cobalt blue ground,
matching dished undertray,
impressed Minton marks & date
code for 1869 on pot & 1895 on
undertray, designed by Baron
Carlo Marochetti, England, overall
14" h., 2 pcs. **2,760.00**
Jardinieres, flattened leaftip-molded
rim, the deep urn-form sides
molded in high-relief w/winged
terms & grotesque masks joined by
swags, William Brownfield,
England, ca. 1875, 12¾" d.,
11¼" h., pr. **6,900.00**
Model of a lion, naturalistically
modeled & glazed, standing on a
rockwork base, impressed Minton
mark, England, ca. 1890, 8½" h. . . **1,840.00**

Majolica Oyster Plate

Oyster Plate, six pale blue wells
divided by yellow, green & brown
sea plants w/center white well, ca.
1875, George Jones, 8¾" d.
(ILLUS.) **1,725.00**

Majolica Revolving Oyster Stand

Oyster stand, revolving, figural oyster shells in four graduated tiers on a rockwork base w/figural eel & two fish knop, impressed date code for 1856, Minton, 10½" h. (ILLUS.) . . **4,312.00**

Pitcher, jug-type, squatty, Water Lily patt. **195.00**

Pitcher, 7" h., Chickens w/Wheat Sheaf patt., probably English **295.00**

Pitcher, 7" h., moon flask-shape, oval foot on a flattened round body w/an upright oblong neck w/pinched spout, angled handle, molded musical design on each side, mottled blue, green, yellow & brown glaze, 19th c. **105.00**

Pitcher, 7½" h., Owl & Fan patt. **250.00**

Pitcher, 7¾" h., figural, modeled as a branch of coral encrusted w/shells & resting on waves, Simon Fielding, England, ca. 1880 . . . . . . **230.00**

Pitcher, 8" h., swelled cylindrical form w/pinched rim spout & C-scroll handle, molded up the sides w/large fish on a cobalt blue ground, England, ca. 1875 . . . . **431.00**

Pitcher, 8¼" h., figural, modeled as a large ovoid pineapple w/flaring molded green leafage forming the neck & spout & continuing to form the curved handle, Minton, impressed marks & dated 1867 . . . **575.00**

Pitcher, caterer's jug-type, 8½" h., glazed in browns, yellow & blues, modeled by Frederick Bret Russell, impressed Wedgwood marks & dated 1872 . . . . **172.00**

Pitcher, jug-type, 10¾" h., tall ovoid body raised on a short ringed pedestal on a round domed foot, the cylindrical neck w/a molded pointed spout, ringed strap handle, molded overall w/designs in the Elizabethan style w/an oval portrait medallion of William Shakespeare in a strapwork oval at the front & strapwork band around the body, the body band molded w/a commemorative inscription for the tercentenary of Shakespeare's birth in 1564, Minton, impressed marks & dated 1864 . . . . **1,035.00**

Pitcher, 11¾" h., figural, modeled as two intertwined Renaissance-style scaly fish w/the upper one's mouth forming opening & spout, William Brownfield, England, 1879, molded mark & registry mark **1,955.00**

Majolica Tower Pitcher

Pitcher, hinged pewter lid w/figural jester head knop, jug-type, 13" h., decorated w/Medieval merrymakers around a rustic stone tower, impressed marks & dated 1872, Minton (ILLUS.) **1,035.00**

Planter, figural, modeled as a sleigh molded w/floral sprays, Europe, ca. 1900, 14" l. **546.00**

Platter, oval w/drip tray, cream center w/alternating bands of geometric designs in green, rust, black, mustard yellow & white, George Jones, England, 12 x 20" . . . **165.00**

Majolica Punch Bowl

Punch bowl, w/figure of Punchinello, recumbent on a cushion & holding a squatty bulbous bowl, decorated w/a band of holly, ca. 1875, George Jones, 9" h. (ILLUS.) . . . **13,800.00**

Punch service stand, in the Louis XVI-Style, round scalloped tray raised on scroll feet & fitted for a punch bowl & twelve cups, England, ca. 1880, stand only, 23" d. **747.00**

Salt dip, figural, Hogarth-style, a figure of a gallant holding an oval basket, impressed Minton marks & date code for 1863, England, 7¾" h. **460.00**

Sardine box, cov., rectangular, molded w/seaweed & applied w/a fish finial, on a cobalt blue ground, England, ca. 1875, 7½" l. **546.00**

Sardine box, cov., rectangular basketweave-molded box w/the cover applied w/overlapping fish, set on a boat-form plant-molded dish, impressed marks of George Jones, England, ca. 1876, 9⅛" l. . . **546.00**

Sardine box, cover & stand, molded w/radiating stiff leaves, the cover molded w/three fish, George Jones, England, ca. 1872, 8½" l., the set **1,150.00**

Sauceboat, modeled as an oval shell w/handle formed as a coiled sea snake, impressed & painted marks of William Brownfield, England, ca. 1870, 7½" l. **431.00**

Shelves, bracket-form, each modeled in the Renaissance taste w/Minerva heads, grotesques & foliage on a robin's-egg blue ground, impressed William Brownfield marks, England, ca. 1870, 10" h., pr. **2,415.00**

Strawberry basket, molded w/fruiting strawberry plants & a stalk handle, England, ca. 1875, 9¼" l. **431.00**

Strawberry plate, shell-form dish patterned w/naturalistic fruiting strawberry plants, Minton, England, impressed marks & date code for "1869," 8" d. **373.00**

Strawberry plates, each decorated w/molded strawberry leaves on a pink & white napkin ground, George Jones, England, three w/painted design number "2284," 8" d., set of 4 . . . . **920.00**

Strawberry server, molded as four mossy oval wells, raised on & bordered w/twigs & molded w/naturalistic blossoming strawberry plants, George Jones, England, painted marks & impressed registry mark, dated 1873, 11¾" l. **1,265.00**

Strawberry server, molded w/strawberry leaves on pink & white napkin ground & fitted w/a pair of cream jugs, George Jones applied cartouche mark, England, ca. 1875, 14½" l. **805.00**

Sugar bowl, cov., naturalistically modeled as a bird's nest, raised on leafy oak branches, the interior glazed robin's-egg blue, impressed Minton marks & date code for 1866, 4" d. **345.00**

Sweetmeat dish, modeled as a putto seated on a conch shell, raised on a dolphin & oval plinth, England, ca. 1870, 7" h. **1,725.00**

Table center, figural, modeled as three storks encircling a clump of reeds supporting a dish patterned w/waterlilies, England, ca. 1870, 9" h. **862.00**

Teapot, cov., Bird & Fan patt. **325.00**

Teapot, cov., modeled as a lemon fruit wrapped in leaves, the cover molded as a mushroom, impressed Minton marks & date code for 1868, 4¾" h. **2,185.00**

Teapot, cov., figural, modeled as a large head of cauliflower molded w/wide green leaves & a green vine spout & handle, England, ca. 1865, 5¼" h. **977.00**

Majolica Monkey Teapot

Teapot, cov., figural, modeled as a monkey wearing a Japanese tunic & clutching a coconut, impressed Minton marks & date code for 1874, 6" h. (ILLUS.) **4,830.00**

Chinese Boy Teapot

Teapot, cov., decorated w/Chinese boy in cobalt blue & yellow robe climbing on a giant coconut, ca. 1875, Joseph Holdcroft, 7½" l. (ILLUS.) **2,070.00**

Teapot, cov., figural, modeled as a Chinese dwarf seated holding a mask, his pigtail forming the handle, impressed Minton marks & dated code for 1876, 7¾" l. **2,300.00**

Teapot, cov., kettle-form, the body w/pineapple molding, England, ca. 1875, 8" h. **373.00**

Teapot, cov., squatty bulbous body molded w/leafy scrolls & garlands joined by mask terminals, impressed Wedgwood marks & date code for 1868, C-scroll handle, 9" l. **575.00**

Teapot, cov., figural, naturalistically modeled as a large blow fish swallowing another small fish which forms the spout, England, ca. 1875, 11½" l. **575.00**

Tile, frieze-type, rectangular, molded w/a Neo-classical relief of Triton & other figures after Clodion, on a cobalt blue ground, set in a molded frame, Wedgwood, England, ca. 1866, 7½ x 14½" **1,092.00**

Tobacco jar, cov., modeled as a rustic tree stump patterned w/oak leaves & acorns, England, ca. 1870, 7½" h. **345.00**

Toiletry box, cov., gentleman's, the base molded w/diaperwork & florettes, the cover molded w/a recumbent lion, England, ca. 1870, 6" l. **805.00**

Tray, dessert-type, molded w/grapes & vine leaves in rich colors, impressed Wedgwood marks, England, dated 1882, 12" l. **488.00**

Umbrella stand, cylindrical w/a flared rim, mottled shades of green w/reddish brown stripes, 11½" d., 21" h. **734.00**

Vase, 5" h., modeled as three stalks of bamboo growing from a round leafy base, England, ca. 1875 . . . . **143.00**

Vase, 9½" h., figural, modeled as a female vintager resting on a basket, impressed Minton marks & date code for 1870, England **1,035.00**

Vase, 9½" h., figural, the base modeled as a large swan w/a trumpet-form vase molded w/cattails emerging from the center of its back, its open neck curving

up & back w/its head attached under the rolled rim, England, dated 1876 . . . . **1,955.00**

Vase, 9½" h., naturalistically modeled as a nautilus shell surmounted by a lizard raised on branching coral, impressed Royal Worcester marks, England, ca. 1875 . . . . **1,610.00**

Vase, 10½" h., figural, naturalistically modeled as an upright ear of corn w/green open leaves forming handles & a stalk base, Europe, ca. 1890 . . . . **747.00**

Rare Rooster Floor Vase

Vase, floor-type, 27" h., Choisy-Le-Roi figural life-size, naturalistically colored cockerel standing against a tree stump overgrown w/wild flowers, modeled by Paul Comolera, ca. 1885, printed mark of Hippolyte Boulanger (ILLUS.). . **6,325.00**

Vase, floor-type, 31" h., figural, modeled as a heron holding a fish in its beak & standing against a clump of reeds, designed by John Henk, impressed Minton marks, England, ca. 1880 . . . . **9,775.00**

Sarreguemines Majolica Wall Fountain

Wall fountain, figural giant tortoise above a shell-form basin, on a fitted painted wood wall bracket, ca. 1890, Sarreguemines, 36" h. overall (ILLUS.) **1,150.00**

Wall plaque, molded in relief w/a tavern scene of two characters playing checkers, England, ca. 1870, 10 x 13" **575.00**

Wall tile, square, modeled w/a round panel of a disguised cupid representing Winter in rich colors, impressed "COPELAND," ca. 1875, 8" w. **258.00**

Wine cooler, cylindrical body w/a molded rim & base band, raised on three tall scroll feet, in the Neo-classical style, the body w/a cobalt blue ground flanked by two molded bail handles, impressed Minton mark & date code for 1867, England, 15¾" h. **2,070.00**

Majolica Wine Cooler & Stand

Wine cooler, w/stand, quatrefoil bowl w/figural mermen handles, raised on a pedestal base molded w/grotesque masks, impressed marks & date of 1859, Minton, 22½" overall (ILLUS.) **3,737.00**

MARBLEHEAD

This pottery was organized in 1904 by Dr. Herbert J. Hall as a therapeutic aid to patients in a sanitarium he ran in Marblehead, Massachusetts. It was later separated from the sanitarium and directed by Arthur E. Baggs, a fine artist and designer, who bought out the factory in 1916 and operated it until its closing in 1936. Most wares were hand-thrown and decorated and carry the company mark of a stylized sailing vessel flanked by the letters "M" and "P."

Marblehead Mark

Bowl, 7¾" d., 4½" h., thin footring supporting the widely flaring trumpet-form body w/a flattened rim, fine matte yellow glaze w/a green shaded to blue interior, ship mark **$303.00**

Trivet, square, decorated w/stylized flowers in matte blue, green, yellow & red, impressed mark & paper label, remnant of original price label, 6" w. **863.00**

Trivet, square, colorful floral basket in blue, red, yellow, green & orange on a black ground, impressed mark & paper label, 6¼" w. **431.00**

Small Marblehead Vase

Vase, 3½" h., 3¼" d., small swelled cylindrical body w/a wide, flat mouth, dripping iridescent red striations on a creamy white & red glossy glazed ground, impressed mark, two paper labels, remnant of original price tag (ILLUS.) **3,450.00**

Vase, 3½" h., 4" d., squatty bulbous ovoid body tapering to a rolled rim, decorated w/a band of tall slender stylized trees in two tones of bluish grey against a lighter grey ground, by Hannah Tuff, ship mark & artist's initials **1,760.00**

Vase, 5¼" h., 3¼" d., simple swelled & gently flaring cylindrical form w/a wide flat mouth, decorated w/tall slender stylized trees & yellow flowers on a matte speckled blue ground, ship mark. **1,650.00**

Vase, 6" h., 4½" d., gently flaring cylindrical body w/a short rounded shoulder tapering to the wide, flattened, flaring rim, smooth matte dark blue glaze, unsigned **165.00**

Vase, 6¼" h., 3¾" d., slightly waisted cylindrical body decorated in wax-resist w/a rim band of stylized trees in brown on a green ground, early ship mark (flaking to rim glaze) . . **1,760.00**

Vase, 6¼" h., 8" w., fan-shaped, matte blue glazes, impressed mark & paper label **316.00**

Marblehead Vase with Trees

Vase, 6½" h., 6" d., wide bulbous baluster-form body w/a wide short neck, incised stylized tree designs on three sides in a light brown on creamy white ground, impressed mark, initials "A.E.B.", two company labels (ILLUS.) **3,450.00**

Vase, 6¾" h., 3¾" d., simple ovoid body swelling to a wide, flat mouth, smooth matte blue glaze, ship mark **413.00**

Vase, 7" h., 4" d., simple ovoid body w/a flat rim, smooth speckled matte green & brown glaze, ship mark ... **440.00**

Vase, 8" h., 4¼" d., gently tapering swelled cylindrical body w/a rolled rim, bluish grey microcrystalline glaze, ship mark **495.00**

Vase, 9" h., 4" d., cylindrical, matte blue glaze, impressed mark **863.00**

Vase, 9" h., 7" d., large gently tapering cylindrical body w/a wide closed rim, smooth matte speckled bluish grey glaze, ship mark **990.00**

Wall pocket, blue matte glaze, impressed mark, 4" w., 5" h. **230.00**

Wall pocket, half-round form w/a three-panel front w/raised border framing indented tapering rectangular panels, the center one embossed w/stylized blossoms on leafy stems, smooth dark blue matte glaze, ship mark & paper label, 7" w., 5½" h. **550.00**

Wall pocket, fluted rim, matte blue glaze, impressed mark, 4" w., 8" h. **288.00**

MC COY

Collectors are now seeking the art wares of two McCoy potteries. One was founded in Roseville, Ohio, in the late 19th century as the J.W. McCoy Pottery, subsequently becoming

Brush-McCoy Pottery Co., later Brush Pottery. The other was also founded in Roseville in 1910 as Nelson McCoy Sanitary Stoneware Co., later becoming Nelson McCoy Pottery. In 1967 the pottery was sold to D.T. Chase of the Mount Clemens Pottery Co. who sold his interest to the Lancaster Colony Corp. in 1974. The pottery shop closed in 1985. Cookie jars are especially collectible today.

A helpful reference book is The Collector's Encyclopedia of McCoy Pottery, *by the Huxfords (Collector Books), and* McCoy Cookie Jars From the First to the Latest, *by Harold Nichols (Nichols Publishing, 1987).*

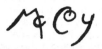

McCoy Mark

Basket, hanging-type, Pine Cone Rustic patt. **$38.00**

Coffee server & stand, El Rancho Bar-B-Que Line, 1960, the set **125.00**

Astronaut Cookie Jar

Cookie jar, Astronaut, 1963, good gold trim (ILLUS.) **750.00**

Freddie the Gleep Cookie Jar

Cookie jar, Freddie the Gleep, 1974 (ILLUS.)..................... **475.00**

Cookie jar, Happy Face,1972-79 ..... **75.00**

Cookie jar, Indian Head, 1954-56 ... **380.00**

Cookie Jar, Little Boy Blue cylinder
w/decal, 1968-70 . . . . **80.00**
Cookie jar, Mammy, yellow glaze . . . **495.00**
Cookie jar, Panda Bear, black &
white w/red & yellow swirl on chest,
1978 . . . . **145.00**

The Plant Entrance Cookie Jar

Cookie jar, Plant Entrance (The), first
of special tribute series, 1992 (ILLUS.) . . **195.00**
Cookie jar, Rocking Chair
(Dalmations), 1961 . . . . **300.00**
Cookie jar, Stage Coach, brown
glaze **600.00**
Cookie jar, Teepee, 1956-59 . . . . . . **425.00**
Cookie jar, Winking Pig, 1972 . . . . . **195.00**
Cookie jar, World Globe, 1960 . . . . . **318.00**
Cookie jar, Wren House w/brown
bird on top, 1958-60 . . . . **125.00**
Creamer & cov. sugar bowl, Elsie
the Cow on creamer, Elmer the
Bull on the sugar, pr. **90.00**
Model of a shoe, Mary Jane-style,
blue glaze **25.00**
Planter, figural, man in barrel **125.00**
Planter, figural, model of
wheelbarrow & rooster, white glaze . . **95.00**
Planter, figural, Mother Duck wearing
bonnet, w/egg, blue glaze, 1950s . . **135.00**
Planter, model of a pear **65.00**
Planter, model of a roadster, No. HN
246 . . . . **25.00**
Planter, model of duck w/umbrella . . **129.00**
Planter, figural, log-shaped w/molded
rifle & saddlebag, 1956, 12¼" l.,
4" h. **55.00**
Tea set: cov. teapot, creamer & open
sugar bowl; Daisy patt., 3 pcs. **75.00**
Vase, 8" h., figural double tulip
blossom, yellow glaze **75.00**
Vase, 8½" h., Triple Lily,1950, yellow
matte glaze **75.00**
Vase, triple lily-form, white glaze, ... **68.00**
Wall pocket, figural, model of a fan,
blue **95.00**
Wall pocket, figural, model of a leaf,
pink **75.00**

Wall pocket, figural, model of
bellows, green **150.00**
Wall pocket, figural, model of
lovebirds, yellow & brown **95.00**
Window box, Pine Cone Rustic patt. . . . **34.00**

MEISSEN

*The secret of true hard paste porcelain,
known long before to the Chinese, was
"discovered" accidentally in Meissen, Germany,
by J.F. Bottger, an alchemist working with E.W.
Tschirnhausen. The first European true
porcelain was made in the Meissen Porcelain
Works, organized about 1709. Meissen marks
have been widely copied by other factories. Some
pieces listed here are recent.*

Meissen Mark

Bowl, 7" sq., serving-type w/ornate
corners & scalloped rims, Blue
Onion patt., "Meissen" incised &
Teichert oval around "Meissen" w/a
star below **$77.00**
Center bowl, the exterior decorated
w/scenes of fishing villages
alternating w/puce panels
decorated w/colorful flowers,
underglaze-blue crossed swords
mark, seconds mark, 19th c.,
9" d. **230.00**
Compote, open, 12" h., figural, the
figures of two nude youths encircle
the stump stem set upon an
applied-floral rocky base,
supporting a double-handled bowl
decorated w/colored applied florals
around the exterior & painted
decoration on the interior,
19th c. **1,100.00**
Cup & saucer, ribbed body
w/enameled floral & insect
decorations, blue crossed swords
mark, 19th c., saucer, 5"d. **230.00**
Figure of a gentleman, standing
wearing a cape, polychrome
decoration, factory marks &
impressed "148," late 19th c.,
4¼" h. **173.00**
Figure of a woman, allegorical,
modeled holding a stringed
instrument & seated on a scrolled
free-form base, polychrome & gilt
trim, incised "#369 - 6," late 19th -
early 20th c., 16½" h. **2,990.00**

Figure of a woman, allegorical, shown seated on a scroll free-form base & holding a staff, the other hand holding the scarf draped across her head, flowing robes w/polychrome florette decoration, gilt-trimmed base, incised "#369 - 5" & printed mark, late 19th - early 20th c., 16½" h. **3,220.00**

Meissen Figures of Children

Figures, young boy & girl, each standing wearing 18th c. attire, he holding a round wreath of flowers, she holding her apron full of flowers & standing beside a vase, each on a round scroll-molded base, painted predominately blue & white, marked, early 20th c., 4¾" h., pr. (ILLUS.) **633.00**

Figures, Flower Sellers, a lady holding a garland, the man w/flowers in his hat, blue crossed swords marks, 19th c., 6¼ & 6⅝" h., pr. (arm repair, losses) **489.00**

Figure group, a winged Cupid standing & holding a disc-form birdbath sideways w/a group of birds applied to it, on a cylindrical swirled scroll-molded pedestal base, polychrome & gilt trim, marked, late 19th c. (minor chip) . . **1,495.00**

Figure group, two men in 18th century costume studying a globe, signed w/underglaze crossed swords mark, ca. 1865-1910, Germany, 9 x 10", 5¾" h. **3,600.00**

Figure group, Monkey Band, composed of a conductor, oboe player, flute player, trumpet player, piano player on monkey-back, cello player, French horn player & violin player, late 19th - early 20th c., tallest 7" h., the set (various chips & small damages). **6,038.00**

Figure group, allegorical, "Spring," a woman holding a bird & a basket of flowers, another seated woman w/a birdcage & a gentleman w/an urn,

all on a rockwork base, underglaze-blue crossed swords mark, 19th c., 9" h. **1,380.00**

Adam & Eve Figure Group

Figure group, Adam & Eve standing among various birds & animals w/the apple tree & serpent behind them, Adam just biting the apple, oblong mound base, polychrome decoration, underglaze-blue crossed swords mark & seconds mark, 19th c., 12" h. (ILLUS.). . . . **4,025.00**

Figure group, allegorical, "North America," modeled as a Native American wearing a feathered headdress & riding his horse while spearing a charging buffalo, underglaze-blue crossed swords mark, modeled in 1903 by Erich Hoesel, 14" l., 14" h. **3,910.00**

Invalid feeder, boat-shaped w/ring handle, Blue Onion patt., numbered "3617," unsigned, 19th c., 6½" l., 2" h. **61.00**

Model of a monkey, seated animal holding an apple, 2¾" h. **2,040.00**

Pastille burner, square form w/raised columns at corners, a pierced scrolled gallery to the stepped cover w/a female bust finial, set in a deep tray, blue crossed swords mark, 19th c., 4½" h. (chips) **690.00**

Serving dishes, each w/gilt trimwork & enamel-decorated fruit cartouches, printed marks, 20th c., 11¾" d., pr. **431.00**

Fine Meissen Tete-a-Tete Tea Set

Tea set, tete-a-tete size: cov. teapot,
cov. sugar bowl, creamer, two cups
& saucers & an oblong tray; each
decorated w/colorful encrusted
flowers w/painted flowers on the
tray, cups w/six feet, underglaze-
blue crossed swords mark, 19th c.,
tray 16" l., the set (ILLUS.) **3,795.00**

Teacup & saucer, cobalt blue ground
decorated w/a topographical
landscape showing the city of
Konigstein, late 19th c., 3⅞" d. . . **1,380.00**

Vase, 15 3/8" h., snake-handled, new
gold decoration & polychrome
enameled floral bouquets on each
side, crossed swords mark,
19th c. **690.00**

METTLACH

*Ceramics with the name Mettlach were
produced by Villeroy & Boch and other potteries
in the Mettlach area of Germany. Villeroy and
Boch's finest years of production are thought to
be from about 1890 to 1910.*

Mettlach Mark

Mettlach Ewer & Punch Bowl Set

Ewer, moon-shaped, a flattened
round disk body w/molded chain
"jeweled" border framing on each
side a polychrome Renaissance-
style bust portrait, raised on a
ringed small domed foot, ringed
neck w/deep cupped rim w/spout &
C-scroll handle to shoulder, No.
1124, 15½" h. (ILLUS. right) **$460.00**

Jardiniere, phanolith, footed oval
wide bowl w/a gadrooned base
band & incurved flaring rim,
decorated w/a continuous band of
white relief cameo figures of
Grecian men & women riding in a

chariot or sitting at a table &
drinking, green ground, No. 7000 &
No. 17 marked on base, 8¾ x 10",
5½" h. **495.00**

Jug w/hinged metal cover, colorful
transfer-printed scenes of several
gnomes sitting atop hops drinking
beer, scattered verses, No. 2332,
10" h. **275.00**

Mettlach "Cameo" Plaque

Plaque, oval, Cameo ware, a white
relief bust portrait of a classical
woman against a green ground,
white border band, dated 1900, No.
7032, 7½ x 8¾" (ILLUS.) **295.00**

Plaque, pierced to hang, round,
etched color design of a knight
carrying a large flag, artist-signed,
No. 1384, 14½" d. **695.00**

Mettlach Scenic Plaque

Plaque, pierced to hang, etched color
scene of a large castle above a
river in a mountainous landscape,
dated 1909, No. 1365, gold border,
17" d. (ILLUS.). **845.00**

Plaques, pierced to hang, decorated
w/exotic colorful peafowl at water's
edge on one, the other w/blue
geese on the bank of a waterway,
each w/golden setting sun & lotus
blossoms, embossed border
repeats lotus & bird design in slate
blue on brick red, No. 1500 & No.
1677, 15" d., pr. **1,760.00**

Punch bowl, cover & undertray, Cameo ware, the deep slightly waisted cylindrical body swelled at the base & raised on a domed flaring base, angular branch side handles, the domed cover also w/a branch handle, white relief classical figures & grapevines around the body ground in blue & green, on a matching round dished undertray w/white relief grape sprigs, signed "Stahl," No. 2602, 13" h., the set (ILLUS. left) **633.00**

Tall Mettlach Tankard with Cyclist

Tankard, tall slightly tapering cylindrical body, decorated around the top & base w/molded narrow bands flanking a wide rosette band, the tall body decorated w/a polychrome scene of an early bicyclist standing next to his high-wheeled bike, signed "Schultz," factory marks, no top, 3 liter, 15" h. (ILLUS.) **978.00**
Vases, 10" h., each w/incised foliate decoration w/enameled trim, impressed marks, No. 1808, pr. . . . **230.00**

Mettlach Portrait Vases

Vases, 18" h., flat-sided tapering rounded body on a flaring scalloped & scroll-molded base, a scalloped crown-form scroll-molded neck flanked by ornate C-scroll handles from the rim to the center

of the sides, each side w/a large round medallion enclosing a bust portrait of a Renaissance era woman wearing a large feathered hat, etched & mosaic work, impressed marks, No. 1416, one w/restored handles & rim, pr. (ILLUS.) **1,495.00**

MINTON

The Minton factory in England was established by Thomas Minton in 1793. The factory made earthenware, especially the blue-printed variety and Thomas Minton is sometimes credited with invention of the blue "Willow" pattern. For a time majolica and tiles were also an important part of production, but bone china soon became the principal ware. Mintons, Ltd., continues in operation today. Also see MAJOLICA in Ceramics.

Minton Marks

Oyster plates, each painted in tones of yellow, pink & green, printed marks, ca. 1900, 9¼" d., set of 12 . . . . **$1,035.00**
Soup tureen, cover & undertray, ironstone china, footed squatty bulbous oval body w/rolled loop end handles, high domed cover w/loop handle, matching dished undertray, decorated w/black transfer-printed Oriental garden landscapes trimmed w/colorful enamels, impressed marks, ca. 1882, handle to handle 14¼" l., the set **403.00**

Minton "Pate-sur-Pate" Moon Flask

Vase, 13" h., moon flask-form, "pate-sure-pate," flattened disk form raised on an oblong foot, w/a short ringed neck & bulbed rim flanked by loop handles to the shoulder, one side decorated w/white slip Chinese figures in a garden setting, the other side w/garden furniture, against a brown background & the body in coral, impressed mark & shape No. 1664, printed factory marks, ca. 1873 (ILLUS.) **1,725.00**

MOCHA

Mocha decoration is found on basically utilitarian creamware or yellowware articles and is achieved by a simple chemical reaction. A color pigment of brown, blue, green or black is given an acid nature by infusion of tobacco or hops. When this acid nature colorant is applied in blobs to an alkaline ground color, it reacts by spreading in feathery seaweed designs. This type of decoration is usually accompanied by horizontal bands of light color slip. Produced in numerous Staffordshire potteries from the late 18th until the late 19th centuries, its name is derived from the similar markings found on mocha quartz. In addition to the seaweed decoration, mocha wares are also seen with Earthworm and Cat's Eye patterns or a marbleized effect.

Grouping of Mocha Pieces

Bowl, 4¾" d., 3½" h., footed bulbous body w/a wide rolled rim, canary yellow ground w/a wide green band decorated in yellow & black w/the Earthworm patt., partial impressed mark "CL & – Mont –," chips, repairs, appears to have had an eared handle (ILLUS. bottom center) **$110.00**

Bowl, 6½" d., yellowware, brown & white stripes (wear & stains w/short rim hairline) **83.00**

Bowl, 7" d., 3½" h., white band w/blue seaweed decoration & brown stripes (minor wear) **385.00**

Bowl, 8⅛" d., 3⅞" h., white band w/green seaweed decoration & brown stripes (wear & small interior flake) **165.00**

Bowl, 10⅛" d., 4⅝" h., white band w/green seaweed decoration & brown stripes (wear, stains & shallow interior flakes) **341.00**

Bowl, 11" d., 5¼" h., footed w/deep, wide bell-form body w/rolled rim, yellowware w/a wide white upper band w/blue seaweed decoration, East Liverpool, Ohio (wear, large foot chip) **220.00**

Bowl, 12½" d., yellowware w/a band of green seaweed decoration, 19th c. (cracks, chips, wear) **316.00**

Bowl, 12¾" d., 5¾" h., bulbous cylindrical on a thin footring, sides tapering to flaring rim, white band w/green seaweed decoration & dark brown stripes, East Liverpool, Ohio (wear, stains & interior w/scratches & surface flakes) **110.00**

Bowl, 13½" d., 6½" h., bulbous cylindrical body on a thin footring, sides tapering to flaring rim, white band w/blue seaweed decoration, East Liverpool, Ohio (wear & chip on foot) **165.00**

Castor, footed baluster-form, seaweed decoration around the sides on a pumpkin orange ground, first half 19th c., 4½" h. (imperfections). . **575.00**

Chamber pot, footed squatty bulbous form w/C-form leaftip handle, a wide two-tone blue band decorated w/a zigzag Earthworm patt. in black & white flanked by narrow double black stripes, 8¾" d. (some wear, edge flakes) **121.00**

Creamer, bulbous body w/ribbed leaftip handle, amber band w/black seaweed decoration, brown & white stripes, 2⅝" h. (hairline & some area of glaze flaking) **220.00**

Creamer, swelled cylindrical body tapering slightly to the flat rim w/rim spout & C-form handle, yellowware w/a white shoulder band w/blue seaweed decoration flanked by three narrow double dark brown bands around the sides, 4¾" h. (shallow flake on inside edge of table ring) **440.00**

Cup, impressed border band above a brown & white Earthworm patt. on a blue band, 19th c., 2⅞" h. (imperfections) **374.00**

Jar, cov., cylindrical w/a flared base & low domed cover w/button finial, the body & cover w/a pale blue band flanked by black stripes & Earthworm or Cat's-eye patt. in white, blue & blue, repairs, hairline in cover, 5" h. (ILLUS. top left) **495.00**

Mixing bowl, footed, deep flaring sides w/long arched spout, yellowware, wide white band decoration w/blue seaweed design, flanked by blue stripes, East Liverpool, Ohio, 11½" d. (wear, hairlines & chips). **440.00**

Mug, barrel-shaped w/applied leaftip handle, black & white geometric design w/yellow-ochre bands, 2¾" h. (hairlines) **50.00**

Mug, cylindrical, yellowware w/wide white band decorated w/blue seaweed design, flanked by narrow blue stripes, 2⅞" h. (small flake on table ring) **385.00**

Mug, wide footed cylindrical leaftip handle, light blue band flanked by black stripes on white ground, 2⅞" h. (minor stains) **99.00**

Mug, cylindrical w/leaftip handle, decorated w/black stripes & grey bands w/black, white & blue Earthworm patt., 3⅝" h. (pinpoint flakes) **248.00**

Mug, ironstone, black & blue stripes & olive grey band w/seaweed decoration, labeled "Half Pint," 3¾" h. (stains & crazing) **105.00**

Mug, low, wide cylindrical body w/C-scroll leaftip handle, heavy double brown bands flanking a center dark brown band decorated w/the Earthworm patt. in blue, white & tan, hairlines, 3¾" h. (ILLUS. bottom left) **550.00**

Mug, cylindrical, blue & brown border bands centering a brown impressed repeating geometric design on a cream ground, 19th c., 5⅝" h. (very minor chips & cracks, minor staining) **978.00**

Mustard pot, cov., low cylindrical body w/narrow flared rim & foot, inset flat cover w/knob finial, C-form handle, the body w/a wide tan band decorated w/looping Earthworm patt. in white, yellow & black, narrow black stripes at top & bottom, 2½" h. (chips on lid, small lid repair) **605.00**

Mustard pot, cov., yellowware, cylindrical w/C-form handle, button finial, white band w/blue seaweed decoration flanked by narrow blue stripes, 3" d. (wear & chips) **468.00**

Mustard pot, cov., bulbous base tapering to flat rim & low-domed cover w/button finial, leaftip handle, wide bluish grey band w/tan & white stripes & Earthworm & Cat's

Eye patt. in blue, tan & white, 4⅛" h. (chips, glaze flakes & colors vary on lid). **220.00**

Pepper pot, cov., footed ovoid body w/domed cap, orangish tan band w/black seaweed decoration, brown stripes, 3⅝" h. (small flakes) . . **990.00**

Pepper pot, cov., footed ovoid body tapering to short cylindrical neck fitted w/a pierced domed top, a wide yellow-ochre band w/Earthworm patt. in white, brown & beige, narrow brown stripes, 3⅞" h. (small chips on dome). . . . **1,100.00**

Three Mocha Pepper Pots

Pepper pot, baluster-form w/flaring foot & domed cover, yellow ochre trimmed w/white, green & dark brown stripes, wide center band w/dark brown seaweed patt., wear, old chips, 4½" h. (ILLUS. center) . . **825.00**

Pepper pot, cylindrical body w/flaring foot & tapering neck to the domed cover, wide grey band decorated w/the Earthworm patt. in brown, tan & white, blue cover w/black edge stripe, edge chips & repair in base, 4½" h. (ILLUS. left) **825.00**

Pepper pot, wide short cylindrical body on a flaring pedestal base, tapering neck to domed cover w/button finial, wide grey band flanked by white & dark brown stripes, decorated in black w/seaweed patt., chips, cover w/glued repair, 4½" h. (ILLUS. right) **385.00**

Pitcher, milk, jug-form, 4⅝" h., C-scroll leaftip handle, decorated w/a dark bluish grey band flanked by black stripes, the center embossed dark band decorated w/green & black seaweed patt., wear, painted-over flake on spout (ILLUS. top right, in group photo) **440.00**

Pitcher, jug-type, 4⅞" h., baluster-form body w/narrow black & blue stripes & a wide blue band decorated w/black, blue & brown Earthworm patt., 19th c. (repairs) . . **193.00**

Pitcher, 5¾" h., white band w/brown seaweed decoration & brown stripes (wear). **550.00**

Pitcher, 6½" h., tapering cylindrical ironstone body, wide central band flanked by narrow stripes & narrow band beneath rim in tan & blue, seaweed decoration in black. **138.00**

Pitcher, 6¾" h., barrel-shaped w/leaftip handle & arched spout, tooled bands w/blue, black & tan stripes & blue band w/Earthworm patt. (short hairlines on bottom & in handle, pinpoint edge flakes) **1,155.00**

Pitcher, 7¼" h., blue ground w/a band of green seaweed design, 19th c. (cracks, staining, minor rim roughness) **403.00**

Salt dip, a low pedestal base supporting a wide shallow cylindrical cup decorated w/wavy white lines on a grey band flanked by thin black stripes, 3" d., 2⅛" h. (stains on foot, hairline in rim) **330.00**

Shaker w/domed top, footed short cylindrical body w/tapering neck to domed top, wide tan body band w/seaweed decoration flanked by narrow black stripes & a narrower tan band at neck, 4⅛" h. (chips) . . . **220.00**

Shaker w/domed top, baluster-form w/small knop finial on top, white ground decorated w/alternating narrow bands in black, tan & blue, 4⅞" h. **330.00**

Shaker w/domed top, footed cylindrical body w/a tapered neck to the top, the body w/a wide blue band decorated w/the Earthworm patt. in brown, black & white flanked by narrow black stripes, blue top, 4⅞" h. (repair) **330.00**

Waste bowl, footed deep gently flaring rounded form, a wide orangish tan band flanked by thin dark brown stripes & an embossed green band, decorated w/the Earthworm patt. in blue, white & dark brown, repairs, 5⅝" d., 2⅞" h. (ILLUS. bottom right, in group photo) . . **550.00**

Waste bowl, round w/deep tapering sides, amber band w/unusual black seaweed patt. separated into five segments by squiggly lines, green molded lip band, 4¾" d. (stains, hairlines) **275.00**

Waste bowl, deep flaring rounded sides above a thick footring, a wide white band w/Earthworm patt. & stripes in blue, black, grey, tan & white, 6½" d., 3½" h. (wear, chips & short hairlines) **165.00**

MOORCROFT

William Moorcroft became a designer for James Macintyre & Co. in 1897 and was put in charge of their art pottery production. Moorcroft developed a number of popular designs, including Florian Ware while with Macintyre and continued with that firm until 1913 when they discontinued the production of art pottery.

After leaving Macintyre in 1913, Moorcroft set up his own pottery in Burslem and continued producing the art wares he had designed earlier as well as introducing new patterns. After William's death in 1945, the pottery was operated by his son, Walter.

MOORCROFT *Moorcroft*

Moorcroft Marks

Bowl, 7¼" d., 1½" h., Clematis patt., signed **$195.00**

Pitcher, 5" h., 6" d., footed bulbous nearly spherical body w/a wide short cylindrical neck w/pinched spout, C-form strap handle, decorated w/yellow & pink irises on a shaded dark blue to light green ground, impressed "MOORCROFT - MADE IN ENGLAND" & script signature **385.00**

Potpourri jar, cov., footed bulbous ovoid shouldered body w/a fitted flat-topped cover pierced w/small holes, the sides of the body w/incised roundels enclosing a cluster of three small heart-shaped leaves, overall cinnabar red glossy glaze, ink script signature, impressed "W225," 3½" d., 3¼" h. (chip to threaded inside rim of cover & base) **440.00**

Vase, 7" h., Wisteria patt. **220.00**

Vase, 7½" h., 4½" d., disc foot below the simple ovoid body flaring to a wide, flat mouth, decorated w/purple grapes & yellow leaves on a shaded green to dark blue ground, die-stamped "Moorcroft - MADE IN ENGLAND" & w/ink signature **660.00**

Vase, 9" h., Clematis patt. **413.00**

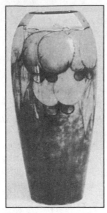

Tall Moorcroft Vase

Vase, 16" h., tall slender ovoid body,
Wisteria patt. w/flambé glaze,
impressed marks, ca. 1930, drilled
(ILLUS.)..................... **978.00**

MULBERRY

Mulberry or Flow Mulberry ironstone wares were produced in the Staffordshire district of England in the period between 1840 and 1870 at many of the same factories which produced its close "cousin," Flow Blue china. In fact, some of the early Flow Blue patterns were also decorated with the dark blackish or brownish purple mulberry coloration and feature the same heavy smearing or "flown" effect. Produced on sturdy ironstone bodies, the designs were either transfer-printed or hand-painted (Brush stroke) with an Asian, Scenic, Floral or Marble design. Some patterns were also decorated with additional colors over or under the glaze; these are designated in the following listings as "w/polychrome."

Quite a bit of this ware is still to be found and it is becoming increasingly sought-after by collectors although presently its values lag somewhat behind similar Flow Blue pieces. The standard references to Mulberry wares is Petra Williams' book, Flow Blue China and Mulberry Ware, Similarity and Value Guide and Mulberry Ironstone - Flow Blue's Best Kept Little Secret, by Ellen R. Hill.

ALBANY (Godwin)
Plate, 10" d..................... **$72.00**

ATHENS (C. Meigh, ca. 1845)
Cup & saucer, handleless **75.00**
Plate, 6" d....................... **75.00**
Plate, 8½" d..................... **50.00**
Plate, 10½" d.................... **75.00**

Platter, 16" l..................... **275.00**
Teapot, cov., vertical -paneled Gothic
shape....................... **495.00**
Vegetable bowl, cov. **350.00**

ATHENS (Wm. Adams & Son, ca. 1849)
Creamer cov., full-paneled Gothic
shape........................ **150.00**
Cup & saucer, handleless,.......... **75.00**
Plate, 7½" d..................... **35.00**
Plate, 8½" d..................... **45.00**
Plate, 9½" d..................... **55.00**
Plate, 10½" d.................... **75.00**
Soup plate, 9½" d. **85.00**
Sugar, cov., full-paneled Gothic
shape........................ **200.00**
Teapot, cov., full-paneled Gothic
shape........................ **300.00**

AVA (T.J. & J. Mayer, ca. 1850)
Cup & saucer, handled,
w/polychrome **85.00**
Plate, 9½" d., w/polychrome **65.00**
Plate, 10½" d., w/polychrome **75.00**
Platter, 16" l..................... **200.00**
Sauce tureen, cover & undertray,
w/polychrome, 3 pcs............. **450.00**
Soup plate, 10" d................. **80.00**

BEAUTIES OF CHINA (Mellor, Venables & Co., ca. 1845)
Plate, 7½" d..................... **40.00**
Plate, 9½" d..................... **60.00**
Plate, 10½" d.................... **85.00**
Platter, 16" l., w/polychrome........ **200.00**
Sauce tureen, cover & underplate,
long octagon, 3 pcs. **475.00**

BIRD OF PARADISE (S. Moore & Co., ca. 1850)
Gravy boat **125.00**
Plate, 10½" d..................... **75.00**
Sauce tureen, 4 pcs. **500.00**

Bird of Paradise Vegetable Bowl

Vegetable bowl, cov. (ILLUS.) **300.00**

BLUEBELL & LEAF - BRUSH STROKE (m.u., ca. 1850)

Cup & saucer, handleless 125.00
Plate, 10½" d. 125.00
Plate, 7½" d. 60.00

Bluebell & Leaf Teapot

Teapot, cov., full-paneled Gothic
    shape (ILLUS.) 350.00
Vegetable bowl, cov. 350.00

BOCHARA (James Edwards, ca. 1850)

Creamer, pedestal, Gothic shape. . . . 125.00
Cup & saucer, handleless 60.00
Platter, 18" l. 300.00
Relish dish, mitten-shaped 125.00
Soup plate, 9½" d. 85.00
Soup undertray, square. 135.00
Sugar bowl, cov. 150.00

Bochara Sugar Bowl

Sugar bowl, cov., full-paneled Gothic
    shape (ILLUS.) 150.00
Teapot, cov., pedestal, Gothic
    shape. 250.00
Vegetable bowl, cov. 350.00

CLEOPATRA (F. Morley & Co., ca. 1850)

Hot water pitcher, w/polychrome. . . . 175.00
Plate, 10½" d. 75.00
Soup plate, 9½" d. 90.00
Soup tureen w/ladle, 2 pcs. 1,500.00
Wash pitcher, w/polychrome 200.00

COREA (J. Clementson, ca. 1850)

Cup & saucer, handlelesss 75.00
Plate, 7½" d. 40.00
Plate, 10½" d. 80.00
Platter, 14" l. 200.00
Vegetable bowl, cov. 250.00

COREAN (Podmore, Walker & Co., ca. 1850)

Creamer, classic Gothic shape. 150.00
Cup plate 65.00
Cup & saucer, handleless 75.00
Pitcher, 1 qt. 160.00
Pitcher, 2 qt. 195.00
Plate, 7½" d. 30.00
Plate, 8½" d. 45.00
Plate, 9½" d. 55.00
Plate, 10½" d. 75.00
Relish, shell-shaped 125.00
Sauce tureen, cover & undertray,
    2 pcs. 425.00
Sugar bowl, cov., lion handles,
    classic Gothic shaped 275.00

Corean Teapot

Teapot, cov., cockscomb handle
    (ILLUS.) 600.00

CYPRUS (Wm. Davenport, ca. 1845)

Creamer, octagon. 150.00
Cup & saucer, handleless 65.00
Plate, 7½" d. 35.00
Plate, 10½" d. 75.00
Platter, 14" l. 200.00

Cyprus Punch Cups

Punch cups, grooved, pr. (ILLUS.) . . 200.00

Cyprus Sugar Bowl

Sugar bowl, cov., six-sided, vertical-
   paneled Gothic shape (ILLUS.). . . . **300.00**
Vegetable bowl, cov. **250.00**

DORA (E. Challinor, ca. 1850)

Cup & saucer, handleless **60.00**
Plate, 8½" d. **45.00**
Plate, 10½" d. **70.00**
Teapot, cov., Baltic shape **600.00**

FLORA (T. Walker, ca. 1847)

Creamer, classic Gothic shape. **175.00**
Cup & saucer, handleless **55.00**
Plate, 7½" d. **45.00**
Plate, 9¾" d. **65.00**

Flora Platter

Platter, 16" l., (ILLUS.) **200.00**
Sugar bowl, cov., classic Gothic
   shape. **200.00**
Teapot, cov., classic Gothic shape. . . **400.00**
Wash bowl **135.00**

GRAPE & SPRIG - BRUSH STROKE (T. Walker, ca. 1847)

Grape & Sprig Creamer

Creamer, w/ cockscomb handle
   (ILLUS.). **185.00**
Platter, 14" l. **250.00**

GRAPE & VINE - BRUSH STROKE (ca. 1850)

Vegetable bowl, cov. **375.00**

GRAPE & VINE - BRUSH STROKE (m.u., ca. 1850)

Basin. **350.00**

Grape & Vine Platter

Platter, 16" l. (ILLUS.). **300.00**
Razor or brush box, cov. **175.00**

HADDON (Scott, ca. 1850)

Haddon Gravy Boat

Gravy boat w/undertray, 2 pcs.
   (ILLUS.). **200.00**
Plate, 8¾" d. **50.00**
Platter, 14" l. **195.00**

JARDINIERE (Villeroy & Boch, ca. 1890)

Creamer **100.00**
Cup & saucer, handled **50.00**
Plate, 7½" d. **25.00**
Plate, 9½" d. **35.00**
Sugar bowl, cov. **150.00**
Teapot, cov. **200.00**

JEDDO (Wm. Adams, ca. 1849)

Jeddo Creamer

Creamer, full-paneled Gothic shape
(ILLUS.)....................... 125.00
Plate, 7½" d....................... 35.00
Plate, 8½" d....................... 45.00
Plate, 9½" d....................... 55.00
Plate, 10½" d...................... 60.00
Platter, 20" l...................... 400.00
Sugar bowl, cov. full-paneled Gothic
shape.......................... 200.00
Teapot, cov., full-paneled Gothic
shape.......................... 300.00

MEDINA (J. Furnival, ca. 1850)

Cup & saucer, handled 65.00
Platter, 16" l...................... 250.00
Punch cup,........................ 95.00
Teapot, cov., child's 225.00
Vegetable bowl, cov.............. 275.00

NANKIN (Wm. Davenport, ca. 1845)

Pitcher, milk, bearded spout........ 175.00
Pitcher, water, 9" h. 275.00
Teapot, cov., Davenport octagon
shape.......................... 350.00

NING PO (R. Hall, ca. 1840)

Cup plate,........................ 75.00
Cup & saucer, handleless 65.00
Plate, 8½" d....................... 45.00
Plate, 9½" d....................... 55.00
Plate, 10½" d...................... 65.00
Soup plate, 9½" d. 85.00
Vegetable bowl, cov.............. 300.00

PANAMA (E. Challinor, ca. 1850)

Cup & saucer, handleless 65.00
Plate, 10½" d...................... 75.00
Platter, 20" l...................... 300.00
Soup plate, 9½" d. 65.00

PELEW (E. Challinor, ca. 1850)

Cup & saucer, handleless 60.00
Plate, 7½" d....................... 45.00

Plate, 9½" d....................... 55.00
Plate, 10½" d...................... 70.00
Platter, 12½" l.................... 145.00
Platter, 16" l..................... 250.00
Teapot, cov., pumpkin-shaped 500.00

PHANTASIA (J. Furnival, ca. 1850)

Chamberpot, cov., w/polychrome ... 450.00
Creamer, Cockscomb handle
w/polychrome 275.00
Plate, 8½" d....................... 75.00

RHONE SCENERY (T.J. & J. Mayer, ca. 1850)

Creamer, full-paneled Gothic shape ... 125.00
Plate, 7½" d....................... 35.00
Plate, 8½" d....................... 45.00
Plate, 9½" d....................... 55.00
Plate, 10½" d...................... 60.00
Platter, 14" l..................... 190.00
Soap dish, cover & drainer........ 200.00
Soup plate, 9½" d. 65.00
Sugar bowl, cov., full-paneled Gothic
shape.......................... 195.00
Teapot, cov., full-paneled Gothic
shape.......................... 275.00
Wash pitcher w/basin,........... 550.00

ROYAL CONSERVATORY (J.& M.P. Bell, ca. 1850)

Royal Conservatory Wash Pitcher

Wash pitcher, 13" h. (ILLUS.) 175.00

SCINDE (T. Walker, ca. 1847)

Plate, 7½" d....................... 35.00
Plate, 9½" d....................... 65.00
Platter, 16" l..................... 195.00
Teapot, cov., Primary shape........ 495.00

SHAPOO (T. & R. Boote, ca. 1850)

Platter, 14" l. 200.00
Sugar bowl, cov., Primary shape 200.00
Teapot, cov., Primary shape 350.00

TEMPLE (Podmore, Walker, & Co., ca. 1850)

Creamer, classic Gothic shape 145.00

Temple Cup & Saucer

Cup & sucer, handled (ILLUS.) 95.00
Pitcher, milk, classic Gothic shape. . . 225.00
Plate, 10½" d. 65.00
Plate, 8½" d. 50.00
Sugar bowl, cov., classic Gothic
    shape. 195.00
Teapot, cov., classic Gothic shape . . . 300.00

VINCENNES (J. & G. Alcock, ca. 1845)

Vincennes Compote

Compote, Gothic Cameo shape
    (ILLUS.). 495.00
Cup & saucer, farmer size 75.00
Platter, 12" l. 125.00
Platter, 15½" l. 175.00
Relish, Gothic Cameo shape 125.00
Sauce tureen, cover & undertray,
    3 pcs. 325.00
Sugar bowl, cov. full-paneled Gothic
    shape. 200.00
Vegetable bowl, cov. 250.00

WASHINGTON VASE (Podmore, Walker, & Co., Ca. 1850)

Creamer, classic Gothic shape. 200.00
Cup plate, ... 100.00
Cup & saucer, handleless, ... 75.00
Gravy boat, ... 150.00
Plate, 6" d. 75.00
Plate, 7½" d. 35.00
Plate, 8½" d. 40.00
Plate, 9½" d. 45.00
Plate, 10½" d. 65.00
Relish dish, mitten-shaped 135.00
Soup plate, 9½" d. 75.00
Sugar bowl, cov., classic Gothic
    shape, strap handles. 275.00

Washington Vase Teapots

Teapot, cov., classic Gothic shape,
    large (ILLUS., left) 400.00
Teapot, cov., classic Gothic shape,
    small (ILLUS., right). 350.00
Vegetable bowl, cov. 300.00

NEWCOMB COLLEGE POTTERY

This pottery was established in the art department of Newcomb College, New Orleans, Louisiana, in 1897. Each piece was hand-thrown and bore the potter's mark & decorator's monogram on the base. It was always a studio business and never operated as a factory and its pieces are therefore scarce, with the early wares being eagerly sought. The pottery closed in 1940.

Newcomb Mark

Bowl, 5¾" d., 3¼" h., small footring below the wide squatty bulbous sides w/a wide sloping shoulder to a wide flat mouth, incised around the shoulder w/pink dogwood blossoms against a shaded blue to pink ground, by Sarah Irvine, marked "NC -260 - KS40" & artist's initials (some glaze spiderwebbing) $935.00

Bowl, 8" d., 3½" h., the shoulder decorated w/yellow, red & green flowers on a matte blue body, impressed "NC - HF - 64 - 259" . . . **978.00**

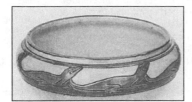

Newcomb Bulb Bowl with Lizards

Bulb bowl, wide squatty rounded bowl w/a flat bottom & incurved sides, incised & surface-painted around the upper half w/a band of lizards in green on a dark blue band on a light blue ground, by M.T. Ryan, 1904, marked "NC - AE73 - MT Ryan - Q - JM," tight 1" line, small base spider, 8¾" d., 3¼" h. (ILLUS.). **5,225.00**

Candleholder, tall flaring cylindrical shaft w/a cupped top centering a cylindrical candle socket, dripping bluish grey matte glaze, impressed mark, 6½" d., 10½" h. **440.00**

Pitcher, 5½" h., 4" d., ovoid shouldered body w/a wide short cylindrical neck w/pinched spout & angular handle, deep greyish green metallic dripping glaze on a brown ground, impressed "CN - GM" **259.00**

Vase, 4" h., 2¾" d., gently tapering ovoid body w/closed rim, decorated w/white bell-shaped flowers against a cobalt & light green ground, by Sadie Irvine, 1914, impressed "NC - SI - JM - C - 51 - GN52" **935.00**

Vase, 4¼" h., 2¾" d., tapering ovoid body w/a wide closed rim, modeled & surface-painted trees in blue & green against a pink sky, by Sadie Irvine, 1918, impressed "NC - JM - SI - JO-3" **1,430.00**

Vase, 4½" h., 2" d., slender ovoid form w/angled tapering neck, crisply modeled flowers in high-relief around the shoulder on a matte blue ground, impressed "NC - RQ3 - IS - JS" **1,380.00**

Vase, 4½" h., 3½" d., slightly ovoid body tapering gently to a wide flat rim, molded around the top w/stylized white & yellow flowers & green leaves w/stems down the sides against a soft blue ground, Sadie Irvine, 1928, impressed "NC - SI - JM - 25 - QS100" **990.00**

Vase, 4½" h., 4¾" d., spherical form on cylindrical rim w/short flat rim, carved matte decorations of pink & yellow blossoms on a green branch, against a cobalt blue ground, impressed "NC - SI- JM - W22 - 271," BY S. IRVIN, 1920 . . **1,760.00**

Vase, 5" h., 6" d., bulbous ovoid form w/flat rim, decorated w/carved moonlight scene of live oaks w/Spanish moss, done in blues & bluish greens, impressed "NC - S26 - 500 - JM - AFS," by A.F. Simpson, 1930 . . . . **4,150.00**

Vase, 5¼" h., 5" d., footring supporting a wide squatty bulbous base below the gently tapering sides to a wide flat mouth, incised clusters of stylized blossoms at the base of wide side panels, in pink & green against a blue ground, 1926, impressed "NC - PW12 - JM" & artist's mark, original paper label . . **990.00**

Vase, 5¼" h., 6½" d., footed spherical body w/a wide flat mouth, molded w/clusters of large bluish white roses & bluish green leaves & stems on a deep blue matte ground, Henrietta Bailey, 1923, impressed "NC - HB - NG88 - 26" . . **2,090.00**

Vase, 6" h., 6¾" d., slab-built, a small footring supporting a wide inverted bell-form bowl w/a crackled glossy glaze, base marked w/monogram of Leoni Nicholson, attributed to Newcomb (minor hairline) **259.00**

Vase, 6½" h., 3½" d., slightly ovoid body w/a rounded shoulder to a short small rolled neck, the upper half decorated w/a continuous band of incised stylized organic designs in blue & white on a light blue, dark blue & green ground, glossy glaze, Sabrina E. Wells, 1904, impressed "NC - S.E. Wells - P64" **2,860.00**

Vase, 6½" h., 6" d., footed wide ovoid body tapering slightly to a wide low cylindrical neck band, enameled decoration of amber, pink & white swirls on a turquoise blue ground, "NC" mark & paper label **715.00**

Vase, 7" h., 4" d., a narrow footring supports a bulbous base tapering gently to a tall cylindrical neck, an incised rim band of stylized yellow peppers pendent from a green leafy vine between bands of dark blue above the glossy light greyish blue lower body, Henrietta Bailey, 1904, ink mark & "NC - LLNN" & artist's initials **4,125.00**

Vase, 7" h., 4½" d., tapering ovoid body w/a wide, flat molded mouth, decorated w/Spanish moss in oak trees in a moonlit landscape, 1920, impressed "NC - KX18 - 147 - JM". . **4,070.00**

Vase, 8" h., 4" d., footed rounded tapering cylindrical body w/a flaring cylindrical neck, molded around the shoulder w/a wide band of crocuses in white & red on a mottled red, blue & green ground, a band of impressed lines near the base, Maria Hoa LeBlanc, 1905, impressed "NC - MHLEB - JM - AV1 -A". **6,050.00**

Vase, 9" h., 3¾" d., slender gently swelled cylindrical body w/a narrow angled shoulder below the gently tapering cylindrical neck, decorated w/tall blue jonquils, leaves & stems & blue rim band on a shaded bluish white to pale blue ground, by Anna F. Simpson, 1925, impressed "NC - JM - AFS - OQ10" **3,575.00**

Vase, 9" h., 4½" d., footed bulbous base below a tall slender, tapering body w/a slightly flared mouth, modeled & painted w/trefoil blossoms in blue & yellow w/green leaves & undulating stems on a medium blue ground, by Sadie Irvine, 1920, impressed "NC - SI - JM - 179 - KW82". **2,970.00**

Early Newcomb Vase

Vase, 9" h., 5" d., baluster-form w/a short, thick rolled rim, incised & surface-painted w/bulbs issuing tall stems topped by berry-style blossoms in cobalt blue on a green & blue striated ground, glossy glaze, by Harriet Joor, 1902, impressed "NC - JM - V-84 - Q," short, tight 1" rim line (ILLUS.) . . . **7,150.00**

Vase, 9" h., 7½" d., hand-built, bulbous ovoid body w/a flaring base & short tapering neck, incised down the sides w/stylized hanging

flowers in black, yellow & green on an orange glossy ground, marked "NC - HB - FR - JM" (small enamel nicks) **2,750.00**

Vase, 9½" h., 3" d., tall slender waisted cylindrical form, deeply incised w/tall green sheaves of wheat on a dark blue ground, Henrietta Bailey, 1909, marked "NC - HB - JM - DC96 - Q" **4,125.00**

Scenic Newcomb Vase

Vase, 11" h., 4½" d., tall slender ovoid body w/a flat rim, carved & painted w/tall pine trees in light blue & feathered green on a soft blue ground, by Anna Francis Simpson, 1915, impressed "NC - AFS - JM - 133 - 307 - HN54" (ILLUS.) **7,150.00**

Newcomb College Vase with Pine Trees

Vase, 12½" h., 5" d., tall slender ovoid body tapering to a flat rim, modeled & painted w/towering pine trees in green & dark blue on a shaded light blue to dark blue ground, glossy glaze, by A.F. Simpson, 1908, impressed "NC - FS - JM - CR-8 - Q" (ILLUS.) **17,600.00**

NIPPON

"Nippon" is a term which is used to describe a wide range of porcelain wares produced in Japan from the late 19th century until about 1921. It was in 1891 that the U.S. implemented the McKinley Tariff Act which required that all wares exported to the United States carry a marking indicating the country of origin. The Japanese chose to use "Nippon," their name for Japan. In 1921 the import laws were revised and the words "Made in" had to be added to the markings. Japan was also required to replace the "Nippon" with the English name "Japan" on all wares sent to the U.S.

Many Japanese factories produced Nippon porcelains and much of it was hand-painted with ornate floral or landscape decoration and heavy gold decoration, applied beading and slip-trailed designs referred to as "moriage." We indicate the specific marking used on a piece, when known, at the end of each listing below. Be aware that a number of Nippon markings have been reproduced and used on new porcelain wares.

Important reference books on Nippon include: The Collector's Encyclopedia of Nippon Porcelain, Series One through Three, *by Joan F. Van Patten (Collector Books, Paducah, Kentucky) and* The Wonderful World of Nippon Porcelain, 1891-1921 *by Kathy Wojciechowski (Schiffer Publishing, Ltd., Atglen, Pennsylvania).*

Bowl, 6¼" d., footed, h.p. daffodils .. **$35.00**
Bowl, 7¾" d., round gently scalloped rim w/long pierced rim handles, gold rim band & handles, the shallow interior decorated in an Imari-style patt. in dark burnt orange, dark blue, yellow & pink on white, green "M in Wreath" mark **39.00**
Bowl, 9½" d., serpentine border decorated w/a wide beaded gold band, the interior decorated w/a turquoise blue tapestry-type ground painted w/large purple violets w/green beaded leaves, centered w/gold centers & stripes, further decoration on the exterior **149.00**
Bowl, 11" w., octagonal w/a gently scalloped rim, relief-molded shape w/large purple orchid blossoms around the interior framed by lacy gold borders, double blossoms in bottom w/lacy gold trim **220.00**
Hair receiver, cov., apple green & creamy beige decorated overall w/applied gold florals, 4½" d. (blue Maple Leaf mark) **44.00**

Fine Quality Nippon Pieces

Humidor, cov., ovoid body w/a short flaring neck w/molded rim, inset cover w/large knob handle, h.p. continuous fox hunt scene in full color, stylized floral & geometric borders in dark green & brown, 7" h., green "M" in Wreath mark (ILLUS. right) **1,760.00**
Luncheon set: six each luncheon plates, dessert plates, chocolate cups & saucers, one master nut bowl w/six individual nut cups, cov. sugar bowl, mustard jar & spoon (no cover), condiment shaker, deep sauce dish & five oblong sandwich trays w/fitted cups; all decorated in a flying geese decoration, white against a pale grey & sea green ground w/heavy gold & jeweling on the edges, 45 pcs. (T.S. Nippon) .. **550.00**
Pitcher, tankard, 14" h., h.p. plush pink roses w/cobalt blue trim **275.00**

Plaque with "Man on Camel" Scene

Plaque, pierced to hang, round, molded in relief w/the "Man on Camel" design w/raised enamel border, 10¾" d., green "M" in Wreath mark (ILLUS.) **1,100.00**
Punch bowl & base, widely flaring pedestal-footed bowl resting on a round gold base w/animal paw feet, the interior of the bowl ornately decorated in the center w/large red, white & yellow roses & green leaves surrounded by a wide raised gold scroll border band, the exterior w/a white ground decorated overall

w/lacy gold, lacy gold on the pedestal foot, 10" d., 2 pcs., blue Maple Leaf mark (ILLUS. center, previous page). **550.00**

Tea set: cov. teapot, cov. sugar bowl, creamer, salt & pepper shakers & 10" d. plate; all decorated w/h.p. red plush roses & green leaves on a mottled green ground w/gold trim, the set (blue Maple Leaf mark) **99.00**

Tea strainer, two-part, decorated w/bright roses on a cobalt blue over white ground, unmarked **110.00**

Urn, cov., large bulbous inverted pear-shaped body raised on a ringed pedestal & flaring round foot, the shoulders mounted w/ornate scrolling gilt handles, short small scrolled neck fitted w/a domed cover w/pointed gold finial, the body centered by an oval color bust portrait of Queen Louise against a wide maroon band w/ornate gilt trim, white & maroon gilt-trimmed narrower bands above & below & on cover & base, the reverse w/an oval medallion of pink & red roses, marked, 15" h. (professional finial repair) **1,210.00**

Vase, 7" h., hexagonal upright body w/narrow inward angled rim, angled scroll gold shoulder handles, peach rim & base bands w/ornate gilt scrolling, the main body w/a continuous h.p. landscape of a lakeside meadow w/a foot bridge over a stream all in naturalistic tones, marked **175.00**

Three Nippon Vases

Vase, 8½" h., moon flask-form, oblong foot supporting a flattened disk pierced through w/an arched opening in the upper half, moriage overall decoration of florals in color w/white beading (ILLUS. left) **248.00**

Vase, 9" h., round cushion base below the tall slender baluster-form body flanked by large loop handles from lower body to rim of base,

overall moriage decoration of purple violets, marked "Royal Moriye Nippon" (ILLUS. center). . . . **193.00**

Vase, 10½" h., slender ovoid body w/short rolled neck, decorated around the upper half w/large clusters of yellow roses on a burnt orange ground, green "M" in Wreath mark (ILLUS. right) **138.00**

Nippon Vase with Egyptian Scene

Vase, 11" h., flaring cylindrical lower body below the wide waist band & short tapering neck flanked by angled gold handle, the waist band h.p. w/an Egyptian Nile River scene w/sailing ship & temple at sunset, the lower body w/gilt-outlined panels w/scrolling gilt drops on a mottled dark green, purple & yellow ground, the neck in dark green trimmed w/heavy gilt scrolling (ILLUS.). **935.00**

Vase, 11½" h., wide ovoid body tapering to a short widely flaring trumpet neck, h.p. w/large life-sized pink & ruby full-blown roses & green leaves on a shaded ground w/heavy gilt trim & separated by small gilt ovals enclosing red roses, white & green neck bands w/delicate gilt scrolling trim, marked **605.00**

Vase, 12" h., pillow-style, a tall flattened ovoid body on a scroll-molded gold-trimmed foot, the rounded shoulder tapering to a short cylindrical flaring neck w/a deeply ruffled gold-trimmed rim, large double loop gold shoulder handles, the body w/a large rectangular central reserve continuing into a band decorated w/a lakeside landscape scene w/high mountains in the distance, painted in shades of purple, yellow, green & brown, ornate gilt scrolling w/dainty colored blossoms above & below the center band, marked "Hand-painted Morimura Nippon" . . **770.00**

Vase, 16" h., footed tall swelled cylindrical body w/a molded cross-form shoulder centered w/a short neck w/a deep cupped rib-molded rim, gold rim & gold leaves painted on the top of the shoulders, the body h.p. w/large orangish red poppies, small black-centered blue blossoms, tall green & small green & yellow leaves all against a shaded blue ground, a gilt scroll band around the base, (Maple Leaf mark) **1,650.00**

Superb Tall Nippon Vase

Vase, 17½" h., tall slender ovoid body, the wide central band finely h.p. w/a mountain scene w/trees & river in the foreground w/a satin finish, shades of green, brown, tan & pale blue, top & bottom cobalt blue bands highlighted w/ornate gilt scroll & floral trim & turquoise jeweling, blue Maple Leaf mark (ILLUS.) **7,480.00**

Wine jug w/mushroom stopper, bulbous tapering ovoid body w/a small neck & tiny spout, loop shoulder handle, decorated in autumnal colors w/the "Elks in Silhouette at Sunset" scene, 8" h., green "M" in Wreath mark (ILLUS. left, in group photo) **935.00**

NORITAKE

Noritake china, still in production in Japan, has been exported in large quantities to this country since early in this century. Though the Noritake Company first registered in 1904, it did not use "Noritake" as part of its backstamp until 1918. Interest in Noritake has escalated as collectors now seek out pieces made between the "Nippon" era and World War II (1921-41). The Azalea pattern is also popular with collectors.

Noritake Mark

Ashtray, figural girl holding out hem of dress w/both hands on rim **$115.00**

Bonbon, Azalea patt., No. 184 . . . . . . **50.00**

Bowl, oatmeal, Azalea patt., No. 55 . . **28.00**

Bowl, salad, Azalea patt., No. 12 . . . . . **21.00**

Bowl, 8" d., Art Deco design, orange lustre interior w/a blue & gold peacock feather design, gold rim & handles **135.00**

Bowl, 9" d., handles, blue floral decoration **23.00**

Butter tub w/insert, Azalea patt., No. 54, 2 pcs. **48.00**

Cake plate, Azalea patt., No. 10 . . . . . **40.00**

Celery dish, Azalea patt., No. 99 . . . . **65.00**

Coffeepot, cov., demitasse, Tree in Meadow patt. **225.00**

Creamer & open sugar bowl, individual size, Azalea patt., No. 449, pr. **450.00**

Gravy boat, Azalea patt., No. 40 . . . . . **55.00**

Jam jar, cover, underplate & ladle, Azalea patt., No. 125, 4 pcs. **170.00**

Plate, breakfast, Azalea patt., No. 98 . . . **28.00**

Plates, 7½" d., the center h.p. w/a large yellow rose & green leaves against a shaded brown, yellow & pale blue ground, the wide border band in cobalt blue w/scrolled panels in grey & black & overall heavy gold trim, ca. 1920s, pr. **193.00**

Platter, 12" oval, Azalea patt., No. 56 . . . . **60.00**

Platter, 14" l., oval, Azalea patt., No. 17 . . . . **60.00**

Powder puff box, cov., round, cover decorated w/a lady in 18th c. costume wearing a black tricorner hat & mask & a billowing skirt w/wide stripes of orange alternating w/black stripes w/colored florals, pale blue edge band, 3¼" d. **220.00**

Relish dish, Azalea patt., No. 18 . . . . . **18.00**

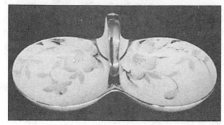

Rare Noritake Azalea Twin Relish

Relish dish, twin-lobe style, center
  handle, Azalea patt., No. 450
  (ILLUS.). **425.00**
Salad serving set: 10" d. bowl,
  underplate, serving spoon & fork;
  bowl exterior in green lustre, the
  interior decorated w/vegetables in
  color, the set **195.00**
Salad set: 10" d. bowl, underplate,
  serving spoon & fork; h.p.
  vegetables on the interior, the set . . **225.00**
Salt & pepper shakers, Azalea patt.,
  No. 11, pr. **30.00**
Teapot, cov., Azalea patt., regular
  size, No. 15 . . . . **110.00**
Vegetable bowl, open, divided,
  Azalea patt., No. 439 . . . . **285.00**

NORTH DAKOTA
SCHOOL OF MINES

*All pottery produced at the University of
North Dakota School of Mines was made from
North Dakota clay. In 1910, the University hired
Margaret Kelly Cable to teach pottery making
and she remained at the school until her
retirement. Julia Mattson and Margaret Pachl
were other instructors between 1923 and 1970.
Designs and glazes varied through the years
ranging from the Art Nouveau to modern styles.
Pieces were marked "University of North Dakota
- Grand Forks, N.D. - Made at School of Mines,
N.D." within a circle and also signed by the
students until 1963. Since that time, the pieces
bear only the students' signatures. Items signed
"Huck" are by the artist Flora Huckfield and
were made between 1923 and 1949. Pieces were
marked with the University name until 1963.*

North Dakota School of Mines Mark

North Dakota School of Mines Pieces

Bowl, 7¼" d., 1¼" h., wide flat low
  form w/incurved sides, black &
  green stylized flowers on a light
  blue ground, decorated by
  M.K.,circular mark & "MK" (ILLUS.
  bottom left) **$1,045.00**
Bowl-vase, nearly spherical body w/a
  wide flat mouth, Bentonite clay w/a
  dark reddish color decorated
  around the upper half w/facing
  pairs of black buffalo between
  double upright stripes, possiby the
  work of Julia Mattson, marked &
  incised "992," 3¼" h. **880.00**
Jar, cov., cylindrical barrel-shaped
  w/a narrow shoulder & short
  cylindrical neck w/a fitted flat cover,
  overall incised oak leaves & acorns
  within large C-scrolls, shaded
  matte green glaze, ink stamp &
  "M.L.M. 1931," 5¾" d., 6" h. **495.00**
Planter-book ends, two half-round
  squatty, bulbous bowls w/closed
  rims, each incised w/an ivy leaf
  design in dark green over a moss
  matte glaze, by Dora Whitman, ink
  mark & incised signature, 5½" d.,
  3¾" h., pr. **825.00**
Plate, 9½" d., decorated in the Art
  Deco style w/a large stylized
  blossom on stem to one side of
  center rings & within an outer
  angle-ended ring band, in yellow &
  brown on a beige ground, ink
  stamp & incised "JCH - 1933" **413.00**
Trivet, circular, carved w/blue &
  green flowers against a yellow
  ground, by BLW, w/circular ink
  stamp & incised "BLW," 5½" d. **248.00**
Vase, 3½" h., 3½" d., ovoid form
  w/closed mouth, excised w/Canada
  geese in flight in a caramel glossy
  glaze against an ivory ground,
  w/circular ink stamp & incised
  "JM869". **660.00**
Vase, 3½" h., 3¾" d., bulbous ovoid
  body w/a closed rim, panels of
  tooled violet flowers between
  vertical bars on a white ground, by
  Huckfield, circular ink mark &
  "Huck - Jill - 9 - 670" (ILLUS. left
  top) **495.00**

Vase, 3½" h., 5½" d., a wide flat bottom w/a low flaring base band below the sharply tapering sides to a molded flat mouth, the sides carved w/a band of large stylized flowers in brown & blue on a tannish green ground, by Lem Tuick, stamped mark & artist's signature, No. 5053 . . . . **715.00**

Vase, 4½" h., wide bulbous ovoid body w/the wide shoulder tapering to a small, short molded rim, the shoulder relief-carved w/a wide band of stylized large fish w/bulging eyes backed by stylized waves & fish hooks, rich medium blue glossy glaze against a terra cotta ground, circular ink mark, incised artist's initials & "3-38" **880.00**

Vase, 5" h., 7½" d., squatty wide bulbous body w/a wide shoulder to the short, wide rolled neck, rose & green matte glaze, marked **303.00**

Vase, 5½" h., 5" d., bulbous ovoid body w/closed rim, carved w/a design of daffodils & leaves in mustard yellow & cream, by Julia Mattson, circular mark & "J.M." (ILLUS. right) **770.00**

Vase, 6" h., simple swelled cylindrical body tapering to a small, flat mouth, deeply carved w/tulip blossoms & buds atop vertical stems & leaves, rich medium green matte glaze, blue circular ink mark, incised "R.M. 5-1-31" **468.00**

Vase, 8" h., simple ovoid body tapering to a flat mouth, decorated w/six panels of cut-out stylized daffodil & leaf design around the body, two-tone chocolate brown glaze, artist-signed "B.J. Anderson" **935.00**

Vase, 8½" h., tall ovoid body tapering to a flat rim, deeply carved shoulder decoration of broad leaves w/prominent veins & jagged edges, tobacco brown matte glaze, blue circular mark, incised "D. O'Brien" **523.00**

OHR (GEORGE) POTTERY

George Ohr, the eccentric potter of Biloxi, Mississippi, worked from about 1883 to 1906. Some think him to be one of the most expert throwers the craft will ever see. The majority of his works were hand-thrown, exceedingly thin-walled items, some of which have a crushed or folded appearance. He considered himself the foremost potter in the world and declined to sell much of his production, instead accumulating a

great horde to leave as a legacy to his children. In 1972 this collection was purchased for resale by an antiques dealer.

GEO. E. OHR
BILOXI, MISS.

Ohr Pottery Marks

Bowl, 6½" w., 3" h., footed wide rounded form w/folded & pinched asymmetrical sides w/incurved rim, speckled amber & gunmetal glaze, impressed "G.E. OHR - Biloxi - Miss." **$2,860.00**

Bowl-vase, footed squatty bulbous body w/large deep rounded dimples around the sides below the short rolled & scalloped rim, exterior w/a glossy raspberry glaze, the interior w/a shimmering gunmetal glaze, die-stamped "G.E. OHR - BILOXI," 3½" d., 2½" h. . . **1,760.00**

Bowl-vase, a thin footring below the wide bulbous body swelling to a rim w/four pinched-up corners & dimples along the incurved rim, mottled gunmetal over green glaze, die-stamped "G.E. OHR - Biloxi, Miss.," 4½" d., 3⅓" h. (restoration to two small rim nicks) **1,100.00**

Chamberstick, wide domed foot w/deep in-body twists tapering to a tapering standard w/a swelled mid-section below the cylindrical cupped socket, looped & folded side handle from mid-neck to side of base, bisque clay, script signature, 4¾" d., 5½" h. **413.00**

Small Ohr Bisque-fired Jug & Vase

Jug, ovoid body w/a small molded neck & C-scroll handle, bisque-fired white clay, from the St. Louis Exposition, signed in script "G.E. Ohr - Expo Day '04," 3" d., 4" h. (ILLUS. left) **495.00**

Pitcher, 3" h., 5½" l., short round pedestal base below the deep bulbous rounded body w/a wide rolled & pinched rim w/end pinched spout & end strap handle, speckled green glossy glaze, marked "G.E. OHR - Biloxi, Miss." **1,760.00**

Pitcher, 3¾" h., 4¾" w., footed flattened bulbous body w/ cut-out handle & flaring almond-shaped rim w/pinched spout, overall gunmetal glaze, marked "G.E. Ohr, Biloxi, Miss." **1,870.00**

Pitcher, 4" h., 5¼" l., short pedestal base supports the pinched & compressed oblong body w/cut-out angular handle & rolled, flaring rim w/pinched tip spout, glossy green & red speckled glaze, incised "G.E. OHR - Biloxi, Miss." **4,950.00**

Vase, 3¼" h., 3¼" d., wide bulbous ovoid tapering toward the base, wide & short rolled neck, mottled pink, white & blue glossy glaze, die-stamped "G.E. OHR - Biloxi, Miss." (ILLUS. right) **1,210.00**

Vase, 3¼" h., 3¾" d., footring below a rounded base below a coggled band at the base of the heavily dimpled cylindrical body w/a pinched & inwardly folded rim, overall gunmetal glaze, marked "G.E. OHR - Biloxi - Miss." (very small rim chip) **935.00**

Vase, 4" h., 4¾" d., round footring below the wide squatty bulbous body tapering to an upright folded, twisted & crinolated neck, bisque scroddled clay, script signature . . **1,210.00**

Vase, 4¾" h., 3¾" d., a footring below the bulbous cylindrical ringed body w/a rounded shoulder tapering to the wide cupped rim, pink, blue & green mottled glossy glaze, impressed "G.E. OHR - Biloxi, Miss." **1,430.00**

Vase, 5" h., 4½" d., footring below a rounded base flaring to a ringed cylindrical wide body w/a rounded shoulder to the folded cylindrical neck, covered in a mahogany, Aventurine & gunmetal glaze, incised "Biloxi" in script **935.00**

Vase, 5¼" h., 4½" d., a footring below the flaring rounded base, a medial band & wide conical sides tapering to a crimped, twisted & folded rim, dark Aventurine & gunmetal glaze, incised "G.E. OHR - Biloxi - Miss." (one very small under-rim chip) . . . **880.00**

Vase, 6¼" h., 3¼" d., disc-footed baluster-form body w/a trumpet-form neck, unusual cobalt blue,

light green & mahogany flambé glaze, die-stamped "G.E. OHR - Biloxi, Miss." **935.00**

Rare Ohr Bottle-form Vase

Vase, 9¼" h., 3¾" d., bottle-form, short flaring foot supporting a cylindrical body w/a curved shoulder to a tall cylindircal neck, upright bar & scroll pierced shoulder handles, rare mottled blue & greenish red & cobalt blue on a pink ground, restoration to rim, hand-incised "Ohr - Biloxi Miss." (ILLUS.) **13,200.00**

OWENS

Owens pottery was the product of the J.B. Owens Pottery Company, which operated in Ohio from 1890 to 1929. In 1891 it located in Zanesville and produced art pottery from 1896, introducing "Utopian" wares as its first art pottery. The company switched to tile after 1907. Efforts to rebuild after the factory burned in 1928 failed and the company closed in 1929.

Owens Pottery Mark

Jardiniere, Cyrano line, 8" d. **$175.00**

Mug, Utopian line, cylindrical w/angled loop handle, bittersweet vines on a shaded olive green & brown ground, glossy finish, impressed mark, 5⅛" h. (minor wear) **105.00**

Owens Lotus Line Pitcher

Pitcher, 8⅝" h., Lotus line, footed ovoid body tapering to a rolled rim & arched spout, D-form handle, dark green shaded to creamy white ground decorated on one wide w/a wading white & blue bird & on the other side w/a lotus blossom, unmarked, some usage staining (ILLUS.)......................358.00

Tankard, Utopian line, tapering cylindrical body w/angled handle, decorated w/red cherries & green leaves, dark brown shading to tan, artist-initialed, impressed "J.B Owens Utopian" & "830," 6⅞" h.....193.00

Owens Utopian Line Vase

Vase, 4¼" h., Utopian line, crescent-shaped bowl raised on four tab feet, decorated w/dark red clover & green & brown stems on a dark brown shaded to moss green ground, glossy glaze, artist monogram on back, base w/impressed mark "Utopian J.B. Owens," shape No. 872 (ILLUS.) .. 220.00

Vase, 6½" h., green matte glaze.....325.00

Vase, 9½" h., jug-form, Aborigine Indian style 315.00

Vase, 12" h., Utopian line, decorated w/yellow tulips................200.00

Vase, 13½" h., Utopian line, squatty wide ringed base below tall slender tapering cylindrical sides below the cupped mouth, flowers & foliage encrusted in beige, white & blue on

a matte blue & beige ground, impressed "Owens 123" (two small flakes on lip) **138.00**

PACIFIC CLAY PRODUCTS

At the beginning of the 1920s William Lacy merged several southern California potteries to form the Pacific Clay Products Company in Los Angeles. However, it was not until the early 1930s that Pacific began producing tableware and that has piqued the interest of today's collectors. Ceramic engineer, Frank McCann, and Matthew Lattie, designer and head of the art department, were largely responsible for Pacific's success. Pottery production ceased in 1942. Today the company has a plant in Corona, California specializing in roofing tiles.

Pacific Clay Products Marks

Cheese server, orange, 15" d.......**$85.00**
Coaster, round, solid glaze, 4" d......**20.00**

Pacific Clay Cornucopia-vase

Cornucopia-vase, 8¼" h., model of upright cornucopia, scalloped rim, turquoise interior, white exterior (ILLUS.).....................**38.00**

Cup & saucer, demitasse, ring-style .. **25.00**

Grease jar w/cover, round w/three rings near middle section of bottom, 5¼" h.................**58.00**

Tray, Hostessware line, Apache Red glaze, 15" l....................**60.00**

Trivet, green glaze **100.00**

Tumbler, Hostessware line, straight sides flaring slightly at rim, two rings near bottom, three rings near top, 4⅛" h....................**15.00**

Pacific Clay George and Martha Washington Wall Pockets

Wall pocket, profile of George Washington, beading around his profile, two pistols on top of pocket, can also sit as a planter, Claire Lerner design, pink high gloss, Model No. 3060L, 5¾" h. (ILLUS. left) **14.00**

Wall pocket, profile of Martha Washington, beading around her profile, bow on top of pocket, can also sit as a planter, Claire Lerner design, pink high gloss, Model No. 3060R, 5¾" h. (ILLUS. right) **14.00**

Water set: carafe & five 5" h. tumblers; Apache Red glaze, 6 pcs. **145.00**

PARIAN

Parian is unglazed porcelain in the biscuit stage, and takes its name from its resemblance to Parian marble used for statuary. Parian wares were made in this country and abroad through much of the last century and continue to be made.

Charles Sumner Parian Bust

Bust of Charles Sumner, mounted on a raised socle base, impressed title, verse & manufacturer's mark of Robinson & Leadbeater, England, ca. 1880, 12⅞" h. (ILLUS.) **$345.00**

Bust of General Robert E. Lee, mounted on a raised circular plinth, sculpted by Roland Morris, manufactured by James & Thomas Berington, impressed marks & title, England, ca. 1870, 12¾" h. **690.00**

Bust of Shakespeare, beaded man wearing cord-tied collared shirt & cloak, on a socle base, name impressed on the back, 19th c., 8" h. **110.00**

Busts of Mozart & Beethoven, each mounted on a raised circular plinth, each titled, attributed to Robinson & Leadbeater, England, ca. 1880, 11¼" h., pr. **748.00**

Figure of a woman, the kneeling maiden wearing a simple costume, her hands clasped in her lap, raised on a separate molded circular base, impressed marks of the Gustafsberg factory, Sweden, late 19th c., overall 16½" h., 2 pcs. **575.00**

Figural Owl Match Holder

Match holder, figural, two owls snuggled together on a tree branch w/a small stump in front for the matches, inscribed across the front of the platform base "Match Making," English registry mark for 1871, 5⅜" w., 7¾" h. (ILLUS.) **195.00**

Pitcher, 10" h., flaring scalloped foot below the rounded tapering conical body w/a scroll-molded narrow neck & high arched spout, forked scroll-molded long handle, relief-molded Naomi patt., group of three woman on the side, attributed to Samuel Alcock, first half 19th c. **110.00**

PARIS & OLD PARIS

China known by the generic name of Paris and Old Paris was made by several Parisian factories from the 18th through the 19th century; some of it is marked and some is not. Much of it was handsomely decorated.

Ice bucket, cylindrical, a blue ground banded w/raised gilt flowers & beadwork & enameled floral panels, festoons & border, retailed by Davis Collamore & Co., Ltd., New York, mid-19th c., 7⅜" d., 7½" h. (gilt wear on footrim) **$575.00**

Tea set: cov. teapot, cov. sugar bowl & creamer; each w/a gilt ground enamel-decorated w/floral bouquets & banding, 19th c., teapot 8⅝" h., the set (sugar cover damaged) **460.00**

Vase, 11½" h., baluster-form footed body w/a short cylindrical neck w/a flared rim, high arched loop gold handles from the rim to the shoulder & down the sides each terminating in a classical bust medallion in turquoise blue, the background in pale lavender pink h.p. down the sides w/colorful clusters of reddish orange, white & blue blossoms & green leaves, black foot band, mid-19th c. **193.00**

Vase, 12" h., portrait decoration on a gilt ground, square enamel-decorated panels on each side, one depicting a female taverner, the other w/an exterior topographical landscape w/building, 19th c. **345.00**

Vase, 14½" h., baluster-form body tapering to a tall flaring flute-molded neck w/a four-scallop rim, long curled & scroll-trimmed handles from the neck down the sides, the neck in pale pink above the main body in dark blue decorated w/delicate green vines w/lavender blossoms framing a gold urn of blossoms above ornate gilt scrolls & further tiny blossoms, black foot band, white & gold handles, mid-19th c. **385.00**

Vases, 14½"h., baluster-form w/wide ovoid body raised on a short pedestal & square foot, the slender trumpet neck w/a tightly ruffled rim, ornate goat head & fruiting grapevine handles, the blue ground decorated w/a large oval medallion

Paris Porcelain Vases

framing a scene of 18th c. ladies in peasant costume in a landscape, gilt trim, restorations, 19th c., pr. (ILLUS.). **575.00**

PATE-SUR-PATE

Taking its name from the French phrase meaning "paste on paste," this type of ware features designs in relief, obtained by successive layers of thin pottery paste, painted one on top of the other. Much of this work was done in France and England, and perhaps the best-known wares of this type from England are those made by Minton, which see.

Box, cov., triangular, the cover molded w/a white nude woman sitting at water's edge silhouetted against blue, trimmed w/gold, marked "Limoges France," late 19th - early 20th c., 5½" w., 2" h. . . . **$220.00**

Box, cov., round, the cover w/a white relief figure on a chariot against a blue ground, cobalt blue rim band & gilt trim lines, illegible printed marks, Europe, late 19th - early 20th c., 7¾" d. **173.00**

Medallion, portrait-type, round, blue ground w/a white slip self-portrait side bust profile of Louis Solon, artist-signed & dated 1892, England, 3⅞" d. **1,265.00**

Plaque, rectangular, brown ground decorated w/white slip depicting a classical female figure holding a candlestick surrounded by three putti in flight, gilt-accented, Solon-type, France, unsigned, 19th c., 3 x 5¾" **1,840.00**

Plaque, oval, blue ground w/white slip decoration of a Cupid figure holding a hammer to an anvil to break a chain, artist-signed by Louis Solon, late 19th c., England, in a giltwood frame, 4¾ x 6" **1,840.00**

Plaque, rectangular, a white relief design of a woman standing w/a large dog silhouetted against deep blue sky, artist-signed "A. Barriere," marked "Limoges," 6 x 8¼" **468.00**

Plaque, oval, a dark blue ground decorated in white slip w/an angelic winged figure among stars w/a tall lily below, artist-signed by Louis Solon, dated 1908, mounted in an ebonized & giltwood rectangular frame, plaque 5½ x 9½" **3,738.00**

Plaque, oval, dark green ground decorated in white slip w/a classical scene of five putti chained by a column, artist monogram of Louis Solon, England, ca. 1885, in an ebonized wood frame, 7½ x 9¾" **4,888.00**

Plaque, rectangular, blue ground decorated w/a white slip scene of a draped maiden offering drinks to numerous cherubs by her feet, artist-signed by Louis Solon, dated 1908, England, mounted in a flat, wide wood frame, 5 x 10½" **4,313.00**

Plaque, rectangular, brown ground decorated w/a white slip classical scene of "The Flight of Love," artist-signed by Louis Solon, ca. 1875, England, in a flat ebonized wood frame, 6½ x 10½" **4,888.00**

Rare Pate-sur-Pate Demi-lune Plaque

Plaque, demi-lune shaped, green ground w/white slip decoration of a central figure of Venus holding a mirror in each hand, fending off two groups of putti w/their reflections, artist-signed by Louis Solon, England, ca. 1885, plaque 15" l., mounted in a rosewood frame (ILLUS.) **9,200.00**

Plaques, rectangular, the dark ground decorated in white slip w/different allegorical scenes of a classical man & woman & cupid representing "The Fall of Love," artist-signed by Louis Solon,

mounted in ebonized & giltwood rectangular frames, chips to back of one, plaques 6 x 8¼", pr. **5,750.00**

Pate-sur-Pate Plate & Vase

Plate, 9⅛" d., round w/dished rim, deep brown ground w/gilt trim & white slip decoration of a nude child behind a net supported by two small trees, monogram of artist Henry Saunders, printed & impressed marks of Moore Brothers, England, ca. 1885 (ILLUS. left) **748.00**

Tea set: cov. teapot, creamer & sugar bowl, six dessert plates, six cups & saucers; yellow ground w/white slip medallions of women's heads, Czecho-Slovakia-Union T Musterschutz No. 5716, 21 pcs. (professional repair) **100.00**

Vases, 6⅞" h., ovoid body tapering to a short neck w/a flaring cupped rim, curved handles from under rim to shoulders, blue ground w/an oval mauve reserve decorated w/a white slip classical female, printed marks, Germany, 20th c., pr. (ILLUS. of one, right)` **748.00**

Vases, 7¼" h., 2½ x 5¾", gold serpent skin twisted handles, nearly identical white floral decoration w/gold trim, front & back, celadon green ground, unmarked, possibly Grainger, Worcester, pr. **995.00**

Vases, 9½" h., tall slender slightly tapering body w/a waisted, forked & widely flaring mouth, looped long gilt handles down the sides, the dark brown ground decorated in white slip w/swirling stylized floral designs, gilt trim at the rim, base & handles, artist monogram of Albione Birks, printed & impressed Minton marks, pr. **4,313.00**

PAUL REVERE POTTERY

This pottery was established in Boston, Massachusetts, in 1906, by a group of philanthropists seeking to establish better conditions for underprivileged young girls of the area. Edith Brown served as supervisor of the small "Saturday Evening Girls Club" pottery operation which was moved, in 1912, to a house close to the Old North Church where Paul Revere's signal lanterns had been placed. The wares were mostly hand decorated in mineral colors and both sgraffito and molded decorations were employed. Although it became popular, it was never a profitable operation and always depended on financial contributions to operate. After the death of Edith Brown in 1932, the pottery foundered and finally closed in 1942.

Paul Revere Marks

Bowl, 4¼" d., 2¼" h., decorated w/a yellow & black band of walking ducks, signed "S.E.G. - 6-21" & initials "B.L." **$518.00**

Bowl, 4¼" d., 2¼" h., deep rounded upright sides on a narrow footring, decorated w/a band of white ducks on a bluish grey ground, 1910, marked "S.E.G. - 553-3 - 10 - I.G." **523.00**

Group of Paul Revere Pieces

Bowl, 6" d., low flaring sides, the interior rim decorated w/a band of clustered trees against a blue ground, marked "S.E.G. - 6-14," w/artist's mark, 1914 (ILLUS. center bottom) **468.00**

Bowl, 6" d., 2½" h., low rounded sides w/closed-in rim, decorated in 'cuerda seca' w/a stylized floral design in green, blue & frothy white on a brown ground, stamped mark **605.00**

Bowl, 6¾" d., 3" h., flaring round sides, decorated w/a band of trees in light green on a light blue ground, remnant of the paper label **523.00**

Bowl, 8½" d., 2½" h., a wide shallow form w/rounded bulbous sides & a wide flat molded rim, white-glazed rim & shoulder over a lotus flower band in white, beige & pale yellow outlined in black, the lower half & interior in a yellow glaze, Fanny Levine, 1921, inscribed marks (short tight hairlines) **403.00**

Bowl, 10" d., 4" h., deep flaring sides, the interior rim decorated in 'cuerda seca' w/two-tone yellow daffodils on a bright yellow ground, marked "S.E.G. - 12-16," w/artist's cipher, restored (ILLUS. bottom right) **880.00**

Cake set: 10" d. cake plate & six 8½" d. plates; each w/a tree pattern w/black outlined scene w/blue sky & green trees, all marked w/initials "J.G. - S.E.G.," three dated "7/15," three dated "1/4/15" & one dated "3/15," the set **1,840.00**

Humidor, cov., flat-bottomed spherical body w/a small domed cover w/knob finial, matte blue glaze w/a pink interior, base signed in slip "P.R.P. 3 - 36," 5¾" d., 6¼" h. (minute inside rim nick) **440.00**

Pitcher, 4½" h., 4½" d., gently tapering cylindrical body w/loop handle & tiny pinched rim spout, a wide green rim band above a dark blue lower body, a round medallion under the spout decorated w/a goose in white, yellow, light blue & green, marked "S.E.G. ELW 3-20," 1920 . . . . **825.00**

Pitcher, tankard, 7¾" h., 5½" d., slightly tapering cylindrical body w/a pointed rim spout & angled long loop handle, decorated w/a continuous band of tall yellow tulips & green leaves & stems on a brown ground against a blue sky, the incised work outlined in black & enamel-glazed, fully-decorated by S. Galner, 1914, minor glaze scaling under base, painted in black "SEG - G - 3-14" **15,400.00**

Ring tray, round w/low dished rim, the interior decorated w/a band of trees in bluish grey & green on a bluish grey ground, signed "S.E.G. - J.G.," 4" d. **303.00**

Teapot, cov., bulbous body w/angled spout & C-form handle, inset cover w/button finial, decorated around

the upper half w/a band of wavy
sailboats in brown & white against
a yellow sky, restored, 1918, 9" l.,
4½" h. (ILLUS. top) **770.00**

Trivet, round, decorated around the
rim w/a band of white rabbits on a
white & mauve ground, marked in
black "AM - 5 - 13 - S.E.G.," 1913,
5½" d. **468.00**

Trivet, round, decorated in 'cuerda
seca' w/a landscape w/a white
house flanked by trees, water in
the distance, marked "S.E.G. - 5-20
- MA," 1920, 5½" d. (ILLUS. bottom
left) **1,430.00**

PEWABIC

*Mary Chase Perry (Stratton) and Horace J.
Caulkins were partners in this Detroit, Michigan
pottery. Established in 1903, Pewabic Pottery
evolved from their Revelation Pottery, "Pewabic"
meaning "clay with copper color" in the language
of Michigan's Chippewa Indians. Caulkins
attended to the clay formulas and Mary Perry
Stratton was artistic creator of forms & glaze
formulas, eventually developing a wide range of
colors for her finely textured glazes. The pottery's
reputation for fine wares and architectural tiles
enabled it to survive the depression years of the
1930s. After Caulkins died in 1923, Mrs.
Stratton continued to be active in the pottery
until her death, at age ninety-four, in 1961. Her
contributions to the art pottery field are
numerous.*

Pewabic Pottery Mark

Bowl, 4" d., 3" h., blue iridescent
glaze **$525.00**

Bowl, 5" d., 2" h., rounded widely
flaring sides w/flat rim, exterior w/a
shimmering burgundy glaze, the
interior w/a richly lustred gold
glaze, stamped mark **495.00**

Bowl, 5" d., 4" h., squatty footed form
w/flared lip, the interior glazed in
cobalt blue, the exterior w/celadon
green w/gold & iridescent dripping
overglaze, circular impressed mark . . **700.00**

Vase, 4" h., 3" d., a squatty bulbous
base tapering to wide gently
tapering cylindrical sides, overall
mottled green, purple & red lustre
glaze, paper label **330.00**

Vase, 4¼" h., 5" d., squatty bulbous
body w/a sharply angled rounded
shoulder tapering to a short
cylindrical neck w/molded rim,
overall mottled gold lustre glaze,
unmarked **413.00**

Vase, 4½" h., 4½" d., a narrow
footring supports the wide squatty
bulbous body centered at the top
by a tiny tapering cylindrical neck,
overall fine dark blue, green &
burgundy lustre glaze, mark
obscured by glaze **385.00**

Vase, 5½" h., 4" d., bulbous ovoid
body tapering to a very short
cylindrical neck, an iridescent
celadon glaze dripping over a
lustred dark blue glaze, impressed
mark (small chip to base in
making) **825.00**

Vase, 6¼" h., 4½" d., bottle-form,
bulbous ovoid body tapering
sharply to a short cylindrical neck,
bluish green iridescent glaze
dripping down over a gold & purple
mottled glaze, impressed mark &
paper label (restoration to rim) **440.00**

Vase, 7" h., 5" d., bulbous body w/a
flaring rim, intense iridescent glaze,
circular impressed mark **863.00**

Vase, 7½" h., 5" d., simple ovoid
body w/a wide, flat molded rim, red
& gold iridescent glaze dripping
over a Chinese blue & red glaze
base, impressed circular mark . . **1,760.00**

Vase, 8¼" h., 5¼" d., wide ovoid
body w/an angled neck to the small
flaring neck, overall lustred gold,
green & burgundy glaze, mark
partially obscured by glaze **1,430.00**

Vase, 9¼" h., 7¼" d., footed bulbous
nearly spherical body tapering to a
short gently flaring cylindrical neck,
overall lustred cobalt blue glaze,
circular stamp mark (slight bruise
to side in making) **1,100.00**

Vase, 9¾" h., 5¾" d., baluster-
shaped w/a short flaring wide neck,
overall dark greenish blue
crystalline glaze, impressed mark &
paper label **2,200.00**

PISGAH FOREST POTTERY

*Walter Stephen experimented with making
pottery shortly after 1900 with his parents in
Tennessee. After their deaths in 1910, he
eventually moved to the foot of Mt. Pisgah in
North Carolina where he became a partner of
C.P. Ryman. Together they built a kiln and a
shop but this partnership was dissolved in 1916.
During 1920 Stephen again began to experiment*

with pottery and by 1926 had his own pottery and equipment. Pieces are usually marked and may also be signed "W. Stephen" and dated. Walter Stephen died in 1961 but work at the pottery still continues, although on a part-time basis.

Pisgah Forest Marks

Bowl-vase, wide squatty bulbous body w/a wide shoulder tapering to a short, wide cylindrical neck, overall celadon flambé glaze w/blue & white crystals, die-stamped mark, 1941, 7" d., 5" h. (large stilt pull on bottom) **$825.00**

Mug, Cameo Ware, cylindrical, medium blue ground w/a white cameo finely detailed design of two clog dancers, the work of Walter Stephen, base w/raised logo, 3⅜" h. **110.00**

Pitcher, 9" h., pale yellow glaze **250.00**

Pisgah Forest Cameo Ware Vase

Vase, 4" h., 4" d., Cameo Ware, squatty bulbous base below a wide cylindrical neck, the neck in dark green w/a white relief design of a wagon train above a glossy lighter green lower body, die-stamped mark (ILLUS.) **330.00**

Vase, 6" h., 4¼" d., simple ovoid body tapering to a short rolled neck w/a molded, flattened rim, fine bluish green crystalline glaze, die-stamped mark, 1936 . . . . **523.00**

Unusual Pisgah Forest Vase

Vase, 6" h., 4½" d., wide ovoid body tapering to a cylindrical neck w/molded rim, overall dark green & red lustred crystalline glaze, die-stamped mark, 1938 (ILLUS.) **935.00**

Vase, 6" h., 6½" d., wide bulbous ovoid body tapering to a short rolled neck, overall dark brown & purple flambé glaze, die-stamped mark, 1935 . . . . **523.00**

Vase, 6½" h., 4½" d., tall deeply corseted cylindrical body w/a widely flaring rim, smooth silver & gold crystalline glaze, glossy pink interior, potter's mark, illegible date **275.00**

Vase, 7½" h., 5" d., baluster-shaped body w/a short wide rolled neck, glossy cream shaded to moss flambé glaze w/blue & white crystals, die-stamped mark, date obscured (in-the-making base chip) **413.00**

Vase, 8" h., 5" d., baluster-shaped body w/flaring rolled short neck, blue, green & white crystalline glaze w/heavy blue spotting around the lower half, die-stamped mark, 1949 . . . . **660.00**

Vase, 8" h., 6½" d., wide bulbous baluster form w/a short slightly flaring cylindrical neck, overall fine celadon crystalline glaze, die-stamped mark, 1936 (base chip, stilt pull) **660.00**

Vase, 10" h., Cameo Ware, baluster-form body w/a short cylindrical neck, the body w/a white relief band showing a farmer plowing w/oxen followed by another man sowing seed, birds flying overhead, against a light blue ground over a rich aqua glossy glaze, the neck decorated w/an applied band of blossoms & heart-shaped leaves, wafer mark & signed in cameo "Stephen," 1953 (minor chip on one figure) **1,210.00**

PRATT WARES

The earliest ware now classified as Pratt ware was made by Felix Pratt at his pottery in Fenton, England from about 1810. He made earthenware with bright glazes, relief sporting jugs, toby mugs and commercial pots and jars whose lids bore multicolored transfer prints. The F. & R. Pratt mark is mid-19th century. The name Pratt ware is also applied today to mid and late 19th century English ware of the same general type as that made by Felix Pratt.

Pratt Wares Mark

Figure, allegorical-type, a lady representing Spring standing half-nude w/a flowering vine wrapped around her neck, wearing draped lower garment, on a colored rockwork round base, decorated in green, yellow, orange, fleshtone, black & brown, ca. 1800, 7" h. (old restoration on some base chips, other unrestored base chips) **$275.00**

Garniture set, a set of three matching vases, a central taller one flanked by two slightly shorter ones, each of classical footed urn form w/widely flaring necks w/lightly scalloped rims, the necks decorated w/an enameled band of stylized flowers & leaves, all molded in relief on one side w/a round vignette scene of a boy w/dogs & on the other a boy, a bird & a dog, each framed by painted sprigs above upright bands of molded & enamel-decorated acanthus leaves rising from the base, highlighted in pink lustre, brown, yellow, black & green, smaller vases 6½" h., large vase 7½" h., the set (smaller vases w/old deteriorating rim restoration, one w/a base crack) **644.00**

Mirror or window rest, figural, pearlware, the bust of a brown-bearded man wearing an orangish ochre turban, his eyes painted pale blue, a dark blue area behind his beard, the base in colorful yellowish ochre, ca. 1800-20, invisible restoration to the base, 5¾" h. **660.00**

Pitcher, 5¼"h., bulbous ovoid body tapering to a wide mouth w/pointed rim spout, C-scroll handle, sporting motif w/relief-molded running dogs among leafy trees, long-haired dog on reverse, dogs w/large spots & other trim in shades of yellow, orange, green, blue & brown, early 19th c. **495.00**

Wall vase, pierced to hang, model of a cornucopia, molded in relief w/a child drinking from a bottle & grapes & leaves, fine coloring in

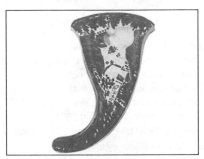

Pratt Ware Wall Vase

green, yellow, blue, brown & orange, early 19th c., small shallow chip on back rim, flake on bottom front rim, 6" w., 10" h. (ILLUS.) **990.00**

QUIMPER

This French earthenware pottery has been made in France since the end of the 17th century and is still in production today. Because the colorful decoration on this ware, predominantly of Breton peasant figures, is all hand-painted and each piece is unique, it has become increasingly popular with collectors in recent years. Most pieces offered today date from about the mid-19th century to the present. Modern potteries continue to operate today and contemporary examples are available in gift shops.

Quimper Marks

Figure group, peasant dancers, signed "Henriot Quimper France 49," 9¼" h. **$90.00**

Jar, cov., two-handled, obverse w/figure of girl, surrounded by floral motifs on yellow ground, signed

"Henriot Quimper France
Entierement Decore Main,"
No. F61 9-201 GA, 7" h. 110.00
Pitcher, milk, 6⅜" h., w/legend "A
Mon Amour" obverse, signed under
handle & impressed "France" &
No. 2 on base (minor rim chips) . . . 120.00
Pitcher, milk, 7½" h., French maiden
on obverse, signed "Henriot
Quimper France 429" 170.00
Soup tureen, cover, matching tray &
soup ladle, signed w/legend
"Entierement Decore Main" & "No.
F324," "D485 MB" (tureen) &
"RH" (tray), the set. 300.00
Tray, octagonal, faience, featuring
parade of couples w/pair of
musicians, signed "Henriot
Quimper France, No. 477," 21" l. . . 490.00

REDWARE

*Red earthenware pottery was made in the
American colonies from the late 1600s. Bowls,
crocks and all types of utilitarian wares were
turned out in great abundance to supplement the
pewter and handmade treenware. The ready
availability of the clay, the same used in making
bricks and roof tiles, accounted for the vast
production. The lead-glazed redware retained its
reddish color though a variety of colors could be
obtained by adding various metals to the glaze.
Interesting effects occurred accidentally through
unsuspected impurities in the clay or uneven
temperatures in the firing kiln which sometimes
resulted in streaks or mottled splotches.*

*Redware pottery was seldom marked by the
maker.*

Batter bowl, w/handle & pouring
spout, Maryland, 7¾" d., 3½" h. $95.00
Bowl, 8½" d., 4½" h., w/green glaze,
Ezra Porter 800.00
Dye pot, flared side, green glazed
interior, Porter, 6" d. , 5" h. 100.00
Herb pot, ovoid, 1½" h. 100.00
Jar, ovoid body w/a molded wide
mouth, overall dark brown glaze,
bottom impressed "W. Smith
Womelsdorf," Pennsylvania, 5½" h.
(minor crazing, possible base
hairline) 94.00
Jar, red ground w/dripping dark &
olive glazes, incised numerals on
base, Corlis, 6¼" h. 3,750.00
Jar, w/slip decorated "7," green glaze
w/peach, 8" h. 2,000.00
Jar, impressed w/variety of star &
snowflake decorations, olive & red
glaze, impressed "John Safford,
Monmouth," 13" h., (cracks, glaze
loss, one ear missing) 3,500.00

Jug, straight sided, w/yellow green
drip decoration, Ezra Porter,
5¾" h. 400.00
Jug, ovoid, various shades of red
brown w/green blush, western
Maine, 6" h. 450.00
Jug, speckle brown to yellow brown,
Essex City, Massachusetts,
6¾" h. 6,750.00
Model of a frog, crouching animal
w/boldly molded details, overall
dark green glaze, 6" h. (chips) 330.00
Muffin cup, green-glazed interior,
3⅛" d. 360.00
Pitcher, cream, 3¾" h., black glaze
w/carved scalloped top . . . 125.00
Pitcher, 7" h., orange & blue glazes,
Pennsylvania. 225.00
Pitcher, milk, 8¼" h., w/reddish
brown glaze w/darker brown
splotches, Corlis. 2,100.00
Pudding mold, fluted, green & red
glaze, 7" l. 125.00
Shaving mug, w/applied soap cup &
handle in olive green w/dark
speckles, southern Maine,
5" d.,4" h. 300.00
Shaving mug, one-handled, medium
brown glaze w/splotching, Corlis,
4½" h. 2,600.00
Shaving mug, w/blown out soap cup,
brown decorations, Pennsylvania
4⅜" d., 7" h. 275.00
Stewpot, w/pouring lip & handle, in
pale olive green glaze & chrome
yellow interior glaze, impressed
"John Safford, Stewpot #3,"
5⅞" h. 4,000.00

RED WING

*Various potteries operated in Red Wing,
Minnesota from 1868, the most successful being
the Red Wing Stoneware Co., organized in 1878.
Merged with other local potteries through the
years, it became known as Red Wing Union
Stoneware Co. in 1894, and was one of the
largest producers of utilitarian stoneware items
in the United States. After a decline in the
popularity of stoneware products, an art pottery
line was introduced to compensate for the loss
and this was reflected in a new name for the
company, Red Wing Potteries, Inc., in 1930.
Stoneware production ceased entirely in 1947,
but vases, planters, cookie jars and dinnerwares
of art pottery quality continued in production
until 1967 when the pottery ceased operation
altogether.*

Red Wing Marks

DINNERWARES & NOVELTIES

Bowl, cereal, Bob White patt. **$20.00**
Bread tray, Bob White patt., 24" l. . . . **105.00**
Butter dish, cov., Bob White patt. **80.00**

Red Wing Bob White Casserole

Casserole, cov., Bob White patt.,
    4 qt. (ILLUS.). **55.00**

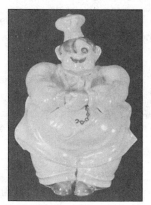

Red Wing French Chef Cookie Jar

Cookie jar, cov., figural French Chef,
    yellow glaze (ILLUS.) **100.00**
Cookie jar, cov., figural Jack Frost,
    tall **695.00**
Cookie jar, cov., Round-Up patt. **450.00**
Creamer & cov. sugar bowl, Bob
    White patt., pr. **55.00**
Cup and saucer, Magnolia patt. **10.00**
Cup & saucer, Bob White patt. **12.00**
Hor d'oeuvres holder, Bob White
    patt., model of a bird pierced for
    picks **45.00**
Marmite, cov., Bob White patt. **30.00**

Mug, Bob White patt. **60.00**
Pitcher, 12" h., Bob White patt. **35.00**
Pitcher, water, Bob White patt., 60 oz. . . . **45.00**
Planter, model of a duck, No. 439 . . . . **95.00**
Planter, model of a seal, No. 941 . . . . **89.00**
Plate, dinner, Town & Country patt. **16.00**
Plate, bread & butter, 6½" d.,
    Bob White patt. **7.00**
Plate, salad, 7½" d., Bob White patt. . . . **8.00**
Plate, dinner, 10½" d., Bob White patt. . . **13.00**
Platter, 13" oval, Bob White patt. **25.00**
Vegetable bowl, Bob White patt. **28.00**
Vegetable bowl, open, divided &
    angled, Bob White patt. **45.00**
Vegetable dish, divided, Round Up
    patt. **165.00**

STONEWARE & UTILITY WARES

Bowl, 5" d., paneled sides, blue &
    rust sponged decoration **525.00**
Bowl, 10" d., paneled, sponged blue
    & red decoration **70.00**
Crock, large wing mark, 1 gal. **350.00**

Red Wing 1 Quart Fruit Jar

Fruit jar, screw-on metal lid, "Stone
    Mason Fruit Jar," 1 qt. (ILLUS.). . . . **150.00**
Model of a pig, medium brown
    glaze, 7½" l. **400.00**

Red Wing Water Cooler

Water cooler w/original lid, small
    wing mark, w/original metal spigot,
    3 gal. (ILLUS. without spigot) **695.00**

ROCKINGHAM WARES

The Marquis of Rockingham first established an earthenware pottery in the Yorkshire district of England around 1745 and it was occupied afterwards by various potters. The well-known mottled brown Rockingham glaze was introduced about 1788 by the Brameld Brothers and became immediately popular. It was during the 1820s that the production of true porcelain began at the factory and continued to be made until the firm closed in 1842. Since that time the so-called Rockingham glaze has been used by various potters in England and the United States, including some famous wares produced in Bennington, Vermont. However, very similar glazes were also used by potteries in other areas of the United States including Ohio and Indiana and only wares specifically attributed to Bennington should use that name. The following listings will include mainly wares featuring the dark brown mottled glaze produced at various sites here and abroad.

Batter jug, cov., molded base & bulbous ovoid body tapering to a ringed rim band, short wide angled cylindrical shoulder spout & eared grip handle on opposite base, inset disk cover w/knob finial, wire bail handle w/wooden grip, relief-molded medallion portraits of a man smoking & woman taking snuff, overall mottled dark brown glaze, 19th c. (chips, especially on cover) **$440.00**

Book flask, molded book-form w/raised bands on binding, opening at the top corner, overall mottled dark brown glaze, 6" h. (edge chips) **50.00**

Bottle, figural Toby Barrel-type, overall dark brown slightly mottled glaze, "No.2" on barrel, probably English, 19th c., 8¾" h. **165.00**

Cow creamer, model of a standing cow w/tail looped for handle & mouth open as spout, overall mottled dark brown glaze, 19th c., 7⅝" l. (one ear & one horn broken off, small edge chips) **110.00**

Pitcher, 9" h., ovoid body tapering to a low arched spout & a scrolled branch handle, the sides molded in relief w/a scene of Cupid & Psyche, dark brown mottled glaze, late 19th c. **99.00**

Rockingham Ware Preserving Jar

Preserving jar, cylindrical, mottled dark brown glaze, filled-in rim chip, small edge chips, short hairlines in base, 7¼" h. (ILLUS.) **50.00**

ROOKWOOD

Considered America's foremost art pottery, the Rookwood Pottery Company was established in Cincinnati, Ohio in 1880, by Mrs. Maria Nichols Longworth Storer. To accurately record its development, each piece carried the Rookwood insignia, or mark, was dated, and, if individually decorated, was usually signed by the artist. The pottery remained in Cincinnati until 1959 when it was sold to Herschede Hall Clock Company and moved to Starkville, Mississippi, where it continued in operation until 1967.

A private company is now producing a limited variety of pieces using original Rookwood molds.

Rookwood Mark

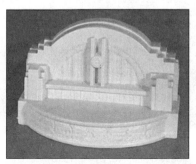

Union Terminal Book End

Book ends, model of Union Terminal, arched Art Deco-style design, ca. 1930s, 4⅝" h., pr. (ILLUS. of one) **$5,500.00**

Book ends, figural, model of a peacock w/a widely opened rounded tail standing on a low pedestal on a stepped half-round base, dark yellow Matte glaze, No. 2445, 1925, 4⅞" h., pr. **495.00**

Book ends, figural, modeled as a galleon under full sail w/clouds behind the sails, on an oblong wave-molded base, green w/rust highlights Matte glaze, No. 2634, 1942, 5" h., pr. **413.00**

Book ends, figural, model of a large rook perched on a rockwork paneled base, rich greenish black Matte glaze, designed by William McDonald, No. 2275, 1925, 5¼" h., pr. **660.00**

Book ends, figural, "Oak Tree," modeled in the half-round as rounded leafy trees on twisted trunks on oblong rockwork bases, fine Coromandel glaze, designed by William McDonald, No. 6023, 1929, 5⅝" h., pr. **880.00**

Book ends, figural, figure of St. Francis, w/a bird & fox, brown & cream glaze, No. 6883, 1945, 5¼" w., 7½" h., pr. **431.00**

Bowl, 7½" d., 2½" h., squatty reticulated form w/closed mouth, relief-molded w/pine cones & pine needles, under a ochre Matte glaze, impressed w/flame mark, 1907 . . . . **550.00**

Bowl, 8¼" d., round petal-form eight-lobed rounded flaring sides w/a 1932 Glaze Effect decoration of dark brown w/streaks of greenish blue & dark blue & a pool of dark blue in the bottom center, done in Michele Blush over creamy grey over Ralphie Brown, No. 6313, 1932 . . . . **275.00**

Bowl-vase, a small round foot supports a wide bulbous ovoid bowl w/a very wide, flat incurved mouth, decorated w/a repeating border of stylized flowers in purple, pink & brown against a mottled dark blue ground, Black Opal glaze, No. 1877, 1928, Sara Sax, 3⅜" h. **880.00**

Bowl-vase, rounded squatty form w/a closed rim, decorated around the mouth w/an incised ring, deep blue glossy glaze, No. 214C, 1915, W.E. Hentschel, 5½" d., 2¾" h. . . . **403.00**

Chocolate pot, cov., tall slender cylindrical body w/a short arched rim spout & large ribbed handle scrolling up from near the base to near the rim, fitted disc cover w/a large pointed finial, dark brown shaded to medium green to orange ground, decorated w/stylized blue violets extending onto the cover over long dark green stems & leaves, Standard glaze, No. 528 C, 1901, Irene Bishop, 8⅛" h. **825.00**

Dealer's sign, blue matte drip glaze, ca. 1926 . . . . **1,100.00**

Ewer, slender baluster-form w/a widely flaring, rolled tricorner rim, slender S-scroll handle, decorated w/yellow & brown pansies trimmed w/silver overlay flowering stems up the sides w/a silver-overlaid rim, handle & base, Standard glaze, No. 510, 1896, silver marked by Gorham Mfg. Co., Josephine Zettel, 4" d., 7" h. (hairline in base, possibly in the making) **1,320.00**

Ewer, slender ovoid body tapering to a tall slender neck w/a tricorner rim, slender C-scroll handle from rim to shoulder, decorated w/dark red & gold rose hips on dark brown stems w/dark green leaves against a dark brown shaded to mottled green to golden brown ground, Standard glaze, No. 851 E, 1899, Jeanette Swing, 7½" h. **550.00**

Ewer, footed spherical body centered by a tall slender cylindrical neck w/a tricorner rim, applied C-scroll strap handle, Limoges-style w/dark red ground decorated in white & black slip w/sea creatures & several spiders, highlighted by fired-on gold, swirls of turbulent water & a small crab near the top of the neck, 1882, Maria Longworth Nichols, 11¼" h. (professionally repaired crack at apex of handle) **1,980.00**

Ewer, footed spherical body centered by a very tall & slender cylindrical neck w/a flaring tricorner rim, long, slender S-scroll applied handle, the body decorated w/a cluster of life-like yellow jonquils w/shaded bright green leaves against a ground shading from bright yellow at the top of the neck down to shaded green to shaded brown on the lower body, Standard glaze, No. 560 A, 1890, Albert Valentien, 16¾" h. (minor glaze bubbles) . . . **1,540.00**

Jar, cov., ovoid body, decorated w/hanging white, yellow & blue flowers on a brown butterfat ground, Carved Matte glaze, No. 2004, 1918, Charles Todd (hairlines in lid) **770.00**

Jug w/original bulbous stopper, wide squatty bulbous body w/a flat bottom, the wide shoulder centered by a short small swelled cylindrical neck & a loop handle from the rim to the shoulder, decorated w/an ear of corn against a shaded brown ground, Standard glaze, No. 676, 1896, Josephine Zettel, 6"d., 7" h. (some crazing) **316.00**

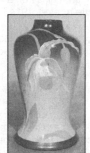

Iris Glaze Lamp Base

Lamp base, baluster-form w/the wide shoulder tapering to a short cylindrical neck, decorated w/a large orchid on a leafy stem against a shaded black to grey ground, Iris glaze, 1906, Carl Schmidt (ILLUS.) **11,000.00**

Loving cup, three-handled, wide ovoid body tapering slightly to a wide flared mouth, large D-form handles, the body divided into three panels each decorated w/finely detailed dark brown fish swimming among dark brown strands of seaweed against a shaded dark green & brown ground, Standard glaze, No. 659 B, 1897, Kataro Shirayamadani, 7⅞" h. (glaze scratches). **1,210.00**

Mug, cylindrical, decorated w/a modeled peacock feather in two tones of green & blue, Incised Matte glaze, No. 587, 1905 . . . . **440.00**

Mug, cylindrical body w/closed rim & heavy D-form handle, relief-molded down the inner side w/a large pendent ear of corn & scrolling leaves, reddish brown exterior Matte glaze & dark green interior glaze, designed by John Dee Wareham, No. 332 Z, 1902, 5⅜" h. . . **275.00**

Paperweight, figural, rook perched on a thick rectangular base, mottled greenish brown Matte glaze, No. 1623, 1921, 2¾" h. **358.00**

Paperweight, figural, modeled as two geese on a molded rectangular base, one w/its head down, the other w/its head resting on the neck of the other, white Matte glaze, No. 1855, 1933, 4⅛" h. **220.00**

Pitcher, 4¾" h., 6" d., tapering swelled cylindrical body w/a tricorner spouted rim & C-form handle, decorated w/incised mottled brown oak leaves on a blue Matte ground, No. 753D, 1900, Albert Pons **468.00**

Pitcher, 7⅛" h., wide bulbous body tapering to a flat mouth w/rim spout & C-scroll handle, creamy ground w/a shaded pale orange area behind a large cluster of orangish white apple blossoms & dark brownish green leaves & branches, Cameo glaze, No. 182, 1887, Matt Daly **935.00**

Pitcher, tankard, 9⅜" h., gently tapering cylindrical body w/a band of thin incised rings near the bottom, a blackish brown shaded to dark brown ground decorated w/a scene of a frightened black man staring in disbelief as a red devil plays a banjo while a yellow-eyed bat flutters overhead, Standard glaze, No. 587, 1891, Harriet Wilcox (professionally repaired rim chip) **1,100.00**

Planter, Jewel Porcelain, deep slightly flaring cylindrical wide body w/a rolled rim, decorated in an overall Art Deco geometric design w/dots, bands & herringbone in chartreuse & purple, No. G165, 1931, Lorinda Epply **880.00**

Planter, round, incised stylized leaves under a frothy brownish green Matte glaze, No. 180C, 1910, 8½" d., 8¾" h. (touch-ups on high points) **550.00**

Plaque, rectangular, a lovely twilight landscape of a tree-lined river bank w/a meadow in the foreground, in shades of dark green, blue, lavender & cream, Vellum glaze, 1919, Lenore Asbury, in original wide flat greenish frame w/a narrow gilt design border, "The River L. Asbury," 7¼ x 9⅛" **2,860.00**

Plaque, rectangular, a scene of tall birch trees in a landscape, in moody greys on an ivory sky, Vellum glaze, 1913, E.T. Hurley, in beveled oak frame, 8½ x 11" **3,960.00**

Rare Vellum Glaze Plaque

Plaque, rectangular, a scene w/the city of Venice in the background & several sailing vessels in the foreground, bright cloud-filled sky in yellow, white & blues, Vellum glaze, 1929, Ed Diers, framed, 14 x 16" (ILLUS.) **49,500.00**

Art Nouveau Rookwood Plaque

Plaque, rectangular, bust portrait of an Art Nouveau lady standing in a field of lilies, Matte glaze, framed, 1902, Albert Valentien, 15 x 21" (ILLUS.) **22,000.00**

Teapot, cov., squatty spherical body w/a C-form handle & swan's-neck spout, the wide flattened overhanging cover centered by a button finial, a deep shaded rose pink ground decorated w/clusters of large stylized white daisies w/red centers on the body & cover, Cameo glaze, No. 554, 1890, Harriet Wilcox, 4⅜" h. **440.00**

Trivet, round, decorated w/carrots & flowers, No. 3077, multicolored, ca. 1922, 6" d. **325.00**

Trivet, round, modeled w/swirling white sea gulls & blue waves against a green ground, No. 2350, 1919, 6" d. **138.00**

Vase, miniature, 2¼" h., 4½" d., squatty bulbous bowl-form w/a wide shoulder to a low molded flat mouth, decorated w/foliate design against a dark ground, Standard glaze, No. 798C, 1894. . . . . **230.00**

Vase, 3½" h., 3½" d., rounded form w/abstract flowers carved under a dripping butterfat glaze on a brown Carved Matte ground, 1914, No. 1064, C.S. Todd **550.00**

Vase, 4½" h., 3½"d., short ovoid body w/a wide rolled rim, decorated w/a wreath of green & yellow flowers outlined in dark blue against a turquoise ground, Wax Matte glaze, No. 63, 1924, E. Barrett **330.00**

Vase, 4½" h., 4½" d., bulbous ovoid body tapering to a wide flat molded mouth, decorated w/a wide band of stylized pink wild roses & pale green leaves on a shaded turquoise blue butterfat ground, Wax Matte glaze, No. 905E, 1928, Margaret McDonald. **660.00**

Vase, 4¾" h., 3¾" d., short ovoid form tapering to cylindrical neck w/flat rim, carved w/a swirling tulip in purple on Matte green glaze, No. 969D, impressed w/flame mark & artist's initials, 1904, Sallie Toohey. **440.00**

Vase, 5" h., 4" d., ovoid body w/a wide rolled rim, decorated w/white roses & green foliage on a light blue ground, Vellum glaze, No. 915F, 1925, Ed Diers **523.00**

Vase, 5" h., 5" d., wide ovoid horizontally-ribbed body tapering slightly to a wide low neck, decorated w/brown seed pods in squeezebag on a brown & blue Modeled Matte ground, No. 1931, 1927, W. Hentschel **413.00**

Vase, 5" h., 7" d., squatty bulbous body incised w/stylized flowers under a mustard glaze, Matte glaze, No. 1929, impressed w/flame mark, 1913. . . . . **440.00**

Vase, 5¼" h., 6" d., spherical form w/closed mouth, decorated w/rows of leaves (like an artichoke) all under a mottled Matte raspberry pink glaze, No. 2354, impressed w/flame makr, 1919 (white clay showing through). **358.00**

Vase, 5½" h., 2¾" d., cylindrical ovoid body w/rolled rim, decorated w/mustard daisies on a shaded bluish green to celadon ground, No. 950D, impressed w/flame mark & artist's initials, 1901, Sallie Coyne **1,540.00**

Vase, 5½" h., 4" d., footed bulbous ovoid body tapering to a short molded mouth, decorated w/a geometric butterfat pattern in brick red, black & light yellow, No.1695F, 1930, Jens Jensen . . . **1,100.00**

Vase, 5¾" h., 2½" d., simple ovoid body tapering to a tall slender 'stick' neck, decorated in shades of light blue w/a sailboat against the horizon scene, Aerial Blue glaze, No. 7623, 1895, Harriet Strafer . . **4,070.00**

Vase, 5¾" h., 4" d., simple ovoid body w/a wide flat mouth, decorated w/purple grapes & green leaves on a shaded green to purple ground, No. 942D, 1910, Charles Todd. **825.00**

Vase, 6" h., 2½" d., slightly tapering cylindrical body tapering to bulbous shoulder w/closed rim, decorated w/tall trees in a flat landscape, in tones of green & brown, Vellum glaze, No. 1656E, impressed flame mark & artist's initials, 1912, Sallie Coyne (hairlines to rim) **825.00**

Two Jewel Porcelain Vases

Vase, 6" h., 3" d., Jewel Porcelain, gently tapering cylindrical body w/a flared rim, decorated w/pink flowers & blue berries on a pink shaded to a blue ground, No. 4660F, 1924, Fred Rothenbush (ILLUS. left) . . **1,760.00**

Vase, 6" h., 3½" d., simple ovoid body w/a molded rim, decorated w/incised fish in blue, white & green, Vellum glaze, No. 913E, 1908, Lorinda Epply **1,610.00**

Vase, 6" h., 3½" d., waisted cylindrical body w/a swelled shoulder w/short, wide cylindrical neck, decorated w/a branch of holly w/pink berries & celadon green leaves against a black shaded to ivory ground, Iris glaze, No. 9355, 1906, E.T. Hurley **770.00**

Vase, 6" h., 4" d., decorated w/stylized foliate design in relief in browns, blues & green, Mat Moderne glaze, No. 2723, 1929, Elizabeth Barrett **489.00**

Vase, 6" h., 4" d., figural, Z-Line, molded w/two female figures languidly draped around the rim, smooth Matte green glaze, No. 128Z, 1910, A.M. Valentien . . . **3,850.00**

Vase, 6" h., 5" d., footed wide rounded cylindrical body tapering to a think molded wide mouth, decorated around the upper half w/a band of large lavender poppies & green leaves & stems on a shaded blue to turquoise blue ground, Wax Matte glaze, No. 6194D, 1931, Sallie Coyne. . . . **880.00**

Vase, 6¼" h., 3" d., slightly tapering cylindrical body, incised around the rim w/large stylized tulip-like blossoms in blue w/the stems down the sides under a flowing aventurine apple green flambé glaze, No. 2136, 1920, Lorinda Epply **2,090.00**

Vase, 6¼" h., 3¼" d., slightly flaring cylindrical body w/a wide flat mouth, decorated w/stylized flowers on a creamy green to pink ground, double Vellum glaze, No. 1369F, 1926, Margaret H. McDonald **805.00**

Vase, 6¼" h., 4¼" d., squaty ovoid body w/short cylindrical neck, incised blossoms around the neck, under mottled green, yellow & brown glaze, against crystalline flambé ground, Matte glaze, No. 927F, impressed w/flame mark & artist's initials, 1924, W. Hentchel . . **770.00**

Vase, 6½" h., gently tapering smooth cylindrical body w/a narrow angled shoulder to the short cylindrical neck flanked by small squared handles, rose Matte glaze, No. 2076, 1926 . . . . **303.00**

Vase, 6½" h., 3½" d., Jewel Porcelain, baluster-shaped body decorated w/cherry blossoms in pink w/green leaves on an evory ground, No. 2720, impressed w/flame mark & artist's initials, 1924, L. Epply **1,100.00**

Vase, 6½" h., 4¾" d., Jewel Porcelain, bulbous ovoid body w/a wide molded mouth, raised on a short round pedestal base, decorated w/the squeezebag technique in the Art Deco style w/stylized leaves & berries in brown against a turquoise ground, Matte glazes, No. 1781, 1927, Elizabeth Barrett **440.00**

Vase, 6¾" h., 3¼" d., slender ovoid body tapering to a flat rim, decorated w/slip-painted pink blossoms & green leaves on a shaded pink ground, Vellum glaze, No. 925E, 1905, Mary Nourse. **440.00**

Vase, 6¾" h., 4¼" d., double gourd-form on a small footring, the top tapering to a tiny flaring neck, decorated w/slip-painted gooseberries in yellow, blue & brown on a green & brown ground, Standard glaze, No. 629, 1892, Harriet Strafer **468.00**

Vase, pillow-type, 6¾" h., 7" w., wide flattened bulbous tapering ovoid form w/a small foot, a wide short flaring neck, decorated w/narcissus-like blossoms & stems against a shaded dark brown ground, Standard glaze, No. 297, 1900, Edward Diers **345.00**

Vase, 7" h. porcelain, simple ovoid body tapering to a small rolled mouth, Matte glaze, olive green ground molded in low-relief w/stylized fish, No. 6215, 1931 . . . . **288.00**

Vase, 7" h., 3" d., slender slightly swelled cylindrical body w/flat rim, decorated w/four detailed fish on a light orange, yellow, green & blue ground, Iris glaze, No. 951E, 1906, initials obscured **2,760.00**

Vase, 7" h., 3¼" d., slender ovoid body tapering to a tall trumpet neck, greenish Aventurine glazed neck above a paneled red flambé-glazed body, No. 6306C, 1932 . . . . **413.00**

Vase, 7" h., 3½" d., slender ovoid body tapering to a short wide slightly rolled neck, decorated w/white narcissus & dark green stems & leaves against a shaded pale mauve to ivory ground, Iris glaze, No. 822D, 1911, Sara Sax . . **1,760.00**

Vase, 7" h., 4" d., bottle-shaped body decorated w/pink tulips & green stems on a feathered pink & red

glaze, Wax Matte glaze, impressed w/flame mark & artist's initials, 1919, L. Lincoln. **523.00**

Vase, 7" h., 4¼" d., cylindrical body swelling at the top w/a closed mouth, heavily embossed around the top w/large dogwood blossoms on tall stems down the sides, green on brown Matte glaze, No. 1370, 1911 . . . . **495.00**

Vase, 7" h., 7" d., Jewel Porcelain, flared foot below inverted bell-shaped body, base w/embossed lotus leaves, covered in glossy black glaze & matte turquoise glaze, No. 2834, impressed w/flame mark, 1926. . . . . **138.00**

Vase, 7¼" h., 3½" d., slender ovoid body w/a flared mouth, incised decoration of stylized white & red flowers ^ green foliage around the top on a royal blue ground, Matte glaze, No. 917, 1917, C.S. Todd. . . **440.00**

Vase, 7½" h., 3" d., slightly swelled cylindrical body tapering slightly at the flat rim, decorated w/a lakeside landscape w/trees in olive & beige, Iris glaze, No. 951E, 1911, Lenore Asbury (three hairlines on rim) **880.00**

Vase, 7½" h., 3" d., slightly tapering cylindrical form w/bulbous shoulder w/closed rim, decorated w/three peacock feathers in blue, rust & green, on a shaded blue to peach ground, impressed w/flame mark & artist's initials, 1910, C. Steinle . . **1,650.00**

Vase, 7½" h., 3¼" d., slightly ovoid body w/short cylindrical neck w/flat rim, decorated w/crisply-rendered Virginia creeper vines in green grey & purple, against a shaded perwinkle to grey ground, No. 901F, impressed w/flame mark & artist's initials, 1921, Fred Rothenbusch **1,320.00**

Vase, 7½" h., 3½" d., slender trumpet shape, decorated w/a landscape of brown trees & green grass against a shade brown, light blue & ivory sky, Vellum glaze, No. 1357E, 1916, Margaret McDonald **1,210.00**

Vase, 7½" h., 3¾" d., tall slightly waisted cylindrical form, decorated w/an underwater scene of swimming fish, against a shaded pink to green ground, Vellum glaze, No. 1358E, 1908, Edith Noonan . . . **1,320.00**

Vase, 7½" h., 4" d., slender waisted cylindrical form, a brown Vellum matte glaze w/three narrow three-

Vase, sided rectangular blue panels of silhouetted soaring birds, No. 1358, 1911, Charles Todd **1,430.00**

Vase, 7½" h., 4" d., slightly waisted cylindrical body tpaering a tthe foot & w/a closed rim, decorated w/a fine seascape w/fishing boats in bluish greens & ivory on a shaded ground, Vellum glaze, No. 2066, 1925, Carl Schmidt. **3,190.00**

Vase, 7½" h., 5" d., bulbous ovoid form tapering to thin tapering rim, decorated w/maroon & yellow flowers & olive green leaves against a shaded dark brown to orange ground, Standard glaze, No. 902D, impressed w/flame mark & artist's initials, 1902, L. Asbury . . **330.00**

Vase, 7¾" h., tall slightly swelled cylindrical body w/a short cylindrical neck, Matte glaze w/light brown rim on a dark brown neck, the shoulder decorated w/incised & overlapping cresents, streaked in blue, beige & light brown w/rose highlighting the tan body, No. 907F, 1919, Charles Todd **863.00**

Vase, 7¾" h., 4¼" d., ovoid form w/rolled lip, painted w/yellow daffodils w/olive green leaves against a shaded green to orange ground. Standard glaze, No. 913D, impressed w/flame mark & artist's initials, 1903, S.E. Coyne **633.00**

Art Deco Vase with Nudes

Vase, 7⅞" h., ovoid body w/a wide, slightly rolled neck, Art Deco stylized design of three nudes, 1931, Jens Jensen (ILLUS.). . . . **13,200.00**

Vase, 8" h., tall ovoid body on a small flaring foot w/a wide, flat incurved mouth, decorated w/a landscape view of a river & wooded banks, Vellum glaze, 1912, Fred Rothenbusch **805.00**

Vase, 8" h., 3½" d., slender ovoid body w/a short gently tapering neck, decorated around the neck & shoulder w/green holly leaves & red berries below a dark brown rim, the body w/a burnt amber ground, Matte glaze, No. 9232E, 1926, Sallie Coyne **770.00**

Vase, 8" h., 3½" d., slightly tapering cylindrical body w/a narrow tapering band at the base & rim, decorated around the rim w/large stylized three-petal flowers, a blue rim band & a rose background, Matte glaze, No. 2067, 1920, Elizabeth Lincoln **605.00**

Vase, 8" h., 4" d., Jewel Porcelain, simple ovoid body tapering to a flared mouth, the lower half incised w/a band of stylized flowers & leaves in purple & green on the black ground, purple interior, uncrazed, No. 536D, 1922, Sarah Sax **8,800.00**

Vase, 8" h., 4" d., slender ovoid body tapering slightly to a flat mouth, incised & embossed cattails on a brown ground, Modeled Matte glaze, No. 80E, 1906, Albert Pons. **1,320.00**

Vase, 8" h., 4" d., slender ovoid body tapering to a widely flaring mough, decorated w/purple flowers & green leaves on a lightly feathered mauve ground, Wax Matte glaze, No. 233, 1925, Cora Crofton **880.00**

Vase, 8" h., 5½" d., Jewel Porcelain, bulbous ovoid body tapering to a short swelled neck, Art Deco decoration in geometrics done w/a green & blue triangular design under a white Butterfat glaze, No. 902D, 1930, Janet Harris (ILLUS. right, with 6" vase). **770.00**

Vase, 8" h., 6¼" d., wide ovoid body tapering to a wide flat mouth, decorated all around w/large realistic red tulips & leaves on a shaded purple ground, Matte glaze, No. 356C, 1910, Harriet Wilcox . . . **15,400.00**

Vase, 8¼" h., gently tapering cylindrical form w/a flat rim, decorated w/a long vine w/berry clusters & foliage in dusty grey, pale pink & seafoam green, Iris glaze, No. 950D, 1900, Edward Diers. **1,035.00**

Vase, 8¼" h., simple ovoid body tapering to a flat rim, decorated w/deep red large cherry blossoms & leaves on a shaded deep red ground, Standard glaze, No. 939C, 1903, Elizabeth Lincoln (small glaze flake off rim) **303.00**

Vase, 8¼" h., 3½" d., ovoid body w/short flared rim, w/carved drooping blue flowers w/green leaves on a raspberry pink ground, Matte glaze, No. 233, impressed w/flame mark & artist's initials, 1917, C.S. Todd **715.00**

Vase, 8¼" h., 4¼" d., slender baluster-form, decorated around the top of the neck w/a cluster of white flowers on a branch against a blue ground, Vellum glaze, No. 2885, 1927, Edward T. Hurley **863.00**

Vase, 8¼" h., 4½" d., simple ovoid body w/low inverted loop handles at the top, decorated w/wild roses in orange & yellow w/green leaves on a shaded brown ground, Standard glaze, No. 77A, 1890, Artus Van Briggle **880.00**

Vase, 8⅜" h., ovoid body w/a rounded shoulder to a short rolled neck, decorated w/a continuous waterside landscape scene w/birch trees & shades of tan, pale green & blues, Vellum glaze, No. 5318, 1946, E.T. Hurley **2,090.00**

Finely Painted Matte Glaze Vase

Vase, 8⅜" h., simple ovoid body tapering to a short cylindrical neck, decorated w/finely detailed large chrysanthemums in shades of yellow & orange on a deep green ground, Matte glaze, 1902, Harriet Wilcox (ILLUS.) **14,300.00**

Vase, 8½" h., a broad gently flaring cylindrical body w/a swelled shoulder & wide flat mouth, molded w/large stylized blossoms atop vertical stems against a dense band of leaves around the rim, covered in a green over rose curdled Matte glaze, No. 1722, 1912 . . . . **550.00**

Vase, 8½" h., 3¾" d. slightly swelled cylindrical body tapering to mouth, crisply painted w/lavender gooseberries & celadon leaves against a shaded black to celadon to ivory ground, Iris glaze, No. 950D, impressed w/flame mark & artist's initals, 1910, O.G. Reed (lightly crazed) **1,540.00**

Vase, 8½" h., 4" d., slender ovoid body w/a short flaring neck, incised design of white, red & black fuchsia blossoms against a deep purple ground, Matte glaze, No. 233, 1922, Louise Abel **715.00**

Vase, 8½" h., 4" d., slender ovoid body w/a slightly flared moded mouth, decorated w/tall green palm trees & tall grasses on a peach ground, Vellum glaze, ca. 1905, E. T. Hurley (drilled base) **905.00**

Vase, 8½" h., 5¼" d., decorated w/cherry blossom branches on a rust shaded to grey butterfat ground, Wax Matte glaze, No. 191B, 1923, Margaret McDonald . . **715.00**

Vase, 8½" h. 6½" d., bulbous ovoid form tapering to flared rim, covered in a deep red & caramel crystalline flambé glaze, Aventurine glaze, No. 6707, impressed w/flame mark, 1938 . . . . **414.00**

Vase, 8½" h., 7½" d., bulbous body decorated w/stylized leaves in black on an olive to moss green ground, Incised Matte glaze, No. 2911, 1926, William T. Hentschel **1,540.00**

Fine Rookwood Landscape Vase

Vase, 8⅝" h., gently flaring cylindrical body w/a narrow angled shoulder to the short cylindrical neck, decorated w/a continuous landscape scene of a castle nestled between a lake & mountains, glossy glaze, Arthur Conant (ILLUS.) **10,450.00**

Vase, 8¾" h., simple ovoid body tapering to a short cylindrical neck, dark grey shaded to white ground decorated w/two large blue irises w/yellow beards on shaded green stems & leaves, Iris glaze, No. 901, 1903, Ed Diers **4,400.00**

Vase, 8¾" h., 1903, slightly ovoid body tapering to cylindrical neck w/flat mouth, painted w/river scene in blue, green & peach, Vellum glaze, No. 30E, impressed w/flame mark & artist's initials, 1921, Fred Rothenbusch (heavy crazing line at bottom corner) **1,210.00**

Vase, 8⅞" h., graceful ovoid body tapering to a short cylindrical neck, decorated w/two large nightblooming cereus flowers in white & creamy yellow on green stems, dark blue shaded to cream to white ground, Iris glaze, No. 900B, 1906, Lenore Asbury . . **9,625.00**

Vase, 9" h., 4" d., cylindrical body w/flared rim on flared foot, decorated w/panels of Viking ships in purple & blue against a green sea & ivory sky, all on dark blue ground, Vellum glaze, No. 1`3??, impressed w/flame mark, 1915, S. Coyne. **1,540.00**

Vase, 9" h., 4" d., gently tapering cylindrical body, decorated w/a waterside landscape w/a Japanese-style inlet scene in muted tones of purples, greys & whites, No. 950D, 1912, Lenore Asbury **1,100.00**

Vase, 9" h., 4¼" d., tall slender trumpet-form body, red roses & green leaves on a yellow ground, Wax Matte glaze, No. 1357, 1926, E. Barrett. **825.00**

Vase, 9" h., 4½" d., slightly swelled cylindrical body tapering slightly at the top, the scalloped rim molded in high-relief w/jonquil blossoms w/leafy stems trailing up the sides, fine green & rose Matte butterfat glaze, No. 1003, 1909 . . . . **660.00**

Vase, 9" h., 5" d., corseted cylindrical body decorated w/a colorful continuous banded landscape scene w/a pale blue rim band above a deep golden yellow & pink band w/white geese in flight above a dark charcoal lower landscape of trees, Vellum glaze, No. 1358D, 1910, Katiro Shirayamadani **4,400.00**

Vase, 9" h., 5" d., Jewel Porcelain, ovoid body w/a low molded rim, decorated w/pink daffodils & green leaves on a blue to violet ground, No. 6869, 1944, Katiro Shirayamadani **1,760.00**

Vase, 9½" h., 5" d., gently flaring cylindrical body w/an angled shoulder to the short, wide flaring neck, decorated w/mauve & white flowers & dark green leaves around the body on a medium green ground, Wax Matte glaze, No. 1320, 1929, Jens Jensen. . . . **1,100.00**

Vase, 9½" h., 4½" d., gently flaring cylindrical body w/an angled shoulder to a short flaring neck, decorated w/a branch of red flowers & green leaves on a dark blue ground, Wax Matte glaze, No. 1920, 1923, Cora Crofton. **743.00**

Fine Standard Glaze Vases

Vase, 9½" h., 5" d., bulbous spherical body tapering to a tall slender neck w/a widely flaring rim, decorated w/leaves & berries on a shaded ground, the lower body & upper neck & rim trimmed w/ornate scrolling openwork silver overlay by Gorham Mfg. Corp., Standard glaze, No. 716C, 1895, Rose Fescheimer (ILLUS. left) **2,090.00**

Vase, 9½" h., 5" d., graceful ovoid body w/a short tapering neck & molded rim, decorated w/blue & white irises on a pink to blue ground, Vellum glaze, 1905, artist-initials (crazing) **2,070.00**

Vase, 9¾" h., expanding cylinder w/narrow shoulder & rolled rim, decorated w/a painted forest landscape in shades of blue, grey, tan & brown reserved against light blue, Vellum glaze, impressed factory marks "XVII/30 D, 1917, E. Diers. **1,840.00**

Rare Black Iris Vase

Vase, 9¾" h., slender ovoid body w/a widely flaring neck, large irises on a black ground, Black Iris glaze, 1907, Carl Schmidt (ILLUS.) . . . **18,700.00**

Vase, 10" h., tapering ovoid body w/a flat mouth, decorated w/Art Nouveau large white poppy blossoms on slender green stems against a light blue shaded to white shaded black to blue ground, Vellum glaze, No. 2033 D, 1913, Katherine Van Horne (minor glaze peppering) **935.00**

Vase, 10" h., 4¼" d., tall slightly tapering cylindrical body, slip-painted w/orange tulips & green leaves on a golden brown to deep blue to mahogany ground, Standard glaze, No. 950C, 1907, Elizabeth Lincoln **550.00**

Vase, 10" h., 5" d., slender ovoid body w/the swelled shoulder tapering to a short cylindrical neck, carved around the shoulder w/crisp red flowers & green leaves on a purple shaded to rust ground, Matte glaze, No. 943C, 1918, Elizabeth Lincoln **1,760.00**

Vase, 10⅛" h., Jewel Porcelain, the narrow disc base w/an angled shoulder tapering gently to a tall cylindrical neck w/a widely flaring rim, a dark bluish grey base below the shoulder & neck w/a white ground decorated around the shoulder w/a wide band of pink blossoms w/yellow centers, green leaves & grey limbs, an intricate band in the same colors encircles the rim, the interior w/a pink glaze, overall glossy glaze, No. 553 C, 1918, Sara Sax. **1,650.00**

Vase, 10½" h., 3¾" d., slightly swelled cylindrical body tpaerin to rolled lip, decoarted w/maple leaves & seedlings in raspberry red against a reddish purple ground, Matte glaze, No. 915C, impressed w/flame mark & artist's initials, 1903, Olga G. Reed **5,500.00**

Vase, 10½" h., 4" d., gently tapering cylindrical body w/a wide, flat mouth, decorated w/branches of pink & white blossoms & green foliage on a shaded green to pink ground, Matte glaze, No. 952C, 1907, Olga G. Reed **3,300.00**

Vase, 10¾" h., 5" d., tall slender ovoid body tapering to a short cylindrical neck, decorated w/a sunset landscape w/charcoal grey cypress trees against a dark blue

shaded to dark green to gold sky w/dark grey & black background, Aventurine glaze, No. 977, 1920, Lorinda Epply **1,650.00**

Rare Sea Green Glaze Vase

Vase, 10⅞" h., bottle-form ovoid body tapering to a short, small flaring neck, decorated w/a school of swimming fish around the sides against a shaded ground, Sea Green glaze, 1896, Albert Valentien (ILLUS.) **14,300.00**

Vase, 11" h., 5¼" d., simple ovoid body tapering to a flat mouth, decorated w/a lakeside landscape w/birch trees in the foreground & low mountains in the distance done in shades of blue, green & white against a shaded periwindle blue to peach shaded sky, Vellum glaze, No. 977, 1942, E. T. Hurley **4,400.00**

Vase, 11" h., 5¾" d., ovoid form tapering to short cylindrical neck w/flat rim, decorated w/harbor scene w/sailboats in blues & greens against a shaded pink to blue to ivory sky, Vellum glaze, No. 900B, impressed w/flame mark & artist's initials, Carl Schmidt **4,730.00**

Vase, 11" h., 7" d., tall waisted cylindrical form, decorated around the rim w/well-defined blue, burgundy & yellow flowers against a burgundy ground, No. 1133, 1915, C.S.Todd **825.00**

Vase, 11⅛" h., slender ovoid body tapering to a short cylindrical neck, decorated w/a large stalk of lily-of-the-valley in bluish white w/shaded bluish green leaves & stem against a shaded black to dark purple ground, Black Iris glaze, No. 295 C, 1912, Carl Schmidt (faint glaze run on the back, two pinhead-size glaze nicks at base) **3,520.00**

Matte-glazed Orchid Vase

Vase, 11⅜" h., baluster-form w/a wide rounded shoulder & flat rim, decorated w/a large white orchid w/yellow trim on the front w/its dark green tendrils undulating around the back, Matte glaze, 1900, Albert Valentien (ILLUS.) **11,000.00**

Vase, 11½" h., gently swelled tall cylindrical body molded w/clusters of long, overlapping leaves w/jagged edges on narrow bowed stems, tobacco brown over tan curdled Matte glaze, No. 2482, 1920 . . . . **440.00**

Vase, 11½" h., 4¾" d., tall slender cylindrical form swelling gently near the flat rim, decorated w/purple columbine & green leaves on a shaded purplish blue to light green ground, Vellum glaze, No. 2039CV, 1912, Ed Diers. **2,420.00**

Vase, 11½" h., 5¾" d., flaring ovoid body tapering to short cylindrical rim, decorated w/stylized blue & yellow flowers w/green leaves on a raspberry flowing ground, Matte glaze, No. 1369C, impressed w/flame mark & artist's initials, 1925, E. McDermott (hole drilled in base) **385.00**

Vase, 11½" h., 7½" d., squatty ovoid body tapering to cylindrical flat rim, carved w/peacock feathers under a superior dark green, brown & dark blue mottled Matte glaze, No. 1007C, impressed w/flame mark, 1915, C.S. Todd **1,430.00**

Vase, 12" h., 5" d., Jewel Porcelain, footed swelled cylindrical tall body w/a narrow shoulder to a short cylindrical neck w/a flaring rim, ddecorated w/blue iris & leaves on a mint green ground, No. 2933,

1928, Lorinda Epley (three flat manufacturing grinding chips on side of base) **880.00**

Vase, 12" h., 5" d., tall slender gently flaring cylindrical body w/a short waisted neck & widely flaring & flattened rim, decorated w/a hilly countryside landscape w/old trees in blues & ochres against a shaded blue to ivory sky, Vellum glaze, No. 2790, 1926, Fred Rothenbusch . . **3,850.00**

Vase, 12" h., 7" d., baluster-shaped w/cylindrical neck, decorated w/large calla lillies in white, celadon & yellow against a shaded black, celadon & lavender ground, Iris glaze, factory-drilled hole in base for lamp, No. 1038, iumpressed flame mark & artist's initials, 1906, Carl Schmidt. **4,125.00**

Arthur Conant Vase

Vase, 12½" h., wide baluster-form body, decorated overall w/exotic birds, fruit & flowers in yellows & oranges against a dark green ground, glossy glaze, repaired drill hole in base, Arthur Conant (ILLUS.) **9,075.00**

Vase, 12½" h., 4½" d., tall slender ovoid body tapering to a slender cylindrical neck w/a tall widely flaring ruffled top, decorated in slip-relief w/a branch of cherry blossoms on a golden brown ground, Standard glaze, No. 2116, 1886, Laura Fry **935.00**

Vase, 12½" h., 5½" d., gently swelled baluster-form body w/a flattened narrow shoulder centered by a short cylindrical neck, decorated w/a landscape at dusk w/old trees silhouetted against a shaded grey, yellow & peach cloudy sky, Vellum glaze, No. 664C, 1909, E.T. Hurley **4,180.00**

Vase, 12½" h., 11" d., footed bulbous ovoid urn-form w/upright loop handles at the wide shoulders centered by a tapering cylindrical neck w/a flared rim, decorated w/large tulips in amber w/green leaves & stems on a shaded dark brown to green ground, first-fire crazing on some flowers, Standard glaze, No. 800A, 1900, Sallie Toohey (ILLUS. right w/silver overlay vase) **880.00**

Rare Vase with Mistletoe

Vase, 13" h., tall slightly swelled cylindrical body w/a short small neck w/flared rim, decorated around the upper half w/a tall band of mistletoe against a dark shaded ground, Black Iris glaze, 1900, Matt Daly (ILLUS.) **16,500.00**

Rare Grouse in Tree Vase

Vase, 14" h., flaring cylindrical body w/a narrow shoulder to the wide, flat mouth, decorated w/a large grouse perched in a leafless tree against a shaded ground, Black Iris glaze, Carl Schmidt (ILLUS.) . . . **46,200.00**

Vase, 14" h., tall gently ovoid body w/a short flaring neck flanked by incurved loop shoulder handles, decorated w/the profile bust portrait of a Native American, Binanset, an Arapaho, Standard glaze, Matt Daly **13,750.00**

Large Vase with Flowing Glaze

Vase, 14⅛" h., ovoid body tapering to a tall cylindrical neck, carved & painted w/stylized flowers in white w/orange centers, flowing clear glaze w/hazy blue striations, incised "F" (ILLUS.) **29,700.00**

Vase, 14½" h., 7" d., tapering cylindrical form w/slightly flared mouth w/lakeside landscape w/tall birch trees on pink, green & violet ground, Vellum glaze, No. 1658B, impressed flame mark w/original paper label, 1913, Lenore Asbury (old repair to rim chip, minor pitting). **1,650.00**

Vase, 17½" h., footed ovoid body tapering to a wide cylindrical short neck, large red poppies w/a blue drip glaze spreading down from the rim, 1926, attributed to Kataro Shirayamadani **12,650.00**

Vase, 19½" h., 10" d., tall slightly ovoid body w/a wide, flat rim, decorated w/a long branch of amber yellow roses & green leaves trailing down the side against a shaded mahogany ground, Standard glaze, No. 139a, 1889, Albert Valentien (ILLUS. center w/silver overlay vase) **3,300.00**

Fine Standard Glaze Vase

Vase, 22½" h., bulbous ovoid body tapering to a short neck w/a widely flaring flattened rim, decorated w/five dragons peering out from dense foliage, Standard glaze, 1891, Kataro Shirayamadani (ILLUS.) **17,600.00**

ROSEMEADE

Laura Taylor was a ceramic artist who supervised Federal Works Projects in her native North Dakota during the Depression era and later demonstrated at the potter's wheel during the 1939 New York World's Fair. In 1940, Laura Taylor and Robert J. Hughes opened the Rosemeade-Wahpeton Pottery, naming it after the North Dakota county and town of Wahpeton where it was located. Rosemeade Pottery was made on a small scale for only about twelve years with Laura Taylor designing the items and perfecting colors. Her animal and bird figures are popular among collectors. Hughes and Taylor married in 1943 and the pottery did a thriving business until her death in 1959. The pottery closed in 1961 but stock was sold from the factory salesroom until 1964.

Rosemeade Mark

Hors d'ouvres server, model of a pheasant, 4½" h. **$125.00**
Salt & pepper shakers, model of a bear, brown glaze, pr. **85.00**

Salt & pepper shakers, model of a cat, multi-colored, pr. **115.00**
Salt & pepper shakers, model of a Dalmatian, pr. **140.00**
Salt & pepper shakers, model of a Fox Terrier, pr. **85.00**
Salt & pepper shakers, model of a Greyhound, pr. **75.00**
Salt & pepper shakers, model of a Pekinese, pr. **75.00**
Salt & pepper shakers, model of a Scottish Terrier, pr. **75.00**
Salt & pepper shakers, model of an elephant, blue glaze, pr. **85.00**
Salt & pepper shakers, model of black bear w/tan face, pr. **30.00**

ROSE MEDALLION & ROSE CANTON CHINA

The lovely Chinese ware known as rose Medallion was made through the past century and into the present one. It features alternating panels of people and flowers or insects with most pieces having four medallions with a central rose or peony medallion. The ware is called Rose Canton if floras and birds or insects fill all the panels. Unless otherwise noted, our listing is for Rose Medallion ware.

Basket & undertray, oval basket w/reticulated sides, on a matching undertray, 19th c., basket 8⅜" l., undertray 9⁵⁄₁₆" l., the set (minor chips, crack) **$489.00**
Charger, large round very slightly dished form, radiating panels alternating figural & floral designs, 16¼" d. **440.00**

Rose Medallion Garden Seat

Garden seat, barrel form & molded w/'studs', the top pierced with a 'cash' motif & sides w/two double 'cash' motifs, decorated w/two large reserves of figures & small panels of figures or flowers, birds & butterflies, 19th c., 19" h., 12" d. at top (ILLUS.) **1,495.00**

Punch bowl, deep rounded sides on a footring, usual palette & design, 13⅝" d. (minor enamel wear) . . . **2,300.00**

Punch bowl, deep rounded sides on a low footring, alternating panels of figures or flowers, fruits & birds, second quarter 19th c., 15½" d. **1,092.00**

Rose Mandarin Punch Bowl

Punch bowl, Rose Mandarin variant, alternating panels of Mandarin figures, 19th c., China, minor rim repair, gilt wear, 15¾" d. (ILLUS.) **2,415.00**

Rice bowls, wide ring foot supporting a wide round gently flaring bowl w/scalloped rim, 19th c., 4⅝" d., set of 4 . . . . **110.00**

Teapot, cov., footed wide squatty body w/low cylindrical sides below the angled shoulder to a small flared mouth w/high domed cover w/knob finial, swan's-neck spout & arched C-form handle, 19th c., 8½" h. **660.00**

Tureen, cov., flaring foot below the tall squatty bulbous oval body w/gilt twisted band end handles, high domed cover w/large gilt mushroom-shaped finial, 13¾" l., 11¼" h. **1,100.00**

Vase, 13½" h., bottle-form, a bulbous slightly squatty body tapering to a tall 'stick' neck, decorated w/alternating panels of figures, birds and insects on a ground of flowers, scrolls & insects w/gilding, mid-19th c. **805.00**

Vases, 24¾" h., tall cylindrical body tapering to a long neck w/a flared rim, decorated w/three rows of alternating panels of figures or flowers & butterflies on a ground of

Tall Rose Medallion Vases

green scrolls, pink flowers & butterflies w/gilt trim, 19th ca., pr. (ILLUS.) **2,875.00**

ROSEVILLE

Roseville Pottery Company operated in Zanesville, Ohio from 1898 to 1954 after having been in business for six years prior to that in Muskingum County, Ohio. Art wares similar to those of Owens and Weller Potteries were produced. Items listed here are by patterns or lines.

Roseville Mark

APPLE BLOSSOM (1948)

White apple blossoms in relief on blue, green or pink ground; brown tree branch handles.

Basket w/overhead handle, blue ground, No. 309-8", 8" h. **$285.00**

Basket w/overhead handle, green ground, No. 309-8", 8" h. **210.00**

Basket w/overhead handle, pink ground, No. 309-8", 8" h. **245.00**

Basket w/low overhead handle, blue ground, No. 310-10", 10" h. . . . . **280.00 to 285.00**

Basket, hanging-type, pink ground, 8" h. **210.00**

Book ends, green ground, No. 359, pr. . . . **198.00**

Book ends, pink ground, No. 359, pr. . . **275.00**
Bowl, 8" d., blue ground,
No. 328-8" **125.00**
Bowl, 8" d., green ground,
No. 328-8" **105.00**
Candlesticks, No. 351-2", 2" h., pr. . . . **80.00**
Console bowl, pink ground,
No. 331-12", 12" l. **175.00**
Console bowl, green ground,
No. 333-14", 8 x 18" oval. **160.00**
Console bowl, pink ground,
No. 333-14", 8 x 18" oval. **175.00**
Cornucopia-vase, blue ground,
No. 323-8". . . . . **150.00 to 175.00**

Apple Blossom Cornucopia-vase

Cornucopia-vase, pink ground, No.
323-8" (ILLUS.) **135.00**
Jardiniere, blue ground, No. 300-4",
4" h. **135.00**
Jardiniere, pink ground, No. 300-4",
4" h. **90.00**
Jardiniere, pink ground,
No. 301-6" **225.00**
Teapot, cov., pink ground,
No. 371-P **260.00**
Vase, 6" h., two-handled, squatty
base, long cylindrical neck, green
ground, No. 381-6" **70.00**
Vase, 7" h., blue ground,
No. 373-7". . . . . **140.00 to 150.00**
Vase, 7" h., pink ground,
No. 373-7" **145.00**
Vase, 7" h., asymmetrical rim &
handles, pink ground,
No. 382-7" **125.00**
Vase, 8¼" h., blue ground,
No. 385-8". . . . . **160.00 to 175.00**
Vase, 8¼" h., green ground,
No. 385-8" **165.00**
Vase, 10" h., base handles, blue
ground, No. 388-10" **170.00**
Vase, 10" h., base handles, pink
ground, No. 388-10" **255.00**
Vase, 10" h., two-handled, pink
ground, No. 389-10" **185.00**
Vase, 12½" h., base handles, pink
ground, No. 390-12" (ILLUS.) **295.00**

Apple Blossom Vase

Vase, 15" h., floor-type, pink ground,
No. 392-15" (ILLUS.) **375.00**
Wall pocket, conical w/overhead
handle, blue ground, No. 366-8",
8" h. . . . . **220.00 to 230.00**
Wall pocket, conical w/overhead
handle, brown ground, No. 366-8",
8" h. **190.00**
Wall pocket, conical w/overhead
handle, green ground, No. 366-8",
8" h. . . . . **235.00 to 250.00**
Window box, end handles, blue
ground, No. 368-8", 2½ x 10½". . . . **115.00**

ARTWOOD (LATE 1940s)

*Realistically molded flowers and woody
branches framed within cut-outs within
geometrically shaped picture planters and vases.*

Planter, grey ground, No. 1061-10",
10" l. **100.00**
Vase, double bud, 8" h.,
No. 1057-8" **150.00**
Vase, triple bud, 8" h., grey ground. . . **150.00**
Vase, double, 12" h., footed upright
rectangular body w/pierced
rectangular center decorated
w/molded pine bough, green
ground, No. 1060-12" **225.00**

BANEDA (1933)

*Band of embossed pods, blossoms and leaves
on green or raspberry pink ground.*

Candleholders, pink ground, No.
1088-4", 4½" h., pr. **575.00**
Jardiniere, pink ground, 9½" h.
(ILLUS. top next page) **1,800.00**
Urn, small rim handles, bulbous,
green ground, 5" h. **555.00**
Vase, 9" h., cylindrical w/short
collared neck, handles rising from
shoulder to beneath rim, green
ground. . . . . **775.00 to 800.00**

Baneda Jardiniere

Vase, 10" h., two handles rising from
shoulder to beneath rim, raspberry
pink ground . . . . **860.00 to 875.00**

BITTERSWEET (1940)

*Orange bittersweet pods and green leaves on
a grey blending to rose, yellow with terra cotta,
rose with green or solid green bark-textured
ground; brown branch handles.*

Basket, hanging-type, green
ground **275.00**
Console bowl, yellow ground,
No. 830-14", 14" l. **175.00**
Jardiniere, green ground, No. 842-7",
7" h. **175.00**
Jardiniere & pedestal base, green
ground, overall 24" h., 2 pcs. **1,295.00**
Vase, 8" h., asymmetrical handles,
bulging cylindrical form, grey
ground, No. 883-8" **135.00**
Vase, 10" h., handles at midsection,
scalloped rim, green ground,
No. 885-10" **165.00**
Vase, 12" h., No. 886-12" **148.00**
Vase, 15½" h., floor-type, baluster-
form body w/trumpet neck & flaring
foot, shoulder handles, green
ground, No. 888-16" **575.00**

BLACKBERRY (1933)

*Band of relief clusters of blackberries with
vines and ivory leaves accented in green and
terra cotta on a green textured ground.*

Blackberry Wall Pocket

Jardiniere, two-handled, No. 623-9",
9" h. **800.00**
Vase, 4" h., sharply compressed
globular base, handles rising from
shoulder to rim, terra cotta ground,
No. 555-4". . . . . **165.00 to 175.00**
Vase, 4" h., two-handled, bulbous . . . **350.00**
Vase, 5" h., tiny rim handles, canted
sides **445.00**
Wall pocket, basket-shaped
w/narrow base & flaring rim, 6¾" w.
at rim, 8½" h. (ILLUS. bottom
left column) . . . . **925.00 to 975.00**

BLEEDING HEART (1938)

*Pink blossoms and green leaves on shaded
blue, green or pink ground.*

Console bowl, blue ground,
No. 382-10", 10" l. **295.00**
Cornucopia-vase, pink ground,
No. 141-6", 6" h. **165.00**
Flower frog, pink ground, No. 40 . . . . **110.00**

Bleeding Heart Jardiniere

Jardiniere & pedestal base, blue
ground, jardiniere 10" h., 2 pcs.
(ILLUS.) **3,500.00**
Vase, 5" h., blue ground,
No. 962-5" **115.00**
Vase, 6½" h., base handles, blue
ground, No. 964-6" **175.00**
Vase, 6½" h., base handles, pink
ground, No. 964-6" **150.00**
Vase, 15" h., two-handled, flaring
hexagonal mouth, pink ground,
No. 976-15" **775.00**
Vase, 18" h., floor-type, blue ground,
No. 977-18" **1,200.00**

BUSHBERRY (1948)

*Berries and leaves on blue, green or russet
bark-textured ground; brown or green branch
handles.*

**Basket w/asymmetrical overhead
handle,** blue ground, No. 369.
6½" h. **195.00**

Basket w/asymmetrical overhead handle, russet ground, No. 369, 6½" h. **180.00**

Basket w/low overhead handle, asymmetric rim, blue ground, No 372-12", 12" h. **400.00**

Basket, hanging-type w/original chains, green ground, No. 465-5", 7" h. **275.00**

Bushberry Cider Set

Cider set: 8¾" h. pitcher w/ice lip & six 1¾" h. mugs; russet ground, the set (ILLUS.) **1,100.00**

Console bowl, two-handled, blue ground, No. 414-10", 10" d. **155.00**

Cornucopia-vase, double, green ground, No. 155-8", 6" h. **120.00**

Cornucopia-vase, double, russet ground, No. 155-8", 6" h. . . . . **160.00 to 175.00**

Ewer, green ground, No. 1-6, 6" h. . . . **150.00**

Jardiniere, two-handled, No. 657-3" **100.00**

Jardiniere, two-handled, russet ground, No. 657-4" **100.00**

Jardiniere & pedestal base, russet ground, No. 657-8", 2 pcs. **855.00**

Mug, green ground, No. 1-3½", 3½" h. **135.00**

Sand jar, green ground, No. 778-14", 14" h. **1,400.00**

Umbrella stand, double handles, blue ground, No. 779-20", 20½" h. . . . . **750.00 to 950.00**

Vase, 6" h., two-handled, green ground, No. 30-6" . . . . **90.00 to 100.00**

Vase, 6" h., angular side handles, low foot, globular w/wide neck, blue ground, No. 156-6" **165.00**

Vase, 6" h., angular side handles, low foot, globular w/wide neck, blue ground, No. 156-6" **145.00**

Vase, 6" h., angular side handles, low foot, globular w/wide neck, russet ground, No. 156-6" **95.00**

Vase, 9" h., two-handled, ovoid, russet ground, No. 35-9" **205.00**

Vase, 9" h., footed cylindrical body w/small angled handles near rim, green ground, No. 36-9" **225.00**

Vase, 12½" h., large asymmetrical side handles, bulging cylinder w/flaring foot, russet ground, No. 38-12" **275.00**

CARNELIAN I (1910-15)

Matte glaze with a combination of two colors or two shades of the same color with the darker dripping over the lighter tone or heavy and textured glaze with intermingled colors and some running.

Candleholder, green ground, No. 1059-2½", 1½" h. **75.00**

Flower frog, blue & grey ground, 6¼" w., 2½" h. **110.00**

Flower frog, green ground, 4½" h. **175.00**

Vase, 6" h., pillow-type, light blue & dark blue . . . . **75.00 to 100.00**

Vase, 10" h., semi-ovoid base & long wide neck w/rolled rim, ornate handles, dark blue & light blue . . . . **125.00 to 175.00**

CARNELIAN II (1915)

Intermingled colors, some with a drip effect.

Bowl, footed, six-sided, w/drip glaze in shades of rose, grey, green & tan, unmarked, small separation at the rim, 4 x 15" **330.00**

Carnelian II Ewer

Ewer, pink, mauve, green & black mottled matte glaze, unmarked, 15" h. (ILLUS.) **1,760.00**

Urn, 5" h. **175.00**

Vase, bud, 6" h., footed trumpet-form w/ornate handles from base to mid-section, blue ground **90.00**

Vase, bud, 6" h., footed trumpet-form
w/ornate handles from base to
mid-section, intermingled shades of
raspberry pink **135.00**

Vase, 7" h. compressed globular
base w/short wide neck, large
handles, purple & rose **225.00**

Vase, 7" h., footed baluster-form
w/small low loop handles from
shoulder to rim, shades of green. . . **240.00**

Vase, 8" h., intermingled shades of
blue **185.00**

Vase, 8" h., intermingled shades of
raspberry pink . . . . **270.00 to 300.00**

CHERRY BLOSSOM (1933)

*Sprigs of cherry blossoms, green leaves and
twigs with pink fence against a combed blue-
green ground or creamy ivory fence against a
terra cotta ground shading to dark brown.*

Bowl-vase, two-handled, globular,
blue-green ground, 6" h. **468.00**

Jardiniere, squatty bulbous body,
two-handled, terra cotta ground,
4" h. . . . . **300.00 to 350.00**

Jardiniere, shoulder handles, terra
cotta ground, 8" h. **605.00**

Vase, 8" h., two-handled, globular,
terra cotta ground . . . . . . **550.00 to 600.00**

Vase, 10" h., slender ovoid body
w/wide cylindrical neck, loop
handles from shoulder to middle of
neck, terra-cotta ground **595.00**

CHLORON (1907)

*Molded in high-relief in the manner of early
Roman and Greek artifacts. Solid matte green
glaze, sometimes combined with ivory. Very
similar in form to Egypto.*

Jardiniere & pedestal base, overall
34" h., 2 pcs. (jardiniere perfect;
tripod pedestal w/chips, no damage
to cameo faces or trim on pedestal
legs) **2,000.00**

Vase, 9" h., squatty bulbous body
tapering to a wide flat mouth, small
loop handle on shoulder w/molded
double curved branch handle on
opposite side rising from base to
neck, molded flower decoration,
signed **525.00**

CLEMATIS (1944)

*Clematis blossoms and heart-shaped green
leaves against a vertically textured ground -
white blossoms on blue, rose-pink blossoms on
green and ivory blossoms on golden brown.*

Basket w/overhead handle,
pedestal base, blue ground, No.
389-10", 10" h. **195.00**

Basket w/overhead handle,
pedestal base, brown ground, No.
389-10", 10" h. **189.00**

Basket w/overhead handle,
pedestal base, green ground, No.
389-10", 10" h. **250.00**

Basket, hanging-type, blue ground,
No. 470-5", 5" h. **225.00**

Basket, hanging-type, green ground,
No. 470-5", 5" h. **195.00**

Candleholders, bulbous w/tiny
pointed handles, green ground,
No. 1158-2", 2½" h., pr. **165.00**

Console bowl, blue ground,
No. 461-14", 14" l. **200.00**

Cookie jar, cov., blue ground,
No. 3-8", 8" h. **400.00**

Cookie jar, cov., brown ground,
No. 3-8", 8" h. **350.00**

Creamer, blue ground, No. 5-C **75.00**

Creamer, green ground, No. 5-C **75.00**

Ewer, green ground, No. 17-10",
10" h. **190.00**

Flowerpot w/saucer, blue ground,
No. 668-5", 5½" h. **140.00**

Jardiniere, blue ground, No. 667-8",
8" h. **395.00**

Teapot, cov., green ground, No. 5 . . . **200.00**

Tea set: cov. teapot, creamer & open
sugar bowl; green ground, No. 5,
3 pcs. **325.00**

Vase, 6" h., two-handled, green
ground, No. 102-6" **55.00**

Vase, 6" h., two-handled, blue
ground, No. 103-6" **110.00**

Vase, 6" h., two-handled, brown
ground, No. 103-6" **85.00**

Vase, 6" h., two-handled, urn-form,
blue ground, No. 188-6" **95.00**

Clematis Vase

Vase, 7" h., blue ground, No. 105-7"
(ILLUS.). **110.00**

Vase, 8" h., two-handled, blue
ground, No. 107-8" . . . . . . **90.00 to 100.00**
Vase, 9" h., blue ground,
No. 109-9" **225.00**
Wall pocket, angular side handles,
green ground, No. 1295-8",
8½" h. **200.00**

COLONIAL (1900S)

Glossy spongeware in shades of blue with gold highlights on embossed detail at base of handles.

Pitcher, 11" h. **380.00**
Toothbrush holder, 5" h.,
unmarked **145.00**

COLUMBINE (1940S)

Columbine blossoms and foliage on shaded ground - yellow blossoms on blue, pink blossoms on pink shaded to green and blue blossoms on tan shaded to green.

Basket, elaborate handle rising from
midsection, blue ground,
No. 365-7", 7" h. **250.00**
Basket, blue ground, No. 366-8",
8" h. **275.00**
Basket, pointed handle rising from
flat base, ovoid w/boat-shaped top
w/shaped rim, blue ground,
No. 368-12", 12" h. **450.00**
Basket, hanging-type **385.00**
Book end planters, blue ground,
No. 8, 5" h., pr. **295.00**
Console bowl, stepped handles
rising from rim, tan ground,
No. 404-10" **125.00**
Ewer, sharply angled handle, pink
ground, No. 18-7", 7" h. **170.00**
Jardiniere, two-handled, blue
ground, No. 655-3", 3" h. . . . **90.00 to 100.00**
Jardiniere, two-handled, pink ground.
No. 655-3", 3" h. . . . . **90.00 to 100.00**
Jardiniere & pedestal base, two-
handled, tan ground, No. 655-10",
10" h., 2 pcs. **1,800.00**
Urn-vase, pink ground, No. 150-6",
6" h. **155.00**
Urn-vase, tan ground, No. 151-8",
8" h. **144.00**
Vase, 7" h., blue ground, No. 16-7". . . **105.00**
Vase, 8" h., handles rising from base,
blue ground, No. 19-8" **125.00**
Vase, 14" h., tan ground,
No. 26-14" **500.00**
Vase, 16" h., floor-type, blue ground,
No. 27-16" **585.00**

CORINTHIAN (1923)

Deeply fluted ivory and green body below a continuous band of molded grapevine, fruit, foliage and florals in naturalistic colors, narrow ivory and green molded border at the rim.

Basket, hanging-type w/chains,
8" d. **260.00**
Bowl, 7" d. **75.00**
Flower frog, No. 14-3½", 3½" h. **50.00**
Jardiniere, 8" h. **325.00**

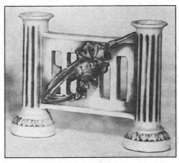

Corinthian Bud Vase

Vase, double bud, 4½" h., 7" w., gate
form (ILLUS.). **150.00**
Wall pocket, 8½" h. **325.00**

COSMOS (1940)

Embossed blossoms against a wavy horizontal ridged band on a textured ground - ivory band with yellow and orchid blossoms on blue, blue band with white and orchid blossoms on green or tan.

Bowl, 4" d., blue ground,
No. 375-4" **185.00**
Bowl, 4" d., tan ground,
No. 375-4" **165.00**
Bowl, 8" d., blue ground,
No. 370-8" **195.00**
Console bowl, green ground,
No. 370-8", 8" l. **150.00**
Cornucopia-vase, blue ground,
No. 136-6", 6" h. **155.00**
Flower frog, pierced globular body
w/asymmetrical overhead handle,
blue ground, No. 39, 3½" h. **145.00**
Flower frog, pierced globular body
w/asymmetrical overhead handle,
tan shaded to green ground,
No. 39, 3½" h. **125.00**
Jardiniere, two-handled, tan ground,
No. 649-4" . . . . **100.00 to 125.00**
Jardiniere, two handled, blue ground,
No. 649-6", 6" h. **195.00**

Rose bowl, two-handled, blue
ground, No. 375-4", 4" h. **175.00**
Rose bowl, green ground,
No. 375-4", 4" h. **120.00**
Urn-vase, green ground, No. 135-8",
8" h. **250.00**
Vase, 8" h., two-handled, cut-out
top edge, tan ground,
No. 950-8". . . . . **275.00 to 350.00**
Vase, 10" h., green ground,
No. 954-10". **385.00**
Wall pocket, double, tan ground,
No. 1285-8", 8½" h. **400.00**

CREMONA (1927)

*Relief-molded floral motifs including a tall
stem with small blossoms and arrowhead leaves,
wreathed with leaves similar to Velmoss or a
web of delicate vines against a background of
light green mottled with pale blue or pink with
creamy ivory.*

Console bowl w/flower frog, green
ground, No. 178-8", 8" l. **200.00**
Vase, 4" h., rectangular mouth
w/pointed ends, slightly canted
sides, stepped foot, pink ground,
No. 72-4". **95.00**

DAHLROSE (1924-28)

*Band of ivory daisy-like blossoms and green
leaves against a mottled tan ground.*

Bowl, 10" oval, two-handled **165.00**
Jardiniere, 4" d. **135.00**
Jardiniere, 6" h. **165.00**
Vase, double bud, 6" h.,
gate-form. . . . . **145.00 to 175.00**
Vase, 8" h., ornate curving
asymmetrical handle, mound base,
No. 78-8". **150.00**
Wall pocket, No. 1258-8", 8" h. **350.00**
Wall pocket, two-handled, conical,
10" h. . . . . **230.00 to 300.00**

DOGWOOD II (1928)

*White dogwood blossoms & black branches
against a smooth green ground.*

Jardiniere, No. 590-7", 7" h. **210.00**
Jardiniere, No. 590-8", 8" h. **385.00**
Jardiniere, No. 490-10", 12" d., 10" h. . . **575.00**
Vase, bud, 8" h., tusk-form w/single
handle rising from base to
midsection. **135.00**
Wall pocket, two handles in the form
of blossoming branches,
1218-10", 10" h. **350.00**

DONATELLO (1915)

*Deeply fluted ivory and green body with wide
tan band embossed with cherubs at various
pursuits in pastoral settings.*

Bowl, 7½" d., low **45.00**
Bowl, 8½" d., 3½" h. **95.00**
Bowl, 9½" d., 3" h. **80.00**
Candlesticks, cylindrical w/flaring
base & candle nozzle, 4" widest d.,
8" h., pr. **200.00**
Compote, No. 231-5", 5" h. **135.00**
Compote, 9½" h. **135.00**
Jardiniere, No. 575-6", 6" h. **150.00**
Jardiniere, 7" d., 6" h. . . . . **100.00 to 125.00**
Vase, 6" h., two-handled **150.00**
Vase, 8" h., expanding cylinder. **175.00**
Vase, 12" h., No. 184-12" **225.00**
Wall pocket, ovoid, 9" h. . . **200.00 to 250.00**
Wall pocket, 10" h. **110.00**

DUTCH (Before 1916)

*Creamware with colorful decal scenes of
Dutch children and adults at various activities.*

Pitcher, tankard, 11½" h. **225.00**
Sugar bowl, cov., 4" h. **120.00**

EARLAM (1930)

*Mottled glaze on various simple shapes. The
line includes many crocus or strawberry pots.*

Bowl, 4" h., canted sides w/scroll
handles, bluish green glaze on
exterior & salmon interior,
unmarked, No. 217-4" **248.00**

Earlam Planter

Planter, two-handled, rectangular
w/shaped rim, curved end handles,
mottled green glaze, No. 89-8",
5 x 10½" (ILLUS.) **275.00**
Urn-vase, two-handled, bulbous
ovoid body, mottled green glaze,
No. 519-7", 7" h. **395.00**

EARLY EMBOSSED PITCHERS (Pre-1916)

Landscape Pitcher

The Bridge, 6" h. **90.00**
Grape, 6" h. **90.00**
Landscape, 7½" h.
   (ILLUS.). . . . . **100.00 to 125.00**

FALLINE (1933)

Curving panels topped by a semi-scallop separated by vertical peapod decorations; blended backgrounds of tan shading to green and blue or tan shading to darker brown.

Console bowl, tan ground,
   No. 244-8", 8" l. **350.00**
Vase, 7" h., ovoid body w/shoulder
   loop handles, shaded brown body,
   No. 648-7" **560.00**

FERELLA (1930)

Impressed shell design alternating with small cut-outs at top and base; mottled brown or turquoise and red glaze.

Console bowl w/attached flower
   frog, deep flaring sides, brown
   glaze No. 87-8", 8" d. . . . **450.00 to 500.00**
Vase, 4" h., angular handles, short
   narrow neck, brown glaze,
   No. 497-4". . . . . **300.00 to 375.00**

Ferella Vase

Vase, 4" h., angular handles,
   bulbous, turquoise & red glaze,
   No. 498-4" (ILLUS.) . . . . **300.00 to 350.00**

Vase, 5" h., two-handled, flaring rim,
   brown glaze, No. 503-5" **400.00**
Vase, 6" h., turquoise & red glaze,
   No. 505-6". **700.00**
Vase, 8" h., slightly ovoid, turquoise &
   red glaze, No. 508-8" . . . **675.00 to 775.00**
Vase, 9¼" h., 5¼" d., footed slender
   ovoid body tapering to a short
   flaring neck, low arched handles
   down the sides, stylized green &
   yellow blossoms on reticulated
   bands, brown glaze,
   No. 507-9". . . . . **600.00 to 650.00**
Wall pocket, half-round basket-form
   w/widely flaring rim & high shaped
   & arched backplate w/hanging
   hole, turquoise & red glaze,
   No. 1266-6½", 6½" h. **1,200.00**

FLORENTINE (1924-28)

Bark-textured panels alternating with embossed garlands of cascading fruit and florals; ivory with tan and green, beige with brown and green or brown with beige and green glaze.

Candleholders, No. 1049-8",
   8" h., pr. **125.00**
Jardiniere & pedestal base,
   2 pcs. **1,350.00**
Wall pocket, overhead handle, brown
   ground, No. 1238-8", 8½" h. **165.00**

Florentine Wall Pocket

Wall pocket, brown ground, 9½" h.
   (ILLUS.). **325.00**

FOXGLOVE (1940S)

Sprays of pink and white blossoms embossed against a shaded matte finish ground.

Basket, hanging-type, blue ground,
No. 466-5", 6½" h.. . . . . . **300.00 to 350.00**
Basket, hanging-type, green ground,
No. 466-5", 6½" h.. . . . . . **250.00 to 300.00**
Book ends, blue ground, No. 10, pr. . **250.00**
Candleholders, blue, No. 1149,
2½" h., pr. **90.00**
Console bowl, blue ground,
No. 421-10", 10" l.. . . . . **150.00**
Console bowl, blue ground,
No. 422-10", 10" l.. . . . . **165.00**

Foxglove Cornucopia-vase

Cornucopia-vase, snail shell-type,
pink ground, No. 166-6" (ILLUS.) . . **135.00**
Ewer, pink ground, No. 4-6½",
6½" h. **178.00**
Ewer, blue ground, No. 5-10",
10" h.. . . . . **270.00**
Jardiniere, green ground, No. 659-5",
5" h.. . . . . **145.00**
Tray, single open handle, leaf-
shaped, green ground,
8½" w.. . . . . **100.00 to 125.00**
Tray, open rim handles, shaped oval,
blue ground, 11" l.. . . . . . **160.00 to 170.00**
Vase, 4" h., angular side handles,
blue ground, No. 42-4" **145.00**
Vase, 4" h., angular side handles,
pink ground, No. 42-4" **60.00**
Vase, 6½" h., two-handled, pink
ground, No. 44-6" . . . . . . **125.00 to 150.00**
Vase, 15" h., two-handled, green
ground, No. 54-15" **550.00**
Vase, 18" h., floor-type, blue
ground. . . . . **725.00 to 750.00**

FREESIA (1945)

Trumpet-shaped blossoms and long slender green leaves against wavy impressed lines - white and lavender blossoms on blended green; white and yellow blossoms on shaded blue or terra cotta and brown.

Basket w/low overhead handle,
green ground, No. 310-10", 10" h.. . **250.00**

Basket, hanging-type, blue ground,
No. 471-5" **250.00**
Bowl, 11" d., two-handled, terra cotta
ground, No. 465-8" **135.00**
Candleholders, tiny pointed handles,
domed base, terra cotta ground,
No. 1160-2", 2" h., pr. **100.00**

Freesia Candlesticks

Candlesticks, disc base, cylindrical
w/low handles, terra cotta ground,
No. 1161-4½", 4½" h., pr.
(ILLUS.). . . . . **125.00 to 130.00**
Console bowl, 16½" l., green
ground, No. 469-14" **165.00**
Console bowl, 16½" l., terra cotta
ground, No. 469-14" **135.00**
Creamer, green ground, No. 6C **100.00**
Ewer, blue ground, No. 19-6", 6" h. . . **125.00**
Ewer, terra cotta ground, No. 20-10",
10" h.. . . . . **160.00**
Ewer, green ground, No. 21-15",
15" h.. . . . . **325.00**
Jardiniere, tiny rim handles, terra
cotta ground, No. 669-4",
4" h.. . . . . **75.00 to 100.00**
Jardiniere, rim handles, blue ground,
No. 669-8", 8" h. **425.00**
Lamp, blue ground,
No. 145 . . . . **400.00 to 450.00**
Pitcher, 10" h., tankard, footed
slender ovoid body w/wide spout &
pointed arched handle, green
ground, No. 20-10" **235.00**
Pitcher, 10" h., swollen cylinder,
terra cotta ground,
No. 20-10". . . . . **150.00 to 200.00**
Teapot, cov., terra cotta ground,
No. 6-T **200.00**
Teapot, cov., green ground,
No. 6-T **295.00**
Urn-vase, two-handled, green
ground, No. 196-8", 8" h.. . . . . **225.00**
Vase, 7" h., two-handled, slightly
expanding cylinder, blue ground,
No. 120-7". **140.00**
Vase, 7" h., two-handled, fan-shaped,
blue, No. 200-7" **125.00**

Vase, 8" h., globular base & flaring rim, handles at midsection, blue ground, No. 122-8" **175.00**

Vase, 8" h., globular base & flaring rim, handles at midsection, terra cotta ground, No. 122-8" **110.00**

Vase, 9½" h., a short ringed pedestal base supporting a flaring half-round base w/an angled shoulder tapering slightly to a tall, wide cylindrical neck, down-curved angled loop handles from center of neck to rim of lower shoulder, blue ground, No. 123-9" **185.00**

Vase, 10" h., base handles, pink ground, No. 389-10" **225.00**

Vase, 10½" h., blended green ground, No. 125-10" (professional repair) **175.00**

Wall pocket, angular handles, green ground, No. 1296-8", 8½" h. **250.00**

Wall pocket, angular handles, terra cotta ground, No. 1296-8", 8½" h. . . . . **200.00 to 225.00**

Window box, two-handled, green ground, No. 1392-8", 10½" l. **150.00**

FUCHSIA (1939)

Coral pink fuchsia blossoms and green leaves against a background of blue shading to yellow, green shading to terra cotta or terra cotta shading to gold.

Basket, hanging-type, brown ground, No. 359-5", 5" h. **350.00**

Basket, hanging-type, green ground, No. 359-5", 5" h. . . . . . . **285.00 to 300.00**

Bowl, 5" d., two-handled, blue ground, No. 348-5" **150.00**

Bowl, 6" d., blue ground, No. 347-6" (w/sticker) **300.00**

Bowl, 6" d., brown ground, No. 347-6" . . . . **250.00 to 275.00**

Console bowl, two-handled, blue ground, No. 349-8", 8" l. **250.00**

Console bowl, blue ground, No. 352-12", 12" l. **335.00**

Console set: 10" bowl & pair of 5" h. candleholders; blue ground, Nos. 351-10" & 1133-5", the set **750.00**

Ewer, terra cotta ground, No. 902-10", 10" h. **300.00**

Flower frog, green ground, No. 37 . . . . **185.00 to 195.00**

Flowerpot, terra cotta ground, No. 646-5", 5" h. **155.00**

Jardiniere, two-handled, green ground, No. 645-3", 3" h. **85.00**

Jardiniere, two-handled, green ground, No. 645-4", 4" h. **135.00**

Pitcher w/ice lip, 8" h., green ground, No. 1322-8" **395.00**

Vase, 6" h., ovoid w/handles rising from shoulder to rim, blue ground, No. 892-6" **125.00**

Vase, 6" h., footed swelled cylindrical body w/long loop handles, blue ground, No. 893-6" **200.00**

Vase, 7" h., terra cotta ground, No. 895-7" **165.00**

Vase, 8" h., handles rising from flat base to shoulder, terra cotta ground, No. 897-8" **225.00**

Vase, 8" h., blue ground, No. 898-8". . **415.00**

Vase, 8" h., footed bulbous base w/tapering cylindrical neck, loop handles, blue ground, No. 898-8". . . . . **350.00 to 400.00**

Vase, 8½" h., pillow-type w/handles rising from base to midsection, blue ground, No. 896-8" **495.00**

Vase, 9" h., two-handled, blue ground, No. 899-9" **495.00**

Vase, 9" h., two-handled, blue ground, No. 900-9" **350.00**

Vase, 10" h., two-handled, blue ground, No. 901-10" . . . . **435.00 to 475.00**

Vase, 10" h., two-handled, terra cotta ground, No. 901-10" **335.00**

Vase, 12" h., two handles rising from above base to neck, blue ground, No. 903-12" . . . . **400.00 to 600.00**

Vase, 12" h., two handles rising from above base to neck, brown ground, No. 903-12" **400.00**

Vase, 15" h., blue ground, No. 904-15" . . . . **650.00 to 700.00**

Vase, 15" h., terra cotta ground, No. 904-15" . . . . **550.00 to 600.00**

Vase, 18" h., 10" d., floor-type, a disc foot supports a tall baluster-form body w/long low C-form handles down the sides, terra cotta ground, No. 905-18" . . . . **850.00 to 1,000.00**

Wall pocket, two-handled, green ground, No. 1282-8", 8½" h. **475.00**

FUTURA (1928)

Varied line with shapes ranging from Art Deco geometrics to futuristic. Matte glaze is typical although an occasional piece may be high gloss.

Jardiniere, angular handles rising from wide sloping shoulders to rim, sharply canted sides, terra cotta ground, No. 616-6", 6" h. **275.00**

Vase, 8" h., bottle-shape w/stepped back bands, No. 384-8" **450.00**

Vase, 8" h., 3¾" d., star-shaped slender tapering body on stepped circular base, pink & grey ground, No. 385-8"........... **475.00 to 500.00**

Vase, 8" h., upright rectangular form on rectangular foot, stepped neck, long square handles, No. 386-8"........... **575.00 to 600.00**

Vase, 8" h., spherical body w/a tiny flared neck raised on a wide flat pedestal foot w/slender buttresses from base to bottom of body, No. 404-8" **1,400.00**

Vase, 8" h., square, slightly tapering body twisting toward the rim, pink ground, No. 425-8" **475.00**

Futura Vase

Vase, 9" h., "Emerald Urn," bulbous base w/tall wide cylindrical neck w/four molded rings, long angled handles from shoulder to rim, green & black, No. 389-9" (ILLUS.)..................... **605.00**

Vase, 9" h., short rectangular mouth above a swelled rectangular body raised on four short rectangular legs, No. 430-9"............... **500.00**

Vase, 9¼" h, 5¼" d., angular handles raising from bulbous base to rim, sharply stepped neck shaded dark to light green high gloss glaze, No. 389-9".................... **675.00**

Vase, 10" h., squatty bulbous base w/molded ring mid-section, wide cylindrical neck w/flaring rim, No. 435-10" **1,575.00**

Vase, 12" h., slightly tapering tall cylindrical body w/flat flared rim, flanked by long tapering buttress handles, No. 437-12" **1,200.00**

Wall pocket, canted sides, angular rim handles, geometric design in blue, yellow, green & lavender on brown ground, No. 1261-8" 6" w., 8¼" h. **400.00**

GARDENIA (1940S)

Large white gardenia blossoms and green leaves over a textured impressed band on a shaded green, grey or tan ground.

Book ends, green ground, No. 659, pr... **250.00**

Candleholders, grey ground, No. 652-4½", 4½" h., pr. **115.00**

Bowl, 10" d., grey ground, No. 628-10".................. **120.00**

Ewer, ovoid base, green ground, No. 617-10", 10" h. **180.00**

Vase, 10" h., green ground, No. 658-10" **160.00**

Vase, 10" h., tall ovoid body w/fanned rim, base handles, grey ground, No. 685-10".................. **198.00**

Vase, 10" h., two-handled, tan ground, No. 924-9" **325.00**

Vase, 14½" h., floral-type, two handles rising from midsection to below rim, tan ground, No. 689-14".................. **375.00**

Wall pocket, large handles, green ground, No. 666-8", 9½" h. **250.00**

Window box, green ground, No. 668-8", 8" l................. **95.00**

Window box, grey ground, No. 669-12", 14" l.............. **115.00**

IMPERIAL I (1916)

Brown pretzel-twisted vine, green grape leaf and cluster of blue grapes in relief on green and brown back-textured ground.

Bowl, 8" d., No. 71-8" **125.00**
Bowl, 9" d., two-handled........... **90.00**
Vase, triple bud, 8" h., No. 25-8"..... **140.00**
Vase, 8" h., bulbous w/pierced handles at shoulder............ **145.00**

IMPERIAL II (1924)

Varied line with no common characteristics. Many of the pieces are heavily glazed with colors that run and blend.

Bowl, 4½" d., ivory ground **75.00**

Imperial II Vase

Vase, 5" h., wide squatty bulbous body w/a wide shoulder to the short rolled neck, embossed designs around the rim, blue flambé ground, marked w/gold foil label & incised "9" (ILLUS.) **220.00**

Vase, 5" h., tapering ovoid ringed body, tan shading to green, No. 467-5" . . . . **225.00 to 235.00**

Vase, 5½" h., tapering cylinder w/horizontal ribbing above base, mottled green ground, No. 468-5" . . . . **185.00 to 200.00**

Vase, 6" h., purple & yellow ground, No. 469-6" . . . . **350.00 to 400.00**

Vase, 7" h., hemispherical w/sloping shoulder & short collared neck, No. 474-7" . . . . **375.00 to 400.00**

Vase, 10" h., baluster form w/short wide cylindrical neck, cobalt blue ground, No. 477-10" **575.00**

Vase, 11" h., tapering ovoid body with short wide rim, blue ground **795.00**

IRIS (1938)

White or yellow blossoms and green leaves on rose blending with green, light blue deepening to a darker blue or tan shading to green or brown.

Bowl, 6" d., blue ground, 360-6" **140.00**

Candlesticks, flat disc base, cylindrical nozzle flanked by elongated open handles, rose ground, No. 1135-4½", 4½" h., pr. **175.00**

Cornucopia-vase, blue ground, No. 130-4", 4" h. **75.00**

Flower frog, blue ground, No. 38 . . . . **125.00**

Jardiniere, two-handled, rose ground, No. 647-3", 3" h. **70.00**

Vase, 4" h., base handles, tan ground, No. 914-4" **100.00**

Vase, 6½" h., two handles rising from shoulder of globular base to midsection of wide neck, rose ground, No. 917-6" . . . . . **175.00 to 225.00**

Vase, 6½" h., two handles rising from shoulder of globular base to midsection of wide neck, tan shading to brown ground, No. 917-6" **225.00**

Vase, 7" h., blue ground, No. 919-7" . . . . **150.00 to 175.00**

Vase, 8" h., urn-form w/pedestal base, tan ground, No. 923-8" **215.00**

Vase, 10" h., rose ground, No. 927-10" **475.00**

Vase, 12½" h., semi-ovoid base w/two handles rising from shoulder to beneath rim of short wide mouth, brown ground, No. 928-12" **350.00**

IXIA (1930S)

Embossed spray of tiny bell-shaped flowers and slender leaves - white blossoms on pink ground; lavender blossoms on green or yellow ground.

Bowl, 4" d., pointed closed handles at rim, pink ground, No. 326-4" **115.00**

Bowl, 6" d., pink ground, No. 387-6" **225.00**

Bowl, 6" d., yellow ground, No. 387-6" **125.00**

Candlesticks, double, No. 1127, 3" h., pr. **138.00**

Console bowl, pink ground, No. 330-9", 9" l. **140.00**

Jardiniere, green ground, No. 640-7", 7" h. **300.00**

Vase, 6" h., elongated closed handles at shoulders, ovoid body, pink ground, No. 853-6" **85.00**

Vase, 7" h., green ground, No. 855-7" **150.00**

Vase, 8" h., pillow-form, green ground, No. 858-8" **265.00**

Vase, 12" h., closed handles, cylindrical, yellow ground, No. 864-12" . . . . **300.00 to 350.00**

JONQUIL (1931)

White jonquil blossoms and green leaves in relief against textured tan ground; green lining.

Candleholders, No. 1082-4", 4" h., pr. **400.00**

Jardiniere, two handled, No. 621-8", 8" h. **425.00**

Jonquil Vase

Vase, 4" h., bulbous spherical form, loop handles from mid-section to rim (ILLUS.) **165.00**

Vase, 8" h., tapering cylinder w/elongated side handles, No. 528-8" . . . . **250.00 to 300.00**

Vase, 10½" h., cylindrical w/narrow shoulder, asymmetrical, branch handles, white ground, No. 583-10" **225.00**

JUVENILE

Transfer-printed and painted on creamware with nursery rhyme characters, cute animals and other motifs appealing to children.

Cup & saucer, Sunbonnet Girl , cup 2" h., saucer 3" d., pr. **125.00**

Sitting Rabbits Feeding Dish

Feeding dish w/rolled edge, sitting rabbits, 6½" d. (ILLUS.) **145.00**

Feeding dish w/rolled edge, nursery rhyme "Bye Baby Bunting," w/cat, 8" d. **110.00**

Feeding dish w/rolled edge, Santa Claus, 8" d. **750.00**

Feeding dish w/rolled edge, Sunbonnet girl, 8" d. **165.00**

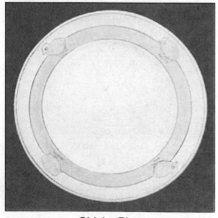

Chicks Plate

Mug, chicks, 3" h. **95.00**
Mug, duck w/hat, 3" h.. . . . . **150.00**
Mug, standing rabbit, 3" h.. . . . . **150.00 to 200.00**
Pitcher, 3" h., chicks **115.00**
Pitcher, 3½" h., duck w/hat **145.00**
Pitcher, 3½" h., fat puppy **85.00**
Pitcher, 3" h., rabbits **175.00**
Pitcher, 3" h., side pour, chicks . . . . **110.00 to 125.00**
Pitcher, 3½" h., side pour, rabbits . . . **145.00**
Plate, 8" d., chicks (ILLUS.) **185.00**
Plate, 8" d., Sunbonnet girl . . . . **190.00 to 200.00**

JUVENILE (1916 on)

Transfer-printed and painted on creamware with nursery rhyme characters, cute animals and other motifs appealing to children.

Egg cup, child's, chicks decoration . . **279.00**
Feeding dish w/rolled edge, chicks, orange band, 8" d. **155.00**
Feeding dish w/rolled edge, nursery rhyme, "Baby Bunting," 8" d. **148.00**
Feeding dish w/rolled edge, nursery rhyme, "Little Jack Horner," 8" d. . . . **170.00**
Feeding dish w/rolled edge, rabbit w/jacket, 8" d. **155.00**
Feeding dish w/rolled edge, sitting rabbits, 8" d. **110.00**
Mug, child's, chicks decoration **128.00**

LA ROSE (1924)

Swags of green leaves and red roses on a creamy ivory ground.

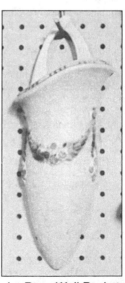

La Rose Wall Pocket

Candleholder, straight handle rising
from base to just below nozzle,
4" h. 120.00
Candlestick, 8" h. 160.00
Vase, double bud, 4½" h., gate-form,
No. 43-4½" 165.00
Wall pocket, 12" h. (ILLUS.). 235.00

LAUREL (1934)

*Laurel branch and berries in low-relief with
reeded panels at the sides. Glazed in deep yellow,
green shading to cream or terra cotta.*

Urn, deep yellow, No. 250-6½",
6½" h. . . . . **265.00 to 350.00**
Vase, 6" h., No. 239-6" 130.00
Vase, 6" h., tapering cylinder w/wide
mouth, closed angular handles at
shoulder, deep yellow, No. 667-6" . . . 150.00
Vase, 6½" h., green, No. 669-6½" . . . 185.00
Vase, 7¼" h., green, No. 670-7¼" . . . 358.00
Vase, 7½" h., tapering cylinder
w/pierced angular handles at
midsection, terra cotta,
No. 671-7¼" 295.00
Vase, 8" h., bulbous ovoid body
w/short collared neck, closed
handles from shoulder to rim,
yellow ground, No. 672-8" 325.00
Vase, 9" h., deep yellow 195.00
Vase, 9¼" h., angular side handles,
globular base w/wide stepped
mouth, green ground,
No. 674-9¼" 475.00

LUFFA (1934)

*Relief-molded ivy leaves and blossoms on
shaded brown or green wavy horizontal ridges.*

Console bowl, green ground,
13" l. . . . . **300.00 to 325.00**
Jardiniere & pedestal base, brown
ground, jardiniere 8" h., 2 pcs. **1,500.00**
Vase, 6" h., two-handled, cylindrical,
green ground 145.00
Vase, 7" h., brown ground. 300.00
Vase, 12" h., brown ground,
No. 691-12" 650.00

MAGNOLIA (1943)

*Large white blossoms with rose centers and
black stems in relief against a blue, green or tan
textured ground.*

Ashtray, two-handled, low bowl form,
blue ground, No. 28, 7" d. 118.00
Basket, blue ground, No. 385-10 ,
10" h. 275.00

Basket, green ground, No. 385-10",
10" h. **225.00**
Basket, asymmetrical overhead
handle, footed, blue ground, No.
386-12", 12" h.. . . . . **330.00**
Basket, asymmetrical overhead
handle, footed, green ground, No.
386-12", 12" h.. . . . . 375.00
Book ends, green ground, No. 13,
pr. 195.00
Bowl, 10" l., two-handled, green
ground, No. 450-10" 145.00
Candleholders, blue ground, No.
H57-4", 4" h., pr. 105.00
Candlesticks, angular handles rising
from flat base to midsection of
stem, blue ground, No. 1157-4½",
5" h., pr. 162.00
Console bowl, blue ground, No.449-
10", 10" l. 133.00
Cookie jar, cov., shoulder handles,
blue ground, No. 2-8", overall
10" h.. . . . . 438.00
Cookie jar, cov., shoulder handles,
green ground, No. 2-8, overall
10" h.. . . . . 479.00
Cornucopia-vase, green ground,
No. 184-6", 6" h. 95.00
Creamer & sugar bowl, blue ground,
Nos. 4C & 4S, pr. 128.00
Ewer, green ground, No. 13-6",
6" h.. . . . . 124.00

Magnolia Jardiniere & Pedestal

Jardiniere & pedestal base, tan
ground, No. 665-10", jardiniere
10" h., 2 pcs. (ILLUS.) **1,250.00**
Model of a conch shell, blue ground,
No. 454-8", 8½" w. 125.00
Mug, tan ground, No. 3-3" 110.00
Pitcher, cider, 7" h., blue ground,
No. 132-7. . . . . 450.00
Pitcher, cider, 7" h., green ground,
No. 132-7. . . . . 325.00
Pitcher, cider, 7" h., tan ground,
No. 132-7" 200.00

Planter, two-handled, tan ground,
No. 389-8", 8" l. **115.00**
Tea set: cov. teapot, creamer & open
sugar bowl; green ground, No. 4,
3 pcs.. . . . . **375.00**
Tea set: cov. teapot, creamer & open
sugar bowl; tan ground, 3 pcs. **460.00**
Teapot, cov., tan ground, No. 4 . . . . . **295.00**
Vase, 4" h., ovoid w/angular handles
at rim, blue ground, No. 86-4" **100.00**
Vase, 4" h., ovoid w/angular handles
at rim, green ground,
No. 86-4". **60.00**
Vase, 4" h., ovoid w/angular handles
at rim, tan ground, No. 86-4" **95.00**
Vase, double bud, 4" h., No. 186-
4½" **135.00**
Vase, 6" h., blue ground,
No. 88-6" **115.00**
Vase, 6" h., two-handled, tan ground,
No. 87-6". **150.00**
Vase, 7" h., green ground,
No. 89-7" **110.00**
Vase, bud, 7" h., blue ground,
No. 179-7" **135.00**
Vase, 8" h., blue ground,
No. 92-8". **130.00**
Vase, 8" h., globular w/large angular
handles, blue ground,
No. 91-8" **213.00**

Magnolia Vase

Vase, 9" h., two-handled, blue
ground, No. 93-9" (ILLUS). **175.00**
Vase, 9" h., two-handled, green
ground, No.93-9". **195.00**
Vase, 12" h., two-handled, blue
ground, No. 96-12" **395.00**
Vase, floor type, 15" h., green
ground, No. 98-15" **550.00**

MATT COLORS (1920s)

*Simple paneled forms in colors of light blue,
turquoise, yellow and pink. Reissued later with a
glossy glaze.*

Basket, hanging-type, tan ground,
No. 364-5", 5" h. **85.00**
Bowl, 5½" d., 4" h., footed squatty
bulbous body w/wide flaring mouth,
small handles at shoulder, yellow
glaze, No. 550-4". **45.00**
Vase, 4" h., slightly canted ribbed
sides, plain color under rim w/four
raised squares, turquoise matt
finish, No. 624-4". **48.00**

MATT GREEN (Before 1916)

*Dark green matt finish. Some pieces plain;
others decorated with various embossed designs
such as leaves or children's faces.*

Basket, hanging-type, No. 364-5" . . . **150.00**
Basket, hanging-type, green ground,
9" h.. . . . . **218.00**

MING TREE (1949)

*Embossed twisted bonsai tree topped with
puffy foliage pink-topped trees on mint green
ground, green tops on white ground and white
tops on blue ground; handles in the form of
gnarled branches.*

Basket, hanging-type, blue
ground, 6" **200.00**
Basket, hanging-type, green
ground, 6" **295.00**
Basket, overhead branch handle,
rounded body w/shaped rim, blue
ground, No. 508-8", 8" h.. . . . . **125.00**
Basket, white ground,
No. 510-14", 14" **275.00**
Candleholders, squat melon-ribbed
body w/angular branch handles at
shoulder, blue ground, No. 551, pr. . . **145.00**
Ewer, white ground,
No. 516-10", 10" h. **140.00**
Model of a conch shell, white glaze,
No. 563-7½" **75.00**
Planter, blue ground, No. 568-8",
4 x 8½" **125.00**
Vase, 8" h., asymmetrical branch
handles, green ground, No. 582-8" . . **110.00**
Vase, 14" h., green ground,
No. 585-14". **525.00**
Wall pocket, overhead branch
handle, white ground, No. 566-8",
8½" h. **275.00**
Wall pocket, overhead branch
handle, green ground, No. 566-8",
8½" h. **275.00**

MOCK ORANGE (1950)

Basket, hanging-type **375.00**
Basket, green ground, No. 911-10",
   10" h. **250.00**

MODERNE (1930s)

Art Deco style rounded and angular shapes trimmed with an embossed panel of vertical lines and modified swirls and circleswhite trimmed with terra cotta, medium blue with white and turquoise with a burnished antique gold.

Vase, 6½" h., urn-form w/slender
   handles, white ground,
   No. 787-6" **125.00**
Vase, 10¼" h., 8" d., large spherical
   body on a small footring, the neck
   composed of stepped bands,
   "Black Flame" on lower half,
   No. 391-10" **750.00**

MONTACELLO (1931)

White stylized trumpet flowers with black accents on a terra cotta bandlight terra cotta mottled in blue or light green mottled and blended with blue backgrounds.

Basket, bulbous base w/wide neck &
   flaring rim, a long curved upright
   handle from shoulder to shoulder
   coming to a point above the neck,
   terra cotta ground, No. 333-6",
   6" h. **595.00**
Vase, 5" h., ovoid w/shoulder
   handles, blue ground, No. 557-5" . . **312.00**
Vase, 5" h., ovoid w/shoulder
   handles, terra cotta ground,
   No. 557-5" **360.00**

MORNING GLORY (1935)

Stylized pastel morning glory blossoms and twining vines in low relief against a white or green ground.

Bowl, 4" d., white ground, No. 268-4" . . . **375.00**
Vase, 6" h., two-handled, waisted
   cylinder, white ground,
   No. 6-6" **375.00**
Vase, 7" h., tapering sides, base
   handles, green ground **475.00**
Vase, 8½" h., trumpet-shaped
   handles at base, white ground **450.00**
Vase, 9" h., green ground,
   No. 728-9" **1,150.00**
Vase, 10" h., two-handled, white
   ground **675.00**

MOSS (1930s)

Spanish moss draped over a brown branch with green leaves against a background of ivory, pink or tan shading to blue.

Bowl, 8" d., blue ground, No. 292-
   8" **200.00**
Candleholders, pink or blue ground,
   No. 1109-2", 2" h., pr., each **160.00**
Candlesticks, angular handles at
   midsection, pink ground,
   No. 1107-4½", 4½" h., pr. **125.00**
Console bowl, No. 294-12", 12" l. . . . **350.00**
Jardiniere, No. 635-8", 8" h. **495.00**
Jardiniere, pink ground, No. 635
   10", 10" h. **1,200.00**
Urn, small angular handles rising
   from base to mid-section, globular,
   pink ground, No. 290-6", 6" h. **175.00**
Urn, small angular handles rising
   from base to mid-section, globular,
   blue ground, No. 290-6", 6" h. **225.00**
Vase, pillow-type, tan ground **245.00**
Vase, 6" h., angular handles, pink
   ground, No. 776-6" **175.00**
Vase, 7" h., pink ground, No. 778-7" . **253.00**
Vase, 8" h., pillow-type w/small
   angular handles rising from
   midsection to rim, blue,
   No. 781-8" **275.00**
Vase, 8" h., pillow-type w/small
   angular handles rising from
   midsection to rim, tan,
   No. 781-8" **468.00**
Vase, 9" h., blue ground,
   No. 782-9" **275.00**

MOSTIQUE (1915)

Incised Indian-type design of stylized flowers, leaves or geometric shapes glazed in bright glossy colors against a heavy, pebbled ground.

Bowl, 7" d., stylized flowers, grey
   ground. **118.00**
Jardiniere, geometric floral design
   w/arrowhead leaves, tan ground,
   No. 606-6", 6" h. **250.00**
Jardiniere, brown ground, 10" h. **550.00**
Vase, 6" h., arrowhead leaves
   design **150.00**
Vase, 6" h., two-handled, brown
   ground. **185.00**
Vase, 15" h., 8" w., floral &
   geometric design, grey ground . . . **525.00**

NORMANDY (1924-28)

Green and ivory vertical fluting with a band of embossed ivory vines, pink grapes and green leaves on a brown ground at the rim.

Normandy Hanging Basket

Basket, hanging-type (ILLUS.) **385.00**
Jardiniere & pedestal base, overall
   28" h., 2 pcs. **895.00**

PANEL (1920)

Recessed panels decorated with embossed naturalistic or stylized florals or female nudes.

Bowl, 6" d., low sides, geometric
   design, grey ground. **125.00**
Vase, 8" h., fan-shaped, nude in
   panel, dark brown ground **400.00**
Vase, 8" h., two small rim handles,
   expanding cylinder, stylized florals,
   dark brown ground **200.00**
Vase, 10" h., cylindrical, nude in
   panel, dark brown ground **365.00**
Vase, 12" h., floral design, brown
   ground **335.00**
Wall pocket, leaves in panel, brown
   ground **295.00**

PEONY (1942)

Peony blossoms in relief against a textured swirling ground–yellow blossoms against rose shading to green, brown shading to gold or gold with green; white blossoms against green.

Basket w/overhead handle,
   hanging-type, green ground,
   No. 467-5" **225.00**
Basket w/overhead handle, gold
   ground, No. 378-10", 10" h. **185.00**
Basket w/overhead handle, green
   ground, No. 378-10", 10" h. **233.00**
Book ends, gold ground, No. 11,
   5½" h., pr. **295.00**

Small Peony Bowl

Bowl, 4" d., rose shading to green
   No. 427-4" (ILLUS) **130.00**
Bowl, 6" d., pink ground, No. 428-6" . . **75.00**
Bowl, 10" l., two-handled, irregular
   rim, green ground, No. 430-10". . . . **125.00**
Candleholders, pink ground,
   No. 1151-2", 2" h., pr. **80.00**
Console bowl, gold ground,
   No. 4-10" (small chip) **180.00**
Cornucopia-vase, gold ground,
   No. 170-6", 6" h. **85.00**
Cornucopia-vase, brown ground,
   No. 171-8", 8" h. **135.00**
Cornucopia-vase, green ground,
   No. 171-8", 8" h. **165.00**
Creamer, gold ground, No. 3-C **75.00**
Creamer, pink ground, No. 3-C **80.00**
Flower arranger, pink ground, No.
   47-4", 4" h. **85.00**
Jardiniere, green ground, No. 661-4",
   4" h. **100.00**
Jardiniere & pedestal, green & gold,
   30" h., 2 pcs. **950.00**
Jardiniere & pedestal base, gold
   ground, No. 661-10", 2 pcs. **1,500.00**
Model of a conch shell, pink ground,
   No. 436, 9½" w. **175.00**
Pitcher w/ice lip, 7½" h., blue
   ground, No. 1326-7½". **275.00**
Tea set: cov. teapot, creamer & open
   sugar; green ground, No. 3,
   3 pcs. **300.00**
Tea set: cov. teapot, sugar bowl &
   creamer; gold ground, Nos. 3, 3C &
   3S, 3 pcs. **375.00**
Teapot, cov., pink shading to green
   ground, No. 3. . . . . **288.00**
Tray, gold ground, 11" l. **150.00**
Vase, 7" h., gold ground, No. 60-7". . . . **95.00**
Vase, 10" h., handles rising from
   midsection to below flaring rim,
   gold ground, No. 66-10" **175.00**
Vase, 14" h., angular handles at
   midsection, gold ground,
   No. 68-14". **245.00**
Wall pocket, gold ground **325.00**

PERSIAN (1916)

Creamware decorated by means of pouncing technique, in bright colors. Water lily and pad most common motif, although a variety of others were also used.

Basket, hanging-type, 9" h. **$575.00**
Bowl, large **195.00**

PINE CONE (1931)

Realistic embossed brown pine cones and green pine needles on shaded blue, brown or green ground. (Pink is extremely rare.)

Ashtray, blue ground or brown ground, No. 499, 4½" l., each **$108.00**
Basket, hanging-type, squatty bulbous body tapering slightly toward the base, w/a short wide cylindrical neck flanked by tiny branch hanging handles, green ground, No. 352-5", 7" d., 5½" h. . . **413.00**
Basket, hanging-type, squatty bulbous body tapering slightly toward the base, w/a short wide cylindrical neck flanked by tiny branch hanging handles, brown ground, No. 352-5", 7" d., 5½" h. . . **488.00**
Basket, hanging-type, squatty bulbous body tapering slightly toward the base, w/a short wide cylindrical neck flanked by tiny branch hanging handles, blue ground, No. 352-5", 7" d., 5½" h. . . **535.00**
Basket, w/overhead branch handle, asymmetrical body, brown ground, No. 408-6", 6" h. . . . . **250.00 to 300.00**
Basket, w/overhead branch handle, green ground, No. 409-8", 8" h. **450.00**
Basket, w/overhead branch handle, boat-shaped, blue ground, No. 410-10", 10" h. **405.00**
Basket, w/overhead branch handle, disc base, flaring rim, blue ground, No. 338-10", 10" h. **513.00**
Book ends, brown ground, No. 1, pr. . . **388.00**
Book ends, brown ground, No. 5, pr. . . **300.00**
Bowl, 4" d., green ground, No. 278-4" . . **175.00**
Bowl, 6" d., brown ground, No. 261-6" **275.00**
Bowl, boat-shaped, 8" l., green ground, No. 427-8" **185.00**
Bowl, 9" d., blue ground, No. 321-9" . . **600.00**
Bowl, 9" l., 4" h., footed oval low body w/fanned sections at each end & small twig end handles, brown ground, No. 279-9" **250.00**
Candleholders, brown ground, No. 451-4", 4" h., pr. **195.00**
Candlestick, blue ground, No. 1099-4½", 4½" h. **75.00**

Candlestick, triple, green ground, No. 1106-5½", 5½" h. **425.00**
Console bowl, brown ground, No. 322-12", 12" l. **373.00**
Console bowl, green ground, No. 322-12", 12" l. **210.00**
Cornucopia-vase, blue ground, No. 126-6", 6" h. **325.00**
Cornucopia-vase, brown ground, No. 126-6", 6" h. **188.00**
Cornucopia-vase, blue ground, No. 128-8", 8" h. **313.00**
Dish, boat-shaped, brown or green ground, No. 427-8", 9" l., each **313.00**
Ewer, brown ground, No. 909-10", 10" h. **450.00**
Ewer, green ground, No. 851-15", 15" h., ... **575.00**
Flowerpot & saucer, No. 633-5BR . . **325.00**
Jardiniere, brown ground, No. 632-3", 3" h. . . . . **150.00 to 175.00**
Jardiniere, brown ground, No. 632-4", 4" h. **218.00**
Jardiniere, green ground, No. 632-4", 4" h. **200.00**
Jardiniere, brown ground, No. 632-5", 5" h. **225.00**
Jardiniere, brown ground, No. 642-6", 6" h. **295.00**
Jardiniere & pedestal base, brown ground, No. 632-10", jardiniere 10" h., 2 pcs. **3,250.00**
Pitcher, brown ground, No. 1321 . . . . **575.00**
Pitcher, 9½" h., ovoid, small branch handle, blue ground, No. 708-9" . . **1,073.00**
Pitcher, 9" h., brown ground, No. 415-9" **675.00**
Pitcher, 9½" h., ovoid, small branch handle, brown ground, No. 708-9" . . . **875.00**
Planter, single side handle rising from base, blue ground, No. 124-5", 5" h. **375.00**
Planter, single side handle rising from base, green ground, No. 124-5", 5" h. **175.00**
Planter, boat-shaped, blue ground, No. 455-6", 6" l. **325.00**
Planter, green ground, No. 456-6", 6" l. **150.00**
Planter, brown ground, No. 457-7", 7" l. **245.00**
Planter-book ends, green ground, pr. **575.00**
Rose bowl, brown ground, No. 278-4", 4" h. **225.00**
Sand jar, green ground, No. 776-14", 14" h. **1,800.00**
Tray, brown ground, No. 430-12", 12" l. **410.00**

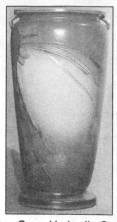

Pine Cone Umbrella Stand

Umbrella stand, blue ground, No.
   777-20", 20" h. (ILLUS.) **3,565.00**
Umbrella stand, brown ground, No.
   777-20", 20" h. **2,342.00**
Urn, green ground, No. 745-7", 7" h. . . **275.00**
Urn-vase, asymmetrical handles,
   footed, brown ground, No. 121-7",
   7" h. **225.00**
Urn-vase, brown ground, No. 908-8",
   8" h. **325.00**
Vase, 6" h., blue ground, No. 472-6" . . . **595.00**
Vase, 6" h., brown ground, No. 839-
   6" **180.00**
Vase, 6" h., trumpet-shaped, brown
   ground, No. 906-6" **200.00**
Vase, 7" h., brown ground, No. 480-
   7" **175.00**
Vase, 7" h., brown ground, No. 840-
   7" **225.00**
Vase, 7" h., green ground, No. 704-7" . . **185.00**
Vase, 7" h., pillow-type, blue ground,
   No. 478-7" **373.00**
Vase, bud, 7" h., brown ground,
   No. 112-7" **265.00**
Vase, 8" h., double, brown ground,
   No. 473-8" . . . . **275.00 to 350.00**
Vase, 8½" h., green ground, No. 490-
   8" **240.00**
Vase, 9" h., blue ground, No. 705-9" . . . **400.00**
Vase, 10" h., brown ground, No. 711-
   10" **450.00**
Vase, 10" h., brown ground, No. 848-
   10" **525.00**
Vase, 10" h., expanding cylinder, blue
   ground, No. 709-10" **388.00**
Vase, 10" h., expanding cylinder,
   brown ground, No. 709-10" **475.00**
Vase, 10" h., green ground, No. 491-
   10" **322.00**
Vase, 10½" h., blue ground, No. 747-
   10" **565.00**

Vase, 10½" h., brown ground,
   No. 747-10" **488.00**
Vase, 12" h., blue ground, No. 493-
   12" **795.00**
Vase, 12" h., blue ground, No. 712-
   12" **50.00**
Vase, 12" h., blue ground, No. 805-
   12" **1,295.00**
Vase, 12" h., brown ground, No. 712-
   12" **495.00**
Vase, 12" h., green ground, No. 712-
   12" **563.00**
Wall pocket, double, two flaring
   conical containers joined by an
   arched pine cone & needle top
   handle, brown ground, No. 1273-
   8", 8½" h. **400.00**
Wall pocket, blue ground, No. 1283-
   9", 9" h. **625.00**

POPPY (1930s)

Embossed full-blown poppy blossoms, buds
and foliage yellow blossoms on green, white
blossoms on blue or soft pink blossoms on a
deeper pink.

Basket, wide trumpet-form w/high &
   wide arched handle, pink ground,
   No. 347-10", 10" h. **450.00**
Basket, green ground, No. 348-12",
   12" h. **385.00**
Bowl, 10" l., blue ground, No. 338-
   10" **158.00**
Bowl, 10" l., pink ground, No. 338-10" . . **160.00**
Ewer, green ground, No. 876-10",
   10" h. **325.00**
Ewer, pink ground, No. 876-10",
   10" h. **213.00**
Jardiniere, tiny handles at rim, pink
   ground, No. 642-4", 4" h. **130.00**
Jardiniere, pink ground, No. 642-5",
   5" h. **130.00**
Jardiniere, green ground, No. 335-6",
   6" h. **225.00**
Vase, 6" h., blue ground, No. 867-6"
   (w/sticker) **150.00**
Vase, 6" h., pink ground, No. 866-6" . . . **95.00**
Vase, 9" h., two-handled, ovoid
   w/wide mouth, green ground, No.
   872-9" **225.00**

PRIMROSE (1932)

Cluster of long-stemmed blossoms and pod-
like leaves in relief on blue, pink or tan ground.

Flower frog, pink ground, No. 22 . . . . **125.00**
Vase, 7" h., two-handled, brown
   ground, No. 762-7" **170.00**

Vase, 8" h., fan-shaped, brown
  ground, No. 767-8" 168.00
Vase, 9" h., pink ground, No. 769-9" . . 265.00
Vase, 12" h., blue ground, No. 771-
  12" 300.00

RAYMOR (1952)

Modernistic design oven-proof dinnerware.

Casserole, cov., Terra Cotta, No.
  185, large 85.00
Celery & olive dish, Contemporary
  White, No. 177, 15½" l. 75.00
Cruets w/original stoppers, vinegar
  & oil, No. 170 & No. 171, Terra
  Cotta, pr. 95.00
Cup & saucer, restyled, Terra Cotta,
  No. 250 . . . . 25.00
Pitcher, water, 10" h., Contemporary
  White, No. 189 . . . . 150.00

ROSECRAFT (1916)

Curving band of brown and yellow grapevine with fruit and foliage at top, usually on a dark brown ground.

Basket, hanging-type, light blue glaze . . 85.00
Bowl, 6½" d., yellow glaze 50.00
Vase, double-bud, No.16-5", 5" h. . . . 185.00

ROZANE (1917)

Honeycomb backgrounds in ivory, light green, pink, yellow, blue; decorated with green leaves and clusters of roses in delicate tints.

Jardiniere, ivory ground, No. 588-8",
  8" h. 225.00
Jardiniere & pedestal, ivory ground,
  jardiniere No. 588-10", 10" h.,
  2 pcs. 850.00
Vase, ivory ground, No. 110-6", 6" h. . . 85.00

ROZANE PATTERN (1940s)

Solid or blended matte glazes on simple shapes. Shaded browns or blues; ivory, turquoise.

Vase, 6" h., blue glaze, No. 1-6" 80.00
Vase, 8" h., blue glaze 125.00
Vase, 8" h., ivory glaze 60.00

SILHOUETTE (1952)

Recessed shaped panels decorated with floral designs or exotic female nudes against a combed background.

Basket, florals, rose ground, No. 708-
  6", 6" h. 145.00
Basket, curved rim & asymmetrical
  handle, florals, rose ground, No.
  710-10", 10" h. 200.00

Bowl, 8" d., florals, rose ground, No.
  727-8" 75.00
Candleholder, florals, white ground,
  No. 751-3", 3" h. 65.00
Ewer, sharply canted sides, florals,
  rose, No. 717-10", 10" h. 185.00
Planter, florals, rose ground, footed
  long rectangular form, No. 756-5",
  5" h. 100.00
Planter, double, florals, turquoise
  ground, No. 757-9", 5½" h. 103.00
Rose bowl, female nudes, rose
  ground, No. 742-6", 6" h. 335.00
Vase, 7" h., fan-shaped, nude lady,
  rose ground, No. 783-7" 400.00
Vase, 9" h., florals, rose ground,
  slender ovoid body w/flaring base
  & rim, No. 785-9" 145.00
Vase, 9" h., florals, turquoise ground,
  No. 786-9" 140.00
Vase, 10" h., small open handles
  between square base & waisted
  cylindrical body, shaped rim,
  female nudes, tan ground, No. 787-
  10" 375.00
Vase, 10" h., small open handles
  between square base & waisted
  cylindrical body, shaped rim,
  female nudes, turquoise ground
  No. 787-10" 500.00

SNOWBERRY (1946)

Clusters of white berries on brown stems with green foliage over oblique scalloping, against a blue, green or rose background.

Ashtray, round dished form, shaded
  blue ground 115.00
Basket, hanging-type, shaded blue
  ground, No. 1HB-5", 5" h. 288.00
Basket, hanging-type, shaded green
  ground, 1HB-5", 5" h. 240.00
Basket, hanging-type, shaded rose
  ground, No. 1HB-5", 5" h. 225.00
Basket, footed fan-shaped body
  w/wide looped & pointed handle,
  shaded rose ground, No. 1BK-7",
  7" h. 190.00
Basket, w/asymmetrical overhead
  handle, shaded green ground, No.
  1BK8", 8" h. 225.00
Basket, w/asymmetrical overhead
  handle, shaded rose ground,
  No. 1BK-8", 8" h. 160.00
Book ends, shaded blue ground,
  1BE, pr. 275.00
Book ends, shaded rose ground,
  No. 1BE, pr. 250.00
Bowl, 6" d., shaded rose ground,
  No. 1BL1-6" 100.00

Candleholders, squatty w/angular handles at shoulder, shaded green ground, No. 1CS1-2", 2" h., pr. **90.00**

Candlesticks, angular side handles, shaded blue ground, No. 1CS2-4½", 4½" h., pr. **135.00**

Candlesticks, angular side handles, shaded rose ground, No. 1CS2-4½", 4½" h., pr. **95.00**

Console bowl, boat-shaped, pointed end handles, shaded rose ground, No. 1BL2-12", 15" l. **150.00**

Cornucopia-vase, shaded rose ground, No. 1CC-8", 8" h. **105.00**

Ewer, shaded rose ground, No. 1TK-6", 6" h. **138.00**

Ewer, shaded rose ground, No. 1TK-10", 10" h. **180.00**

Ewer, shaded green ground, 1TK-15, 16" h. **450.00**

Jardiniere, two-handled, shaded blue ground, No. 1J-4", 4" h. **130.00**

Jardiniere, two-handled, shaded green ground, No. 1J-6", 6" h. **550.00**

Jardiniere & pedestal, shaded green ground, No. 1 J-8, 2 pcs. **900.00**

Jardiniere & pedestal, shaded rose ground, No. 1J-8", overall 25" h., 2 pcs. **1,088.00**

Rose bowl, two handled, shaded blue ground, No. 1RB-5", 5" d. **105.00**

Sugar bowl, open, shaded green or shaded rose ground, No. 1-S, each . . **73.00**

Tea set: cov. teapot, open sugar bowl & creamer; shaded green ground, Nos. 1TP, 1S & 1C, 3 pcs. **375.00**

Teapot, cov., shaded green ground, No. 1TP **255.00**

Tray, long leaf-shaped, shaded blue ground, No. 1BL1-12", 14" l. **150.00**

Vase, 6" h., shaded green ground, No. 1V-6". **75.00**

Vase, 6½" h., pillow-type, shaded green ground, No. 1FH-6" **140.00**

Vase, 7" h., fan-shaped, shaded blue ground, No. 1FH-7" **190.00**

Vase, 7" h., fan-shaped, shaded rose ground, No. 1FH-7" **150.00**

Vase, 7" h., two-handled, shaded rose ground, No. 1V1-7" **110.00**

Vase, bud, 7"h., slender w/irregular rim & small angled base handle, shaded blue ground, No. 1BV-7". . . . **90.00**

Vase, 7½" h., bulbous base w/tall cylindrical neck, pointed shoulder handles, shaded rose ground, No. 1V2-7". **105.00**

Vase, 7½" h., bulbous base w/tall cylindrical neck, pointed shoulder handles, shaded green ground,

No. 1V2-7". **125.00**

Vase, 8½" h., urn-shaped w/pointed shoulder handles, shaded rose ground, No. 1UR-8". **225.00**

Vase, 9" h., base handles, shaded green ground, No. 1V1-9" **95.00**

Vase, 9" h., shaded blue ground, No. 1V2-9" **175.00**

Vase, 9" h., shaded rose ground, No. 1V2-9". **145.00**

Vase, 10" h., shaded rose ground, No. 1V2-10". **275.00**

Vase, 12" h., floor-type, shaded blue ground, No. 1V2-12" **230.00**

Vase, 12" h., floor-type, shaded rose ground, No. 1V2-12" **275.00**

Vase, 18" h., floor-type, shaded rose ground, 1V1-18" **650.00**

Wall pocket, wide half-round form tapering to a pointed base, low angled handles along the lower sides, shaded blue ground, No. 1WP-8", 8" w., 5½" h. . . **225.00 to 250.00**

Wall pocket, wide half-round form tapering to a pointed base, low angled handles along the lower sides, shaded rose ground, No. 1WP-8", 8" w., 5½" h. **225.00**

Window box, rectangular, shaded blue ground, No. 1WX-8", 8" l. **155.00**

Window box, rectangular, shaded rose ground, No. 1WX-8, 8" l. **100.00**

SUNFLOWER (1930)

Long-stemmed yellow sunflower blossoms framed in green leaves against a mottled green textured ground.

Bowl, 5" d., No. 208-5" **695.00**

Jardiniere & pedestal base, jardiniere No. 619-10", 10" h., 2 pcs. **6,900.00**

Urn-vase, nearly spherical w/tiny rim handles, 4" h. **405.00**

Urn-vase, nearly spherical w/short wide neck, 7" **400.00**

Vase, 5" h. **350.00**

Vase, 5½" h., 5¼" d., bulbous ovoid body tapering to a wide flat mouth, small loop handles at the shoulder . . **660.00**

Vase, 6" h., cylindrical w/small pointed angled rim handles **563.00**

Vase, 8" h., bulbous base, wide tapering cylindrical neck, No. 491-8". **925.00**

Vase, 10" h., swelled cylindrical body w/tiny shoulder handles, No. 492-10" **2,500.00**

TEASEL (1936)

Gracefully curving long stems and delicate pods.

Bowl, 8" d., blue ground, No. 344-8" . . **155.00**
Vase, 6" h., closed handles at
  midsection, cut-out rim, beige
  shading to tan ground, No. 881-6" . . **130.00**
Vase, 8" h., closed handles at
  shoulder, low foot, beige shading to
  tan, No. 884-8" **175.00**
Vase, 14" h., ovoid w/double open
  handles at shoulder, low foot, small
  mouth, beige shading to tan,
  No. 889-15" **525.00**

THORN APPLE (1930s)

White trumpet flower and foliage one side, reverse with thorny pod and foliage against shaded blue, brown or pink ground.

Book ends, pink & green ground,
  No. 3, pr. **240.00**
Bowl, 6" d., pointed handles, shaded
  blue ground, No. 307-6" **175.00**
Bowl, 12" d., shaded blue ground,
  No. 311-12" **250.00**
Jardiniere, shaded brown ground,
  No. 638-10", 10" h. **625.00**
Urn, footed spherical body flanked by
  stepped, angled handles, shaded
  brown ground, No. 305-6", 6½" h. . . **295.00**
Vase, 4" h., jug-form, shaded brown
  ground, No. 808-4" **140.00**
Vase, 4" h., squatty body w/short
  narrow neck, angular pierced
  handles rising from midsection,
  pink & green ground, No. 308-4". . . **133.00**
Vase, 5½" h., double-bud, shaded
  brown ground, No. 1119-5" **195.00**
Vase, bud, 7" h., shaded brown
  ground, No. 813-7" **145.00**

TOPEO (1934)

Four evenly spaced vertical garlands beginning near the top and tapering gently down the sides.

Bowl, 6" d., shaded blue ground,
  No. 245-6" **165.00**
Vase, 9" h., squared ovoid body,
  glossy deep red glaze **290.00**
Vase, 9¼" h., ovoid w/short collared
  neck, shaded blue ground,
  No. 661-9¼" **460.00**

TOURMALINE (1933)

Produced in various simple shapes and a wide variety of glazes including rose and grey, blue-green, brown or azure blue with green and gold, and terra cotta with yellow.

Bowl, 8" d., low incurved sides,
  mottled turquoise glaze **75.00**
Urn-vase, compressed globular base
  w/short collared neck, mottled
  glaze, No. 200-4", 4" h. **125.00**
Vase, 6" h., ovoid body tapering to a
  cylindrical neck flanked by loop
  handles to the shoulder, mottled
  dark blue glaze **135.00**
Vase, 7" h., shaded orange glaze,
  No. 318-7" **135.00**

TUSCANY (1927)

Simple forms with gently curving handles ending in leaf and grape clusters. Mottled finish found in shiny pink with pale bluish green leaves, overall greyish blue or dull turquoise.

Console bowl, rectangular
  w/rounded ends, mottled turquoise
  glaze, No. 174-12", 12" l. **200.00**
Cornucopia-vase, 9" h., mottled pink
  glaze **175.00**
Vase, 6" h., two-handled, mottled pink
  glaze **210.00**
Vase, 9" h., two-handled, globular
  base, short wide neck, mottled grey
  glaze **180.00**
Vase, 9" h., two-handled, globular
  base, short wide neck, mottled pink
  glaze **210.00**
Vase, 10" h., shoulder handles,
  bulbous, mottled pink glaze. **238.00**
Wall pocket, long open handles,
  rounded rim, mottled pink glaze,
  No. 1255-8", 8" h. **280.00**

VELMOSS (1935)

Embossed clusters of long slender green leaves extending down from the top and crossing three wavy horizontal lines. Some pieces reverse the design with the leaves rising from the base.

Jardiniere, footed spherical body
  w/short wide neck & pointed
  shoulder handles, mottled green
  glaze, No. 264-5", 5" h. **140.00**
Jardiniere, footed spherical body
  w/short wide neck & pointed
  shoulder handles, mottled blue
  glaze, No. 264-5", 5" h. **180.00**

Jardiniere, footed spherical body
w/short wide neck & pointed
shoulder handles, mottled blue
glaze, No. 265-6", 6" h. **175.00**
Planter, rectangular w/shaped sides,
pointed end handles, mottled blue
glaze, No. 266, 6 x 12" **378.00**
Planter, rectangular w/shaped sides,
pointed end handles, mottled green
glaze, No. 266, 6 x 12" **250.00**
Vase, 6" h., swelled cylindrical body
w/pointed shoulder handles, blue &
brown glaze, No. 714-6" **225.00**
Vase, 6" h., swelled cylindrical body
w/pointed shoulder handles,
mottled raspberry red glaze,
No. 714-6" **225.00**
Vase, 8" h., footed swelled cylindrical
body tapering at the short neck,
pointed shoulder handles, mottled
blue glaze, No. 718-8". **295.00**
Vase, 9½" h., ovoid body w/pointed
shoulder handles, mottled blue
glaze, No. 719-9". **325.00**
Vase, 9½" h., ovoid body w/pointed
shoulder handles, mottled green
glaze, No. 719-9". **385.00**
Vase, 10" h., slender trumpet-form
body on a round foot
w/asymmetrical scroll loop handles,
mottled blue glaze, No. 119-10" . . . **325.00**
Vase, 14½" h., tall trumpet-form body
w/low foot, angular pointed
handles, mottled green glaze,
No. 722-14" **375.00**

VELMOSS SCROLL (1916)

*Incised stylized red roses and green leaves on
a creamy ivory matte glaze.*

Basket, hanging-type **375.00**
Bowl, 7" d., 3" h., canted sides,
No. 117-6" **145.00**

Velmoss Scroll Jardiniere & Pedestal

Jardiniere & pedestal base,
unmarked, slightly dirty crazing,
interior, 29½" h., 2 pcs. (ILLUS.) . . **1,045.00**
Wall pocket, elongated oviform,
No. 1226-11", 11" h. **273.00**

VISTA (1920s)

*Embossed green coconut palm trees and
lavender blue pool against grey ground.*

Bowl, 7" d.. **225.00**
Jardiniere, bulbous form, strong
mold in colors of green, purple &
grey, 12" d., 10¼" h. **546.00**

Vista Umbrella Stand

Umbrella stand, unmarked, 19¾" h.
(ILLUS.) **1,760.00**
Vase, 10" h., conical w/arms **495.00**
Vase, 12" h.. **600.00**
Vase, floor-type, 14" h. **785.00**

WATER LILY (1940s)

*Water lily blossoms and pods against a
horizontally ridged ground. White lilies on green
lily pads against a blended blue ground, pink
lilies on a pink shading to green ground or
yellow lilies against a gold shading to brown
ground.*

Basket, hanging-type, gold shading
to brown ground, 9" l. (chains
missing). **175.00**
Basket, conch shell-shaped w/high
arched handle, gold shading to
brown ground, No. 381-10",
10" h.. . . . . **175.00 to 225.00**
Basket, conch shell-shaped w/high
arched handle, shaded blue
ground, No. 381-10", 10" h.. . . . . . **245.00**
Basket, w/asymmetrical overhead
handle,curved & sharply scalloped
rim, pink shading to green ground,
No. 382-12", 12" h. **260.00**

Book ends, pink shading to green ground, No. 12, pr. 250.00

Bowl w/flower frog, 8" l., pointed end handles, shaded blue ground, No. 440-8" 165.00

Bowl-vase, pink shading to green ground, No.437-4", 4" h., ... 95.00

Candleholders, flat base, angular handles rising from base to midsection of nozzle, shaded blue ground, No. 1155-4½", 5" h., pr. 165.00

Console bowl, oblong w/pointed end handles, pink shading to green ground, No.443-12", 12" l. 140.00

Cookie jar, cov., angular handles, blended blue ground, No. 1-8", 8" h........................... 403.00

Cookie jar, cov., angular handles, gold shading to brown ground, No. 1-8", 8" h. 650.00

Cornucopia-vase, gold shading to brown ground, No. 176-6", 6" h. 90.00

Flower holder, two-handled, fan-shaped body, pink shading to green ground, No. 48, 4½" h. 115.00

Jardiniere, gold shading to brown ground, No. 663-10", 10" h........ 725.00

Model of a conch shell, shaded blue ground, No. 445-6", 6" h............ 85.00

Model of a conch shell, pink shading to green ground, No. 438-8", 8" h. 175.00

Urn-vase, gold shading to brown ground, No. 175-8", 8" h.......... 180.00

Vase, 4" h., gold shading to brown ground, No. 71-4" 75.00

Vase, 6" h., shaded blue ground, No. 174-6" 175.00

Vase, 8" h., two-handled, gold shading to brown, No. 77-8" 145.00

Vase, 9" h., footed ovoid body flanked by pointed downswept handles, shaded blue ground, No. 78-9" 245.00

Vase, 15" h., pink shading to green ground, No. 83-15" 450.00

Vase, 18" h., floor-type, tall baluster-form w/pointed shoulder handles, pink shading to green ground, No. 85-18" 650.00

WHITE ROSE (1940)

White roses and green leaves against a vertically combed ground of blended blue, brown shading to green or pink shading to green.

Basket, hanging-type, blended blue ground, No. 463-5" 280.00

Basket, oblong flaring bowl w/high heart-form pointed overhead handle, brown shading to green ground, No. 362-8", 8" h. 140.00

Book ends, brown shading to green ground, No. 7, pr. 250.00

Bowl, 6" d., handled, brown shading to green ground, No. 389-6" 125.00

Bowl, 8" d., pink shading to green ground, No. 390-8" 100.00

Candleholders, two-handled, low, blended blue ground, No. 1141-2", 2" h., pr.................... 88.00

Candleholders, two-handled, low, brown shading to green ground, No. 1141-2", 2" h., pr............ 135.00

Candleholders, double, blended blue ground, No. 1143-4", 4" h., pr...... 188.00

Candleholders, double, pink shading to green ground, No. 1143-4", 4" h., pr.................... 110.00

Console bowl, brown shading to green ground, No. 391-10", 10" l. ... 185.00

Console bowl, pink shading to green ground, No. 391-10", 10" l. 150.00

Console bowl, pink shading to green ground, No. 394-14", 14" l 250.00

Console bowl, elongated pointed handles, blended blue ground, No. 393-12", 16½" l. 140.00

Cornucopia-vase, blended blue ground, No. 143-6", 6" h.......... 120.00

Cornucopia-vase, double, No. 145-8", 8" h. 120.00

Ewer, footed wide rounded lower body w/an angled shoulder taerping to a forked, long spout & loop handle, blended blue ground, No. 981-6", 6" h. 110.00

Ewer, globular base w/long neck & sweeping lip, blended blue ground, No. 993-15", 15" h. 365.00

Flower frog, basket-shaped w/overhead handle, pink shading to green ground, No. 41 .... 135.00

Flowerpot, No. 654-5" 95.00

Jardiniere, spherical w/small shoulder loop handles, brown shading to green ground, No. 653-3", 3" h....................... 80.00

Jardiniere, spherical w/small shoulder loop handles, pink shading to green ground, No.653-3", 3" h....................... 150.00

Jardiniere, spherical w/small shoulder loop handles, blended blue ground, No. 653-5", 5" h. 150.00

Jardiniere & pedestal base, brown shading to green ground, overall 25" h., 2 pcs. (small chip on base of jardiniere) 625.00

Rose bowl, spherical body, two-handled, blended blue ground, No. 387-4", 4" d. 60.00

Urn-vase, spherical body on footring w/small loop handles flanking the flat mouth, blended blue ground, No. 388-7", 7" h. **198.00**

Vase, 5" h., footed trumpet-form body w/notched rim & asymmetrical base loop handles, blended blue ground, 980-6". **128.00**

Vase, 7" h., blended blue ground, No. 983-7" **185.00**

Vase, 7" h., handled, pink shading to green ground, No. 982-7" **130.00**

Vase, 8" h., flattened ovoid body on a rectangular foot, small pointed shoulder handles, brown shading to green ground, No. 984-8" **195.00**

Vase, 8½" h., small footring below a squatty bulbous base & tall, wide cylindrical body w/notched flat rim, long loop handles from rim to edge of base, pink shading to green ground, No. 985-8" **185.00**

Vase, 10" h., brown shading to green ground, No. 988-10" **240.00**

Vase, 12½" h., ovoid, angular handles at rim, blended blue ground, No. 991-12" **340.00**

Vase, 12½" h., ovoid, angular handles at rim, pink shading to green ground, No. 991-12" **418.00**

Vase, 18" h., floor-type, two-handled, blended blue ground, No. 994-18" . . **488.00**

WINCRAFT (1948)

Shapes from older lines such as Pine Cone, Cremona, Primrose and others, vases with an animal motif, and contemporary shapes. High gloss glaze in bright shades of blue, tan, yellow, turquoise, apricot and grey.

Basket, hanging-type, blue ground, No. 261-6", 6" h. **135.00**

Basket, hanging-type, tan ground, No. 261-6", 6" h. **145.00**

Book ends, swelled leaf-form, blue ground, No. 259-6", 6½" h., pr. **160.00**

Candlesticks, brown ground, No. 251, pr. **60.00**

Candlesticks, triple, green ground, No. 253-3", 3" h., pr. **250.00**

Console bowl, rectangular foot supporting a long, low serpentine bowl w/pointed ends, green ground, No.227-10", 13½" l., 4" h., . . **49.00**

Console bowl, blue ground, No. 229-14", 14" l **115.00**

Ewer, bell-form body below a tall neck w/upright tall spout & angled shoulder handle, tan ground, No. 216-8", 8" h. **95.00**

Tray, rectangular, No. 230-8", each color. **90.00**

Vase, 6" h., asymmetrical fan shape, pine cones & needles in relief on shaded blue ground, No. 272-6" . . . **130.00**

Vase, 6" h., tan ground, No. 241-6" . . . **75.00**

Vase, 6" h., tan ground, No.281-6" . . . **40.00**

Vase, 8" h., flowing lily form w/asymmetrical side handles, tulip & foliage in relief on glossy green & yellow ground, No. 282-8" **175.00**

Vase, 10" h., cylindrical, tab handles, black panther & green palm trees in relief on blue ground, No. 290-10". **550.00**

Vase, 10" h., ovoid base & long cylindrical neck w/wedge-shaped closed handle on one side & long closed column-form handle on the other, glossy mottled blue, No. 284-10". **150.00**

Vase, 10" h., wide disc foot below the tall cylindrical body joined to the foot w/a leaf-form handle, blue ground, No. 285-10" **150.00**

Vase, 16" h., thick disc foot below the tall cylindrical body w/a fanned rim, blue ground, No. 288-15" **400.00**

Wall pocket, rectangular box-like holders w/horizonotal ribbing & ivy leaves as rim handle, brown ground, No. 266-4", 8½" h. **250.00**

Window box, two-part, lime ground, No. 268-12", 12" l. **235.00**

WINDSOR (1931)

Stylized florals, foliage, vines and ferns on some, others with repetitive band arrangement of small squares and rectangles, on mottled blue blending into green or terra cotta and light orange blending into brown.

Low Windsor Bowl

Bowl, 12" d., 2¾" h., low compressed body w/wide molded rim, strap handles, stylized leaf & berry decoration around the shoulder in green, brown & red, terra cotta ground (ILLUS) **275.00**

Vase, 6" h., canted sides, handles rising from shoulder to rim, geometric design against mottled blue ground, No. 547-6" **280.00**

Windsor Vase

Vase, 6⅛" h., bulbous body w/wide flaring rim, mottled blue matte glaze w/embossed rectangles around the collar in alternating yellow & green, unmarked (ILLUS.) . . **413.00**

Vase, 7" h., large handles, globular base, stylized ferns against mottled blue ground, No. 548-7" **375.00**

WISTERIA (1933)

Lavender wisteria blossoms and green vines against a roughly textured brown shading to deep blue ground, rarely found in only brown.

Bowl-vase, squatty bulbous form tapering sharply to a flat mouth flanked by small loop handles, brown ground, No. 242-4", 4" h. . . . **359.00**

Bowl-vase, squatty bulbous form tapering sharply to a flat mouth flanked by small loop handles, blue ground, No. 242-4", 4" h. **425.00**

Console bowl, narrow oblong form w/upright sides & small pointed end handles, brown ground, No. 243-12", 12" l. **545.00**

Jardiniere & pedestal base, brown & purple ground, 2 pcs. **2,300.00**

Vase, 6" h., ovoid body tapering to short cylindrical neck flanked by small loop handles, blue ground, No. 631-6" **570.00**

Vase, 6½" h., 4" d., bulbous ovoid body w/a wide shoulder tapering up to a small mouth, small angled shoulder handles, mottled blue & brown ground, No. 630-6" **353.00**

Vase, 7" h., bulbous waisted ovoid body w/small pointed shoulder handles, brown ground, No. 634-7" . . **545.00**

Vase, 7" h., bulbous waisted ovoid body w/small pointed shoulder handles, blue ground, No. 634-7" . . **795.00**

Vase, 8" h., pear-shaped body w/short cylindrical neck & tiny angled shoulder handles, blue ground, No. 636-8" **723.00**

Vase, 8" h., 6½" d., wide tapering cylindrical body w/small angled handles flanking the flat rim, blue ground, No. 633-8" **795.00**

Vase, 8½" h., slender base handles, conical body bulging slightly below rim, blue ground, No. 635-8" **759.00**

Wall pocket, fan-shaped, blue ground, 8" h. **1,650.00**

ZEPHYR LILY (1946)

Deeply embossed day lilies against a swirl-textured ground. White and yellow lilies on a blended blue ground; rose and yellow lilies on a green ground; yellow lilies on terra cotta shading to olive green ground.

Ashtray, shallow lobed blossom-form, blue ground, No. 27 . . . . **65.00**

Basket, footed half-round body w/curled-in rim tabs & high arched handle, blue ground, No. 393-7", 7" h. **150.00**

Basket, footed half-round body w/curled-in rim tabs & high arched handle, terra cotta ground, No. 393-7", 7" h. **175.00**

Basket, hanging-type, blue or terra cotta ground, No. 472-5", 7½" w., each. **233.00**

Basket, hanging-type, green ground, No. 472-5", 7½" w. **280.00**

Basket, footed flaring rectangular body w/upcurved rim & long asymmetrical handle, blue ground, No. 394-8", 8" h. **200.00**

Basket, w/low wide overhead handle, disc foot, cylindrical body flaring slightly to an ornate cut rim, terra cotta ground, No. 395-10", 10" h. . . . **275.00**

Book ends, green ground, No. 16, pr. . . **225.00**

Bowl, 6" d., blue ground, No. 472-6" . . . **100.00**

Bowl, 8" l., low oblong form w/curved end tab handles, terra cotta ground, No. 474-8" **115.00**

Candleholders, low tapering sides w/two-handles, blue ground, No. 1162-2", 2" h., pr. **85.00**

Candleholders, terra cotta ground, No. 1163-4½", 4½" h., pr. **155.00**

Compote, open, green ground, No. 8-10", 10" h. **150.00**

Compote, opwn, terra cotta ground, No. 8-10", 10" h. **195.00**

Console bowl, blue ground, No. 478-12", 12" l. **165.00**

Console bowl, terra cotta ground,
No. 478-12", 12" l. **145.00**

Cookie jar, cov., terra cotta ground,
No. 5-8", 8" h. **395.00**

Cornucopia vase, terra cotta ground,
No. 204-8", 81/2" h. **130.00**

Creamer, terra cotta ground, No. 7-C . . **75.00**

Ewer, green ground, No. 22-6", 6" h. . . . **125.00**

Ewer, footed flaring lower body
w/angled shoulder tapering to a tall
folked neck w/upright tall spout,
long low arched handle, terra cotta
ground, No. 23-10", 10" h. **200.00**

Ewer, footed baluster-form w/a tall
neck w/tall forked rim & upright
spout, handle from rim to shoulder,
terra cotta ground, No. 24-15",
15" h. **298.00**

Ewer, footed baluster-form w/a tall
neck w/tall forked rim & upright
spout, handle from rim to shoulder,
green ground, No. 24-15", 15" h. . . . **370.00**

Flowerpot w/saucer, terra cotta
ground, No. 672-5" **200.00**

Jardiniere & pedestal base, green
ground, No. 671-8", overall 25" h.,
2 pcs. **875.00**

Planter, green ground, No. 470-5" . . . **135.00**

Tea set: cov. teapot, creamer & open
sugar bowl; green ground, 3 pcs. . . **475.00**

Tray, leaf-shaped, blue ground,
No. 479-14", 16½" l. **185.00**

Tray, leaf-shaped, terra cotta ground,
No. 479-14", 16½" l. **140.00**

Vase, 7" h., footed pillow-type w/base
handles, green ground, No. 206-7" . . **175.00**

Vase, 7" h., green ground, No. 132-7" . . **140.00**

Vase, 7" h.,squatty flat-shouldered
base centered by a tall cylindrical
neck, arched base handles, green
ground, No. 131-7" **135.00**

Vase, 7" h., squatty flat-shouldered
base centered by a tall cylindrical
neck, arched base handles, blue
ground, No. 131-7" **158.00**

Vase, 7" h., terra cotta ground,
No. 132-7" **140.00**

Vase, 8½" h., a disc foot & short
pedestal support a tall slightly
swelled cylindrical body w/a thin-
rolled rim, low curved handles from
mid-body to the base of the
pedestal, terra cotta ground,
No. 133-8" **130.00**

Vase, 8½" h., a disc foot & short
pedestal support a tall slightly
swelled cylindrical body w/a thin-
rolled rim, low curved handles from
mid-body to the base of the
pedestal, blue ground, No. 133-8". . **158.00**

Vase, 9½" h., footed waisted
cylindrical body w/low side
handles, blue ground, No. 135-9" . . **215.00**

Vase, 9½" h., footed waisted
cylindrical body w/low side
handles, terra cotta ground,
No. 135-9" **145.00**

Vase, 10" h., bulbous base tapering
to a tall trumpet neck, low curved
handles at center of the sides, terra
cotta ground, No. 137-10" **195.00**

Vase, 10" h., handles at midsection,
cylindrical w/slightly bulging base,
terra cotta ground, No. 138-10". . . . **225.00**

Vase, 10" h., handles at midsection,
cylindrical w/slightly bulging base,
blue ground, No. 138-10" **245.00**

Vase, 12" h., wide disk foot below the
tall trumpet-form body, low base
handles, terra cotta ground,
No. 139-12" **225.00**

Vase, 15" h., floor-type, blue ground,
No. 141-15" **368.00**

Vase, 15" h., floor-type, terra cotta
ground, No. 141-15" **795.00**

Vase, 18" h., floor-type, blue ground,
No. 142-18" **775.00**

Wall pocket, pointed conical form
w/base handles, green ground,
No. 1297-8", 8" h. **295.00**

Wall pocket, pointed conical form
w/base handles, terra cotta ground,
No. 1297-8", 8" h. **245.00**

Window box, green ground,
No. 1393-8", 8" l. **165.00**

ROYAL BAYREUTH

*Good china in numerous patterns and
designs has been made at the Royal Bayreuth
factory in Tettau, Germany since 1794. Listings
below are by the company's lines, plus
miscellaneous pieces. Interest in this china
remains at a peak and prices continue to rise.
Pieces listed carry the company's blue mark
except where noted otherwise.*

Royal Bayreuth Mark

DEVIL & CARDS

Creamer, full-bodied red devil **$285.00**

Devil & Cards Creamer

Creamer (ILLUS.) **175.00**

MOTHER-OF-PEARL

Creamer, Murex Shell patt., white
pearlized finish, 4½" h. **175.00**
Mustard jar, cov., Murex Shell patt.
white pearlized finish, 3½" h. **165.00**
Nappy, Poppy mold, white satin **110.00**

ROSE TAPESTRY

Creamer, ovoid body w/flared base &
long pinched spout, three-color
roses, 3½" h. **193.00**

Rose Tapestry Creamer

Creamer, swelled cylindrical body
w/a long pinched spout, angled
loop handle, 4" h. (ILLUS.) **193.00**
Dish, leaf-shaped, 3-color roses, 5" l. . . **180.00**
Plate, 6" d. **120.00**
Plate, 10½" d., overall colorful roses
w/four gilded scrolls around the
rims **138.00**
Vase, 7" h., bulbous ovoid body
tapering to a short tiny flared neck . . **275.00**

SAND BABIES

Trivet. **95.00**

SNOW BABIES

Pitcher, 3½" h. **75.00**

MISCELLANEOUS

Cake Plate with Polar Bears

Cake plate, decorated w/snowy
scene & two polar bears, gold
trimmed scalloped border
(ILLUS.) **1,900.00**
Candleholder, figural Bassett hound,
brown **425.00**
Candleholder, figural rose **600.00**
Compote, open, pastoral cow scene . . **110.00**
Creamer, figural alligator **323.00**
Creamer, figural apple **100.00**
Creamer, figural black cat **245.00**
Creamer, figural butterfly, open wings . . **225.00**
Creamer, figural cat handle **295.00**
Creamer, figural coachman **265.00**
Creamer, figural crow, brown beak . . **150.00**
Creamer, figural dachshund **225.00**
Creamer, figural lamplighter **250.00**
Creamer, figural lemon **150.00**
Creamer, figural monkey **400.00**
Creamer, figural mountain goat **275.00**
Creamer, figural owl **225.00**
Creamer, figural parakeet, green **250.00**
Creamer, figural poodle, black **245.00**
Creamer, figural poodle, grey **225.00**
Creamer, figural rooster **375.00**
Creamer, figural seal **250.00**
Creamer, figural strawberry **150.00**

Figural Trout Creamer

Creamer, figural trout, standing on
tail, shaded brown to white
w/reddish dots (ILLUS.) **2,090.00**

Creamer, figural clown, orange outfit, 3⅝" h. (minor enamel flakes) **358.00**

Creamer, figural Murex Shell, colored glaze, 3¾" h. **150.00**

Creamer, figural lobster, 4" h. **75.00**

Creamer & open sugar bowl, each decorated w/a mountain landscape w/a boy & donkey, 3" h., pr. **175.00**

Cup & saucer, floral decoration on the inside & outside, gold handle on cup, scalloped standard saucer, ca. 1916 . . . . **22.00**

Dresser tray, rectangular w/rounded corners, "tapestry" decoration of a young courting couple wearing early 19th c. attire, 11½" l. **248.00**

Royal Bayreuth Flower Holder

Flower holder, bulbous ovoid body w/domed flower holder top w/holes, color Hunt Scene decoration, 3¾" h. (ILLUS.) **190.00**

Hatpin holder, footed baluster-form body w/a scalloped rim & top pierced w/holes, "tapestry" design of a youth & maiden in early 19th c. costume, 4½" h. **303.00**

Mug, beer, figural elk **325.00**

Pipe holder, figural Bassett hound, black **395.00**

Pitcher, milk, figural coachman **300.00**

Pitcher, milk, figural dachshund **425.00**

Pitcher, water, figural robin **550.00**

Pitcher, 5" h., double handles, scene of fisherman in boat w/sails **125.00**

Figural Sunflower Pitcher

Pitcher, water, 6½" h., figural sunflower (ILLUS.) **4,450.00**

Pitcher, 6¾"h., wide ovoid body w/a flaring lightly scalloped base & a long pinched spout, tapestry finish w/a color landscape "Don Quixote" scene **523.00**

Pitcher, 7½" h., figural Conch Shell, brownish amethyst & yellow mottled body, orange angled coral handle **303.00**

Plate, 9" d., Cavalier Musicians scene . . **75.00**

Relish dish, figural Murex shell **175.00**

Salt & pepper shakers, figural Poppy, red, pr. **295.00**

String holder, hanging-type, figure rooster head **620.00**

Sugar bowl, cov., figural rose **250.00**

Teapot, cov., figural orange **350.00**

Vase, bud, 4½" h., two handles, Babes in Wood scene, cobalt blue & white **170.00**

Vase, 7" h., "tapestry," a bulbous ovoid body w/the rounded shoulder centering a tiny flared neck, a shaded pastel ground centered on one side w/a three-quarters length portrait of a lady in 18th c. attire w/a large feathered hat & large muff, on the reverse w/a landscape scene **550.00**

Vase, 8¼" h., footed squatty bulbous bottom tapering to a tall waisted base w/a gently scalloped flaring rim, polychrome boy & two donkeys decoration **165.00**

Vase, 9" h., tall slender waisted cylindrical body w/a gently scalloped flaring rim, three long green scroll & bead loop handles down the sides, the top body w/a band decorated w/a toasting Cavaliers scene in color on one side & "Ye Old Bell" scene on the other, the lower body all in dark green, ca. 1902 . . . . **138.00**

ROYAL BONN & BONN

Bonn and subsequently Royal Bonn china were produced in Bonn, Germany, in a manufactory established in 1755. Later wares made there are often marked Mehlem or bear the initials FM or a castle mark. Most wares were of the hand-painted type. Clock cases were also made in Bonn.

Royal Bonn & Bonn Mark

Centerpiece, bowl-form h.p w/flowers outlined in raised gold against a matte cream ground, brushed gold rims, late 19th c., 13½" l., 6" h. **$400.00**

Ornate Royal Bonn Clock

Clock, mantel-type, upright ornately scroll-molded case w/a scroll cartouche crest above the round enameled dial w/Arabic numerals & a gilt-metal bezel, waisted scroll-molded sides & floral & scrolling leaf-decorated lower front, on mold hoof feet, late 19th - early 20th c., 15½" h. (ILLUS.). **1,035.00**

Ewer, slender ovoid shouldered body tapering to a short slender neck w/a tall upright petal-form spout & a high arched gilt handle, the cream ground decorated w/polychrome flowers & gilt trim, late 19th c., 12½" h. **110.00**

Vase, 8¼" h., spherical body w/a short cylindrical neck, decorated w/a painted central vignette of a female surrounded by a floral landscape, printed mark, ca. 1900 . . **575.00**

Vase, 8½" h., tapering cylindrical body w/a short flaring neck, overall sand tapestry decoration, four tall arch-topped narrow panels w/a cream ground decorated w/multicolored scrolls & blossoms, dividing bands in dark maroon w/gold trim & patterned gold around the shoulder & neck, a narrow & white chain band around the base, one in gold on maroon, the other w/maroon on green, marked, ca. 1890 . . . . **330.00**

ROYAL DUX

This factory in Bohemia was noted for the figural porcelain wares in the Art Nouveau style which were exported around the turn of the century. Other notable figural pieces were produced through the 1930s and the factory was nationalized after World War II.

Royal Dux Marks

Royal Dux Figural Bowl & Compote

Bowl, 18½" l., figural, oval shell-form bowl w/sloping rim molded w/water plants & a fishing net w/the figure of an Art Nouveau maiden tending the next seated at the upper rim, naturalistic coloring, impressed mark, early 20th c. (ILLUS. left). . . **$489.00**

Centerpiece, figural, a rectangular round-edged platform base molded at the corners w/olive brown branches & molded on the top to represent a pond w/the figures of two young girls, one kneeling & the other sitting & pulling a large jug out of the water, jug & girls' costumes in golden brown w/pastel floral trim on a cream ground, pink triangle mark, 12½" l., 10" h. (minor floral flakes) **770.00**

Compote, 14½" h., figural, the top molded as a conch-type shell w/an Art Nouveau maiden seated at one end, raised on a wave-molded pedestal base w/another figure below the bowl, naturalistic coloring, impressed mark, early 20th c. (ILLUS. right) **748.00**

Compote, 20¼" h., figural, the wide shallow rounded bowl molded w/flowers & leaves & pierced branch handles raised on a tall spiral-twisted tree trunk-form

Tall Figural Royal Dux Compote

central pedestal surrounded by three dancing Art Nouveau maidens, delicate coloring, impressed & printed marks, early 20th c. (ILLUS.) **633.00**

Figure of a lady w/a harp, incised scroll banding on the raised base, impressed mark, early 20th c., 14¼" h. **173.00**

Royal Dux "Tragedy" Figure

Figure of "Tragedy," a standing classical woman wearing a flowing salmon robe trimmed w/gilding & falling from her right shoulder, a laurel wreath in her hair, beside a column on an architectural plinth, holding an actor's mask in one hand & a dagger in the other, some minute chips, early 20th c., 16⅝" h. (ILLUS.) **1,035.00**

Royal Dux Shepherd & Shepherdess

Figures of a shepherd & shepherdess, each standing beside a goat, raised on a rectangular plinth w/notched corners, colored in moss green & tan, pr. (ILLUS.) **1,250.00**

Model of a bird, perched on stylized thistles on a domed foot, decorated in shades of yellow & brown, 5⅝" h. **83.00**

Vase, 19¼" h., bisque, figural, an Art Nouveau style female figure on one side of the leaf- and floral-molded body, impressed mark, early 20th c. **288.00**

ROYAL RUDOLSTADT

This factory began as a faience pottery established in 1720. E. Bohne made hard paste porcelain wares from 1852 to 1920, when the factory became a branch of Heubach Brothers. The factory is still producing in the former East Germany.

Royal Rudolstadt Mark

Bust of an old woman, wearing a polk bonnet & shawl around her shoulders, a small jar in one hand, raised on a square waisted plinth w/scroll feet, shaded beige glaze, 19th c., 7" h. **$138.00**

Ewer, ivory ground decorated w/multicolored floral sprays strewn around the sides, gold scroll handle, marked **138.00**

Ewer, a narrow footring below the wide squatty bulbous lobed base below a deeply waisted band below an lobed conical shoulder to the tall slightly tapering ribbed & ringed columnar neck w/an upright pointed split spout, long angled bamboo handle from top of neck to shoulder, creamy ground w/all ribbing outlined in gold & delicate painted florals around the lower waisted band, signed, 15" h. **220.00**

Ewer, bulbous body w/cylindrical neck & ribbed angular handle, the body decorated w/fall-colored branch flowers w/gold trim on an ivory ground, autumn green swirl neck band w/lilac rings, peach-colored handle, marked, 15" h. . . . **121.00**

Vase, 12¼" h., bulbous ovoid shoulder body w/overall swirled ribbing, a small domed section at the base of the cylindrical molded swirl & ring neck topped by a scalloped & reticulated cupped rim, ornate flattened pierced scroll gold handles flanking the neck, creamy beige ground, the body decorated w/a large bouquet of purple flowers w/golden leaves & stems, late 19th c. **193.00**

ROYAL VIENNA

The second factory in Europe to make hard paste porcelain was established in Vienna in 1719 by Claud Innocentius de Paquier. The factory underwent various changes of administration through the years and finally closed in 1865. Since then, however, the porcelain has been reproduced by various factories in Austria and Germany, many of which have also reproduced the early beehive mark. Early pieces, naturally, bring far higher prices than the later ones or the reproductions.

Royal Vienna Mark

Bust, "Child with Bonnet," relief-molded floral ornamentation, mid-third quarter 19th c., Austria, 5¾" h. . . . **$110.00**

Cabinet cups, covers & underplates, the slightly flaring cylindrical cup w/two gilt scroll side handles & a domed cover w/a gold knop finial, the round dished underplate w/a central raised cylindrical reticulated ring for holding the cup, the cup decorated w/a round color scene of classical figures framed by dark green & maroon w/gilt trim, the cover w/matching green, maroon & white panels w/gilt trim, underplate matching, blue overglaze shield mark, late 19th c., 2 sets **83.00**

Exquisite Royal Vienna Charger

Charger, round dished form w/wide flanged rim, dark greenish black ground, the center h.p. w/a color scene of a seated classical maiden being dressed by her three maids while Cupid holds up a string of pearls before her, the wide border w/ornate lacy gold trim w/reserves trimmed w/turquoise 'jeweling,' 16" d. (ILLUS.) **2,750.00**

Chocolate pot, cov., tall cylindrical form gilted & painted on a cobalt blue ground w/an oval reserve & gilded foliage, shield mark, 19th c., 8¾" h. (minor wear) **978.00**

Elegant Royal Vienna Figure

Figure of a lady, standing elegant lady in 18th c. dress, wide flower-decorated gown, holding a Pug dog at her waist w/another peeking out from under the gown, raised on a waisted plinth base, underglaze-blue beehive mark, 8" h. (ILLUS.) . . **460.00**

Model of a buffalo, painted green w/brown highlights, early 20th c., 11" l. **460.00**

Plate, 9½" d., the wide rim in blackish green ornately decorated w/small gold panels of either a wreathed crown or crossed military emblems alternating w/long panels of pointed arches w/delicate scrolling trim, the center h.p. w/a colorful battlefront scene apparently depicting Napoleon on horseback surrounded by officers on foot, a fallen horse in the foreground, marked **440.00**

Vase, 5⅛" h., Classical Grecian motif revolving around Neptune on entire body w/red, pink & tan borders & gold trim, late 19th c., Austria **155.00**

Tall Royal Vienna Floor Vase

Vase, floor-type, 33" h., tall classical urn-form, the ovoid body painted in the center w/an oval reserve framing a half-length portrait of a young dark-haired woman wearing an off-the-shoulder gown & holding flowers, ornate overall large gilt flowers & leaves on a green, blue & lavender mottled ground, wide cylindrical neck w/flaring rim, ornate gold inwardly scrolled shoulder handles, the body raised on a slender gold-decorated

pedestal on a high round plinth base w/further gold florals & a molded leaf band, factory marks, ca. 1900, slight wear (ILLUS.) . . . **7,475.00**

ROYAL WORCESTER

This porcelain has been made by the Royal Worcester Porcelain Co. at Worcester, England, from 1862 to the present. Royal Worcester is distinguished from those wares made at Worcester between 1751 and 1862 that are referred to as only Worcester by collectors.

Royal Worcester Marks

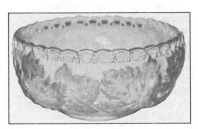

Royal Worcester Bowl with Leaves

Bowl, 9" d., 4½" h., footed deep rounded wide body w/a pierced arched lattice gilt rim above basketweave and grape leaf-molded exterior, beige ground w/the leaves shading from lavender pink to green, date mark for 1896 (ILLUS.) **$295.00**

Cracker jar, cov., ribbed barrel shape, ivory ground decorated w/colorful scattered flowers w/gilt highlights, maroon mark, impressed "#1282," 7½" h. **275.00**

Cracker jar, cover & underplate, barrel-shaped melon-lobed body w/a small low domed cover w/angular loop gold handle, creamy ground decorated around the body w/clusters of pastel flowers w/further flowers on the cover, cover gold rim band, scalloped gold rim band on body & narrow band at the base, matching round underplate, No. 1412, the set **1,210.00**

Ewer, bulbous ivory body w/a slender bronze-colored figural dragon handle wrapping around the neck, the body decorated w/scattered colorful floral sprigs, maroon mark, 7" h. **275.00**

Ewer, footed bulbous ovoid body tapering to a short tapering cylindrical neck w/an upright split spout, gold ribbed C-scroll handle, beige matte ground decorated overall w/delicate pastel florals w/gold trim, Rd. 29115, base incised "R3-6-15," 7¾" h. **193.00**

Figure, "First Dance," No. 3629, lavender dress, pink stole **135.00**

Figure, "Grandmother's Dress," little girl standing wearing a long dress & gold cap, designed by F.G. Doughty, Rd. 799938, 6½" h. **248.00**

Figure, standing Egyptian female musican holding a tambourine, standing beside a short obelisk, round rockwork base, pastel naturalistic tones on a cream ground, No. 1084, date mark for 1886, name "Hadley" incised on top of the base, 13" h. **660.00**

Pitcher, 6" h., jug-type, squatty bulbous molded basketweave body tapering to a short neck & upright arched spout, gold neck ring continues to large angular gold bamboo handle, cream ground w/a relief-molded gold lizard on the sides, No. 1714, ca. 1912 .... **385.00**

Fine Royal Worcester Plate

Plate, 10½" d., lightly scalloped edge on the wide flanged rim, h.p. overall in color w/a scene of Scottish mountain cattle in a hazy mountainous landscape, by John Stinton, mounted in a shadowbox frame, ca. 1900 (ILLUS.) **1,540.00**

Sugar bowl, open, Wicker patt., footed squatty bulbous body w/a low rolled rim, No. 1881, 3½" d., 2" h. **39.00**

Vase, 8" h., swelled cylindrical body, ivory ground molded w/Oriental dancing figures, Ming trees & a mountainscape, raised mark **209.00**

Vase, 8¼" h., 'Nautilus Shell on Coral,' a large lustre-glazed parian shell-form flower holder raised on a molded bronze-colored coral stem w/molded seaweed & small shells, domed rockwork base w/gilt-trimmed reticulated border band, No. 1145, ca. 1886 .... **880.00**

Vase, 12" h., bulbous body w/a tall 'stick' neck, decorated w/assorted multicolored garden flowers strewn upon an ivory ground, reticulated floral handles trimmed w/gold, molded gilt netted neck, maroon mark, impressed "#942" **248.00**

Vase, 12" h., Sabina Ware, a small footring supporting the wide squatty bulbous base tapering sharply to a tall slender cylindrical neck swelled at the top, bluish green polychrome decoration, glossy glaze **220.00**

Vase, 14½" h., baluster-form w/a flaring foot below the bulbous wide ovoid body tapering sharply to a slender cylindrical neck topped by a deep cupped rim, integral pointed tab reticulated handles at the shoulder w/gold trim, gold trim teardrop band around the rim & gold panels & trim on the lower neck, all w/a creamy beige ground, the main body decorated w/large maroon & gold fern leaves, date mark for 1878 .... **660.00**

Vase, 16¾" h., footed bottle-form, the low flaring foot below the tapering ovoid body w/a tall flaring 'stick'

Tall Royal Worcester Vase with Bird

neck flanked by pointed pierced long tab handles, the body decorated w/a large bird perched on a branch before a moonlit sky, gold handles & gilt & enamel-trimmed upper neck & footring, retailed by Bigelow, Kennard & Co., Boston, late 19th c. (ILLUS.) . . . **920.00**

R.S. PRUSSIA & RELATED WARES

R.S. Prussia & Related Wares Marks

Ornately decorated china marked "R.S. Prussia" and "R.S. Germany" continues to grow in popularity. According to the Third Series of Mary Frank Gaston's Encyclopedia of R.S. Prussia (Collector Books, Paducah, Kentucky), these marks were used by the Reinhold Schlegelmilch porcelain factories located in Suhl in the Germanic regions known as "Prussia" prior to World War I, and in Tillowitz, Silesia, which became part of Poland after World War II. Other marks sought by collectors include "R.S. Suhl," "R.S. " steeple or church marks, and "R.S. Poland."

The Suhl factory was founded by Reinhold Schlegelmilch in 1869 and closed in 1917. The Tillowitz factory was established in 1895 by Erhard Schlegelmilch, Reinhold's son. This china customarily bears the phrase "R.S. Germany" and "R.S. Tillowitz." The Tillowitz factory closed in 1945, but it was re-opened for a few years under Polish administration. The "R.S. Poland" mark is attributed to that later time period.

Prices are high and collectors should beware of the forgeries that sometimes find their way onto the market. Mold names and numbers are taken from Mary Frank Gaston's books on R.S. Prussia.

We illustrate three typical markings. The "R.S. Prussia" and "R.S. Suhl" marks have been reproduced so buy with care.

Collectors are also interested in the porcelain products made by the Erdmann Schlegelmilch factory. This factory was founded by three brothers in Suhl in 1861. They named the factory in honor of their father, Erdmann Schlegelmilch. A variety of marks incorporating the "E.S." initials were used. The factory closed circa 1935. The Erdmann Schlegelmilch factory was an earlier and entirely separate business from the Reinhold Schlegelmilch factory. The two were not related to each other.

R.S. GERMANY

Cheese server, a slightly dished round plate centered by a short pedestal supporting a small dished plate, each section decorated w/large blossoms joined by green tendrils on a shaded ground, 8½" d. **$39.00**

Chocolate set: cov. pot & five cups & saucers; white flower decoration, blue mark, the set **450.00**

Lilac-decorated R.S. Germany Plate

Plate, 11¼" d., smooth round form w/gold rim band, white, green & pink lilac clusters between curved panels of small gold leaves on a pale green ground (ILLUS.). **110.00**

R.S. PRUSSIA

Bowl, 10" d., Icicle mold (Mold 7), red & gold border around the creamy satin interior decorated w/large gold roses **495.00**

Bowl, 10" d., Mold 202, gold beaded rim, double swans center scene in shades of beige & white, unmarked **165.00**

Bowl, 10½" d., Mold 101, Tiffany finish around rim, orchid & cream trim on molded border blossoms, central bouquet of pink, yellow & white roses w/green leaves **248.00**

R.S. Prussia Swans Decorated Bowl

Bowl, 11" d., Icicle mold (Mold 7),
Swans decoration w/clouds &
autumn foliage in the background
(ILLUS.). **500.00**
Bowl, 11" d., Mold 155, Sheepherder
scene decoration in shades of
green w/gold & pink. **220.00**

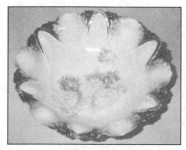

R.S. Prussia Roses & Snowballs Bowl

Bowl, 11" d., Mold 96, pink roses &
white snowballs decoration on a
pale creamy yellow ground
w/shaded dark green & white rim
panels w/shadow flowers (ILLUS.). . . **400.00**
Bread tray, Mold 428, wide oval form
w/low flared sides w/a narrow
flanged rim, pierced end rim
handles, decorated w/a large
cluster of roses in peach, pink &
green, traces of gold edging,
9 x 12½" **154.00**
Cake plate, open handles, Mold 256,
satin ground decorated w/flowers in
blue, pink & white w/gold trim,
11½" d. **110.00**
Celery dish, Mold 25, oblong,
pearlized finish w/Surreal Dogwood
blossoms w/gold trim, 6 x 12¼" . . . **110.00**
Chocolate set: tankard-style covered
pot & six cups & saucers; Mold
510, laurel chain decoration,
the set **1,100.00**
Cracker jar, cov., Mold 540a, beige
satin ground w/floral decoration in
orchid, yellow & gold, 9½" w.

handle to handle, overall 5½" h. . . . **303.00**
Creamer & cov. sugar bowl, Mold
505, pink & yellow roses, pr. **135.00**
Hair receiver, cov., Mold 814,
Surreal Dogwood decoration **150.00**
Lemonade pitcher, Mold 501, relief-
molded turquoise blue on white
w/pink Surreal blossoms & fans
around scalloped top & base,
unmarked, 6" h. **248.00**
Nut dish, Carnation mold (Mold 28),
floral decoration w/pearlized finish . . **200.00**

Tankard Pitcher with LeBrun Portrait

Pitcher, tankard, 15" h., Mold 517,
bronzed finish rim & base bands
centering a LeBrun II portrait
against a shaded brown & green
ground, gold handle (ILLUS.). . . . **3,000.00**
Plate, 8½" d., Medallion mold (Mold
14), Reflecting Lilies patt. **135.00**
Plate, 8½" d., Mold 300, beaded gold
band around the lobed rim, Old Mill
Scene decoration in center against
a shaded dark green to yellow &
blue ground **138.00**

OTHER MARKS

Prov. Saxe Scenic Bowl

Bowl, 10" d., Irregular Border mold, colorful magenta border band around gold-bordered pointed dark green panels, the center w/a round reserve w/a colorful romantic scene w/18th c. lovers, Prov. Saxe (ILLUS.) **165.00**

R.S. Suhl Coffeepot from a Set

Coffee set: cov. coffeepot, cov. sugar bowl, creamer & six cups & saucers; the tall ovoid pot w/a long swan's-neck spout, domed cover w/flame finial & ornate scrolled handle, each piece decorated w/an oval color central reserve w/a classical scene based on Angelica Kauffmann, borders in dark burgundy & green on white w/scattered delicate gold trim,coffeepot 9" h., R.S. Suhl, the set (ILLUS. of coffeepot) **1,675.00**

R.S. Suhl Ornate Cup & Saucer

Cup & saucer, deep bell-form cup w/ornate pierced scrolling handle, the sides decorated w/an oval reserve w/a color scene of an 18th c. courting couple, within a maroon panel w/deep red & green border bands, overall delicate gilt trim, saucer 4⅞" d., cup 2¼" h., R.S. Suhl (ILLUS.) **100.00**

Match holder, hanging-type on attached backplate decorated w/a scene of a man w/mug of beer & pipe (E.S. Prov. Saxe) **125.00**

Plate, 7" d., scene of girl w/rose, trimmed w/gold flowers, beading & a burgundy border **85.00**

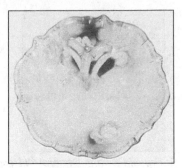

R.S. Poland Center-handle Server

Server, center handle w/three loops, dished paneled base w/a lightly scalloped rim, lavender & pink roses & green leaves on a pale creamy green ground & gilt border trim, 11" d., 8" h., R.S. Poland (ILLUS.) **515.00**

R.S. Tillowitz Golden Pheasant Vase

Vase, 6" h., simple ovoid body w/flaring rim, decorated in color w/golden pheasants against a dark green shaded forest background, R.S. Tillowitz - Silesia (ILLUS.) **260.00**

Vase, 9¼" h., gently tapering cylindrical body w/a wide cupped rim w/gilt scalloped rim, pierced gold serpentine handles from rim to center of sides, decorated around the body w/large blossoms in purple, pink, yellow & green on a shaded brownish green ground (Prove. Saxe) **110.00**

RUSSEL WRIGHT DESIGNS

The innovative dinnerwares designed by Russel Wright and produced by various companies beginning in the late 1930s were an immediate success with a society that was turning to a more casual and informal lifestyle. His designs, with their flowing lines and unconventional shapes, were produced in many different colors which allowed the hostess to arrange a creative table. Although not antique, these designs, which we list below by line and manufacturer, are highly collectible. In addition to dinnerwares, Wright was also known as a trend-setter in the design of furniture, glassware, lamps, fabric and a multitude of other household goods.

Russel Wright Design Marks

AMERICAN MODERN (Steubenville Pottery Co.)

Bowl, fruit, lug handle, coral $15.00
Bowl, fruit, lug handle, granite grey ... 10.00
Bowl, soup, lug handle, granite grey .. 10.00
Butter dish, cov., granite grey 245.00
Casserole, cov., stick handle, coral ... 25.00
Celery tray, slender oblong shape
  w/asymmetrical incurved sides,
  seafoam blue, 13" l. 18.00
Coffeepot, cov., demitasse, cedar
  green 150.00
Coffeepot, cov., demitasse, granite
  grey 250.00
Creamer, coral 12.00
Creamer & cov. sugar bowl, white,
  in original box, pr. 135.00
Cup & saucer, chartreuse 8.00
Cup & saucer, coral 9.00
Cup & saucer, granite grey 8.00
Cup & saucer, seafoam blue 9.00
Cup & saucer, demitasse, bean
  brown 26.00
Cup & saucer, demitasse,
  chartreuse 18.00
Pitcher, water, 12" h., bean brown ... 125.00
Pitcher, water, 12" h., granite grey ... 50.00
Plate, bread & butter, 6¼" d., coral ... 4.00
Plate, bread & butter, 6¼" d., granite
  grey 3.00
Plate, salad, 8" d., coral 12.00
Plate, dinner, 10" d., bean brown 12.00
Plate, dinner, 10" d., coral 10.00
Plate, dinner, 10" d., granite grey 7.00
Plate, dinner, 10" d., seafoam blue ... 7.00
Plate, chop, 13" sq., chartreuse 24.00
Plate, chop, 13" sq., granite grey 24.00
Platter, 13¾" l., oblong, coral 18.00
Relish dish, divided, raffia handle,
  chartreuse 225.00
Salt & pepper shakers, coral, pr. ... 12.00
Sugar bowl, cov., coral 15.00
Vegetable dish, open, oval,
  chartreuse, 10" l. 26.00

CASUAL CHINA (Iroquois China Company)

Bowl, cereal, ice blue 45.00
Carafe, cov., pink sherbet 225.00
Cup & saucer, cantaloupe 20.00
Mug, pink sherbet 85.00
Plate, bread & butter, 6" d.,
  cantaloupe 14.00
Plate, bread & butter, 6" d., pink
  sherbet 2.00
Plate, luncheon, 9" d., ice blue 5.00
Plate, dinner, 10" d., pink sherbet ... 6.00
Platter, 14½" l., pink sherbet 18.00
Vegetable bowl, cov., divided,
  avocado yellow............... 30.00
Vegetable bowl, cov., divided,
  nutmeg brown, 10" d. 40.00
Vegetable bowl, cov., divided, ripe
  apricot, 10" d. 40.00

SATSUMA

These decorated wares have been produced in Japan since the end of the 18th century. The early pieces are scarce and high-priced. Later Satsuma wares are plentiful and, with prices rising, as highly collectible as earlier pieces.

Tall Satsuma Vase

Vase, 22" h., deep rounded lower body below a wide flat shoulder centered by a tall cylindrical neck flanked by square bamboo-form handles wa bird perched on each, the rim formed into a pierced domed cage, decorated in low-relief w/chrysanthemums & leaves, Meiji Period, minor restoration to top cage (ILLUS.) $330.00
Vase, 43" h., elaborately decorated & ascribed to depict "Kaguyahima" (featuring Shogun w/Courtiers & Samurai), late 19th c., Japan (two minor chips on one handle)....... 850.00

Vases, 10¼" h., baluster-shaped,
cobalt blue ground decorated w/gilt
trim, the front w/a rectangular
polychrome landscape scene, late
19th - early 20th c., pr.
(gilt worn) **578.00**

SEVRES & SEVRES-STYLE

*Some of the most desirable porcelain ever
produced was made at the Sevres factory,
originally established at Vincennes, France, and
transferred, through permission of Madame de
Pompadour, to Sevres as the Royal Manufactory
about the middle of the 18th century. King Louis
XV took sole responsibility for the works in 1759
when production of hard plastic waste began.
Between 1850 and 1900, many biscuit and soft-
paste pieces were made again. Fine early pieces
are scarce and high-priced. Many of those
available today are late productions. The various
Sevres marks have been copied and pieces listed
as "Sevres-Style" are similar to actual Sevres
wares, but not necessarily from that factory.
Three of the many Sevres marks are illustrated
below.*

Sevres & Sevres Marks

Sevres-Style Breakfast Set

Breakfast set: cov. teapot, cov.
sugar bowl, creamer & two coffee
cups & saucers; Sevres-Style,
slightly flaring cylindrical forms
w/domed covers & pointed angled
gold handles, each decorated w/a
titled bust portrait, the teapot &
sugar w/a panel on the reverse
enclosing a lyre & weapons of war,
each panel gilt-framed against a
pink ground w/gilt laurel borders,
minor gilt wear, fake red printed
Sevres mark, second half 19th c.,
teapot 5½" h., the set
(ILLUS.) **$1,840.00**

Centerpiece, bisque, figural,
modeled as four youths in a
procession, each supporting a
basket & mounted to a free-form
base, impressed mark, early 20th
c., 20¼" l. **316.00**

Sevres Console Bowl with Ormolu

Console bowl, large oblong squatty
bulbous footed bowl decorated w/a
large colorful panel showing 18th c.
peasants in a landscape within gilt
borders & against a medium blue
ground w/gilt scroll trim, mounted
w/an ormolu scroll-pierced rim, end
handles & a footed flaring base,
19th c. (ILLUS.) **6,000.00**

Vase, bud, 6" h., Art Nouveau style
w/a gilt ground enameled
w/stylized leaf & flower designs,
printed mark, ca. 1900 . . . . **633.00**

Sevres Covered Vase with Cherubs

Vase, cov., 22" h., tall baluster-form,
the ovoid body painted w/winged
cherubs hovering w/garlands of
flowers on a white ground, the
waisted neck & domed cover
decorated in pink w/gilt trim, a gilt
ribbed pedestal & round foot raised
on a gilt-bronze squared footed
base, signed "PouPanger 1762,"
(ILLUS.) **3,795.00**

Very Large Scenic Sevres Vase

Vase, cov., 36" h., tall baluster-form, the ovoid body decorated w/a large oval reserve showing Venus holding a garland full of flowers w/two cupids & doves, the reverse w/a landscape reserve, ornate gilt trim on the celeste blue ground, the trumpet-form neck w/cameo-style portrait reserves, the domed, ribbed cover w/pine cone finial, on a rings waisted pedestal base painted w/ribs & gold trim, Chateau de Tuileries mark, 19th c. (ILLUS.) **5,175.00**

SHAWNEE

The Shawnee Pottery operated in Zanesville, Ohio, from 1937 until 1961. Much of the early production was sold to chain stores and mail-order houses including Sears, Roebuck, Woolworth and others. Planters, cookie jars and vases, along with the popular "Corn King" oven ware line, are among the collectible items which are plentiful and still reasonably priced. Reference numbers used here are taken from Mark E. Supnick's book, Collecting Shawnee Pottery, The Collector's Guide to Shawnee Pottery *by Duane and Janice Vanderbilt, or* Shawnee Pottery – An Identification & Value Guide *by Jim and Bev Mangus.*

Shawnee
U.S.A.

Shawnee Mark

Bank, figural Mugsey Dog, commemorative **$275.00**

Jo-Jo the Clown Cookie Jar

Cookie jar, figural Jo-Jo the Clown (ILLUS.) **500.00**
Cookie jar, figural Mugsey Dog **420.00**

Gold-decorated Puss 'n Boots

Cookie jar, figural Puss 'n Boots, floral decals & gold trim (ILLUS.) **425.00**
Cookie jar, figural Smiley Pig, decorated w/shamrocks, gold trim on base only **200.00**
Cookie jar, figural Smiley Pig, gold rose decoration **495.00**
Cookie jar, figural Smiley Pig, shamrock decoration **150.00**
Cookie jar, figural Winnie Pig, clover bud decoration **400.00**
Creamer, figural Little Boy Blue **150.00**
Creamer, figural Puss 'n Boots **75.00**
Creamer, figural Puss 'n Boots, heavy gold trim **240.00**
Creamer, figural sunflower **65.00**
Match box holder, embossed Fern patt. **115.00**
Pitcher, figural Chanticleer Rooster . . . **90.00**
Pitcher, figural Little Bo Peep, green decoration **100.00**
Pitcher, figural Little Boy Blue **130.00**
Pitcher, figural Smiley Pig, clover bud decoration **250.00**

Pitcher, figural Smiley Pig, peach
  flower decoration **195.00**
Pitcher, figural Smiley Pig, pink &
  maroon floral decoration **175.00**
Pitcher, milk, figural Smiley Pig,
  apple blossom decoration **185.00**
Pitcher, milk, figural Smiley Pig,
  three-flowers decoration **165.00**
Pitcher, figural Little Bo-Peep patt.,
  blue hat, 8" h. **135.00**
Planter, model of a black locomotive . . **50.00**
Planter, model of a grist mill, No.
  769 . . . . **26.00**
Planter, train engine & three cars,
  white decorated, 4 pcs. **325.00**
Salt & pepper shakers, figural Boy
  Blue & Bo Peep, pr. . . . . . . **35.00 to 50.00**
Salt & pepper shakers, figural
  Chanticleer Rooster, large, pr. **55.00**
Salt & pepper shakers, figural
  Chanticleer Rooster, small, pr. **40.00**
Salt & pepper shakers, figural Chef,
  "S" & "P" on top, gold trim, pr. **50.00**

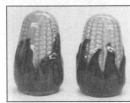

Corn King Shakers

Salt & pepper shakers, figural Corn
  King, No. 76, 3¼" h., pr.
  (ILLUS.). . . . . **25.00 to 30.00**
Salt & pepper shakers, figural Corn
  Queen, large, pr. **40.00**
Salt & pepper shakers, figural
  Cottage, pr. **275.00**
Salt & pepper shakers, figural Duck,
  pr. **45.00**
Salt & pepper shakers, figural Dutch
  Boy & Dutch Girl, large, pr. **65.00**
Salt & pepper shakers, figural Dutch
  Boy & Dutch Girl w/gold trim &
  decals, large, pr. **145.00**
Salt & pepper shakers, figural
  Farmer Pig, pr. **42.00**
Salt & pepper shakers, figural
  Flowerpot, pr. **24.00**
Salt & pepper shakers, figural Fruit,
  large pr. **35.00**
Salt & pepper shakers, figural Fruit,
  small, pr. **25.00**
Salt & pepper shakers, figural Jack
  & Jill, large, pr. **53.00**
Salt & pepper shakers, figural
  Lobster claw, pr. **30.00**

Salt & pepper shakers, figural
  Lobster, full body, pr. **125.00**
Salt & pepper shakers, figural Milk
  Can, pr. **43.00**
Salt & pepper shakers, figural
  Mugsey Dog, large
  pr. . . . . **165.00 to 200.00**
Salt & pepper shakers, figural Mugsey
  Dog, small, pr. **66.00**
Salt & pepper shakers, figural Owl,
  decorated w/gold trim, pr. **75.00**
Salt & pepper shakers, figural Owl,
  white w/blue eyes, pr. **55.00**
Salt & pepper shakers, figural
  Pennsylvania Dutch jugs, pr. **89.00**
Salt & pepper shakers, figural Puss
  'n Boots, regular decoration, pr. **38.00**
Salt & pepper shakers, figural Puss
  'n Boots, small, pr. **30.00**
Salt & pepper shakers, figural Puss
  'n Boots w/gold trim,
  pr. . . . . **110.00 to 120.00**
Salt & pepper shakers, figural "S" &
  "P," pr. . . . . **25.00 to 35.00**
Salt & pepper shakers, figural Sailor
  boy & girl, pr. **30.00**
Salt & pepper shakers, figural
  Smiley Pig, floral decals & gold
  trim, pr. **135.00**
Salt & pepper shakers, figural
  Smiley Pig & Winnie Pig, clover
  bud decoration, large, pr. **225.00**
Salt & pepper shakers, figural
  Smiley Pig & Winnie Pig, heart
  decoration, large, pr. **110.00**
Salt & pepper shakers, figural
  Stylized Black Cat, 2¼" h. & 4¼"h.,
  pr. **150.00**
Salt & pepper shakers, figural
  Sunflower, large pr. **45.00**
Salt & pepper shakers, figural Swiss
  Kids, large, pr. **60.00**
Salt & pepper shakers, figural
  Watering Can, pr. **19.00**
Salt & pepper shakers, figural
  Wheelbarrow, pr. **18.00**
Teapot, cov., figural Granny Ann **153.00**
Teapot, cov., Pennsylvania Dutch
  patt., 10 oz. **225.00**

SHELLEY CHINA

*Members of the Shelley family were in the
pottery business in England as early as the 18th
century. In 1872 Joseph Shelley formed a
partnership with James Wileman of Wileman &
Co. who operated the Foley China Works. The
Wileman & Co. name was used for the firm for*

the next fifty years, and between 1890 and 1910 the words "The Foley" appeared above conjoined "WC" initials.

Beginning in 1910 the Shelley family name in a shield appeared on wares, although the firm's official name was still Wileman & Co. The company's name was finally changed to Shelley in 1925 and then Shelley China Ltd. after 1965. The firm changed hands in the 1960s and became part of the Doulton Group in 1971.

At first only average quality earthenwares were produced but in the late 1890s new shapes and better quality decorations were used.

Bone china was introduced at Shelley before World War I and these fine dinnerwares became very popular in the United States and are increasingly popular today with collectors. Thin "eggshell china" teawares, miniatures and souvenir items were widely marketed during the 1920s and 1930s and are sought-after today.

Shelley China Mark

Bowl, cream soup, Begonia patt. **$35.00**
Cake plate, Anemone Bunch patt. . . . **155.00**
Cake plate, pedestal base, Regency
  patt. **125.00**
Cheese dish, cov., Cloisello patt. . . . **450.00**
Coffeepot, cov., Melody Chintz patt. . . **700.00**
Coffeepot, cov., Blue Rock patt.,
  8½" h. **695.00**
Creamer, Queen Anne patt., Sunrise
  shape, tall trees **120.00**
Creamer & open sugar bowl,
  Melody Chintz patt., pr. **200.00**
Cup & saucer, Begonia patt., Dainty
  shape. **59.00**
Cup & saucer, Blue Daisy patt. **65.00**
Cup & saucer, Blue Daisy patt.,
  Oleander shape **95.00**
Cup & saucer, Blue Rock patt. **45.00**
Cup & saucer, Crochet patt., pink &
  blue flower w/gold trim **50.00**
Cup & saucer, Dainty Blue patt., ... **50.00**
Cup & saucer, Dainty patt., black &
  gold exterior. **175.00**
Cup & saucer, Dainty Pink patt. **40.00**
Cup & saucer, demitasse, Harebell
  patt. **45.00**
Cup & saucer, demitasse, Rosebud
  patt. **45.00**
Cup & saucer, demitassse, Begonia
  patt., blue trim **58.00**
Cup & saucer, Heather patt., Perth
  shape. **55.00**
Cup & saucer, Melody patt. **103.00**

Cup & saucer, Rock Garden patt. **145.00**
Cup & saucer, Wild Anemone patt. **65.00**
Demitasse cup & saucer, Blue Rock
  patt. **50.00**
Demitasse cup & saucer, Dainty
  Blue patt. **50.00**
Demitasse set: creamer, open sugar
  & eight cups & saucers; Six Flutes
  patt., white & gold, ca. 1920s, the
  set **138.00**
Dish, oval, Blue Rock patt., 5½" l. **38.00**

Cape Gooseberry Luncheon Set

Luncheon set: six dessert plates, six
  tea cups & saucers, six demitasse
  cups & saucers, open sugar,
  creamer, waste bowl & handled
  cake plate; Cape Gooseberry patt.
  in white w/orange, green & yellow,
  conical cups & squared plates
  w/notched corners, marked, the
  set (ILLUS.) **275.00**
Mug, Poppy patt., blue **78.00**
Mug, Wild Anemone patt. **78.00**
Pin dish, Maytime patt. **50.00**
Pitcher, milk, Anemone Bunch patt.,
  ca. 1932 . . . . **125.00**
Plate, dinner, Sheraton patt. **55.00**
Plate, 7" d., Begonia patt. **36.00**
Plate, 7" d., Heather patt. **38.00**
Plate, 7" d., Tearose patt. **30.00**
Plate, 8" d., Melody patt. **125.00**
Plate, 8" d., Rock Garden patt. **125.00**
Sugar bowl, cov., Anemone Bunch
  patt., ca. 1932 . . . . **125.00**
Tea cup & saucer, Melody Chintz
  patt. **85.00**
Teapot, cov., individual size, Dainty
  Blue patt. **395.00**
Teapot, cov., Melody Chintz patt. . . . **850.00**

SLIPWARE

This term refers to ceramics, primarily redware, decorated by the application of slip, or semi-liquid paste made of clay. Such wares were made for decades in England and Germany and elsewhere on the Continent, and in the

Pennsylvania Dutch country and elsewhere in the United States. Today, contemporary copies of early Slipware items are featured in numerous decorator magazines and offered for sale in gift catalogs.

Bowl, 13" d., 2¾" h., wide shallow form w/coggled rim, three triple-bands of wavy yellow slip across the interior, 19th c. **$770.00**

Slipware Jar with Sgraffito Decoration

Jar, cov., redware, bulbous ovoid body w/applied branch handles w/tooled flower ends at sides & flat lid w/applied tooled handle, yellow slip w/sgraffito decoration, wide bands of vertical lines at top & base w/center band of continuous squggled design, wear, edge chips & hairlines in jar, 8" h. (ILLUS.) **715.00**

Slipware Loaf Dish

Loaf dish, rectangular w/coggle wheel rim, redware, w/yellow triple-quill slip decoration, Pennsylvania, 19th c., 11¼ x 16" (ILLUS.) **1,725.00**
Pie plate, coggled rim, wavy three-line yellow slip stripe across the center, yellow slip feather three at opposite edges, 19th c., 9¾" d. **220.00**

SPATTERWARE

This ceramic ware takes its name from the "spattered" decoration, in various colors, generally used to trim pieces hand-painted with rustic center designs of flowers, birds, houses, etc. Popular in the early 19th century, most was imported from England.

Related wares, called "stick spatter," had free-hand designs applied with pieces of cut sponge attached to sticks, hence the name. Examples date from the 19th and early 20th century and were produced in England, Europe and America.

Some early spatter-decorated wares were marked by the manufacturers, but not many. 20th century reproductions are also sometimes marked, including those produced by Boleslaw Cybis

Bowl, 6½" d., Schoolhouse patt., free-hand red & yellow building w/green spatter on a black field & blue spatter flanking (hairline) **$1,150.00**
Bowl, 7" d., Castle patt., free-hand castle in grey, black & red w/a green spatter ground & trees & blue spatter background **460.00**

Rainbow Spatter Compote

Compote, footed, Rainbow spatter, octagonal w/broad molded rim, decorated w/alternating blue & red bands with center red star decoration, 11½" (ILLUS.) **1,725.00**
Creamer, child's, Townhouse patt., free-hand black house w/blue doors & trellis flanked by green spatter trees & foreground, overall red & purple spatter ground, 5" h. **2,530.00**
Cup & saucer, handleless, child's, Tree patt., light green-leaved tree w/black line trunk on a green ground, blue spatter border **259.00**

Cup & saucer, handleless, Rooster patt., free-hand blue, red & yellow bird on an overall blue spatter ground **1,150.00**

Cup & saucer, handleless, Shed patt., free-hand red shed w/yellow door & blue roof, red spatter background **633.00**

Cup & saucer, handleless, Deer patt., central brown transfer-printed & spatter deer on saucer, green spatter background on saucer & cup, saucer 5½" d. **1,495.00**

Cup & saucer, handleless, Peafowl patt., free-hand bird in red, yellow & blue perched on a black branch, border of alternating red & purple spatter banding, saucer 5¾" d. **863.00**

Cup & saucer, handleless, Chevron patt., the cup w/alternating red & green chevron design, the saucer w/a star design, saucer 6" d. **3,738.00**

Cup & saucer, handleless, Thistle patt., free-hand red thistle & leaf stem, alternating bands of red & yellow spatter border, 6" d. **1,840.00**

Mug, cylindrical w/C-form leaftip handle, Peafowl patt., free-hand bird in red, yellow, green & black, blue spatter overall background, 3 1/8" h. (stains) **715.00**

Pitcher, 7¾" h., paneled body, Rainbow spatter w/alternating bands of blue & red, applied handle **1,380.00**

Plate, child's, 5" d., Schoolhouse patt., free-hand red school on a brown & green spatter ground within a red spatter border **4,140.00**

Plate, toddy, 6½" d., paneled rim, Tulip patt., free-hand green, purple, black & yellow flower, red spatter rim band (minor wear) **770.00**

Plate, 7¼" d., Parrot patt., free-hand bird in green, red & black w/a blue spatter border (minor age crack) **345.00**

Plate, 7½" d., Peafowl patt., free-hand red, green & blue bird on a black branch w/green leaves, red spatter border **575.00**

Plate, 7½" d., Rooster patt., free-hand red, blue & yellow bird w/yellow fence flanked by green spatter trees, blue spatter border w/black banding **489.00**

Plate, 7½" d., Schoolhouse patt., free-hand schoolhouse scene in red, dark brown & green w/a red spatter border **1,955.00**

Schoolhouse Plate

Plate, 8" d., Schoolhouse patt., blue school on brown field, green tree, red spatter border, ca. 1840 (ILLUS.) **863.00**

Plate, 8" d., Tulip patt., paneled rim, free-hand blossom in red, green & black, yellow spatter border band (wear, stains) **1,980.00**

Plate, 9" w., Tulip patt., paneled sides, free-hand central flower in red, green & black, red spatter border (stains, small flakes, short hairline) **248.00**

Plate, dinner, 9½" d., Peafowl patt., free-hand green, yellow & red bird on a black branch, blue spatter border **690.00**

Plates, dinner, 8½" d., Wigwam patt., red wigwams flanked by red spatter trees, set of 5 . . . . **1,380.00**

Spatter Fort Platter

Platter, 13½" l., octagonal, Fort patt., center decoration of brown & black fort flanked by green trees on a grassy field, blue spatter rim, ca. 1840 (ILLUS.) **2,300.00**

Soup plate, flanged rim, Rainbow spatter border, alternating bands of blue & black, 8¼" d. (minor edge flakes) **935.00**

Sugar bowl, cov., Parrot patt., free-hand bird in red, green & black, crimson red & blue spattered border, 4½" h. **403.00**

Sugar bowl, cov., Castle patt., free-hand grey, black & red castle flanked by green spatter trees w/black branches against a blue spatter ground, domed cover w/blue & green spatter, 5" h. **518.00**

Sugar bowl, cov., Thistle patt., free-hand red thistle w/green leaves, alternating bands of grey & yellow spatter, matching bands on the domed cover, 5" h. (repaired) **1,840.00**

Tea set, child's: cov. teapot, cov. sugar bowl, creamer & three handleless cups & one saucer; Peafowl patt., free-hand bird in blue, yellow & red against a green spatter ground, edged in ochre, the set (repairs) **978.00**

Teapot, cov., child's, bulbous footed body w/flaring rim & inset cover w/button knop, swan's-neck spout & C-form handle, Townhouse patt. free-hand house in black & blue flanked by green spatter trees in foreground, overall red spatter background, 3¼" h. (repairs) **1,265.00**

Stick & Cut Sponge Spatter

Plate, 8½" d., the center h.p. w/a large red rose w/green leaves & blue & black trim, the flanged rim w/a cut-sponge figure-eight design in blue **275.00**

Plate, 8½" d., the center painted w/a large red rose w/green leaves & blue & black trim, the flanged rim w/a cut-sponge figure-eight design band in green **303.00**

Plate, 9¼" d., Rabbit patt. in center, flanged border w/large free-hand leaves & large & small cut-sponge blossoms in red, blue & green **385.00**

Plates, dinner, 9¼" d., Rabbit patt., transfer-printed center scene of rabbits & frogs w/a wide border of

Cut-sponge Rabbit Plate

free-hand polychrome leaf & cut-sponge blossoms, late 19th c. set of 5 (ILLUS. of one) **1,380.00**

Plates, 9½" d., red & green cut-sponge design border & center, set of 8 . . . . **660.00**

Platter, 12¼" l., oval, Black Beauty patt., central section w/a free-hand polychrome floral decoration, Adams, England, late 19th c. **259.00**

Cut Sponge Platter

Platter, 16¼" l., oval, brown cut-sponge repeating leaf sprig border band & ring of matching leaf sprigs in the center, thin blue circle at center of leaf ring & thin blue border band (slight internal hairline (ILLUS.). **193.00**

Tea set: cov. teapot, cov. sugar bowl, creamer, five handleless cups, six saucers, six plates & a waste bowl; all in a blue cut-sponge diamond design w/brown striping, marked "Staffordshire, England," late 19th c., the set (hairlines) **316.00**

SPONGEWARE

Spongeware's designs were spattered, sponged or daubed on in colors, sometimes with a piece of cloth. Blue on white was the most common type, but mottled tans, browns and greens on yellowware were also popular. Spongeware generally has an overall pattern with a coarser look than Spatterwares, to which it is loosely related. These wares were extensively produced in England and America well into the 20th century.

Spongeware Bank

Bank, bulbous bottle-shaped w/blue polka dot sponging & "J.W.B." stenciled in blue, lip chips, 6" h. (ILLUS.)................... **$743.00**

Bean pot, bulbous flat-bottomed body tapering to a flat mouth, small loop handle at shoulder, wide spiral bands of blue sponging on white, 4⅝" h. **413.00**

Bowl, 8½" sq., 2⅜" h., deep slightly flaring sides, overall heavy mottled blue sponging on white **358.00**

Bowl, 8½" d., 4" h., heavy wide molded rim on a deep rounded body, overall heavy blue bands of sponging on white, wire bail handle (wear, pinpoint flakes) **72.00**

Bowl, 10¼" d., 5¼" h., deep flaring sides w/a wide molded rim w/ears, overall molded basketweave & flower design, star on the bottom for the Star Pottery, Arkon, Ohio, overall bold blue sponging on white (one ear chipped, other w/professional repair) **193.00**

Butter crock, cov., deep cylindrical sides w/relief-molded band of swastikas & the word "Butter," flattened lid w/inset button handle, wire bail handle w/turned wood grip, overall light blue sponging on stoneware, 7½" d. **220.00**

Butter crock, wide cylindrical body w/heavy molded rim, scattered vertical bands of blue sponging on white w/"Butter" stenciled in blue, 9¼" d. **220.00**

Crock, deep cylindrical sides w/narrow molded rim w/rim spout, wire bail handle w/turned wooden grip, overall dark blue sponging on white, 6¾" d. (rim chips) **330.00**

Crock, cylindrical, decorated w/three wide bands of dark blue sponging on white, brown Albany slip-glazed interior, 7¾" d., 7¼" h. (small chips & hairline) **110.00**

Cuspidor, miniature, squatty bulbous round base below a deep flat & flaring neck, three thin blue stripes around the base w/overall blue sponging around the base & neck, 3¼" d. (repaired rim chips) **275.00**

Dish, cov., miniature, flat bottom w/low flaring sides & heavy molded flat rim, fitted domed cover wbutton finial, overall heavy blue sponging on white, 3¼" d. **935.00**

Dish, rectangular w/low flaring serpentine sides, blue sponging on white, 6½ x 8½" **193.00**

Mush cup & saucer, heavy blue banded sponging on white, worn gilt trim (slight hairline in base of cup) **83.00**

Pitcher, tall cylindrical body w/a small rim spout & C-form handle, relief-molded oval reserve w/a child & dog, overall blue sponging on white **275.00**

Pitcher, 6½" h., bulbous base, overall blue sponging on white, base marked "Uhl Pottery" **770.00**

Pitcher, 7½" h., barrel-shaped, overall blue sponging on white (small edge flakes) **193.00**

Pitcher, 7½" h., slightly tapering cylindrical body w/wide pointed rim spout & squared loop handle, relief-molded floral designs covered overall w/heavy blue sponging on white (crazing, hairline in handle) **303.00**

Pitcher, 7½" h., wide cylindrical body w/pointed rim spout & C-form handle, stripes of blue sponging alternating w/wide stripes of plain white (chip on spout) **220.00**

Pitcher, 8¼" h., swelled ovoid body tapering to a flaring neck w/pointed rim spout, small C-form shoulder handle, overall blue sponging on yellowware **138.00**

Pitcher, 8¼" h., wide cylindrical body tapering at the shoulder to a wide flat mouth w/rim spout, small loop handle at shoulder, overall banded blue sponging on white (rim flakes) **468.00**

Spongeware Pitcher

Pitcher, 8¾" h., cylindrical body tapering to a flat rim w/a pinched spout, C-form handle, chip on table ring, blue on white (ILLUS.) **468.00**

Pitcher, 8⅞" h., swelled base below a tall slightly tapering cylindrical body w/a large rim spout & angled loop handle, overall heavy blue sponging on white (two rim hairlines, small chip on base) **193.00**

Pitcher, 9" h., cylindrical body w/a rim spout & small C-form handle, the side w/relief-molded blossom on leafy stem decorated in dark blue, lighter sponged sawtooth bands around the rim & base (chip on base) **336.00**

Pitcher, 9" h., slightly tapering tall cylindrical body w/lightly molded horizontal ribs, rim spout & angled loop handle, overall light blue sponging on white (rim hairline at handle) **193.00**

Pitcher, 9" h., tall slender cylindrical body w/pointed rim spout & small C-form handle, heavy overall blue sponging on white **330.00**

Pitcher, 9" h., tall slender slightly tapering cylindrical body w/a molded band at base & rim, small C-form handle, overall dark blue sponging on white (small base chips) **330.00**

Pitcher, 9" h., tall slender tapering cylindrical body w/a molded base & rim band, pointed rim spout, C-form handle, overall mottled bands of vertical blue sponging on white **303.00**

Pitcher, 9½" h., cylindrical w/bulbous base, overall blue sponging on white **715.00**

Pitcher, 9⅞" h., tall slender ovoid body w/pinched rim spout & C-form low handle w/thumbrest, overall light blue banding on white (spout chipped) **171.00**

Platter, 13" l., oval, wide flanged rim, overall light blue sponging on white (some crazing) **259.00**

Platter, 15" l., oval, wide flanged rim, heavy dark blue sponging on white (wear) **303.00**

Teapot, cov., miniature, bulbous cylindrical body w/a short cylindrical neck, inset low-domed cover w/knob handle, swan's-neck spout & C-form handle, overall swirled bands of blue sponging on white, 4¼" h. (small flakes, professional handle repair) **578.00**

Spongeware Teapot

Teapot, cov., bulbous body w/C-form handle, swan's-neck spout, blue sponging on white, lid chipped & glued, 5½" h. (ILLUS.) **633.00**

Teapot, cov., blue sponging on white, 7" h. (chips on table ring, professional repair) **825.00**

Umbrella stand, slender cylindrical form, wide blue & white bands around the top & base w/overall banded blue sponging on white, 15½" h. **770.00**

Umbrella stand, tall cylindrical form, the front center w/an oval reserve w/a blue transfer-printed scene of a Dutch girl & boy, wide blue bands near the top & base w/overall banded blue sponging on white, 22¼" h. (hairlines) **825.00**

Spongeware Water Cooler

Water cooler, cov., bulbous
cylindrical body w/wooden cover &
spigot, applied blue spongeware
decoration overall, "No. 9", 19th c.,
minor chips, cracks to base,
13½" h. (ILLUS.) **230.00**

STAFFORDSHIRE FIGURES

*Small figures and groups made of pottery
were produced by the majority of the
Staffordshire, England potters in the 19th
century and were used as mantel decorations or
"chimney ornaments," as they were sometimes
called. Pairs of dogs were favorites and were
turned out by the carload, and 19th century
pieces are still available. Well-painted
reproductions also abound and collectors are
urged to exercise caution before investing.*

Bust of George Washington, on a
socle base, polychrome decoration,
19th c., 7⅝" h. **$275.00**
Dog, Spaniel, seated position, white
w/tan head, ears & portion of back,
lock & chain collar, glass eyes,
worn gold trim, 13½" h. **250.00**
Dogs, Spaniel in seated position,
sleek body w/long curly ears & coat
w/curled-up tail, large red spots on
the white body w/polychrome facial
features, 19th c., 13" h., pr. (one
cracked) **495.00**
Figure of Benjamin Franklin,
standing on oblong base
w/incorrect inscription
"Washington," first half 19th c.,
15½" h. (cracks, very minor chips) .. **920.00**
Figure of Little Red Riding Hood,
standing girl in polychrome outfit,
oblong base, 19th c., 10⅛" h.
(minor losses & paint wear) **173.00**

Figure group, a seated mother
Poodle & two puppies, all in white
w/sanded fur trim, painted facial
details, deep blue oblong base,
19th c., 4" h. **385.00**
Figure group, a man wearing
kneebreeches & a long jacket
standing behind a seated young
lady wearing a long cape &
sprigged dress & styling her hair,
flowering bocage behind them, on
a stepped rockwork base, early
19th c., 9" h. (restoration, minor
chips & enamel loss) **460.00**

Man with Rooster & Dog Group

Figure group, man wearing a
cavalier costume seated beneath a
wide openwork arch trimmed
w/small applied blossoms, holding
a colorful rooster on one knee,
petting a spotted dog w/his other
hand, molded scroll oval base,
decorated in bright red, green, dark
blue, orange & yellow, glaze
hairline, 19th c., 9¾" h.
(ILLUS.)..................... **187.00**
Figure group, Dick Turpin on
horseback, ca. 1840, England,
12¼" h. **350.00**

Staffordshire Hen on Nest

Hen on nest, white hen trimmed w/black & brown w/red wattle on light brown basketweave base, bisque finish, 5⅜ x 7", 7" h. (ILLUS.). **650.00**

Horse, yellowware, the standing animal wearing reins, head lowered, on a molded oval base, body heavily splashed w/dark brown, attributed to The Don Pottery, England, ca. 1800-22, 6¼" h. (tail & both ears restored) **1,100.00**

Rabbits, each recumbent animal w/long ears decorated in polychrome & shown nibbling on lettuce leaves, 19th c., 10¼" l., pr. **4,025.00**

Sheep, a horned ram & a ewe, each standing on an oblong tree-root & grass base in front of an open tree stump, each w/a sanded white coat & long tail, decorated in green & brown, 5¼" h., pr. (one w/tiny base flake, other w/hairline to a reglued piece on rim) **424.00**

Sheep, pearlware, standing animal, white w/brick red spots, a small sheep below it on the stepped base, flower-and-leaf bocage behind, further decorated in blue, red & green, 4½ & 5¼" h., facing pr. (damages to bocage, ear chips, base chips on one, base hairlines in other) **385.00**

STAFFORDSHIRE TRANSFER WARES

The process of transfer-printing designs on earthenwares developed in England in the late 18th century and by the mid-19th century most common ceramic wares were decorated in this manner, most often with romantic European or Oriental landscape scenes, animals or flowers. The earliest such wares were printed in dark blue but a little later light blue, pink, purple, red, black, green and brown were used. A majority of these wares were produced at various English potteries right up till the turn of the century but French and other European firms also made similar pieces and all are quite collectible. The best reference on this area is Petra Williams' book Staffordshire Romantic Transfer Patterns - Cup Plates and Early Victorian China *(Fountain House East, 1978). Also see HISTORICAL & COMMEMORATIVE WARES.*

Rural Scenery Footed Bowl

Bowl, 11" d., 4½" h., footed, deep sides w/lightly scalloped rim, Rural Scenery patt. w/sheep, cow & horse, light blue, Adams, unseen foot rim chip, chip on extreme rim edge (ILLUS.) **$303.00**

Brush box, cov., long oblong form, Wild Rose patt., lakeside landscape on cover, medium blue, 7¼" l. (very small unseen base flake) **275.00**

Coffeepot, cov., tall baluster-form body w/bulbous tapering neck w/rolled rim & high domed cover w/acorn finial, swan's-neck spout & angled & pointed handle, dark blue scene of two men talking beside a horse near a stable, ca. 1830, 11½" h. (chip on edge of spout) . **1,100.00**

Creamer, footed bulbous ovoid body tapering to a flat rim w/pointed rim spout, C-form handle, Pomona patt., brown, mid-19th c. (tiny footrim flake) **88.00**

Creamer, wide flared base ring below the jug-form ovoid body tapering to a flat rim & arched rim spout, C-form handle, brown transfer scenes titled "Robin Hood and The Sheriff" & "Robin Hood and the Butcher," trimmed in blue, green, orange & red, blue base band, first half 19th c., 4¼" h. **66.00**

Cup & saucer, handleless, dark blue transfer of bird & flowers, marked "Stone China," ca. 1830 (wear, small flakes) **105.00**

Cup & saucer, handleless, Horse patt., dark blue, Stubbs & Kent (small unseen table ring flake on saucer, cup w/mellowing) **385.00**

Cup & saucer, handleless, Hunter w/Dogs patt., dark blue, cup 5¼" d., 2¼" h. (small unseen table ring chip) **176.00**

Dish, round w/a scalloped rim & small embossed fruit & leaf rim handle, Filigree patt., medium blue, Spode, 7½" d. (unseen foot rim flake, tight rim hairline) **198.00**

Egg cup, pedestal foot, Eastern Scenery patt., light blue, ca. 1830s, 2⅛" h. (small inner rim chip) **66.00**

Egg cup, pedestal base, English Pasture & Ruins patt., light blue, ca. 1830s, 2⅝" h. (light to moderate mellowing) **143.00**

Frog mug, cylindrical mug w/C-scroll handle, small figure of a frog applied inside the bottom, the exterior w/a reserve of a black transfer-printed ship under sail framed by a band of orange lustre & trimmed in polychrome, the Sailor's Lament on the reverse, ca. 1830, 4" h. (wear, crazing, hairline) **165.00**

Gravy boat, sailboat on lake in tree-filled landscape, brown, mid-19th c. **66.00**

Pitcher, jug-type, 8½" h., wide ovoid body tapering to a short, rolled neck w/long rim spout & C-scroll handle, scene of a large manor house w/covered walkway, a stream w/sailboat in foreground, large leaves around rim, ochre line around mouth rim, dark blue, ca. 1830s unknown maker (small spout tip chip, traces of two small spiders in base) **385.00**

Pitcher, 9⅛" h., 8¾" d., jug-form, wide footed ovoid body w/a short cylindrical neck w/pointed spout & C-scroll handle, Peruvian Horse Hunters patt., black, inscribed under spout "J Buckley 1853," Anthony Shaw (invisible restoration to base exterior) **308.00**

Pitcher, 10¼" h., ornate baroque-style w/tapering bulbous footed body, wide arched spout & ornate S-scroll handle, Rural Scenery patt. w/sheep, cow & horse, light blue, Adams, ca. 1840 . . . . **385.00**

Plate, toddy, 5⅛" d., Running Setter patt., Quadrupeds series, dark blue, Hall, ca. 1830s **275.00**

Plate, toddy, 5½" d., scalloped rim, brown printed central rectangular cartouche & floral wreath enclosing wording "A Trifle For Charles," embossed rim scale & rope trimmed in dark blue, impressed Enoch Wood mark, early 19th c. . . **413.00**

Plate, 7¼" d., Mastiff (Guard Dog) patt., Quadrupeds series, dark blue, Hall, ca. 1830s (stacking wear) **165.00**

Plate, 8" d., rounded 12-paneled rim, dark greyish blue center decoration of an mountainous landscape, the rim band w/a finely dotted ground w/small building & tree vignettes & a narrow floral edge band, Charles Meigh, 1851-61 . . . . **61.00**

Plate, 8½" d., Hunter & Fox patt., Zoological series, dark blue, Wood, ca. 1830s **330.00**

Plate, 8¾" d., Christmas Eve patt., central scene of family in interior, floral border, Wilkie Series by Clews, ca. 1830s **314.00**

Plate, 9¼" d., Caledonia patt., purple, Adams **108.00**

Spode Castle Plate

Plate, 9¾" d., Castle patt., medium blue, Spode, first half 19th c., few light scatches (ILLUS.) **105.00**

Plate, 9¾" d., Lion patt., Quadrupeds series, dark blue, Hall, ca. 1830s **330.00**

Plate, 9¾" d., Shepherd Piping patt., medium blue, ca. 1830s **88.00**

Plate, 10⅜" d., Fox Hunters patt., scalloped rim, floral border, medium blue, ca. 1840 . . . . **165.00**

Plate, 10⅜" d., lightly scalloped rim, Tyrolean patt., Wm. Ridgway, ca. 1840 . . . . **66.00**

Plate, 10½" d., Romantic Castles patt., medium blue, Davenport **66.00**

Plates, 10½" d., Acropolis patt., purple, ca. 1840, pr. (small areas of mellowing) **154.00**

Platter, 12¼" l., oval, Fountain Scenery patt., medium blue, Adams **176.00**

Platter, 12¼" l., oval w/lightly
scalloped rim, Caledonia patt.,
purple, Adams, ca. 1840 (overall
mellowing) **308.00**

Platter, 13¼" l., oval, lightly scalloped
rim, Palestine patt., light blue,
Adams, ca. 1840 . . . . **248.00**

Platter, 13⅜" l., oval, Duck Hunting
patt., dark blue, ca. 1830s **770.00**

Platter, 15" l., oval, Caledonia patt.,
purple, Adams (tiny pit on back
rim) **468.00**

Platter, 15" l., oval, lightly scalloped
rim, Palestine patt., light blue,
Adams, ca. 1840 . . . . **303.00**

Platter, 15¼" l., oval, Moose patt.,
Quadrupeds series, dark blue, Hall,
ca. 1830s (crack off rim, some
inner rim wear, light
scratches) **550.00**

Platter, 15½" l., oval, Oriental patt.,
purple, ca. 1840 (slight edge
wear) **330.00**

Platter, 16" l., oval, Aurora patt.,
brown, ca. 1850 . . . . **83.00**

Fine Palestine Pattern Platter

Platter, 17" l., oval, lightly scalloped
rim, Palestine patt., light blue,
Adams (ILLUS.). **330.00**

Platter, 19" l., oval, lightly scalloped
rim, Tyrolean patt., light blue, Wm.
Ridgway, ca. 1840 . . . . **358.00**

Platter, 19⅝" l., oval, lightly scalloped
rim, Delhi patt., brown, ca.
1840 . . . . **468.00**

Lakeside Meeting Platter

Platter, 20" l., oval, Lakeside Meeting
patt., medium dark blue, unknown
maker, ca. 1830, some scratches &
stains on face, few tiny outer rim
flakes (ILLUS.). **605.00**

Platter, 20" l., oval, medium blue
central scene of an England
riverscape w/boats & cottage in the
distance, wide floral border, mid-
19th c. (wear, crazing) **275.00**

Early Staffordshire Platter

Platter, 20¾" l., oval well-and-tree
style, Ruins with Horseman in
Foreground patt., dark blue, ca.
1830s, unseen foot chip
(ILLUS.) **1,210.00**

**Sauce tureen, cover, ladle &
undertray,** squatty bulbous oblong
tureen body w/upturned loop end
handles, stepped & domed cover
w/squared loop finial, matching
dished undertray, Royal Cottage
patt., light blue, ca. 1830-40, 8¾" l.,
the set (mismatching plain white
ladle) **220.00**

Sauce tureen, cover & undertray,
Hare & Pointer patt. on base,
Rooster & Fox patt. on undertray,
tureen w/footed bulbous body
w/rolled rim & domed cover w/berry
finial, loop shoulder handles,
Quadrupeds series, dark blue, Hall,
the set **1,430.00**

Sauce tureen, cover & undertray,
bulbous oblong deep body
w/indented wide corners & a flaring
rim, raised on tall heavy scroll legs,
inset high domed cover w/flower
finial & ladle rim notch, English
landscape scenes in dark blue w/a
grapevine border, E. Wood, ca.
1835, undertay 7⅛" l., 6¼" h., the
set (hairline in cover, unseen rim
chips & short hairline, tray w/large
spider crack) **1,210.00**

Sauce tureen undertray, oval,
Hyena patt., Zoological series, dark
blue, Wood, ca. 1830s, 8" l. (slight
scratching). **330.00**

Shaker, footed w/bulbous body, tall cylindrical neck & domed top, Oriental or Arabian scene, light blue, ca. 1840, 4¼" h. (shallow chip under top, slight mellowing) **132.00**

Soup plate, Common Wolf Trap patt., Oriental Sports series, dark blue, Edward Challinor, ca. 1830s, 8⅜" d. **303.00**

Soup plate, Shells patt., dark blue, Stubbs & Kent, ca. 1830s, 9¾" d. (small unseen table ring flake) **386.00**

Soup plate, Llama patt., Quadrupeds series, dark blue, Hall, 10" d. **330.00**

Rare Caledonia Soup Tureen

Soup tureen, cov., bulbous oval tapering deep ribbed body on four peg feet, upturned loop end handles, high domed cover w/squared ropetwist handle, Caledonia patt., purple, Adams, ca. 1840, in-the-making separations in base & ladle hole, 14" l., 9¾" h. (ILLUS.) **660.00**

Sugar bowl, cov., small footring under the bulbous body w/flared rim & pointed loop handles, high domed cover, Water Girl patt., medium blue, Spode, ca. 1830s, 4¼" h. **182.00**

Sugar bowl, cov., boat-shaped w/angled loop end handles, The Rooster & The Fox patt., Aesop's Fables series, medium blue, unknown maker, ca. 1830s, 7½" l., 4½" h. (unseen chip inside cover) **176.00**

Undertray, round, Zebra patt., floral border, dark blue, impressed Rogers mark & underglaze 'Seal of the U.S.' mark, ca. 1830s, 7⅛" d. **187.00**

Vegetable dish, cov., Caledonia patt., rectangular w/wide notched corners, angled loop end handles, domed cover w/blossom finial,

purple, Adams, ca. 1840 (small area of mellowing, slight rim wear) **605.00**

Vegetable dish, cov., rectangular w/incurved sides & wide notched corners, angled loop rim handles, high domed & stepped cover w/blossom finial, Abbey Ruins patt., light blue, T. Mayer, ca. 1840 (two foot rim chips) **176.00**

Vegetable dish, cov., squared form w/rounded corners, flaring base w/flanged rim & rounded rim tab handles, high domed cover w/fruit finial, Wild Rose patt., medium blue, unknown maker, ca. 1840, 10¼" w., 5¾" h. **187.00**

Waste bowl, Ducks patt., medium blue, ca. 1830s, 4¼" d., 2⅝" h. **72.00**

Waste bowl, wide flat flaring sides, scene of a woman w/child talking to a man w/a bundle on his stick, dark blue, ca. 1830s, 5¾" d., 3" h. **132.00**

STANGL POTTERY

Johann Martin Stangl, who first came to work for the Fulper Pottery in 1910 as a ceramic chemist and plant superintendent, acquired a financial interest and became president of the company in 1926. The name of the firm was changed to Stangl Pottery in 1929 and at that time much of the production was devoted to a high grade dinnerware to enable the company to survive the Depression years. One of the earliest solid-color dinnerware patterns was their Colonial line, introduced in 1926. In the 1930s it was joined by their Americana pattern. After 1942 these early patterns were followed by a wide range of hand-decorated patterns featuring flowers and fruits with a few decorated with animals or human figures.

Around 1940 a very limited edition of porcelain birds, patterned after the illustrations in John James Audubon's "Birds of America," was issued. Stangl subsequently began production of less expensive ceramic birds and these proved to be popular during the war years, 1940-46. Each bird was handpainted and each was well marked with impressed, painted or stamped numerals which indicated the species and the size.

All operations ceased at the Trenton, New Jersey plant in 1978.

Two reference books which collectors will find helpful are The Collectors Handbook of Stangl Pottery *by Norma Rehl (The Democrat Press, 1979), and* Stangl Pottery *by Harvey Duke (Wallace-Homestead, 1994).*

Stangl Pottery Mark

BIRDS

Bluebird, No. 32765 . . . . **$125.00**
Blue Jay, No. 3716,
  10¼" h. . . . . **450.00 to 500.00**
Chestnut Chickadee, No. 3811 . . . . . **82.00**
Cock Pheasant, No. 3492, 6¼ x 11" . . **185.00**
Double Parakeets, No. 3582 . . . . **175.00**
Duck, flying, No. 3443 . . . . **300.00**
Key West Dove, No. 3454, one wing
  up **260.00**
Magnolia Warbler, No. 3582 . . . . . . **1,100.00**
Parrot, No. 2449 . . . . **145.00**
Verdin, No. 3921 . . . . **625.00**
Yellow Hen, No. 3446. . . . . **115.00**

DINNERWARES & ARTWARES

Bowl, salad, Golden Harvest patt. **28.00**
Bowl, soup, 5½" d., Apple Delight
  patt. **7.00**
Bowl, soup, 7½" d., Apple Delight
  patt. **11.00**
Bowl, 8" d., Apple Delight patt. **28.00**
Coaster, Country Garden patt. **6.00**
Creamer, Apple Delight patt. **8.00**
Cup & saucer, Bittersweet patt. **11.00**
Cup & saucer, Golden Harvest patt. . . . **18.00**

Garden Flower Dinner Service

Dinner service: thirteen 9½" plates,
  seven 6" plates, two 5¼" plates,
  one 12½" plate, fifteen saucers, six
  soup bowls, three cups, one small
  & one large pitcher, small
  casserole, eight goblets, two 9"
  bowls, cov. teapot, creamer & cov.
  sugar bowl, salt & pepper shakers
  & one cruet; some damage,
  Garden Flower patt., Terra Rose
  line, the set (ILLUS. of part) **358.00**
Plate, bread & butter, 6" d., Apple
  Delight patt. **4.00**
Plate, bread & butter, 6" d., Golden
  Harvest patt. **4.00**

Plate, bread & butter, 6" d., Orchard
  Song patt. **3.00**
Plate, luncheon, 8" d., Apple Delight
  patt. **6.00**
Plate, dinner, 10" d., Apple Delight
  patt. **10.00**
Plate, dinner, 10" d., Bittersweet patt. . . **14.00**
Plate, dinner, 10" d., Golden Harvest
  patt. **9.00**
Plate, 12" d., Orchard Song patt. **20.00**
Relish dish, Blueberry patt. **35.00**
Server, center-handled, Orchard
  Song patt. **12.00**
Tea tile, Apple Delight patt. **13.00**
Tray, bread, Country Garden patt. **32.00**
Tray, bread, Orchard Song patt. **22.00**
Vegetable bowl, divided, Golden
  Harvest patt. **30.00**

STONEWARE

Stoneware is essentially a vitreous pottery, impervious to water even in its unglazed state, that has been produced by potteries all over the world for centuries. Utilitarian wares such as crocks, jugs, churns and the like, were the most common productions in the numerous potteries that sprang into existence in the United States during the 19th century. These items were often enhanced by the application of a cobalt blue oxide decoration. In addition to the coarse, primarily salt-glazed stonewares, there are other categories of stoneware known by such special names as basalt, jasper and others.

Butter churn, tall slender slightly
  tapering cylindrical form w/short
  flared neck & eared handles, cobalt
  blue slip-quilled large sunflower-
  style blossom on stem w/four
  leaves below an "8," impressed
  label "J. Burger, Rochester, N.Y.,"
  late 19th c., 8 gal., 22¾" h. (minor
  lime deposits) **$990.00**
Crock, cylindrical w/flaring molded
  rim, impressed oval label
  highlighted in blue reads "H.J.
  Heinz Co., Pittsburgh USA," narrow
  impressed dot bands around top &
  base also highlighted in blue,
  brown Albany slip-glazed interior,
  6¾" d. (rim chip) **248.00**
Crock, two-handled, slip-quilled
  cobalt blue bird on branch,
  impressed "F.A. Plaisted, Gardiner,
  Maine," 11½" h **400.00**
Crock, cylindrical w/molded rim &
  eared handles, cobalt blue
  stenciled "4" within a circle of stars
  near the rim, 4 gal., 11⅝" h. **165.00**

Stoneware Crock with Codfish Decoration

Crock, ovoid w/flared mouth & eared handles, incised w/horizontal lines & two codfish on front, "Boston" & "JF" on reverse, Jonathan Fenton, Boston, ca. 1794-97, minor chips, 13" h. (ILLUS.) **6,325.00**

Crock, cylindrical w/eared handles, cobalt blue slip-quilled design of two large stylized blossoms issuing from a squiggle stem, impressed label "M. Woodruff & Co. Cortland 6," label highlighted in blue, late 19th c., 6 gal., 13¼" h. (rim chips & flaking) **248.00**

Cobalt Decorated Crock

Crock, semi-ovoid w/eared handles & molded rolled mouth, cobalt blue slip-quilled decoration of two large daisy-like blossoms on a central squiggle stem below dot & arch bands at the shoulder, impressed mark of Somerset Pottery, Pottersville & Boston, Massachusetts, 1882-1909, 4 gal., chip on one handle, firing crack, 14½" h. (ILLUS.) **345.00**

Foot warmer, ovoid, marked "P.L. Rider Boston, Mass.," printed in blue "Dorchester Pottery" **100.00**

Jar, ovoid w/wide flaring rim & eared handles, cobalt blue brushed design of two large leaves flanking "II," impressed rim label "S.S. Perry, Troy" highlighted in blue, 19th c., 11" h. (small base chip) **83.00**

Jar, ovoid body w/thick molded neck, brushed cobalt blue wide band of leafy scrolls & blossoms around the sides, 12¼" h. (hairlines) **330.00**

Jar, ovoid, impressed eagle & cannon, Charlestown, 12½" h. **125.00**

Jar, tall swelled cylindrical body w/short cylindrical neck & eared handles, cobalt blue large stenciled flower & leaf upright wreath flanking a central scroll band above a large '4,' late 19th c., 4 gal., 15¼" h. **440.00**

Jug, semi-ovoid, molded mouth, strap handle, cobalt blue large brushed stylized blossom on leafy stem, impressed label "-M. Harris, Easton, Pa.," 19th c., 10¾" h. (chip on base) **303.00**

Jug, ovoid, Charlestown, 12" h. **250.00**

Jug, semi-ovoid w/a wide flat bottom & wide rounded shoulders tapering to the small molded mouth, applied strap handle, cobalt blue brushed large three-leaf sprig below two "2" numerals, impressed shoulder label "Whitteman, Havana, N.Y.," late 19th c., 2 gal., 12" h. (small base flakes) **110.00**

Jug, ovoid, w/ochre decorated flower, impressed "Lyman and Clark, Gardiner," 12½" h. **1,900.00**

Jug, ovoid, slip-quilled cobalt floral decoration, impressed "R. Thompson, Gardiner, Maine," 2 gal., 13½" h. **400.00**

Jug, tall slender ovoid body w/a small neck & loop handle, cobalt blue stenciled label "Louis P. F---, Wines and Liquors. Wheeling, W.Va. - 2," late 19th c., 2 gal., 14" h. (base chips) **171.00**

Jug, tall ovoid body w/a small molded rim & strap shoulder handle, brushed cobalt blue large stylized flower on the front & a "2" near the top, 2 gal., 14¼" h. (hairlines) **165.00**

Jug, ovoid, two handled, impressed "Lyman and Clark," 4 gal., 14½" h. **650.00**

Jug, semi-ovoid w/small molded
mouth & strap handle, cobalt blue
slip-quilled large blossom w/leaves
& scrolls on the front, impressed
label "---Gale, Gale-Ville, NY 2,"
19th c., 2 gal., 14½" h. (small
flakes, short hairlines) **303.00**

Jug, ovoid, w/handles, impressed
"Lyman and Clark, Gardiner, #3,"
w/a free-hand "3" in ochre in
center, 3 gal., 15" h. **450.00**

Jug, ovoid, w/strap handle, brushed
cobalt blue "3" flanked by short
wavy lines, 19th c., 3 gal., 15½" h.
(minor lip chip) **94.00**

Jug, ovoid, in ochre, impressed
"Lyman and Clark Gardiner," dated
1837, 16" h.................. **400.00**

Jug, ovoid, slip-quilled cobalt blue
flower, impressed "Thompson &
Company, Gardiner," 3 gal.,
16" h....................... **300.00**

Jug, ovoid, impressed "Boston,"
16½" h. **100.00**

Jug, ovoid, Orcutt and Crafts, 3 gal.,
17½" h. **150.00**

Jug, ovoid tapering to a molded
mouth & applied handle, slip-
quilled cobalt blue primitive bird,
impressed label "J. Fisher & Co.,
Lyons," 19th c., 17½" h. (minor
hairlines) **358.00**

Jug, slip-quilled cobalt blue bird o
stump decoration, 5 gal., 18" h..... **850.00**

Jug, ovoid, decorated w/cobalt blue
swags, impressed "C. Croleus
Stonemaker New York" **1,750.00**

Pitcher, 14½" h., ovoid, slip-quilled
cobalt zigzag & flower
decoration.................. **700.00**

Iowa Stoneware Preserving Jar

Preserving jar, cylindrical w/applied
eared handles & rolled rim,
brushed cobalt blue floral motif &
"2", impressed "Tolman, Eldora,
IA," 2 gal. (ILLUS.) **3,250.00**

Preserving jar, cylindrical w/heavy
molded flat rim, vertical stripes of
cobalt blue stenciled stars, 19th c.,
9" h. **660.00**

Preserving jar, semi-ovoid w/molded
rim, cobalt blue stenciled label
"T.F. Reppert, Greensboro, Pa.,"
late 19th c., 9½" h. **94.00**

Preserving jar, slightly ovoid
w/molded rim, cobalt blue stenciled
& free-hand decoration, printed
"Excelsior Works, Isaac Hewitt, Jr.
Rices Landing, PA," 9½" h. **330.00**

TECO

*Teco Pottery was actually the line of art
pottery introduced by the American Terra Cotta
and Ceramic Company of Terra Cotta (Crystal
Lake), Illinois in 1902. Founded by William D.
Gates in 1881, American Terra Cotta originally
produced only bricks and drain tile. Because of
superior facilities for experimentation, including
a chemical laboratory, the company was able to
develop an art pottery line, favoring a matte
green glaze in the earlier years but eventually
achieving a wide range of colors including a
metallic lustre glaze and a crystalline glaze.
Though some hand-thrown pottery was made,
Gates favored a molded ware because it was less
expensive to produce. By 1923, Teco Pottery was
no longer being made and in 1930 American
Terra Cotta and Ceramic Company was sold. A
book on the topic is* Teco: Art Pottery of the
Prairie School, *by Sharon S. Darling (Erie Art
Museum, 1990).*

Teco Mark

Teco Tea Set

Tea set: 6" h. cov. teapot, creamer,
sugar bowl & lemon pot; all
designed w/embossed Art

Nouveau on grey/beige matte glaze, all pieces are stamped w/the vertical Teco logo, small flake off the spout of the lemon pot, the set (ILLUS.) **$715.00**

Vase, 4½" h., 2¾" d., simple ovoid body w/a molded rim, matte green glaze, stamped mark **660.00**

Vase, 5½" h., 2¾" d., swelled cylindrical form w/small squared rim handles continuing as thin buttresses down to the base, smooth matte light green glaze, marked "Teco - 428" **770.00**

Vase, 7⅝" h., triangular w/flat broad sides, a flat shoulder & short triangular rim, yellow/green matte glaze, designed by Fritz Albert, Shape No. 336, impressed marks . . . **495.00**

Vase, 8" h., 4" d., swelled cylindrical body w/a flattened shoulder centering a small molded mouth, smooth matte green glaze, impressed mark, original paper label & price tag **1,045.00**

Lobed Teco Vase

Vase, 9" h., 4" d., four protruding lobes on a tapering base, matte green & gunmetal glaze, impressed "TECO 1-86" (ILLUS.) **1,430.00**

Vase, 13" h., 5 1/4" d., tall slender slightly tapering cylindrical form, embossed up around the sides w/calla lilies, smooth matte green & gun-metal glaze, impressed "Teco - 134" **935.00**

TEPLITZ - AMPHORA

These wares were produced in numerous potteries in the vicinity of Teplitz in the Bohemian area of what is now The Czech Republic during the late 19th and into the 20th century. Vases and figures, of varying quality, were the primary products of such firms as

Riessner & Kessel (Amphora), Ernst Wahliss and Alfred Stellmacher. Although originally rather low-priced items, today collectors are searching out the best marked examples and prices are soaring.

Teplitz-Amphora Marks

Ewer, footed spherical body tapering to a short neck below a short conical segment below the tall cylindrical upright spout w/a high curved rim, an upswept angled handle above a smaller loop handle down the neck, glossy cobalt blue ground decorated around the body w/heavy gilt fruiting vines, flowers & a bird, dusted gold on the handles & spout, unmarked Teplitz, 13" h. **$138.00**

Jardiniere, bulbous form w/four loop handles, textured gold ground w/applied green leaves & agate flowers bordered in black, Amphora mark & crown w/"57-8890," 30" d., 7" h. **475.00**

Pitcher, tankard, 15" h., shades of violet w/relief-molded clusters of grapes & leaves, gold trim, Ernst Wahliss mark, ca. 1900 . . . . **525.00**

Vase, 4¾" h., a reverse swirl conical body w/double free-form branch handles extending across the body, iridescent blue glaze, Amphora mark **138.00**

Vase, 7" h., free-form gourd body in iridescent blue glaze w/overlapped rims forming four open handles & trailing vines, Amphora mark. **220.00**

Vase, 8½" h., squatty bulbous body tapering to wide cylindrical neck w/thick rolled rim, w/a figure of a pouncing lioness on the shoulder, honeycombed ground, glazed in shades of pink, gold & black reserved against a mottled ochre

Jeweled Amphora Vase

surface & applied w/multicolored glass 'jewels,' impressed "AMPHORA/AUSTRIA 508/52," ca. 1900 (ILLUS.) **4,025.00**

Amphora Vase

Vase, 11" h., 5" d., slender baluster-form, the short flaring pedestal foot w/four tiny loop handles below the bulbous double-lobed body tapering to a slender neck flanked by long curved handles below the cupped rim above four more tiny loop handles, decorated down the body w/two raised leaves in pinks, green & blue, impressed crown & "Amphora - Austria" (ILLUS.) **460.00**

Vase, 14" h., tall ovoid body tapering to a short cylindrical tapering neck w/flat rim, the main body in dark green w/a gold-trimmed forest scene & two white & black flying geese in relief, a narrow gold honeycomb band around the base & the shoulder decorated w/a wide gold honeycomb & triangle band set w/dark green triangular 'jewels,' rust Amphora crown mark & numbered "9041 - D 1906" **2,420.00**

Vase, 17" h., bulbous ovoid body w/a flaring rim, decorated w/four masques of felines & stylized leafage, modeled in high-relief, glazed in cream & gold, impressed "AMPHORA/TURN/FAIENCE/AUS TRIA," ca. 1900 . . . . **4,600.00**

Ornate Amphora Vase

Vase, 17¾" h., tall ovoid body tapering to rolled neck, applied branch handles, basketweave design w/three molded cherubs climbing floral applied drapery, impressed & printed marks, restoration, Czechoslovakia, early 20th c. (ILLUS.) **230.00**

TILES

Tiles have been made by potteries in the United States and abroad for many years. Apart from small tea tiles used on tables, there are also decorative tiles for fireplaces, floors and walls and this is where present collector interest lies, especially in the late 19th century American-made art pottery tiles.

Grueby Pottery, Boston, Massachusetts, shaded green & brown matte glaze, shows two pine trees in foreground w/blue sky & rolling hills in background, marked "MD" in green slip on reverse, 6" sq. (edge chips & a few surface nicks) **$1,980.00**

Hamilton Tile Works Company, woodland scene of two deer, green high glaze, marked on reverse "The Hamilton Tile Works Co. Hamilton Ohio," 6 x 12" (minor roughness on edges) **413.00**

Marblehead Pottery, Marblehead, Massachusetts, a colorful still life w/stylized flowers in a large vase, impressed on back w/the Marblehead logo & signed in black slip " Arthur Baggs" & "Hannah Tutt," uncrazed, 5⅞ sq. (minor edge chips covered by a very new frame) **935.00**

Moravian & Weller Tiles

Moravian, depicting an artist's palette in the center w/a Latin inscription around the border reading "Pictura Ornat-Domum Ornat," unmarked, minor edge flakes, 3¾" sq. (ILLUS. left) **83.00**

Northwestern Terra Cotta Company, advertising tile cold painted in gold, showing two putti holding up a heavy cloth border, embossed message on front reads "Northwestern Terra Cotta Comp. Chicago Ill.," 4⅛ x 5½" (minor wear to gilt paint & a small edge chip) **220.00**

Paul Revere Pottery, Boston, Massachusetts, square, a scene depicting Washington Street in blue, white, green & brown, marked "H.S. - S4-9/1/10," 3¾" w. (edge chips) **403.00**

Tiffany Mosaic Tile

Tiffany Studios, New York, New York, square, architectural-type, heavy composition inlaid w/opal, green & gold glass squares & rectangular small tiles, jewels & tesserae in stylized geometric squared design, 17 x 18" (ILLUS.) **1,840.00**

Trent Tile Company, Trenton, New Jersey, square, molded head of Michelangelo, sea green glaze, signed by Isaac Broome, impressed marks, 6" w. **115.00**

Van Briggle Pottery, Colorado Springs, Colorado, square, worked in cuenca technique w/a stylized landscape w/tall trees in the foreground in polychrome matte glazes, Shape No. 113B, in an Arts & Crafts style wood frame, 6" sq. **2,530.00**

Weller Pottery, Zanesville, Ohio, hand carved in green, blue, yellow, brown & pink matte glazes depicting what is probably the original Weller Pottery building under a full moon., incised "Weller Art Tiles" enclosed in a square, "2026-79" in black slip on reverse, 4¼" sq. (ILLUS. right) **992.00**

Weller, bisque, shaded brown & tan, w/the embossed image of a classical female figure, stamped "Weller" in small block letters on reverse, 16⅞" h. (repair of a small chip on lower left corner) **468.00**

TOBY MUGS & JUGS

The Toby is a figural jug or mug usually delineating a robust, genial drinking man. The name has been used in England since the mid-18th century. Copies of the English mugs and jugs were made in America.

For listings of related Character Jugs see DOULTON & ROYAL DOULTON.

Prattware Toby, seated Mr. Toby, blue, brown & ochre, pearlware glaze, ca. 1800, 9¼" h. (small chips throughout) **$403.00**

Ralph Wood-type Toby, seated Mr. Toby wearing a black tricorn hat & holding a frothing jug, translucent glazes, ca. 1770, England, 9¾" h. **1,035.00**

Staffordshire Black Slave Toby, a figure of a woman or boy house slave kneeling in prayer, hands together & chained at the wrists, wearing a green coat w/gold trim, white shirt w/blue, & gold, blue, red & white pants & a yellow bandanna w/yellow, red, & blue polka dots,

Rare Black Slave Toby

'crabstock' handle w/gold trim,
probably England, ca. 1850, few
small spots of flaking, 10¾" h.
(ILLUS.) **2,860.00**

Staffordshire Creamware Toby,
seated Mr. Toby holding a jug,
mottled & translucent glazes, 18th
c., England, 9¾" h. (small foot rim
chips) **460.00**

VAN BRIGGLE

*The Van Briggle Pottery was established by
Artus Van Briggle, who formerly worked for
Rookwood Pottery, in Colorado Springs,
Colorado at the turn of the century. He died in
1904 but the pottery was carried on by his widow
and others. From 1900 until 1920, the pieces
were dated. It remains in production today,
specializing in Art Potttery.*

Van Briggle Mark

Bowl-vase, spherical form
w/hexagonal paneled sides &
closed rim, embossed around the
rim w/peacock feathers, matte
brown glaze, Shape No. 851, dated
1905, 6" d., 5½" h. **$1,540.00**

Plate, 8½" d., molded in bold relief
w/a large poppy blossom on
swirling leafy stem, red on a bluish
green ground, 1907-11 . . . . **990.00**

Vase, 7¼" h., 3¾" d., simple ovoid
body w/a small molded mouth,
molded around the shoulder w/a
row of dragonflies w/the bodies

extending down the sides, mauve,
green & turquoise feathered glaze,
1907-11 . . . . **990.00**

"Dos Cabezos" Vase

Vase, 7½" h., "Dos Cabezos" model,
an ovoid form molded in relief on
each side w/a standing Art
Nouveau woman reaching around
& clinging to the sides of the vase,
under a light green matte glaze,
three lines in base, from firing,
incised "AA -Van Briggle - 1902 -
III" (ILLUS.). **20,900.00**

Vase, 7½" h., 4¼" d., simple ovoid
body tapering to a short cylindrical
neck, embossed w/flowers around
the neck, the stems down the
sides, dark bluish green matte
glaze, incised mark, dated 1916 . . . **550.00**

Vase, 7½" h., 5¼" d., bulbous body
below a tapering cylindrical neck,
the sides molded w/wide sharply
pointed leaves, matte raspberry
glaze, Shape No. 742, marked **770.00**

Vase, 8½" h., 9" d., bulbous ovoid
body tapering to a flat mouth,
molded around the center band w/a
row of stylized wide triangular
ribbed leaves, dark blue on a
turquoise blue ground, marks, ca.
1930s **523.00**

Vase, 9½" h., 4" d., "Lorelei," swelled
cylindrical form w/a figure of a
maiden draped around the rim,
blue & turquoise matte glaze,
1920-25, marked **1,430.00**

Vase, 12" h., 10½" d., broad ovoid
body w/an angled shoulder to the
wide flat mouth, smooth medium
matte green glaze, incised mark,
Shape No. 340, dated 1905
(restoration to small hole on base
side) **715.00**

Vase, 11" h., 12" d., large wide
bulbous body tapering slightly to
the flat mouth, embossed up
around the sides w/stylized daisies

around the rim on swirling stems &
leaves, matte purple to red glaze,
dated 1918 . . . . **1,650.00**

Van Briggle Vase with Daffodils

Vase, 14" h., footed cylindrical body
tapering to a short molded neck,
decorated w/embossed daffodils
under a frothy periwinkle blue
glaze, impressed "AA - Van Briggle
- 1903 - III - 100" (ILLUS.) **5,225.00**

VERNON KILNS

The story of Vernon Kilns Pottery begins with the purchase by Mr. Faye Bennison of the Poxon China Company (Vernon Potteries) in July 1931. The Poxon family had run the pottery for a number of years in Vernon, California, but with the founding of Vernon Kilns the product lines were greatly expanded.

Many innovative dinnerware lines and patterns were introduced during the 1930s, including designs by such noted American artists as Rockwell Kent and Don Blanding. In the early 1940s items were designed to tie in with Walt Disney's animated features "Fantasia" and "Dumbo." Various commemorative plates, including the popular "Bits" series, were also produced over a long period of time. Vernon Kilns was taken over by Metlox Potteries in 1958 and completely ceased production in 1960.Disney "Fantasia" & Other Items

Vernon Kilns Mark

DISNEY "FANTASIA" & OTHER ITEMS

Bowl, 7 x 12" rectangular, 2" h.,
'Mushroom' patt., No. 120, pink
glaze **$350.00**
Platter, 12½" l., Fantasia patt.,
brown, Ultra shape **350.00**

DON BLANDING DINNERWARES

Plate, chop, 12½" d., Hawaiian
Flowers patt., maroon **150.00**
Salt & pepper shakers, Hawaiian
Flowers patt., blue, pr. **55.00**

ROCKWELL KENT DESIGNS

Plate, salad, "Our America" series,
brown glaze **45.00**
Plate, chop, 12½" d., Moby Dick
patt. **150.00**
Plate, chop, 14" d., Moby Dick patt. . . . **125.00**
Vegetable bowl, open, "Our
America" series, 8" d. **200.00**

WATT

Founded in 1922, in Crooksville, Ohio, this pottery continued in operation until the factory was destroyed by fire in 1965. Although stoneware crocks and jugs were the first wares produced, by 1935 sturdy kitchen items in yellowware were the mainstay of production. Attractive lines like Kitch-N-Queen (banded) wares and the hand-painted Apple, Cherry and Pennsylvania Dutch (tulip) patterns were popular throughout the country. Today these hand-painted utilitarian wares are "hot" with collectors.

A good reference book for collectors is Watt Pottery, An Identification and Value Guide, by Sue and Dave Morris (Collector Books, 1933)

Watt Mark

Baker, individual, tab-handled,
Starflower patt. **$45.00**
Baker, cov., Double Apple patt., No.
96, 8½" d., 5¾" h. **295.00**
Bean pot, cov., American Red Bud
(Tear Drop) patt. **95.00**
Bean pot, cov., Campbell Kids
decoration **153.00**

Bean pot, cov., two-handled, Autumn
Foliage patt., No. 76, 7½" d.,
6½" h. 145.00
Bean server, individual, American
Red Bud (Tear Drop) patt., No. 75.,
3½" d. 35.00
Bowl, 5½" d., cereal, Apple patt., No.
74 . . . . 45.00
Bowl, cov., 7½"d., Dutch Tulip patt.,
No. 66 . . . . 325.00
Bowl, cov., 8¾"d., ribbed, Eagle patt.,
No. 601 . . . . 210.00

Starflower Tea Canister

Canister, cov., Starflower patt., four-
petal, "Tea," (ILLUS.). 175.00
Casserole, cov., individual, oval
handles, Moonflower patt., pink on
black (old style) 120.00
Chip N' Dip set, Apple patt.,
No. 73. . . . . 100.00
Cookie jar, cov., Rooster patt.,
No. 503 . . . . 275.00
Creamer, Apple (two-leaf) patt.,
No. 62 . . . . 128.00

Rooster Pattern Creamer

Creamer, Rooster patt., No.62,
4¼" h. (ILLUS.) 219.00
Creamer, Starflower patt., No. 62,
4¼" h. 275.00
Creamer & cov. sugar bowl,
Morning Glory patt., Nos. 97 & 98,
pr. 650.00
Fondue pot, cov., handled, Apple
patt., 9" l., 3" h. 500.00
Goodies jar, cov., Apple patt., No.
59, 8½" h. 295.00

Grease jar, cov., American Red Bud
(Tear Drop) patt. 185.00
Grease jar, cov., Apple patt.,
No. 01 . . . . 375.00
Mixing bowls, Apple patt., Nos. 5,6,
8 & 9, the set 220.00
Mug, Apple patt., No. 121, 3¾" h. 195.00
Pie plate, Apple patt., No. 33, 9" d. . . . 140.00
Pitcher, Cherry patt., No. 16 . . . . . . 210.00
Pitcher, Pennsylvania Dutch patt.,
No. 15 . . . . 158.00
Pitcher, Tulip patt., No. 16 . . . . 200.00
Pitcher, Tulip patt., No. 17 . . . . 350.00
Pitcher, Tulip patt., No. 62 . . . . 250.00
Pitcher, 5½" h., American Red Bud
(Tear Drop) patt., No. 15 . . . . 50.00
Pitcher, 5½" h., Cherry patt., No. 15.,
w/advertising 145.00

Rooster Pattern Pitcher

Pitcher, 6½" h., Rooster patt., No. 16
(ILLUS.). 138.00
Pitcher w/ice lip, 8" h., Starflower
patt., four-petal, No. 17 . . . . 160.00
Plate, chop, Apple patt., No. 49 . . . . . 375.00
Refrigerator pitcher, square-shaped,
Dutch Tulip patt., No. 69, 8½" w.,
8" h. 525.00
Salt & pepper shakers, Rooster
patt., barrel-shaped, pr. 450.00
Salt & pepper shakers, American
Red Bud (Tear Drop) patt., barrel-
shaped, 4" h., pr. 200.00

Dutch Tulip Spaghetti Bowl

Spaghetti bowl, 13" d., Dutch Tulip
patt., No. 39, (ILLUS.) **185.00**
Spaghetti bowl, 13" d., Starflower
patt., No. 39 . . . . **78.00**
Sugar bowl, cov., Apple patt.
w/advertising, No. 98 . . . . **395.00**
Teapot, cov., Autumn Foliage patt.,
No. 112, 6" h **1,500.00**

WEDGWOOD

*Reference here is to the famous pottery
established by Josiah Wedgwood in 1759 in
England. Numerous types of wares have been
produced through the years to the present.*

WEDGWOOD

Wedgwood Mark

BASALT

Bust of Locke

Bust of Locke, raised on a round
socle base, impressed title & mark,
ca. 1865, 7¾" h. (ILLUS.) **$518.00**
Figure group, Cupid & Psyche, the
seated figures mounted to a free-
form oval base, 19th c., impressed
title & mark, 8" h. **1,265.00**
Vase, 8¾" h., Krater form, encaustic
decoration of iron red & black
enamel classical figures on each
side, early 19th c., impressed
mark, England **2,070.00**
Vase, 9" h., ovoid body tapering to
wide flaring rim, C-form handles
from rim to shoulder, encaustic
decoration of white & black

Basalt Vase

classical figure w/borders in iron
red, blue, white & black, early 19th
c., impressed mark
(ILLUS.) **2,990.00**
Vase, 12½, classical urn-form,
upswept loop handles, encaustic
decoration of iron red, black &
white designs w/classical figures to
one side, a stylized palmette
design to the reverse, borders of
gadroon & dot, palmette, laurel &
dot & spearhead & dot, , ca. 1800,
impressed mark **4,313.00**

CREAMWARE

Plate, 9⅛" d., "Buns! Buns! Buns!,"
man selling buns to lady & child
h.p. center scene, gold border,
artist-signed "E. Lessore," date
mark of 1863 . . . . **325.00**
Vase, 6" h., molded w/grapevines &
foliate, painted w/a band of
strawberries, mid-19th c. **86.00**

JASPER WARE

Cheese dome, cov., the high
cylindrical domed top w/an upright
white acorn finial, white relief
classical figures separated by
upright flared bands on lavender,
dished base w/heavy rolled rim in
lavender w/white relief blossom &
leaf bands, late 19th c. **275.00**
Pitcher, 5⅝" h., barrel-shaped, white
relief classical figures alternating
w/vertical bands between leaf
bands at the top & bottom, on blue,
impressed "Wedgwood
England" **94.00**

Pitcher, 6¼" h., tankard-type, white relief decoration of classical figures on blue, marked "Wedgwood" only **94.00**

Wedgwood Sugar bowl

Sugar bowl, cov., spherical body w/inset domed cover & button finial, upswept handles, white relief classical figures around sides on dark blue, marked for 1892-1915 & "Wedgwood - England," 5" d., 4" h. (ILLUS.) **80.00**

Tea set: cov. teapot, cov. sugar bowl & creamer; spherical forms w/white relief classical figures & trees on dark blue, the teapot w/a pyramidal cover, marked "Made in England," 3 pcs. **358.00**

MISCELLANEOUS

Bust of Stephenson

Bust of Stephenson, carrara, designed by E.W. Wyon, on raised circular base, impressed title, factory mark & "E.W. Wyons.F. - 1853," England, 14¾" h. (ILLUS.) **518.00**

Cake stands, "Argenta Ware," Fan patt., impressed marks & date code for 1879, pr. **460.00**

Fish set: 6 plates & large oval serving platter; "Argenta Ware," each piece decorated w/a salmon on a bed of leaves, impressed marks & date code for 1875, platter 25" l., the set **977.00**

Jar, cov., Fairyland Lustre, a squatty bulbous body fitted w/a domed cover, decorated w/a continuous scene of an enchanted forest full of nymphs & mythical creatures in a variety of oranges, blue & greens w/gold outlines, the cover w/a solitary spider in web bordered w/multicolored foliage, 3½" h. **5,775.00**

Plate, 9" d., commemorative-type, "Fort Dearborn," black center, 20th c. **50.00**

Plate, 9" d., commemorative-type, "Home of Emerson," cabbage rose border, blue & white, 20th c. **40.00**

Plate, 9" d., commemorative-type, "Saratoga Monument," cabbage rose border, blue & white, 20th c. **40.00**

Plate, 10" d., Ivanhoe series, "Rebecca Repelling the Templar," blue & white, early 20th c. **95.00**

Plates, college commemorative, "Princeton," black on cream, 1952, set of 8 . . . . **150.00**

Strawberry service: 6 plates & a 16½" l. serving tray; "Argenta Ware," each decorated w/strawberry plants & ribbons on a reed-molded ground, impressed marks & date code for 1876, the set **977.00**

WELLER

This pottery was made from 1872 to 1945 at a pottery established originally by Samuel A. Weller at Fultonham, Ohio, and moved in 1882 to Zanesville. Numerous lines were produced and listings below are by the pattern or lines.

Reference books on Weller include The Collectors Encyclopedia of Weller Pottery, *by Sharon & Bob Huxford (Collector Books, 1979) and* All About Weller *by Ann Gilbert McDonald (Antique Publications, 1989).*

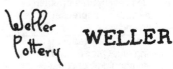

Weller Marks

AURELIAN (1898-1910)

Similar to Louwelsa line but brighter colors and a glossy glaze. With bright yellow/orange brush-applied background along with brown and yellow transparent glaze.

Lamp, kerosene table-type, a wide baluster-form body on small knob feet, the deep shoulder w/a wide short molded neck supporting a collar w/a kerosene burner & glass globe shade, the body decorated w/bold grape clusters & leaves on a fiery gold, green & mahogany ground, decorated by Eugene Roberts, incised "Aurelian" on the base, electrified, base only 9½" d., 11" h.. . . . . **$600.00 to 660.00**

Plaque, rectangular, decorated w/life-sized red apples hanging on leafy branches against a streaky brown, orange & yellow background, decorated by Frank Ferrell, ca. 1898, w/old metal framework & hanging chain, 10⅞ x 16½" (several glaze scratches, small patch of glaze loss, some bubbles in glaze). **935.00**

Vase, 5½" h., 5¾" d., spherical w/pinched neck, decorated w/yellow, brown & green roses on a fiery yellow & brown ground. . . . . **375.00 to 450.00**

Vase, 7" h., bulbous ovoid body tapering to a trumpet neck, decorated w/yellow & orange rose blossoms & green leaves against a dark brown ground, the neck & rim mounted w/a foliate-case sterling silver mount, decorated by Hattie Mitchell, artist-initials & impressed "WELLER - 838 - 6," silver impressed "STERLING - 634" w/hallmark, ca. 1900-10. . . . . **2,000.00 to 2,500.00**

Aurelian Vase

Vase, 14¾" h., baluster form w/flared foot & incurved cupped rim, large floral decoration, artist-signed, incised "Aurelian," "X" & "K," impressed "Weller" & the numbers "56" & "2" (ILLUS.) **2,090.00**

BONITO (1927-33)

Hand-painted florals and foliage in soft tones on cream ground. Quality of artwork greatly affects price.

Bowl, 5¾" d., 3⅜" h., squatty round form, h.p. w/leafy swags & colorful flower clusters on the ivory ground, incised mark **61.00**

Bowl, 8½" d.. . . . . **60.00 to 70.00**

Vase, urn shape decorated overall w/red roses & buds, artist-signed "C". **125.00**

Vase, 4" h., large pansy decoration by Naomi Walch, artist-signed "N". **125.00**

Vase, 5⅞" h., bulbous ovoid body w/small tab handles at shoulder, tapering to wide flaring rim, h.p. bluebell decoration **110.00**

Vase, 6" h., slightly flaring cylindrical body on short flaring foot, artist-signed . . . . **80.00 to 90.00**

Vase, 6¾" h., wide baluster-form body w/upright open scroll handles from shoulder to flared rim, decorated w/h.p. polychrome flowers & dots around the rim against an ivory ground, marked **121.00**

Vase, 7" h., handled, decorated w/red flowers & leaves on front & back, artist-signed "L". **135.00**

Vase, 7⅞" h., wide cylinder flaring toward base & then tapering to round foot, ornate scrolled handles from shoulder to rim, floral decoration **165.00**

BRIGHTON (1915)

Various bird or butterfly figurals colorfully decorated and with glossy glazes.

Flower frog, model of a Kingfisher, 9" h.. . . . . **350.00 to 375.00**

Model of a parakeet, on tapering cylindrical pedestal perch, bird in polychrome colors of pink, yellow &

Brighton Parakeet

blue, on a green perch, 5¾" d.,
7½" h., unmarked
(ILLUS.). . . . . **1,000.00 to 1,200.00**

Brighton Parrot

Model of a parrot, bright raspberry
red & blue, yellow & green, on a tall
swirled brown upright perch, die-
stamped mark, 9" w., 14" h.
(ILLUS.). . . . . **1,400.00 to 1,600.00**

Model of a woodpecker, perched on
a base of entwined branches, blue
& orange bird on a green perch,
glossy glaze, unmarked, 3½" d.,
6¼" h. . . . . **150.00 to 185.00**

Model of parakeets, perched on a
curving branch, birds brightly
colored in red, yellow & blue,
brown perch, glossy finish,
unmarked, 5¾ x 9" . . **1,100.00 to 1,400.00**

Name card holder w/figural butterfly
& attached bud vase **395.00**

BURNT WOOD (1910)

*Molded designs on an unglazed light tan
ground with dark brown trim. Similar to
Claywood but no vertical bands*

Vase, 9" h., 4" d., decorated w/three
mocking birds **299.00**

CLOUDBURST (1921)

*Overall "crackle" design with a high gloss
lustre finish on simple shapes.*

Vase, 6" h., red ground. . . . . **85.00 to 100.00**
Vase, 7" h., red ground. . . . . **95.00 to 110.00**
Vase, bud, 7" h.. . . . . **65.00**

Large Cloudburst Vase

Vase, 10¾" h., ovoid body w/short
cylindrical mouth, purple, grey &
white, unmarked (ILLUS.) **523.00**

COPPERTONE (Late 1920s)

*Various shapes with an overall mottled
bright green glaze on a "copper" glaze base. Some
pieces with figural frog or fish handles. Models
of frogs also included.*

Bowl, 9" d., 3¾" h., two raised open
square handles on flat rim, mottled
green & brown matte glaze (two
pinhead glaze nicks to
rim) . . . . **100.00 to 125.00**

Bowl, 9¾" l., 5½" h., deep rounded
sides w/an undulating oblong
molded rim molded at one side w/a
frog, each side embossed w/a
carp, rich mottled green & brown
glaze, ink kiln mark
"191-G". . . . . **900.00 to 1,250.00**

Candleholders, model of a turtle
w/lily blossom, 3" h., pr. . . **450.00 to 600.00**

Card tray, in the form of a lily pad
leaf w/shallow dished sides,
molded at one side w/a crouching
frog on the rim, ink kiln mark, 6" l.,
2¼" h. . . . . **250.00 to 285.00**

Center bowl, deep w/irregular rim, frog perched on one edge, mottled green & brown glaze, 10½" w., 5½" h.,; . . . . 525.00 to 650.00

Coppertone Cigarette/Match Holder

Cigarette or match holder, model of a lily pad bloom w/seated frog, 5½" w., 4½" h. (ILLUS.). 330.00

Cigarette stand, model of a frog, 5" h. . . . . 250.00 to 275.00

Console bowl w/figural lily pad & frog flower frog, oblong bowl, 8 x 10½", 2 pcs. . . . . 900.00 to 1,100.00

Console bowl, long narrow oblong form w/undulating rim, molded at one end w/a small figural frog & at the opposite end w/a water lily & leaves, ink kiln mark, 15½" l., 3½" h. 990.00

Flower frog, model of a frog sitting in front of a lily pad blossom, 4½" h. 171.00

Fountain, tall boy holding fishing pole standing on pedestal surrounded by four upright fish on flared base, rich mottled green & brown semi-gloss finish glaze, boy & fish are fitted w/water nozzles. 5,000.00

Model of a frog, 2" h. 200.00
Model of a frog, 4" h. . . . . . 300.00 to 350.00
Model of a frog, large animal w/a hole in its mouth to accommodate a sprinkler, dark mottled green & brown w/ivory chest, 10¼" l., 8½" h. . . . . 2,800.00 to 3,500.00

Vase, bud, 9" h., 3¼" d., slender body w/flaring irregular rim, frog crawling up the side, mottled green & brown glaze 350.00

Vase, 10" h., trumpet-shaped w/molded lily pads. 325.00

Vase, 19" h., floor-type 750.00

DICKENSWARE 1st Line (1897-98)

Underglaze slip-decorated designs on a brown, green or blue ground. Glossy glaze.

Jardiniere & pedestal, the squatty bulbous jardiniere w/a wide, rolled rim & tapering to a flared foot, the sides in black decorated w/a flock of walking yellow geese, the tall cylindrical pedestal flared at the rim & base & decorated w/a scene of a little girl feeding geese all against a black ground, glossy glaze, signed, ca. 1907, 41½" h., 2 pcs. . . . . 2,500.00 to 3,500.00

Lamp base, kerosene-type, lily of the valley decoration on dark green ground, artist-signed, 12" h.. . . . . 450.00 to 600.00

Mug, h.p. deer head, tall, artist-signed . . . . 125.00 to 150.00

Vase, 11½" h., waisted cylindrical body w/short wide rim, Art Nouveau style decoration of bright orange poppies & orange stylized leaves on a deep blue ground, impressed "Dickensware - Weller 581" artist-signed, (crudely drilled through the bottom & slightly scuffed) 275.00

DICKENSWARE 2nd Line (early 1900s)

Various incised "sgraffito" designs usually with a matte glaze. Quality of the artwork greatly affects price.

Ewer, tall slender cylindrical body w/flaring ringed foot, C-form handle, decorated w/a bust profile portrait of "Chief Hollowhorn Bear," shaded tan to dark green ground, 16" . . . . 750.00 to 1,250.00

Mug, depicts detailed image of deer. . . . . 175.00 to 250.00

Mug, 5½" h., decorated w/scene of monk drinking from mug, green ground 385.00

Mug, bust portrait of American Indian "Tame Wolf," artist-signed, 6¼" h. . . . . 625.00 to 750.00

Pitcher, 10½" h., portrait of monk, blue & white, marked "X". . 625.00 to 750.00

Vase, 5¼" h., 5¼" w., pocket-form, flattened bulbous ovoid sides tapering to a short flaring rim pinched together at the center, sgraffito marsh scene w/a duck & reeds by a lake in shades of brown & green, die-stamped "Dickensware - Weller - X352" . . . . 220.00 to 250.00

Vase, 8⅞" h., ovoid body w/short wide flaring neck, shows scene of a young woman wearing blue gown, sitting in a crescent moon playing a long-necked mandolin, green & yellow, decorated by Anthony

Dunlavy, impressed "Dickensware - Weller" & "X31" w/"M" incised on base, artist-initialed (glaze nicks on rim) **385.00**

Vase, 9¼" h., slightly expanding cylindrical body w/wide flaring rim, golfing scene featuring a golfer & caddy, trees & a fence, brown, gold & blue, marked "Dickensware - Weller" & impressed "X 169," "12" & "KVV" **2,200.00**

Two Scenic Dickensware Vases

Vase, 11⅞" h., tall waisted cylindrical body w/narrow shoulder & short flaring neck, depicts an intricately carved & colorfully painted scene of Colonial life w/seven people, three horses & two statues in a densely wooded area, all in 18th c. costume, brown, green, grey & black glossy glaze, rim chip has been professionally repaired, impressed marks "Dickensware - Weller" & "X 48," "8" & "W" (ILLUS. right) **1,540.00**

Vase, 12½" h., tall cylindrical body w/a narrow shoulder to the short rolled rim, continuous landscape scene of white mounted knights in deep woods, blue sky above, glossy glaze . . . . **3,100.00 to 3,750.00**

Vase, 14" h., tall slender ovoid body w/short narrow flared neck, decorated w/an outdoor scene showing a young mother walking through a wooded area w/her two daughters, all dressed in white, shaded brown ground w/green trees in background, artist-initialed, small chip on rim, die-stamped "Dickensware - Weller X 290 0" (ILLUS. left) **990.00**

Vase, 16" h., etched scene w/hunting dogs . . . . **1,400.00 to 2,500.00**

Vase, 17⅞" h., very tall slender cylindrical body w/a narrow rounded shoulder to the short rolled neck, decorated w/a standing monk tasting wine, in browns & yellow against a shaded brown to gold ground, glossy glaze, decorated by Mary Gellier, ca. 1900, marked & artist-signed. **1,650.00**

EOCEAN and EOCEAN ROSE (1898-1925)

Early art line with various hand-painted flowers on shaded grounds, usually with a clear glossy glaze. Quality of artwork varies greatly.

Vase, 5⅛" h., squared shape, pink, white & blue flowers on slate blue ground, ca. 1910 . . . . **165.00**

Vase, 5⅛" h., squatty bulbous body on a narrow footring, tapering to a cylindrical neck w/rolled rim, decorated around the shoulder w/large maroon & grey Virginia creeper leaves & berries, against a grey/green to pale green ground, decorated by Claude Leffler, incised "Eocean Rose Weller" & stamped "9056," artist-initialed (professionally repaired small glaze nicks on rim & foot) **303.00**

Vase, bud, 5½" h., slip-painted florals on shaded pale blue to grey ground **75.00**

Vase, 6" h., 5" d., swelled cylindrical body w/a wide flat shoulder to the short cylindrical neck, decorated w/dogwood branches in white & purple against a shaded dark blue to ivory ground, glossy glaze, marked, Eocean Rose. **330.00**

Vase, 6½" h., 3" d., simple cylindrical body, decorated w/a large polychrome stork standing on one leg against a shaded dark grey to white ground, incised "Eocean - Weller" (crazed) . . . . . . **900.00 to 1,100.00**

Vase, 8" h., 2½" d., slender cylindrical body w/a narrow round shoulder & short rolled neck, decorated w/purple & green lily-of-the-valley against a shaded black to light green ground, die-stamped circle mark . . . . **400.00 to 425.00**

Vase, 10⅜" h., gently tapering cylindrical body w/a swelled shoulder tapering to a short cylindrical rim, decorated w/pink wild roses on shaded green glossy ground, decorated by Levi J. Burgess, artist-signed, stamped "Weller" & incised "Eocean," "X" & "501" **935.00**

Vase, 10⅝" h., wide slightly tapering cylindrical body w/a wide shoulder to the compressed incurved short neck, decorated w/a band of swimming green fish against a shaded dark green to cream ground, signed, ca. 1905, Eocean Rose . . . . **2,500.00 to 2,800.00**

Tall Eocean Vase with Tulips

Vase, 12¾" h., tall ovoid form w/wide rolled rim, decorated w/red & white tulips & green leaves on glossy white ground, incised "Eocean - Weller," "F" & impressed "X 467," artist-signed (ILLUS.) **1,320.00**

Vase, 12¾" h., 4¾" d., slender tapering body w/six open handles rising from narrow shoulder to flared rim, decorated w/large green & violet leaves against a shaded pale pink & dark green ground . . . . **900.00 to 1,400.00**

Vase, 12⅞" h., slender ovoid body w/wide flat mouth, wisteria decoration on shaded brown to yellow ground, glossy glaze, marked & incised "X," artist-initialed (tight 2" hairline from rim) **468.00**

Vase, 14⅛" h., tall cylindrical body w/the narrow flat shoulder tapering to a short rolled neck, decorated w/two finely detailed fish swimming among lily pads & flowers, dark greyish green to pale green ground, decorated by Eugene Roberts, incised "Eocean Rose Weller" & impressed with shape number 579, artist-signed. **3,850.00**

ETNA (1906)

Similar colors as Early Eocean line but designs are molded in low-relief and colored.

Lemonade set: a 14" h. tankard pitcher & two cylindrical mugs; each w/an angled handle

decorated w/a large cluster of deep reddish purple grapes & green leaves at the top against a shaded grey to pink ground, signed, 3 pcs. (hairline in one mug) . . . . **400.00 to 450.00**

Vase, 6½" h., footed angular bulbous body tapering to a wide cylindrical neck w/slightly flaring rim, slip-painted floral design **125.00**

Vase, 7" h., cylindrical, decorated w/yellow dandelions on grey ground **165.00**

Vase, 8⅜" h., gently flaring cylindrical body tapering to a short wide neck, decorated w/embossed flowers in pink & yellow on a shaded grey to pink ground **220.00**

Vase, 10⅞" h., tall gently flaring cylindrical body w/flat shoulder tapering to a short rolled rim, embossed pink carnation decoration on dark blue shaded to pink ground **220.00**

Vase, 11" h., tall ovoid body w/bulbous short neck w/closed rim flanked by short twisted strap handles, low-relief floral bouquet in rosey red & pale green leafy stems against a shaded grey ground **300.00**

Tall Etna Vase with Roses

Vase, 13⅜" h., gently swelled cylindrical body tapering to a short cylindrical neck, decorated w/embossed pink roses, grey to ivory ground (ILLUS.) **550.00**

FLEMISH (mid-Teens to 1928)

Clusters of pink roses and green leaves, often against a molded light brown basketweave ground. Some pieces molded with fruit or small figural birds. Matte glaze.

Basket, hanging-type w/chains,
7" h. **125.00**
Jardiniere, birds on wire scene,
7½" h. **250.00**
Jardiniere, wide slightly swelled
cylindrical body, pink floral
decoration on cream ground,
8½" h. **175.00**
Jardiniere, decorated w/four lion
heads & garlands, 13" d.,
10" h. **250.00**
Planter, figural log, 4½" h. **35.00**
Tub, basket-shaped w/rim handles,
rose swag on front, 8½" d.,
5½" h. **165.00**

GLENDALE (early to late 1920s)

*Various relief-molded birds in their natural
habitats, life-like coloring.*

Vase, 6" h., cylindrical, large standing
marsh bird **400.00**
Vase, 6½" h., ovoid body w/slightly
tapering neck & a flat rim,
decorated w/outdoor scene of a
bird in flight **450.00**
Vase, 7" h., baluster-form body
w/gently flaring rim, decorated w/a
brown bird standing beside its
ground nest w/eggs, green grass &
white & yellow daisies under a blue
sky in background **450.00**
Vase, double-bud, 7" h., tree trunk-
form vases flank a panel embossed
w/a bird & nest w/four eggs,
original label . . . . **325.00 to 350.00**
Wall pocket, bird w/chicks in nest,
long conical form w/curved &
pointed base, 12½" h. . . . **395.00 to 450.00**

HOBART (early to late 1920s)

*Figural women, children and birds on
various shaped bowls in solid pastel colors.
Matte glaze.*

Flower frog, figure of a girl w/a duck,
blue, 4½" h. **140.00**
Flower frog, bathing beauty, 6" h. **325.00**
Flower frog, two figural mermaids
splashing in waves, white, 8" h. . . . **325.00**
Vase, double bud, 10" h., figural
female nude standing between two
tree trunks forming vase w/leafy
branches overhead, blue, 10" h. . . . **395.00**

HUDSON (1917-34)

*Underglaze slip-painted decoration,
"parchment-vellum" transparent glaze.*

Candlestick, cylindrical w/flaring
base & cupped socket w/floral
decoration by Mae Timberlake,
pink & shaded grey ground, artist-
initialed in black slip among the
flowers, 8⅝" h. **303.00**
Vase, 7" h., swelled cylindrical body
w/a flaring base & widely flaring
rim, decorated around the top w/a
pink, yellow & blue blossom
against a group of pale green
leaves all against a shaded white
to pale green ground, decorated by
Sara Timberlake, ca. 1920,
marked . . . . **250.00 to 275.00**
Vase, 7" h., 3½" d., ovoid, decorated
w/white & pink dogwood blossoms
against a blue shading to cream to
pink ground, artist-signed . . **300.00 to 350.00**
Vase, 8¼" h., 3½" d., baluster-form,
decorated w/slip-painted trefoil
blossoms in dark & light blue
w/green leaves on a blue to cream
ground, die-stamped
"WELLER". . . . . **350.00 to 400.00**

Hudson Vase with Sailboats

Vase, 8½" h., cylindrical form
decorated w/several sailboats
plying quiet blue sea while sea
gulls fly overhead, shaded pink
ground, decorated by Sarah Reid
McLaughlin, artist-signed on side
w/"A" in black slip on base
(ILLUS.) **3,850.00**
Vase, 8⅝" h., decorated w/a Spanish
caravel under full sail moving over
blue sea w/white-capped waves,
two other crafts behind, flying sea
gulls accompany the boats, shaded
blue to pink ground w/red & yellow
designs on sails, decorated by
Hester Pillsbury, artist-signed on
side, the base marked w/the letter
"A" in black slip **4,510.00**

Vase, 8⅞" h., swelled cylindrical body w/a short molded mouth, decorated w/large white jonquils on pale green leafy stems against a green to pale cream ground, stamped "Weller" in block letters . . **450.00 to 500.00**

Vase, 9⅜" h., swelled cylindrical shouldered body w/a short rounded neck w/flat rim, decorated around the top half w/large creamy white nasturtium blossoms & green leaves & vines against a shaded blue to pale green ground, decorated by Sarah McLaughlin, ca. 1920, artist-signed & marked . . . . **500.00 to 550.00**

Vase, 9½" h., 4" d., decorated w/a blooming iris in white, blue & green on a blue ground, signed "Walch," marked "Weller Pottery" **546.00**

Vase, 9½" h., 5" d., swelling cylindrical body w/a wide shoulder tapering to a short wide mouth, decorated around the upper half w/large white & blue morning glories & green leaves against a shaded blue to green ground, decorated by Hester Pillsbury, artist's initials on side, black kiln mark on base . . . . **600.00 to 650.00**

Vase, 11" h., 'Hudson Light,' tall slender ovoid body tapering to a molded rim, decorated w/large pastel pink & white iris blossoms w/pale green leaves & stems against a shaded dark to light green ground, signed (few small glaze imperfections in the making) **385.00**

Vase, 12⅛" h., ovoid body tapering to flaring rim, red & blue hollyhocks on a medium blue ground, decorated by Mae Timberlake, artist-signed on side in dark blue slip, impressed "Weller" (professional repair to rim chip). . . . **770.00**

Vase, 12¼" h., bulbous ovoid body tapering to a cylindrical neck w/flaring rim, decorated w/a scene depicting a distant city across a bay, tall bamboo shoots & leaves tower over sea gulls flying toward wood pilings in the bay, impressed "Weller" (a½" drill hole in bottom professionally repaired) **2,200.00**

Vase, 13" h., 4¼" d., tall cylindrical body decorated w/white floral blossoms on a pink to blue ground, painted paper label, impressed "Weller" & signed "Pillsbury" **690.00**

Vase, 13½" h., urn-form, the wide ovoid body tapering to a short cylindrical neck w/rolled rim, wide strap handles from neck to shoulder, decorated w/a scenic design of a large peacock resting near a large wrought-iron gate & stone fence in shades of blue, white, yellow, green & black against a mottled blue-green to tan ground, attributed to Mae Timberlake, the base marked w/a letter "A" in black slip. . **4,500.00 to 6,000.00**

HUNTER (Before 1910)

Brown with under-the-glaze slip decoration of ducks, butterflies and probably other outdoor subjects. Signed only "HUNTER." high gloss glaze. Usually incised decoration.

Mug, tankard, slightly tapering cylindrical w/C-form handle, decorated w/incised & h.p. scene of several sea birds & crashing waves, brown & yellow, decorated by Charles B. Upjohn, impressed "562" & "7," incised artist-initials just below handle, 5⅝" h. **385.00**

Vase, 4¼" h., 6" w., a squatty bulbous body formed as six incurved panels, the wide top centered by a short flaring neck, sgraffito decoration on three panels w/a fish under water in brown & greens, glossy glaze, by Upjohn, incised "UJ" on the side, die-stamped "N36-2" on the base **500.00**

Vase, 6" h., flattened tapering three-sided body w/rounded corners below an incurvate round rim, three applied strap handles, decorated w/swimming fish in bluish water against a shaded green ground, incised "Hunter" & stamped "356 - 3 -X," artist-initialed **385.00**

IVORY (1910 to late 1920s)

Ivory-colored body with various shallow embossed designs with rubbed-on brown highlights.

Jardiniere & pedestal, tapering jardiniere bowl on scrolled feet w/molded Art Nouveau women & scrolling on sides, on matching pedestal, 2 pcs. **2,090.00**

Vase, 11" h., decorated w/molded peacocks design **80.00**

Vase, 12" h., decorated w/peacocks. . **110.00**

Window box, embossed Victorian nudes, 7 x 13" . . . . **275.00 to 350.00**

Ivory Window Box

Window box, w/relief-molded classic
scenes of cherubs, putti, griffins &
horses, "Weller" impressed in large
block letters, repair to small chips
at high points & to one handle,
20⅜" l, 8" h. (ILLUS.). **550.00**

LASA (1920-25)

*Various landscapes on a banded reddish and
gold iridescent ground. Lack of scratches and
abrasions important.*

Vase, 4" h., lakeside scene w/three
pines, lake & mountains, iridescent
glaze **350.00**
Vase, 6¼" h., scenic decoration
w/mountains, ocean, palm trees . . . **350.00**
Vase, 7¼" h., wide disc foot
supporting a slender trumpet-form
body, decorated w/a landscape of
bare trees (small nick on base) **138.00**
Vase, 7⅝" h., slender trumpet-shaped
body w/widely flaring foot,
decorated w/landscape done in
gold, reddish & green gold,
iridescent metallic glaze . . **325.00 to 400.00**
Vase, 8½" h., slender ovoid body
tapering to a short flaring neck,
decorated w/a stylized landscape
scene w/tall leafy trees on a
rainbow iridescent ground, marked . . **374.00**

Lasa Vase with Palm Trees

Vase, 16" h., ovoid body tapering to
cylindrical neck w/slightly flaring
rim, decorated w/water scene, two
palm trees in the foreground, on an
iridescent ground (ILLUS.) **2,070.00**

LOUWELSA (1896-1924)

*Hand-painted underglaze slip decoration on
dark brown shading to yellow ground; glossy
yellow glaze.*

Candlestick, decorated w/pansies,
10" h. **225.00**

Louwelsa Table Clock

Clock, table model, scalloped case
decorated w/yellow daffodils, artist-
signed, tiny base repair
(ILLUS.). . . . . **650.00 to 700.00**
Lamp base, wide squatty baluster-
form body on scrolled tab feet,
decorated w/large yellow iris &
green leaves on a shaded dark
brown to yellow ground, early 20th
c., original oil font & burner
adapted for electricity, marked on
the base, 10⅞" h. **880.00**
Mug, slightly tapering cylindrical body
w/a thick D-form handle, decorated
w/the bust portrait of a smiling
monk in dark brown, rust & blue
against a dark brown ground,
decorated by Levi J. Burgess,
ca. 1898, marked, 5⅞" h. (very
minor glaze scratches) . . **250.00 to 300.00**
Vase, 'Green Louwelsa,' tall very
slender cylindrical body w/a slightly
flaring foot, the narrow shoulder
tapering to a short flaring neck,
decorated w/a long swirled school
of grey & white fish down the sides
against a shaded black to dark
green to pale yellowish green
ground **4,000.00**
Vase, 3½" h., jug-shaped, bright
yellow floral decoration on dark
brown ground **175.00**

Vase, 5" h., wide squatty bulbous body, wide shoulder tapering to flared rim w/inbody handles from shoulder to rim, Virginia creeper decoration in light blue to white on dark blue ground, decorated by Hattie Mitchell, impressed "Louwelsa Weller" on base, artist-initialed just below flowers **1,100.00**

Vase, 5½" h., globular body w/stick neck, decorated w/wild rose, artist-signed **250.00**

Vase, 6⅝" h., 'Blue Louwelsa,' plain cylindrical body decorated in shades of dark blue w/large poppies, base stamped "Louwelsa Weller" & "X 516" & incised "7," ca. 1900 . . . . **600.00 to 650.00**

Vase, 13½" h., tall slender cylindrical body w/a narrow flat shoulder to a short rolled neck, h.p. bust portrait of a Cavalier in brown, black, tan & cream against a black shaded to green shaded to brown ground . . **3,300.00**

Vase, 14¼" h., ovoid body w/the wide shoulder tapering to a short flaring neck, Golden Retriever decoration, decorated by Albert Wilson, "X 635" & "Louwelsa Weller" marked on base, artist-signed on side in white slip (professional repair to rim) **550.00**

Vase, 24" h., 8¾" d., floor model, baluster-shaped body w/a tall flaring neck, decorated w/yellow & orange carnations w/green foliage, on a shaded brown ground, decorated by Eugene Roberts, artist's initials. . . . . . . **1,500.00 to 2,000.00**

MAMMY LINE (1935)

Figural black mammy pieces or pieces with figural black children as handles.

Batter bowl, large . . . . **900.00 to 975.00**
Cookie jar, cov., 11" **2,225.00**
Creamer, little black boy figural handle, 3½" h. . . . . **500.00 to 650.00**
Creamer & cov. sugar bowl, pr. . . **1,650.00**
Sugar bowl, cov., 3½" h. . . . **700.00 to 975.00**
Syrup pitcher, cov., 6" h. . . . **700.00 to 775.00**
Teapot, cov. . . . . **800.00 to 1,100.00**

MATT GREEN (ca. 1904)

Various shapes with slightly shaded dark green matte glaze and molded with leaves and other natural forms.

Ewer, spherical body molded w/a lizard around the sides below a cylindrical neck w/pinched spout &

long angled handle, rich mottled matte greenish blue glaze, die-stamped "WELLER," 3¼" d., 5" h. . . . . **600.00 to 750.00**

Matt Green Jardiniere

Jardiniere, bulbous ovoid body w/a wide molded mouth flanked by four small ribbon handles, molded around the shoulder w/stylized florals, unmarked, 7¼" h. (ILLUS.). . . . . **500.00 to 575.00**

Jardiniere, decorated w/embossed hosta leaves, 8" h. . . . . . **250.00 to 300.00**

Jardiniere, wide, cylindrical body w/molded rim flanked by four small loop handles, four wide ribs down the sides to the rounded bottom edge, embossed w/a wide center band of repeating herringbone, unmarked, 11" d., 8¼" h. . . . . **350.00 to 425.00**

Lamp base, wide bulbous multi-lobed gourd-form body tapering sharply to a slender cylindrical neck w/a molded rim, embossed on each side of the base w/grotesque 'devil' heads, raised on a narrow flaring base w/four 'knob' feet, smooth matte green glaze, complete w/original gas fittings, unmarked, 8½" d., 14½" h. . . . . **440.00 to 600.00**

Umbrella stand, cylindrical w/a flattened flaring rim flanked by low angular loop handles, decorated w/two impressed stylized bushes w/Glasgow roses, dark matte green glaze, unmarked **1,210.00**

Vase, 11" h., 10" d., compressed globular lower section on a low foot, broad stovepipe neck, covered in a leathery green to terra cotta matte glaze. . . . . . . **375.00 to 425.00**

PATRICIA (Early 1930s)

Glossy pale cream glaze, sometimes tinted, with leaf decoration, swan handles.

Planter, figural swan, white, 6" l., 4" h. **50.00**

Vase, 7" h., 4" d., footed bulbous body w/short wide cylindrical neck, figural swan neck handles, green . . . **65.00**

Vase, 11⅝" h., squatty bulbous base w/trumpet neck, relief-molded duck's head on each side at base w/embossed leaves at base & neck, gold, tan & green crystalline glaze **770.00**

ROMA (1912-late 20s)

Cream-colored ground decorated with embossed floral swags, bands or fruit cluster.

Compote open, an oblong bowl w/shaped rim & scroll end handles raised on a low pedestal, decorated w/garlands of leaves & small plaques on each side w/bright yellow birds & flowers, unmarked, 11" l., 4⅞" h. **220.00**

Weller Roma Vase

Vase, 10" h., slightly swelled cylindrical body w/a wide flattened rim, a paneled decoration of carved leaves, twisting stems & berries in pale pink & pale green against a bone white ground, marked (ILLUS.). . . . . **140.00 to 170.00**

Wall pocket, conical, decorated w/flowers on a trellis w/bumble bee near rim, cream ground, stamped "WELLER," on back, 5⅝" h. **303.00**

Wall pocket, conical, incised vertical lines & decorated w/roses & grape cluster near top, green leaves w/yellow center at base, cream ground, unmarked, 8⅜" h. **138.00**

SICARDO (1902-07)

Various shapes with iridescent glaze of metallic shadings in greens, blues, crimson, purple or coppertone decorated with vines, flowers, stars or free-form geometric lines.

Candlestick, sharply tapering conical base below the wide conical socket, small loop handles from base of socket to sides, socket w/electric fitting & a small domed reverse-painted shade, signed **385.00**

Jardiniere, very wide bulbous body raised on short arcaded feet, the sides boldly embossed w/large Moorish arabesques, tapering to a wide short flaring scalloped neck, iridescent purple, gold & green glaze, painted "Weller SICARD" on the side, 14½" d., 12½" h. . . . . **1,500.00 to 2,000.00**

Vase, miniature, 1⅞" h., squatty bulbous form w/wide shoudlers tapering to closed rim, in body loop handles from shoulder to rim, deep purple ground, impressed "15" **330.00**

Vase, 3¼" h., 5¾" d., footed wide & low cushion-form body centered by a short widely flaring trefoil neck, bright satiny decoration of gold arabesques against a lustred green & burgundy ground, signed on the side . . . . **700.00 to 800.00**

Weller Sicardo Vase

Vase, 4⅜" h., inverted pear-shaped body w/flat rim, decorated w/relief-molded arrowroot leaves, iridescent glaze in shades of green, burgundy & gold, marked "Weller Sicard" on side (ILLUS.) **660.00**

Vase, 4¾" h., ovoid body tapering to a short thick rim, embossed ears of corn on iridescent ground of purple & gold, decorated by Jacques Sicard, signed "Weller Sicard" on the side **770.00**

Vase, 5" h., baluster-form, a multicolored iridescent glaze decorated w/mistletoe branches, signed . . . . **400.00 to 450.00**

Vase, 6½" h., 4¼" d., tapering ovoid body w/a bulbous compressed & closed neck flanked by small loop handles, iridescent gold flowers on a deep purple ground, unmarked . . . . **850.00 to 1,100.00**

Vase, 7" h., tall tri-lobed upright undulating body, floral designs on sides, covered in iridescent glaze in shades of green & gold . . . . **1,150.00 to 1,300.00**

Vase, 8⅝" h., wide bulbous ovoid body tapering sharply to a molded flat mouth, incurved loop handles on the sides, decorated w/several snails amid leafy vegetation, base cut "36," glaze flaw from bottom up side½", signed "Weller Sicard," ca. 1905 . . . . **950.00 to 1,100.00**

Vase, 9" h., wide ovoid shouldered body tapering to a short rounded neck w/flat rim, decorated w/flowing chrysanthemums & buds against a background of scattered dots, ca. 1904 . . . . . **2,200.00 to 2,600.00**

Vase, 9½" h., expanding cylinder w/rounded shoulders & rolled rim, a profusion of daisies encircle the body, iridescent gold, blue, burgundy & green glaze, decorated by Jacques Sicard, signed "Sicard Weller" on side (pinhead size glaze flake off rim) **1,650.00**

Vase, 10⅛" h., slender, slightly swelled cylindrical body w/short flaring rim, decorated overall w/stylized arrowroot decoration, iridescent glaze, signed "Weller Sicard" on side & bears older paper label which reads "Whitlow Collection," stamped numbers on base are not legible **770.00**

Tall Sicardo Vase

Vase, 13" h., 5¾" d., bulbous top w/closed small mouth above tapering cylindrical sides, embossed w/large, tall irises, rich burgundy & gold lustre glaze, unmarked (ILLUS.) . . **7,700.00 to 8,500.00**

Vase, 14⅜" h., tall slender slightly tapering cylindrical body w/a flared foot & a widely flared & flattened rim, iridescent mottled green, blue & gold design of stars & butterflies, signed low on the side "Weller Sicard," base embossed w/two rectangles, one above the other, top one w/"12" & lower one w/"Weller" **1,430.00**

Vase, 19½" h., 13" d., Art Nouveau style, ovoid body on scroll-molded feet, the sides tapering to a bulbous, pierced rim molded w/whiplash swirls above large pendent blossoms above the relief-molded figures of two swirling Art Nouveau maidens flanked by long scrolls, the body flanked by large, long pierced scrolling handles continuing down to the scrolled feet, gold, green, blue & purple iridescent glaze, signed "Weller - Sicard". . . . . **7,700.00 to 9,500.00**

Vase, floor-type, 21¾" h., wide ovoid body w/a molded mouth, decorated w/large Art Nouveau stylized poppies against a streaked ground, ca. 1905, signed **12,100.00**

WHITE & DECORATED HUDSON (1917-34)

A version of the Hudson line usually with dark colored floral designs against a creamy white ground always with a black line on rim. Almost never artist-signed.

Vase, 7" h., fruit blossoms decoration on white ground **275.00**

Vase, 8" h., ovoid body w/wide closed rim, black & pale green slip decoration of grapes, grape leaves & vines, cream ground, stamped "Weller" in large block letters **358.00**

Weller White & Decorated Vase

Vase, 8¼" h., tapering cylindrical body w/closed rim, hand-thrown w/horizontal lines & decorated w/repeating floral sprays of heavy slip-painted stylized blue flowers, green leaves & narrow green band around rim, cream ground, unmarked (ILLUS.) **468.00**

Vase, 8⅝" h., cylindrical, decorated w/yellow jonquils & green stems, stamped "Weller" in small block letters. **330.00**

Vase, 9⅜" h., bulbous base tapering to wide cylindrical neck, decorated w/mauve & blue Virginia creeper leaves, vines & berries & narrow band near rim & wide band at top portion of base, cream ground, unmarked **523.00**

Vase, 10" h., overall floral decoration on white ground. **550.00**

Vase, bud, 10" h., slender waisted cylinder w/flaring base, decorated w/trailing blossoms on grey to glossy pink ground **325.00**

Vase, 10" h., 5¼" d., octagonal, decorated w/stylized blossoms in black, burgundy & grey in slip relief on a cream ground, die-stamped "WELLER". . . . . **275.00 to 350.00**

Vase, 11⅛" h., hexagonal w/Oriental prunus blossoms decoration in red, yellow, green & black on cream ground, impressed "Weller" in large block letters **330.00**

Wall pocket, decorated w/roses, 10" h.. . . . . **450.00 to 500.00**

WOODCRAFT (1917)

Rustic designs simulating the appearance of stumps, logs and tree trunks. Some pieces are adorned with owls, squirrels, dogs and other animals. Matte finish.

Candlestick, double, modeled as an owl perched at the top of an apple tree between candle nozzles, 8" w., 13½" h. . . . . **325.00 to 350.00**

Flower frog, figural lobster. . **120.00 to 170.00**

Lamp, table-type, w/double branched tree trunk & two electric lights w/lampshades, owl sitting in center of branched fixtures, 15" h. **499.00**

Lawn ornament, figural, model of a large squirrel seated & holding an acorn, mottled brown & green, stamped "WELLER POTTERY," 11½" w., 11¾" h. (restoration to ears, tight hairline in tail) . . . . **2,000.00 to 2,500.00**

Woodcraft Mug

Mug, cylinderical tree trunk form w/three small molded foxes peeking out of trunk opening, double loop branch handle, large loop above smaller loop, small flake off nose of one fox, 6" h. (ILLUS.). **193.00**

Nut dish, wide shallow dish w/round sides, leaf & branch rim w/figural squirrel eating a nut perched on one side, impressed "WELLER," 5¼" (professional repair to small nick on squirrel's left ear) **468.00**

Planter, log-form w/molded leaf & narrow strap handle at top center, 11" l. **75.00 to 95.00**

Vase, 12" h., smooth tree trunk form w/molded leafy branch around rim & down sides w/hanging purple plums . . . . **175.00 to 225.00**

Vase, 13" h., waisted cylindrical tree trunk form w/relief-molded branch, apple & leaves down the front. . . . . **250.00 to 300.00**

Wall hanging, model of a large climbing squirrel, matte brown & green glaze, black ink kiln mark, 4¾" w., 13½" h.. . . . . . **1,200.00 to 1,500.00**

Wall pocket, conical w/applied figural squirrel **375.00**

WHEATLEY POTTERY

Thomas J. Wheatley was one of the original founders of the art pottery movement in Cincinnati, Ohio in the early 1880s. In 1879 the Cincinnati Art Pottery was formed and after some legal problems it operated under the name T.J. Wheatley & Company. Their production featured Limoges-style hand-painted decorations and most pieces were carefully marked and often dated.

In 1882 Wheatley disassociated himself from the Cincinnati Art Pottery and opened another pottery which was destroyed by fire in 1884. Around 1900 Wheatley finally resumed making art pottery in Cincinnati and in 1903 he founded the Wheatley Pottery Company with a new partner, Isaac Kahn.

The new pottery from this company featured colored matte glazes over relief work designs and green, yellow and blue were the most often used colors. There were imitations of the well-known Grueby Pottery wares as well as artware, garden pottery and architectural pieces. Artwork was apparently not made much after 1907. This plant was destroyed by fire in 1910 but was rebuilt and run by Wheatley until his death in 1917. Wheatley artware was generally unmarked except for a paper label.

Wheatley Pottery Marks

Lamp base, wide tapering cylindrical body raised on four small block feet, the thick squared rim molded w/four extended rim blocks above tapering buttress brackets, overall curdled matte green glaze, complete w/x-ray of the mark, 9½" d., 11½" h. (glaze scrape, small nicks to feet bottoms) **$2,860.00**

Vase, 7¾" h., Arts & Crafts style, w/bulbous base decorated w/overlapping embossed leaves, tapering to a long flaring neck, decorated w/embossed thin flower buds, matte green glaze, logo partially obscured by glaze **990.00**

Vase, 12¾" h., 7" d., large ovoid body, decorated w/white & green flowers on a mottled brown & green glossy glaze ground, inscribed "T.J. Wheatley, Cincinnati, 1879" **863.00**

Vase, 12¾" h., ovoid body, decorated w/white & green flowers on a mottled blue & light blue glossy glaze ground, inscribed "T. J. Wheatley, Cincinnati, 1879" (minor base chip) **863.00**

Large Wheatley Vase

Vase, 20⅝" h., Arts & Crafts style, bulbous ovoid body w/wide cylindrical neck & buttressed bat wing handles, decorated w/overlapping leaves w/buds, cafe'-au-lait bumpy glaze, professional repair to chip on handle & side of vase, unmarked (ILLUS.) **5,775.00**

YELLOW-GLAZED EARTHENWARE

In the past this early English ware was often referred to as "Canary Lustre," but recently a more accurate title has come into use.

Produced in the late 18th and early 19th centuries, pieces featured an overall yellow glaze, often decorated with silver or copper lustre designs or black, brown or red transfer-printed scenes.

Most pieces are not marked and today the scarcity of examples in good condition keeps market prices high.

Creamer, footed tapering bulbous body below the wide cylindrical neck w/pointed rim spout & C-scroll handle, yellow ground w/large round brick red h.p. blossoms & green leaves around the body & vining flowers & leaves around the neck, 3½" h. (small chips) **$605.00**

Cup plate, decorated w/a polychrome bird perched on a branch w/greenspatter foliage, early 19th c., 4¼" d. **316.00**

Cup & saucer, handleless, each transfer-printed in brick red w/a fishing scene & castle & windmill in background all on the yellow ground **495.00**

Cup & saucer, handleless, footed cup w/flaring sides & scalloped rim, matching deep saucer, each h.p. w/large rounded brick red blossoms alternating w/smaller blossom buds among green leaves, green rim bands **1,073.00**

Cup & saucer, handleless, yellow ground transfer-printed in orange & brown w/a scene of a mother & children, early 19th c. **328.00**

Flowerpot & saucer, tapering cylindrical pot w/rounded thick rim band, conforming deep saucer, each w/h.p. large stylized flowers, vines & leaves in red, green & brick

Early Yellow-glazed Flowerpot

red, brick red rims, light spots of
wear, early 19th c., saucer 4½" d.,
1¼" h., pot 4½" d., 4" h. (ILLUS.) . . **1,045.00**

Garniture set: a pair of vases & a
slightly taller vase; each of trumpet-
form w/a flaring foot & widely
flaring, flattened rim, decorated at
the rim & base w/two thin brown
stripes, the body decorated w/h.p.
flower clusters on leafy vines
around the sides, in red, brown &
green, two vases 4¼" h., third one
4⅞" h., the set (wear, repair,
decoration slightly varies) **1,430.00**

Mug, child's, cylindrical, transfer-
printed scene of a coach within an
oval wreath w/inscription "A New
Carriage For Ann," 2" h. **484.00**

Mug, child's, cylindrical, brick red
transfer-printed scene of a woman
& two children in the wood, printed
across the top w/"A Present For My
Dear Girl," 2¼" h. (worn lettering,
professional restoration to foot
chip) **220.00**

Mug, child's, cylindrical w/applied
handle, decorated w/stylized multicolored flowers & leaves w/lustre
trim, 2¼" h. **825.00**

Mug, child's, cylindrical w/C-scroll
leaftip handle, the front w/a
rectangular scroll-trimmed reddish
brown transfer-printed cartouche
enclosing the motto "My Son, if
sinners entice thee, consent thou
not lest disgrace come upon thee,"
2⅜" h. (small lip flakes) **413.00**

Mug, child's, cylindrical w/a brick red
transfer-printed wreath enclosing a
box reading "Esteem Truth Above
All Things," pink lustre band around
the base, rim & handle, 2½"
(pinpoint nick on rim, light lustre
wear) **440.00**

Mug, child's, cylindrical, yellow
ground h.p. w/a pink lustre cottage
scene, applied handle, 2½" h. **330.00**

Mug, child's, cylindrical w/applied
handle, the yellow ground
decorated w/delicate sprigs of
small brick red blossoms on leaf
stems, green rim band, 3" h. **743.00**

Pitcher, 4¾" h., mask-form, the front
molded in relief w/the face of a
man w/flesh-toned skin, black hair
& beard, the sides molded overall
w/large rounded knobs painted
brick red w/a green sprigged
ground on the yellow ground,
angled handle & gently flaring rim
& spout w/green band **935.00**

Floral-decorated Yellow-Glazed Pitcher

Pitcher, 7¼" h., ovoid wide-lobed
body tapering to a flat rim
w/pointed spout & molded feather-
edging, C-form handle, sides h.p.
w/large delicated stylized scrolling
brown flowers & leaves w/brown
band at rim, fine restoration along
side of handle, few spots on spout
rim, early 19th c. (ILLUS.) **550.00**

Plate, 6½" d., h.p. central design of
stylized reddish orange blossoms &
green leafy branches on a white
ground, yellow-glazed border band . . **248.00**

Plate, 6½" d., scalloped flanged rim
w/embossed bird & butterfly design
trimmed in brick red, the center w/a
large stylized flower & leaf design
in brick red & green, all on a yellow
ground (repaired) **440.00**

Plate, 8¼" d., yellow ground w/the
flanged rim embossed w/fruits &
flowers painted in brick red &
green, the center w/a large h.p.
brick red blossom framed by
smaller pointed blossoms & green
leaves **413.00**

Platter, 9½ x 11", oval w/gently
scalloped rim, h.p. King's Rose
center design in reddish orange,
yellow & green, reticulated border
w/yellow (hairline) **825.00**

Soup plate w/flanged rim, the rim h.p. w/clusters of small brick red blossoms & green leaves, the center h.p. w/a large brick red pinwheel-form blossoms framed by smaller blossoms & green leaves, 8¼" d. **2,750.00**

Tea cup, handleless, raised footring, the flaring rounded sides decorated w/a continuous undulating band of orange blossoms & green leaf bands on the yellow ground, 4⅜" d., 2¾" h. (repair on base rim) **413.00**

Teapot, cov., child's, bulbous body w/a short cylindrical neck & inset flat cover, C-form handle & straight angled spout, the body h.p. w/a band of large brick red blossoms & green leaves on the yellow ground, 3½" h. (spout repaired, hairline) . . . **633.00**

Whistle, model of a bird perched on a round base, the angled tail forming the blow-hole, early 19th c., 3" h. (small flake near wing) **385.00**

ZSOLNAY

This pottery was made in Pecs, Hungary, in a factory founded in 1862 by Vilmos Zsolnay. Utilitarian earthenware was originally produced but by the turn of the century ornamental Art Nouveau style wares with bright colors and lustre decoration were produced and these wares are especially sought today. Currently Zsolnay pieces are being made in a new factory.

Zsolnay Marks

Figure group, two bears walking on a rockwork platform base, overall green iridescent glaze, marked "Zsolnay - Made in Hungary," 7⅝" l. **$110.00**

Figurine, figure of a partially clad reclining female w/green, gold & pink lustre glaze, clothing & rectangular base a blue & green iridescent glaze, stamped company mark, 10" l. **990.00**

Zsolnay Floral Design Vase

Vase, 8" d., wide squatty bulbous base centered by a short cylindrical neck & slightly flared rim, elaborate foral design in red, tan & gold w/overall iridescence, signed w/wafer mark **1,210.00**

Scenic Zsolnay Vase

Vase, earthenware, wide ovoid base w/broad flattened shoulder centered by a short cylindrical rim, decorated w/a caravan of men on camels carrying guns & spears, in an oasis w/palm trees, below a wavy edged border of scattered flowerheads, iridescent red, brown & blue glaze, ca. 1900-10, molded factory seal, impressed "8868" & "19," imperfection at edge of foot, 8" w. **2,300.00**

Vase, 9" h., baluster form w/form of draped woman molded in full relief at shoulder, tall cylindrical neck w/flaring scalloped rim, metallic green & blue glaze, stamped company mark **660.00**

Vase, 10" h., tall slender double-gourd body w/a flat rim, overall iridescent bluish green & gold glaze on molded flowers & leaves, 19th c. (minor base rim chip) **110.00**

CHALKWARE

So-called chalkware available today is actually made of plaster of Paris, much of it decorated in color and primarily in the form of busts, figurines and ornaments. It was produced through most of the 19th century and the majority of pieces were originally quite inexpensive when made. Today even 20th century "carnival" pieces are collectible.

Fine Chalkware Cat

Model of a cat, seated animal, hollow-bodied, painted w/black, red & yellow markings on a white ground, probably Pennsylvania, mid-19th c., 15¾" h. (ILLUS.). . . **$6,325.00**

Early Chalkware Dog

Model of a dog, standing w/open legs, head turned to the side, molded chest hair, long dark ears, short tail, on a rectangular base, worn red, black, yellow & green paint, wear & repair, 19th c., 7⅞" h. (ILLUS.) **248.00**

Model of a ewe & lamb, the recumbent animals on a rectangular base, white w/original painted details in red, yellow & black, 19th c., 8¾" l. (repaired cracks). **523.00**

Model of a horse, the solid molded animal w/front leg raised mounted on a yellow ovoid plinth w/red & black painted trim, Pennsylvania, 19th c., 1¾ x 5½", 6½" h. **173.00**

Scarce Early Chalkware Ram

Model of a ram, standing w/open legs, head turned to side, on a rectangular mound base, painted in red, olive green, yellow & black, chips on base, some edge wear, small flakes on ears, unfilled bubbled on chin, 19th c., 9" h. (ILLUS.). **935.00**

Model of a squirrel, seated animal holding nut in his paws, on a high domed foot, worn red & green paint, 5" h. (flakes on base). **248.00**

Model of a stag, recumbent animal w/head turned to side & one front leg raised, on an oblong base, old worn black & brown repaint, 10" h. (one antler damaged) **209.00**

Watch hutch, shrine-form, an arched alcove flanked by pillars enclosing the wax figures of a Mary & Baby Jesus w/polychrome decoration behind the glass front, the arched crest w/an open ring to hold a watch, raised on a rectangular plinth, back w/penciled inscription dated "1817," 15" h. (mold on glass, worn polychrome on outer case) **292.00**

CHARACTER COLLECTIBLES

Numerous objects made in the likeness of or named after comic strip and comic book personalities or characters abounded from the 1920s to the present. Scores of these are now being eagerly collected and prices still vary widely. Also see RADIO & TELEVISION MEMORABILIA and TOYS.

Andy Gump game, board-type, "The Gumps at the Seashore," ca. 1920s. **$75.00**

Andy Panda doll, stuffed cloth, 1940s. **600.00**

Blondie game, board-type, "Blondie Goes to Leisureland," advertising promotion for Westinghouse, original illustrated packaging & colorful 21 x 29" game board, the set **65.00**

Bluey Blooper, Kosmic Kiddle, pink hair w/attached yellow plastic cap w/two antenna, yellow coat, black & white removable disc eyes, red plastic stand & spaceship **200.00**

Buttercup toy, wind-up tin, the crawling baby lithographed in color, Germany, mid-1920s, 7½" l. (paint loss to right side) **259.00**

Captain America toy, wind-up tin Captain America on tricycle, excellent original condition **330.00**

Dennis the Menace book, "Babysitter's Guide," paperback, 1954 . . . . **15.00**

Dionne Quintuplets dress, girl's, size 3, 1930s **55.00**

Dionne Quintuplets magazine, "Look," October 11, 1938, Dr. Dafoe & the Quints on the cover **15.00**

Felix the Cat color-by-number set, "Mr. Big". **96.00**

Felix the Cat figure, bisque, 2" h. **90.00**

Felix the Cat Schoenhut Figure

Felix the Cat figure, jointed wood, painted black & white w/leather ears, decal on chest & trademark under foot, Schoenhut, ca. 1924, slight face paint wear, needs restringing, 8⅛" h. (ILLUS.). **374.00**

Foxy Grandpa figure, nodder-type, painted cast iron, Kenton Hardware, ca. 1910, 6¼" l. **345.00**

Greenie Meenie doll, Kosmic Kiddle, green curl w/attached pink plastic cap, blue coat w/two buttons, black & white removable disc eyes, purple plastic stand & spaceship (one antenna missing). **115.00**

Happy Hooligan figure, china, reclining figure w/full-color under-glaze paint, early 20th c., 3" l. **65.00**

Katzenjammer Kids figure, "Hans," Syroco pressed wood, 1944 King Features Syndicate copyright, 3" h. . . **55.00**

Laurel & Hardy game, Magnetic Pie Toss. **100.00**

Little Lulu doll, stuffed cloth, pressed cloth face w/painted features, yarn hair, red dress, Georgine Averill, 1930s, 36" (doll fair condition, dress faded) **201.00**

Little LuLu perfume bottle **102.00**

Maggie & Jiggs (Bringing Up Father comic) salt & pepper shakers, figural chalkware, full original paint, ca. 1920s, pr. **85.00**

Mutt (Mutt & Jeff comics) pitcher, milk-type, figural, porcelain w/full-color underglaze decoration, ca. 1920s, mint, 5¼" h. **150.00**

Nancy & Sluggo (comics) sewing set, 1949, original box, box 16" l. . . . **100.00**

Orphan Annie tea set: cov. teapot, cov. sugar bowl, creamer & two cups & saucers; porcelain, lustre trim, Japan, ca. 1930s, the set **295.00**

Orphan Annie & Sandy dolls, Freundlich, marked "Harold Gray" on paper hand tag, composition head, pale blue painted eyes, closed mouth, molded & painted hair, original red dress, orange composition dog, 12" Annie, pr. . . . **575.00**

Orphan Annie & Sandy teapot, cov., child's, porcelain, color decoration of Annie & Sandy on a lustre ground, Japan, ca. 1930s **95.00**

Popeye bank, ceramic, figural, American Bisque **450.00**

Popeye bank, dime-type, lithographed tin, ca. 1929 . . . . **99.00**

Popeye bubble pipe, 1950s, mint in package. **50.00**

Popeye Cookie Jar

Popeye cookie jar, cov., ceramic, figural head, American Bisque (ILLUS.). **825.00**

Popeye game, "Pin the Pipe" party game, 1937 . . . . **95.00**

Popeye pencil sharpener, Bakelite, ca. 1930s. **125.00**

Shirley Temple doll, marked "Ideal Doll, ST - 35 - 38 - 2," vinyl head, hazel eyes w/real lashes, feathered brows, painted lower lashes, open-closed mouth w/six upper teeth, rooted hair, original yellow nylon dress w/attached slip, 36" h. **1,300.00**

Spider-Man toy, pogo stick, ca. 1960s, excellent original condition. . **450.00**

Super Hero Express Toy

Super Hero toy, wind-up tin train, "Super Hero Express," lithographed in color, a two-wheeled locomotive & three hinged cars featuring scenes of the various Marvel characters, 1960s, mint in box (ILLUS.) **9,075.00**

Superman game, "Calling Superman," board-type, 1954 . . . . . . **95.00**

Tarzan action figure, 1984, Dakin, 4" h. **75.00**

Tarzan action figure, 1972, Mego, 8" h. **350.00**

Tarzan action figure, Tarzan, The Epic Adventures "Kerchak" action figure, 1995, Trendmasters, 12" h. . . **25.00**

Tarzan action figures, young Tarzan & Kala, 1984, Dakin. **25.00**

Tarzan Aurora kit, #181, 1974. . . . . . **100.00**

Tarzan Belt Buckle

Tarzan belt buckle, limited edition, #233 of 1,000, Smokey Mountain Knife Works, 1995 (ILLUS.). **7.00**

Tarzan Big Little Book

Tarzan Big Little Book, #2005, "Tarzan and the Mark of the Red Hyena," 1967 (ILLUS.) **5.00**

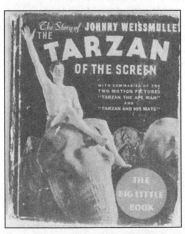

Tarzan Big Little Book

Tarzan Big Little Book, #778, "Tarzan of the Screen," 1934 (ILLUS.). 35.00

Tarzan book, "Tarzan and the Amazons," cover by Burne Hogarth, Superscope Story Teller, 1977 . . . . 6.00

Tarzan book, "Tarzan and the Lost Empire," cover by A. W. Sperry, hardcover, 1931-1940, Grosset & Dunlap. 50.00

Tarzan book, "Tarzan of the Apes," first edition, cover by Fred Arting, hardcover, 1914, McClurg 19,550.00

Tarzan book, "Tarzan of the Apes," four volumes in one, cover by J. Allen St. John, hardcover, 1988, Avenal Books 15.00

Tarzan book, "Tarzan of the Apes," hardcover, 1927, Grosset & Dunlap . 50.00

Tarzan book, "Tarzan of the Apes in the Land That Time Forgot," undated, Treasure Hour Books, art by Russ Manning. 20.00

Tarzan book, "Tarzan of the Apes/Return of Tarzan," hardcover, 1995, Book of the Month Club. 15.00

Tarzan book, "Tarzan of the Movies," Gabe Essoe, hard cover, Cadillac Publishing, 1968 . . . . 20.00

Tarzan book, "Tarzan The Invincible," cover by Studly Burroughs, hardcover, 1933-1940, Grosset & Dunlap 50.00

Tarzan book, "The Beasts of Tarzan," cover by J. Allen St. John, hardcover, 1927-1940, Grosset & Dunlap. 50.00

Tarzan book, "The Return of Tarzan," hardcover, 1927-1940, Grosset & Dunlap 50.00

Tarzan book, "The Son of Tarzan," cover by J. Allen St. John, hardcover, 1927-1940, Grosset & Dunlap. 50.00

Tarzan calendar, artwork by Boris Vallego, Ballantine Books, 1978 . . . . 15.00

Tarzan card #1, Banner Prods., 1966 . . 2.00

Tarzan comic book, "Dell #1," February 1948, cover by Jesse March 600.00

Tarzan comic book, "Dell #21," June 1951, Lex Barker photo cover 100.00

Tarzan comic book, "Jungle Tales of Tarzan #3," May 1965, Charlton Comics 7.00

Tarzan comic book, "Korak #9," July 1965, Gold Key 9.00

Tarzan comic book, "Korak, Son of Tarzan," #22, Gold Key, April, 1968 . . 2.00

Tarzan comic book, "Limited Collectors Edition (large format) #C-22," 1973, DC, cover by Joe Kubert 8.00

Tarzan comic book, "Love, Lies and the Lost City," #1 of 3, 1992, Malibu Comics. 2.00

Tarzan comic book, "March of Comics #114," 1954, K.K. Publications. 15.00

Tarzan comic book, "Sparkler Comics #42," March 1945, cover by Burne Hogarth 150.00

Tarzan comic book, "Tarzan #138," October 1963, Gold Key 9.00

Tarzan comic book, "Tarzan #16," September 1978, Marvel. 2.00

Tarzan comic book, "Tarzan," #168, June, 1967, signed by Ron Ely (Tarzan), Gold Key 20.00

Tarzan comic book, "Tarzan #2," August 1996, Dark Horse Comics, cover by Art Suydam. 3.00

Tarzan comic book, "Tarzan #224," October 1973, DC 4.00

Tarzan comic book, "Tarzan Family #60," November-December 1975, DC . . 4.00

Tarzan British Comic Book

Tarzan comic book, "Tarzan Summer Special," British, 1979 (ILLUS.). 5.00

Tarzan comic book, "Tarzan, The Lost Adventure," #2 of 4, by ERB and Joe Lansdale, 1995, Dark Horse Comics 3.00

Tarzan comic book, "Tarzan's Jungle World," Dell #25, 1959 . . . . . . 20.00

Tarzan comic book, "Weird Worlds #1," DC, September 1972 . . . . 2.00

Tarzan figure, ceramic, 1930s, Foulds, 4" h. 75.00

Tarzan Flicker Ring

Tarzan flicker ring, Vari Vue, 1960s (ILLUS.)...................... **12.00**

Tarzan game, Tarzan, The Epic Adventures "City of Gold Tarzan," 1995, Trendmasters **10.00**

Tarzan Knife Set

Tarzan knife set, Smokey Mountain Knifeworks, boxed, 1995 (ILLUS.)... **25.00**

Tarzan movie lobby card, "Greystoke," 1984, Warner Bros. **5.00**

Tarzan movie lobby card, "Tarzan and the Huntress," 1947, RKO **275.00**

Tarzan Movie Lobby Card

Tarzan movie lobby card, "Tarzan Goes to India," Jock Mahoney in title role, MGM, 1962, set of 8 (ILLUS.)...................... **15.00**

Tarzan movie lobby card, "Tarzan The Magnificent," 1960, Paramount Pictures...................... **10.00**

Tarzan movie lobby card, "Tarzan The Mighty," 1928, Universal Pictures..................... **300.00**

Tarzan movie lobby card, "Tarzan's Hidden Jungle," 1955, RKO **35.00**

Tarzan movie lobby card, "Tarzan's Jungle Rebellion," 1970, National General Pictures **25.00**

Tarzan movie lobby card, "Tarzan's Secret Treasure," 1941, MGM..... **185.00**

Tarzan movie lobby card, "The New Adventures of Tarzan," 1935, Burroughs/Tarzan Productions **75.00**

Tarzan movie poster, "Tarzan and the Slave Girl," 1950, RKO **75.00**

Tarzan movie poster, "Tarzan the Ape Man," 1981, MGM **40.00**

Tarzan movie poster, "Tarzan's Greatest Adventure," 1959, Paramount.................... **35.00**

Tarzan movie poster, Tarzan's Revenge," 1938, Twentieth Century Fox **3,000.00**

Tarzan Movie Pressbook

Tarzan movie pressbook, "Tarzan and the Valley of Gold," Mike Henry in title role, American International Pictures, 1966 (ILLUS.)...................... **15.00**

Tarzan Movie Pressbook Repro

Tarzan movie pressbook (repro), "The New Adventrues of Tarzan," 1965 autographed by Bruce Bennett (Herman Brix) (ILLUS.) **50.00**

Tarzan paperback book, "King of the Apes," by Joan Vinge, 1983, Random House **2.00**

Tarzan Paperback Book

Tarzan paperback book, "Tarzan and the Castaways," 1978, Ballantine, cover by Boris Vallejo (ILLUS.). **4.00**

Tarzan paperback book, "Tarzan and the Cave City," by Barton Werper, 1964, Gold Star **15.00**

Tarzan paperback book, "Tarzan and the City of Gold," Ace #F-205, cover by Frank Frazetta **5.00**

Tarzan paperback book, "Tarzan and the Jewels of Opar," 1984, Ballantine, cover by Neal Adams **3.00**

Tarzan paperback book, "Tarzan and the Jewels of Opar," Ballantine, 19th printing, May 1991, cover by Barclay Shaw (signed) **10.00**

Tarzan paperback book, "Tarzan and the Lion Man," Ace f-#212, cover by Frank Frazetta **5.00**

Tarzan paperback book, "Tarzan and the Lion Man," Mark Goulden, Ltd. (British), 1950 . . . . **5.00**

Tarzan paperback book, "Tarzan and the Lost Empire," 1949 Dell, #436 . . . . **65.00**

Tarzan paperback book, "Tarzan and the Tower of Diamonds," by Richard Reinsmith, TSR Inc., 1985 . . . **3.00**

Tarzan paperback book, "Tarzan and the Valley of Gold," by Fritz Leiber, 1966, Ballantine. **8.00**

Tarzan paperback book, "Tarzan Lord of the Jungle," 1963, Ballantine, cover by Dick Powers **4.00**

Tarzan paperback book, "Tarzan of the Apes," 1943, Armed Forces edition **500.00**

Tarzan paperback book, "Tarzan of the Apes," adapted by Harold & Geraldine Woods, 1982, Random House **3.00**

Tarzan paperback book, "Tarzan Triumphant," Ballantine, cover by Dick Powers, 1964 . . . . **5.00**

Tarzan photo, then and now, signed by Denny Miller (Tarzan, 1959) **15.00**

Tarzan picture puzzle, H-G Toys Inc., 1975. . . . . **10.00**

Tarzan toy, plastic knife, Japan **65.00**

Tarzan toy, Tarzan bow & arrow play set, 1976, Fleetwood. **75.00**

Tarzan toy, Tarzan & gorilla clicker, Japan. **30.00**

Tarzan toy, Tarzan Thingmaker Accessory Kit, 1966, Mattel. **125.00**

Tarzan toy, tin whistle, Japan, 1930s . . **75.00**

Tarzan toy, "Tarzan and the Giant Ape," 1977, Mattel, 15" h. **300.00**

Tarzan video 4 pack, Glenn Morris on cover, 1995, Madacy Music Group **25.00**

The Three Stooges coloring book, Lowe, 1959, fine **92.00**

The Three Stooges display card, "Flying Cane," Empire, 1959, very good **35.00**

The Three Stooges hand puppet, Curly, blue cloth, 1950s, very fine . . **150.00**

The Three Stooges hand puppet, Larry, 1950s, very fine. **150.00**

The Three Stooges hand puppet, Moe, pink cloth, 1950s, very fine. . . **150.00**

The Three Stooges ring, flasher-type, Curly, 1960s, near mint **15.00**

The Three Stooges ring display card, 1960s, near mint **40.00**

Tom & Jerry "Tom" Pez Candy Container

Tom & Jerry "Tom" candy container, Pez, 1960s (ILLUS.). **35.00-65.00**

Tom & Jerry Transistor Radio

Tom & Jerry transistor radio, MI, 1960s (ILLUS.) 75.00-100.00

Toni Tennile doll, Mego, never removed from box, ca. 1977, 12¼" h. (ILLUS.) **45.00**

Twiggy clothing set, "Twiggy-Do's," No. 1725, yellow, green & white knit short dress, yellow socks, yellow pointed-toe shoes, yellow purse w/chain strap, two-strand white & green bead necklace, no fading or wear, the set. **115.00**

Twiggy clothing set, "Twigster," No 1727, yellow & orange knit short dress, matching scarf w/fringe trim, orange cut-out shoes, no fading or wear, the set **95.00**

Twiggy doll, 1967, blonde, never removed from box (ILLUS.) **330.00**

Uncle Wiggily doll, unmarked, cloth swivel head w/mask face, black glass eyes, multi-stroke brows, painted upper & lower lashes, open-closed mouth w/two teeth, cloth ears attached to black felt hat, cloth body, original white collar, red felt jacket w/black snap buttons, blue pants w/red & white striped cuff, 13" h. **155.00**

Toni Tennile Doll

Boxed Twiggy Doll

Uncle Wiggily doll, marked "A Georgene Product" on doll, "Uncle Wiggily (Long Ears), The Famous Story Book Character, Copyright 1943 Howard R. Garis, Trade Mark Reg." on one side paper tag, "Georgene Novelties, Inc. New York, Executive Licensed Manufacturers" on the other, cloth body, applied long ears, original white shirt, gold felt vest, blue felt jacket w/red lapels, blue pants w/red poka dot cuffs, blue ribbon tie, holding black felt hat, 20" h. . . . **550.00**

Woody Woodpecker cap, cloth, 1950s. **60.00**

Yellow Kid (early comics) pincushion, metal figure w/cushion, ca. 1890s, 3½" h. **350.00**

Yellow Kid toy, Yellow Kid in goat cart, cast iron, Kenton Hardware, early 20th c., 7½" l. (overpainted) . . **345.00**

CHILDREN'S DISHES

During the reign of Queen Victoria, dollhouses and accessories became more popular and as the century progressed, there was greater demand for toys which would subtly train a little girl in the art of homemaking. Also see CHARACTER COLLECTIBLES *and* DISNEY COLLECTIBLES *and, under* Glass, DEPRESSION GLASS *and* PATTERN GLASS.

Butter dish, cov., pressed glass, Tappan patt., clear **$75.00**

Butter dish, cov., pressed glass, Tulip & Honeycomb patt., clear **32.00**

Creamer, pressed glass, Tulip & Honeycomb patt., clear **17.00**

Creamer & covered sugar bowl, earthenware, footed boat-shapes w/flaring rims, light blue transfer-printed design of an Oriental landscape on each, ca. 1840, pr. (unseen chip on lid rest of sugar base) **165.00**

Cup & saucer, handleless, earthenware, Casino patt., transfer-printed in light blue, Adams, England, ca. 1830-40 . . . . **50.00**

Cups & saucers, handleless, earthenware, transfer-printed light blue decoration of a lake w/towers, geometric border w/medallions of the view, England, ca. 1830-50, five sets & one extra saucer, the group **303.00**

Dinner service: 15 dinner plates, four soup plates, four platters, one well-and-tree platter, two gravy boats, two soup tureens w/undertrays & ladles, one cov. soup tureen, undertray & ladle; transfer-printed design w/geometric & Greek key banding, blue on white, Staffordshire, England, 19th c., platter 5¾" l., the set (minor chips, cracks, restoration) **230.00**

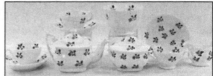

Monopteros Children's Dinner Service

Dinner service: two 2⅜" d. plates, one 3" d. plate, three 3" d. soup plates, one 5½" l., 3½" h. cov. soup tureen, two 3¼" l., 2½" h. square cov. vegetable dishes, two 1⅜" h. gravy boats & one 3¼" l. oval platter; earthenware, Monopteros patt., medium dark blue design of ancient ruins, Rogers, ca. 1830, the set, some damages (ILLUS.). . . **660.00**

Gravy boat, earthenware, transfer-printed light blue floral designs, England, ca. 1830-40 . . . . **55.00**

Plate, round w/flanged rim, the center w/a relief-molded turkey, lightly embossed rim w/six green enamel dots, turkey lightly colored in black & brown, first half 19th c., 4" d. **94.00**

Plate, round w/flanged rim, center w/a blue transfer-printed sheep, the border embossed w/a monkey, dogs & foxes highlighted in blue, green & bluish green, probably Adams, first half 19th c., 4¾" d. . . . **220.00**

Plate, octagonal, center red transfer-printed scene of four men sitting around a table & drinking, titled "Pot Boys," flanged rim embossed w/stars & florets, 5½" w. (two tiny chips) **110.00**

Plate, round, flanged rim, center w/a black transfer-printed scene of a British soldier titled "A Soldier Visiting Home," the rim embossed & crudely painted in red, green, blue & purple, mid-19th c., 5½" d. (two minute nicks on rim) **66.00**

Plate, octagonal, flanged rim, central black transfer-printed scene w/the Farmer's Arms including wheat, farming tools, flowers, hay, etc., banner w/"Our Bread - Untaxed - Our Commerce - Free," trimmed in blue, yellow & red, border band of embossed stars & florets w/pink lustre rim band, first half 19th c., 6" w. **220.00**

Plate, round w/flanged rim, the center w/a dark blue transfer-printed design of three men fishing, border embossed w/flower clusters trimmed in red, green, black & orange, first half 19th c., 6" d. (two unseen chips on the back) **88.00**

Punch bowl, pressed glass, Wild Rose patt., clear **45.00**

Punch set: punch bowl & six cups; pressed glass, Nursery Rhyme patt., blue opaque, the set **460.00**

Punch set: punch bowl & six cups; pressed glass, Nursery Rhyme patt., milk white, the set **225.00**

Table set: cov. sugar, creamer, spooner & cov. butter dish; Vine & Beads patt., clear, the set **175.00**

Table set: creamer, cov. sugar, cov. butter & spooner; pressed glass, Wild Rose patt., milk white, 4 pcs.. . **275.00**

Table set: creamer, sugar, cov. butter & spooner; pressed glass, Arrowhead in Ovals patt., clear, the set **100.00**

Children's Porcelain Tea Service

Tea service: 3½" h. cov. teapot, 2⅞" h. cov. sugar bowl, 2½" h. creamer, 3½" d., 2½" h. waste bowl & six handled cups & saucers; porcelain, boat-shaped serving pieces, all decorated w/overall h.p. enameled floral sprigs in blue, brick red & orange, ca. 1820, the set, some damages (ILLUS.) **440.00**

Tea set: cov. teapot, cov. sugar bowl, creamer & four cups & saucers; pearlware w/a light blue transfer-printed Willow-like patt., boat-shaped serving pieces, marked "Semi China," ca. 1840, teapot 3¼" h., the set (teapot spout chip, chips on sugar lid, surface flakes or pinpoints on saucers) **220.00**

Tea set: cov. teapot, cov. sugar, creamer, waste bowl, six handled cups & saucers & six 5½" d. plates; overall red spatter decoration, serving pieces w/tall cylindrical bodies, marked "Staffordshire, England," ca. 1900, teapot 5¼" h., the set (teapot spout chip, small hairline in creamer) **358.00**

CHILDREN'S MUGS

The small sized mugs used by children first attempting to drink from a cup appeal to many collectors. Because they were made of such diverse materials as china, glass, pottery, graniteware, plated silver and sterling silver, the collector can assemble a diversified collection or single out a particular type around which to base a collection. Also see CHILDREN'S DISHES, PATTERN GLASS, and YELLOW-GLAZED EARTHENWARE under Ceramics.

Rare Washington-Lafayette Mug

Staffordshire pottery, cylindrical w/C-form handle, black transfer-printed decoration, one side w/an oval leafy medallion w/the words "Washington - His Countrys Father" enclosing a bust portrait of Washington, the reverse w/a similar wreath w/the words "Fayette

- the Nations Guest" enclosing a bust of the Marquis de Lafayette, on the front the Seal of the United States w/the wording "Republicans Are Not Always Ungrateful," base rim chip, unseen table ring flake, minute rim nick, 2⅜" h. (ILLUS.). . **$1,540.00**

Staffordshire pottery, cylindrical w/C-form handle, pearlware, red transfer-printed American eagles on a shell on the sides, the front w/a scroll cartouche enclosing "Prosper Freedom," 2⅜" h. (overall mellowing) **440.00**

Staffordshire pottery, cylindrical, brown transfer-printed scene of a cat & her kittens, trimmed in green, red & yellow, 2½" h. (chip on base). . **99.00**

Staffordshire pottery, cylindrical w/molded base & C-form handle, black transfer-printed medallion enclosing a bust profile of Benjamin Franklin within a leafy wreath, reverse w/a farm scene of three men talking, highlighted in blue, red & green, 2¾" h. (minor rim flakes) . **550.00**

CHRISTMAS COLLECTIBLES

Christmas collecting is extremely popular today, with both old and new Christmas-related pieces being sought by collectors around the country. In the following listing we present a selection of old and scarce Christmas collectibles which are especially desirable and can sometimes be quite expensive.

Card, fold-out die-cut figure of Santa in a yellow robe, mint. **$125.00**

Christmas tree fence, painted wood, rectangular board base w/a short picket fence, stenciled mark "Meany & Co., Phila., Pa.," 35 x 36" (bottom is an addition w/a hole towards one end, some replaced pickets) **193.00**

Feather tree w/ornaments, green tree decorated w/blown glass sphericals, celluloid figures, hand-crafted packages, crepe paper figures & an all-bisque baby, early 20th c., 28" h. (some wear) **345.00**

Figure of Belsnickel, papier-mâché, molded & painted, wearing a white outfit sprinkled w/mica flecks, gold accents, black boots, early 20th c., 11" h. (minor crackling back of head & shoulders) **546.00**

Figure of Santa Claus, nodder-type, papier-mâché, sheepskin hair & beard, replaced outfit of synthetic red fleece w/sheepskin trim, Germany, 1930s, 25½" h. (some face & hands damage) **633.00**

Papier-Mâché Santa Claus Figure

Figure of Santa Claus, papier-mâché, standing wearing a fur-trimmed hat, cloak, gloves & fur-trimmed boots, worn old polychrome paint, made to hold a pole or tree, 41" h. (ILLUS.) **550.00**

CHRISTMAS TREE ORNAMENTS

Barbie, 1993 Holiday Barbie, Hallmark, blonde Barbie wearing red dress, first of ornament series, in box, 3½" **85.00**

Barbie, 1994 Holiday Barbie, Hallmark, blonde Barbie wearing gold dress, in box, 3½" **60.00**

Barbie, 1995 Holiday Barbie, Hallmark, blonde Barbie wearing green dress, in box, 3½" **30.00**

Dresden-type, dromedary camel, three-dimensional brown & tan standing animal, 2" l............. **86.00**

HALLMARK KEEPSAKE ORNAMENTS

Christmas Carousel, 1979 .... **75.00**
Dove, 1978 .... **40.00**
Heavenly Sounds, 1980 .... **40.00**
Soldier, 1976 .... **45.00**
Tin Locomotive, second edition, 1983, 3" h..................... **250.00**
Weather House, 1977 .... **40.00**

CIRCUS COLLECTIBLES

The romance of the "Big Top," stirred by memories of sawdust, spangles, thrills and chills, has captured the imagination of the American public for over 100 years. Though the heyday of the traveling circus is now past, dedicated collectors and fans of all ages eagerly seek out choice memorabilia from the late 19th and early 20th centuries, the "golden age" of circuses.

Poster, Adam Forepaugh & Sells Bros. Big United Shows, "The Hazardous, Terrific Automobile Double Forward Somersault," excellent graphics **$210.00**

Poster, Barnum & Bailey for Berta Beeson, "Sensational High Wire Artist, The Mad-Cap Whirlwind of the Mid-Air," shows the high wire artist in a variety of poses, balancing with the aid of fans & parasols, Strobridge, 1920s **920.00**

Poster, Barnum & Bailey Greatest Show on Earth (The), printed in 1897 by Strobridge, 30 x 40" **1,380.00**

Poster, Barnum & Bailey, promoting a troupe of Equestrians, "Versatile Performers Executing a Series of Intensely Interesting and Absolutely Original and Very Astonishing Equestrain Exploits," showing several circus performers atop horses in acrobatic poses, 1898 .... **1,725.00**

Poster, Forepaugh & Sells Brothers Enormous Shows United, dominated by a real estate shot of New York City's Madison Square Garden, "The World Famous Metropolitan Home of These Combined Stupendous Shows," Strobridge, 1900.............. **1,150.00**

Poster, Hagenbeck-Wallace Circus, features Dare Devil Wilno being shot out of a cannon, 28 x 42"..... **450.00**

Poster, Hagenbeck-Wallace Circus, featuring "Colossal Display Of Living Statues," by Erie, 28 x 42" .. **400.00**

Poster, John Robinson's Circus, featues two clowns one holds a banner w/the words "John Robinson's," by Erie, 27 x 41"..... **375.00**

Poster, John Robinson's Circus, features four clowns pointing their fingers up, 27 x 40½" **375.00**

Poster, John Robinson's Circus, features "Judy Rudynoff & her prize Waltzing Horses," by Erie, 28 x 42" **700.00**

Poster, John Robinson's Circus, features "Miss Billie Ward," by Erie, 20 x 27" **850.00**

Poster, John Robinson's Circus, features older bearded gentleman & the legend "Oldest & Best," by Erie, 27 x 41" **700.00**

Poster, John Robinson's Circus, features seven performing horses plus several riders, by Erie, 27 x 40" **450.00**

Poster, John Robinson's Circus, features two hippos including "Tinymite The Smallest Hippo," 27 x 40" **600.00**

Poster, Ringling Bros. and Barnum & Bailey Circus, features nine-dog act in the center ring, by Illinois Litho, 21 x 28" **800.00**

Poster, Ringling Bros. and Barnum & Bailey Combined Circus, featuring "World's Biggest Menagerie," 21 x 27" **125.00**

Poster, Ringling Bros. and Barnum & Bailey Combined Circus, w/legend "India" & a three-person mounted unit of drummer & two buglers dressed as hussars, 21 x 28" **400.00**

Poster, Ringling Bros. and Barnum & Bailey Combined Circuses, features "Miss Dorothy Herbert," 20 x 53" **500.00**

Poster, Ringling Bros. and Barnum & Bailey Combined Circuses, features "The Great Alloys," 20 x 53" **600.00**

Poster, Ringling Bros. and Barnum & Bailey Combined Circuses, featuring "Antalek Troupe," 20 x 54" **375.00**

Modern Circus Poster

Poster, "Ringling Bros. and Barnum & Bailey," lithographed cardboard, ferocious lion & tiger leaping out of the center, advertising above & veneered rectangular door on base w/crossbanding & flaring French below, printed in red, yellow, blue, green & other colors, copyrighted 1974, 13½ x 21¼" (ILLUS.) **44.00**

Poster, Shrine Charity Big 3 Ring Circus, features three clowns, 28 x 42" **150.00**

Poster, Shrine Charity Big 3 Ring Circus, featuring clown & elephant, 28 x 42" **110.00**

Program, Ringling Bros. and Barnum & Bailey Circus, 1951, colorful cover & Howdy Doody centerfold, mint **35.00**

Program, souvenir, Ringling Bros. and Barnum & Bailey, 1961 . . . . **35.00**

CLOCKS

Federal Mahogany Banjo Clock

Banjo clock, Aaron Willard Jr., Boston, Federal-style mahogany, the case w/molded circular brass bezel enclosing the white painted iron dial inscribed "2076 A. Willard, Jr. Boston", brass eight-day weight-driven movement impressed "A. Willard Jr. Boston", the trapezoidal eglomisé throat tablet w/scrolled red & green designs & "patent" on a banner, above the pendulum box w/table showing a gentleman & young girl pulling a carriage w/two children, both tablets framed by half-round moldings flanked by pierced brackets, ca. 1820, 33" h.,imperfections (ILLUS.) . . . **$9,200.00**

Banjo clock, Massachusetts or New
Hampshire, Federal mahogany &
gilt gesso, the molded brass bezel
enclosing a white painted metal
dial above the gilt rope molded
framed throat & pendulum
eglomisé tablets, the lower
showing a woman playing a harp,
eight-day weight-driven movement,
ca. 1820, 33¼" h. including finial
(restored) **1,150.00**

Banjo clock, probably New
Hampshire, Federal-style mahogany
case, the molded brass bezel
enclosing a white painted dial above
the flat veneered framed throat,
eglomisé tablet inscribed "Patent" &
the pendulum tablet "Constitutions
Escape," w/flanking brass pierced
brackets w/eight-day weight-driven
movement, ca. 1820, 34" h.
including finial (imperfections) **1,610.00**

Banjo clock, Simon Willard,
Roxbury, Massachusetts, Federal
style, inlaid mahogany case w/a
top round brass molded bezel
enclosing a white painted dial
w/Roman numerals & an eight-day
brass weight-driven movement
w/T-bridge above the long
trapezoidal throat, lower case
w/white eglomisé tablet &
pendulum box tablet inscribed "S.
Willards Patent," both framed by
mahogany cross-banding &
stringing w/flanking pierced brass
brackets, old finish, ca. 1815,
32¼" h. (restoration). **1,955.00**

Carriage clock, brass & glass,
engaged columnar brass supports,
scrolled base w/subsidiary alarm
dial & bell, glass front & sides,
France, ca. 1900, 5" h. (wear). **403.00**

Carriage clock, brass & glass, the
upright rectangular brass case
w/turned brass loop swing handle
on the top, molded base, glass
form over the dial w/Roman
numerals & a seconds dial,
repeating movement, France,
overall 6" h. **1,200.00**

Cartel clock, French classical revival
style, gilt bronze, the drum-shaped
movement & egg-and-dart- molded
borders flanked by fruiting
cornucopia w/a ribbon-tied
backplate, ca. 1900, 15" h. **633.00**

Grandfather, Samuel Best,
Cincinnati, Ohio, Federal-style
cherry case, broken-arch pediment
w/carved floral rosettes above the
arched frieze above the conforming

inset glazed door opening to a
white-painted dial w/Roman
numerals & moon phases dial,
calendar movement seconds hand
& signature "Samuel Best," hood
flanked by four small slender free-
standing colonettes above the tall
raised-panel case w/reeded
quarter-round corner columns
above the outset panels base on
small cabriole feet, interior
w/original instructions & signature
dated "1806," 95½" h. (feet
replaced, repairs, restoration) . . . **8,250.00**

Grandfather, Daniel Burnap, East
Windsor, Connecticut, carved
cherry Federal-style case, the
arched hood w/pierced fretwork
joining square plinths above an
arched molded cornice & glass
arched door opening to a silver
engraved dial w/Roman numerals
& signed "Danl Burnap E.
Windsor," seconds hand &
calendar dial, flanked by free-
standing columns, the waisted
case w/arched, molded long door
flanked by reeded quarter columns,
stepped-out base on ogee bracket
feet, old refinish, late 18th c., 93" h.
(restored) **7,475.00**

Grandfather, Silas Hoadley,
Plymouth, Connecticut, painted
pine Federal-style, arched hood
w/pierced fretwork joining reeded
plinths & brass urn finials above
the glazed arched door flanked by
freestanding reeded columns,
opening to a polychrome & gilt
wooden dial w/Arabic numerals &
shell spandrels & sidewheeler in
arch inscribed w/maker's name,
central case w/a tall narrow door
above the stepped-out base on
shaped French feet, thirty-hour
wooden movement, old black paint,
ca. 1825, 91" h. **2,530.00**

Grandfather, New England,
Chippendale-style butternut, the
hood w/fretwork joining three
reeded plinths above the
tombstone glazed door enclosing a
painted iron dial w/a portrait of
bearded man in the arch
w/articulated eyes, the dial flanked
by free-standing base stop, fluted
columns above the molded
tombstone waist door flanked by
brass stop, fluted reeded quarter
columns on base & ogee bracket
feet, old finish, late 18th c., 93" h.
(imperfections) **4,025.00**

Grandfather, New England & England, cherry wood, the hood w/a flat molded cornice above a glazed tombstone door enclosing an engraved brass dial w/cast metal spandrels, arch engraved boss "James Atfield Brontford," brass eight-day weight-driven movement, the waist w/thumb-molded tombstone door on base w/applied molding, Spanish brown paint, 18th c., 81½" h. (restored, works of different origin) **3,105.00**

Grandfather, possibly New Hampshire, maple case, the hood w/pierced fretwork joining square plinths above the molded arched cornice & glazed tombstone door flanked by turned columns, the brass dial w/cast metal spandrels, engraved pewter boss, engraved arch, engraved chapter ring & seconds indicator w/brass eight-day weight-driven movement, the waist w/thumb-molded tombstone door on double-stepped molded base & platform feet, old refinish, late 18th c., 86" h. (restored, works of different origin) **3,335.00**

Grandfather, Paul Rogers, Berwick, Maine, Federal-style cherry & mahogany inlaid case, the hood w/molded arched cresting & three reeded plinths joining pierced fretwork above the glazed tombstone door enclosing the painted iron dial w/floral designs, seconds hand w/spurious signature "Simon Willard & Son Boston," the waist w/molded mahogany feet, old refinish, ca. 1810, 94½" h., imperfections & restoration, feet & finials replaced, patches to veneer in waist & part of base missing skirt (ILLUS.) **4,312.00**

Federal Mahogany Grandfather Clock

Grandfather, Samuel Rogers, Plymouth, Massachusetts, Federal-style mahogany inlaid case w/inlaid stringing & crossbanding, brass stop fluted hood columns & waist w/quarter columns, the dial w/polychrome floral decorations, with seconds hand inscribed "SamL Rogers," brass eight-day weight-driven movement, old refinish, ca. 1810, 89¼" h., restoration (ILLUS.) **10,350.00**

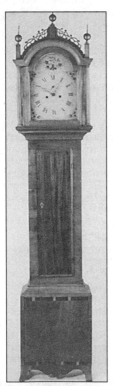

Paul Rogers Grandfather Clock

Looking glass clock, Daniel Pratt, Reading, Massachusetts, mahogany & mahogany veneer case, the scrolled cresting above a glazed door enclosing painted wooden dial w/painted spandrels, Arabic numerals, brass alarm wheel, thirty-hour wooden weight-driven movement, the mirror below flanked by square tapering pilasters, 1837, 6 x 16", 35" h.. . . . . . **374.00**

Shelf or mantel, Ansonia Clock Co., New York, New York, cast metal, a figural cherub holding a wreath seated atop the scroll-embossed case adorned w/floral garlands & framing a porcelain dial, late 19th c., 13" h. **110.00**

Shelf or mantel, E. and G.W. Bartholomew, Bristol, Connecticut, classical-style mahogany, the flat molded cornice above a glazed door w/flanking black painted & stenciled columns, enclosing a painted wood dial w/gilt spandrels & elgomisé tablet of a landscape, thirty-hour wooden weight-driven movement, ca. 1830, 16½" w., 29¾" h. **690.00**

Beehive Mahogany Veneer Shelf Clock

Shelf or mantel, Connecticut, rare "beehive" style case, the mahogany veneer case w/glazed shaped door enclosing a painted circular wooden glazed dial, brass eight-day fusee movement, stamped no. 2752, the tablet below showing an American eagle & shield design, refinished, ca. 1845, 4¼ x 10¾", 19" h., minor imperfections (ILLUS.) **1,725.00**

French Marble & Brass Mantel Clock

Shelf or mantel, French design, black marble w/gilt brass figural cast lovebirds & fruit clusters on arched top flanked by seated putti figures, dial w/Roman numerals, all raised on stepped rectangular marble base w/incised decoration & gilt banding flanking a central leaf swag & scroll cartouche w/classical mask, raised on scroll cast gilt metal paw feet, last quarter 19th c., some damage (ILLUS.) . . **1,025.00**

Shelf or mantel, French Napoleon III period, gilt bronze, figure of Eros seated w/a lyre on base molded w/a portrait roundel, scrolling foliate on knot, upturned nozzle-form feet, ca. 1840, 14" h. **1,380.00**

Shelf or mantel, Gothic Revival-style, gilt-bronze & glass, the tall columned framework modeled as a Gothic spire w/a steeple-pointed roof w/ornate finial & a Gothic finial at each corner of the front above the gilt-bronze column capitals above the ropetwist clear glass columns flanking the ornate rose window-form dial above the ornately cast & trimmed pendulum, the stepped square base w/Gothic lattice trim & raised on figural beast-form feet, France, mid-19th c., 23½" h. (minor chips) **6,900.00**

Shelf or mantel, Jeromes, Gilbert, Grant & Co., Bristol, Connecticut, magogany case, the rectangular ogee molded case w/glazed door enclosing a painted zinc dial & thirty-hour striking weight-driven movement, w/label of manufacturer, the lower tablet depicting a classical building, ca. 1840, 4½ x 15½", 26" h. (minor imperfections) **288.00**

Rare Papier-Mâché Mantel Clock

Louis XV-Style Mantel Clock

E. Terry and Sons Mantel Clock

Shelf or mantel, Litchfield Manufacturing Co., Litchfield, Connecticut, papier-mâché polychrome & gilt, the shaped case of two birds above brass bezel & circular dial framed by mother-of-pearl inlay & an oval reserve below showing a cottage, spring-driven tension balance movement, the scrolled feet on molded platform base on bracket feet, ca. 1850, 5¼ x 14", 17" h. (ILLUS.) **2,070.00**

Shelf or mantel, Louis XV-style, glass & silvered metal, the ornate scroll-embossed top above glass door, sides raised on scroll-embossed footed base, the dial w/Arabic numerals, early 20th c., 14½" h. (ILLUS.) **345.00**

Shelf or mantel, E. Terry and Sons, Plymouth, Connecticut, Federal-style mahogany pillar & scroll case, the painted wooden dial above an eglomisé tablet showing two classical buildings, ca. 1825, 4 x 16½", 30½" h., restored (ILLUS.) **978.00**

Shelf or mantel, Seth Thomas, Plymouth, Connecticut, classical style carved mahogany, the eagle & foliate carved crest above a glazed door w/eglomisé tablet enclosing a polychrome & gilt floral-decorated dial, flanked by stenciled columns on carved hairy paw feet, labeled "Invented by Eli Terry made and sold by Seth Thomas Plymouth Connecticut," ca. 1825, old finish, 30" h., some imperfections (ILLUS.). **748.00**

Seth Thomas Mantel Clock

Shelf or mantel, Seth Thomas, Plymouth, Connecticut, mahogany pillar & scroll case, the arched broken-scroll crest w/wavy birch plinths & brass urn finials above the glazed two-panel door w/the upper panel opening to the white-painted dial w/Roman numerals & polychrome gilt corners, the lower door panel decorated w/a polychrome landscape w/a small house & trees, door flanked by slender colonettes, molded base w/a shaped apron & slender French feet, thirty-hour weight-driven movement w/off-center escapement, ca. 1820, 30" h. (restoration) **2,415.00**

Table clock, Tiffany & Company, New York, gilt-bronze & enamel, offset triangular cast bronze frame w/geometric design enhanced by red & pink enameling, round dial w/Arabic numerals, base impressed "Louis C. Tiffany Furnaces Inc. 360," housing keywind Chelsea movement w/key, dial impressed "Tiffany & Co., New York," 5½" h. **1,495.00**

Brass Wag-on-the-Wall Alarm Clock

Wag-on-the-wall alarm clock, Wynn Frimley, England, brass, the brass tombstone dial w/cast spandrels & a boss in the arch engraved "Wynn Frimley" above the engraved chapter ring & alarm wheel, weight-driven brass movement, 4¼ x 4¾", 7½" h. (ILLUS.). **1,725.00**

Wall clock, Baird Manufacturing Co., advertising-type, cast metal case w/large ring around dial, embossed with "EL CAZA & HONEYMOON CIGARS," the dial w/Roman numerals, lower smaller ring further embossed with "CREME DE LA CREME Cigar Factory J.M. Fortier Montreal" (ILLUS.) **1,000.00**

Baird Advertising Clock

CLOTHING

Recent interest in period clothing, uniforms and accessories from the 18th, 19th and through the 20th century compels us to include this category in our compilation. While style and fabric play an important role in the values of older garments of previous centuries, designer dresses of the 1920s and '30s, especially evening gowns, are enhanced by the original label of a noted couturier such as Worth or Adrian. Prices vary widely for these garments which we list by type, with infant's and children's apparel so designated.

Bathing suit, adult's, black, wool-blend knit, size 38, ca. 1930s **$34.00**

Bathing suit, child's, navy blue, wool-blend knit, size 32-36, ca. 1930s. **29.00**

Blouse, lace w/wire collar & silk under-blouse, Victorian **165.00**

Bonnet, lady's, finely woven poplar, green gauze band trim across the top & a long ruffled gauze bottom border, mid-19th c. (worn, some damage) **138.00**

Boots, lady's, black kid leather, Buster Brown................. **145.00**

Boots, lady's black leather lace-up-type w/pointed toes **125.00**

Boots, lady's, white bucks, pointed toes **118.00**

Paisley shawl, shades of red & black, fringe on two sides, machine-woven, 19th c., 68 x 69" (some edge wear & fringe loss). ... **215.00**

Shoes, boy's, brown leather mesh w/pointed toes, size 13½, ca. 1950s-60s **15.00**

Shoes, child's, Mary Jane-type, caramel kid leather, two-strapped w/side buttons, Buster Brown, ca. 1930s **42.00**

Shoes, child's, Oxford-type, black kid leather, Buster Brown, ca. 1930s . . . **40.00**

Shoes, child's, rust-colored faux crocodile & suede w/side buckles, ca. 1930s **36.00**

Shoes, child's, T-strap-type, brown leather w/black, rust & tan suede, Red Goose, ca. 1930s. **40.00**

Shoes, girl's, saddle shoes, black & white, size 3, ca. 1950s-60s **33.00**

Shoes, lady's, high top, brown leather w/ornate toe, size 7-8, pr. **135.00**

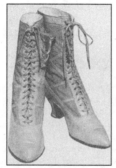

Lady's Lace-up Shoes

Shoes, lady's lace-up style, Walkover custom made, light tan & brown, pointed toe, "37/12/248743K/2796," very minor soiling, 9½" h., pr. (ILLUS.) **110.00**

Wedding gown, eggshell taffeta w/seed pearl decoration, hand-made, includes headpiece of faux pearls & clear stones, 1941, the set . . **275.00**

COCA-COLA ITEMS

Coca-Cola promotion has been achieved through the issuance of scores of small objects through the years. These, together with trays, signs and other articles bearing the name of this soft drink, are now sought by many collectors. The major reference in this field is Petretti's Coca-Cola Collectibles Price Guide, 10th Edition, *by Allan Petretti (Antique Trader Books).*

Advertisement, round, celluloid over metal w/cardboard backing for hanging or standing, red w/bottle of Coca-Cola in center, reads "Coca-Cola" across diameter, 9" d. (scratches & soiling) **$198.00**

Advertisement, stand-up cardboard, autographed picture of baseball player Ernie Banks swinging a bat & reading "Swing to the Real Thing!", 1960, 10" w., 20" h. (minor chipping at edges & some fading) . . **303.00**

Red Tin Dispenser Bank

Bank, tin, battery-operated, painted red, designed to look like Coke dispenser, window at top front to view money, reads "Drink Coca-Cola" on window, other lettering reads "Refresh Yourself" & "Ice Cold", 1950s (ILLUS.) **440.00**

Bottle opener, in original box, white plastic front w/picture of "Sprite Boy" & bottle of Coke, metal hardware for mounting, box is marked "The Starr Bottle Opener," 2¾"w., 6" h. (soiling & wear to box, opener faded) **28.00**

Bottles & carrier, glass bottles & debossed metal carrier w/metal handle, four bottles have embossed lettering & two have decals, 5 x 8", 8" h. (denting & wear to carrier, scratches & soiling to bottles) **44.00**

1896 Coca-Cola Calendar

Calendar, 1896, color lithographed
cardboard, color bust portrait of a
beautiful lady holding a mug of
Coca-Cola, rare, 6½ x 10½"
(ILLUS.) **20,000.00**

Calendar, 1899, color lithographed
cardboard, central oval reserve of
lovely lady seated at table writing a
letter, pink roses along one side,
calendar below, rare, 7⅜ x 13". . **10,000.00**

1901 Coca-Cola Calendar

Calendar, 1901, color lithographed
cardboard, lovely lady wearing
feathered hat & holding a glass of
Coca-Cola in a scroll-trimmed
central reserve surrounded by
yellow & purple pansies,
7⅜ x 13" (ILLUS.). **7,500.00**

Calendar, 1904, color lithographed
cardboard, a full-length portrait of a
handsome lady standing in front of
an ornate screen, the product on
an ornate stand to the left,
7¾ x 15¼" **4,500.00**

Calendar, 1906, color lithographed
cardboard, bust portrait of pretty
young lady wearing a lacy white
blouse w/a corsage of violets &
drinking a glass of Coca-Cola,
calendar below, 7¾ x 14¼" **6,500.00**

Calendar, 1909, color lithographed
cardboard, portrait of a young lady
seated at a table w/a glass of
Coca-Cola, the lights of a World's
Fair in the background, rare,
11 x 20½" **8,500.00**

Calendar, 1910, color lithographed
cardbard, Hamilton King artwork
w/the head of a young lady wearing
a large feathered hat, 8¾ x 17½" . . **6,500.00**

Calendar, 1913, color lithographed
cardboard, lovely lady seated &
leaning on a railing while sipping
from a bottle of Coca-Cola, wearing
large white & red hat & a white
dress trimmed in red, bottlers'
calendar, 16 x 28" **8,500.00**

Calendar, 1914, color lithographed
cardboard, three-quarter length
portrait of young lady "Betty"
wearing a pink & white dress &
bonnet, 13 x 32" **2,000.00**

1915 Coca-Cola Calendar

Calendar, 1915, color lithographed
cardboard, full-length portrait of a
young lady wearing a pale pink
dress & hat seated on a large
boulder, holding a glass in one
hand & leaning on a closed parasol
w/the other, 13 x 32" (ILLUS.) . . . **4,800.00**

Calendar, 1918, color lithographed
cardboard, beachside scene of a
young lady in white carrying a
glass & open umbrella & standing
beside a second young lady seated
wearing a yellow & red bathing
outfit, 13 x 32" **5,000.00**

Calendar, 1922, color lithographed
cardboard, three-quarter length
portrait of a young lady wearing a
pink dress & hat & holding a glass

1922 Coca-Cola Calendar

while leaning on a bench, baseball
players in background, 12 x 32"
(ILLUS.) **2,400.00**

Calendar, 1928, color lithographed
cardboard, a seated flapper in a
satiny gown & a wrap w/a white fur
collar holding a glass of Coca-Cola,
12 x 24" **1,200.00**

Calendar, 1931, color lithographed
cardboard, Norman Rockwell
artwork of a young boy in straw hat
seated by tree eating sandwich &
drinking from a bottle, his dog
watching, 12 x 24" **1,000.00**

Calendar, 1936, color lithographed
cardboard, seaside scene of an old
fisherman & young girl & boy by a
rowboat, 12 x 24" **900.00**

1943 South American Calendar

Calendar, 1943, color lithographed
cardboard, half-length portrait of
pretty dark-haired lady surrounded
by flowering branches & holding a
glass of Coca-Cola, text in Spanish
for the South American market,
14 x 29" (ILLUS.). **500.00**

1946 Boy Scout Rockwell Calendar

Calendar, 1946, color lithographed
paper, Boy Scout version
w/Norman Rockwell artwork of a
Boy Scout helping a Cub Scout
learn to tie a knot, 6½ x 11½"
(ILLUS.). **375.00**

Calendar, 1947, color lithographed
paper, bust portrait of a pretty
young lady holding skis, two
months on each page, six pages. . . **350.00**

Calendar, 1954, color lithographed
paper, a month at the top & bottom
w/the bust portrait of a young lady
holding a bottle of Coca-Cola in the
center w/a background portrait of a
leaping basketball player to the
right, six pages **165.00**

1958 Rockwell Boy Scout Calendar

Calendar, 1958, color printed paper,
Boy Scout version w/Norman
Rockwell artwork showing a Cub

Scout, Boy Scout & Eagle Scout standing & saluting, 11 x 23" (ILLUS.)...................... **400.00**

Calendar, 1960, color printed paper, scene of a young couple standing & holding skis, each w/a bottle of Coca-Cola.................... **60.00**

Calendar, 1966, color printed paper, color photo scene of a couple working in a flower garden, a wheelbarrow full of flowers, he drinking from a bottle, six pages **60.00**

Calendar, 1972, color printed paper, a large photo close-up of a yellow daisy, six pages................. **20.00**

Can, "diamond" style, 12 oz. unopened, 2½" d., 4¾" h. (scratches & soiling) **83.00**

Clock, counter-type, rectangular metal w/reverse-painted glass, "Lunch With Us" in embossed green lettering at bottom, "Drink Coca-Cola" in white lettering next to dial, gold Arabic numerals, lights up, hook for hanging, working condition, 5 x19", 9" h. (edge wear, scratching & soiling)........... **1,018.00**

Cooler, metal, painted silver w/metal handle & embossed lettering reading "Drink Coca-Cola" on front, inside tray, 9½ x 19", 18" h. (denting, scratching & soiling)..... **149.00**

Cooler, metal w/galvanized interior & tray, chest-type w/handle, in original box, 17 x 12", 19" h. (very minor scratches & soiling to cooler, wear to box).................. **418.00**

Cooler, metal, single case, junior size, red chest on brown frame legs, sides of chest read "Drink Coca-Cola," 1929, 17½ x 17½" sq., 27½" h. (casters missing, edge wear, rust spotting, scratches, soiling & paint chips to frame & signs)........... **852.00**

Coupon, cardboard, entitles customer to one free Coca-Cola, central lettering flanked by two bottles of Coke, reverse side reads "Millions Drink Coca Cola 7,000,000 Sold a Day," 1929, 2⅜ x 3 5/8" .... **30.00 to 60.00**

Lighter, gold-plated, metal & plastic in original bag w/lettering "Gold Plated Lighter Reg. $1.00 Value Only $.49 When you buy a carton of Coca-Cola King Size," 2½" h. (lettering on bag faded)........... **94.00**

Menu board, wall-type, tin, Coca-Cola logo at top, 1960s, 20" w., 28" h. (scratches, soiling & dent to chalkboard) **93.00**

"Drink Coca-Cola" Plate

Plate, 7½" d., china w/lettering reading "Drink Coca-Cola," bottle & glass in green, yellow, red, brown, & cream w/red, black & yellow lettering, marked "Vitreous/Edwin M. Knowles China Co./31-2-1," crazing (ILLUS.) **385.00**

Coca-Cola Framed Poster

Poster, colorful cardboard litho in green wooden frame, depicts a smiling girl standing behind table laden w/cookies & bottles of Coke, reads "Come Over For Coke", Forbes-Boston Litho, 1947 The Coca-Cola Co., 36½" l., 20¾" h., hole in middle (ILLUS.) **253.00**

Girl on the Calendar Sign

Sign, cardboard, lettering in center reads "The Girl on the Calendar-Through the Years" w/ small round Coca-Cola logo underneath, surrounded by twelve different pictures of ladies from previous calendars on a blue background, gold metal frame, 1939, 56" w., 27½" h. (ILLUS.) ..... **500.00 to 1,000.00**

Girl With Horse Sign

Sign, cardboard, shows girl in riding outfit standing near flowers next to horse, holding Coke in right hand, blue & white sky w/round Coca-Cola logo in upper left corner, 1940s, framed, 30" w., 50" h. (ILLUS.) . . . **1,320.00**

Coca-Cola Die-Cut Sign

Sign, die-cut porcelain in shape of Coca-Cola bottle, brown, gray, green, red & white, 5" w., 16½" h., minor scratches, some chipping at edges (ILLUS.) . . . . **200.00 to 250.00**

Sign, flange-type, metal, rectangular reading "Drink Coca-Cola," picture of bottle of Coke w/yellow background underneath rectangle, 1940s, 24" w., 20½" h. (scratches, touch-up under "C" in "Coca" on one side) **605.00**

Sign, flange-type, porcelain, reading "Coca-Cola" in white lettering & "Iced Here" in yellow on red

background, 1949, 17¾" w., 19" h. (scratches, fading & chips to edges) **550.00**

Sign, neon glass w/transformer, blue letters reading "Coca-Cola" on black plastic background w/orange border, 26" w., 14" h. **330.00**

Sign, one-sided self-framed tin, painted yellow, depicting "Sprite Boy" (boy wearing Coca-Cola cap & pointing to a bottle of Coke resting on a small red Coca-Cola sign,) made in USA & used for exporting, 1947, 13" d. **1,430.00**

Sign, porcelain, rectangular, green & red w/tan lettering reading "Fountain Service" & white lettering reading "Drink Coca-Cola Delicious and Refreshing," 60 x 45½" (chips to raised border) **2,420.00**

Sign, porcelain, rectangular, left side light green background w/dark green lettering reads "Fountain Service," w/words separated by white wavy lines, right side red background w/white lettering reads "Drink Coca-Cola," 1950s, 12 x 28" (chips to edges & creases, scratches) **231.00**

Sign, round, one-sided porcelain, painted dark blue, reading "Drink Coca Cola Ice Cold", allegedly foreign fridge sign, 14" d. (minor fading) **357.00**

Very Rare Hilda Clark Sign

Sign, tin, oval self-framed, featuring picture of Hilda Clark, popular Victorian beauty, surrounded w/floral border & "Coca-Cola" written on bottom of border, very rare, 1903 (ILLUS.). **83,375.00**

Sign, tin, painted white w/green border, top half w/red logo reading "Drink Coca-Cola - Sign of Good Taste," bottom half showing a bottle of Coke, 1963, 17½" w., 53½" h. (scratches to edges) **300.00**

Sign, two-sided wood w/metal base, yellow, green, white & red, one side showing silhouette of a little girl in pigtails, w/lettering "Slow School Zone, Enjoy Coca-Cola, Drive Safely," reverse side depicting a bottle of Coke & reading "Thank You, Resume Speed, Enjoy Coca-Cola, Drive Refreshed," reflective paint to top portion & words "Coca-Cola," ca. 1950s-1960s, 24" d., 49½" h. (edge wear, crayon markings, minor paint chips) **715.00**

Stand-up advertisement, die-cut, one-sided cardboard, depicting little boy sleeping, dreaming of a toy train & helicopter painted white w/red lettering "Enjoy Coca Cola," w/Santa waving & holding a bottle of Coke, reads "Season's Greetings" at lower edge, 31½" w., 47" h. (edge wear, scratches, soiling, paper starting to separate from lower corner) **215.00**

Thermometer, embossed metal, bottle-shaped, 17" h. **140.00**

Thermometer, tin, embossed bottle shape, 1958, 8½" w., 29½" h. (very minor scratches & paint chips) **83.00**

1934 "Tarzan & Jane" Tray

Tray, 1934, Johnny Weismuller & Maureen O'Sullivan (Tarzan & Jane), 10½ x 13¼" rectangle (ILLUS.) **660.00**

1940 Fishing Girl Coca-Cola Tray

Tray, 1940, Girl Fishing, 10½ x 13¼" rectangle (ILLUS.) **154.00**

Coca-Cola "Lois" Serving Tray

Tray, 1953-1960, smiling woman w/arm propped up & chin resting on hand, holding a bottle of Coke in other hand, multi-colored litho w/various scenes on sides, handwritten "Lois" on woman's forehead, 10½" w., 13½" h., minor scratches (ILLUS.) . . . . **40.00 to 60.00**

Truck, metal cab & frame w/wood bed containing fourteen wood block Coca-Cola cases, Smitty Toys, Smith-Miller, California, 13½" l. (scratches & soiling, chips to sides of truck bed) **715.00**

Urn, cov., ceramic, 1970s reproduction miniature used for display purposes, white w/red lettering & gold design (ILLUS., left) **132.00**

Large & Small Reproduction Urns

Urn, cov., ceramic, 1970s reproduction used for display purposes (1896 originals were syrup dispensers,) white w/red lettering & gold design, approximately 18" h. (ILLUS., right) **935.00**

COMMEMORATIVE PLATES

BING & GRONDAHL

CHRISTMAS

1895	$5,379.00
1896	1,571.00
1897	1,411.00
1898	624.00
1899	1,212.00
1900	803.00
1901	348.00
1902	357.00
1903	315.00
1904	120.00
1905	137.00
1906	87.00
1907	118.00
1908	75.00
1909	84.00
1910	92.00
1911	75.00
1912	82.00
1913	78.00
1914	79.00
1915	123.00
1916	79.00
1917	80.00
1918	73.00
1919	64.00
1920	65.00
1921	61.00
1922	71.00
1923	70.00
1924	69.00

1925 Bing & Grondahl Christmas Plate

1925 (ILLUS.)	75.00
1926	75.00
1927	93.00
1928	71.00
1929	66.00
1930	79.00
1931	79.00
1932	72.00
1933	67.00
1934	62.00
1935	71.00
1936	71.00
1937	76.00
1938	118.00

1939 Bing & Grondahl Christmas Plate

1939 (ILLUS.)	144.00
1940	151.00
1941	228.00
1942	193.00
1943	151.00
1944	91.00
1945	160.00
1946	76.00
1947	92.00
1948	72.00
1949	84.00
1950	105.00
1951	85.00
1952	80.00
1953	79.00
1954	84.00
1955	114.00
1956	135.00
1957	125.00
1958	85.00
1959	104.00
1960	142.00
1961	100.00
1962	52.00
1963	81.00
1964	33.00
1965	37.00
1966	33.00
1967	30.00
1968	27.00
1969	19.00
1970	17.00
1971	11.00
1972	13.00
1973	18.00
1974	14.00
1975	20.00
1976	21.00
1977	18.00
1978	22.00

1979	26.00
1980	24.00
1981	23.00
1982	29.00
1983	28.00
1984	28.00
1985	33.00
1986	34.00
1987	44.00
1988	40.00
1989	46.00
1990	58.00
1991	57.00
1992	65.00

MOTHER'S DAY

1969, Dog & Puppies	342.00
1970, Birds & Chicks	18.00
1971, Cat & Kitten	10.00
1972, Mare & Foal	11.00
1973, Duck & Ducklings	13.00
1974, Bear & Cubs	13.00
1975, Doe & Fawns	13.00
1976, Swan Family	17.00
1977, Squirrel & Young	20.00
1978, Heron	16.00
1979, Fox & Cubs	34.00
1980, Woodpecker & Young	25.00
1981, Hare & Young	26.00
1982, Lioness & Cubs	26.00
1983, Racoon & Young	25.00
1984, Stork & Nestlings	37.00
1985, Bear with Cubs	26.00
1986, Elephant with Calf	29.00
1987, Sheep with Lambs	54.00

HUMMEL (GOEBEL WORKS)

ANNIVERSARY

1975, Stormy Weather	55.00
1980, Spring Dance	77.00
1985, Auf Wiedersehen	124.00

ANNUAL

1971, Heavenly Angel	427.00
1972, Hear Ye, Hear Ye	54.00
1973, Globe Trotter	70.00
1974, Goose Girl	38.00
1975, Ride into Christmas	45.00
1976, Apple Tree Girl	37.00
1977, Apple Tree Boy	48.00
1978, Happy Pastime	29.00
1979, Singing Lesson	27.00
1980, School Girl	40.00
1981, Umbrella Boy	42.00
1982, Umbrella Girl	88.00
1983, The Postman	157.00
1984, Little Helper	45.00
1985, Chick Girl	68.00
1986, Playmates	122.00
1987, Feeding Time	287.00

ROYAL COPENHAGEN

1955 Royal Copenhagen Christmas Plate

CHRISTMAS

1908	2,746.00
1909	162.00
1910	117.00
1911	121.00
1912	139.00
1913	117.00
1914	155.00
1915	158.00
1916	104.00
1917	98.00
1918	98.00
1919	96.00
1920	92.00
1921	79.00
1922	75.00
1923	82.00
1924	106.00
1925	101.00
1926	77.00
1927	116.00
1928	104.00
1929	92.00
1930	121.00
1931	124.00
1932	106.00
1933	169.00
1934	160.00
1935	242.00
1936	174.00
1937	201.00
1938	246.00
1939	329.00
1940	330.00
1941	293.00
1942	285.00
1943	491.00
1944	195.00
1945	383.00
1946	153.00

1947	204.00
1948	176.00
1949	187.00
1950	122.00
1951	253.00
1952	109.00
1953	158.00
1954	128.00
1955 (ILLUS.)	140.00
1956	147.00
1957	91.00
1958	113.00
1959	113.00
1960	105.00
1961	99.00
1962	184.00
1963	57.00
1964	41.00
1965	38.00
1966	28.00
1967	29.00
1968	21.00
1969	24.00
1970	25.00
1971	18.00
1972	18.00
1973	21.00
1974	23.00
1975	17.00
1976	20.00
1977	17.00
1978	21.00
1979	39.00
1980	23.00
1981	21.00
1982	47.00
1983	37.00
1984	32.00
1985	47.00
1986	45.00
1987	47.00
1988	43.00
1989	50.00
1990	54.00
1991	43.00
1992	54.00

MOTHER'S DAY

1971, American Mother	75.00
1972, Oriental Mother	39.00
1973, Danish Mother	38.00
1974, Greenland Mother	30.00
1975, Bird in Nest	35.00
1976, Mermaids	33.00
1977, The Twins	25.00
1978, Mother & Child	26.00
1979, A Loving Mother	10.00
1980, An Outing with Mother	14.00
1981, Reunion	15.00
1982, Children's Hour	14.00

COMPACTS & VANITY CASES

Bakelite necessaire, black & ivorene, front lid decorated w/rhinestones, front opening reveals mirror & compartments for rouge & powder, back pocket for change, keys, etc., carrying cord & tassel, 1¾ x 4" **$350.00-450.00**

Brushed goldtone compact, opens when attached lipstick is pressed back, lid enhanced w/band of turquoise & red stones, beveled mirror, K & K, 2¼ x 3" **100.00-150.00**

Brushed goldtone compact, square, dime centered on lid, Volupte, 2½" sq. **40.00-60.00**

Brushed goldtone compact, designed to resemble artist's palette, lid decorated w/paint tube, paint brush & colors of paint, Volupte, 3 x 2¾" **125.00-175.00**

Brushed goldtone compact, purse-shaped, polished goldtone flap opens to reveal opening for picture or rouge, tango chain lipstick tube suspended by two chains, sticker on mirror reads "Genuine Collectors Item by Volupte," 3½ x 2¾" **135.00-160.00**

Celluloid & brass compact, round, celluloid top has image of train coming out from behind trees, advertising "Frisco Line", on brass box, 2" d. **138.00**

Cloisonné enameled goldtone compact, lid decorated w/French scene, Schildkraut, 2½" d. . . . **50.00-70.00**

Compact w/matching pill box, lids decorated w/mother-of-pearl, enhanced w/goldtone bands & raised painted flowers set w/sparkle, Marhill, 2¾ x 2½", pill box 1½" sq. **50.00-60.00**

Compact/bracelet combination, polished satin finish, lid of compact set w/red & clear crystal stones, K & K, 2 x 1½" **250.00-300.00**

Compact/cane combination, hallmarked sterling, cane handle is a compact, lid decorated w/black island scene, dark brown wood shaft designed to resemble bamboo, metal ferrule protector at end of stick, wrist cord under compact handle, 1¾" d. . . . **375.00-500.00**

Compact/perfume/lipstick combination, Goldtone, pearl & rhinestone, lipstick tube attached to side of mini-compact & mini-

perfume holder, compact &
perfume holder attached back-to-
back, mirror on exterior of perfume
holder, 2 x 2½ x 1¼" **100.00-150.00**

Compact/watch combination, White
cloisonné enhanced w/hand-
painted roses on lid, interior metal
swinging mirror conceals watch,
Evans, 2½ x 2½" sq. **50.00-200.00**

**Compact/watch/music box
combination,** watch centered on
embossed sunburst design lid,
interior reveals powder well &
music box, Evans, 3 x 2". . . **175.00-195.00**

"Crystell" (plastic) compact,
butterfly-shaped, black, blue &
silver design on lid, mirrors on
interiors of both wings, puff &
powder compartment on one side,
other side for pills, Wadsworth,
4¼ x 2¾" **150.00-225.00**

Enameled compact, Art Deco-style,
geometric pattern in shades of
blue, rose-cut diamond closure &
front motifs, in yellow gold (14k),
signed "Flato," boxed (minor wear
to enamel) **2,875.00**

Enameled compact, round, blue
w/multicolored Eastern Star
decoration, Stratton, England,
2¼" d. **60.00-80.00**

Enameled compact, round, white,
decorated w/red anchor & blue
rope, Volupte, 2½" d. **50.00-70.00**

Enameled compact, round, white,
designed to resemble baseball,
team name "Giants" centered on
front lid decorated w/blue & white
painted stitching, 3" d. **60.00-100.00**

Gilded Silver Compact

Gilded silver blue enamel compact,
front lid w/hand-painted scene,
back lid engraved, interior has
deeply beveled mirror & powder
well, 4 x 3" (ILLUS.) **450.00-550.00**

Gold (14k yellow) compact, bi-
colored w/alternating reeded &
textured panels, diamond
thumbpiece **805.00**

Gold (14k yellow) compact, ribbed
finish w/mirror, suede case,
2¾" sq. **920.00**

Goldtone compact, round, top lip
decorated w/profile of woman, a
rose & star on dark blue & black
background framed w/goldtone
bars, silvertone back lid, Karess,
1¾" d. **80.00-150.00**

Goldtone compact, ball-shaped,
exterior engraved w/beautiful floral
design, plastic interior, Pygmalion,
2⅛" d. **150.00-200.00**

Goldtone compact, round, designed
to resemble train conductor's
pocket watch, lid decorated
w/paper transfer of watch face
w/Roman numerals, back lid
decorated w/old-fashioned
steam locomotive, Wadsworth,
2¼" d. **40.00-60.00**

Goldtone compact, Coty trademark
(stylized white puffs on orange
background) on lid, Coty,
2½" d. **60.00-80.00**

Goldtone compact, designed to
resemble padlock, has picture
locket under flower-decorated lid,
Zell, 2½" d. **75.00-125.00**

Goldtone compact, round, lid has
picture of female flamenco dancer
w/applied lace skirt protected by
beveled glass dome, beveled glass
bottom lid, 2¾" d. **80.00-100.00**

Goldtone compact, square
w/matching lipstick, compact lid &
lipstick top decorated w/pale
orange cabochon stones, interior
mirror & powder well, gold threads
decorate black fitted case, Ciner,
2¾" **150.00-175.00**

Goldtone compact, w/matching
lipstick/perfume combination
designed to resemble book,
embossed basketweave design on
lid, cartouche on polished goldtone
spine, lipstick/perfume combination
designed to resemble pencil, one
side of tube contains creamy
lipstick, other side small bottle of
Chypre perfume, "Memo" by Coty,
3½ x 2¼" & the lipstick,
3½" **175.00-225.00**

Goldtone compact, designed to
resemble purse, overall engraved
design, push-back handle reveals
powder compartment, lid centered

"Prinzess" Goldtone Compact

w/colored stone & raised enameled flowers, "Prinzess," Czechoslavkia, 3½ x 3" (ILLUS.) 150.00-200.00

Volupte Goldtone Compact

Goldtone compact, shaped to resemble hand, lid decorated w/enameled black lace mitt, faux diamond engagement ring, faux diamond bracelet, Volupte, 4½ x 2" (ILLUS.) 450.00-500.00

Goldtone vanity case, shaped as hand mirror, filigree lid, lipstick tube set w/red stones, interior reveals mirror, powder, rouge compartments, lipstick slides out of handle, 2 x 4" 200.00-250.00

Lucite compact, square, clear, sterling repoussé medallion of two doves centered on lid, 2⅞" sq. 150.00-175.00

Lucite compact, sunburst medallion molded & painted separately & hand-applied to lid, Roger & Gallet, 4 x 4" sq. 125.00-225.00

Mohair compact, miniature teddy bear, opens to reveal powder compartment, head lifts off to reveal lipstick tube, Schuco, 3¾" h. 600.00-800.00

Mother-of-pearl compact, swing-out lipstick on back lid, interior mirror, beveled mirror on exterior lid, 2" sq. 60.00-80.00

Necessaire, textured goldtone w/goldtone tassel, top lid decorated w/filigree leaves, pearls, rhinestones & colored stones, top opens to reveal mirror & powder

well, bottom pulls out to reveal tube for cigarettes or other small items, "Bon Bon" by Wadsworth, 1¾ x 4¾" 150.00-175.00

Plastic compact, round, silvertone Scottie dog centered on top of ivorene lid, black bottom, Astor-Pak, 3½" d. 100.00-125.00

Polished goldtone compact, round, designed to resemble tambourine, lid decorated w/incised birds, 8 movable rings on outer rim, interior mirror, powder compartment & puff, Lucien Lelong, 2½" d. 175.00-275.00

Polished goldtone compact, lid decorated w/crown set w/five red stones & lady sitting on chair, banner underneath reads "Queen for a Day," beveled mirror, "American" by Elgin, 3½ x 2¼" 100.00-150.00

Presentation boxed set, red velvet, contains matching mother-of-pearl vanity & locket w/chain, interior of compact reveals metal mirror that separates powder & rouge compartments, La Mode, compact 2¼" d., box 4¾ x 3¾ x 1" 100.00-125.00

Presentation boxed set, black faille fitted, matching goldtone lipstick tube, perfume bottle, compact & rouge case, interior white satin, Avon, compact 2¾" sq., box 8 x 4 x 1¾" 100.00-125.00

Silver-plated compact, heart-shaped, designed by Elsa Peretti, Halson, 3 x 3¾". 150.00-200.00

Silvertone compact/bridge indicator combination, round, enambled blue & white front lid, reverse side reveals center dial indicating raised number 1,2,3,4,5, or 6, spinning selector displays heart, diamond, spade, club, or NT, suits in black or red enamel, interior reveals mirror & powder well, H.W.K. Co., 1¾" d. 150.00-175.00

Sterling & gold (14k) compact, Art Deco style, alternating engine-turned & reeded panel, lapis lazuli sides, signed "Cartier," 2⅞" sq. 375.00

Sterling silver compact, interior mirror & powder well, case signed, Tiffany & Co., 2¾ x 1¼" . . . 100.00-125.00

Sterling silver vanity case, designed to resemble cigarette lighter, front opens to reveal mirror, powder & rouge compartments, top lifts to reveal sliding lipstick, Alfred Dunhill, 1⅞ x ⅞" 225.00-300.00

COOKIE JARS

All sorts of charming and whimsical cookie jars have been produced in recent decades and these are increasingly collectible today. Many well known American potteries such as McCoy, Hull and Abingdon produced cookie jars and they are included in those listings. Below we are listing cookie jars produced by other companies.

Current reference books for collectors include: The Collectors Encyclopedia of Cookie Jars by Fred and Joyce Roerig (Collector Books, 1991); Collector's Encyclopedia of Cookie Jars, Book II by Fred and Joyce Roerig (Collector Books, 1994); and The Complete Cookie Jar Book by Mike Schneider (Schiffer, Ltd. 1991). Also see: CERAMICS, CHARACTER COLLECTIBLES and DISNEY COLLECTIBLES

AMERICAN BISQUE

Baby Elephant	$145.00
Baby Girl Elephant	220.00
Bear w/Honey, flasher-type	400.00
Boy Pig, gold trim	125.00
Chalkboard Girl	
Cow Jumped Over the Moon (The), flasher-type	945.00
Dog on quilted base	250.00
Grandma	100.00

Kittens and Yarn Cookie Jar

Kittens and Yarn (ILLUS.)	275.00
Liberty Bell	195.00
Oaken Bucket w/dipper	258.00
Olive Oyl	1,500.00
Peasant Girl	750.00
Pennsylvania Dutch Girl, blue	450.00
Popeye	584.00

Professor Ludwig Von Drake Cookie Jar

Professor Ludwig Von Drake (ILLUS.)	1,100.00
Saddle Blackboard	145.00
Sailor Elephant	115.00
Spaceship, "Cookies Out of the World"	225.00
Spool of Thread w/thimble finial	335.00
Treasure Chest	135.00
Yarn Doll	95.00

Yogi Bear Cookie Jar

Yogi Bear (ILLUS.)	350.00

BRAYTON - LAGUNA

Brayton-Laguna Mammy Cookie Jar

Mammy, blue dress (ILLUS.)	8,000.00
Mammy, red dress	1,150.00

Ring Master Cookie Jar

Ring Master, Pinocchio series,
stamped "GEPPETTO POTTERY"
(ILLUS.) **3,100.00**

BRUSH - MCCOY

Bear, feet together **125.00**
Cow w/cat finial, brown **65.00**
Davy Crockett **175.00**

Formal Pig Cookie Jar

Formal Pig, black coat, blue vest
(ILLUS.) **235.00**
Granny, green dress **300.00**

Cinderella Pumpkin Coach

Pumpkin Coach (ILLUS.) **200.00**

CALIFORNIA ORIGINALS

Juggling Clown **80.00**
Old-fashioned Phonograph **150.00**
Raggedy Ann **85.00**
Yellow Cab, unmarked **260.00**

CARDINAL

Castle, "Cardinal USA 307" **200.00**

METLOX

Ali Cat **260.00**
Clown, black & white **90.00**
Clown, standing, yellow **130.00**
Drummer Boy **500.00**

Ferdinand Calf Cookie Jar

Ferdinand Calf (ILLUS.) **650.00**
Humpty Dumpty **350.00**
Panda w/lollipop **475.00**
Pine Cone w/bluebird finial **95.00**
Purple Cow **65.00**
Raggedy Ann **140.00**
Teddy Bear, unmarked **118.00**
Walrus **150.00**

MOSAIC TILE

Mammy, blue dress **520.00**

NAPCO

Cinderella **175.00**
Little Bo Peep **175.00**
Little Red Riding Hood **175.00**

PURINTON POTTERY

Pig **595.00**

REGAL

Cat, unmarked **375.00**

Goldilocks Cookie Jar

Goldilocks (ILLUS.) **244.00**
Majorette, bust **415.00**
Majorette Head, w/gold trim **355.00**

Miss Muffet Cookie Jar

Miss Muffet (ILLUS.) **325.00**
Quaker Oats **85.00**

ROBINSON RANSBOTTOM

Bud, unmarked, ca. 1943 . . . . **190.00**
Peter Pumpkin Eater **135.00**

SIERRA VISTA

Poodle **170.00**
Smiling Train **225.00**
Spaceship **795.00**
Squirrel. **65.00**

TREASURE CRAFT

Howdy Doody, full figure standing by
& leaning on television set w/ "The
HOWDY DOODY Show" on the
screen **250.00**
Pick-up Truck. **48.00**

TWIN WINTON

Barrel w/mouse finial **140.00**
Coach **150.00**
Cookie Nut **35.00**
Donkey **55.00**
Friar Tuck **75.00**
Gorilla **550.00**
"Gun Fighter Rabbit" **225.00**
Hen on Nest **45.00**
Mother Goose **125.00**
Porky Pig **115.00**
Rooster **65.00**
Squirrel. **55.00**
Tepee **265.00**

Tommy Turtle Cookie Jar

Tommy Turtle (ILLUS.) **60.00**

VANDOR

Betty Boop, head w/top hat **110.00**
Fred Flintstone **168.00**
Fred Flintstone, sitting in chair
w/Pebbles **325.00**
Popeye Head **350.00**

WISECARVER ORIGINALS

Geronimo, 10½" h. **75.00**
Pickers, 7¼ x 14½". **95.00**
Tepee w/gold trim **110.00**

MISCELLANEOUS

Airplane, "DCJ 34, 1987 NAC USA,"
North American Ceramics **575.00**
**Basket Handle Mammy w/yellow
rose finial,** "Maruhon Ware (K),
Hand Painted, Japan". **1,200.00**
Bear, Pearl China **75.00**
Betsy Ross, Enesco. **177.00**
Chef, Pearl China **550.00**
Christmas Car, Robert C. Floyd
Signature Collection, Fitz & Floyd . . **995.00**
Clock, unmarked, Pfaltzgraff Co. **250.00**
Darth Vader turn-around, Sigma **75.00**
Funfetti, The Pillsbury Company,
made in Taiwan **45.00**
Gigantic Chef head **150.00**
Good Humor Ice Cream Truck
Cavanagh **450.00**
Homer Simpson, England, Harry
James Design **950.00**
Hound Dog, yellow, Doranne of
California **30.00**
Lamb w/red suspenders, American
Pottery Company. **145.00**
Little Girl, Pottery Guild, unmarked . . **125.00**
Mammy, grey dress, Mosiac
Tile Co. **825.00**
Mammy, National Silver Company . . . **300.00**
Mammy, Pearl China **700.00**
**Mother-in-the-Kitchen (Prayer
Lady),** Enesco. **250.00**

Mrs. Fields Cookie Sack, "Made in Taiwan" paper label. **45.00**
Mrs. Potts. **35.00**
Noah's Ark, Starnes of California. . . . **175.00**
Nummy Cookies, Haeger Pottery **78.00**
Packard Convertible, Appleman **795.00**

Appleman Taxi Cookie Jar

Sid's Taxi, Appleman (ILLUS.) **850.00**
Spirit of St. Nicholas,
Fitz & Floyd **1,750.00**
Tat-L-Tale, "Helen Hutula Original,"
Supnick **950.00**

CURRIER & IVES PRINTS

This lithographic firm was founded in 1835 by Nathaniel Currier with James M. Ives becoming a partner in 1857. Current events of the day were portrayed in the early days and the prints were hand-colored. Landscapes, vessels, sport and hunting scenes of the West all became popular subjects. The firm was in existence until 1906. All prints listed are hand-colored unless otherwise noted. Numbers at the end of the listings refer to those used in Currier & Ives Prints, An Illustrated Checklist, *by Frederick A. Conningham (Crown Publishers).*

Across the Continent - "Westward the Course of Empire Takes Its Way," large folio, 1868, framed (33) **$230.00**
American Farm Scenes - No. 1 (Spring), large folio, N. Currier, 1853, framed, 134 (slight overall discoloration, other stains in margins, few edge tears) **1,725.00**
American Farm Scenes - No. 2 (Summer), large folio, 1853, N. Currier, framed, 135 (slight discoloration in margins) **2,070.00**
American Game Fish, large folio, 1866, framed, 164 (unobtrusive toning & staining) **978.00**

American Winter Scenes - Evening

American Winter Scenes - Evening, large folio, 1854, framed, some minor damages & stains (ILLUS.) **2,760.00**
Brush on the Homestretch (The), large folio, 1869, framed, 711 (faint foxing, water stain on outer right margin, mat stain). **1,099.00**
Camping Out "Some of the Right Sort," large folio, 1856, framed, 777 (minor toning & staining, possible retouch to some coloring) **2,415.00**
Celebrated Trotting Mares Maud S. and Aldine (The), large folio, 1883, framed, 925 (slight lightstain) **977.00**

The Celebrated Trotting Stallion George Wilkes

Celebrated Trotting Stallion George Wilkes, Formerly "Robert Fillingham," (The), large folio, 1866, framed, 20 mm. repaired tear in lower margin, 932 (ILLUS.). **1,150.00**
Central Park, The Drive, medium folio, 1862, framed, 951(slight lightstain, surface soiling, scattered pale foxing) **1,380.00**
Central Park, The Lake, medium folio, 1862, framed, 952 (overall staining from applied varnish, several small scuffs, soiling & foxing, tears to margins) **345.00**

City of New York (The), large folio,
1876, framed (1107) **5,175.00**

Clipper Ship "Flying Cloud," large
folio, N. Currier, 1852, framed,
1145 (discoloration & specks of
black paint in margins) **2,587.00**

Clipper Ship "Sweepstakes," large
folio, N. Currier, 1853, framed,
1168 (slight background stain,
specks of black paint in margins,
faint foxing) **3,450.00**

**Eventide - October - The Village
Inn,** large folio, 1867, framed, 1780
(faint water stains, a few skinned
areas on verso, mat stain) **2,185.00**

Farm-Yard in Winter (The), large
folio, 1861, framed, 1881 (mat
stain, fox marks, repaired tears &
losses top of sheet edge) **5,175.00**

Fashionable "Turn-Outs" in Central Park

**Fashionable "Turn-Outs" in Central
Park.,** large folio, 1869, framed,
slight soiling & discoloration on
verso, 1896 (ILLUS.) **2,587.00**

**Futurity Race at Sheepshead Bay
(The),** large folio, 1889, framed,
2209 (lightstain inside mat) **1,725.00**

**Going To The Trot - A Good Day
and Good Track** large folio, 1869,
framed (2409) **1,265.00**

**Grand Racer Kingston (The), by
Spendthrift,** large folio, 1891,
framed, 2521 (overall toning &
lightstain) **1,035.00**

**Grandest Palace Drawing Room
Steamers in the World (The),**
large folio, 1878, framed, 2541
(overall slight discoloration, various
punctures, tears & scuffs, tear in
upper center) **2,760.00**

Great Ocean Yacht Race (The),
large folio, 1867, framed, 2634
(toning, subtle staining, areas of
possible retouch) **920.00**

Great Salt Lake, Utah, small folio,
undated, framed, 2649 (few fox
marks & timestain) **690.00**

**Home From the Brook - The Lucky
Fisherman,** large folio, 1867,
period frame, 2856 (unobtrusive
toning & staining) **1,150.00**

**Hudson Highlands (The), From the
Peekskill and Cold Spring Road,
near Garrison's Landing,** large
folio, 1867, framed, 2973 (slight
overall discoloration, some surface
mold in margins) **1,495.00**

**King of the Turf (The) St. Julien
Driven by Orrin A. Hickok,** large
folio, 1880, framed, 3339 (faint
spots of foxing in margins) **1,150.00**

Lady Suffolk and Lady Moscow,
large folio, N. Currier, 1850,
framed, 3390 (short tear extreme
lower right margin, faint foxing) . . **1,495.00**

Life of a Fireman (The) - The Fire,
large folio, N. Currier, 1854,
framed, 3515 (discolored paper
tone, crease in each top sheet
corners) **977.00**

*The Life of a Fireman -
The Metropolitan System*

**Life of a Fireman (The) - The
Metropolitan System,** large folio,
1866, framed, discoloration, foxing,
lower margin water stains, nicks to
extreme edge, 3516 (ILLUS.) **2,875.00**

**Life of a Fireman (The) - The New
Era,** large folio, 1861, framed, 3517
(discoloration, water stains in
margins, tiny nicks to extreme
edges) **1,840.00**

**Life of a Fireman (The) - The Night
Alarm,** large folio, N. Currier, 1854,
framed, 3518 (discoloration,
repaired tears in image at top &
margins, stains) **460.00**

Life of a Fireman (The) - The Ruins,
large folio, N. Currier, 1854,
framed, 3520 (scuffs in image at
center, small tear in bottom sheet
edge) **977.00**

**Midnight Race on the Mississippi
(A),** large folio, 1860, 4116
(repaired tears in outer image, tiny
scuff in sky at right) **8,050.00**

Mr. August Belmont's - Potomac and Masher, large folio, 1891, framed, 4249 (overall toning & lightstaining) **862.00**

New York Bay From Bay Ridge, L.I., medium folio, 1860, framed, 4435 (overall timestain verso, minor defects in margins, trimmed at bottom) **1,380.00**

Niagara Falls, medium folio, undated, framed, 4456 (slight discoloration, minor soiling & staining). **345.00**

Pride of the West (The), small folio, bust portrait of lovely lady, 1870, Victorian criss-cross frame (4916). . . **72.00**

Queen of the Turf "Maud S.," large folio, 1880, framed, 5016 (slight soiling & discoloration, overall verso mat stain, occasional edge tears). **488.00**

Return From the Woods, medium folio, undated, framed, 5131 (30 mm. repaired tear in right margain, backboard stain on verso) **1,098.00**

Road (The) - Winter, large folio, N. Currier, 1853, framed, 5171 (four repaired tears extending into margins, mat stain, soiling in margins). **6,900.00**

Sleigh Race (The), small folio, undated, framed, 5554 (timestain, water staining, repaired tear) **977.00**

Staten Island and the Narrows from Fort Hamilton, large folio, 1861, framed, 5715 (slight mat stain, pale foxing, few pinholes in edge) **1,380.00**

"Stopping Place" on the Road (A), large folio, 1868, framed, 5821, (waterstains & other defects in margins, some spotting & foxing in image) **1,092.00**

"Trotting Cracks" on the Snow, large folio, 1858, framed, a few short tears in lower margin (6170). **3,162.00**

View on the Harlem River, N.Y. - The High Bridge in the Distance, large folio, N. Currier, 1852, framed, 6441 (some discoloration) **1,092.00**

View on the Potomac Near Harper's Ferry, large folio, 1866, framed, 6449 (slight margin soiling) **1,035.00**

Whale Fishery, (The) - Attacking a "Right Whale"—and "Cutting In," large folio, undated, 6623 (surface scuffs, foxing, repaired losses in corners, repaired nicks & minor staining in margins) **5,175.00**

Whale Fishery, (The) - Sperm Whale "In a Flurry," large folio, 1852, 6627 (repaired loss & crease in upper right margin corner, minor staining in margins) **4,887.00**

The Yacht Henrietta

Yacht Henrietta (The), large folio, 1867, 6801 framed, minor scuffs & edge tears (ILLUS.) **2,185.00**

DECOYS

Decoys have been utilized for years to lure flying water fowl into target range. They have been made of carved and turned wood, papier-mâché, canvas and metal, and some are in the category of outstanding folk art and command high prices.

Barnacle Goose, carved wood, 19½" l., 12¼" h. (repair to bill, minor cracks to base) **$633.00**

Black Bellied Plover, by A. Elmer Crowell, East Harwich, Massachusetts, carved wood, rectangular stamp, 8½" l., 9" h. (very minor paint wear to bill & legs) **6,325.00**

Standing Black Duck Decoy

Black Duck, standing position w/head raised, carved wood, glass eyes, from Marshfield, Massachusetts (ILLUS.) **55,000.00**

Black Duck, carved wood, marked
on the base "BLTX Chas. Shang
Wheeler Ken Peck 1920," 17¼" l.,
6¾" h. (areas of repaint, minor
paint wear & loss). **1,955.00**

Black-Bellied Plover, carved &
painted wood, 11¼" l., 6" h. (bill
probably replaced). **748.00**

Black-Bellied Plover, carved &
painted wood, possibly Martha's
Vineyard, Massachusetts, 8" l.,
10½" h. (bill possibly replaced, very
minor paint wear) **2,760.00**

Ward Bros. Bluebill Drake

Bluebill Drake, Ward Bros., Crisfield,
Maryland, carved wood w/good
used paint, glass eyes, signed
(ILLUS.) **10,450.00**

Bluebill Drake & Hen, by Harold
Dinham Waubaushone, Ontario,
Canada, carved wood w/original
paint & glass eyes, 13" l., pr. **72.00**

Canada Goose, by Miles Smith,
carved wood, hollow-carved
w/open bottom, original paint
w/stamped feather design & glass
eyes, 17¾" l. **61.00**

Canada Goose, alert head position,
carved wood w/original paint,
branded "Castle Haven," 22" l.
(minor age cracks) **303.00**

Canada Goose, by John Castle,
Birmingham, Michigan, carved
wood w/bluish black stain & glass
eyes, unsigned, 25½" l. **204.00**

Canvasback Drake, carved wood in
flying pose, Tuveson Mfg. Co.,
Saint James, Minnesota, patent-
dated "May 17, 1927," w/pressed
brass label, 24" l., 4¼" h. (cracks,
paint wear on wings) **575.00**

Canvasback Drake, by Alex Meldrum,
Marine City, Michigan, carved hollow
block, old working repaint, glass
eyes, unsigned,16¾" l. **160.00**

Canvasback Hen, hollow-carved
wood, Dodge factory, Detroit,
Michigan, 15" l., 6¾" h. (areas of
repaint) **748.00**

Common Pintail Drake, carved &
painted wood, Ward Brothers,
Crisfield, Maryland, marked on
base "made and painted by Lem
Ward 1930," 17½" l., 7¾" h. (old
repaint, crack to neck) **1,840.00**

Dowitcher, by John Dilley, Quoque,
Long Island, carved wood, 10¼" l.
(very minor paint wear). **9,200.00**

Eider Drake, carved wood, probably
Maine, 17½" l., 7" h. (minor cracks,
minor losses to tail & bill) **920.00**

Goldeneye Drake, by Shang
Wheeler, Stratford, Connecticut,
carved wood, 18" l., 6" h.
(imperfections). **633.00**

Goldeneye Drake, by Joe Wooster,
carved wood w/original paint &
glass eyes, signed "Good Hunting,
Josef Wooster '70," 14½" l. **358.00**

Goldeneye Drake & Hen, hollow-
carved wood w/open bottoms &
keels, old paint & glass eyes, by an
anonymous Ontario, Canada
carver, 15¾" l., pr. **55.00**

Green Heron, by E. Elmer Crowell,
East Harwich, Massachusetts,
carved wood, retangular stamp, 13"
l., 12⅛" h. (very minor paint wear to
tail & bill, minor bill crack). **6,325.00**

Herring Gull, carved wood
w/delineated wing tips, New Jersey
style, 18¾" l., 6½" h. (very
minor paint wear) **2,760.00**

Long Bill Curlew, by Chief Coffey,
Long Island, New York, carved
wood, 15½" l., 8" h. (replaced bill,
wear to wing tips) **1,380.00**

Mallard Drake, carved wood w/old
working repaint & tack eyes, from
the Duck Creek Hunt Club, Lake
Erie, Ontario, Canada, 17½" l. (age
crack in block) **88.00**

Mallard Hen, by Charles Perdew,
Henry, Illinois, carved wood w/later
varnish, 17½" l., 7" h. (paint
imperfections). **2,013.00**

Merganser Drake, by H. Keyes
Chadwic, Martha's Vineyard,
Massachusetts, carved wood, 19¾"
l., 6¼" h. (old repaint, cracks to
base) **978.00**

Merganser Hen, by Joe Wooster,
carved wood w/original paint &
glass eyes w/good detail, signed
"Good Hunting Josef 'Buckeye Joe'
Wooster," 2½" l. (minor paint
separation at top of neck dowel) . . . **193.00**

Pigeon, carved & painted wood, late
19th - early 20th c., 12¼" l. (minor
paint wear) **575.00**

Crowell Pintail Drake

Pintail Drake, by Elmer Crowell, Cape Cod, Massachusetts, carved wood w/good paint, glass eyes (ILLUS.) **55,000.00**

Red-Breasted Merganser Drake, carved wood, marked "L.B." on base, 14" l., 9¾" h. (minor cracks, paint wear). **374.00**

Red-Breasted Merganser Drake, carved wood, in the style of Monhegan Island, 15½" l., 10" h. (cracks, paint flaking) **518.00**

Sandpiper, carved wood, signed on base "Dr. B.," 8¾" l., 5¼" h. (bill possibly replaced, very minor paint wear to tail) **403.00**

Shorebird, carved wood, paint decorated, impressed on underside "Stevens," 20th c., 12" l., 15¾" h. . . . **230.00**

White-Winged Scoter Drake, by Roswell Bliss, Stratford, Connecticut, carved wood, stamped on base "R. Bliss," 16" l., 5½" h. (minor crack to base) **288.00**

White-Winged Scoter Drake, carved wood, Monhegan Island, 17½" l., 7½" h. (cracks to base, minor losses, original patch). **1,495.00**

Widgeon Drake, by Madison Mitchell, Havre de Grace, Maryland, carved wood, 13⅝" l., 6¾" h. (very minor paint wear, chips to bill) **316.00**

Wigeon Drake, by Joe Lincoln, Accord, Massachusetts, carved wood, stamped on base "F.B. Rice," 15½" l., 7" h., (old weathered surface, crack to base, chip to tail) . . **1,380.00**

Wood Duck, by A. Elmer Crowell, East Harwich, Massachusetts, carved wood, raised crossed wings, two rectangular stamps, 12¾" l., 5¾" h. (very minor paint wear, minute chips to bill). **7,188.00**

Yellow Legs, by Elisha Burr, Hingham, Massachusetts, carved wood, 11½" l. (minor paint wear, possibly old replaced bill) **2,760.00**

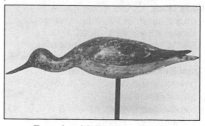

Running Yellowlegs Decoy

Yellowlegs, running pose, carved wood, old paint, glass eyes, from Nantucket Island, Massachusetts (ILLUS.) **55,000.00**

DISNEY COLLECTIBLES

Scores of objects ranging from watches to dolls have been created showing Walt Disney's copyrighted animated cartoon characters, and an increasing number of collectors now are seeking these, made primarily by licensed manufacturers.

Alice in Wonderland cookie jar, ceramic, marked "Walt Disney Productions," Regal China, 1950s . . **$425.00**

Alice in Wonderland doll, Alice, Duchess Doll Co., mint in box **145.00**

Alice in Wonderland figurines, "Tweedle Dum and Tweedle Dee" - Evan K. Shaw Co., pair **700.00**

Alice in Wonderland marionette, Alice, wood, early 1950s, original box. **145.00**

Alice in Wonderland sheet music, "I'm Late". **25.00**

Alice in Wonderland wrist watch, U.S. Time, ca. 1950, w/teacup in box. **450.00**

Bambi candy container, PEZ **55.00**

Bambi charm, metal, 1940s **55.00**

Bambi figurine, ceramic, American Pottery Co., 4½" h. **145.00**

Bambi pencil sharpener, Bakelite. . . . **35.00**

Bambi pin, sterling silver, Art Deco style, Bambi in rectangular frame, "Coro" **90.00**

Bambi planter, ceramic, butterfly on the tail, American Pottery **200.00**

Bambi & friends coat hangers, set of 5. . . . . **45.00**

Bambi & Thumper planter, china, marked "Walt Disney," 7" **60.00**

Big Bad Wolf alarm clock (from "Three Little Pigs & The Big Bad Wolf"), Ingersoll, 1930s **675.00**

Big Bad Wolf (from "Three Little Pigs") doll, cloth, felt face w/toothy open mouth & button eyes, plus body, wearing red pants w/patches at the knees, foot stamped w/mark of Knickerbocker Toy Company, 1930s, 18" h. **1,000.00**

Big Bad Wolf (from "Three Little Pigs") figure, rubber, standing position, brown w/painted details, Seiberling Products, 1930s, w/original box, 10" h. (some cracking) **900.00**

Big Bad Wolf (from "Three Little Pigs") sheet music, "Who's Afraid of the Big Bad Wolf," 1932 . . . . **50.00**

Cinderella apron, uncut J. C. Penney pattern, Disney copyright . . . **40.00**

Cinderella hand puppet, Walt Disney Productions, 1956 . . . . **28.00**

Cinderella marionette, Hazelle's Marionettes, mint in box **140.00**

Cinderella sheet music, "Bibbidi-Bobbidi-Boo" **38.00**

Cinderella tea set: cov. teapot, sugar bowl, tray & six plates, cups & saucers; tin, Ohio Art Co., the set . . **260.00**

Cinderella toy, wind-up plastic, dancing w/the prince, Irwin Mfg. Box, Inc. **225.00**

Cinderella toy, windup tin "Cinderella Railcar," a handcar driven by the composition figures of Gus & Jaq, complete w/track, Well-Brimtoy, England, in original box **1,500.00**

Cinderella wrist watch, w/glass slipper case, U. S. Time, 1950, mint in box **480.00**

Cinderella & Prince planter, ceramic, Evan Shaw **400.00**

Clarabelle Cow book, "The Story of Clarabell Cow," Whitman, 1938 . . . . . **60.00**

Early Clarabelle & Horace Glasses

Clarabelle Cow tumbler, clear slightly tapering glass decorated w/black enamel, Clarabelle seated looking in a mirror (ILLUS. right) . . . **151.00**

Davy Crockett bank, "Davy Crockett Shoot-A-Bear," metal, mechanical . . . **400.00**

Davy Crockett bedspread, chenille, pictures Davy fighting a bear **205.00**

Davy Crockett chair, folding-type, aluminum w/canvas seat & back, illustration of Davy & signature in script on back **60.00**

Davy Crockett clock, wall-type, Davy on face & pendulum, 1955, w/original box **400.00**

Davy Crockett coloring book, colorful cover, Saalfield, 1955, unused, 16 pp. to color, 10½ x 14" . . **20.00**

Davy Crockett Cookie Jar by Regal

Davy Crockett cookie jar, cov., bust of Davy wearing coonskin cap & "Davy Crockett" embossed on his collar, base marked "Translucent Vitrified China, copyright, C. Miller 55-140 B," Regal China (ILLUS.) . . **600.00**

Davy Crockett coonskin cap, mint in box, Walt Disney Productions **85.00**

Davy Crockett equipment set, powder horn, belt & compass, colorful, mint in original box, the set . . **125.00**

Davy Crockett flashlight, original box **55.00**

Davy Crockett game, "Davy Crockett Indian Scouting Game," board-type, 1955, unused **75.00**

Davy Crockett lamp, ceramic base w/figure of Davy & bear by tree, glossy green & brown-toned glaze, Premco Mfg. Co., Chicago, 1955, 8" h. **400.00**

Davy Crockett mug, milk white glass, red graphics **32.00**

Davy Crockett sheet music, "Ballad of Davy Crockett," w/Fess Parker's picture on cover. **40.00**

Davy Crockett tray, tin, lithographed picture of Davy Crockett & scenes from Alamo & Congress around him. **55.00**

Disney characters book, "Peculiar Penguins," published by David McKay, 1934 . . . . **120.00**

1942 Disney Characters Calendar

Disney characters calendar, 1942, color lithographed paper, advertising promotion for Morrell's Ham, each month w/a different color scene of various Disney characters, each page shrinkwrapped individually, minor soiling & edge creasing, each 8¼ x 17¾" (ILLUS. of part) **1,150.00**

Disney characters card game, "Silly Symphony Mickey Snap," includes Mickey & several Disney characters, England, 1930s **120.00**

Disney characters ceiling globe, glass, illustration includes Mickey & Minnie Mouse, Donald Duck & Pluto **205.00**

Disney characters chalkboards, Mickey Mouse, Donald Duck, Pinocchio & Ludwig Von Drake, child size, copyright Walt Disney Productions, 1961, unused, each, 16 x 23", set of 4 . . . . **300.00**

Disney Characters Chamber Pot

Disney characters chamber pot, child's, ceramic, molded in relief on one side w/Mickey & Minnie Mouse running off to Dreamland & Huey, Dewey & Louie in the reverse, trimmed in color, marked "141" on the bottom, 6" d. (ILLUS.) **3,000.00**

Disney characters charm bracelet, 14k gold, w/Dumbo, Bambi, Jiminy Cricket, Thumper, Pluto & Flower, the skunk, together w/an enameled piano, key & heart, 7" l. **550.00**

Disney characters Christmas card, Mickey Mouse & several other characters, 1949 . . . . **45.00**

Disney characters Christmas tree lights, Silly Symphony series by NOMA, original box **405.00**

Disney characters doll, cloth, from "Babes in Toyland," features "Mary, Mary Quite Contrary," w/printed features, dressed in original dress, 18" **205.00**

Disney characters music box, "Melody Player" w/five paper rolls, J. Chein & Co., 6½" x 7" **125.00**

Disney characters pillow, pictures Mickey Mouse, Donald Duck, Goofy & others riding rocket ships **55.00**

Disney characters rug, Mickey & Minnie in airplane, Donald in parachute, label reads "Alexander Smith–Good Housekeeping," 27 x 45" **350.00**

Disney characters rug, area-type, featuring a host of Disney characters including Mickey & Minnie Mouse, Goofy, Lady, Tramp, Bambi, Thumper, Chip 'n Dale, Gus, Jaq, The Seven Dwarfs, Donald Duck & his nephews, ca. 1950s, 68 x 100" **700.00**

Disney characters Silly Symphonies book, pop-up type, King Neptune/Babes in Woods, Walt Disney Enterprises, 1934, hard cover, w/dust jacket. . . . **575.00**

Disney characters toy, pull-type, "Disney Easter Parade," Fisher-Price No. 205, 1936, complete set with five figures, set **1,600.00**

Donald Duck alarm clock, Bayard Co., France, dated 1956 . . . . **145.00**

Donald Duck ashtray, china, trapezoidal dish w/two cigarette indentations at front edge & two Donald Duck figures perched on back edge, glossy glaze w/painted trim, Japan, ca. 1935, 3½" h. **725.00**

Donald Duck bank, dime register, lithographed tin, Louis Marx & Co. . . **300.00**

Donald Duck bicycle, 1950s, restored **1,500.00**

Donald Duck book, "Donald Duck & Ghost Morgan's Treasure," Big Little Books, 1946 . . . . **105.00**

Donald Duck book, "Donald Duck's Adventure," Little Golden Book, 1950 . . . . **60.00**

Donald Duck camera, pictures Donald, Huey, Dewey & Louie, Walt Disney Productions & Herbert George Co., Chicago, Illinois, uses 127 film, 12 exp. **250.00**

Donald Duck cola bottle, 1953, 7 oz. **60.00**

Donald Duck cookie jar, cov., ceramic, cylindrical, California Originals **130.00**

Donald Duck doll, cloth, long-billed Donald dressed in a blue & green sailor suit, red bow tie & blue cap, w/original Knickerbocker tag, ca. 1930s, 13" h. (some stains) **900.00**

Large Donald Knickerbocker Doll

Donald Duck doll, stuffed cloth & felt, Donald dressed in a red bandleader's uniform w/gold trim & brass buttons, w/a "bearskin" tall black hat & wooden baton, Knickerbocker, ca. 1930s, 21" h. (ILLUS.) **1,200.00**

Donald Duck figure, bisque, long-billed Donald, 1930s, 1¾" h. **105.00**

Donald Duck figure, bisque, w/horn, ca. 1930, 3" h. **110.00**

Donald Duck figure, rubber, Seiberling, 5½" h. **105.00**

Donald Duck game, "Bean Bag Party," Parker Bros., original box, dated 1939 . . . . **135.00**

Donald Duck lemonade pack, colorful cardboard pack w/Donald's face on the side, holds six 7-oz. full bottles **125.00**

Donald Duck paint box, Transogram, 1938. . . . . **65.00**

Donald Duck phonograph record, "Donald Trick or Treat," 78 rpm, Golden Records, 1951, w/dust cover, 6" d. **30.00**

Donald Duck projector, metal case, Stephens Products Co., Middletown, Connecticut, mint w/box. **95.00**

Donald duck ring, sterling silver, full-figure raised image of Donald waving, late 1930s. **105.00**

Donald Duck salt & pepper shakers, ceramic, figural, marked "McCoy," pr. **60.00**

Donald Duck sand pail, tin, Disneyland candy-type, 1950s **125.00**

Donald Duck sheet music, "Der Fuehrer's Face," 1942. . . . . **38.00**

Donald Duck sign, tin, "Donald Duck Bread" over picture of Donald & loaf of bread in colorful wrapper over "Oven Fresh Flavor" **400.00**

Donald Duck toothbrush holder, bisque, modeled as two long-billed Donalds standing side to side, Japan, ca. 1935, 4" h. **400.00**

Donald Duck toy, friction-type, "Disney Flivver" car, features a long-necked Donald Duck driver in a yellow convertible lithographed w/Mickey Mouse, Thumper, Dopey & others. **605.00**

Donald Duck toy, pull-type, "Donald Duck Choo Choo," Fisher-Price No. 450, early version, 1940 . . . . **350.00**

Donald Duck toy, keywind tinplate, waddling figure covered in plush sailor suit w/bobbing head, Line Mar, Japan, w/original box, 6" h. . . . **660.00**

Donald Duck toy, carousel, wind-up celluloid, long-billed Donald on wheeled metal base rolls forward as the carousel turns, Japan, 7" h. (arms glued in place) **1,250.00**

Donald Duck toy, friction-type, tinplate rocket, features Donald steering a friction-drive wheeled missile, w/original box, 7" l. **775.00**

Donald Duck Bosco Tumbler

Donald Duck tumbler, clear glass tapering cylindrical form w/blue enameled decoration, Bosco premium (ILLUS.) **25.00**

Donald Duck umbrella, figural Donald head handle, yellow silk, Louis Weiss Company, ca. 1930s. . **125.00**

Donald Duck valentine card, dated 1939, mint condition **40.00**

Donald Duck wrist watch, oblong or round, U. S. Time, 1948 . . . . **250.00**

Donald Duck & Ludwig Von Drake salt & pepper shakers, 1961, pr. **135.00**

Donald Duck & Mickey Mouse book, "Donald Duck & Mickey Mouse Cub Scouts," Walt Disney Productions, 1950 . . . . **45.00**

Donald Duck & nephew cookie jar, turnabout-type **90.00**

Donald Duck & Pluto toy, composition, metal & wood, h.p. figures riding a railroad flatcar on which Pluto's doghouse is placed, The Lionel Corporation, 1938, w/original box, 10" l. **1,400.00**

Dumbo the Elephant bank, china, marked "W. Disney U. S. A.," 1940s. **75.00**

Dumbo the Elephant figure, pottery, American Pottery, w/paper label, 6" h. **145.00**

Dumbo the Elephant planter, ceramic, American Pottery, 4" l. . . . **145.00**

Dwarf Bashful doll, composition head, cloth body, Knickerbocker Toy Co. . . . . **195.00 to 225.00**

Dwarf Bashful figure, bisque, 3¼" h. **75.00**

Dwarf Dopey doll, composition, movable arms, original paint & cloth costume, marked "Walt Disney, Knickerbocker Toy Co.," 9" h. (some wear) **400.00**

Dwarf Dopey pin, plastic, Dopey on skis, 1940s, on original card **75.00**

Dwarf Dopey toy, windup tin, eyes moving up & down as he walks from side to side, Louis Marx & Co., ca. 1938, 8" h. **375.00**

Dwarf Grumpy figure, bisque, Walt Disney Enterprises, 3" h. **40.00**

Dwarf Happy Birthday card, "Disney Birthday Card," 1938, excellent condition **80.00**

Dwarf Sleepy doll, Ideal, w/original 1937 tag, 12" **550.00**

Dwarf Sneezy charm, silver, movable head **65.00**

Dwarfs Grumpy & Dopey hairbrush set, large & small brush, pr. **140.00**

Eeyore (from Winnie the Pooh) cookie jar, cov., dark grey w/pink cover, ceramic, large, California Originals **750.00**

Elmer Elephant book, "Elmer Elephant", 1936, McKay **78.00**

Elmer Elephant toy, pull-type, "Elmer Elephant," Fisher-Price No. 206A, 1936 . . . . **295.00**

Faline (from Bambi) figure, ceramic, American Pottery Co., 4¼" h. **125.00**

Fantasia book, "Fantasia Paint Book", 1939, #689. . . . . **120.00**

Fantasia figure, china, Centaurette, black, Vernon Kilns, No. 24 . . . . . **1,000.00**

Fantasia figure, ceramic, Ostrich, Vernon Kilns, 9" h. **1,400.00**

Fantasia book, "The Sorcerer's Apprentice," 1940, w/dust jacket **40.00**

Ferdinand the Bull book, 1939, linen-like cover **45.00**

Ferdinand the Bull costume, mask includes horns, by Fishbach, New York, ca. 1940, w/original box **85.00**

Ferdinand the Bull figure, rubber, Seiberling, 1938-40, 5½" l. **125.00**

Ferdinand the Bull toy, windup tin, Ferdinand & the matador, Louis Marx & Co., 1938, mint in box **950.00**

Figaro (Pinocchio's cat) doll, mohair w/oilcloth face, ca. 1939 . . . **150.00**

Figaro (Pinocchio's cat) figure, ceramic, Figaro w/bowl, Brayton Laguna **280.00**

Flower the Skunk (Bambi) figure, ceramic, American Pottery Co., 3" h. **105.00**

Flower Salt & Pepper Shakers

Flower the Skunk (Bambi) salt & pepper shakers, china, figural, paper sticker "Walt Disney Flower Character W. D. P. F Fm copyright," marked on bottom "W. Goebel" w/full bee and (R) in parenthesis, also printed "Germany" mint condition w/cork stoppers, 2 2/3" h., pr. (ILLUS.). . . . **400.00**

Geppetto (from Pinocchio) figure, pressed wood, Multi Products, 1943, 5" h. **118.00**

Goofy book, "Dippy the Goof," hardbound, Whitman, 1938 . . . . **65.00**

Goofy candy container, PEZ, Walt Disney Productions **40.00**

Goofy flasher pin, red, from Disneyland, 2½" **80.00**

Goofy rug, colorful scene of Goofy riding on a go-cart, fringed ends . . . **185.00**

Goofy toy, windup plastic, standing figure of Goofy w/a little dog biting the seat of the pants, Marx **105.00**

Goofy toy, windup tin, Goofy w/twirling tail, brightly lithographed figure hobbles & hops in circles when wound, w/original lithographed box, Line Mar, Japan, 5½" h. **695.00**

Haley Mills paper doll, "Moon-Spinners," Whitman, 1964, very fine. **40.00**

Horace Horsecollar tumbler, clear cylindrical glass w/red & blue enamel decoration of Horace playing a flute (ILLUS. left w/Clarabelle Cow) **151.00**

Jiminy Cricket (from Pinocchio) doll, made by Knickerbocker Toy Company, paper wrist tag, composition character head w/large painted eyes, closed smiling mouth, composition cricket body, painted yellow gloves & black shoes, original black jacket w/long tails, orange felt vest, blue felt hat w/yellow band, ca. 1939, 10" h. **1,100.00**

Jiminy Cricket (from Pinocchio) "Soakey" container **15.00**

Jiminy Cricket (from Pinocchio) toy, windup tin, a smiling Jiminy Cricket wearing a black & white tuxedo w/blue top hat bobs up & down when wound, Line Mar, ca. 1960, 6" h. **400.00**

Joe (Jose) Carioca toy, balancing-type, lithographed paper on metal Joe Carioca balances on a metal base finished in black, France, 1940s, 12" h. . . . . **185.00 to 225.00**

King Louie (from "The Jungle Book") doll, stuffed plush, Steiff, original button in ear, 12" h. **325.00**

Lady & The Tramp hand puppets, Gund, pr. **75.00**

Lady & The Tramp tape dispenser, metal, 1950s **60.00**

Ludwig Von Drake card game, Walt Disney Productions, 1963, w/box . . . **18.00**

Ludwig Von Drake lunch box w/thermos, Aladdin, 1962 . . . . **275.00**

Ludwig Von Drake toy, friction-type, Ludwig seated on an open car carriage, Marx **300.00**

Ludwig Von Drake toy, windup tin walker, figure wearing cap, jacket & checked vest & carrying a cane, Line Mar, Japan, ca. 1961 . . . . **220.00**

Mad Hatter (from Alice in Wonderland) counter display, advertising hats & the movie "Alice in Wonderland," cardboard, 10 x 12" **85.00**

Maleficent (witch from Sleeping Beauty) tumbler, clear glass, No. D2405 . . . . **28.00**

Mary Poppins card game, Whitman, 1966, w/box. **25.00**

Mary Poppins doll, vinyl, Hasbro, 1964, very fine. **40.00**

Mary Poppins paint set, 1960s, unused. **105.00**

Mickey Mouse alarm clock, animated, Ingersoll, 1930s **2,700.00**

Mickey Mouse alarm clock, Ingersoll, ca. 1950, w/original box (stain on clock face, edge wear & staining on box) **230.00**

Mickey Mouse ashtray, ceramic, triangular dish base w/figure of Mickey standing at short end playing the saxaphone, hand-painted, Japan, 5" w. **300.00**

Mickey Mouse baby rattle, wood, pie-cut eyes, ca. 1930 . . . . **95.00**

Mickey Mouse bank, book-shaped, red leather & brass, Zell Products Co., 1930s, (Moore No. 197) **175.00**

Mickey Mouse bank, dime register,
lithographed tin, dated 1939,
2½ x 2½" 195.00
Mickey Mouse bell toy, Mickey on
roller-skates painted on wood, 6" d.
metal wheels w/large paper
lithograph of Mickey on hubs,
marked "WD Ent.," Mickey 7 x 8",
overall 7 x 14" 600.00
Mickey Mouse blocks, picture-type,
Germany, ca. 1950, in original
carrying case 230.00
Mickey Mouse book, "Hello
Everybody," Bibo and Lang, 1930 . . 875.00
Mickey Mouse book, "King Arthur's
Court," pop-up type, 1933 . . . . . . 1,050.00
Mickey Mouse book, "Mickey Mouse
Pictures to Paint", 1931, #210,
Saalfield Publishing Co. of Akron,
Ohio. 240.00
Mickey Mouse book, "Mickey Never
Fails," hardbound, Heath, 1939 . . . . 125.00
Mickey Mouse booklet, "Sun Oil
Automotive" premium, 1938 . . . . 25.00
Mickey Mouse bowl, Beetleware,
w/alphabet & numerals on rim,
Walt Disney Ent., ca. 1930s, large . . . 105.00
Mickey Mouse buttons, dress-type,
Walt Disney Enterprises, ca. 1930,
on original card, set of 4 . . . . 95.00
Mickey Mouse candy box,
lithographed tin, elliptical shape
w/colorful images of Mickey w/top
hat & cane bowing to Minnie on the
lid, & ice skating around the sides,
4½ x 8" 705.00
Mickey Mouse card games, "Library
of Games," five volumes of card
games, 1946, the set 125.00
Mickey Mouse Christmas card, die-
cut, Walt Disney Enterprises, 1936 . . . 200.00
Mickey Mouse clothes bag, cloth,
shows Mickey pointing at a pair of
pants on the clothes line
w/"Mickey" on the pocket, Vogue
Designs, 14 x 20" 125.00
Mickey Mouse clothes hanger,
wooden, marked "Walt Disney
Enterprises" 65.00
Mickey Mouse cookie jar, cov.,
ceramic, model of a tall birthday
cake w/Mickey seated on top,
made to celebrate his 60th
Anniversary in 1988, Walt Disney
Productions (ILLUS.) 650.00
Mickey Mouse cookie jar, cov.,
Mickey Clock, pictures Mickey &
"Mickey Mouse Cookie Time" on
the clock face of a Big Ben-type
alarm clock, marked "Enesco
WDE-219" 450.00

Mickey 60th Anniversary Cookie Jar

Mickey Mouse costume, orange
w/red pants, plastic mask, ca.
1950s, child's size large 12-14,
original size paper tag sewn in
(mask slightly pushed in, minor soil
on one arm & leg) 75.00
Mickey Mouse costume, cloth &
rubber, includes mask, skull cap,
long-sleeved shirt w/Mickey Mouse
patch, shorts w/four metal buttons,
red scarf & rubber tail, Wornova
Play Clothes, New York, New York,
ca. 1930s, size 6, w/original box,
box 11½ x 12", 7" h. (shorts faded,
box w/edge wear & tears) 431.00
Mickey Mouse decals, "Mickey
Mouse Transfer-O-S for Easter
Eggs," Paas Dye Co., Newark,
N.J., Walt Disney Enterprises, ca.
1930 . . . . 80.00
Mickey Mouse doll, cowboy, made
by Knickerbocker Toy Company,
paper wrist tag, swivel cloth
character head w/large "pie" eyes,
string whiskers, painted open-
closed mouth, applied felt ears,
large orange hands w/three fingers
& a thumb, original red bandanna,
white leather fur chaps w/red belt,
two metal guns, holding rope lariat
& felt cowboy hat, ca. 1936,
11" h. 3,900.00

Mickey Mouse doll, plush, stockinette mask face, painted black eyes, painted upper lashes & black nose, open-closed mouth, black felt ears, unjointed black plush body w/white felt hands, yellow felt feet, original red felt short pants, tag on foot w/"Merrythought Ironbridge Shops, Made in England," 12" h. (nose touched up) **90.00**

Mickey Mouse doll, stuffed cloth, velour face w/pie-cut eyes, sharp nose, long whiskers & felt ears, dressed in double-button shorts, gold gloves & orange shoes, distributed by George Borgfeldt, ca. 1936, 15" h. **900.00**

Mickey Mouse egg cup, china, 1930s. **162.00**

Mickey Mouse feeding dish, heavy white china, center w/pie-eyed Mickey wearing red pants & yellow shoes & playing one-string guitar, border w/alphabet in black, marked "Mickey Mouse China, Authorized by Walter E. Disney, Made in Bavaria," excellent condition, 7¾" d. . . **190.00**

Mickey Mouse figure, celluloid, Mickey on ball, 2½" h. **295.00**

Mickey Mouse figure, bisque, Mickey riding Pluto, 1930s, 3¼" h. . . **150.00**

Mickey Mouse figure, bisque, playing French horn, 3½" h. **600.00**

Mickey Mouse figure, jointed wood, two decals on feet, marked "A Fun-e-Flex Toy," excellent paint, 1930s, 7" h. (minor flaking on chest decal) . . . **650.00**

Mickey Mouse flatware set: knife, fork & spoon; stainless steel, 1959, mint in original box, the set **400.00**

Mickey Mouse game, "Mickey Mouse Target," includes target, guns & darts, Louis Marx Bros., in original box **575.00**

Mickey Mouse handkerchief, Mickey playing football, 1940s, 8½" sq. **18.00**

Mickey Mouse lamp, table model, soft rubber figure of Mickey sits on the round base, paper shade decorated w/various Disney characters, ca. 1950s . . . **275.00 to 350.00**

Mickey Mouse lunch kit, lithographed tin, an oval box & cover w/hinged wire bail side handles, green ground decorated on the cover w/a picture of Mickey walking to school, marked "Walt Disney Enterprises," 1930s, some paint wear, (ILLUS.) **500.00**

Early Mickey Mouse Lunch Kit

Mickey Mouse napkin rings, wooden, painted Mickey Mouse head w/ring body & feet, stand upright, 3" h., pr. **69.00**

Mickey Mouse paint book, "Mickey Mouse & The Beanstalk," 1948 . . . . . **60.00**

Mickey Mouse pen knife, bone handle, "Chicago World Fair, 1933" souvenir, 4" l. **89.00**

Mickey Mouse pencil sharpener, celluloid, figure of Mickey, 1930s . . **125.00**

Mickey Mouse pocket watch, die-stamped picture of a standing Mickey on the back, Ingersoll, 1933, mint in box **1,400.00**

Mickey Mouse rocker, wooden, each side painted w/an early Mickey lying in a pool of water, the sides connected by a seat & play rack, the Mengel Company, ca. 1935, w/a photo of the toy & its original owner, 35" l. (some flaking on one side). **550.00**

Mickey Mouse sheet music, "The Wedding Party of Mickey Mouse," 1936 . . . . **80.00**

Mickey Mouse slot machine, life-size figural Mickey Mouse, wood cased w/aluminum front cast as Mickey's chest & waist, 5-cent play, 62" h. **4,888.00**

Mickey Mouse table set: cov. sugar bowl, salt & pepper shakers & tray; china, each modeled as a long-nosed Mickey on a shaped triangular tray, black & white w/yellow shoes, marked "Made in Germany," mint condition, sugar bowl 4" h., the set **3,000.00**

Mickey Mouse toy, pull-type, "Mickey Mouse Safety Patrol," Fisher-Price, No. 733, ca. 1956. . . . . **175.00**

Mickey Mouse toy, train car, Lionel
No. 69672, Mickey Mouse 50th
Anniversary commemorative, mint
in original box **400.00**

Mickey Mouse toy, windup celluloid,
Mickey riding a bucking bronco,
ca. 1930s, 5½" l. **2,800.00**

Mickey Mouse toy, pull-type,
wooden, Mickey Mouse Xylophone,
Fisher-Price, 1939, 9 x 11" **375.00**

Mickey & Minnie Mouse coin purse,
metal mesh w/metal frame
decorated w/Mickey & Minnie
Mouse in yellow, red & green,
fringed bag painted w/an
impressionistic design in pink &
yellow, Whiting-Davis Co., 4¼" l. . . **300.00**

Mickey & Minnie Mouse creamer,
china, blue luster glaze, Japan,
1930s. **235.00**

Mickey & Minnie Mouse dolls,
flannel, each w/flannel bodies, felt
ears, swirling tails & stitched
smiles, Mickey dressed in red
flannel shorts, Minnie wearing a
bubble & dot print green dress,
Mickey 15" h., Minnie 14" h., pr. . . . **950.00**

Mickey & Minnie Mouse figures,
glazed china, Mickey wearing long
pants & Minnie wearing balloon
skirt, ca. 1940, 3" h., pr. **155.00**

Mickey & Minnie Mouse figures,
wooden, w/decals on front,
Borgfeldt, 1934, 3½" h., pr. **195.00**

**Mickey & Minnie Mouse
marionettes,** composition & wood,
composition heads & wooden
bodies, Mickey w/painted pie-cut
eyes, rat teeth grin, gold plush hands
& red velvet pants, Minnie w/painted
closed eyes & closed mouth smile,
wearing a white & red polka dot skirt
& green shoes, each 9" h., pr. **2,760.00**

**Mickey & Minnie Mouse pencil
case,** Dixon No. 2909, depicts
Minnie Mouse waving from balcony
to Mickey in car, includes newer
Disney pencils & some original
crayons, pull-out drawer w/original
protractor, 6" w., 10¾" h. **58.00**

Mickey & Minnie Mouse plate,
lithographed metal, depicts Mickey
& Minnie doing dishes, 4" d. **60.00**

**Mickey Mouse & Donald Duck
lunch box,** scene of Pluto pulling a
cart filled w/Donald's nephews &
Mickey running behind, near mint
condition, 1954. . . . . **1,250.00**

**Mickey & Minnie Mouse & Donald
Duck toothbrush holder,** marked
"Walt Disney," original paint, 1930s . . **325.00**

Mickey Mouse Club costume,
Mouseketeer, mint in box **185.00**

Mickey Mouse Club lunch box,
w/metal thermos, excellent
condition **65.00**

**Mickey Mouse Club Mouseketeer
ears.** **28.00**

Mickey Mouse Club toy, moving van,
the red cab w/articulated trailer
lithographed w/portraits of Mickey &
friends, also marked "Mickey's
Mousekemovers," friction action, Line
Mar, w/original box,12½" l. **1,050.00**

Minnie Mouse cookie cutter,
aluminum, 4" **85.00**

Minnie Mouse doll, black cloth body
& tail, black felt ears, white felt face
w/stitched smile & eyebrows, pie-
cut eyes, dressed in white
pantaloons & red velvet skirt, red
felt high heel shoes & flesh-colored
felt hands, 16" h. **585.00**

Minnie Mouse earrings, lacquered
wood, 1940s **145.00**

Minnie Mouse figure, jointed wood,
w/cloth skirt, marked "Walt E.
Disney," 1934, 3½" h. **325.00**

Minnie Mouse figure, bisque, Minnie
carrying purse & umbrella, 1930s,
4½" h. **150.00**

Minnie Mouse lawn chair, wood &
canvas, 1930s, child's size **440.00**

Minnie Mouse pillow cover, pictures
Minnie powdering her nose, 1930s . . **105.00**

Minnie Mouse toy, windup celluloid,
Minnie on a trapeze, Borgfeldt,
1930s, w/box **1,800.00**

101 Dalmatians puzzles, 1961, set
of 4 . . . . **125.00**

Peter Pan book, colorfully illustrated
w/24 characters including
Tinkerbell, die-cut cover w/plastic
sword & feather, Spain, 1944 . . . . . **45.00**

Peter Pan Christmas card, Disney
Productions, 1953 . . . . **35.00**

Peter Pan hand puppet, Gund Mfg.
Co., Walt Disney Productions **35.00**

Peter Pan phonograph record, 78
r.p.m., Golden Records, 1952,
w/dust cover, 6" d. **8.00**

Peter & the Wolf candy mold, tin,
marked "Belgium," 1946, 8 x 12". . . . **175.00**

Pinocchio bank, composition,
Pinocchio leaning on tree, signed
"Disney Enterprises," 1940s **233.00**

Pinocchio book, Cocomalt premium,
1939 . . . . **65.00**

Pinocchio book, "Pinocchio," Little
Golden Books, Walt Disney
Productions, 1948 . . . . **20.00**

Pinocchio cookie jar, bust of Pinocchio, pottery, marked "CJ46-Copyright USA" on two lines, Doranne of California **650.00**

Pinocchio doll, stuffed plush w/mask face, Gund, 1960s **38.00**

Pinocchio doll, made by Knickerbocker Toy Company, paper wrist tag, composition character head w/large painted blue eyes w/shadow, closed smiling mouth, molded & painted hair, molded & painted yellow gloves & green shoes, original red romper w/blue sleeves & white collar, yellow felt hat w/red trim & blue band, ca. 1939, 10" h. **900.00**

Pinocchio figure, jointed wood, "Fun-e-Flex," colorfully painted, marked "Pinocchio copyright Walt Disney - Geo. Borgfeldt Corp., New York," 4¾" h. **285.00**

Pinocchio Carnival Chalk Figure

Pinocchio figure, carnival-type chalkware, 16" h. (ILLUS.) **65.00**

Pinocchio lunch box, tin, cylindrical, Walt Disney Productions, Libbey Glass Co. **300.00**

Pinocchio record album, original movie sound track, cover decorated w/movie scenes, Walt Disney Enterprises, 1939, 3 records **195.00**

Pinocchio sand pail, tin, green background w/two pictures of Pinocchio, 4½" d. **175.00**

Pinocchio toy, battery-operated, "Pinocchio Playing Xylophone," Rosko, w/box. **275.00**

Pinocchio toy, pull-type, "Plucky Pinocchio," Pinocchio on donkey, Fisher-Price No. 494 . . . . **275.00 to 325.00**

Pinocchio tumbler, clear glass w/a single color picture of Pinocchio, part of a dairy promotions series, 1940 . . . . **40.00**

Pluto alarm clock, scene of Pluto in front of his doghouse surrounded by baby chicks, blue case, Bayard, France, 1964 . . . . **195.00**

Pluto book, "Story of Pluto the Pup," 1938, hardbound **48.00**

Pluto doll, plush velveteen, featuring a seated Pluto w/pie-cut eyes, stitched snout, black velveteen nose & red tongue, original Gund tag affixed to one long, droopy wire-framed ear, 17½" h. **140.00**

Pluto figure, ceramic, reclining Pluto w/legs crossed, American Pottery . . **225.00**

Pluto lamp, ceramic, figural, soft brown tones, Leeds, marked "Walt Disney Productions" on base, late 1940s, 4 x 4 x 6" **145.00**

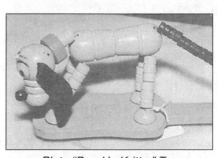

Pluto "Pop-Up Kritter" Toy

Pluto toy, "Mickey's Pal Pluto Pop-Up Kritter," yellow dog w/black tail, red collar & black oilcloth ears on a guitar-shaped base, Model 210, Fisher-Price, Inc., 1936, mint condition (ILLUS.) **400.00**

Pluto toy, friction-type, Pluto driving a four-wheel car w/lever action handlebars, Marx, Japan, 6" l. **395.00**

Snow White book, "Snow White Storybook," Walt Disney Productions, 1938 . . . . **60.00**

Snow White candy container, glitter covered papier-maché, Walt Disney Productions **68.00**

Snow White figure, bisque, Goebel, Germany, full bee & crown mark . . . **400.00**

Snow White flour sack, pictures Snow White rolling dough (unused) . . . **40.00**

Snow White pencil sharpener, Bakelite, late 1930s **65.00**

Snow White planter, ceramic, Leeds China Company, late 1940s, 6½" h. . . . **60.00**

Snow White toothbrush or toothpick holder, china, figural, S. Maw & Sons, England, ca. 1938, 6" h. **450.00**

Snow White & the Seven Dwarfs blocks, "Safety Blocks," painted wood, a different character on each block, Halsam, 1938, in original box, the set **275.00**

Snow White & the Seven Dwarfs dolls, felt, each doll w/a painted felt face, wearing clothes w/felt shoes, each w/original paper label w/name except for Sleepy who had a control number, each Dwarf w/original box, Chad Valley, England, (16" Snow White, 6" Dwarfs), set of 8 . . . . **3,500.00**

Snow White & the Seven Dwarfs figures, bisque, figures range from 2" to 2¾" h., set of 8 . . . . **525.00**

Snow White & the Seven Dwarfs lunch pail, lithographed tin, rectangular w/double swing handles on top, colorful scenes around the sides & top, 1940s (light wear) **2,500.00**

Snow White & the Seven Dwarfs napkin ring, Bakelite, Plastic Novelties of New York, late 1930s, 2½" h. **95.00**

Snow White & the Seven Dwarfs tea set, aluminum, Aluminum Goods Company produced for Walt Disney Enterprises, 1937, w/box. . . **425.00**

"That Darn Cat" book, pictorial highlights of the movie w/shots of Hayley Mills & the cast, spiral-bound, 1965 . . . . **45.00**

Three Caballeros sheet music, "Saludos Amigos" **18.00**

Three Little Pigs figure, bisque, pig playing violin, 1930s, 3½" h. **58.00**

Three Little Pigs ashtray, china w/lustre finish, figures of the three pigs on the back edge of the ashtray, Japan, 1930s, 4½" w., 3" h. **140.00**

Three Little Pigs sand pail, Ohio Art, 3" h. **125.00**

Three Little Pigs toy, windup celluloid, acrobat-type w/three celluloid figures of pigs swinging on a trapeze, in original box w/decorative label on the lid, Japan, 10" h. **275.00**

Thumper (from Bambi) figure, ceramic, American Pottery **65.00**

Thumper (from Bambi) figure, ceramic, w/original paper label, American Pottery, 4" h. **70.00**

Thumper (from Bambi) salt & pepper shakers, ceramic, Goebel, w/label, pr. **175.00**

Tweedle Dee & Tweedle Dum (from Alice in Wonderland) salt & pepper shakers, Walt Disney Productions, 1950s, pr. **375.00**

20,000 Leagues Under the Sea coloring book, 1953. . . . . **40.00**

Wendy (from Peter Pan) hand puppet, Gund Mfg. Co., Walt Disney Productions **45.00**

Zorro coloring book, Whitman, 1958, very fine. **31.00**

Zorro gloves, w/original tag, mint, pr. . . **25.00**

Zorro half-mask & wrist flashlight, in original box, 2 pcs. **150.00**

Zorro toy, windup tin, masked figure of Zorro riding his horse, Marx, w/original box **225.00**

Zorro Wrist Watch & Box

Zorro wrist watch, U. S. Time, 1957, original box (ILLUS.) . . . . **225.00 to 300.00**

DOLL FURNITURE & ACCESSORIES

Bathroom set: toilet, bathtub & sink; cast iron, Arcade Mfg. Co., the set (toilet worn) **$250.00**

Bed, wooden, tall tapered posts, w/mattress, sheet & patchwork quilt, 19th c., 11¼ x 16½", 14" h. . . **115.00**

Bed, birch cannonball posts w/old natural finish, rope support for mattress made from old ticking, 12¼ x 19½" (glued break in headboard) **248.00**

Bed, Federal tall-poster tester-style, mahogany, a scrolled headboard & reeded baluster-turned posts, 17 x 29¼", 29¼" h. **1,495.00**

Carriage, soft metal sleigh-style w/pink cardboard insert supporting maroon velvet cushion, ornate parasol on bracket, large spoked wheels, 3½" h.................. **225.00**

Carriage, metal frame & wheels, wire mesh body, fine wire wound over metal handle & side curled pieces, painted gold, 12½" h. **115.00**

Carriage, wicker & iron, Southbend Toys, 13 x 19" (some wicker broken, frame slightly bent)........ **40.00**

Carriage, metal frame, wire seat & foot rest, coil swirls on sides & back, wire wrapped w/coiled wire on handle & wheels, painted white, unmarked, 23" h................ **210.00**

Carriage, wood w/steel & cast metal fittings, sun shade w/fringe, original light blue paint w/brown stain & reddish striping, 29" l., 26" h. (damage to one wooden wheel & fringe) **165.00**

Carriage, wood & metal, Joel Ellis-type, 26 x 30", red paint, black fringe (chipping on wood) **230.00**

Chairs, kitchen, cast iron, Arcade Mfg. Co., pr.................... **100.00**

Chest of drawers, refinished ash, cut out apron, applied bamboo turnings & three drawers, nail construction, 9 x 17½", 14" h....................... **83.00**

Clothing set, Barbie's "After Five," No. 934, never removed from box.. **135.00**

Clothing set, Barbie's "Arabian Nights," No. 0874 (discolored metal on necklace & gold bracelet) **105.00**

Clothing set, Barbie's "Ballerina," No. 989, never removed from box.. **155.00**

Barbie's Fur Fashion From Europe

Clothing set, Barbie's "Barbie Fur Fashion from Europe," 1979, never removed from box (ILLUS.)........ **30.00**

Clothing set, Barbie's "Beautiful Bride," No. 1698 (some wear & soil) **200.00**

Clothing set, Barbie's "Belle Dress," Barbie Pak item, pink dress w/bow accent, "pearl" necklace, attached hanger, booklet, paper Barbie label, never removed from cardboard **145.00**

Clothing set, Barbie's "Bermuda Holidays," No. 1810 (frayed tag) ... **125.00**

Clothing set, Barbie's "Best Bow, Best Pak," complete w/red cotton top dress, matching bow accent, blue & white floral print skirt **130.00**

Clothing set, Barbie's "Cardigan," Barbie Pak item, black sweater w/white angora collar, attached hanger, booklet, paper Barbie label, never removed from cardboard **50.00**

Clothing set, Barbie's "Check the Suit," No. 1794 .... **95.00**

Clothing set, Barbie's "Cinderella," No. 0872 (slightly discolored program & dress sleeves) **145.00**

Clothing set, Barbie's "Country Fair," No. 1603, never removed from box.. **85.00**

Clothing set, Barbie's "Country Music," No. 1055 (frayed inseams on blouse & skirt, staining & wear to boots) **75.00**

Clothing set, Barbie's "Daisy Crazy," No. 1732 .... **45.00**

Clothing set, Barbie's "Day in Town," No. 1712, Barbie Sew-Free Fashion, never removed from box.. **110.00**

Clothing set, Barbie's "Day 'N Night," No. 1723, Barbie Sew-Free Fashion, never removed from box.. **135.00**

Clothing set, Barbie's "Debutante Party," No. 1711, Barbie Sew-Free Fashion, never removed from box......................... **105.00**

Clothing set, Barbie's "Dress Up Hats," Barbie Pak, never removed from cardboard (wear & discoloration to package) **140.00**

Clothing set, Barbie's "Drum Major," No. 9755, never removed from box .. **125.00**

Clothing set, Barbie's "Fancy Dancy," No. 1858 .... **35.00**

Clothing set, Barbie's "Firelights," No. 1481 .... **45.00**

Clothing set, Barbie's "Firelights," No. 1481 (frayed trim end on inside left pant leg)................... **35.00**

Clothing set, Barbie's "From Nine to Five," No. 1701, Barbie Sew-Free Fashion, never removed from box... **75.00**

Clothing set, Barbie's "Garden Party," No. 931, never removed from box 130.00

Clothing set, Barbie's "Glowin' Out," No. 3404 . . . . 40.00

Clothing set, Barbie's "Golden Ball," No. 1724, Barbie Sew-Free Fashion, never removed from box . . . 175.00

Clothing set, Barbie's "Happy Go Pink," No. 1868 . . . . 40.00

Clothing set, Barbie's "Helenca Swimsuit," Barbie Pak item, never removed from cardboard 105.00

Clothing set, Barbie's "Hootenanny," No. 1707, Barbie Sew-Free Fashion, never removed from box. . . 75.00

Clothing set, Barbie's "Invitation to Tea," No. 1632 (slight wear) 150.00

Clothing set, Barbie's "Let's Dance," never removed from box 145.00

Clothing set, Barbie's "Lovely Lingerie," Barbie Pak item, blue slip, panties, bra, scuffs w/pompons, mirror, attached hanger, paper Barbie label, never removed from carton 125.00

Clothing set, Barbie's "Moonlight 'n Roses," No. 1721, Barbie Sew-Free Fashion, never removed from box. 170.00

Clothing set, Barbie's "Patio Party," No. 1708, Barbie Sew-Free Fashion, never removed from box . . 75.00

Clothing set, Barbie's "Pretty Traveler," No. 1706, Barbie Sew-Free Fashion, never removed from box. 55.00

Clothing set, Barbie's "Red Flare," No. 393, never removed from box. . 115.00

Clothing set, Barbie's "Red Flare," No. 939 . . . . 45.00

Clothing set, Barbie's "Registered Nurse," No. 991 (slightly aged & discolored diploma, small soil areas on cap) 70.00

Clothing set, Barbie's "Satin Coat," Barbie Pak item, rose coat w/"diamond" accents, attached hanger, booklet, paper Barbie label, never removed from cardboard 95.00

Clothing set, Barbie's "Senior Prom," No. 951, never removed from box . . . 155.00

Clothing set, Barbie's "Sightseeing," No. 1713, Barbie Sew-Free Fashion, never removed from box. . 145.00

Clothing set, Barbie's "Ski Queen," No. 948 (two small scuffs on skis). . . 35.00

Clothing set, Barbie's "Skin Diver," No. 1608, never removed from box. . 85.00

Clothing set, Barbie's "Sorority Tea," No. 1703, Barbie Sew-Free Fashion, never removed from box. . . 80.00

Clothing set, Barbie's "Sparkle Squares," No. 1814 . . . . 150.00

Clothing set, Barbie's "Stardust," No. 1722, Barbie Sew-Free Fashion, never removed from box 140.00

Clothing set, Barbie's "Tropicana," No. 1460, never removed from box . . 145.00

Clothing set, Barbie's "Two Piece Pajamas," Barbie Pak item, yellow top w/matching pants, attached hanger, booklet, paper Barbie label, never removed from cardboard 35.00

Clothing set, Francie, "The Yellow Bit," No. 1223 (partially loose upper stitching on hose) 55.00

Clothing set, Francie's "Satin Happenin'," No. 1237 . . . . 40.00

Clothing set, Francie's "Snappy Snoozers," No. 1238, never removed from box 65.00

Clothing set, Francie's "The Silver Cage," No. 1208 . . . . 70.00

Clothing set, Julia's "Pink Fantasy," No. 1754 (several faded ink spots on right front robe, frayed ribbon ends) 50.00

Clothing set, Ken's "American Airlines Captain," No. 0779 (slight wear to silver trim). 115.00

Ken's Army & Air Force Clothing Set

Clothing set, Ken's "Army and Air Force," No. 797, never removed from box (ILLUS.) 175.00

Clothing set, Ken's "Campus Hero," No. 770, never removed from box. . . 55.00

Clothing set, Ken's "Casuals," No. 782, never removed from box 55.00

Clothing set, Ken's "Hiking Holiday," No. 1412, never removed from box . . 115.00

Clothing set, Ken's "Holiday," No. 1414, never removed from box 160.00

Clothing set, Ken's "Loungin' Around," Ken Pak item, includes shorts, red & tan print shirt, booklet, cellophane bag, never removed from cardboard **40.00**

Clothing set, Ken's "Rally Day," No. 788, never removed from box **60.00**

Clothing set, Ken's "Terry Togs," No. 784, never removed from box **40.00**

Clothing set, Ricky's "Lights Out," No. 1501, never removed from box (box slightly discolored & worn). **45.00**

Clothing set, Skipper's "Land and Sea," No.1917, never removed from box (box slightly discolored) . . **110.00**

Clothing set, Skipper's "Ship Ahoy!," No.1918, never removed from box. **200.00**

Clothing set, Skipper's "Under-Pretties," No. 1900, never removed from box **40.00**

Clothing set, Tutti's "Puddle Jumpers," No. 3601, never removed from box (box discolored & scuffed) **45.00**

Cookbook, Barbie's "Easy-As-Pie" Cookbook, 1964, by Cynthia Lawrence, Randon House (age discolored w/slightly worn corners & edges) **75.00**

Cradle, old alligatored yellow green paint w/orange geometric decoration (shows blue beneath), 13½" l. (one rocker is replaced) **83.00**

Cupboard, primitive, two doors above & beneath a drawer, 15" h.. . . . **40.00**

Cupboard, stepback wall-type, walnut & pine w/old finish, square nail construction, 15¾" h. **385.00**

Cupboard base, pine w/old finish, raised panel doors & three dovetailed drawers w/porcelain knobs, 10¾" h., (one drawer front is damaged & adjoining stile is missing). **248.00**

Dish set, marked "Germany" on bottom of all pieces, includes 5" teapot w/lid, sugar w/lid, six cups, six saucers & six plates w/picture & flower decals of various Dutch children & scenes, a boxed baby spoon & a boxed fork & knife both depicting bear on front, 21 pcs. . . . **225.00**

Doll carriage, woven wicker, articulated bonnet, natural finish, metal chassis on wheels, Whitney Carriage Co., Leominster, Massachusetts, 1920s-30s, 40" l., 37" h. (slight wicker damage) **201.00**

Doll case, "Midge, Barbie's Best Friend" doll case, 1963, black vinyl w/picture of Midge on cover wearing pink dress & "Red Flare" outfit, includes metal clothing hanger & cardboard drawer (small scuff, slight discoloration of cardboard drawer). **35.00**

Dollhouse & accessories, 1920s bungalow-style house w/a red gambrel roof, front porch that opens, front dormer, two-room first floor, one-room second floor, opens at either end, together w/assorted wood & lacquered board furniture for the living room, dining room, kitchen, bath & bedrooms as well as metalwares, china & wood accessories, pieces in ¾ - 1" scale, house 10½ x 19¼", 18¾" h., the set (some lot damages) **1,150.00**

Dress, Barbie's "Color Magic," green, yellow, blue & white plaid w/yellow waistband & pleated skirt **45.00**

Dresser, wooden w/oak-type finish, three drawers w/large original wooden knobs, wood-framed mirror w/decorative piece at top, curved decorative pieces at bottom, unmarked, 4" h.. . . . . **75.00**

Dresser, oak w/three large drawers on bottom, three smaller drawers on top, all w/turned knobs, pressed design on drawer fronts & mirror frame, original swivel mirror w/ornate turned brackets, cut-out skirt & top piece on upper drawers, 22½" h.. . . . **350.00**

Dresser, oak, three drawers w/curved fronts, white porcelain pulls, solid front skirt, cut-out bottom at sides, replaced mirror in oak frame w/curved decorative piece at top, 25" h.. . . . . **275.00**

Dresser, unmarked, three-drawer, mirror w/ornately carved frame w/applied columns to cornice, candle brackets on each side, black decorative stenciling on frame & drawers, original wooden pulls, 25" h. (replaced mirror, some wear to stenciling) **220.00**

Hair styling kit, Barbie's "Color 'n Curl," includes four colored wigs & hair salon accessories, in box (some wear & discoloration) **145.00**

High chair, wooden w/spiral-cut straight legs forming frame, decorative-cut back w/three round dowels, plain plank bottom & tray w/round edges, painted black w/rose

design on back & seat, brown trim &
stenciling on back, seat foot rest &
frame, unmarked, 23" h. **95.00**

House, Wishnik Troll House, vinyl,
Ideal, 1965, near mint **25.00**

Ice cream set: table & four chairs;
metal w/bent wire legs & heart
design on chair backs, white
repaint, table 15" d., 10" h., chairs
16" h., 5 pcs. **138.00**

Parasol, unmarked, metal shaft &
frame w/decorative bone handle &
tip, original pink silk w/white lace
trim, 7¼" l. **185.00**

Parasol, pale green silk w/scalloped
edges, ecru silk ruffle, fringe &
lining marked "The Watteau,
(crown), Sangster & Co.,
Patentees" on metal shaft w/ivory
handle & top, 25" l. **190.00**

School master's desk, painted pine,
low crestrail above a hinged
sloping rectangular top opening to
an interior w/three drawers &
original red stain, decorative brass
trim, on ring- and baluster-turned
legs, old brown graining over
yellow repaint, 19th c., 9 x 14½",
12¼" h. (some skillful restoration) . . . **413.00**

Stove, cast iron, green "Roper,"
Arcade Mfg. Co. **200.00**

Stroller, wicker, round spiral-cut
wooden-frame seat on metal frame
w/springs, metal wheels w/rubber
tires, metal brackets holding
original parasol, ornate body
w/adjustable back & foot rest,
original pillow upholstery,
unmarked, 33½" h. **350.00**

Table, kitchen-type, cast iron, Arcade
Mfg. Co. (missing drawer) **50.00**

Trunk, domed top, paper leatherette
pattern, colorful tray w/covers in
place, w/key. **150.00**

Trunk w/accessories, unmarked,
covered w/maroon paper, black tin
panels on corners, metal slat w/metal
corner, tin strips along edges, brown
leather straps, leather straps &
handles, inside lined w/tan paper
w/red print trim, cardboard-covered
compartment in lid, wooden paper
covered tray w/covered compartment,
red print trim on cover, 14" doll clothing
includes beige sailor dress w/matching
hat, white lace-trimmed dress w/yellow
ribbon, pink wool flapper-style dress
trimmed w/fringe, light blue dress
w/white scalloped trim, dark blue
jumper w/button trim & white blouse,
full-length flannel slip, two white half
slips, one pair pants, two chemise

tops, corset & garters, 18" doll clothing
includes white dress w/lace inserts,
red satin dress w/white crocheted trim,
three full-length slips, one w/matching
pants, one pair newer pants, half slip,
chemise, crocheted cap, black
stockings, white leather shoes, corset,
7¼" x 8 x 14" the set. **400.00**

Wall cupboard, painted pine &
poplar, one-piece construction, a
narrow rectangular top over two
cupboard doors w/small wood
knobs over an open pie shelf
above the stepped-out lower
section w/a pair of small drawers
over two cupboard doors, all
w/turned knobs, short stile feet,
painted grey, wire nail construction,
early 20th c., 8¼ x 13½", 18¼" h. . . . **193.00**

Wicker basket w/accessories,
marked "Toys - G.A. Schwarz -
1006 Chestnut St. - Philadelphia"
on bottom paper label, mid basket
woven w/pale blue ribbon, lined
w/blue silk & edged w/chenille,
elastic holders for accessories,
includes bone-handled brush,
sponge & manicure accessory, 3½
x 6", the set (basket in excellent
condition, some accessories
missing). **115.00**

DOLLS

**A.B.G. (Alt, Beck & Gottschalck)
bisque shoulder head girl,**
marked "23, 1365/23" brown sleep
eyes w/feathered brows, painted
upper & lower lashes, open mouth
w/three upper teeth, mohair wig,
kid body, long lace-trimmed calico
dress, 13½" **$125.00**

A.B.G. bisque socket head baby,
marked "ABG (entwined), 1361,
35.36, Made in Germany, 10,"
brown sleep eyes w/real lashes,
feathered brows, painted upper &
lower lashes, open mouth w/two
upper teeth & molded tongue,
mohair wig, white eyelet baby dress,
diaper, bonnet w/lace trim, 15" **300.00**

A.B.G. bisque socket head baby,
marked "ABG (entwined), 1361/50,
Made in Germany, 15," blue sleep
eyes w/heavily feathered brows,
painted upper & lower lashes, open
mouth w/two upper teeth & tongue,
h.h. (human-hair) wig, blue lace-
trimmed baby dress, 21" **450.00**

A.B.G. bisque socket head "Bebe,"
marked "911 #0," brown paperweight eyes
w/feathered brows, painted upper & lower
lashes, closed mouth, pierced ears,
replaced mohair wig, gold silk dress w/gold
embroidery trim, gold striped sash,
16" **1,400.00**

A.B.G. bisque socket head girl,
marked "1123½ #8," brown sleep
eyes w/heavily feathered brows,
painted upper & lower lashes, open
mouth w/six upper teeth, original
blonde mohair wig, kid body,
antique white blouse, teal blue silk
skirt & matching vest, 20" **220.00**

A.B.G. bisque socket head girl,
marked "12. 154. Dep.," blue sleep
eyes w/feathered brows, painted
upper & lower lashes, open mouth
w/four upper teeth, pierced ears,
brunette mohair wig, blue & white
silk dress, 22" **250.00**

Alt, Beck & Gottschalck Girl

A.B.G. bisque socket head girl,
marked "ABC (entwined), 1362,
Made in Germany," brown sleep
eyes w/feathered brows, painted
upper & lower lashes, open mouth
w/four upper teeth, pierced ears,
synthetic wig, white dress, 26"
(ILLUS.). **275.00**

A.B.G. bisque socket head girl,
marked "12," large set brown eyes
w/heavily feathered brows, painted
upper & lower lashes, open mouth
w/six upper teeth, replaced h.h.
wig, kid body, antique white long
dress w/lace inserts & tucks, 28" . . **650.00**

A.B.G. bisque socket head toddler,
marked "ABG (entwined), 1361/45,
Made in Germany, 19", set blue
eyes w/remnants of real lashes,

feathered brows, painted lower
lashes, open mouth w/two upper
teeth & tongue, replaced synthetic
wig, toddler body, white baby
romper, 22½" **350.00**

**A.M. (Armand Marseille) bisque
socket head boy,** marked "1894,
A.M. 10 DEP," brown sleep eyes
w/feathered brows, painted upper
& lower lashes, open mouth w/four
upper teeth, mohair wig, blue two-
piece velvet suit, 23" **400.00**

**A.M. bisque socket head
"Florodora" girl,** marked "A. O. M.
Florodora, Armand Marseille, Made
in Germany," brown sleep eyes
w/single-stroke brows, painted
upper & lower lashes, open mouth
w/four upper teeth, kidette body,
original pink & white gingham
dress & bonnett, 20" **125.00**

A.M. bisque socket head girl,
marked "Made in Germany, Armand
Marseille, 390n, A. 13 M.," brown
sleep eyes w/feathered brows,
painted upper & lower lashes, open
mouth w/four upper teeth, replaced
wig, antique dress, 30". **300.00**

A.M. bisque socket head girl,
marked "1894 A.M. 6 DEP, made
in Germany," brown sleep eyes
w/molded & feathered brows,
painted upper & lower lashes, open
mouth w/four upper teeth, original
h.h. wig, pink & white print dress
trimmed w/lace, new pants,
19" **285.00**

A.M. bisque socket head girl,
marked "1894, A.M. 10 DEP," dark
brown eyes w/heavily feathered
brows, painted upper & lower
lashes, open mouth w/four upper
teeth, h.h. wig, rose dress,
underclothing, 25" **275.00**

A.M. bisque socket head girl,
marked "A. 15.," blue sleep eyes
w/feathered brows, painted upper
& lower lashes, open mouth w/four
upper teeth, original mohair wig,
pink nylon dotted Swiss dress,
33" **650.00**

**A.M. bisque socket head "Just Me"
girl,** marked "Just Me, Registered,
Germany, A. 310/7/0 M.," blue
sleep eyes looking to side, single-
stroke brows, painted upper &
lower lashes, closed "rosebud"
mouth, replaced mohair wig, blue
dotted Swiss dress w/white lace-
trimmed pinafore, 9" **1,050.00**

A.M. bisque socket head "Nobbi Kid," marked "A. 253. M., Nobbi Kid, Reg. U.S. Pat. Off., Germany, 10/0," blue sleep eyes, single-stroke brows, painted upper & lower lashes, closed smiling mouth, original mohair wig, factory original print dress, white bonnet, 7" **550.00**

A.M. bisque socket head "Nun," marked "Armand Marseille, 390n, Germany, A. 5. M.," brown sleep eyes w/feathered brows, painted upper & lower lashes, open mouth w/four upper teeth, nun's habit w/black dress, black belt w/rosary, 20" **295.00**

A.M. bisque socket head "Queen Louise" girl, marked "29, Queen Louise, 100, Germany," set brown eyes w/real lashes, feathered brows, painted upper & lower lashes, open mouth w/four upper teeth, original mohair wig, pink taffeta dress w/lace trim, 25" **200.00**

A.M. bisque socket head Scottish child, marked "Armand Marseille, Germany, 390, A. 10/0 M.," brown sleep eyes w/single-stroke brows, painted upper & lower lashes, open mouth w/four upper teeth, original Scottish outfit w/plaid wool skirt, red wool jacket w/white belt & gold trim, plaid wool scarf, black fur hat, 9" **130.00**

A.M. Bisque Welsh Child

A.M. bisque socket head Welsh child, marked "Germany, 390, A. 10/0 M.," blue sleep eyes w/single-stroke brows, painted upper & lower lashes, open mouth w/four upper teeth, original mohair wig, original black cape Welsh outfit, 9" (ILLUS.) **375.00**

Alexander (Madame) "Ballerina," marked "Alex," plastic body, blue sleep eyes w/real lashes, painted lower lashes, single-stroke brows, closed mouth, original synthetic wig & pink satin tutu, 14" **205.00**

Alexander (Madame) "Caroline," marked "Alexander, 1961," vinyl head, blue sleep eyes w/real lashes, single-stroke brows, painted lower lashes, open-closed mouth, original rooted hair, original red & white dress, original box, 15" **300.00**

Alexander (Madame) Dionne Cecile baby, marked "Dionne, Alexander," composition head w/painted brown eyes looking to side, single-stroke brows, painted upper lashes, closed mouth, molded & painted brown hair, yellow baby dress & bonnet, 7" **95.00**

Alexander (Madame) Dionne Quintuplet "Cecile" toddler, marked "Dionne, Alexander," composition head, brown sleep eyes w/real lashes, single-stroke brows, painted lower lashes, open mouth w/four upper teeth, original brunette h.h. wig, original organdy green dress w/matching bonnet, 11" **375.00**

Alexander (Madame) "Emelie" toddler, marked "Alexander," composition head w/painted brown eyes looking to side, single-stroke brows, painted upper lashes, closed mouth, molded & painted brown hair, original lavender dress, 7" **200.00**

Alexander (Madame) "Little Shaver," marked "Little Shaver, Madame Alexander, New York, All Rights Reserved," pressed-cloth face w/painted eyes & upper lashes, closed mouth, original yarn wig, original dress w/maroon taffeta top & organdy skirt, 15" **220.00**

Alexander (Madame) "Mary Ellen" marked "Mme. Alexander," plastic head, blue sleep eyes w/real lashes, painted lower lashes, feathered brows, closed mouth, head attached to walking mechanism, original saran wig & clothing, 31" **215.00**

Alexander (Madame) "Princess," marked "Every Little Girl's Dream Come True, Princess, A Madame Alexander Creation" on paper wrist tag, "Madame Alexander, New York" on dress tag, composition head, brown sleep eyes w/real lashes &

feathered brows, painted lower lashes, open mouth w/four upper teeth & tongue, original mohair wig, pink taffeta dress, 19" **425.00**

Alexander (Madame) "Quiz-Kin," marked "Alex," marked clothing tag, plastic body w/walking mechanism, blue sleep eyes w/molded mouth, molded & painted hair, original romper, 7½" **225.00**

Alexander (Madame) "Sonja Henie," marked "Genuine Sonja Henie," composition head, brown sleep eyes w/real lashes, open mouth w/four upper teeth, original mohair wig, tagged skating dress w/flower print, 14" **425.00**

Alexander (Madame) "Sonja Henie," marked "Madame Alexander, Sonja Henie," composition head, brown sleep eyes w/real lashes, painted lower lashes, single-stroke brows, open mouth w/six upper teeth, original mohair wig, gold satin skating dress & matching panties, white skates, 17" **400.00**

Alexander (Madame) "Wendy Bride," marked "Madame Alexander, New York, U.S.A.," composition head, brown sleep eyes w/real lashes, painted lower lashes, eye shadow, mohair wig, original satin white wedding gown, 20" **125.00**

Sandy & Betsy McCall

American Character "Betsy McCall," marked "McCall, 1961, Corp.," vinyl socket head, blue sleep eyes w/real lashes, feathered brows, painted upper lashes, closed smiling mouth, rooted red hair, original blue & white dress trimmed w/black velvet ribbon, silver sandals, 30"(ILLUS. left) **275.00**

American Character "Sandy McCall," marked "McCall, 1959, Corp.," vinyl socket head, blue sleep eyes w/real lashes, feathered brows, painted upper lashes, freckles on bridge of nose, closed smiling mouth, molded & painted hair, original white shirt, black bow tie, red corduroy shorts, white shoes, 35" (ILLUS. right) **530.00**

American Character "Sweet Sue Sophisticate," marked "Sweet Sue Sophisticate, Your Grown Up Doll," vinyl head, blue sleep eyes w/real lashes, feathered brows, painted lower lashes, closed mouth, pierced ears w/original pearl drop earrings, rooted saran hair, original red & white dress w/pearl circle pin holding white netting over shoulders, 19" **305.00**

American Character "Tiny Tears" w/layette, marked "American Character Doll, Pat. No. 2675644," hard plastic head, blue sleep eyes w/real lashes, single-stroke brows, painted lower lashes, open mouth w/hole for bottle, original playsuit & accessories, boxed, 12" **250.00**

Art Fabric Mills "Topsy Doll," printed uncut cotton pattern, shrinkwrapped, patented in 1900, 19" **345.00**

Bahr & Proschild bisque socket head baby, marked "678, 3/0, BP (in heart), Made in Germany," brown sleep eyes w/real lashes, single-stroke brows, painted upper & lower lashes, open mouth w/two upper teeth, original blonde mohair wig, white baby dress w/blue smocking, 9½" **175.00**

Barbie, "1920s Flapper Barbie," 1993, The Great Eras Collection Second Edition, No. 4063, boxed **225.00**

Barbie, "American Girl Barbie" on straight-leg body, long dark hair, 1965, coral lips, painted finger & toe nails, wearing black & white striped swimsuit, black wire stand (some rubs & scratches) **800.00**

Barbie, "Antique Rose Barbie," 1996, FAO Schwarz Limited Edition Floral Signature Collection, first in series, No. 15814, never removed from box **180.00**

Barbie, "City Sophisticate Barbie," 1994, Service Merchandise Limited Edition, No. 12005, never removed from box **45.00**

Barbie, "Dorothy in The Wizard of Oz," 1994, Hollywood Legends Collection Special Edition, No. 12701, boxed **125.00**

Barbie, "Happy Holidays Barbie," 1989, Special Edition, white dress w/fur trim, No. 3523, boxed **250.00**

Barbie, "Happy Holidays Barbie," 1990, Special Edition, fuchsia gown w/silver design, No. 4098, boxed. **125.00**

Barbie, "Jewel Princess Barbie," 1996, The Winter Princess Collection Limited Edition (Disney's brunette edition), No. 16400, never removed from box **175.00**

Barbie, "Kimono Barbie," short blonde hair, wearing pink floral kimono, accessories, Tarkara, Japanese, never removed from box. **105.00**

Barbie, "Matinee Today Barbie," 1996, Barbie Millecent Roberts Limited Edition, No. 16079, includes extra outfit, never removed from box **75.00**

Barbie, "Mrs. P.F.E. Albee," 1997, first in series, Avon Special Edition, No. 17690, never removed from box **90.00**

Barbie, No. 3, blonde ponytail, 1960, red lips, faint eyeshadow, painted fingers & toe nails, straight leg, wearing black & white striped swimsuit, white-rimmed glasses w/blue lenses (discoloring, wear & staining). **625.00**

Barbie, No. 4, blonde ponytail in original set w/hard curl, 1960, red lips, eyeshadow, finger & toe paint, wearing black & white striped swimsuit, "pearl" earrings, black open-toe shoes, Barbie & Ken pink cover booklet, in box labeled "Ash Blonde Ponytail" w/black pedestal stand base. **400.00**

Barbie, No. 4, brunette ponytail in original set, red lips, eyeshadow, finger & toe paint, straight leg, wearing black & white striped swimsuit, "pearl" earrings, black open-toe shoes, boxed w/pedestal stand & pink cover Ponytail Barbie booklet. **400.00**

Barbie, "Pink Ice Barbie," 1996, Toys R Us Limited Edition, first in series, No. 15141, never removed from box. **125.00**

Barbie, "Radiant Rose Barbie," 1996, Society Style Collection Limited Edition, second in series, Toys R Us Special Edition, No. 15140, never removed from box **45.00**

Barbie, "Sapphire Dream Barbie," 1995, Society Style Collection Limited Edition, first in series, Toys R Us Special Edition, No. 13255, never removed from box **65.00**

Barbie, "Silver Screen Barbie," 1993, FAO Schwartz Limited Edition, No. 11652, boxed. **215.00**

Barbie, "Starlight Waltz Barbie," 1995, Ballroom Beauties Collection Limited Edition (Disney's brunette edition), No.14954. . . . . **225.00**

Barbie, "Swirl Ponytail Barbie," 1964, dark blonde hair in original set w/yellow ribbon tie & hair pin, coral lips, painted fingers & toes, straight leg, wearing red nylon swimsuit, in box w/cardboard liner, gold wire stand & pink cover booklet (some wear & fading) **400.00**

Belton-type bisque socket head girl, marked "183, 15," set brown eyes w/heavily feathered brows, painted upper & lower lashes, closed mouth, pierced ears, h.h. wig, antique white blouse, maroon wool jumper w/matching coat & hat, 24" **275.00**

Bergmann (C.M.) bisque socket girl, marked "Simon & Halbig, C.M. Bergmann, 1," blue sleep eyes w/feathered brows, painted upper & lower lashes, open mouth w/four upper teeth, original mohair wig, antique knit dress w/ribbon trim, 22". **400.00**

Bisque shoulder head German girl, marked "901, TR," set light blue eyes w/feathered brows, painted upper & lower lashes, closed mouth, pierced ears, original blonde mohair wig, original rose colored dress w/lace & ribbon trim, kid body, 12" **475.00**

Kestner Baby & German Child Doll

Bisque socket head German child,
marked "2/0," blue eyes w/single-
stroke brows, painted upper &
lower lashes, closed mouth,
original mohair wig, original ecru
dress w/lace collar, 3" (ILLUS.
w/11" h. Kestner baby) **145.00**

Bisque socket head German girl,
marked "449, 5/0," painted upper &
lower lashes, open mouth w/five
upper teeth, original blonde mohair
wig, beige dress w/maroon trim,
red felt embroidered vest, colorful
apron, gold trimmed head piece
w/glass bead trim, 9" **425.00**

Bisque socket head German girl,
marked "R, Germany," blue sleep
eyes w/single-stroke brows, open
mouth w/five upper teeth, original
mohair wig, crude five-piece body,
original Welsh costume of red
dress, black & white striped apron,
red felt cape, black paper hat
trimmed w/white lace, 13" **85.00**

**Borgfeldt (George) bisque socket
head child,** marked "Germany,
G.B.," blue sleep eyes w/real
lashes, open mouth w/four upper
teeth, original mohair wig & mauve
two-piece outfit, 24½" **350.00**

Buddy Lee composition boy,
molded & painted features, jointed
shoulders & one hip, wearing blue
denim engineer's outfit w/cloth
label, made for H.D. Lee Mercantile
Co., San Francisco, 1920s, 13" (left
arms needs reattaching, paint wear
on back of head, hands &
boots) **316.00**

Bye-Lo Baby, marked "Copr. Grace
S. Putnam Made in Germany,"
bisque flange head w/blue sleep
eyes, cloth body & legs, celluloid
hands, original lawn christening
dress w/cloth label, 13" **374.00**

Bye-Lo Baby, marked "Corp. by
Grace S. Putman, Made in
Germany, 1360 45," bisque socket
head w/tiny blue eyes, softly
brushed brows, painted upper &
lower lashes, closed mouth, lightly
molded & painted hair, original white
organdy long baby dress, 14" **600.00**

Bye-Lo Baby with wardrobe,
marked "(c) 1923 by Grace S.
Putnam, Made in Germany,
1372/30," bisque flange head
w/brown sleep eyes, painted upper
& lower lashes, closed mouth,
lightly molded & painted hair,
dressed in original flannel

undershirt & diaper, includes 31 pc.
complete original wardrobe &
bedding, 10" c., 12", the set **2,500.00**

Princess Elizabeth as Child

Chad Valley "Princess Elizabeth,"
marked "Hygienic Toys, Made in
England by Chad Valley Co. Ltd.,"
pressed-felt swivel head, blue
glass eyes w/single-stroke brows,
painted upper & lower lashes,
original blonde mohair wig, original
peach felt coat & shoes, pink print
dress, 18" **400.00**

China head lady, marked "1867,"
china shoulder head, painted blue
eyes w/red accent line & molded
eyelid, single-stroke brows, closed
mouth, molded & painted black
hair, cloth body, old two-piece
green checked outfit, 34" **625.00**

China shoulder head lady,
unmarked, painted blue eyes w/red
accent line, single-stroke brows,
accented nostrils, closed mouth,
molded blonde hair w/deep curls &
exposed ears, cloth body, dressed
in brown homemade dress, 21" **145.00**

China shoulder head lady,
unmarked, painted blue eyes w/red
accent lines, single-stroke brows,
closed mouth, molded & painted
black hair w/center part & ten
vertical curls, cloth body w/china
lower arms, blue lower legs w/kid
boots, redressed in two-piece blue
dress, 18" **175.00**

China shoulder head lady,
unmarked, painted blue eyes w/red
accent lines, single-stroke brows,
closed mouth, molded & painted
black hair w/center part & twenty-
three vertical curls, homemade cloth

body w/no hands, large oversized legs, blue & white plaid dress w/lace-trimmed apron, 25" **150.00**

Cochran (Dewees) "Angela Appleseed" lady, marked "A.A.-'58, 11," latex socket head w/painted brown eyes, molded lids & real upper lashes, multi-stroke brows, open-closed mouth w/painted upper & lower teeth, original blonde wig, red calico long dress w/white trim, white eyelet apron, 17" **775.00**

Danbury Mint "The Princess Diana Bride," blue glass eyes, open-closed mouth, replication of original wedding dress & flower bouquet, original box, 18". **385.00**

Dressel (Cuno & Otto) bisque socket head girl, marked "1913, Made in Germany, 1912 - 5," blue sleep eyes w/real lashes, feathered brows, painted upper & lower lashes, open mouth w/four upper teeth, original h.h. wig, blue flowered dress, 24" **250.00**

Dressel (Cuno & Otto) bisque socket head girl, marked "9, Cuno & Otto Dressel, Germany," brown sleep eyes w/feathered brows, painted upper & lower lashes, open mouth w/four upper teeth, mohair wig, antique white dress w/rosebud trim, 28". **400.00**

Eden Bebe bisque socket head girl, marked "Eden Bebe, Paris, L," large blue paperweight eyes, feathered brows, painted upper & lower lashes, open-closed mouth, pierced ears, replaced synthetic wig, torso w/crier, mama & papa pull strings, redressed in pale blue dress w/tiny flowers & lace trim, 20". **750.00**

Effanbee "Barbara Ann"

Effanbee "Barbara Ann," marked "Effanbee, Anne Shirley," composition head, green sleep eyes w/real lashes, single-stroke brows, open mouth w/four upper teeth, original h.h. wig, pink trimmed dress w/white panties, 16" (ILLUS.). **450.00**

Effanbee "Marilee," marked "Effanbee Marilee, Copyr. Doll," composition shoulder head w/blue tin sleep eyes w/real lashes, feathered brows, painted upper & lower lashes, open mouth w/two upper teeth, h.h. wig, original pale yellow dress trimmed w/ruffles & black velvet ribbons, 29" **650.00**

Effanbee "Patsy Lou," composition head w/light green sleep eyes w/real lashes, feathered brows, painted lower lashes, closed "rosebud" mouth, molded & painted bobbed hair, original pink organdy dress trimmed w/ruffle, 22" **525.00**

Farnell's "King George VI," marked "Farnell's, Alpha Toys, Made in England," pressed felt swivel head w/painted blue eyes w/red accent line, single-stroke brows, closed mouth, applied ears, molded & lightly painted hair, original Royal Air Force uniform, 15" (moth damage to left cheek, nose & brows) **150.00**

French-type all-bisque girl, marked "1," solid dome head w/painted blue eyes, single-stroke brows, closed mouth, mohair wig, original lace trimmed silk dress, tiny straw bonnet, 6" child's wicker purse w/lace & taffeta lining, 3½". **400.00**

Freundlich "Red Riding Hood" set, consists of Red Riding Hood, Grandmother & Wolf, each w/jointed composition head, shoulders & hips, molded & painted heads, wolf head on human body, cotton outfits, in original lithographed cardboard schoolhouse box, box 10 x 11 3/8", 2⅞" h., dolls, 9", 9¼" & 9½", the set **805.00**

Frozen Charlie, china, unmarked, head w/stiff neck & light pink tint, painted brown eyes w/single-stroke brows, closed mouth, painted black hair, knit dark green pants & cap, 14½". **300.00**

Frozen Charlie, china, unmarked, head w/stiff neck & light pink tint, painted blue eyes w/single-stroke eyes, molded mouth, molded & painted blond hair, unclothed, 15".........................**325.00**

German "Googlie" character boy, marked "Germany, BN . 27-15, D.R.G.M.," bisque socket head, painted eyes to side, single-stroke brows, watermelon mouth, molded & painted hair, original Dutch outfit w/black wool jacket, red felt skirt, white cotton shawl, white apron & Dutch hat, wooden shoes, 7".........................**600.00**

Gibbs (Ruth) Godey's "Little Lady," marked "Ruth Gibb's Godey's Little Lady Dolls, Flemington, New Jersey," pink china shoulder head w/painted blue eyes, painted upper lashes, open-closed mouth, molded & painted hair, original pale blue brocade taffeta dress & blue felt lace-trimmed bonnet, boxed, 7".........................**225.00**

Handwerck (Heinrich) bisque socket head child, marked "Germany, Heinrich Handwerck, Simon & Halbig, 2½," brown sleep eyes w/real lashes, feathered brows, painted lower lashes, open mouth w/four upper teeth, pierced ears, h.h. wig, antique off-white dress, 21".........................**425.00**

Handwerck (Heinrich) bisque socket head girl, marked "Germany, Heinrich Handwerck, Simon & Halbig, 6½" & "W," blue sleep eyes w/molded & feathered brows, painted lower lashes, open mouth w/four upper teeth, pierced ears, original mohair wig, antique white dress w/embroidery & lace trim, 31".........................**700.00**

Happifats all-bisque boy & girl, marked w/copyright symbol on foot of man, both w/painted brown eyes, painted upper lashes, open-closed mouths w/two painted upper teeth, molded & painted wisps of hair, lady w/molded & painted ruffled dress w/pink highlights, molded blue sash & painted shoes, man w/molded & painted dark green jacket w/white collar, white tie, brown pants, painted green shoes, 4", pr.........................**375.00**

Hertel, Schwab & Co. bisque socket head baby, marked "4, 151," blue sleep eyes w/feathered brows, painted upper & lower lashes, open mouth w/two upper teeth & molded tongue, lightly molded hair, antique white long baby dress w/lace inserts, bonnet, slip & flannel diaper, 12".........**160.00**

Hertel, Schwab & Co. bisque socket head baby, marked "Made In Germany, 152 2," bluish grey sleep eyes w/feathered brows, painted upper & lower lashes, open mouth w/molded tongue & two upper teeth, blonde mohair wig, white dotted Swiss baby dress, antique underclothing, handmade booties, new pink sweater & bonnet, 12".................**130.00**

Heubach (Ernst) bisque socket head baby, marked "Heubach, 267 . 11, Koppelsdorf, D.R.G.M., Thuringia," blue sleep eyes w/feathered brows, painted upper & lower lashes, open mouth w/four upper teeth, mouth & chin dimples, mohair wig, antique christening dress, embroidered baby coat w/cape, knit bonnet w/ribbon ties, 26".........................**275.00**

Heubach (Ernst) bisque socket head child, marked "DEP, (horseshoe) K, 0½," set brown eyes w/feathered brows & long painted lashes, open mouth w/four upper teeth, pierced ears, original mohair blonde wig, pink & blue plaid dress, straw hat, 15½".......**275.00**

Heubach (Ernst) bisque socket head toddler, marked "Heubach-Koppelsdorf, 320 .8/0, Germany," blue sleep eyes w/feathered brows, painted upper & lower lashes, open mouth w/two upper teeth, mohair wig, redressed, 12½".............**225.00**

Heubach (Gebruder) bisque character head baby, marked "Heubach," blue intaglio eyes w/single-stroke brows, open-closed mouth w/two lower teeth, molded & painted hair, original factory pink lace-trimmed dress & bonnet, walking mechanism w/key, 6".....**500.00**

Heubach (Gebruder) bisque character head girl, marked w/illegible number (possibly 7303), "1, (sunburst), DEP," set blue eyes w/multi-stroke brows, painted upper & lower lashes, open-closed mouth w/two upper teeth, original mohair wig, walking mechanism w/key, white lace dress w/bonnet, 11"...............**2,000.00**

Heubach (Gebruder) bisque head character child, marked "2, Germany" incised & stamped "46" in green on back, "4" on front of neck socket, blue intaglio eyes w/single-stroke brows, closed pouty mouth, molded & painted blond hair, blue romper w/red piping trim, 11½" **500.00**

Heubach (Gebruder) bisque head character child, marked "Germany, 7" & "Holz-Masse," molded string loop, blue intaglio eyes w/single-stroke brows, molded & painted hair, redressed in blue velvet suit w/lace collar, 17" **1,000.00**

Heubach (Gebruder) bisque head Scottish girl, marked "8192, Germany, Gebruder Heubach, Heubach," brown sleep eyes w/feathered brows, painted upper & lower lashes, open mouth w/four teeth, original mohair wig, original black velvet & plaid Scottish outfit, 12" (no shoes) **400.00**

Heubach (Gebruder) bisque socket head girl, marked "6971, 59, 0, Germany, 2," blue intaglio eyes w/single-stroke brows, open-closed mouth w/two lower teeth, molded dimples, original blonde mohair wig w/coiled braids, original factory pink lace trim & ribbon trimmed dress, 10½" **925.00**

Hoyer (Mary) composition head girl, marked "The Mary Hoyer Doll," blue sleep eyes w/real lashes, single-stroke brows, painted lower lashes, closed mouth, mohair wig, tagged blue & yellow silk dress, boxed, 14" **450.00**

Huss (Adolf) bisque socket head toddler, marked "X, Simon & Halbig, AH, W, Made in Germany, 156/6," blue sleep eyes w/real lashes, feathered brows, original blonde mohair wig, painted upper & lower lashes, two upper teeth, yellow dress w/flower print, 14" (ILLUS.) **700.00**

Ideal's Mary Hartline

Ideal's Mary Hartline, marked "P-91, Ideal Doll, Made in U.S.A.," hard plastic head, blue sleep eyes w/real lashes & eye shadow, feathered brows, painted lower lashes, closed mouth, original wig, original marked dress, boxed, 16" (ILLUS.) **700.00**

Izannah Walker girl, unmarked oil painted cloth head, painted brown eyes w/single-stroke brows, closed mouth, applied ears, painted hair, cloth body w/painted arms, legs, & shoes, old striped dress, 18" **700.00**

Adolf Huss Toddler

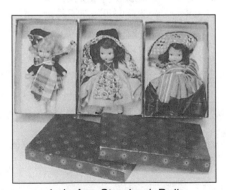

Judy-Ann Storybook Dolls

Judy-Ann Storybook Dolls, ceramic head & body, each in a different costume, "Scotland," "Portugal," & "Mexico," mid-20th c., w/original boxes, set of 3 (ILLUS.) **3,600.00**

Undocumented Jumeau Character

Jumeau bisque head character girl, No. 200 series, undocumented, head w/glass paperweight eyes, brown h.h. wig, puckered open mouth, jointed composition body, German peasant-style costume (ILLUS.) **66,000.00**

Rare "Portrait" Jumeau

Jumeau bisque head "Portrait" lady, glass paperweight eyes, closed mouth, blonde h.h. wig, jointed composition body, wearing period style hat & gown, first period (ILLUS.) **53,000.00**

Jumeau bisque socket head "Bebe" girl, marked "E. 6. D." & "Bebe, paperweight eyes w/heavily feathered brows, long painted lashes, closed mouth, pierced ears, h.h. wig, new peach frilly silk dress w/lace trim, 16½" **2,600.00**

Jumeau bisque socket head "Bebe" girl, marked w/artist marks, "scrubbed" mark area & "France" label above "Bebe Jumeau, Diplome d'honneur" in oval on back, large blue paperweight eyes, heavily feathered brows, long painted upper & lower lashes, closed mouth, pierced ears, h.h. wig, rust colored dress w/lace trim, 17" . . . **2,800.00**

Jumeau bisque socket head girl, marked "8" on back, "Jumeau, Medaille d' Or, Paris" blue stamp on rear torso, blue paperweight eyes w/feathered brows, painted upper & lower lashes, open mouth w/six upper teeth, pierced ears, replaced h.h. wig, new pink dress w/lace inserts & gathers, 20" **1,900.00**

Jumeau bisque socket head girl, marked "DEP, 11," & "Tete Jumeau," set original sleep eyes w/missing rocker, molded & feathered brows, painted lower lashes, open mouth w/four upper teeth, pierced ears, h.h. wig, pale green silk dress, 24" **675.00**

Jumeau bisque socket head girl, marked "12" & "Bebe Jumeau, Bte. S.G.D.G. - Depose," blue paperweight eyes w/heavily feathered brows, painted upper & lower lashes, open mouth w/six upper teeth, pierced ears, replaced wig, ecru lace & embroidery dress, 27" **1,800.00**

Jumeau Bisque Socket Head Girl

Jumeau bisque socket head girl,
marked "15," blue sleep eyes
w/feathered brows, painted upper
& lower lashes, open mouth w/six
upper teeth, pierced ears, replaced
wig, antique white dress
w/embroidery & tucks, 31"
(ILLUS.) **2,900.00**

K * R bisque socket head baby,
marked "K * R, Simon & Halbig,
126, 42," forehead marked "W,"
painted upper & lower lashes, open
mouth w/two upper teeth & spring
tongue, mohair wig, white baby
dress w/blue jacket & matching
bonnet, 17" **350.00**

K * R bisque socket head girl,
marked "Halbig, K * R, 21," brown
sleep eyes w/single-stroke brows,
painted upper & lower lashes, open
mouth w/three upper teeth, h.h.wig,
white dress w/blue flowers,
8¼" **275.00**

K * R bisque socket head girl,
marked "L, S & H, K * R, 30," blue
sleep eyes w/feathered brows,
painted upper & lower lashes,
accented nostrils, open mouth
w/four upper teeth, mohair wig, five-
piece composition body w/walking
mechanism, molded & painted
black socks w/brown two-strap
shoes, white eyelet dress w/lace
trim, white organdy bonnet, 11½" .. **575.00**

K * R bisque socket head girl,
marked "192, 14," blue sleep eyes
w/feathered brows, painted upper
& lower lashes, open mouth w/four
upper teeth, pierced ears, replaced
wig, antique white embroidered
dress, 27" **1,100.00**

K * R bisque socket head girl,
marked "Simon & Halbig, K * R,
68," blue sleep eyes, molded &
feathered brows, painted upper &
lower lashes, open mouth w/three
upper teeth, pierced ears, replaced
wig, ecru silk lacy dress, peach
silk bonnet, 27" **600.00**

K * R bisque socket head girl,
marked "Simon & Halbig, K * R,
73," brown sleep eyes w/molded &
feathered brows, painted upper &
lower lashes, open mouth
w/accented lips & four upper teeth,
pierced ears, replaced h.h. wig,
ecru lace dress, 28" **600.00**

K * R bisque socket head girl,
marked "Simon & Halbig, K * R,
85," blue sleep eyes w/real lashes,
molded & feathered brows, painted
upper & lower lashes, open mouth

w/four upper teeth, pierced ears,
original mohair wig w/rope curls,
antique white Swiss dress w/ribbon
trim, 33" **2,300.00**

K * R bisque socket head toddler,
marked "K * S, Simon & Halbig,
121, 36," blue sleep eyes w/real
lashes, open mouth w/two upper
teeth, mohair wig, blue
embroidered baby jacket &
underclothing, 16" **525.00**

K * R celluloid socket head toddler,
marked "K * R, 1728/6," blue flirty
eyes w/tin lids & real lashes,
feathered brows, painted upper &
lower lashes, open mouth w/two
upper teeth, original mohair wig, white
crocheted dress, 15"............ **325.00**

*K * R "Karl" Character Boy*

**K * R bisque head "Karl" character
boy,** painted side-glancing eyes,
short brown h.h. wig, pouty open
mouth, wearing Victorian-style
boy's costume &
hat, 21" (ILLUS.)............ **46,000.00**

Ken, 1961, flocked brunette hair, pink
lips, straight leg, wearing red shorts
w/white stripe, cork sandals w/red
straps, in box w/black wire stand,
cardboard neck & foot inserts, pink
cover booklet (some wear &
discoloring) **130.00**

Kestner (J.D.) all-bisque girl,
marked "150, 4½ 0," brown sleep
eyes w/single-stroke brows,
painted upper & lower lashes,
closed mouth, original mohair wig,
peach dress & bonnet, 5" **250.00**

Kestner (J.D.) all-bisque girl,
marked "150, 5/0," brown sleep
eyes, single-stroke brows, painted
upper & lower lashes, closed

mouth, original mohair wig, unclothed w/painted socks & one-strap shoes, original box, 4½"..... **275.00**

Kestner (J.D.) all-bisque girl, marked "208, 1" w/illegible red stamp, brown sleep eyes w/single-stroke brows, painted upper & lower lashes, original mohair wig, red silk dress made from ribbon & panties, molded & painted socks & black one-strap shoes, original box w/paper reading "Dolly Dimples, for sale, 334 Luck Ave., Zanesville, O.," 4½"..................... **160.00**

Kestner (J.D.) all-bisque girl, marked "150, 4½ 0," brown sleep eyes w/single-stroke brows, painted upper & lower lashes, closed mouth, original mohair wig, peach dress & bonnet, 5" **250.00**

Kestner (J.D.) all-bisque girl in wicker basket, umarked, tiny blue sleep eyes w/fine feathered brows, painted upper & lower lashes, closed mouth, mohair wig, clenched fists, crocheted dress trimmed w/tiny flowers, matching hat & panties, 6" wicker basket w/lid, 4¾"................... **800.00**

Kestner "Googlie" Girl

Kestner (J.D.) bisque head "Googlie" character girl, marked "F. made in Germany 10., J.D.K., 221., Ges. gesch.," large oversize brown sleep eyes looking to side, short feathered brows, tiny painted upper lashes, brunette mohair wig, silk & lacy dress w/straw & lace bonnett, 12½" (ILLUS.)........ **7,200.00**

Kestner (J.D.) bisque shoulder head girl, marked "C" & "made in Germany," brown sleep eyes w/feathered brows, painted upper

& lower lashes, open mouth w/four upper teeth, original blonde mohair wig, original red dress w/black velvet bodice & sash, 12" **400.00**

Kestner (J.D.) bisque shoulder head girl, marked "Dep. 154 2¼," brown sleep eyes w/molded & feathered brows, painted upper & lower lashes, open mouth w/four upper teeth, original mohair wig, kid body, antique ecru skirt & blouse w/red embroidered trim, 13"...... **110.00**

Kestner (J.D.) bisque shoulder head girl, marked "X," set blue eyes w/feathered brows, painted upper & lower lashes, closed mouth, replaced skin wig, off-white satin shirt trimmed w/lace, blue velvet pants & cap, 15" **400.00**

Kestner (J.D.) bisque shoulder head girl, marked "H" & "Made in Germany," set dark brown eyes w/heavily feathered brows, turned head, painted upper & lower lashes, closed mouth, h.h. wig, kid body, pale pink antique silk dress w/lace bodice & ribbon trim, 20" **375.00**

Kestner (J.D.) bisque shoulder head girl, marked "12. 154. Dep.," brown sleep eyes w/heavy molded & feathered brows, long painted upper & lower lashes, open mouth w/four upper teeth, original auburn mohair wig, antique white dress & matching underclothing, 24½"..... **450.00**

Kestner (J.D.) bisque shoulder head girl, marked "Made in Germany," turned head, set blue eyes w/feathered brows, painted upper & lower lashes, open mouth w/four upper teeth, h.h. wig, kid body, antique white dress, 24½" ... **450.00**

Kestner (J.D.) bisque socket head baby, marked "7," solid dome head, painted blue eyes w/single-stroke brows, open-closed mouth, lightly molded & brush-stroked hair, dressed in antique white romper & diaper, 10½" **250.00**

Kestner (J.D.) bisque socket head baby, unmarked, solid dome head w/painted blue eyes, feathered brows, open-closed mouth, lightly molded & painted hair, original pink & white knit romper w/matching cap & sweater, 11" (ILLUS. w/3" German child doll) previous page .. **300.00**

Kestner (J.D.) bisque socket head girl, marked "M1/2 made in Germany," blue sleep eyes w/real lashes, molded & feathered brows, painted upper & lower lashes, open mouth w/four upper teeth, h.h. wig, antique white dress w/lace insert & tucks, straw-type bonnet, 32" **1,200.00**

Kestner (J.D.) bisque socket head girl, marked "K. made in Germany 6/0, 155," brown sleep eyes w/feathered brows, painted upper & lower lashes, open mouth w/four upper teeth, mohair wig, low-waisted dress w/lace iserts, 6¾" . . . **450.00**

Kestner (J.D.) bisque socket head girl, marked "4," pale blue sleep eyes w/feathered brows, closed mouth, original blonde mohair wig w/plaster pate, pale green silk dress w/lace trim, 11½" **1,600.00**

Kestner (J.D.) bisque socket head girl, marked "7," dark brown sleep eyes w/feathered brows, open mouth w/two upper square teeth, dark brown h.h. wig, antique white dress w/pastel flowers, blue belt & trim, 16½" **1,400.00**

Kestner (J.D.) bisque socket head girl, marked "13" & "Germany, 3361," blue sleep eyes w/feathered brows, painted upper & lower lashes, closed mouth, replaced pale blonde mohair wig, antique pale green French-style silk dress w/flower design, 20" **3,100.00**

Kestner (J.D.) bisque socket head girl, marked "H¼ made in Germany 12¼, 167," blue sleep eyes w/molded & feathered brows, painted upper & lower lashes, open mouth w/four upper teeth, h.h. wig, antique white eyelet dress w/ribbon trim, 24" **425.00**

Kestner (J.D.) bisque socket head girl, marked "K made in Germany" & "7," dark brown sleep eyes w/heavily feathered brows, painted upper & lower lashes, open mouth w/four upper teeth, replaced wig, redressed in dark green taffeta dress & dark green velvet coat w/ribbon trim, 25" **800.00**

Kestner (J.D.) bisque socket head girl, marked "L½ made in Germany 15½, 171, 6," brown sleep eyes w/molded & feathered brows, painted upper & lower lashes, open mouth w/four upper teeth, original blonde h.h. wig, antique white dress w/lace inserts, 29" **800.00**

Kestner (J.D.) bisque socket head "Hilda" baby, marked "H. made in Germany 12., 245. J.D.K. jr., 1914, Hilda, 2 Ges. gesch. N....," brown sleep eyes w/feathered brows, painted upper & lower lashes, open

mouth w/two upper teeth & tongue, original mohair wig, white baby dress, 16" **2,900.00**

Gibson Girl With Dog

Kestner (J.D.) "Gibson Girl," marked "6/9 172, made in Germany," brown sleep eyes w/feathered brows, painted upper & lower lashes, closed smiling mouth, original blonde mohair wig, salmon colored organdy dress trimmed w/white lace & black velvet ribbon, 10" (ILLUS.) **650.00**

Kruse (Kathe) "Mimerle" girl, marked "Kathe Kruse" on dress seam, hard plastic head w/painted blue eyes, single-stroke brows, closed mouth, original h.h. wig & navy blue dress w/white flowers, boxed, 14" **155.00**

LeConte & Alliot bisque socket head girl, marked "Depose, L. 15 C.," & "Bebe A. Gesland, Brevet S.G.D.G., S. Rue Beranger 5, Paris" stamped on Gesland stockinette body, brown sleep eyes w/real lashes, heavily feathered brows, painted lower lashes, open mouth w/six upper teeth, pierced ears replaced synthetic wig, antique white dress w/lace inserts, 31" **1,100.00**

Lenci girl, marked "3" on bottom of right foot, "Bambola Italia, Lenci, Torino, Made in Italy" on paper tag, pressed felt swivel head w/painted brown eyes to side, feathered brows, painted upper & lower lashes, closed mouth, original blonde mohair wig & red felt dress, black matching raincoat & boots, 16" **450.00**

Lenci Lady

Lenci lady, unmarked, pressed felt swivel head w/painted brown eyes looking to side, multi-stroke brows, painted upper & lower lashes, closed two-tone mouth, applied ears, mohair wig, original organdy skirt & underclothing, green felt jacket & flower-trimmed hat, black "lace" gloves, 35" (ILLUS.) **1,800.00**

Lenci "Mascotte" girl, pressed felt swivel head w/painted blue eyes looking to side, single-stroke brows, painted upper lashes, open-closed mouth, original felt hair in braids, original green felt dress, white organdy pinafore w/flower trim, yellow & green felt hat, 10" . . . **245.00**

Lenci Opium Smoker

Lenci Oriental opium smoker, unmarked, pressed felt swivel head w/painted closed eyes, single-stroke brows, closed mouth, applied ears, yarn hair, original yellow felt top w/green trim & black felt pants w/gold trim, 12" (ILLUS.) **375.00**

Little Kiddle, "Kiddle Kone" doll, vinyl, 1960s **35.00**

Martha Chase baby, painted stuffed fabric, painted blonde hair, brown eyes, jointed arms & legs, wearing early white dress, 24" (some paint retouch on face & arms, knee joints repaired) **374.00**

Martha Chase stockinette head girl, marked w/incomplete Chase stamp on front upper left leg, oil painted, brown eyes w/single-stroke brows, painted upper lashes, closed mouth, blonde hair, applied ears, cloth body, original pink low-waisted dress, 13" **300.00**

"Merrie Marie" doll, printed uncut cotton, shrinkwrapped, patented in 1900, Selchow & Richter, 25" **230.00**

Morimura Brothers bisque socket head child, marked "1, M B, Japan, 8," blue sleep eyes w/real lashes, feathered brows, painted lower lashes, open mouth w/four upper teeth, original mohair wig, original pink silk dress w/pink bonnet, 25" **375.00**

My Girlie III bisque head girl, marked "My Girlie, III, Germany," blue sleep eyes w/real lashes, feathered brows, painted upper & lower lashes, open mouth w/four teeth, h.h. wig, composition body, original ecru lace wedding dress w/matching veil, 24" **235.00**

Queen Louise bisque socket head girl, marked "29, Queen Louise, 10, Germany," brown sleep eyes w/real lashes, feathered brows, painted lower lashes, open mouth w/four upper teeth, original mohair wig, antique white dress, 24". **375.00**

Redmond (Kathy) "Edward VIII" baby, marked "Edward VIII, R" (in cat), unjointed all bisque w/molded & painted features, glazed hair w/molded bonnet, molded clothing & shoes, lace skirt w/sequins, pearls & beads, 6¼" **200.00**

Redmond (Kathy) "Prince Albert," marked "Albert R" (in cat), bisque shoulder head, molded & painted character features, hair, sideburns, mustache & gold collar w/medallion, red velour jacket w/gold epaulets & buttons, beige breeches, blue ribbon sash, 14" . . . **400.00**

Redmond (Kathy) "Princess Royal," marked "Princess Royal, R" (in cat), all bisque body, molded & painted features, molded clothing w/ruffles & ribbons w/rosebuds, long white christening gown w/lace inserts & embroidered red overlay, 5".... **275.00**

Redmond (Kathy) "Queen Victoria," marked "Queen Victoria, R" (in cat), bisque shoulder head, molded & painted character features, glazed hair w/snood & gold crown, jewels on shoulder plate, black taffeta dress w/sequin trimmed net overlay, 15".... **575.00**

Redmond (Kathy) young "Queen Victoria," marked "Queen Victoria, R" (in cat), bisque shoulder head, molded & painted features, hair & crown, jewelry on shoulder plate, light mauve dress w/net overlay, blue velvet sash, 14".... **550.00**

S.F.B.J. bisque socket head girl, marked "S.F.B.J., 301, Paris, -12-," blue sleep eyes w/real lashes, molded & feathered brows, painted lower lashes, open mouth w/six upper teeth, pierced ears, original h.h. wig, antique white dress w/lace insert trim, 29".... **725.00**

Sasha "Blonde Gingham" girl, marked "Sasha Doll" in "crayon" on tube, "Sasha" on circular wrist tag, vinyl head, painted blue eyes w/single-stroke brows, painted upper lashes, closed mouth, blonde rooted hair, original blue gingham dress, includes clothes set #4-201 plus crayon tube & original paper bag, 16".... **300.00**

Schmitt & Fils bisque socket head girl, marked "0, Sch, Sch," blue threaded paperweight eyes, feathered brows, painted upper & lower lashes, closed mouth, pierced ears, original skin wig, maroon & ecru silk dress, 14"... **2,000.00**

Schoenau & Hoffmeister bisque head infant, marked "Made in Germany, S PB (instar) H," solid dome head w/flange neck, blue sleep eyes, painted upper & lower lashes, closed mouth, lightly molded & softly brushed hair, original white baby dress, 12".... **200.00**

Schoenau & Hoffmeister bisque socket head girl, marked "S PB (in star) H, 1909, 5½, Germany," brown sleep eyes w/real lashes, feathered brows, painted upper & lower lashes, open mouth w/four upper teeth, old mohair wig, antique white dress w/large collar, 24".... **325.00**

Schoenau & Hoffmeister brown-painted bisque toddler, marked "SHPB Hanna," brown glass sleep eyes, open mouth w/teeth, black mohair wig, wearing Hawaiian lei & grass skirt, 1920s, 8".... **230.00**

Schoenhut Wooden Head Doll

Schoenhut character girl, marked "Schoenhut Doll, Pat. Jan. 17 - '11 U.S.A. & Foreign Countries," jointed wood body, carved wooden head, blue intaglio eyes w/feathered brows, carved hair w/blue ribbon, closed mouth, grey low-waisted dress, 14" (ILLUS.).... **525.00**

Schoenhut character girl, marked "Schoenhut Doll, Pat. Jan. 17 '11- U.S.A. & Foreign Countries," jointed wood body, carved wooden socket head w/blue intaglio eyes, feathered brows, replaced old h.h. wig, blue sailor-type dress w/red trim & matching hat, 16".... **750.00**

Schoenhut character girl, marked "Schoenhut Doll, Pat. Jan. 17, '11, U.S.A. & Foreign Countries," jointed wood body, carved wooden head, decal eyes w/feathered brows, painted upper & lower lashes, accented nostrils, open-closed mouth w/four painted teeth, mohair wig, original knit underwear & socks, old blue lace-trimmed dress, replaced shoes, 17".... **250.00**

Schoenhut character girl, jointed wood body, carved wooden head, painted brown eyes, original blonde mohair wig, wearing a floral print long dress, white shoes & socks, sober facial expression, 18½" (some retouch on face).... **374.00**

Shirley Temple, vinyl, Ideal, 1957, unused, near mint in box, 12" **220.00**

Shirley Temple, Ideal, marked "Shirley Temple" on head, "Shirley Temple, 11" on back, original "starburst" dress, dress tag & button, original mohair wig, 11" h. **750.00**

Shirley Temple, Ideal, marked "13, Shirley Temple, Cop. Ideal N & T Co." on back of head, "Shirley Temple NRA" tag on back of dress, original red & white dress, original mohair wig, 13" h. **550.00**

Shirley Temple, Ideal, marked "Shirley Temple" on back of head, "Shirley Temple, 13" on back, original white dress w/red Scottie dogs, original mohair wig, 13" **675.00**

Shirley Temple, Ideal, marked "Shirley Temple, 17, Cop. Ideal N & T Co." on back of head, "Shirley Temple, 17" on back, original tagged blue & white dress, original mohair wig, 17" h. **550.00**

Shirley Temple, Ideal, marked "18, Shirley Temple, Cop. Ideal N & T Co." on back of head, "Shirley Temple 18" on back, tagged navy blue sailor dress w/matching hat, original mohair wig, 18" h. **850.00**

Shirley Temple, Ideal, marked "Shirley Temple, Cop. Ideal N & T Co." on back of head, "Shirley Temple, Ideal" in diamond on back, "Genuine Shirley Temple Doll" on dress tag, original red dress & mohair wig, 22" h. **400.00**

Shirley Temple Baby

Shirley Temple baby, Ideal, marked "Shirley Temple" on back of head, white organdy dress w/pink bonnet, original mohair wig, 20" h. (ILLUS.) **1,100.00**

Simon & Halbig bisque head automation girl, marked "1300-6, DEP, S & H," blue eyes, feathered brows, painted lower lashes, open mouth w/four upper teeth, pierced ears, replaced skin wig, carton torso w/mechanism, mauve silk lace-trimmed dress & matching bonnet, right-hand feathers fan doll as music plays, 21" **2,700.00**

Simon & Halbig bisque shoulder head girl, marked "Germany, S H 1080 - 12 DEP," brown sleep eyes w/real lashes, molded & feathered brows, painted lower lashes, open mouth w/four upper teeth, pierced ears, original h.h. wig, purple velvet dress w/embroidered velvet panel, 29". **350.00**

Simon & Halbig bisque socket head baby, marked "1498, 6," solid dome head, set blue eyes w/feathered brows, painted upper & lower lashes, closed mouth, lightly molded & painted hair, christening gown w/lace trim & embroidery, 13" **1,100.00**

Simon & Halbig bisque socket head girl, marked "S&H 1249," blue glass sleep eyes, pierced ears, open mouth w/teeth, original blonde mohair wig, red velvet dress covered w/large variety of buttons, 18" (body paint wear) **748.00**

Simon & Halbig bisque socket head girl, marked "1229, Halbig, S & H, 8½" & "Heinrich Handwerck, Germany," brown sleep eyes, molded & feathered brows, painted upper & lower lashes, open mouth w/four upper teeth, pierced ears, antique mohair wig, antique white low-waisted dress, 20½" **1,200.00**

Simon & Halbig bisque socket head girl, marked "1039, Germany, Simon & Halbig, S & H. 10½," blue flirty eyes w/cotton lashes, molded & feathered brows, painted upper & lower lashes, open mouth w/four teeth, pierced ears, replaced h.h. wig, antique white dress w/lace & tucks, working crier, 22". **1,100.00**

Simon & Halbig bisque socket head girl, marked "S12H - 719," blue sleep eyes, open mouth, pierced ears, original light brown mohair wig, long dress & ruffled bonnet, 23¾" (some wear & paint scuffing) **1,495.00**

Simon & Halbig bisque socket head girl, marked "S & H, Halbig, 9½", blue sleep eyes w/feathered brows, painted upper & lower lashes, open mouth w/four upper teeth, pierced ears, original blonde mohair wig, white antique dress w/crocheted insert & trim, blue ribbon sash, 24" **375.00**

Simon & Halbig bisque socket head girl, marked "S.H. 1079 DEP, 14," dark brown sleep eyes w/heavily feathered brows, painted upper & lower lashes, open mouth w/four upper teeth, pierced ears, dark brown h.h. wig, antique white dress w/embroidery & eyelet trim, 28" **550.00**

Simon & Halbig bisque socket head girl, marked "S & H 1079, DEP, Germany, 15," brown sleep eyes w/molded & feathered brows, painted upper & lower lashes, open mouth w/four upper teeth, pierced ears, replaced wig, antique white child's dress w/embroidery, print pink pinafore, 31" **675.00**

Special (A.W.) bisque socket head child, marked "A.W. Special," blue sleep eyes, feathered brows, painted upper & lower lashes, open mouth w/four teeth, synthetic wig, blue & white checked dress w/white trim, 22" **275.00**

Steiner (Herm) bisque socket head girl w/wardrobe trunk, marked "Made in Germany, Herm Steiner, 20/0," blue sleep eyes w/single-stroke brows, painted upper & lower lashes, open mouth w/four upper teeth, original mohair wig, original factory blue & white print dress w/blue ribbon trim, original brown trunk w/two original factory print dresses, extra underclothing, lace on cardboard tray, 6¾" **575.00**

Steiner (Jules) bisque socket head girl, marked "a - 13, Paris," large paperweight eyes w/heavily feathered brows, painted upper & lower lashes, open mouth w/six upper teeth, pierced ears, original h.h. wig, ecru dress w/net & ribbon overlay, 20" **3,500.00**

Steiner (Jules) bisque socket head "Le Parisien," marked "A. 4.5" w/"Le Parisien" stamped in red, "Paris" on back of head, "Bebe Le Parisien, Medaille d'Or, Paris" on left hip, set brown eyes w/feathered brows, painted upper & lower

Jules Steiner "Le Parisien"

lashes, closed mouth, pierced ears, original blonde mohair wig, antique white dress, 11½" (ILLUS.) **1,850.00**

Taft Bisque Socket Head Girl

Taft bisque socket head girl, marked "X, D., Taft, 1910, 6," blue sleep eyes w/real lashes, feathered brows, painted upper & lower lashes, open mouth w/four upper teeth, replaced wig, rose colored dress w/matching bonnet, 24" (ILLUS.). **300.00**

Terri Lee with trunk, hard plastic head, brown eyes w/real lashes, single-stroke brows, closed mouth, original brunette wig, tagged blue & green plaid dress, includes plaid trunk w/six tagged outfits, coat, sunsuit, roller skates & silver shoes, 10" **425.00**

Dwight & Mamie Eisenhower

Thompson (Martha) "Dwight & Mamie Eisenhower," bisque shoulder heads w/painted blue eyes, Mamie, marked "Martha Thompson, Mamie Eisenhower, 1956," smiling open mouth, pierced ears, molded & painted brown hair, pale pink silk dress w/matching shawl, Dwight marked "Murry T.," molded & painted hair, black tuxedo w/white shirt, vest & bow tie, 17", pr. (ILLUS.). **450.00**

Thompson (Martha) "Prince Charles" boy, marked "MDT, 53" & "Martha Thompson," bisque shoulder head, painted blue eyes w/molded lids, molded & painted brown hair, beige shorts & shirt w/red accent stitching, 10" **425.00**

Thompson (Martha) "Prince Phillip," marked "Martha Thompson," bisque shoulder head, painted deep eyes, closed well-molded mouth, dressed in white naval uniform w/gold trim & buttons, blue sash, matching cap, ca. 1952, 21" **200.00**

Thompson (Martha) "Princess Anne" as child, marked "1960, Princess Anne," bisque shoulder head, painted blue eyes w/molded lids, multi-stroke brows, closed mouth, molded & painted hair, white dress w/embroidery trim, 12". . **525.00**

Thompson (Martha) "Princess Anne" girl, marked "MDT 53" & "Martha D. Thompson," bisque shoulder head w/tiny painted blue eyes, multi-stroke brows, closed mouth, molded & painted curly blonde hair, original light blue smocked dress, 10". **425.00**

Thompson (Martha) "Princess Margaret," marked "M. Thompson, Princess Margaret, 1958," bisque shoulder head, painted blue eyes w/molded lids, closed mouth, pierced ears, molded & painted dark hair, molded gold crown, pearl necklace, off-white gown w/flower trim, 20" **550.00**

Wax over composition girl, unmarked, brown sleep eyes w/feathered brows, closed mouth, blonde mohair wig, cloth body w/kid arms, individually stitched fingers, gussets at elbows, antique black silk taffeta two-piece outfit w/jet black trim, black lace bonnet, 24" . . **300.00**

Wax over composition lady, unmarked, rounded head w/shoulder plate fitted w/glass eyes, brown hair & tinted cheeks, cloth body w/kid forearms & hands, wearing old long blue & white print dress, early 19th c., 15¼" (repairs, repaint to wax). **220.00**

Wax over composition lady, pink-tinted wax, stationary brown pupil-less eyes, painted mouth, brown glued-on h.h. wig, cloth body w/tan leather arms, original pink tarlatan & white lace costume, England or Germany, mid-19th c., 21½" (fine cracks in wax) **230.00**

Wright (R.John) "Lillian," marked "R. John Wright," pressed felt swivel head w/painted brown eyes, single-stroke brows, painted upper & lower lashes, closed mouth, auburn mohair wig, original blue sailor dress w/white tie, 20" **725.00**

DOORSTOPS

All doorstops listed are flat-back cast iron unless otherwise noted. Most names are taken from Doorstops—Identification & Values, *by Jeanne Bertioa (Collector Books, 1985).*

Bear w/Honey, full figure, standing on back legs, holding honeycomb in paws, 6½ x 15" **$3,740.00**

Cat, "Fireside Cat," original paint, signed Hubley **225.00**

Cat, seated cat, glass eyes, cleaned down surface except for eyes & mouth which have old repaint, 9¾" h. **248.00**

Cat, seated on cushion, ribbon around neck, old black & red repaint, 7¾" h. **193.00**

Cat Scratch Fever Doorstop

Cat Scratch Fever, standing little girl looking at cat scratch on her arm w/cat clawing at her dress, worn original polychrome paint (ILLUS.) **1,760.00**

Charleston Dancers, stylized dancing couple, original polychrome paint **2,970.00**

Dog, Boston Terrier, small, old black & white paint, old added leather collar, 8¼" h. (paint wear) **61.00**

Dog, Bulldog, looking to the left **250.00**

Dog, English Bulldog, full-bodied standing form w/head turned to side, old polychrome paint, Hubley & other companies, 9" l. (wear, touch up, light rust) **138.00**

Dog, English Bulldog, three-square view standing stance on a stepped base w/angled front corners, original polychrome paint, marked "LAGS," 7¾" h. (some paint wear) **220.00**

Dog, French Bulldog, seated animal looking upward w/long angled upright ears, old black & white paint, Hubley, National Foundry & others, 7¾" h. (some wear, light rust) **187.00**

Dog & Duck, sitting dog w/duck's bill near his ear, AM Greenblatt, Boston, Massachusetts, copyright 1925, 8¾ x 10" **2,310.00**

Flower Basket, figural white basket w/basketweave design, overhead handle w/bow at the top, polychrome flowers, round base, 10" h. **132.00**

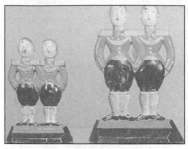

Large & Small Footmen Doorstops

Footmen, large, two standing side by side on a rectangular platform, worn original paint, by Hubley, marked "Fish," 12" h. (ILLUS. right) . . . . **1,775.00 to 1,875.00**

Footmen, small, two standing side by side on a rectangular platform, worn original paint, by Hubley, marked "Fish," 9⅛" h. (ILLUS. left), ... **1,045.00**

Giraffe, tan w/black spots, Hubley, 9 x 12½" **4,070.00**

Girl w/pom-pons, full figure holding a floral pom-pon in each hand, old polychrome repaint, marked "821," 9" h. **193.00**

Major Domo, standing man in doorman's uniform, original paint. **225.00**

Man on Cotton Bale Doorstop

Man on Cotton Bale, an African-American gentleman wearing a white suit & top hat seated on a brown bale of cotton w/black bands (ILLUS.) **3,410.00**

Monkey, sitting, w/tail in front **250.00**

Penguin, No. 1, ca. 1930, Taylor Cook, 5¼ x 9½" **3,520.00**

Popeye, full figure, ca. 1929 Hubley (King Features Syn. Made in USA) 4½ x 9" **2,310.00**

Sheep, white ram w/curved horn standing on a green mound-form narrow rectangular base, 9 5/8" l., 7¼" h. (worn polychrome repaint) 303.00

Whistling Boy, full figure boy standing on figural rock base, hands in pockets, green pants & jacket & red cap, rubber knobs on back, Bradley & Hubbard, 5½ x 10" 4,290.00

DRUGSTORE & PHARMACY ITEMS

The old-time corner drugstore, once a familiar part of every American town, has now given way to a modern, efficient pharmacy. With the streamlining and modernization of this trade, many of the early tools and store adjuncts have become outdated and now fall into the realm of "collectibles." Listed here are the variety of tools, bottles, display pieces and other ephemera once closely associated with the druggist's trade.

Apothecary bottle, cylindrical, embossed "Liq. Potas Arsenit" in oval, tooled lip, "Phila Whitall Tatum & Co New York" on smooth base, original ground glass stopper, ca. 1890-1910, cobalt blue, 4¼" h $770.00

Apothecary bottle, square, "Silver Nitrate 5%" on label-under-glass, wide tooled lip, smooth base, original notched glass stopper & "Poison" label, ca. 1890-1910, amber, 4⅝" h. 44.00

Apothecary bottle, cylindrical w/ribbed neck, footed pedestal smooth base, original ribbed ground glass stopper, ca. 1900-1920, clear, 5⅝" h. to top of lid (ILLUS.) 1,650.00

Apothecary bottle, rectanglar w/beveled edging, embossed "Benjamin Green Apothecary Portsmouth, N.H.," tooled lip w/long ringed neck, "W.T. & Co. U.S.A." on smooth base, ca. 1885-1900, cobalt blue, 7¼" h. 165.00

Apothecary bottle, cylindrical, "Tr. Cannab. Ind." on label-under-glass, tooled mouth, "W.T. & Co." on smooth base, original ground glass stopper, ca. 1880-1900, cobalt blue, 7¾" h 330.00

Apothecary bottle, cylindrical, "Benzine Rect:" on label-under-glass, tooled lip, smooth base, original ground glass stopper, ca. 1865-1890, 8" h. 121.00

Apothecary bottle, cylindrical, "Syr. Sarasp. Co." on label-under-glass, tooled mouth, "Pat Apr 2 1883 W.T. & Co." on smooth base, period clear notched stopper, ca. 1883-1890, cobalt blue, 8⅞" h. 143.00

Apothecary bottle, cylindrical, "Acidum Tannic" on label-under-glass, smooth lip, smooth base, original tin lid, France, ca. 1875-1885, turquoise, 10¼" h. 143.00

Apothecary bottle, cylindrical, "Ferri Subcarb." on label-under-glass, flared lip, "W.N. Walton Patd Sept 23d 1862" on smooth base, ca. 1865-1875, cobalt blue, 11⅛" h. 242.00

Counter Display Apothecary Jar

Large Apothecary Bottle

Apothecary bottle, cylindrical, "Creta C: Camph:" on label-under-glass, applied mouth, polished pontil, original ground glass stopper, England, ca. 1875-1890, pink amethyst, 11⅝" h. (ILLUS.) **633.00**

Apothecary bottle, cylindrical w/ribbed neck, footed pedestal smooth base, label reading "1378 Anise 'Anis' Pimpinella anisum L. Umbelliferae," original ribbed ground glass stopper, filled w/anise, ca. 1900-1920, clear, 13" h. **303.00**

Apothecary cabinet, hardwood w/tin front, marked "Humphreys' Specifics (two side-by-side lists) Humphreys' Witch Hazel Oil, The Pile Ointment" in yellow lettering on blue background, hinged door on reverse opens to 36 individual dovetailed drawers, 21¾" w., 9½" deep., 27¾" h. (missing eight drawers, some discoloration to front tin) **633.00**

Apothecary Globe

Apothecary globe, cylindrical stained glass leaded globe tapering to point, open-top w/metal edging & three-chain attached hanger, cast-iron eagle flange, one cracked square in globe, globe 21" l., eagle 19" l. (ILLUS.) **2,300.00**

Apothecary jar, cylindrical, impressed "J. Milhau Druggist, 183 Broadway N-Y," dark brown glazed stoneware, ca. 1820-1830, 6½" h. . . **207.00**

Apothecary jar, flared lip w/short cylindrical neck, bulbous body tapering to bottom ring, applied stem & foot, original round tapering

stopper w/bottom ring, light powder blue milk glass, ca. 1870-1890, 13" h. **495.00**

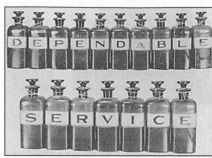

Apothecary Jar Set

Apothecary jars, labels-under-glass w/letters "D-E-P-E-N-D-A-B-L-E-S-E-R-V-I-C-E," tooled lips, "Wt. & Co. U.S.A." on smooth bases, all w/original ground glass stoppers & in original shipping boxes, ca. 1890-1910, 8¾" h., set of 18 (ILLUS.) **715.00**

Bottle, rectangular w/beveled edges, embossed "Jacob's Pharmacy (motif of eagle on mortar & pestle) Atlanta GA," tooled mouth, "W.T. Co. U.S.A." on smooth base, 70% original label for "Strychnine Sulphate," ca. 1885-1910, amber, 2½" h. **77.00**

Bottle, rectangular w/sloping shoulder, embossed "Jozeau" & "Pharmacien" on opposite ends, rolled lip, pontil-scarred base, ca. 1840-1855, deep olive green, 4½" h. **165.00**

Bottle, cylindrical, embossed "Strong, Cobb & Co. Wholesale Druggists Cleveland, O," applied mouth, smooth base, ca. 1875-1885, cobalt blue, 6¼" h. **110.00**

Bottle, brown slip stoneware w/slightly formed pour spout, debossed "R.H. Lackey Pharmacies Philda," ca. 1845-1860, 7½ " h. **165.00**

Bottle, cylindrical, embossed "G.W. Merchant Chemist Lockport N.Y.," applied sloping collar mouth, iron pontil, ca. 1845-1855, medium Lockport green, 7½" h. **330.00**

Bottle, cylindrical, embossed "J & C Maguire Chemists And Druggists St. Louis. Mo.," applied double collar mouth, smooth base, ca. 1855-1865, medium cobalt blue, 7½" h. **330.00**

Rare Druggist Bottle

Bottle, rectangular, embossed "J & C Maguire Chemists And Druggists St. Louis. Mo.," applied double collar mouth, iron pontil, ca. 1845-1855, cobalt blue, 7⅞" h. (ILLUS.) **2,145.00**

Muegge's Druggist Bottle

Bottle, rectangular w/beveled edges, embossed "We Never Sleep Muegge The Druggist Baker Ore. - Muegge's," tooled lip, smooth base, ca. 1885-1900, rich yellowish green, 8¼" h. (ILLUS.) **143.00**

Bottle, cylindrical, embossed "Strong, Cobb & Co Wholesale Druggists Cleveland," applied mouth, marked "C & I" on smooth base, ca. 1875-1885, cobalt blue, 10⅜" h. **121.00**

Leech Jar

Leech jar, white porcelain w/black transfer reading "Sangsues," base marked "J. Mourier & Cie. 15. rue Pastourelle, Paris, Depose, Gandois Successeur," includes jar, insert & lid, France, ca. 1890-1910, 12¾" h. (ILLUS.) **3,960.00**

Medicine chest, cherry wood w/purple felt-lined lid, brass fittings & plaque engraved "Carl's Drug Store Greencastle, PA Est. 1825," stamped "Whitall Tatum & Co. Makers" on base, includes 14 labeled clear glass apothecary jars, two Lattice & Diamond patt. poison bottles w/labels & stoppers, two ointment jars w/metal lids & one dose glass, all w/original ground glass stoppers, original skeleton key, ca. 1890-1910 . . . . **468.00**

Sign, rectangular w/rounded ends, metal, painted "The Rexall Store" in green, red & blue enamel, ca. 1915-1930, 38¾" l., 8" h. (some minor chipping to edges) **242.00**

Drugstore Sign

Sign, beveled glass w/ornate filigree background, reads "Drugs," copper frame, 47" l., 7½" h. (ILLUS.) **460.00**

Owl Drug Wall Advertisment

Wall advertisement, round, plaster, painted orange w/high relief decoration of flowers around owl & words "The Owl Drug Co." at bottom, 12¾" d. (ILLUS.). **358.00**

ENAMELS

Enamels have been used to decorate a variety of substances, particularly metals. The best-known small enameled wares such as patch and other small boxes and napkin rings, are the Battersea Enamels made by the Battersea Enamel Works in the last half of the 18th century. However, the term is often loosely applied to other English enamels. Russian enamels, usually on a silver or gold base, are famous and expensive. Early 20th century French enamel on copper wares and those items produced in China at the turn of the century in imitation of the early Russian style are also drawing dealer and collector attention.

Fine Russian Enameled Bowl

Bowl, enamel & silver-gilt, low-footed boat-shaped vessel w/figural bear-head handles at each end, the sides w/elaborate scrolling stylized florals & geometric designs highlighted in green, yellow, blue, white, red & black enamel, silver maker Fyodor Ruckert, Russia, late 19th - early 20th c., 8" l (ILLUS.)............ **$9,487.00**

Medallion, oval, profile bust portrait of King George II painted *en grisaille* & flanked by the inscription "Georgius - II Rex," mounted in a narrow gilt-metal oval frame, Battersea, England, third quarter 18th c., 4" l. **1,265.00**

French Limoges Portrait Plaque

Plaque, rectangular, painted w/a half-length portrait of a man in 17th c. costume, based on a self-portrait by Peter Paul Rubens, mounted in an ornate rectangular bronze frame w/outset corners & topped by a large ribbon bow, the flat sides cast w/wreath & leafy scroll swags, Limoges, France, 19th c., 4 x 5½" (ILLUS.)..................... **633.00**

Enameled Russian Salt Dip

Salt dip, silver-gilt & enamel w/glass liner, small tapering cylindrical form w/low metal buttress legs & a ringed rim, the sides enameled w/a red & white enamel "fishscale" design, Russia, ca. 1940, 1⅝" d., 1¼" h. (ILLUS.) **95.00**

Snuff box, cov., Battersea-type, the top modeled as a spaniel & a landscape painted on the base, England, 3" l. (lines) **1,265.00**

Vase, footed bulbous ovoid body tapering to a tiny rimmed mouth, metal thickly enameled overall w/an Art Deco design of stylized sawtooth leaves & scrolled tendrils in purple, lavender & white, marked in gilt "C. Faure, Limoges," France, ca. 1930s, 5½" d., 6½" h. **1,380.00**

Vase, footed large ovoid body tapering to a short, small flared neck, Art Deco design thickly enameled on metal w/graduated lappet design w/curved "sawtooth" bands in red, pink & white, inscribed in gilt "C. Fauré Limoges," France, 1930s, 7" d., 10" h. **1,725.00**

EPERGNES

Blue overlay glass, single lily, trumpet-form lily w/blue ruffled rim & interior of lower wide blue ruffled bowl each decorated w/green & maroon flowers & lacy foliage, white undersides, ring-trimmed pedestal base, 10¾" d., 16" h. (ILLUS.).................... **$395.00**

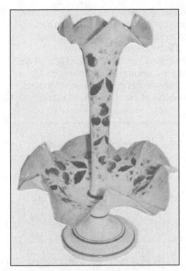

Decorated Blue & White Epergne

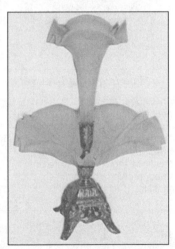

Blue & White Satin Glass Epergne

Blue shaded to white, single lily, satin-finished tall trumpet vase w/squared ruffled & flaring blue rim shading to white set in a leaf-form silvered metal socket above the matching ruffled bowl, raised on a silvered metal stem above the squared pierced & footed base w/a cast face at each corner, 10" d., 14½" h. (ILLUS.) **350.00**

Coin Spot opalescent glass, single lily, a silver plated conical base supports a wide frosted clear Coin Spot patt. bowl w/a pink ruffled rim & centered by a matching Coin Spot lily w/ruffled rim, 13" d., 21" h. **220.00**

Cranberry glass, three-lily, a widely flaring & fluted cranberry bowl base w/a brass top socket supporting a tall cranberry lily-form vase w/a deeply rolled & fluted rim pulled into points & supported on a twisted clear stem w/an applied clear leaf up the side, center lily flanked by two tall clear twisted curled hooks each supporting a small cranberry lily-form basket suspended from an applied clear handle, late 19th c., overall 15" h. . . . **440.00**

Striped & threaded glass, four-lily, a deeply ruffled & flaring centerbowl of clear internally striped in pink & white & overlaid w/progressive yellow threading, a central metal & glass mount supporting a tall matching central lily w/crimped & rolled rim above three clear arms supporting three matching smaller lilies, England, late 19th c., overall 18½" h. (minor chips to center holder at rim) **978.00**

Yellow & blue opalescent glass, four-lily, the round ribbed & dished base w/a raised center supporting a metal fitting issuing a tall upright tall center lily w/a crimped & rolled rim framed by three shorter curved lilies w/jack-in-the-pulpit rims, swirled alternatiing stripes of yellow & blue opalescent color in each section, England, late 19th c., overall 13" h. **248.00**

FIRE FIGHTING COLLECTIBLES

Ceremonial Fire Bucket

Bucket, painted leather, tapering cylindrical form w/stitched rim & base, the front painted w/spread-winged American eagle perched on a framed portrait w/a banner in its beak, flanked by acanthus leaves, inscribed "Franklin Fire Society" & "Wm. Caban" signed on the base, leather swing handle, late 18th c., probably New England, overall cracking & darkening of painted surface, 12" h. (ILLUS.) **$5,750.00**

Leather Fire Bucket

Bucket, painted leather, slightly swelled cylindrical form w/swing handle & stitched rim & base, the front painted w/the inscription "Pro: Bono: Publico" & "No. 3" above a pair of clasped hands & "Thomas Briggs 1802" below, possibly Duxbury, Massachusetts, original paint, losses to handle & base, paint wear & loss, 13½" h. (ILLUS.) **2,760.00**

Fire buckets, painted & decorated leather, each decorated w/clasped hands & banners w/inscription "Mutual Fire Society, Duncan McB Thayer," & brand "C. Lincoln," dated 1805, 13" h., pr. **1,600.00**

Parade Fire Hat

Fire hat, parade-type, painted leather, polychrome decoration on green ground, front w/eagle & harp w/banner above "Hibernia," inscribed in gilt on back "1752" & on top "1," underside of brim red, 19th c., some age cracks & small losses to edge of brim, 6½" h. (ILLUS.) . . **3,335.00**

FIREARMS

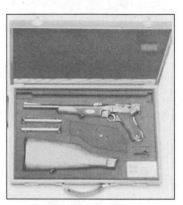

Rare Luger Carbine Set

Carbine, Luger Model 1902, hand-model w/adaptable stock, complete w/accessories in original hinged case (ILLUS.) **$11,500.00**

Carbine, Smith percussion model, .50 caliber, legible signature on framed, browned barrel finish, Serial No. 13611, overall 39" l. **990.00**

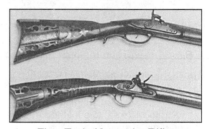

Fine Early Kentucky Rifles

Long rifle, Kentucky-type, curly maple stock w/ornate pierced brass inlay & brass patch box, steel fittings & octagonal barrel, unsigned, barrel 43" l. (ILLUS. bottom) **8,050.00**

Long rifle, Kentucky-type, walnut stock w/ornate pierced brass inlay & engraved patch box, steel fittings & octagonal barrel, signed by

Christian Hawken, Kentucky, late
18th - early 19th c., overall 45½" l.
(ILLUS.) **8,050.00**

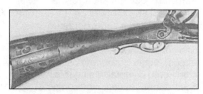

Pennsylvania Long Rifle

Long rifle, Pennsylvania-type, curly
maple stocks w/incised carving
around cheek piece, behind tang &
on either side of ramrod entry pipe,
brass hardware includes a pierced
& engraved patchbox, silver barrel
pin escutcheons, engraved "S.B."
on top of barrel w/carving
characteristic of maker Samuel
Baum, Columbia County,
Pennsylvania, restored breaks at
wrist & around lock, w/leather
pouch w/D-shaped flag & restored
handle, w/8½" l. powder horn,
overall 60" l. (ILLUS.) **6,050.00**

Musket, Springfield Model 1863, type
1, percussion style, lock w/bold
signature w/eagle & "1863," round
barrel w/proof marks & eagle head
w/date "63," areas of fine pitting,
few scrapes in stock, barrel 40" l. . . . **660.00**

Musket, Whitney 1833 contract
musket by "P. & E.W. Blake,"
percussion conversion, lock
stamped "1830," walnut stock
w/dark patina & inspector's stamps
including "Ohio," plate inlaid
w/"Jeffries & Van Allen, Coshocton,
Ohio," chip near lock mortise,
overall 57½" l. **440.00**

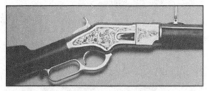

Fine Winchester Musket

Musket, Winchester Model 1886,
scroll-engraved fittings, walnut
stock, factory-engraved "M. 1886"
(ILLUS.) **18,400.00**

Pistol, Allen & Thurber six-short
"pepper box" model, .28 caliber,
bar hammer w/Allen's 1845 patent
date, worn simple scroll engraving,
overall 7⅜" l. **303.00**

Record-setting System Mauser Pistol

Pistol, System Mauser "conehammer
broomhandle" model, six-shot,
wooden grip w/fine turned rings,
world-record price (ILLUS.) **45,245.00**

Pistol, U.S. Aston Model 1842,
percussion-type, brass hardware,
lock w/good signature & address
w/"1847," walnut stock w/hairline in
grip, round barrel 8½" l. **413.00**

Pistol, Waters (A.H.) Model 1836, .54
caliber percussion conversion, all
steel surfaces carefully cleaned to
dull grey, lock w/good signature
w/eagle head & "1844," heavily
pitted at bolster & ramrod replaced,
overall 14" l. **303.00**

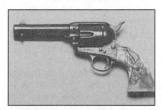

Rare Colt Revolver, One of a Pair

Revolvers, Colt single-action model,
fancy factory engraving on metal,
long-horned steerhead carved on
pearl grips, matching pr.
(ILLUS. of one) **15,525.00**

Revolver, Lefaucheux (French)
pinfire model, .44 caliber, browned
finish w/areas of pitting, found in
Tennessee, Serial No. 38398 . . . . . **220.00**

Revolver, Manhattan Firearms
model, .36 caliber, octagonal
barrel, faint cylinder scenes
w/traces of silver plate on grip
straps, simple engraving along
barrel w/ "J.W. Baillie 1892" &
drum, small grip chip, Serial No.
22320, barrel 6½" l. **303.00**

Revolver, Manhattan percussion
pocket-style, 5" l. octagonal barrel
w/browned finish, matching serial
number & cylinder scenes, Serial
No. 65457 . . . . **495.00**

Revolver, Massachusetts Arms Co. Adams, .36 caliber, percussion model, checkered grips w/browned finish on metal, leading lever & cylinder heavily pitted, barrel 6" l. . . **440.00**

Revolver, Rogers & Spencer percussion model, .44 caliber, lightly cleaned metal w/some areas of light pitting, grip shows bold inspector's mark w/a few chips, Serial No. 3390, octagonal barrel 7½" l. **358.00**

Revolver, Smith & Wesson Old Model, .32 caliber, 6" l. octagonal barrel, surface w/light pitting & holster wear, Serial No. 47103 . . . . **193.00**

Revolver, Smith & Wesson #2 Old Model, .32 caliber, 6" l. octagonal barrel, as-found w/blued finish & some surface rust, Serial No. 13602 . . . . **193.00**

Rifle, Remington 03-A3 bolt-action model, blued & parkerized finish, muzzle w/ "R.A." & flaming bomb stamp w/ "6 - 43," Serial No. 3896610 . . . . **165.00**

Rifle, Springfield Model 1888 "trapdoor" model, w/ramrod bayonet, faint cartouche on stock, bold stampings in metal, stamped "28" on top of comb **248.00**

Rifle, Springfield Model 1888 "trapdoor" model, w/ramrod bayonet, walnut stock w/old dark patina & stamped numbers "7" & "812," lock shows signature & eagle mark, metal lightly cleaned w/some pitting, small chip on buttplate, Serial No. 531743 . . . . . . **303.00**

Rifle, Springfield Model 1898 bolt-action, all metal surfaces w/brown finish w/some rust, stock shows 1907 stamp above trigger guard, no bayonet, Serial No. 321538 . . . . **110.00**

Rifle, Springfield Model 1898 bolt-action, bold cartouche & "1899" date on stock, serial number 192995 . . . . **110.00**

Rifle, Springfield "trapdoor" model, walnut stock w/bold proof mark w/1887 date & stamped "Co. A5" on comb, blued hardware & minor surface rust on door, door stamped "Model 1884," Serial No. 461361 . . . . **248.00**

Rifle, Springfield Model 1873 "trapdoor," walnut stock w/trace of the cartouche, browned barrel, block marked "model 1873," worn lock stampings, Serial No. 373605, barrel 32¼" l. **303.00**

Rifle, half-stock percussion model by "B. Rickets, Mansfield, Ohio," walnut (fish belly) stock w/brass hardware, octagonal barrel, refinished stock, barrel 36" l. **385.00**

Shotgun, LeFever Arms double-barrel model, damascus barrels, fine condition w/case colors on lock plates, trigger guard, etc., stock checkered & metal w/simple scroll & border engraving, worn original leather case, Serial No. 34684F, barrels 30" l. **193.00**

FIREPLACE & HEARTH ITEMS

Andirons, brass, belted ball-top w/slender knob-topped & ring-turned finial & pedestal above the square plinth engraved w/urn & willow motif above the spurred cabriole front legs w/knob feet, stepped iron log bar, attributed to R. Wittingham, New York, New York, early 19th c., 22" h., pr. **$4,888.00**

Andirons, brass, Federal style, belted ball & slender steeple top on a columnar shaft above the spurred cabriole front legs, iron log bar, probably New York, early 19th c., 18½" h., pr. **489.00**

Andirons, brass & iron, Federal style, an urn-form top w/finial above a columnar standard above a plinth engraved w/an urn & willow tree, on arched & spurred legs w/pad feet, iron log bar, early 19th c., 26½" h., pr. **2,400.00**

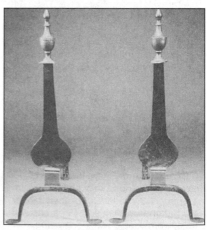

Federal Style Andirons

Andirons, brass & wrought iron, Federal style, urn-shaped finials above blade shaped uprights raised on penny feet, one brass shield marked "I.C.," last quarter 18th c., America, 22½" h., pr. (ILLUS.) **1,840.00**

Ornate Figural Andirons

Andirons, bronze, figural, bare-breasted female bust above a mask applied standard on a scrolled base w/cavorting putti, ca. 1890-1900, probably French, lacking log supports, 38" h., pr. (ILLUS.) **2,990.00**

Andirons, cast iron, a large ball finial above two graduated rings over the baluster-form shaft on a ring-turned connector to the cabriole front legs, curved log bar, marked "B&H" for Bradley & Hubbard, early 20th c., 18" h., pr. **55.00**

Andirons, cast iron, figural, standing Native American w/a small feathered headdress, cloak & holding a tomahawk, late 19th c., 19¼" h., pr. (corrosion) **748.00**

Andirons, wrought iron, Arts & Crafts style, heavy square shaft w/a flared square top w/pyramidal tip, raised on angular arched front strap legs w/penny feet, slender angled log bar, unmarked, 12" w., 18½" h., pr. . . . **110.00**

Andirons, wrought iron, Arts & Crafts style, heavy square shaft w/each side decorated w/two hammered buttons flanking a hammered diamond, the square cap w/pyramidal top also trimmed w/diamonds, shaft raised on heavy arched legs w/square feet, curved

log bar, covered in a brass wash, Bradley & Hubbard, early 20th c., 12½" w., 22" h., pr. **275.00**

Andirons, wrought iron, Arts & Crafts style, heavy squared wide low-arched front legs centered by an upright bar w/an open pointed loop top, log back extending back from base, each w/impressed mark of Gustav Stickley, Model No. 315, 16" h., pr. **9,775.00**

Andirons, wrought iron, Baroque-Style, twisted shaft w/connecting rod & associated log carrier, Europe, 19th c., 27" h. pr. **748.00**

Bellows, painted wood & leather, original red paint w/vintage grape design in two-tone gold & black, sheet brass nozzle, old worn releathering, 19th c., 17¾" l. **220.00**

Bellows, painted wood & leather, original smoked yellow paint w/stenciled & free-hand fruit & foliage in gold, green, black & red, brass nozzle, professionally releathered, 19th c., 18" l. **880.00**

Bellows, turtle-back type, original cream paint w/stenciled & free-hand fruit & foliage decoration in various shades of bronze powder w/gilt & black, brass nozzle, releathered, 18¼" l. (some wear) . . **358.00**

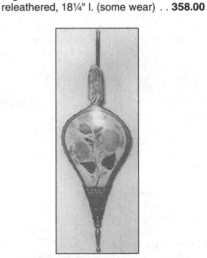

Bellows with Floral Decoration

Bellows, turtle-back type, painted & decorated wood & leather, original smoked white paint w/stenciled & freehand floral decoration in red, green, black & gold, sheet brass nozzle, back handle replaced & professionally releathered, some wear, 17½" l. (ILLUS.) **358.00**

Figural Fireboard

Fireboard, painted sheet metal, figural dog, Papillon spaniel, 19th c., areas of repaint, minor paint loss, 18¾" l., 12¼" h. (ILLUS.) **518.00**

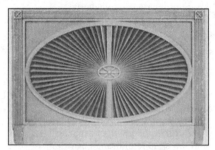

Louvered Fireboard

Fireboard, painted wood, an oval louvered panel centering a carved rosette framed by molded & reeded border joining two square carved corner rosettes, light green, probably American-made, minor imperfections, 43¼" w., 30" h. (ILLUS.) **1,840.00**

Fireplace fender, brass & wire, a curved form w/a brass rim & finials above a vertical wire screen w/a meadering horizontal scrolling wire, 55" w. (top rail has damage & repair) **660.00**

Fireplace tool set, brass andirons w/sphere & steeple finials, ball feet & matching shovel & tongs, andirons 22½" h., the set **2,585.00**

Fireplace tool set, brass & iron, Federal style, bulbous urn-turned finial above turned stand raised on spurred arched front legs on ball feet, curved brackets ending in small urn-turned finials in front of iron log supports, w/matching brass & iron tongs & shovel, early 19th c., New York, minor loss to one log stop, andirons 19" h., the set (ILLUS.) **2,070.00**

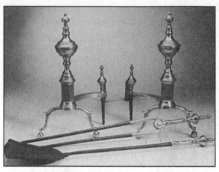

Brass & Iron Fireplace Tool Set

Fireplace tool set, gilt-bronze, Egyptian Revival style, andirons w/a female Egyptian bust wearing a flaring headdress w/serpent finial above a lotus blossom & columnar block shaft above a winged scarab above the front feet cast w/Egyptian masks, King Tut-style figural Egyptian busts at the ends of the log rests, a set of matching tools in a rack topped by an Egyptian pharoah bust & ending in a tray w/early Egyptian designs, late 19th or early 20th c., the set. . . **2,760.00**

Fireside trivet, wrought iron, a half-round flat top rack raised on two slender rear legs & a wider front leg all joined by narrow stretchers, on penny feet, 15 x 17½", 12" h. (old damage, one penny foot incomplete) **220.00**

Toaster, wrought iron, rotary-type w/ornately wrought spiral twist & scrolling sides, probably American-made, 18th c., 29⅞" l **259.00**

FISHING COLLECTIBLES

LURES

Creek Chub "Wiggler"

Creek Chub "Wiggler," No. 100, in
original box (ILLUS.)......... **$1,100.00**

Heddon "Near Surface Wiggler"

Heddon "Near Surface Wiggler"
(ILLUS.) **1,980.00**

Hedden "Punkinseed"

Heddon "Punkinseed," rainbow
finish (ILLUS.)............... **1,320.00**

Heddon "Spindiver"

Heddon "Spindiver," crackle back
green finish (ILLUS.) **1,650.00**

REELS

Atwood Patent Reel

Atwood (Lenard) patent reel,
patent-dated 1907, w/original
illustrated box (ILLUS.)........ **1,400.00**

Silver Presentation Reel

**Conroy-attributed multiplying trout
reel,** presentation Civil War era
model, silver New York style, mid-
19th c. (ILLUS.) **2,255.00**

Gates Patent Trout Reel

Gates (George S.) trout reel, patent-
dated 1885, Athol, Massachusetts
(ILLUS.) **2,319.00**

Milam Bait Casting Reel

Milam (B.C.) bait casting reel, small
No. 2 size, German silver, 1881-96
(ILLUS.) **1,760.00**

MISCELLANEOUS

Meek Reel Oil Bottle & Box

Bottle, "Meek Reel Oil," cylindrical
body tapering to cylindrical neck
w/molded lip, paper label, w/worn
original box (ILLUS.) **550.00**

Milam Reel Oil Bottle

Bottle of reel oil, "Milam's Reel Oil,"
square w/cylindrical neck & paper
label, clear (ILLUS.). **935.00**

Pflueger Fishing Tackle Poster

Poster, "Pflueger Fishing Tackle,"
rectangular w/various species of
fish w/descriptions around the
border, central fishing scene, early
20th c. (ILLUS.) **550.00**

Early Walsh Fishing Print

Print, hand-tinted lithograph,
"American Sporting Scene: Trout
Fishing," Victorian couples along a
small river in a wooded landscape,
John Walsh, New York, New York,
1870, framed (ILLUS.) **1,045.00**

Meek Reel Oiler & Screwdriver Kit

Reel oiler & screwdriver kit, pocket-
sized, cylindrical two-part style,
B.F. Meek & Sons, Louisville,
Kentucky, ca. 1910 (ILLUS.) **825.00**

Realistic Brook Trout Carving

Wooden carving, a carved full-
bodied leaping brook trout
realistically painted & mounted
against a large hand-decorated
silhouette map of the state of
Maine, by Lawrence Irvine,
Winthrop, Maine (ILLUS.) **750.00**

FOOT & BED WARMERS

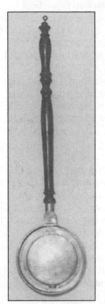

Small Copper Bedwarmer

Bed warmer, brass, tooled floral design on lid, turned & shaped maple handle w/old finish, 40¾" l. . **$248.00**

Bed warmer, copper pan w/hinged cover w/a simple punched star design, brass ferrule to the long knob- and rod-turned handle (minor damage to handle, dents in ferrule) . . **165.00**

Bed warmer, copper, w/engraved peacock lid & turned wooden handle, 31" l. (ILLUS.) **523.00**

Bed warmer, wrought iron w/punched brass lid decorated w/starflower design, Europe, 34" l. . . . **55.00**

Foot warmer, hardwood & punched tin, a wooden frame w/double-baluster-turned corner posts enclosing tin panels punched w/diamonds & the date "1800" on the door, old worn refinishing, 8 x 9", 6" h. **226.00**

Foot warmer, hardwood & tin, the mortised wooden frame w/turned corner posts & old red stain encloses tin sides punched w/a design of circles & hearts, 19th c., 7¾ x 9" **138.00**

Foot warmer, wood & punched tin, a mortised wooden frame w/baluster-turned corner posts framing the tin sides punched in a circle & heart design, traces of red on the wood, 19th c., 8 x 9", 5¾" h. **193.00**

FRAKTUR

Fraktur paintings are decorative birth and marriage certificates of the 18th and 19th centuries and also include family registers and similar documents. Illuminated family documents, birth and baptismal certificates, religious texts and rewards of merit, in a particular style, are known as "fraktur" because of the similarity to the 16th century type-face of that name. Gay watercolor borders, frequently incorporating stylized birds, angels, animals and flowers, surrounded the hand-lettered documents, which were executed by local ministers, school masters or itinerant penman. Most are of Pennsylvania Dutch origin.

Baptismal certificate fraktur for Johannes Umman, pen & ink & water-color on paper, a yellow-bordered double-band central horizontal cartouche reserve centered by a block w/the inscription, small starflowers between the borders & large curving vines of starflowers along each side in the border, done in red, blue, green & purple, pinpricking highlighting the paper, dated 1804, framed, 7⅝ x 12¾" **$1,725.00**

Early Birth & Baptismal Fraktur

Birth & baptismal fraktur for Susanna Oberl(in) pen & ink & water-color on paper, rectangular, a large oval central reserve w/round stylized small blossoms & vines above a pagoda-form roof over an inscribed reserve w/curved blue borders above a stemmed base, all within blue borders, the center highlighted w/red & white stripes & red & white blossoms, dated 1823, attributed to Samuel Bentz (The Mount Pleasant Artist), beveled veneer frame, 7¼" x 9 (ILLUS.) **3,450.00**

Birth record for Maria Grager, pen
& ink & water-color on wove paper,
rectangular, brown, black & green
flourishes across the top including
"cyclone-shaped" designs above
the large German lettering which
translates "Maria Grager - 1850 -
Born June 4th, AD 1833 in State of
Ohio," framed, 6½ x 9½" (minor
paper damage) **825.00**

Book plate, pen & ink & water-color
on laid paper, rectangular,
decorated w/a large tulip blossom
w/a checked diamond design
above a large heart enclosing the
name "Barbara Hallern 1790,"
small tulip blossoms down the
sides & in the bottom corners, in
red, yellow & black, probably Berks
County, Pennsylvania, framed, 5
3/8 x 6 7/8" (some damage &
repair) **1,540.00**

Book plate, pen & ink & water-color
on wove paper, rectangular, a large
starburst tree on a leafy trunk
w/flaring base issuing further leafy
branches, in red, orange, blue,
olive green & yellow, dated "1830,"
Pennsylvania, framed, 6½ x 9"
(edge damage, stains, tape stains) . . **660.00**

Drawing, pen & ink & water-color on
paper, the large flaring stylized
lollipop blossoms on leafy stems
above two small blossoms below
resting on striped pyramids, in red,
green & yellow, by Sarah Bryan,
dated 1813, framed, 6½ x 8" **2,300.00**

Fine Fraktur Drawing with a Cat

Drawing, pen & ink & water-color on
paper, the top w/a large reclining
brown cat w/a red collar resting on
a grassy ground w/a quarter star in
each corner & a half star at top
center, all above a large panel

decorated w/a large colorful
pineapple in brown, green, red &
yellow & flanked by vertical
blossoming vines in red & green,
by Cecilia E. Smith, New England,
ca. 1830 & signed across the
center, in old flat wood-grained
frame, 9½ x 12¾" (ILLUS.). **14,950.00**

Family record, pen & ink & water-
color on paper, rectangular, a
central vertical rectangular box
inscribed w/the names of Robert &
Betsy Mayberry followed by their
children, all framed by large
clusters of colorful flowers &
flowing vines along the sides above
a bottom rectangular panel w/the
oval reverses, gilt highlights,
scattered staining, minor tears,
some tape repairs & creases, early
19th c., probably Windham, Maine,
11¼ x 15¼" **460.00**

House blessing, printed & hand-
colored, an angel head & cloud at
the top flanked by two rectangles
w/printing above a long central
rectangular box flanked by pairs of
angels & birds w/fruit & leaves
across the bottom, colored in
orange, green, blue, yellow, brown
& black, printed by Johann Ritter,
Reading, Pennsylvania, early 19th
c., old stenciled wood frame, 14 3/8
x 18¼" (professionally repaired &
rebacked on cloth). **495.00**

Fraktur Reward of Merit

Reward of Merit fraktur, pen & ink &
water-color on paper, rectangular,
an oversized sunflower-style
blossom raised on a short leaf stalk
w/two drooping branches w/small
blossom buds all within a thin
rectangular band, in red, yellow &

green, in a molded painted wood
frame, early 19th c., 4¼ x 6⅝"
(ILLUS.) **2,587.00**

Vorschrift fraktur, pen & ink &
water-color on paper, rectangular,
two birds & a large horizontal tulip
blossom above a band of small
blossoms over the lengthy
inscription in color & black ink w/a
tulip blossom in the lower left
corner, in red, yellow & green, early
19th c., old painted wood frame,
8¼ x 13" **3,450.00**

FRAMES

Cast iron, wall-type, a gilt eagle crest
above an elaborately decorated
frame w/C-scrolls & foliate designs,
19th c., 6 x 8½" **$575.00**

Easel-form Frame

Giltwood, oval, easel-form, glass
mounted w/micromosaic floral
decoration & "Venezia" at base,
Italy, 16" h. (ILLUS.) **690.00**

Metal & glass, flat rectangular form,
Pine Needle patt., pierced metal
frame over amber slag glass
inserts, easel stand, impressed
mark "Tiffany Studios New York
918," 9¼ x 11¾" **1,265.00**

Oak, Mission-style (Arts & Crafts
movement), rectangular w/a narrow
flat crestboard w/two metal hanging
loops above the narrow flat top &
sides w/a wide bottom board

w/arched border, original medium
finish, unmarked L. & J. G.
Stickley, early 20th c., 30 x 33" **990.00**

Painted & decorated pine,
rectangular, rust & ochre designs
on a mottled ochre & dark brown
ground, attributed to John Colvin,
Scituate, Rhode Island, early 19th
c., 12¾ x 16⅞" **489.00**

Painted & decorated pine,
rectangular, decorated w/red &
blue heart & foliate & geometric
designs on an ochre ground,
attributed to John Colvin, Scituate,
Rhode Island, early 19th c., 13¼ x
17½" (minor paint wear) **4,313.00**

Sterling silver, double-type,
horizontal rectangular form
w/serpentine edges, the center
divider cast w/a winged female
figure w/her head & wings above
the upper rim & her body down the
center, the two vertical rectangular
openings framed by wide borders
embossed w/trailing floral sprays &
architectural scrollwork corners
w/reclining putti, American-made,
early 20th c., 11¼ x 13¼" **288.00**

Sterling Mirror Frame

Sterling silver, rectangular,
decorated w/high-relief bird & floral
design, beveled mirror, maker,
J.R., 15⅝ x 19⅝" (ILLUS.) **1,150.00**

Wood, rectangular stepped design
w/inlaid parquetry scrolled leaf
outer band around wider band of
stylized floral design featuring a
bird at each corner and a narrow
inner band w/leaf design and

Parquetry Inlaid Frame

stylized star at each corner &
center of each side, 19th c.,
probably England, old surface,
minor cracks & loses, 31 x 36"
(ILLUS.)...................... **978.00**

FRATERNAL ORDER COLLECTIBLES

**G.A.R. (Grand Army of the
Republic) booklet,** Women's
Corps, 1889.................. **$15.00**

G.A.R. tintype, sixth-plate, older
gentleman & his wife, he wearing
G.A.R. badges & coat, late 19th c. ... **95.00**

Motto of the Odd Fellows

**I.O.O.F. (Independent Order of Odd
Fellows) painting,** oil on canvas
American School rendering of the
fraternal motto, unsigned, framed,
19th c., 20 x 23¼" (ILLUS.) **2,645.00**

I.O.O.F. sign, carved & gilded pine,
three interlacing ovals, retaining
much of the original gilding, late
19th - early 20th c., 12¼" l........ **402.00**

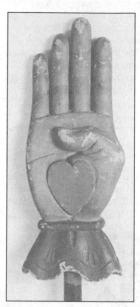

Odd Fellows Staff

I.O.O.F. staff, folk-carved & painted
heart-in-hand (ILLUS.) **1,100.00**

Masonic Plaque

Masonic plaques, polychrome
patriotic theme w/relief-carved
decoration of eagle & shield near
top & striped shield w/Masonic
symbol beneath & inscribed in
center "Jr OUAM", pr. (ILLUS. of
one) **1,980.00**

Masonic Pocket Watch

Masonic pocket watch, gold (14k), Dudley openface w/display back, serial number appears to be 888, engine-turned radiating dial (ILLUS.) **2,070.00**

Shriner wine, clear glass w/various symbols & gold buffalo, marked "Buffalo - 1899" **95.00**

FRUIT JARS

American (motif of eagle w/flag) Fruit Jar, ground lip, smooth base, original lid & lightning closure, Australian, ca. 1885-1895, pale green, ½ gal. **$88.00**

Arthur Burham & Gilroy 10th & Geo. Sts. Philadelphia - R. Arthur's Patent Jany 2nd 1855, ground lip w/press-down groove ring wax sealer, smooth base, ca. 1855-1860, rare, bluish aqua, 7¼" h. (¾" stress crack on shoulder) **550.00**

Atlas Fruit Jar

Atlas Strong Shoulder Mason, smooth lip & base, original zinc screw lid, ca. 1915-1925, deep smoky cornflower blue, qt. (ILLUS.) . . **110.00**

Ball Perfect Mason, smooth lip & base, original zinc screw lid, ca. 1915-1925, deep yellowish-olive amber, qt. **77.00**

Ball (The) Pat Apl'd For, ground, lip, smooth base, ca. 1899-1900, original metal lid & lightning closure, aqua, qt.. . . . . **303.00**

Banner, Patd Feby 9th 1864, Reisd Jan 22d 1867, ground lip, smooth base, correct glass lid, ca. 1867-1875, aqua, qt. **210.00**

Bee, ground lip, smooth base, reproduction closure, ca. 1869-1875, rare, aqua, ½ gal. **770.00**

Bellerjeaus Simplicity Fruit Jar Patd Mar 31st 1869, ground lip, smooth base, ca. 1868-1870, very rare, aqua, qt. **798.00**

Stoneware Fruit Jar

Bennett's Patent Dec 2, 1856, stoneware, impressed "Bennett's Patent Dec 2, 1856" below series of horizontal rings & on underside of original lid, ca. 1856-1865, minor chips on side of lip & on lid, beige, qt. (ILLUS.) **385.00**

Bloeser, ground lip, smooth base, original glass lid embossed "Pat Sept 27 1887" & metal closure, ca. 1887-1895, aqua, qt.. . . . . **303.00**

Buckeye, ground lip, smooth base, original lid w/reproduction metal closure, ca. 1870-1885, bluish, aqua, qt. **187.00**

Clarke Fruit Jar Co Cleveland, O., ground lip, smooth base, original glass lid & metal closure, ca. 1880-1890, aqua, qt. **142.00**

Clarke Fruit Jar Co Cleveland, O., ground lip, smooth base, original glass lid & metal closure, impressed "Pat. M'ch 17 1885," ca. 1885-1895, aqua, qt.. . . . . **83.00**

Cohansey Glass Mfg. Pat. Feb. 12 1861, ground lip, smooth base, original metal lid & wire closure, ca. 1870-1880, aqua, pt. **116.00**

Crystal Fruit Jar

Crystal Food Holder (motif of jar in use) Trade Mark, ground lip, smooth base marked "Patents-Pending," original metal screw lid w/slide opening & glass funnel, motif depicts woman's hand operating jar, ca. 1890-1910, clear, 10¾" total h. (ILLUS.) **330.00**

Dexter, ground lip, smooth base, original glass insert, ca. 1875-1890, rare, aqua, midget (missing screw band, two ¼" stress cracks in lip) **198.00**

E.G. Co. (The) Imperial w/monogram, ground lip, smooth base, correct glass insert, metal screw band, Canada, ca. 1865-1885, aqua, midget pt.. . . . . **72.00**

Eagle Patd 28th 1858 Reisd June 16th 1868, ground lip, smooth base, original glass lid & metal yoke, ca. 1858-1865, aqua, qt. (1" sliver chip inside contour of lip) **165.00**

Eclipse (The), applied groove ring wax sealer, tin lid, smooth base, ca. 1875-1895, bluish aqua, qt. (iridescent bruise inside wax ring) . . . **50.00**

Fink & Nasse St. Louis, ground lip, smooth base marked "Cohansey Glass Co Philada," original glass lid & metal closure, ca. 1875-1885, deep bluish aqua, qt. (two ⅛" stress cracks on base) **198.00**

Globe, ground lip, "70" embossed on smooth base, "Patented May 25th 1886" on original glass lid, metal closure, golden amber, qt. **94.00**

Griffin's Patent Oct 7 1862, ground lip, smooth base, original glass lid & metal closure, ca. 1862-1870, bluish aqua, ½ gal. **193.00**

Hartell's Glass Air Tight Cover (on rim) - Patented Oct 19 1858, ground lip, smooth base, original embossed glass lid, pale bluish green, pt. **253.00**

Howe (The) Jar Scranton Pa, ground lip, smooth lip, original glass lid embossed "Pat, Feby, 28/88" & wire closure, ca. 1888-1895, aqua, qt. **55.00**

Howe (The) Jar Scranton Pa, ground lip, smooth lip, original glass lid embossed "Pat, Feby, 28/88" & wire closure, ca. 1888-1900, clear, qt.. . . . . **100.00**

Johnson & Johnson Fruit Jar

Johnson & Johnson New York, square, ground lip, smooth base, marked "Made in U.S.A." on aqua glass lid, metal screw band, ca. 1900-1915, deep cobalt blue (ILLUS.). **385.00**

King (The) Pat. Nov. 2. 1860, ground lip, smooth base, original lid & metal closure, ca. 1860-1870, aqua, qt. **275.00**

Mansfield, ABM lip, smooth base marked "Mansfield Glass W'K'S. Knowlton's May 03" on smooth base, original embossed glass insert & correct zinc screw lid, ca. 1903-1910, clear, qt. **330.00**

"Mascot" (The) Trade Mark Pat'd Improved, ground lip, smooth base, original milk glass "pickle pusher" insert & zinc screw band, clear, qt. (two 3/8" iridescent bruise on lower jar) **110.00**

Mason (keystone inside circle), ground lip, smooth base, zinc screw lid, ca, 1875-1895, medium amber, qt. **440.00**

Mason (The) Jar of 1858 Trade Mark, ground lip, embossed "Patented By Jno. Mason Nov 30 1858" on smooth base, zinc screw lid, ca. 1875-1895, aqua, qt. 303.00

Mason's 400 Patent Nov 30th 1858, ground lip, smooth base, zinc screw lid, ca. 1865-1885, aqua, qt.. . . . . . . 176.00

Mason's 5 Patent Nov 30th 1858, ground lid, smooth base, zinc screw lid, ca. 1875-1885, medium cobalt blue, qt. (3/4" chip out of lip) 2,420.00

Mason's C.F.J. Co. (monogram) Patent Nov 30th 1858, ground lip, smooth base, zinc screw lid, ca. 1865-1885, medium yellowish green, ½ gal. 264.00

Mason's (cross) Patent Nov 30th 1858, ground lip, smooth base marked "Pat Nov 26 67," zinc screw lid, ca. 1865-1885, yellow w/hint of olive, qt.. . . . . 935.00

Mason's (keystone in circle) Patent Nov 30th 1858, ground lip, smooth base, correct zinc screw lid, ca. 1875-1895, medium amber, qt.. . . . 935.00

Mason's (keystone in circle) Patent Nov 30th 1858, ground lip, smooth base, original zinc screw lid, ca. 1865-1885, aqua, midget pt. 33.00

Mason's Patent Nov 30th 1858, ABM lid, smooth base, zinc screw lid, deep olive green, qt. (⅜" vertical stress crack from top of lid) . . . 743.00

Rare Mason Jar

Mason's Patent Nov 30th 1858, ground lip, "A 17 V" on smooth base, zinc screw lid, ca. 1875-1895, bright yellowish green, qt. (ILLUS.) 3,410.00

Mason's Patent Nov 30th 1858, ground lip, smooth base marked "Pat Nov 26 67," correct zinc screw lid, ca. 1865-1885, amber, qt. 770.00

Mason's Patent Nov 30th 1858, ground lip, smooth base, zinc screw lid, ca. 1865-1885, dark tobacco amber, qt.. . . . . 578.00

Mason's Patent Nov 30th 1858, ground lip, smooth base, zinc screw lid, ca. 1875-1895, black olive amber, qt. 660.00

Mason's Patent Nov 30th 1858, ground lip, smooth base, zinc screw lid, ca. 1875-1895, light sapphire, qt. 2,090.00

Mason's Patent Nov 30th 1858, ground lip, smooth base, zinc screw lid, ca. 1875-1895, light yellowish amber w/olive tone, qt.. . . . 715.00

Mason's Patent Nov 30th 1858 - C.F.J. Co., ground lip, smooth base, correct zinc screw lid w/embossed amber insert, ca. 1875-1895, amber, qt. 2,640.00

Mason's Patent Nov 30th 1858 - N.C. L. Co., ground lip, smooth base, zinc screw lid, ca. 1875-1895, amethyst, qt. 231.00

Mason's Patent Nov 30th 1858 - (Tudor rose), ground lip, smooth base, correct screw lid w/immerser stamped "Trade atd Nov. 30. 1880," ca. 1875-1895, deep bluish aqua, qt. 880.00

Millville Atmospheric Fruit Jar - Whitall's Patent June 18th 1861, applied groove ring wax sealer, original glass lid & metal yoke, smooth base, ca. 1865-1870, bluish aqua, qt. (several small chips). 55.00

Moore's Patent Dec 3d 1861, applied mouth, smooth base, original "Patent, Dec. 23rd. 1861" glass lid & yoke, ca. 1861-1870, deep aqua, qt. 209.00

Newman's Patent Dec. 20th 1859, ground lip, smooth base, ca. 1859-1865, deep bluish aqua, qt. (a few minor scratches in shoulder area). . 358.00

Penn (The), applied groove ring wax sealer, tin lid, marked "Beck Phillips & Co Pitts. PA." on smooth base w/three raised "feet,", ca. 1875-1895, aqua, qt. (shallow ⅜" chip on lip). 94.00

Protector, six-sided, ground lip, smooth base, correct metal lid, ca. 1885-1895, aqua, qt. 165.00

Salem (The) Jar, ground internal screw thread lip, original glass lid embossed "Wm Grange & Son 711 Nth 2nd St Phila," smooth base, ca. 1870-1880, aqua, ½ gal. **1,320.00**

San Francisco Glass Works, applied groove ring wax sealer, tin lid, smooth base, ca. 1875-1895, bluish aqua, qt. (repaired chips on applied wax seal ring) **220.00**

Standard, applied groove ring wax sealer, correct tin embossed "Wm. Mc.Cully & Co. Glass Pittsburgh," smooth base, ca. 1880-1895, amber, qt. **468.00**

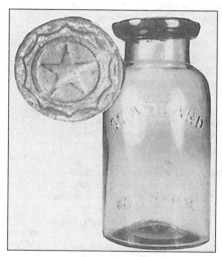

Standard Fruit Jar

Standard - W. McC & Co, applied groove ring wax sealer, correct tin lid w/embossed star, smooth base, ca. 1880-1895, light emerald green, qt. (ILLUS.). **990.00**

Standard - W. McC & Co, applied grove ring wax sealer, correct tin lid embossed "McCully Co. Glass Pittsburgh," smooth base, ca. 1880-1895, light to medium cobalt blue, (½ chip on wax seal ring) **855.00**

Stark Jar Patented, smooth lip & base, original glass lid & spring-loaded metal closure, ca. 1910-1920, clear, qt.. . . . . **110.00**

Steven Tin Top Patd July 17, 1873, applied groove ring wax sealer, tin lid, smooth base marked "S.K. & Co" around "N" within star, ca. 1875-1895, aqua, qt. (⅜" chip outer edge of wax seal ring) **55.00**

Sun Fruit Jar

Sun (inside motif of sun) Trade Mark, ground lip, marked "J.P. Barstow" on smooth base, original glass lid & metal closure embossed "Monier's Pat Apr. 1 90 Mar 12 96," ca. 1895-1900, aqua, pt. (ILLUS.). **120.00**

Van Vliet (The) Jar of 1881, ground lip, original glass lid metal yoke, smooth base, tapering cylindrical, ground lip, smooth base, original glass lid w/reproduction wire & metal closure, ca. 1881-1890, aqua,½ gal. (ILLUS.) **908.00**

Van Vliet Jar of 1881

Van Vliet (The) Jar of 1881, tapering cylindrical, ground lip, smooth base, original glass lid w/reproduction wire & metal closure, ca. 1881-1890, aqua, ½ gal. (ILLUS.) **468.00**

Winslow, ground lip, smooth base, original glass lid embossed "Patented Nov. 29th 1870 Patented Feb 25 1973" & wire closure, ca. 1873-1880, bluish aqua, ½ gal.. . . . . **176.00**

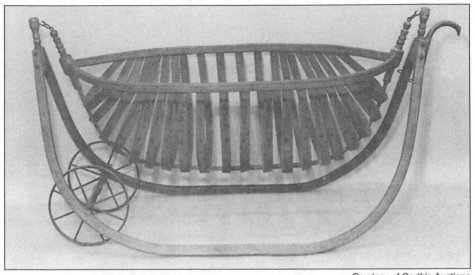

Patent-dated "Harvest" Cradle

Courtesy of Garth's Auctions

FURNITURE

Furniture made in the United States during the 18th and 19th centuries is coveted by collectors. American antique furniture has a European background, primarily English, since the influence of the Continent usually found its way to America by way of England. If the style did not originate in England, it came to America by way of England. For this reason, some American furniture styles carry the name of an English monarch or an English designer. However, we must realize that, until recently, little research has been conducted and even less published on the Spanish and French influences in the area of the California missions and New Orleans.

After the American revolution, cabinetmakers in the United States shunned the prevailing styles in England and chose to bring the French styles of Napoleon's Empire to the United States and we have the uniquely named "American Empire" style of furniture in a country that never had an emperor.

During the Victorian period, quality furniture began to be mass-produced in this country with its rapidly growing population. So much walnut furniture was manufactured, the vast supply of walnut was virtually depleted and it was of necessity that oak furniture became fashionable as the 19th century drew to a close.

For our purposes, the general guidelines for dating will be:

Pilgrim Century - 1620-85
William & Mary - 1685-1720
Queen Anne - 1720-50

Chippendale - 1750-85
Federal - 1785-1820
   Hepplewhite - 1785-1820
   Sheraton - 1800-20
American Empire (Classical) - 1815-40
Victorian - 1840-1900
   Early Victorian - 1840-50
   Gothic Revival - 1840-90
   Rococo (Louis XV) - 1845-70
   Renaissance - 1860-85
   Louis XVI - 1865-75
   Eastlake - 1870-95
   Jacobean & Turkish Revival - 1870-95
   Aesthetic Movement - 1880-1900
Art Nouveau - 1890-1918
Turn-of-the-Century - 1895-1910
Mission (Arts & Crafts movement) - 1900-15
Art Deco - 1925-40

All furniture included in this listing is American unless otherwise noted.

BEDROOM SUITES

Victorian Eastlake substyle: double bed & chest of drawers; walnut & burl walnut, the chest of drawers w/a tall superstructure w/a stepped crown-form crest w/hole-pierced scallops & a decorated central raised panel, the reeded side stiles w/small candle shelves flank the tall rectangular mirror, angled lower stile brackets w/raised burl panels, the base w/small rectangular white

Victorian Eastlake Chest of Drawers

marble top sections over small drawers & flanking a marble-topped drop well all above two long lower drawers, each drawer w/blocked rectangular raised burl panel, matching bed, bed 55 x 79", chest 18 x 40", 7' 2" h. (ILLUS. of chest) **$2,200.00**

Victorian turn-of-the century: double bed, chest of drawers w/mirror & washstand; Golden Oak, the bed & chest w/high backs & slightly shaped crestrails trimmed w/applied central leafy scrolls & fanned corner carving between the stepped & reeded stiles, the bed headboard & lower footboard divided into horizontal panels, the chest w/a large rectangular swivel mirror above a rectangular top overhanging a case of three long drawers, the top one slightly overhanging the lower two, the washstand w/raised towel bar above a case w/a long & two short drawers & a small door, the set . . **1,045.00**

BEDS

Art Nouveau bed, bronze-mounted fruitwood marquetry, the high arched headboard crested w/stylized pierced whiplash designs & a repoussé bronze flower flanked by outset small rounded shelves above a rectangular panel inlaid in various woods w/poppies & leafage flanked by carved whiplash pierced designs, a short matching

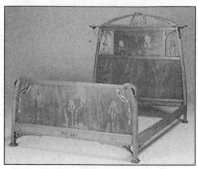

Fine Art Nouveau Inlaid Bed

footboard, by Leon Benouville, France, ca. 1900, 60 x 80", headboard 5' 2" h. (ILLUS.) **4,025.00**

Classical country-style low-poster bed, carved maple & pine, the pineapple-carved & star-punched posts flanking a shaped headboard, New England, ca. 1840, 42 x 72¼", 44¼" h. (some height loss, restoration) **259.00**

Classical country-style rope bed, cherry, maple & curly maple, matching head & footboards w/a cylindrical crestrail above a headboard w/two recessed curly maple panels flanked by ring & tapering cylindrical side posts w/ring- and cylindrical-turned finials above blocked sections also joined by a heavy medial rail, raised on tapering, turned legs w/peg feet, refinished, replaced steel side rails, 75½" l., 47½ h. **330.00**

Classical Low Poster Bed

Classical low poster bed, carved mahogany & mahogany veneer, the scrolled & paneled headboard w/leaf-carved finials flanked by posts w/pineapple finials & acanthus leaves above spiral-carved & ring-turned posts, original side rails, bed bolts & covers, refinished, imperfections, probably Middle Atlantic States, ca. 1835-45, 58½ x 78", 4' 8" h. (ILLUS.) **1,093.00**

Classical single bed, curly & bird's-eye maple, the even head- and footboards w/rolled crestrails above wide panels of bird's-eye maple flanked by square stiles ending in tapering ring- and rod-turned legs w/peg feet, original rails, found in Zoar, Ohio, 19th c., 32½ x 72", 31½" h. (minor age cracks, one repaired rail) **825.00**

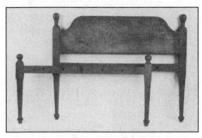

Country Low Poster Bed

Country-style low poster bed, painted birch, the low arched headboard flanked by block-turned tapering legs w/ball-turned finials, the footrail w/matching legs & ball finials, original red paint, New England, 18th c., 49 x 75½", 39¼" h. (ILLUS.) **863.00**

Country-style trundle bed, cherry, low head- and footboards w/scrolled top edge, turned feet, original side rails, old finish, 19th c., 62 x 64½", 16" h. **110.00**

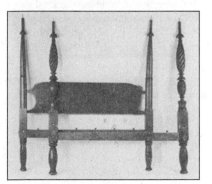

Country Federal Tall Poster Bed

Federal country-style tall poster bed, painted & turned wood, the turned & tapering headposts flanking a shaped & gently arched headboard, the spiral-turned footposts joined by rails fitted for roping, w/accompanying tester, old red paint, New England, ca. 1820, restored, 54 x 79", 5'½" h. (ILLUS.) **1,380.00**

Federal country-style tall poster bed, maple & pine, tall turned tapering head- & footposts, a scroll-shaped pine headboard, an arched tester & rails, New England, early 19th c., 55 x 82", 5' 4¼" h. (restored, cracked headboard) **460.00**

Federal country-style tall poster bed, maple, the pine scrolled headboard flanked by turned posts on bulbous turned legs, matching footposts, w/arched tester, side rails & bed bolts, New England, 1830s, refinished, 54½ x 72", 5' 4½" h. (minor restoration) **1,380.00**

Federal country-style tall poster bed, curly maple, the plain gently arched headboard flanked by urn turnings below the tall turned reeded tapering posts, rope end rails w/matching posts, old mellow refinishing, early 19th c., 52½ x 70", 6' 10" h. (pine headboard old replacement, replaced side rails) . . **4,400.00**

Federal country-style tall poster canopy bed, birch & pine, a wide low arched pine headboard between urn turnings below the tall turned tapering reeded posts w/peg finials to support the arched canopy frame, end rails w/matching posts, original hinged canopy, original rails, old reddish brown finish, New England, early 19th c., 56½ x 69½", 5' 6¼" h. (damage to some turnings) **4,950.00**

Federal tall poster tester bed, mahogany, a low arched & peaked headboard flanked by vase- and ring-turned tapering posts, matching footposts on square tapering legs, arched tester frame, probably Southern, first quarter 19th c., 52¾" w., 5' 3" h. **978.00**

George III-Style full-tester bed, decorated satinwood, the rectangular headboard panel decorated w/a painted rectangular band between the square headposts, the lower footboard w/a rectangular reserve decorated w/a central oval reserve of putti framed by long leafy scrolls all between the ring-, knob- and rod-turned footposts ending in ring-turned short legs, a full cornice-form tester decorated w/a continuous band of small floral swags, complete w/slats, England, late 19th c., 71 x 83¼", overall 7' 9" h. (missing bolt covers) **8,625.00**

Mission-style (Arts & Crafts movement) twin beds, oak, headboard w/heavy crestrail above seven square spindles joined by a medial rail between the square through-tenon stiles, matching lower footboard, new dark finish, early 20th c., headboard 47 x 47½", pr. **2,420.00**

George Nakashima Platform Bed

Modern style platform bed, walnut, upright rectangular headboard w/block dovetail top & doweled sides w/two sliding doors, plywood back w/holes for wire, wide rectangular bed raised on set-back platform base w/flush tenons & dowels, original finish, designed by George Nakashima, mid-20th c., platform 60 x 74", 10" h. plus 36" h. headboard (ILLUS.) **5,175.00**

Fine Victorian Aesthetic Bed

Victorian highback bed, Aesthetic Movement substyle, ebonized & gilt-incised wood w/marquetry, the high stepped headboard crest w/notched rails & gilt-incised blocks flanked by brackets & pierced w/rows of short baluster-turned spindles, the blocked stiles w/gilt-incised decoration & beehive-

turned finials, simple lower panels w/line-incised trim, the lower footboard w/a top round bar over short spindles & panels, deep side rails w/spindled & plain gilt-incised corner brackets, on short turned feet, late 19th c., 64½ x 76", 6' 1" h. (ILLUS.) **3,163.00**

Aesthetic Movement Twin Bed

Victorian twin beds, Aesthetic Movement substyle, carved mahogany, the tall squared headboard w/scroll-carved finials centered by rectangular upper panel w/reeded pilasters flanking looping leafy swags centered by a face, the lower footboard w/an arched crest & scrolled ears above a raised beaded rectangular panel, deep siderails, block feet, ca. 1880, 35¾ x 78", 5' h., pr. (ILLUS. of one) **690.00**

BENCHES

Bucket (or water) bench, painted pine, a narrow rectangular top shelf above a medial open shelf w/curved edges & applied molding between board upright ends on angled shoe feet, worn yellow repaint, renailed, 19th c., 7½ x 22¾", 22¼" h. **275.00**

Bucket (or water) bench, painted pine, a narrow rectangular top above a low shelf over a deep shelf above wide apron boards joining the bootjack ends, closed back, old worn mustard yellow repaint, second half 19th c., 11¾ x 30½", 30" h. **385.00**

Bucket (or water) bench, painted poplar, a rectangular well top w/beaded board sides above solid end boards & an open back supporting two open shelves, some old red paint, 19th c., 16 x 37½", 29½" h. (age cracks in shelves) . . . **715.00**

Country-style bench, painted pine, narrow rectangular top w/rounded end corners above wide side aprons w/shaped bracket ends, bootjack ends w/arched cut-outs, old grey paint, 68" l., 11½" h. (wear, some edge damage, top weathered) **138.00**

Country-style bench, painted wood, long rectangular top on cut-out end legs joined by shaped brackets, painted blue, New England, 19th c., 10½ x 72", 18" h. **460.00**

Country-style bench, stained pine, the long narrow plank seat w/notched ends raised on shaped & tapered cut-out bootjack legs w/arched feet, curved braces from legs to underside of seat, worn old red finish, found in Massachusetts, 19th c., 8¾ x 46", 19" h. **660.00**

Country-style bench, a straight board crestrail painted w/numbers above a spindled back & shaped arms over a rectangular plank seat on turned legs, mid-19th c., 108" l. . **345.00**

William & Mary joint bench, walnut, rectangular top (lacking upholstery) over turned legs joined by a turned H-stretcher, England, late 17th - early 18th c., 16 x 26½", 16" h. . . . **633.00**

Window benches, Classical style, mahogany & mahogany veneer, the beaded rolled end rail panels on scrolled supports continuing to outswept legs joined by the rectangular seatrail w/an upholstered slip seat, old finish, probably Boston, ca. 1820, 20½ x 33½", 23½" h., pr. (imperfections) **4,945.00**

BOOKCASES

Art Deco French Bookcase

Art Deco bookcase, rosewood, the rectangular slightly stepped top above two sliding glass doors opening to three wooden shelves flanked by tall narrow end doors opening to shelves, w/plaque reading "J. Leleu," Jules Leleu, France, ca. 1930, 13¾ x 82¾", 5' h. (ILLUS.) **5,175.00**

Arts & Crafts Revolving Bookcase

Arts & Crafts bookcase, oak, revolving-type, a square top above sides w/three small open shelves beside a board w/keyed tenon construction for supporting the shelves, raised & revolving on a cross-form base on casters, dark finish, early 20th c., 20¾" w., 44" h. (ILLUS.). **575.00**

Biedermeier-Style bookcase, fruitwood & part-ebonized, rectangular top over a narrow drawer & three open shelves flanked by ebonized columns, elongated ball feet, Europe, late 19th c., small **316.00**

Empire-Style Bookcase

Empire-Style bookcase, gilt-bronze mounted mahogany, rectangular top stepped above molded border over a frieze band carved w/palmettes above a pair of wire mesh-covered doors opening to shelves & flanked by carved square tapering pilasters topped by carved classical heads over leaf drops, deep base frieze w/gilt-bronze rosettes & leaf bands flanked by blocked corners on knob-turned feet, Europe, late 19th c., 16¼ x 58¾", 4' h. (ILLUS.) . . . **3,105.00**

Federal Country-Style Bookcase

Federal country-style bookcase, walnut, two-part step-back style: the upper section w/a rectangular top above the widely flaring angled cornice above a pair of tall 6-pane glazed doors opening to four shelves; the stepped-out lower section w/two pairs of paneled doors w/thumb latches & wooden knobs, simple cut-out feet, from Ohio, refinished, some restoration & shelves altered, first half 19th c., 15½ x 58¾", 8' 1" h. (ILLUS.).... **2,420.00**

Lawyer's bookcase, hardwood, five-stack style, each section w/a lift-front glass door, by Globe Wernike, early 20th c. **700.00**

Mission Oak Bookcase

Mission-style (Arts & Crafts movement) bookcase, oak, rectangular top above a pair of tall glazed doors w/panels of six panes above two lower panes, glass sides, slightly arched apron, short style legs on casters, early 20th c. (ILLUS.) **1,100.00**

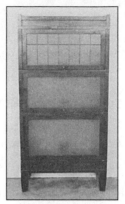

Stacking Mission Bookcase

Mission-style (Arts & Crafts movement) bookcase, oak, stacking-type, a rectangular top w/paneled frieze band above a leaded glass lift-front door above two lower stacks w/lift-front glazed doors, heavy square stiles legs, square wooden knobs, early 20th c. (ILLUS.) **715.00**

Mission-style (Arts & Crafts movement) bookcase, oak, rectangular top above a single 12-pane glazed door opening to shelves, slightly arched apron, square stile feet, J. M. Young Company, 14 x 33¾", 4' 2½" h. (refinished) **1,725.00**

Mission-style (Arts & Crafts movement) miniature bookcase, oak, rectangular top w/a gently arched three-quarter gallery & through-tenons above a single 6-pane glazed cupboard door w/metal pull opening to three shelves, added varnish, unmarked Lifetime Furniture Company, 12¼ x 30¼", 44" h. **2,750.00**

Victorian bookcase, Renaissance Revival substyle, oak, the rectangular top w/a molded cornice above a pair of tall single-pane glazed top-locking sliding doors opening to three shelves & flankedby reeded pilasters, the slightly stepped-out base w/a pair

Renaissance Revival Oak Bookcase

of drawers w/pairs of pierced brass pulls & molded base flanked by blocking & raised on casters, by R. J. Horner, third quarter 19th c. (ILLUS.) **2,500.00**

Fine Renaissance Revival Bookcase

Victorian bookcase, Renaissance Revival substyle, walnut & burl walnut, the rectangular top w/deep flaring molded cornice above a burl frieze band above three tall glazed arch-topped cabinet doors opening to three shelves, each door separated by a carved scroll block (one missing) & narrow burl panels & rondels, the stepped-out lower section w/a molded edge above three doors w/raised rectangular molded panels w/notched corners enclosing matching burl panels, molded base (ILLUS.) **2,500.00**

Victorian Oak Bookcase

Victorian bookcase, country-style, oak, a rectangular top w/deep molded flaring cornice above a pair of tall 2-pane glazed cupboard doors opening to shelves, the stepped-out lower section w/a pair of deep drawers w/bail pulls, late 19th c., 20 x 48", 6' 7" h. (ILLUS.) . . **495.00**

William IV bookcase, mahogany, two-part construction: the upper section w/a domed cornice above two bow-front 8-pane cupboard doors opening to three shelves; the lower protruding conforming section w/two faux tambour front panel doors, raised on flattened bun feet, early 19th c., England, 18 x 46", 7' 2" h. **4,887.00**

BUREAUX PLAT

Provincial Louis XV-Style Bureau Plat

Louis XV-Style, Provincial style, parcel-gilt & green paint, rectangular top w/leather inset above a serpentine kneehole flanked by drawers in front opposing false drawer fronts in back, ornate scrolling gilt-metal drawer pulls, raised on simple cabriole legs carved w/foliage at the knees & feet, paint wear, France, 19th c., 25¼ x 56", 29½" h. (ILLUS.). **5,462.00**

Louis XV-Style Bureau Plat

Louis XV-Style, ormolu-mounted inlaid wood, the rectangular top inset w/a leather surface over a beaded edge above the shaped apron w/a row of three drawers w/ornate ormolu pulls & keyhole escutcheons, scroll mounts between drawers, on simple cabriole legs w/ormolu caryatid figural mounts continuing down each leg, Europe, 19th c., 27 x 49" (ILLUS.) **2,990.00**

Louis XV-Style, bronze-mounted hardwood, the shaped top w/inset leather writing surface & glass top, bronze foliate & scallop shell mounts, apron w/one long drawer & two short drawers, raised on cabriole legs w/female terms & ending in sabots, 19th c., 30 x 68", 31" h. **5,750.00**

CABINETS

Mission Oak China Cabinet

China cabinet, Mission-style (Arts & Crafts movement), oak, rectangular top above a molded frieze over a pair of tall single-pane glazed doors w/arched tops opening to an half-mirrored interior & three wooden shelves, top corner blocks above incised side stiles, glass sides w/arched tops, shaped apron, square stile legs on casters, ca. 1910-20 (ILLUS.) **1,100.00**

"Side-by-Side" China Cabinet

China cabinet, turn-of-the-century "side-by-side" style, oak, one side w/a tall cabinet section w/a flat top w/curved front above a conforming long single-pane glazed door opening to four wooden shelves & flanked by glass sides, molded apron raised on two cabriole legs ending in paw feet, the conjoined cabinet w/a large arched beveled mirror w/carved grotesque head crest above a rectangular top w/curved front above a conforming case w/a long drawer over two small deep drawers beside a scroll-carved cabinet door, molded base, raised on additional matching cabriole legs, ca. 1900 (ILLUS.). . **1,300.00**

China cabinet, Mission-style (Arts & Crafts movement), oak, curved-front style, a D-form top above a conforming case w/curved glass sides flanking a flat lattice-glazed single door opening to three adjustable wooden shelves, on short square stile legs, two interior mirrored panels, original finish, unmarked Lifetime Furniture Co., early 20th c., 14 x 51½", 4' 7" h. **4,950.00**

Classical Revival China Cabinet

China cabinet, Classical Revival-Style, oak, rectangular top above a pair of tall single-pane glazed doors opening to four wooden shelves, shaped smooth side pilasters ending in C-scroll front feet, glass sides, on casters, ca. 1910-20, 15 x 37", 4' 10" h. (ILLUS.). **495.00**

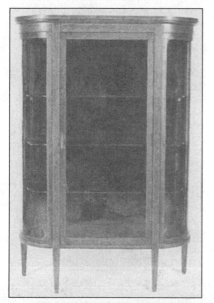

Curved-front China Cabinet

China cabinet, turn-of-the-century curved-front style, mahogany, D-form top above a conforming case w/curved glass sides flanking the flat single-pane center door opening to three wooden shelves, slender square tapering legs, ca. 1910-20, 14 x 42", 5' 2" h. (ILLUS.). **440.00**

China cabinet, Mission-style (Arts & Crafts movement), oak, a rectangular top w/a flat crestrail above a case w/two tall 8-pane cupboard doors above a flat apron, raised on slender square legs, four panes on each end, original finish, paper label of Gustav Stickley, 15¼ x 42", 5' 2½" h. (one pane cracked) **5,175.00**

Display cabinets, Federal country-style, rectangular heavy top above a pair of large 12-pane glazed cupboard doors opening to four shelves above a low stepped-out base w/two double-panel wide doors opening to a shelf, old brown wood graining, Massachusetts, mid-19th c., 16 x 70¾", 6' 6" h., pr. (imperfections) **5,175.00**

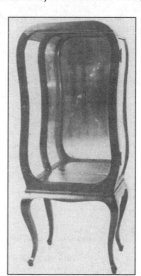

Unusual Display Cabinet

Display cabinet, turn-of-the-century, mahogany, an upright kidney bean-shaped framework w/single-pane front door & undulating glass sides, opening to a mirror-backed compartment & two glass shelves, simple cabriole legs, curved top veneer separated on curves, ca. 1900 (ILLUS.) **468.00**

Unique Oak File Cabinet

File cabinet, turn-of-the-century, oak, stack-type, a curved upper cornice above a section w/a row of seven upright narrow file drawers over a section of three large file drawers above another section of seven upright file drawers, a stepped-out base section w/a pair of paneled cupboard doors, ogee molded base (ILLUS.)..................... **825.00**

Rare Rohlfs File Cabinet

File cabinet, Arts & Crafts style, oak, a square top slightly overhanging an upright case w/a long door w/heavy raised & serpentined wooden strap hinges & latch & pierced serpentine slot w/pull-out writing surface, each side w/two pierced rectangular panels, the bottom section w/a pull-out file drawer w/pierced hand hole & tack trim, designed by Charles Rohlfs, ca. 1900, burned-in mark, 18" sq., 38" h. (ILLUS.) **12,650.00**

Hardware cabinet, country store-type, floor model, pine & hardwood, upright octagonal form, octagonal top w/molded edges above eight sides each w/nine numbered small drawers w/porcelain knobs, molded base band above raised swiveling inset base, original varnish & black transfer labels, late 19th c., 32½" h. **1,650.00**

Gallé Marquetry Music Cabinet

Music cabinet, Art Nouveau, fruitwood marquetry, the molded rectangular top w/outset corners above a pair of arched cabinet doors inlaid in various woods w/trailing clematis blossoms & leafage & a group of butterflies, above a drawer also inlaid w/butterflies, continuing to an arcaded open shelf; the lower door inlaid w/a tranquil landscape, the sides also inlaid w/dragonflies & falling leaves, signed in marquetry "Gallé," ca. 1900, 18½ x 31", 63¼" h. (ILLUS.)............. **6,900.00**

Turn-of-the-Century Record Cabinet

Record cabinet, turn-of-the-century, oak, the rectangular top w/low backrail & molded edges above a single-pane glazed door w/wooden knob opening to four wooden shelves, simple cabriole front legs, square back legs, 20" w., 38" h. (ILLUS.). **165.00**

Smoker's cabinet, Mission-style (Arts & Crafts movement), oak, rectangular top overhanging the upright case w/a single drawer w/hammered copper plate & bail pull above a single cabinet door, branded mark of Gustav Stickley, 15 x 20", 29" h. (cleaned finish, veneer chips) **2,420.00**

Classical Vitrine Cabinet

Vitrine cabinet, Classical style, mahogany & mahogany veneer, the rectangular top w/a cockbeaded pedimented backboard above two large 2-pane glazed doors flanked by turned half-engaged columns, continuing to baluster-turned short legs, refinished, Middle Atlantic States, 1815-25, 12½ x 28¾", 33" h. (ILLUS.) **1,840.00**

Vitrine cabinet, Louis XV-Style, giltwood & "Vernis Martin" decorated, the arched cornice w/an ornate scroll- and shell-cast pediment continuing down to rounded sides, the front arched frieze band decorated w/cherubs above the tall shaped single-pane glazed door opening to shelves & a mirrored back, the sides w/glass, the lower front & sides decorated w/elaborate scrollwork enclosing

Ornate Louis XV-Style Vitrine

romantic 18th c. landscape scenes w/couples, simple tapering cabriole legs, France, late 19th c., 14 x 35", 5' 11½" h. (ILLUS.) **2,760.00**

CHAIRS

Art Deco armchairs, *ebene de Macassar* & burled walnut, each w/a U-form seat frame forming the arms done in burled walnut & frame the padded upholstered arm interiors & the deep seat, the squared back upholstered, raised on an inverted U-form wide *ebene de Macassar* base, France, ca. 1930, pr. **3,162.00**

Arts & Crafts "cube" chair, oak, even flat back & side crestrails w/through-tenons above four vertical back slats & three slats on each side, newly covered cushion seat, new medium finish, early 20th c., 26 x 33", 33" h. **550.00**

Charles Rohlfs "Barrel" Chair

Arts & Crafts style "barrel" chair, oak, the flat U-form crestrail above sides composed of full-length flat baluster-form slats, scroll-cut brackets under the arm fronts, heavy plank seat above flat apron, designed by Charles Rohlfs, early 20th c. (ILLUS.) **18,700.00**

Bentwood armchairs, beechwood, Modern style w/a curved central crestrail above U-form frame arms above the upholstered back panel raised above the conforming upholstered seat, six slender square legs to the U-form base rail, medium brown stain, upholstered in a Secessionist reprint fabric, each branded "J. & J. Kohn," Josef Hoffmann, Model No. 728, Vienna, Austria, ca. 1906, pr. **2,875.00**

Chippendale corner chair, carved mahogany, the shaped back rest curving & continuing to scrolled flat arms, raised on three turned columnar stiles flanking two loop-pierced vase-form splats, the square upholstered slip seat on carved frontal cabriole legs ending in a claw-and-ball foot & three square chamfered legs joined by box stretchers, refinished, New England, ca. 1780, 31" h. (restored) **2,530.00**

Chippendale country-style side chair, mahogany, the arched crestrail ending in scrolled ears above gently racked stiles flanking the loop-pierced back splat, molded upholstered slip seat, square tapering legs joined by stretchers, old original surface, western Massachusetts, 18th c., 36¾" h. **1,265.00**

Chippendale country-style side chair, cherry, ladder-back style, the tall back w/three oxbow splats

Country Chippendale Side Chair

& back seatrail flanked by eared flat stiles, woven rush seat, square legs joined by box stretchers, Deerfield, Massachusetts area, 1785-1810, old surface, minor height loss to rear legs, 39¼" h. (ILLUS.) **690.00**

Chippendale country-style side chairs, painted, serpentine crestrail above a pierced baluster splat, the overupholstered seat raised on molded straight legs joined by molded stretchers, New England, late 18th - early 19th c., pr. **747.00**

Chippendale country-style side chairs, mahogany, serpentine crestrail above a loop-pierced vase-form splat above an inset upholstered seat framed by a molded seatrail, square legs joined by flat box stretchers, old refinish, possibly Portsmouth, New Hampshire, 18th c., 37½" h., pr. **1,610.00**

Philadelphia Chippendale Chair

Chippendale side chair, carved mahogany, the oxbow-shaped crestrail w/molded ears & scroll-carved central crest above a pierced scroll-carved splat between beaded raked stiles, trapezoidal slip seat, seatrail w/central carved shell, on cabriole front legs w/claw-and-ball feet, canted turned rear legs, refinished, minor imperfections, Philadelphia, 1760-90, 40" h. (ILLUS.) **9,200.00**

Chippendale side chair, mahogany, the serpentine crest w/molded ears above a pierced strapwork splat, the overupholstered seat raised on angular cabriole legs joined by turned stretchers & ending in pad feet, New England, third quarter 18th c. **1,092.00**

Chippendale side chair, carved mahogany, the serpentine oxyoke crestrail w/carved upturned ears above a pierced splat, joined raked stiles to the trapezoidal slip seat on front cabriole legs ending in pad feet on platforms, chamfered rear legs, old refinish, Massachusetts, ca. 1780, 37" h. **2,300.00**

Chippendale "Writing Arm" Armchair

Chippendale "writing arm" armchair, painted, the molded crestrail on the U-form crest w/one end terminating in a scrolled arm & the other end w/a wide rectangular paddle-form writing surface, the ring-turned back spindles above the square seat raised on four block- and baluster-turned legs joined by ring- and baluster-turned double front stretchers & plain rear stretchers, black over red paint, old surface, late 19th c. alterations, height loss, surface imperfections, New England, mid-18th c., 29" h. (ILLUS.) **1,035.00**

Chippendale-Style corner chair, mahogany, a raised molded crestrail on the U-form flat backrail ending in scrolled hand holds, the

Chippendale-Style Corner Chair

columnar supports flanking two wide pierced back splats above the square upholstered slip seat, cabriole front leg ending in a claw-and-ball foot & three turned & swelled back legs, 19th c., 31" h. (ILLUS.) **209.00**

Chippendale-Style dining chairs, hardwood w/mahogany finish, "ladder-back" style, each back w/four gently arched & pierced back slats w/a center cut-out loop between the gently flaring stiles, shaped & curved open arms, overupholstered seat, square molded legs joined by a square H-stretcher, 20th century reproductions, two arm- & six side chairs, the set **1,320.00**

Chippendale-Style Side Chairs

Chippendale-Style side chairs, walnut, ornate shell-carved oxyoke crestrail above a pierced & looped vasiform splat, upholstered slip seat, shell-carved seatrail raised on cabriole front legs w/acanthus leaf-carved knees & ending in claw-and-ball feet, turned canted rear legs, ca. 1930, set of 6 (ILLUS.) . . . **605.00**

Chippendale-Style Wingchair

Chippendale-Style "wingback" armchair, walnut, the high upholstered back w/a serpentine crestrail flanked by rounded, rolled side wings continuing to rolled upholstered arms, wide overupholstered seat, simple cabriole front legs on pad feet joined by a swelled H-stretcher to the plain rear legs, 19th c., 45" h. (ILLUS.) **275.00**

Classical country-style side chairs, tiger stripe maple & maple, each w/a flat curved crestrail at the top of the square stiles joined by a lower horizontal rail above the rectangular caned seat, ring-turned front legs joined by a flat, curved stretcher w/simple turned side & back stretchers, old finish, probably New England, ca. 1830, 33½" h., set of 8 (minor imperfections). . . . **2,645.00**

Country-style rocking chair w/arms, stencil- and paint-decorated wood, the scrolled splat w/stenciled compote of fruit above six spindles, scrolled open arms & seat painted burnt sienna & mustard yellow, probably New England, ca. 1830, 45" h. (minor wear) **1,035.00**

Country-style sewing rocker without arms, maple, the tall turned round back stiles w/turned acorn finials flanking two horizontal rails joined by four slender vertical slats raised above the original woven rush seat, late 19th - early 20th c. **61.00**

Country-style side chairs, child-size, painted & decorated, the wide rounded crestrail above three bamboo-turned spindles & canted ring- and baluster-turned stiles above the shaped plank seat, canted ring-turned legs joined by ring-turned box stretchers, worn original light green paint w/black striping, gold stenciling & polychrome floral decoration on the crestrail & seat edge, mid-19th c., 22" h., pr. **605.00**

Early American child's "ladder-back" armchair, painted, turned finials on the back stiles flanking shaped horizontal slats, a plank seat & turned posts, old red paint, old replaced seat, New England, ca. 1790, 23½" h. (surface imperfections) **978.00**

Early American country-style "ladder-back" side chair, maple, the tall back w/five arched & graduated slats between round stiles topped w/turned ball finials, woven rush seat on rod- and ball-turned front legs w/ball feet joined by a ball- and ring-turned front stretcher, plain double side stretchers, refinished, early 19th c., 41½" h. **715.00**

Early Ladder-back Armchair

Early American "ladder-back" armchair, maple & ash, the tall back w/three arched slats flanked by ring- and rod-turned stiles w/long knob-turned finials above simple turned open arms w/mushroom-turned hand rests above the ring-, baluster- and rod-turned arm supports continuing to form the front legs, woven rush seat, simple turned double stretchers in the front & plain double stretchers at the sides, old refinish, minor imperfections, probably New England, 18th c., 38½" h. (ILLUS.). **2,415.00**

Early American "ladder-back" armchair, painted maple & ash, the four arched slats joining turned stiles w/ball finials to the high turned open arms w/large mushroom handholds on vase- and ring-turned supports continuing to turned legs joined by double front & side stretchers, original salmon red paint, old splint seat, New England, early 18th c., 44¾" h. (imperfections) **5,175.00**

Early American "ladder-back" rocking armchair, painted & decorated, the tall back w/four arched slats between the knob- and rod-turned stiles w/knob finials above the open scrolled arms on baluster-turned arm supports over the old woven rush seat, simple turned legs w/wide inset rockers, original olive green paint striped w/mustard yellow, Providence, Rhode Island, early 19th c., 39" h. (minor repair) **748.00**

Fine Empire-Style Armchair

Empire-Style armchair, gilt bronze-mounted mahogany, the square back w/rolled crestrail w/gilt bronze mounts above the upholstered back panel over shaped open arms w/gilt metal mounts raised on gilded figural sphinx arm supports, overholstered seat on a flat seatrail w/gilt metal mounts, gilded winged griffin front legs ending in gilded paw feet, square canted rear legs, late 19th - early 20th c., 35" h. (ILLUS.) **4,025.00**

Federal country-style "fancy" side chairs, painted & decorated, an arched & shaped crestrail supported by ring-turned & tapering stiles enclosing a rectangular slat above four ring-turned short spindles, shaped plank seat raised on ring-turned legs joined by turned box stretchers, decorated overall in brown w/green & red floral decoration on the crest & slat & yellow banding, probably Pennsylvania, ca. 1825, set of 6 (each w/repairs & paint touch-up) . . **374.00**

Federal country-style rocking chair w/arms, painted & decorated, the scrolled crestrail decorated w/a stenciled compote of fruit above six spindles, scrolled arms & seat painted burnt sienna & mustard yellow, probably New England, ca. 1830, 45" h. (minor wear) **1,035.00**

Federal "lolling" armchair, inlaid mahogany, the tall rectangular upholstered back w/a serpentine crest above the trapezoidal overupholstered seat flanked by serpentine open arms on interrupted inlaid concave tapering supports continuing to square tapering legs joined by stretchers, probably Massachusetts, ca. 1790, 45½" h. **3,738.00**

Carved Federal Side Chair

Federal side chairs, mahogany, upright rectangular back w/stepped crestrail above a central pierced swag-draped urn w/plumes flanked by carved straight spindles raised above a serpentine-fronted overupholstered seat, raised on square tapering legs ending in spade feet, New York, ca. 1810, pr. (ILLUS. of one) **1,955.00**

Federal side chairs, mahogany veneer, each w/a flat curved crestrail w/raised veneered panels above shaped stiles & a lower rail over the upholstered slip seat, raised on sabre legs, Boston, 1815-25, 32¾" h., set of 8 (repairs) **4,313.00**

Federal side chairs, mahogany, shield-back style, the molded arched crestrail above a pierced urn & drape splat flanked by outward curving stiles, the trapezoidal overupholstered seat on molded square tapering legs joined by box stretchers, old finish, probably Rhode Island, ca. 1790, 38" h., set of 4 (imperfections) . . **2,530.00**

Federal "wingback" armchair, mahogany, serpentine crestrail above the upholstered back flanked by vertically scrolled upholstered wings & outscrolled arms, loose cushion seat, on molded tapering legs, early 19th c. **2,070.00**

Federal "wingback" armchair, mahogany base w/inlay, upholstered back w/an arched crestrail flanked by flaring rounded wings above rolled upholstered arms above the cushion seat, serpentine seatrail raised on square tapering legs joined by an H-stretcher, reupholstered in gold damask, Philadelphia, late 18th c., 44" h. **7,150.00**

George II Corner Chair

George II corner chair, walnut, U-form crestrail carved w/shell & foliage, above two vasiform pierced

splats between three baluster-turned supports, serpentine-sided slip-seat, shell- and scroll-carved front cabriole leg, three swelled turned rear legs, England, mid-18th c. (ILLUS.) **4,600.00**

George III-Style dining chairs, mahogany, ladder-back style w/four pierced serpentine back rails between the slightly outswept stiles, overupholstered trapezoidal seat, square tapering legs joined by an H-stretcher, beige faux leather upholstery, two arm- and eight side chairs, 19th c., the set . . **5,750.00**

Mission-style (Arts & Crafts movement) armchair, oak, the back w/three vertical slats raised above the upholstered rectangular seat above an arched apron above open arms, original finish w/old overcoat, red Gustav Stickley mark, Model No. 353A, 21 x 25", 41½" h. **288.00**

Mission-style (Arts & Crafts movement) dining chair, oak, rectangular back panel & seat completely upholstered in original hard leather, the wide seatrails w/large round tack trim, original dark finish, L. & J.G. Stickley "Work of..." label, 17 x 20", 34¼" h. (tears to leather on back) **880.00**

Mission-style (Arts & Crafts movement) dining chairs, oak, two flat horizontal rails flanking three vertical slats in the back raised above the leather-upholstered rectangular seat above an arched seatrail, slender square tapering legs, original finish w/old overcoat, red Gustav Stickley mark, Model No. 353, 39½" h., pr. . . **863.00**

Mission-style (Arts & Crafts movement) "ladder-back" rocker, oak, three wide horizontal back slats between rectangular stiles over flat arms w/corbels over five vertical slats on each side, deep cushion seat over wide aprons, refinished, Gustav Stickley Model No. 323, 29 x 34", 38" h. . . . **1,650.00**

Mission-style (Arts & Crafts movement) Morris chair, oak, slatted adjustable back above flat shaped open arms over corbels at the front & rear, back pad & drop-in spring seat w/new saddle tan leather, lightened original finish, paper label of The Sykes Company, early 20th c., 29 x 31½", 37" h. **660.00**

Mission-Style Pool Hall Chair

Mission-style (Arts & Crafts movement) pool hall chairs, oak, rectangular back w/a wide curved crestrail above five vertical slats between the square stiles, flat paddle arms over corbels, arm supports continue to form tall legs, shaped rectangular seat, wide flat front stretcher, rectangular side & rear stretchers, foot rest at front, early 20th c., pr. (ILLUS. of one)... **715.00**

Mission-style (Arts & Crafts movement) rocking chair w/arms, oak, flat crestrail over six tall slats flanked by flat stiles over flat arms over six slats, corbels under arms on front legs, drop-in spring seat, light overcoat on reddish brown finish, "The Work of..." decal of L. & J.G. Stickley, 28½ x 29", 37¼" h. **1,760.00**

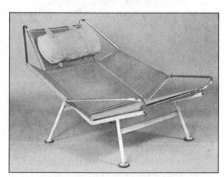

Wegner "Flag Line" Chair

Modern style armchair, "Flag Line" style, flaring metal bar framework w/stretched fabric strands forming the seat, back & arms, cushion headrest, designed by Hanz Wegner, ca. 1950 (ILLUS.)...... **1,400.00**

Charles Eames Lounge Chair

Modern style armchair & ottoman, upholstered rosewood, the lounge armchair w/black leather clip-on cushions & headrest on a rosewood shell, rotating on a cast aluminum five-part base, the matching rectangular ottoman on a four-part base, designed by Charles Eames, Model No. 670, made by Herman Miller, mid-20th c., chair 31½" h., 2 pcs. (ILLUS.) **1,610.00**

Modern style rocking chair, "Eames" chair, molded fiberglas body raised on metal legs w/rockers, designed by Charles & Ray Eames for the Herman Miller Furniture Company, 1950 .... **400.00**

Modern "Barcelona" Chair

Modern style side chair, 'Barcelona' chair, wide upholstered cushion back & seat on a chrome frame w/crossed outswept legs, worn green upholstery (ILLUS.) **150.00**

Modern Side Chair with Naugahyde

Modern style side chair, pale green Naugahyde-upholstered back & seat, raised on square tapering wood legs, 1950s (ILLUS.) **50.00**

Modern style side chairs, cloth on metal framework, wide C-form seat tapering to top of back & front of seat, the seat in yellow, green or blue fabric stretched on a metal frame & raised on canted & interlaced straight wires forming the legs & stretchers, designed by Charles Eames, manufactured by Herman Miller, ca. 1950s, 32" h., set of 4 (fabric wear) **374.00**

Modern style 'wire basket' chair, an open ring seat frame w/tapering wire back spindles, tied upholstered back pad & upholstered seat cushion, on canted metal legs joined by metal stretchers, 1950s **50.00**

Pilgrim Century "Great" Chair

Pilgrim Century armchair, joined & turned oak, the back w/deep turned finials above ring-turned stiles joined by an upper rail & a pair of turned rails centered by three knob- and baluster-turned spindles, simple turned open arms to ring-turned arm supports forming front legs, replaced rush seat, double knob- and baluster-turned front rungs & plain side & back rungs, Massachusetts, 17th c., minor losses including tops of finials, 43" h. (ILLUS.) **5,175.00**

Queen Anne side chair, maple, the yoked crest above a vase-form splat, the slip seat raised on cabriole legs joined by turned stretchers & ending in turned feet, New England, 18th c. **920.00**

Queen Anne "Crooked-back" Chair

Queen Anne side chair, painted crooked-back style, the yoked carved crestrail above a vasiform splat & raked molded stiles, the trapezoidal upholstered slip seat on a scrolled frame w/frontal cabriole legs ending in square pad feet, joined to chamfered rear legs by block-, vase- and ring-turned stretchers, grain-painted dark brown, imperfections, Massachusetts, ca. 1760, 41" h. (ILLUS.) **3,738.00**

Queen Anne side chairs, maple, each w/a yoked crest above a vase-form splat between molded stiles, over an overupholstered seat, raised on block- and baluster-turned legs w/a turned front stretcher, New England, second half 18th c., pr. **690.00**

Queen Anne side chairs, walnut, an oxyoke crestrail above spooned stiles flanking a solid vase-form splat, upholstered slip seat, cabriole front legs ending in raised pad feet, turned & blocked canted rear legs, legs joined by turned stretchers, old finish, Massachusetts, 18th c., 40¾" h., set of 4 (minor repairs) **23,100.00**

Queen Anne transitional country-style side chair, birch, oxbow crestrail w/eared ends above a simple pierced vase splat on a lower rail above the woven rush seat, block- and knob-turned front legs ending in raised pad feet & joined by a ball- and ring-turned front stretcher, swelled side & back stretchers, old cherry finish, 18th c., 38¾" h. (replaced rush seat) **935.00**

Victorian armchair, Renaissance Revival substyle,walnut, the high upholstered back between slender backswept stiles above round molded & scroll-pierced half-arms above the wide rectangular upholstered seat on a wide seatrail carved w/large bottons, cabriole front legs ending in paw feet, scrolled back legs, attributed to Pottier & Stymus, New York, New York, ca. 1870, 38" h. **1,093.00**

Rare Egyptian Revival Armchair

Victorian armchair, Egyptian Revival substyle, ebonized & parcel-gilt wood, the thick upholstered back w/a rolled crest flanked by rolled square stiles w/heavy turned projecting crest knobs, heavy padded open arms w/a half-round hand grip above the carved full-

figural sphinx arm support, the overupholstered seat flanked by deep side rails w/pierced arched bands of gilt-incised palmette devices, heavy paw front feet, on casters, ca. 1870, 39½" h. (ILLUS.) **8,050.00**

Victorian country-style side chairs, painted & decorated, the back w/two arched & shaped rails decorated w/florals above the balloon-front caned seat, knob-and-ring-turned front legs joined by two ring-turned stretchers, plain turned side & back stretchers, overall h.p. decoration & gilt trim, New England, ca. 1850, set of 6 (two seats damaged, three chairs repaired) **345.00**

Victorian country-style side chairs, balloon-back style, painted & decorated, the rounded crestrail continuing to tapering stiles flanking the wide vase-form splat, shaped plank seat on slightly canted ring-turned legs joined by turned stretchers, decorated w/original brown painted stencilled & free-hand decorated w/a fruit basket & scrolls on the crest & fruit cluster & banding on the splat, striping trim, in yellow, pink, gold, blue, red & green, Pennsylvania, mid-19th c., 33½" h., set of 6 . . . **1,485.00**

Victorian lady's parlor chair, Rococo substyle, walnut, the tall "balloon" back w/a finger-carved frame surrounding the tufted upholstered back curving down to swelled sides above the over-upholstered spring seat, demi-cabriole front legs, on casters, reupholstered, ca. 1860, 37" h. . . . **220.00**

Victorian Sewing Rocker

Victorian rocker without arms,
Renaissance Revival substyle,
walnut & burl walnut, the stepped
crestrail w/a burl panel above
reeded slightly flaring stiles framing
a caned back, angled open skirt
guards on the round caned seat
w/a small front shaped drop, ring-
turned front legs joined by a
matching stretcher, plain side &
back stretchers, recaned, late
19th c. (ILLUS.) **145.00**

Victorian "Grecian" Rocker

Victorian rocking chair, walnut,
country-style "Grecian" rocker
w/arms, the gently arched crestrail
above a row of short turned
spindles over the rectangular
caned back panel between the
curved stiles continuing to form
looped & scrolled open arms,
rounded cane seat, turned front
legs & stretcher, plain side & rear
stretchers, ca. 1880, 40" h.
(ILLUS.) **165.00**

Victorian Cane-seat Side Chair

Victorian side chair, Renaissance
Revival country-style, walnut, the
arched crestrail above a row of
ring-turned spindles above a lower
rail & a bottom back rail, long S-
form angular skirt guards on the
rounded caned seat, ring- and rod-
turned front legs w/double turned
front stretchers, plain side & back
stretchers, recaned, ca. 1890
(ILLUS.) **94.00**

American Cattle Horn Side Chair

Victorian side chair, cattle horn
construction, the crestrail formed
by a pair of long downturned cattle
horns joined by a rectangular back
pad to the long S-form cattle horn
side rails & back supports, rounded
upholstered seat raised on
intertwined curved cattle horns
forming the legs, late 19th c.,
39½" h. (ILLUS.) **920.00**

Unusual Baroque Revival Chairs

Victorian side chairs, Baroque
Revival substyle, walnut, tall back
topped by an ornately carved
crestrail w/a raised central arched
pediment above a carved face
flanked by carved griffins, scroll-
carved frieze band above an

arched central upholstered panel flanked by free-standing square stiles ending in short seat brackets at the overupholstered seat, deep apron w/line-incised decoration, shoulder knob- and rod-turned front legs, late 19th c., set of 12 (ILLUS. of part) **17,600.00**

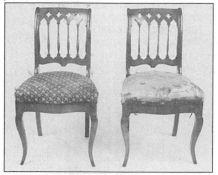

Victorian Gothic Revival Side Chairs

Victorian side chairs, Gothic Revival substyle, mahogany, the gently curved flat crestrail pierced w/a row of quatrefoils above Gothic arch openings separated by slender baluster-turned spindles, serpentine back base rail raised above the overupholstered spring seat, serpentine front seatrail & simple cabriole front legs w/canted square rear legs, old refinish, minor imperfections, New York City, ca. 1850, 33¾" h., pr. (ILLUS.) **978.00**

Bust-carved Victorian Side Chairs

Victorian side chairs, Renaissance Revival substyle, carved walnut, the arched & scroll-carved crestrail centered by full-relief Renaissance-style portrait busts of a man or a woman, ached padded back panel, low S-form skirt guards flank the

overupholstered spring seat, curved seatrail w/carved drop, ring- and rod-turned front legs on casters, ca. 1875-85, 37" h., pr. (ILLUS.) **248.00**

Renaissance Revival Side Chairs

Victorian side chairs, Renaissance Revival substyle, walnut, the arched scroll-carved crestrail centered by a palmette over burl panels & rondel corners above the shaped stiles enclosing the upholstered back panel, curved skirt guards flank the overupholstered spring seat w/a burl panel & carved drop on the seatrail, ring- and rod-turned tapering front legs on casters, velour upholstery, ca.1875-85, 39" h., pr. (ILLUS.) **193.00**

Belter "Cornucopia" Side Chair

Victorian side chairs, Rococo substyle, laminated & pierce-carved rosewood, the balloon back w/a tall, wide pierce-carved frame of florals, leafy vines & scrolls enclosing the oblong upholstered back panel, overupholstered spring seat w/a serpentine seatrail further carved w/florals & continuing to demi-cabriole front legs, on casters, the "Cornucopia" patt. by John H. Belter, New York, ca. 1850, pr. (ILLUS. of one) . . . **20,100.00**

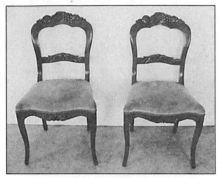

Victorian Rococo Side Chairs

Victorian side chairs, Rococo substyle, walnut, balloon-back type w/the arched crestrail carved w/fruits & nuts above a scroll-carved lower rail, serpentine-sided overupholstered seat above a scroll-carved seatrail, simple cabriole front legs & canted rear legs, mid-19th c., set of 10 (ILLUS. of two) **1,320.00**

Victorian Aesthetic Slipper Chair

Victorian slipper chair, Aesthetic Movement substyle, inlaid & parcel-gilt rosewood, the arched crestrail w/fine stylized floral inlay flanked by square tapering inlaid stiles enclosing the upholstered back pad above a row of short turned spindles, wide spring overupholstered seat, turned tapering & decorated front legs & canted square rear legs all on casters, attributed to the Herter

Brothers, New York, ca. 1880, no seat upholstery, 30¼" h. (ILLUS.) **3,450.00**
William & Mary "Heart-and-Crown" armchair, the scrolled arched crestrail pierced w/a heart above molded spindles between turned stiles, the shaped open arms above horizontal turned sides, all raised on turned legs joined by turned stretchers, painted black, New England, second half 18th c. **2,875.00**

William & Mary "Banister-back" Chair

William & Mary side chair, painted & turned "banister-back," the arched crestrail above four split banisters flanked by block-, baluster- and ring-turned stiles w/acorn finials, raised above the trapezoidal woven rush seat, block- and baluster-turned front legs joined by a double-knob turned front stretcher & plain side & back stretchers, front knob feet, Massachusetts, 18th c., 46" h. (ILLUS.) **1,380.00**
Windsor "arrow-back" armchair, the back w/three small arrow spindles above five large spindles, shaped seat raised on bamboo-turned canted legs joined by bamboo-turned stretchers, early 19th c. **632.00**
Windsor "arrow-back" armchair, painted & decorated, the flat crestrail above a back w/vertical arrow slats, plank seat & canted, turned legs w/stretchers, original yellow paint w/free-hand floral & fruit decoration, New England, early 19th c., 33½" h. **1,380.00**

Windsor "Arrow-back" Rocker

Windsor "arrow-back" rocker, painted & decorated, the very tall back w/bamboo-turned slightly canted stiles flanking three graduated slats, the narrow lower slat above four arrow-form spindles, the shaped arms each over two arrow-form spindles & a canted bamboo-turned arm support, wide squared thick plank seat w/rounded corners, slightly canted bamboo-turned legs joined by an arrow front rung & plain back rungs, on tapering rockers, painted brown & black graining bordered by gold & green striping, possibly Maine, ca. 1830 (ILLUS.) **575.00**

Windsor "arrow-back" side chair, painted, a wide arched crestrail above three arrow slats between the tapering 'rabbit-ear' stiles, shaped plank seat, canted turned & tapering legs joined by plain turned rungs, old black finish, mid-19th c., 33¾" h. **165.00**

Windsor "arrow-back" side chairs, the wide arched crest flanked by canted tapering stiles w/three arrow slats in the back above the shaped saddle seat, on canted bamboo-turned legs joined by simple turned box stretchers, original red & brown mottled paint w/free-hand yellow-painted foliate designs, New England, ca. 1830, 33¼" h., set of 6 . . . . **4,313.00**

Windsor "bamboo-turned" side chair, painted & decorated, the wide flat crestrail decorated w/h.p. floral reserve between canted &

tapering stiles flanking four slender turned & tapering spindles, shaped plank seat on canted bamboo-turned legs joined by bamboo-turned box stretchers, original red & black graining w/green & yellow striping & yellow floral decoration, branded "Kilburn," Stephen Kilbourn or Kilburn, New London, Ohio, first half 19th c., 34¾" h. (some wear) **1,360.00**

Windsor "bamboo-turned" tall-back rocker w/arms, the tall back w/a slightly stepped solid crestrail w/cut-out end sections attached to the gently outswept turned stiles flanking the seven tall curved bamboo-turned spindles, S-scroll arms on a bamboo-turned spindle & canted arm support, wide shaped plank seat, raised on canted bamboo-turned legs on rockers joined by stretchers, old worn mustard yellow graining over earlier red, early 19th c., 43½" h. . . . **660.00**

Windsor "birdcage" side chair, decorated, the double rail "birdcage" crestrail w/three short spindles over seven tall bamboo-turned spindles between canted bamboo-turned stiles over the shaped plank seat, canted bamboo-turned legs joined by bamboo-turned box stretchers, old black paint w/yellow striping & yellow & red stenciled decal, early 19th c., 35" h. **193.00**

Windsor "birdcage" side chairs, painted, each w/a double bamboo-turned crestrail centered by three short spindles above seven tall bamboo-turned spindles flanked by canted bamboo-turned stiles, shaped plank seat raised on slightly canted bamboo-turned legs joined by bamboo-turned box stretchers, old black paint, New England, 1800-20, 32½" h., set of 6 (minor imperfections) **6,325.00**

Windsor "bow-back" side chairs, ash & pine, bowed & incised crestrail above seven slender turned spindles over the shaped saddle seat, raised on canted bamboo-turned legs joined by a bamboo-turned H-stretcher, old refinish, New England, early 19th c., 38¾" h., pr. (repair) **1,150.00**

Windsor "bowed brace-back" armchair, the arched backrail over seven slender baluster-turned spindles & a pair of turned back

Windsor "Bowed Brace-back" Chair

braces, shaped open arms on a small turned spindles & baluster- and ring-turned canted arm support, shaped saddle seat, canted baluster-, ring- and rod-turned legs joined by a swelled H-stetcher, Rhode Island, ca. 1800 (ILLUS.) **2,530.00**

Windsor "braced fan-back" side chair, the narrow serpentine crestrail w/rounded ears over six plain turned spindles & a brace support w/two spindles all flanked by slender canted baluster- and ring-turned stiles, shaped saddle seat raised on canted baluster-, ring & tapering rod-turned legs joined by a swelled H-stretcher, old brown paint, possibly Connecticut, ca. 1780, 37¼" h. **2,990.00**

Windsor "Comb-back" Armchair

Windsor "comb-back" armchair, maple & ash, the shaped curved upturned crestrail above seven

slender spindles continuing through a medial rail ending in slender shaped arms above a canted spindle & baluster- and ring-turned arm support, shaped saddle seat raised on widely canted baluster-, ring & rod-turned legs joined by a swelled H-stretcher, old dark surface, imperfections, rear height loss, Connecticut, 1780-1800, 36¼" h. (ILLUS.). **1,610.00**

Windsor "comb-back" armchair, bamboo-turned wood, a stepped & curved crestrail raised on six tall turned spindles above a bowed backrail above seven slender bamboo-turned spindles w/shaped mahogany arms over two shorter spindles & canted bamboo-turned arm supports, simple shaped plank seat raised on slightly canted bamboo-turned legs joined by a bamboo-turned H-stretcher, old black paint, New England, ca. 1810, 46" h. (repairs) **748.00**

Windsor "comb-back" rocking chair w/arms, painted wood, a serpentine crestrail above seven long slender spindles continuing down through a bowed rail connected to a medial rail continuing to form flat arms w/rounded handholds, two canted bamboo-turned spindles & arm support under the arms, shaped oblong plank seat, canted bamboo-turned legs joined by a bamboo-turned H-stretcher above mortised rockers, black repaint w/yellow striping & stenciled floral design on top crest, old marriage record under seat, early 19th c., 43½" h. . . **880.00**

"Continuous-arm" Windsor

Windsor "continuous arm" armchair, painted wood, the arched crestrail continuing to slender hand holds all above simple turned spindles & baluster- and ring-turned canted arm supports, shaped saddle seat raised on canted baluster-, ring- and rod-turned legs joined by a swelled H-stretcher, old worn green repaint, breaks, repair to one arm, late 18th c., 36½" h. (ILLUS.) **2,090.00**

Windsor "continuous-arm" armchair, pine & hickory, a bowed crestrail continuing to shaped arm rails above seven turned & tapering back spindles & six arm supports above a shield-shaped seat raised on tapering bamboo-turned canted legs joined by a swelled H-stretcher, New England, late 18th c. (repair to crestrail) **1,035.00**

Windsor "fan-back" armchair, the serpentine crestrail w/scrolled ears above seven tall spindles continuing through the flattened medial rail that extends to form flat arms w/scroll-carved handgrips above two short spindles & a canted baluster- and ring-turned arm support, wide shaped saddle seat on canted baluster- and ring-turned legs joined by a swelled H-stetcher, old mellow refinishing, underside of seat w/traces of old paint & stamped "P.S. Byrn 1708," 43½" h. (variation in leg turnings, portion of one handgrip replaced) **3,960.00**

Rare Windsor Highchair

Windsor "fan-back" highchair, painted, the curved serpentine crestrail w/round terminals above five tall plain spindles between tall baluster- and ring-turned stiles, bamboo-turned arms on a turned spindle & baluster-, ring- and rod-turned arm support, shaped saddle seat, on very tall canted baluster-, ring- and rod-turned legs joined by a swelled H-stretcher, old worn red umber & black graining & free-hand yellow decoration, possibly southeastern Massachusetts, ca. 1780, 35¾" h. (ILLUS.) **28,750.00**

Windsor "Fan-back" Side Chair

Windsor "fan-back" side chair, ash, cherry & maple, the serpentine crestrail w/scroll-carved terminals above seven plain spindles & canted baluster-, ring- & rod-turned stiles w/plain forked brace spindles at the back, shaped saddle seat raised on canted baluster-, ring- and rod-turned legs joined by a swelled H-stretcher, New England, ca. 1780, 36" h. (ILLUS.) **1,150.00**

Windsor "fan-back" side chairs, serpentine crestrail w/rounded ears above eight slender spindles flanked by canted baluster- and ring-turned stiles, shaped saddle seat above canted baluster- and ring-turned legs joined by a swelled H-stretcher, old refinishing, 36" h., pr. (age cracks in seat, minor damage to one stile). **1,320.00**

Windsor "fan-back" side chairs, maple, pine & ash, a serpentine crestrail ending in scrolls above seven turned spindles & slender baluster- and ring-turned canted stiles over the shaped saddle seat, canted ring- and baluster-turned legs joined by a swelled H-stretcher, New England, ca. 1780, 36½" h., pr. **2,990.00**

Low-back Windsor Armchair

Windsor "low-back" armchair,
turned wood, a curved molded
crest above the U-form crestrail
continuing to form shaped flat arms
all above numerous simple turned
spindles & baluster- and ring-
turned arm supports, wide shaped
saddle seat, canted baluster- and
ring-turned legs joined by a swelled
H-stretcher, Pennsylvania, late
18th c. (ILLUS.) **2,990.00**

Windsor "low-back" armchair,
maple, ash & poplar, the low
curved & shaped crest centered on
the U-form flat crestrail continuing
to form shaped arms all above
numerous simple turned spindles &
baluster- and ring-turned arm
supports, wide shaped saddle seat
on canted & turned legs joined by a
swelled H-stretcher, old refinish,
late 18th c., 29½" h.
(imperfections) **1,265.00**

Windsor "Rod-back" Highchair

Windsor "rod-back" highchair,
painted wood, the slightly arched
crestrail above four bamboo-turned
spindles & canted bamboo-turned
stiles, turned open arm rods on
canted bamboo-turned arm
supports, shaped saddle seat, tall
canted bamboo-turned legs joined
by a swelled H-stretcher, old red
paint, minor surface imperfections,
New England, early 19th c., "TH"
carved on underside of seat,
32½" h. (ILLUS.). **1,150.00**

Windsor "sack-back" armchair, the
bowed crestrail over six long
spindles continuing through a flat
medial rail that extends to form flat
shaped arms over canted ring- and
baluster-turned arm supports,
shaped saddle seat on canted ring-
and baluster-turned legs joined by
a swelled H-stretcher, painted
black, a plaque attached under the
seat identifying owners from 18th c.
to early 20th c., late 18th - early
19th c. **3,737.00**

Windsor "Sack-back" Armchair

Windsor "sack-back" armchair, the
bowed crestrail over seven plain
spindles continuing through the
medial rail which terminates in
scrolled hand grips above a short
spindle & canted baluster-, ring-
and rod-turned arm supports,
shaped saddle seat, canted
baluster-, ring- and rod-turned legs
joined by a swelled H-stretcher, old
worn brown finish, attributed to
Connecticut, 18th c., 28½" h.
(ILLUS.) **2,750.00**

Windsor "sack-back" armchair,
ash, pine & maple, the arched
crestrail continuing to a medial rail
continuing to form slender arms,
nine slender turned spindles from
the seat to the crestrail, canted
baluster- and ring-turned arm
supports above the wide shaped
saddle seat raised on canted
baluster- and ring-turned legs
joined by a swelled H-stretcher, old
refinish, New England, ca. 1780,
38½" h. **1,380.00**

Windsor "sack-back" armchair,
painted, the high bowed crestrail
above seven spindles continuing
down through the medial rail
extending to four scrolled arms
above spindles & canted baluster-
and ring-turned arm supports, wide
shaped saddle seat, canted
baluster-, ring- and rod-turned legs
joined by a swelled H-stretcher, old
black paint, New England, ca.
1780, 39½" h. **3,335.00**

Windsor-Style "Sack-back" Armchair

Windsor-Style "sack-back"
armchair, hardwood, the bowed
crestrail above plain spindles
continuing through the medial rail
which ends in shaped flat arms
over short spindles & canted
baluster- and ring-turned arm
supports, oblong shaped seat on
canted baluster-, ring- and rod-
turned legs joined by a swelled
H-stretcher, mahogany finish, ca.
1930, 36" h. (ILLUS.). **66.00**

CHESTS & CHESTS OF DRAWERS

Adirondack-style Blanket Chest

Adirondack-style blanket chest,
painted & twig-decorated, the
hinged rectangular top opening to a
deep well, the front & sides
decorated w/applied designs
centering moons, stars & planets
on the front, shaped aprons &
bracket feet w/bands of applied
twigs, old light red paint, New York,
early 20th c. minor paint loss,
16⅞ x 33¾", 23½" h. (ILLUS.). **633.00**

Decorated Pennsylvania Blanket Chest

Blanket chest, Chippendale country-
style, painted & decorated pine &
poplar, rectangular hinged top
w/molded edges opening to a deep
well, the dovetailed case decorated
on the front w/original brown & blue
graining in oblong panels flanking a
large white central heart decorated
w/flowers & the inscription "Johan
Witmer 1799," a mid-molding over
two drawers at the bottom, each
w/two simple bail pulls, molded
base on scroll-cut ogee bracket
feet, Pennsylvania (ILLUS.) **22,000.00**

Blanket chest, country-style, painted,
the hinged rectangular top w/a
molded edge opening to a well
fitted w/a till, plain case raised on
bracket feet, first quarter 19th c.,
20 x 33", 19" h. **517.00**

Blanket chest, country-style, painted & decorated pine, six-board construction, the rectangular top w/shaped end brackets opening to a deep well w/a lidded till above the dovetailed case on a molded base & a flat apron w/a central double drop & simple bracket feet, decorated overall w/a grained design in orange & burnt sienna done in an arrangement of large fans & clusters of ovals, New England, 19th c., 17¼ x 37½", 21⅛" h. (imperfections) **1,495.00**

Blanket chest, country-style, painted, six-board construction, molded rectangular hinged top opening to a well w/a molded lidded till, shaped sides, nailed case, original red paint, New Durham, New Hampshire, 18th c., 17 x 47", 23" h. **1,150.00**

Blanket chest, country-style, painted & decorated poplar, the rectangular lid w/molded edges opening to a well w/a lidded till, dovetailed case above two drawers at the bottom on a base molding & simple cut-out bracket feet, the case w/original red & black graining & black trim, simple stenciled detail on the feet, the case w/three small floral transfer-printed decals across the front, till lid inscribed in pencil "D.S. Yoder, Scalpland, Cumbria Co. Pa. Apr. 10, 1882," 20¼ x 44¼", 27¼" h. (till lid damage) **3,300.00**

Blanket chest, painted & decorated pine & poplar, rectangular hinged lid w/molded edge opening to a well w/a lidded till, dovetailed case w/base molding, raised on turned bulbous tapering feet, decorated w/original red graining on a light colored ground, 19th c., 43¼" l. . . . **440.00**

Blanket chest, painted & decorated pine & poplar, rectangular hinged top w/molded edges opening to a well w/till above the dovetailed case on a molded base w/scroll-cut ogee bracket feet, original brown brushed graining on an orangish red ground, back dated "1852" in red paint, professionally cleaned, Berks County, Pennsylvania, late 18th - early 19th c., 20½ x 44¾", 26½" h. **3,300.00**

Blanket chest, child's, painted & decorated pine, six-board construction, the hinged top w/molded edge opening to a deep well in the dovetailed case raised

on bracket feet, painted light blue, the front w/free-hand decoration in yellow inscribed "J.J. H. 1820" in a wreath flanked by tulips & meandering vines at the ends above a pinwheel, Schoharie County, New York, 1820, 13¾ x 37", 15½" h. (imperfections) **2,645.00**

Blanket chest, William & Mary country-style, painted, a rectangular hinged top w/molded edge opening to a deep well above a case w/two long false drawers above two long real drawers all w/brass quatrefoil plates w/teardrop pulls & matching keyhole escutcheons, wide molded base raised on short slender legs ending in large turnip-form turned feet, New England, early 18th c., 21 x 41½", 40" h. **1,265.00**

Carpenter's chest, cherry, a thick rectangular hinged top opening to a deep well, heavy edge moldings around the top & bottom edges of the dovetailed base, interior tray & saw holder, old finish, late 19th c., 13 x 28¾", 12" h. **220.00**

Carpenter's chest, poplar, rectangular hinged top opening to a fitted interior, dovetailed case w/old worn dark patina, base molding, 19th c., 22¾ x 48½", 23" h. (age cracks, some edge damage, front lid molding replaced) **193.00**

Chippendale chest of drawers, cherry, a rectangular top above molded band over the case w/fluted quarter columns flanking the four long graduated drawers w/simple bail pulls & inlaid ivory keyhole escutcheons, molded base above scroll-cut ogee bracket feet, refinished, Pennsylvania, late 18th c., 22¾ x 42½", 38½" h. (feet & brasses replaced) **2,200.00**

Chippendale chest of drawers, cherry, a rectangular top w/molded edges & notched corners above a case of four long graduated cockbeaded drawers w/simple bail pulls & brass keyhole escutcheons, molded base on scroll-cut ogee bracket feet, old refinish, restoration, probably Connecticut. ca/ 1780, 19 x 39¼", 33½" h. **2,645.00**

Chippendale country-style chest of drawers, cherry, a rectangular top w/molded edges above a case w/four long graduated thumb-molded drawers w/simple bail handles flanked by fluted quarter-round corner columns, molded base raised on ogee bracket feet, replaced brasses, old refinish, Pennsylvania, 18th c., 19¼ x 38", 34⅛" h. (repairs) **4,313.00**

Chippendale country-style chest of drawers, painted cherry, the rectangular top above a case of four long graduated drawers w/simple turned wood knobs, molded base on simple shaped bracket feet, red paint, replaced pulls, New England, late 18th c., 18¾ x 40¼", 42½" h. (minor imperfections). **1,265.00**

Chippendale "serpentine-front" chest of drawers, cherry, the rectangular top w/molded edges & a serpentine front overhanging a conforming case w/four long graduated cockbeaded drawers w/oval brass pulls & keyhole escutcheons, molded base on scroll-cut ogee bracket feet, old finish, pulls may be early replacements, probably Massachusetts, ca. 1780, 19¾ x 36¼", 33½" h. (minor imperfections) **42,550.00**

Chippendale "serpentine-front" chest of drawers, mahogany & mahogany veneer, a rectangular top w/a serpentine front above a conforming case of four long graduated cockbeaded drawers w/simple bail pulls, molded base on ogee bracket feet, old refinish, some old brasses, Massachusetts, ca. 1780, 19½ x 40", 35¾" h. (restoration) **2,875.00**

Tall Chippendale Chest of Drawers

Chippendale tall chest of drawers, carved cherry, a rectangular top w/a deep coved cornice carved w/a dentil band above a case fitted w/two pairs of short drawers flanking a deep central fan-carved drawer over three long thumb-molded drawers all flanked by engaged, fluted & stop-fluted quarter columns w/bases & capitals, molded base on scroll-cut bracket feet, butterfly brasses, old refinish, replaced brasses, repairs, Connecticut, mid- to late 18th c., 19¼ x 38", 43½" h. (ILLUS.). **2,070.00**

Chippendale tall chest of drawers, carved maple, rectangular top w/a deep flaring molded cornice above a case of six thumb-molded long graduated drawers w/butterfly pulls, the top drawer w/central fan carving & a faux three-drawer facade, the case w/a molded base raised on tall bracket feet, old refinish, replaced brasses, New England, last quarter 18th c., 18 x 36", 4' 10¾" h. (restoration) **5,060.00**

Chippendale tall chest of drawers, maple, the rectangular top w/a narrow flaring cornice over stepped dentil frieze bands above a row of three small thumb-molded drawers over a pair of matching longer drawers above a stack of five long graduated drawers, simple bail pulls & rectangular keyhole escutcheons, molded base w/a flat apron centered by a drop pendant & raised on scroll-cut bracket feet, old brasses, refinished, Rhode Island, late 18th c., 16¾ x 36", 5' 11" h. (imperfections) **8,338.00**

Chippendale tall chest of drawers, painted pine, the rectangular top above a stepped cornice over a case w/five long, graduated thumb-molded drawers w/simple bail pulls, molded base w/scroll-cut bracket feet, old red paint, back dated "1802," New England, late 18th c., replaced brasses, 17 x 35½", 44¼" h. (imperfections) **4,313.00**

Chippendale chest-on-chest, cherry, two-part construction: the upper section w/a rectangular top w/a deep flaring coved cornice above a case w/five long graduated overlapping drawers w/simple bails & brass keyhole escutcheons; the lower section w/a mid-molding over a case of four long graduated overlapping drawers, molded base

Chippendale Chest-on-Chest

on tall cut-out bracket feet, refinished, minor age cracks, replaced brasses, Connecticut, 18th c., 19 x 38½", 6' 1½" h. (ILLUS.) **7,700.00**

Chippendale chest-on-chest, maple, two-part construction: the upper section w/a rectangular top over a deep flaring molded cornice over a stack of five long graduated thumb-molded drawers w/brass butterfly pulls & keyhole escutcheons; the lower section w/a mid-molding over a stack of four long graduated drawers w/ matching pulls, molded base w/scroll-cut bracket feet, old refinish, original brasses, Massachusetts or New Hampshire, 18th c., 18½ x 38½", 6' 4½" h. **11,500.00**

Chippendale country-style chest over drawers, painted & decorated, the rectangular hinged top w/molded edges opening to a deep well above a case of two thumb-molded false long drawers over three long graduated working drawers, all w/simple bail pulls, high scroll-cut bracket feet, original reddish orange grain paint resembling exotic wood, Massachusetts, late 18th c., 19¼ x 35¼", 46" h. (replaced brasses, very minor imperfections) **4,485.00**

Classical Tiger Stripe Maple Chest

Classical (American Empire) chest of drawers, tiger stripe maple, a rectangular top above a deep long drawer slightly overhanging a case w/three long graduated drawers flanked by ring-turned side columns on blocks, flat apron raised on ring- and knob-turned legs on casters, old round embossed brass pulls, old refinish, very minor imperfections, probably New England, ca. 1825, 22½ x 47", 41 1¾" h. (ILLUS.) **2,415.00**

Fine Classical Chest of Drawers

Classical chest of drawers, decorated cherry, a rectangular top above a long, deep drawer w/light veneer banding & a pair of early pressed glass knobs above a narrow rounded drawer over a veneer band above the set-back set of three long drawers w/glass pulls flanked by black-painted &

gilt-stenciled pilasters above base blocks over baluster- and ring-turned legs on casters, ca. 1840 (ILLUS.) **770.00**

Classical chest of drawers,
mahogany, a rectangular top above a molded frieze drawer & three setback long drawers between fluted pilasters, on turned feet, second quarter 19th c. **517.00**

Mahogany Classical Chest of Drawers

Classical chest of drawers,
mahogany & mahogany veneer, a high flat crestrail above a narrow shelf over a pair of small handkerchief drawers on the stepped-out rectangular top above an overhanging round-fronted long drawer over three long flat drawers flanked by free-standing ring-turned columns above tall turned double-knob feet, one drawer stenciled "Walter Corey, Furniture Warehouse...Portland, ME," w/Egyptian Revival mounts, early 19th c., 20¼ x 43½", 4' 3½" h. (ILLUS.) **1,495.00**

Classical chest of drawers, child's,
painted & decorated, a high rectangular splashboard across the top centered by a short shelf over two small handkerchief drawers on the stepped-out rectangular top overhanging the case w/a deep long top drawer overhanging three long graduated drawers flanked by cyma-curve pilasters w/C-scroll feet, tapering turned rear legs, painted ground decorated on top surfaces w/a compote of fruit,

Child's Classical Chest of Drawers

wreathed landscape reserves & floral sprays, the drawers w/wood graining, wear, age crack, ca. 1840, 13 x 20", 22" h. (ILLUS.) **863.00**

Classical chest of drawers w/mirror, a narrow rectangular stepped top above three aligned short drawers supporting a pair of tall S-scroll acanthus-carved uprights flanking a molded-edge rectangular swiveling mirror, the case w/a rectangular slightly overhanging top above a central drawer flanked by two short drawers over a single long drawer, raised on ring-turned & spiral-leaf carved tapering legs w/peg feet in brass casters, Massachusetts, ca. 1820, 21 x 40½", 5' 2" h. (molding losses & repairs, top cracked) . . . **1,495.00**

Classical country-style chest of drawers, cherry, a rectangular top over a long round-fronted drawer w/two wooden pulls overhanging a stack of three additional flat long drawers w/wooden pulls flanked by long ogee side pilasters ending in C-scroll front feet, old worn refinishing, ca. 1840, 22 x 43¼", 46¼" h. **220.00**

Classical country-style chest of drawers, cherry & bird's-eye maple, the rectangular top fitted w/a narrow row of three serpentine-fronted handkerchief drawers each separated by a half-round ring-turned column & faced w/crotch-grain mahogany veneer, the case w/a long deep drawer overhanging three long graduated drawers all w/pairs of leaf-carved pulls, a scroll-cut apron & bracket feet, the

Fine Country-Style Classical Chest

facade in bird's-eye maple, paneled sides, short S-curve brackets at sides below top drawer applied w/half-round turned drops over outset sides, refinished, 23¼ x 42½", 46½" h. (ILLUS.) . . . **1,265.00**

Classical Country Chest of Drawers

Classical country-style chest of drawers, grained & mahogany-veneered, a flat low crestrail above a narrow shelf over a pair of mahogany-veneered small handkerchief drawers on the stepped-out rectangular top over a case w/a deep long drawer overhanging a stack of three long drawers flanked by cyma-curve side pilasters w/C-scroll feet, turned back feet, original orange & yellow graining w/mahogany veneer on drawers & pilasters, original turned wood pulls, minor surface imperfections, northern New England, ca. 1835-45, 17 x 41", 47" h. (ILLUS.) **288.00**

Classical country-style chest of drawers, curly & bird's-eye maple & mahogany veneer, the long stepped crestrail in curly maple w/mahogany veneer edge banding above the rectangular top w/mahogany edge banding above a deep long top drawer faced in bird's-eye maple w/mahogany banding & two turned wood knobs slightly overhanging a case w/three long graduated matching drawers flanked by long cyma-curve pilasters, short baluster- and ring-turned front legs, ca. 1840, 21¾ x 43¾", overall 4' 8" h. (age cracks, edge & veneer damage) **715.00**

Country Storage Chest

Country-style storage chest, painted pine, a square top w/applied beaded edge above a tall case of four incised beaded drawers, paneled sides joining square corners on short ring-turned legs, old brown varnish, imperfections, New England, early 19th c., 18½" sq., 29¼" h. (ILLUS.) **690.00**

Federal "bow-front" chest of drawers, cherry & mahogany veneer, the rectangular top w/gently bowed front above a conforming case w/four long, graduated drawers w/original oval brasses & keyhole escutcheons above a molded base & scalloped apron raised on tall French feet, old surface, New Hampshire, early 19th c., 20¾ x 41¾", 37½" h. . . . **2,185.00**

Federal "bowfront" chest of drawers, mahogany & tiger stripe maple, rectangular top w/molded edges & a bowfront & ovolo corners w/edge crossbanding over a case w/four long cockbeaded graduated drawers w/central tiger stripe maple inlaid panel flanked by mahogany panels & bordered by contrasting stringing & crossbanding, the quarter - engaged ring-turned reeded posts continuing to short baluster-turned legs w/peg feet, old refinish, turned wood pulls, probably Massachusetts, 1815-25, 20¾ x 40¼", 38¼" h. (minor imperfections) **2,530.00**

Federal chest of drawers w/mirror, a rectangular mirror w/a flat frame swivels between S-scroll uprights above a pair of stepped-back handkerchief drawers on the rectangular top, the case w/two long graduated drawers, raised on ring-, knob- and rod-turned legs w/knob feet, replaced small round brass pulls, old refinish, New England, 1810-20, 19¼ x 38¼", 4' 10¾" h. (restoration) **863.00**

Federal "Bow-Front" Chest of Drawers

Federal country-style "bow-front" chest of drawers, cherry w/curly maple facade, the rectangular top w/a bowed front above a conforming case w/four long graduated drawers w/applied edge beading raised on ring- and knob-turned legs w/knob feet, old but not original round brasses & keyhole escutcheons, minor veneer damage, age cracks & pieced repairs, refinished, early 19th c., 22½ x 40", 40¾" h. (ILLUS.). **1,595.00**

Federal country-style chest of drawers, cherry & bird's-eye maple, rectangular top above a molded edge over a narrow case of three deep graduated bird's-eye

maple drawers w/two turned wood knobs each, paneled ends, inlaid brass keyhole escutcheons, short swelled turned legs ending in knob & peg feet, old red stain, found in Pennsylvania, first half 19th c., 16¾ x 29½", 38¾" h. **7,700.00**

Federal country-style chest of drawers, cherry & tiger stripe maple, a rectangular cherry top above a cherry case fitted w/four long tiger stripe maple drawers w/replaced oval brasses & keyhole escutcheons, the top deep drawer above three graduated drawers, flat apron & tall tapering flat feet, refinished, New England, early 19th c., 18¾ x 43", 40¼" h. (imperfections) **1,380.00**

Federal country-style chest of drawers, cherry, rectangular top above a case w/four long graduated drawers w/two turned wood knobs each, paneled ends, on ring- and baluster-turned legs w/knob feet, old dark worn finish, early 19th c., 20¾ x 40½", 44½" h. (replaced knobs, some age cracks & edge damage) **550.00**

Federal country-style chest of drawers, cherry & curly maple, the rectangular cherry top above a cherry case w/a pair of narrow curly maple drawers above a deep, long curly maple drawer over three long graduated curly maple drawers, all w/turned wood knobs, serpentine apron & tall outswept French feet, mahogany veneer trim, early 19th c., 19¾ x 46½", 47¼" h. (feet & apron edge damage, old repairs to veneer & facings) **825.00**

Federal country-style chest of drawers, painted pine, the rectangular top above a case w/two narrow drawers above four long, graduated thumb-molded drawers w/turned wood knobs, scalloped apron above simple French feet, light yellow paint, ca. 1790-1810, 18 x 35¼", 37½" h. (imperfections) **2,185.00**

Federal country-style chest of drawers, tiger stripe maple, the rectangular top slightly overhanging the case w/four long graduated beaded drawers w/oval brasses, applied reeded base band above the shaped apron & tall

Federal Tiger Stripe Chest of Drawers

French feet, refinished, New England, ca. 1810, 19 x 40½", 39¾" h. (ILLUS.). **5,750.00**

Federal country-style chest of drawers, walnut & cherry, the rectangular top w/a three-quarter gallery, the high crestboard cut w/facing scrolls & points, the side rails composed of a slender shaped rail over a row of short baluster-turned spindles, the case w/a deep long top drawer above three long graduated drawers, raised on baluster-turned legs w/peg feet, paneled ends, clear pressed glass pulls, old finish, ca. 1820, 20½ x 43¼", overall 4' 4¼" h. (some foot damage) **605.00**

Federal country-style tall chest of drawers, cherry & maple, rectangular top w/a high crestrail w/scroll-cut ends above a case fitted w/six long, graduated thumb-molded drawers w/butterfly brasses & keyhole escutcheons, molded base over a shaped apron & simple bracket feet, old refinish, replaced brasses, New England, ca. 1800, 17½ x 36", 4' 5" h. (restoration) . . **1,840.00**

Federal tall chest of drawers, satinwood-inlaid mahogany, a rectangular top slightly overhanging a case of five long graduated cockbeaded drawers w/satinwood-inlaid keyhole escutcheons above a satinwood line-inlaid base continuing to a scalloped apron raised on French feet, probably Baltimore, Maryland, ca. 1810, 20½ x 38¼", 44" h. (one foot & portions of apron repaired, losses to veneer) **1,495.00**

Federal chest-on-chest, inlaid cherry, two-part construction: the upper section w/a rectangular top w/a narrow coved cornice over a narrow geometrically-inlaid frieze band over a row of three small drawers above four long graduated drawers; the lower section w/a medial-molding above two long deep drawers, raised on slender French feet, round brass knobs & oval keyhole escutcheons, New England, early 19th c., 20¼ x 39¼", 6' 6" h. **7,475.00**

Jacobean blanket chest, carved oak, a rectangular hinged four-panel insert top above a conforming case, raised straight legs, England, 17th c., 25¼ x 48½", 23¾" h. **1,150.00**

Mission-style (Arts & Crafts movement) chest of drawers, oak, a slightly peaked crestrail on the rectangular top above a case w/two short drawers over three long drawers all w/metal pulls, Stickley Craftsman paper label, ca. 1910, 19¼ x 36", 43" h. **2,990.00**

Early Child's Mule Chest

Mule chest (box chest w/one or more drawers below a storage compartment), child's, painted pine & poplar, a rectangular hinged top w/molded edges opening to a deep well above a single long drawer w/simple turned knobs across the bottom, arched cut-out ends & scallop-cut apron, old dark green paint, imperfections, probably New England, ca. 1800, 11½ x 26¾", 22" h. (ILLUS.). **2,530.00**

Mule chest (box chest w/one or more drawers below a storage compartment), Federal country-style, painted & decorated, a rectangular hinged top w/molded edges opening to a deep well over two long bottom drawers w/replaced round brass knobs, shaped end skirts & shaped front tall bracket feet, original polychrome vinegar painting in bands of fanned designs, New England, early 19th c., 18¾ x 42⅛", 36" h. (imperfections) **20,700.00**

Mule chest (box chest w/one or more drawers below a storage compartment), country-style, painted pine & poplar, a rectangular hinged lid w/molded edges opening to a deep well , the front case w/half-round thin corner moldings above the single deep bottom drawer w/two small turned wood knobs, tall scroll-cut bracket feet, original paint, New England, early 18th c., 18½ x 36", 37" h. (minor imperfections) **4,600.00**

Mule chest (box chest w/one or more drawers below the storage compartment), painted pine, the rectangular molded hinged top opening to a deep well over two flush drawers w/simple turned wood knobs, bootjack cut-out ends & a front apron cut-out w/a band of small Gothic arches, original red paint & pulls, original surface finish, Milton, New Hampshire area, ca. 1830, 16 x 38", 38¼" h. **3,450.00**

Pilgrim Century Chest of Drawers

Pilgrim Century chest of drawers, joined oak & pine, the rectangular pine thumb-molded top above a case w/a pair of drawers over three long drawers all w/varied designs of applied raised moldings & split spindles, paneled sides & heavy molded base on large ball feet, split spindles & turned pulls ebonized maple, old Spanish brown color w/black accents, restoration, New England, late 17th c., 21½ x 39", 39½" h. (ILLUS.). **20,700.00**

Pilgriim Century chest-over-drawer, painted & decorated pine, rectangular thumb-molded cleated top opening to a deep well above a long drawer in a case w/double arched edge moldings, a straight molded front skirt & arched cut-out sides, original Spanish brown paint w/white scrolling vines accented w/vermilion red flowers, Taunton, Massachusetts area, early 18th c., 17¼ x 44", 32½" h. (minor imperfections) **31,050.00**

Queen Anne tall chest of drawers, maple, the rectangular top w/a narrow stepped flaring cornice over a pair of drawers above four long graduated drawers each w/butterfly brasses & keyhole escutcheons, molded base on cut-out tall bracket feet, old refinish, New England, 18th c., 18¾ x 36", 44½" h. (replaced brasses, restoration) . . **3,738.00**

Queen Anne tall chest of drawers, maple, a rectangular top w/a molded edge above a tall case w/a pair of small drawers above four long graduated drawers, molded base on tall scroll-cut bracket feet, engraved butterfly brasses, old refinish, probably Rhode Island, ca. 1750, 18 x 33¾", 45½" h. (repairs, imperfections) **2,645.00**

Turn-of-the-Century Tall Chest

Turn-of-the-century tall chest of drawers, oak, a serpentine crestrail above the rectangular top w/molded edge above a tall case w/five graduated drawers w/simple bail pulls, serpentine apron & short square legs, signed by the Larkin Company, ca. 1910, 18 x 33", 4' 2" h. (ILLUS.). **215.00**

Victorian chest of drawers, child's, Eastlake substyle, walnut, the tall superstructure w/a crestrail pierced & cut as a band of fleur-de-lis alternating w/pointed arches above a line-incised rail over a frieze band of pierced diamonds & rondels flanked by end blocks atop the line-incised stiles flanking the tall rectangular swiveling mirror in a reeded frame, shaped sides, atop a rectangular white marble top over a case of three long drawers each w/a narrow raised burl band & two turned wood knobs all flanked by blocked & line-incised side rails on a deep molded base, ca. 1880, 13½ x 27¼", 4' 5" h.(reconstructed top drawer) **550.00**

Victorian Small Chest of Drawers

Victorian Renaissance Revival substyle chest of drawers, walnut, a rectangular top w/molded edges above a long drawer w/two oblong incised panels slightly overhanging three long graduated drawers, carved leaf pulls, paneled sides, scroll-cut bracket feet, late 19th c., 19 x 38", 39" h. (ILLUS.). . . **303.00**

Victorian Renaissance Revival chest of drawers, walnut, an arched & scroll-cut molded crestrail above a narrow shelf over a pair of handkerchief drawers each w/two raised lozenge-shaped raised burl panels & ring-turned quarter-round corner spindles above the stepped-out rectangular top, the case w/four long reverse-graduated drawers each w/two raised lozenge-shaped burl panels w/carved fruit & leaf pulls, three short ring-turned quarter-round spindles along each canted front corner, ornate pierced & scroll-cut foot brackets, ca. 1875, 17⅞ x 40½", overall 4' 3" h. **479.00**

Fine Renaissance Revival Chest

Victorian Renaissance Revival chest of drawers w/mirror, walnut & burl walnut, the superstructure w/a high pierced & scroll-carved crest above further scrolls & arched rails w/further carving flanking a recessed round burl reserve & small burl panels over the tall rectangular mirror flanked by small candle shelves & shaped sides over small white marble tops over two small handkerchief drawers flanking a white marble top well over two long base drawers w/raised burl panels & teardrop pulls, molded base, ca. 1875, 20 x 46", 7' 10" h. (ILLUS.) **825.00**

Victorian Renaissance Revival substyle chest of drawers w/mirror, walnut & burl walnut, the superstructure w/a high arched, scalloped & scroll-cut crest above curved side rails w/applied cut-out scrolls centered by a rondel over the tall rectangular mirror w/rounded top flanked by turned drops & shaped side brackets, the top w/a pair of small handkerchief drawers flanking a white marble top well over a case w/three long drawers each w/two raised burl panels flanking a shield-form

Renaissance Revival Chest

center panel, split spindle side trim & lightly scalloped apron to bracket feet, repairs, ca. 1875, 17½ x 40¾", 6' 9" h. (ILLUS.) **330.00**

Victorian Rococo Chest of Drawers

Victorian Rococo substyle chest of drawers w/mirror, carved mahogany, the superstructure w/a high scroll-carved arched crestrail over a carved leafy vine & continuing to shaped side rails w/small turned drops & small candle shelves framing the round-topped molded swiveling mirror frame, white marble top w/serpentine sides & front above a conforming case w/outset corners w/half-round turnings flanking the four long graduated drawers w/applied oval reserves, pierced scrolls & leaf-carved pulls, deep molded base & shaped apron, ca. 1860, 24 x 55", 7' 8" h. (ILLUS.) **1,650.00**

Victorian transitional chest of drawers, cherry & mahogany veneer, the rectangular top w/rounded front corners fitted w/a pair of small handkerchief drawers w/pairs of small wooden knobs & connected by a back crestrail, the case w/three deep mahogany-veneered drawers w/turned & reeded knobs & scroll-carved keyhole escutcheons, scroll-cut bracket feet, ca. 1840-50, 20 x 39", overall 41" h. **358.00**

William & Mary Chest of Drawers

William & Mary chest of drawers, painted wood, joined construction w/a rectangular top w/molded deep edge above a case of four long drawers w/narrow half-round rail trim & small butterfly brasses & keyhole escutcheons, molded base on short square feet, old black paint, imperfections, loss of height, Deerfield, Massachusetts, ca.1700-15, 19 x 36", 38" h. (ILLUS.) **3,450.00**

William & Mary Painted Chest

William & Mary chest of drawers, oak & poplar, the rectangular overhanging top w/molded cornice above the arch-molded case w/four long drawers, recessed end panels w/chamfered borders, applied base molding on turned turnip-form feet & rear stile feet, original red paint, original engraved brasses & keyhole escutcheons, imperfections, probably Connecticut, first quarter 18th c., 21¾ x 40", 40½" h. (ILLUS.). **7,475.00**

William & Mary chest of drawers, maple, rectangular top w/a stepped flaring cornice above a case of five long graduated drawers w/butterfly brasses & keyhole escutcheons, flaring molded base raised on turnip-turned feet, old mellow finish, replaced brasses, Massachusetts, 19¾ x 37¾", 42½" h. (minor renailing, edge damage, surface scratches) **5,225.00**

William & Mary tall chest of drawers, painted pine, rectangular top w/molded edges above a tall case w/five long graduated drawers simple butterfly brasses, molded base above a deeply scalloped apron & stile legs, New England, early 18th c., 17½ x 35½", 4' 2½" h. (ILLUS. top next column). . . **3,910.00**

William & Mary chest over drawer, painted, the rectangular hinged top w/molded edge opening to a well above a plain dovetailed case w/a long drawer within a molded opening across the bottom, base molding & turned bun feet, New England, early 18th c., 17½ x 29½", 22" h. **2,990.00**

Tall William & Mary Chest

William & Mary tall chest over drawers, painted wood, a rectangular chamfered cotter pinned hinged top over a deep well & a double-arch molded case of two false over two working drawers above a molded base, tall turned ovoid front feet & cut-out rear feet, original reddish brown paint, New England, first half 18th c., replaced simple bail brasses, 17⅞ x 35¼", 33½" h. **4,313.00**

CRADLES

Country-style cradle on rockers, walnut & curly maple, low scrolled head- and footboards between square canted stiles w/turned finials, folding blanket rest at head, canted even sides, scroll-edged removable rockers w/wrought-iron thumb screws, old soft finish, Pennsylvania, 19th c., 40½" l. (bottom missing) **880.00**

Country-style low cradle on rockers, painted walnut, flat slightly canted sides w/bands of incised lines, raised scrolls cut at arched headboard w/heart cut-out between square stiles w/knob finials, lower arched footboard w/matching cut-out, stiles & knobs, on inset scrolled rockers, old worn green repaint, 19th c., 38½" l. (age cracks, wear, part of bottom framed & one slat replaced) **204.00**

Country-style low cradle on rockers, painted poplar, the slightly canted sides w/the tall ends scroll-cut & stepped above the flat sides, high arched headboard & lower arched footboard each w/heart-shaped cut-outs, dovetailed sides on scrolled rockers, old brown grained repaint, 40½" l. (crests w/nailed breaks) . . . **150.00**

Country-style low cradle on rockers, cherry, dovetailed construction, the high arched headboard flanked by shaped downswept & canted sides w/small rim cut-outs, lower arched footboard, on wide shaped rockers, old finish, 19th c., 42½" l. (old rocker repairs) **220.00**

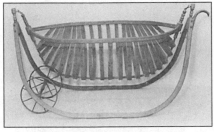

Patent-dated "Harvest" Cradle

"Harvest" cradle, bentwood, a oblong tapering basket-form cradle w/bentwood sides suspended between long, high bentwood rails joined at the ends & connected by a turned stretcher mounted w/two small iron wheels, original red paint w/silver striping & gold stenciling including "Ford Johnson & Co. Manufacturers, Michigan - Indiana - Patent Oct. 17th '76," minor wear, third quarter 19th c., 54" l. (ILLUS.). **605.00**

CUPBOARDS

Chimney cupboard, painted pine, a rectangular top w/a molded cornice above a tall narrow case w/a single narrow board & batten door over cut-out feet, very worn old blue, late 19th c., 18 x 23¾", 5' 7½" h. (renailing, age cracks, one foot & cornice old replacements) **396.00**

Chimney cupboard, painted pine, the rectangular top w/a molded cornice above a single triple-raised panel door opening to six shelves, front & side shaping, early H-hinges & original red paint, New England, 18th c., 15½ x 26½", 5' 7¼" h. (some hardware changes, minor wear) **4,888.00**

Cherry Country Corner Cupboard

Corner cupboard, country-style, cherry, one-piece construction, the flat top w/a cove-molded cornice above a pair of tall 3-pane glazed cupboard doors w/cast-iron latch opening to two shelves above a mid-molding over a pair of tall paneled lower doors w/cast-iron latch, scroll-cut bracket feet, old mellow refinishing, 19th c., cornice 50" w., 6' 10¼" h. (ILLUS.). **2,035.00**

Corner cupboard, country-style, pine, two-part construction: the upper section w/a coved cornice above a dentil frieze band above the single tall 12-pane glazed cupboard door opening to three scalloped shelves; the lower section w/a mid-molding over a large single double-paneled cupboard door w/a small wooden knob, flat molded base, original wrought-iron rattail door hinges, old mellow refinishing, late 18th - early 19th c., 49" w., 7'¼" h. (some edge damage, repair to left stile of bottom door) **1,760.00**

Corner cupboard, country-style, pine & poplar, one-piece construction, the deep cornice w/a dentil-carved top border above molded frieze band continuing to frame the case, two tall 8-pane cupboard doors opening to three shelves above a

Early Pine & Poplar Corner Cupboard

pair of paneled lower doors, molded flat base, upper shelves w/butterfly cut-outs, two panes cracked, some replaced, minor edge damage & pieced repair, refinished, early 19th c.. 53" w. cornice, 6' 11¼" h. (ILLUS.) **2,200.00**

Tiger Stripe Maple Corner Cupboard

Corner cupboard, country-style, tiger stripe maple & walnut, two-part construction: the upper section w/a cove-molded cornice above a pair of 8-pane glazed cupboard doors w/turned wood knob opening to three shelves; lower section w/a mid-molding over a pair of narrow drawers w/wood knobs above a pair of paneled cupboard doors w/wood knobs, simple cut-out bracket feet, 19th c. (ILLUS.) **4,510.00**

Walnut Corner Cupboard

Corner cupboard, country-style, walnut, one-piece construction, coved cornice above a pair of tall paneled cupboard doors w/a cast-iron thumb latch w/porcelain knob above a pair of shorter paneled doors w/a matching latch, flat apron, tall tapering bracket feet, old soft finish, 19th c., 49½" w., 7' h. (ILLUS.) **1,815.00**

Corner cupboard, Federal country-style, cherry, one-piece construction, the flat top w/a deep sharply curved coved cornice above a pair of tall double-panel cupboard doors above a pair of short paneled cupboard doors, simple cut-out apron, shiny varnish finish, first half 19th c., 46" w., 6' 6¾" h. (interior & back boards stripped, crack in a door panel) **990.00**

Federal Cherry Corner Cupboard

Federal Two-Piece Cupboard

Federal Country Corner Cupboard

Corner cupboard, Federal country-style, cherry, one-piece construction, the flat top w/a heavy ogee cornice above a pair of narrow 8-pane glazed cupboard doors w/a brass thumb latch opening to shelves above a row of three dovetailed drawers w/turned wood knobs above a pair of double-paneled cupboard doors w/a brass thumb latch, serpentine apron w/bracket feet, old refinishing, first half 19th c., hinges replaced, center drawer front cracked, 49½" w., 7' 3¼" h. (ILLUS.) **3,410.00**

Corner cupboard, Federal country-style, cherry, two-piece construction: the upper section w/a deep coved cornice above a tall 12-pane glazed cupboard door opening to three shelves; the lower section w/a mid-molding over a pair of small drawers flanking a longer center drawer above a pair of paneled cupboard doors, flat apron, simple bracket feet, old replaced pulls, refinished, New York state, ca. 1830, minor imperfections, 21¼ x 43", 7' 4" h. (ILLUS.) **4,600.00**

Corner cupboard, Federal country-style, inlaid cherry, one-piece construction, molded broken-scroll pediment w/central acorn-turned finial above a frieze molding over a band of delicate band & undulating line inlay over the tall single 12-pane glazed door w/fan-inlaid corners opening to three shelves above further checkered inlay over the single paneled door w/a band of herringbone inlay around the panel, low scroll-cut feet, cornice old addition, possibly Virginia, late 18th - early 19th c., 48" w., 7' 8½" h. (ILLUS.). **4,950.00**

Corner cupboard, Federal country-style "turkey breast" style, cherry, one-piece construction, the center of the case coming to a gentle peak, the flat top w/a coved cornice over applied picture frame moldings over a pair of 6-pane glazed cupboard doors opening to shelves over a mid-molding & a pair of raised panel cupboard doors, molded flat base, old refinishing, Ohio, 19th c., 51¼" w., 6' 8" h. (some edge damage & repairs, one pane missing, some termite damage on back) **1,650.00**

Federal Painted Corner Cupboard

Corner cupboard, Federal country-style, painted, one-piece construction, the flat molded coved cornice above four tall narrow paneled cupboard doors, the upper two w/a small panel above a long panel, the doors flanked by matching recessed paneling, ogee bracket base centering a drop pendant, old dark brown paint, New England, ca. 1790, 20 x 49", 6' 5½" h. (ILLUS.). **4,025.00**

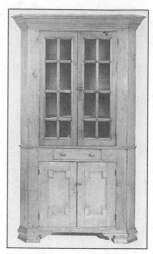

Fine Pine Corner Cupboard

Corner cupboard, Federal country-style, pine, two-piece construction: the upper section w/a deep flaring & stepped cornice above a pair of tall, narrow 8-pane glazed cupboard doors w/molded muntins & wooden knob opening to three shelves; the lower section w/a mid-molding over a single cockbeaded drawer w/two wooden knobs above a pair of cross-form paneled cupboard doors w/brass latch, molded base on scroll-cut ogee bracket feet, Middle Atlantic states, early 19th c., restoration, 21½ x 48½", 7' 3" h. (ILLUS.) **2,415.00**

Corner cupboard, Federal country-style, walnut, two-part construction: the upper section w/a wide ogee cornice above a pair of 3-pane glazed cupboard doors opening to two shelves; the lower section w/a mid-molding above a small centered drawer w/round brass knob above a pair of paneled cupboard doors opening to one shelf, flat apron & stile feet, Mid-Atlantic States, early 19th c., 23¼ x 49", 6' 5" h. **1,265.00**

Corner cupboard, Federal country-style, walnut, one-piece construction, the top w/a flat flaring cornice above a pair of 6-pane glazed cupboard doors opening to shelves above a mid-molding over a pair of small drawers w/turned wood knobs above a pair of paneled cupboard doors w/original brass thumb latch w/porcelain knob, base molding above square

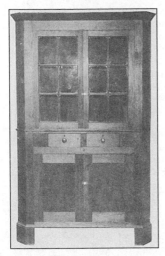

Country Walnut Corner Cupboard

bracket feet, old soft finish, early 19th c., 52½" w., 6' 10" h. (ILLUS.) **3,025.00**

Corner cupboard, Federal country-style, walnut, two-piece construction: the upper section w/a wide coved cornice above a pair of tall double-paneled cupboard doors w/a short panel over a tall panel; the lower section w/a mid-molding over a pair of paneled cupboard doors, molding around the base above the shaped bracket feet, first half 19th c., old refinishing, 46" w., 6' 11" h. (replaced feet, edge damage & age cracks) **1,320.00**

Federal Walnut Corner Cupboard

Corner cupboard, Federal, walnut, one-piece construction, the top w/a cove-molded cornice above a pair of 8-pane glazed cupboard doors opening to butterfly shelves w/worn old red paint, the base w/a pair of paneled cupboard doors above a curved apron & bracket feet, worn & partially removed old finish, found in Pennsylvania, first half 19th c., 53½" w. plus cornice, one pane cracked, one end of cornice missing, 7' 4½" h. (ILLUS.) **2,750.00**

Hutch cupboard, country-style, stained pine, the upper section w/a rectangular top w/a straight molded cornice above three open shelves, the lower section w/a sliding work surface opening to a well over a small drawer & two paneled doors, resting on bracket feet, 19th c., 21½ x 43", 6' 11" h. **862.00**

Grain-painted Hutch Cupboard

Hutch cupboard, painted & decorated, country-style, one-piece construction, a rectangular top w/a narrow molded cornice above three open shelves flanked by molded front stiles, tall narrow double-raised panel cupboard drawer w/cast-iron latch below, flat base, grain-painted in grey w/dark grey swirl design & reddish orange interior, paint wear, New England, early 19th c., 15 x 28", 6' 8" h. (ILLUS.) **5,463.00**

Hutch cupboard, pine, two-part construction: the upper section w/a rectangular top over open shelves; the lower section w/two drawers &

a dry sink over two cupboard doors, on bracket feet, 19th c., 18 x 50", 7½" h. **2,530.00**

Jelly cupboard, cherry, rectangular top above a pair of drawers w/small turned knobs over a pair of tall paneled doors w/a wooden thumb latch & small wood knob, flat apron & tapering stile feet, 19th c., 18½ x 44½", 4' 7" h. **880.00**

Jelly cupboard, painted pine, a rectangular top above a wide two-board door w/molded edging flanked by wide flat stile boards continuing down to form high tapering front feet, old worn bluish grey, 19th c., 13¾ x 41½", 47" h. . . **413.00**

Painted Pine Jelly Cupboard

Jelly cupboard, painted pine, rectangular top above a pair of plain board & batten doors w/beaded framing opening to two shelves, scalloped deep apron, old salmon red, wear & edge damage, one end of top w/water damage, interior shelves replaced, interior repainted greyish green, 19th c., 17½ x 44½", 4' 7½" h. (ILLUS.). . . . **715.00**

Jelly cupboard, painted pine, a serpentine crestrail w/a flat center section above the rectangular top above the tall narrow case w/a single drawer above a pair of tall narrow board & batten doors w/small wooden thumb latches & pulls, curved bracket feet, wire nail construction, worn yellow repaint, late 19th - early 20th c., 17¾ x 37½", overall 6' ⅞" h. **1,150.00**

Jelly cupboard, stained poplar, a scroll-cut rounded crestrail above the rectangular top above a pair of deep drawers w/simple turned knobs above two board and batten

doors w/wood knobs & thumb latch, flat base, bootjack ends, old worn brown finish over weathered white, 14 x 39½", 4' 2" h. (age cracks, wear & edge damage) **578.00**

Jelly cupboard, walnut, rectangular top w/a flaring molded cornice above a single long drawer w/two turned wood knobs above a pair of tall, narrow cock-beaded cupboard doors w/wooden knobs, molded base w/simple cut-out feet, refinished, 19th c., 19½ x 46¾", 5'½" h. (replaced pulls & feet) . . . **1,100.00**

Grain-painted Linen Press

Linen press, country-style, painted poplar, two-piece construction: the upper section w/a rectangular top w/flat, flaring cornice above a pair of tall, narrow paneled cupboard doors w/brass latches; the lower section w/a mid-molding over a row of three drawers w/wooden pulls over a pair of short paneled doors w/brass latches, molded base on low bracket feet, original brown combed graining, minor edge damage, mid-molding replaced, 19th c., 17½ x 56½", 7' 1¼" h. (ILLUS.) **1,540.00**

Linen press, Federal, walnut, two-part construction: the upper section w/a removable rectangular stepped & cove-molded cornice above a 14-pane geometrically-glazed pair of cupboard doors opening to four shelves; the slightly stepped-out lower section w/a rectangular top w/rounded edges above a pair of large paneled cupboard doors opening to two shelves, on short ring- and ball-turned legs w/peg feet, Petersburg, Virginia, ca. 1810, 22¾ x 45¾", 7' 7" h. (cracks in several panes, one upper door warped) **3,910.00**

Dutch Neoclassical Linen Press

Linen press, Neoclassical style, mahogany & marquetry, the rectangular top w/notched front corners above a frieze band w/swag inlay above a pair of tall raised-panel cupboard doors w/florettes in each corner & ribbon & swag inlay above central classical urn inlay on a veneered ground flanked by reeded curved pilasters, a mid-molding above the lower section w/a pair of drawers over two long drawers, all w/cross-banded & line-inlay, round brass pulls & keyhole escutcheons, molded base & bracket feet, Holland, late 18th c., 21 x 63", 7' 3" h. (ILLUS.) **9,200.00**

Pewter cupboard, red-washed pine, one-piece construction, the rectangular top above flat board stiles flanking the open cupboard w/two shelves above a slightly stepped-out base w/two tall narrow board doors w/wooden thumb latches & tiny wood knobs separated by wide board stiles, low

cut-out feet, red wash over traces of earlier paint, 19th c., 16 x 50", 5' 11" h. (base stiles, doors & top board replaced) **385.00**

Early Painted Pewter Cupboard

Pewter cupboard, painted wood, two-part construction: the upper section w/a rectangular top w/a deep molded flaring cornice above corner blocks above reeded pilasters flanking an arched frieze border over a large open compartment w/three long shelves; the stepped-out lower section w/a pair of four-panel cupboard doors flanking a stack of three central drawers, flat base, old red paint, New York state or New Jersey, early 19th c., restoration, 20 x 72½", 7' 3½" h. (ILLUS.). **5,175.00**

Pharmacy cupboard, painted walnut & cherry, a raised crestrail shelf above a low raised two-panel back flanked by scalloped end brackets over a long narrow rectangular top over two long narrow drawers w/wooden knobs over two pairs of raised-panel cupboard doors w/small wood knobs, molded flat base, old mustard yellow paint, 19th c., 15 x 86", 4' 8½" h. (drawers rebuilt, some edge damage & age cracks) **2,090.00**

Pie safe, painted wood, a rectangular top above a pair of three-panel doors w/punched-tin panels featuring a central four-lobe florette flanked by starbursts & corner scrolls, wooden thumb latches, three matching tin panels down

Early Painted Pie Safe

each side, raised on tall turned & tapering legs, old worn red paint & rust on tins, Pennsylvania or Virginia, 19th c. (ILLUS.) **1,100.00**

Pie safe, painted yellow pine, rectangular top above a pair of tall cupboard doors each w/three punched-tin panels decorated w/a central six-point star in a scalloped circle w/quarter-round bands in each corner, three matching tin panels down each side, on tall square stile legs, old worn blue over green paint, 19th c., 19 x 39", 4' 6¾" h. (some rust, loose frame, one back foot ended out) **660.00**

Pie safe, pine & punched tin, rectangular top w/stepped cornice above a mortised frame w/two narrow tall punched tin panels at the front decorated w/alternating stars in circles & large curved leaves flanking the single rectangular wide door w/a punched tin panel decorated w/an oval reserve filled w/circles, stars & other designs, the side tin panels w/Gothic arch designs, some rust damage & renailing, 19th c., top 17 x 38¾", 45" h. (some door edge repair, old fastener repair) **1,265.00**

Pie safe, poplar, the rectangular top above a pair of tall three-panel doors opening to two shelves, each panel w/a punched tin insert decorated w/a star in circle design, three matching tin panels on each side, the square stiles continuing to form tall legs, mortised rail construction, refinished w/soft surface, 19th c., 18 x 40½", 4' 9½" h. **825.00**

Pie safe, walnut, a rectangular top above a long dovetailed drawer w/two wooden knobs above a pair of tall cupboard doors each w/three punched-tin panels in a heart & star design, solid ends & square stile legs, refinished, 14½ x 40½", 4' 10" h. (edge damage on one corner) **990.00**

Pie safe, walnut, a rectangular top above a pair of wide drawers w/turned wood knobs above a pair of tall cupboard doors each fitted w/two punched tin panels, the two door panels forming a single design of a large handled pot of flowers holding leafy flowering flower stock, single side panels punched w/matching design, raised on ring-turned & tapering short legs, probably Virginia, 19th c., refinished, 16½ x 53", 6' 2¾" h. (some light rust on tins & one w/old pieced corner repair) **3,300.00**

Fine Early Side Cupboard

Side cupboard, country-style, painted & carved pine, rectangular top w/flaring molded cornice above a frieze band of a central raised diamond & narrow panels flanked by reeded end blocks above a pair of paneled cupboard doors w/brass pulls flanked by reeded pilasters above a long drawer at the bottom, scalloped apron & reeded bracket feet, three-shelved interior, old red wash, New Jersey area, early 19th c., replaced hardware, minor imperfections, 17¼ x 40½", 4' h. (ILLUS.) **3,450.00**

Side cupboard, painted & decorated poplar, rectangular top w/a shaped three-quarter gallery above a wide single board-and-batten door w/cast-iron thumb latch, one-board ends, curved bracket front feet, old brown graining, interior shelves, found near Richmond, Indiana, second half 19th c., 19¼ x 27¾", overall 32½" h. (strip added to door) **715.00**

Step-back wall cupboard, Chippendale, walnut, two-part construction: the upper section w/a deep stepped & cove-molded rectangular cornice above a pair of paneled cupboard doors opening to three shelves w/plate grooves & spoon racks over an open pie shelf w/curved end brackets; the stepped-out lower section w/a pair of short drawers w/simple bail pulls above a pair of paneled cupboard doors opening to a shelf, molded base on slender ogee bracket feet, Pennsylvania, ca. 1770 (replaced brasses, repaired rear feet) **6,900.00**

bone frieze band over a pair of tall, narrow 8-pane glazed cupboard doors opening to three shelves; the lower section w/a projecting front above a pair of deep end drawers flanking two small central drawers all overhanging a stack of three long drawers flanked by ring- and knob-turned columns, block feet & flat base, paneled sides, old refinish, replaced oval brasses, New York or New Jersey, ca. 1825, damages, feet missing, 20½ x 40", 7' 4"h. (ILLUS.) **5,175.00**

Butternut Step-back Cupboard

Step-back wall cupboard, country-style, butternut, two-piece construction: the upper section w/a rectangular top w/a deep ogee cornice above a pair of 6-pane glazed cupboard doors opening to two shelves over a open scalloped pie shelf; the lower stepped-out section w/a pair of drawers above a pair of paneled cupboard doors, paneled sides, scalloped apron on simple bracket feet, refinished, added Rockingham-glazed pulls, one drawer old replacement, some edge damage & repair, mid-19th c., cornice 14¾ x 52", 7' 4¼" h. (ILLUS.) **1,870.00**

Fine Tiger Maple Cupboard

Step-back wall cupboard, Classical style, tiger stripe maple, two-part construction: the upper section w/a rectangular top over a deep coved cornice above a carved herring-

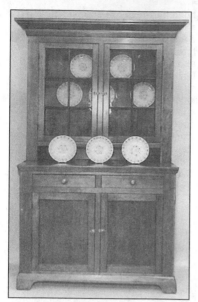

Cherry Step-back Wall Cupboard

Step-back wall cupboard, country-style, cherry, two-piece construction: the upper section w/a rectangular top w/a widely flaring flat cornice above a pair of 6-pane cupboard doors opening to three shelves above an open pie shelf; the lower section projecting w/two long narrow drawers w/wooden knobs over a pair of paneled cupboard doors, molded base on simple bracket feet, original brass thumb latches, old door glass, refinished, mid-19th c., cornice 14½ x 58", 7' 5" h. (ILLUS.) **4,070.00**

Pine Step-back Wall Cupboard

Step-back wall cupboard, country-style, pine, one-piece construction, rectangular top w/a deep coved cornice above a pair of paneled cupboard doors w/wooden thumb latch opening to shelves above a high open pie shelf, the stepped-out lower section w/a single double-panel cupboard door w/wooden thumb latch, shaped apron & bracket feet, 19th c. (ILLUS.) **2,860.00**

Fine Pine Step-back Cupboard

Step-back wall cupboard, country-style, pine, two-part construction: the upper section w/a rectangular top & simple cove-molded cornice above a pair of 6-pane glazed cupboard doors w/arched upper panes opening to two shelves over a row of four very narrow small drawers over an open pie shelf w/shaped ends; the stepped-out lower section w/two curved-end drawers above a pair of paneled cupboard doors flanked by half-round column pilasters above turned bulbous tapering feet, second half 19th c., 20 x 53½", 6' 11" h. (ILLUS.) **4,887.00**

Step-back wall cupboard, country-style, painted poplar, two-part construction: the upper section w/a rectangular top over a deep flaring ogee cornice above a pair of tall paneled doors w/a cast-iron thumb latch w/porcelain knob above an open pie shelf; the stepped-out lower section w/a pair of drawers w/wooden knobs above a pair of paneled cupboard doors w/a cast-iron thumb latch, flat apron & short bracket feet, old light green repaint w/black trim, 19th c., 14¼ x 50½", 6' 11¾" h. **990.00**

Step-back wall cupboard, country-style, walnut, two-piece construction: the upper section w/a rectangular top w/a deep stepped & cove-molded cornice above a pair of two two-board raised-panel cupboard doors fitted w/a cast-iron thumb latch above a mid-molding over an open pie shelf w/shaped side brackets; the stepped-out lower section w/a pair of drawers w/small knobs above a pair of two-board raised panel doors w/a cast-iron thumb latch (missing brass knob) above a simple cut-out base, old worn refinishing, 19th c., 14 x 48½", 6' 11¾" h. (separation in one lower door panel) **1,650.00**

Step-back wall cupboard, country-style, walnut, two-piece construction: the upper section w/a rectangular top & narrow molded cornice above a pair of geometrically-glazed cupboard doors w/curved mullions forming diamonds & Gothic arches & opening to scalloped shelves above an open pie shelf; the stepped-out lower section w/a pair of long drawers above a pair of raised diamond panel doors, molded base on bracket feet, wrought-iron pintel hinges & old replaced brass hardware, old dark worn finish, early 19th c., wear & damage, 17 x 52", 7' 2" h. **9,350.00**

Step-back wall cupboard, painted & decorated pine, one-piece construction, a rectangular top w/a flaring coved cornice over a pair of tall paneled cupboard doors w/a cast-iron thumb latch w/porcelain knob above a narrow stepped-out ledge above a wide single two-panel door in the bottom w/a cast-iron thumb latch w/porcelain knob, flat apron on short feet, ornate old brown & yellow grained repaint, found in Maine, second half 19th c., top 14 x 41¼", 6' 6" h. (one front foot facing gone, one replaced) **880.00**

Step-back wall cupboard, painted pine, one-piece construction, a rectangular top w/a molded cornice above a pair of tall, narrow raised

Early Small Step-back Cupboard

panel cupboard doors w/a looped brass pull opening to three shelves above a stepped-out lower case w/molded top above a single large raised panel door w/brass pull, molded base on simple bracket feet, painted red, hardware replaced, imperfections, New England, early 19th c., 15½ x 36", 6' 8½" h. (ILLUS.) **2,415.00**

Rare Spanish "Vargueno" Cupboard

Vargueno, iron-mounted walnut w/bone inlay & parcel-gilt, the rectangular top above a wide hinged fall-front over the top half opening to a section of numerous ornately carved & inlaid interior compartments, the ends w/wrought-iron loop carrying handles, a mid-molding above the lower section w/four long rectangular diamond-carved cupboard doors, on small square tapering feet, Baroque style, Spain, 17th c., 16 x 44½", 5' 2" h. (ILLUS.) **10,925.00**

Country Eastlake Wall Cupboard

Victorian Wall cupboard, Victorian country Eastlake substyle, oak, one-piece construction, the rectangular top w/an arched & knobbed cornice board above a molded cornice over a pair of one-pane glazed cupboard doors opening to two shelves over a pair of drawers w/metal knob & ring pulls over a lower pair of cupboard doors w/simple incised leafy scrolls, flat apron & angled bracket feet, ca. 1890s, 16 x 41¼", 6' 7¼" h. (ILLUS.) **468.00**

Tall Country Victorian Cupboard

Wall cupboard, Victorian country-style, walnut & ash, one-piece construction, the rectangular top above a deep molded cornice over a pair of tall paneled cupboard doors w/chamfered inside edges over a single long drawer above a pair of small cupboard doors matching upper pair, side front stiles w/carved pointed drops at top & chamfered outer corners, replaced iron hardware, shaped base replaced, refinished, ca. 1880-1900, cornice 16 x 44½", 7' 7¾" h. (ILLUS.) **935.00**

Wall cupboard, painted & decorated pine, a rectangular top w/a narrow cornice above a tall, narrow four-panel door w/a turned wood knob & metal turn latch, flat base raised on short ball feet, original simulated crotch mahogany graining in ochre & reddish brown, Maine, mid-19th c., 17¼ x 41½", 7' 1" h. (minor imperfections) **2,300.00**

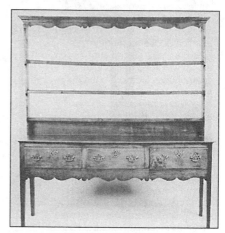

Early English Welsh Cupboard

Welsh cupboard, oak & elm, the tall superstructure w/a narrow top w/molded cornice & scalloped crest board above shaped sides flanking the open back w/two long shelves over a lower shelf above a backed compartment, the widely stepped-out lower section above three large, deep drawers w/pierced brass butterfly pulls & keyhole escutcheons, square tapering legs, George III period, England, late 18th - early 19th c., 16½ x 76", 6' 9⅛" h. (ILLUS.) **4,025.00**

DESKS

Fine Art Deco Desk

Art Deco desk, mahogany, the long rectangular slightly bowed top w/a center leather writing surface above a narrow center drawer & kneehole flanked on each side by stacks of four drawers, the front set w/four bronze-trimmed columns, metal-trimmed narrow platform base, w/ivory plaque signed "J. Leleu," Jules Leleu, France, ca. 1930, 34 x 79", 29½" h. (ILLUS.) **5,750.00**

Art Nouveau desk, mahogany & rosewood, the galleried top w/flanking cabinets w/curved tambour doors opening to fitted interior, the tooled leather writing surface above two long & two short drawers, all raised on buttressed forked legs heavily carved w/foliage, designed by Louis Majorelle, France, ca. 1900, 43 x 75", 43" h. **31,050.00**

Art Nouveau writing desk, wood & gilt mounts, the superstructure w/a wide down-curved crestrail w/rounded ends above a pair of small raised end shelves flanking a stepped down long top shelf over an open compartment above a pair of drawers w/curved scroll-cast gilt-metal pulls over the central pull-out writing surface flanked by rounded, molded projecting ends w/molded incurved supports joining the gently outswept front legs, backswept rear legs, L. Majorelle, France, ca. 1900, 30 x 48", 4' h. **17,250.00**

Chippendale "block-front" desk, carved mahogany, a narrow rectangular top above a wide slant front opening to reveal an interior of fan-carved prospect door flanked by document drawers w/flame-carved finials on columns & valanced compartments plus fan-carved concave drawers, the blocked cockbeaded case of four

long graduated drawers w/butterfly pulls above a molded base raised on ball-and-claw feet w/scroll-cut corner brackets & a central shaped pendant, old refinish, replaced brasses, Massachusetts, last quarter 18th c., 22 x 41¾", 44¼" h. (minor imperfections) **25,300.00**

Chippendale country-style slant-front desk, tiger stripe maple, a narrow rectangular top above a wide slant lid w/breadboard ends opening to an interior fitted w/open valanced compartments & drawers, the case w/four long, graduated cock-beaded drawers w/replaced butterfly brasses & keyhole escutcheons, molded base on shaped bracket feet, refinished, New England, late 18th c., 19½ x 40", 41" h. (restored) **2,760.00**

Chippendale country-style slant-front desk, painted maple, a narrow rectangular top above a wide slant front opening to a stepped interior of compartments & drawers above a case of four long graduated thumb-molded drawers w/turned wood knobs, molded base on scroll-cut bracket feet & flat apron centered by a carved fan pendant, old red grain painting, probably Massachusetts, ca. 1750, 18½ x 38", 43½" h. (replaced pulls, imperfections) **4,313.00**

Chippendale Desk-on-Frame

Chippendale desk-on-frame, mahogany, two-part construction: the upper case w/a long hinged slant front w/pen rail opening to an interior of open cubbyholes w/shaped dividers above compartments & small drawers; set into a molded frame w/square legs joined by square stretchers, original surface, probably New England, late 18th c., 18⅝ x 36¾", 37½" h. (ILLUS.) **2,875.00**

Chippendale slant-front desk, child's, birch, a narrow top above the slant-front opening to an interior fitted w/four drawers & four valanced compartments, the cockbeaded case w/four long graduated drawers w/small turned wood knobs, molded base w/shaped bracket feet, old refinish, southeastern New England, late 18th c., 11¼ x 15", 21¼" h. (minor imperfections) **4,313.00**

Chippendale slant-front desk, walnut, a narrow rectangular top above a wide hinged slant lid opening to an interior fitted w/valanced pigeonholes & eight small drawers centering a paneled prospect door opening to reveal a small drawer, the case w/a narrow long drawer over a pair of short drawers over two long drawers, molded base on scroll-cut bracket feet, Mid-Atlantic States, late 18th c., 21½ x 38½", 43¼" h. **7,475.00**

Chippendale-Style Slant-front Desk

Chippendale-Style slant-front desk, mahogany & mahogany veneer, a narrow rectangular top above a hinged slant-front opening to a fitted interior above a double-serpentine case w/four long drawers, molded base & short cabriole front legs w/claw-and-ball feet, early 20th c. (ILLUS.) **495.00**

Country-style fall-front desk, painted pine, the top w/a narrow rectangular top above a hinged flat fall-front opening to an interior fitted w/pigeonholes & three small drawers, the stepped-out lower case w/two long deep drawers w/turned wood knobs, arched apron w/bracket feet, old white paint covered w/green wash, old white paint on interior, age cracks, 19th c., 18 x 36", 4' ½" h. **495.00**

Country-style post office desk on frame, painted pine, the top w/seven open storage compartments above two hinged & rimmed desk tops which open to two interiors, each w/an upper & lower set of seven open compartments, set in a molded frame raised on square tapering legs, original green paint, New England, early 19th c., 33¼ x 63", 5' 5½" h. (surface imperfections) .. **805.00**

Country-style school desk, painted & decorated pine, a low rounded crestboard above a narrow shelf over a hinged slant lid opening to an interior w/pigeonholes above a single long drawer w/two wooden knobs, raised on ring- and rod-turned tapering legs w/baluster-turned feet, old yellow wood graining on a white ground over a dark red earlier finish, 19th c., 22¾ x 33", overall 39½" h. (wear, pieced drawer repair) **550.00**

Country-style schoolmaster's desk, walnut, a narrow rectangular top above a wide hinged slant top w/breadboard ends opening to an interior fitted w/pigeonholes, the apron w/a single long, narrow drawer raised on ring-, knob- and baluster-turned slender legs on knob feet, refinished, first half 19th c., 24¼ x 39", 38¼" h. (lid hinge rail restored, pigeonhole brackets replaced) **825.00**

Country-style schoolmaster's desk, pine, a low crestrail over a narrow shelf above a wide hinged slant top w/edge molding opening to a compartment above an apron w/a single drawer w/turned wood knob, raised on square tapering legs, old red stain, 19th c., 20½ x 41½", 38¾" h. (gallery ends missing) **220.00**

Country-style slant-front lady's desk, carved & stained pine, the arched three-quarter gallery top w/serrated edges joined by spool-turned stiles continuing down to knob finials, the narrow top shelf w/half-round turned crosses above a wide fall-front w/spool-turned borders & half-round spool-turned cross designs w/a central rectangular shelf, opening to a fitted interior, a long drawer

Unique Country-style Lady's Desk

w/spool-turned borders & cross designs above curved serrated aprons & raised on spool-turned legs w/a medial shelf on short rows of spindles, probably New England, ca. 1900, 4' 4½" h. (ILLUS.) **863.00**

Country-style 'stand-up' desk, butternut, a rectangular hinged slant lid opening to a well above a single long drawer, raised on tall square legs, refinished, New England, 19th c., 23¾ x 40", 38" h. ... **518.00**

Country-style 'Stand-up' Desk

Country-style 'stand-up' desk, painted, the scroll-cut crestboard above a narrow shelf & a wide hinged slant-front opening to an interior w/compartments, the apron w/a single long drawer w/incised scrolling panel & two turned wood

knobs, on square tapering stile legs, old red paint, New England, early 19th c., 21⅝ x 26⅜", 44¾" h. (ILLUS.) **863.00**

Federal desk, cherry & tiger stripe maple, rectangular top above a hinged slant lid opening to a fitted interior w/a central molded door flanked by document drawers, valanced compartments & drawers, the case w/four thumb-molded graduated long drawers w/oval brasses, molded base w/bracket feet & a central drop pendant, old refinish, old replaced brasses, possibly Massachusetts, last half 18th c., 18¾ x 35⅝", 41⅝" h. (minor imperfections) **4,313.00**

Federal desk, inlaid cherry, a narrow rectangular top above a wide hinged line-inlaid slant front opening to an interior fitted w/valanced pigeonholes flanking a prospect door, the case w/four graduated line-inlaid long drawers above a serpentine apron continuing to splayed bracket feet, early 19th c., 21½ x 39", 45½" h. **3,450.00**

Federal Slant-front Desk

Federal desk, mahogany & inlaid mahogany veneer, a narrow rectangular top above a wide hinged slant front opening to an interior w/a central prospect door flanked by three drawers & four valanced compartments, the case w/four long graduated cockbeaded drawers w/oval pulls, shaped skirt w/stringing & crossbanding, tall French feet, old finish & brasses, minor imperfections, probably Massachusetts, ca. 1800, 20 x 41½", 42½" h. (ILLUS.) **3,105.00**

Federal desk, walnut, a narrow rectangular top shelf w/a very low gallery above a raised section w/a row of three small drawers w/turned wood knobs above the stepped-out slanted hinged writing surface opening to a deep well, all above a long apron drawer, raised on baluster, knob- and ring-turned legs, Mid-Atlantic States, ca. 1820, 22 x 34", 39¾" h. (patches to veneer) **431.00**

Federal 'butler's' desk, walnut, a rectangular top slightly overhanging a cockbeaded wide fall-front drawer w/a sliding central door hinged at the top & opening to reveal a single short drawer above a valanced document slot flanked on each side by a single long drawer above two short drawers & four valanced pigeonholes, all above three long graduated & cockbeaded drawers flanked by reeded pilasters, raised on ring-turned legs, Mid-Atlantic States, ca. 1820, 22¼ x 42", 48¼" h. (wooden knobs replaced, two veneer patches) **1,495.00**

George III-Style partner's desk, mahogany, the rectangular top w/gilt tooled leather inset writing surface, three frieze drawers above a pair of raised stacks of three drawers each flanking the kneehole, all backed by working drawers & doors, England, late 19th c., 34 x 59½", 30½" h. **5,175.00**

George III-Style writing desk, mahogany, rectangular molded top inset w/gilt tooled leather, over three drawers, each pedestal w/three graduated drawers, plinth base, England, 19th c., 26½ x 48", 29 ½" h. **1,840.00**

George III-Style Writing Desk

George III-Style writing desk, mahogany, rectangular top inset w/green tooled leather above an apron w/two long front drawers w/pairs of round brass pulls, square tapering reeded legs w/square cuffs, England, second half 19th c., 28 x 52¼", 30½" h. (ILLUS.) **3,450.00**

Mission-style (Arts & Crafts movement) drop-front desk, oak, a narrow rectangular top w/a high three-quarter gallery above the wide slant-front w/long pointed strap hinges opening to a full gallery interior, case w/a pair of drawers over a long drawer above a pair of short rectangular cupboard doors w/long pointed strap hinges & square pulls, flat apron, new ebonized finish, large red decal mark of Gustav Stickley, 14 x 32¾", 4' h.. .... **3,300.00**

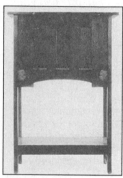

Rare G. Stickley Lady's Desk

Mission-style (Arts & Crafts movement) fall-front lady's desk, oak, rectangular top overhanging a case w/a paneled fall-front w/hand-wrought iron trim opening to an interior of 11 pigeonholes & a drawer, original black finish, large Gustav Stickley red mark, Model No. 724, 12 x 32", 46" h. (ILLUS.) **29,900.00**

Mission-style (Arts & Crafts movement) "postcard" desk, oak, rectangular flush top over sides w/through-tenon rails flanking two banks of two small drawers each flanking a longer central drawer above the kneehole w/a set-back shelf w/through-tenons, recent dark finish, large red box decal of Gustav Stickley, 24¼ x 36½", 29¼" h. **1,870.00**

Queen Anne desk-on-frame, child's, maple, two-part construction: the upper section w/a hinged slant-front opening to an interior of eight

Queen Anne Child's Desk-on-Frame

valanced compartments & four drawers above the case w/four long graduated thumb-molded drawers, set into a lower section w/a mid-molding above the deeply arched skirt on four block-turned legs ending in pad feet, old varnish stain, restored, probably southeastern New England, last half 18th c., 13½ x 23½", 35¾" h. (ILLUS.) **4,313.00**

Queen Anne Slant-front Desk

Queen Anne slant-front desk, tiger stripe maple & cherry, a narrow rectangular top above a hinged slant-front opening to an interior w/a central fan-carved drawer & two valanced compartments flanked by molded document drawers, four valanced compartments & three drawers above a case w/four long graduated thumb-molded drawers w/bail pulls, molded base & simple bracket feet & center drop, old refinish, replaced brasses, imperfections, repairs, possibly Vermont, ca. 1750, 18 x 36", 41½" h. (ILLUS.). **5,175.00**

Queen Anne slant-front desk, inlaid walnut, a narrow rectangular top above a wide hinged slant front w/two inlaid stellate devices opening to an interior fitted w/open valanced compartments over small drawers centered by a stellate-inlaid prospect door flanked by half-round columns, the lower case w/four long graduated line-inlaid drawers on a molded base w/cut-out bracket feet, old surface, replaced brasses, Massachusetts, 1730-50, 19½ x 38", 43" h. (surface imperfections & repairs) **5,463.00**

Italian Renaissance-Style Desk

Renaissance-Style desk, walnut, a narrow top shelf flanked at each end by stepped-out compartments carved at the front w/grotesque faces above the writing surface w/a carved egg-and-dart border, the apron w/a row of three small paneled drawers flanked by rondels above turned columns flanking a paneled door on each side of the kneehole, wide molded base, Italy, late 19th c., 28½ x 61¼", 39" h. (ILLUS.) **2,530.00**

Early Store Keeper's Desk

Store keeper's desk, country-style, grain-painted pine, a narrow galleried top above a hinged wide slant lid opening to valanced compartments & a single drawer set onto a stand w/two long drawers w/small turned wood knobs, shaped skirt, square stile legs & square H-stretcher, brown & gold graining, New England or New York state, early 19th c., 20 x 33", 4' h. (ILLUS.) **1,840.00**

Fine Rolltop Desk

Turn-of-the-century "rolltop" desk, quarter-sawn oak, a rectangular top above an S-scroll roll opening to an interior fitted w/raised drawers, letter slots & cubbyholes, the molded top above a case w/a center drawer over the kneehole flanked on the right by a stack of four drawers w/wide wood finger pulls & on the left by a hinged door w/carved scrolls & swags opening to a typewriter platform above two lower drawers, molded base, center base drawer replaced, ca. 1900, 34½ x 60", 4' 1½" h. (ILLUS.) **2,420.00**

Ornate Venetian Writing Desk

Venetian writing desk, painted & decorated, kidney-shaped, the oblong top w/ molded edge above a conforming case w/a long scroll-trimmed drawer above the central kneehole flanked by pairs of small drawers w/scroll trim, each drawer

decorated w/flowers, birds & scrolls on a yellow ground, on cabriole legs w/scroll & peg feet, early 20th c., 20 x 49", 30" h. (ILLUS.) **1,840.00**

Victorian country-style fall-front desk, walnut, a narrow rectangular top overhanging a wide hinged slightly angled fall-front opening to an interior fitted w/two central small drawers over an opening flanked on one side by pigeonholes & on the other by letter slots, the lower case w/a pair of paneled cupboard doors, scalloped apron & short bracket feet, cast-iron hinges on lid, old dark finish, mid-19th c., 18 x 33¾", 46" h. **550.00**

Unusual Victorian Walnut Desk

Victorian desk, Renaissance Revival substyle, walnut & walnut veneer, the rectangular top w/notched corners inset w/green beize above an apron w/a long burl-paneled drawer & a small swing-out side inkwell w/porcelain knob, raised on pairs of heavy squared supports joined by a pierced upper stretcher above the trestle base w/arched end legs & a stepped stretcher w/small center spindles, top tilts for use as drafting table, made by H. Closterman, Cincinnati, Ohio & patent-dated "February 12, 1878," refinished (ILLUS.) **715.00**

Victorian desk, Renaissance Revival substyle, walnut & walnut veneer, an eclectic variation of William & Mary style, a carved shingled Mansard-style top canopy rising above an open shelf w/two enclosed locking drawers flanking a finely carved back panel above another long open compartment raised on short ring-turned supports above the overhanging writing surface w/molded edges & decorated w/satinwood medallions of the American eagle & shield, the

Very Ornate Victorian Desk

apron w/two long narrow drawers, on knob-, and ring-turned legs joined by curved flat stretchers, a drawer signed "Adolf Kelsch, ca.1870," 25 x 42", 4' 10" h. (ILLUS.) **3,575.00**

Unique Victorian Bamboo-turned Set

Victorian lady's desk & side chair, faux bamboo bird's-eye maple, the desk w/an ornate stepped superstructure w/a tall central panel w/bamboo-turned trim & spindles framing a small shelf over a rectangular mirror flanked by short side panels w/matching bamboo-turned trim & open shelves supported on bamboo-turned columns, the hinged slanted leather-inset writing surface opening to a fitted interior, bamboo-turned edge trim, corner brackets & legs joined by a

bamboo-form H-stretcher, the matching bamboo-turned chair w/caned seat, late 19th c., desk 22½ x 32", 4' 7" h., 2 pcs. (ILLUS.) **3,738.00**

DINING ROOM SUITES

Art Deco: table w/two leaves & eight side chairs; bronze & iron-mounted inlaid oak, the table w/an oval top inlaid w/a basketweave design & raised on a fluted heavy oval pedestal decorated w/applied bronze mounts cast w/stylized flowerheads above a foot applied w/hammered iron plates; each chair w/an arched molded crestrail over the upholstered back & inset upholstered seat, raised on tapering round legs ending in ball feet, front legs mounted w/bronze rings cast w/florals, France, ca. 1925, table open 44 x 101", 30½" h., the set **21,850.00**

Art Nouveau: dining table, two armchairs & eight side chairs; ash & mahogany, the table top w/a molded oblong top raised on four carved & molded legs joined by wide curved stretchers, the chairs w/arched & pierced crestrails above tall oblong upholstered back panels, crestrail continues down to form rounded open arms on the armchairs, over-upholstered seats, molded V-form front legs joining back stiles, back legs joined by an arched stretcher, brown leather upholstery, designed by L. Majorelle, France, ca. 1900, table 50¼ x 62", 29" h. (two modern leaves) **39,100.00**

Art Nouveau Dining Suite

Art Nouveau: dining table & six side chairs; "Chicoree" patt., mahogany, the table w/a rectangular split-top w/heavy molded edges & rounded corners above buttressed legs elaborately carved w/leafage, each chair w/a conforming frame enclosing upholstered tapering back panels & seats, table w/five leaves, Louis Majorelle, France, ca. 1900, table 50 x 60", 29½" h., the set (ILLUS.) **9,200.00**

Rare Danish Modern Dining Suite

Danish Modern: two-leaf dining table & six armchairs, teak, the rectangular top w/draw ends raised on tapering legs, each chair w/an arched backrail continuing to form shaped flattened arms raised on round tapering stile supports & legs w/matching rear legs, gently curved upholstered seat, designed by Hans Wegner, produced by Johannes Hansen, Copenhagen, Denmark, chairs impressed "Johannes Hansen Copenhagen - Denmark," ca. 1950, table open, 42 x 106", 29" h., the set (ILLUS.) **13,800.00**

1950s Modern Dining Set

Modern style: rectangular-topped pedestal table & four dining chairs; the table w/a red Formica top trimmed in metal raised on a black metal column on a wide disc foot, each chair w/a pale green Naugahyde-upholstered back & seat on square, tapering wood legs, the set (ILLUS.) **300.00**

DRY SINKS

Decorated oak, rectangular well w/serpentine splashboard & molding edging slightly overhanging a case w/a pair of drawers w/porcelain knobs over a pair of cupboard doors w/recessed cartouche-shaped panels & cast-iron thumb latches, flat apron w/simple cut-out feet, overall old yellow wood graining, late 19th c., 20¼ x 44½", 34" h. plus crest (replaced latches, knobs damaged) **495.00**

Painted pine, a rectangular shallow well w/a flat-molded rim above flat board front stiles tapering to form curved bracket feet flanking a single open shelf, worn blue paint, 19th c., 17½ x 38¾", 30½" h. (signs of some restoration) **770.00**

Poplar, a raised narrow back shelf above the beaded vertical board back above the long rectangular well w/a small work shelf at one end above a small drawer w/a turned wood knob, two double-paneled doors below, slender curved bracket feet, refinished, 19th c., 20 x 54", 42¾" h. **523.00**

Walnut, rectangular top w/shallow galleried sides overhanging a small case w/a single square paneled door w/a cast-iron thumb latch w/damaged porcelain knob, on simple bracket feet, old red finish, found in Sugar Creek, Ohio, mid-19th c., 14¾ x 24", 26" h. (damage to one rear foot) **3,850.00**

GARDEN & LAWN

(Cast Iron Unless Otherwise Noted)
Armchair, rounded crestrail continuing to form rounded arms all above pierced flaring fern fronds, pierced seat, slender canted legs w/fern frond brackets at the sides, seat labeled "James W. Carr, Richmond, Va.," worn silver repaint, 19th c., 30" h. (some old repairs & damage). **413.00**

Settee, double-arched crestrail continuing down to form rounded arms all above panels of arching fern fronds, pierced seat, slender curved legs w/fern frond brackets at the ends, seat labeled "James W. Carr, Richmond, Va.," 19th c., worn silver paint, 39" l. (some damage) **660.00**

Garden Settee from a Set

Settee & two armchairs, the backs & arms composed of an overall pierced fern & blackberry design, pierced seat, arched end legs, painted white, minor imperfections, probably England, last quarter 19th c., settee 16 x 52", 34" h. (ILLUS. of settee) **3,738.00**

HALL RACKS & TREES

Hall rack, Mission-style (Arts & Crafts movement), oak, a wide flat top crossbar mounted w/five brass hooks above a narrow brace bar both between the tall square end stiles resting on shoe feet joined by a bar stretcher, original finish w/some nicks & scratches, early 20th c., 20 x 45", 5' 10" h. **495.00**

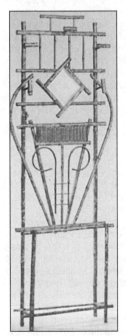

Unique Victorian Bamboo Hall Rack

Hall rack, bamboo, the tall back composed of a latticework of bamboo pieces w/bamboo hooks & curving bamboo braces flanking a small upper diamond-shaped mirror above a small woven wicker backet, an open wicker framework below for holding umbrellas & canes, late 19th c., 32" w., 6' 10" h. (ILLUS.) **300.00**

Bear & Tree Hall Tree

Hall tree, carved walnut, figural, a large full-figure standing bear grasping a tree trunk w/a bear cub perched in the upper bare branches, branch-form oval rack above another cub at the bottom behind the round dished drip tray, Black Forest region of Germany, late 19th c., oiled finish, 7' h. (ILLUS.) **4,600.00**

HIGHBOYS & LOWBOYS

HIGHBOYS

Queen Anne "bonnet-top" highboy, cherry, maple & birch, two-part construction: the upper section w/a broken-arch pediment centered by a flattened finial topped w/a ball-and urn-turned cap raised above a

Early Queen Anne Highboy

row of three drawers w/a deep
sunburst-carved center drawer
flanked by small drawers above a
stack of five long, graduated cockbeaded drawers w/butterfly pulls &
keyhole escutcheons; the lower
section w/a mid-molding above a
long drawer over a row of three
drawers, the center fan-carved, two
turned drops on apron, carbiole
legs ending in raised pad feet,
possibly Massachusetts, some
repairs, 6' 8¾" h. (ILLUS.) **8,250.00**

Queen Anne "bonnet-top" highboy,
cherry, two-part construction: the
upper section w/a broken-scroll
swan's-neck crest w/three flame-
turned slender finials above a pair
of small short drawers flanking a
deep center drawer above three
long graduated drawers; the lower
section w/a mid-molding over a
long narrow drawer over a row of
three deep drawers, shaped apron
w/two turned pointed drops,
cabriole legs ending in pad feet,
most brasses appear to be original,
old refinish, Concord,
Massachusetts, late 18th c.,
20¼ x 38", 7' 3" h. (minor
imperfections). **17,250.00**

Queen Anne "flat-top" highboy,
cherry, two-part construction: the
mismatched upper section w/a
rectangular top & deep cornice
above pairs of short drawers

flanking a deep center drawer
carved w/a sunburst above a stack
of four long graduated drawers; the
lower section w/a mid-molding over
a long drawer above a row of three
deep drawers, apron w/two turned
drops raised on angled cabriole
legs ending in pad feet, replaced
butterfly brasses, old mellow
refinishing, 18th c., 18½ x 37", 6'
¾" h. (repaired leg break, cornice
replaced) **6,050.00**

Queen Anne "flat-top" highboy,
cherry, two-part construction: the
upper section w/a rectangular top
over a deep stepped flaring cornice
over a row of three drawers, the
center one arch-carved, above
three long graduated drawers; the
lower section stepped-out w/a mid-
molding over a single long drawer
over a row of three drawers, the
center one arch-carved, front apron
w/two pendent drops, simple
cabriole legs ending in raised pad
feet, New England, second quarter
18th c., 21¾ x 40", 6' 1" h. **9,775.00**

Queen Anne "flat-top" highboy,
tiger stripe maple, two-part
construction: the upper section w/a
rectangular top w/a coved cornice
above a deep center fan-carved
drawer flanked by pairs of small
drawers over four long graduated
drawers; the lower section w/a mid-
molding over a long drawer above
a row of three deep drawers, the
center one fan-carved, serpentine
apron above cabriole legs ending
in pad feet on platforms, original
butterfly brasses, old refinish,
Newburyport, Massachusetts, ca.
1760, 21⅛ x 38⅜", 6' 2¼" h. (very
minor imperfections) **20,700.00**

Queen Anne "flat-top" highboy,
curly maple, two-part construction:
the top section w/a rectangular top
above a deep stepped & flaring
cornice above a row of three small
drawers, the center w/fan-carving,
above a stack of four long
graduated drawers; the lower
section w/a mid-molding over two
long drawers over a row of three
deep drawers, the center one
w/fan-carving, shaped apron w/two
pendent drops, cabriole legs
w/scroll-cut corner blocks ending in
raised duck feet, original butterfly
brasses & keyhole escutcheons,
New Hampshire, 18th c., 21¾ x
40⅜", 6' 7¼" h. **23,100.00**

Queen Anne-Style Highboy

Queen Anne-Style highboy,
mahogany, two-part construction:
the upper section w/a broken-crest
pediment w/a central urn-turned
finial above an edge molding over
a stack of four long graduated
drawers w/bail pulls; the lower
section w/a wide mid-molding over
two long drawers flanked by
quarter-round reeded columns,
molded base & slightly shaped
apron raised on cabriole legs
ending in pad feet, early 20th c.
(ILLUS.). 385.00

William & Mary "flat-top" highboy,
burled walnut, two-part
construction: the upper section w/a
rectangular top w/a narrow molded
cornice above a case w/a pair of
burl-veneered drawers over three
long graduated matching drawers,
each w/butterfly brasses & keyhole
escutcheons; the lower section w/a
flaring mid-molding above a pair of
short deep drawers flanking a
center narrow drawer above the
deeply scalloped & arched apron
raised on four front ball-and-
baluster-form legs & two back legs
joined by a flat serpentine stretcher
at the front & sides, on 'turnip' feet,
19¼ x 36½", 5' 1¼" h. (sides
cracked) 1,840.00

LOWBOYS

Chippendale-Style lowboy,
mahogany, rectangular top
w/molded edge above a case w/a
pair of drawers above a pair of
smaller square drawers flanking a

deeply arched & scalloped apron ,
on cabriole legs ending in ball-and-
claw feet, early 20th century hand-
made reproduction, 20¾ x 36",
32¼" h. 550.00

Chippendale-Style Lowboy

Chippendale-Style lowboy, walnut,
the rectangular top w/molded
edges above a long drawer
w/butterfly pulls over a row of three
deep drawers, the center one shell-
carved, scalloped & shell-carved
apron above the cabriole legs
w/acanthus-carved knees & ending
in claw-and-ball feet, ca. 1930, 20 x
31", 36" h. (ILLUS.) 248.00

LOVE SEATS, SOFAS & SETTEES

Chaise longue, Art Deco,
upholstered stained mahogany,
one end w/a squared curved
backrail continuing on one side to
form a short arm w/a tapered,
reeded arm support & the other
side forming a long, low back
ending in a tapering reeded arm
support, long shaped cushion, arm
supports continue to form two legs
w/two other short reeded support
legs, upholstered in striped beige
cotton, France, ca. 1925, 52" l. . . 4,025.00

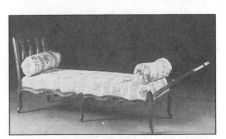

Louis XV Chaise Longue

Chaise longue, Louis XV style, beechwood, the serpentine molded crestrail on each end centered by a foliate cartouche above later baluster-shaped splats, the upholstered long seat raised on six cabriole legs w/a serpentine foliate-carved apron, one end fitted w/a ratchet mechanism to recline, restorations, France, mid-18th c., 74" l. (ILLUS.) **2,300.00**

Daybed, Mission-style (Arts & Crafts movement), oak, the angled end back w/five vertical slats, original finish, early Gustav Stickley mark, Model No. 191, 30 x 74", 29" h. (minor wear)................ **2,990.00**

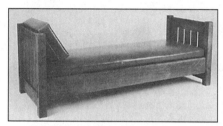

Gustav Stickley Mission Daybed

Daybed, Mission-style (Arts & Crafts movement), oak, each upright end w/a flat heavy crestrail over five vertical slats between square heavy stiles, wide side rails fitted w/a replaced brown leather cushion & pillow, original finish, Gustav Stickley Model No. 216, 31 x 80", 29" h. (ILLUS.) **4,025.00**

French Empire Daybed

Daybed, Empire style, ormolu-mounted mahogany, the foot- & headboards w/outscrolled supports, the downswept sides continuing to a neoclassically decorated ormolu-mounted rail raised on a molded plinth, France, first quarter 19th c., 31¼ x 78½", 34" h. (ILLUS.) **4,600.00**

Loveseat, Modern style, walnut, a heavy walnut plank back w/undulating rim raised on back post legs above the rectangular seat frame w/double through-tenons supporting a long green vinyl cushion, short & slightly tapering square legs, by George Nakashima, ca. 1950s, 91" l., 36" h. **6,325.00**

Mammy's bench on rockers, painted & decorated, a long flat board crestrail above the back composed of multiple arrow slats flanked by S-scroll arms on turned & canted arm supports, shaped plank seat w/a removable board insert guard at one end, turned tapering legs joined by flat front & rear stretchers on rockers, black repaint w/yellow striping, mid-19th c., 73" l. (minor repairs) **550.00**

Louis XV-Style Recamier

Recamier, Louis XV-Style, carved walnut, one end w/a raised scroll-carved serpentine crestrail w/an upholstered panel over a caned panel, a lower scroll-carved serpentine back of similar construction, a long cushion seat, end bolster & three large pillows, on a scroll-carved serpentine seatrail & short scroll-carved legs, France, late 19th c. (ILLUS.) **1,925.00**

Nice Classical Style Settee

Settee, Classical style, decorated mahogany, the back-curved crestrail w/gilt-trimmed ends above shaped rail over the upholstered back panel flanked by incurved arms w/padded C-scroll upholstered tops & cornucopia & leaf-carved fronts w/enclosed bolsters on the upholstered seat, plain low rounded seatrail raised on leafy scroll-carved & animal paw gilt-trimmed feet & a gadrooned edge band (ILLUS.) **1,045.00**

Settee, Classical country-style, painted & decorated wood, the long flat, wide crestrail w/a scroll-cut center section & rounded ends decorated w/long bands of colorful fruit & flower stenciling above three stiles joined by two narrow decorated rails each above five slender turned short spindles, S-scroll end arms above two turned spindles & a turned, canted arm support, long plank seat over four pairs of ring-turned tapering legs joined by simple turned box stretchers, worn original light green background paint w/black & grey striping, first half 19th c., 69" l. . . **1,375.00**

Settee, Federal country-style, painted & decorated, triple-back form w/a long three section shaped decorated crestrail above four turned & tapering stiles joined by three lower rails over knob-turned spindles, S-scroll arms over three turned spindles & a canted, turned arm support, long plank seat raised on four pairs of ring-turned canted legs joined by turned stretchers, old light green ground paint accented by gold & green striping w/polychrome fruit & leaf stenciling on the crest- and backrails, Pennsylvania, 1830s, 16¼ x 72", 32¼" h. (minor paint wear) **1,955.00**

George III-Style Settee

Settee, George III-Style, paint-decorated satinwood, a flat crestrail on the upholstered back flanked by slightly downcurved upholstered

arms w/scrolled hand grips on ring- and baluster-turned & leaf-carved arm support columns, overupholstered seat above a paint-decorated seatrail w/a central block w/two figures, square corner blocks above the square tapering legs w/blocked ankles, striped silk upholstery, England, late 19th c., 54" l., 35" h. (ILLUS.) **3,738.00**

Settee, Mission-style (Arts & Crafts movement), oak, a wide V-form crestrail above twelve vertical slats to the lower rail flanked by flat shaped arms w/corbels above the rectangular original leather seat, square stile legs joined by flat stretchers, worn original finish, Gustav Stickley Model 212, 24 x 41½", 36" h. **1,955.00**

L. & J.G. Stickley Settee

Settee, Mission-style (Arts & Crafts movement), oak, the wide crestrail slightly curved along the top above two lower rails between the square stiles above the wide, flat shaped arms w/through-tenons above corbels & square arm supports continuing to form the front legs, flat seatrail & flat lower stretcher, double stretchers at the ends, upholstered box cushion, original medium finish, "The Work of..." decal mark of L. & J.G. Stickley, Model No. 226, ca. 1912, 52½" l., 36½" h. (ILLUS.) **1,150.00**

Settee, Modern style, walnut, the canted flat rectangular back frame enclosing a long row of tall, slender square spindles above the rectangular seat frame w/a long cushion pad, raised on short canted turned & tapering legs, original finish, by George Nakashima, ca. 1950s, 48" l., 30" h. **1,955.00**

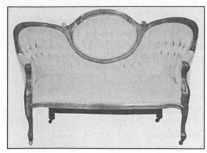

Medallion-back Victorian Settee

Settee, Victorian Rococo substyle, walnut, an oval medallion-back framed by a finger-carved rail continuing around the curved crestrails & down to the padded, closed arms, tufted medallion, back & arms above the overupholstered seat w/a slightly curved, molded seatrail continuing into the demi-cabriole front legs, on casters, repairs, reupholstered, 57½" l. (ILLUS.)....................**330.00**

Settee, Windsor "arrow-back" style, a long flat board crestrail above numerous arrow slats between the turned & tapering stiles & S-scroll arms over three turned spindles & a turned & canted arm support, long plank seat raised on four pairs of turned & tapering legs joined by horizontal front arrow stretchers & plain turned side & back stretchers, black repaint, first half 19th c., 78" l. **495.00**

Settee, Windsor, bamboo-turned wood, the long stepped flat crestrail above numerous bamboo-turned spindles & bamboo-turned stiles w/bamboo-turned rod arms over bamboo-turned spindles & arm supports, long plank seat on eight slightly canted bamboo-turned legs joined by bamboo-turned stretchers, old mellow refinishing, early 19th c., 77" l., 36" h. (old repaired seat age cracks, puttied joints) **1,045.00**

Classical-Style Sofa

Sofa, Classical-Style, carved mahogany, a flat reeded crestrail above curved side rails above the upholstered back flanked by outswept arms w/S-scroll arm supports, three-cushion seat over the rolled & reeded seatrail raised on outswept reeded legs ending in brass paw feet, reupholstered, ca. 1920s, 77¾" l. (ILLUS.)..........**248.00**

Sofa, Classical-Style, mahogany, the long backrail above an upholstered back & outscrolled acanthus-carved arms, raised on paw feet w/cornucopiae brackets, late 19th c., 84" l. **920.00**

Sofa, Classical-Style, mahogany, a shaped & scrolling crestrail above an upholstered back & seat w/bolsters flanked by incurved scroll arms w/cornucopia- and acanthus-carved arm supports w/brass rosette terminals, a half-round seatrail w/blocked ends above short legs topped by carved cornucopia & acanthus-capped lion's paw feet, late 19th - early 20th c., 93" l., 34" h...........**1,610.00**

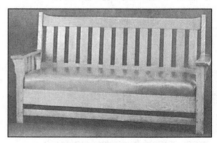

Limbert Mission Sofa

Sofa, Mission-style (Arts & Crafts movement), oak, the wide crestrail w/a curved top edge above a slatted back flanked by square stiles over shaped paddle arms w/through-tenons over corbels & square stile legs, wide seatrail & lower rail, replaced brown leather drop-in spring seat, new light finish, unmarked Charles Limbert Co., 27½ x 74 ½", 40½" h. (ILLUS.)...**3,575.00**

Sofa, Modern style, "Marshmallow Sofa," designed by George Nelson, produced by Herman Miller Furniture Company, vinyl naugahyde cushions, 1956, 52" l., 32" h. **17,000.00**

Sofa, Victorian Rococo substyle, carved rosewood, triple-back style, an oval tufted upholstered center

Fine Victorian Rococo Sofa

medallion w/an ornate scroll- and floral-carved crestrail & frame flanked by a pair of matching round medallions raised above the long upholstered spring seat flanked by serpentine padded open arms on scrolled arm supports, gently shaped seatrail w/further scroll & floral carving continuing to demi-cabriole front legs, on casters, minor restorations, ca. 1850-60, 67" l., 41" h. (ILLUS.) **2,070.00**

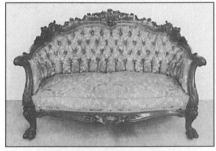

Ornate Late Victorian Sofa

Sofa, Victorian Late Rococo style, the gently arched & ornately scroll-carved crestrail curving around to form the arms w/scrolled hand grips above incurved leaf-carved arm supports, curved tufted back above an upholstered spring seat, serpentine shell- and scroll-carved seatrail continuing to short, heavy carved cabriole legs ending in large paw feet, ca. 1890-1900 (ILLUS.) **1,870.00**

MIRRORS

Bentwood dressing table mirror, Modern style, beechwood & bronze, the exterior bentwood frame enclosing bentwood & bronze discs, spheres & tubular bronze columns, surrounding an interior bentwood frame, all raised on bronze ball feet, mahogany

brown stain, designed by Koloman Moser, produced by J. &. J. Kohn, Model No. 1147, Vienna, Austria, ca. 1902, 35½" w., 4' 10½" h. . . . **6,900.00**

Chippendale Wall Mirror

Chippendale wall mirror, mahogany, high arched & scroll-cut crest above serrated upright ears over the rectangular molded frame & mirror plate, scroll-cut & scalloped bottom frame, molded parcel gilt liner, repairs, America, late 18th c., 14¼ x 35" (ILLUS.) . . . **546.00**

Chippendale-Style wall mirror, mahogany & mahogany veneer, an arched & scrolled crest above a pierced circle enclosing a gilt flying bird flanked by side crest scrolls & serrated corner ears above the rectangular mirror plate, scroll-carved & arched bottom frame, old glass, refinished, 19th c., 19½ x 38" **413.00**

Classical girandole wall mirror, a circular cove-molded spherule-decorated frame continuing to a black reeded inner border & a convex round mirror, surmounted by a spread-winged eagle atop a rock formation, the base w/a cluster of bowknot-tied leafy branches flanked by scrolling candle arms w/sockets, American or English, first quarter 19th c., 18¾" d., 33¼" h. (cracks to frame, silvering & branches loose) **5,750.00**

Classical overmantel mirror, gilt gesso, rectangular w/a molded cornice w/a split-baluster frame w/acanthus leaf decoration & reeded ebony liner, probably New York, ca. 1820, 43¼" l., 25¾" h. (imperfections). **863.00**

Classical overmantel mirror, giltwood, long & low three-part rectangular frame divided by bulbous & half-round ring-turned columns, the outer columns w/foliate- and ball-carved capitals & bases, raised on a shaped & molded base, first quarter 19th c., 66" l., 26¼" h. **633.00**

Classical pier mirror, gilt-stenciled mahogany, rectangular frame w/applied half-baluster pilasters, inset w/an upper églomisé panel depicting a country house, second quarter 19th c., 16 x 35" **690.00**

Classical pier mirror, giltwood, rectangular frame w/half-columns & rosette corners, the frieze applied w/a grape branch, second quarter 19th c., 20 x 43" **920.00**

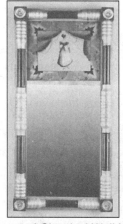

Decorated Classical Wall Mirror

Classical wall mirror, gilded & black-painted wood, rectangular frame w/turned split-baluster borders & corner blocks w/rondels, a reverse-painted rectangular tablet at the top showing a lady standing under draperies, leaftip & blossom borders, rectangular mirror plate, New England, minor imperfections, ca. 1830, 16 x 32" (ILLUS.) **748.00**

Classical wall mirror, carved mahogany & mahogany veneer, a deep stepped cornice above a wide veneered frieze flanked by blocks w/lyre designs above acanthus leaf & spiral-twist carved split balusters flanking the divided mirror plate, bottom corner blocks w/rondels, minor imperfections, New York City, 1820-35, 21½ x 40¼" (ILLUS.) **633.00**

Classical Mahogany Wall Mirror

Country-style wall mirror, curly maple flat rectangular frame w/simple corner blocks, old finish & original mirror w/worn silvering, 19th c., 12⅜ x 15¼" **743.00**

Federal "Girandole" Wall Mirror

Federal "girandole" wall mirror, gilt gesso, the tall crest w/a figure of a spread-winged eagle above foliate & grapevine cresting above a molded round framed w/ebonized liner, each w/a curved candlearm & socket, repainted, imperfections, England or America, early 19th c., 28½" w., 41½" h. (ILLUS.) **2,530.00**

Federal wall mirror, gilt gesso, narrow stepped cornice w/applied spiral molding & foliate banding above a narrow rectangular reverse-painted tablet w/an oval central scene of ruins within a

Federal Gilt Gesso Wall Mirror

white & blue rectangle w/fanned leaf spandrels, rectangular mirror plate below, fluted half-columns down the sides, minor imperfections, possibly Massachusetts, ca. 1810, 24 x 45" (ILLUS.) **2,415.00**

Federal wall mirror, inlaid & parcel-gilt mahogany, the curved & gilded swan's-neck cresting surmounted by a gilded urn w/wheat ears & flowers, the crest & pendant inlaid w/oval reserves, flanked by giltwood drapery, old refinish & regilding, New York City, 1790-1810, 24½" w., 5' 2" h. (restoration, losses) **3,105.00**

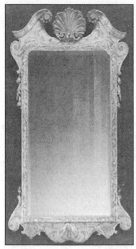

George I-Style Wall Mirror

George I-Style wall mirror, gilt gesso & giltwood, the beveled rectangular mirror plate w/swan's-neck cresting centering a shell, w/scrolled ears & pendent foliage, the shaped pendant w/a central shell, missing candlearms, England, 19th c., 22 x 41" (ILLUS.) **3,450.00**

Mission-style (Arts & Crafts movement) wall mirror, oak, rectangular w/inverted-V crestrail, two-color glass, original finish, Lifetime Furniture Co., similar to Model No. 512, 48¾" l., 28¼" h. **489.00**

Queen Anne wall mirror, walnut, a scroll-cut crest above a molded shaped liner enclosing the mirror plate, old refinish, England, ca. 1750, 17 x 36" (minor imperfections). **1,725.00**

Queen Anne wall mirror, walnut, the high gently arched & scroll-cut crestrail above a molded mirror frame w/rounded top corners enclosing the conforming mirror plate, deeply scalloped bottom rail fitted w/scrolled brass candlearms w/cylindrical sockets & drip pans, 18th c., 17 x 36" **1,300.00**

Regency Giltwood Wall Mirror

Regency wall mirror, giltwood & part-ebonized, a convex mirror plate within a beaded frame mounted w/spherules, the pendant w/a leaf spray flanked by foliage & continuing to exotic serpentine beasts, missing cresting, losses, England, early 19th c., 47" d., 4' 7" h. (ILLUS.) **7,475.00**

Classical Revival Cheval Mirror

Victorian cheval mirror, Classical Revival style, oak, a long rectangular frame w/rounded top corners holding a beveled mirror & swiveling between two knob-topped uprights joined by a cross-stretchers & C-scroll high feet on casters, ca. 1900, 27" w., 5' 9" h. (ILLUS.). **440.00**

Renaissance Revival Pier Mirror

Victorian pier mirror, Renaissance Revival substyle, walnut & burl walnut, the crestrail w/a large wheel-form rondel above a wide swag flanked by small pierced panels & small wheels at each corner above blocked & incised panels above a narrow burl panel over the long rectangular beveled mirror plate, slender columns over

long incised blocks down the sides, ca. 1880, 23" w., 4' 9" h. (ILLUS.). **275.00**

Simple Victorian Giltwood Mirror

Victorian wall mirror, giltwood, simple oval form w/beaded edge bands, mid-19th c. (ILLUS.) **220.00**

PARLOR SUITES

French Art Deco Parlor Suite

Art Deco: sofa & two armchairs; tapestry-upholstered, each w/an arched, scalloped back & gently rolled closed arms, deep upholstered seatrails w/fringe border, colorful floral design on cream ground, designed by Jules Leleu, France, ca. 1930, sofa 84" l., 33" h. (ILLUS.) **10,350.00**

Art Nouveau: settee, two armchairs & two side chairs; carved mahogany, each w/tall squared backs carved w/hawthorns in the frame & w/upholstered backs, closed arms & spring seats, slender squared & tapering gently flaring legs, matching carved apron, upholstered in original stamped velvet fabric in red or orange, Louis Majorelle "Sieges Aubegine," France, ca. 1900, the set **9,200.00**

Hoffmann Bentwood Parlor Suite

Bentwood: settee & two armchairs; bent beechwood in the Modern style, each w/a bentwood raised crestrail continuing to form the arms over two long spindles & an arm support leg, rectangular upholstered back panels & upholstered seat, U-form base stretcher, dark brown stain, designed by Josef Hoffmann, produced by J. & J. Kohn, Model No. 728, ca. 1906, settee 46" l., the set (ILLUS.) **9,775.00**

Italian Baroque-Style: two sofas, four armchairs & seven side chairs; giltwood frame w/round upholstered backs on chairs & curved crestrail on the sofas, each rail centered at the top by pierced scroll clusters centered by a cupid head on the chairs & a full-figure cupid on the sofas, beaded band trim around frame to scroll-molded & florette-decorated back supports flanking the upholstered seat, scroll-molded padded open arms, wide leaf-molded seatrail above reeded & gadrooned tapering cylindrical legs, sofa 80" l., side chairs 44" h., late 19th c., the set **6,900.00**

Victorian Baroque Parlor Suite

Victorian Baroque: sofa, armchair & rocker; carved mahogany, each w/a wide ornately scroll-carved crestrail centered by a winged cupid head, S-scroll heavy open arms above scroll-carved lyre-form splats & raised on heavy scroll-

carved arm supports continuing to form the front legs ending in paw feet, upholstered back & upholstered spring seats, ca. 1890, the set (ILLUS.) **1,100.00**

Renaissance Revival Chair Set

Victorian Renaissance Revival: armchair & two side chairs; walnut, each w/an arched crestrail centered by a pierced-cut central reserve w/palmette finial over narrow burl panels & round corners w/pendent drops, the tall waisted upholstered back above a rounded upholstered seat, the armchair w/rolled closed arms, curved seatrail w/burl trim & front drop, ring- and rod-turned tapering front legs on casters, ca. 1875, 3 pcs. (ILLUS.)...................... **660.00**

Fine Renaissance Revival Suite

Victorian Renaissance Revival: two settees, two armchairs & two side chairs; rosewood & marquetry, each piece w/a pointed & scroll-carved crest w/pointed finial above a round medallion flanked by pierced lattice & scroll carving above the upholstered back, the side chairs w/a round upholstered back between ornate rolled & inlaid frames above the round upholstered seats, the armchairs w/squared or flared upholstered back & closed upholstered arms, curved inlaid seatrails on knob- and reeded rod-turned tapering front legs on casters, ca. 1875, the set (ILLUS. of part) **7,475.00**

Renaissance Revival Sofas

Victorian Renaissance Revival: two
sofas, two pairs of armchairs & a
pair of side chairs; marquetry-inlaid
walnut; arched crestrail centered
by a large inlaid medallion framed
by an arched & pointed framework
& pierced carving, pointed corner
finials over pierce-carved corner
brackets above the inlaid back
framework enclosing an oblong
upholstery panel, deep upholstered
arms w/curved arm supports,
oblong serpentine seatrails
w/further inlay & raised panels
above short knob- and tapering
turned legs, some on casters,
probably New York City, ca. 1870-
80, the set (ILLUS. of part) **4,125.00**

Fine Victorian Rococo Sofa

Victorian Rococo: sofa & armchair;
carved rosewood, each w/an
ornate pierce-carved crest on the
arched crestrail, the armchair w/a
tall waisted tufted upholstered back
& rolled arms, curved arm supports
continuing to the scroll-carved
serpentine seatrail & demi-cabriole
front legs, the triple-back sofa
w/matching crest & tufted back &
arms, long serpentined & scroll-
carved seatrail above demi-
cabriole front legs, golden velvet
upholstery, ca. 1860, 2 pcs.
(ILLUS. of sofa) **1,320.00**

SCREENS

Fine Classical Fire Screen

Fire screen, Classical, carved
rosewood & rosewood-grained
w/parcel-gilt ormolu, a round
crestbar on the frame w/simulated
gilt-painted stringing, the
rectangular needlework panel
flanked by turned columns on
acanthus-carved outswept legs
w/cast foliate cap fire gilt casters,
old finish, very minor imperfections,
probably New York City, ca. 1830,
24" w., 38" h. (ILLUS.) **21,850.00**
Fire screen, Victorian Rococo
substyle, carved rosewood, the
large rectangular flat frame
w/rounded corners & molded
edges topped by a long pierced &
ornately scroll-carved crest, the
frame enclosing a needlepoint
panel of two people w/horses
outside a stable, the frame raised
on a trestle-form base w/scroll-
carved arched end legs on casters
joined by a ring-turned cross-
stretcher, ca. 1850-70, 4' h. **575.00**
Folding screen, three-fold, Arts &
Crafts style, painted wood, two
narrow & a wide central panel
decorated w/a continuous river
valley landscape w/a large tree in
the foreground & mountains in the
distance, decorated in shades of
dark & light green, rust red &
purple, V-notches at the top of
the panel joints, overall 96" w.,
72¼" h. **660.00**
Folding screen, five-fold, painted
fabric, Louis XV-Style, each panel
within a cartouche-shaped
decoration, decorated w/foliate
wreaths, classical urns, rocaille
elements, scantily clad classical
figures & hunt & harvest trophies in
tones of greyish blue & cream,

Louis XV-Style Folding Screen

highlighted w/white & dark grey & painted on the reverse w/cartouches & arabesques, France, 19th c., minor tears throughout, each panel 29" w., 9' 7½" h. (ILLUS.) **10,925.00**

Folding screen, six-fold, inlaid & decorated black lacquer, each panel w/an inlaid quatrefoil frame at the top surrounding applied Oriental figures, square bottom frames on each panel decorated w/exotic birds, the two end panels divided into three frames surround Chinese motifs & calligraphy, the four center panels w/long central frames decorated w/various applied Chinese designs, decorations in carved stone, ivory, wood & cloisonne, China, 19th c., each panel 15¾ x 72" (minor edge damage) **2,475.00**

Dutch Rococo-Style Screen

Folding screen, six-fold, painted & embossed leather, Rococo style, a continuous scene of large exotic trees in the foreground & temple-like buildings in the distance, decorated base border band, scalloped top, Holland, 19th c., areas of burn damage at base, each panel 15½" w., 6' 7" h. (ILLUS.) **2,645.00**

Folding screen, six-fold, painted leather, decorated w/a continuous landscape scene w/exotic birds w/an architectural surround hung w/floral garlands, the verso w/chinoiserie scenes, Europe, 19th c., each panel 21" w., 7' 6" h. **8,050.00**

French Painted Paper Screen

Folding screen, seven-fold, painted paper, decorated w/a continuous landscape scene of country folk in native costume dancing in a wooded mountainous landscape, w/two well-dressed gentlemen hunters looking on, painted *en grisaille*, within an applied brown Greek key border, now fitted onto a hardwood backing, France, 19th c., some tearing, restorations, each panel 19" w., 6' 6" h. (ILLUS.) ... **2,875.00**

Chinese Coromandel Screen

Folding screen, eight-fold, Coromandel-type, black & polychrome lacquer, decorated w/a continuous scene of Immortals within extensive landscapes w/pavilions & rockwork & a dragon above, the borders w/stylized Chinese characters, the reverse w/a riverscape w/Chinese figures in a mountainous landscape within floral borders, China, late 18th - early 19th c., each panel 14¾" w., 5' 10½" h. (ILLUS.) **9,200.00**

SECRETARIES

Rare Harvey Ellis Secretary

Arts & Crafts secretary, oak, a long rectangular top overhanging a case w/a pair of tall, slender doors w/four small glass panes above a single tall pane opening to shelves & fitted w/long strap hinges & a metal plate & bail pulls, the doors flanking an upper open compartment above a paneled fall-front w/large long strap hinges opening to a fitted interior above two long drawers over a lower open compartment, arched apron, designed by Harvey Ellis for Gustav Stickley, early 20th c. (ILLUS.) **66,000.00**

Chippendale Walnut Secretary

Chippendale secretary-bookcase, walnut, two-part construction: the upper section w/a broken-scroll pediment centered by a flame-turned finial above a pair of arched, raised panel cupboard doors; the lower section w/a hinged slant-lid opening to an interior fitted w/valanced slots & small drawers centered by a prospect door, the lower case w/four long graduated cockbeaded drawers w/butterfly brasses & keyhole escutcheons, molded base w/bracket feet, one drawer top signed "Chloe Dunbar," Massachusetts, late 18th c. (ILLUS.) **17,600.00**

Cherry Chippendale Secretary

Chippendale secretary-bookcase, cherry, two-part construction: the upper section w/a rectangular top w/a deep coved cornice above a pair of tall paneled doors; the lower section w/a hinged slant-front opening to an interior fitted w/pigeonholes, two drawers & four drawers disguised as scalloped brackets, the lower case w/four long graduated cockbeaded drawers w/simple bail pulls, molded base on scroll-cut ogee bracket feet, old mellow finish, original brasses, replaced escutcheons on upper doors, minor repairs, 18th c., 11½ x 41¾", 6' 11" h. (ILLUS.) . . . **8,800.00**

Chippendale secretary-bookcase, carved mahogany, two-part construction: the upper section w/a scrolled pediment w/carved rosettes & three flame-turned finials above a pair of cyma-curved paneled doors flanked by reeded pilasters & opening to an interior of

Fine Chippendale Secretary

open bookshelves surrounded by small valanced compartments & pigeonholes; the lower section w/a hinged slant-front opening to an interior fitted w/blocked & shell-carved drawers, pigeonholes & open compartments, the lower blocked case w/four long drawers, molded base w/scroll-cut bracket feet & center drop, restoration, 7' 11½" h.(ILLUS.) **14,950.00**

Chippendale-Style Secretary

Chippendale-Style secretary-bookcase, mahogany veneer, two-part construction: the upper section w/a broken-scroll pediment centered by a pointed ball finial above a pair of tall geometrically-glazed doors opening to two shelves; the lower section w/a hinged slant lid opening to a fitted interior above a double-serpentine

fronted case of four long graduated drawers w/butterfly pulls, molded base on short cabriole legs w/claw-and-ball feet, ca. 1920s (ILLUS.) . . **550.00**

Classical 'butler's' secretary-bookcase, mahogany, two-part construction: the upper section w/a rectangular top w/molded & stepped cornice over a wide plain frieze band above a pair of 9-pane triple Gothic arch-glazed doors opening to two shelves; the stepped-out lower section w/an overhanging rounded edge mid-molding above a large, deep cockbeaded fall-front drawer enclosing a beize-lined writing surface & fitted interior all overhanging three long graduated cockbeaded drawers flanked by free-standing ring-turned columns, double-ball & ring-turned legs, metal rosette & ring pulls, New York, ca. 1825 (veneer & other losses) **2,300.00**

Classical secretary-bookcase, mahogany, two-part construction: the upper section w/a rectangular top w/a straight concave cornice above a pair of tall geometrically-glazed doors; the lower section w/a paneled fitted desk drawer over three stepped-back long drawers flanked by free-standing columns, resting on bun feet, New York, second quarter 19th c., 22¼ x 44", overall 6' h. **2,300.00**

New England Classical Secretary

Classical secretary-bookcase, mahogany & mahogany veneer, two-part construction: the upper section w/a rectangular top w/a very deep widely flaring stepped cornice above a pair of Gothic arch-glazed cupboard doors opening to three shelves above a row of three small drawers; the lower section w/a fold-out writing surface above a long ogee-molded drawer over a pair of paneled cupboard doors, molded base on ogee bracket feet, New England, ca. 1830, refinished, very minor imperfections, 25 x 45½", 6' 11½" h. (ILLUS.) **4,600.00**

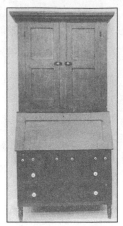

Country Secretary-Bookcase

slant-front opening to an interior fitted w/nine drawers, a center door & pigeonholes above a case w/a pair of drawers above two long, graduated drawers all w/porcelain knobs, short ring-turned tapering legs, old dark red repaint, wear, edge damage, 19th c., 21 x 40", 7' 2" h. (ILLUS.) **2,420.00**

Federal country-style secretary-bookcase, painted pine & poplar, two-part construction: the upper section w/a rectangular top w/a coved cornice above a single large raised panel cupboard door above an arched opening; the lower section w/a slanted hinged writing surface w/molded edges opening to an interior fitted w/four drawers & pigeonholes above a single long drawer, raised on square tapering slender legs, worn old brown graining on a yellow ground, early 19th c., 25 x 31¾", 6' 2¼" h. (replaced brasses & lock, wear & edge damage, some moldings missing) **2,640.00**

Federal lady's secretary, mahogany & mahogany veneer, two-part construction: the upper section w/a rectangular top & narrow cornice above a pair of simple cupboard doors opening to an interior fitted w/small drawers & valanced compartments plus full-sized compartments w/scrolled dividers; the stepped-out lower section w/a fold-out writing surface above a case of three long cockbeaded drawers w/round replaced brass pulls, scalloped & scroll-cut apron, baluster- and ring-turned legs

Fine Classical Secretary-Bookcase

Classical secretary-bookcase, mahogany & mahogany veneer, two-part construction: the upper section w/a rectangular top w/a flaring stepped cornice over a plain frieze band above a pair of tall geometrically-glazed cupboard doors opening to shelves & flanked by free-standing long columns above a row of three small drawers; the stepped-out lower section w/a fold-out writing surface above a pair of raised panel cupboard doors flanked by free-standing columns, wide tapering octagonal blocks on knob feet, probably New York, ca. 1830, refinished, 26 x 45½", 7' 7" h. (ILLUS.) **5,463.00**

Country-style secretary-bookcase, painted poplar, two-part construction: the upper section w/a rectangular top w/a wide stepped, flaring cornice above a pair of tall double-paneled cupboard doors w/cast-iron latches w/porcelain knobs opening to shelves; the lower section w/a paneled, hinged

Simple Federal Lady's Secretary

w/knob feet, old surface, imperfections, New England, early 19th c., 17 x 39¼", 4' 3" h. (ILLUS.). **1,725.00**

Attractive New England Secretary

Federal secretary-bookcase, carved mahogany & mahogany veneer, two-part construction: the upper section w/a rectangular top w/a flat, flaring cornice above a pair of geometrically-glazed cupboard doors opening to shelves above a row of three small cockbeaded drawers w/round brass pulls; the stepped-out lower section w/a fold-down writing surface above a pair of stepped-out drawers over two long drawers flanked by acanthus leaf-carved & ring-turned columns, round brass pulls, scalloped apron, on acanthus-carved, knob- and ring-turned legs w/peg feet, New England, 1815-25, old refinish, restoration (ILLUS.) **1,495.00**

Federal secretary-bookcase, mahogany, two-part construction: the upper section w/a scrolled pediment w/a central oval-inlaid

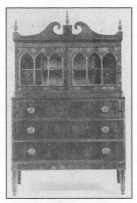

Federal Mahogany Secetary

block & three brass urns above a pair of long triple Gothic arch glazed doors opening to a fitted interior; the lower section w/a fold-out writing surface above a case w/pull-out supports & three long graduated drawers w/oval brass pulls, on ring-turned & reeded legs, early 19th c., 18½ x 40½", 5' 4½" h. (ILLUS.) **1,265.00**

Massachusetts Federal Secretary

Federal secretary-bookcase, mahogany & mahogany veneer, two-part construction: the upper section w/a broken-scroll crest & three reeded blocks above a pair of rectangular cupboard doors each w/two arched glass panes opening to an interior w/shelves & small drawers above a pair of drawers w/turned wood knobs; the stepped-out lower section w/a fold-out writing surface above a long projecting drawer above two long drawers flanked by spiral-turned columns, all w/wooden knobs, raised on baluster- and ring-turned legs w/peg feet, Massachusetts, ca. 1820, old refinish, imperfections, 5' 5½" h. (ILLUS.) **1,610.00**

Tall Federal Secretary-Bookcase

Federal secretary-bookcase, mahogany, two-part construction: the upper section w/a rectangular top w/a wide coved cornice above a pair of tall paneled doors; the lower section w/a slant-front hinged writing surface opening to a fitted interior above a case w/three long graduated drawers w/oval brass pulls, scalloped apron & slender French feet, Mid-Atlantic States, early 19th c., 19½ x 45½", 6' 10" h. (ILLUS.) **2,300.00**

Victorian "Cylinder-front" Secretary

Victorian "cylinder-front" secretary-bookcase, Golden Oak, two-part construction: the upper section w/a rectangular top & flaring stepped cornice above a pair of tall single-pane glazed cupboard doors w/stamped scrolling reserves in the upper corner opening to shelves; the lower section w/a paneled cylinder-front w/brass knobs opening to a fitted interior above a long drawer over a stack of two small drawers beside a paneled cupboard door w/stamped scrolling, reeded & half-round turned frame trim, scroll-stamped apron, ca. 1890s (ILLUS.) **1,045.00**

Fine Victorian Secretary-Bookcase

Victorian "cylinder-front" secretary-bookcase, Renaissance Revival substyle, walnut & walnut burl, two-part construction: the upper section w/a high arched crestboard w/carved & paneled decoration above a band of carved stylized fans above a thin burl-veneer band w/curved ends raised on an openwork band above a veneered frieze band over the pairs of single-pane tall glazed doors opening to three adjustable shelves; the lower section w/a two-panel cylinder front opening to a fitted interior above a case w/a narrow long drawer over two stepped-back drawers flanked by colonettes, 23 x 44", 7' h. (ILLUS.) **2,750.00**

Wooton "Patent" Secretary

Victorian "patent" secretary, walnut & walnut veneer, a "Wooton" patent model w/the front hinged to open to an ornately fitted desk interior, each door w/a curved paneled top above an arched raised panel below, paneled ends, raised on heavy molded feet, some veneer damage & losses, ca. 1870s (ILLUS.) **2,500.00**

SHELVES

Floor shelves, painted pine, two-part construction: the upper section w/three shelves w/the lower two divided into compartments; the projecting lower section w/two open shelves, grain-painted, probably New England, early 19th c., 10 x 37", 4' 10" h. **575.00**

Floor shelves, painted pine, the five open shelves joined by shaped sides on a cut-out base, yellow paint over earlier red & grey, New England, 19th c., 10 x 51½", 6' 2¼" h. (imperfections) **1,093.00**

Grain-painted Floor Shelves

Floor shelves, grain-painted pine, gently tapering shaped tall sides framing eight open shelves above a serpentine apron & cut-out feet, New England, mid-19th c., minor imperfections, 10½ x 48", 7' 9" h. (ILLUS.) **3,450.00**

Wall corner shelf, pine, the curved-front shelf w/triangular back brackets, old finish, attributed to the Shakers, 19th c., 13" h. **248.00**

Unique Decorated Corner Shelves

Wall corner shelves, painted pine, the wide deep base w/edge moldings & a narrow hinged door w/an applied diamond, the tall set-back scalloped back w/two quarter-round graduated shelves, two-tone brown stained & natural finish, beaded detail incomplete, 19th c., 24½" w., 37" h. (ILLUS.) **4,400.00**

Mahogany Wall Shelves

Wall shelves, mahogany, long shaped sides w/tapering ends enclosing a top open shelf w/a scroll-cut crest above a second open shelf above a lower shelf above a row of three small drawers w/turned wood knobs, glue & wire nail construction, old dry worn brown patina, 19th c., 6½ x 23¾", 36 ½" h. (ILLUS.) **3,740.00**

Wall shelves, mahogany, whale-end, the shaped dovetailed ends joining four open shelves, old refinish, New England, early 19th c., 8 x 31½", 36" h. (imperfections) . . . **920.00**

Wall shelves, painted pine, board ends tapering gradually to top small hanging hooks, two open shelves, dovetailed construction, old blue paint, 7 x 31½", 25" h. . . **2,090.00**

Wall shelves, painted pine, four open shelves joined by rectangular ends, painted turquoise blue, probably New England, 19th c., 11½ x 35", 39" h. (imperfections) **575.00**

Early Painted Wall Shelves

Wall shelves, painted wood, a bowed molded medial shelf between two conforming shaped shallow shelves joined by shaped sides terminating in spade cut-outs centering a rectangular hanger terminating in a spade cut-out, original dark blue paint, left side repair, probably New England, first third 19th c., left side repaired, 10½ x 13", 20½" h. (ILLUS.). **1,380.00**

Wall shelves, walnut, shaped whale-end sides joining four long open shelves & two short shelves below, old refinish, New England, mid-19th c., 7½ x 25¾", 34¼" h. (imperfections) **863.00**

SIDEBOARDS

Arts & Crafts sideboard, oak, the superstructure w/a low crestboard on a rectangular shelf raised on square front supports forming an open compartment backed by a rectangular mirror, the stepped-out rectangular top above a pair of geometrically-glazed cupboard doors flanking a center stack of three drawers above a single long

Arts & Crafts Oak Sideboard

drawer at the base, on square stile legs, original finish, early 20th c., 20 x 46", 4' 7" h. (ILLUS.) **690.00**

Grain-Painted Classical Server

Classical country-style server, grain-painted wood, the rectangular top w/a three-quarters high gallery, the back w/chamfered corners & the side front edges step-cut, the case w/a pair of deep drawers w/beveled edges & pairs of turned wood knobs above a pair of paneled doors, raised on turned double-knob feet, paneled ends, old red paint & burnt sienna graining, possibly New England, early 19th c., minor imperfections, 21 x 40¾", 44½" h. (ILLUS.). **1,840.00**

Classical server, mahogany, a flat rectangular crestboard above the rectangular top slightly overhanging the case w/a pair of two drawers w/small lacy glass knobs above a pair of set-back paneled cupboard doors opening to a single shelf & flanked by free-standing columns w/acanthus-carved & scrolling capitals, flat base raised on ball feet, New York, ca. 1820, 23¾ x 50", 44¾" h. (cracks in top, crestboard not attached, minor veneer loss) **690.00**

Small Classical Sideboard

Classical sideboard, mahogany & mahogany veneer, the high peaked backboard & scrolled gallery ends on the rectangular top w/rounded front edge above a case w/a pair of cockbeaded drawers w/oval brasses above a pair of paneled cupboard doors, paneled ends, short turned & tapering knob & peg legs, replaced brasses, old refinish, minor imperfections, probably New England, ca. 1820, 21 x 58", 44" h. (ILLUS.) **3,105.00**

Impressive Classical Sideboard

Classical sideboard, carved mahogany & mahogany veneer, the high serpentine ornately carved crestrail w/scrolling leafage centering a fruit-filled basket above two rectangular platforms flanking a central drop well, each platform above a round-fronted drawer

w/pressed glass knob, each drawer above pairs of free-standing columns flanking a narrow paneled door, a central drawer above an arch-paneled wide center door, plinth base raised on four leaf-carved front paw feet, old refinish, minor imperfections, New York State, ca. 1830s, 21 x 60", 4' 2½" h. (ILLUS.) **2,530.00**

Unique Inlaid Sideboard

Country-style sideboard, inlaid walnut, the rectangular top w/a central rectangular inlay outlined w/a double row of light & dark inlays & stringing above a case w/a pair of short drawers & a long drawer each w/diamond & checkerboard inlay above two similarly inlaid paneled cupboard doors above the deeply scalloped & star-inlaid apron on ogee bracket feet, old refinish, probably North or South Carolina, 1850-75, imperfections, 19¾ x 44", 37" h. (ILLUS.) **3,738.00**

Small Federal Inlaid Sideboard

Federal sideboard, carved & inlaid mahogany & mahogany veneer, the rectangular top w/a bowed front & ovolo corners over a conforming case w/two long cockbeaded central drawers inlaid w/oval bands flanked by narrow wine drawers w/similar inlay above two lower cupboard doors also w/oval inlay &

banded veneering, reeded quarter-round corner posts continuing to tapering reeded legs, old refinish, restored, probably Massachusetts, ca. 1815, 21½ x 44¼", 39½" h. (ILLUS.) **4,888.00**

Federal sideboard, inlaid walnut, the rectangular top w/line-inlaid edge above a case w/a single center drawer above a small cupboard door flanked by deep end drawers, raised on tall slender square tapering legs w/inlaid cuffs, probably Virginia, early 19th c., 21½ x 57", 39½" h. **8,050.00**

Federal sideboard, satinwood-inlaid mahogany, the rectangular top w/a serpentine front w/a line-inlaid edge above a conforming case w/a line-inlaid long central drawer veneered to resemble two drawers & flanked at each end by a line-inlaid working drawer, each drawer separated by a stile inlaid w/a floral medallion all above a pair of central recessed doors flanked by deep concave-front drawers, supports on four front square tapering legs w/banded cuffs, possibly Charleston or Georgetown, South Carolina, ca. 1810, 25¼ x 70¼", 40½" h. (some veneer loss, cracks in center doors & sides) **8,050.00**

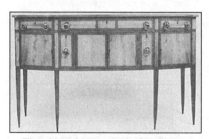

Fine New Hampshire Sideboard

Federal sideboard, mahogany & flame birch veneer, the rectangular top w/long bowed front w/an inlaid edge above a pair of small drawers flanking a long central drawer all outlined in crossbanded mahogany veneer & stringing over two central cupboard doors flanked by sectioned bottle drawers & end cabinets, on six double tapered square cuff-inlaid legs, the front legs w/bellflower inlay, old surface, replaced round pulls, imperfections, Portsmouth, New Hampshire, 1800-15, 26 x 68¾", 41⅝" h. (ILLUS.). **16,675.00**

French Provincial Buffet

French Provincial buffet, oak, rectangular top above a pair of narrow cockbeaded drawers w/simple pulls above a pair of raised panel cupboard doors, paneled ends, scalloped apron & short cabriole front legs, France, ca. 1760, 23 x 57", 42" h. (ILLUS.) **1,640.00**

Mission-style (Arts & Crafts movement) server, oak, rectangular top w/low backsplash overhanging an apron w/two drawers w/copper V-pulls, fine original medium dark finish, red decal mark of Gustav Stickley, 18 x 42", 38" h. **3,080.00**

Gustav Stickley Mission Server

Mission-style (Arts & Crafts movement) server, oak, a low crestboard on the rectangular top overhanging an apron w/a pair of drawers w/metal plate & bail pulls above the arched apron, on square tapering legs joined by side rails & a lower medial shelf, original dark chocolate finish w/some wear, original hardware, large red decal Gustav Stickley mark, Model No. 802, 18 x 41¾", 39½" h. (ILLUS.) **7,475.00**

Mission-style (Arts & Crafts movement) sideboard, oak, a low crestboard on the rectangular top overhanging a case w/two pairs of small drawers flanking a deep central drawer above a single long drawer, plate & bail metal hardware, square tapering stile legs joined by a lower medial shelf, original hardware w/dark patina, original dark chocolate finish, two top drawers w/original suede lining, large red Gustav Stickley decal mark, Model No. 800, early 20th c., 21 x 53½", 43" h. **4,025.00**

Fine Aesthetic "Gothic" Sideboard

Victorian sideboard, Aesthetic Movement "Gothic" substyle, walnut, the superstructure w/a rectangular backboard & pointed crest framing a galleried shelf above a pair of paneled cupboard doors w/long angular strap hinges & square animal-decorated panels above an open shelf above narrow sectioned compartments over a hinged slant-front w/long angular hinges & incised & paneled decoration opening to a fitted interior above a center drawer above an open shelf w/back spindled rail flanked by a pair of narrow cupboard doors w/similar design, curved base brackets, Kimbel & Cabus, New York, ca. 1875, 17¾ x 39¼", 6' 1" h. (ILLUS.) **9,775.00**

Victorian sideboard, Baroque Revival, carved walnut, the tall arched backboard ornately carved

Victorian Baroque Sideboard

in bold relief w/central figures flanked by scrolls & smaller figures w/a winged lion seated at each end above the rectangular top w/a breakfront w/three projecting sections, the case w/a pair of long figural-carved drawers between three paneled raised blocks w/grotesque masks above a pair of paneled, figure-carved cupboard doors separated by three full-figure semi-nude males, heavy conforming scroll-carved base on grotesque mask feet, Europe, late 19th c. (ILLUS.) **5,000.00**

Outstanding Victorian Sideboard

Victorian sideboard, Renaissance Revival substyle, gilt bronze-mounted rosewood & marquetry, the pedimented crestboard centered by a raised panel w/a bold relief-carved classical woman's head flanked by gilt-incised pilasters & scrolls, the rectangular top w/stepped, molded front & central raised platform above a band of three narrow drawers above three paneled doors each w/ornate marquetry panels & raised borders & separated by four ornately carved & mounted columns, stepped & molded decorated base, backboards w/"WHW," probably New York, ca. 1875, 74" l. (ILLUS.) **11,500.00**

Fine Victorian Eastlake Sideboard

Victorian sideboard, Eastlake
substyle, the tall superstructure w/a
stepped, molded crestboard w/a
band of leaf carving above a
paneled frieze supported by square
reeded posts forming two small
open shelves w/diamond ray
carved backboards & flanking a
large central beveled mirror all on a
rectangular brown marble top over
a pair of narrow drawers & a long
drawer all w/pierced brass pulls
over a pair of paneled, ray-carved
cupboard doors, molded base on
casters, ca. 1885, 22 x 54", 7' 6" h.
(ILLUS.) **2,200.00**

STANDS

Federal Revival Book Stand

Book stand, Federal Revival style,
rotating-type, the round scalloped
top w/reeded edge above three
pierced dividers on a round lower
shelf all rotating above a short ring-
turned pedestal & four downswept
reeded legs ending in brass claw
feet, ca. 1930, 23" d., 29" h.
(ILLUS.) **116.00**

Arts & Crafts Book Stand

Book stand, Arts & Crafts style, oak,
the tall tapering round-topped key-
pierced sides flanking a top angled
shelf above three graduated open
shelves, early 20th c., 10 x 22",
47" h. (ILLUS.). **220.00**

Cherry Classical Candlestand

Candlestand, Classical, carved
cherry, the rectangular top w/notch-
cut corners above a vase-, ring-
and spiral-turned pedestal on a
tripod base w/three long slender
outstretched S-scroll legs, New
England, ca. 1825, refinished,
16⅜ x 22", 25" h. (ILLUS.) **1,150.00**
Candlestand, country-style, painted
& turned wood, the round thick top
w/chamfered edge above a boldly
knob-turned post terminating in a
drop ball pendant raised on three
splayed vase-, ring- and rod-turned
legs, old brown paint over several
earlier layers, 18th c., 12¾" d.,
26" h. **2,300.00**
Candlestand, country-style, carved &
painted wood, adjustable, tin
candleholders w/crimped drip pans
& end mounts raised on a circular
base on three ball feet, green,
yellow & cream banded paint
decoration, Scandinavia, 19th c.,
33" h. (paint wear, minor losses) . . **633.00**

Candlestand, country-style, a heavy square foot w/chamfered sides centered by a tall slender post fitted w/an adjustable cross-arm w/a tall cylindrical candle socket post at each tip, old finish, old but not period, 33¾" h. **303.00**

Early Primitive Candlestand

Candlestand, country-style, painted maple & pine, screw-form, a tall slender screw shaft w/adjustable two-socket candlearm above a small round platform on a ring-, knob- and columnar-turned pedestal on a tripod base w/flattened cabriole legs, painted apple green, probably New England, late 18th c., imperfections, 11" d., 40" h. (ILLUS.). **2,300.00**

Candlestand, Federal country-style, maple, oblong coffin-shaped top raised on a baluster- and ring-turned pedestal over a tripod base w/spider legs, old surface, New England, early 19th c., 16¾ x 19¼", 26¾" h. (very minor surface imperfections) **518.00**

Federal Country-style Candlestand

Candlestand, Federal country-style, tiger stripe maple & cherry, the rectangular top w/notched corners above a baluster-turned maple pedestal on a tripod base w/angular flat cabriole cherry legs, old refinish, imperfections, New England, early 19th c., 16 x 18", 27½" h. (ILLUS.) **403.00**

Candlestand, Federal country-style, red-stained birch, the octagonal top tilting above a ring-turned pedestal on a tripod base w/spider legs ending in spade feet, original surface, Portsmouth, New Hampshire, early 19th c., 16 x 23¼", 28¼" h. (minor surface imperfections) **2,300.00**

Candlestand, Federal country-style, cherry, a nearly square top w/a scratch-beaded edge on a ring-turned pedestal over a tripod base w/three cabriole legs w/sharply angled knees & ending in snake feet, Connecticut, late 18th c., 16 x 16 ½", 28½" h. (repairs) **863.00**

Candlestand, Federal, inlaid cherry, the octagonal top w/an inlaid central oval reserve outlined w/diagonal inlaid banding, tilting above a vase- and ring-turned pedestal w/incised bands above the tripod base w/cabriole legs ending in pad feet, old finish, Concord, Massachusetts, ca. 1780, 14½ x 18", 27¼" h. . . . **5,463.00**

Candlestand, Federal, mahogany "tilt-top," the serpentine top tilting above a vase- and ring-turned pedestal on a tripod base w/cabriole legs ending in arris pad feet on platforms, old finish, Massachusetts, ca. 1790, 19 x 19¾", 27" h. (very minor imperfections). **5,175.00**

Candlestand, Queen Anne, mahogany, round dished top tilting above a birdcage mechanism w/baluster-turned spindles above a ring- and rod-turned pedestal on a squashed turned ball above the tripod base w/flattened cabriole legs ending in slipper feet, Philadelphia, ca. 1760, 18¾" d., 29¼" h. (repairs to birdcage) **9,200.00**

Candlestand, Windsor-style, cherry, the round top above a slender vase- and ring-turned pedestal raised on four splayed block- and baluster-turned legs joined by a matching H-stretcher, old refinish,

Early Windsor Candlestand

minor imperfections, New England, early 19th c., 18½" d., 28½" h. (ILLUS.) **1,840.00**

Candlestand w/drawer, Federal, mahogany, the square top on a chamfered platform containing a small drawer above a vase- and ring-turned pedestal on a tripod base w/flat cabriole legs ending in arris pad feet on platforms, old refinish, probably Connecticut, ca. 1790, 14 ½ x 14¾", 29½" h. **2,990.00**

Drink stand, Mission-style (Arts & Crafts movement), oak, round top overhanging square legs joined by arched cross-stretchers w/a round medial shelf, refinished top, unmarked L. & J. G. Stickley, 18" d., 29" h. **1,045.00**

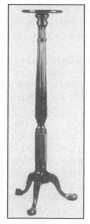

Fine Victorian Fern Stand

Fern stand, Victorian, mahogany, a small round top raised on a very tall reeded column above a spiral-turned cylinder above the tripod base w/cabriole legs ending in claw-and-ball feet, late 19th c., 4' 8¾" h. (ILLUS.) 518.00

Unusual Lacemaker's Stand

Lacemaker's stand, mahogany, the rectangular box-form w/a tapering, rounded rectangular top above a tapering rectangular case w/a compartmented side drawer containing numerous bobbins, on an applied ripple molded base, old surface, first half 19th c., 9⅜ x 18⅝", 11⅝" h. (ILLUS.). **978.00**

Magazine stand, Mission-style (Arts & Crafts movement), oak, rectangular top overhanging narrow arched aprons & three open shelves, slender square stile legs joined by side stretchers, designed by Harvey Ellis, original reddish brown finish, new finish on top, branded Gustav Stickley mark, 13 x 22", 42" h. **2,640.00**

Magazine stand, Mission-style (Arts & Crafts movement), oak, a rectangular top w/a low three-quarter gallery w/a pointed backrail & chamfered closed back & sides framing three lower shelves, arched aprons, some refinishing, unmarked, L. & J.G. Stickley - Onondaga Shops, 12 x 19", 45" h. **1,210.00**

Decorated Classical Music Stand

Music stand, Classical, grain-painted, the rectangular two-sided rack w/lyre-shaped pierced center w/brass strings & adjustable end candlearms adjusting on a thumbscrew collar above the tapering ring-turned & gold stencil-decorated pedestal ending in a tripod base w/outswept reeded legs ending in brass paw feet, overall rosewood graining trimmed w/gilt striping, original surface, repair to candle drip pans, very minor surface imperfections, probably England, ca. 1800, 45½" h. (ILLUS.) **4,600.00**

Rosewood Classical Music Stand

Music stand, Classical, carved rosewood & rosewood veneer, the two-sided rectangular top rack w/metal stringing raised on a slender turned shaft above a large paneled & leaf-carved pedestal on a tripartite platform base w/bun feet, old finish, imperfections, probably England, ca. 1830, overall 4' h. (ILLUS.) **1,955.00**

Nightstand, Federal country-style, cherry, a square top above an apron w/a singled cockbeaded drawer w/metal drop pull, on simple round tapering legs, New England, early 19th c., 17⅛" w., 28¾" h. **230.00**

Mission-style Nightstand

Nightstand, Mission-style (Arts & Crafts movement), oak, a rectangular top overhanging a single drawer w/a hammered copper pull above a narrow arched apron, raised on square legs joined by a lower medial shelf, refinished w/a varnish coat, unmarked Lifetime Furniture Co., numbered Model No. 1203, early 20th c., 15 x 20", 29¾" h. (ILLUS.) **660.00**

Plant stand, Mission-style (Arts & Crafts movement), oak, square deep well top w/cut-out handholds between square stiles ending in MacMurdo feet, box stretchers w/three central slats on each side, varnish overcoat, paper label of Lakeside Craft Shops, 15" sq., 20½" h. **633.00**

Plant stand, decorated wood, the square top trimmed around the apron w/a band of old wooden sewing spools, the tall slender canted legs composed of rows of old wooden sewing spools, a low square shelf trimmed below w/further wooden spools, old yellow wood graining w/yellow striping & gold stenciled decoration w/red trim, late 19th c., 14½" sq., 28½" h. **99.00**

Smoking stand, Arts & Crafts style, oak w/square copper-covered top trimmed w/twenty pyramidal tacks, pointed caned panels in the upper sides above a small square medial shelf over a tall cane-paneled door w/ push-button lock, quarter-sawn oak, unmarked, 9¼" sq., 25" h. . . . **1,093.00**

Decorated Cherry Telephone Stand

Telephone stand, Victorian-Style, decorated cherry, the oval dished top over a narrow drawer raised on lyre-form supports joined by a flat stretcher above arched legs joined by a narrow stretcher, polychrome fruit decoration, signed "Flint & Horner, New York," ca. 1920s, 13 x 19", 27" h. (ILLUS.) **220.00**

Umbrella stand, Mission-style (Arts & Crafts movement), oak, four square posts tapering at the tops & joined near the top & bottom by box stretchers, original metal drip pan in base, original finish, early 20th c., 11¾" sq., 29" h. **193.00**

Classical Washstand

Washstand, Classical, cherry & mahogany veneer, a scalloped splashboard ending w/turned towel bars w/scrolled front supports above the rectangular top above a long ogee-fronted drawer over two deep flat drawers w/turned wood knobs, scroll-cut bracket feet, the case in cherry, the drawers w/mahogany veneering, top appears to be replaced, ca. 1840, 17⅛ x 30⅛", 28" h. (ILLUS.) **303.00**

Classical Tiger Maple Washstand

Washstand, Classical country-style, tiger stripe maple, the high arched & scalloped backboard flanked by low side gallery boards on the long rectangular top above a single long drawer w/small turned wood knobs, heavy knob- and block-turned

supports to the rectangular medial shelf w/serpentine front, raised on short turned & tapering legs w/knob feet, probably New York State, first half 19th c., minor imperfections, 18 x 34", 29" h. (ILLUS.). **2,415.00**

Washstand, Classical country-style, painted & decorated, the arched three-quarter gallery w/scrolled sides on the rectangular top & shelf & a single drawer, raised on turned legs, green & yellow striping w/stenciled decoration, ca. 1840, 13 x 20½", 35¼" h. **690.00**

Painted Country Corner Washstand

Washstand, country corner-style, painted pine & maple, the high scrolled backsplash above a quarter-round small shelf & small drawer w/brass pull above a square top w/an off-center round hole, raised on slender square legs joined by a medial shelf over a thin drawer w/simple bail pull, original red paint, New England, 1820s, very minor surface imperfections, 16¾" sq., 34½" h. (ILLUS.). **2,415.00**

Washstand, Federal country-style, painted & decorated pine & poplar, a rectangular top w/a large round cut-out below the high arched three-quarter gallery decorated at the back w/a large cluster of grapes & grapevine, the top raised on four ring- and baluster-turned supports to a medial shelf over a small drawer w/a round brass pull, on ring- and baluster-turned legs w/ball feet, original yellow painted w/black & gold striping & stenciled & free-hand crest decoration, early 19th c., 17 x 18½", 30½" h. plus gallery (minor wear & shelf age crack). **688.00**

Washstand, Federal country-style, painted & decorated pine, the rectangular top w/a cut-out round bowl opening below the high three-quarter gallery w/an arched & scroll-cut backboard w/small corner shelves joining the scroll-cut sides, a decorated frieze band & corner blocks raised on ring- and baluster-turned supports to the medial shelf above a narrow decorated drawer w/two round metal pulls, baluster- and ring-turned legs w/knob feet, original red & black graining w/yellow & green striping & gilt stenciled trim, Maine, early 19th c., 16¼ x 18¼", overall 36½" h. **440.00**

Washstand, Federal, inlaid mahogany, bowfront corner-style, a high back gallery w/a small corner shelf above the quarter-round top w/a large & two small round cut-outs all trimmed w/ebony line inlay, three square supports above the medial shelf over a narrow curve-fronted drawer above a shaped apron & three outswept legs joined by a flat three-armed stretcher w/turned ring, refinished, early 19th c., 19 x 25", 41¾" h. **990.00**

Washstand, Victorian cottage-style, painted & decorated, a rectangular hinged lift lid w/a molded edge opening to a deep well over a small drawer, a heavy mid-molding above a small paneled door in the bottom, scroll-cut apron & simple bracket feet, original brown wood graining on a yellow ground w/red, brown & green striping & foliage & berry decoration, second half 19th c., 18¼ x 29", 29½" h. **358.00**

Country Victorian Washstand

Washstand, Victorian country-style, cherry & poplar w/cherry finish, a serpentine splashboard w/turned

end towel bars w/shaped front supports above the rectangular top over a single drawer w/a wooden knob, raised on bobbin-turned supports to a serpentine-fronted medial shelf on blocked & bobbin-turned legs, ca. 1850-70, 17 x 27½", 33½" h. (ILLUS.) **165.00**

Washstand, Victorian Eastlake substyle, walnut, a rectangular white marble top w/molded edges & a high rounded marble backsplash above the case w/a long line-incised drawer above a pair of small deep line-incised drawers beside a line-incised paneled cupboard door, line-incised bands down the side stiles, molded base, old finish, ca. 1890, 15 x 30", overall 34" h. (stains & short crack in splashback) **303.00**

Victorian Marble-topped Washstand

Washstand, Victorian Renaissance Revival substyle, walnut & burl walnut, the tall white marble splashback w/chamfered corners & two angled shelves on brackets above the rectangular white marble top above a long drawer w/burl panel & black pear-shaped pulls above a pair of paneled doors w/raised burl panels all flanked by blocked & carved side stiles, flat molded base, ca. 1875, 17 x 27½", 28½" h. (ILLUS.) **424.00**

Washstand, Victorian Renaissance Revival substyle, walnut & burl walnut, the rectangular white marble top w/a molded edge & a tall arched white marble backsplash w/two small braced marble shelves, the case w/three long drawers each w/pairs of shaped raised burl panels w/black pear-shaped pulls, deep molded base on flat square feet, old finish, ca. 1875, 16¼ x 30", 29" h. plus backsplash **523.00**

Washstand, Victorian Renaissance Revival substyle, walnut, a high arched & stepped backsplash above the rectangular top w/a molded edge & rounded front corners, the case w/a single long drawer w/a raised molding ring around the keyhole flanked by half-oval raised molding panels above a pair of arched molded panel doors, deep molded base on flat block feet on casters, ca. 1870, 15½ x 29½", 30½" h. plus backsplash . . . **385.00**

Classical Country-style Stand

Classical country-style one-drawer stand, walnut, retangular top slightly overhanging an apron w/a single drawer & two turned wood knobs, raised on block- and knob-turned legs w/knob feet, mid-19th c., 18 x 22", 28" h. (ILLUS.). **165.00**

Classical country-style two-drawer stand, cherry, rectangular top slightly overhanging a deep case w/two ogee-fronted drawers w/pairs of small round brass pulls, raised on tapering ring-, knob- and rod-turned legs ending in ball feet, refinished, first half 19th c., 22½ x 22⅞", 29½" h. (edge wear, top replaced) **550.00**

Fine Classical Two-Drawer Stand

Classical two-drawer stand, curly maple & mahogany, the thin rectangular top above an apron w/two mahogany-trimmed drawers w/turned wood knobs flanked by corner blocks w/disc-turned pendants, raised on a heavy ring- and urn-turned pedestal on a center ring raised on four C-scroll legs w/applied mahogany rondels & ending in mahogany knob feet, ca. 1840, refinished (ILLUS.) **1,430.00**

Classical Drop-leaf Stand

Classical two-drawer stand, curly maple & mahogany veneer, the rectangular top flanked by two rounded drop leaves above the apron w/two round-fronted mahogany-veneered drawers w/small round knobs, raised on ring-, knob- and baluster-turned legs ending in baluster-turned feet, ca. 1840 (ILLUS.) **715.00**

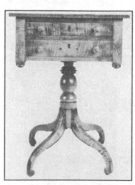

Classical Tiger Stripe Maple Stand

Classical two-drawer stand, tiger stripe maple, rectangular top above an apron w/two narrow drawers w/round brass pulls & block stiles w/turned base buttons, raised on a heavy ball- and ring-turned pedestal over four outswept S-scroll legs, refinished, minor imperfections, Middle Atlantic states, ca. 1825, 17¾ x 21", 29" h. (ILLUS.) **1,093.00**

Classical two-drawer stand, mahogany veneer, a rectangular marble top above a single cockbeaded drawer w/turned wooden pulls, raised on ring-turned tapering legs & feet flanking a medial shelf, refinished, New England, 1830s, 17 x 24", 32" h. (restoration) **460.00**

Federal country-style one-drawer stand, cherry, a rectangular one-board top slightly overhanging an apron w/a single drawer w/a turned wood knob, raised on ring-, ball-and tapering rod-turned legs ending in ball feet, good old finish, early 19th c., 17½ x 19¾", 28" h. . . . **440.00**

Federal country-style one-drawer stand, bird's-eye maple & cherry, a rectangular top w/applied beaded edge widely overhanging an apron w/a single drawer w/a round brass pulls, raised on four simple slighting tapering ring-turned legs, old finish, New England, early 19th c., 19 x 20", 26¼" h. (imperfections) **863.00**

Federal country-style one-drawer stand, curly & bird's-eye maple, rectangular two-board top above a single dovetailed drawer w/original brass pull, turned legs, old mellow refinishing w/wear, early 19th c., 20 x 20¼", 27¼" h. **715.00**

Federal country-style one-drawer stand, cherry, rectangular top above an apron w/a single drawer w/a turned wood knob, tall slender ring- and baluster-turned tapering legs w/button feet, old finish, early 19th c., 18¾ x 19½", 28" h. (some edge damage on legs) **358.00**

Federal country-style one-drawer stand, painted & decorated pine & poplar, rectangular top overhanging an apron w/a single drawer w/a turned knob, raised on slender ring- and rod-turned tapering legs w/peg feet, original brown flame graining, New England, early 19th c., 17¼ x 19½", 28½" h. (strip on one top edge loose) **1,045.00**

Federal country-style one-drawer stand, cherry, rectangular two-board top above an apron w/a single beaded drawer w/a

damaged lacy glass pull, ring-, baluster- and knob-turned legs w/peg feet, old finish, early 19th c., 19 x 21", 29" h. **358.00**

Federal country-style stand, cherry, nearly square one-board top w/beveled edges widely overhanging the angled apron & tall slender canted & tapering legs, old dark varnish finish, early 19th c., 19½ x 20", 25¾" h. **605.00**

Federal country-style stand, pine, the square one-board top above a mortised & nailed deep apron raised on square tapering legs, traces of old red, 19th c., 15" w., 27" h. (top wear, old edge repair) . . **295.00**

Federal country-style stand, poplar, the nearly square top widely overhanging the deep tapering apron above tall canted ring- and rod-turned legs w/peg feet, dark finish w/traces of old blue, Pennsylvania, 19th c., 17 x 17½", 28½" h. **660.00**

Federal Country-Style Stand

Federal country-style two-drawer stand, tiger stripe maple, the rectangular top above a narrow drawer over a deeper drawer each w/pairs of large turned wood knobs, raised on ring-, knob- and baluster-turned legs ending in knob feet, ca. 1820-30 (ILLUS.) **2,090.00**

Federal country-style two-drawer stand, walnut, rectangular top flanked by two hinged rectangular drop leaves over a deep apron w/two drawers w/turned wood knobs, ring-, baluster- and rod-turned legs w/knob feet, old dark varnish stain finish, first half 19th c., closed 17¼ x 22¼", 28" h. **303.00**

Federal country-style two-drawer stand, walnut & mahogany veneer, rectangular top overhanging

slightly a deep apron w/two
reverse-graduated drawers
w/turned wood knobs, on ring-,
knob- and tapering rod-turned legs
w/knob feet, old worn finish, first
half 19th c., 20¼ x 21½", 28¼" h.
(surface damage on refastened
top) **248.00**

**Federal country-style two-drawer
stand,** cherry, curly & bird's-eye
maple, the rectangular one-board
top above a deep apron w/a bird's-
eye maple drawer above a deeper
curly maple drawer, each w/a
single turned knob, cherry case
w/ring- and bobbin-turned legs
w/tapering peg feet, refinished,
early 19th c., 18½ x 20", 29¾" h.
(top & drawer bottoms replaced) . . **495.00**

Federal one-drawer stand, curly
maple, nearly square two-board top
w/ovolo corners above an apron
w/a single drawer w/an oval brass
pull, on tall slender square tapering
legs, old brass, refinished, early
19th c., 18 x 18¼", 25¾" h. **1,210.00**

Federal one-drawer stand, maple &
birch, the rectangular top
overhanging an apron w/a single
drawer, on tall slender square
tapering legs, refinished, New
Hampshire, early 19th c., 15 x
17¾", 27½" h. (brass pull may not
be original) **805.00**

Federal one-drawer stand, birch, the
rectangular top slightly
overhanging the apron w/a single
drawer constructed without pulls,
square tall slender tapering legs,
original surface, Loudon, New
Hampshire, early 19th c., 14¾ x
17¾", 28⅜" h. (very minor
imperfections) **748.00**

Federal two-drawer stand, cherry &
curly maple, the rectangular curly
maple top w/rounded edges above
a deep curly maple case w/two
matching drawers w/turned wood
knobs, ring- and ropetwist-turned
cherry legs, early 19th c., 17¼ x
19½", 29¾" h. (dividers missing in
top drawer, one section of back
panel old replacement) **2,200.00**

Federal two-drawer stand, curly &
bird's-eye maple, the rectangular
top w/a molded edge above a case
w/two small drawers w/old brass
pulls raised on tall ring- and
baluster-turned legs w/ball feet, top
drawer w/fitted interior, early 19th
c., 17½ x 18", 30" h. (minor top age
cracks, one pull incomplete) **825.00**

STOOLS

Classical Footstool

Classical footstool, mahogany, the
deep overupholstered rectangular
top raised on a double C-scroll
base centering rosettes joined by a
turned stretcher, attributed to
Hancock, Holden and Adams,
Boston, ca. 1830s, old refinish,
15½ x 16½", 14" h. (ILLUS.) **920.00**

Classical footstool, mahogany, the
rectangular concave over-
upholstered top on a conforming
frame & curule-form base centering
a circular boss & joined by a turned
medial stretcher, old finish, New
York City, 1810-15, 15½ x 21",
15" h. (imperfections) **978.00**

Classical footstools, mahogany &
mahogany veneer, the rectangular
upholstered top in a conforming
frame raised on demi-lune legs, old
finish, possibly Boston, ca. 1825,
13 x 20", 7¾" h., pr. (minor veneer
loss) **575.00**

Simple Classical Piano Stool

Classical piano stool, rosewood, the
round adjustable molded seat on a
tapering paneled column & a
tripartite base w/C-scroll feet on
knobs, probably New England, ca.
1830, 18" h. (ILLUS.). **460.00**

Fine Classical Piano Stool

Classical piano stool, carved mahogany & mahogany veneer, the back w/a curving veneered crestrail above a lyre-form splat w/brass strings over a carved stay rail flanked by molded & carved curved stiles, upholstered seat raised on a heavy ornately carved pedestal on outswept dolphin-carved legs on casters, New York, ca. 1810-15, very minor imperfections, 32" h. (ILLUS.) . . . **4,888.00**

Federal piano stool, Federal, mahogany, round seat w/reeded seatrail above four spiral-carved & turned legs flanking a platform, old mahogany surface & dark stain accenting the turnings, New York state, 1820s, unupholstered, 13½" d., 19" h. **403.00**

Footstool, crude oval bird's-eye maple top on slender turned & canted tapering maple legs, old refinishing, 19th c., 7¾ x 12¼", 5¾" h. **303.00**

Footstool, curly maple, rectangular top above deeply scalloped sides & slightly canted squared pine legs, old finish, 19th c., 6 x 11¼", 6" h. **770.00**

Footstool, an oval padded & needlepoint-upholstered top raised on curved pairs of forked stag antlers, 19th c., 11 x 12", 11" h. **110.00**

Footstool, painted & decorated pine, a rectangular upholstered top above deeply scalloped side aprons decorated in old black paint & striping in yellow, red, & green, bootjack legs, top recovered w/old brown & white check homespun, 19th c., 8 x 15" (some damage, wear & small holes in fabric) **248.00**

George I Giltwood Stool

George I stool, giltwood, the rectangular overupholstered seat raised on cabriole legs carved w/crosshatching & flowerheads, adapted, England, early 18th c., 16 x 23", 14½" h. (ILLUS.). **7,475.00**

Mission-style (Arts & Crafts movement) footstool, oak, rectangular black leather drop-in seat framed by arched seatrails on square legs joined by box stretchers, wear & added varnish to dark finish, Lifetime Furniture Company paper label, 16½" sq., 13" h. (some loose joints) **275.00**

Regency stools, gilt & black-painted wood, X-form frame w/the upcurved side frames terminating in griffin head finials & joined by a round stretcher, fitted w/a square padded seat, the downcurved legs ending in paw feet, England, early 19th c., 28" l., pr. **9,200.00**

Victorian Beadwork Footstool

Victorian footstools, beadwork & giltwood, an upholstered round giltwood frame covered w/a domed top of multicolored beadwork designs, the giltwood base w/a trelliswork band over a cabochon band, on porcelain ball feet, losses, areas of minor restoration, ca. 1880, 11½" d., pr. (ILLUS. of one) **978.00**

Victorian Renaissance Revival substyle stool, ebonized & gilt-trimmed mahogany, the deep round top w/needlepoint upholstery above the round line-incised apron raised on four slender ring- and rod-turned legs w/button feet, ca. 1875, 14½" d., 17½" h. **193.00**

William & Mary Stool

William & Mary stool, turned maple, the rectangular overupholstered seat on four block- and ring-turned legs joined by a block- and knob-turned H-stretcher, on knob feet, old refinish, imperfections, possibly French Canada, 18th c., 15½ x 19", 14½" h. (ILLUS.) **2,415.00**

Windsor footstool, painted & decorated wood, rectangular board top raised on four slightly canted swelled & tapering turned legs, worn dark paint w/floral design in the center top surrounded by yellow banding, further banding on the legs, 19th c., 7½ x 13", 8¾" h. . **138.00**

Windsor stool, round plank seat on tall canted bamboo-turned legs joined by simple turned rungs, old dark brown varnish stain finish, bottom of seat stamped "J.C. Hubbard, Boston," early 19th c., 32" h. (one rung missing) **413.00**

TABLES

Art Nouveau side table, fruitwood marquetry, two-tier, the rectangular top inlaid in various woods w/irises & leaves above a conformingly-inlaid oversized lower shelf w/notched corners, raised on buttressed, molded legs, signed in marquetry "L. Majorelle," France, ca. 1900, 24 x 32", 31" h. **3,220.00**

Baroque Revival-Style parlor table, carved walnut, a black & brown octagonal marble top resting on a scroll-cut & carved conforming

Baroque Revival Parlor Table

apron raised on eight spiral-turned legs w/ball feet joined by arched pierced and scroll-carved stretchers, ca. 1910-30, 35½" w., 30" h. (ILLUS.). **715.00**

Baroque-Style trestle table, oak, a long narrow rectangular top w/wide edge moldings, raised near each end on heavy shaped cross-braces on heavy square legs flanked by scroll-cut brackets above the stepped cross-form feet, late 19th - early 20th c., 32 x 114¼", 30½" h. **1,955.00**

Chinese Export Lacquer Tables

Chinese Export nesting tables, black lacquer & parcel-gilt, each graduated table w/a rectangular top raised on ring- and rod-turned end legs on scrolled shoe feet, each painted on the top w/figures in a courtyard, carved dragon masks on the feet, first half 19th c., China, largest 13¼ x 21½", 28" h., set of 4 (ILLUS.) **6,325.00**

Chippendale Pembroke table, mahogany, a boldly grained wide rectangular top flanked by two narrow hinged drop leaves above an apron w/an end drawer w/a butterfly brass, square legs w/inside chamfered corners joined by shaped flat cross-stretchers, old finish, original brass, Connecticut River Valley, ca. 1780, 34¾ x 35", 27" h. (top slightly warped) **2,875.00**

Chippendale tea table, mahogany, the square top w/molded serpentine edges tilting above a vase- and ring-turned pedestal on a tripod base w/cabriole legs ending in arris pad feet on platforms, old refinish, Massachusetts, ca. 1780, 28¾ x 29½", 27½" h. **1,610.00**

Chippendale tea table, walnut, wide round dished top tilting above a birdcage platform on a vase- and ring-turned pedestal continuing to the tripod base w/cabriole legs w/paneled knees & ending in pad feet on platforms, old refinish, Pennsylvania, ca. 1780, 35½" d., 28 ½" h. (minor imperfections) .. **2,300.00**

Chippendale-Style Tea Table

Chippendale-Style tea table, mahogany, a round dished top tilting above a ring-turned column on a bulbous knop above the tripod base w/cabriole legs ending in inlaid paw feet, late 19th c., 26" d. (ILLUS.)..................... **121.00**

Chippendale-Style tea table, mahogany, a round top w/a piecrust rim tilting on a birdcage support on a turned standard raised on a tripod base w/cabriole legs ending in claw-and-ball feet, 19th c., 32" d., 31" h. **1,495.00**

Classical breakfast table, mahogany, a rectangular top flanked by wide drop leaves w/serpentine corners above the bowed apron w/turreted corners, raised on a leaf-carved pedestal continuing to four leaf-carved

downswept legs ending in carved paw feet on casters, New York, ca. 1825, 22½ x 38", 28" h. **1,380.00**

Classical breakfast table, carved mahogany & mahogany veneer, rectangular top flanked by drop leaves above a straight apron fitted w/two cockbeaded drawers at the ends, on turned & spiral-carved post & rectangular platform on four scrolled legs w/brass rosettes ending in cast brass hairy paw feet, probably Massachusetts, ca. 1820, closed 18 x 42", 28" h. (imperfections) **1,150.00**

Classical breakfast table, carved mahogany veneer, rectangular top flanked by two hinged drop leaves w/rounded corners above a cockbeaded veneered apron w/ring- and ball-turned corner drops, raised on four columnar ring-turned & leaf-carved supports on a platform raised on four downswept sabre legs carved along the top w/a leafy band & ending in brass paw feet on casters, old refinish, New England, 1810-20, open 39 x 44", 28" h. (imperfections) **1,093.00**

Classical Mahogany Breakfast Table

Classical breakfast table, carved mahogany, a rectangular top flanked by wide D-form drop leaves w/notched corners flanking an apron w/inlay & a single end drawer, raised on a turned & acanthus-carved pedestal above the four shaped acanthus-carved legs ending in hairy paw feet on casters, original drawer brass, old worn refinishing, some edge & veneer damage & repairs, attributed to Boston or New York, ca. 1825, 24 x 42" plus 15½" leaves, 29" h. (ILLUS.)......... **1,870.00**

Classical card table, rectangular hinged top w/rounded front corners above a gilt-decorated convex frieze w/a gadrooned apron, raised on a columnar pedestal continuing to a shaped base on paw feet, Philadelphia, ca. 1830, 18 x 36", 27½" h. **1,150.00**

Classical card table, mahogany, the oblong fold-over top w/canted corners above a conforming concave apron, raised on a leaf-carved & gadrooned pedestal continuing to a square base on leaf-carved molded legs ending in brass paw casters, probably Philadelphia, ca. 1825, 17¾ x 35¾", 29½" h. **1,150.00**

Classical console tables, mahogany, each w/a brown & white-veined grey marble rectangular top w/serpentine sides & front above a conforming apron w/beaded scroll edges, raised on scroll-form front supports w/a closed lower back centering a large rectangular mirror w/beaded border band & flanked by pointed arch panels above the shaped platform stretcher & scroll feet, Boston, ca. 1840, 18 x 40¼", 35½" h., pr. ... **9,200.00**

Classical country-style dressing table, cherry, high flat-topped crestrail w/scroll-cut ends above the rectangular top above a case w/a long narrow drawer over a slightly deeper long drawer, on ring-, knob & baluster-turned legs ending in knob feet on casters, ca. 1830-40, 16¾ x 39", overall 36¼" h. (age cracks) **1,815.00**

Classical Pedestal Dining Table

Classical dining table, carved mahogany, two-part, each section w/a wide D-form top w/molded edge & raised on two heavy ring- and knob-turned pedestals on tripod bases w/three molded outswept legs ending in brass hairy paw feet on casters, a large central rectangular leaf joins the top end sections, old refinish, alterations,

possibly New England, ca. 1825, open 47 x 74½", 27¾" h. (ILLUS.) **4,600.00**

Classical dining table, cherry & mahogany flame veneer, two-parts, each half w/a rectangular top w/a wide hinged drop leaf along one side, the other three sides w/a deep veneered ogee apron above four ring- and rod-turned tapering legs ending in baluster-turned feet w/brass knob tips, first half 19th c., opens to 43¾ x 79", 30" h. (repairs to tops & leaves) **770.00**

Fine Classical Pembroke Table

Classical Pembroke table, inlaid mahogany, the rectangular top flanked by two rectangular drop leaves w/cut corners & rosewood banding above a molded apron w/one end drawer, turned corner pendants, raised on a reeded vasiform pedestal on four downswept reeded legs ending in brass paw casters, New York, ca. 1820, 24½ x 36", 28¾" h. (ILLUS.) **1,495.00**

Painted Classical Sofa Table

Classical sofa table, painted & decorated, the rectangular top w/a hinged drop leaf at each end, the apron w/a pair of short drawers painted w/gilt foliate designs, on lyre-shaped end supports painted w/gilt acanthus leaves & continuing to outswept scroll legs bordered by pinstriping & centering an anthemion & painted rosette, a baluster- and ring-turned cross stretcher, on casters, Baltimore, Maryland, ca. 1830, paint wear, 20½ x 21" closed, 28" h. (ILLUS.) **1,725.00**

Country-style card table, painted & decorated, a rectangular top overhanging an apron w/a single drawer over turned legs, early red & yellow graining to simulate mahogany, original brass pulls, Maine, 1830s, 17½ x 36", 30" h. (some surface imperfections) **345.00**

Country-style side table, pine, the rectangular top w/breadboard ends above a long apron drawer, raised on turned legs joined by a box stretcher, 19th c., 26 x 41", 23½" h. **460.00**

Country-style work table, painted pine & poplar, four-board rectangular top w/a scrubbed finish widely overhangs the deep apron w/two drawers w/turned wood knobs, raised on ring-, knob- and rod-turned legs w/peg feet, base w/old worn blue repaint, late 19th c., 38½ x 67½", 28¾" h. (one drawer replaced, top wear, age cracks & damage) **358.00**

Early American work table, painted pine & maple, the long rectangular top w/breadboard ends widely overhangs an apron w/a single full-length drawer w/simple turned knob, on block- and baluster-turned legs on button feet joined by low rectangular stretchers, old painted surface w/traces of red & black top paint & black on the base, New England, 18th c., 32¾ x 69¼", 27⅜" h. **10,925.00**

Federal Mahogany Breakfast Table

Federal breakfast table, mahogany, a rectangular top flanked by scalloped D-form drop leaves above an apron w/one working & one simulated end drawer, raised on four slender tapering reeded legs w/knob-turned ankles on brass

knob feet, replaced ring pulls, imperfections, probably New York area, ca. 1815, 22 x 34", 29" h. (ILLUS.) **1,610.00**

Federal card table, inlaid mahogany, demi-lune form w/a hinged top, line inlay around the apron & bellflowers & ovals w/flowers down the four square tapering legs, early 19th c., 17½ x 35½", 28¾" h. (veneer & inlay damage, pieced top repair, leaf hinge repair) . . . **2,090.00**

Federal card table, inlaid cherry, rectangular hinged top w/fluted edge & undercut inner top above an apron w/a central inlaid stellate device & two paterae at the corners, a small drawer at one end, raised on square molded legs w/curved pierced frontal brackets, old surface, Massachusetts, 1750-80, closed 13½ x 3¼", 29¼" h. (imperfections) **5,750.00**

Federal card table, inlaid mahogany, folding top w/half-serpentine ends, D-front & squared corners, edge inlaid w/stringing & crossbanding above a conforming skirt centering an oval panel within a mahogany mitered frame, flanked by satinwood panels bordered by stringing & crossbanding joining four slender ring-turned, reeded & tapering legs, old refinish, Massachusetts, ca. 1815, 17¼ x 35½", 29½" h. **8,625.00**

Federal card table, mahogany & flame birch veneer, the hinged rectangular top w/an inlaid edge & ovolo corners above an apron w/rounded corner reeding flanking a pair of rectangular birch inlay panels & a long oval central birch inlay panel, on ring- and rod-turned tapering legs w/slender peg feet, old refinish, Massachusetts, ca. 1800, 17¾ x 36", 30" h. (minor imperfections) **1,955.00**

Federal country-style dining table, curly maple & pine, a rectangular curly maple top flanked by rectangular curly maple drop leaves above a pine apron, square tapering legs w/swing-out support legs, early 19th c., 13¼ x 42" plus 12" leaves, 27" h. (hinged replaced, leaves w/square butt joints, leaves & top warped) **825.00**

Federal country-style dining table, mahogany, a rectangular top flanked by two wide rectangular drop leaves, raised on ring-, knob-

and tapering rod-turned legs w/knob feet, old refinish, New England, early 19th c.,open 41¾ x 46¼", 28¾" h. (very minor imperfections) **460.00**

Federal country-style dining table, cherry, a rectangular top flanked by wide rectangular hinged drop leaves above a plain apron, on ring-, baluster- and knob-turned legs w/a disc angle above the ball & peg feet, Mid-Atlantic States, ca. 1820, open 39¼ x 47¼", 29¾" h. (crack to rule joint, repaired crack in apron) **460.00**

Faux-Painted Federal Pier Table

Federal county-style pier table, painted & decorated pine, a rectangular top decorated w/painted marbleizing overhanging an apron w/a long drawer painted to simulate bamboo trim, raised on square tapering legs, the top in grey & white, the base in yellow accented w/orange, cream & black striping simulating inlay, minor paint loss, ca. 1810, 19½ x 30¼", 32¾" h. (ILLUS.) **2,875.00**

Federal dining table, child's size, walnut, a rectangular top flanked by two wide drop leaves w/scallop-notched corners above an apron w/one end drawer, simple turned legs w/double-knob turned feet, old finish, early 19th c., 12½ x 23½" plus 10¾" w. leaves, 19" h. (minor edge damage, hinges replaced, top age crack) **1,100.00**

Federal dining table, 'plum-pudding' mahogany, a rectangular top flanked by a pair of wide D-form hinged drop leaves all w/reeded edges, above a concave single apron drawer flanked by spiral-turned half-columns, opposite end w/a false drawer, raised on a bulbous ring-turned pedestal raised

on four downswept tapering reeded legs terminating in brass animal paw feet w/casters, Ducan Phyfe school, New York, ca. 1815, 49¾ x 59¼", 28½" h. (patches to veneer, repairs to rule joint at hinges, pedestal repair) **1,725.00**

Federal dining table, cherry & figured mahogany, two-part, each section w/a D-shaped end & a rectangular hinged drop leaf above a flame mahogany-veneered & cockbeaded apron, raised on ring- and rod-turned tapering legs w/ball-and-peg feet, blocks at top of legs w/veneered Gothic arches, New England, ca. 1815, open 42¾ x 73¾", 28¾" h. (one small top repair, cracks in veneer) **1,840.00**

Federal dining table, cherry & walnut veneer, two-part, each section w/a D-form top w/a scallop-cut end opposite a wide drop leaf over a reveneered wide skirt, raised on four ring-, baluster-, and spiral-turned legs ending in knob feet w/a fifth swing-out support leg, old refinish, New England or New York, ca. 1825, open 44 x 84¼", 29⅝" h. (restoration) **1,380.00**

Federal dining table, mahogany veneer, two-part construction, each D-shaped section w/a reeded edge & a single wide drop leaf above a veneered skirt, raised on ring-, knob-turned & reeded legs on casters, old refinish, New England, early 19th c., open 45¾ x 89¼", 30½" h. (minor imperfections) . . . **4,025.00**

Federal dining table, mahogany, rectangular top flanked by two wide hinged drop leaves above an apron & six turned & reeded legs w/two swinging-out to support leaves, Virginia, early 19th c., closed 20 x 46½" w/21" w. leaves (minor edge damage) **935.00**

Rare Federal Mixing Table

Federal mixing table, inlaid mahogany & bird's-eye maple, the rectangular white marble-inset top above a bird's-eye maple veneered apron w/a long narrow cock-beaded drawer w/round brass knobs, raised on very slender ring- and knob-turned reeded legs w/tall peg feet on brass casters, Boston, early 19th c., 21¼ x 25¾", 29½" h. (ILLUS.) **4,312.00**

Federal Pembroke table, inlaid mahogany, a rectangular top w/rounded, molded ends flanked by two hinged D-shaped drop leaves above an apron w/a single end drawer, banded inlay around the apron, square tapering legs, old finish, old brass bail, late 18th - early 19th c., 17¾ x 31" plus 9¾" leaves, 28" h. (minor repairs & some edge damage) **3,300.00**

Federal Revival Dressing Table

Federal Revival-Style dressing table & bench, mahogany veneer, a round framed mirror swiveling between two ring-turned columnar uprights w/turned urn finials above the long rectangular top over an apron w/a single long beaded drawer w/polychrome floral decoration & gold accents, raised on lyre-form pierced end legs joined by a turned stretcher, the rectangular bench w/an upholstered seat flanked by low open outswept arms, ca. 1930, 17 x 55", 44" h., pr. (ILLUS.) **220.00**

Federal work table, cherry, the mahogany-banded square top above a single apron drawer, raised on square tapering legs, New England, early 19th c., 19'" sq., 26" h. **460.00**

Federal work table, carved bird's-eye maple & mahogany veneer, rectangular top w/bird's-eye maple veneer bordered by mahogany veneer cross-banding above a case of two drawers w/bird's-eye maple veneer joining fluted corners, on ring-turned reeded tapering legs on casters, old round brass pulls, refinished, Massa-chusetts, 1815-20, 17 x 20½", 29" h. (minor imperfections) **2,875.00**

Federal work table, mahogany, a square top flanked by two D-form hinged drop leaves above an apron w/two flame-veneered narrow drawers w/small turned wood knobs raised on ring-,rod- and knob-turned tapering legs, Massachusetts, ca. 1820, 18 x 19½", 29½" h. **431.00**

Federal-Style dining table, satinwood-inlaid mahogany, a narrow rectangular top flanked by two wide hinged drop leaves above a plain apron w/a checkerboard-inlaid edge, raised on four square tapering line-inlaid legs ending in brass casters, last quarter 19th c., open 46 x 64¼", 30¼" h. (distress to finish, minor inlay losses) **288.00**

George II Mahogany Tea Table

George II tea table, mahogany, the round dished top raised on a ring- and knob-turned pedestal on a tripod base w/three cabriole legs ending in claw-and-ball feet, England, second quarter 18th c., 17" d., 26½" h. (ILLUS.) **3,162.00**

George III Tea Table

George III tea table, mahogany, the wide molded round top w/a low spindle-inset gallery tilting above a scrolled urn- and column-turned pedestal on a tripod base w/three foliate-carved cabriole legs ending in foliate-carved pad feet, England, mid-18th c., repairs to gallery, 31" d., 30½" h. (ILLUS.) **3,162.00**

George III-Style dining table, mahogany, triple-pedestal extension-type, the drop-leaf center section & each D-shaped end section raised on a turned circular pedestal continuing to splayed legs ending in cast brass animal paws on casters, England, late 19th c. **4,600.00**

Georgian-Style Dining Table

Georgian-Style dining table, mahogany & beech, two-pedestal type, w/wide D-form ends overhanging a veneered apron, each section raised on a leaf-carved knobbed pedestal on four outswept leaf-carved legs ending in brass hairy paw feet on casters, w/two additional leaves, England, 19th c., closed 47 x 72", 29½" h. (ILLUS.) **5,175.00**

"Harvest" table, pine & cherry, a long, narrow rectangular top flanked by long drop leaves over the apron, raised on four square tapering legs on casters, vestiges of old red paint, New England, early 19th c., open 37½ x 72", 28¾" h. (ILLUS.) **4,025.00**

New England "Harvest Table"

Hutch (or chair) table, hardwood & pine, rectangular three-board top tilting above a rectangular plank seat w/deep aprons & square tapered legs, chamfering, mortised & pinned construction, old refinishing w/traces of old red, 19th c., 42 x 47", 26½" h. **880.00**

Hutch (or chair) table, maple, the round top tilting above a deep well w/rectangular ends ending in shoe feet, old refinish, probably New England, late 18th c., 41¾" d., 28" h. (minor imperfections) **3,738.00**

Hutch (or chair) table, painted & decorated, the rectangular top w/rounded corners tilting above baluster- and ring-turned supports on a box base w/drawer & baluster- and ring-turned legs, red & black graining simulating rosewood, probably New England, 19th c., 42¼ x 42½", 28½" h. **4,888.00**

Hutch (or chair) table, painted pine, long rectangular three-board top tilting above a rectangular bench seat w/a wide board apron, on bootjack ends, old worn dark green paint, 19th c., 35 x 70", 29½" h. . . . **1,375.00**

Hutch (or chair) table, painted pine, rectangular three-board top tilting above a bench seat w/lift lid flanked by one-board ends w/curved cut-out tops, worn yellow repaint w/striping & stencilled design over earlier red, 33¼ x 51¾", 30" h. (feet ended out) . . . **1,100.00**

Hutch (or chair) table, pine & ash, the circular top widely overhanging a deep box seat on plank sides incurved in the lower half & w/demi-lune cut-out legs on molded shoe feet, old surface, New England, late 18th c., 46¾" d., 22¼" h. **16,100.00**

Mission-style (Arts & Crafts movement) dining table, oak, round split top above a square split pedestal w/ four long corbels on the cross-form legs, two hide-away legs, branded mark of L. & J. G. Stickley, Model No. 713, refinished, w/one leaf, 54" d., 29" h. **3,105.00**

Mission-style (Arts & Crafts movement) dining table, oak, a round divided top above a deep apron raised on four heavy square legs w/through-tenon flat stretchers joining them to the central square split-pedestal, w/six leaves, large Gustav Stickley red decal, Model No. 634, closed 48" d., 30" h. . . **13,750.00**

Mission-style (Arts & Crafts movement) dining table, oak, round divided top raised on a heavy square split pedestal w/cross-form legs w/rounded ends & joined by corbels to the pedestal, original finish, signed by Gustav Stickley, w/four leaves, 54" d. (veneer missing from apron seams) **3,738.00**

Mission-style (Arts & Crafts movement) hall table, oak, rectangular top overhanging an arched apron on square legs w/tapered feet, end stretchers w/two slats at each end, new dark finish, unmarked Stickley Brothers, 18 x 24", 26½" h. **825.00**

Mission-style (Arts & Crafts movement) library table, oak, rectangular top overhanging an apron w/a single long drawer w/two metal ring pulls, heavy square legs w/shaped feet joined by through-tenon slats & slatted sides w/a medial shelf, refinished, metal tag of The Lifetime Furniture Company, 28 x 42", 29" h. **1,045.00**

Mission-style (Arts & Crafts movement) library table, oak, an oval top over four flat flaring legs & an oval medial shelf resting on cross-stretchers w/two rectangular cut-outs each, mint original finish, branded mark of the Limbert Furniture Company, 37¼ x 47½", 29¼" h. **13,750.00**

Mission-style (Arts & Crafts movement) side table, oak, oval w/square cut-outs & arched apron, original finish w/some color added, branded Charles Limbert mark, Model No. 146, 30 x 45", 29" h. . . **2,990.00**

Modern style coffee table, kidney-shaped plywood top raised on three canted looped wire legs, 1950s (ILLUS.) **50.00**

Modern Style Coffee Table

Queen Anne dining table, walnut, a rectangular top flanked by two wide drop leaves w/knob-cut corners above the scalloped apron, cabriole legs ending in drake feet, swing-leg supports drop leaves, Pennsylvania, 18th c., 15½ x 47¾" w/17" w. leaves, 27½" h. (repairs, leg returns replaced, repaired cracks in top) **4,400.00**

Queen Anne dining table, maple, a rectangular top w/rounded ends flanked by two D-form hinged drop leaves above a shaped skirt, raised on four cabriole legs ending in high pad feet, refinished, Massachusetts, mid-18th c., open 46 x 47½", 29¼" h. (repairs) **2,530.00**

Queen Anne dining table, maple, rectangular narrow top w/rounded ends flanked by two D-form hinged drop leaves, shaped apron raised on simple cabriole legs ending in high pad feet, refinished, Massachusetts, mid-18th c., open 46 x 47½", 29¼" h. (repairs) **2,530.00**

Queen Anne tavern table, hardwood & pine, rectangular breadboard top above a deep apron above baluster- and ring-turned legs ending in block feet joined by flat mortised & pinned box stretchers, old mellow patina, 18th c., minor age cracks, 21½ x 30¼", 25¾" h. **3,025.00**

Queen Anne tea table, cherry & maple, the oval top on a deep shaped skirt joining pegged corner blocks raised on straight turned legs ending in pad feet on platforms, refinished, New England, 18th c., 26 x 34¾", 25¾" h. (imperfections) **4,888.00**

Queen Anne tea table, maple, the oval top widely overhanging the deeply scalloped apron, four turned tapering legs ending in button feet,

Queen Anne Oval Tea Table

old refinish, New England, mid-18th c., minor imperfections, 21¾ x 28", 26" h. (ILLUS.) **2,875.00**

Queen Anne "Tray-Top" Tea Table

Queen Anne "tray-top" tea table, carved walnut, dished rectangular tray top over a slightly shaped apron raised on four cabriole legs w/shell carvings, bellflowers below & deeply carved elongated flanking scrolls above paneled trifid feet, old surface, minor imperfections, Williamsburg, Virginia area, mid-18th c., 18¾ x 27½", 29¼" h. (ILLUS.) **5,750.00**

Queen Anne-Style side table, mahogany, a rectangular top w/molded edge over two drawers, raised on cabriole legs ending in pad feet on casters, late 19th c., 18¼ x 26", 30¼" h. **374.00**

Queen Anne-Style "tray-top" tea table, mahogany, the dished rectangular top w/molded edges above a deep apron w/a finely scalloped bottom edge, raised on simple cabriole legs ending in raised pad feet, Williamsburg reproduction by Kittinger, branded mark & metal label, 20th c., 17¾ x 29¼", 26½" h. **990.00**

Regency sofa table, rosewood & burl walnut, the rectangular long cross-banded top w/two small D-form end hinged drop leaves above the apron w/three drawers each w/two metal rosette pulls, raised on rectangular end supports continuing to splayed legs joined by a rectangular stretchers & ending in cast brass paw feet on casters, England, early 19th c., 27 x 51½", 27" h. **5,750.00**

"Sawbuck" table, painted pine, rectangular top above an apron w/a drawer above the crossed "sawbuck" base w/horizontal rails, old lime green paint worn on the top, New England, late 19th c., 15 x 30¼", 15" h. **863.00**

"Sawbuck" table, stained pine, rectangular three-board top w/breadboard ends above crossed narrow rectangular legs w/wide flat board cross-braces, red stain on base, old varnish on top, 19th c., 30½ x 49½", 28¾" h. **880.00**

Tavern table, painted pine & maple, scrubbed rectangular top w/breadboard ends widely overhanging the deep apron w/a side-opening drawer, on baluster- and ring-turned legs joined by square stretchers & block feet, old red paint, northern New England, mid-18th c., 23⅝ x 37¾", 23½" h. (probable height loss) **1,840.00**

Early Walnut Tavern Table

Tavern table, walnut, a rectangular top overhanging a deep apron w/a large thumb-molded drawer on the left & a small drawer on the right, raised on ring, knob- and rod-turned legs w/turned tapering knob feet set under the flat rail box stretcher, refinished, minor imper-fections, Pennsylvania, early 18th c., 21½ x 32", 28¼" h. (ILLUS.). **2,530.00**

Turn-of-the-Century dining table, mahogany, round top slightly overhanging a deep apron raised on a heavy central round pedestal

Turn-of-the-Century Dining Table

centered on a four-part platform on
heavy carved claw feet on casters,
ca. 1900, 48" d. (ILLUS.). **495.00**

Turn-of-the-Century Parlor Table

Turn-of-the-Century parlor table,
quarter-sawn oak, the oval top
above a deep apron raised on two
end columns atop an oblong
platform raised on four C-scroll feet
on casters, ca. 1900-10, 30 x 44",
27" h. (ILLUS.). **275.00**

Victorian Butcher Block Table

**Victorian country-style butcher
block table,** hardwood, a long low
crestrail w/rounded corners above
the very thick dovetails, worn block
top set atop a case w/a pair of

deep drawers w/wooden hand-
pulls, raised on five heavy ring- and
baluster-turned legs ending in peg
feet, late 19th c., 55" w. (ILLUS.) . . **715.00**
Victorian country-style side table,
walnut, a round top w/beveled
edges tilting above a ring-turned
bulbous pedestal w/shaped pierced
loops joining it to the tripod base
w/flat scroll-cut legs w/scroll feet,
late 19th c., 33½" d., 28¾" h.
(distress to finish, crack in top) **316.00**

Folk Art Table

Victorian country-style side table,
carved & painted wood in folk art
style, a round carved top w/a
sawtooth edge & centering a
carved star & bordered by a leafy
meandering vine, the underside of
the rim decorated w/applied ball-in-
cage pointed pendants, raised on
four ring-carved square supports
tapering down to a central ball over
pointed finials above four square
ring-carved canted legs, old finish
w/polychrome decoration, possibly
Pennsylvania, late 19th c., 21" d.,
30" h. (ILLUS.) **805.00**

Gothic Revival Library Table

**Victorian Gothic Revival substyle
library table,** mahogany, the
rectangular sienna marble top
w/cut-corners & molded edges over
a narrow apron w/two long drawers

w/raised oblong moldings on one side w/matching molded panels on the other sides, raised on pairs of shaped Gothic-style end legs w/arched shoe feet joined by a Gothic-form long stretcher w/a carved central Gothic spire finial, in the manner of Alexander Jackson Davis, ca. 1840-50, 29 x 50¼", 30¼" h. (ILLUS.) **5,175.00**

Fine Renaissance Revival Table

Victorian parlor center table, Renaissance Revival substyle, walnut & walnut veneer, the oblong top w/notched corners & molded rim & inset marble top above a deep molded & burl paneled apron w/scroll-cut brackets raised on four blocked curved supports continuing to downswept curved flat supports w/burl trim & scroll-carved ends each topped by a full-figure bust of a lady, the supports all joined to a ring- and knob-turned central column w/block- and ring-turned straight cross-spindles joining it to the curved supports, legs ending in rosette-carved blocks on compressed knob feet, attributed to J. Jelliff, ca. 1880 (ILLUS.) **5,225.00**

Ornate Renaissance Revival Table

Victorian Renaissance Revival parlor center table, gilt-bronze-mounted carved rosewood, marquetry & marble, the

rectangular top w/wide rounded ends & ovolo corners framing the inset white marble top above a conforming apron w/gilt-trimmed loop & florette bands & each long side centered by a panel w/a central hand-painted figural round reserve, heavy square cabriole corner legs carved w/a caryatid & ending in a hairy paw foot, lower pierced key-form flat stretcher centered by a round tazza w/marble-inset top, possibly Pottier & Stymus, New York, ca. 1875, 30 x 51½", 30½" h. (ILLUS.) . . . **19,550.00**

Victorian Renaissance Revival parlor table, walnut, the oval white marble top w/molded edge set upon a deep molded apron w/long scallop-cut drops, raised on a quadripartite base w/the four flat angular supports continuing to outswept legs on casters, the supports joined by a central columnar-turned post w/a pointed turned drop finial, old dark finish, ca. 1870, 21 x 29" **413.00**

Victorian Renaissance Revival parlor table, walnut & burl walnut, the rectangular top w/rounded notched corners & heavy border molding framing inset white marble, the deep line-incised apron w/four pointed & carved drops, raised on a quatrapartite base w/four flat angular supports continuing to outward-angled legs decorated w/small burl panels & raised on porcelain casters, the four supports joined to a central heavily turned post w/a turned & pointed base finial, paper label marked "From James Moriarty & Bro...Cleveland, O.," ca. 1875, 22 x 30", 30" h. **715.00**

Renaissance Revival Side Table

Victorian Renaissance Revival side table, walnut, the rectangular top w/rounded corners & a wide molded edge framing an inset white marble top above the line-incised apron w/triangular drops, raised on four molded serpentine supports tapering down & then flaring out to form legs ending in casters, the four legs joined at the center by a long ring- and rod-turned spindle w/an acorn-turned drop finial, ca. 1875, old finish, 18 x 24", 29¾" h. (ILLUS.). **248.00**

Victorian Rococo Rosewood Table

Victorian Rococo substyle parlor center table, carved rosewood, the black & brown "turtle-form" marble top above a conforming deep apron ornately carved w/blossoms & leafy scrolls, four square incurving S- and C-scroll legs w/leaf carving raised on casters & joined by serpentine scroll-carved cross-stretchers w/a central urn-turned finial, one leg repaired, ca. 1860, 26 x 36" (ILLUS.). **660.00**

William & Mary "butterfly" drop-leaf table, cherry, rectangular top w/rounded ends flanked by two D-form drop leaves, beaded apron w/one thumb-molded end drawer w/wooden pull, raised on four splayed block-, vase- and ring-turned legs ending in turned feet & joined by rectangular box stretchers, swing-out "butterfly" leaf supports, old refinish, probably Connecticut, early 18th c., 36¼ x 40", 25½" h. (restored) **2,415.00**

William & Mary dining table, a rectangular top w/rounded ends flanked by two half-round hinged drop leaves above swing gate-legs, the apron w/a single end drawer, raised on double-baluster-turned legs joined by conforming stretchers, New England, early 18th c., 17½ x 41", 24½" h. **26,450.00**

William & Mary side table, maple, a rectangular two-board top w/breadboard ends above an apron w/a single drawer, raised on baluster-turned legs joined by box stretchers, 18th c., 26½ x 36", 26" h. **747.00**

William & Mary tavern table, painted wood, the wide rectangular top w/breadboard ends widely overhanging the apron raised on block-, vase- and ring-turned legs w/knob feet joined by rectangular box stretchers, old grey paint over earlier colors, New England, early 18th c., 27¼ x 43", 25½" h. (imperfections, one foot w/minor repair) **6,325.00**

William & Mary tavern table, maple, the long rectangular top w/breadboard ends widely overhanging the apron w/a single long thumb-molded drawer w/wooden knob, raised on baluster-, ring- and block-turned legs w/ovoid knob feet joined by box stretchers, refinished, New England, 18th c., 27 x 38½", 27" h. **2,415.00**

William & Mary Revival Library Table

William & Mary Revival-Style library table, mahogany-finished hardwood, the long rectangular top w/a molded edge above a deep apron w/a dentil-carved band & two drawers, raised on pierced lyre-form end legs & two baluster- and ring-turned central legs alternating w/turned drops all resting on a trestle-form base w/heavy shoe feet & a shaped flat medial stretcher, signed "Imperial, Grand Rapids," ca. 1920-30, 31 x 54", 28" h. (ILLUS.). **275.00**

WARDROBES & ARMOIRES

Fine Biedermeier Armoire

Armoire, Biedermeier, birch & ebonized wood, the rectangular top w/a stepped flaring cornice above a pair of tall paneled doors above a conforming plinth on later block feet, Europe, first quarter 19th c. (ILLUS.) **4,600.00**

Decorated French Provincial Armoire

Armoire, French Provincial, decorated oak, the rectangular top w/a flaring cornice above a deep frieze band decorated w/flowering leafy scrolling bands over a medial molding above the pair of tall double-raised panel doors, flat molded base on blocked shaped feet, each door panel decorated w/a vase of flowers or large flowerhead, France, 18th c. (ILLUS.) **1,430.00**

Louis XVI Revival Armoire

Armoire, Louis XVI Revival-Style, hardwood inlay, the block-fronted rectangular top w/an arched center section w/an ormolu floral mount on the molded cornice, the wide arched center door w/a beveled mirror, side front panels w/herringbone veneering & inlaid oval medallions w/urns of flowers, raised on a plinth base w/ormolu corner mounts above the tapering cylindrical short legs, Europe, ca. 1900, 19 x 65", 6' 10" h. (ILLUS.) . . **825.00**

William & Mary Gumwood Kas

Kas, (American version of the Netherlands Kast or wardrobe), William & Mary style, gumwood, the rectangular top w/a widely flaring deep, stepped cornice above a pair of tall raised panel doors separated by three narrow double-paneled stiles, a mid-molding above a pair of small molded base drawers separated by three raised diamond designs, molded base band on large turnip-turned ball feet, Hudson River Valley, New York, 18th c., 23½ x 61½", 5'½" h. (ILLUS.) **6,900.00**

Hudson River Valley Kas

Kas, cherry, the rectangular top w/a widely flaring heavy stepped cornice above a pair of tall bordered panel doors opening to a two-shelved interior & flanked by flat pilasters, a wide mid-molding above a long base drawer w/applied molding to resemble a pair of drawers, heavy molded base raised on turned feet, replaced pulls, refinished, restored, Hudson River Valley, New York, 18th c., 21 x 62", 5' 9¾" h. (ILLUS.)....................**2,415.00**

Early Ohio Kas

Kas, painted poplar, the rectangular top w/a flaring stepped cornice above a wide plain frieze over the two tall raised panel doors above an applied molding & wide base band on molded flat base, interior w/shelves on one side & an open compartment on the other, removable cornice, old worn varnish over earlier red, found in New Bremen, Ohio, 19th c., 23½ x 72¾", 6' 1½" h. (ILLUS.) . . **3,025.00**

Walnut Pennsylvania Schrank

Schrank (massive Germanic wardrobe), walnut, originally made in two sections, the rectangular top w/a deep flaring & stepped cornice above a case w/a pair of tall double-raised panel doors flanking a double panel central panel above a mid-molding over a row of three paneled drawers, molded base w/three low feet across the front, doors w/wrought-iron rattail hinges, interior w/added shelves on one side & a bar on the other, drawer hardware missing, Pennsylvania, 18th c., 27 x 80", 7' 4½" h. (ILLUS.) **4,400.00**

Victorian Country Wardrobe

Wardrobe, Victorian country-style, walnut, the rectangular top w/a low gallery on knob-turned short spindles above a narrow cornice over a pair of tall recessed panel doors w/rounded corners, a pair of drawers below w/small turned wood knobs & round keyhole escutcheons above the scallop-cut apron w/a central rondel, refinished, second half 19th c., 18¼ x 52¾", 7' 3¼" h. (ILLUS.).... **688.00**

Wardrobe, Victorian country-style, stained pine, a rectangular top w/a pointed molded cornice above a wide conforming frieze band over a pair of tall raised-panel cupboard doors opening to an added shelf above a single long deep drawer at the bottom, flat base, old dark red finish, 19th c., 20 x 45", 6' 10" h. (edge damage & damage around door) **413.00**

Impressive Victorian Wardrobe

Wardrobe, Victorian Rococo substyle, carved mahogany, the very high arched, pierced & scroll-carved crestrail centered by a large cartouche & flanked by urn-turned finials atop the arched cornice above a frieze band w/a large scroll-carved cartouche over a pair of tall cupboard doors w/triple-arch tops & mirror panels flanked by narrow sides w/raised panels w/rounded tops, the base section w/a pair of molding-trimmed drawers w/scroll-carved pulls & keyhole escutcheons, deep plinth base, ca. 1850, 20 x 55", overall 9' 9" h. (ILLUS.) **2,640.00**

WHATNOTS & ETAGERES

Etagere, Regency-Style, mahogany, three-tier, rectangular molded top w/ring-turned suports over two open shelves, raised on casters, England, late 19th c., 19 x 42", 39½" h. **633.00**

Huge Victorian Etagere

Etagere, Victorian Renaissance Revival substyle, carved oak, the high arched & molded central cornice centered by a full-relief carved figure of a seated goddess flanked by heavy arched cornices over panels of carved grapevines above a frieze band of leafy scrolls & a griffin, the large arched central mirror flanked on each side by a stack of three quarter-round open glass shelves w/turned supports, each side topped w/carved full-figure putti & lower back panels carved in relief w/dead game & hunting trophies, stepped-out & block-fronted plinth base w/a scroll-carved base band, ca. 1875, 85" w., 10' 4" h. (ILLUS.) **9,200.00**

Whatnot, Mission-style (Arts & Crafts movement), oak, the arched & scalloped crestrail above two slats w/round holes continuing to form the back slats, the case w/five open shelves between slatted sides & back, early 20th c. **770.00**

Whatnot, Victorian country-style, walnut, corner-style, three quarter-round open shelves between pierced & spearpoint-carved sides raised on flat angular legs, last quarter 19th c., 41" h. **105.00**

GAMES & GAME BOARDS

"Das Belagerungspliel" (The Game of Besieging), hand-colored engraving w/original slipcase, Germany, ca. 1800-20, 12⅝ x 13¼" (scattered foxing, wear, some case staining) **$259.00**

Domino set, whalebone & exotic wood, the 28 pieces in a slide-top rectangular box, 19th c., each piece ⅞ x 1¹³⁄₁₆", the set (lacking slide top) **288.00**

Dominoes, miniature painted bone, the set in a marbleized wooden egg-shaped case, 19th c., egg 2½" l., the set (paint wear, very minor losses) **345.00**

Game board, painted poplar, square w/large bull's-eyes in each corner w/a six-arm starburst in the center, triple-band block bands forming central cross design, original black, yellow & red paint, back initialed "S.W." & "A.W.," from Ohio, 19th c., 24¾" sq. **1,265.00**

"Game of Auto Race," board-type, graphic racing game w/six early 1" die-cast vehicles, including Saxon & Maxwell, manufacturer's name on roof, box includes dice & instructions, Orotech Co., USA **58.00**

"Game of Boy Scouts"

"Game of Boy Scouts," board-type, lithographed paper, missing all but two playing pieces, ca. 1910, No. 4405, Milton Bradley Company,

10½ x 22", minor staining & some edge wear to box, torn interior strip (ILLUS.) **288.00**

"Game of Merry Christmas," board-type, folding game board, three wooden tokens, rules & spinner card, J.H. Singer (New York, New York), box 7 x 13½", 1½" h. (box & bottom w/edge damage) **920.00**

"Game of Robbing the Miller," board-type, McLoughlin Bros., 1888, box 8 x 15½" (missing some playing pieces) **374.00**

"Going to Market," card game, 52 cards advertising real products from 13 companies of the era, 1915 (box in poor condition) **75.00**

"Military Ten Pins," painted wood & lithographed paper, five soldiers w/red uniforms & blue legs & hats, five w/blue uniforms & red legs & hats, patented May 5, 1885, w/original wood box, 8" h. (some paper loss, box missing lid, major label loss, ball missing) **978.00**

"The Game of Jack and the Beanstalk"

"The Game of Jack and the Beanstalk," board-type, ca. 1898, McLoughlin Bros., edge wear & minor staining to box, 10½ x 19¾" (ILLUS.). **863.00**

"The New Howard H. Jones Collegiate Football Game," board-type, folding board, instructions, goal posts, two play cards, play indicators, etc., ca. 1927-31, box 13 x 26", 2" h. (slight edge wear on box) **86.00**

GARDEN FOUNTAINS & ORNAMENTS

Bench, marble, the rectangular seat w/a chamfered leaftip-carved border raised on scroll & griffin-carved end supports on narrow oval feet, Italy **$5,462.00**

Fountain, cast iron, two-tier, a wide shallow lower tier joined by a knob- and baluster-form reeded pedestal to the upper tier w/a crown-form center finial, both basins cast w/athemia, raised on a reeded columnar pedestal w/round base, late 19th - early 20th c., 140" h. **12,650.00**

Little Boy & Umbrella Lead Fountain

Fountain, cast lead, figural, a little boy standing atop a rocky base & looking up while opening an umbrella, plumbed for water, 16" h. (ILLUS.) **2,875.00**

Fountain, marble, a stepped triangular foot supporting a fluted tapering cylindrical standard supporting a wide rounded gadrooned basin fitted in the center w/a figure of a putto blowing a conch shell, plumbed for water, early 20th c., 73" h. **8,050.00**

Painted Metal Models of Lions

Models of lions, painted metal, the recumbent animals w/front paws hanging over the rectangular base, hollow eyes, stamped "J.W. Fiske Ironworks, New York - Made in U.S.A.," early 20th c., 52" l., pr., (ILLUS. prev. column) **7,475.00**

Plant holder, wrought iron, the pierced-scroll frame fitted w/four circular pot holders surmounted by a spiral-twist arch hung w/a small iron bowl, the stretcher base w/two pot holders, raised on arched scrolling legs, early 20th c., 48" w., 66" h. **2,875.00**

Statue, marble, figure of Hercules, a youthful male leaning against a slender tree stump, nude except for a lion skin around his shoulder & a fig leaf, restorations, 19th c., 46" h. **4,887.00**

Urns, cast iron, campana-form, slender flaring tall bowls w/wide rolled egg-and-dart molded rims, the sides cast w/winged putti supporting a floral festoon, the gadroon lower body raised on a short flaring pedestal above the tall tapering stepped square base w/each side cast w/a panel of winged kissing putti, 65" h., pr.. . . . **1,495.00**

Victorian Cast-Iron Garden Urns

Urns, cast iron, deep swelled cylindrical body w/an upswept scroll-cast arched rim, the body centered by opposing cartouches flanked by scrolled angular loop handles, raised on a stepped rectangular base w/egg-and-dart borders, late 19th c., 23" h., pr. (ILLUS.) **1,265.00**

Urns, terra cotta, wide bulbous body w/incurved shoulder to an egg-and-dart rim, the shoulder modeled w/four crowned female masks joined by floral garlands, raised on a fluted leaftip-decorated pedestal on a square foot, 20th c., 30" h., pr. **3,737.00**

Russian Cut Ice Cream Set

Courtesy of Skinner, Inc.

GLASS

AGATA

Agata was patented by Joseph Locke of the New England Glass Company in 1887. The application of mineral stain left a mottled effect on the surface of the article. It was applied chiefly to the Wild Rose (Peach Blow) line but sometimes was applied as a border on a pale opaque green. In production for a short time, it is scarce. Items listed below are of the Wild Rose line unless otherwise noted.

Juice tumbler, slightly tapering cylindrical body, old Maude Feld sticker, 3¾" h. **$248.00**

Pitcher, 7" h., bulbous ovoid body tapering to a short squared neck, applied reeded pink handle, uniform mottling **4,070.00**

Toothpick holder, cylindrical w/a tricorner incurved rim, fine mottling, 2" h. **688.00**

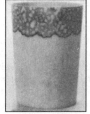

Fine Green Opaque Tumbler

Tumbler, cylindrical, Green Opaque, strong rim mottling, sticker of Maude B. Feld, 3¾" h. (ILLUS.) . . . **605.00**

Tumbler, cylindrical, heavy overall blue 'oil spotting' on the mottled ground, 3¾" h. **550.00**

Tumbler, cylindrical, scattered blue 'oil spots' on a finely mottled surface, 3¾" h. **440.00**

Tumbler, nicely mottled, sticker of Maude B. Feld, 3¾" h. **399.00**

Whiskey tumbler, cylindrical, fine mottling, 2½" h. **193.00**

AMBERINA

Amberina was developed in the late 1880s by the New England Glass Company and a pressed version was made by Hobbs, Brockunier & Company (under license from the former). A similar ware, called Rose Amber, was made by the Mt. Washington Glass Works. Amberina-Rose Amber shades from amber to deep red or fuchsia and cut and plated (lined with creamy white) examples were also made. The Libbey Glass Company briefly revived blown Amberina, using modern shapes, in 1917.

Amberina Label

Basket, ruffled rim, applied amber feet & handle, New England, 4" d., 9" h. **$475.00**

Large Amberina Basket

Basket, tall flaring 'poke bonnet' form w/swirled Optic Rib patt., applied amber wishbone feet & applied amber rigaree handle, 7" w., 10¾" h. (ILLUS.) **395.00**

Fine Amberina Bowl

Bowl, 8¾" d., 4" h., squatty bulbous wide base w/high ruffled & flaring sides, Diamond Quilted patt., ground base pontil (ILLUS.) **468.00**

Bowl, 10½" l., Reverse Amberina, Diamond Quilted patt. in a rounded heart-form bowl w/a rolled & tightly crimped rim, a curved, looped clear applied thorn handle at one side, late 19th c. **495.00**

Cruet w/original stopper, spherical body tapering to short pedestal base & to a slender cylindrical neck w/a high, arched spout, Inverted Thumbprint patt., blue floral enamel decoration, applied angled amber handle & amber facet-cut stopper, 7¾" h. **688.00**

Finger bowl, fluted rim, fine color. . . . **365.00**

Lemonade glass, slightly tapering tall cylindrical body w/a small applied reeded ring handle near the base. **138.00**

Lemonade glass, tall slightly flaring cylindrical form, Plated Amberina, applied amber loop handle near base, 4¾" h. **4,400.00**

Pitcher, 5⅝" h., spherical body w/a cylindrical neck & pinched spout, Inverted Thumbprint patt., applied ribbed amber handle, 19th c. **193.00**

Pitcher, 8½" h., bulbous ovoid body w/four pinched-in sides below a cylindrical neck w/pinched spout, applied angled clear handle, Inverted Thumbprint patt., 19th c. **220.00**

Tall Amberina Water Pitcher

Pitcher, water, 10" h., 4¾" d., tall cylindrical Optic Ribbed patt. body w/rounded shoulder to the wide cylindrical neck w/pinched spout, applied amber handle (ILLUS.) **210.00**

Salt & pepper shakers w/original metal lids, cylindrical, Inverted Thumbprint patt., 3½" h., pr. **220.00**

Pressed Amberina Sauce Dish

Sauce dish, pressed Daisy & Button patt., square w/rounded corners, Hobbs, Brockunier & Co., Wheeling, West Virginia, 1880s, 5" w., 1⅝" h. (ILLUS.) **85.00**

Sugar bowl, open, Plated Amberina, squatty bulbous form tapering to a wide flat mouth, applied amber loop handles at shoulder, fine coloring, 2" h. **15,400.00**

Toothpick holder, cylindrical body w/infolded tricorner rim, Venetian Diamond patt. **275.00**

Toothpick holder, pressed Daisy & Button patt., cylindrical sides w/rounded bottom raised on three small peg feet **220.00**

Toothpick holder, Venetian Diamond patt., Libbey, ca. 1917 . . . **195.00**

Toothpick holder, cylindrical w/incurved tricorner rim, Diamond Quilted patt., 2¼" h. **248.00**

Tumbler, cylindrical, Diamond
Quilted patt., enamel-decorated
around the body w/large shaded
white daisies & multicolored
leaves **193.00**
Tumbler, cylindrical, Diamond
Quilted patt., 3½" h.. . . . . **61.00**

Diamond Quilted Amberina Tumbler

Tumbler, cylindrical, Diamond
Quilted patt., New England Glass
Co., 2½" d., 3⅝" h. (ILLUS.) **90.00**
Tumbler, cylindrical, a plain rim
above a body cut overall in the
Russian patt., 3¾" h. **2,530.00**
Tumbler, cylindrical, Optic Ribbed
patt., 3¾" h.. . . . . **77.00**
Tumbler, cylindrical, Optic Ribbed
patt., attributed to Libbey, ca. 1917,
3¾" h. **105.00**
Tumbler, cylindrical, optic Swirled
Coin Spot patt., 3¾" h. **94.00**
Tumbler, cylindrical, Plated
Amberina, 4" h.. . . . . **1,650.00**
Vase, 8" h., lily-form, tall slender body
w/rolled flaring rim, teardrop
enclosed in lower stem, round foot,
unmarked Libbey, ca. 1917. . . . . . . **275.00**
Vase, 9" h., ribbed swirled body
tapering to a flared rim, applied
amber rigaree trim. **176.00**
Vase, 10" h., Plated Amberina, lily-
form, slender trumpet-form body
w/flaring tri-corner rim, applied
round amber foot **4,400.00**

APPLIQUED

*Simply stated, this is an art glass form with
applied decoration. Sometimes master glass
craftsmen applied stems or branches to an art
glass object and then added molded glass
flowers or fruit specimens to these branches or
stems. At other times a button of molten glass
was daubed on the object and a tool pressed over
it to form a prunt in the form of a raspberry,
rosette or other shape. Always the work of a
skilled glassmaker, applied decoration can be
found on both cased (two-layer) and single layer
glass. The English firm of Stevens and Williams
was renowned for the appliqued glass they
produced.*

Appliqued Ewer

Ewer, baluster-form w/widely flaring
crimped & ruffled rim, opaque white
body w/applied amber rim, loop
handle & three long leaves in
green, amber & cranberry & an
amber acorn under the handle,
3¼" d., 8" h. (ILLUS.) **$110.00**

Ovoid Appliqued Vase with Leaves

Vase, 5¾" h., 3⅞" d., ovoid swirled
white opalescent body w/a fluted
rose-cased rim, applied w/three
large ruffled amber leaves up the
sides continuing to form the feet
(ILLUS.). **135.00**

Decorated Blue Appliqued Vase

Vase, 6⅜" h., 5⅛" d., sapphire blue
bulbous body tapering to a short
cylindrical neck, applied clear
ruffled rim band & three pointed
feet, decorated w/a gold bird in
flight & colored flowers & leaves
(ILLUS.). **150.00**
Vase, 6½" h., 5½" d., spherical
creamy opaque body cased in rose
red, the rim applied w/an amber
ruffle, the sides applied w/swirled
tapering ruffled amber leaves

Two Appliqued Vases

ending in amber loop feet, clear
applied blossom prunt, attributed to
Stevens & Williams (ILLUS. left) . . . **295.00**

Vase, 6¾" h., 3⅞" d., bulbous body
tapering to a three-lobed curled &
crimped rim, opaque white body
w/a thin applied amber rim band, a
large applied cranberry oak leaf
around the sides & an amber
acorn, raised on applied amber leaf
feet (ILLUS. right) **145.00**

Square Vase with 'Icicle' Decoration

Vase, 8¾" h., 6" w., tall, wide square
deep amethyst body applied
around the rim w/clear overshot
'icicle' decoration (ILLUS.). **795.00**

Ribbon-decorated Appliqued Vase

Vase, 12½" h., 6½" d., tall waisted
ovoid sapphire blue body w/clear
appliqued spines down the sides &

clear feet, ornate colored enamel
ribbon decoration w/pink & white
flowers, further crystal applied
around rim (ILLUS.). **265.00**

Tall Soft Green Appliqued Vase

Vase, 15" h., 4¾" d., slender
baluster-form body w/a swirled
optic rib design, soft green
opalescent ground, applied w/large
pale pink leaves & stems w/a large
dark peach-centered four-petal
flower w/opalescent edges
(ILLUS.). **450.00**

Slender Tree Trunk Appliqued Vase

Vase, 16" h., 5" d., tree-trunk form, a
slender cylindrical rich orangish red
body w/white opalescent thorns &
applied w/slender vaseline
branches & greenish leaves up the
sides w/pink bell-like flowers on the
sides & at the base, swirled
greenish applied feet, gilt trim
(ILLUS.). **550.00**

ART GLASS BASKETS

Blue, wide squatty bulbous body w/a swirled optic rib design tapering up to a wide rolled & crimped rim w/one side turned up, an applied clear handle from side to side, 5½" d., 6" h. **$135.00**

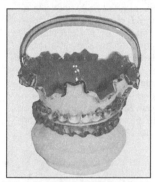

Pink & White Cased Basket

Cased, ringed squatty bulbous base tapering to a tall flaring neck w/crimped & ruffled rim, white exterior w/dark pink interior, applied amber rim band & wide amber & pink crimped leaf wrapped around center & continuing up to the applied amber handle, attributed to Stevens & Williams, 6" d., 7½" h. (ILLUS.) **225.00**

Cased Blue Basket

Cased, widely flaring gently ruffled body on a ring of applied clear 'shell' feet, applied clear angular handle continuing down the sides of the body, shaded shiny blue exterior, white interior, 2¾ x 5", 4⅝" h. (ILLUS.) **89.00**

Cased satin, squatty melon-lobed bluish white exterior enameled in color w/tiny blossoms & branches below the rolled & crimped rim, lavender interior, applied frosted clear handle, England, 6¼" h. **138.00**

Emerald Green Basket

Green, flaring cylindrical emerald green Optic Ribbed patt. body w/a clear applied ribbed petal band rim & clear twisted tall handle, 4⅝" d., 6¾" h. (ILLUS.) **110.00**

Overshot, green shaded down to clear w/an overshot finish, bulbous tapering ovoid body w/a wide flaring ruffled rim, applied dark green twisted loop handle, applied green rim band & an applied green vine w/red blossom wrapping around the body, 6" h. **83.00**

Rose red & blue, the deep bulbous basket w/a deep rose red interior cased w/pale pink under a clear Hobnail patt. casing, a widely flaring ruffled & crimped rim pulled in on two sides & w/a folded rim design, applied pale blue rim band & high arched & twisted applied blue handle, raised on four reeded curved tapering applied pale blue feet, 11½" w., 12½" h. **330.00**

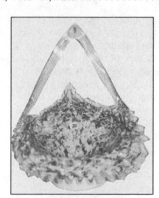

Large Spangled Basket

Spangled, deep rounded body w/a wide rolled crimped rim, the back side pulled-up into a point, applied clear reeded tall pointed handle, white exterior, blue, yellow, brown & white spatter interior w/silver mica flecks, 8½" d., 11½" h. (ILLUS.) **265.00**

Spangled, footed shallow form w/widely flared ruffled & crimped edge, shaded pink interior w/silver mica flecks, white exterior, applied clear ropetwist handle, 8" d., 8" h. (tiny nick at top of handle) **165.00**

Spangled, low rounded & ribbed body w/a deeply fluted & crimped rim, golden yellow, green, pink & white spatter interior w/mica flecks, white exterior, applied clear ribbed handle, 6⅝ x 7⅝", 6½" h. **195.00**

Spangled, rounded body w/an eight-crimp rim, blue exterior w/stripes of silver mica flecks, cased in white, applied clear looped thorn handle, 5¼" d., 8¼" h. **195.00**

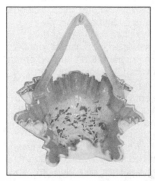

Shaded Pink Spangled Basket

Spangled, rounded body w/flaring deeply ruffled & crimped sides, applied clear reeded tall pointed handle, white exterior, dark pink shaded interior w/pale blue, yellow & brown spatter w/silver mica flecks, 8 x 10", 10½" h. (ILLUS.) . . . **295.00**

Spangled, rounded w/crimped & ruffled rim, pink spangled ground applied w/red cherries on a clear leafy stem continuing to form an arched handle, 8" h. **110.00**

Green with White Spatter Basket

Spatter, cylindrical sides w/two sides pulled up & two rolled out, dark green covered on the exterior

w/fine white spatter, applied clear pointed handle & raised on tall pointed, ribbed & pointed applied petal feet, 4½" d., 6⅜" h. (ILLUS.). . . **85.00**

Spatter, heart-shaped w/crimped rim, royal blue, tan & opal white spatter, clear applied twisted thorn handle, 8½" d., 8" h. **248.00**

Spatter, rounded body flaring to a triangular crimped rim, pink, maroon, yellow, white & blue spatter exterior, white interior, applied clear looped thorn handle . . **175.00**

Spatter, rounded ribbed body w/an upright crimped & ruffled rim, mottled teal blue, pink, yellow, maroon & peach spatter exterior, white interior, applied clear thorn handle, 5¾" d., 6¾" h. **175.00**

BACCARAT

Baccarat glass has been made by Cristalleries de Baccarat, France, since 1765. The firm has produced various glassware of excellent quality and paperweights. Baccarat's Rose Teinte is often referred to as Baccarat's Amberina

Baccarat "Rose Teinte" Lamp Base

Lamp base, kerosene-type, footed ovoid font in Rose Teinte Swirl patt. metal collar w/original brass European burner, late 19th - early 20th c., 3⅝" d., 8½" h. (ILLUS.). . . **$145.00**

Vase, 10" h., footed tall clear cylindrical body w/optic ribbing, decorated w/large gold fern leaves up the sides & two gold butterflies, gold rim band, partial paper label. **303.00**

Wine glasses, cut-overlay, squatty rounded bowl in smoky brown cut to clear w/alternating upright & inverted fans, raised on a tall slender clear zipper-cut hexagonal stem & round foot, one marked w/embossed signature, early 20th c., 7½" h., set of 6 . . . . **275.00**

BLOWN THREE MOLD

This type of glass was entirely or partially blown in a mold and was popular from about 1820 to 1840. The object was formed and the decoration impressed upon it by blowing the glass into a metal mold, usually of three but sometimes more sections, hinged together. Mold-blown glass actually dates back to ancient times. Recent research reveals that certain geometric patterns were reproduced in the 1920s and some new pieces, usually sold through museum gift shops, are still available. Collectors are urged to read all recent information available. Reference numbers are from George L. and Helen McKearin's book, American Glass.

Creamer, geometric, ovoid body tapering to a wide flaring rim w/pinched spout, applied ribbed solid handle w/end curl, clear, half-pint (GII-32) **$413.00**

Creamer, miniature, geometric, ovoid body tapering to a flaring rim w/pinched spout, applied solid handle w/end curl missing, clear, 2⅞" h. (GIII-21) **143.00**

Creamer, geometric, ovoid ribbed body w/widely flaring neck & spout, applied strap handle w/curl end, clear, 3⅛" h. (GI-29) **660.00**

Decanter w/hollow patterned stopper, geometric, ovoid body tapering to a flared rim, clear, 10¼" h. (GIII-5) **132.00**

Decanter w/original pressed wheel stopper, geometric, cylindrical body below the angled shoulder to the tapering cylindrical neck w/a folded lip, clear, pint, 9" h.(GIV-5) **187.00**

Decanter w/original pressed wheel stopper, geometric, swelled cylindrical ringed & ribbed body w/a rounded ribbed shoulder tapering to the ringed tapering neck, clear, quart, 10¾" h. (GI-29) **110.00**

Decanter w/period pressed waffle stopper, geometric, ovoid body tapering to a cylindrical neck w/flanged rim, clear, GIII-26 (trace of light stain on inside base) **110.00**

Decanter w/period pressed wheel stopper, geometric, barrel-shaped w/a short cylindrical neck & flanged rim w/one side formed into a pouring spout, clear, 7" h., GII-7 (some interior haze in base) **132.00**

Decanter w/period pressed wheel stopper, geometric, cylindrical body sharply tapering to a flanged rim, clear w/hint of blue, pint, GIII-9 (lightly ground lip) **154.00**

Decanter w/pressed waffle stopper, geometric, ovoid body tapering to a plain neck w/flaring flattened rim, clear, pint, without stopper 7⅛" h. (GIII-6) **83.00**

Decanter w/pressed wheel stopper, miniature, geometric, bulbous body tapering to a flared rim, diamond base w/pontil, slightly weak impression, clear, 5" h. (GII-18) . . . **303.00**

Decanter w/pressed wheel stopper, geometric, ovoid body tapering to a cylindrical neck w/a flattened rim, clear, 9½" h. (GIII-6) **110.00**

Dish, geometric, shallow round form w/a folded rim, clear, 5¾" d., GII-18 (few small under rim chips) **165.00**

Dish, geometric, shallow round form w/folded rim, clear, 5¹³⁄₁₆" d., GIII-24 (slightly lopsided) **77.00**

Rare Blown Three Mold Hat

Model of a top hat, geometric, flared brim, dark sapphire blue, 2¼" h., GII-18 (ILLUS.) **468.00**

Model of a top hat, geometric, rolled & folded rim, rayed base w/pontil, double-molded, clear, 2½" h. (GIII-18) **660.00**

Blown Three Mold Mustard Jar

Mustard jar, cov., geometric, cylindrical body w/short flared neck, ribbed tam-o-shanter lid, clear, 4¼" h., GI-24 (ILLUS.) **132.00**

Geometric Blown Three Mold Pitcher

Pitcher, 6¾" h., geometric, ovoid body w/short cylindrical neck & pinched spout, applied ribbed strap handle w/end curl , clear,GII-18 (ILLUS.) **880.00**

Salt dip, geometric, round w/a widely flaring flattened rim above the rounded bowl molded w/panels of beaded Roman arches w/beading between an upper bead band & tapering to a round beaded foot, deep opalescent white, embossed "R. & G. A. WRIGHT - PHILADELPHIA," 3½" d., 2" h., GV-24 (discolored in-the-making line off the rim) **550.00**

Salt dip, geometric, wide rounded bowl on a short footed base, clear, 2¾" h. (GII-18) **495.00**

Sugar bowl, cov., geometric, wide cylindrical body w/galleried rim & rounded bottom raised on a ribbed funnel foot w/a folded rim, the domed inset cover w/a drawn-out ribbed finial, clear, 6¼" h., GII-22 (ground chip on cover) **3,300.00**

Tumbler, geometric, barrel-shaped, clear, 2½" h. (GII-19) **165.00**

Tumbler, geometric, barrel-shaped, clear, 2¾" h. (GII-18) **171.00**

Tumbler, geometric, barrel-shaped, tooled rim, rayed base w/pontil, clear, 3½" h., GIII-21 (rim lightly ground) **165.00**

Tumbler, geometric, flaring cylindrical form, sheared plain rim, plain base w/pontil, clear, 3¾" h. (GII-33 . . . . . **110.00**

Wine, geometric, conical bowl on a bladed stem & round foot, clear, 4" h., GII-19 (small shallow base flake) **165.00**

BOHEMIAN

Numerous types of glass were made in the once-independent country of Bohemia and fine colored, cut and engraved glass was turned out. Flashed and other inexpensive wares also were made and many of these, including amber-and ruby-shaded glass, were exported to the United States last century and in the present one. One *favorite pattern in the late 19th and early 20th centuries was Deer & castle. Another was Deer and Pine Tree.*

Bowl, cov., 6½" d., 5½" h., deep round stepped-in sides w/a wide flat rim fitted w/a slightly domed cover w/a knob finial, crystal w/translucent studio enamels in gold, red, blue & green foliate elements w/delicate black outlining throughout, decoration repeated on the cover, in the manner of Steinschonau. **$633.00**

Jar, cov., wide paneled goblet-form bowl w/a rounded base band, fitted w/a domed cover w/rounded rim band & topped by a bulbous pointed finial, raised on a faceted large knob above a thick star-cut foot, amber, attributed to Moser or Kulka, 10¾" h. **345.00**

Fine Engraved Bohemian Pokal

Pokal, cov., flashed & engraved, a tall slightly flaring cylindrical bowl flashed in ruby & engraved w/an ornate scene of deer in a forest, the bowl raised on a faceted & knopped tall stem w/further engraving on the foot, the top fitted w/a high paneled pagoda-form domed cover w/a facet-cut knop & oblong finial, 19th c., 22" h. (ILLUS.) **1,150.00**

Ornate Bohemian Punch Bowl

Punch bowl, cover & underplate, all in frosted clear, the tall swelled cylindrical bowl decorated around the sides w/red glass jewels centering gold enameled medallions joined by beaded swags, w/presentation engraving dated "1875," the wide low-domed cover w/similar decoration & a long curved metal handle, set into a dished widely flaring matching underplate, underplate 11" d., 11" h. (ILLUS.). 345.00

Elaborate Bohemian Covered Urns

Urns, cov., cut overlay, classical form w/deep bowl raised on a short paneled & ringed pedestal on a square foot, a tapering cover w/large faceted pointed knop finial, ruby etched to clear frosted w/oval & squared panels of baskets of flowers or floral swags around the center, ornate gilt border panels & trim, swag engraving around the cover, some wear, 19th c., 9¼" h., pr. (ILLUS.). 1,725.00

Vase, 6" h., flora-form deep bowl w/a six-ruffle rim, raised on a wafer on a short pedestal foot, iridescent gold interior, gold oil spotted iridescent exterior, polished base, late 19th - early 20th c. 288.00

Vase, 8¾" h., simple ovoid body tapering to a short cylindrical neck, cased w/opal lined in turquoise blue, the exterior w/striated bands of blue, green & burgundy red down the sides also highlighted w/scattered gilt enamel medallions centered by red glass "jewels". 316.00

Vase, 10" h., tall cylindrical body w/a widely flaring rim, purple w/a broad medial band of etched griffins, urns & swags enameled in gold in the Moser style, polished pontil. 374.00

Vase, 12" h., a squatty compressed bulbous base tapering to a tall slender swelled cylindrical body w/a narrow shoulder below an urn-form cupped rim section, Czechoslovakian-style in apple green w/the lower half enhanced w/spotted reddish amber decoration, polished top rim 173.00

Ornate Bohemian Portrait Vase

Vases, 13½" h., tall slender baluster form w/a tall trumpet neck, dark green w/overall delicate dotted & banded gilt trim framing central oval portrait medallions of ladies, slight wear, early 20th c., pr. (ILLUS. of one) 690.00

Vases, 19¼" h., cut overlay, tall cylindrical pedestal base supporting a slender tall urn-form vase w/wide faceted trumpet neck, dark ruby engraved on the vase & base w/floral swags, oval reserves or leaf & blossom bands in frosted clear, highlighted w/ornate delicate

Elaborate Pedestal-based Vases

gilt trelliswork, scrolls, banding &
panels, base of one cracked,
19th c., pr. (ILLUS.) **2,300.00**

BRIDE'S BASKETS & BOWLS

*These berry or fruit bowls were popular late
Victorian wedding gifts, hence the name. They
were produced in a variety of quality art
glasswares and sometimes were fitted in ornate
silver plate holders.*

Shaded Purple Bride's Bowl

Cased bowl, purple shaded to pale
lavender interior on a squared bowl
w/a notched & crimped rim, lacy
golden orange scrolls on the
interior, white exterior, 7⅛" d.,
2⅝" h. (ILLUS.) **$165.00**
Cased bowl, deep shaded pink
Peach Blow exterior w/crimped rim,
decorated w/raised gold floral
branches, white interior, in an
ornate Victorian silver plate
handled stand, bowl attributed to
Thomas Webb, bowl 9" d., 2¾" h. . . **303.00**

Decorated Pink Satin Bride's Bowl

Cased bowl, pink satin interior
w/crimped & ruffled rim around a
ring of indented wells & a central
round indentation, dainty enameled
decoration of a ring of golden
orange flowers & leaves, white
exterior, 10⅜" d., 2⅝" h. (ILLUS.) . . **265.00**

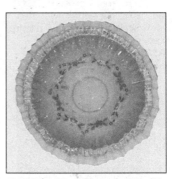

Shaded Pink Bowl with Applied Bands

Cased bowl, shaded pink interior
w/an applied crimped white & clear
border band, center enamel-
decorated w/a swagged band of
white, brown, orange & green
florals, white exterior, 9¾" d.,
2¾" h. (ILLUS.) **165.00**

Maroon & Cream Bride's Bowl

Cased bowl, maroon shaded to cream interior, crimped & ruffled rim w/molded ring & U-form designs around the sides, delicate enameling on pink flowers & gold leaves of the interior, white exterior,11⅜" d., 3¼" h. (ILLUS.) .. **195.00**

Blue Cased Bride's Bowl

Cased bowl, blue interior w/wide down-turned rib sides w/a double-lobed & crimped upturned section at the back, overall dainty white & yellow enameled blossoms on branches, white exterior, 10¾" d., 3½" h. (ILLUS.) **195.00**

Cased bowl, pink satin glass interior, applied crystal rim, silver pedestal base, 7¾" d., 5½" h. **210.00**

Cased bowl, heavily fluted & ruffled bowl, pink interior w/amber border, white exterior, enameled floral decoration inside & out, in an ornate Middletown silver plate frame, 9" d. **715.00**

Cased bowl, apricot interior & white exterior, the interior finely enameled w/vining florals & butterfly band, in an ornate skirted silver plate footed stand w/scrolled acanthus leaf loop handles, marked "Reed & Barton #4643," bowl probably by Thomas Webb, 10" d. **605.00**

Cased bowl, shallow tightly crimped & ruffled bowl w/a blue interior w/enameled decoration, white exterior, signed "Thomas Webb & Sons," on an ornate silver plate stand w/lacy looped handles flanking the bowl above a short pedestal & domed, stepped base w/scroll-cast borders & feet, stand marked by E. B. Webster & Sons, 11" w. **935.00**

Cased bowl, deep rounded form w/upright crimped rim, deep pink interior & white opal exterior,

applied amber rim band, raised on a silver plate base w/a tall slender flaring pedestal & engraved domed round foot, bowl 8" d., 4" h., overall 11" h. **198.00**

Cased bowl, pink shading to amber interior, white exterior, the interior enameled w/polychrome florals, deeply fluted & crimped rim, footed silver plate stand w/high scroll-cast arched handle, late 19th c., 11" d., 11" h. **275.00**

Decorated Maroon Bride's Basket

Cased bowl, maroon interior decorated w/enameled white flowers & green leaves, white exterior, applied clear rim band on crimped border w/two turned-up sides, in an ornate silver plate Rockford frame, bowl 6½ x 10", overall 13½" h. (ILLUS.) **450.00**

Monet Stumpf Bride's Bowl

Opalescent pink bowl, gold lustred interior, low rounded bottom w/squared upturned fluted & crimped sides, Monet Stumpf, Pantin, France, 7½" d., 3¾" h. (ILLUS.) **195.00**

Pale green bowl, decorated w/dainty white enameled flowers, turned-in pleated rim, flared footed base, 10¾" d., 3¾" h. **300.00**

Pigeon blood bowl, deeply lobed flaring sides w/a tightly crimped rim, white enameled florals around the interior, satin finish, 19th c., 11" d. **330.00**

BRISTOL

A number of glasshouses operated in Bristol, England over the years and they produced a variety of wares. Today, however, the generic name Bristol refers to a type of semi-opaque glass, often accented with ornate enameling. Such wares were produced in England, Europe and America in the 19th and early 20th centuries.

Cracker jar, cov., cylindrical pale green body finely decorated w/a scene of a stork standing among cattails & water plants, silver plate rim, bail handle & cover w/strawberry finial **$220.00**

Bristol Cracker Jar

Cracker jar, cov., slightly tapering cylindrical glossy soft green body enameled w/a walking stork & a large stylized tree, silver plate rim, cover & bail handle, 3¼" d., 4⅜" h. (ILLUS.) **125.00**

Dresser bottles w/original tulip-shaped stoppers, tapering cylindrical form, opaque blue enameled w/morning glories, leaves & other florals, late 19th c., 10½" h., pr. **175.00**

Pink & Gold Bristol Ewer

Ewer, footed ovoid body w/a neck ring & cupped rim, satin pink decorated w/an ornate gold

palmette band w/leaf sprigs & gilt line trim & a gold handle from the rim to the shoulder, 2⅝" d., 6⅜" h. (ILLUS.) **125.00**

Finger bowl, narrow footring under the deep rounded upright sides w/a flat rim, clambroth w/colored enamel floral & leaf sprigs around the sides, 19th c., 4½" d., 3" h. **33.00**

Unusual Bristol Teapot

Teapot, cov., slightly tapering cylindrical body w/low domed cover w/knob finial, slender angled spout & applied C-form handle, creamy opaque white decorated around the body w/a wading stork among water plants, 4½" d., 5¼" h. (ILLUS.) **295.00**

Pair Blue Bristol Vases

Vases, 10½" h., 4" d., baluster-form w/a four-lobed rolled & crimped rim, glossy turquoise blue decorated boldly w/dark blue blossoms on leafy gold stems, pr. (ILLUS.) **225.00**

Vases, 12" h., baluster-form w/a ringed pedestal & trumpet neck, h.p. in enamel w/birds & flowers in green, brown & white on a pink ground, late 19th c., pr. (minor lip flakes) **165.00**

Vases, 17" h., simple classic baluster-form, cushion foot & ovoid body tapering to a slightly flaring wide cylindrical neck, pink ground w/black & gilt trim bands & a central oval reserve in white h.p. w/a bust portrait of a lovely young lady bordered in black w/gilt

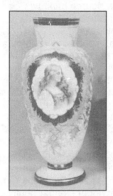

Fine Bristol Portrait Vase

squigglework all enclosed by a gold serrated leaf wreath & green leafage & purple blossoms, Europe, third quarter 19th c., pr. (ILLUS. of one) **990.00**

BURMESE

Burmese is a single-layer glass that shades from pink to pale yellow. It was patented by Frederick S. Shirley and made by the Mt. Washington Glass Co. A license to produce the glass in England was granted to Thomas Webb & Sons, which called its articles Queen's Burmese. Gundersen Burmese was made briefly about the middle of this century, and the Pairpoint Crystal Company is making limited quantities at the present time.

Bowl, 4" d., 2¼" h., rounded bottom w/flaring, crimped star-shaped rim, paper label w/"Thomas Webb & Sons - Queen's Burmese," satin finish **$413.00**

Bowl, 5¾" d., 2¾" h., rounded base below the flaring ruffled star-shaped rim, Mt. Washington, satin finish **303.00**

Bowl, 12" d., 3½" h., rounded base below the widely flaring 10-flute rim, glossy finish, late 19th c. **385.00**

Compote, open, 7" d., 4" h., a wide shallow bowl w/a gently ruffled rim, raised on a baluster-form stem on a round foot, glossy finish,19th c. ... **330.00**

Creamer, footed spherical body w/a wide cylindrical neck w/pinched spout, applied pale yellow handle, glossy finish, Mt. Washington, 4" h........................ **440.00**

Cruet w/original stopper, enameled white & blue flowers w/green leaves & vines, Mt. Washington .. **2,950.00**

Cup & saucer, flaring cylindrical cup w/applied angular yellow handle, deeply dished saucer, saucer w/original Mt. Washington paper label, saucer 4¾" d., cup 2" h...... **440.00**

Cup & saucer, deep rounded cylindrical cup w/an applied angular yellow handle, deeply dished saucer, glossy finish, Mt. Washington, saucer 5" d., cup 2¼" h. **468.00**

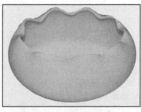

Burmese Finger Bowl

Finger bowl, wide shallow rounded shape w/an incurved crimped rim, satin finish, Mt. Washington, 4½" d., 2½" h. (ILLUS.) **195.00**

Ginger jar, cov., ovoid body tapering to a short cylindrical neck w/a fitted domed cover, decorated w/white enamel clumps of asters on delicate leafy vines w/raised gold berries, Mt. Washington, 5" h. **2,090.00**

Rose bowl, miniature, satin finish, Mt. Washington, 2¼" h.......... **110.00**

Rose bowl, miniature, spherical body enamel-decorated w/green & brown blossoms, leaves & twigs, six-crimp rim, 2¼" h. **220.00**

Rose bowl, miniature, spherical w/a six-crimp rim, enamel-decorated w/lavender blue flowers, satin finish, 3" h.................... **275.00**

Toothpick holder, model of a hat, fine blue glass threading around the brim, glossy finish, 2⅛" h. **220.00**

Toothpick holder, spherical body w/a short hexagonal neck, undecorated, 2½" h. **237.00**

Tumbler, cylindrical, decorated around the body in the Queen's patt. w/yellow or white dotted enamel daisies & green leaves, enhanced w/raised gold grasses, Mt. Washington, 3¾" h. **1,430.00**

Tumbler, cylindrical, glossy finish, Mt. Washington, 3¾" h.......... **138.00**

Vase, miniature, 2¼" h., rounded bottom below a widely flaring crimped & ruffled rim, satin finish, Mt. Washington **193.00**

Vase, miniature, 2¾" h., a spherical base below the squared & gently flaring upright neck, enamel-decorated around the neck w/a band of reddish brown blossoms & green leaves **330.00**

Vase, miniature, 3" h., footed squatty bulbous body tapering to a upward flaring, ruffled neck, enamel-decorated w/variegated green ivy vine, satin finish, signed "Thomas Webb & Sons - Queen's Burmese". **319.00**

Vase, miniature, 3" h., spherical body below a widely flaring crimped & flattened rim, enamel-decorated w/fall leaves & red berries, satin finish,Thomas Webb **240.00**

Vase, miniature, 3" h., squatty bulbous base tapering to a flaring, incurved star-shaped rim, decorated w/finely enameled lavender blue flowers & fall foliage, stamped mark "Queen's Burmese - Thomas Webb & Sons" **330.00**

Vase, miniature, 3⅛" h., squatty bulbous base & waisted body to the flaring rim pinched & folded into five points, enamel-decorated w/a running leafy vine w/red berries around the middle, Thomas Webb, England **286.00**

Vase, miniature, 3¼" h., spherical body tapering to an upturned tricorner rim, attributed to Thomas Webb, satin finish **193.00**

Vase, miniature, 3¼" h., tapering cylindrical body w/a wide flaring & ruffled rim, attributed to Libbey, satin finish **295.00**

Small Webb Burmese Vase

Vase, miniature 3⅝" h., 2⅜" d., squatty spherical base below a tall cylindrical six-sided neck, Thomas Webb, glossy finish (ILLUS.) **195.00**

Vase, miniature, 4½" h., lightly ribbed squatty bulbous bag-form body tapering to a widely flaring, lightly ruffled neck, the neck applied w/a yellow rigaree band w/a button & tassels at the front, Mt. Washington **2,090.00**

Vase, 6½" h., double-gourd form, a spherical bottom below a small ovoid section at the base of the slender 'stick' neck, enamel-decorated around the base & neck w/a leafy vine of red trumpet flowers, acid-stamped "Thomas Webb & Sons Queen's Burmese" . . **880.00**

Vase, 6½" h., lily-form, round foot & tricorner flaring rim, Mt. Washington, satin finish **275.00**

Vase, 6¾" h., jack-in-the-pulpit-form, round foot under slender gently flaring cylindrical body w/a crimped & rolled rim **230.00**

Vase, 7¼" h., ovoid body, Japanesque style decoration on the 'white burmese' body w/pink at the top, decorated overall w/delicate Oriental scenes in sepia tones, Thomas Webb, England. . . . **345.00**

Vase, 8" h., simple ovoid body tapering to a short, wide cylindrical neck, a variegated enameled green vine cascades across the body w/a single large blue clematis blossom & several buds, satin finish, attributed to Webb **1,540.00**

Vase, 8¼" h., trumpet-form w/large ruffled rim, fitted w/metal handles & base, creamy background decorated w/flowers, attributed to Thomas Webb. **515.00**

Vase, lily-form, 10" h., tri-corner rim, Mt. Washington **385.00**

Fine Decorated Burmese Vase

Vase, 10¼" h., 5" d., spherical base centered by a tall slender 'stick' neck w/slightly flared rim,

decorated around the body & neck w/green & brown ivy vines, satin finish, impressed Thomas Webb Queen's Burmese base mark (ILLUS.) **895.00**

Vase, 11" h., jack-in-the-pulpit-form, a round foot & tall very slender flaring body w/a wide rolled & crimped rim, Mt. Washington, satin finish . . . **990.00**

Vase, 12" h., decorated w/a scene of pyramids, sacred ibis & desert oasis, Mt. Washington Glass Co. **1,750.00**

Vase, 12½" h., lily-form, tricorner rim, satin finish, Mt. Washington (base slightly out of round) **230.00**

Vase, 18" h., lily-type, tri-corner rim, Mt. Washington, satin finish **690.00**

Vases, 5½" h., rolled-up flared tops, undecorated, Mt. Washington Glass Co., pr. **895.00**

Whiskey tumbler, cylindrical body w/squared rim, Diamond Quilted patt., glossy finish, Mt. Washington, 2½" h. **275.00**

Whiskey tumbler, cylindrical w/squared rim, satin finish, 2½" h. . . **193.00**

CAMBRIDGE

The Cambridge Glass Company was founded in Ohio in 1901. Numerous pieces are now sought, especially those designed by Arthur J. Bennett, including Crown Tuscan. Other productions included crystal animals, "Black Amethyst," "blanc opaque," and other types of colored glass. The firm was finally closed in 1954. It should not be confused with the New England Glass Co., Cambridge, Massachusets.

  NEAR CUT TUSCAN

Various Cambridge Marks

Basket, etched Chantilly patt., Crystal, 6" h. **$28.00**

Bowl, 9" d., 3" h., round flaring bowl on a low standard, Azurite, ca. 1922 . . . . **28.00**

Bowl, 12" d., footed, etched Rose Point patt., No. 3400, Crystal **129.00**

Bowl, 13" d., crimped rim, four-footed, Caprice patt., Crystal. **25.00**

Butter dish, cov., etched Elaine patt., No. 3400/52, Crystal **219.00**

Candlestick, three-light, etched Wildflower patt., Crystal. **45.00**

Candlestick, three-light, etched Wildflower patt., No. 638, Crystal . . . **77.00**

Candlesticks, pressed Caprice patt., Crystal, 2½" h., pr. **25.00**

Candlesticks, shape No. 639, ringed stem, Cobalt blue, 4" h., pr. **150.00**

Candlesticks, Corinth (No. 3900) line, Crystal, 5" h., pr. **100.00**

Candy dish, cov., Decagon line, No. 864, Ebony **95.00**

Candy dish, cov., blown Line No. 3121, Crystal, 6" d. **275.00**

Champagne, etched Wildflower patt., No. 3121, Crystal. **24.00**

Coaster, Caprice patt., Moonlight Blue, No. 20, 5½" d. **29.00**

Cocktail, engraved Lynbrook patt., Crystal **10.00**

Cocktail, etched Chantilly patt., No. 3625, Crystal. **24.00**

Cocktail, tall, Rose Point etching, Crystal **23.00**

Cocktail, Tally-Ho line, Cobalt blue . **44.00**

Cocktail, blown Caprice patt., No. 300, Crystal, 3 oz. **19.00**

Cocktail, Line No. 3121, Crystal, 3 oz. **30.00**

Compote, open, four-toed, etched Apple Blossom patt., No. 3400, yellow **59.00**

Compote, open, etched Elaine patt., No. 3500/36, Crystal, 6" h. **59.00**

Cordial, No. 1066, Royal blue **45.00**

Cordial, etched Wildflower patt., Crystal, 1 oz. **70.00**

Cordial, footed, Mt. Vernon line, Crystal, 1 oz. **17.00**

Creamer & open sugar bowl, etched Elaine patt., No.1402/33, Crystal, pr. **65.00**

Creamer & open sugar bowl, individual, etched gold-encrusted Rose Point patt., Crystal, pr. **65.00**

Creamer & open sugar bowl, individual size, Gadroon (No. 3500 line), Crystal, pr. **45.00**

Flying Lady Cambridge Bowl

Crown Tuscan bowl, flower or fruit, 10½" l., footed, Statuesque line, Flying Lady patt., seashell bowl w/nude lady at one end, h.p. roses & floral bands, No. 30011/40 (ILLUS.). **173.00**

Crown Tuscan bowl, 10½ x 11½", oblong body raised on four small tab feet, the widely flared rim deeply ruffled, the interior & exterior decorated w/an ornate scrolling gold floral design, marked **165.00**

Crown Tuscan compote, footed, shell-form bowl **45.00**

Cup & saucer, Caprice patt., Mocha **36.00**

Cup & saucer, etched Apple Blossom patt., Crystal **25.00**

Decanter in Farberware

Decanter w/stopper, Emerald body in Farberware metal holder, 8" h. (ILLUS.). **95.00**

Figural flower holder, "Draped Lady," green, 13" h. **350.00**

Fruit saucer, crimped, Caprice patt., Moonlight Blue. **89.00**

Goblet, water, Caprice patt., Crystal. . . **14.00**

Goblet, water, etched Elaine patt., No. 3121, Crystal. **39.00**

Goblet, Decagon line, No. 3077, Moonlight Blue, 9 oz.. . . . . **20.00**

Ice bucket, etched Chantilly patt., Martha blank, Crystal **189.00**

Ice pail, etched Cleo patt., No. 851, yellow **169.00**

Oyster cocktail, Caprice patt., No. 300, Crystal. **18.00**

Parfait, Caprice patt., No. 300, pink, 5 oz.. . . . . **169.00**

Pickle tray, etched Apple Blossom patt., No. 3400/59, yellow, 9" l. **69.00**

Pitcher, Doulton-style w/chrome base, handled, Amber **35.00**

Pitcher, ball-shaped, etched Apple Blossom patt., pink, 80 oz. **495.00**

Plate, 6" d., Rose Point etching, Crystal **12.00**

Plate, 7" d., etched Cleo patt., green . . **18.00**

Plate, 7" d., etched Cleo patt., pink. . . . **16.00**

Plate, 8" d., Line No. 3400, Crystal. . . . **20.00**

Plate, 8½" d., etched Apple Blossom patt., pink. **20.00**

Plate, 8½" d., etched Appled Blossom patt., Amber **16.00**

Plate, 14" d., Alpine Caprice patt., Moonlight Blue. **119.00**

Relish dish, oval, etched Chantilly patt., Crystal, 8¼" l. **18.00**

Relish dish, three-part, Mt. Vernon line, Royal blue **45.00**

Relish dish, three-part, handled, Gadroon (No. 3500) line, Crystal, 6½" l. **45.00**

Relish dish, two-part, two-handled, Line No. 3400, Crystal, 8¾" l. **75.00**

Sherbet, Rose Point etching, Crystal . . **15.00**

Sherbet, blown Caprice patt., No. 300, Moonlight blue, 6 oz.. . . . . . **35.00**

Sherbet, tall, Caprice patt., No. 300, clear, 6 oz.. . . . . **10.00**

Sherbet, tall, etched Wildflower patt., Crystal, 6 oz.. . . . . **16.00**

Tumbler, juice, footed, pressed Caprice patt., No. 300, Crystal, 5 oz.. . . . . **18.00**

Tumbler, juice, footed, Square Line, Crystal, 5 oz. **15.00**

Tumbler, etched Diane patt., Crystal, 9 oz. **32.00**

Tumbler, footed, Decagon line, green, 12 oz. **30.00**

Tumbler, iced-tea, footed, pressed Caprice patt., Crystal, 12 oz.. . . . . . . **22.00**

Tumbler, low footed, etched Rose Point patt., No. 3121, Crystal, 12 oz.. . . . . **42.00**

Vase, 5½" h., pressed Caprice patt., Moonlight Blue. **189.00**

Vase, 8" h., bulbous-shape, No. 1431, Cobalt blue **165.00**

Vase, 8½" h., ball-shaped, pressed Caprice patt., Amber **195.00**

Water set: pitcher & six tumblers; Inverted Thistle patt., green w/gold trim, the set **280.00**

Wine, Decagon line, No. 3077, pink . . . **18.00**

Wine, Caprice patt., Crystal, 2½ oz. . . . **18.00**

Wine, Line No. 3121, Crystal, 2½ oz. . . **55.00**

Wines, Statuesque line, clear bowl, Ebony Nude Lady stem, 6½" h., set of 8. . . . . **345.00**

CARNIVAL

Earlier called Taffeta glass, the Carnival glass now being collected was introduced early in this century. Its producers gave it an iridescence that attempted to imitate that of some Tiffany glass. Collectors will find available books by leading authorities Donald E. Moore, Sherman Hand, Marion T. Hartung, Rose M. Presznick, and Bill Edwards

For a more extensive listing of Carnival Glass, please refer to Antique Trader Books American Pressed Glass & Bottles Price Guide.

Acanthus

Bowl, 7" d., marigold	$48.00
Bowl, 7¾" d., marigold	48.00
Bowl, 7¾" d., smoky	50.00
Bowl, 8" to 9" d., green	86.00
Bowl, 8" to 9" d., marigold	106.00
Bowl, 8" to 9" d., purple	115.00
Bowl, 8" to 9" d., smoky	88.00
Bowl, 9" d., ice cream shape, marigold	50.00
Plate, 9" to 10" d., marigold	194.00
Plate, chop, marigold	135.00
Plate, chop, smoky	155.00

Acorn (Fenton)

Bowl, 6" d., aqua	139.00
Bowl, 6" d., ruffled, sapphire blue	90.00
Bowl, 6" d., vaseline	113.00
Bowl, 7" d., ruffled, amber	110.00
Bowl, 7" d., aqua	84.00
Bowl, 7" d., blue	68.00
Bowl, 7" d., marigold	41.00
Bowl, 7" d., red	544.00
Bowl, 7" d., ice cream shape, red	300.00
Bowl, 7" d., ice cream shape, sapphire blue	400.00
Bowl, 7" d., ruffled, vaseline	105.00
Bowl, 7½" d., blue	48.00
Bowl, 7½" d., ruffled, blue	105.00
Bowl, 7½" d., marigold	43.00
Bowl, 7½" d., purple	140.00
Bowl, 8" d., amber	165.00
Bowl, 8" to 9" d., blue	55.00
Bowl, 8" to 9" d., marigold	42.00
Bowl, 8" to 9" d., ribbon candy rim, purple	113.00
Bowl, 8" to 9" d., ruffled, red	775.00
Bowl, deep, red	425.00
Bowl, flat, red	950.00
Bowl, ice cream shape, aqua	170.00
Bowl, ice cream shape, blue	48.00
Bowl, ice cream shape, green	105.00
Bowl, ice cream shape, vaseline	195.00

Bowl, ruffled, sapphire blue	675.00
Bowl, white	185.00
Compote, vaseline (Millersburg)	1,625.00

Acorn Burrs (Northwood)

Berry set: master bowl & 5 sauce dishes; purple, 6 pcs.	475.00
Berry set: master bowl & 6 sauce dishes; marigold, 7 pcs.	255.00
Berry set: master bowl & 6 sauce dishes; purple, 7 pcs.	525.00

Acorn Burrs Butter Dish

Butter dish, cov., purple (ILLUS.)	263.00
Pitcher, water, green	400.00
Pitcher, water, marigold	425.00
Pitcher, water, purple	463.00
Punch set: bowl, base & 6 cups; marigold, 8 pcs.	2,125.00
Punch set: bowl, base & 6 cups; purple, 8 pcs.	1,325.00
Sauce dish, marigold	30.00
Table set, purple, 4 pcs.	800.00
Water set: pitcher & 6 tumblers; green, 7 pcs.	950.00

Advertising & Souvenir Items

Basket, "Feldman Bros. Furniture, Salisbury, Md.," open edge, marigold	68.00
Basket, "Miller's Furniture," marigold	94.00
Bell, souvenir, BPOE Elks, "Atlantic City, 1911," blue	2,000.00
Bell, souvenir, BPOE Elks, "Parkersburg, 1914," blue	2,000.00
Bowl, "Isaac Benesch," 6¼" d., purple (Millersburg)	425.00
Bowl, "H. Mayday & Co., 1910," 8½" d., Wild Blackberry patt., purple	270.00
Bowl, "Dreibus Parfait Sweets," ruffled, smoky lavender	567.00
Bowl, "Horlacher," Peacock Tail patt., green	108.00

Bowl, "Horlacher," Thistle patt.,
green **175.00**
Bowl, "Horlacher," Vintage patt.,
marigold. **120.00**
Bowl, "Morris Smith," ruffled,
purple **1,250.00**
Bowl, souvenir, BPOE Elks, "Atlantic
City, 1911," blue, one-eyed Elk . . **1,295.00**
Bowl, souvenir, BPOE Elks, "Detroit,
1910," blue, one-eyed Elk **875.00**
Bowl, souvenir, BPOE Elks, "Detroit,
1910," green, one-eyed Elk. **900.00**
Bowl, souvenir, BPOE Elks, "Detroit,
1910," purple, two-eyed Elk
(Millersburg) **2,750.00**
Bowl, souvenir, "Millersburg
Courthouse," purple **738.00**
Card tray, "Isaac Benesch," Holly
Whirl patt., marigold **106.00**
Hat, "Miller's Furniture - Harrisburg,"
Basketweave, marigold **125.00**
Paperweight, souvenir, BPOE Elks,
green **3,500.00**
Plate, "Central Shoe," flat, purple. . . **1,200.00**
Plate, "Fern Brand Chocolates," 6" d.,
purple **900.00**
Plate, "Gervitz Bros., Furniture &
Clothing," w/handgrip, 6" d.,
purple **1,690.00**
Plate, "Season's Greetings - Eat
Paradise Soda Candies," 6" d.,
purple **500.00**
Plate, "Spector's Department Store,"
Heart & Vine patt., 9" d.,
marigold **1,025.00**
Plate, souvenir, BPOE Elks, "Atlantic
City, 1911," blue **1,600.00**
Plate, souvenir, BPOE Elks,
"Parkersburg, 1914," 7½" d.,
blue. **1,225.00**
Plate, "E. A. Hudson," w/handgrip,
purple **1,450.00**

Amaryllis (Dugan)

Compote, marigold. **325.00**
Compote, purple. **313.00**

Apple Blossoms

Bowl, 5" d., marigold. **40.00**
Bowl, 7" d., collared base, purple **78.00**
Bowl, 7" d., ribbon candy rim,
marigold **38.00**
Bowl, 9" d., three-in-one edge, peach
opalescent **130.00**
Rose bowl, marigold. **65.00**
Tumbler, enameled, blue **85.00**
Water set: pitcher & 1 tumbler;
enameled, blue, 2 pcs. **300.00**

Apple Blossom Twigs

Banana boat-shaped bowl, ruffled,
purple **190.00**
Bowl, 8" to 9" d., ice cream shape,
Basketweave exterior, blue **200.00**
Bowl, 8" to 9" d., peach opalescent . . **170.00**
Bowl, 8" to 9" d., purple **240.00**
Bowl, 8½" d., ice cream shape,
peach opalescent **188.00**
Bowl, 9" d., ice cream shape, white . . **170.00**
Bowl, low, ruffled, peach
opalescent. **325.00**
Plate, 9" d., blue **313.00**
Plate, 9" d., ruffled, marigold. **92.00**
Plate, 9" d., peach
opalescent. **425.00**
Plate, 9" d., purple. **315.00**
Plate, 9" d., flat, smooth edge,
purple **750.00**
Plate, 9" d., white **240.00**
Plate, 9" d., ruffled, white **213.00**

Apple Tree

Pitcher, water, marigold **213.00**
Pitcher, water, white. **470.00**
Tumbler, blue **63.00**
Tumbler, marigold **52.00**
Water set: pitcher & 1 tumbler; white,
2 pcs.. . . . . **575.00**
Water set: pitcher & 2 tumblers;
marigold, 3 pcs. **410.00**
Water set: pitcher & 4 tumblers;
marigold, 5 pcs. **375.00**
Water set: pitcher & 4 tumblers;
white, 5 pcs. **1,250.00**
Water set: pitcher & 6 tumblers; blue,
7 pcs. **1,250.00**
Water set: pitcher & 6 tumblers;
marigold, 7 pcs. **325.00**

April Showers (Fenton)

Vase, 7½" h., purple **55.00**
Vase, 8" h., marigold **53.00**
Vase, 9" h., pie crust edge, blue **60.00**
Vase, 9¾" h., Peacock Tail interior,
green **95.00**
Vase, 10" h., blue **50.00**
Vase, 10" h., purple. **55.00**
Vase, 10" h., teal. **70.00**
Vase, 10½" h., Peacock Tail
interior, blue. **78.00**
Vase, 11" h., blue **83.00**
Vase, 11" h., Peacock Tail interior,
green **90.00**
Vase, 11" h., Peacock Tail interior,
purple **63.00**
Vase, 11½" h., marigold **42.00**

Vase, 11½" h., Peacock Tail
   interior, green 108.00
Vase, 12" h., blue 65.00
Vase, 12" h., green 65.00
Vase, 12" h., Peacock Tail interior,
   marigold. 40.00
Vase, 12" h., Peacock Tail interior,
   purple 53.00
Vase, 13" h., green 35.00
Vase, 13½" h., marigold 48.00
Vase, purple opalescent 725.00

Australian

Berry set: master bowl & 6 sauce
   dishes; Magpie, marigold,
   7 pcs.. . . . . 325.00
Bowl, 9" to 10" d., Emu, aqua 550.00
Bowl, 9" to 10" d., Emu, purple. 600.00
Bowl, 9" to 10" d., Kangaroo, black
   amethyst 650.00
Bowl, 9" to 10" d., Kangaroo,
   purple 160.00
Bowl, 9" to 10" d., Kingfisher,
   purple 175.00
Bowl, 9" to 10" d., Kiwi, ruffled,
   marigold. 243.00
Bowl, 9" to 10" d., Kookaburra,
   purple 188.00
Bowl, 9" to 10" d., Magpie,
   marigold. 179.00
Bowl, 9" to 10" d., Swan, marigold . . . 170.00
Bowl, 9" to 10" d., Swan, purple 145.00
Bowl, 9" to 10" d., Thunderbird,
   marigold. 215.00
Bowl, 11" d., ice cream shape,
   Kookaburra, marigold 193.00

Australian Kookaburra Bowl

Bowl, 11" d., ice cream shape,
   Kookaburra variant, marigold
   (ILLUS.). 135.00
Compote, Butterflies & Waratah,
   marigold. 200.00
Sauce dish, Kangaroo, purple 57.00
Sauce dish, Magpie, purple 300.00

Autumn Acorns (Fenton)

Bowl, 8" to 9" d., blue 79.00
Bowl, 8" to 9" d., marigold 55.00
Bowl, 8" to 9" d., purple 125.00
Bowl, 8½" d., three-in-one edge,
   green. 73.00
Bowl, 9" d., ribbon candy edge,
   purple 75.00
Bowl, ribbon candy edge, green. 80.00
Plate, purple 525.00

Basket or Bushel Basket (Northwood)

Aqua, 4½" d., 4¾" h. 625.00
Aqua opalescent, 4½" d.,
   4¾" h. 350.00
Blue. 214.00
Blue opalescent. 195.00
Green 425.00
Purple. 129.00
Sapphire blue 1,700.00
Smoky. 725.00
White. 188.00

Beaded Bull's Eye (Imperial)

Vase, 5¼" h., green. 325.00
Vase, 7" to 12" h., marigold. 65.00
Vase, 7" to 12" h., purple 180.00

Beaded Cable (Northwood)

Candy dish, marigold 43.00
Candy dish, purple. 65.00
Rose bowl, aqua 345.00
Rose bowl, aqua opalescent 318.00
Rose bowl, blue 160.00
Rose bowl, green. 133.00
Rose bowl, ice blue 775.00
Rose bowl, ice green. 1,125.00
Rose bowl, lavender. 375.00
Rose bowl, marigold. 84.00

Beaded Cable Rose Bowl

Rose bowl, purple (ILLUS.) 103.00
Rose bowl, white 470.00

Big Fish Bowl (Millersburg)

Green 600.00
Green, square 950.00
Marigold 588.00
Marigold, ice cream shape 500.00
Purple, ice cream shape 575.00
Purple, ruffled 780.00

Birds & Cherries

Bonbon, blue 75.00
Bonbon, marigold 85.00
Compote, blue 123.00
Compote, marigold 50.00
Compote, purple 150.00

Blackberry Bramble

Compote, ruffled, green 54.00
Compote, ruffled, marigold 55.00
Compote, ruffled, olive green 80.00
Compote, ruffled, purple 43.00
Compote, ruffled, sq., purple 75.00

Blackberry Miniature Compote

Blue 63.00
Green 275.00
Marigold 63.00
Purple 75.00

Blackberry Wreath (Millersburg)

Berry set: master bowl & 6 sauce
  dishes; green, 7 pcs 413.00
Bowl, 5" d., candy ribbon edge,
  purple 100.00
Bowl, 5" d., fluted, marigold variant . . 100.00
Bowl, 5" d., green 90.00
Bowl, 5" d., ice cream shape, fluted,
  purple variant 208.00
Bowl, 5" d., marigold 50.00
Bowl, 5" d., ruffled, marigold 80.00
Bowl, 5" d., purple 70.00
Bowl, 6" d., ruffled, marigold 60.00
Bowl, 6" d., three-in-one edge,
  green 138.00
Bowl, 6" d., three-in-one edge,
  purple 188.00
Bowl, 7" d., green 90.00
Bowl, 7" d., marigold 65.00
Bowl, 7" d., purple 85.00
Bowl, 7½" d., ruffled, purple 100.00
Bowl, 8" d., ruffled, green 65.00
Bowl, 8" d., three-in-one edge,
  marigold 103.00
Bowl, ice cream, large, purple 213.00
Bowl, triangular, large, marigold 110.00
Plate, 6" to 7½" d., marigold 750.00

Blueberry (Fenton)

Pitcher, water, marigold 625.00

Tumbler, blue 75.00
Tumbler, marigold 50.00
Tumbler, white 115.00
Water set: pitcher & 6 tumblers; blue,
  7 pcs 1,525.00
Water set: pitcher & 6 tumblers;
  marigold, 7 pcs 913.00

Broken Arches (Imperial)

Punch bowl, marigold, 12" d 140.00
Punch bowl & base, marigold,
  12" d., 2 pcs 450.00
Punch cup, marigold 25.00
Punch cup, purple 30.00

Butterflies (Fenton)

Bonbon, blue 65.00
Bonbon, green 60.00
Bonbon, marigold 48.00
Bonbon, purple 64.00

Butterfly & Berry (Fenton)

Berry set: master bowl & 5 sauce
  dishes; marigold, 6 pcs . . 200.00 to 250.00
Bowl, master berry, four-footed,
  blue 207.00
Bowl, master berry, four-footed,
  green 260.00
Bowl, master berry, four-footed,
  marigold 89.00
Bowl, master berry, four-footed,
  purple 220.00
Bowl, master berry, four-footed,
  white 625.00
Butter dish, cov., blue 250.00
Butter dish, cov., green 875.00
Butter dish, cov., marigold 150.00
Creamer, blue 85.00
Creamer, marigold 80.00
Creamer, purple 145.00
Creamer & cov. sugar bowl,
  marigold, pr 190.00
Hatpin holder, blue 1,900.00
Hatpin holder, marigold 1,600.00
Pitcher, water, green 595.00

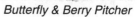

Butterfly & Berry Pitcher

Pitcher, water, marigold (ILLUS.) **221.00**
Sauce dish, blue. **63.00**
Sauce dish, green **113.00**
Sauce dish, marigold **29.00**
Sauce dish, purple **77.00**
Spooner, marigold **57.00**
Spooner, purple **140.00**
Sugar bowl, cov., marigold. **75.00**
Table set: cov. butter dish, creamer
   & spooner; marigold, 3 pcs. **225.00**
Table set, marigold, 4 pcs. **413.00**
Tumbler, blue **45.00**
Tumbler, green. **113.00**
Tumbler, marigold **35.00**
Tumbler, purple **138.00**
Vase, 6" to 10" h., amber. **163.00**
Vase, 6" to 10" h., blue **80.00**
Vase, 6" to 10" h., green **160.00**
Vase, 6" to 10" h., marigold. **40.00**
Vase, purple **138.00**
Water set: pitcher & 5 tumblers;
   marigold, 6 pcs. . . . . **350.00 to 400.00**
Water set: pitcher & 6 tumblers; blue,
   7 pcs. **850.00**
Water set: pitcher & 6 tumblers;
   purple, 7 pcs. **1,050.00**

Butterfly (Northwood)

Bonbon, green **163.00**
Bonbon, purple. **68.00**

Butterfly Bonbon

Bonbon, threaded exterior, blue
   (ILLUS.). **260.00**
Bonbon, threaded exterior, emerald
   green. **575.00**
Bonbon, threaded exterior, ice
   blue. **2,850.00**

Butterfly & Tulip

Bowl, 9" w., 5½" h., footed,
   marigold. **315.00**
Bowl, 10½" square flat shape,
   footed, marigold. **450.00**

Captive Rose

Bonbon, two-handled, blue,
   7½" d. **85.00**
Bowl, 8" d., three-in-one edge,
   blue **75.00**

Bowl, 8" d., three-in-one edge,
   purple **106.00**
Bowl, 8" to 9" d., candy ribbon edge,
   blue **80.00**
Bowl, 8" to 9" d., candy ribbon edge,
   green. **70.00**
Bowl, 8" to 9" d., candy ribbon edge,
   marigold. **66.00**
Bowl, 8" to 9" d., candy ribbon edge,
   purple **92.00**
Bowl, 8" to 9" d., blue **102.00**
Bowl, 8" to 9" d., green. **75.00**
Bowl, 8" to 9" d., marigold **93.00**
Bowl, 8" to 9" d., purple **75.00**
Compote, candy ribbon edge,
   purple **130.00**
Compote, green **58.00**
Compote, ice blue **138.00**
Compote, marigold. **75.00**
Compote, purple. **100.00**
Compote, white **166.00**
Plate, 9" d., blue **482.00**
Plate, 9" d., green **695.00**
Plate, 9" d., marigold. **325.00**
Plate, 9" d., purple. **550.00**

Caroline

Banana bowl, peach opalescent **65.00**
Basket w/applied handle, peach
   opalescent. **388.00**
Bowl, 8" d., handgrip, ruffled, peach
   opalescent. **133.00**
Bowl, 8" to 9" d., peach opalescent . . . **77.00**
Bowl, 8" to 9" w., tricornered, peach
   opalescent. **90.00**
Bowl, 9" d., pie crust edge, shallow,
   peach opalescent **65.00**
Bowl, 9" d., ruffled, peach
   opalescent. **139.00**
Bowl, 9" sq., peach opalescent **108.00**

Cherry Chain (Fenton)

Bowl, 5" d., blue **40.00**
Bowl, 5" d., Orange Tree exterior,
   marigold. **35.00**
Bowl, 6" d., blue **70.00**
Bowl, 8" to 9" d., white **75.00**
Bowl, 9" d., ice cream shape, white . . **155.00**
Bowl, 10" d., ice cream shape,
   Orange Tree exterior, white. **138.00**
Bowl, 10" d., Orange Tree exterior,
   marigold. **63.00**
Bowl, 10" d., Orange Tree exterior,
   red **1,750.00**
Bowl, 10" d., three-in-one edge,
   blue **245.00**
Bowl, 10½" d., blue. **125.00**
Bowl, ruffled, large, green. **300.00**
Plate, 6" d., Orange Tree exterior,
   blue **300.00**

Plate, 6" d., Orange Tree exterior,
marigold. **88.00**
Plate, 6" d., Orange Tree exterior,
white **160.00**
Plate, 6" to 7" d., marigold **108.00**

Chrysanthemum or Windmill & Mums

Bowl, 8" to 9" d., three-footed, blue . . **128.00**
Bowl, 10" d., collared base, red. . . . **2,250.00**
Bowl, 10" d., three-footed, blue **145.00**
Bowl, 10" d., three-footed, green **350.00**

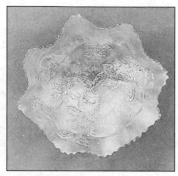

Chrysanthemum Bowl

Bowl, 10" d., three-footed, marigold
(ILLUS.). **93.00**
Bowl, 11" d., three-footed, blue **220.00**
Bowl, 11" d., three-footed, marigold . . . **95.00**
Bowl, 11" d., three-footed, purple **250.00**
Bowl, 12" d., three-footed, vaseline . . **260.00**
Bowl, collared base, marigold. **75.00**

Concord (Fenton)

Bowl, 9" d., ruffled, blue **363.00**
Bowl, 9" d., three-in-one edge,
green. **500.00**
Bowl, candy ribbon edge, blue **225.00**
Bowl, green. **363.00**

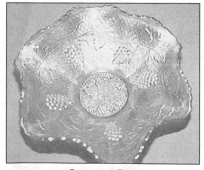

Concord Bowl

Bowl, marigold (ILLUS.) **102.00**
Bowl, ruffled, marigold **275.00**

Bowl, purple **163.00**
Bowl, three-in-one edge, purple **324.00**
Plate, green **4,250.00**
Plate, marigold. **1,625.00**
Plate, purple. **3,250.00**

Constellation (Dugan)

Compote, clambroth. **150.00**
Compote, green **95.00**
Compote, marigold. **108.00**
Compote, purple. **310.00**
Compote, white **507.00**
Compote, marigold. **108.00**

Coral (Fenton)

Bowl, 8" to 9" d., collared base,
green. **170.00**
Bowl, 8" to 9" d., collared base,
marigold. **335.00**
Plate, 9" d., marigold **1,338.00**

Crab Claw (Imperial)

Bowl, 4½" d., green **25.00**
Bowl, 8" to 9" d., clambroth **100.00**
Bowl, 8" to 9" d., marigold **38.00**
Bowl, 10" d., ruffled, marigold. **70.00**
Bowl, 10" d., purple. **100.00**
Bowl, fruit, w/base, marigold. **90.00**
Cruet, w/original stopper, marigold. . . **798.00**
Sauce dish, marigold **29.00**
Tumbler, marigold **65.00**

Double Stem Rose

Bowl, 7" d., dome-footed, marigold. . . . **75.00**
Bowl, 8" to 9" d., dome-footed,
aqua **450.00**
Bowl, 8" to 9" d., dome-footed,
blue **225.00**
Bowl, 8" to 9" d., dome-footed,
purple **100.00**
Bowl, 8" to 9" d., dome-footed,
white **125.00**
Bowl, 10" d., peach opalescent **175.00**
Plate, dome-footed, marigold **95.00**
Plate, dome-footed,
purple . . . . **260.00 to 375.00**
Plate, dome-footed,
white . . . . **100.00 to 160.00**

Fanciful (Dugan)

Bowl, 8" to 9" d., ruffled, blue **195.00**
Bowl, 8" to 9" d., marigold . . . **40.00 to 75.00**
Bowl, 8" to 9" d., piecrust rim,
marigold. **113.00**
Bowl, 8" to 9" d., peach opalescent . . **213.00**

Fanciful Bowl

Bowl, 8" to 9" d., ruffled, purple
　(ILLUS.). **165.00**
Bowl, 8" to 9" d., ruffled, white **155.00**
Bowl, 9" d., three-in-one edge,
　white **225.00**
Bowl, 10" d., ruffled, white **165.00**
Bowl, ice cream shape, peach
　opalescent. **144.00**
Bowl, ice cream shape, purple **255.00**
Bowl, ice cream shape, white. **190.00**
Plate, 9" d., blue **400.00**
Plate, 9" d., marigold. **120.00**
Plate, 9" d., peach opalescent **288.00**
Plate, 9" d., purple . . . . . . **200.00 to 250.00**
Plate, 9" d., white . . . . **200.00 to 250.00**
Plate, 9½" d., ruffled, white **200.00**

Field Thistle (English)

Compote, marigold. **210.00**
Plate, 6" d., marigold. **255.00**
Plate, 9" d., marigold. **375.00**
Spooner, marigold **70.00**
Tumbler, marigold **46.00**
Vase, 7" h., marigold. **65.00**
Water set: pitcher & 4 tumblers;
　marigold, 5 pcs. **775.00**

Fisherman's Mug

Black amethyst **195.00**
Marigold **230.00**
Pastel marigold **225.00**
Peach opalescent **1,233.00**

Purple Fisherman's Mug

Purple, (ILLUS.) **143.00**
Purple, w/advertising **148.00**

Good Luck (Northwood)

Bowl, 8" d., ruffled, Basketweave
　exterior, green. **300.00**
Bowl, 8" d., ruffled, Basketweave
　exterior, marigold . . . . . . **200.00 to 225.00**
Bowl, 8" d., ruffled, Basketweave
　exterior, purple **250.00**
Bowl, 8" d., ruffled, blue w/electric
　iridescence **405.00**
Bowl, 8" d., ruffled, green **250.00**
Bowl, 8" d., ruffled, lavender. **350.00**
Bowl, 8" d., ruffled,
　marigold . . . . **140.00 to 145.00**
Bowl, 8" d., ruffled, purple. **265.00**
Bowl, 8" d., ruffled, stippled,
　blue. . . . . **300.00 to 375.00**
Bowl, 8" d., ruffled, stippled, blue
　w/electric iridescence **405.00**
Bowl, 8" d., ruffled, stippled,
　marigold. **190.00**
Bowl, 8" to 9" d., piecrust rim, aqua
　opalescent. . . . . **1,700.00 to 1,800.00**
Bowl, 8" to 9" d., piecrust rim,
　Basketweave exterior, marigold . . . **175.00**

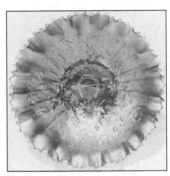

Good Luck Bowl

Bowl, 8" to 9" d., piecrust rim, blue
　(ILLUS.). . . . . **375.00 to 400.00**
Bowl, 8" to 9" d., piecrust rim, blue
　w/electric iridescence **630.00**
Bowl, 8" to 9" d., piecrust rim,
　marigold. **225.00**
Bowl, 8" to 9" d., piecrust rim,
　purple **220.00**
Bowl, 8" to 9" d., piecrust rim,
　stippled, blue **321.00**
Bowl, 8" to 9" d., piecrust rim,
　stippled, marigold . . . . . . **200.00 to 250.00**
Bowl, 8" to 9" d., piecrust rim, teal
　blue. **2,750.00**
Bowl, 8" to 9" d., ruffled, aqua
　opalescent **1,025.00**
Bowl, 8" to 9" d., ruffled, blue **475.00**

Bowl, 8" to 9" d., ruffled, green 650.00
Bowl, 8" to 9" d., ruffled, ice
  blue . . . . 3,500.00 to 4,000.00
Bowl, 8" to 9" d., ruffled, lavender . . . 225.00
Bowl, 8" to 9" d., ruffled, marigold . . . 170.00
Bowl, 8" to 9" d., ruffled, purple 297.00
Bowl, 8" to 9" d., ruffled, stippled,
  marigold. 225.00
Bowl, 8" to 9" d., ruffled, teal blue . . 1,350.00
Bowl, piecrust rim, ribbed exterior,
  purple 450.00
Bowl, piecrust rim, stippled, ribbed
  exterior, blue w/electric
  iridescence 675.00
Bowl, ruffled, purple 400.00
Bowl, stippled, marigold iridescence . 380.00
Plate, 9" d., blue w/electric
  iridescence . . . . 1,250.00 to 1,275.00
Plate, 9" d., green 1,650.00
Plate, 9" d., marigold . . . . . 425.00 to 450.00
Plate, 9" d., purple. 475.00
Plate, 9" d., Basketweave exterior,
  purple . . . . 525.00 to 575.00
Plate, 9" d., stippled, purple 600.00
Plate, 9" d., white. 1,600.00
Plate, Basketweave exterior, green . . 475.00
Plate, marigold 188.00

Greek Key (Northwood)

Bowl, eight-sided, 6½" w., 4" h.,
  purple 75.00
Bowl, 8" to 9" d., fluted,
  green. . . . . 150.00 to 175.00
Bowl, 8" to 9" d., ruffled, marigold . . . 152.00
Bowl, 8" to 9" d., purple 110.00
Bowl, 8" to 9" d., ruffled,
  purple . . . . 175.00 to 200.00
Bowl, dome-footed, green 75.00
Bowl, piecrust rim, green 400.00
Bowl, piecrust rim, purple 200.00
Pitcher, water, green . . 1,300.00 to 1,350.00
Pitcher, water, marigold . . . 800.00 to 875.00
Plate, 9" d., blue. 2,800.00

Greek Key Plate

Plate, 9" d., green (ILLUS.) 1,150.00

Plate, 9" d., marigold . . . . 825.00 to 850.00
Plate, 9" d., purple . . . . . . 300.00 to 400.00
Tumbler, green. 145.00

Kittens (Fenton)

Bowl, cereal, aqua 725.00
Bowl, cereal, blue. . . . . 425.00 to 475.00

Kittens Cereal Bowl

Bowl, cereal, marigold (ILLUS.) 195.00
Bowl, four-sided, ruffled,
  marigold . . . . 200.00 to 225.00
Bowl, ruffled, blue. 775.00
Bowl, ruffled, marigold . . . . 120.00 to 150.00
Bowl, six-sided, ruffled,
  marigold . . . . 250.00 to 300.00
Cup, blue. 550.00
Cup, marigold . . . . 135.00 to 150.00
Cup & saucer, blue 2,025.00
Cup & saucer, marigold. . . 250.00 to 260.00

Kittens Dish

Dish, turned-up sides, marigold
  (ILLUS.). . . . . 145.00 to 165.00
Dish, turned-up sides,
  purple . . . . 450.00 to 500.00
Plate, 4½" d., marigold . . . . 150.00 to 200.00
Saucer, marigold. 190.00
Toothpick holder, blue . . . 375.00 to 475.00
Toothpick holder,
  marigold . . . . 165.00 to 185.00
Vase, child's, ruffled, marigold 143.00
Vase, marigold 223.00

Nippon (Northwood)

Bowl, 8" d., piecrust rim, blue, electric
iridescent **225.00**
Bowl, 8" d., piecrust rim, ice
blue . . . . **200.00 to 300.00**
Bowl, 8" d., piecrust rim, ice
green . . . . **600.00 to 900.00**
Bowl, 8" d., piecrust rim, marigold . . . **250.00**
Bowl, 8" d., piecrust rim, pastel lime
green w/opal tips **2,950.00**
Bowl, 8" d., piecrust rim,
purple . . . . **300.00 to 350.00**
Bowl, 8" d., piecrust rim, white **270.00**
Bowl, 8" to 9" d., blue **275.00**
Bowl, 8" to 9" d., fluted, white **235.00**
Bowl, 8" to 9" d., ice green **1,000.00**
Bowl, 8" to 9" d.,
marigold . . . . **100.00 to 125.00**
Bowl, 8" to 9" d., purple **180.00**

Nippon Bowl

Bowl, 8" to 9" d., 2¼" h., ice blue
(ILLUS.) . . . . **300.00 to 350.00**
Bowl, 8" to 9" d., 3" h.,
green . . . . **275.00 to 325.00**
Plate, 9" d., green . . . . **600.00 to 750.00**
Plate, 9" d., purple . . . . **800.00 to 900.00**

Open Rose (Imperial)

Berry set: master bowl & 6 sauce dishes,
purple, 7 pcs. . . . . **280.00 to 290.00**
Bowl, 5" d., blue **125.00**
Bowl, 5" d., purple . . . . **40.00 to 45.00**
Bowl, 5" d., smoky **45.00**
Bowl, 6" d., ice cream shape,
amber **125.00**
Bowl, 7" d., footed, blue **55.00**
Bowl, 7" d., footed, marigold **35.00**
Bowl, 7" d., footed, purple **75.00**
Bowl, 8" to 9" d., amber **55.00**
Bowl, 8" to 9" d., aqua **45.00**
Bowl, 8" to 9" d., green **40.00**
Bowl, 8" to 9" d., marigold **37.00**
Bowl, 8" to 9" d., purple . . . **100.00 to 125.00**
Bowl, 8" to 9" d., footed, vaseline **150.00**
Bowl, 8" to 9" d., white **95.00**
Bowl, 10" d., amber . . . . . **175.00 to 200.00**

Bowl, 10" d., smoky . . . . **65.00 to 75.00**
Bowl, 11" d., marigold **60.00**
Bowl, 11" d., smoky **75.00**
Fernery, three-footed, blue **90.00**
Plate, 9" d., amber . . . . **100.00 to 125.00**
Plate, 9" d., green . . . . **120.00 to 125.00**
Plate, 9" d., marigold . . . . . **90.00 to 100.00**
Plate, 9" d., purple **850.00**
Rose bowl, amber **70.00**
Rose bowl, green . . . . **70.00 to 90.00**
Rose bowl, marigold **48.00**
Tumbler, marigold **35.00**

Oriental Poppy (Northwood)

Pitcher, water, green **1,250.00**
Pitcher, water, marigold . . . **450.00 to 500.00**
Pitcher, water, purple **800.00**
Pitcher, water, white . . . **1,500.00 to 2,000.00**
Tumbler, green . . . . **65.00 to 75.00**
Tumbler, ice blue **185.00**
Tumbler, ice green . . . . . . **325.00 to 375.00**
Tumbler, marigold . . . . **45.00 to 55.00**
Tumbler, purple . . . . **50.00 to 60.00**
Tumbler, white **160.00**
Tumblers, marigold, set of 4 . . . . **170.00**
Tumblers, purple, set of 6 . . . . **300.00**
Water set: pitcher & 5 tumblers,
purple, 6 pcs. **1,400.00**
Water set: pitcher & 6 tumblers,
marigold, 7 pcs. **838.00**

Peacock, Fluffy (Fenton)

Pitcher, water, green . . . . . **650.00 to 700.00**
Pitcher, water, marigold . . . **450.00 to 500.00**
Pitcher, water, purple . . . . . **575.00 to 600.00**
Tumbler, purple . . . . **60.00 to 70.00**

Fluffy Peacock Water Set

Water set: pitcher & 6 tumblers;
purple, 7 pcs. (ILLUS.) **1,025.00**

Peacock & Urn (Millersburg, Fenton & Northwood)

Berry set: master bowl & 5 sauce
dishes; purple, 6 pcs.
(Northwood) . . . . **750.00 to 800.00**

Berry set: master bowl & 6 sauce
dishes; marigold, 7 pcs.
(Northwood). **700.00**
Bowl, 6" d., ice cream shape, blue
(Northwood). **125.00**
Bowl, 6" d., ice cream shape, green
(Millersburg) **325.00**
Bowl, 6" d., ice cream shape, purple
(Millersburg) . . . . **275.00 to 300.00**
Bowl, 6" d., ice cream shape, purple
satin. **195.00**
Bowl, 6" d., ice cream shape,
white . . . . **120.00 to 150.00**
Bowl, 7" d., ruffled, blue
(Millersburg) **400.00**
Bowl, 7" d., ruffled, green
(Millersburg) **250.00**
Bowl, 7" d., ruffled, marigold
(Millersburg) **395.00**
Bowl, 7" d., ruffled, purple
(Millersburg) **350.00**
Bowl, 8" d., ice cream shape, Beaded
Berry exterior, purple (Fenton) **275.00**
Bowl, 8" d., ice cream shape, green
(Fenton) . . . . **250.00 to 300.00**
Bowl, 8" d., ice cream shape,
marigold (Fenton) . . . . . . **125.00 to 150.00**
Bowl, 8" to 9" d., blue
(Fenton) . . . . **275.00 to 300.00**
Bowl, 8" to 9" d., green (Fenton) **300.00**
Bowl, 8" to 9" d., green
(Millersburg) . . . . **375.00 to 400.00**
Bowl, 8" to 9" d., marigold
(Fenton) . . . . **140.00 to 160.00**
Bowl, 8" to 9" d., ruffled, marigold
(Millersburg) **225.00**
Bowl, 8" to 9" d., purple
(Fenton) . . . . **200.00 to 225.00**
Bowl, 8¾" d., ice cream shape,
purple (Millersburg) **1,000.00**
Bowl, 9" d., ruffled, purple
(Millersburg) **3,500.00**
Bowl, 9" d., ruffled, white **175.00**
Bowl, 9½" d., berry, purple
(Millersburg) . . . . **550.00 to 600.00**
Bowl, 10" d., fluted, green
(Millersburg) **350.00**
Bowl, 10" d., ruffled, marigold. **145.00**
Bowl, 10" d., ruffled, pastel marigold
(Northwood). **650.00**
Bowl, 10" d., ruffled,
purple . . . . **400.00 to 450.00**
Bowl, 10" d., three-in-one edge,
purple (Millersburg). . . . . **650.00 to 700.00**
Bowl, ice cream shape, 10" d., aqua
opalescent (Northwood) **25,000.00**
Bowl, ice cream shape, 10" d., blue
(Northwood) . . . . **900.00 to 1,000.00**
Bowl, ice cream shape, 10" d., blue
(Northwood) **3,650.00**

Bowl, ice cream shape, 10" d., blue,
stippled (Northwood) **1,250.00**
Bowl, ice cream shape, 10" d., green
(Northwood) . . . . **2,500.00 to 3,000.00**
Bowl, ice cream shape, 10" d., green
w/bee (Millersburg) . . . **950.00 to 1,000.00**
Bowl, ice cream shape, 10" d., ice
blue (Northwood) . . . . . . **800.00 to 900.00**
Bowl, ice cream shape, 10" d., ice
green (Northwood) . . **1,000.00 to 1,125.00**
Bowl, ice cream shape, 10" d.,
marigold (Millersburg) . . . **375.00 to 425.00**
Bowl, ice cream shape, 10" d.,
marigold (Northwood) . . . **400.00 to 450.00**
Bowl, ice cream shape, 10" d., pastel
marigold (Northwood) . . . **650.00 to 700.00**
Bowl, ice cream shape, 10" d., purple
(Millersburg) . . . . **1,075.00 to 1,125.00**

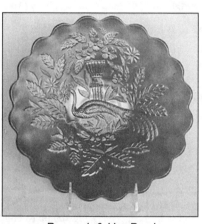

Peacock & Urn Bowl

Bowl, ice cream shape, 10" d.,
purple, Northwood
(ILLUS.). . . . . **550.00 to 600.00**
Bowl, ice cream shape, 10" d.,
stippled, honey amber
(Northwood) **1,400.00**
Bowl, ice cream shape, 10" d.,
stippled, marigold
(Northwood) . . . . **600.00 to 700.00**
Bowl, ice cream shape, 10" d.,
stippled, pastel marigold
(Northwood) . . . . **550.00 to 600.00**
Bowl, ice cream shape, 10" d., white
(Northwood) . . . . **550.00 to 575.00**
Bowl, 10½" d., ruffled, green
(Millersburg) . . . . **325.00 to 350.00**
Bowl, 10½" d., ruffled, marigold
(Millersburg) . . . . **225.00 to 250.00**
Bowl, 10½" d., ruffled, purple
(Fenton) . . . . **250.00 to 300.00**
Bowl, 10½" d., ruffled, purple
(Millersburg) **400.00**

Bowl, ruffled, marigold (Northwood) . . **245.00**
Bowl, ruffled, white
(Fenton) . . . . **150.00 to 175.00**
Compote, 5½" d., 5" h., aqua
(Fenton). **165.00**
Compote, 5½" d., 5" h., blue
(Fenton) . . . . **120.00 to 150.00**
Compote, 5½" d., 5" h., marigold
(Fenton) . . . . **55.00 to 65.00**
Compote, 5½" d., 5" h., white
(Fenton). **245.00**
Compote, green (Millersburg
Giant) . . . . **1,350.00 to 1,400.00**
Compote, marigold (Millersburg
Giant) **1,700.00**
Compote, purple (Millersburg
Giant) **2,000.00**
Compote, violet (Fenton) **150.00**
Goblet, blue (Fenton) **90.00**
Ice cream dish, blue w/electric
iridescence **180.00**
Ice cream dish, purple, small **95.00**
Ice cream dish, white, small. **200.00**
Plate, 6½" d., green
(Millersburg) **1,500.00**

Peacock & Urn Plate

Plate, 6½" d., marigold, Millersburg
(ILLUS.) **1,000.00**
Plate, 6½" d., purple
(Millersburg) . . . . **1,000.00 to 1,200.00**
Plate, 9" d., blue (Fenton). . **400.00 to 450.00**
Plate, 9" d., marigold
(Fenton) . . . . **400.00 to 500.00**
Plate, 9" d., purple (Fenton) **150.00**
Plate, 9" d., white
(Fenton) . . . . **400.00 to 500.00**
Plate, chop, 11" d., purple
(Millersburg) **2,250.00**

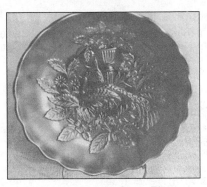

Peacock & Urn Chop Plate

Plate, chop, 11" d., purple,
Northwood (ILLUS.) **1,400.00**
Sauce dish, blue
(Millersburg) . . . . . . **1,000.00 to 1,200.00**
Sauce dish, blue (Northwood) **120.00**
Sauce dish, ice blue (Northwood) . . . **200.00**
Sauce dish, lavender (Millersburg). . . **100.00**
Sauce dish, marigold (Northwood). . . . **95.00**
Sauce dish, purple
(Millersburg) . . . . **150.00 to 175.00**
Sauce dish, purple
(Northwood) . . . . **100.00 to 125.00**
Sauce dish, stippled, blue
(Northwood) . . . . **150.00 to 160.00**
Whimsey sauce dish, purple,
5¼" d. . . . . **275.00 to 300.00**

Peter Rabbit (Fenton)

Bowl, 8" d., blue . . . . . . **1,000.00 to 1,100.00**
Bowl, 8" d., green . . . . . . **950.00 to 1,000.00**
Bowl, 8" d., marigold **1,500.00**
Plate, blue **1,900.00**

Peter Rabbit Plate

Plate, green (ILLUS.) . . **3,000.00 to 3,500.00**

Rambler Rose (Dugan)

Pitcher, water, blue . . . . 95.00 to 125.00
Tumbler, blue . . . . 40.00 to 45.00
Tumbler, marigold 25.00
Water set: pitcher & 8 tumblers;
   marigold, 9 pcs 350.00

Scroll Embossed

Bowl, 5½" d., File exterior, purple 25.00
Bowl, 6½" d., Hobstar exterior, purple . 65.00
Bowl, 7" d., purple 45.00
Bowl, 8" d., clambroth 35.00
Bowl, 8" to 9" d., green 40.00
Bowl, 8" to 9" d., marigold . . . 30.00 to 40.00
Bowl, 8" to 9" d., purple . . . . . 80.00 to 85.00
Bowl, 8" to 9" d., ruffled, File exterior,
   purple 68.00
Bowl, 9" d., ruffled,
   lavender . . . . 100.00 to 125.00
Compote, green . . . . 30.00 to 40.00
Compote, marigold 45.00
Compote, File exterior, marigold 50.00
Compote, purple . . . . 100.00 to 125.00
Compote, miniature, purple 325.00
Plate, 9" d., green . . . . 90.00 to 100.00
Plate, 9" d., marigold . . . . . 125.00 to 150.00
Plate, 9" d., pastel marigold 85.00
Plate, 9" d., purple 260.00
Sauce dish, purple, 5½" d 40.00
Sauce dish, ruffled, purple, 5¾" d 75.00

Shell (Imperial)

Bowl, 5" d., footed, green 35.00
Bowl, 5" d., purple 25.00
Bowl, 7½" d., amber 190.00
Bowl, 7¾" d., ruffled, smoky 60.00
Bowl, 8" d., ruffled, green 50.00
Bowl, 8" d., marigold . . . . 40.00 to 45.00
Bowl, 8" d., purple 95.00
Bowl, footed, marigold 20.00
Bowl, ruffled, green 35.00
Plate, marigold 350.00
Plate, smoky 300.00

Singing Birds (Northwood)

Butter dish, cov., purple 400.00
Creamer, green 150.00
Creamer, marigold . . . . 65.00 to 75.00
Creamer, purple . . . . 125.00 to 150.00
Mug, aqua opalescent 1,150.00
Mug, blue . . . . 200.00 to 250.00
Mug, blue w/electric
   iridescence . . . . 200.00 to 250.00
Mug, green . . . . 250.00 to 275.00
Mug, ice blue . . . . 700.00 to 750.00
Mug, lavender . . . . 250.00 to 300.00
Mug, marigold . . . . 95.00 to 125.00

Singing Birds Mug

Mug, purple (ILLUS.) 125.00
Mug, purple, w/advertising, "Amazon
   Hotel" . . . . 175.00 to 200.00
Mug, stippled, blue . . . . . . 625.00 to 650.00
Mug, stippled, green . . . . . . 400.00 to 450.00
Mug, stippled, marigold . . . 175.00 to 250.00
Mug, stippled, Renniger blue 1,500.00
Mug, white . . . . 600.00 to 625.00
Pitcher, green 300.00
Pitcher, marigold 350.00
Pitcher, purple . . . . 450.00 to 500.00
Sauce dish, blue w/electric
   iridescence 225.00
Sauce dish, green . . . . 30.00 to 45.00
Sauce dish, marigold 36.00
Sauce dish, purple 45.00
Spooner, marigold 56.00
Spooner, purple . . . . 100.00 to 125.00
Sugar bowl, cov.,
   marigold . . . . 90.00 to 110.00
Tumbler, green . . . . 75.00 to 125.00
Tumbler, green w/marigold
   overlay . . . . 60.00 to 65.00
Tumbler, marigold 50.00
Tumbler, purple . . . . 50.00 to 60.00
Tumblers, green, set of 4 . . . . 500.00
Tumblers, marigold, set of 6 . . . . 300.00

Singing Birds Water Set

Water set: pitcher & 6 tumblers;
   green, 7 pcs.
   (ILLUS.) . . . . 1,000.00 to 1,200.00
Water set: pitcher & 6 tumblers;
   marigold, 7 pcs . . . . 550.00 to 600.00

Single Flower

Basket, handled, ruffled, peach
   opalescent . . . . 750.00 to 1,000.00

Bowl, 7½" d., candy ribbon edge,
   peach opalescent . . . . **85.00 to 90.00**
Bowl, 8¾" d., ruffled, peach
   opalescent. **57.00**
Bowl, 9" d., peach opalescent **55.00**
Bowl, 9" d., three-in-one edge, peach
   opalescent. **135.00**
Bowl, 9", framed, tricornered, peach
   opalescent. . . . . **85.00 to 95.00**
Bowl, 9" d., purple. **50.00**
Bowl, candy ribbon edge, peach
   opalescent. . . . . **125.00 to 150.00**
Bowl, framed, candy ribbon edge,
   peach opalescent **113.00**
Plate, 7" d., framed, crimped rim,
   peach opalescent . . . . **50.00 to 100.00**
Plate, framed, w/hand grip, peach
   opalescent. . . . . **90.00 to 100.00**

Soda Gold (Imperial)

Bowl, 9" d., marigold. **48.00**
Console set: bowl & pr. candlesticks;
   smoky, 3 pcs. **100.00**
Cuspidor, marigold. **50.00**
Pitcher, water, marigold . . . **175.00 to 180.00**
Pitcher, water, smoky. . . . . **275.00 to 300.00**
Salt & pepper shakers w/original
   tops, marigold, pr. **95.00**
Salt & pepper shakers w/original
   tops, smoky, pr. **125.00**
Tumbler, clambroth **35.00**
Tumbler, marigold . . . . **35.00 to 40.00**
Tumbler, pastel marigold . . . . **60.00 to 70.00**
Tumbler, smoky . . . . **50.00 to 60.00**
Urn, marigold **30.00**

Soda Gold Water Set

Water set: pitcher & 6 tumblers;
   smoky, 7 pcs. (ILLUS.) . . **600.00 to 650.00**

Strawberry (Fenton)

Bonbon, Amberina **200.00**
Bonbon, reverse
   Amberina. . . . . **325.00 to 400.00**

Bonbon, two-handled,
   amber . . . . **75.00 to 100.00**
Bonbon, two-handled,
   blue . . . . **65.00 to 70.00**
Bonbon, two-handled,
   green. . . . . **65.00 to 75.00**
Bonbon, two-handled, ice green
   opalescent. . . . . **450.00 to 500.00**
Bonbon, two-handled, marigold **36.00**
Bonbon, two-handled, purple **32.00**
Bonbon, two-handled,
   red. . . . . **350.00 to 400.00**
Bonbon, two-handled,
   vaseline w/marigold
   iridescence . . . . **100.00 to 125.00**

Sunflower Bowl (Northwood)

Sunflower Bowl

Bowl, 8" d., footed, blue (ILLUS.) **650.00**
Bowl, 8" d., footed, blue w/electric
   iridescence . . . . **650.00 to 700.00**
Bowl, 8" d., footed, green **127.00**
Bowl, 8" d., footed, ice blue **1,000.00**
Bowl, 8" d., footed, lavender. **90.00**
Bowl, 8" d., footed, marigold. **65.00**
Bowl, 8" d., footed, pastel marigold . . **300.00**
Bowl, 8" d., footed, Meander exterior,
   purple . . . . **150.00 to 160.00**
Bowl, 8" d., footed,
   purple . . . . **100.00 to 125.00**

Target Vase (Dugan)

6" h., purple **75.00**
7" h., squatty, peach
   opalescent. . . . . **75.00 to 100.00**
7" h., white **75.00**
9½" h., marigold **40.00**
10" h., peach opalescent **80.00**
11" h., purple **55.00**
11" h., vaseline
   opalescent. . . . . **400.00 to 500.00**
11" h., white **100.00**
11½" h., peach opalescent **60.00**
12" h., white . . . . **100.00 to 125.00**

Ten Mums (Fenton)

Bowl, 8" to 9" d., ribbon candy rim,
blue . . . . **140.00 to 250.00**
Bowl, 8" to 9" d., ribbon candy rim,
green . . . . **275.00 to 300.00**
Bowl, 8" to 9" d., ribbon candy rim,
purple . . . . **180.00 to 250.00**

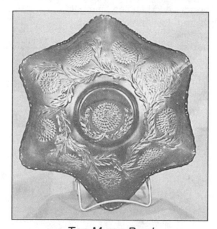

Ten Mums Bowl

Bowl, 10" d., footed, green (ILLUS.) . . **200.00**
Bowl, 10" d., ribbon candy rim,
green . . . . **150.00 to 175.00**
Bowl, 10" d., ribbon candy rim,
marigold **300.00**
Bowl, 10" d., ribbon candy rim,
purple . . . . **250.00 to 300.00**
Bowl, 10" d., ruffled, blue **190.00**
Bowl, 10" d., ruffled, marigold **200.00**
Bowl, 10" d., ruffled,
purple . . . . **250.00 to 300.00**
Pitcher, water,
marigold . . . . **750.00 to 1,000.00**
Tumbler, blue **75.00**
Tumbler, marigold **65.00**
Water set: pitcher & 1 tumbler;
marigold, 2 pcs.. . . . . **1,000.00 to 1,200.00**

Three Fruits (Northwood)

Bowl, 5" d., marigold **30.00**
Bowl, 5" d., purple **48.00**
Bowl, 6" d., marigold **30.00**
Bowl, 7" d., dome-footed,
Basketweave & Grapevine exterior,
purple **150.00**
Bowl, 8" d., dome-footed,
Basketweave & Grapevine exterior,
white . . . . **250.00 to 275.00**
Bowl, 8" d., ruffled, green **70.00**
Bowl, 8" d., ruffled,
marigold . . . . **75.00 to 100.00**

Bowl, 8" d., ruffled, purple **100.00**
Bowl, 8¼" d., dome-footed, ruffled,
Basketweave & Grapevine exterior,
marigold **150.00**
Bowl, 8½" d., collared base,
Basketweave & Grapevine exterior,
green **90.00**
Bowl, 8½" d., dome-footed,
green . . . . **170.00 to 190.00**
Bowl, 8½" d., purple **80.00**
Bowl, , 8½" d., piecrust rim,
Basketweave exterior, purple **105.00**
Bowl, 8½" d., piecrust rim,
green . . . . **125.00 to 150.00**
Bowl, 8½" d., piecrust rim,
marigold . . . . **65.00 to 75.00**
Bowl, 8½" d., piecrust rim, purple **68.00**
Bowl, 8½" d., piecrust rim, stippled,
green . . . . **600.00 to 625.00**
Bowl, 8½" d., ruffled, blue **95.00**
Bowl, 9" d., dome-footed,
Basketweave & Grapevine exterior,
green **135.00**
Bowl, 9" d., dome-footed,
Basketweave & Grapevine exterior,
ice green **675.00**
Bowl, 9" d., dome-footed,
Basketweave & Grapevine exterior,
marigold . . . . **85.00 to 90.00**
Bowl, 9" d., dome-footed,
Basketweave & Grapevine exterior,
purple . . . . **140.00 to 145.00**
Bowl, 9" d., dome-footed,
Basketweave & Grapevine exterior,
white . . . . **350.00 to 380.00**
Bowl, 9" d., footed, Meander reverse,
black amethyst **750.00**
Bowl, 9" d., green **67.00**
Bowl, 9" d., piecrust rim, collared
base, blue w/electric iridescence . . . **700.00**
Bowl, 9" d., piecrust rim, smoky **500.00**
Bowl, 9" d., piecrust rim, stippled,
ribbed exterior, green **735.00**
Bowl, 9" d., purple . . . . **100.00 to 125.00**
Bowl, 9" d., ruffled, blue **175.00**
Bowl, 9" d., ruffled, collared base,
marigold **60.00**
Bowl, 9" d., ruffled, green . . **150.00 to 175.00**
Bowl, 9" d., ruffled, pastel marigold . . . **95.00**
Bowl, 9" d., ruffled, stippled, aqua
opalescent . . . . **600.00 to 675.00**
Bowl, 9" d., spatula-footed, aqua
opalescent . . . . **600.00 to 725.00**
Bowl, 9" d., spatula-footed, emerald
green **425.00**
Bowl, 9" d., spatula-footed, ice
green . . . . **1,045.00 to 1,075.00**
Bowl, 9" d., spatula-footed, marigold . . **95.00**
Bowl, 9" d., spatula-footed, Meander
exterior, marigold **145.00**

Bowl, 9" d., spatula-footed, pastel
   honey amber (smoke tint) **275.00**
Bowl, 9" d., spatula-footed, purple . . . **189.00**
Bowl, 9" d., spatula-footed, ruffled,
   green. . . . . **70.00 to 75.00**
Bowl, 9" d., spatula-footed, white **360.00**
Bowl, 9" d., stippled,
   marigold . . . . **100.00 to 125.00**
Bowl, 9" d., stippled,
   purple . . . . **200.00 to 250.00**
Bowl, 10" d., ruffled, ice green **375.00**
Bowl, collared base, aqua
   opalescent. . . . . **1,100.00 to 1,200.00**
Bowl, collared base, stippled,
   white . . . . **700.00 to 750.00**
Bowl, dome-footed, Basketweave &
   Meander exterior, white. **325.00**
Bowl, dome-footed, ruffled, Vintage
   exterior, ice green **300.00**
Bowl, dome-footed, ruffled,
   white **245.00**
Bowl, piecrust rim, stippled,
   green **1,425.00**
Bowl, piecrust rim, stippled,
   marigold. **235.00**
Bowl, ruffled, footed, Meander
   exterior, ice blue . . . . . . **500.00 to 600.00**
Bowl, ruffled, spatula-footed,
   Meander exterior, ice
   blue . . . . **500.00 to 600.00**
Bowl, ruffled, spatula-footed,
   Meander exterior,
   purple . . . . **140.00 to 150.00**
Bowl, ruffled, spatula-footed
   w/Meander exterior, aqua
   opalescent **1,150.00**
Bowl, ruffled, stippled, footed, ice
   blue . . . . **800.00 to 1,000.00**
Bowl, spatula-footed, stippled,
   purple **175.00**
Bowl, stippled, blue w/electric
   iridescence **475.00**
Bowl, stippled, footed, blue. **450.00**
Bowl, stippled, footed, ice
   green **1,025.00**
Bowl, stippled, ruffled, ribbed
   exterior, marigold. **175.00**
Plate, 7¼" d., Basketweave &
   Grapevine exterior, green **175.00**
Plate, 8" d., stippled, purple **425.00**
Plate, 8" d., w/handgrip, ribbed
   exterior, purple **150.00**
Plate, 9" d., Basketweave exterior,
   green. . . . . **135.00 to 175.00**
Plate, 9" d., Basketweave exterior,
   marigold. **185.00**
Plate, 9" d., Basketweave exterior,
   purple **245.00**

Three Fruits Plate

Plate, 9" d., blue
   (ILLUS.). . . . . **400.00 to 425.00**
Plate, 9" d., green. . . . . . . **200.00 to 225.00**
Plate, 9" d., horehound **295.00**
Plate, 9" d., lavender. **325.00**
Plate, 9" d., marigold . . . . . **150.00 to 200.00**
Plate, 9" d., purple . . . . **150.00 to 160.00**
Plate, 9" d., stippled, aqua
   opalescent. . . . . **1,900.00 to 1,975.00**
Plate, 9" d., stippled, blue w/electric
   iridescence . . . . **800.00 to 850.00**
Plate, 9" d., stippled,
   lavender . . . . **1,250.00 to 1,400.00**
Plate, 9" d., stippled,
   marigold. . . . . **325.00 to 350.00**
Plate, 9" d., stippled, pastel
   marigold. **750.00**
Plate, 9" d., stippled,
   purple . . . . **375.00 to 425.00**
Plate, 9" d., stippled, ribbed exterior,
   marigold . . . . **275.00 to 300.00**
Plate, 9" d., stippled, ribbed exterior,
   purple **590.00**
Plate, 9" d., stippled, teal blue **2,600.00**
Plate, 9" d., stippled, w/ribbed
   exterior, aqua
   opalescent. . . . . **3,650.00 to 4,000.00**
Plate, 9" d., stippled, w/ribbed
   exterior, honey amber **2,400.00**
Plate, 9½" w., 12-sided, blue
   (Fenton) . . . . **175.00 to 225.00**
Plate, 9½" w., 12-sided, green
   (Fenton) . . . . **250.00 to 300.00**
Plate, 9½" w., 12-sided, marigold
   (Fenton). **150.00**
Plate, 9½" w., 12-sided, purple
   (Fenton) . . . . **150.00 to 175.00**
Plate, Basketweave exterior, green . . **195.00**
Plate, Basketweave exterior, marigold. . **125.00**
Plate, Basketweave exterior, purple . . . **258.00**
Plate, plain back, marigold **100.00**
Plate, plain back, stretch "electric"
   finish, purple . . . . **275.00 to 300.00**

Tiger Lily (Imperial)

Tiger Lily Pitcher

Pitcher, water, green
   (ILLUS.) . . . . **200.00 to 250.00**
Pitcher, water, marigold . . . **100.00 to 125.00**
Tumbler, aqua . . . . **165.00 to 175.00**
Tumbler, blue **250.00**
Tumbler, green. . . . . **55.00 to 65.00**
Tumbler, marigold . . . . **30.00 to 40.00**
Tumbler, olive green. **115.00**
Tumbler, purple . . . . **100.00 to 120.00**
Water set: pitcher & 2 tumblers;
   green, 3 pcs. **390.00**
Water set: pitcher & 4 tumblers;
   marigold, 5 pcs. **305.00**

Town Pump Novelty (Northwood)

Town Pump Novelty

Green (ILLUS.). **3,450.00**
Marigold . . . . **2,000.00 to 2,500.00**
Purple **1,000.00**

Tracery (Millersburg)

Bonbon, handled, oval, purple **550.00**

Tracery Bonbon

Bonbon, handled, square, green
   (ILLUS.) . . . . **950.00 to 1,000.00**

Tree Trunk Vase (Northwood)

6" h., squatty, purple . . . . **50.00 to 75.00**
6¼" h., squatty, marigold . . . . **55.00 to 60.00**
6¾" h., marigold **75.00**
7" h., green. . . . . **45.00 to 75.00**
7" h., ice blue **500.00**
7½" h., squatty, green. **145.00**
8" to 10" h., blue. **81.00**
8" to 11" h., green . . . . **80.00 to 100.00**
8" to 11" h., purple. . . . . . . **110.00 to 120.00**
9" to 10" h., marigold **45.00**
9" to 10" h., purple. . . . . **70.00 to 80.00**
9" to 12" h., aqua
   opalescent. . . . . **500.00 to 600.00**
10" h., green. . . . . **125.00 to 150.00**
10½" h., blue w/electric
   iridescence **126.00**
11" h., ice blue **350.00**
11" h., ice green **285.00**
11" h., marigold. **70.00**
11" h., purple **90.00**
11½" h., blue. **60.00**
12" h., blue . . . . **150.00 to 175.00**
12" h., green. **35.00**
12" h., ice blue **275.00**
12" h., marigold . . . . **130.00 to 150.00**
12" h., purple **185.00**
12" h., purple, w/elephant foot,
   funeral. . . . . **2,900.00 to 2,975.00**
12" h., white **175.00**
13" h., green. . . . . **250.00 to 275.00**
13" h., purple **275.00**
13½" h., blue. **473.00**
13½" h., purple **130.00**
14" h., blue w/electric iridescence,
   funeral. . . . . **1,375.00 to 1,500.00**
14" h., marigold. **125.00**
14" h., purple, funeral **1,700.00**
15" h., purple, w/elephant foot. **1,300.00**
18" h., purple, w/elephant foot **375.00**
19" h., purple, funeral **1,800.00**

Twins or Horseshoe Curve (Imperial)

Bowl, 5" d., ruffled, smoky 65.00
Bowl, 6" d., green 45.00
Bowl, 6" d., marigold. 23.00
Bowl, 10" d., marigold. 35.00
Fruit bowl, marigold 67.00
Fruit bowl & base, clambroth, 2 pcs. . . 80.00
Fruit bowl & base, marigold, 2 pcs. . . 108.00
Fruit bowl & base, white, 2 pcs. 650.00

Two Fruits

Banana boat, marigold 95.00
Bonbon, divided, blue . . . . 100.00 to 125.00
Bonbon, divided, green 240.00
Bonbon, divided, marigold . . . 50.00 to 60.00
Bowl, large, in metal holder,
    marigold . . . . 125.00 to 150.00

Vineyard

Pitcher, water, marigold . . . 100.00 to 125.00
Pitcher, water, peach opalescent . . 1,200.00
Pitcher, water, purple . . . . . 320.00 to 350.00
Tumbler, lavender 79.00
Tumbler, marigold 26.00
Tumbler, purple . . . . 60.00 to 70.00
Water set: pitcher & 1 tumbler;
    marigold, 2 pcs. . . . . 125.00 to 175.00

Water Lily (Fenton)

Banana boat, blue 160.00
Banana boat, marigold 70.00
Bonbon, white 60.00
Bowl, 5" d., aqua. 95.00
Bowl, 5" d., blue 70.00
Bowl, 5" d., marigold. 28.00
Bowl, 6" d., amber 60.00
Bowl, 6" d., aqua. 145.00
Bowl, 6" d., footed, green . . 150.00 to 175.00
Bowl, 6" d., footed, honey amber 60.00
Bowl, 6" d., footed, marigold. 44.00
Bowl, 6" d., footed, purple. 150.00
Bowl, 6" d., footed, red 1,900.00
Bowl, 6" d., footed, red
    opalescent. . . . . 1,025.00 to 1,050.00
Bowl, 6" d., footed, vaseline 108.00
Bowl, 6" d., green 145.00
Bowl, 9" d., footed, black amethyst. . . . 75.00
Bowl, 9" d., footed, ice cream shape,
    lavender . . . . 175.00 to 200.00
Bowl, 9" d., footed, lavender. 235.00
Bowl, 9" d., footed,
    marigold . . . . 75.00 to 100.00
Bowl, 10" d., footed, fluted,
    blue. . . . . 95.00 to 100.00
Bowl, 10" d., footed, marigold. 100.00
Butter dish, cov.,
    marigold . . . . 100.00 to 125.00
Whimsey, toothpick, marigold 65.00

Whirling Leaves Bowl (Millersburg)

9" d., green 70.00
9" d., marigold. 82.00
9" d., purple . . . . 350.00 to 400.00
9½" w., tricornered,
    green. . . . . 350.00 to 400.00
9½" w., tricornered, marigold 317.00
9½" w., tricornered, purple 225.00
10" d., green. . . . . 50.00 to 75.00
10" d., marigold. 100.00
10" d., purple 120.00

Wild Rose

Wild Rose Bowl

Bowl, 7" d., three-footed, open heart
    rim, green, Northwood
    (ILLUS.). . . . . 75.00 to 85.00
Bowl, 7" d., three-footed, open heart
    rim, marigold (Northwood). 44.00
Bowl, 7" d., three-footed, open heart
    rim, purple (Northwood) . . . 70.00 to 80.00
Bowl, 8" to 9" d., green (Northwood) . . 38.00
Candy dish, open edge, green. 68.00
Candy dish, open edge, purple 75.00
Lamp, w/original burner & etched
    chimney shade, green, medium
    (Millersburg) . . . . 1,250.00 to 1,450.00

Wishbone & Spades

Banana bowl, ruffled, peach
    opalescent, 10" l. 148.00
Berry set: master bowl & 4 sauce
    dishes; purple, 5 pcs. 500.00
Bowl, 5" d., peach opalescent 80.00
Bowl, 6" d., ruffled, peach
    opalescent. 55.00
Bowl, ice cream shape, 9" d., peach
    opalescent. . . . . 160.00 to 175.00
Bowl, 10" d., purple. 270.00
Bowl, footed, green. 85.00
Bowl, ruffled, purple 100.00
Plate, 6" d., purple . . . . . . 345.00 to 375.00
Plate, 6½" d., peach opalescent 325.00
Plate, 6½" d., purple 150.00
Plate, chop, 11" d.,
    purple. . . . . 950.00 to 1,000.00
**Whimsey from 10½" ruffled chop
    plate,** sides folded up like a napkin
    holder, peach opalescent 1,400.00

CHOCOLATE

This glass is often called Carmel Slag. It was made by the Indiana Tumbler and Goblet Company of Greentown, Indiana, and other glasshouses, beginning at the turn of this century. Various patterns were produced, highly popular among them being Cactus and Leaf Bracket.

Animal covered dish, Dolphin,
   w/sawtooth rim, Greentown **$200.00**
Bowl, master berry, 10½" d.,
   Geneva patt., Greentown **450.00**
Butter dish, cov., Shuttle patt.,
   Greentown **1,100.00**
Compote, jelly, Pleat Band patt.,
   Greentown **150.00**
Cruet w/original stopper,
   Chrysanthemum Leaf patt....... **1,275.00**
Pitcher, water, Shuttle patt.,
   Greentown **3,500.00**
Plate, 8½" d., Serenade patt. **125.00**

Chocolate Cactus Shakers

**Salt & pepper shakers w/original
   metal lids,** Cactus patt.,
   Greentown, pr. (ILLUS.) **275.00**

Chocolate Cactus Table Set

Table set: cov. butter, cov. sugar,
   creamer & spooner; Cactus patt.,
   Greentown, 4 pcs. (ILLUS.)....... **413.00**

CHRYSANTHEMUM SPRIG, BLUE

The Chrysanthemum Sprig pattern, originally called "Pagoda," was one of several patterns produced by the Northwood Glass Company at the turn-of-the-century in their creamy white Custard glass (which see). A limited amount of this pattern was also produced in a blue opaque color, sometimes erroneously called 'blue custard.'

Bowl, master berry **$573.00**
Butter dish, cov. **1,250.00**
Celery dish **1,495.00**
Compote, jelly **525.00**
Creamer **385.00**

Blue Chrysanthemum Sprig Cruet

Cruet w/original stopper, 6½" h.
   (ILLUS.) **1,250.00**
Pitcher **1,450.00**
Sauce dish **195.00**
Spooner **325.00**
Tumbler **225.00**

CONSOLIDATED

The Consolidated Lamp and Glass Company of Coraopolis, Pennsylvania was founded in 1894 and for a number of years was noted for its lighting wares but also produced popular lines of pressed and blown tablewares. Highly collectible glass patterns of this early era include the Cone, Cosmos, Florette and Guttate lines.

Lamps and shades continued to be good sellers but in 1926 a new "art" line of molded decorative wares was introduced. This "Martelé" line was developed as a direct imitation of the fine glasswares being produced by René Lalique of France and many Consolidated patterns resembled their French counterparts. Other popular lines produced during the 1920s and

1930s were "Dancing Nymph," the delightfully Art Deco "Ruba Rombic," introduced in 1928, and the "Catalonian" line, imitating 17th century Spanish glass, which debuted in 1927.

Although the factory closed in 1933, it was reopened under new management in 1936 and prospered through the 1940s. It finally closed in 1967. Collectors should note that many later Consolidated patterns closely resemble wares of other competing firms, especially the Phoenix Glass Company. Careful study is needed to determine the maker of pieces from the 1920-40 era.

A recent book which will be of help to collectors is Phoenix & Consolidated Art Glass, 1926-1980, *by Jack D. Wilson (Antique Publications, 1989).*

Consolidated Martelé Label

Cone

Pickle castor, silver plate frame
w/Pigeon Blood insert **$600.00**
Sugar shaker w/original lid, squatty
form, blue **100.00**
Sugar shaker w/original lid, squatty
form, pink **125.00**

Florette

Cracker jar, cov., barrel-shaped,
cased pink satin, silver plate rim,
cover & bail handle **330.00**
Cracker jar, cov., pink satin w/white
interior, 6½" h. **225.00**
Cruet w/original stopper, pink
satin **225.00**

Guttate

Cruet w/original stopper,
cranberry **425.00**
Syrup pitcher w/original lid, pink
satin, applied clear frosted
handle **275.00**

Later Lines

Bowl, cupped shape, Ruba Rombic,
smokey topaz, 8" d. **1,200.00**
Cigarette box, cov., Santa Maria
patt., green wash **795.00**
Cookie jar, cov., Regent Line,
Florette patt., rose pink cased in
white opal, No. 3758, 6½" h. **369.00**

Pitcher, jug-type, Five Fruits patt.,
Martelé line, French Crystal,
½ gal.. . . . . **259.00**
Planter, Nuthatch patt., oblong shape
w/serpentine rim, relief-molded
small birds & tree branches in blue,
green & brown on an ivory ground,
10¼" l. **160.00**
Vase, 8¼" h., Katydid patt., No. 212,
white frosted **129.00**

Rare Ruba Rombic Vase

Vase, 9¼" h., 7" w., Ruba Rombic
patt., jagged Art Deco Cubist form
tapering toward the base,
translucent jade green
(ILLUS.) . . . . **2,000.00 to 3,000.00**
Vase, 12" h., Florentine patt., collared
flat form, green **289.00**
Vases, 8" h., Catalonian line, squatty
bulbous body tapering to a wide
cylindrical neck, wavy irregular
form in translucent pinkish opal,
ground pontil, pr. **138.00**

CORALENE

Coralene is a method of decorating glass, usually satin glass, with the use of beaded-type decoration customarily applied to the glass with the use of enamels, which were melted. Coralene decoration has been faked with the use of glue.

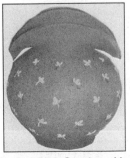

Shaded Pink Coralene Vase

Vase, 5½" h., 4⅝" d., footed spherical body w/a folded-up fan-shaped rim, soft opaque pink shading to frosted clear, decorated overall w/scattered small yellow Coralene beaded three-leaf sprigs (ILLUS.) **$225.00**

Vase, 7½" h., slender ovoid body tapering to a short trumpet neck, shaded pink to red satin ground, overall yellow "seaweed" coralene beading, 19th c. **193.00**

Vase, 8⅛" h., clear bulbous base w/a tall gently flaring sapphire blue neck & tri-lobed tightly crimped & curled flaring rim, overall yellow "seaweed" coralene beading, 19th c. **193.00**

Vases, 7" h., simple ovoid body tapering to a short cylindrical neck, shaded pink satin cased exterior w/an overall diamond & cross design in gold coralene beading, opal white linings, pr. **489.00**

CRANBERRY

Gold was added to glass batches to give this glass its color on reheating. It has been made by numerous glasshouses for years and is currently being reproduced. Both blown and molded articles were produced. A less expensive type of cranberry was made with the substitution of copper for gold.

Cranberry Music Box Bottle

Bottle w/clear facet-cut stopper, bulbous rib-molded base tapering to a knob-ringed tall cylindrical neck w/a flared rim, rich engraved decoration, non-working music box fitted into the base, 5¼" d., 12¼" h. (ILLUS.) **$245.00**

Butter dish, cov., footed squatty round base w/an applied skirt band of clear rigaree, flattened domed cover w/optic ribbing & an applied clear twisted leaf finial, 19th c., 6½" d. (minor edge flakes) **193.00**

Celery vase, cylindrical Inverted Thumbprint body enameled w/flowers & birds, fitted in a footed silver plate base w/ornate handles, good original plating, base marked by Jas. Tufts Co., late 19th c., 10" h. **550.00**

Cologne bottle w/swirl flame stopper, the corset-form body molded w/four ribs & tapering to a rim applied w/a marked sterling silver band embossed w/a single leaf, 9½" h. **110.00**

Decorated Cranberry Decanter

Decanter w/clear facet-cut stopper, optic-ribbed tapering cylindrical body w/a wide rounded shoulder tapering to a cylindrical neck w/flared rim, enamel-decorated around the shoulder w/white & yellow daisies on green & yellow leafy stems, 3" d., 7⅞" h. (ILLUS.) **125.00**

Decanter w/flat-topped bubble stopper, bulbous spherical optic ribbed body tapering to a short cylindrical neck, early 20th c., 10" h. **138.00**

Finger bowl, rounded form w/heavily applied clear rigaree around the rim, 6" d., 2½" h. **77.00**

Liqueur set: 9¾" h. tapering bulbous footed decanter w/crystal stopper, six 3" h. footed tumblers & a 11 x 13" cranberry tray; decanter & tumblers decorated w/gold-outlined grasshoppers, wasps & dragonflies, the set **845.00**

Small Decorated Cranberry Pitcher

Pitcher, 4" h., 2⅜" d., ovoid body w/a wide cylindrical neck & pinched spout, applied clear gilt-trimmed handle, the body decorated w/a large gilt & white scroll cartouche flanked by large leaf & berry sprigs (ILLUS.) **75.00**

Ripple-molded Cranberry Pitcher

Pitcher, 6¼" h., 4⅜" d., bulbous nearly spherical body tapering to a wide cylindrical neck w/pinched spout, overall ripple-molded design, applied clear angled handle (ILLUS.) **98.00**

Large Cranberry Rose Bowl

Rose bowl, spherical w/optic ribbed sides, six-crimp rim, 5¼" d., 5⅛" h. (ILLUS.) **100.00**

Salt & pepper shakers w/original metal lids, cylindrical Tapered Pillar patt., enameled floral decoration, fitted in a silver plate frame w/diamond-shaped base, bar sides & center upright handle w/loop grip, frame marked by Webster Co., the set **385.00**

Sugar shaker w/metal lid, tapering cylindrical optic ribbed form w/a swelled base band, 6" h. **176.00**

Sugar shaker w/metal top, tapering twelve-panel form, 5½" h. (small base chip) **165.00**

Sugar shaker w/original lid, Diamond Quilted patt. **190.00**

Syrup pitcher w/original lid, Inverted Thumbprint patt., applied clear handle **303.00**

Greek Key-decorated Cranberry Vase

Vase, 6" h., 3" d., ovoid body tapering to a short flaring neck, decorated around the middle w/a wide white sanded Greek key design w/a matching scalloped band around the shoulder & a band of points around the base, set on a gilt-metal ring base w/scroll-stamped legs (ILLUS.) **135.00**

Vase, 12" h., frosted cylindrical body w/a fold-down crimped rim **165.00**

Water set: pitcher w/clear applied reeded handle & four matching tumblers; Inverted Thumbprint patt., enameled polychrome Coreopsis blossom decoration, 5 pcs. **375.00**

Wine, cranberry bowl w/clear stem & foot, 4 oz., 4½" h. **35.00**

CROWN MILANO

This glass, produced by Mt. Washington Glass Company late last century, is opal glass decorated by painting and enameling. It appears identical to a ware termed Albertine, also made by Mt. Washington.

Crown Milano Mark

Stunning Crown Milano Bride's Bowl

Bride's bowl, deep rounded triangular form w/a crimped tricorner rim, the sides decorated w/large yellow & purple pansies & gilt edging, set on an ornate Pairpoint silver plate stand w/a round knopped pedestal above a domed triangular base w/embossed grapevines raised on three pierced & pointed floral-decorated feet, signed, 11½" h. (ILLUS.) **$3,630.00**

Cracker jar, cov., squatty bulbous, nearly spherical body w/a low-relief molded overall hobnail design, decorated w/white lotus blossoms & pod leaves enhanced w/raised gold outlining, design repeats in pale green on the molded ground, decorative silver plate rim & domed, floral-embossed cover w/applied butterfly at rim, marked 660.00

Ewer, Colonial Ware line, wide squatty bulbous body tapering to a short cylindrical neck w/an arched spout, applied S-scroll reeded gilt shoulder handle, the sides decorated w/two bouquets of assorted garden flowers in pink, purple & yellow, encircled w/raised gold scrolls & connected w/gold netting above an ivory white ground, glossy finish, 6" h. **550.00**

Crown Milano Ewer

Ewer, wide squatty bulbous body tapering to a small short neck w/an upright curved spout, slender serpent handle down the shoulder, gold lotus blossoms & green & gold pods outlined in raised gold on a light green ground, gold handle, spout w/aqua & scrolled leaves, No. 0567, ca. 1894, 8" d., 8" h. (ILLUS.) **1,650.00**

Ewer, tall ovoid body tapering to a short cylindrical neck w/a cupped rim w/a pinched spout, rope-wrapped neck continuing to form rope handle, beige, tan & rust ornately decorated w/jeweled shadow flowers outlined in heavy gold scrolls, ca. 1893, 10½" h. . . **1,375.00**

Jardiniere, wide bulbous flat-bottomed body w/a wide short cylindrical neck, almond white ground decorated around the body w/colorful pastel pansies among grey & tan lacy medallions, pink gold-trimmed neck, marked, 10" d., 7" h. 605.00

Sweetmeat jar, cov., barrel-shaped w/an embossed overall swirled diamond quilted design, decorated w/a biscuit-colored ground enameled w/earthtone holly leaves outlined in raised gold & enhanced by clumps of ruby-jeweled berries & tan shadow coiled designs, original paper label, silver plated domed cover w/twig handle & embossed floral design, 4" h. . . . **1,100.00**

Tumbler, cylindrical, Colonial Ware line w/a white glossy ground decorated around the body w/two raised gold bows suspending garlands of assorted flowers, crown & wreath mark on bottom, 3¾" h. . . **440.00**

Vase, 4½" h., wide squatty bulbous body w/the top centered by a short small cylindrical neck, almond brown ground decorated overall w/scattered heavy gilt spider mum blossoms & light brown shadow blossoms **825.00**

Vase, 5" h., footed squatty bulbous ovoid body molded w/lightly molded swirled ribs up the sharply tapering sides to small neck w/a four-lobed upturned rim, decorated w/tan shadow ferns overlaid w/gold fern fronds outlined w/raised gold, gold-trimmed rim, unmarked **770.00**

Vase, 6½" h., 7½" d., large spherical body centered at the top by a small, cylindrical neck, decorated w/three scattered multicolored floral bouquets bordered in ornate raised gold scrolls, strewn bluish grey shadow floral sprigs upon white ground, blue collar molded w/beading & painted w/golden stars, signed **853.00**

Crown Milano Vase with Cacti

Vase, 7¼" h., 6½" d., squatty bulbous swirl-molded body tapering to a short neck flaring into four fluted lobes, decorated w/life-like flowering cacti outlined in heavy gold on a beige background, unmarked (ILLUS.) **1,715.00**

Vase, 7½" h., cylindrical, blue wash decoration w/heavy gold floral design, white interior, gold detailing on wavy rim, marked "1556/1210" on base, original silver plated holder stamped "P" in diamond & "Pairpoint Mfg. Co." **450.00**

Vase, 7½" h., 3¾" d., cylindrical w/blue wash & overlapping heavy gold floral decoration in original Pairpoint silver plated holder **650.00**

Vase, 8" h., bulbous wide four-sided body tapering to a short cylindrical neck w/a flared rim flanked by two almond applied pointed arch shoulder handles, the body lavishly decorated w/peach & yellow shadow foliage overlaid w/raised gold branches of wild roses w/jewel stamens, buds & leaves, unmarked **523.00**

Vase, 8¼" h., ovoid teardrop-shaped w/a small flat mouth, double decoration w/heavy applied gold roses on the front & back below a delicate tracery & beaded band around the rim **1,380.00**

Vase, 8½" h., footring below the large egg-form ovoid body tapering to a small flat mouth, apricot-tinted ground decorated w/colorful floral bouquets scattered around the body w/raised gold trim, marked . . **770.00**

Vase, 8½" h., tall tapering melon-lobed body w/a small tricorner incurved mouth, the ivory ground decorated w/raised gold stylized flowers & leaves accented w/multicolored enameled dots **825.00**

Vase, 9" h., gourd-form w/large neck ring, bell-shaped top, decoration of pansies outlined in gold & a circle filled w/matte gold scrolls on a creamy white background **860.00**

Vase, 9½" h., wide low squatty bulbous body centered by a tall slender 'stick' neck swelled at the bottom & w/a gently flaring rim, white satin ground decorated overall w/wrapped raised gold fern leaves, original paper label **468.00**

Vase, 11" h., tall slender ovoid body w/pulled-out loop handles from the small mouth & attached to the shoulder, gold decorated scrolling borders enclosing a h.p. scene of a dancing couple in 18th c. attire, glossy finish, base w/red crown-in-wreath mark & "1001" (some gild rim wear) **805.00**

Vase, 11¾" h., tall slender conical body w/a flaring, gently ruffled rim, glossy white ground decorated around the rim & base w/delicate gilt scrolls & four bands of three large gold prunts applied up around the lower body, marked **770.00**

Vase, 12" h., bulbous ovoid melon-lobed body tapering to a tall slender twisted cylindrical neck w/flared rim, golden applied arched & reeded handles at the base of the neck, the body decorated in pastel fall colors w/large teasel leaves & floral buds against a biscuit ground, gold scrolls & pink blush on the neck, marked **2,090.00**

Vase, 15" h., wide squatty bulbous base centered by a very tall slender slightly flaring cylindrical neck w/a deeply forked rim w/notched edges, completely covered w/raised gold overlapped fern fronds in exceptional detail, painted tan shadow leaves, paper label marked "Mt. Washington, Crown Milano" **523.00**

CRUETS

Amber, mold-blown, cylindrical w/three embossed raised rings on body, white flower & leaf enameling, applied amber handle, bubble stopper w/white enamel trim **$110.00**

Amber, blown, footed bulbous body tapering to a short cylindrical neck, decorated w/pink & gold flowers, applied sapphire blue handle & teardrop stopper, 6¾" h. **265.00**

Three Varied Cruets

Amber, blown, bulbous cylindrical body w/a wide shoulder tapering to a cylindrical neck w/a tricorner rim, applied amber handle, the shoulder decorated w/tiny white dot flowers & green leafy branches, original facet-cut amber stopper, 3⅛" d., 7¼" h. (ILLUS. right) **115.00**

Amber, blown, short cylindrical body w/sapphire blue stopper & applied handle, lions' heads above sapphire blue feet, 7½" h. **200.00**

Amber, mold-blown, spherical optic-ribbed body tapering to a tall slender cylindrical neck w/a pinched spout, applied pale blue ropetwist handle & blue optic-ribbed bubble stopper, 3½" d., 7⅝" h. (ILLUS. left) **75.00**

Blue frosted, blown, tall slender conical body w/a tricorner mouth, the sides enameled w/large pink, white & lavender daisy-like flowers w/green leaves & salmon pink branches, applied clear long handle & clear facet-cut stopper, 3¾" d., 10" h. (ILLUS. center) **125.00**

Cameo glass, clear frosted & textured ground overlaid w/ruby shading to yellowish green at the neck, the ruby cut w/floral branches, scrolls & netting w/gilt highlights, cut neck, clear applied handle & facet-cut stopper, St. Louis, France, 9" h. **440.00**

Clear w/enamel decoration pressed glass, Nevada patt. **195.00**

Cranberry, blown, ovoid w/clear wafer foot, spun rope clear applied handle, original clear bubble stopper, 2¾" d., 8¼" h. **118.00**

Fireglow, blown, tapered cylinder, enameled blue & white flowers & green leaves w/sprays of white flowers & leaves, marked "St. Raphael," frosted applied handle w/blue enamel dots, original clear ball stopper w/gold trim, 2¼" d., 6¾" h. **195.00**

Green, pressed glass, Beveled Star patt. **375.00**

Green, pressed glass, Zipper Dart patt. **195.00**

Green w/gold trim, pressed glass, Empress patt. **375.00**

Green w/gold trim, pressed glass, Ivy Scroll patt. **195.00**

Sapphire blue, squared body w/bottom half w/flat outward flaring sides & the upper half w/pyramidal sides tapering to a cylindrical neck w/flared rim, some side panels w/a relief-molded oval medallion, decorated overall w/enameled woodland flowers, melon-ribbed amber bubble stopper, straight square zipper-cut amber applied handle, attributed to Moser, 6" h. ... **468.00**

Smokey blue, footed ovoid Optic Rib patt. body w/a cylindrical neck & pinched spout, decorated w/heavy raised gold wild roses & a butterfly, clear bubble stopper & pale blue ropetwist , 6" h. **110.00**

CUP PLATES

Produced in numerous patterns beginning some 170 years ago, these little plates were designed to hold a cup while the tea or coffee was allowed to cool in a saucer. Cup plates were also made of ceramics. Where numbers are listed below, they refer to numbers assigned these plates in the book, American Glass Cup Plates, *by Ruth Webb Lee and James H. Rose. Plates are of clear glass unless otherwise noted. A number of cup plates have been reproduced.*

L & R-77, round, a three spearpoint center cluster surrounded w/a band of swirled leaves w/another vining leaf band & rope border, clear, very rare **$990.00**

L & R-95, 10-sided, ornate scrolled design, opaque white, 3½" d. (mold roughness) **154.00**

L & R-95, twelve-sided, central large florette surrounded by a band of florettes & shields within an outer border of shields & pine trees, rope border, deep fiery opalescent (large chip on front, few on rope border) **77.00**

L & R-179, round, center w/a large stylized flowerhead w/small round & long pointed petal within outer rings & a rim w/wide lobes, clear, 3⁷⁄₁₆" d. (shallow spall, minor flakes) **55.00**

L & R-191B, round, large flowerhead center design w/a rim band of large pointed petals, blue, 3" d. (six large & small rim flakes) **187.00**

L & R-211, round, small starburst center framed by three concentric beaded rings within a leaf & bud outer band, clear, 3⅝" d. (minor nicks, area of rim underfill) **110.00**

L & R-212, round, large quatrefoil w/spearpoints in center, narrow ruffled & ribbed bands around the rim, clear, 3⅝" d. (three small rim flakes) **165.00**

L & R-215A, round, Basketweave patt. center & rim, clear, 3⅝" d. (three large chips, multiple small nicks) **308.00**

L & R-251, round, center w/pairs of adorsed C-scrolls framed by an outer border of fans alternating w/points, clear, 3⅞" d. (four small spalls & some flakes) **248.00**

L & R-251, round, center w/pairs of adorsed C-scrolls framed by an outer border of fans alternating w/points, clear, 3⅞" d. (four small spalls & some flakes) **248.00**

L & R-262, round, center w/four-point star alternating w/paired scrolls, cross & fleur-de-lis border, greyish blue (three tipped scallops, four surface spalls) **198.00**

L & R-272, round, scroll design, opal opaque (one scallop tipped, mold roughness) **149.00**

L & R-323, round, center sunburst w/four long rays framed by four small sunbursts, rayed outer border & scalloped rim, amber (two chips, few nicks) **110.00**

L & R-374, round, Bull's-eye center, scalloped rim, golden amber (five scallops tipped) **209.00**

L & R-374, round, Bull's-eye center, scalloped rim, light green (heavy mold roughness, loss of five scallops) **66.00**

L & R-440, round, Valentine patt., harp border, peacock blue (one scallop tipped) **303.00**

L & R-440B, round, Valentine patt., harp & scroll border, deep blue (few nicks on scallops) **275.00**

L & R-455, round, Heart patt., loop & lancet center, unlisted emerald green, probably Boston & Sandwich, 3¾" d. (two non-disfiguring shallow chips) **1,980.00**

L & R-455B, round, Heart patt. border, loop & lancet center, electric blue (one scallop tipped) . . . **825.00**

L & R-459Q, round, Heart patt. border, loop & lancet center, opal (mold roughness, tiny underside flake) **66.00**

L & R-465J, round, Heart patt. border, loop & lancet center, opal (one tipped scallop) **77.00**

L & R-465L, round, Heart patt. border, loop & lancet center, violet blue (seven scallops tipped or partially gone) **275.00**

L & R-477, round, Heart patt., four-heart center, fiery opalescent (two scallops missing, several tightly tipped) **110.00**

L & R-500, round, starburst center, plain rim, blue, 3 1/4" d. (three rim spalls) **55.00**

L & R-511, round, starburst center, plain border & scalloped rim, amethyst (heavy mold roughness, one point missing, slight rim underfill) **187.00**

L & R-522, round, starburst center, ringed border, light amethyst (three tipped scallops) **94.00**

L & R-524, round, starburst center, plain rim, amethyst, 3¹⁄₁₆" d. (three scallops w/spalls, few w/minute nicks) **193.00**

Starburst Cup Plate

L & R-531, round, starburst center & beaded rim, yellowish green, four lightly tipped beads (ILLUS.) **275.00**

L & R-531, round, sunburst in center, plain inner band, bull's-eye scalloped border, light green (two short refracting lines, few flakes & a chip) **138.00**

L & R-564, round, Henry Clay patt., pronounced lavender tint (three tipped scallops) **66.00**

L & R-565B, round, Henry Clay patt., deep peacock blue, 3½" d. (three scallops missing, three tipped) **138.00**

L & R-571, round, Queen Victoria center bust framed by ring w/her name, crown & wreath border, clear (one tipped scallop, mold roughness) **165.00**

L & R-573, round, Henry Clay patt., yellowish green tint (mold roughness, four scallops tipped) . . . **154.00**

L & R-585A, round, Ringgold - Palo Alto patt., clear, 3½" d. (chip w/loss of a large & two small rim scallops, slight rim underfill) **385.00**

L & R-592, round, Log Cabin patt. center, plain border, clear (six scallops missing, others tipped) . . . **165.00**

L & R-594, round, Log Cabin patt., golden amber, 3 1/4" d. **523.00**

L & R-604A, round, Ship patt., clear (four tipped scallops) **88.00**

L & R-607, round, Maid of the Mist patt., clear (some mold roughness, tiny rim flakes) **77.00**

L & R-610b, round, Cadmus (so-called) patt., scroll border, peacock blue (underfill, some rim flaking) . . . **303.00**

L & R-615A, round, Steamboat patt., hairpin border, light pink tint (several points & scallops disfigured) **248.00**

L & R-619, round, Ship Benjamin Franklin patt., floral scroll border, fiery opalescent **605.00**

L & R-643, round, Bunker Hill Monument patt., fiery opalescent . . **880.00**

L & R-654A, round, Eagle patt., leafy band border, clear, probably Midwestern **275.00**

L & R-662, round, Eagle patt. w/"1832," violet blue (four tipped or partially missing scallops) **605.00**

L & R-670B, round, Eagle patt., clear, 3½" d. (few tipped scallops) **220.00**

L & R-676A, round, Eagle patt. center, bull's-eyes around rim, clear w/long swirl of olive green . . . **154.00**

L & R-677A, round, Eagle patt., blue (only two minute scallop nicks) **605.00**

L & R-689, round, Plow patt., clear, 3½" d. (few tiny flakes) **281.00**

CUSTARD

This ware takes its name from its color and is a variant of milk white glass. It was produced largely between 1890 and 1915 by the Northwood Glass Co., Heisey Glass Company, Fenton Art Glass Co., Jefferson Glass Co., and a few others. There are 21 major patterns and a number of minor ones. The prime patterns are considered Argonaut Shell, Chrysanthemum Sprig, Inverted Fan and Feather, Louis XV and Winged Scroll. Most custard glass patterns are enhanced with gold and some have additional enameled decoration or stained highlights. Unless otherwise noted, items in this listing are fully decorated.

For an expanded listing of Custard Glass see Antique Trader Books American & European Decorative & Art Glass.

ARGONAUT SHELL (Northwood)

Creamer $150.00
Spooner 150.00

BEADED CIRCLE (Northwood)

Butter dish, cov. 450.00
Creamer 165.00
Cruet w/original stopper 650.00
Pitcher, water 625.00
Spooner 125.00
Sugar bowl, cov. 175.00

Tumbler 130.00

BEADED SWAG (Heisey)

Butter dish, cov. 115.00
Goblet. 65.00
Goblet, souvenir 75.00
Sauce dish 25.00
Sauce dish, souvenir 45.00
Sugar bowl, open. 45.00
Wine 48.00
Wine, souvenir 60.00

Carnelian - See Everglades Pattern

CHERRY & SCALE or FENTONIA (Fenton)

Berry set, master bowl & 6 sauce
   dishes, 7 pcs. 390.00
Bowl, master berry or fruit 115.00
Butter dish, cov. 235.00

Cherry & Scale Spooner

Spooner (ILLUS.) 95.00
Tumbler 75.00

CHRYSANTHEMUM SPRIG (Northwood's Pagoda)

Butter dish, cov. 365.00
Compote, jelly. 135.00
Creamer 139.00
Cruet w/original stopper. 495.00
Pitcher 495.00
Salt & pepper shakers w/original
   lids, pr. 195.00
Spooner 117.00
Sugar bowl, cov. 235.00
Tray, cruet. 650.00
Tumbler 69.00

DIAMOND MAPLE LEAF (Dugan)

Banana boat. 235.00
Bowl, master berry 145.00
Butter dish, cov. 325.00
Creamer 145.00

Sugar bowl, cov., w/gold trim. 275.00
Water set, pitcher & 6 tumblers,
   7 pcs.. . . . . 700.00

DIAMOND WITH PEG (Jefferson)

Butter dish, cov. 265.00
Creamer 60.00
Creamer, individual size 30.00
Creamer, individual size, souvenir 45.00
Mug, rose decoration 45.00
Mug, souvenir 40.00
Napkin ring. 145.00
Pitcher, water, tankard, decorated . . . 395.00
Pitcher, 5½" h. 140.00
Pitcher, tankard, 7½" h. 250.00
Pitcher, tankard, 7½" h., souvenir . . . 230.00
Salt shaker w/original top. 60.00
Spooner 95.00
Sugar bowl, cov. 138.00
Toothpick holder 75.00
Toothpick holder, h.p. rose
   decoration & souvenir inscription . . . 61.00

Diamond with Peg Tumbler

Tumbler (ILLUS.) 75.00
Tumbler, souvenir. 39.00
Wine, souvenir 64.00

EVERGLADES or CARNELIAN (Northwood)

Bowl, master berry or fruit, footed . . . 175.00

Everglades Jelly Compote

Compote, jelly (ILLUS.) 265.00
Creamer 125.00
Sauce dish 60.00
Spooner 130.00
Sugar bowl, cov. 175.00
Table set, 4 pcs. 850.00
Tumbler 125.00

FAN (Dugan)

Bowl, master berry or fruit 185.00
Creamer 95.00
Ice cream dish 50.00
Pitcher, water 285.00
Sauce dish 60.00
Spooner 65.00
Tumbler 75.00

FLUTED SCROLLS or KLONDYKE (Northwood)

Berry set: master bowl, 2 decorated
   sauces & 4 undecorated sauces,
   7 pcs. 375.00
Bowl, master berry or fruit, footed . . . 150.00
Creamer 65.00
Spooner 48.00

GENEVA (Northwood)

Butter dish, cov. 125.00
Spooner 80.00

GEORGIA GEM or LITTLE GEM (Tarentum)

Bowl, master berry, decorated 117.00
Bowl, master berry, undecorated 65.00
Butter dish, cov., decorated 195.00
Butter dish, cov., undecorated 110.00
Creamer, decorated 95.00
Creamer & cov. sugar bowl,
   breakfast size, decorated, pr. 95.00
Creamer & cov. sugar bowl,
   souvenir, pr. 100.00
Creamer & open sugar bowl,
   breakfast size, souvenir, pr. 90.00
Cruet w/original stopper 295.00
Pitcher, water, undecorated 175.00
Sauce dish, decorated 35.00
Spooner 65.00
Sugar bowl, cov., decorated 105.00
Sugar bowl, cov., undecorated 45.00
Sugar bowl, open, breakfast size. 45.00
Sugar bowl, open, breakfast size,
   souvenir. 38.00
Table set, decorated, 4 pcs. 400.00
Toothpick holder 25.00
Tumbler, souvenir. 35.00

GRAPE & GOTHIC ARCHES (Northwood)

Goblet, nutmeg stain 66.00

Sugar bowl, cov., blue stain 195.00
Table set, 4 pcs. 375.00
Tumbler 58.00
Vase, ruffled hat shape 55.00
Vase, 10" h. "favor" (vase made from
   goblet mold). 75.00

INTAGLIO (Northwood)

Pitcher, blue & gold trim 250.00

INVERTED FAN & FEATHER (Northwood)

Berry set, master bowl & 6 sauce
   dishes, 7 pcs. 650.00
Bowl, master berry or fruit, 10" d.,
   5½" h., four-footed. 225.00
Butter dish, cov. 216.00
Compote, jelly. 475.00
Creamer 110.00
Pitcher, water 650.00
Punch cup 265.00
Salt & pepper shakers w/original
   tops, pr. 500.00
Sauce dish 60.00
Spooner 138.00
Sugar bowl, cov. 250.00
Table set, 4 pcs. 825.00
Toothpick holder 625.00
Tumbler 100.00

LOUIS XV (Northwood)

Salt & pepper shakers w/original
   lids, pr. 350.00
Sugar bowl, cov. 145.00

MAPLE LEAF (Northwood)

Banana bowl 175.00
Butter dish, cov. 318.00
Compote, jelly. 440.00

Maple Leaf Creamer

Creamer 143.00
Pitcher, water 448.00
Sauce dish 80.00
Spooner 143.00
Sugar bowl, cov. 215.00
Toothpick holder 650.00
Tumbler 90.00

NORTHWOOD GRAPE, GRAPE & CABLE or GRAPE & THUMBPRINT

Creamer & open sugar bowl,
breakfast-size, pr. 100.00
Plate, nutmeg decoration 60.00

PUNTY BAND (Heisey)

Creamer, individual size, souvenir 35.00
Cuspidor, lady's 75.00
Mug, souvenir 55.00
Mug, 4½" h. 32.00
Toothpick holder, souvenir 45.00
Tumbler, floral decoration, souvenir . . . 45.00

RIBBED DRAPE (Jefferson)

Bowl, master berry 295.00
Compote, jelly. 150.00
Compote, jelly, no decoration. 125.00
Creamer 125.00
Pitcher, water 255.00
Sauce dish 40.00
Sauce dish, decorated 65.00
Sauce dishes, set of 6 . . . . 250.00
Spooner 125.00

Ribbed Drape Sugar Bowl

Sugar bowl, cov. (ILLUS.) 225.00
Toothpick holder, rose decoration . . 195.00
Tumbler 90.00

RING BAND (Heisey)

Berry set, master bowl & 6 sauce
dishes, 7 pcs. 480.00
Butter dish, cov. 225.00
Compote, jelly. 160.00
Condiment tray 150.00
Pitcher, water 350.00

Salt shaker w/original top,
undecorated 50.00
Sauce dish 38.00
Spooner 125.00
Sugar bowl, cov. 165.00
Syrup pitcher w/original top 350.00
Table set, creamer, cov. sugar & cov.
butter dish, 3 pcs. 425.00
Toothpick holder, decorated 115.00
Toothpick holder, souvenir 75.00
Toothpick holder, undecorated 85.00
Tumbler, decorated 75.00
Tumbler, undecorated 70.00
Water set, pitcher & 4 tumblers,
decorated, 5 pcs. 895.00

VICTORIA (Tarentum)

Butter dish, cov. 300.00
Celery vase 175.00
Spooner, decorated 135.00
Spooner, undecorated 70.00
Vase, bud 325.00

WINGED SCROLL (Heisey)

Bowl, master berry 100.00
Butter dish, cov. 150.00
Sauce dish, gold trim, 5¾" d. 61.00
Spooner 80.00
Sugar bowl, cov. 100.00
Water set, pitcher & 9 tumblers,
10 pcs. 750.00

MISCELLANEOUS PATTERNS

Delaware

Berry set, master bowl & 5 sauce
dishes, 6 pcs. 190.00
Card tray, 5" 145.00
Creamer, individual size 45.00
Creamer, w/rose decoration 67.00
Pin tray, w/blue decoration 65.00
Pin tray, w/rose stain, 4½" 68.00
Pin tray, w/green decoration, 7" l. 70.00
Punch cup 40.00
Ring tree, 4" h. 90.00
Spooner 65.00
Sugar bowl, open, breakfast size. 45.00
Tumbler, w/blue decoration 70.00
Tumbler, w/green decoration 54.00

Heart With Thumbprint

Lamp, kerosene-type 400.00

Peacock and Urn

Bowl, master berry 200.00
Ice cream bowl, undecorated,
master 320.00

Ice Cream Bowl

Ice cream bowl, master w/nutmeg
  stain, 9¾" d. (ILLUS.) 350.00
Ice cream dish, individual w/nutmeg
  stain 56.00

Vermont

Bowl, master berry 115.00
Butter dish, cov., ... 110.00
Candlestick, finger-type 65.00
Celery vase 225.00
Creamer, w/blue decoration 98.00
Creamer, w/green & pink florals 95.00
**Salt & pepper shakers w/original
  tops,** blue decoration, pr. 135.00
Salt shaker w/original top,
  enameled decoration. 78.00
Spooner 95.00
Spooner, w/green decoration 75.00
Toothpick holder, w/blue trim &
  enameled decoration. 95.00
Toothpick holder, w/green
  decoration 135.00
Tumbler, w/blue decoration 75.00
Vase, w/enameled decoration. 135.00

Wild Bouquet

Bowl, master berry 225.00
Butter dish, cov. 575.00
Creamer 115.00
Cruet w/original stopper,
  w/enameling & gold trim 1,000.00
Sauce dish, small, grey, rare 295.00
Sauce dish, undecorated 46.00
Spooner, undecorated 72.00
Spooner, w/gold trim & colored
  decoration 165.00
Toothpick holder, decorated 475.00
Tumbler, undecorated 86.00

OTHER MISCELLANEOUS
PIECES

Alba, sugar shaker w/original lid 125.00
Basket (Northwood), w/nutmeg
  stain. 65.00

Beaded Cable, rose bowl, w/nutmeg
  stain. 88.00
Beaded Scroll, butter dish, cov.,
  enameled floral top 175.00
Blackberry Spray, hat-shape, ribbon
  candy edge 35.00
Butterfly & Berry, vase, 7" h. 25.00
Canadian, compote 30.00
Chrysanthemum, tray, 4½ x 8½" 40.00
Creased Bale, condiment set
  w/original tops 125.00
Cut Block, sugar bowl, open,
  individual size 35.00
Dandelion, mug, w/nutmeg stain 135.00
Drapery, vase, 10" h., w/nutmeg
  stain 55.00
Drapery, vase, 12" h., w/nutmeg
  stain. 65.00
Drapery, vase, swung-type. 55.00
Finecut & Roses, rose bowl,
  w/nutmeg stain 63.00
Footed Wreath, bowl 85.00
Fruits & Flower (N), bowl, 7¼" d.,
  flared 65.00
Gothic Arches, goblet 35.00
Grape Arbor, hat shape, w/nutmeg
  stain. 42.00
Grape Arbor, vase, No.200 . . . . 40.00
Grape Arbor, vase, 3¾" h. 85.00
Heart, salt shaker w/original top 45.00
Honeycomb, cordial 70.00
Honeycomb, wine 60.00
Horse Medallion, bowl, grapes
  exterior, 6½" d. 50.00
Horse Medallion, bowl, green stain,
  7" d. 60.00
Iris, cruet w/original stopper,
  undecorated 290.00
Jefferson Optic, berry set, master
  bowl & 6 sauce dishes, 7 pcs. 350.00
Jefferson Optic, butter dish, cov. 50.00
Jefferson Optic, creamer 150.00
Jefferson Optic, pitcher, tankard,
  souvenir. 275.00
Jefferson Optic, salt dip, w/rose
  decoration 65.00
Jefferson Optic, salt shaker
  w/original top, roses decoration,
  souvenir. 35.00
Jefferson Optic, spooner. 65.00
Jefferson Optic, sugar bowl, cov. 85.00
Jefferson Optic, table set, bases
  w/gold, 4 pcs. 350.00
Jefferson Optic, toothpick holder,
  souvenir. 40.00
Jefferson Optic, tumbler 32.00
Lacy Medallion, tumbler. 38.00
Ladder w/Diamond, butter dish, cov. . . 85.00
Ladder w/Diamond, creamer 60.00
Ladder w/Diamond, spooner 60.00
Ladder w/Diamond, sugar bowl,
  cov. 70.00

Lamp, kerosene, finger-type,
greenish color w/embossed tulip
design 185.00
Lion, plate, 7" d., w/green stain 150.00
Little Shrimp, salt shaker w/original
top 45.00
Lotus, nappy, handled, 6½" w. 35.00
Lotus & Grape, bonbon, handled,
red stain. 45.00
Lotus & Grape, bonbon, nutmeg
stain. 115.00
Lotus & Grape, bonbon, w/green
stain. 65.00
Lotus & Grape, nappy, handled. 65.00
Many Lobes, sugar shaker w/original
top 95.00
Melon Rib, lamp base, kerosene-
type 55.00
Nine Panels, lamp, miniature,
kerosene-type 65.00
Panelled Teardrop, sugar shaker
w/original top 140.00
Pansy, pitcher, milk. 50.00
Peacock & Dahlia, plate, 7¾" d.,
flat,. 75.00
Peacock & Urn, ice cream bowl,
9¾" d., nutmeg stain 265.00
Pineapple & Fan, pitcher, 5½" h.,
souvenir. 65.00
Pods & Posies, butter dish, cov.,
w/gold trim. 125.00
Poppy, relish tray, w/nutmeg stain 45.00
Prayer Rug, nappy, two-handled,
ruffled rim, nutmeg stain, 6" w. 40.00
Ribbed Thumbprint, toothpick
holder, w/floral decoration 82.00
Ribbed Thumbprint, tumbler,
souvenir. 70.00
Rings & Beads, pitcher, 2¾" h.,
souvenir. 25.00
Rings & Beads, toothpick holder,
souvenir. 45.00
Shell & Scroll, spooner, 3½" d.,
4¼" h. 150.00
Singing Birds, mug 85.00
Smocking, bell w/original clapper. 45.00
Spool, spooner 32.00
Strawberry, compote 75.00
Sunset, toothpick holder. 98.00
Three Fruits, bowl, 6¾" d., flared rim,
nutmeg stain 95.00
Three Fruits, plate 95.00
Tiny Thumbprint, goblet, souvenir. . . . 62.00
Tiny Thumbprint, pitcher, 5" h.,
souvenir. 30.00
Tiny Thumbprint, table set, 4 pcs. . . . 650.00
Tiny Thumbprint, toothpick holder,
souvenir. 85.00
Trailing Vine, sauce dish, footed 30.00
Trailing Vine, spooner, blue
decoration 65.00
Twigs, plate 70.00

Water Lily, cracker jar, cov. 190.00
Woven Cane, salt shaker w/original
top 30.00

CUT GLASS

*Cut glass most eagerly sought by collectors is
American glass produced during the so-called "Brilliant
Period" from 1880 to about 1915. Pieces listed below are
by type of article in alphabetical order.*

*Hawkes, Hoare, Libbey and
Straus Marks*

BASKETS

Fry signed, round low cylindrical
form w/notched rim & notched
applied handle, cut w/pinwheels
alternating w/spearpoints & fans,
small $385.00

BOTTLES

Bitters, Dorflinger's Marlboro patt.,
sterling top, 8" h. 300.00
Jug, Hoare's Monarch patt., triple-
notched side strap handle,
15" h. 3,750.00
Lady's flask, basketweave design,
sterling holder & screw flip lid,
marked by Tiffany & Co., 6" h. 500.00
Smelling salts, buzzstar & cross-cut
diamond, w/matching stopper,
5½" h. 300.00
Whiskey w/original stopper, overall
deep cutting of hobstars, fans,
cross-hatching w/same cutting on
stopper, neck w/eight flutes
separated by zipper cutting, cut
hobstars around lip, 13¾" h. 295.00
Worcestershire, hobstars & file
cutting w/mushroom-cut stopper,
7¾" h. 300.00
Worcestershire, Prism patt., 8" h. 425.00

BOWLS

Banana, Fry's Trojan patt., cut in
pinwheels w/notched prism panels
around the bottom hobstar 237.00

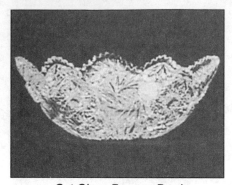

Cut Glass Banana Bowl

Banana, oval w/deeply scalloped & notched rim, four buzzstars alternating w/four large hobstars, four sections of shooting-star style cutting from base up lower sides, minor use flaking, 8¼ x 11½", 4½" h. (ILLUS.) **220.00**

Bergen's 'Goldenrod' patt., round w/lobed & notched rim, cut w/three rosettes & three blazing stars w/strawberry diamond & crosshatch cutting, cane cutting in base, 8" d. **110.00**

Center hobstar, surrounded by cut fans & a mesh of hobnail & crosshatching, sawtooth rim, 8¼" d. **115.00**

Chrysanthemum patt., very large hobstars alternate w/pairs of flaring spearpoints flanking a teardrop hobstar around the deeply scalloped & notched rim, late 19th c., 12⅛" d., 6" h. **374.00**

Cross design, the cross composed of three facet-cut bands alternating w/panels centered by a hobstar surrounded by a ring of smaller hobstars, notched & scalloped rim, large hobstar in the bottom, 9" d. **345.00**

Fans around the rim, alternating w/large triangles composed of small diamonds enclosing hobstars or strawberry diamond, 9" d. **83.00**

Fruit bowl, deeply scalloped notched rim, cut w/four large "shooting stars" & a hobstar in the center bottom, 8" d., 4" h. **138.00**

Fry signed, cut w/alternating hobstars inside a horseshoe or crescent moon alternating w/cross branches of flashed fans w/three hobstars. **127.00**

Hawkes' Venetian patt., 9" d. **237.00**

Hobstars, alternating w/panels of stars & pinwheels, 8" d. **264.00**

Cut Bowl with Hobstars

Hobstars, four around the sides & a large one in the bottom, side hobstars alternate w/twelve small ones w/fans & crosshatching, scalloped & notched rim, 9" d., 8½" h. (ILLUS.) **138.00**

Hobstars, alternating w/strawberry diamond & fan cutting, shallow, 9" d. **94.00**

Large hobstars, alternating w/panels of crosshatching enclosing small hobstars, a band of fans around the bottom, scalloped & notched rim, 8" d. **127.00**

Large hobstars, alternating w/smaller five-sided panels of cane cutting, plain scalloped & notched rim, 8" d. **110.00**

Large panels of crosshatching, scalloped & notched rim w/fan cutting, large hobstar in base, 9" d. **110.00**

Libbey-signed, cut w/hobstars, fans & finecut sections, 8" d., 4" h. **330.00**

Libbey-signed, cut w/hobstars & crosshatchings, 8" d. **149.00**

Orient patt., footed, cut w/flashed pinwheels, notchings & fans, 9" d. **424.00**

Pinwheels, large hobstar in the base, 8" d. **110.00**

Raised diamond, crosshatching & star designs, alternating w/notching, hobstar & strawberry diamond cuts, 9" d. **230.00**

Roden Bros. signed, Alhambra patt., Toronto, Canada, 8" d. **495.00**

Russian cut, 9" d., 4¼" h. **275.00**

Small hobstars, cut overall w/hobstar clusters divided by a looping band enclosing further hobstars, shallow, 9" d. **165.00**

Fine Amber Cut Glass Bowl

Union Glass-attributed, wide upper body w/a smooth eight-scalloped rim above a body cut w/a large overall cane design, the bottom tapering to a facet-cut low pedestal foot w/star-cut base, golden amber, probably Somerville, Massachusetts, 9¼" d., 5" h. (ILLUS.) **3,450.00**

Whipped cream bowl, squatty bulbous form w/an applied Gorham sterling silver rim band, cut in a vesica design alternating w/variants of vesica w/alternating sections of flat-topped diamond cutting & a 24-point cut hobstar in the base, unsigned, 6½" d. **275.00**

BOXES

Dresser box, square w/notched corners & hinged cover, the top cut in a circle of hobstars, the sides cut w/stars within squares, a rayed star in the base, 5" w............... **275.00**

Dresser box, square w/notched corners, the cover cut in the center w/a large sunburst framed by a wide Harvard-cut border, banded stepped bottom, 7" w. **330.00**

BUTTER DISHES & TUBS

Covered dish, domed cover w/large engraved daisy-like blossoms w/brilliant-cut centers alternating w/fan cutting, facet-cut knob, dished base w/matching design & notched rim, 8" d. **303.00**

CANDLESTICKS & CANDLEHOLDERS

Hawkes signed, heavy flute cut, rayed star base, 9" h., pr. **475.00**

Rock crystal, engraved, base & candle cup w/bobeche rim joined together w/a wafer, 7" h., pr....... **235.00**

Russian patt., candelabrum, standard cut w/teardrop stem & swirl design................. **9,500.00**

CARAFES

Border of hobstars around the body, notching below w/large hobstar in base, waisted cylindrical neck ring- and panel-cut **171.00**

Dorflinger, hobstars in diamonds & engraved florals................ **95.00**

Dorflinger, hobstars in diamonds overall **135.00**

Eight bull's-eye punties & sections of mitered cutting around the squatty bulbous body, star cutting above each punty, tall slightly flaring panel-cut neck, 32 cut rays in the base, 8" h. **110.00**

Brilliant Cut Carafe

Mitered & zipper cutting around bulbous base, paneled flaring cylindrical neck w/zipper cutting, star-cut base, 8½" h. (ILLUS.)..... **165.00**

CHAMPAGNES, CORDIALS & WINES

Hoare signed, champagne, Comet patt. **3,600.00**

Liquors, St. Regis patt. by Hawkes, pedestal base, set of 10 .... **275.00**

Sherry glasses, strawberry diamond & fan design, notched stem & rayed foot, cranberry cut to clear, set of 4 .... **1,000.00**

Wine glass, hobstars & elongated zippered ovals................. **38.00**

Wine glasses, Baccarat signed, Fleur-de-Lis patt., green cut to clear, set of 4................. **550.00**

Wine glasses, Dorflinger's Patt. No. 210, triple mitre trellis cutting, cut feet in same pattern, pr. (small chip on one bowl)................ **1,400.00**

Wine glasses, double-mitre & cross-cut hobnail design, cranberry cut to clear, rayed bases & notched stems, 5" h., pr................ **400.00**

Wine glasses, Hawkes-signed, bowl
cut w/a raised diamond border,
circles & spheres above the
beaded stem & square foot, 6½" h.,
set of 5. . . . . **173.00**

CLOCKS

Boudoir, Harvard-type cutting,
intaglio cut satin tulip on front,
6¼" h. **145.00**
Pairpoint's Colias patt., 5½" h. **395.00**

COMPOTES

Buzzstar, cane & finecut cutting,
round bowl on tall slender stem &
foot, 5¾" d., 8" h. **66.00**
Hobstar-cut dish, raised on a notch-
cut pedestal & foot, 9" h. **546.00**

CREAMERS & SUGAR BOWLS

Hoare-signed, cut w/hobstars
alternating w/crosshatching,
2½" h., pr. **83.00**

DECANTERS

Bull's-eye & Prism patt., sterling
spout & stopper, elk horn handle,
10" h. **525.00**
Clark signed, bulbous ovoid body
tapering to a tall panel-cut neck w/a
flattened rim, cut w/large buzzstars
alternating w/fan cutting,
compressed ball stopper
w/matching cutting, 11" h., pr. **358.00**
Cordial, Parisian patt., 9" h. **375.00**

Cranberry Cut to Clear Decanter

Cranberry cut to clear, flattened
oval body w/a short slender
cylindrical neck fitted w/a cut knob
stopper, the base cut around the
edges w/large leaf bands enclosing
rings of cut printies, one side
centered by a medallion engraved
"Mollies Pony 1869," the other
sides w/a scene centering a horse,
some internal bubbles,
10" h. (ILLUS.). **978.00**

Cranberry Cut to Clear Decanter

Cranberry cut to clear, tall slender
tapering cylindrical body,
crosshatched large diamonds
alternating w/large fans below
starbursts in triangles below the tall
slender panel-cut neck, tall panel-
cut pointed clear stopper, 3⅝" d.,
16½" h. (ILLUS.) **210.00**
Decanter, Hobstars, fan & nailhead
cutting **138.00**
Decanter w/original stopper,
cranberry cut to clear, bulbous
body w/fan & diamond cutting,
notched paneled neck, applied cut
handle, faceted stopper, star-cut
base, 13" h. **3,450.00**
Diamond point cut overall, squared
form w/matching cut stoppers,
13¼" h., pr. **468.00**

Green Cut to Clear Decanter

Green cut to clear, overall large plain diamond cutting w/panel cuts around the base & fan cuts above, the tall tapering panel-cut neck w/a flattened rim, panel- and fan-cut teardrop stopper, 3⅝" d., 16⅛" h. (ILLUS.) **195.00**

Hawkes signed, Greek key & flutes design, 13" h. **160.00**

Hoare's Wedding Ring patt., 16" h. **1,900.00**

Libbey signed, teardrop design cut in flutes, 13" h. **150.00**

Mt. Washington's Triple Miter Trellis patt., handled **950.00**

Ship-style, short squatty bulbous body centered by a tall cylindrical neck w/a flaring notched spout, sides cut in hobstars w/cross-cut diamonds in hob points, triple-notched handle, 32-point hobstar in base **550.00**

Teepee-shape, body cut overall w/starred buttons, hexagonal buttons w/cross-hatching, neck cut w/step cutting, 13" h. **295.00**

DISHES, MISCELLANEOUS

Cheese, cov., the domed cover w/facet-cut knob handle above sides cut w/hobstars, the dished base w/a center cut hobstar surrounded by hobstar & fan cutting, plate 8" d., 2 pcs. **460.00**

Cheese, cov., the domed cover cut w/hobstars, crosshatching & fans w/a facet-cut handle, the dished underplate cut w/hobstars, fans & crosshatching w/a sawtooth rim, 9½" d., 2 pcs. **546.00**

Relish, hobstar & mitre cutting, 5¾ x 7¾", 2" h. **75.00**

Relish, oblong, four feathered vesicas w/hobstars, hobstars in tab ends, Straus signed, 4½ x 12" **220.00**

FERNERS

Fluted zipper cutting on upright sides, star & diamond cutting in bottom, 9" d. **165.00**

ICE TUBS & BUCKETS

Cylindrical w/a sterling silver rim & handle, the sides cut w/hobstars, crosshatching & fans, 6" h. **345.00**

Diamond point cutting overall, cylindrical three-footed body w/base drainage opening, 5¾" d., 6" h. **121.00**

Wedding Ring Ice Bucket

Ice bucket, Wedding Ring patt., engraved "Orienta" for Harvey S. Ladew's famous yacht, sterling silver handle & rim, ca. 1891 (ILLUS.) . . **9,500.00**

Ice tub, Hoare's Wedding Ring patt. **1,200.00**

JARS

Cracker jar, cov., barrel-shaped, a band of cross-cut diamonds, silver plate rim, cover & bail handle, 4½" h. **248.00**

Tobacco, cov., paneled cylindrical body w/fine cut Cane panels alternating w/panels of large thumbprints, narrow shoulder to the wide short neck w/rolled rim, matching cut mushroom cover & star-cut base, 6" d., 9" h. **1,150.00**

KNIFE RESTS

Barbell-shaped, facet-cut ends & zipper-cut crossbar, 5¼" l. **39.00**

Cut six-panel "bar," w/honeycomb-cut faceted ball at each end, canary yellow, 4⅜" l. **150.00**

LAMPS

Lamp with Daisy-etched Shade

Table, domed shaded w/etched daisy-like blossoms & pressed leaf sprigs on a metal ring suspending pointed facet-cut prisms, tall tapering cylindrical base w/panel cutting above a section of hobstar & fan cutting over a large face ted knob on the fan-cut domed & scalloped foot (ILLUS.) **990.00**

Russian Cut Ice Cream Set

Ice cream set: 11" d. cake plate, 8½" d. bowl w/upright sides & eight 7" d. plates; Russian cut w/starburst centers, some edge chips, 10 pcs. (ILLUS.) **489.00**

Silver-mounted Cut Glass Lamp

Table, baluster-form body w/bands of strawberry diamond cutting around the rim, center & base alternating w/wide bands of leafy bands w/etched daisy-like blossoms, set on a stepped silver plated floral-pierced base, electrical fittings, w/matching faceted finials, early 20th c., base 14" h., pr. (ILLUS. of one) **489.00**

Table, domed shade above a baluster-form tall base, cut w/crosshatching & notching w/a floral pattern, 22" h. **690.00**

MISCELLANEOUS

Bell, Bergen's Premier patt., 6" h. **400.00**

Fork & spoon, Dorflinger signed, block diamond design handles, pr. **900.00**

Fork & spoon, Dorflinger signed, star diamond design handles, pr. **1,200.00**

Ice cream set: tray & six plates; Libbey signed Sultana patt., tray w/fishtail handles, plates signed w/Libbey sword trademark, tray 13" l., plates 7" d., set of 7 . . . . . . **1,800.00**

Wedding Ring Loving Cup with Silver

Loving cup, Wedding Ring patt., wide ornately stamped sterling silver rim band & two sterling handles, w/original time sheets & documents (ILLUS.) **8,000.00**

Loving cup, three triple-notched handles, prism cutting, sterling silver below rim, 6½" h. **575.00**

Martini shaker, Hawkes signed, engraved Chinese Pheasant w/sterling top **375.00**

Paperweight, model of a closed book, the front cut w/a cross & the initials "C.M.," the back cut w/large squares w/dots **204.00**

Rose bowl, spherical body on an integrated foot, cut overall w/a tiny starburst in diamond design, top rim polished, cut base, 10" d., 9½" h. **575.00**

Scent bottle, lay-down type, slender tapering cylindrical form w/a hinged sterling silver rim & cap, cut w/an overall Cane patt., rim marked "Tiffany & Co. Sterling," 6¼" l. (cover misaligned, glass dauber missing) **173.00**

NAPPIES

Clark's El Paso patt., round w/three facet-cut applied loop handles, feather leaf & vine panels between cut triangular sections, 6" d. **358.00**

Fry signed, round w/scalloped & notched rim, three large flashed hobstars alternating w/three large spearpoints enclosing small hobstars w/a fan cut at the rim, applied ring handle, 6" d.......... **77.00**

Heart-shaped, cut w/three large hobstars above fan-cut corners & divided by panels w/cane cutting, curved triangles & rim fans, fan-cut tab handle at the top (minor flakes) **94.00**

PITCHERS

Hawkes signed, engraved floral band around center, cut nailhead bands at top & base **300.00**

Jug-form, cut w/pinwheels, fans, strawberry diamonds & a central star, notched spout & thumbprint-cut applied handle, 10" h. **105.00**

Tankard, Fry signed, waisted cylindrical form w/large pinwheels above notched prisms, triple-notched applied handle, 8" h. **374.00**

Tankard, waisted cylindrical form, hobstars alternating w/stars & notched prisms, notched applied handle, 8" h. **149.00**

Tankard, waisted cylindrical form, pair of large hobstars alternating w/vesicas enclosing a small hobstar flanked by fans, notched rim w/arched spout, notch-cut applied handle, 8" h. **94.00**

Tankard, Libbey signed, tall waisted cylindrical shape cut w/two large hobstars above a band of feather cutting alternating w/large triangular panels of notch cutting beside fan cuts, 9" h............ **358.00**

Wreath Pattern Pitcher

Tankard, Wreath patt., waisted cylindrical shape w/notched angled rim & wide spout, notched applied handle, cut in hobstars w/panels of large cane cutting, 10" h. (ILLUS.)..................... **143.00**

Water, bulbous body cut w/large hobstars alternating w/small hobstars above diamond panels, tapering step-cut neck w/fans at the sides below the notch-cut rim, facet-cut applied handle, 8" h........................ **468.00**

Water, large hobstars above pairs of triangular panels & panels of zipper cutting, alternating w/vertical bands of three small hobstars w/fans at top & base, facet-cut applied handle, notched rim, 9" h........................ **193.00**

Water, pedestal-based, ovoid body tapering to a flaring plain neck w/rolled spout, applied handle, the body cut w/narrow flutes above & below a medial band of strawberry diamond, possibly early Dorflinger, 10½" h. **358.00**

PLATES

Empire's Berkshire patt., paneled rounded form cut w/large hobstars alternating w/small panels w/two small hobstars, a large center hobstar within a hexagonal panel, notched rim, 9" d. **154.00**

Ice cream, round w/scalloped border of hobstars alternating w/crosshatching, the center w/a large ring-encircled hobstar, similar to Hunt's Royal Variant, 7" d., set of 6...................... **462.00**

PUNCH BOWLS, CUPS & SETS

Bowl & base, each section cut w/large Hobstars alternating w/tusks of buttons & w/hexagonal bars of cane cutting flanking each hobstar, the flaring pedestal base w/a top band of strawberry diamond above smooth bands over the design, the deep bowl w/a scalloped & notched rim cut w/small blazing stars flanked by fan cutting, attributed to Libbey, 12" d., overall 11½" h., 2 pcs. (minor flake on upper side of bowl) **295.00**

Floral & Cane Cut Punch Bowl

Floral & cane cutting, the bulbous incurved bowl w/wide panels of large engraved blossoms w/pressed leafy vines alternating w/engraved vesicas below the wide Harvard-cut rim, on a conical matching base, 12" d., overall 13½" h., 2 pcs. (ILLUS.) **770.00**

Florence hobstars, cut in panels alternating w/four thumbprints, then triangle of stars, border of fans alternating w/squares of crosshatcing & hobstars, bowl & base, 14" d., 13" h., 2 pcs. **2,310.00**

Punch bowl, round bowl w/sawtooth rim above sides cut w/a center hobstar, strawberry diamonds, pinwheels & crosshatching, raised on a tapering pedestal base cut w/hobstars, crosshatching & fans, 9¾" d., 2 pcs. **460.00**

Punch cups, Florence hobstars in panels alternating w/four thumbprints w/crosshatching, then triangle of stars, border of fans w/alternating squares of crosshatching & hobstars, set of 11 (three damaged) **187.00**

Punch ladle, handle cut in hobstars, crosshatching & cane cutting w/internal teardrop, in silver plate handle & bowl by Pairpoint, 15" l. **468.00**

Silver-mounted bowl, deep rounded sides cut w/four large hobstars alternating w/panels of zipper cutting, the rim mounted w/a wide rolled Wilcox silver rim w/grapevine-embossed border marked "Sterling," 12¼" d., 5" h. **1,035.00**

SALT & PEPPER SHAKERS
Zipper & thumbprint cutting, silver lids, 3¼" h., pr. **66.00**

SPOONERS
Harvard patt., deep cut **168.00**

TOOTHPICK HOLDERS
Pitkins & Brooks, strawberry diamond & fan, notched rim, pedestal base **75.00**

TRAYS
Bread, sled-shape, four hobstars w/diamond & fans **90.00**

Dorflinger, intricate vesica, hobstar w/chain of hobstar border, 10½ x 11½" **725.00**

Fry signed, round three-footed form w/slightly dished scalloped & notched edges, three large flashed hobstars alternating w/vesicas & fans, 10½" d. **165.00**

Hawkes Gladys patt., round, 13" d. . . **625.00**

Hawkes signed, lattice & rosette design, 15" h. **16,000.00**

Ice cream, rectangular, Dorflinger, star & diamond design, 8 x 14" **750.00**

Ice cream, oval w/a chain of hobstars around the sides w/crosshatching, 32 point hobstar at each end, rayed center, 8½ x 14" **385.00**

Hawkes Ice Cream Tray

Ice cream, rectangular, Hawkes signed, hobstar center surrounded by small hobstars alternating w/crosshatched diamonds & fans, a large eight-point star in each corner, heavy blank, 10 x 14" (ILLUS.) **425.00**

Ice cream, oblong w/large rounded scallops around the sides each enclosing a large hobstar alternating w/crosshatching, rectangular center panel w/fine facet cutting surrounding a large round central hobstar, similar to Hunt's Royal Variant, 11 x 15" **715.00**

Libbey's Ellsmere patt., round, center hobstar w/large six-point star surrounded by six smaller hobstars alternating w/panels of cane cutting, outer border of fine notched ribbings, 12" d. **3,000.00**

Perfume tray, oval, Chrysanthemum patt. variant, 7 x 10" **225.00**

Relish dish, canoe-shaped, Harvard patt., 5 x 12" **275.00**

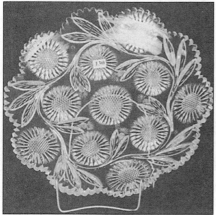

Sunflower Design Tray

Sunflower design, flower-shaped cut w/eleven flowers & vining stems, scalloped & notched rim, 14" d. (ILLUS.)................... **625.00**

Tuthill's Four Fruits patt., oranges, cherries, pears & berries cutting, 12" d. **2,200.00**

Tuthill's Vintage patt., round, 10" d....................... **975.00**

TUMBLERS

Libbey-signed, Hobstars at top above band of feather cutting alternating w/a large triangle of notched cutting & fans, set of 9.... **523.00**

Overall cutting, detailed bird on branches of oak leaves & primrose, hexagonal buttons around base, late 19th c., set of 4............. **112.00**

Two hobstars & two ovals, flanked by fans & strawberry diamond, 16-rayed base, early 20th c., 3⅛" h..... **22.00**

VASES

Bud-type, tall slender trumpet-form body w/vertical narrow bands of rainbow colors cut w/crosshatching & swirls, on a flat clear star-cut foot, 12" h.................... **358.00**

Cylindrical, flaring foot & mouth, large cut thumbprints above cut hobstars at top & bottom w/bands of crosshatching & notching up the sides, 20" h. **1,150.00**

Cylindrical tapering body, flared & notched rim, cut w/vertical tapering bands of hobstars alternating w/deep grooves, 16" h....................... **633.00**

Cylindrical w/distended midsection, w/three rayed sunflowers, fans & cross-cut diamonds, 8" h................. **94.00**

Fry signed, trumpet-form, tall flaring sides w/two-lobed notched rim, cut w/hobstars alternating w/small panels of cane cutting, 18" h........................ **413.00**

Harvard cutting overall, tall footed waisted cylindrical body w/a flaring scalloped rim, 16" h........ **660.00**

Hobstars, corset-shaped w/large hobstars at the rim & base joined by a band of three small hobstars all alternating w/narrow bands of notch cutting, rayed base, 11" h........................ **105.00**

Hobstars & florals, trumpet-shaped w/scalloped & notched rim & widely flaring base, the rim cut w/hobstars above bands of zipper cutting alternating w/full-length pointed arch panels of engraved flower heads & pressed leaf bands, 12" h........................ **66.00**

Libbey signed, tall waisted cylindrical form w/a four-lobed flaring notched rim, cut w/long alternating panels of hobstars & notched prism, 12" h. **138.00**

Pinwheels, trumpet-shaped w/large pinwheels around the rim alternating w/smaller flashed stars all above crosshatching & a paneled zipper-cut stem on a round tar-cut foot, 12" h.......... **66.00**

Tapered form w/a faceted foot, the neck cut w/notching & the body cut w/strawberry diamonds, crosshatching, fans & hobstars, 10" h........................ **690.00**

Trumpet-form, the slender flaring body cut w/narrow vesicas w/three small hobstars flanked by a cut flower leaf design & diamonds & fans, knopped stem on round foot, approximately 15" h........................ **690.00**

Fine Tall Cut Glass Vase

Waisted tall body, the wide rounded shoulder w/a notched & scalloped rim tapering in & flaring out at the base, large hobstars above long stripes of small diamond & hobstar clusters alternating w/full-length stripes of diamond & hobstar clusters, unsigned, some small interior rim chips, 16" h. (ILLUS.) **1,840.00**

Wide ovoid body, short flaring & scalloped neck cut w/panels & narrow bands above the panel-cut shoulder & the body cut w/large almond-shaped pinwheels alternating w/small hobstars, fans & crosshatching, large (chip to slightly ground rim) **805.00**

WATER SETS

Water set: pitcher & 10 tumblers; Libbey signed Florence patt., 11 pcs. **650.00**

CUT VELVET

This mold-blown, two-layer glassware is usually lined in white with a colored exterior with a molded pattern. Pieces have a satiny finish, giving them a 'velvety' appearance. The Mt. Washington Glass Company was one of several firms which produced this glass.

Cut Velvet Rose Bowl & Vase

Rose bowl, ovoid egg-shaped w/six-crimp rim, deep blue satin Diamond Quilted patt., white lining, 3½" d., 3½" h. (ILLUS. left) **$135.00**

Vase, 6" h., 3⅜" d., bottle-form, ovoid body tapering to a tall slender cylindrical neck, heavenly blue satin Diamond Quilted patt., white lining (ILLUS. right) **125.00**

Vase, 6¾" h., footed bottle-form, bulbous ovoid body tapering to a slender cylindrical neck, blue Diamond Quilted patt., satin finish **110.00**

Vase, 7" h., footed squatty bulbous body centered by a swelled ring at the base of the tall slender flaring cylindrical neck w/a widely flaring four-lobed crimped rim, rose pink . . **138.00**

Cut Velvet Bottle-form Vase

Vase, 7½" h., 3½" d., bottle-form, bulbous base tapering to a tall slender cylindrical neck w/a twist in the ribbing, blue Diamond Quilted patt. (ILLUS.). **98.00**

Vase, 9" h., ovoid body tapering to a tall gently flaring cylindrical neck w/a flat rim, blue Ribbon patt. **138.00**

Vase, 9½" h., 6" d., bright yellow satin Diamond Quilted patt., crimped frosted clear edge flaring over rim **325.00**

CZECHOSLOVAKIAN

At the close of World War I, Czechoslovakia was declared an independent republic and immediately developed a large export industry. Czechoslovakian glass factories produced a wide variety of colored and hand-painted glasswares from about 1918 until 1939, when the country was occupied by Germany at the outset of World War II. Between the wars, fine quality blown glasswares were produced along with a deluge of cheaper, vividly colored spatterwares for the American market. Subsequent production was primarily limited to cut crystal or Bohemian-type etched wares for the American market. Although it was marked, much Czechoslovakian glass is mistaken for the work of Tiffany, Loetz, or other glass artisans it imitates. It is often misrepresented and overpriced.

With the recent break-up of Czechoslovakia into two republics, such wares should gain added collector appeal.

Czechoslovakian Jade Bowl

Bowl, 10½" d., 5" h., footed, a half-round bottom below the deep & widely flaring upper half, raised on three large knob feet, the body in green Jade w/applied black feet & rim band, attributed to Michael Powolny (ILLUS.) **$288.00**

Candelabrum, three-light, overlay, cranberry cut to clear, a heavy cut square domed foot below the baluster stem cut w/a band of crosshatching & supporting a panel-cut small bowl w/an upright scalloped rim centered by a tall slender shaped cylindrical post w/a panel-cut rolled socket fitted w/a clear pointed facet-cut insert, two clear ropetwist arms extending from the base bowl & flanking the central post, each arm ending in a cut bobeche & tulip-form socket, clear teardrop prisms from bobeche & chains of clear bead swags from top socket to side sockets, signed, 24" h. **2,090.00**

Candlesticks, tortoiseshell design in browns, marked, 8½" h., pr. **350.00**

Chalice, black amethyst w/silver overlay decoration of figures, signed, 7½" h. **300.00**

Vase, 5⅛" h., a wide bullet-form bowl w/incurved rim in mottled red internally striped in black, raised on three canted red applied legs w/support struts to the vase sides, polished at the top **259.00**

Glass & Wrought-Iron Vase

Vase, 9" h., squatty double-lobed body w/a low widely flaring neck, glass free-blown into a reticulated wrought-iron frame, glass in splotched blue, orange & green cased in white, stamped on base "Czechoslovakia" (ILLUS.) **460.00**

Vase, 13½" h., jack-in-the-pulpit form, a bell-form base below the tall slender cylindrical body topped by a jack-in-the-pulpit rim w/the back pulled into a point, brilliant yellow w/clear overlay, a black rim band **201.00**

Vase, 14¾" h., tall tapering ovoid body w/a small flattened shoulder centered by a short flaring neck, clear case in white opal w/an internal layer of bright red, orange & olive green overall splotched decoration, exterior iridized finish, base stamped "Czechoslovakia" . . . **518.00**

D'ARGENTAL

Glass known by this name is co-called after its producer, who fashioned fine cameo pieces in St. Louis, France late last century and up to 1918.

D'Argental Mark

Cameo atomizer, cylindrical amber bottle overlaid in green & brown w/an etched landscape of leafy trees w/wild geese in flight, signed on the side, w/a gilt-metal fitting marked "Le Parisien Made in France" & "BTE. S.G.D.G.," 4" h. **$805.00**

Cameo vase, 6¾" h., slender ovoid body tapering to a short cylindrical neck, frosted pastel green layered in greyish black & etched as blossoms, pods & leafy poppy plants, signed at the side. **431.00**

Cameo vase, 8" h., ovoid body w/a tapering neck, yellow ground overlaid in cranberry, etched to depict maple branches laden w/pods & foliage, cameo signature **403.00**

D'Argental Scenic Cameo Vase

Cameo vase, 10" h., simple ovoid body tapering to a flat rim, fiery opalescent amber layered in burgundy red & maroon, etched overall w/an expansive landscape w/distant buildings & a castle beyond, signed at lower edge (ILLUS.) **1,150.00**

Cameo vase, 11 7/8" h., footed tapering cylindrical form w/a short everted rim, frosted orange overlaid in green, cut w/a tall leafy tree against a marshy landscape, the foot of solid green, cameo signature (minor foot rim polishing) **1,431.00**

DAUM NANCY

This fine glass, much of it cameo, was made by Auguste and Antonin Daum, who founded a factory in 1875 in Nancy, France. Most of their cameo and enameled glass was made from the 1890s into the early 20th century.

Daum Nancy Marks

Bowl, 6¾" d., 3⅛" h., deep flaring sides, mottled yellowish pink w/metal foil inclusions, blown into a simple lattice-form wrought-iron framework, signed "Daum Nancy - L. Majorelle" on base **$1,093.00**

Daum Cameo Glass Ewer

Cameo ewer, 12" h., tall ovoid body tapering to a flaring neck w/arched spout, clear frosted body layered in bright rose red & deeply etched as convolvulus blossoms w/matching flowers & decorated on the silver mounts at the round foot, scrolled loop handle, rim & hinged domed cover, impressed silver hallmarks & "Sterling," base signed "Daum - Nancy" & the cross of Lorraine (ILLUS.) **4,888.00**

Cameo vase, 16" h., a bulbous cushion foot tapering sharply to a slender stem gradually swelling to an ovoid upper body w/a closed rim, opalescent grey overlaid w/bright orange & deep forest green, finely cut w/daisies above leafage, the blossoms finely wheel-carved, the ground selectively *martelé*, signed in cameo & the Cross of Lorraine, ca. 1900 . . . . . **6,325.00**

Cameo vase, 19¼" h., a wide cushion foot below the tall gently tapering cylindrical body, grey streaked w/tangerine & overlaid in charcoal grey & umber, cut w/a verdant riverside landscape w/leafy trees & grasses in the foreground, signed in cameo "DAUM NANCY" w/the Cross of Lorraine, ca. 1900 . . . . . . **3,450.00**

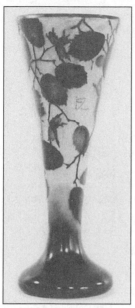

Daum Nancy Cameo Vase

Cameo vase, 21" h., tall trumpet-form body on a cushion foot, grey mottled w/orange & yellow, overlaid in brown & cameo-cut w/pendent leafy branches, signed in cameo "Daum Nancy France" (ILLUS.) . . **5,175.00**

Flowerpot, tapering cylindrical body w/a flatted flaring rim, heavy walled clear molded form internally decorated by tiny overall bubbles, engraved on the lower edge "Daum - Nancy - France" w/the Cross of Lorraine, 5¾" h. **345.00**

Vase, 4⅜" h., a cushion foot supports a slender ovoid body tapering to a small flared mouth, grey streaked w/pale blue, white & grass green, cut w/a cluster of trees in the foreground, a broad lake, forest & rolling hills in the background, enameled in shades of green, brown & grey, signed in enamel "DAUM NANCY" w/the Cross of Lorraine, ca. 1910 . . . . **2,070.00**

Vase, 4½" h., footed squatty bulbous base w/a wide shoulder centered by a tall cylindrical neck, fiery opalescent amber w/red striations, etched w/thistle pods & thorny stems, enameled in burgundy red, signed on the side **805.00**

Vase, 4¾" h., a flared foot tapering to a swelled ovoid body w/a wide flat mouth, grey internally shaded w/opalescence, mottled w/pink & green, textured & cut w/dandelions & leafage & the phrase "Comme la plume au vent," enameled in charcoal & brown, the whole trimmed w/gilt, signed in gilt "DAUM NANCY" w/the Cross of Lorraine, ca. 1900 . . . . **2,300.00**

Vase, 5½" h., bulbous baluster form tapering to a flaring foot & w/a short, wide neck, four pinched-in sides, enamel-painted on yellow & amethyst frosted ground w/orange blossoms on tall spiked leaves, painted signature on side **1,610.00**

Vase, 5½" h., footed spherical body, monochromatic translucent yellow w/alternating glossy & etched narrow panels up the sides, inscribed mark on the base **345.00**

Vase, 6¾" h., a cushion foot & cylindrical pedestal supporting a wide squatty bulbous body tapering to a short neck w/a widely flaring flattened mouth, clear frosted body enamel-decorated w/emerald green nuts on a leafy branch highlighted in gold, etched signature **880.00**

Vase, 7" h., short round pedestal foot supporting a deep cup-form body w/a wide, flat rim, clear w/rose red mottled powders below bright royal blue border, inscribed mark on base edge **431.00**

Vase, 7⅜" h., tall rectangular block form, grey walls w/rose pink shaded interior, cut w/oleander blossoms & leafage & trimmed in gilt, signed in enamel "Daum - Nancy" w/a Cross of Lorraine, ca. 1900. **690.00**

Vase, 9½" h., flattened cylindrical mouth tapering to a bulbous base, grey mottled w/pale blue, carved & enameled w/an early spring landscape, signed in enamel **4,025.00**

Vase, 10¼" h., tall swelled cylindrical body in grey mottled w/pale blue & cut & enameled w/a fall landscape of tall colorful trees, signed in enamel **5,160.00**

Rare Daum Nancy Vase

Vase, 10¾" h., tall slender slightly
swelled cylindrical body w/a thick
cushion foot, slightly tapered at the
top to a flattened flaring mouth,
mottled white, clear & deep
purplish blue, etched overall &
enameled w/naturalized stalks of
wheat & grasses w/gold accents &
trim, base marked in gold "Daum"
(ILLUS.) **5,750.00**

Vase, 13" h., wide ovoid body
tapering slightly to a short flaring
wide neck, grey internally mottled
w/pale salmon & decorated w/black
speckles, overlaid in orange &
acid-etched & cut w/overall large
stylized round flowers & large
leaves, signed in intaglio "DAUM
NANCY - FRANCE" w/the Cross of
Lorraine, ca. 1925 . . . . **3,450.00**

Vase, 14⅜" h., a cushion foot
tapering to a slender stem gently
flaring to a tall body w/a swelled
shoulder tapering inward to a
small, flat mouth, green shading up
to yellow & blue w/grey at the top,
cut w/stems of primroses enameled
in shades of green, brown, pink &
yellow, engraved signature,
ca. 1900 . . . . **3,450.00**

Vase, 15¼" h., a rectangular thick
foot w/notched corners supporting
a tall trumpet-form body, palest
yellow decorated up the sides
w/acid-etched bands of rectangular
geometric designs, inscribed

Acid-etched Daum Nancy Vase

"DAUM - NANCY - FRANCE" w/the
Cross of Lorraine, ca. 1925
(ILLUS.) **3,105.00**

DEPRESSION

*The phrase "Depression Glass" is used by
collectors to denote a specific kind of transparent
glass produced primarily as tablewares, in
crystal, amber, blue, green, pink, milky-white,
etc., during the late 1920s and 1930s when this
country was in the midst of a financial
depression. Made to sell inexpensively, it was
turned out by such producers as Jeannette,
Hocking, Westmoreland, Indiana and other
glass companies. We compile prices on all the
major Depression Glass patterns. Collectors
should consult Depression Glass references for
information on those patterns and pieces which
have been reproduced.*

*For a more extensive listing of Depression
Glass, please refer to* Antique Trader Books
American Pressed Glass & Bottles Price Guide.

ADAM, Jeanette Glass Co., 1932-34 (Process-etched)

Ashtray, clear, 4½" sq. $11.00
Ashtray, green, 4½" sq. 24.00
Ashtray, pink, 4½" sq. 30.00
Bowl, dessert, 4¾" sq., pink 18.00
Bowl, cereal, 5¾" sq., green. 44.00
Bowl, cereal, 5¾" sq., pink 54.00
Bowl, nappy, 7¾" sq., green. 26.00
Bowl, nappy, 7¾" sq., pink 26.00
Bowl, 9" sq., green 28.00
Bowl, 9" sq., pink 20.00
Bowl, cov., 9" sq., green. 68.00
Bowl, cov., 9" sq., pink 67.00

Bowl, 10" oval vegetable, green 25.00
Bowl, 10" oval vegetable, pink 33.00
Butter dish, cov., green 307.00
Cake plate, footed, green, 10" sq. 29.00
Cake plate, footed, pink, 10" sq. 26.00
Candlestick, green, 4" h. 42.00
Coaster, green, 3¼" sq. 21.00
Coaster, pink, 3¼" sq. 23.00
Creamer, green 21.00
Creamer, pink 23.00
Cup, green 21.00
Cup, pink. 27.00
Cup & saucer, green 28.00
Cup & saucer, pink. 33.00
Pitcher, 32 oz., round base, clear. 19.00
Pitcher, 32 oz., round base, pink 53.00
Pitcher, 8" h., 32 oz., cone-shaped,
    clear. 35.00
Pitcher, 8" h., 32 oz., cone-shaped,
    green. 43.00
Pitcher, 8" h., 32 oz., cone-shaped,
    pink 38.00
Plate, grill, 9" sq., green. 20.00
Plate, salad, round, pink 60.00
Plate, salad, round, yellow. 110.00
Plate, sherbet, 6" sq., green. 24.00
Plate, sherbet, 6" sq., pink. 9.00
Plate, salad, 7¾" sq., green. 16.00
Plate, salad, 7¾" sq., pink 19.00
Plate, dinner, 9" sq., green. 28.00
Plate, dinner, 9" sq., pink. 37.00
Relish dish, two-part, green, 8" sq. . . . 25.00
Relish dish, two-part, pink, 8" sq.. . . . . 25.00
Salt & pepper shakers, footed,
    green, 4" h., pr. 88.00
Salt & pepper shakers, footed, pink,
    4" h., pr. 81.00
Saucer, round, green 7.00
Saucer, round, pink. 8.00
Saucer, pink, 6" sq.. . . . . 8.00
Sherbet, green, 3" h.. . . . . 38.00
Sherbet, pink, 3" h. 32.00
Sugar bowl, cov., green 25.00
Sugar bowl, cov., pink 42.00
Tumbler, cone-shaped, green,
    4½" h., 7 oz. 29.00
Tumbler, cone-shaped, pink, 4½" h.,
    7 oz.. . . . . 31.00
Tumbler, iced tea, green, 5½" h.,
    9 oz.. . . . . 57.00
Tumbler, iced tea, pink 5½" h., 9 oz. . . 74.00
Vase, 7½" h., green. 68.00
Vase, 7½" h., pink. 300.00

AMERICAN SWEETHEART, MacBeth-Evans Glass Co., 1930-36 (Process-etched)

Bowl, cream soup, 4½" d., Monax . . . 123.00
Bowl, cream soup, 4½" d., pink 86.00
Bowl, cereal, 6" d., Cremax 8.00
Bowl, cereal, 6" d., Monax 16.00

Bowl, cereal, 6" d., pink 16.00
Bowl, berry, 9" d., Cremax 29.00
Bowl, berry, 9" d., Monax 63.00
Bowl, berry, 9" d., pink 56.00
Bowl, soup w/flanged rim, 9½" d.,
    Monax. 78.00
Bowl, soup w/flanged rim, 9½" d.,
    pink 69.00
Bowl, 11" oval vegetable, Monax 79.00
Bowl, 11" oval vegetable, pink 78.00
Console bowl, blue, 18" d. 850.00
Console bowl, Monax, 18" d. 574.00
Console bowl, ruby red, 18" d. 2,250.00
Creamer, footed, blue. 95.00
Creamer, footed, Monax. 11.00
Creamer, footed, pink 15.00
Creamer, footed, ruby red. 106.00
Creamer & cov. sugar bowl,
    Monax, pr. 233.00
Cup, Monax. 10.00
Cup, pink. 17.00
Cup, ruby red 91.00
Cup & saucer, blue 121.00
Cup & saucer, Monax 13.00
Cup & saucer, pink. 22.00
Cup & saucer, ruby red 121.00
Lamp shade, Monax. 630.00
Pitcher, 7½" h., 60 oz., jug-type,
    pink 615.00
Pitcher, 8" h., 80 oz., pink. 622.00
Plate, bread & butter, 6" d., Monax. . . . 6.00
Plate, bread & butter, 6" d., pink. 6.00
Plate, salad, 8" d., blue 110.00
Plate, salad, 8" d., Monax. 9.00
Plate, salad, 8" d., pink 12.00
Plate, salad, 8" d., ruby red. 68.00
Plate, luncheon, 9" d., Monax 14.00
Plate, dinner, 9¾" d., Monax. 25.00
Plate, dinner, 9¾" d., pink. 39.00
Plate, dinner, 10¼" d., Monax. 27.00
Plate, dinner, 10¼" d., pink. 40.00
Plate, chop, 11" d., Monax 17.00
Plate, salver, 12" d., blue 159.00
Plate, salver, 12" d., Monax 19.00
Plate, salver, 12" d., pink 24.00
Plate, 15½" d., w/center handle,
    blue 725.00
Plate, 15½" d., w/center handle,
    Monax. 223.00
Plate, 15½" d., w/center handle,
    ruby red. 242.00
Platter, 13" oval, Monax 87.00
Platter, 13" oval, pink 57.00
Salt & pepper shakers, footed,
    Monax, pr.. . . . . 364.00
Salt & pepper shakers, footed, pink,
    pr. 218.00
Saucer, blue 31.00
Saucer, Monax 2.00
Saucer, pink 4.00
Saucer, ruby red. 25.00
Sherbet, metal holder, clear 14.00

Sherbet, footed, pink, 3¾" h. **21.00**
Sherbet, footed, Monax, 4¼" h. **22.00**
Sherbet, footed, pink, 4¼" h. **17.00**
Sugar bowl, cov., Monax (only) **355.00**
Sugar bowl, open, blue **90.00**
Sugar bowl, open, Monax **7.00**
Sugar bowl, open, pink **15.00**
Sugar bowl, open, ruby red **90.00**
Tidbit server, three-tier, Monax **241.00**
Tidbit server, three-tier, ruby red . . . **813.00**
Tidbit server, two-tier, Monax **99.00**
Tidbit server, two-tier, pink **56.00**
Tidbit server, two-tier, ruby red **220.00**
Tumbler, pink, 3½" h., 5 oz. **101.00**
Tumbler, pink, 4¼" h., 9 oz. **87.00**
Tumbler, pink, 4¾" h., 10 oz. **95.00**
Water set: 7½" h. pitcher & four 9 oz.
   tumblers; pink, 5 pcs. **525.00**

AUNT POLLY, U.S. Glass Co., late 1920s

Bowl, 4¾" d., berry, blue. **16.00**
Bowl, 4¾" d., berry, green **7.00**
Bowl, 4¾" d., 2" h., blue **18.00**
Bowl, 4¾" d., 2" h., green. **8.00**
Bowl, 7¼" d., oval, handled pickle,
   blue **29.00**
Bowl, 7¼" d., oval, handled pickle,
   green **10.00**
Bowl, 7⅞" d., large berry, blue. **40.00**
Bowl, 7⅞" d., large berry, green **16.00**
Bowl, 8⅜" d., oval, blue. **113.00**
Butter dish, cov., blue **203.00**
Butter dish, cov., green **225.00**
Candy dish, footed, two-handled,
   blue **30.00**
Candy dish, footed, two-handled,
   green **22.00**
Creamer, blue. **46.00**
Pitcher, blue, 8" h., 48 oz. **200.00**
Plate, sherbet, 6" d., blue **11.00**
Plate, sherbet, 6" d., iridescent. **13.00**
Plate, luncheon, 8" d., blue. **10.00**
Sherbet, blue **13.00**
Sherbet, green **11.00**
Sherbet, iridescent **6.00**
Sugar bowl, cov., blue **210.00**
Sugar bowl, cov., green **38.00**
Sugar bowl, cov., iridescent. **65.00**
Tumbler, water, blue, 3⅝" h., 8 oz.. . . **29.00**
Vase, 6½" h., blue. **47.00**
Vase, 6½" h., green. **26.00**
Vase, 6½" h., iridescent **24.00**

BLOCK or Block Optic, Hocking Glass Co., 1919-33 (Press-mold)

Bowl, berry, 4¼" d., green **9.00**
Bowl, berry, 4¼" d., pink. **2.00**
Bowl, berry, 4½" d., green **29.00**
Bowl, cereal, 5¼" d., green. **15.00**
Bowl, cereal, 5¼" d., pink. **32.00**

Bowl, salad, 7" d., green. **39.00**
Bowl, salad, 7" d., pink **11.00**
Bowl, large berry, 8½" d., green. **29.00**
Bowl, large berry, 8½" d., pink **22.00**
Butter dish, cov., rectangular, green,
   3" x 5" **42.00**
Butter dish, cov., rectangular, green
   clambroth, 3" x 5" **350.00**
Candlesticks, amber, 1¾" h., pr. **89.00**
Candlesticks, green, 1¾" h., pr. **112.00**
Candlesticks, pink, 1¾" h., pr. **79.00**
Candy jar, cov., green, 2¼" h. **59.00**
Candy jar, cov., pink, 2¼" h. **51.00**
Candy jar, cov., yellow, 2¼" h. **61.00**
Candy jar, cov., clear, 6¼" h. **23.00**
Candy jar, cov., green, 6¼" h. **61.00**
Candy jar, cov., pink, 6¼" h. **128.00**
Compote, 4" d., cone-shaped, green. . **27.00**
Compote, 4" d., cone-shaped, pink . . . **17.00**
Creamer, various styles, green. **14.00**
Creamer, various styles, pink **14.00**
Creamer, various styles, yellow **12.00**
Cup, various styles, green **6.00**
Cup, various styles, pink. **6.00**
Cup, various styles, yellow **7.00**
Cup & saucer, green **16.00**
Cup & saucer, pink. **11.00**
Cup & saucer, yellow. **11.00**
Goblet, wine, pink, 3½" h. **35.00**
Goblet, cocktail, clear, 4" h. **8.00**
Goblet, cocktail, green, 4" h. **32.00**
Goblet, cocktail, pink, 4" h. **33.00**
Goblet, wine, clear, 4½" h. **9.00**
Goblet, wine, green, 4½" h. **32.00**
Goblet, wine, pink, 4½" h. **32.00**
Goblet, clear, 5¾" h., 9 oz. **12.00**
Goblet, green, 5¾" h., 9 oz. **29.00**
Goblet, pink, 5¾" h., 9 oz. **31.00**
Goblet, yellow, 5¾" h., 9 oz. **31.00**
Goblet, clear, 7¼" h., 9 oz. **12.00**
Goblet, green, 7¼" h., 9 oz. **19.00**
Goblet, pink, 7¼" h., 9 oz. **27.00**
Goblet, yellow, 7¼" h., 9 oz. **36.00**
Ice bucket, w/metal bail handle,
   clear. **24.00**
Ice bucket, w/metal bail handle,
   green. **37.00**
Ice bucket, w/metal bail handle, pink . . **61.00**
Ice tub, tab handles, clear **16.00**
Ice tub, tab handles, green. **47.00**
Ice tub, tab handles, pink **86.00**
Mug, green **38.00**
Pitcher, 7⅝" h., 54 oz., bulbous,
   green. **67.00**
Pitcher, 8" h., 80 oz., clear **37.00**
Pitcher, 8" h., 80 oz., green **54.00**
Pitcher, 8½" h., 54 oz., clear **22.00**
Pitcher, 8½" h., 54 oz., green. **48.00**
Pitcher, 8½" h., 54 oz., pink. **38.00**
Plate, sherbet, 6" d., green **3.00**
Plate, sherbet, 6" d., pink **3.00**
Plate, sherbet, 6" d., yellow. **3.00**

Plate, luncheon, 8" d., clear 3.00
Plate, luncheon, 8" d., green. 6.00
Plate, luncheon, 8" d., pink 5.00
Plate, luncheon, 8" d., yellow 6.00
Plate, dinner, 9" d., clear. 5.00
Plate, dinner, 9" d., green 25.00
Plate, dinner, 9" d., pink 21.00
Plate, dinner, 9" d., yellow. 34.00
Plate, grill, 9" d., clear. 5.00
Plate, grill, 9" d., green 16.00
Plate, grill, 9" d., yellow. 45.00
Plate, sandwich, 10¼" d., clear. 10.00
Plate, sandwich, 10¼" d., green 38.00
Plate, sandwich, 10¼" d., pink 26.00
Salt & pepper shakers, footed, clear,
    pr. 22.00
Salt & pepper shakers, footed,
    green, pr. 43.00
Salt & pepper shakers, footed, pink,
    pr. 81.00
Salt & pepper shakers, footed,
    yellow, pr. 68.00
Salt & pepper shakers, squat,
    green, pr. 90.00
Sandwich server w/center handle,
    green 65.00
Sandwich server w/center handle,
    pink 47.00
Saucer, green, 5¾" d. 9.00
Saucer, pink, 5¾" d. 7.00
Saucer, green, 6⅛" d. 10.00
Saucer, pink, 6⅛" d. 5.00
Saucer, yellow, 6⅛" d. 7.00

Block Sherbet

Sherbet, cone-shaped, footed, green
    (ILLUS.). 5.00
Sherbet, cone-shaped, footed, pink . . . 12.00
Sherbet, cone-shaped, footed, yellow . . 9.00
Sherbet, stemmed, clear, 3¼" h.,
    5½ oz. 6.00
Sherbet, stemmed, green, 3¼" h. ,
    5½ oz. 6.00
Sherbet, stemmed, pink, 3¼" h. ,
    5½ oz. 6.00
Sherbet, stemmed, yellow, 3¼" h.,
    5½ oz. 8.00
Sherbet, stemmed, clear, 4¾" h.,
    6 oz. 6.00
Sherbet, stemmed, green, 4¾" h.,
    6 oz. 15.00

Sherbet, stemmed, pink, 4¾" h.,
    6 oz. 15.00
Sherbet, stemmed, yellow, 4¾" h.,
    6 oz. 15.00
Sugar bowl, open, various styles,
    clear. 9.00
Sugar bowl, open, various styles,
    green 12.00
Sugar bowl, open, various styles,
    pink 15.00
Sugar bowl, open, various styles,
    yellow 12.00
Tumble-up set: bottle & 3" h.
    tumbler: green, 2 pcs. 68.00
Tumbler, whiskey, clear, 2¼" h.,
    2 oz. 9.00
Tumbler, whiskey, green, 2¼" h.,
    2 oz. 21.00
Tumbler, whiskey, pink, 2¼" h., 2 oz.. . 30.00
Tumbler, footed, green, 2⅝" h., 3 oz. . . 20.00
Tumbler, footed, pink, 2⅝" h., 3 oz. . . . 26.00
Tumbler, juice, clear, 3½" h., 5 oz. 6.00
Tumbler, juice, green, 3½" h., 5 oz. . . . 20.00
Tumbler, juice, pink, 3½" h., 5 oz. 24.00
Tumbler, footed, clear, 9 oz. 5.00
Tumbler, footed, green, 9 oz. 23.00
Tumbler, footed, pink, 9 oz. 16.00
Tumbler, footed, yellow, 9 oz. 21.00
Tumbler, clear, 3⅞" h., 9½ oz. 5.00
Tumbler, green, 3⅞" h., 9½ oz. 18.00
Tumbler, pink, 3⅞" h., 9½ oz.. . . . . 15.00
Tumbler, iced tea, footed, green,
    6" h., 10 oz. 32.00
Tumbler, green, 5" h., 10 to 11 oz. 18.00
Tumbler, pink, 5" h., 10 to 11 oz. 17.00
Tumbler, green, 4⅞" h., 12 oz. 23.00
Tumbler, yellow, 4⅞" h., 12 oz. 7.00
Tumbler, green, 5¼" h., 15 oz. 26.00
Tumbler, pink, 5¼" h., 15 oz. 37.00
Tumbler-up bottle, green. 17.00
Vase, 5¾" h., green. 288.00

BUBBLE, Bullseye or Provincial, Anchor-Hocking Glass Co., 1940-65 (Press-mold)

Bowl, berry, 4" d., blue 16.00
Bowl, berry, 4" d., clear. 6.00
Bowl, berry, 4" d., green 10.00
Bowl, berry, 4" d., milk white. 4.00
Bowl, berry, 4" d., pink 15.00
Bowl, fruit, 4½" d., blue. 12.00
Bowl, fruit, 4½" d., clear 4.00
Bowl, cereal, 5¼" d., blue. 14.00
Bowl, cereal, 5¼" d., clear 6.00
Bowl, cereal, 5¼" d., green. 12.00
Bowl, soup, 7¾" d., blue. 14.00
Bowl, soup, 7¾" d., clear 6.00
Bowl, soup, 7¾" d., pink. 9.00
Bowl, 8⅜" d., clear 16.00
Bowl, 8⅜" d., green 16.00

Bowl, 8⅜" d., milk white 5.00
Bowl, 8⅜" d., pink. 7.00
Bowl, 8⅜" d., ruby red 19.00
Bowl, 9" d., flanged, blue 13.00
Bowl, 9" d., flanged, milk white. 30.00
Candlesticks, clear, pr. 13.00
Creamer, blue. 34.00
Creamer, clear 6.00
Creamer, green. 12.00
Creamer, milk white 4.00
Cup, blue 4.00
Cup, clear 4.00
Cup, green 9.00
Cup, ruby red 8.00
Cup & saucer, blue 6.00
Cup & saucer, clear 5.00
Cup & saucer, green 11.00
Cup & saucer, milk white 3.00
Cup & saucer, pink. 4.00
Cup & saucer, ruby red 13.00
Dinner service, 4 dinner plates, 4
  cups & saucers, four 5½" d. bowls,
  creamer & sugar bowl, 18 pcs.,
  green 190.00
Dinner service for 4 w/serving
  pieces, blue, 31 pcs. 200.00
Lamps, clear (electric), pr. 56.00
Pitcher w/ice lip, 64 oz., clear. 65.00
Plate, bread & butter, 6¾" d., green 4.00
Plate, dinner, 9⅜" d., blue. 10.00
Plate, dinner, 9⅜" d., clear 6.00
Plate, dinner, 9⅜" d., green 23.00
Plate, dinner, 9⅜" d., ruby red 22.00
Plate, grill, 9⅜" d., blue. 18.00
Plate, grill, 9⅜" d., clear 8.00
Platter, 12" oval, blue 13.00
Platter, 12" oval, clear. 13.00
Saucer, blue 4.00
Saucer, green. 4.00
Saucer, milk white. 2.00
Saucer, ruby red 5.00
Sugar bowl, open, blue 20.00
Sugar bowl, open, clear 6.00
Sugar bowl, open, green 11.00
Sugar bowl, open, milk white 5.00
Tidbit server, two tier, blue 44.00
Tidbit server, two-tier, ruby red 50.00
Tumbler, juice, clear, 6 oz. 7.00
Tumbler, juice, green, 6 oz. 11.00
Tumbler, juice, ruby red, 6 oz. 10.00
Tumbler, old fashioned, ruby red,
  3¼" h., 8 oz. 12.00
Tumbler, ruby red, 9 oz. 11.00
Tumbler, water, clear, 9 oz. 7.00
Tumbler, iced tea, clear, 4½" h.,
  12 oz.. . . . . 16.00
Tumbler, iced tea, ruby red, 4½" h.,
  12 oz.. . . . . 16.00
Tumbler, lemonade, clear, 5⅞" h.,
  16 oz. 14.00
Tumbler, lemonade, ruby red, 5⅞" h.,
  16 oz.. . . . . 16.00

CAMEO or Ballerina or Dancing Girl, Hocking Glass Co. 1930-34 (Process-etched)

Bowl, sauce, 4¼" d., clear 5.00
Bowl, cream soup, 4¾" d., green 178.00
Bowl, cereal, 5½" d., clear 6.00
Bowl, cereal, 5½" d., green. 36.00
Bowl, cereal, 5½" d., yellow 34.00
Bowl, salad, 7¼" d., green 56.00
Bowl, large berry, 8¼" d., green 39.00
Bowl, large berry, 8¼" d., pink 125.00
Bowl, soup w/flange rim, 9" d., green. . 57.00
Bowl, 10" oval vegetable, green 32.00
Bowl, 10" oval vegetable, yellow 44.00
Butter dish, cov., green 246.00

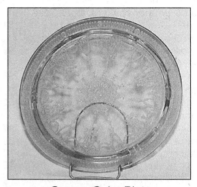

Cameo Cake Plate

Cake plate, three-footed, green,
  10" d. (ILLUS.). 23.00
Cake plate, handled, green, 10½" d. . . 32.00
Candlestick, green, 4" h. 51.00
Candlesticks, green, 4" h., pr. 120.00
Candy jar, cov., green, 4" h. 70.00
Candy jar, cov., yellow, 4" h. 98.00
Candy jar, cov., green, 6½" h. 215.00
Compote, mayonnaise, 5" d., 4" h.,
  cone-shaped, green 31.00
Compote, mayonnaise, 5" d., 4" h.,
  cone-shaped, pink. 21.00
Console bowl, three-footed, green,
  11" d. 74.00
Console bowl, three-footed, pink,
  11" d. 65.00
Console bowl, three-footed, yellow,
  11" d. 95.00
Cookie jar, cov., green 60.00
Creamer, green, 3¼" h. 22.00
Creamer, yellow, 3¼" h. 22.00
Creamer, green, 4¼" h. 23.00
Creamer, pink, 4¼" h. 65.00
Cup, clear 5.00
Cup, green 14.00
Cup, yellow 8.00

Cameo Cup & Saucer

Cup & saucer, green (ILLUS.) 22.00
Cup & saucer, pink. 8.00
Cup & saucer, yellow 10.00
Decanter, no stopper, green. 68.00
Decanter w/stopper, green, 10" h.. . . 161.00
Decanter w/stopper, green frosted,
  10" h. 36.00
Dinner set: service for six, green,
  46 pcs. 400.00
Domino tray, clear, 7" d. 85.00
Domino tray, green, 7" d. 172.00
Domino tray, pink, 7" d. 185.00
Goblet, wine, green, 3½" h. 58.00
Goblet, wine, green, 4" h. 78.00
Goblet, water, green, 6" h. 61.00
Goblet, water, pink, 6" h. 164.00
Jam jar, cov., closed handles, green,
  2". 196.00
Juice set: pitcher & four 3 oz. footed
  tumblers; green, 5 pcs. 200.00
Pitcher, syrup or milk, 5¾" h., 20 oz.,
  green. 207.00
Pitcher, syrup or milk, 5¾" h., 20 oz.,
  yellow 32.00
Pitcher, juice, 6" h., 36 oz., green. 56.00
Pitcher, water, 8½" h., 56 oz., jug-
  type, clear 35.00
Pitcher, water, 8½" h., 56 oz., jug-
  type, green 67.00
Pitcher, water, 8½" h., 56 oz., jug-
  type, pink. 18.00
Plate, sherbet (or ringless saucer),
  6" d., clear 2.00
Plate, sherbet (or ringless saucer),
  6" d., green 5.00
Plate, sherbet (or ringless saucer),
  6" d., pink 35.00
Plate, sherbet (or ringless saucer),
  6" d., yellow 4.00
Plate, salad, 7" d., clear 4.00
Plate, luncheon, 8" d., clear 3.00
Plate, luncheon, 8" d., green. 14.00
Plate, luncheon, 8" d., yellow 10.00
Plate, 8½" sq., green. 47.00
Plate, 8½" sq., yellow 310.00
Plate, dinner, 9½" d., green 21.00
Plate, dinner, 9½" d., yellow 9.00
Plate, sandwich, 10" d., green 20.00
Plate, sandwich, 10" d., pink. 61.00
Plate, 10½" d., closed handles, green . 24.00

Plate, 10½" d., closed handles, yellow . 27.00
Plate, dinner, 10½" d., rimmed, green . 12.00
Plate, dinner, 10½" d., rimmed, yellow . . 9.00
Plate, grill, 10½" d., closed handles,
  green. 77.00
Plate, grill, 10½" d., closed handles,
  yellow 7.00
Plate, grill, 10½" d., green. 12.00
Plate, grill, 10½" d., yellow 8.00
Platter, 10½" oval, green 23.00
Platter, 10½" oval, yellow 38.00
Platter, 12", closed handles, green. . . . 24.00
Platter, 12", closed handles, yellow . . . 41.00
Relish, footed, three-part, green, 7½". . 36.00
Salt & pepper shakers, green, pr. . . . 71.00
Salt & pepper shakers, pink, pr. 950.00
Server w/center handle, green. . . . 1,495.00
Sherbet, green, 3⅛" h. 15.00
Sherbet, pink, 3⅛" h. 83.00
Sherbet, yellow, 3⅛" h. 42.00
Sherbet, thin, high stem, green,
  4⅞" h. 35.00
Sherbet, thin, high stem, yellow,
  4⅞" h. 39.00
Saucer w/cup ring, green 178.00
Sugar bowl, open, green, 3¼" h. 22.00
Sugar bowl, open, yellow, 3¼" h. 15.00
Sugar bowl, open, green, 4¼" h. 25.00
Sugar bowl, open, pink, 4¼" h. 81.00
Tumbler, juice, footed, green, 3 oz. . . 72.00
Tumbler, juice, green, 3¾" h., 5 oz. . . . 28.00
Tumbler, juice, pink, 3¾" h., 5 oz. . . . 185.00
Tumbler, water, clear, 4" h., 9 oz. 10.00
Tumbler, water, green, 4" h., 9 oz. 29.00
Tumbler, water, pink, 4" h., 9 oz. 95.00
Tumbler, footed, green, 5" h., 9 oz. . . . 30.00
Tumbler, footed, pink, 5" h., 9 oz.
Tumbler, green, 4¾" h., 10 oz. 27.00
Tumbler, pink, 4¾" h., 10 oz. 160.00
Tumbler, yellow, 4¾" h., 10 oz. 83.00
Tumbler, green, 5" h., 11 oz. 32.00
Tumbler, yellow, 5" h., 11 oz. 58.00
Tumbler, footed, green, 5¾" h., 11 oz. . 75.00
Tumbler, green, 5¼" h., 15 oz. 69.00
Tumbler, footed, green, 6⅜" h., 15 oz. 108.00
Vase, 5¾" h., green. 257.00
Vase, 8" h., green 40.00
Vegetable bowl, oval, green 25.00
Water bottle, dark green "White
  House Vinegar" base, 8½" h. 35.00
Water set: pitcher & 6 tumblers;
  green, 7 pcs. 250.00

CHERRY BLOSSOM, Jeannette Glass Co., 1930-38 (Process-etched)

Bowl, berry, 4¾" d., Delphite 15.00
Bowl, berry, 4¾" d., green 16.00
Bowl, berry, 4¾" d., pink. 16.00
Bowl, cereal, 5¾" d., green. 44.00
Bowl, cereal, 5¾" d., pink. 44.00

Bowl, soup, 7¾" d., green. 71.00
Bowl, soup, 7¾" d., pink. 72.00
Bowl, berry, 8½" d., Delphite 44.00
Bowl, berry, 8½" d., green 42.00
Bowl, berry, 8½" d., pink. 53.00
Bowl, 9" d., two-handled, Delphite 32.00
Bowl, 9" d., two-handled, green 57.00
Bowl, 9" d., two-handled, pink 58.00
Bowl, 9" oval vegetable, Delphite. 38.00
Bowl, 9" oval vegetable, green. 43.00
Bowl, 9" oval vegetable, pink 49.00
Bowl, fruit, 10½" d., three-footed,
    green. 92.00
Bowl, fruit, 10½" d., three-footed, pink . 92.00
Butter dish, cov., green 80.00
Butter dish, cov., pink 77.00
Cake plate, three-footed, green,
    10¼" d. 31.00
Cake plate, three-footed, pink, 10¼" d. 30.00
Coaster, green. 14.00
Coaster, pink. 15.00
Creamer, Delphite. 20.00
Creamer, green. 19.00
Creamer, pink. 20.00
Cup, Delphite 19.00
Cup, green 20.00
Cup, pink. 21.00
Cup & saucer, Delphite 24.00
Cup & saucer, green 24.00
Cup & saucer, pink. 25.00
Mug, green, 7 oz. 194.00
Mug, pink, 7 oz.. . . . . 180.00
Pitcher, 6¾" h., 36 oz., overall patt.,
    Delphite. 92.00
Pitcher, 6¾" h., 36 oz., overall patt.,
    green. 58.00
Pitcher, 6¾" h., 36 oz., overall patt.,
    pink. 59.00
Pitcher, 8" h., 36 oz., footed, cone-
    shaped, patt. top, green 59.00
Pitcher, 8" h., 36 oz., footed, cone-
    shaped, patt. top, pink. 67.00
Pitcher, 8" h., 42 oz., patt. top, green. . 58.00
Pitcher, 8" h., 42 oz., patt. top, pink . . . 55.00
Plate, sherbet, 6" d., Delphite 8.00
Plate, sherbet, 6" d., green 8.00
Plate, sherbet, 6" d., pink 8.00
Plate, salad, 7" d., green. 20.00
Plate, salad, 7" d., pink 22.00
Plate, dinner, 9" d., Delphite 22.00
Plate, dinner, 9" d., green 21.00
Plate, dinner, 9" d., pink 24.00
Plate, grill, 9" d., green 26.00
Plate, grill, 9" d., pink 27.00
Plate, grill, 10" d., green 250.00
Platter, 11" oval, Delphite 36.00
Platter, 11" oval, green. 47.00
Platter, 11" oval, pink 47.00
Platter, 13" oval, green. 63.00
Platter, 13" oval, pink 64.00
Platter, 13" oval, divided, pink 70.00

Sandwich tray, handled, Delphite,
    10½" d. 23.00
Sandwich tray, handled, green,
    10½" d. 28.00
Sandwich tray, handled, pink,
    10½" d. 28.00
Saucer, Delphite. 4.00
Saucer, green. 5.00
Saucer, pink 6.00
Sherbet, Delphite 12.00
Sherbet, green 18.00
Sherbet, pink 18.00
Soup bowl, flat, green 80.00
Sugar bowl, cov., clear. 18.00
Sugar bowl, cov., Delphite 35.00
Sugar bowl, cov., green 40.00
Sugar bowl, cov., pink 39.00
Sugar bowl, open, Delphite 18.00
Sugar bowl, open, green 15.00
Sugar bowl, open, pink 10.00
Tumbler, patt. top, green, 3½" h.,
    4 oz.. . . . . 25.00
Tumbler, juice, footed, overall patt.,
    Delphite, 3¾" h., 4 oz. 18.00
Tumbler, juice, footed, overall patt.,
    green, 3¾" h., 4 oz. 21.00
Tumbler, juice, footed, overall patt.,
    pink, 3¾" h., 4 oz. 20.00
Tumbler, footed, overall patt.,
    Delphite, 4½" h., 8 oz. 20.00
Tumbler, footed, overall patt., green,
    4½" h., 8 oz. 33.00
Tumbler, footed, overall patt., pink,
    4½" h., 8 oz. 35.00
Tumbler, patt. top, green, 4¼" h.,
    9 oz.. . . . . 23.00
Tumbler, patt. top, pink, 4¼" h., 9 oz.. . 24.00
Tumbler, footed, overall patt.,
    Delphite, 4½" h., 9 oz. 23.00
Tumbler, footed, overall patt., green,
    4½" h., 9 oz. 32.00
Tumbler, footed, overall patt., pink,
    4½" h., 9 oz. 35.00
Tumbler, patt. top, green, 5" h.,
    12 oz.. . . . . 58.00
Tumbler, patt. top, pink, 5" h., 12 oz. . . 75.00

Junior Set:
14 pc. set, Delphite. 322.00
14 pc. set, pink 322.00
Creamer, Delphite. 43.00
Creamer, pink 48.00
Cup, pink. 37.00
Cup & saucer, Delphite 45.00
Cup & saucer, pink. 43.00
Plate, 6" d., Delphite 14.00
Plate, 6" d., pink 13.00
Saucer, Delphite. 6.00
Saucer, pink 8.00
Sugar bowl, Delphite 42.00
Sugar bowl, pink 44.00

CLOVERLEAF, Hazel Atlas Glass Co., 1931-35 (Process-etched)

Ashtray w/match holder in center,
    black, 5¾" d. 78.00
Bowl, dessert, 4" d., green 23.00
Bowl, cereal, 5" d., yellow. 25.00
Bowl, salad, 7" d., deep, yellow 47.00
Bowl, 8" d., green 47.00
Candy dish, cov., green 47.00
Creamer, footed, black, 3⅝" h. 19.00
Creamer, footed, green, 3⅝" h. 10.00
Cup & saucer, black. 23.00
Cup & saucer, green 10.00
Cup & saucer, pink. 10.00
Cup & saucer, yellow 14.00
Plate, sherbet, 6" d., black 36.00
Plate, sherbet, 6" d., green 10.00
Plate, sherbet, 6" d., yellow. 8.00
Plate, luncheon, 8" d., clear 5.00
Plate, luncheon, 8" d., green. 8.00
Plate, luncheon, 8" d., pink. 9.00
Plate, luncheon, 8" d., yellow 14.00
Plate, grill, 10¼" d., green. 23.00
Plate, grill, 10¼" d., yellow 25.00
Sherbet, footed, black, 3" h. 19.00
Sherbet, footed, green, 3" h. 9.00
Sugar bowl, open, footed, black,
    3⅝" h. 18.00
Sugar bowl, open, footed, green,
    3⅝" h. 10.00
Sugar bowl, open, footed, yellow,
    3⅝" h. 15.00
Tumbler, flared, green, 3¾" h.,
    10 oz. 40.00
Tumbler, footed, green, 5¾" h.,
    10 oz. 23.00
Tumbler, footed, yellow, 5¾" h.,
    10 oz. 32.00

COLONIAL or Knife & Fork, Hocking Glass Co., 1934-39 (Press-mold)

Bowl, berry, 3¾" d., pink. 53.00
Bowl, berry, 4½" d., clear 5.00
Bowl, berry, 4½" d., green 17.00
Bowl, berry, 4½" d., pink. 15.00
Bowl, cream soup, 4½" d., green 66.00
Bowl, cereal, 5½" d., clear 33.00
Bowl, cereal, 5½" d., green. 66.00
Bowl, cereal, 5½" d., pink. 31.00
Bowl, soup, 7" d., clear. 22.00
Bowl, soup, 7" d., green 57.00
Bowl, soup, 7" d., pink 61.00
Bowl, 9" d., clear. 18.00
Bowl, 9" d., green 30.00
Bowl, 9" d., pink 30.00
Butter dish, cov., pink 700.00
Celery or spooner, clear 62.00

Colonial Celery or Spooner

Celery or spooner, green
    (ILLUS.). 114.00
Celery or spooner, pink. 119.00
Cheese dish, wooden base w/green
    dome cover 65.00
Creamer or milk pitcher, clear, 5" h.,
    16 oz. 18.00
Creamer or milk pitcher, green,
    5" h., 16 oz. 16.00
Creamer or milk pitcher, pink, 5" h.,
    16 oz. 15.00
Cup, clear 7.00
Cup, green 10.00
Cup, milk white 5.00
Cup, pink. 10.00
Cup & saucer, clear 10.00
Cup & saucer, green 18.00
Cup & saucer, pink. 17.00
Goblet, cordial, clear, 3¾" h., 1 oz. . . . 16.00
Goblet, cordial, green, 3¾" h., 1 oz. . . 28.00
Goblet, wine, clear, 4½" h., 2½ oz. . . . 15.00
Goblet, green, 5¾" h., 8½ oz. 31.00
Goblet, pink, 5¾" h., 8½ oz. 17.00
Mug, green, 4½" h., 12 oz. 750.00
Pitcher, ice lip or plain, 7" h., 54 oz.,
    clear. 33.00
Pitcher, ice lip or plain, 7" h., 54 oz.,
    green 54.00
Pitcher, ice lip or plain, 7" h., 54 oz.,
    pink. 56.00
Plate, sherbet, 6" d., clear. 4.00
Plate, sherbet, 6" d., green 8.00
Plate, sherbet, 6" d., pink 7.00
Plate, luncheon, 8½" d., clear 5.00
Plate, luncheon, 8½" d., green 10.00
Plate, luncheon, 8½" d., pink 10.00
Plate, dinner, 10" d., clear. 26.00
Plate, dinner, 10" d., green 63.00
Plate, dinner, 10" d., pink 56.00
Plate, grill, 10" d., clear 12.00
Plate, grill, 10" d., green 25.00
Plate, grill, 10" d., pink 26.00
Platter, 12" oval, clear. 14.00
Platter, 12" oval, green. 23.00
Platter, 12" oval, pink 31.00
Salt & pepper shakers, clear, pr. 46.00

Colonial Salt & Pepper Shakers

Salt & pepper shakers, green, pr.
  (ILLUS.)....................145.00
Salt & pepper shakers, pink, pr. 112.00
Saucer, green.....................6.00
Saucer, pink....................6.00
Sherbet, pink, 3" h...............19.00
Sherbet, clear, 3⅜" h...............5.00
Sherbet, green, 3⅜" h..............14.00
Sherbet, pink, 3⅜" h. 11.00
Sugar bowl, cov., clear.............23.00
Sugar bowl, cov., green...........26.00
Sugar bowl, cov., pink............60.00
Tumbler, pink, 2½" h., 1½ oz.......12.00
Tumbler, whiskey, clear, 2½" h.,
  1½ oz......................11.00
Tumbler, whiskey, green, 2½" h.,
  1½ oz......................15.00
Tumbler, cordial, footed, clear, 3¼" h.,
  3 oz........................12.00
Tumbler, cordial, footed, green, 3¼" h.,
  3 oz........................24.00
Tumbler, cordial, footed, pink, 3¼" h.,
  3 oz........................15.00
Tumbler, juice, clear, 3" h., 5 oz.......4.00
Tumbler, juice, green, 3" h., 5 oz......24.00
Tumbler, juice, pink, 3" h., 5 oz.......20.00
Tumbler, footed, clear, 4" h., 5 oz....13.00
Tumbler, footed, green, 4" h., 5 oz. ...43.00
Tumbler, footed, pink, 4" h., 5 oz.....31.00
Tumbler, water, clear, 4" h., 9 oz.....14.00
Tumbler, water, green, 4" h., 9 oz.....21.00
Tumbler, water, pink, 4" h., 9 oz. 21.00
Tumbler, footed, clear, 5¼" h.,
  10 oz.......................22.00
Tumbler, footed, green, 5¼" h.,
  10 oz.......................44.00
Tumbler, footed, pink, 5¼" h., 10 oz. ...46.00
Tumbler, clear, 5 1/8" h., 11 oz.......19.00
Tumbler, pink, 5 1/8" h., 11 oz........36.00
Tumbler, iced tea, clear, 12 oz. 15.00
Tumbler, iced tea, green, 12 oz.......32.00
Tumbler, iced tea, pink, 12 oz........45.00
Tumbler, lemonade, clear, 15 oz......11.00
Tumbler, lemonade, green, 15 oz.....73.00
Tumbler, lemonade, pink, 15 oz. 60.00

COLUMBIA, Federal Glass Co., 1938-42 (Press-mold)

Bowl, cereal, 5" d., clear............16.00
Bowl, soup, 8" d., clear.............20.00

Bowl, salad, 8½" d., clear...........17.00
Bowl, 10½" d., ruffled rim, clear 20.00
Butter dish, cov., clear.............19.00
Cup, clear 7.00
Cup & saucer, clear 11.00
Cup & saucer, pink 40.00
Plate, bread & butter, 6" d., clear 4.00
Plate, bread & butter, 6" d., pink......9.00
Plate, luncheon, 9½" d., clear.......11.00
Plate, luncheon, 9½" d., pink 36.00
Plate, chop, 11" d., clear............10.00
Saucer, clear.....................3.00
Saucer, pink 10.00
Snack plate, handled, clear 32.00
Snack plate, handled, w/cup, clear ...39.00

CUBE or Cubist, Jeannette Glass Co., 1929-33 (Press-Mold)

Bowl, 4½" d., deep, green 5.00
Bowl, 4½" d., deep, pink............6.00
Bowl, salad, 6½" d., clear...........5.00
Bowl, salad, 6½" d., green..........14.00
Bowl, salad, 6½" d., pink 11.00
Bowl, salad, 6½" d., ultramarine......55.00
Butter dish, cov., green............59.00
Butter dish, cov., pink 53.00
Candy jar, cov., green, 6½" h. 30.00
Candy jar, cov., pink, 6½" h.........28.00
Coaster, green, 3¼" d 8.00
Coaster, pink, 3¼" d. 6.00
Creamer, clear, 2⅝" h.............2.00
Creamer, pink, 2⅝" h..............4.00
Creamer, open sugar bowl & tray,
  clear, 3 pcs....................7.00
Creamer, clear, 3½" h..............1.00
Creamer, green, 3½" h.............8.00
Creamer, pink, 3½" h..............7.00
Cup, green 8.00
Cup, pink.......................7.00
Cup & saucer, green..............12.00
Cup & saucer, pink 11.00
Pitcher, 8¾" h., 45 oz., green.......226.00
Pitcher, 8¾" h., 45 oz., pink........215.00
Plate, sherbet, 6" d., clear..........1.00
Plate, sherbet, 6" d., green...........4.00
Plate, sherbet, 6" d., pink 4.00
Plate, luncheon, 8" d., green.........8.00
Plate, luncheon, 8" d., pink 7.00
Powder jar, cov., three-footed, clear ...8.00
Powder jar, cov., three-footed, green...26.00
Powder jar, cov., three-footed, pink ...25.00
Salt & pepper shakers, green, pr.....31.00
Salt & pepper shakers, pink, pr. 34.00
Saucer, footed, green..............8.00
Saucer, footed, pink 7.00
Saucer, green....................3.00
Saucer, pink.....................3.00
Sugar bowl, open, clear, 2⅜" h........2.00
Sugar bowl, open, pink, 2⅜" h. 5.00
Sugar bowl, cov., green, 3" h. 20.00
Sugar bowl, cov., pink, 3" h..........20.00

Tray for 3 1/2" h. creamer & open
  sugar bowl, clear, 7½" 7.00
Tumbler, green, 4" h., 9 oz. 70.00
Tumbler, pink, 4" h., 9 oz.. . . . . 65.00

DAISY or Number 620, Indiana Glass Co., 1933-40, 1960s-80s (Press-mold)

Bowl, berry, 4½" d., amber 8.00
Bowl, berry, 4½" d., clear 5.00
Bowl, cream soup, 4½" d., amber. 10.00
Bowl, cereal, 6" d., amber. 25.00
Bowl, cereal, 6" d., clear. 9.00
Bowl, berry, 7⅜" d., amber 14.00
Bowl, berry, 7⅜" d., clear 6.00
Bowl, berry, 9⅜" d., amber 28.00
Bowl, berry, 9⅜" d., clear 13.00
Bowl, 10" oval vegetable, amber 15.00
Creamer, footed, amber 8.00
Cup, amber. 5.00
Cup, clear 3.00
Cup & saucer, amber. 6.00
Cup & saucer, clear 6.00
Plate, sherbet, 6" d., amber 3.00
Plate, sherbet, 6" d., clear. 2.00
Plate, salad, 7⅜" d., amber 11.00
Plate, salad, 7⅜" d., clear 5.00
Plate, luncheon, 8⅜" d., amber. 5.00
Plate, dinner, 9⅜" d., clear 4.00
Plate, grill, 10⅜" d., amber 13.00
Plate, grill, 10⅜" d., clear 5.00
Plate, 11½" d., clear 7.00
Platter, 10¾" l., amber 15.00
Relish dish, three-part, amber, 8⅜" . . . 28.00
Relish dish, three-part, clear, 8⅜" 10.00
Saucer, amber 2.00
Sherbet, footed, amber. 6.00
Sherbet, footed, clear 5.00
Sugar bowl, open, footed, amber. 7.00
Sugar bowl, open, footed, clear 4.00
Tumbler, footed, amber, 9 oz. 16.00
Tumbler, footed, amber, 12 oz. 43.00
Tumbler, footed, clear, 12 oz.. . . . . 20.00

DIAMOND QUILTED or Flat Diamond, Imperial Glass Co., late 1920s-early 1930s (Press-Mold)

Bowl, cream soup, 4¾" d., black 18.00
Bowl, cream soup, 4¾" d., blue 18.00
Bowl, cream soup, 4¾" d., green 13.00
Bowl, cream soup, 4¾" d., pink 9.00
Bowl, cereal, 5" d., pink 5.00
Bowl, 5½" d., single handle, black 16.00
Bowl, 5½" d., single handle, blue 18.00
Bowl, 5½" d., single handle, green. 9.00
Bowl, 5½" d., single handle, pink 8.00
Bowl, 7" d., crimped rim, amber 9.00
Bowl, 7" d., crimped rim, black 22.00
Bowl, 7" d., crimped rim, blue. 19.00
Bowl, 7" d., crimped rim, green. 11.00
Bowl, 7" d., crimped rim, pink 7.00

Candlesticks, flat or domed base,
  amber, pr. 10.00
Candlesticks, flat or domed base,
  black, pr. 37.00
Candlesticks, flat or domed base,
  blue, pr. 43.00
Candlesticks, flat or domed base,
  green, pr.. . . . . 25.00
Candlesticks, flat or domed base,
  pink, pr. 22.00
Candy jar, cov., footed, green 20.00
Candy jar, cov., footed, pink. 135.00
Candy jar, cov., footed, pink w/gold
  trim 75.00
Compote, open, 7¼" d.,6" h., green . . 40.00
Console bowl, rolled edge, pink. 33.00
Creamer, amber 6.00
Creamer, black 16.00
Creamer, blue. 15.00
Creamer, green. 9.00
Creamer, pink. 8.00
Creamer, red. 35.00
Cup, black. 15.00
Cup, blue. 17.00
Cup, green 11.00
Cup, pink. 9.00
Cup & saucer, amber. 8.00
Cup & saucer, black. 20.00
Cup & saucer, green 12.00
Cup & saucer, pink. 17.00
Goblet, wine, green, 3 oz.. . . . . 14.00
Goblet, champagne, green, 6" h.,
  9 oz.. . . . . 14.00
Goblet, champagne, pink, 6" h.,
  9 oz.. . . . . 12.00
Ice bucket, black 73.00
Ice bucket, blue 64.00
Mayonnaise set: three-footed dish,
  plate & ladle; green, 3 pcs. 27.00
Mayonnaise set: three-footed dish,
  plate & ladle; pink, 3 pcs. 38.00
Pitcher, 64 oz., green. 42.00
Plate, sherbet, 6" d., black 5.00
Plate, sherbet, 6" d., blue 6.00
Plate, sherbet, 6" d., green 4.00
Plate, sherbet, 6" d., pink 5.00
Plate, salad, 7" d., black 5.00
Plate, salad, 7" d., blue. 6.00
Plate, salad, 7" d., green. 4.00
Plate, salad, 7" d., pink. 4.00
Plate, luncheon, 8" d., black 13.00
Plate, luncheon, 8" d., blue 15.00
Plate, luncheon, 8" d., green. 7.00
Plate, luncheon, 8" d., pink 5.00
Plate, sandwich, 14" d., green 21.00
Plate, sandwich, 14" d., pink 18.00
Punch bowl w/stand, green,
  2 pcs.. . . . . 275.00
Punch set: bowl w/stand & 12 cups;
  pink, 14 pcs. 400.00
Saucer, black. 4.00

Saucer, blue. 8.00
Sherbet, amber. 3.00
Sherbet, black. 11.00
Sherbet, blue. 12.00
Sherbet, green 7.00
Sherbet, pink 7.00
Sugar bowl, open, amber. 8.00
Sugar bowl, open, black. 17.00
Sugar bowl, open, blue 16.00
Sugar bowl, open, green 8.00
Sugar bowl, open, pink 9.00
Tumbler, whiskey, green, 1½ oz. 7.00
Tumbler, footed, pink, 6 oz. 6.00
Tumbler, footed, clear, 9 oz. 3.00
Tumbler, iced tea, green, 12 oz. 9.00
Vase, 7½" flip, blue 172.00

DORIC, Jeannette Glass Co., 1935-38 (Press-mold)

Bowl, berry, 4½" d., green 10.00
Bowl, berry, 4½" d., pink. 8.00
Bowl, large berry, 8¼" d., green 29.00
Bowl, large berry, 8¼" d., pink 24.00
Bowl, 9" d., two-handled, green 14.00
Bowl, 9" d., two-handled, pink 16.00
Bowl, 9" oval vegetable, green. 36.00
Bowl, 9" oval vegetable, pink 34.00
Butter dish, cov., green 87.00

Doric Butter Dish

Butter dish, cov., pink (ILLUS.) 70.00
Cake plate, three-footed, green,
    10" d. 21.00
Cake plate, three-footed, pink,
    10" d. 24.00
Candy dish, three-section, Delphite,
    6". 8.00
Candy dish, three-section, green, 6" . . 11.00
Candy dish, three-section, pink, 6" . . . 9.00
Candy jar, cov., green, 8" h. 38.00
Coaster, pink, 3" d. 19.00
Creamer, green, 4" h. 14.00
Cup & saucer, green 9.00
Cup & saucer, pink. 14.00
Pitcher, 5½" h., 32 oz., green 45.00
Pitcher, 5½" h., 32 oz., pink. 45.00
Pitcher, 7½" h., 48 oz., footed,
    pink 425.00
Plate, sherbet, 6" d., green 6.00

Relish or serving tray, green,
    8" x 8" 21.00
Relish or serving tray, pink,
    8" x 8" 24.00
Relish tray, green, 4" x 4" 12.00
Relish tray, pink, 4" x 4" 11.00
Salt & pepper shakers, green, pr. 38.00
Salt & pepper shakers, pink, pr. 35.00
Sandwich tray, handled, green,
    10" d. 20.00
Sandwich tray, handled, pink,
    10" d. 15.00
Sherbet, footed, Delphite. 7.00
Sherbet, footed, green. 18.00
Sherbet, footed, pink 16.00
Sugar bowl, cov., green 17.00
Sugar bowl, cov., pink 21.00
Tumbler, green, 4½" h., 9 oz. 86.00
Tumbler, pink, 4½" h., 9 oz. 63.00
Tumbler, footed, pink, 4" h., 10 oz. . . . 63.00
Tumbler, footed, green, 5" h., 12 oz. . . 91.00
Tumbler, footed, pink, 5" h., 12 oz. . . . 82.00

FLORAL or Poinsettia, Jeannette Glass Co., 1931-35 (Process-etched)

Bowl, salad, 7½" d., pink 24.00
Bowl, cov. vegetable, 8" d., green 49.00
Bowl, cov. vegetable, 8" d., pink. 47.00
Bowl, 9" oval vegetable, green. 21.00
Bowl, 9" oval vegetable, pink 19.00
Butter dish, cov., pink 83.00
Candlesticks, green, 4" h., pr. 87.00

Floral Candy Jar

Candy jar, cov., green (ILLUS.) 40.00
Candy jar, cov., pink. 42.00
Coaster, green, 3¼" d. 13.00
Coaster, pink, 3¼" d. 14.00
Creamer, green. 15.00
Creamer, pink. 14.00
Cup & saucer, green 26.00
Cup & saucer, pink. 25.00

Pitcher, 8" h., 32 oz., cone-shaped,
   pink **42.00**
Plate, sherbet, 6" d., green **7.00**
Plate, sherbet, 6" d., pink **5.00**
Plate, salad, 8" d., green **11.00**
Plate, salad, 8" d., pink **15.00**
Plate, dinner, 9" d., green **20.00**
Plate, dinner, 9" d., pink **23.00**
Platter, 10¾" oval, green **20.00**
Platter, 10¾" oval, pink. **23.00**
Relish, two-part, oval, green. **19.00**
Relish, two-part, oval, pink **20.00**
Sherbet, green **19.00**
Sherbet, pink **16.00**
Sugar bowl, cov., green **33.00**
Sugar bowl, cov., pink **30.00**
Tumbler, water, footed, green,
   4 ¾" h., 7 oz. **20.00**
Tumbler, water, footed, pink, 4 ¾" h.,
   7 oz.. . . . . **18.00**
Tumbler, green, 4½" h., 9 oz. **188.00**
Tumbler, lemonade, footed, green,
   5¼" h., 9 oz. **57.00**
Tumbler, lemonade, footed, pink,
   5¼" h., 9 oz. **47.00**

Floral Water Set

Water set: cone-shaped pitcher & 6
   footed tumblers; green, 7 pcs.
   (ILLUS. of part) . . . . **160.00 to 175.00**

GEORGIAN or Lovebirds, Federal Glass Co., 1931-36 (Process-etched)

Bowl, berry, 4½" d. **10.00**
Bowl, cereal, 5¾" d. **22.00**
Bowl, berry, 7½" d. **58.00**
Bowl, 9" oval vegetable **63.00**
Creamer, footed, 3" h. **12.00**
Creamer, footed, 4" h. **15.00**

Georgian Cup & Saucer

Cup & saucer (ILLUS.). **14.00**
Plate, sherbet, 6" d. **6.00**
Plate, luncheon, 8" d. **13.00**
Plate, dinner, 9¼" d. **24.00**
Sherbet. **13.00**
Sugar bowl, cov., footed, 3" h. **44.00**
Sugar bowl, open, footed, 3" h. **9.00**
Tumbler, 4" h., 9 oz. **58.00**

HOLIDAY or Buttons and Bows, Jeannette Glass Co., 1947-mid '50s (Press-mold)

Holiday Bowl

Bowl, berry, 5⅛" d. (ILLUS.) **12.00**
Bowl, flat soup, 7¾" d. **59.00**
Bowl, berry, 8½" d. **29.00**
Bowl, 9½" oval vegetable **25.00**
Butter dish, cov. **38.00**
Candlesticks, 3" h., pr. **105.00**
Console bowl, 10¾" d. **116.00**
Creamer, footed **11.00**
Cup & saucer, plain or rayed base. . . . **12.00**
Pitcher, milk, 4¾" h., 16 oz., pink **62.00**

Holiday Pitcher

Pitcher, 6¾" h., 52 oz. (ILLUS.) **36.00**
Plate, sherbet, 6" d.. . . . . **6.00**
Plate, dinner, 9" d.. . . . . **23.00**

Plate, chop, 13¾" d. 98.00
Platter, 8" x 11⅜" oval, pink 21.00
Sandwich tray, 10½" d. 20.00
Sugar bowl, cov. 32.00
Sugar bowl, open. 9.00
Tumbler, footed, pink, 4" h., 5 oz. 45.00
Tumbler, footed, 6" h., 9 oz. 163.00
Tumbler, 4" h., 10 oz. 20.00

LACE EDGE or Open Lace, Hocking Glass Co., 1935-38 (Press-mold)

Bowl, cereal, 6½" d., pink 21.00
Bowl, salad or butter dish bottom,
  7¾" d., pink 26.00
Bowl, 9½" d., plain or ribbed, pink 25.00
Butter dish or bonbon, cov., pink 66.00
Candlesticks, pink, pr. 437.00
Candy jar, cov., ribbed, pink, 4" h. 51.00
Compote, cov., 7" d., footed, clear 28.00
Compote, cov., 7" d., footed, pink 57.00
Compote, open, 7" d., footed, pink. . . . 25.00
Console bowl, three-footed, pink,
  10½" d. 200.00
Cookie jar, cov., pink, 5" h. 74.00
Creamer, pink 21.00
Cup, pink 25.00
Cup & saucer, pink. 32.00
Flower bowl w/crystal block, pink . . . 35.00
Flower bowl without crystal block,
  pink 20.00
Plate, salad 7¼" d., pink 23.00
Plate, salad, 7¼" d., clear 5.00
Plate, luncheon, 8¾" d., pink 22.00
Plate, dinner, 10½" d., clear 17.00
Plate, dinner, 10½" d., pink. 37.00
Plate, grill, 10½" d., pink 23.00
Plate, 13" d., solid lace, pink. 47.00
Platter, 12¾" oval, pink. 31.00
Platter, 12¾" oval, five-part, pink 30.00
Platter, 12¾" oval, pink. 31.00
Relish dish, three-part, deep, pink,
  7½" d. 67.00
Relish plate, three-part, pink,
  10½" d. 24.00
Relish plate, four-part, solid lace,
  pink, 13" d. 58.00
Saucer, pink 13.00
Sherbet, footed, pink 103.00
Sugar bowl, open, pink 21.00
Tumbler, pink, 4½" h., 9 oz. 19.00
Tumbler, footed, pink, 5" h., 10½ oz. . . 76.00
Vase, 7" h., pink frosted 50.00

LORAIN or Basket or Number 615, Indiana Glass Co., 1929-32 (Press-etched)

Bowl, cereal, 6", green 38.00
Bowl, cereal, 6", yellow. 65.00
Bowl, salad, 7¼", green 48.00

Bowl, salad, 7¼", yellow. 58.00
Bowl, berry, 8", green 81.00
Bowl, berry, 8", yellow 142.00
Bowl, 9¾" oval vegetable, green 44.00
Bowl, 9¾" oval vegetable, yellow 48.00
Creamer, footed, green. 16.00

Lorain Creamer

Creamer, footed, yellow
  (ILLUS.). 24.00
Cup & saucer, green 15.00
Cup & saucer, yellow 20.00
Plate, sherbet, 5½", green 7.00
Plate, sherbet, 5½", yellow 12.00
Plate, 7¾", green 11.00
Plate, 7¾", yellow 15.00
Plate, salad, 7¾", clear. 10.00
Plate, luncheon, 8⅜", green 17.00
Plate, luncheon, 8⅜", yellow 26.00
Plate, dinner, 10¼", clear 36.00
Plate, dinner, 10¼", green 48.00
Plate, dinner, 10¼", yellow 62.00
Platter, 11½", green 29.00
Platter, 11½", yellow. 42.00
Relish, four-part, clear, 8". 13.00
Relish, four-part, yellow, 8". 35.00
Sherbet, footed, green 20.00
Sherbet, footed, yellow. 30.00

Lorain Sugar Bowl

Sugar bowl, open, footed, yellow
  (ILLUS.). 22.00
Tumbler, footed, green, 4¾" h., 9 oz. . . 22.00
Tumbler, footed, yellow, 4¾" h., 9 oz. . . 29.00

MADRID, Federal Glass Co., 1932-39 (Process-etched)

Ashtray, amber, 6" sq. 264.00
Bowl, cream soup, 4¾" d., amber. 16.00
Bowl, sauce, 5" d., amber. 6.00
Bowl, sauce, 5" d., clear 7.00
Bowl, sauce, 5" d., green 9.00
Bowl, sauce, 5" d., pink 11.00
Bowl, soup, 7" d., amber. 16.00
Bowl, soup, 7" d., clear. 6.00
Bowl, soup, 7" d., green 18.00
Bowl, salad, 8" d., amber 14.00
Bowl, salad, 8" d., clear 10.00
Bowl, salad, 8" d., green 16.00
Bowl, large berry, 9⅜" d., amber 22.00
Bowl, salad, 9½" d., deep, amber 28.00
Bowl, 10" oval vegetable, amber 21.00
Bowl, 10" oval vegetable, blue 34.00
Bowl, 10" oval vegetable, green 19.00
Butter dish, cov., amber. 68.00
Butter dish, cov., clear. 52.00
Butter dish, cov., green 86.00
Cake plate, amber, 11¼" d. 16.00
Candlesticks, amber, 2¼" h., pr. 19.00
Candlesticks, clear, 2¼" h., pr. 15.00
Candlesticks, iridescent, 2¼" h., pr. . . 22.00
Candlesticks, pink, 2¼" h., pr. 25.00
Console bowl, flared, amber, 11" d. 14.00
Console bowl, flared, iridescent,
    11" d. 16.00
Console set: bowl & pair of
    candlesticks; amber, 3 pcs. 38.00
Console set: bowl & pair of
    candlesticks; pink, 3 pcs. 36.00
Cookie jar, cov., amber 49.00
Cookie jar, cov., pink 37.00
Creamer, amber 7.00
Creamer, blue. 14.00
Creamer, clear 7.00
Creamer, green. 11.00
Cup & saucer, amber. 8.00
Cup & saucer, blue 23.00
Cup & saucer, clear 9.00
Cup & saucer, green 12.00
Cup & saucer, pink. 13.00
Gelatin mold, amber, 2⅛" h. 14.00
Gravy boat platter, amber 650.00
Hot dish coaster, amber, 5" d. 40.00
Hot dish coaster, clear, 5" d. 36.00
Hot dish coaster w/indentation,
    amber 35.00
Hot dish coaster w/indentation,
    clear. 28.00
Hot dish coaster w/indentation,
    green. 37.00
Jam dish, amber, 7" d. 20.00
Jam dish, blue, 7" d. 33.00
Jam dish, clear, 7" d. 10.00
Jam dish, green, 7" d. 25.00

Madrid Pitcher

Pitcher, juice, 5½" h., 36 oz. amber
    (ILLUS.). 39.00
Pitcher, 8" h., 60 oz., square, amber . . 48.00
Pitcher, 8" h., 60 oz., square, blue . . . 173.00
Pitcher, 8" h., 60 oz., square, green. . 133.00
Pitcher, 8½" h., 80 oz., jug-type,
    amber 58.00
Pitcher w/ice lip, 8½" h., 80 oz.,
    amber 63.00
Plate, sherbet, 6" d., amber 4.00
Plate, sherbet, 6" d., blue 12.00
Plate, sherbet, 6" d., clear. 4.00
Plate, salad, 7½" d., pink 9.00
Plate, luncheon, 8⅞" d., amber. 7.00
Plate, luncheon, 8⅞" d., blue 18.00
Plate, luncheon, 8⅞" d., clear. 6.00
Plate, luncheon, 8⅞" d., green 13.00
Plate, dinner, 10½" d., amber 37.00
Plate, dinner, 10½" d., blue. 66.00
Plate, dinner, 10½" d., clear 21.00
Plate, dinner, 10½" d., green 34.00
Plate, grill, 10½" d., amber 8.00
Plate, grill, 10½" d., green 18.00
Platter, 11½" oval, amber. 17.00
Platter, 11½" oval, blue. 29.00
Platter, 11½" oval, green 19.00
Sherbet, clear. 7.00
Sherbet, green 11.00
Sugar bowl, cov., amber 46.00
Sugar bowl, cov., clear. 33.00
Sugar bowl, cov., green. 48.00
Sugar bowl, open, amber. 5.00
Sugar bowl, open, blue 19.00
Sugar bowl, open, green 9.00
Tumbler, juice, amber, 3⅞" h., 5 oz. . . 16.00
Tumbler, juice, blue, 3⅞" h., 5 oz. . . . 34.00
Tumbler, footed, amber, 4" h., 5 oz. . . 22.00
Tumbler, amber, 4½" h., 9 oz. 14.00
Tumbler, blue, 4½" h., 9 oz. 24.00
Tumbler, green, 4½" h., 9 oz. 24.00
Tumbler, pink, 4½" h., 9 oz. 20.00
Tumbler, footed, amber, 5¼" h.,
    10 oz. 32.00
Tumbler, footed, clear, 5¼" h., 10 oz. . . 11.00
Tumbler, footed, green, 5¼" h.,
    10 oz. 34.00

Madrid Tumbler

Tumbler, amber, 5½" h., 12 oz.
(ILLUS.) 23.00
Tumbler, blue, 5½" h., 12 oz. 32.00
Tumbler, clear, 5½" h., 12 oz. 18.00
Tumbler, green, 5½" h., 12 oz. 33.00

MANHATTAN or Horizontal Ribbed, Anchor Hocking Glass Co., 1938-43 (Press-mold)

Ashtray, clear, 4" d. 10.00
Ashtray, clear, 4½" sq. 19.00
Bowl, sauce, 4½" d., two-handled,
clear. 8.00
Bowl, berry, 5⅜" d., two-handled,
pink 16.00
Bowl, cereal, 5½" d., clear 56.00
Bowl, large berry, 7½" d., clear. 15.00
Bowl, fruit, 9½" d., clear 36.00
Bowl, fruit, 9 ½" d., pink 41.00
Candleholders, clear, 4½" sq., pr. 14.00
Candy dish, cov., clear. 35.00
Candy dish, open, three-footed,
pink 10.00
Coaster, clear, 3½" d. 13.00
Compote, 5¾" h., clear. 32.00
Compote, 5¾" h., pink 35.00
Cup & saucer, clear 24.00
Pitcher, juice, 24 oz., ball tilt-type,
clear. 32.00
Pitcher w/ice lip, 80 oz., ball tilt-type,
clear. 36.00
Plate, sherbet or saucer, 6" d., clear. . . . 6.00
Plate, salad, 8½" d., clear 14.00
Plate, dinner, 10¼" d., clear 18.00
Plate, sandwich, 14" d., clear 23.00
Relish tray, four-part, clear, 14" d. 17.00
Relish tray insert, clear 5.00
Salt & pepper shakers, square,
clear, 2" h., pr. 27.00
Sugar bowl, open, oval, pink 11.00
Tumbler, footed, clear, 10 oz. 16.00
Tumbler, footed, pink, 10 oz. 19.00
Vase, 8" h., clear. 19.00
Wine, clear, 3½" h. 7.00

MISS AMERICA, Hocking Glass Co., 1935-38 (Press-mold)

Bowl, berry, 4½"d., green 13.00
Bowl, berry, 6¼" d., clear 8.00
Bowl, berry, 6¼" d., green 18.00
Bowl, berry, 6¼" d., pink. 24.00
Bowl, fruit, 8" d., curved in at top,
clear. 40.00
Bowl, fruit, 8" d., curved in at top,
pink 84.00
Bowl, fruit, 8¾" d., deep, pink. 73.00
Bowl, 10" oval vegetable, clear. 13.00
Bowl, 10" oval vegetable, pink 32.00
Butter dish, cov., clear. 198.00
Cake plate, footed, clear, 12" d. 31.00
Cake plate, footed, pink, 12" d. 52.00
Candy jar, cov., clear, 11½" h. 52.00
Candy jar, cov., pink, 11½" h. 164.00
Celery tray, clear, 10½" oblong 13.00
Celery tray, pink, 10½" oblong. 32.00
Coaster, clear, 5¾" d. 15.00
Coaster, pink, 5¾" d. 36.00

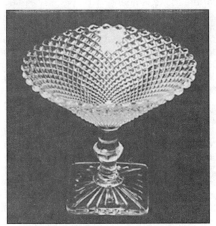

Miss America Compote

Compote, 5" d., clear (ILLUS.) 19.00
Compote 5" d., pink 27.00
Creamer, footed, clear 13.00
Creamer, footed, pink 21.00
Cup & saucer, clear 21.00
Cup & saucer, pink. 33.00
Goblet, wine, clear, 3¾" h., 3 oz. 21.00
Goblet, wine, pink, 3¾" h., 3 oz. 89.00
Goblet, juice, clear, 4¾" h., 5 oz. 22.00
Goblet, juice, pink, 4¾" h., 5 oz. 99.00
Goblet, water, clear, 5½" h., 10 oz. . . . 28.00
Goblet, water, pink, 5½" h., 10 oz. 50.00
Pitcher, 8" h., 65 oz., clear 60.00
Pitcher, 8" h., 65 oz., pink. 174.00
Pitcher w/ice lip, 8½" h., 65 oz.,
clear. 58.00

Miss America Pitcher

Pitcher w/ice lip, 8½" h., 65 oz., pink
    (ILLUS.).................... **168.00**
Plate, sherbet, 5¾" d., clear **5.00**
Plate, sherbet, 5¾" d., pink.......... **10.00**
Plate, 6¾" d., green **8.00**
Plate, salad, 8½" d., clear............ **8.00**
Plate, salad, 8½" d., pink **27.00**
Plate, dinner, 10¼" d., clear **17.00**
Plate, dinner, 10¼" d., pink.......... **36.00**
Plate, grill, 10¼" d., clear **16.00**
Plate, grill, 10¼" d., pink **26.00**
Platter, 12¼" oval, clear **12.00**
Platter, 12¼" oval, pink............ **31.00**
Relish, four-part, clear, 8¾" d. **10.00**

Miss America Relish

Relish, four-part, pink, 8¾" d.
    (ILLUS.)..................... **26.00**
Relish, divided, clear, 11¾" d. **21.00**
Salt & pepper shakers, clear, pr...... **29.00**
Salt & pepper shakers, green, pr.... **279.00**
Salt & pepper shakers, pink, pr. **61.00**
Sherbet, clear.................... **10.00**
Sherbet, pink **16.00**
Sugar bowl, open, footed, clear....... **6.00**
Sugar bowl, open, footed, pink **20.00**
Tumbler, juice, clear, 4" h., 5 oz. **18.00**
Tumbler, juice, pink, 4" h., 5 oz....... **46.00**

Tumbler, water, clear, 4½" h.,
    10 oz...................... **16.00**
Tumbler, water, green, 4½" h.,
    10 oz...................... **14.00**
Tumbler, water, pink, 4½" h.,
    10 oz...................... **30.00**
Tumbler, iced tea, clear, 6¾" h.,
    14 oz...................... **29.00**
Tumbler, iced tea, pink, 6¾" h.,
    14 oz...................... **85.00**

MODERNTONE, Hazel Atlas Glass Co., 1934-43, late 1940s & early 1950s (Press-mold)

Moderntone Pieces

Ashtray w/match holder, cobalt
    blue, 7¾" d.................. **209.00**
Bowl, cream soup, 4¾" d., amethyst .. **15.00**
Bowl, cream soup, 4¾" d., cobalt
    blue **22.00**
Bowl, cream soup, 4¾" d., platonite.... **6.00**
Bowl, berry, 5" d., amethyst **24.00**
Bowl, berry, 5" d., cobalt blue........ **25.00**
Bowl, berry, 5" d., platonite........... **6.00**
Bowl, cream soup w/ruffled rim, 5" d.,
    cobalt blue.................. **56.00**
Bowl, cream soup w/ruffled rim, 5" d.,
    platonite..................... **7.00**
Bowl, cereal, 6½" d., cobalt blue **85.00**
Bowl, cereal, 6½" d., platonite **6.00**
Bowl, soup, 7½" d., cobalt blue **178.00**
Bowl, soup, 7½" d., platonite **12.00**
Bowl, large berry, 8¾" d., amethyst ... **46.00**
Bowl, large berry, 8¾" d., cobalt
    blue **57.00**
Bowl, large berry, 8¾" d., platonite..... **9.00**
Butter dish w/metal lid, cobalt blue.. **104.00**
Cheese dish w/metal lid, cobalt
    blue, 7" d. **416.00**
Creamer, amethyst................ **11.00**
Creamer, cobalt blue (ILLUS. right) ... **11.00**
Creamer, platonite **5.00**
Cup & saucer, amethyst............ **13.00**
Cup & saucer, cobalt blue **17.00**
Cup & saucer, platonite **6.00**
Custard cup, amethyst............. **11.00**
Custard cup, cobalt blue **19.00**
Plate, sherbet, 5⅞" d., amethyst....... **6.00**
Plate, sherbet, 5⅞" d., cobalt blue **6.00**

Plate, salad, 6¾" d., amethyst 5.00
Plate, salad, 6¾" d., cobalt blue 12.00
Plate, salad, 6¾" d., platonite 4.00
Plate, luncheon, 7¾" d., amethyst 9.00
Plate, luncheon, 7¾" d., cobalt
   blue 13.00
Plate, luncheon, 7¾" d., platonite 5.00
Plate, dinner, 8⅞" d., amethyst. 12.00
Plate, dinner, 8⅞" d., cobalt blue 20.00
Plate, dinner, 8⅞" d., platonite 5.00
Plate, sandwich, 10½" d., amethyst . . . 48.00
Plate, sandwich, 10½" d., cobalt
   blue 60.00
Plate, sandwich, 10½" d., platonite 20.00
Platter, 11" oval, cobalt blue 45.00
Platter, 11" oval, platonite. 8.00
Platter, 12" oval, amethyst 44.00
Platter, 12" oval, platonite. 14.00
Salt & pepper shakers, amethyst,
   pr. 43.00
Salt & pepper shakers, cobalt blue,
   pr. (ILLUS. center). 46.00
Salt & pepper shakers, platonite,
   pr. 19.00
Saucer, 3⅞" d., dark. 8.00
Saucer, 3⅞" d., pastel. 8.00
Sherbet, amethyst 12.00
Sherbet, cobalt blue 13.00
Sherbet, platonite 4.00
Sugar bowl, open, amethyst 12.00
Sugar bowl, open, cobalt blue
   (ILLUS. left) 11.00
Sugar bowl, open, platonite 4.00
Sugar bowl, 1¾" h., dark 13.00
Sugar bowl, 1¾" h., pastel 15.00
Sugar bowl w/metal lid, cobalt
   blue 45.00
Teapot, cov., 3½" h., dark. 100.00
Teapot, cov., 3½" h., pastel 60.00
Tumbler, whiskey, clear, 1½ oz. 12.00
Tumbler, whiskey, cobalt blue,
   1½ oz. 45.00
Tumbler, whiskey, platonite, 1½ oz. 11.00
Tumbler, juice, cobalt blue, 5 oz. 49.00
Tumbler, juice, platonite, 5 oz. 11.00
Tumbler, water, amethyst, 4" h.,
   9 oz. 24.00
Tumbler, water, cobalt blue, 4" h.,
   9 oz. 39.00
Tumbler, water, platonite, 4" h., 9 oz. . . . 8.00
Tumbler, iced tea, amethyst, 12 oz. 16.00

Little Hostess Party Set
Creamer, 1¾"h., dark 14.00
Creamer, 1¾" h., pastel 17.00
Cup, 1¾" h., dark 12.00
Cup, 1¾" h., pastel 11.00
Cup & saucer, dark 18.00
Cup & saucer, pastel 10.00
Plate, 5¼" d., dark. 10.00
Plate, 5¼" d., pastel 9.00

MOROCCAN AMETHYST, Hazel Ware, Division of Continental Can, 1960s - (not true Depression)

Ashtray, 3¾" triangle 7.00
Ashtray, 6" triangle. 10.00
Ashtray, 6⅞" triangle 12.00
Bowl, fruit, 4¾" w. octagonal 8.00
Bowl, cereal, 5¾" sq., deep 11.00
Bowl, 6" d.. . . . . 10.00
Bowl, 6" d., w/metal center handle 33.00
Bowl, 6" sq., w/metal center handle . . . 23.00
Bowl, 7¾" oval 17.00
Bowl, 7¾" oval w/center handle 16.00
Bowl, 7¾" rectangle 15.00
Bowl, 9½" oval, low. 13.00
Bowl, 9½" oval, w/metal center
   handle 40.00
Bowl, 10¾" 31.00
Candy jar, cov., short 33.00
Candy jar, cov., tall. 33.00
Celery dish, 9½". 12.00
Chip & dip set, w/metal holder
   (5¾" & 10¾" bowls). 41.00
Cocktail shaker w/chrome lid,
   32 oz. 25.00
Cocktail stirrer, w/pouring lip,
   6¼" h., 16 oz. 25.00

Moroccan Amethyst Cup & Saucer

Cup & saucer (ILLUS.). 9.00
Goblet, wine, 4" h., 4½ oz. 10.00
Goblet, juice, 4⅜" h., 5½ oz. 10.00
Goblet, water, 5½" h., 10 oz. 11.00
Plate, 5¾" w. octagonal 5.00
Plate, salad, 7¼" w. 9.00
Plate, sandwich, w/center handle,
   8" oval 8.00
Plate, dinner, 9¾" w. 12.00
Plate, sandwich, 12" w. 19.00
Sandwich server, w/metal center
   handle, 12" 19.00
Sherbet, footed, 4¼" h.. . . . . 7.00
Tidbit server, three-tier 33.00
Tidbit server, two-tier. 19.00
Tumbler, juice, 2½" h., 4 oz.. . . . . 7.00

Tumbler, Old Fashioned, 3¼" h.,
8 oz.. . . . . **13.00**
Tumbler, water, crinkled bottom,
4¼" h., 11 oz. **11.00**
Tumbler, water, 4⅝" h., 11 oz.. . . . . . **11.00**
Tumbler, iced tea, 6½" h., 16 oz. **16.00**
Vase, 8½" h., ruffled **38.00**

NORMANDIE or Bouquet & Lattice, Federal Glass Co., 1933-40 (Process-etched)

Bowl, berry, 5" d., amber **5.00**
Bowl, berry, 5" d., pink **8.00**
Bowl, berry, 5" d., Sunburst iridescent . . **4.00**
Bowl, cereal, 6½" d., amber **16.00**
Bowl, cereal, 6½" d., cereal,
Sunburst iridescent **7.00**
Bowl, 8½" d., pink. **39.00**
Bowl, 8½" d., Sunburst iridescent. **15.00**
Bowl, large berry, 8½" d., amber **17.00**
Bowl, 10" oval vegetable, Sunburst
iridescent **16.00**
Creamer, footed, amber **8.00**
Creamer, footed, Sunburst iridescent. . . **7.00**
Cup & saucer, amber. **10.00**
Cup & saucer, pink. **12.00**

Normandie Cup & Saucer

Cup & saucer, Sunburst iridescent
(ILLUS.) **8.00**
Pitcher, 8" h., 80 oz., amber. **74.00**
Plate, sherbet, 6" d., amber **5.00**
Plate, sherbet, 6" d., pink **7.00**
Plate, sherbet, 6" d., Sunburst
iridescent. **3.00**
Plate, salad, 8" d., amber **9.00**
Plate, salad, 8" d., pink **11.00**
Plate, luncheon, 9¼" d., amber. **10.00**
Plate, luncheon, 9¼" d., pink **15.00**
Plate, luncheon, 9¼" d., Sunburst
iridescent. **15.00**
Plate, dinner, 11" d., Sunburst
iridescent. **17.00**
Plate, grill, 11" d., amber. **16.00**
Plate, grill, 11" d., Sunburst iridescent . . **9.00**
Platter, 11¾" oval, amber. **21.00**
Salt & pepper shakers, amber, pr. . . . **49.00**
Sherbet, amber. **6.00**
Sherbet, clear. **6.00**

Sherbet, pink **8.00**
Sherbet, Sunburst iridescent **8.00**
Sugar bowl, cov., amber **81.00**
Sugar bowl, open, amber. **7.00**
Sugar bowl, open, Sunburst
iridescent **6.00**
Tumbler, water, amber, 4½" h., 9 oz.. . **21.00**
Tumbler, water, pink, 4½" h., 9 oz.. . . . **49.00**
Tumbler, iced tea, amber, 5" h.,
12 oz.. . . . . **37.00**
Tumbler, iced tea, pink, 5" h.,
12 oz.. . . . . **108.00**

NUMBER 612 or Horseshoe, Indiana Glass Co., 1930-33 (Process-etched)

Bowl, 4½" d., yellow **18.00**
Bowl, berry, 4½" d., green **21.00**
Bowl, cereal, 6½" d., green. **23.00**
Bowl, cereal, 6½" d., yellow **21.00**
Bowl, salad, 7½" d., green **24.00**
Bowl, salad, 7½" d., yellow. **23.00**
Bowl, vegetable, 8½" d., yellow **30.00**
Bowl, large berry, 9½" d., green. **39.00**
Bowl, large berry, 9½" d., yellow **40.00**
Bowl, 10½" oval vegetable, green **22.00**
Candy in metal holder, motif on lid,
green. **165.00**
Candy in metal holder, motif on lid,
pink **175.00**
Creamer, footed, green. **15.00**
Creamer, footed, yellow **18.00**
Cup & saucer, green **14.00**
Cup & saucer, yellow. **15.00**

Number 612 Pitcher

Pitcher, 8½" h., 64 oz., green
(ILLUS.). **302.00**
Pitcher, 8½" h., 64 oz., yellow **365.00**
Plate, sherbet, 6" d., green **8.00**
Plate, sherbet, 6" d., yellow. **7.00**
Plate, salad, 8⅜" d., green **13.00**
Plate, salad, 8⅜" d., yellow. **10.00**
Plate, luncheon, 9⅜" d., green **13.00**
Plate, luncheon, 9⅜" d., yellow. **14.00**

Plate, dinner, 10⅜" d., green 19.00
Plate, dinner, 10⅜" d., yellow 18.00
Plate, grill, 10⅜" d., green. 76.00
Plate, grill, 10⅜" d., yellow 24.00
Plate, sandwich, 11" d., green 22.00
Plate, sandwich, 11" d., yellow 15.00
Platter, 10¾" oval, green 24.00
Platter, 10¾" oval, yellow 19.00
Relish, three-part, footed, green. 22.00
Relish, three-part, footed, yellow 29.00
Sherbet, green 15.00

Number 612 Sherbet

Sherbet, yellow (ILLUS.). 15.00
Sugar bowl, open, footed, green 13.00
Sugar bowl, open, footed, yellow. 15.00
Tumbler, footed, green, 9 oz. 24.00
Tumbler, footed, yellow, 9 oz. 23.00
Tumbler, footed, green, 12 oz. 147.00
Tumbler, footed, yellow, 12 oz. 159.00

OLD CAFE, Hocking Glass Co., 1936-40 (Press-mold)

Bowl, berry, 3¾" d., clear 4.00
Bowl, berry, 3¾" d., pink. . . . . : 6.00
Bowl, nappy, 5" d., handled, clear 4.00
Bowl, nappy, 5" d., handled, pink 8.00
Bowl, cereal, 5½" d., clear 8.00
Bowl, cereal, 5½" d., pink. 9.00
Bowl, cereal, 5½" d. ruby 17.00
Bowl, 9" d., handled, clear 9.00
Bowl, 9" d., handled, pink. 9.00
Bowl, 9" d., handled, ruby. 13.00
Candy dish, clear, 8" d 9.00
Candy dish, pink, 8" d. 10.00
Candy dish, ruby, 8" d. 14.00
Cup & saucer, pink. 13.00
Cup & saucer, ruby cup, clear
  saucer 13.00
Lamp, pink 13.00
Olive dish, clear, 6" oblong 6.00
Olive dish, pink, 6" oblong 6.00
Pitcher, 6" h., 36 oz., pink. 74.00
Pitcher, 8" h., 80 oz., pink. 165.00
Plate, sherbet, 6" d., clear. 4.00
Plate, dinner, 10" d., pink 45.00
Sherbet, low foot, pink 11.00
Sherbet, low foot, ruby 13.00
Tumbler, juice, clear, 3" h. 12.00
Tumbler, juice, pink, 3" h. 13.00
Tumbler, water, pink, 4" h. 12.00
Tumbler, water, ruby, 4" h. 14.00

(OLD) FLORENTINE or Poppy No. 1, Hazel Atlas Glass Co., 1932-35 (Process-etched)

Ashtray, clear, 5½". 18.00
Ashtray, green, 5½" 21.00
Ashtray, pink, 5½" 27.00
Ashtray, yellow, 5½". 28.00
Bowl, berry, 5" d., clear. 11.00
Bowl, berry, 5" d., green 11.00
Bowl, berry, 5" d., yellow 13.00
Bowl, cereal, 6" d., clear. 20.00
Bowl, cereal, 6" d., pink 20.00
Bowl, 8½" d., clear 22.00
Bowl, 8½" d., green 28.00
Bowl, 8½" d., yellow 22.00
Bowl, cov., vegetable, 9½" oval,
  clear. 47.00
Bowl, cov., vegetable, 9½" oval, pink . . 54.00
Bowl, cov., vegetable, 9½" oval,
  yellow 85.00
Butter dish, cov., clear 118.00

(Old) Florentine Butter Dish

Butter dish, cov., green (ILLUS.) 116.00
Butter dish, cov., pink 153.00
Butter dish, cov., yellow. 162.00
Coaster-ashtray, yellow, 3¾" d. 26.00
Creamer, plain rim, clear 7.00
Creamer, plain rim, green. 14.00
Creamer, plain rim, pink 16.00
Creamer, plain rim, yellow 12.00
Creamer, ruffled rim, clear 30.00
Creamer, ruffled rim, cobalt blue 71.00
Cup & saucer, clear 9.00
Cup & saucer, green 14.00
Cup & saucer, pink. 14.00
Cup & saucer, yellow 16.00
Nut dish, handled, ruffled rim, clear . . . 15.00
Nut dish, handled, ruffled rim, cobalt
  blue 45.00
Nut dish, handled, ruffled rim, green . . 24.00
Nut dish, handled, ruffled rim, pink. . . . 17.00
Nut dish, handled, ruffled rim, yellow . . 17.00
Pitcher, 6½" h., 36 oz., footed, clear . . 42.00
Pitcher, 6½" h., 36 oz., footed, green . . 45.00
Pitcher, 6½" h., 36 oz., footed, pink . . . 45.00
Pitcher, 6½" h., 36 oz., footed,
  yellow 43.00
Pitcher, 7½" h., 48 oz., clear 66.00
Pitcher, 7½" h., 48 oz., green. 75.00

Pitcher, 7½" h., 48 oz., pink **125.00**
Pitcher, 7½" h., 48 oz., yellow **155.00**
Plate, sherbet, 6" d., clear **5.00**
Plate, sherbet, 6" d., green **6.00**
Plate, sherbet, 6" d., pink **7.00**
Plate, salad, 8½" d., clear **7.00**
Plate, salad, 8½" d., green **10.00**
Plate, salad, 8½" d., pink **12.00**
Plate, salad, 8½" d., yellow **14.00**
Plate, dinner, 10" d., yellow **19.00**
Plate, grill, 10" d., clear **11.00**
Plate, grill, 10" d., green **14.00**
Plate, grill, 10" d., pink **16.00**
Plate, grill, 10" d., yellow **18.00**
Platter, 11½" oval, clear **15.00**
Salt & pepper shakers, footed,
  green, pr. **36.00**
Salt & pepper shakers, footed,
  pink, pr. **57.00**
Salt & pepper shakers, footed,
  yellow, pr. **55.00**
Sherbet, footed, clear, 3 oz. **7.00**
Sherbet, footed, green, 3 oz. **11.00**
Sherbet, footed, pink, 3 oz. **10.00**
Sherbet, footed, yellow, 3 oz. **11.00**
Sugar bowl, cov., yellow **30.00**
Sugar bowl, open, clear **9.00**
Sugar bowl, open, green **8.00**
Sugar bowl, open, pink **12.00**
Sugar bowl, open, ruffled rim, cobalt
  blue **45.00**
Sugar bowl, open, ruffled rim, green . . **30.00**
Sugar bowl, open, ruffled rim, pink . . . **37.00**
Sugar bowl, open, yellow **12.00**
Tumbler, juice, footed, clear,
  3¾" h., 5 oz. **10.00**
Tumbler, juice, footed, green,
  3¾" h., 5 oz. **16.00**
Tumbler, juice, footed, pink,
  3¾" h., 5 oz. **19.00**
Tumbler, juice, footed, yellow,
  3¾" h., 5 oz. **20.00**
Tumbler, pink, 4" h., 9 oz. **15.00**
Tumbler, ribbed, clear, 4" h., 9 oz. **14.00**
Tumbler, water, footed, green,
  4¾" h., 10 oz. **22.00**
Tumbler, water, footed, pink,
  4¾" h., 10 oz. **25.00**
Tumbler, water, footed, yellow,
  4¾" h., 10 oz. **23.00**

OYSTER & PEARL, Anchor Hocking Glass Corp., 1938-40 (Press-mold)

Bowl, 5¼" heart-shaped, w/handle,
  clear. **9.00**
Bowl, 5¼" heart-shaped, w/handle,
  pink **11.00**
Bowl, 5¼" heart-shaped, w/handle,
  white w/green **8.00**

Bowl, 5¼" heart-shaped, w/handle,
  white w/pink. **9.00**
Bowl, 5½" d., w/handle, clear **9.00**
Bowl, 5½" d., w/handle, ruby **12.00**
Bowl, 6½" d., handled, pink **14.00**
Bowl, 6½" d., handled, ruby **20.00**
Bowl, fruit, 10½" d., clear **19.00**
Bowl, fruit, 10½" d., pink **31.00**
Bowl, fruit, 10½" d., ruby. **50.00**
Bowl, fruit, 10½" d., white w/green **14.00**
Bowl, fruit, 10½" d., white w/pink **14.00**
Candleholders, clear, 3½" h., pr. **18.00**
Candleholders, pink, 3½" h., pr. **31.00**
Candleholders, ruby, 3½" h., pr. **51.00**
Candleholders, white w/green,
  3½" h., pr. **14.00**
Candleholders, white w/pink,
  3½" h., pr. **12.00**
Plate, sandwich, 13½" d., clear. **13.00**
Plate, sandwich, 13½" d., ruby **45.00**
Relish, divided, clear, 10¼" oval. **9.00**
Relish, divided, pink, 10¼" oval **13.00**

PETALWARE, MacBeth-Evans Glass Co., 1930-40 (Press-mold)

Bowl, cream soup, 4½" d., decorated
  Cremax or Monax **12.00**
Bowl, cream soup, 4½" d., pink **15.00**
Bowl, cream soup, 4½" d., plain
  Cremax or Monax **14.00**
Bowl, cereal, 5¾" d., clear **5.00**
Bowl, cereal, 5¾" d., decorated
  Cremax or Monax **7.00**
Bowl, cereal, 5¾" d., Florette **11.00**
Bowl, cereal, 5¾" d., pink **12.00**
Bowl, cereal, 5¾" d., plain Cremax or
  Monax **9.00**
Bowl, large berry, 9" d., decorated
  Cremax or Monax **29.00**
Bowl, large berry, 9" d., Florette **25.00**
Bowl, large berry, 9" d., pink **20.00**
Bowl, large berry, 9" d., plain
  Cremax or Monax **20.00**
Creamer, footed, decorated Cremax
  or Monax **9.00**
Creamer, footed, Florette **11.00**
Creamer, footed, pink **12.00**
Creamer, footed, plain Cremax or
  Monax **7.00**
Cup & saucer, clear **4.00**
Cup & saucer, decorated Cremax or
  Monax **12.00**
Cup & saucer, Florette. **13.00**
Cup & saucer, pink. **10.00**
Cup & saucer, plain Cremax or
  Monax **9.00**
Cup & saucer, Red Trim Floral
Lamp shade, Cremax, 9" h. **12.00**
Lamp shade, Monax, 11" h. **18.00**

Plate, sherbet, 6" d., decorated
Cremax or Monax 4.00
Plate, sherbet, 6" d., pink 4.00
Plate, sherbet, 6" d., plain Cremax or
Monax 4.00
Plate, salad, 8" d., clear 2.00
Plate, salad, 8" d., decorated Cremax
or Monax 9.00
Plate, salad, 8" d., Florette 8.00
Plate, salad, 8" d., pink 7.00
Plate, salad, 8" d., plain Cremax or
Monax 8.00
Plate, dinner, 9" d., decorated
Cremax or Monax 13.00
Plate, dinner, 9" d., pink 10.00
Plate, dinner, 9" d., plain Cremax or
Monax 11.00
Plate, salver, 11" d., decorated
Cremax or Monax 16.00
Plate, salver, 11" d., Florette 16.00
Plate, salver, 11" d., pink 15.00
Plate, salver, 11" d., plain Cremax or
Monax 11.00
Plate, salver, 12" d., decorated
Cremax or Monax 15.00
Plate, salver, 12" d., Red Trim Floral . . 44.00
Platter, 13" oval, plain Cremax or
Monax 18.00
Sherbet, low foot, decorated Cremax
or Monax, 4½" h. 12.00
Sherbet, low foot, plain Cremax or
Monax, 4½" h. 10.00
Sugar bowl, open, footed, decorated
Cremax or Monax 9.00
Sugar bowl, open, footed, Florette 10.00
Sugar bowl, open, footed, plain
Cremax or Monax 6.00
Sugar bowl, open, pink 11.00

PINEAPPLE & FLORAL or Number 618 or Wildflower, Indiana Glass Co., 1932-37 (Press-mold)

Ashtray, clear, 4½" l. 15.00
Bowl, cream soup, 4⅝" d., amber. 18.00
Bowl, berry, 4¾" d., clear 42.00
Bowl, cereal, 6" d., clear. 22.00
Bowl, salad, 7" d., clear 7.00
Bowl, 10" oval vegetable, clear. 23.00
Compote, diamond-shaped, clear 4.00
Creamer, diamond-shaped, amber. 9.00
Cup & saucer, amber. 13.00
Cup & saucer, clear. 14.00
Plate, sherbet, 6" d., amber 5.00
Plate, sherbet, 6" d., clear. 6.00
Plate, salad, 8⅜" d., amber. 8.00
Plate, salad, 8⅜" d., clear. 8.00
Plate, dinner, 9⅜" d., amber 13.00
Plate, dinner, 9⅜" d., clear 16.00
Plate, sandwich, 11½" d., amber 16.00

Plate, sandwich, 11½" d., clear. 20.00
Platter, 11", closed handles, clear 17.00
Relish, divided, clear, 11½" 18.00
Sherbet, footed, clear. 19.00
Sugar bowl, open, diamond-shaped,
clear. 7.00
Tumbler, clear, 4¼" h., 8 oz. 38.00
Tumbler, iced tea, clear, 5" h., 12 oz. . . 46.00

PRINCESS, Hocking Glass Co., 1931-35 (Process-etched)

Ashtray, green, 4½" 68.00
Bowl, berry, 4½", green 26.00
Bowl, berry, 4½", pink. 30.00
Bowl, berry, 4½", yellow 42.00
Bowl, cereal, 5", amber. 20.00
Bowl, cereal, 5", green 37.00
Bowl, cereal, 5", pink 36.00
Bowl, cereal, 5", pink frosted 20.00
Bowl, cereal, 5", yellow 30.00
Bowl, salad, 9" octagon, green. 43.00
Bowl, salad, 9" octagon, pink 44.00
Bowl, salad, 9" octagon, yellow 109.00
Bowl, 9½" hat shape, green 46.00
Bowl, 9½" hat shape, pink 41.00
Bowl, 9½" hat shape, pink frosted 25.00
Bowl, 10" oval vegetable, green. 29.00
Bowl, 10" oval vegetable, pink 39.00
Bowl, 10" oval vegetable, yellow 55.00
Butter dish, cov., green 107.00
Butter dish, cov., pink 95.00
Cake stand, green, 10". 31.00
Cake stand, pink, 10" 31.00
Candy jar, cov., green 67.00
Candy jar, cov., pink. 69.00
Coaster, green, 4" 38.00

Princess Cookie Jar

Cookie jar, cov., green (ILLUS.). 58.00
Cookie jar, cov., pink 64.00
Creamer, oval, amber. 13.00
Creamer, oval, green 13.00
Creamer, oval, pink. 20.00
Creamer, oval, yellow 15.00
Cup & saucer, green 22.00
Cup & saucer, pink. 24.00
Cup & saucer, yellow 12.00

Pitcher, 6" h., 37 oz., jug-type, green . . **51.00**
Pitcher, 6" h., 37 oz., jug-type, pink . . . **68.00**
Pitcher, 8" h., 60 oz., jug-type, pink . . . **67.00**
Pitcher, 8" h., 60 oz., jug-type,
  yellow **100.00**
Plate, sherbet, 5½" , green **9.00**
Plate, sherbet, 5½" , pink **10.00**
Plate, sherbet, 5½" , yellow. **4.00**
Plate, salad, 8" d., green. **15.00**
Plate, salad, 8", pink **15.00**
Plate, salad, 8", yellow **10.00**
Plate, dinner, 9", green **30.00**
Plate, dinner, 9", pink **28.00**
Plate, dinner, 9", yellow. **14.00**
Plate, grill, 9", amber. **7.00**
Plate, grill, 9", pink **12.00**
Plate, grill, 9", yellow. **8.00**
Plate, grill, 10½", closed handles,
  amber **5.00**
Plate, grill, 10½", closed handles,
  yellow **6.00**
Plate, sandwich, 11¼", handled,
  green **16.00**
Plate, sandwich, 11¼", handled, pink . . **31.00**
Platter, 12" oval, closed handles,
  green **28.00**
Platter, 12" oval, closed handles, pink . **25.00**
Platter, 12" oval, closed handles,
  yellow **52.00**
Relish, divided, green, 7½". **24.00**
Relish, divided, pink, 7½". **32.00**
Relish, green, 7½" **103.00**
Salt & pepper shakers, green,
  4½" h., pr. **52.00**
Salt & pepper shakers, pink, 4½" h.,
  pr. **52.00**
Salt & pepper shakers, yellow,
  4½" h., pr. **78.00**
Salt & pepper (or spice) shakers,
  green, 5½" h., pr. **45.00**
Sherbet, footed, green **22.00**
Sherbet, footed, pink **24.00**
Sugar bowl, open, amber. **9.00**
Sugar bowl, open, green **9.00**
Sugar bowl, open, yellow. **9.00**
Tumbler, juice, green, 3" h., 5 oz.. . . . . **28.00**
Tumbler, juice, pink, 3" h., 5 oz. **32.00**
Tumbler, juice, yellow, 3" h., 5 oz. **23.00**
Tumbler, water, green, 4" h., 9 oz. **31.00**
Tumbler, water, yellow, 4" h., 9 oz. . . . **23.00**
Tumbler, footed, green, 5¼" h., 10 oz. . **34.00**
Tumbler, footed, pink, 5¼" h. 10 oz.. . . **27.00**
Tumbler, footed, yellow, 5¼" h.,
  10 oz.. . . . . **23.00**
Tumbler, footed, green, 6½" h.,
  12½ oz. **99.00**
Tumbler, footed, pink, 6½" h.,
  12½ oz. **95.00**
Tumbler, iced tea, green, 5¼" h.,
  13 oz.. . . . . **41.00**

Tumbler, iced tea, pink, 5¼" h.,
  13 oz.. . . . . **43.00**
Tumbler, iced tea, yellow, 5¼" h.,
  13 oz.. . . . . **28.00**
Vase, 8" h., green **36.00**
Vase, 8" h., pink **44.00**

SAILBOATS or Ships or Sportsman Series, Hazel Atlas Glass Co., late 1930s

Ashtray. **25.00**
Cocktail mixer w/stirrer. **27.00**
Ice bowl **31.00**
Plate, bread & butter, 5⅞" d. **22.00**
Plate, salad, 8" d. **40.00**
Plate, dinner, 9" d. **44.00**
Tumbler, shot glass, 2¼" h., 2 oz. . . . **145.00**
Tumbler, juice, 3¾" h., 5 oz.. . . . . **13.00**
Tumbler, roly poly, 6 oz. **10.00**
Tumbler, old fashioned, 3⅜" h., 8 oz.. . **15.00**
Tumbler, water, straight sides, 3¾" h.,
  9 oz.. . . . . **15.00**
Tumbler, water, 4⅝" h., 9 oz. **12.00**
Tumbler, iced tea, 4⅞" h., 10½ oz.. . . . **16.00**

SHARON or Cabbage Rose, Federal Glass Co., 1935-39 (Chip-mold)

Bowl, berry, 5" d., amber **7.00**
Bowl, berry, 5" d., green. **17.00**
Bowl, berry, 5" d., pink **14.00**
Bowl, cream soup, 5" d., amber **23.00**
Bowl, cream soup, 5" d., pink. **49.00**
Bowl, cereal, 6" d., amber. **20.00**
Bowl, cereal, 6" d., pink **31.00**
Bowl, soup, 7½" d., pink. **48.00**
Bowl, berry, 8½" d., amber **7.00**
Bowl, berry, 8½" d., pink. **33.00**
Bowl, 9½" oval vegetable, amber. **18.00**
Bowl, 9½" oval vegetable, green **35.00**
Bowl, fruit, 10½" d., amber **19.00**
Bowl, fruit, 10½" d., green **40.00**
Bowl, fruit, 10½" d., pink. **41.00**
Butter dish, cov., amber. **42.00**
Butter dish, cov., green **90.00**
Butter dish, cov., pink **55.00**
Cake plate, footed, amber, 11½" d. . . . **21.00**
Cake plate, footed, clear, 11½" d. **14.00**
Cake plate, footed, pink, 11½" d **38.00**
Candy jar, cov., amber. **43.00**
Candy jar, cov., green **174.00**
Candy jar, cov., pink. **59.00**
Cup & saucer, amber. **10.00**
Cup & saucer, green **32.00**
Cup & saucer, pink. **25.00**
Jam dish, amber, 7½" d., 1½" h. **36.00**
Pitcher, 9" h., 80 oz., amber. **105.00**
Pitcher w/ice lip, 9" h., 80 oz.,
  amber. **120.00**
Pitcher w/ice lip, 9"h., 80 oz., pink. . . **164.00**

Plate, bread & butter, 6" d., amber 4.00
Plate, bread & butter, 6" d., green. 9.00
Plate, bread & butter, 6" d., pink. 9.00
Plate, salad, 7½" d., amber. 13.00
Plate, salad, 7½" d., green 25.00
Plate, dinner, 9¼" d., amber 9.00
Plate, dinner, 9¼" d., pink. 20.00
Platter, 12¼" oval, amber. 16.00
Platter, 12¼" oval, green 33.00
Platter, 12¼" oval, pink. 32.00
Salt & pepper shakers, amber, pr. . . . 36.00
Salt & pepper shakers, green, pr. 76.00
Salt & pepper shakers, pink, pr. 49.00
Sherbet, footed, amber. 8.00
Sherbet, footed, green 38.00
Sherbet, footed, pink 17.00
Sugar bowl, cov., amber 31.00
Sugar bowl, cov., pink. 42.00
Sugar bowl, open, pink 13.00
Tumbler, amber, 4" h., 9 oz. 27.00
Tumbler, pink, 4" h., 9 oz. 43.00
Tumbler, pink, 5¼" h., 12 oz. 51.00
Tumbler, footed, pink, 6½" h., 15 oz. . . 60.00

SIERRA or Pinwheel, Jeannette Glass Co., 1931-33 (Press-mold)

Bowl, cereal, 5½" d., green. 15.00
Bowl, cereal, 5½" d., pink. 14.00
Bowl, berry, 8½" d., green 31.00
Bowl, berry, 8½" d., pink. 30.00
Bowl, 9½" oval vegetable, green 91.00
Bowl, 9½" oval vegetable, pink. 41.00
Butter dish, cov., green 70.00
Butter dish, cov., pink 59.00
Creamer, green. 21.00
Cup & saucer, green 22.00
Cup & saucer, pink. 17.00
Plate, dinner, 9" d., green. 21.00
Platter, 11" oval, green. 41.00
Salt & pepper shakers, pink, pr. 43.00
Serving tray, two-handled, green. 19.00
Sugar bowl, cov., green. 36.00
Tumbler, footed, green, 4½" h., 9 oz. . . 83.00

SWIRL or Petal Swirl, Jeannette Glass Co., 1937-38 (Press-mold)

Bowl, cereal, 5¼" d., Delphite. 12.00
Bowl, cereal, 5¼" d., pink. 10.00
Bowl, cereal, 5¼" d., ultramarine 16.00
Bowl, 9" d., rimmed, pink. 18.00
Bowl, 9" d., rimmed, ultramarine. 26.00
Bowl, salad, 9" d., Delphite. 30.00
Bowl, salad, 9" d., pink. 18.00
Bowl, salad, 9" d., ultramarine 28.00
Bowl, fruit, 10" d., closed handles, footed, ultramarine 29.00
Butter dish, cov., pink 185.00
Butter dish, cov., ultramarine. 260.00
Candleholders, double, ultramarine, pr. 46.00
Candy dish, cov., pink 120.00

Swirl Candy Dish

Candy dish, cov., ultramarine (ILLUS.). 120.00
Candy dish, open, three-footed, pink, 5½" d. 13.00
Candy dish, open, three-footed, ultramarine, 5½" d. 19.00
Coaster, pink, 3¼" d., 1" h. 15.00
Coaster, ultramarine, 3¼" d., 1" h. 13.00
Console bowl, footed, pink, 10½" d. . . 16.00
Console bowl, footed, ultramarine, 10½" d. 30.00
Creamer, Delphite. 11.00
Creamer, pink. 9.00
Creamer, ultramarine 16.00
Cup & saucer, Delphite 16.00
Cup & saucer, pink. 12.00
Cup & saucer, ultramarine 21.00
Plate, sherbet, 6½" d., Delphite 7.00
Plate, sherbet, 6½" d., pink. 5.00
Plate, sherbet, 6½" d., ultramarine 7.00
Plate, 7¼" d., ultramarine 14.00
Plate, salad, 8" d., ultramarine 13.00
Plate, dinner, 9½" d., Delphite 14.00
Plate, dinner, 9½" d., pink. 12.00
Plate, dinner, 9½" d., ultramarine 19.00
Plate, sandwich, 12½" d., pink 17.00
Plate, sandwich, 12½" d., ultramarine. . 29.00
Platter, 12" oval, Delphite 35.00
Salt & pepper shakers, Delphite, pr. . . 95.00
Salt & pepper shakers, ultramarine, pr. 41.00
Sherbet, pink 11.00
Sherbet, ultramarine. 22.00
Soup bowl w/lug handles, pink. 19.00
Sugar bowl, open, Delphite. 9.00
Sugar bowl, open, pink 10.00
Sugar bowl, open, ultramarine 15.00
Tumbler, footed, pink, 9 oz. 14.00
Tumbler, footed, ultramarine, 9 oz. . . . 43.00
Tumbler, pink, 4" h., 9 oz. 11.00
Tumbler, ultramarine, 4" h., 9 oz. 38.00
Tumbler, pink, 4⅝" h., 9 oz. 16.00
Tumbler, ultramarine, 5⅛" h., 13 oz. 124.00
Vase, 6½" h., pink 17.00

Swirl Vase

Vase, 8½" h., ultramarine (ILLUS.) **27.00**

TEA ROOM, Indiana Glass Co., 1926-31 (Press-mold)

Banana split dish, flat, green, 7½" . . . **99.00**
Banana split dish, footed, clear,
7½" **43.00**
Banana split dish, footed, green,
7½" **78.00**
Bowl, salad, 8¾" d., green **115.00**
Bowl, 9½" oval vegetable, green **69.00**
Candlesticks, green, pr. **66.00**
Candlesticks, pink, pr. **64.00**
Celery or pickle dish, green, 8½" **30.00**
Creamer, pink, 3¼" h. **26.00**
Creamer, footed, green, 4½" h. **20.00**
Creamer, footed, pink, 4½" h. **15.00**
Creamer, rectangular, green. **16.00**
Creamer, rectangular, pink **15.00**
Creamer & open sugar bowl on
rectangular tray, green **96.00**
Creamer & open sugar bowl on
rectangular tray, pink. **60.00**
Cup & saucer, green **62.00**
Cup & saucer, pink. **76.00**
Finger bowl, green **85.00**
Finger bowl, pink. **62.00**
Goblet, green, 9 oz. **78.00**
Goblet, pink, 9 oz. **70.00**
Ice bucket, green **85.00**
Ice bucket, pink **67.00**
Lamp, electric, pink, 9" **84.00**
Mustard, cov., clear **79.00**
Parfait, clear **65.00**
Parfait, green **64.00**
Pitcher, 64 oz., green **160.00**
Pitcher, 64 oz., pink **150.00**
Plate, sandwich, w/center handle,
green **194.00**
Plate, sandwich, w/center handle,
pink **163.00**
Plate, 10½" d., two-handled, green. . . . **50.00**
Relish, divided, green **25.00**
Relish, divided, pink **13.00**
Salt & pepper shakers, green, pr. **70.00**

Salt & pepper shakers, pink, pr. **63.00**
Sherbet, low, flared edge, clear **19.00**
Sherbet, low, flared edge, green **30.00**
Sherbet, low, flared edge, pink **25.00**
Sherbet, low footed, green **30.00**
Sherbet, low footed, pink **23.00**
Sherbet, tall footed, clear **28.00**
Sherbet, tall footed, green **44.00**
Sherbet, tall footed, pink. **40.00**
Sugar bowl, open, rectangular,
green **23.00**
Sugar bowl, open, rectangular, pink . . **15.00**
Sugar bowl, cov., green, 3" h. **100.00**
Sugar bowl, open, green, 4" h. **20.00**
Sugar bowl, open, pink, 4" h. **16.00**
Sugar bowl, open, footed, green,
4½" h. **22.00**
Sugar bowl, open, footed, pink,
4½" h. **17.00**
Sundae, footed, ruffled, clear **48.00**
Sundae, footed, ruffled, green **115.00**
Tray, rectangular, for creamer &
sugar bowl, green **48.00**
Tray, rectangular, for creamer &
sugar bowl, pink **52.00**
Tray w/center handle, for creamer &
sugar bowl, green **175.00**
Tray w/center handle, for creamer &
sugar bowl, pink **163.00**
Tumbler, footed, clear, 6 oz. **28.00**
Tumbler, footed, green, 6 oz. **42.00**
Tumbler, footed, pink, 6 oz. **32.00**
Tumbler, footed, green, 5¼" h.,
8 oz. **41.00**
Tumbler, footed, pink, 5¼" h., 8 oz. . . . **36.00**
Tumbler, green, 4 3/16" h., 8½ oz. . . . **105.00**
Tumbler, footed, clear, 11 oz. **33.00**
Tumbler, footed, green, 11 oz. **49.00**
Tumbler, footed, pink, 11 oz. **46.00**
Tumbler, footed, clear, 12 oz. **45.00**
Tumbler, footed, green, 12 oz. **63.00**
Tumbler, footed, pink, 12 oz. **79.00**
Vase, 6½" h., ruffled rim, green. **230.00**
Vase, 6½" h., ruffled rim, pink **113.00**
Vase, 11" h., ruffled rim, clear **120.00**
Vase, 11" h., straight, green **151.00**
Vase, 11" h., straight, pink **165.00**

WATERFORD or Waffle, Hocking Glass Co., 1938-44 (Press-mold)

Ashtray, clear, 4" **8.00**
Bowl, berry, 4¾" d., clear **7.00**
Bowl, berry, 4¾" d., pink. **18.00**
Bowl, cereal, 5¼" d., clear **19.00**
Bowl, cereal, 5¼" d., pink. **35.00**
Bowl, berry, 8¼" d., clear **10.00**
Bowl, berry, 8¼" d., pink. **25.00**
Butter dish, cov., clear. **24.00**
Butter dish, cov., pink **217.00**
Cake plate, handled, clear, 10¼" d. . . . **10.00**
Cake plate, handled, pink, 10¼" d. **19.00**

Coaster, clear, 4" d. 4.00
Creamer, oval, clear 5.00
Creamer, oval, pink. 12.00
Cup & saucer, clear 10.00
Cup & saucer, pink 19.00
Goblet, clear, 5¼" h. 16.00
Goblet, clear, 5½" h. (Miss America
    Style). 33.00
Lamp, clear, 4" h. 28.00
Pitcher, juice, 42 oz., tilt-type, clear . . . 25.00
Pitcher w/ice lip, 80 oz., clear 34.00
Pitcher w/ice lip, 80 oz., pink. 173.00
Plate, sherbet, 6" d., clear. 4.00
Plate, sherbet, 6" d., pink 8.00
Plate, salad, 7½" d., clear. 7.00
Plate, salad, 7½" d., pink 10.00
Plate, dinner, 9⅝" d., clear 10.00
Plate, dinner, 9⅝" d., pink. 25.00
Plate, sandwich, 13¾" d., clear. 10.00
Plate, sandwich, 13¾" d., pink 26.00
Relish, five-section, clear, 13¾" d. 16.00
Salt & pepper shakers, clear,
    short, pr. 8.00
Salt & pepper shakers, clear,
    tall, pr. 9.00
Sherbet, footed, clear 4.00
Sherbet, footed, pink 14.00
Sugar bowl, cov., oval, clear 10.00
Sugar bowl, cov., oval, pink 19.00
Tumbler, footed, clear, 5" h., 10 oz. . . . 11.00
Tumbler, footed, pink, 5" h., 10 oz.. . . . 24.00

DEVEZ & DEGUÉ

The Saint-Hilaire, Touvier, de Varreaux and Company of Pantin, France used the name De Vez on their cameo glass earlier this century. Some of their examples were marked "Degué," after one of their master glassmakers. Officially the company was named "Cristallerie de Pantin."

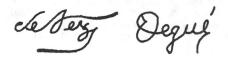

DeVez & Degué Marks

Cameo bell, amber overlaid on red & cut w/daisy flowers & leaves, metal handle, tassel-shaped clapper on chain, 6½" diagonal opening, 8¼" h. $8,025.00
Cameo vase, 3½" h., 4" d., round slightly flaring cylindrical body w/a wide squared rim, frosted shaded pale yellow to burgundy overlaid in blackish green & cut w/a silhouetted landscape w/large evergreens against a waterway w/islands & skimming birds,

mountains in the distance, signed "deVez" 715.00
Cameo vase, 4¾" h., 4½" d., bulbous body w/flaring foot & rim, blue cut to red cut to cream w/a scene of palm trees & a city by the sea 795.00

Degué Scenic Cameo Vase

Cameo vase, 6½" h., 2⅞" d., swelled cylindrical body tapering to a cylindrical neck, mottled orange & red overlaid in deep maroon & cut w/an Arabic desert scene of a camel standing beside a man & a watery oasis, pointed lancet top border, signed "Degué" (ILLUS.). 695.00
Cameo vase, 7¾" h., blue cut to yellow cut to white w/a scene of a girl standing on top of a rocky crag wearing a dress w/a patch & a cape, her hand raised shielding her eyes, a goat at her side, background shows mountains, water, village & trees 4,050.00
Cameo vase, 8" h., 3¾" d., base tapering upwards to a tiny top, cameo-cut w/water, buildings, mountains & foliage including hanging vines, frosted ground overlaid in light & dark blues & pale yellow, signed 950.00
Cameo vase, 8½" h., slightly swelled cylindrical body tapering to a short cylindrical neck fitted w/a gilt-metal rim w/embossed fruit & nut decoration, the sides cameo-cut w/a harbor scene w/dark brown boats w/full sails & a man w/oar backed by detailed buildings & trees extending into calm red & yellow water against a distant deep red, pink & yellow mountain range & a yellow sky w/red clouds, dark brown long stems & leaves w/clumps of deep violet blossoms suspended from the metal rim, in ring-embossed round, flaring gilt-

metal foot, signed in cameo
"DeVez" **1,210.00**
Cameo vase, 9" h., compressed
bulbous base w/tall, slender
tapering sides to a small mouth, a
bluish grey ground overlaid in
cobalt blue & cut w/a landscape
w/a leafy tree in the foreground &
trees & cactus on a distant rocky
island & ivory blue colored
mountains, signed "DeVez" **990.00**
Cameo vase, 19" h., Art Deco-style,
tall waisted trumpet-form body on a
cushion foot, mottled white & clear
layered in bright royal blue &
etched w/repeating stylized foliate
designs up the sides, signed on the
side "Degué," marked on the base
"Made in France" **1,380.00**
Vase, 4¼" h., baluster-form w/flaring
flat rim, yellowish amber top
shading to bluish opalescent
bottom half, etched & enameled
w/burgundy cascading flowering
vines around the rim above a
scene of several sailing vessels in
a harbor, signed "deVez". **495.00**

DORFLINGER

Dorflinger Cocktail Set

Cocktail set: mixing beaker & six
martini glasses; clear w/the tall
flaring cylindrical beaker decorated
w/a large enameled cock, each
stemmed glass w/pairs of cocks,
each glass 4¾" h., beaker 6" h.,
the set (ILLUS.) **$288.00**
Vase, 10¼" h., "Kalana" line, ovoid
body tapering to a short, widely
flaring neck, clear iridescent
surface etched w/butterflies, poppy
blossoms & buds highlighted in
pink w/silver & gold accents
(some gilt wear). **345.00**

DUNCAN & MILLER

*Duncan & Miller Glass Company, a
successor firm to George A. Duncan & Sons
Company, produced a wide range of pressed
wares and novelty pieces during the late 19th
century and into the early 20th century. During
the Depression era and after, they continued
making a wide variety of more modern patterns,
including mold-blown types and also introduced
a number of etched and engraved patterns. Many
colors, including opalescent hues, were produced
during this era and especially popular today are
the graceful swan dishes they produced in the
Pall Mall and Sylvan patterns. The numbers
after the pattern name indicate the original
factory pattern number. The Duncan factory was
closed in 1955. Also see ANIMALS and
PATTERN GLASS in the Glass section.*

Ashtray, model of a duck, clear, large . **$40.00**
Ashtray, model of a duck, clear, small. . **14.00**
Banana boat, Early American
Sandwich patt. (No. 41), milk white,
w/label, 9½" l **250.00**
Basket, handled, Hobnail patt.
(No. 118), clear, 7" h. **22.00**
Basket w/loop handle, Early American
Sandwich patt. clear. **95.00**
Bonbon, round, two-part, two-
handled, Diamond patt. (No. 75),
amber, 6½" l. **15.00**
Bowl, flower, 11½" d., crimped rim,
Early American Sandwich patt.,
clear **38.00**
Bowl, 12" d., flared, flower, etched
First Love patt. (No. 6), clear. **65.00**
Bowl, salad, 12" d., shallow, Hobnail
patt., clear **30.00**
Bowl, 13" oval, flared, etched First
Love patt., clear. **65.00**
Candelabra, one-light w/prisms,
Early American Sandwich patt.,
clear, 11" h., pr. **200.00**
Candelabra, one-light w/prisms,
No. 65 patt., clear, 11½" h. pr. **95.00**
Candlesticks, two-light, etched First
Love patt. (No. 30), clear, pr. **85.00**
Candy jar, cov., footed, etched First
Love patt. (No. 25), clear, 5" h. **55.00**
Celery tray, oval, Teardrop patt.,
(No. 301), clear, 11" l **15.00**
Champagne, Hobnail patt., clear,
5 oz.. . . . . **12.00**
Claret, Teardrop patt., clear **18.00**
Compote, 5½" d., etched First Love
patt., clear **49.00**
Compote, 7" d., Terrace patt.
(No. 111), amber **45.00**
Cornucopia vase, footed, Three
Feathers patt. (No. 117), pink
opalescent, 8" h. **129.00**

Cruet w/original stopper, Caribbean
   patt., clear **69.00**
Cruet w/original stopper, Hobnail
   patt., clear **35.00**
Goblet, water, Hobnail patt., clear **14.00**
Nappy, Canterbury patt., (No. 115),
   clear, 5¼" d. **7.00**
Nut dish, two-part, handled,
   Teardrop patt., clear, 6" l. **17.00**
Plate, 7½" d., Hobnail patt., clear **7.00**
Plate, 8¼" d., Canterbury patt. (No.
   115) w/Lily of the Valley cutting. **15.00**
Plate, 8½" d., Sanibel patt., pink
   opalescent. **45.00**

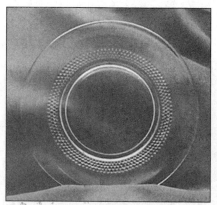

Teardrop Pattern Plate

Plate, 8½" d., Teardrop patt.
   (No. 301), clear (ILLUS.) **8.00**
Punch bowl, Caribbean patt., clear,
   1½ gal.. . . . . **90.00**
Relish dish, five-part, round, Terrace
   patt. (No. 111), clear **40.00**
Relish dish, two-part, round, ring-
   handle, Early American Sandwich
   patt., clear, 6" d. **17.00**
Relish dish, three-part, three-
   handled, etched Language of
   Flowers patt. (No. 115), clear, 9" l. . . **25.00**
Relish dish, two-part, Sanibel patt.,
   pink opalescent, 9" l. **30.00**
Relish dish, four-part, two-handled,
   Early American Sandwich patt.,
   clear, 10" l. **38.00**
Relish dish, three-part oval,
   Canterbury patt., clear, ca. 1950,
   11" l. **24.00**
Relish dish, square, four-part, four-
   handled, Teardrop patt., clear,
   12" d. **45.00**
Relish dish, three-part, Teardrop
   patt., clear, 12" l. **28.00**
Rose bowl, Canterbury patt., clear. . . . **20.00**
Salt & pepper shakers, Hobnail
   patt., clear, 3" h., pr. **20.00**

Sweetmeat, center-handle, Teardrop
   patt., clear, 6½" l. **30.00**
Tray, mint, Sanibel patt. (No. 130),
   blue opalescent, 7" l. **40.00**
Tray, mint, Sanibel patt. ,
   pink opalescent, 7" l. **40.00**
Tray, celery, oblong, etched First Love
   patt. (No. 30), clear, 12" l. **69.00**
Tumbler, juice, footed, Teardrop
   patt., clear, 5 oz. **12.00**
Tumbler, water, footed, Early
   American Sandwich patt., clear,
   4¾" h., 9 oz. **13.00**
Tumbler, iced-tea, footed, Teardrop
   patt., clear, 5½" h., 12 oz. **16.00**
Vase, 5" h., crimped rim, footed, Early
   American Sandwich patt., clear **25.00**
Wine, Teardrop patt., clear **17.00**
Wine, Canterbury patt. (No. 115),
   clear, 5" h., 4 oz. **15.00**
Wine, Canterbury patt., clear, 5 oz. . . . **10.00**

DURAND

Fine decorative glass similar to that made by Tiffany and other outstanding glasshouses of its day was made by the Vineland Flint Glass Works Co. in Vineland, New Jersey, first headed by Victor Durand, Sr., and subsequently by his son Victor Durand, Jr., in the 1920s.

Boudoir lamps, a tapering ovoid
   body in deep orange w/pinkish
   silver iridescent 'King Tut' patt.
   fitted on a brass connector to a
   matching cylindrical glass pedestal
   on a flaring ringed brass foot, brass
   collar & electric socket w/a clear &
   frosted glass chimney fitted w/a
   wide conical pierced filigree silver
   plate Gorham shade, early 20th c.,
   glass unmarked, 15" h., pr. **$1,430.00**
Bowl, 4¼" d., 2" h., wide squatty
   lower body tapering slightly to an
   upright smooth rim, overall blue
   iridescence w/white heart & vine
   decoration, base marked in silver
   "V Durand #3" **575.00**
Bowl, footed, 6½" d., 4¼" h., wide
   bulbous acorn-form body w/closed
   rim in iridescent cobalt blue
   decorated w/iridescent blue leaves
   & entwined vines, raised on a short
   ambergris pedestal & round
   foot **1,870.00**
Compote, cov., 10½" h., "Bridgeton
   Rose" design, a round disc foot
   below a short knopped stem
   supporting a tall inverted pear-form
   body w/a short rim fitted w/a tall
   bell-form cover w/a knob finial,

Durand "Bridgeton Rose" Compote

Spanish yellow cased body w/etched & wheel-cut floral sprig decoration cut to clear, matching cover, marked w/Durand in "V" mark possibly added (ILLUS.) **374.00**

Lamp, torchere-type, black wrought-iron frame w/three long scrolling legs w/applied long acanthus leaves centering a large ball drop below three upward scrolling acanthus leaves framing an inverted slightly flaring cylindrical trumpet shade in iridescent gold w/long pointed opal leaves w/gold veining & emerald green tips, wrapped w/random gold iridescent threading, shade 10" h., overall 15" h. **770.00**

Plate, 8" d., round w/turned-up rim, the center w/a wide circle of opalescent white King Tut pulled swirl design w/lightly iridized finish, the opalescent yellow wide border band w/spaced stripes of blue pulled design **1,320.00**

Rose bowl, short pedestal base below the spherical bowl, iridescent yellowish amber w/the exterior etched overall w/a design of fern wreath & fringed blossoms, early 20th c., signed, 4¾" h. **1,100.00**

Sherbet, wide deep round orangish gold iridescent bowl wrapped w/golden threading, raised on a short stem & disc foot in bluish green iridescence, 4¼" d., 3" h. ... **385.00**

Sherbet & underplate, footed emerald green sherbet w/widely flaring optic-ribbed bowl w/a gently ruffled rim trimmed w/an applied white band, matching underplate w/white rim, underplate 6¼" d., sherbet 2½" h., the set **193.00**

Vase, 6" h., wide ovoid body tapering to a wide mouth w/a low rolled rim, overall iridescent blue decorated around the body w/random white opal webbed vines & scattered heart-shaped leaves, signed "V. Durand 1968-6" **990.00**

Vase, 6" h., wide ovoid body w/the rounded shoulder tapering to a short widely flaring flattened neck, overall ambergris gold iridescence, signed "V. Durand 1710-6" **374.00**

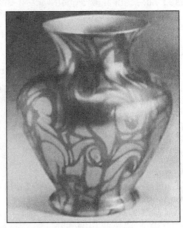

Durand "King Tut" Pattern Vase

Vase, 6¼" h., bulbous baluster-form w/wide flaring neck, overall King Tut design in iridescent green swirls & coils on a warm orange ground cased in white w/lustered orange interior, Larson foot (ILLUS.)...................... **690.00**

Vase, 6½" h., bulbous nearly spherical body w/a small short trumpet neck, gold iridescent ground overlaid w/horizontal bands of random pale red w/frosted webbed vines & bubbles, unmarked **1,045.00**

Vase, 7½" h., a wide squatty bulbous body w/a wide flat shoulder centered by a short waisted neck w/a large bulbous upper section below the rolled & flattened mouth, overall peacock blue iridescence, signed & numbered "1977-8" **1,375.00**

Vase, 7½" h., flaring cylindrical body w/a rounded shoulder tapering to a short wide cylindrical neck w/a flaring flattened rim, dark iridescent blue entirely wrapped w/random blue threading, signed in silver "Durand 1812-8" (threading nearly perfect) **908.00**

Vase, 7½" h., simple ovoid body tapering to a short, wide flaring neck, overall dark blue iridescence decorated w/random white opal entwined vines w/scattered heart-shaped leaves, signed "Durand #1812-7".................... **1,100.00**

Vase, 7½" h., slender cylindrical body w/a flaring foot & rim, overall blue iridescence, signed "Durand #1714" **743.00**

Vase, 8" h., tapering cylindrical body, cased iridescent blue, signed "V. Durand #1970-8"........... **660.00**

Vase, 8" h., wide squatty bulbous body w/the wide rounded shoulder centering a short cylindrical neck under w/deep rolled rim, ambergris w/overall blue iridescence, signed "V. Durand 20161-8" **1,265.00**

Vase, 8½" h., a flaring cylindrical body w/a rounded shoulder tapering to a short cylindrical neck w/a wide flattened, flaring rim, the exterior in greenish aqua decorated overall in the King Tut design w/iridescent silvery gold swirls, gold iridescent interior **1,045.00**

Vase, 9½" h., 11½" d., large spherical body tapering to a small, short flaring neck, overall Egyptian craquelle design w/scattered emerald green & white raised patches on a silvery amber ground **1,980.00**

Vase, 9¾" h., gently swelled ovoid body tapering to a short flaring trumpet neck, "Lady Gay Rose," orange lining cased w/white decorated w/a rose red surface covered w/a swirled King Tut iridescent design in gold & silver **1,495.00**

Vase, 12" h., round foot below a bulbous lower segment tapering sharply to a tall, slender baluster-form body w/flaring rim all in iridescent peacock blue, applied ambergris foot & curved handles from the lower body to the top of the bulbous segment **2,310.00**

Vase, 12" h., tall slender slightly waisted cylindrical body w/a flared rim, bright transparent green shaded to clear w/five green & white striped pulled feathers **748.00**

Vase, 12¼" h., footed slender trumpet-form body, shaded purplish blue iridescence w/overall gold heart & vine design & an aplied gold pedestal foot, marked "Durand 20120-12" **1,725.00**

Bottle-form Durand Vase

Vase, 15" h., bottle-form, squatty bulbous wide-shouldered base w/flattened side indentation, below a tall slender tapering 'stick' neck w/flared rim, overall gold iridescence, signed on base "V Durand 1974-15" (ILLUS.).... **1,150.00**

Vase, 17" h., large spherical body topped by a tall flaring trumpet neck, the emerald green exterior covered in the King Tut design w/iridescent silvery & golden banding, iridescent gold interior, silver company signature w/"#1716-167½" h." **3,795.00**

FENTON

Fenton Art Glass Company began producing glass at Williamstown, West Virginia, in January 1907. Organized by Frank L. and John W. Fenton, the company began operations in a newly built glass factory with an experienced master glass craftsman, Jacob Rosenthal, as their factory manager. Fenton has produced a wide variety of collectible glassware through the years, including Carnival. Still in production today, their current productions may be found at finer gift shops across the country. William Heacock's three-volume set on Fenton, published by Antique Publications, is the standard reference in this field.

Fenton Mark

Basket, looped handle, canary
    opalescent Daisy & Fern patt..... **$190.00**
Basket, Peach Crest, milk white
    applied handle.................. **65.00**
Basket, Hobnail patt., cranberry
    opalescent, 4½" h............... **53.00**
Basket, Black Rose patt., black
    handle, 7" h. **225.00**
Basket, milk white w/matching
    handle, Hobnail patt., 12" d. **54.00**
Bonbon, crimped rim, Hobnail patt.,
    cranberry opalescent............. **20.00**
Bonbon, double crimped rim, Hobnail
    patt., blue opalescent **22.00**
Bowl, fruit, pedestal-footed, square,
    Silver Crest **70.00**
Bowl, heart-shaped, Apple Blossom
    Crest **48.00**
Bowl, 6" d., No. 1092, open-edge
    basket design w/cupped bowl,
    Topaz Opalescent, ca. 1963 ...... **25.00**
Bowl, 8" d., Burmese, footed, deep
    lobed sides w/a tall, flaring ruffled
    rim, No. 7422. .... **150.00**
Bowl, 9½" d., crimped rim, Black
    Rose patt. **90.00**
Bowl, 9½" d., double crimped rim,
    Hobnail patt., blue opalescent...... **60.00**
Bowl, 10" d., cupped rim,
    Silver Crest **40.00**
Bowl, 10" d., double crimped rim,
    Peach Crest, No. 1522 .... **95.00**
Bowl, 13" d., double crimped rim,
    Peach Crest. **145.00**
Cake plate, high-footed, Silver Crest,
    13" d. **40.00**
Candlestick, crimped rim, footed,
    Hobnail patt., milk white **25.00**
Candlesticks, cornucopia-form,
    Silver Crest, pr. **58.00**
Candlesticks, low, Diamond Optic
    patt., green, pr. **35.00**
Candy jar, cov., No. 643, stretch-
    type, Celeste Blue **75.00**
Cigarette holder, hat-shaped, Hobnail
    patt., blue opalescent, 2½" h. **35.00**
Cocktail shaker, cov., Georgian
    patt., cobalt blue **135.00**
Cookie jar, cov., Big Cookies patt.,
    black, w/handle **100.00**
Cookie jar, cov., Big Cookies patt.,
    Jade green **94.00**
Creamer & open sugar bowl,
    Hobnail patt., No. 3906, French
    Opalescent, pr. **35.00**
Creamer, open sugar bowl & tray,
    Hobnail patt., No. 3917, milk white,
    the set **25.00**
Epergne, three-lily, apartment size,
    Hobnail patt., milk white, No. 1948A ... **25.00**
Epergne, four-lily, Hobnail patt., milk
    white, 8" h. **35.00**

Ginger jar, cov., Crystal Ming patt.... **165.00**
Goblet, Hobnail patt., blue opalescent. . . **22.00**
Hurricane lamps & bases, Black
    Rose patt., black bases, pr....... **550.00**
Lamp, Peacock patt., chimney shade
    w/flaring ruffled rim centered on a
    low wide cushion-form base, No. G-70,
    satin black & crystal, 10½" h. **175.00**
Model of a top hat, French
    Opalescent Swirl patt., 7 x 10" **175.00**
Mug, Georgian patt., ruby, 10 oz...... **65.00**
Nut dish, flaring bell-form bowl raised
    on slender stem & round foot,
    Cactus patt., Topaz Opalescent,
    No. 3428, ca. 1959-60, 5½" h. **50.00**
Perfume atomizer, Dot Optic patt.,
    blue **95.00**
Perfume atomizer, Hobnail patt.,
    blue opalescent................ **75.00**
Perfume atomizer, Spiral Optic patt.,
    blue opalescent, tall. **125.00**
Pitcher, Hobnail patt., milk white **60.00**
Pitcher, indented ice lip, Coin Dot patt.
    No. 1353, cranberry opalescent..... **325.00**
Pitcher, cream, 4" h., Dot Optic patt.,
    No. 1924, cranberry opalescent **60.00**
Pitcher, jug-type, 5" h. Diamond
    Optic patt., No. 192, mulberry **195.00**
Pitcher, jug-type, 5½" h., squatty body,
    Hobnail patt., blue opalescent **50.00**
Plate, 7¼" square, No. 1639, etched,
    cobalt blue.................... **80.00**
Plate, 8½" d., Aqua Crest **25.00**
Plate, 8½" d., Silver Crest........... **25.00**
Plate, 12" d., Silver Crest **29.00**
Rose bowl, Inverted Thumbprint
    patt., cranberry **60.00**
**Salt & pepper shakers w/original
    lids,** footed, Hobnail patt., Topaz
    Opalescent, pr. **110.00**
**Salt & pepper shakers w/original
    lids,** Hobnail patt., cranberry
    opalescent, pr.................. **85.00**
Tidbit tray, two-tier, Silver Crest,
    large **45.00**
Tumbler, barrel-shaped, Dot Optic
    patt., cranberry opalescent **45.00**
Tumbler, juice, Hobnail patt., blue
    opalescent, 5 oz................ **14.00**
Tumbler, Coin Dot patt., cranberry,
    12 oz.. .... **40.00**
Vase, 4" h., flared ruffled rim
    w/bulbous base, Beaded Melon
    patt., No. 711, green overlay....... **30.00**
Vase, 4" h., footed, Hobnail patt., blue
    opalescent.................... **28.00**
Vase, 4½" h., Hobnail patt., cranberry
    opalescent.................... **50.00**
Vase, 4½" h., Spiral Optic patt.,
    cranberry..................... **85.00**
Vase, 5" h., fan-shaped, stretch-type,
    Velva Rose **80.00**

Vase, 6" h., fan-shaped, footed,
Hobnail patt., blue opalescent **35.00**

Vase, 6" h., swirled bulbous base
w/slender neck & flared ruffled rim,
Silver Jamestown blue, No. 6056,
ca. 1957-59 . . . . **45.00**

Vase, 6½" h., waisted cylindrical body
w/a four-lobed flattened crimped
rim, No. 1923, Aqua Crest **40.00**

Vase, 6¾" h., Vessel of Gems patt.,
footed tapering cylindrical body
molded w/large berry prunts, from
a Verlys mold, reddish orange,
No. 8253, 1968 . . . . **220.00**

Vase, 7" h., footed bulbous base
w/slender neck & flared rim,
Burmese, No. 7252, decorated **95.00**

Vase, 7½" h., footed, rounded cylindrical body w/flaring trumpet neck,
Heart & Hanging Vine patt., pink on
custard, molded Fenton mark **127.00**

Vase, 7½" h., squared body w/pinched
sides on flaring foot, slender
trumpet neck w/deeply flared &
crimped rim, Hanging Heart patt.,
turquoise, molded Fenton mark **55.00**

Vase, 7½" h., squatty bulbous knobby
lobed body w/a short ringed neck &
a widely flaring crimped & ruffled
rim, Ruby Overlay, Diamond Optic
patt., No. 192 . . . . **40.00**

Vase, 8" h., fan-shaped, stretch-type,
Velva Rose **95.00**

Vase, 8" h., ovoid body w/flared rim,
Hanging Heart patt., bittersweet
w/rare experimental satin finish,
Robert Barber Collection **330.00**

Vase, 8" h., ovoid body w/flaring
trumpet neck, Hanging Heart patt.,
custard iris, Robert Barber
Collection, etched "Fenton 1976" . . **193.00**

Vase, 8" h., Peach Crest, No. 7258 . . . **45.00**

Vase, 8" h., scalloped rim, footed,
Hobnail patt., yellow opalescent **75.00**

Vase, 8" h., Wild Rose line, footed
cylindrical body w/pinched panels
below the short cylindrical neck
w/flaring crimped rim, deep pink
exterior w/trapped air bubbles, white
lining, No. WR1358, ca. 1961-62 . . . . **83.00**

Vase, 8½" h., Coin Dot patt.,
cranberry **110.00**

Vase, 8½" h., tulip-type w/jack-in-the-
pulpit rim, Black Rose line, No.
7250, ca. 1953-54 . . . . **175.00**

Vase, 9" h., Mandarin patt.,
milk white **85.00**

Vase, 9" h., Mandarin patt., Peking
blue **68.00**

Vase, 10" h., gently tapering cylindrical
round body w/trumpet neck,
Hanging Heart patt., custard w/satin
finish, Robert Barber Collection **165.00**

Vase, 11" h., ovoid body tapering to a
long flared neck, Hanging Heart patt.
turquoise iris, Robert Barber Collection,
etched "Fenton 351/600DGS" **182.00**

Vase, 12" h., fan-shaped,
Silver Crest **95.00**

Vases, 8" h., jack-in-the-pulpit-style,
Black Rose, pr. **77.00**

Water set: pitcher & five tumblers;
blue opalescent Christmas
Snowflake patt., 6 pcs. **395.00**

FINDLAY ONYX & FLORADINE

*In January, 1889, the glass firm of Dalzell,
Gilmore & Leighton Co. of Findlay, Ohio began
production of these scarce glass lines. Onyx ware
was a white-lined glass produced mainly in onyx
(creamy yellowish white) but also in bronze and
ruby shades sometimes called cinnamon, rose or
raspberry. Pieces featured raised flowers and
leaves that are silver-colored or, less often,
bronze. By contrast the Floradine line was
produced in ruby and autumn leaf (gold) with
opalescent flowers and leaves. It is not lined.*

Bowl, master berry, 8" d., 2¾" h.,
wide squatty bulbous flat-bottomed
form w/upright crimped rim, creamy
white w/silvery flowers & leaves . . **$385.00**

Celery vase, creamy white w/silver
flowers & leaves **450.00**

Spooner, creamy white w/silver
flowers & leaves **375.00**

Sugar shaker w/original lid,
platinum lustre on creamy ground,
5⅜" h. . . . . **500.00 to 575.00**

**Syrup pitcher w/original hinged
metal lid,** creamy white w/silver
flowers & leaves, 6½" h. **685.00**

Toothpick holder, creamy white
w/platinum staining on flowers &
leaves, 2½" h. (normal rim chips) . . **475.00**

Findlay Onyx Water Set

Water set: pitcher & four barrel-
  shaped tumblers; creamy white
  w/silver flowers & leaves, 5 pcs.
  (ILLUS.) **2,400.00**

FOSTORIA

*Fostoria Glass company, founded in 1887,
produced numerous types of fine glassware over
the years. Their factory in Moundsville, West
Virginia closed in 1986.*

Fostoria Mark

Bowl, 4½" d., Colony patt., clear. **$22.00**
Bowl, dessert, 4½" d., Jamestown
  patt., No. 421, amber. **8.00**
Bowl, fruit, 5" d., Lafayette patt,
  Wisteria **47.00**
Bowl, fruit, 5" d., Mayfair patt., Topaz. . **16.00**
Bowl, 7" d., round, cupped, three-
  footed, Baroque patt., clear. **18.00**
Bowl, 7⅛" d., triangular, three-footed,
  Century patt. clear. **15.00**
Bowl, lemon, 9" d., two-handled,
  Fairfax patt., Azure (light blue
  w/hint of green) **17.00**
Bowl, 9½" l., oval, Century patt.,
  clear. **65.00**
Bowl, 10" l., oval, two-handled,
  Century patt., clear **37.00**
Bowl, fruit, 10½" d., low-footed,
  Colony patt., Queen Ann etching,
  clear. **95.00**
Bowl, 10½" d., 3⅜" h., flared,
  handled, Navarre etching,
  No. 2496, clear **60.00**
Bowl, 11" d., rolled edge, footed,
  Century, clear **45.00**
Bowl, fruit, 13" d., shallow, American
  patt., clear **60.00**
Bowl w/handle, 10" d., Chintz
  etching, clear. **55.00**
Bowl, jelly, two-handled, Mayfair
  patt., Topaz **27.00**
Bowl, sweetmeat, two-handled,
  Fairfax patt., Azure **22.00**
Cake plate, two-handled, Colony
  patt., clear, 10" d. **22.00**
Cake salver, footed, Century patt.,
  clear, 12¼" d. **60.00**
Candelabrum, two-light, bell-form
  base, American patt., clear,
  6½" h. **130.00**
Candleholders, socket on a three-
  footed base w/six scallops, No.

2394, cobalt blue, ca. 1928, pr. **39.00**
Candleholders, three-light, Navarre
  etching, clear, 6" h., pr. **80.00**
Candlestick, two-light, Baroque patt.,
  Azure, 4½" h. **65.00**
Candlestick, two-light, Mayflower
  etching, Line 2496, clear, 8" w.,
  4½" h., ... **96.00**
Candlesticks, one-light, figural sea
  horse stem, clear, pr. **40.00**
Candlesticks, Vesper etching, green,
  4" h., pr. **47.00**
Candlesticks, two-light, Century
  patt., clear, 7" h., pr. **65.00**
Candlesticks, three-light, Century
  patt., clear, 7¾" h., pr. **125.00**
Candlesticks, Coin patt., frosted,
  ruby, 8" h., pr. **125.00**
Candy dish, cov., footed, Colony
  patt., clear,½ lb. **60.00**
Celery dish, Hermitage patt., Topaz,
  11" l. **24.00**
Celery dish, Colony patt., clear,
  11½" l. **32.00**
Champagne, saucer-type, Navarre
  etching, clear, 6 oz. **19.00**
Cigarette box, cov, Coin patt.,
  frosted, blue. **135.00**
Cocktail, June etching, clear, 3 oz. . . . **20.00**
Cocktail, Colony patt., clear, 3½ oz.. . . **12.00**
Compote, low-footed, Vesper
  etching, green **27.00**
Console bowl, Baroque patt., clear,
  12" d. **35.00**
Console bowl, Baroque patt., Topaz,
  12" d. **48.00**
Console bowl, Shirley etching, clear,
  12" d. **74.00**
Cordial Chintz etching, Line No.
  6026, clear, 1 oz. **47.00**
Cream soup & underplate, Baroque
  patt., Topaz, pr. **47.00**
Creamer & open sugar bowl, etched
  Chintz patt., clear, pr. **40.00**
Creamer & open sugar bowl,
  Fairfax patt., Azure, pr. **42.00**
Creamer & open sugar bowl,
  footed, Chintz etching, clear, pr. **38.00**
Creamer & open sugar bowl,
  individual size, Baroque patt.,
  clear, pr. **24.00**
Cup & saucer, Chintz etching, clear. . . **28.00**
Cup & saucer, Colony patt., clear **6.00**
Cup & saucer, June etching, Azure . . . **45.00**
Cup & saucer, Lafayette patt.,
  Wisteria **35.00**
Cup & saucer, Pioneer patt., Topaz. . . . **8.00**
Fruit stand, flat, on pedestal base,
  American patt., 17½" d. **150.00**

Goblet, American patt., hexagonal
foot, clear, 10 oz............... **13.00**
Goblet, Baronet etching, water,
clear........................ **17.00**

Chintz Short-stemmed Goblet

Goblet, Chintz etching, short stem,
No. 6026, clear, 6⅛" h., 9 oz.
(ILLUS.)..................... **23.00**
Goblet, Chintz etching, No.
6026, tall stem, clear, 7⅝" h., 9 oz... **32.00**
Goblet, Circlet patt., clear.......... **10.00**
Goblet, Colony patt., clear **12.00**
Goblet, Hermitage patt.,water,
Topaz **15.00**
Goblet, Navarre etching, water, clear,
10 oz....................... **24.00**
Goblet, Rose cutting, water, clear **25.00**
Goblet, Shirley etching, water clear ... **26.00**
Ice bucket, Beverly etching, green.... **68.00**
Ice bucket, June etching, pink **150.00**
Ice bucket, w/tongs & rest, Versailles
etching, Rose, 3 pcs............. **175.00**
Mustard jar, cover & spoon,
Century patt., clear, 3 pcs. **30.00**
Novelty, model of a top hat,
American patt., clear, 3" h. **25.00**
Novelty, model of a top hat,
American patt., clear, 4" h. **45.00**
Oyster cocktail, Versailles etching,
Azure....................... **32.00**
Parfait, June etching, Topaz, 5¼" h.... **75.00**
Plate, cake, Mayfair patt., pink **33.00**
Plate, dinner, Chintz etching, clear.... **45.00**
Plate, 6" d., Versailles etching, Azure.. **14.00**
Plate, 6" d., Vesper etching, amber **7.00**
Plate, salad, 6" d., Pioneer patt.,
Topaz **3.00**
Plate, lemon, 6½" d., handled,
Colony patt., clear **14.00**
Plate, 7" d., Mayfair patt., amber....... **8.00**
Plate, 7" d., Mayfair patt., Azure **11.00**
Plate, 7" d., Mayfair patt., green **8.00**
Plate, 7" d., Mayfair patt., Topaz....... **9.00**
Plate, salad, 7" d., Baroque patt.,
Azure....................... **16.00**
Plate, 7¼" d., Vernon etching, clear **7.00**
Plate, 7½" d., June etching, clear **7.00**

Plate, 7½" d., Lafayette patt.,
Wisteria **27.00**
Plate, 7½" d., Mayflower etching,
Rose **11.00**
Plate, salad, 7½" d., Century patt.,
clear....................... **8.00**
Plate, salad, 7½" d., Pioneer patt.,
Topaz **4.00**
Plate, 8" d., Jamestown patt., clear.... **12.00**
Plate, 8" d., Mayfair patt., Azure **22.00**
Plate, luncheon, 8" d., Colony patt.,
clear....................... **12.00**
Plate, dinner, 9" d., Baroque patt.,
Azure....................... **75.00**
Plate, dinner, 9½" d., Pioneer patt.,
Topaz **7.00**
Plate, chop, 13" d., June etching,
Rose **110.00**
Plate, torte, 13" d., Colony patt., clear . **28.00**
Plate, torte, 14" d., Baroque patt.,
Topaz **30.00**
Plate, torte, 14" d., Century patt.,
clear....................... **45.00**
Plate, torte, 14" d. Chintz etching,
clear....................... **50.00**
Plate, torte, 14" d., Romance etching,
clear....................... **65.00**
Plate, torte, 15" d., Colony patt., clear . **52.00**
Platter, 10½" d., Vesper etching,
green....................... **35.00**
Platter, 12" oval, Century patt., clear .. **75.00**
Punch set: bowl & twelve cups;
American patt., 13 pcs. **250.00**
Relish dish, five-part, Mayfair patt.,
Topaz **68.00**
Relish dish, four-part, Baroque patt.,
clear....................... **38.00**
Relish dish, three-part, etched
Chintz patt., clear **38.00**
Relish dish, three-part, Pioneer patt.,
amber **18.00**
Relish dish, two-part, Lafayette patt.,
amber **24.00**
Relish dish, Victoria patt., clear **38.00**
Relish dish, two-part, handled,
Lafayette, Topaz, 6½" d........... **24.00**
Relish dish, three-part, Lafayette
patt., Mayflower etching, Rose,
7½" d....................... **48.00**
Relish dish, three-part, Lafayette
patt., Topaz, 7½" d.............. **28.00**
Relish dish, four-part, Mayfair patt.,
Topaz, 8½" l.................. **38.00**
Relish dish, two-part, Fairfax patt.,
green, 8½" l. **9.00**
Relish dish, three-part, Baroque
patt., clear, 10" l............... **38.00**
Relish dish, three-part, Baroque
patt., Topaz, 10" l.............. **38.00**

Relish dish, three-part, handled,
Colony patt., clear, 10½" l. **20.00**
Relish dish, three-part, Century patt.,
clear, 11⅛" l. **24.00**
**Salt & pepper shakers w/original
tops,** footed, Fairfax patt., Azure,
pr. **79.00**
**Salt & pepper shakers w/original
tops,** Raleigh patt., clear, pr. **18.00**
Saucer, Pioneer patt., Topaz **3.00**
Sherbet, Circlet patt., clear. **10.00**
Sherbet, Colony patt., clear **6.00**
Sherbet, low stem, Versailles
etching, green **26.00**
Sherbet, tall, Mayflower etching,
Rose **28.00**
Sherbet, tall, Navarre etching, Line
No. 6016, clear **24.00**
Sherbet, tall stem, Versailles
etching, green **32.00**
Sherbet, tall, Pioneer patt., Topaz,
14" h. **10.00**
Sherbet, tall stem, Versailles
etching, Rose, 12 oz.. . . . . **24.00**
Tidbit tray, Mayflower etching, Rose . . **38.00**
Tidbit tray, three-footed, upturned
edge, Century patt., clear **18.00**
Toothpick holder, Frisco patt., clear,
ca. 1900. . . . . **45.00**
Tray, center-handled, Morning Glory
etching, clear. **30.00**
Tray, muffin, handled, Century patt.,
clear, 9½" d. **30.00**
Tumbler, iced tea, Rambler etching,
clear. **26.00**
Tumbler, juice, footed, Rose cutting,
clear. **15.00**
Tumbler, water, Baroque patt., clear . . **16.00**
Tumbler, juice, Colony patt., clear,
5 oz.. . . . . **16.00**
Tumbler, juice, footed, Century patt.,
clear, 5 oz. **22.00**
Tumbler, juice, footed, Jamestown
patt., green, 5 oz. **16.00**
Tumbler, juice, footed, Navarre
etching, 5 oz.. . . . . **19.00**
Tumbler, water, Colony patt., clear,
9 oz **16.00**
Tumbler, water, Navarre etching,
clear, 10 oz.. . . . . **19.00**
Tumbler, water, footed, Midnight
Rose etching, Line No. 6009, clear,
12 oz.. . . . . **20.00**
Tumbler, iced tea, footed, Chintz
etching, Line No. 6026, clear,
13 oz.. . . . . **32.00**
Vase, 7½" h., flared, Colony patt.,
clear. **40.00**
Wedding bowl, cov., Coin patt.,
frosted, emerald green **95.00**

FRY

Numerous types of glass were made by the
H.C. Fry Company, Rochester, Pennsylvania.
One of its art lines was called Foval and was
blown in 1926-27. Cheaper was its milky-
opalescent ovenware (Pearl Oven Ware) made for
utilitarian purposes but also now being collected.
The company also made fine cut glass.

Collectors of Fry Glass will be interested in
the recent publication of a good reference book,
The Collector's Encyclopedia of Fry Glassware,
by The H.C. Fry Glass Society (Collector Books,
1990).

Fry Foval Candlestick

Candlesticks, Foval, pearl white
wide disc foot w/a jade green
connector to the tall slender
cylindrical white shaft wrapped w/a
thin thread of jade green below a
green wafer supporting the pearl
white cylindrical socket w/flattened
rim, 12" h., pr. (ILLUS. of one) . . **$1,380.00**
Compote, open, 8½" d., 5" h., white
opalescent w/royal blue baluster-
form stem & foot **220.00**
Compote, open, 9⅞" d., 5¼" h., a
Delft blue applied disc foot &
compressed knop stem supporting
a pearl white bowl w/a rippled
flaring base below the narrow
upright rim **518.00**
Console bowl, rolled edge,
controlled bubbles, Emerald Green,
14" d. **95.00**
Platter in metal holder, oval well-
and-tree-type, floral-cut border,
Pearl Oven Ware, 2 pcs. **45.00**

GALLÉ

Gallé glass was made in Nancy, France, by
Emile Gallé, a founder of the Nancy School and
a leader in the Art Nouveau movement in
France. Much of his glass, both enameled and
cameo, is decorated with naturalistic motifs. The
finest pieces were made in the last two decades of

the 19th century and the opening years of the present one. Pieces marked with a star preceding the name were made between 1904, the year of Gallé's death, and 1914.

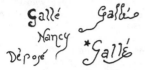

Gallé Marks

Bowl, 5¼" d., footed squatty bulbous body tapering gently to a wide hexagonal rim, tinted aquamarine & cut w/a floral spray & a star & enameled in translucent pink, puce & pale green all trimmed in gilt, signed in intaglio "Gallé deposé GesGesch" within a leaf-form cartouche, gilt rubbed, minor enamel flaking, ca. 1900 . . . . . . **$1,092.00**

Bowl, 7¾" d., rounded sides on a ring foot, green flecked w/gold & orange, carved on the exterior w/flowering stems & large leaves, the interior enameled w/two white orchid blossoms, signed in cameo "Emile Gallé fecit - Nancy," ca. 1900 . . . . **1,092.00**

Cameo bowl, 5" l., 2½" h., oval upright gently flared sides, greenish grey cased to pink & layered w/mauve, acid-etched w/stylized leafy plants, signed on the side **633.00**

Cameo bowl, 10⅜" d., deep rounded sides, cut from claret to clear w/a design of fruiting grapevine, signed in cameo, ca. 1900 . . . . **1,265.00**

Cameo bowl-vase, coupe-form w/sharply tapering sides & a closed wide rim, frosted turquoise overlaid in magenta red & crisply etched w/leafy blossoming plants, signed at the side, 4¾" d., 2¼" h. **748.00**

Cameo bowl-vase, squatty bulbous body tapering to a small base, w/a short wide rolled rim, grey tinted w/amber, overlaid in brown & green, cut w/pendent branches of olives & small leaves, signed in cameo, ca. 1900, 4⅛" d **632.00**

Cameo bowl-vase, canoe-shaped w/pointed ends, dark yellow overlaid in amethyst & dark blue & cut w/a landscape scene of trees & a lake w/distant hills, 11" l., 4⅝" h. (ILLUS. next column, bottom left) **3,025.00**

Fine Gallé Cameo Lamp

Cameo lamp, table model, 10" d. conical pointed shade above an ovoid base, each in clear cased to fiery yellow & layered in dark maroon under burnt umber, cameo etched & cut as exotic blossoms & leafy stems, signed "Gallé" on the shade & base, to "Gallé - Nancy - Paris" paper labels on base, overall 10½" h. (ILLUS.) **8,625.00**

Cameo vase, 3¾" h., flaring cylindrical body w/a wide rounded shoulder centering a short trumpet neck, frosted brick red overlaid in maroon & etched w/a polished stylized floral design, signed at the side **633.00**

Three Gallé Cameo Pieces

Cameo vase, 3¾" h., small footring supporting the bulbous slightly tapering body w/a wide mouth, frosted clear shading to blue overlaid w/pale orange & cut w/a continuous scene of water lilies & leaves, marked w/name & star (ILLUS. top) **880.00**

Cameo vase, 4¼" h., small slender ovoid body, bright frosted red layered in aubergine-black & etched as a wild geranium blossom & leafy stems, signed in the design, a collar ridge at the neck for an atomizer cap **431.00**

Cameo vase, 5⅛" h., gently flaring wide cylindrical sides w/a narrow shoulder to the low flaring orchid-form lip, mottled grey & lemon yellow w/a broad band of light blue around the lower half, underlaid w/splashes of brownish orange, overlaid in violet shading to pale blue & cut w/pond lilies, leaves, grasses & lily pads, signed in cameo, ca. 1900 (burst air bubble, small internalized crack). **1,150.00**

Cameo vase, 6" h., simple slender ovoid body w/a short trumpet neck, greenish grey layered in purple & etched w/leafy branches laden w/berries, signed "Gallé" on the reverse (some interior stain) **748.00**

Cameo vase, 6" h., 6" d., sharply tapering trumpet form body w/closed rim, ending in a small cushion foot, frosted yellow overlaid in wine & cut w/a stylized flower & leaf design (ILLUS. bottom right, previous page). **2,640.00**

Cameo vase, 6⅝" h., bulbous spherical body tapering sharply to a tall, slender slightly flaring 'stick' neck w/a rolled rim, grey tinted on the interior w/vibrant red, overlaid in dark red & cut w/a blossoming plant & windblown flowers, signed in cameo, ca. 1900 . . . . **977.00**

Two Gallé Cameo Vases

Cameo vase, 6⅞" h., compressed bulbous base centered by a tall, slender 'stick' neck, shaded yellowish green ground overlaid in dark green & cut up the sides w/ginko-like leaves & stems (ILLUS. right). **825.00**

Cameo vase, 7" h., banjo-form w/a bulbous flattened bottom tapering to a tall slender 'stick' neck w/a flared rim, overlaid in purple & cut to pale yellow & opaque white w/a large dragonfly descending to a lotus pond, signed in intaglio, ca. 1900 (minor chip on lower section). **1,955.00**

Cameo vase, 7¹⁄₁₆" h., footed slender tapering cylindrical body w/a flaring mouth, grey mottled w/peach & overlaid in purple, cut w/two flowering plants, signed in cameo, ca. 1900 . . . . **1,092.00**

Gallé Cameo Vases

Cameo vase, 8" h., footed baluster-form w/a short flaring neck, shaded frosted white to yellow ground overlaid in amber, green & orange & cut overall w/large swirling leaves (ILLUS. right,) **1,430.00**

Cameo vase, 8" h., graceful baluster-form body, olive green over clear cased to bright orange, acid-etched w/water lilies & water grasses, signed on the side **1,380.00**

Cameo vase, 8⅛" h., slender ovoid body tapering to a tiny flared neck, shaded yellow & white ground overlaid w/brown & orange & cut w/an overall leafy thistle design (ILLUS. left, previous column) . . . **1,100.00**

Cameo vase, 8⅛" h., tapering ovoid body on a low flaring quatrefoil foot & tapering to a quatrefoil lobed flaring neck, grey w/a thin interior coating of pumpkin, overlaid in brown & cut w/pendent berries, leaves & vine tendrils, signed in cameo, ca. 1900. . . . . **1,150.00**

Cameo vase, 8¼" h., squatty bulbous base below tall slightly flaring cylindrical sides, shaded yellow to pale green ground overlaid in dark ambers & orange & cut w/a continuous landscape w/tall leafy trees (ILLUS. left, above) **1,650.00**

Cameo vase, bud-type, 8¾" h., compressed wide base w/a narrow angled shoulder tapering sharply to a tall slender trumpet neck, fiery amber layered in blue & purple, cameo-etched & cut as detailed blossoms & buds w/leaf border below, signed in design **1,380.00**

Cameo vase, 10" h., a round pedestal foot supports a spherical delicately ribbed body w/a short, wide trumpet neck, pale green w/subtle grey highlights overlaid in smoky grey & cameo cut w/morning glory blossoms & buds on twisting vines w/curled, pointed leaves, Chinese-style signature .. **4,125.00**

Cameo vase, bud-type, 11" h., flattened bottle-form w/a bulbous ovoid base tapering to a very tall slender neck w/a flaring rim, frosted pink w/amethyst overlay, cameo-etched w/blossom, bud & vines, signed on reverse **1,150.00**

Cameo vase, 11½" h., bulbous cushion base centered by a very tall slender 'stick' neck, frosty grey splashed w/purple, overlaid in olive green & cut w/branches issuing clusters of seed pods & leafage, signed in cameo, lip & base ground slightly, ca. 1900 .... **690.00**

Cameo vase, 11½" h., tall slender tapering cylindrical body, rounded at the base & w/a short flaring neck, bluish grey overlaid in blue, green, lavender & purple & cameo etched w/a continuous riverside landscape w/mountains beyond tall fir trees in the foreground, signed at the side.................. **2,645.00**

Iris-decorated Gallé Cameo Vase

Cameo vase, 12½" h., tall swelled cylindrical body, frosted translucent ground overlaid in amethyst & etched as a large iris blossom, buds & spiked leaves, polished overall, partial martelé background, signed "Gallé" at lower side (ILLUS.) **2,300.00**

Cameo vase, 13" h., flattened footed ovoid form, clear shaded to blue layered in bright pink & olive green, cameo etched & cut overall as decumbent bleeding heart blossoms on naturalistic leafy stems, signed on the side....... **5,175.00**

Cameo vase, 13¼" h., squatty cushion foot below a tall slender 'stick' neck, grey shaded in pale pink on the interior, overlaid in purple & cut w/pendent boughs of wisteria blossoms & leafage, signed in cameo, ca. 1900 ...... **1,380.00**

Large Gallé Cameo Vase

Cameo vase, 13¼" h., tall tapering cylindrical body w/a small cushion foot & wide incurved mouth, frosted clear layered in pale green & dark green, cameo cut & carved as tall iris blossoms on spiked leaves, Oriental-style "Gallé" signature, four tiny chips on leaf edges (ILLUS.) **1,380.00**

Cameo vase, 13¾" h., footed gently flaring cylindrical body w/a narrow rounded shoulder to the short lobed neck, grey shading to pale yellow, overlaid in purple, cut w/pendent wisteria blossoms & leafage, signed in cameo after a star, ca. 1904-10 .... **1,955.00**

Cameo vase, 16" h., flared trumpet-form ovoid body, frosted pale blue & clear layered in amethyst & mauve-green, cameo etched as hydrangea blossom clusters arising from leafy stems overall, signed on reverse **2,645.00**

Cameo vase, 17⅜" h., squatty cushion foot below a tall slender cylindrical neck, frosted grey

overlaid in pale purple & cut w/a
pendent cluster of wisteria
blossoms & leafage, signed in
cameo, ca. 1900. . . . . **1,725.00**

Cups & saucers, flaring cylindrical
cups w/applied ropetwist handles
on matching flattened scallop-
rimmed saucers, pale topaz
decorated in enamel w/matching
pastel stylized florals, two cups
inscribed "E. Gallé - Nancy" on
base, saucer 5" d., cup 2¼" h.,
set of 4 . . . . **1,495.00**

Decanter w/original stopper, figural,
model of a plump bird, transparent
topaz bird-form body w/applied disc
foot & applied notched handle
curving up from the tail, the body
enamel-decorated w/scrolling multicolored designs & a golden stylized
bird w/the phrase "Je Suis ill Roi,"
engraved on base "E. Gallé -
Nancy," small topaz stopper
forming top of head above beak,
5½" l., 5¼" h. **3,105.00**

Vase, 4¾" h., spherical form in clear
w/applied snake-form ropetwist
collar, the sides decorated
w/japonesque fish over blue waves
among floral designs w/gold
painted "ocean" ripples, inscribed
on the base "E. Gallé a Nancy"
(two sliver chips under rim
collar) **1,380.00**

Vase, 6¼" h., spherical optic-ribbed
body center w/a slightly flaring
cylindrical neck, raised on three
pointed legs, topaz crystal
decorated in the japonesque style
w/florals in pastel tones, base
marked "E. Gallé - Nancy"
(rim polished) **316.00**

Vase, 8" h., a squatty bulbous
cushion-form base centered by a
wide, tall cylindrical neck slightly
tapering to a flat rim, carved &
enameled w/a purple & an orange
yellow poppy & leafy green stems,
all on a pale green acid-etched
ground, incised "Gallé deposé,"
ca. 1900 . . . . **1,150.00**

GREENTOWN

*Greentown glass was made in Greentown, Indiana,
by the Indiana Tumbler & Goblet Co. from 1894 until
1903. In addition to its famed Chocolate and Holly
Amber glass, it produced other types of clear and
colored glass. Miscellaneous pieces are listed here. Also
see PATTERN GLASS, HOLLY AMBER, and
CHOCOLATE GLASS.*

Animal covered dish, Dolphin,
emerald green, sawtooth rim. **$675.00**

Animal covered dish, Robin
w/berry in beak, blue **375.00**

Bowl, 6¼" d., No. 11 patt., blue **200.00**

Creamer, figural Indian Head,
amber **650.00**

Goblet, Austrian patt., clear w/gold
trim on rim **55.00**

Goblet, Diamond Prisms patt., clear. . . **75.00**

Model of a wheelbarrow,
Nile green **350.00**

Pitcher, water, Fleur de Lis patt.,
clear. **265.00**

Toothpick holder, No. 11 patt.,
emerald green **85.00**

Tumblers, Brazen Shield patt.,
cobalt blue, set of 6 . . . . **450.00**

HANDEL

*Lamps, shades and other types of glass by
Handel & Co., which subsequently became The
Handel Co., Inc., were produced in Meriden,
Connecticut, from 1893 to 1941. Also see
LIGHTING DEVICES.*

Handel Mark

Two Handel Vases

Cameo vase, 11" h., baluster-form
w/a tall, wide trumpet neck, clear
overlaid in golden amber & double-
etched in a repeating stylized floral
design, etched "Palme" in design,

base signed "Handel 4258," some rim skips, interior etching (ILLUS. right) **$1,150.00**

Tobacco jar, cov., simple cylindrical body w/silver plate hinged rim fitting w/a flat glass cover insert, opal glass molded w/raised foliate scrollwork in green & mahogany brown w/a rare scene of a lioness & her cubs, base w/Handel shield mark & "40060 - J," 6" h. **1,150.00**

Tobacco jar, cov., wide cylindrical body w/rounded base & shoulder, silver plated hinged fitting w/a domed glass cover w/wide knob handle, opal molded glass decorated w/raised leafy gilt scrollwork against a green shading to mahogany brown ground centered by a bust portrait of a Native American chief in a feathered headdress, base marked w/Handel shield mark, 7¼" h.. . . . **1,495.00**

Vase, 8" h.,"Teroma," tall slender waisted body, the etched exterior surface h.p. in muted colors w/a wooded landscape scene, unsigned, tiny chip near base (ILLUS. left) **690.00**

HEISEY

Numerous types of fine glass were made by A.H. Heisey & Co., Newark, Ohio, from 1895. The company's trade-mark – an H enclosed within a diamond – has become known to most glass collectors. The company's name and molds were acquired by Imperial Glass Co., Bellaire, Ohio, in 1958, and some pieces have been reissued. The glass listed below consists of miscellaneous pieces and types. Also see PATTERN GLASS under GLASS.

Heisey Diamond "H" Mark

Basket, Banded Picket patt., No. 461, Flamingo, (pink) 7" h. **$525.00**

Beer mug, Old Sandwich patt., Moongleam, (green) 12 oz.. . . . . **310.00**

Berry set: master bowl & six sauce dishes; Prison Stripe patt., No. 357, clear w/some worn gold trim, marked, 7 pcs.. . . . . **55.00**

Bowl, large oval, pressed Pineapple & Fan patt., in original fancy silver plate frame w/tongs, late 19th c., clear. **175.00**

Bowl, mint, 6" d., dolphin-footed, Queen Ann patt., clear **15.00**

Bowl, jelly, 6½" d., footed, Waverly patt., Orchid etching **40.00**

Bowl, jelly, 7" d., footed, Orchid etching, clear. **75.00**

Bowl, 8" d., Lodestar patt., Dawn (light grey) **55.00**

Bowl, 8½" d., Lariat patt., clear. . . . **22.00**

Bowl, gardenia, 9" d., Queen Ann patt., Orchid etching, clear **60.00**

Bowl, 9½" d., crimped rim, Queen Ann patt., Orchid etching, clear. **60.00**

Bowl, gardenia, 12" oval, Crystolite patt., clear **45.00**

Bowl, gardenia, 13" d., Orchid etching, clear. **70.00**

Butter dish, cov., Orchid etching, clear. **150.00**

Butter dish, cov., Orchid etching, figural pony finial, clear **145.00**

Butter dish, cov.,oblong, Plantation patt., clear, ¼ lb. **125.00**

Butter dish, cov., Rose etching, clear, 6" d. **188.00**

Cake stand, footed, Waverly patt., Orchid etching, clear, 13" d. **175.00**

Candleholders, single, Sunflower patt. clear pr. **33.00**

Candleholders, Ridgeleigh patt., clear, 2" h., pr. **50.00**

Candlesticks, three-light, Lariat patt., clear, pr. **76.00**

Candlesticks, two-light, Kohinoor patt., No. 1488 (no bobeche), pr. . . . **145.00**

Candlesticks two-light, Lariat patt., pr.. . . . . **49.00**

Candlesticks, two-light, Warwick patt., No. 1428, Sahara, (yellow) pr.. **225.00**

Candlesticks, two-light, Trident patt, Orchid etching, clear, 5" h., pr. **90.00**

Candlesticks, Old Sandwich patt., clear, 6" h., pr.. . . . . **79.00**

Candlesticks, Colony patt., flared socket on a swelled six-paneled stem on a ground hexagonal foot, clear, 9" h., pr.. . . . . **61.00**

Candlesticks, Grape Cluster patt., No. 1445, ca. 1935, clear, 5¾" d., 10½" h., pr. **83.00**

Champagne, Victorian patt., clear **13.00**

Champagne, Kohinoor patt., clear, 3 oz.. . . . . **22.00**

Champagne, saucer-type, Kohinoor patt., clear, 5½" h., ... **45.00**

Champagne, Rose etching, clear,
6 oz................................. **28.00**
Cheese stand, Crystolite patt., clear,
5½" d. **22.00**
Chip & dip set, Saturn patt., clear,
2 pcs................................. **35.00**
Cigarette holder, Ridgeleigh patt. **13.00**
Claret, Colonial No. 300 patt., clear,
4¼ oz................................ **15.00**
Cocktail, Kohinoor patt., clear, 3 oz. ... **18.00**
Cocktail, Rose etching, clear, 4 oz. ... **35.00**
Compote, 5" h., tall stem w/flaring
paneled foot, Greek Key patt.,
clear.................................. **50.00**
Compote, open, 6" d., Old Sandwich
patt. No. 1404, Moongleam....... **165.00**
Compote 7" oval, Orchid etching **119.00**

Heisey Cobalt Blue Warwick Vase

Cornucopia-vase, Warwick patt.,
cobalt blue, 9" h. (ILLUS.)........ **265.00**
Cornucopia-vases, Crystolite patt.,
ornate Calcutta overall cutting,
notching & crosshatching, signed,
9" h., pr............................. **650.00**
Creamer & cov. sugar bowl,
Pineapple & Fan patt., green
w/gold trim, pr...................... **125.00**
Creamer & open sugar bowl,
Waverly patt., Rose etching,
clear, pr. **75.00**
Creamer & sugar bowl, individual
size, Crystolite patt., clear, pr....... **25.00**
Creamer & sugar bowl, individual
size, Ridgeleigh patt., pr........... **19.00**
Creamer & sugar bowl, Saturn patt.,
Zircon (pale blue), pr. **395.00**
Cruet w/original stopper, Punty &
Diamond Point patt., clear, 6 oz..... **95.00**
Cup & saucer, Saturn patt., Zircon... **250.00**
Decanter w/original spire stopper,
No. 367, Moongleam, marked..... **325.00**
Goblet, Rose etching, clear **32.00**
Goblet, claret, Rose etching, 4 oz.... **120.00**

Goblet, water, New Era patt., clear,
10 oz................................ **32.00**
Goblet, water, Old Dominion
patt., clear 10 oz................. **55.00**
Goblet, water, Orchid etching, clear,
10 oz................................ **45.00**
Goblet, water, Provincial patt., clear,
10 oz................................ **15.00**
Goblet, water, Spanish patt., cobalt
blue, 10 oz. **119.00**
Oil cruet w/original stopper, Twist
patt., pink........................ **75.00**
Oil cruet w/stopper, Crystolite patt.,
clear, 3 oz........................ **33.00**
Pitcher, Sunburst patt., No. 343,
clear, ½ gal.................... **195.00**
Pitcher, tankard, Greek Key patt.,
No. 433, clear, 1 qt............. **245.00**
Pitcher, footed, Empress patt.,
Sahara , 3 pt................... **220.00**
Pitcher, Sunburst patt., No. 343,
clear, 3 pt. **195.00**
Pitcher, tankard, clear, Orchid
etching, 64 oz................. **650.00**
Pitcher, Rose etching, clear, 73 oz. ... **675.00**
Pitcher w/ice lip, Old Sandwich patt.,
Sahara,½ gal. **195.00**
Plate, salad, 7" d., Waverly patt.,
Rose etching **40.00**
Plate, luncheon, 8" d., Minuet
etching, clear................... **20.00**
Plate, salad, 8" d., Empress patt.,
Sahara......................... **19.00**
Plate, 8½" d., Saturn patt., Zircon..... **75.00**
Plate, 9" d., Greek Key patt., No. 433,
clear........................... **95.00**
Plate, server, 10½" d., Lariat patt.,
clear........................... **50.00**
Plate, sandwich, 14" d., Plantation
patt., clear **65.00**
Plate, torte, 14" d., Waverly patt.,
Orchid etching, clear **50.00**
Plate, torte, 14" d., Waverly patt.,
Rose etching, clear **93.00**
Plate, deviled egg, 15" oval, Lariat
patt., clear..................... **190.00**
Punch bowl, Crystolite patt., clear
7½ qt. **99.00**
Punch bowl & base, Greek Key
patt., clear, 14½" d., 15" h., 2 pcs. . **260.00**
Punch cup, Crystolite patt., clear...... **6.00**
Relish dish, three-part, Orchid
etching......................... **53.00**
Relish dish, three-part, Queen Anne
patt., Orchid etching,7" d. **55.00**
Relish dish, two-part, Ridgeleigh
patt., clear, 7" l................. **35.00**
Relish dish, three-part, oval, Rose
etching, clear, 11" l............. **75.00**

Relish tray, three-part, Ridgeleigh
   patt., clear, 10½" l. **45.00**
Sherbet, Plantation patt., clear **30.00**
Sherbet, Stanhope patt., Zircon **175.00**
Sherbet. Provincial patt., clear, 5 oz. . . **15.00**
Sherbet. Rose etching, clear,
   6 oz. **27.00**
Sherry, Orchid etching, clear,
   2 oz. **125.00**
Sugar bowl, cov., Plain Band patt.,
   No.1225, clear w/gold trim, ca.
   1900 . . . . **35.00**
Syrup pitcher, cov., Colonial Panel
   patt., No. 331, clear w/clear applied
   handle, marked, 5½" h. **28.00**
Tumbler, footed, Old Dominion patt.,
   Sahara , 5 oz. **16.00**
Tumbler, footed, Plantation patt.,
   clear 5 oz. **39.00**
Tumbler, juice, footed, Rose patt.,
   clear 5 oz. **52.00**
Tumbler, iced tea, footed, Lariat
   patt., Moonglo cutting, clear, 12 oz. . **25.00**
Tumbler, iced tea, footed, Rose
   etching, clear, 12 oz. **52.00**
Vase, 7" h., footed, Orchid etching,
   clear. **150.00**
Wine, Rose etching, clear. **90.00**
Wine, Saxony patt., Sahara,
   2½ oz. **50.00**
Wine, Victorian patt., clear 2½ oz. **17.00**
Wine, Rose etching, clear, 3 oz. **105.00**

HISTORICAL &
COMMEMORATIVE

*Reference numbers are to Bessie M. Lindsey's
book,* American Historical Glass.

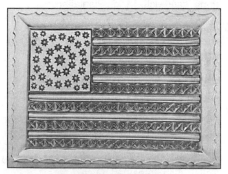

American Flag Platter

American Flag platter, rectangular
   w/scalloped rim, clear, No. 51
   (ILLUS.). **$325.00**
Buddha statuette, seated, amber
   w/fine opalescence, signed
   "Gillinder," 6" h. **325.00**

Columbia Bread Tray

Columbia bread tray, shield-shaped,
   Columbia superimposed against 13
   vertical bars, blue, 9½ x 11½",
   No. 54 (ILLUS.) **475.00**

Admiral Dewey Dish on Tile Base

Dewey (Admiral) dish, cov., tile
   base, No. 390, milk white, 6¾" l.,
   4½" h. (ILLUS.) **89.00**
Emblem creamer, eagle w/shield
   alternates w/ordnance, clear,
   No. 64 . . . . **175.00**
Emblem spooner, eagle w/shield
   alternates w/ordnance, clear,
   No. 64 . . . . **125.00**
Emblem sugar bowl, cov., bullet
   finial, eagle w/shield alternates
   w/ordnance, clear, 4½" d., 6" h.,
   No. 64 . . . . **200.00**
Garfield plate, frosted bust of
   Garfield center, 1-0-1 border, clear,
   9" d., No. 300 . . . . **56.00**
Grant Peace plate, bust portrait of
   Grant center, maple leaf border,
   amber, 10½" d., No. 289 . . . . **56.00**
Grant Peace plate, bust portrait of
   Grant center, maple leaf border,
   blue, 10½" d., No. 289. . . . . **70.00**

Old Abe Butter Dish

Old Abe (eagle) butter dish, cov.,
   clear & frosted, No. 478 (ILLUS.) . . **175.00**
Old Abe (eagle) compote, cov.,
   clear & frosted, No. 478. . . . . **200.00**
Plymouth Rock paperweight, dated
   "1620," Pilgrim landing inscription
   embossed on base, 3¼" l., 4⅛" h.,
   No. 19 . . . . **65.00**
Railroad train platter, Union Pacific
   Engine No. 350, clear, 9 x 12",
   No. 134 . . . . **80.00**
Rock of Ages bread tray, clear
   w/milk glass center, No. 236 . . . . . . **125.00**

Three Presidents Platter

Three Presidents platter, bust
   portraits of Garfield, Washington &
   Lincoln, inscribed "In
   Remembrance," clear, 10 x 12½",
   No. 249 (ILLUS.) **125.00**

HOLLY AMBER

   *Holly Amber, originally marketed under the
name "Golden Agate," was produced for only a
few months in 1903 by the Indiana Tumbler and
Goblet Company of Greentown, Indiana. When
this factory burned in June 1903 all production
of this ware ceased, making it very rare today.
The same "Holly" pressed pattern was also
produced in clear glass by the Greentown
factory. Collectors should note that the St. Clair
Glass Company has reproduced some Holly
Amber pieces.*

Holly Amber Butter Dish

Butter dish, cov. (ILLUS.) **$1,813.00**
Compote, open **1,250.00**
Cruet w/original stopper **1,850.00**
Toothpick holder, 2½" h. **509.00**
Tumbler, cylindrical, 4" h. (minor
   bead chip on base) **275.00**

IMPERIAL

   *Imperial Glass Company, Bellaire, Ohio was
organized in 1901 and was in continuous
production, except for very brief periods, until its
closing in June 1984. It had been a major
producer of Carnival Glass earlier in this
century and also produced other types of glass,
including an Art Glass line called "Free Hand
Ware" during the 1920s and its "Jewels" about
1916. The company acquired a number of molds
of other earlier factories, including the
Cambridge and A.H. Heisey Companies, and
reissued numerous items through the years. Also
see CARNIVAL GLASS under GLASS.*

Imperial Marks

CANDLEWICK

Candlewick No.400/40/0 Basket

Basket, No. 400/40/0, clear, 6½" h.
   (ILLUS.) **$35.00**

Bowl, 9" w., heart-shaped,
No. 400/49H, clear **165.00**
Bowl, 10½" d., bell-shaped,
No. 400/63B, clear. **47.00**
Bowl, 11" d., float-type, cupped edge,
footed, No. 400/75F, clear. **38.00**
Cake stand, No. 400/103D, high-
footed, 11" d., clear **75.00**
Deviled egg server, center handle,
w/factory label, No. 400/154,
12" d. **145.00**
Goblet, No. 3400, water, clear, 9 oz. . . **19.00**
Jam set: oval tray w/two cov.
marmalade jars w/ladles;
No. 400/1589, clear, 5 pcs. **125.00**
Mayonnaise set: bowl & underplate;
No. 400/23, clear, 2 pcs. . . . **40.00**

Rare Candlewick Pastry Tray

Pastry tray, center heart-shaped
handle, ruby red, 11½" d.
(ILLUS.) . . . . **500.00 to 650.00**
Pitcher, bead-footed, No. 400/18,
clear, 80 oz. **270.00**
Pitcher, No. 400/24, clear, 80 oz. **170.00**
Plate, 5½" d., two-handled,
No. 400/42D, clear **13.00**
Plate, dinner, 10½" d., No. 400/10D,
clear. **38.00**
Plate, torte, 12½" d., cupped edge,
No. 400/75V, clear. **35.00**
Punch set: punch bowl, underplate,
12 cups & ladle; No. 400/20, bowl
& cups w/cut Mallard patt.,
15 pcs. **400.00**
Relish, four-part, oblong,
No. 400/215, clear, 12" l. **80.00**
Relish dish, three-part, No. 400/208,
three-toed, clear **130.00**
Relish dish, two-part, oval,
No. 400/268, clear, 8" l. **24.00**
Relish dish, four-part, No.400/55,
clear, 8½" l. **30.00**
Relish dish, five-part, No. 400/102,
clear, 13" l. **85.00**
Sherbet, tall, No. 400/190, clear,
5 oz. **18.00**
Sherbet, tall, No. 3800, clear, 6 oz. . . . **43.00**
Tidbit server, two-tier, cupped,
No. 400/2701, clear. **85.00**

Tray, upturned handles, No. 400/42E,
clear, 5½" l. **18.00**
Vase, 6" h., fan-shaped, beaded
handle, No. 400/287F, clear **60.00**

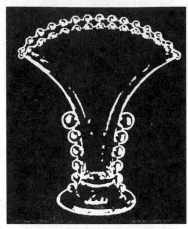

Candlewick Fan Vase

Vase, 8" h., fan-shaped, beaded
handles, No. 400/87F, clear
(ILLUS.) **30.00**

CAPE COD PATTERN

Bowl, spider, 4½" d., handled,
No. 160/180, clear. **25.00**
Bowl, 5" w., heart-shaped,
No. 160/49H, clear **20.00**
Bowl, spider, 6½" d., divided,
handled, No. 160/187, clear **32.00**
Cake stand, No. 160/103D, clear,
11" d. **115.00**
Compote, 7" d., No. 160/48B, clear . . . **28.00**
Cordial, No. 1602, milk white, 1½ oz. . . **15.00**
Creamer & open sugar bowl,
No. 160/30, clear, pr. **24.00**
Cruet w/original stopper,
No. 160/119, Verde green, 4 oz. **30.00**
Cruet w/original stopper,
No. 160/70, clear, 5 oz. **27.00**
Cruet w/original stopper,
No. 160/241, clear, 6 oz. **55.00**
Decanter w/original stopper,
square-shaped, No. 160/212,
clear, 24 oz. **65.00**
Goblet, water, No. 1602, Amber,
9 oz. **12.00**
Goblet, water, No. 1600, clear,
10 oz. **15.00**
Goblet, magnum, No. 160, clear,
14 oz. **28.00**
Oyster cocktail, No. 1602, clear **10.00**
Pitcher, No. 160/24, clear, 2 qt. **85.00**

Relish dish, three-part, oval,
No. 160/55, clear, 9½" l. **18.00**

**Salt & pepper shakers w/original
tops,** individual, No. 160/251,
clear, pr. **18.00**

**Salt & pepper shakers w/original
tops,** individual, original factory
label, No. 160/251, clear, pr. **25.00**

Sherbet, tall, No. 1602, Verde green,
6 oz.. . . . . **15.00**

Tray, for creamer & sugar,
No. 160/29, clear, 7" l. **15.00**

Tumbler, juice, footed, No. 1602,
clear, 6 oz.. . . . . **12.00**

Tumbler, juice, footed, No. 1602,
Verde green, 6 oz.. . . . . **15.00**

Tumbler, juice, No. 1600, clear,
6 oz.. . . . . **12.00**

Tumbler, water, footed, No. 1602,
clear, 10 oz.. . . . . **8.00**

Tumbler, water, No. 160, clear,
10 oz.. . . . . **12.00**

MISCELLANEOUS PATTERNS & LINES

Animal covered dish, Lion laying
down on lacy-rimmed base,
caramel slag, copy of antique
original, 6 x 7½" base, 7" h.. . . . . **95.00**

Ashtray, Caramel Slag, No. 1608/1,
7" d.. . . . . **20.00**

Bowl, berry, 4½" d., Reeded (Spun)
patt., amber. **13.00**

Candy box, cov., footed, Vintage
Grape patt., No. 1950/727, milk
white **35.00**

Figurine, Venus Rising, figure
w/original sticker, 6" h. **32.00**

Tumbler, Little Shot, green, 2½ oz. . . . **19.00**

Vanity jar, Reeded (Spun) patt., pink,
7⅝" d. **95.00**

Imperial Free-Hand Vases

Vase, 7" h., Free-Hand ware, squatty
bulbous ovoid form tapering to a
trumpet neck, opal white iridized
ground w/bright blue heart & vine
decoration, applied cobalt blue rim
wrap, subtle orange lustred interior
(ILLUS. center) **805.00**

Vase, 7¼" h., Free-Hand ware, ovoid
body tapering to a widely flaring
trumpet neck, brilliant orange
iridescent cased to white w/lustred
green pulled decoration overall,
unsigned polished white pontil
(ILLUS. left) **345.00**

Vase, 7¾" h., ovoid body tapering to
a widely flaring trumpet neck, white
w/a mirror bright grayish blue
surface & deep orange iridescent
interior (ILLUS. right). **316.00**

KELVA

*Kelva was made early in this century by the
C.F. Monroe Co., Meriden, Connecticut, and was
a type of decorated opal glass very like the same
company's Wave Crest and Nakara wares. This
type of glass was produced until about the time
of the first World War. Also see NAKARA and
WAVE CREST.*

Box, cov., Crown mold, decorated
w/blue, grey & white flowers on
pinkish rose ground, 6¼" d.,
4¼" h.. **$1,225.00**

Fine Blue Kelva Box

Box w/hinged cover, round mold,
bright blue ground w/pink daisies,
6" d. (ILLUS.). **815.00**

Dish, open-handled, green ground,
6" h.. . . . . **575.00**

Dresser box w/hinged cover, round,
the cover & base decorated w/pink
floral bouquets on a mottled slate
grey ground, marked, 6" d., 3" h.. . . **770.00**

Planter w/original liner, embossed
borders, green ground w/large pink
flowers around body, 8½" l.. . . . . . . **875.00**

Vase, 7¾" h., short cylindrical neck
on swelled cylindrical body w/white
& pink flowers w/brown stems &
green leaves on a bluish ground,
beige beaded pastel ribbon around
lower russet-colored base set on a
round four-footed gilt-metal base . . **725.00**

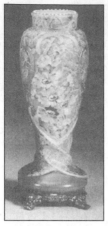

Lovely Kelva Vase on Base

Vase, 8½" h., slender baluster-form body raised on an ornate scroll-cast silver plate foot, the body w/a mottled blue background of pink blossoms & gold scrolls, marked "Kelva Trade - Mark" (ILLUS.) **489.00**

Vase, 11" h., tall ovoid body tapering slightly to a wide flat mouth w/a silver plate rim band, raised on a silver plate three-footed holder, a dark green mottled ground decorated w/soft pink roses, red 1904 mark **1,650.00**

Vase, 13½" h., footed, green mottled ground w/pink flowers **795.00**

KEW BLAS

In the 1890s the Union Glass Works, Somerville, Massachusetts, produced a line of iridescent glasswares closely resembling Louis Tiffany's wares. The name was derived from an anagram of the name of the factory's manager, William S. Blake.

Compote, open, 4½" d., 3½" h., wide round domed foot below a short baluster-form stem supporting a wide squatty bulbous bowl w/a widely flaring rim, overall gold iridescence, signed "Kew Blas" on base **$460.00**

Console set: compote & pair of candlesticks; Alexandrite wide shallow bowl on compote on matching stem, matching baluster-form candlesticks w/tall candle sockets, each piece on a clear "bubble" base knob on an Alexandrite foot, the heat reactive glass in red shaded to blue w/'chocolate' shading, experimental color, compote 6¾" h., candlesticks 10" h., the set **1,265.00**

Cordial, inverted pear-shaped bowl w/a widely flaring rim, raised on a slender swelled stem & round foot, overall reddish gold iridescence, signed, 5" h. **358.00**

Rose bowl, spherical form w/a closed lightly scalloped rim, cased, the exterior in green w/vertical "zipper" stripes alternating w/orange stripes, orange iridescent interior, base inscribed "Kew Blas," 4" h. **690.00**

Tumbler, swelled cylindrical body w/flaring rim & large dimples around the sides, overall gold iridescence, signed, 3" h. **303.00**

Vase, 4¼" h., 5¼" d., simple flared ribbed trumpet form in amber w/pulled emerald green internal decoration, engraved mark on base. **805.00**

Fine Kew Blas Vase

Vase, 7" h., simple ovoid body tapering to a short cylindrical neck, cased ambergris w/gold iridescent pulled feather design on an opal ground, folded gold iridescent rim, signed "Kew-Blas" on base (ILLUS.). **978.00**

KIMBLE

Evan K. Kimble took over the Vineland Flint Glass Works, Vineland, New Jersey in 1931, after the death of Victor Durand, Jr. Most art glass production ceased except for a line of Cluthra-style wares featuring various colors and embedded air bubbles.

Vase, 8½" h., Cluthra, tall slender ovoid body w/a swelled shoulder tapering to a short flaring neck, mottled & swirled bittersweet orange & opalescent white on a clear round foot, No. 2011-8 . . . . . **$330.00**

Vase, 14¼" h., Cluthra, spherical body centered by a tall slightly flaring cylindrical neck, mottled opal white, yellow & tangerine, marked "#20167-14 - Dec. 31" **550.00**

Vases, 11¾" h., Cluthra, footed tall slender ovoid body w/a rounded shoulder tapering to a short wide flaring rim, mottled tangerine, mocha brown & opal on a clear foot, marked, pr. **660.00**

KOSTA

The Kosta Glassworks were founded in the Smaland region of Sweden in 1742 and have grown over the past two centuries to become one of that country's leading makers of fine glassware. Originally their products were utilitarian but by the 19th century they were producing decorative and tablewares. In the 20th century they produced fine crystal wares in modern designs by noted glass artists. In 1970 they merged with several other Swedish glasshouses and continue to produce high quality cut glass and tableware.

Bowl, 6" d., 4¼" h., flaring cylindrical thick-walled form w/a heavy ground rim, clear w/purplish amethyst stripes swirled to the right, base inscribed "Kosta L. #1385," designed by Vicke Lindstrand **$489.00**

Bowl-vase, thick-walled deep bowl-form w/upright sides & wide flat rim, teal blue surface decorations cut to clear in polished oval & circular facets, signed "Kosta 56693 Lindstrand," designed by Vicke Lindstrand, 6½" d., 4¼" h. **575.00**

Decanter w/stopper, figural, crystal model of a fat pheasant forming the body, engraved feathers around the neck, the knob head forming the stopper, designed by Vicke Lindstrand, signed "Kosta 8218 - V. Lindstrand," 8" l., 8¼" h. **403.00**

Sculpture, obelisk formed as a solid triangular tapering wedge w/two blue vitrified surfaces engraved w/petroglyphs revealed through polished front surface, designed by Ann Warff, base signed "Kosta 95689 Warff," 4¾" h. **690.00**

Vase, 5⅜" h., tall slightly tapering square form w/beveled corners & rim, clear w/a small central cavity surrounded by slender purple swirled stripes, inscribed "Kosta L S 637," designed by Vicke Lindstrand **288.00**

Vase, 5¾" h., flattened round body of clear w/opaque white exterior decorated by slender stripes of color on the front & back, signed "Kosta Boda - B. Vallien," by Bertil Vallien **173.00**

Vase, 6" h., tapering cylindrical form w/a wide, flat mouth, thick clear body w/internal black dots & cut & polished windows, designed by Vicke Lindstrand, engraved "Kosta LS 604," ca. 1957 . . . . **138.00**

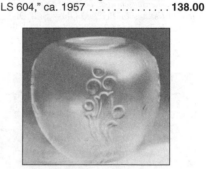

Kosta Art Deco Style Vase

Vase, 7" h., wide bulbous nearly spherical form w/a small closed mouth, Art Deco design in clear w/an etched surface & raised stylized floral panels, signed "Kosta 1936 Came 4" (ILLUS.) **489.00**

Vase, 9" h., flattened & sharply tapering ovoid body w/a small mouth, clear w/internal green striations & bubbles, engraved w/a tropical fish on each side, designed by Vicke Lindstrand, engraved "Kosta LG 2349," ca. 1960s **193.00**

Vase, 10½" h., ovoid body tapering to a wide, flat rim, clear engraved w/a gondolier & his gondola, unusual technique known as "vibrogravur," designed by Vicke Lindstrand, engraved "Kosta LG 155," ca. 1960. **275.00**

Vase, 13" h., very tall slender tapering teardrop form, clear internally decorated w/a black trail from the top to a puddle at the base, designed by Vicke Lindstrand, engraved "Kosta L111291" **275.00**

LACY

Lacy Glass is a general term developed by collectors many years ago to cover the earliest type of pressed glass produced in this country. "Lacy" refers to the fact that most of these early patterns consisted of scrolls and geometric designs against a finely stippled background which gives the glass the look of fine lace. Formerly this glass was often referred to as "Sandwich" for the Boston & Sandwich Glass Company of Sandwich, Massachusetts which produced a great deal of this ware. Today, however, collectors realize that many other factories on the East Coast and in the Pittsburgh, Pennsylvania and Wheeling, West Virginia areas also made lacy glass from the 1820s into the 1840s. All pieces listed are clear unless otherwise noted. Numbers after salt dips refer to listings in Pressed Glass Salt Dishes of the Lacy Period, 1825-1850, *by Logan W. and Dorothy B. Neal. Also see CUP PLATES and SANDWICH GLASS.*

Two Lacy Bowls

Bowl, 6¼" d., "Industry" patt., center scene of a log cabin & barrel, the wide border w/two vignettes, a scene of a man plowing alternating w/a sailing ship, possibly New England Glass Company, probably produced for the 1840 presidential campaign, one scallop missing (ILLUS. right) **$204.00**

Bowl, 8¼" d., Hairpin patt. (mold roughness) **385.00**

Bowl, 8½" d., 1¾" h., Princess Feather patt. (six tipped scallops) . . . **66.00**

Bowl, 9" d., geometric design w/a cross-form center design w/two arms filled w/large strawberry diamonds alternating w/arms filled w/scrolls, wedges of small strawberry diamond between each arm, probably New England Glass Company, ca. 1825-30, one nondisfiguring chip (ILLUS. left) **440.00**

Bowl, 10½" d., round, a center design of a quatrefoil framed by a ring of tulip-form acanthus leaf clusters, wide outer border of tulip-form leaf clusters flanked by long scrolled acanthus leaves, probably Boston & Sandwich Glass Co. (moderately disfiguring rim chip, few scallops tipped) **198.00**

Bowl, 7¾ x 10½", 2" h., rectangular w/notched corners, Peacock Feather & Diamond patt., attributed to New England, ca. 1830-45, clear. **880.00**

Compote, open, 6" d., 3" h., shallow widely flaring Roman Rosette patt. bowl w/a scalloped rim, attached to a flaring Hairpin patt. pedestal base w/a scalloped rim, probably Midwestern, few small bowl chips **523.00**

Compote, open, 7½" d.; 4¾" h., round flaring bowl in Tulip patt., wafer pedestal joins bowl to Plume patt. base (three tipped rim scallops) **413.00**

Compote, open, 8½" w., 4" h., scalloped Crossed Peacock Eye patt. bowl, plain wafer standard on a round patterned foot (one large chip & several minor chips, tiny shallow chips on base) **413.00**

Dish, rectangular w/rounded corners & a deeply scalloped rim, Gothic Arch border patt., center w/a large diamond & pointed quatrefoil, cobalt blue, 6¼" l. (slight rim underfill, few small flakes) **5,500.00**

Dish, deep round form w/flanged rim, florette & four-point star center w/inner ring of swirled ribbed panels, sawtooth design in rim, violet w/light fiery opalescence, attributed to the Boston & Sandwich Glass Co., ca. 1840, five scallops halfway chipped, others tipped, 9⅜" d. **7,425.00**

Plate, 5⅝" d., Roman Rosette patt., round w/scalloped rim, golden amber (overall mold roughness) **358.00**

Plate, 6" d., Acorn & Oak patt., fiery opalescent. **248.00**

Plate, 6" d., pointed scallops form rim, Pine Tree & Shield patt., pre-lacy **110.00**

Plate, 6" w., octagonal Eagle patt., leafy scroll border, attributed to New England, ca. 1830-45 (three tipped scallops) **88.00**

Salt dip, eagle salt, in the form of a Grecian sofa w/the scrolled ends molded at each corner w/a perched eagle looking back over its shoulder, an American shield centered on each side, probably Boston & Sandwich, deep fiery opalescent, EE-3b (½" line off rim) **1,045.00**

Salt dip, Grecian sofa-form, S-scroll
ends & C-scroll feet, beaded edge
trim, violet blue, BS-3 (few tiny
nicks, shallow sliver on one corner) **385.00**

Salt dip, model of a Grecian sofa
w/high scrolled ends & scroll feet,
smooth thick sides, deep cobalt
blue (flaking & shallow chips
on rim) **248.00**

Salt dip, model of a Grecian sofa
w/scrolled ends & feet, eagle
design on each side (EE-7) **358.00**

Salt dip, model of a Grecian sofa
w/scrolled ends & feet, sides
w/baskets of flowers, NE-4
(mold roughness) **94.00**

Salt dip, model of a sidewheeler,
marked on side paddle wheel
casing "Lafayet," Boston &
Sandwich Glass Co., fiery
opalescent medium blue, BT-8
(light mold roughness, tiny spall
on rudder) **1,870.00**

Salt dip, model of a wagon, deep
rectangular sides w/slightly curved
side rims, diamond & starburst
design on the sides above the
molded small wheels, probably
Boston & Sandwich Glass Co.,
WN-1 (light mold roughness) **495.00**

Salt dip, oblong deeply molded bowl
w/a rounded rectangular scalloped
rim, small rounded rectangular
footring, deep blue, OL-18 . . . . **660.00**

Salt dip, oval on a thin footring,
curved sides w/rounded panels
below an upright scalloped &
ribbed rim, probably Pittsburgh
area, OL-34 (small area of rim
underfill) **770.00**

Salt dip, rectangular boat-shaped
bowl on a flaring rectangular foot,
floral clusters on the sides,
probably Boston & Sandwich Glass
Co., golden amber, SN-1 (chip on
corner of base) **132.00**

Salt dip, rectangular pedestal base
on knob feet, the curved oval sides
below a deeply scalloped rim, an
overall diamond design below the
beaded rim band, attributed to
Boston & Sandwich, purplish blue,
OP-2 (minute flake & trace of mold
roughness on rim) **1,320.00**

Salt dip, rectangular sides w/corner
posts ending in small knob feet,
bouquet of flowers on long sides,
scalloped rim, New England Glass
Company, light green, NE-5 (mold
roughness) **143.00**

Salt dip, rectangular w/corner posts
continuing to form short legs,
notched rim, overall strawberry
diamond patt. on sides, probably
Boston & Sandwich Glass Co.,
deep violet (SD-7) **1,100.00**

Salt dip, thick scalloped rectangular
rim w/rounded corners above
incurved rounded panel sides,
bright sapphire blue (mold
roughness) **303.00**

Rare Lacy Pedestal Salt

Salt dip, pedestal-type w/a round
bowl w/a flaring scalloped rim,
peacock eyes around the sides of
the exterior, low pedestal on a plain
round foot w/a sunburst beneath,
probably Boston & Sandwich, ca.
1830-40, opaque violet, very minor
flakes to outside rim, PP-3,
3" d., 2" h. (ILLUS.) **2,750.00**

Lacy Acanthus Leaf Sugar Bowl

Sugar bowl, cov., footed octagonal
form w/a galleried rim inset w/a
domed cover w/a florette finial,
Acanthus Leaf patt., New England,
probably Boston & Sandwich, ca.
1830-40, deep bluish purple, lid
finial chip, two rim chips, small chip
on base foot, 3¾" h. (ILLUS.) **2,475.00**

Sugar bowl, cov., Gothic Arch patt.,
footed octagonal body w/a galleried
rim, inset domed cover w/button
finial, attributed to New England,
ca. 1840-60, fiery opalescent,
5¼" h. **1,210.00**

Gothic Arch Lacy Sugar Bowl

Sugar bowl, cov., Gothic Arch patt.
diamond point arches alternating
w/ribbed arches, scalloped foot,
electric blue, shallow spall & mold
roughness on cover, 5" h.
(ILLUS.) **2,420.00**

Toy Lacy Tureen & Undertray

Tureen, cover & undertray,
miniature toy-size, the footed deep
oval tureen w/small scroll end
handles, the low domed cover
w/a knob finial, each w/a fanned
shell & scroll design, the oval
undertray w/double heart-shaped
center scrolls & a border of tiny
florals, probably Boston &
Sandwich, few flakes on cover &
one on base, 2½" l., 2¾" h., the set
(ILLUS.) **198.00**

Tureen, cover & undertray, toy-size,
deep footed oval body w/small
scroll end handles, slightly domed
cover w/knob finial, matching oval
undertray, overall scrolling design,
probably Boston & Sandwich Glass

Co., mid-19th c., 3¼" h., 3 pcs.
(mold roughness, small chip on
foot of tureen) **198.00**

Rare "Ritchie" Window Pane

Window pane, rectangular, a central
cartouche showing a paddle-wheel
steamer & the name "Ritchie"
framed by tall ovoid vining flowers
above a pair of cornucopia w/shell
at the bottom, clear, bit of flaking
on edges, 5 x 7" (ILLUS.) **11,550.00**

LALIQUE

*Fine glass, which includes numerous
extraordinary molded articles, has been made by
the glasshouse established by René Lalique early
in this century in France. The firm was carried
on by his son, Marc, until his death in 1977 and
is now headed by Marc's daughter, Marie-
Claude. All Lalique glass is marked, usually on,
or near, the bottom with either an engraved or
molded signature. Unless otherwise noted, we
list only those pieces marked "R. Lalique"
produced before the death of René Lalique in
1945.*

R. Lalique France N°3152

R LALIQUE
FRANCE

R. LALIQUE
FRANCE

Lalique Marks

Bowl, 8½" d., 2⅛" h., "Vernon," round press-molded design of large sunflower blossoms, opalescent, "R. Lalique France" molded below rim **$690.00**

Bowl, 9¼" d., 3⅝" h., "Dahlia No. 1," uneven rounded sides w/a wide flat rim, press-molded design of large blossoms & leaves around the sides w/blossom feet, circular center mark "R. Lalique France". . **1,093.00**

Bowl, 9⅜" d., 3¼" h., "Vases No. 1 Coupe," wide shallow form in clear w/a repeating band of large polished pointed leaf-form panels alternating w/frosted stylized bouquets, leafy branches in the bottom, molded "R. Lalique" **230.00**

Lalique "Perruches" Bowl

Bowl, 9¾" d., "Perruches," wide flattened bottom below gently rounded sides w/a wide flat rim, opalescent w/a blue patine on the repeating band of twenty molded love birds in high-relief, blossoms in recessed panels, the base acid-stamped "R. Lalique - France" (ILLUS.) **2,990.00**

Bowl, 10" d., "Nemours," thick deep rounded frosted & enameled sides molded on the exterior w/graduated bands of stylized inset flowerheads, each w/a glossy black enameled center, inscribed "Lalique - France," reissued model after 1945 . . . . **632.00**

Bowl & underplate, "Poissons," the wide shallow bowl w/matching wider dished underplate both in opalescent molded w/a design of repeating swirled fish around a bubbly center, each marked "R. Lalique" in raised letters in the interior, 9⅛" d. & 11¾" d., 2 pcs. . **1,150.00**

Box, cov., "Quatre Papillons," round w/low cylindrical sides in frosted clear, the top molded w/four butterflies circling the center, delicate floral design around the sides, faint molded mark "Lalique Depose" on base, 3⅛" d., 2" h. . . . **920.00**

Dresser jar w/stopper, "Epines," dome-form body center w/a short cylindrical neck fitted w/a

mushroom-form stopper, clear w/a sepia patine molded overall w/a thorny bramble design, raised "R. Lalique" & "France" on base, 3½" h. **460.00**

Jewelry suite: necklace & bracelet; "Dahlias," each formed by bands of molded frosted clear glass in a petal design, the necklace w/adjustable spacer, the bracelet extendable, pr. **1,725.00**

Lalique "Suzanne" Lamp

Lamp, table model, "Suzanne," frosted amber molded in full-relief as a nude dancer w/outstretched arms holding lengths of drapery, w/gilt-bronze base & silk shade, molded "R. Lalique," inscribed "France," ca. 1925, 8⅞" h. (ILLUS.) **6,612.00**

Medallion, round, "Dans Les Fleurs," frosted clear low-relief figure of a nude female under blossoms, made for a Fioret perfume box, marked "R. Lalique - Fioret - Paris," 1⅜" d. **518.00**

Perfume bottle w/stopper, "Le Jade," flattened ovoid snuff bottle-form molded w/a jungle bird design in bright green crystal, matching stopper, marked "Le Jade - Roger et Gallet Paris - R. Lalique," 3¼" h. **2,185.00**

Perfume flacon, w/original stopper, "Salamandres," clear flattened oval w/polished rondels surrounded by curving lizards, greyish green patina in recesses, design repeated on the stopper, base marked "R. Lalique France," 3¾" h. **1,495.00**

Rare Lalique Perfume Flacon

Lalique "Ormeaux" Vase

Perfume flacon, w/ornate stopper, "Bouchon Mures," the clear tall barrel-shaped bottle w/black ribbing, fitted w/a molded flawlesstiara stopper of matte black w/berry clusters, molded "R. Lalique" on the base, 5½" h. (ILLUS.) **9,200.00**

Vase, 4½" h., "Eglantines," frosted clear ovoid form w/polished thorny branches & rose blossoms in relief, inscribed "R. Lalique" on the base. **403.00**

Vase, 5" h., "Chamois," frosted amber ovoid body w/a short flaring neck, molded in bold relief w/two overlapping tiers of stylized gazelles w/long curving antlers, reserved against a thick tan patine, engraved "R.Lalique - France," ca. 1931 . . . . **2,300.00**

Vase, 6⅛" h., "Cogs et Raisins," slightly swelled cylindrical frosted clear body w/a flat rim, molded in low-relief w/a continuous design of pairs of confronting longtailed roosters perched beneath scrolling grapevines heavy w/fruit, inscribed "R. Lalique," introduced in 1928 . . . **1,150.00**

Vase, 6½" h., "Eucalyptus" small knobby feet below a swelled cylindrical body w/a widely flaring, flattened rim, frosted opalescent grey molded on the exterior w/a band of tall, slender vertical overlapping leaves, resting on clusters of seed pods forming the feet, molded "R. LALIQUE," & inscribed "FRANCE," introduced in 1925 . . . . **1,380.00**

Vase, 6½" h., "Ormeaux," frosted deep amber spherical body w/a small trumpet neck, molded overall w/a design of overlapping leaves,

traces of white patine, inscribed "R. Lalique France No. 984," small rim chip, ca. 1926 (ILLUS.) **1,265.00**

Vase, 6⅝" h., "Gui," small footring below a large bulbous ovoid body w/a short cylindrical neck, translucent white molded in low- and medium-relief w/an overall design of overlapping mistletoe leaves, stems & berries, molded mark, introduced in 1920 . . . . **690.00**

Vase, 6¾" h., "Druide," footed large spherical body w/a small rolled neck, milky opalescent molded in medium-relief and low-relief w/an overlapping network of berried branches, engraved "R. Lalique - France - No. 937," introduced in 1924 . . . . **862.00**

Vase, 6¾" h., "Formose," large spherical body on a tiny footring & w/a small, short cylindrical neck, translucent white w/a pale blue tint, molded in medium- and low-relief w/an overall design of large Japanese goldfish w/long delicate tails & fins, retains traces of original aquamarine patine, molded mark, introduced in 1924 . . . . **1,610.00**

Vase, 7⅛" h., "Soucis," ovoid body molded in medium- and low-relief w/stylized flowers & leaves growing from a meandering vine, on a low tapering circular foot, flaring inverted conical neck, frosted blue, etched "R. LALIQUE," inscribed "France," introduced in 1930 (two rim chips) **3,220.00**

Vase, 8¼" h., "Ronsard," frosted clear spherical body w/a small rolled neck flanked by applied ringed shoulder handles each molded in the center w/a nude seated woman supporting the wreath ring, traces of original greyish patine, molded mark, introduced in 1926 (rim chip) **1,610.00**

Blue Lalique "Perruches" Vase

Vase, 10" h., "Perruches," bulbous ovoid body w/a low flat mouth rim, electric blue molded w/fourteen pairs of love birds perched on flowering branches, frosted & polished to enhance the design, possible minor restoration to rim, signed "R. Lalique - France," label w/"H.H. Battles - Philadelphia" (ILLUS.) **9,775.00**

LEGRAS

Cameo and enameled glass somewhat similar to that made by Gallé, Daum Nancy and other factories of the period was made at the Legras works in Saint Denis, France, late last century and until the outbreak of World War I.

Legras Mark

Bowl, 4¾" d., 3" h., rounded upright sides w/a pinched quartreform rim, clear decorated w/green & aubergine leaves & berries against a mustard yellow-colored ground, marked "Leg." on side, "Made in France" stamped on base **$173.00**

Cameo vase, 8¾" h., bulbous ovoid body tapering to a short flared neck, a textured frosted ground, overlaid in shades of purple, cut w/pendent flowers, signed in cameo, ca. 1900 . . . . **345.00**

Vase, 3½" h., short cylindrical base w/a flaring squared rim, frosted clear w/overall shallow etching & enamel painting of a waterfront scene w/sailboats, signed at the side **316.00**

Vase, 4¾" h., cylindrical w/dimpled sides & slightly closed flat rim, shaded peach to chartreuse

ground enameled & cut w/autumn green holly branches dotted w/wine red berries, signed **1,320.00**

Vase, 8" h., tapering cylindrical body w/a small, short waisted neck, variegated butterscotch ground acid-cut & enameled w/dark branches up the sides, signed. **385.00**

Vase, 8¼" h., ovoid form, moss green ground enameled in silver to depict pendent leafy branches w/pod clusters, trimmed w/gilding, cameo signature "Legras" & engraved "Made in France exclusively for Paris Decorators" **633.00**

Vase, 8½" h., bulbous ovoid body tapering to a short cylindrical neck, frosted clear ground etched overall & enamel-decorated w/pink & maroon flowering branches, signed "Legras" at mid-section & stamped by retailer "Ovington New York - France" **575.00**

Legras Enameled Landscape Vase

Vase, 8½" h., tall squared body enameled & cut-back w/a continuous design of silhouetted trees w/a lake & mountains in the distance, signed (ILLUS.). **1,485.00**

Vase, 9¼" h., tall slender waisted cylindrical form, shepherd & sheep & woods in orange, grey & off green, signed. **800.00**

Vase, 14" h., very slender waisted cylindrical form, enameled w/a continuous landscape scene, the base w/an ebony shepherd & flock atop a green grassy hillside, tall slender leafy trees up the sides silhouetted against distant lavender blue mountains against a shaded sunset sky of peach, cream & light orange, signed. **660.00**

Vase, 25¼" h., bulbous ovoid body tapering to a very tall slender 'stick' neck, grey acid-etched ground, cut w/a leafy tendrilous vine heavily laden w/seed pods, highlighted in plum enamel, signed in cameo, ca. 1910 . . . . **2,070.00**

LE VERRE FRANCAIS

Glassware carrying this marking was produced at the French glass factory founded by Charles Schneider in 1908. A great deal of cameo glass was exported to the United States early in this century and much of it was marketed through Ovingtons in New York City.

Le Verre Francais Marks

Atomizer, a mottled yellow pear-shaped vessel w/etched purple & rose pink Art Deco designs, inscribed "Le Verre Francais," fitted w/a gilt-metal atomizer top w/cigarette lighter, overall 7½" h. **$374.00**

Cameo lamp, wide shallow 11¾" d. domical shade w/a knobbed center raised on metal fittings above the slender ovoid base w/a wide disc foot, shades of grey mottled w/blue, overlaid in deep blue & cut w/rondels flowers, wrought-iron mount, acid-stamped indistinctly "FRANCE," 19" h. **2,990.00**

Cameo night light, the glass base w/a squatty bulbous body below a short, thick trumpet-form neck, cased red to yellow layered in tortoiseshell & etched as stylized blossoms, rim inscribed "Le Verre Francais," fitted w/a metal light cap, 3¼" h. **374.00**

Cameo vase, 4" h., ovoid body w/flaring rim, pink layered in amethyst shaded to purple & etched w/stylized sunflowers, inscribed on lower edge **518.00**

Cameo vase, 7" h., 9" d., wide bulbous double-gourd form, bright orange frosted & layered in tortoiseshell brown, etched & polished in stylized repeating geometric designs, marked "Charder" at side & "Le Verre Francais" below **920.00**

Cameo vase, 10" h., chalice-form w/a deep bell-form bowl on a short knopped stem & cushion foot, mottled layered ground cut-back w/stylized orange leaves & berries, etched signature "Le Verre Francais" & cameo signature "Charder" **1,100.00**

Cameo vase, 10¾" h., a thick cushion foot & slender short stem support a large bulbous spherical body tapering to a short thick flaring neck, mottled lavender & grey overlaid in mottled orange shading to purple, cut w/over-lapping pedent clusters of larvae-like decorative designs, signed in intaglio "Le Verre Francais," ca. 1900 . . . . **632.00**

Le Verre Francais Floral Cameo Vase

Cameo vase, 11¾" h., a cushion foot & knob stem support a flaring ovoid body w/a wide, flat mouth, grey streaked w/orange & splashed w/lemon yellow, overlaid in mottled purple & cut w/stylized dahlia blossoms on slender stems, signed in intaglio "Charder - Le Verre Francais," acid-stamped "FRANCE," ca. 1925 (ILLUS.) . . . **1,035.00**

Cameo vase, 11¾" h., long tapering ovoid body raised on a short ringed pedestal & spreading round foot, yellow-speckled orange layered in Tango Red shaded to the aubergine foot, etched w/stylized Art Deco blossoms & dots, "Le Verre Francais" on disk, "France" on base. **1,380.00**

Cameo vase, 12" h., bulbous ovoid body tapering to a widely flaring trumpet neck, mottled red & yellow overlaid in purple & etched w/stylized leaves & berries in long bands down the sides, two applied purple handles at the neck, lower edge inscribed "Le Verre Francais" & base marked "France - Ovington" **1,380.00**

Cameo vase, 15¾" h., thick cushion foot below the slender flaring body w/a swelled shoulder tapering to a flat rim, mottled pink, white & orange layered in lavender & aubergine, etched & polished as stylized rose blossoms on thorny stems, marked "Charder" at the side, "Le Verre Francais" on the foot & "France - Ovington" on the base **1,093.00**

Le Verre Francais Cameo Vases

Cameo vase, 16" h., tall slender ovoid body above a thick cushion pedestal foot, bright mottled orange overlaid in spotted tortoiseshell brown etched & polished w/three tall beetles below & between Art Deco border designs, striped candy cane mark on one side, "Le Verre Francais" mark on other side (ILLLUS. center) **1,150.00**

Cameo vase, 16¼" h., a tapering cushion foot supporting a tall slender flaring body below a bulbous shoulder tapering to a small flat mouth, lemon-tinted grey streaked w/tangerine, overlaid in mottled orange shading to purple, cut w/stylized blossoms on slender leafy stems, signed in cameo "Charder," in intaglio "Le verre francais," & acid-stamped "FRANCE," ca. 1925 . . . . **1,265.00**

Cameo vase, 17½" h., a thick cushion foot tapering to a tall elongated inverted pear-shaped body w/a closed rim, bright orangish red shading down to dark purplish brown & cameo-cut to mottled yellow w/large poppy blossoms on long budded stems tapering to a honeycomb-cut band above the plain foot, signed **3,410.00**

Cameo vase, 21¾" h., tall slender baluster-form body on a thick cushion foot, orange & yellow layered in mottled tortoiseshell brown shading to the aubergine foot, etched & polished w/stylized Art Deco blossoms & seed pods above a leafy border, marked "Le Verre Francais" on the foot (ILLUS. right) **1,495.00**

Cameo vase, 22" h., tall slender baluster-form on a thick cushion foot, translucent orange layered in mottled aubergine w/bluish white spots, etched & polished w/convoluted leaf & vine designs, striped candy cane edge, signed on foot "Le Verre Francais" (ILLUS. left) **1,380.00**

Very Tall Le Verre Francais Vase

Cameo vase, 28" h., tall slender swollen body w/a flat mouth & cushion foot, grey internally mottled & streaked w/orange, red & yellow, overlaid w/maroon & cut w/stylized Art Deco flowers & leaves drooping around the top half, signed in cameo "Charder," signed in intaglio "Le Verre Francais" (ILLUS.) **3,737.00**

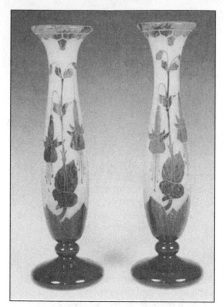

Pair Le Verre Francais Cameo Vases

Cameo vases, 17¾" h., very slender
tall baluster-form body on a
knopped stem & cushion foot,
cream shading to mottled light blue
overlaid w/mottled dark orangish
red & blue shading to cobalt blue &
cut w/stylized pendent flowers &
leaves, signed, early 20th c., pr.
(ILLUS.) **4,180.00**

Vase, 6" h., bulbous base & tapering
cyindrical sides to a short
cylindrical neck, dark tortoiseshell-
type glass acid-cutback w/three
large upright scarabs around the
body, incised signature & candy
cane filigrane, early 20th c. **880.00**

Vase, 10¼" h., footed ovoid body,
pink mottled & layered in amethyst
shaded to purple, etched repeating
design of stylized sunflowers,
marked "Le Verre Francais" on the
foot & "France - Ovington" on the
base **1,035.00**

Vase, 13" h., a broad, bulbous ovoid
body w/a sharply angled shoulder
to a small neck w/a widely flaring
rim, stylized frond of black & teal
blue on mottled pale yellow
overlaid in dark brown & vivid
orange & cameo cut w/a stylized
geometric vertical "Ming Tree"
design of long stems in dark brown
supporting circular pods of brown &
orange, candy cane signature, by
Charles Schneider **1,210.00**

LOETZ

Iridescent glass, some of it somewhat
resembling that of Tiffany and other
contemporary glasshouses, was produced by the
Bohemian firm of J. Loetz Witwe of Klostermule
and is referred to as Loetz. Some cameo pieces
were also made. Not all pieces are marked.

Loetz,
Austria

Loetz Mark

Bowl, 6½" d., 3" h., squatty bulbous
hexagonal form tapering slightly to
a widely flaring ruffled rim, lustrous
iridized rippled pattern, olive green
interior, resting on a bronze Art
Nouveau design four-stemmed
base w/dangling pierced flowers
around the rim, the four stem legs
joined at the base by a continuous
undulating leafy band, overall
8½" h. **$1,100.00**

Center bowl on stand, the
rectangular boat-form bowl
w/gently swelled sides, incurved
rims & the corners pulled into
points, deep purple shading to
amber iridescence decorated
overall w/swirls, raised on a narrow
gilt-metal rectangular frame raised
on four slender columnar supports
above the lower rectangular open
frame on four
paw feet, ca. 1900 . . . . **2,300.00**

Creamer, ovoid melon-lobed body in
iridescent mottled opal w/random
black amethyst trailings, the rim
fitted w/a silver neck, wide arched
spout & high arched open-loop
handle, 4" h. **275.00**

Inkwell w/hinged brass cap, square
chartreuse body applied overall
w/iridescent amethyst random
threading, 2½" w., 2½" h. **176.00**

Persian water sprinkler bottle,
squatty bulbous base w/dimpled
sides tapering to a tall slender neck
w/a jack-in-the-pulpit rim, overall
spotted gold iridescent papillon
surface decoration, polished pontil,
10" h. **633.00**

Vase, 4⅛" h., a thick round foot below
the ovoid body tapering to a six-
pointed star-form flared rim, grey
decorated w/olive green trailings &
overall ruby red oil spotting,
unsigned, ca. 1900 . . . . **2,070.00**

Vase, 4½" h., a tiny footring supporting a wide bulbous body w/double pinched sides & a wide flaring mouth, applied looped branch handles, fine iridescent gold w/bluish gold pulled design w/lavender hues overall, signed "Loetz Austria" **1,980.00**

Vase, 5" h., cased emerald green w/a paneled white lining, the footed sharply waisted body overlaid around the lower body w/an entwined silver overlay flowering leafy vine **165.00**

Vase, 5" h., gently flaring cylindrical body w/a pronounced shoulder & undulating triangular lip, green molded on the interior w/triangular ribs, the iridescent exterior overlaid in sterling silver w/scrolling foliage, unsigned ca. 1900 . . . . **862.00**

Vase, 5½" h., bulbous nearly spherical body tapering to deep indentations around the shoulder below the deeply fluted undulating flaring rim, amber decorated w/iridescent silvery blue leafage & horizontal striations, inscribed "Loetz - Austria," ca. 1901 . . . . . . **2,990.00**

Vase, 6½" h., a bulbous tapering base w/a slender cylindrical neck ending in a widely flaring funnel rim, the neck wrapped w/a band of aqua glass w/gold iridescence, the body in pale green w/violet, blue & orange iridescent highlights, design attributed to Koloman Moser, unsigned **253.00**

A Short and Tall Loetz Vase

Vase, 6½" h., simple ovoid body tapering to a ruffled trefoil rim, ambergris symmetrically decorated w/three gold & silvery iridescent pulled feather designs, base signed "Loetz Austria" (ILLUS. left) **863.00**

Vase, 6¾" h., simple ovoid body tapering to a short flared neck, reddish amber ground decorated overall w/rainbow iridescent 'oil spot' finish **990.00**

Vase, 7" h., bulbous melon-lobed body centered by a tall slender waisted neck, iridescent looped & draped design in blue, green & silver **440.00**

Vase, 7" h., ovoid body tapering to a narrow neck w/flaring rim, bright pink decorated around the lower half w/deep blue overall oil spottings, unsigned, ca. 1920 . . . . **1,725.00**

Vase, 7½" h., gently tapering cylindrical body below a wide squatty bulbous shoulder tapering to a short rolled neck, orange decorated w/greenish blue iridescent swirls & encased in clear, overlaid in sterling silver w/a diamond lattice design around the lower portion & loops, rings, florettes & ribbons around the shoulder, unsigned, ca. 1900 . . . . **3,737.00**

Vase, 8⅛" h., double-gourd form w/large indentations around the lower body, tapering to a short cylindrical neck, deep ruby red decorated up the sides w/large silvery blue pulled feathering, unsigned, ca. 1900 . . . . **4,715.00**

Vase, 8¾" h., "Marmorierte," ovoid body tapering to a short cylindrical neck, marbleized green, aubergine & turquoise blue body striations, cased in opal & lined in blue, decorated w/gilt-enamel scattered sunbursts centered by red glass 'jewels' **460.00**

Rare Signed Loetz Vase

Vase, 9½" h., tapering ovoid double-gourd footed body w/a short trumpet neck & flattened rim, lemon yellow decorated w/pale silvery blue dashes, the neck & shoulder w/dripping trailings of silvery blue & lavender, signed "Loetz - Austria," ca. 1900 (ILLUS.) **19,550.00**

Vase, 9⅞" h., tapering ovoid double-waisted body w/a short neck w/flattened rim, lemon yellow decorated w/overall loopings of silvery blue & purple pulled diagonal feathering in the middle section, the lower section w/deep purple & silvery blue loopings, incribed "Loetz - Austria," ca. 1900 . . . . **18,400.00**

Vase, 11¼" h., tall swelled cylindrical optic ribbed body w/a folded-in crimped rim, set into a cluster of slender bluish gold iridescent glass tubes encircled by a gold iridescent band, spiral veined cushion foot, designed by Eduard Prochaska, ca. 1906 (tiny maker's fracture in spiral band) **1,540.00**

Vase, 11½" h., swelled cylindrical form w/in-body heavy twist below the wide flaring & crimped mouth, shaded green to amethyst lustre ground decorated w/silver overlay swirled flowers & leaves, unmarked (tiny piece of silver missing) **1,100.00**

Vase, 12⅝" h., tall cylindrical body w/a narrow flared base band, clear ribbed form decorated in fine detail w/blue, green & gold combed iridescent horizontal striping, signed on the base w/a circular crossed arrow mark & "Austria". . . . **978.00**

Vase, 16" h., footed squatty bulbous body w/a wide rounded shoulder tapering to a very tall 'stick' neck, orange w/pulled & coiled gold iridescent decoration w/fine lustre, polished pontil & base (ILLUS. right, previous page). **6,900.00**

LUSTRES

Lustres were Victorian glass vase-like decorative objects often hung around the rim with prisms. They were generally sold as matched pairs to be displayed on fireplace mantels. A wide range of colored glasswares were used in producing lustres and pieces were often highlighted with colored enameled decoration.

Three Pairs of Fine Lustres

Amber cut-back, deep bowl-shaped top w/scalloped rim, the sides cut to clear w/large crosshatched diamonds, a ringed pedestal & domed ring foot, long facet-cut prisms suspended from the top bowl, 12¾" h., pr. (ILLUS. back left) **$330.00**

Cranberry, wide rounded top w/upright sides & pointed scalloped rim decorated w/fancy gold stenciling, the slender ringed stem on a domed gilt-trimmed foot, replaced long triangular prisms, signed "Moser," 13½" h., pr. **770.00**

Cranberry, bulbous top w/scalloped rim above a pedestal base & round foot, gold & colored enamel floral decoration, facet-cut prisms, 14½" h., pr. **550.00**

Blue Cut-overlay Lustre

Cut-overlay, cobalt blue cut to clear, a tall slender trumpet-form body w/scalloped rim suspending long triangular prisms, on a domed, scalloped & printie-cut foot, Bohemian, 19th c., minor chips, 12" h., pr. (ILLUS. of one) **1,265.00**

Cut-overlay, white cut to cranberry & trimmed w/an enameled diamond band around the bulbous top w/a flaring scalloped neck trimmed w/enameled florettes, raised on a swelled pedestal & cushion foot, cut w/bands of small ovals, gold trim, hung w/clear facet-cut prisms, 20th c., 12½" h., pr. (minor flakes) **226.00**

Green, the top bowl w/a pointed scalloped rim & swelled base ring, the sides enameled w/delicate florals above the band of facet-cut prisms, the baluster-form pedestal w/a swelled ring top & cushion foot, 14" h., pr. (ILLUS. back right) **440.00**

Pink cased, the squatty bulbous top tapers to a slightly flaring low cylindrical neck w/a scalloped rim, ringed pedestal above the cushion foot, long facet-cut prisms suspended from base of top, decorated overall w/colored floral enameling & gilt trim, 10¾" h., pr. (ILLUS. front) **330.00**

Ruby Glass Lustres

Ruby glass, deep cylindrical bowl w/a scalloped rim above a baluster-form stem on a bell-form foot, the bowl & foot enameled w/delicate beaded reserves & tiny blossoms, suspending triangular cut prisms, 19th c., pr. (ILLUS.) **660.00**

MARY GREGORY

Glass enameled in white with silhouette-type figures, primarily of children, is now termed "Mary Gergory" and was attributed to the Boston and Sandwich Glass Company. However, recent research has proven conclusively that this was not decorated by Mary Gregory, nor was it made at the Sandwich plant. Miss Gregory was employed by Boston and Sandwich Glass Company as a decorator; however, records show her assignment was the painting of naturalistic landscape scenes on larger items such as lamps and shades, but never the charming children for

which her name has become synonymous. Further, in the inspection of fragments from the factory site, no paintings of children were found.

It is now known that all wares collectors call "Mary Gregory" originated in Bohemia beginning in the late 19th century and were extensively exported to England and the United States well into this century.

For further information, see The Glass Industry in Sandwich, Volume #4, *by Raymond E. Barlow and Joan E. Kaiser, and the book,* Mary Gregory Glassware, 1880-1900, *by R. & D. Truitt.*

Mary Gregory Barber Bottle

Barber bottle, bulbous ovoid body tapering to a lady's leg neck, cobalt blue w/white enameled scene of a young girl holding a tennis racket & standing near a net, 8⅛" h. (ILLUS.) **$286.00**

Barber Bottle with Tennis Girl Scene

Barber bottle, bulbous ovoid body tapering to a lady's leg neck, cobalt blue w/white enameled scene of a young girl serving a tennis ball, 8⅛" h. (ILLUS.) **308.00**

Box w/hinged cover, round, golden amber w/white enameled young boy, 3⅜" d., 3¼" h. **245.00**

Ornate Mary Gregory Box

Box w/hinged cover, round, cranberry, white enameled boy w/flowers within a gold & white ring framed by a large diamond panel w/white dots & four white & gold radiating & small white dotted bands, on a squatty gilt-metal base & feet, 5¾" d., 5½" h. (ILLUS.) . . . **1,065.00**

Cruet w/original clear bubble stopper, cranberry bulbous ovoid body tapering to a cylindrical neck w/a pinched spout, white enameled young girl feeding large rooster in garden setting, applied clear handle, 7" h. **468.00**

Cruet w/original clear bubble stopper, ovoid cranberry body tapering to a cylindrical neck w/pinched spout, white enamel boy w/drum in garden setting, applied clear handle, 7" h. **468.00**

Mary Gregory Decanter

Decanter w/original stopper, lavender-stained, cylindrical body w/rounded shoulder to a swelled shoulder & rings, cylindrical neck w/a flared mouth, clear facet-cut stopper, white enameled girl in garden, 2⅞" d., 9½" h. (ILLUS.) . . . **145.00**

Pitcher, 9" h., black amethyst, white enameled girl swinging, applied clear reeded handle. **530.00**

Pitcher, tankard, 11½" h., footed tall baluster-form body w/a wide arched spout & applied arched blue handle, dark blue w/a white enamel scene of a man leaning on a rail fence w/trees & bushes behind, gold band trim **248.00**

Vase, cylindrical ribbed body, Amberina w/white enamel decoration of a young lady w/sprig. **187.00**

Vase, 5" h., pedestal base, cranberry, white enameled girl w/basket **225.00**

Two Mary Gregory Vases

Vase, 8¼" h., 3½" d., amber, footed ovoid optic-ribbed body tapering to a short cylindrical neck w/a deeply crimped & rolled rim, white enameled girl in a garden (ILLUS. right). **175.00**

Vase, 10⅝" h., 4" d., lime green, tall slightly tapering optic-ribbed body, white enameled girl carrying a butterfly net in a landscape setting (ILLUS. left) **188.00**

Vase, 11¾" h., sapphire blue, tapering bell-form w/a ringed neck, white enameled scene of boy on knees holding out a heart to a standing girl. **460.00**

Scarce Mary Gregory Warmer

Warmer in silvered metal frame, a
pale lavender cylindrical glass
insert w/white enamel scenes of
five children in various poses &
ducks, silvered metal pierced-work
frame w/simple bail handle, fanned
side supports continuing to form
blocked feet, late 19th c.
(ILLUS.). **440.00**

Fine Mary Gregory Water Set

Water set: 12" h. footed tankard
pitcher & six 6½" h. matching
goblets; sapphire blue pitcher
w/white enameled woman gazing
at flying birds, applied amber
handle, the blue goblet bowl on an
applied amber-stemmed base,
each w/white enameled decoration,
three w/a girl & three w/a boy,
7 pcs. (ILLUS. of part) **1,345.00**

MILK GLASS

Elephant with Rider Dish

*Opaque white glass, or "opal," has been
called "milk-white glass" perhaps to distinguish
it from transparent or "clear-white glass."
Resembling fine white porcelain, it was viewed
as an inexpensive substitute. Opacity is obtained
by adding bone ash or oxide of tin to clear
molten glass. By the addition of various coloring
agents, the opaque mixture can be turned into
blue milk glass, or pink, yellow, green, caramel,
even black milk glass. Collectors of milk glass
now accept not only the white variety but
virtually any opaque colors and color mixtures,
including slag or marbled glass. It has been
made in numerous forms and shapes in this
country and abroad from about the first quarter
of the 19th century. It is still being produced,
and there are many reproductions of earlier
pieces. Pieces are all-white unless otherwise
noted. Also see HISTORICAL, PATTERN
GLASS and WESTMORELAND.*

Animal covered dish, Baboon on
Fleur-de-lis base, attributed to
Flaccus **$600.00**
Animal covered dish, "British Lion"
on base **210.00**
Animal covered dish, Chick
emerging from egg on basket base . . . **80.00**
Animal covered dish, Dog on wide
rib base, half white & half blue,
Westmoreland Specialty Company,
5½" l. **55.00**
Animal covered dish, Duck w/blue
head, Atterbury, marked "Pat.
March 15, 1887," 11" l. (no eyes,
several minor rim checks) **675.00**
Animal covered dish, Elephant
w/rider, signed "Vallerystahl,"
France (ILLUS.). **700.00**
Animal covered dish, Entwined
Fish, ruby eyes, round lattice-
edged base, Atterbury, ca. 1889,
6" d. **225.00**

Animal covered dish, Fish on Skiff,
7½" l. **43.00**
Animal covered dish, Hen on
Sleigh **90.00**

Rare Monkey On Grass Mound Dish

Animal covered dish, Monkey on
Grass Mound w/leaf & scroll
patt. base, 6¼" l.
(ILLUS.) . . . . **1,800.00 to 2,000.00**
Animal covered dish, Rabbit on
Egg, small rabbit on textured egg
w/pedestal base, Vallerysthal,
5¼" l., 5" h. **190.00**
Animal covered dish, Rabbit,
marked "Portieux," France, 7" l. **475.00**
Animal covered dish, Swan
w/closed neck on basketweave
base, Westmoreland Specialty
Company, 5½" l., 4¾" h. **75.00**
Animal covered dish, Wooly Lamb
on Bo Peep base, Flaccus, 6⅛" l.,
3¾" h. **350.00**
Bowl, 6" d., 2½" h., Blackberry patt. . . . **35.00**
Covered dish, Car, Vallerysthal,
5½" l., 4¾" h. **500.00**
Covered dish, Crate with straps,
Vallerysthal, France, 5½" l., 4" w. . . . **125.00**
Covered dish, Moses in Bulrushes,
5½" l. . . . . **150.00 to 200.00**
Epergne-compote, Tree of Life patt.
bowl, figural Enfant Samuel
pedestal base **310.00**
Jar, cov., tall Owl, Atterbury,
7" h. . . . . **125.00 to 130.00**
Jar, cov., tall Owl, Atterbury, blue
opaque, 7" h. . . . . **350.00 to 400.00**
Lamp, miniature, oil-type, Columbus
bust w/beard base, 4¾" h. **1,250.00**
Models of dogs, Mantel Dogs,
recumbent animal on an oval
serrated base, attributed to
England, 7" l., 5" h., pr. **1,700.00**
Mug, "Tavern Scene" patt. **35.00**
Plate, 5½" d., Woof Woof **45.00**
Plate, 6" d., Dog and Cats, open leaf
border, Gillinder. **125.00**

Three Owls Plate

Plate, 7½" d., Three Owls patt.,
looped border halfway around
plate, Westmoreland Specialty
Company, ca. 1901 (ILLUS.). **48.00**
Shaker w/original top, figural
Columbus bust, beardless. **450.00**
Sugar shaker w/original top, Melligo
patt., decorated **85.00**

Alba Decorated Syrup Pitcher

Syrup pitcher w/metal lid, Alba
patt., colored floral decoration . . .
(ILLUS.). **65.00**

MONT JOYE

*Cameo and enameled glass bearing this
mark was made in Pantin, France, by the same
works that produced pieces signed De Vez.*

Vase, 6" h., small ovoid base tapering
to a tall slender trumpet-form neck,
frosted etched surface in clear
w/naturalistic purple violet
blossoms highlighted in gold, base
marked "Dimier Geneve". **$259.00**
Vase, 12¼" h., ringed foot below the
tall gently tapering cylindrical body
w/a flared rim, pale green textured
surface enamel-decorated up the
sides w/large vines of flowering

sweetpeas w/leaves & tendrils, a
wide rim band in gilt decorated
w/lacy lattice & florals 330.00

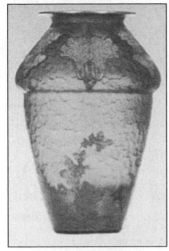

Mont Joye Vase

Vase, 13" h., elongated acorn-form
body w/a short wide mouth w/a
flattened flaring rim, heavily scale-
textured emerald green decorated
around the shoulder & base
w/heavily gilt Art Nouveau style oak
leaves & silver acorns, signed
(ILLUS.) 2,200.00

Vase, 15" h., tall form w/a cylindrical
neck, white opalescent decorated
w/mums & leaves, gold mark 425.00

Vases, 12½" h., cylindrical, each in
sea green enameled
w/chrysanthemums in pink,
yellow & gold, pr. 575.00

Vases, 30" h., tall swelled cylindrical
body w/a pinched rim, deep ruby
shading down to clear, decorated
w/lifesized enameled yellow, lilac &
white mum flowers, pr. 1,430.00

MOSER

*Ludwig Moser opened his first glass shop in
1857 in Karlsbad, Bohemia (now Karlovy Vary,
in the former Czechoslovakia). Here he engraved
and decorated fine glasswares especially to
appeal to rich visitors to the local health spa.
Later other shops were opened in various cities
and throughout the 19th and early 20th century
lovely, colorful glasswares, many beautifully
enameled, were produced by Moser's shops and
reached a wide market in Europe and America.
Ludwig died in 1916 and the firm continued
under his sons. They were forced to merge with*

*the Meyer's Nephews glass factory after World
War I. The glassworks were sold out of the Moser
family in 1933.*

Bowl, 6¾" l., 5" h., rectangular
w/scalloped rim, sapphire blue
w/enameled florals in pastel colors,
in original brass frame $245.00

Bowl, 7½" l., 2½" h., intaglio-carved
florals, leaves & stems on a purple
shaded to clear ground, signed
"Karlsbad" 480.00

Bowl, 9" l., 5" h., cut overlay,
amethyst cut to clear, oblong w/the
body cut in intaglio w/roses & leafy
stems, marked "Moser Karlsbad" . . 303.00

Bowl, 9½" d., 8" h., sixteen-paneled
base, cranberry w/raised gold
ornamentation 485.00

Box, cov., round, amber ground acid-
cut around the low cylindrical body
w/a gilt -trimmed band of warriors &
on the slightly domed cover w/an
acid-cut gilt-trimmed floral vine
band, signed "Moser Karlsbad
Made in Czechoslovakia," 3½" d.,
1¾" h. 275.00

Box, cov., squatty bulbous round
body w/a fitted flattened cover,
green, the cover decorated w/a
large high-relief gold sunflower
w/the stem & leaves wrapping
around the body, original paper
label w/"Glasfabrik Karlsbad,"
6" d., 4" h. 275.00

Cameo vase, 8" h., a footed bulbous
body tapering to a tall, wide
cylindrical neck, pale opaque
yellowish green overlaid in Bahama
brown & cut-back w/a design of a
sailing ship, windmill & large
leaves, base incised "Moser -
Karlsbad," side incised "MK" 1,540.00

**Cologne bottle, stopper &
underplate,** cut-overlay, pink cut to
white cut to clear, the wide tapering
cylindrical body cut w/bands of
trefoils & quatrefoils & bull's-eyes
below the slender waisted neck
w/flaring rim cut w/oval panels & a
band of dots, a clear tall faceted
pointed stopper, underplate cut to
match the bottle, script signature,
late 19th c., bottle 10" h., the set. . . 275.00

Compote, open, 8½" d., 6¾" h., cut-
overlay widely flaring shallow bowl
in white cut to cranberry w/ribs
w/cut printies alternating w/ribs
decorated w/grapes, raised on a
knopped silver plate stem &
squared, stepped foot 330.00

Cracker jar, cov., simple ovoid
  barrel-shaped optic-ribbed
  cranberry body, silver plate rim,
  cover & bail handle, base signed
  "Moser Karlsbad". **275.00**
Cruet w/facet-cut clear stopper,
  mold-blown optic ribbed bulbous
  sapphire blue body tapering to a
  short neck & spout, applied clear
  base & handle, signed in script **88.00**
Ewer, slender panel-cut clear body,
  entirely decorated w/elaborate
  enameled yellow netted scrolls
  surrounding oval ruby panels, gold-
  washed collar, spout & handle,
  12½" h. **303.00**
Pitcher, tankard, 7½" h., cranberry
  w/gold & pink enameling **188.00**

Intaglio-Cut Moser Pitcher

Pitcher, tankard, 12¼" h., intaglio-cut
  floral design, apple green shading
  to clear, applied clear handle
  (ILLUS.). **765.00**
Punch cup, cut overlay, amber cut to
  clear, gilt scissor-cut rim, applied
  handle, the body ornately
  decorated w/enameled & silver
  floral bouquets w/scrolls **132.00**
Tumbler, decorated w/a nude maiden
  w/long flowing hair, 4" h. **400.00**
Vase, 6" h., Radon glass, vaseline-
  colored slender paneled & waisted
  body w/a scalloped rim & gold
  medial band of etched Amazon
  women, raised on a short flaring
  stem & square foot, signed "Moser
  Czecko - Slovakia Karlsbad". **403.00**
Vase, 6½" h., overlay, opaque white
  cut to cranberry, pedestal base
  w/eight cut-back panels & a cut-
  back chalice-form bowl
  w/enameled florals overall. **165.00**

Moser Vase with Amazon Decoration

Vase, 7" h., amber paneled baluster-
  form body w/a wide flat medial
  band of etched Amazon warriors,
  signed on base "Made in
  Czechoslovakia - Moser Karlsbad"
  (ILLUS.). **546.00**
Vase, 8" h., bell-form body w/a
  smooth rim, raised on a knopped
  pedestal w/a round foot, cranberry
  decorated w/multicolored
  enameled leaves & flowers **990.00**
Vase, 8" h., 3" d. top, cranberry
  enamel-decorated w/gold leaves &
  branches w/berries, gold medallion
  of a young lady in white playing a
  flute **195.00**
Vase, 8¾" h., slightly flaring
  cylindrical form, emerald green
  acid cutback w/an overall stylized
  design of large tulip-like blossoms
  & leaves, signed "Moser"
  & "MM" **1,100.00**
Vase, 10" h., heavy walled dark
  amethyst faceted body w/etched &
  gilded medial scene of a bear hunt
  w/spear-armed men & dogs
  pursuing the large bear **345.00**
Vase, 11" h., a round foot & short
  ringed stem supporting a tall
  slightly flaring cylindrical body w/a
  narrow shoulder tapering to a wide
  trumpet neck, amber decorated
  overall w/colored enameled
  flowers, a tree, bee & bird, early
  20th c., script signature **385.00**
Vases, 6" h., upright paneled oblong
  body inset in a gilt-metal pierced
  base & pierced framework w/the
  figure of an Art Deco-style dancing
  lady on each side, pr. **1,100.00**

Ornate Moser Water Set

Water set: 9¼" h. tapering ovoid
pitcher w/a raised ring band near
the rim & base & six 4" h. tumblers;
each decorated w/sanded gold
leaves & tiny blue & white
enameled twigs & blossoms on a
crystal ground, applied clear gilt-
trimmed handle, 7 pcs.(ILLUS. of
part) **1,020.00**

Wine glasses, hock-type, color cut-
back to clear in a flute design, cut
paneled stems w/a cut knop at the
base, in cobalt blue, cranberry,
green, citron, amethyst & topaz,
signed, 7½" h., set of 6 . . . . **395.00**

MT. WASHINGTON

*A wide diversity of glass was made by the
Mt. Washington Glass Company of New Bedford,
Massachusetts, between 1869 and 1900. It was
succeeded in 1900 by the Pairpoint Corporation.
Miscellaneous types are listed below.*

Cracker jar, cov., Shell mold,
decorated w/gold enameling
w/touches of colored enamels,
silver plate rim, cover & bail
handle **$475.00**

Cracker jar, cov., large squared body
w/rounded corners ornately
decorated w/raised gold spider
mums & meandering leafy stems
on the pale peach & ivory ground,
silver-gilt embossed rim, ribbed
pointed cover & bail handle,
6" h. **660.00**

Cracker jar, cov., barrel-shaped,
cased rose satin exterior decorated
overall w/pale blue blossoms
outlined in yellow enamel, white
interior, silver plate rim, floral-
embossed domed cover & twisted
rope bail handle, 7½" h. **523.00**

Cruet w/original stopper, soft yellow
shaded ground enameled w/blue &
white flowers, satin finish **1,950.00**

Flower frog, mushroom-shaped, the
wide domed top in pale shaded
blue satin enameled w/delicate
colored florals, the top raised on a
slender trumpet foot, 5" d., 3¼" h. **220.00**

Hatpin holder, mushroom-shaped,
wide domed round top pierced
w/holes & raised on a trumpet
base, shaded pale blue ground
enameled w/sprigs of blue & white
forget-me-nots on the top, 5½" d.,
3¼" h. **495.00**

Jewel box w/hinged lid, squared
form, the base w/rounded
shoulders above relief-molded
wreaths of roses & tied bows &
garlands of roses in white against a
pale green ground further
decorated w/painted roses & baby
asters, the conforming lid
w/matching molded decoration & a
white central medallion w/painted
flowers, original "MTW" factory
numbers on the base "3 2 12/26,"
ca. 1885, 7½" w., 4¼" h. **1,210.00**

Mt. Washington Cameo Lamp

Lamp, table model, Cameo-type,
10" d. open-topped domical shade
in opal white overlaid in bright rose
pink & acid-etched w/butterflies,
ribbons & bouquets centering
cameo classical portrait
medallions, matching squatty
bulbous base, silver plated burner,
shoulder ring & round knob-footed
base marked "Pairpoint Mfg. Co.
3013," electrified, needs rewiring,
overall 17" h. (ILLUS.) **3,105.00**

Lamp, table model, 10" d. Mt. Washington Cameo shade in rose pink cut to white w/four beaded ovals w/a repeated portrait of woman wearing a Roman helmet, alternating w/floral & scrolled fern designs, resting on a reeded columnar metal base w/a triple pod leaf foot, overall 17½" h. **605.00**

Lamp, kerosene banquet-type, 12" d. melon-ribbed domical shade finely decorated w/pink & white full-blown pink roses & leafy stems on a ivory ground, set in a metal ring above the burner & embossed brass shoulder of the matching squatty bulbous melon-lobed font raised on an ornate gilt-metal figural base w/tall full-figure maidens standing w/arms raised & flanking an embossed funnel on the center standard above a domed floral & scroll-embossed base raised on wide stepped feet & a scrolled apron, overall 24" h. **2,860.00**

Salt & pepper shakers w/original metal lids, lobed tomato-shape, one w/a pink satin ground, the other w/a blue ground, each enamel-decorated w/a leaf & berry design, pr. **193.00**

Salt & pepper shakers w/original metal lids, cockle shell-shaped, one a Burmese color w/pale pink enameled flowers, the other in white opal painted w/a pastel pink floral bouquet, 2¾" l., pr. **2,200.00**

Salt & pepper shakers w/original metal tops, upright egg shape, one w/pink-tinted ground, the other w/a green-tinted ground, each enamel-decorated w/pink & white flowers, 2¼" h., pr. **165.00**

Salt & pepper shakers w/original metal tops, fig-shaped, almond tan ground enameled w/green ferns & light blue flowers highlighted w/small berries & blossoms, 2½" h., pr. **358.00**

Salt shaker w/original lid, model of a fig, pink ground w/enameled flowers. **100.00**

Salt shaker w/original metal top, fig-shaped, ivory textured ground decorated w/tan pine cones on green needled boughs, 2½" h. **220.00**

Scent bottle w/original stopper, milk white ground w/an overall decoration of color enameled florals, acid-etched on the base "Trademark of Mt. Washington Glass Co.," late 19th c., 9" h. **116.00**

Sugar shaker w/original metal lid, melon-lobed tomato shape, pale green shoulder decorated w/pink & white enameled flowers, embossed floral lid, 2½" h. **495.00**

Sugar shaker w/original metal lid, fig-shaped, frosted clear Royal Flemish-style body decorated w/colorful pansies, 4" h. **1,870.00**

Sugar shaker w/original metal lid, figural cockle shell, the ribbed flattened body decorated w/a mottled wine red ground painted w/clumps of white enameled flowers w/colorful pastel leafy branches trimmed w/yellow highlights, 4" l. **5,720.00**

Sugar shaker w/original metal lid, large ovoid egg shape, pale blue ground decorated w/large pointed maroon & moss green leaves, 4¼" h. **523.00**

Toothpick holder, Fig mold, opaque satin w/salmon coloring & blue enameled floral sprays, 1¾" h. **743.00**

Vase, 8" h., eight-ribbed body w/a flared rim, colored base w/green thistle decoration outlined in gold in the Verona manner **201.00**

MULLER FRERES

The Muller Brothers made acid-etched cameo and other fine glass at Luneville, France, starting in 1910 and until the outbreak of World War II in Europe.

Muller Freres Mark

Cameo vase, 11¼" h., wide squatty bulbous body w/a sloping shoulder to a short rolled neck, grey opalescent infused w/lemon yellow, overlaid in crimson & deep red & cut w/full-blown peony blossoms, buds & leaves, signed in cameo "Muller Freres - Luneville," ca. 1925 . . . . **$4,600.00**

Lamp, mantel-type, the pressed pale frosted pink ovoid shade w/a wide flat top, relief-molded stylized Art Deco designs, mounted on a black wrought-iron foliate decorated shaft w/a thick square foot, overall 11½" h. **431.00**

Vase, 3½" h., 6" d., squatty form in mottled golden orange, tangerine & cobalt blue, signed "Muller Fres - Luneville". **148.00**

Vase, 12¾" h., tall slender ovoid body raised on a knop above a disk foot, the top tapering to a short cylindrical neck w/a flattened flaring rim, bright reddish orange shaded to royal blue encased in clear, foot inscribed "Muller Fres - Luneville" . . **748.00**

NAILSEA

Nailsea was another glassmaking center in England where a variety of wares similar to those from Bristol, England were produced between 1788 and 1873. Today most collectors think of Nailsea primarily as a glass featuring swirls and loopings, usually white, on a clear or colored ground. This style of glass decoration, however, was not restricted to Nailsea and was produced in many other glasshouses, including some in America.

Bellows bottle, upright bellow-form body w/tall slender neck w/flaring mouth, clear w/overall delicate red & white looping & clear applied rigaree down the sides & rings around the neck, raised on a knobbed pedestal on a round foot, probably Boston & Sandwich Glass Co., 19th c., 13½" h. **$825.00**

Nailsea Amber Decanter

Decanter w/ribbed matching bubble stopper, yellowish amber w/white looping, conical body tapering to a slender cylindrical neck w/flared rim, stopper w/etched "76" on bottom, 9¾" h. (ILLUS.) . . . **358.00**

Flask, medium red loopings in clear, 19th c. **125.00**

Flask, pink & white loopings in clear, 19th c. **125.00**

Vase, 11½" h., clear w/white loopings, a thick applied round foot w/several wafers supporting the tall cylindrical vase w/a bulbous base & a deeply rolled tooled rim, probably Pittsburgh (some interior stain) **550.00**

Vase, 11⅝" h., bulbous base tapering to a tall cylindrical neck w/a widely rolled rim, clear w/long white loopings, raised on an applied clear disc pedestal & round foot, probably Pittsburgh, mid-19th c.. . **1,265.00**

Nailsea Vase & Witch Ball

Vase w/witch ball, clear w/white & fiery opalescent looping, the tall slender trumpet-form vase w/a swelled base on an applied clear foot, the large witch ball sitting atop the flared rim, probably South Jersey, vase 11" h., overall 16½" h., 2 pcs. (ILLUS.) **4,290.00**

NAKARA

Like Kelva, Nakara was made early in this century by the C.F. Monroe Company. For details see WAVE CREST.

Nakara Box with Pansy Lid

Box w/hinged lid, molded Pansy lid, green ground, 3¾" h. (ILLUS.) . . . **$765.00**

Nakara "Collars & Cuffs" Box

Box w/hinged lid, round, the side decorated w/"Collars & Cuffs" outlined w/white enamel dots on a pinkish to lavender ground, the lid w/a color scene of a Grecian garden in a paneled reserve, 7¼" d., 5½" h. (ILLUS.) **2,500.00**

Box w/hinged lid, Octagonal mold, low paneled base & conforming lid, each half decorated w/purple iris on a yellowish tan ground, 6" w. . . . **990.00**

Box w/hinged lid, peach colored ground, the lid decorated w/a color scene of a 18th c. courting couple, trimmed w/blue flowers, original lining, marked, 6" d. (missing clasp) **1,370.00**

Ornate Nakara Box

Box w/hinged lid, Crown mold, lid & sides w/a green ground w/swirled panels decorated w/pink roses, gold trim & enameled beading, gilt-metal base & scroll feet, clasp missing, 8" d., 6¼" h. (ILLUS.) . . . **2,100.00**

Box w/hinged lid, shaded peach ground, the lid decorated w/two cupids, one w/a palette before an easel painting a lady's portrait, floral decoration around the base, original lining, 8" d **2,315.00**

Dresser box w/hinged cover, squatty bulbous base w/wide decorative gilt-metal fittings, flattened domed cover, mauve

ground, the cover centered by a large reserve featuring a color scene of three Kate Greenaway-style girls having a tea party flanked by daisy bouquets at the rim, the base w/white enameled beaded overlapping lappet panels, marked, 6" d., 3" h **1,155.00**

Dresser box w/hinged cover, octagonal rib-paneled shape, the biscuit yellow ground decorated on the flattened cover w/large purple iris blossoms & elongated green leaves, design repeated on squatty bulbous base, signed, 6" w., 3¼" h. **770.00**

Dresser tray, squatty rounded tapering sides w/a decorative gilt-metal rim band & lacy tab handles, autumn green ground decorated w/a garland of pink mums highlighted w/white enamel, 6"d., 2¼" h. **248.00**

Ferner, cylindrical base below a bulbous shoulder, molded w/bands of leafy scrolls around the top & base, raised on a gilt-metal base w/scrolled feet (no metal liner) **650.00**

Humidor w/brass lid, wide bulbous baluster-form body w/a fitted domed metal lid w/wide knob, the shaded deep red to tan sides decorated w/a colorful bust portrait of a Native American in headdress, 6" d., 5½" h. **1,270.00**

"B.P.O.E." Tobacco Humidor

Humidor w/hinged lid, flaring cylindrical body w/a swelled shoulder, a wide flattened domed cover, the side decorated w/a brown & white elk head & "B.P.O.E.," & "Tobacco" on the cover, shaded dark green to tan ground (ILLUS.) **1,495.00**

Humidor w/hinged lid, low wide tapering cylindrical base w/a wide low domed cover, the side decorated w/a color portrait of a Native American in full headdress w/h.p. trim & the word "Cigars" on the cover, brass holder for moistener inside cover, 6½" d., 5¾" h. **525.00**

Small Nakara Ring Box

Ring box w/hinged lid, squared flat top w/notched corners, squatty rounded base w/corner notches, the lid w/a white diamond decorated w/a romantic couple in costume framed by pale blue w/small daisy-like flowers, the shoulder in creamy white & the base sides in pale blue, 2½" h. (ILLUS.). **880.00**
Vase, 15¾" h., ovoid top tapering to a slightly flared base w/footring, pink & white flowers on a shaded green ground **1,900.00**

NASH

A. Douglas Nash, a former employee of Louis Comfort Tiffany, purchased Tiffany's Corona Works in December 1928 and began his own operation there. For a brief period Nash produced some outstanding glasswares but the factory closed in March of 1931 and Nash then became associated with Libbey Glass of Toledo, Ohio. This quality glass is quite scarce.

Bowl, 8¾" d., footed low squatty round form w/upright optic ribbed fluted sides decorated w/a gold iridescent finish, signed "NASH" . . **$303.00**
Compote, open, 7½" d., 4½" h., "Chintz" line, a domed wide foot & short pedestal supporting a deep rounded bowl w/a very wide, flattened rim, aquamarine transparent bowl & base w/the flat rim of red & greyish green controlled stripe decoration, base inscribed "Nash RD89" **863.00**

Goblet, round foot centerd by a small compressed knop & a slender waisted stem supporting a tall tulip-form bowl w/slightly flaring rim, iridescent gold w/orange, blue & violet highlights, signed "Nash," 7" h. **275.00**
Vase, 5½" h., "Chintz" line, wide ovoid body w/a wide angled shoulder tapering to a short rolled neck, clear internally striped w/pastel orange alternating w/yellow Chintz decoration **173.00**

Fine Nash "Chintz" Vase

Vase, 5½" h., "Chintz" line, wide-shouldered heavy ovoid body w/a short flaring neck, deep rose red w/alternating wide & narrow vertical silver lustre stripes, base signed "Nash RD 66" (ILLUS.) **978.00**
Vase, 5½" h., wide bulbous ovoid body w/the wide rounded shoulder centered by a short rolled neck, brilliant red w/controlled blackish brown striped decoration, base signed **863.00**
Vase, 9" h., "Polka Dot" style, gently swelled ovoid body tapering to a wide trumpet neck, deep opaque red molded w/sixteen prominent ribs, decorated by spaced white opal dots overall, base inscribed "Nash GD154" **1,093.00**

NORTHWOOD

Harry Northwood (1860-1919) was born in England, the son of noted glass artist John Northwood. Brought up in the glass business, Harry immigrated to the United States in 1881 and shortly thereafter became manager of the La Belle Glass Company, Bridgeport, Ohio. Here he was responsible for many innovations in colored and blown glass. After leaving La Belle in 1887 he opened The Northwood Glass Company in Martins Ferry, Ohio in 1888. The company moved to Ellwood City, Pennsylvania in 1892 and Northwood moved again to take over a glass plant in Indiana, Pennsylvania in 1896. One of his major lines made at the Indiana, Pennsylvania plant was Custard glass (which he called "ivory"). It was made in several patterns and some pieces were marked on the base with "Northwood" in script.

Harry and his family moved back to England in 1899 but returned to the U.S. in 1902 at which time he opened another glass factory in Wheeling, West Virginia. Here he was able to put his full talents to work and under his guidance the firm manufactured many notable glass lines including opalescent wares, colored and clear pressed tablewares, various novelties and probably best known of all, Carnival glass. Around 1906 Harry introduced his famous "N" in circle trade-mark which can be found on the base of many, but not all, pieces made at his factory. The factory closed in 1925.

In this listing we are including only the clear and colored tablewares produced at Northwood factories. Specialized lines such as Custard glass, Carnival and Opalescent wares are listed under their own headings in our Glass category.

Northwood Marks

Berry set: master bowl & 6 sauce
dishes; Leaf Mold patt., canary
w/cranberry spatter, 7 pcs. **$675.00**

Bowl, master berry, Chrysanthemum
Swirl patt., speckled canary. **125.00**

Bowl, master berry, Leaf Mold patt.,
canary w/cranberry spatter **150.00**

Bowl, 6" d., cupped form, stretch-
type, russet **65.00**

Bowl, master berry, 7½" d., footed,
Intaglio patt., emerald green
w/gold **60.00**

Bowl, 8" d., rolled rim, stretch-type,
Jade blue..................... **75.00**

Bowl, master berry, 9" d., footed,
Leaf Medallion patt., emerald
green........................ **75.00**

Bowl, master berry, 9" d., 4⅜" h.,
Leaf Medallion patt., green w/gold . **110.00**

Bowl, 10" d., 3¼" h., footed, Grape
Frieze patt., purple w/gold trim **99.00**

Bowl, 11" d., rolled rim, stretch-type,
Jade blue..................... **95.00**

Butter dish, cov., Apple Blossom
patt., milk white w/decoration **265.00**

Butter dish, cov., Leaf Medallion
patt., purple w/gold trim.......... **250.00**

Compote, open, 7" d., footed,
stretch-type, topaz.............. **55.00**

Cracker jar, cov., Cherry Thumbprint
patt., ruby & gold trim **150.00**

Leaf Medallion Green Creamer

Creamer, Leaf Medallion patt., green
w/gold (ILLUS.) **90.00**

Creamer, Leaf Mold patt., canary
w/cranberry spatter, satin finish.... **245.00**

Panelled Holly Opalescent Creamer

Creamer, Paneled Holly patt., white
opalescent w/enameled decoration
(ILLUS.)...................... **70.00**

Cruet w/original stopper, Apple
Blossom patt., milk white
w/decoration **395.00**

Cruet w/original stopper, Leaf
Medallion patt., green w/gold **275.00**

Cruet w/original stopper, Leaf
Medallion patt., purple w/gold trim ... **695.00**

Cruet w/original stopper, Netted
Oak patt., milk white w/decoration. . **295.00**

Pickle caster, cranberry Paneled
Sprig patt. insert, fancy silver plate
Meriden frame w/cover, cover
inscribed "Libbie from Nelson,
Christmas 18--" **633.00**

Pitcher, water, Leaf Medallion patt.,
green w/gold **105.00**

Pitcher, Leaf Umbrella patt., blue
opaque, 72 oz.................. **650.00**

**Salt & pepper shakers w/original
lids,** Paneled Sprig patt.,
cranberry, pr.................. **193.00**

Sauce dish, Cherry Thumbprint patt.,
  ruby & gold trim **15.00**
Sauce dish, Chrysanthemum Swirl
  patt., white-speckled cranberry **62.00**
Spooner, Leaf Medallion patt., green
  w/gold **66.00**
Spooner, Leaf Mold patt., cased lime
  green **150.00**
Sugar bowl, cov., Cherry Thumbprint
  patt., ruby & gold trim **100.00**
Sugar bowl, cov., Chrysanthemum
  Swirl, white-speckled cranberry. . . . **345.00**
Sugar bowl, cov., Peach patt.,
  emerald green w/gold trim. **105.00**
Sugar shaker w/original lid, Apple
  Blossom patt., milk white
  w/decoration **110.00**
Sugar shaker w/original, Leaf
  Mold patt., blue satin **275.00**
Sugar shaker w/original lid, Leaf
  Umbrella patt., canary w/cranberry
  spatter **410.00**
Sugar shaker w/original lid, Leaf
  Umbrella patt., cased yellow **325.00**
Sugar shaker w/original lid, Leaf
  Umbrella patt., cased yellow,
  satin finish **275.00**
Sugar shaker w/original lid, Leaf
  Umbrella patt., cranberry. **475.00**
Sugar shaker w/original lid, Parian
  Swirl patt., cranberry **120.00**
Sugar shaker w/original lid,
  Parian Swirl patt., green opaque. . . . **95.00**
Sugar shaker w/original lid, Quilted
  Phlox patt., amethyst. **335.00**
Sugar shaker w/original lid, Quilted
  Phlox patt., cased pink **150.00**
Sugar shaker w/original lid, Ribbed
  Pillar patt., frosted spatter **250.00**
Syrup pitcher w/original lid,
  cranberry & white spatter, Ring
  Neck mold **250.00**
Syrup pitcher w/original lid, Leaf
  Mold patt., canary w/cranberry
  spatter **475.00**
Toothpick holder, Leaf Mold patt.,
  canary w/cranberry spatter **175.00**
Toothpick holder, Leaf Mold patt.,
  red & white spatter w/mica flecks,
  glossy finish. **110.00**
Tumbler, Leaf Medallion patt., green
  w/gold **39.00**
Tumbler, Leaf Mold patt., canary
  w/cranberry spatter, satin finish. . . . **148.00**
Tumbler, Leaf Umbrella patt., cased
  blue **75.00**
Water set: pitcher & four tumblers;
  Leaf Mold patt., canary w/cranberry
  spatter, 5 pcs. **550.00**

Peach Pattern Water Set

Water set: water pitcher & six
  tumblers; Peach patt., clear w/gold
  trim & rose stain, 7 pcs. (ILLUS. of
  part) **303.00**

OPALESCENT

Presently, this is one of the most popular areas of glass collecting. The opalescent effect was attained by adding bone ash chemicals to areas of an item while still hot and refiring the object at tremendous heat. Both pressed and mold-blown patterns are available to collectors and we distinguish the types in our listing below. Opalescent Glass from A to Z *by the late* William Heacock *is the definitive reference book for collectors.*

For an expanded listing of Opalescent Glass see Antique Trader Books American & European Decorative & Art Glass Price Guide.

MOLD-BLOWN OPALESCENT PATTERNS

BUTTONS & BRAIDS

Pitcher, blue **$220.00**
Water set: pitcher & six tumblers,
  blue, 7 pcs. **400.00**

CHRISTMAS SNOWFLAKE

Pitcher, water, cranberry **2,100.00**

COIN SPOT

**Salt & pepper shakers w/original
  lids,** cranberry, pr. **373.00**
Sugar shaker w/original lid, nine-
  panel mold, cranberry **265.00**
Sugar shaker w/original lid, ring
  neck mold, blue **160.00**
Sugar shaker w/original lid, wide
  waist mold, blue. **165.00**

DAISY & CRISS CROSS

Syrup pitcher w/original lid, white . . **545.00**

DAISY & FERN

Cruet w/original stopper, Apple
    Blossom mold, blue 295.00
Sugar shaker w/original lid, Apple
    Blossom mold, blue 360.00
Sugar shaker w/original lid,
    bulbous, cranberry 375.00
Sugar shaker w/original lid, ovoid
    body, cranberry 220.00

Daisy & Fern Sugar Shaker

Sugar shaker w/original lid, Parian
    Swirl mold, blue (ILLUS.). 295.00
Syrup pitcher w/original lid,
    bulbous mold, blue 285.00

FERN

Cruet w/original stopper, blue 335.00
Sugar shaker w/original lid, blue . . . 450.00
Sugar shaker w/original lid, green . . 150.00

LATTICE (Buckeye)

Creamer, cranberry. 450.00

POINSETTIA

Pitcher, tankard, blue 400.00-500.00
Pitcher, tankard, cranberry 2,500.00

REVERSE SWIRL

Cruet w/original stopper, blue 375.00
Mustard jar, cov., cranberry 375.00
Sugar shaker w/original lid, blue . . . 325.00
Sugar shaker w/original lid,
    cranberry 495.00

Reverse Swirl Syrup Pitcher

Syrup pitcher w/original lid,
    cranberry (ILLUS.) 1,145.00

RIBBED LATTICE

Celery vase, cranberry 250.00
Sugar shaker w/original lid, blue . . . 185.00
Sugar shaker w/original lid,
    cranberry 330.00

SEAWEED

Barber bottle, conical shape,
    cranberry 495.00
Celery vase, cranberry 235.00
Sugar shaker w/original lid, blue . . . 425.00
Sugar shaker w/original lid,
    cranberry 500.00
Tumbler, cranberry 150.00
Water set: pitcher w/triangular
    crimped mouth & six tumblers;
    cranberry, 7 pcs.. . . . . 1,850.00

SPANISH LACE

Sugar shaker w/original lid,
    bulbous, blue. 255.00
Sugar shaker w/original lid,
    canary 285.00

Spanish Lace Sugar Shaker

Sugar shaker w/original lid,
    cranberry (ILLUS.) 540.00
Tumbler, green 65.00
Water set: pitcher & four tumblers;
    cranberry, 5 pcs.. . . . . 1,450.00

STARS & STRIPES

Stars & Stripes Pitcher

Pitcher, water, cranberry
(ILLUS.) **2,100.00**

STRIPE

Salt shaker w/original lid, ring-neck
mold, blue **110.00**

SWIRL

Cruet w/original stopper, blue **179.00**
Pitcher, water, short ball shape,
cranberry **475.00**
Sugar shaker w/original lid, blue . . . **375.00**

WINDOWS SWIRL

Windows Swirl Water Pitcher

Pitcher, water, cranberry
(ILLUS.) **685.00**
Sugar shaker w/original lid, blue . . . **350.00**
Syrup pitcher w/original metal lid,
cranberry **1,275.00**

PRESSED OPALESCENT PATTERNS

ARGONAUT SHELL

Sauce dish, blue. **40.00**

CIRCLED SCROLL

Cruet w/original stopper, blue **575.00**
Table set, creamer, cov. sugar &
spooner, blue, 3 pcs. **200.00**

DIAMOND SPEARHEAD

Compote, jelly, cobalt blue **195.00**

EVERGLADES

Water set: water pitcher & six
tumblers; blue w/gold trim,
the set **605.00**

FLUTED SCROLLS

Fluted Scrolls Butter Dish

Butter dish, cov., canary (ILLUS.) . . . **160.00**
Cruet w/original stopper, blue **250.00**
Pitcher, canary **295.00**

HOBNAIL & PANELED THUMBPRINT

Water set: pitcher & four tumblers;
8¼" h. water pitcher w/square
mouth & applied smooth clear
handle & four 10-row tumblers;
cranberry, 5 pcs. **600.00**

INTAGLIO

Compote, jelly, blue **27.00**
Cruet w/original stopper, blue **250.00**

SUNBURST ON SHIELD

Sugar, open, breakfast-size, blue. **70.00**

WILD BOUQUET

Cruet w/original stopper, blue **425.00**

WREATH & SHELL

Berry set: master berry bowl & five
sauce dishes; white, set of 6 . . . . . . **99.00**
Butter dish, cov., canary **250.00**
Celery vase, blue **225.00**
Celery vase, canary **225.00**
Creamer, blue, decorated. **235.00**

Wreath & Shell Creamer

Creamer, canary (ILLUS.). **145.00**

Cuspidor, canary 150.00
Pitcher, water, canary. 525.00
Rose bowl, blue 95.00
Rose bowl, canary 139.00
Sauce dish, canary. 40.00
Spooner, blue. 135.00
Spooner, blue, decorated. 225.00
Spooner, canary. 118.00
Spooner, canary, decorated. 175.00
Toothpick holder, canary 225.00
Tumbler, blue 79.00
Tumbler, canary 85.00
Water set: water pitcher & six
  tumblers; white w/painted floral
  decoration, 7 pcs. (small base chip
  on pitcher) 413.00

OPALINE

*Also called opal glass (once a name applied
to milk-white glass), opaline is a fairly opaque
glass with a color resembling the opal; however,
pieces in such colors as blue, pink, green and
others, also are referred to now as opaline glass.
Many of the objects were decorated.*

Box w/hinged cover, rectangular
  w/cut corners, apple green
  w/gilt-metal fittings & a gold
  fleur-de-lis flanked by scrolls
  centered on the flat cover,
  France, ca. 1900, 3¼ x 5¼",
  2⅛" h. $110.00
Decanter w/ball stopper, sky
  blue, spherical body tapering
  to a tall slender 'stick' neck
  w/flared rim, polished pontil,
  11" h. 66.00
Pitcher, cushion foot supporting
  a squatty bulbous ovoid body
  tapering to a tall slightly flaring
  cylindrical neck w/an angled
  flat mouth, shaded pink w/an
  applied pink loop handle on the
  neck, decorated around the
  waist w/a delicate band of white
  dotted swags between tiny red
  jewels, gold band around the
  foot, 19th c., France,
  12½" h. 248.00
Vase, 6" h., a blue satin finished
  cylindrical body w/the curved rim
  pulled into two points, decorated
  w/white enameled lacy bands,
  florettes & beading, fitted in a fancy
  silver plate footed round holder
  w/loop side handle, holder marked
  by Meriden Silver Plate Co., late
  19th c., vase alone 4⅛" h. ,
  2 pcs. 440.00

ORREFORS

*This Swedish glass house, founded in 1898
for production of tablewares, has made
decorative wares as well since 1915. By 1925,
Orrefors had achieved an international
reputation for its Graal glass, an engraved art
glass developed by master glassblower Knut
Berquist and artist-designers Simon Gate and
Edward Hald. Ariel glass, recognized by a
design of controlled air traps and the heavy
Ravenna glass, usually tinted, were both
developed in the 1930s. While all Orrrefors glass
is collectible, pieces signed by early designers
and artists are now bringing high prices.*

Orrefors

Orrefors Mark

Bowl-vase, "Ariel," a heavy applied
  blue foot below the deep thick-
  walled rounded bowl in aubergine,
  bright blue & clear vertical trapped
  air stripes, foot signed "Orrefors -
  Ariel 246 F -Edvin Ohrstrom,"
  4½" d., 2¾" h. $403.00
Center bowl, wide shallow half-round
  crystal bowl raised on a heavy solid
  cylindrical foot, open at the center
  base w/a teardrop aperture,
  labeled "Orrefors Sweden,"
  12" d., 6¾" h. 345.00

Orrefors "Romeo & Juliet" Decanter

Decanter w/large flattened
  rectangular stopper, tall squared
  crystal form w/a rounded shoulder
  to a short cylindrical neck
  w/flattened rim, a figure of Romeo
  engraved on one side & Juliet
  engraved on the opposite side,
  signed "Orrefors - Lundberg 1880 -
  111 - F5," 11¾" h. (ILLUS.) 173.00

Decanter w/original stopper, tall clear baluster-form body tapering to a cylindrical neck w/two small pinched side spouts, fitted w/a specially slotted stopper w/a tall, large mushroom knob, finely engraved w/a pair of fighting cocks & flying feathers, engraved "Orrefors N. 12.53 9," designed by Nils Landberg, ca. 1954, 13" h. **110.00**

Sphere, blown glass clear hollow ball in the form of a volleyball engraved w/laces & seams centering a leaping athlete, raised on a black glass stand marked "Of F. 106.32 WE," design attributed to Vicke Lindstrand, 3⅝" h. **690.00**

Vase, 4½" h., "Graal," bulbous heavy ovoid body w/a small opening, clear w/internal aquatic scene of black & emerald green swimming fish among seaweed, marked "#2265D II-Hd." **660.00**

Vase, 5" h., "Graal", bulbous ovoid body w/a small mouth opening, thick pale greenish crystal walls internally decorated & colored in an underwater scene w/fish & aquatic plants, base signed "Orrefors Sweden - Graal N. 231D - Edward Hald". **978.00**

Vase, 5½" h., "Graal," simple bulbous ovoid body tapering to a small mouth, aquarium design in greenish brown w/fish & aquatic plants throughout the clear body, base inscribed "Orrefors Sweden - Graal No. 313C Edward Hald". **575.00**

Vase, 6" h., "Graal," heavy clear ovoid body encasing black-outlined green fish swimming among aquatic plants, signed "Orrefors Graal" **880.00**

A Group of Orrefors Vases

Vase, 6½" h., "Graal," solid clear cylindrical foot supporting a clear bulbous ovoid body tapering to a flared mouth, internally decorated w/spiral alternating between lines & oval windowed sections of deep amber & grey, designed by Nils Landberg, ca. 1958, engraved "Orrefors S. Graal Nr278 O N. Landberg" (ILLUS. center). **825.00**

Vase, 7" h., 6¾" d., wide thick-walled cylindrical form in transparent teal blue, base signed "Orrefors Expo. Pa. 245-62 Sven Palmqvist" **173.00**

Orrefors "Feather" Vase

Vase, 7½" h., "Ariel," wide ovoid thick-walled body tapering to a small cylindrical neck, clear internally decorated by vertical trapped air panels alternating subtle grey feather panels, base signed "Orrefors Ariel No. 111F - Edvin Ohrstrom" (ILLUS.). **2,530.00**

Vase, 7¾" h., "Graal," simple thick-walled ovoid form, clear internally decorated w/central royal blue vertically lined network horizontally banded by pale peach colored divisions in perfect symmetrical alignment, base signed "Orrefors S. Graal No. 194 N Edward Hald" **2,070.00**

Vase, bud, 8¼" h., clear bulbed ovoid form w/internal topaz lined oval pocket, base inscribed "Orrefors - 3538 - 28" **259.00**

Vase, 9½" h., "Graal," clear disc foot supporting a gently flaring tall cylindrical body internally decorated w/spiraling lines of deep amber & light green, designed by Edward Hald, ca. 1952, engraved "ORREFORS Sweden S. Graal Nr1172L Edward Hald" (ILLUS. right) **880.00**

Vase, 9¾" h., clear bucket-form internally decorated by bright blue powders w/several Cluthra bubbles, applied black rim wrap, base pontil inscribed "Of...70" **230.00**

Vase, 13" h., "Kraka," tall slender ovoid body tapering to a very slender neck, heavy clear base, the body internally decorated w/blue overlapping swags, each square created containing a single fine bubble, designed by Sven Palmqvist, ca. 1952, engraved "ORREFORS KRAKA Pu3364 Sven Palmqvist" (ILLUS. left) **1,100.00**

PADEN CITY

The Paden City Glass Manufacturing Company began operations in Paden City, West Virginia in 1916, primarily as a supplier of blanks to other companies. All wares were handmade, that is, either hand-pressed or mold-blown. The early products were not particularly noteworthy but by the early 1930s the quality had improved considerably. The firm continued to turn out high quality glassware in a variety of beautiful colors until financial difficulties necessitated its closing in 1951. Over the years the firm produced, in addition to tablewares, items for hotel and restaurant use, light shades, shaving mugs, perfume bottles and lamps.

Bowl, cream soup, 5" d., Wotta line, red **$20.00**

Candlesticks, two-light, round, Crow's Foot (No. 890) line, red, pr. . . **60.00**

Candy dish, cov., Crow's Foot (No. 412) line, red **85.00**

Candy dish, cov., flat, Nora Bird etching, green **375.00**

Candy dish, cov., flat, Nora Bird etching, pink **375.00**

Candy dish, cov., three-part, Crow's Foot line, cobalt blue **175.00**

Cheese plate, Peacock & Rose etching, pink **60.00**

Compote, open, 6⅝" d., Crow's Foot (No. 412) line, Orchid etching, yellow **175.00**

Compote, open, 7" d., Peacock & Rose etching, green **68.00**

Compote, open, 11" d., footed, Party Line (No.191) line **35.00**

Console bowl, Crow's Foot (No. 412) line, Orchid etching, yellow, 11" d. . **185.00**

Creamer, Black Forest etching, green **60.00**

Ice tub, Black Forest etching, pink . . . **160.00**

Ice tub, Peacock & Rose etching, green **185.00**

Mayonnaise dish, Peacock & Rose etching, pink **55.00**

Mayonnaise dish & ladle, Nora Bird etching, green, 2 pcs. **110.00**

Napkin holder, Party Line (No. 191) line, green **200.00**

Night set: pitcher & tumbler; Black Forest etching, pink, pitcher 6½" h., 42 oz., 2 pcs.. .... **625.00**

Plate, 6" d., Wotta line, red **10.00**

Plate, dinner, 9" d., Wotta line, red **25.00**

Plate, 10½" d., Peacock & Rose etching, green **75.00**

Server, swan-necked center handle, Gazebo etching, Line 1504, clear, 10" l. **45.00**

Sherbet, stemmed, Wotta line, red, 4" h.......................... **20.00**

Tray, center-handled, Mrs. "B" (No. 411) line, Ardith etching, yellow. **50.00**

Tray, center-handled, etched Lela Bird patt., pink, 10½" l. **110.00**

Tumbler, cone-shaped, Party Line (No. 191) line, pink, 5¾" h. **10.00**

Vase, 8" h., Gothic Garden etching, pink **210.00**

Vase, 8½" h., elliptical, etched Lela Bird patt., ebony **175.00**

Vase, 9" h., square, Gothic Garden etching, yellow............... **135.00**

Vase, 10" h., Lela Bird etching, green....................... **135.00**

Vase, 10" h., Peacock & Rose etching, pink **140.00**

Vase, 12" h., Lela Bird etching, ebony....................... **225.00**

PAIRPOINT

Originally organized in New Bedford, Massachusetts in 1880, as the Pairpoint Manufacturing Company, on land adjacent to the famed Mount Washington Glass Company, this company first manufactured silver and plated wares. In 1894, the two famous factories merged as the Pairpoint Corporation and enjoyed great success for more than forty years. The company was sold in 1939 to a group of local businessmen and eventually bought out by one of the group who turned the management over to Robert M. Gundersen. Subsequently, it operated as the Gundersen Glass Works until 1952 when, after Gundersen's death, the name was changed to Gundersen-Pairpoint. The factory closed in 1956. Subsequently, Robert Bryden took charge of this glassworks, at first producing glass for Pairpoint abroad and eventually, in 1970, beginning glass production in Sagamore, Massachusetts. Today the Pairpoint Crystal Glass Company is owned by

Robert and June Bancroft. They continue to manufacture fine quality blown and pressed glass.

Pairpoint Gravic Cut Bowl

Bowl, 4 x 12", 8" h. deep widely flaring sides w/two sides pulled up to make a basket form, Gravic cut w/a swirling design of flowers & leafy vines, unsigned (ILLUS.) . . . **$248.00**

Candleholder-vase, Gravic cut w/an overall vining floral design, clear connecting ball between stem & foot, early 20th c., 12" h. **116.00**

Candlesticks, emerald green standards & sockets raised on a clear controlled bubble ball stem & green foot, 12" h., pr. **275.00**

Compote, open, 7½" d., 4" h., engraved Vintage Grape design, amethyst **110.00**

Dish, three-lobed sides forming three sections, green engraved w/the Colias patt., leaves, spider web & butterflies, early 20th c., 9" w. **138.00**

Dresser box w/hinged cover, round, the flattened radiating rib cover decorated w/colorful pansies framing a molded scroll center all within a gilt brass border, the low squatty bulbous pleated rib base decorated w/scattered floral sprigs, 6" d., 2" h. **358.00**

Vase, jack-in-the-pulpit-type, 9" h., tall footed trumpet-form w/upturned pointed back top rim & downturned front rim, the exterior in opalescent white cased inside w/pink enameled near the center w/rings of small white blossoms, signed on outside of tip w/a "P" in a triangle. **165.00**

Vases, 12" h., red bowl & foot w/clear ball connector, pr. **300.00**

PATE DE VERRE

Pate de Verre, or "paste of glass," was molded by very few artisans. In the pate de verre technique, powdered glass is mixed with a liquid to make a paste which is then placed in a mold and baked at a high temperature. These articles have a finely-pitted or matte finish and are easily distinguised from blown glass. Duplicate pieces are possible with this technique.

Pate De Verre Marks

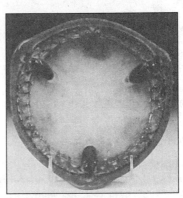

Walter Pate de Verre Bowl

Bowl, 4 x 8¾", rounded triangular form molded in bluish green w/yellow at the center, green around the border, w/three brown scarab beetles w/long black antennae, inscribed "A. Walter - Nancy" & "J. Cayettte," "Made in France," designed by Jules Cayette (ILLUS.) **$4,600.00**

Bowl-vase, flat rim on a swelled shoulder tapering to a flat base, mottled mustard yellow petal-molded ground decorated around the base w/three life-sized snails w/yellow shells & light yellow bodies, signed "A. Walter Nancy - Berge," 3¾" h. **3,300.00**

Coupe, wide footed bowl-form w/deep flaring sides & a wide rolled rim, grey streaked w/golden amber & deep amber, molded around the outer rim w/pairs of facing birds, the exterior w/three rows of vertical slashes, molded "G. ARGY-ROUSSEAU," ca. 1927, 4⅛" h. . . . **3,450.00**

Paperweight, figural, a domed base topped by a figural black-spotted salamander parent w/a single offspring atop a yellow mound covered w/green leaves, signed "A. Walter Nancy - Berge," 3¾" h. **3,025.00**

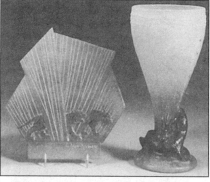

Pate de Verre Plaque and Vase

Plaque, angular upright sheet of glass designed as a lighting plate on electrolier stand, in amber w/two stalking black striped orange tigers emerging from tall stylized panels ribbed to resemble tall grass, signed "G. Argy-Rousseau," 6½" l., 7¼" h. (ILLUS. left) **5,750.00**

Vase, 4¾" h., Spiders & Brambles patt., footed spherical body w/a wide incurved mouth, molded w/two black spiders spinnning webs from yellow, orange, amber & black bramble bushes, the white webs in intricate designs, molded on side "A. Argy-Rousseau," "France" on the base (internal half-inch fracture at mid-center) **2,990.00**

Vase, 9" h., tall goblet-form bowl on a thick round foot w/a finely detailed & realistic greenish black lizard wrapped around the base, the body in yellowish amber shaded to green to orange at the base, impressed "A. Walter" & "H. Berge SC," original thin rim area (ILLUS. right) **6,325.00**

Veilleuse (night light), a press-molded ovoid lamp shade in frosted mottled grey bordered by elaborate purple arches w/three

Argy-Rousseau Veilleuse

teardrop-shaped windows of yellow centered teal green stylized blossoms on black swirling stems, impressed at lower edge "G. Argy-Rousseau," mounted in a wrought-iron frame w/three ball feet centering an internal lamp socket, matching disk cover w/knob finial, 8½" h. (ILLUS.). **6,900.00**

Pate de Verre "Veilleuse"

Veilleusse (night light), the ovoid molded glass shade of mottled greyish lavender decorated by three repeating red-centered purple blossoms within black V-shaped design, raised upon four ball feet on a wrought-iron base, fitted w/a night light & topped w/a conforming cap, shade molded "G. Argy-Rousseau," 8¼" h. (ILLUS.) **5,290.00**

PATTERN

Though it has never been ascertained whether glass was first pressed in the United States or abroad, the development of the glass pressing machine revolutionized the glass industry in the United States and this country receives the credit for improving the method to make this process feasible. The first wares pressed were probably small flat plates of the type now referred to as "lacy," the intricacy of the design concealing flaws.

In 1827, both the New England Glass Co., Cambridge, Massachusetts and Bakewell & Co., Pittsburgh, took out patents for pressing glass furniture knobs and soon other pieces followed. This early pressed glass contained red lead which made it clear and resonant when tapped (flint.) Made primarily in clear, it is rarer in blue, amethyst, olive green and yellow.

By the 1840s, early simple patterns such as Ashburton, Argus and Excelsior appeared. Ribbed Bellflower seems to have been one of the earliest patterns to have had complete sets. By the 1860s, a wide range of patterns was available.

In 1864, William Leighton of Hobbs, Brockunier & Co., Wheeling, West Virginia, developed a formula for "soda lime" glass which did not require the expensive red lead for clarity. Although "soda lime" glass did not have the brilliance of the earlier flint glass, the formula came into widespread use because glass could be produced cheaply.

An asterisk (*) indicates a piece which has been reproduced.

For an expanded listing of Pattern Glass, see Antique Trader Books American Pressed Glass & Bottles Price Guide.

ARGUS (Bakewell) — See Thumbprint, Early Pattern

ARGUS (McKee & Brother, Pittsburgh)

Celery vase, flint. $83.00
Champagne, flint 75.00
Champagne, flint, cut panels w/gilt
   florals. 95.00
Compote, cov., 6¼" d., 7½" h.,
   flint, clear. 175.00
Compote, cov., 9" d., high stand, flint,
   clear. 200.00
Compote, cov., 12" d., high stand,
   flint, clear. 175.00
Compote, open, 6" d., 4½" h., flint . . . 121.00
Cordial, flint 65.00

Creamer, applied handle, flint. 105.00
Decanter, flint, pt. 120.00
Decanter, flint, qt. 130.00
Egg cup, flint . . . . 25.00 to 35.00
Egg cup, handled, flint 55.00
Goblet, five-row 75.00
Goblet, flint 80.00
Lamp, oil-type. 125.00
Mug, applied handle, flint 60.00
Pickle dish, oval. 23.00
Pitcher, water, w/cut Thumbprints,
   flint. 225.00
Pitcher, water, 8¼" h., applied
   handle, flint 200.00
Punch bowl, pedestal base,
   scalloped rim, 11½" d., 9½" h.. . . . . 160.00
Punch bowl, pedestal base,
   scalloped rim, 14½" d., 9½" h.. . . . . 180.00
Salt dip, cov., master size, flint. 90.00
Salt dip, open, master size, flint 35.00
Sauce dish, flint 20.00

Argus Spooner

Spooner, flint (ILLUS.) . . . . . . 45.00 to 55.00
Sugar bowl, cov., flint. 68.00
Sweetmeat dish, cov.. . . . . 85.00
Syrup jug w/pewter top, applied
   handle, flint 150.00
Tumbler, bar-type, flint 60.00
Tumbler, (Barrel Argus), flint 60.00
Tumbler, whiskey, handled . . 70.00 to 75.00
Tumbler, footed, flint, 4" h.. . . . . 36.00
Tumbler, footed, flint, 5" h.. . . . . 60.00
Wine, (Hotel Argus), flint. 40.00
Wine, knob stem, flint 110.00

AZTEC

Bowl, cov., 8½" d., clear. 73.00
Butter dish, cov.. . . . . 40.00
Carafe, water 60.00
Champagne 35.00
Claret 40.00
Cordial 20.00
Cracker jar, cov.. . . . . 40.00

Aztec Creamer

Creamer (ILLUS.) 27.00
Cruet w/original stopper 48.00
Dresser bottle w/original stopper . . . 38.00
Goblet 33.00
Pitcher, lemonade 50.00
Pitcher, water, jug-type 50.00
Pitcher, water, tankard-type 50.00
Punch cup 5.00
Relish 15.00
Salt shaker w/original top 25.00
Sauce dish 10.00
Sugar bowl, cov. 35.00
Syrup pitcher w/original nickeled
    silver tin top 75.00
Toothpick holder 30.00
Tray 15.00
Tumbler, ice tea 20.00
Tumbler, water 20.00
Tumbler, whiskey 20.00
Wine 25.00

BABY FACE

Butter dish, cov., 5¼" d. 150.00
Celery vase . . . . 100.00 to 130.00
Champagne 140.00
Compote, cov., 5¼" d., 8½" h. 150.00
Compote, cov., 6" d., 9½" h. 160.00
Compote, cov., 7" d., high stand 180.00
Compote, cov., 8" d., high stand,
    scalloped rim . . . . 350.00 to 425.00

Baby Face Compote

Compote, open, 8" d., 4¾" h.
    (ILLUS.) 85.00

Cordial 275.00
Creamer . . . . 100.00 to 200.00
Goblet 135.00
Knife rest 105.00
Pitcher, water 300.00
Salt dip 50.00
Spooner 75.00
Sugar bowl, cov. . . . . 150.00 to 175.00

BEADED BAND

Butter dish, cov. 41.00
Cake stand, 9" 29.00
Compote, cov., 8" d. 85.00
Creamer 29.00
Goblet 29.00
Pitcher, water 90.00
Relish, 5¼ x 8½" . . . . 10.00 to 20.00
Sauce dish, flat, 4¼" d. 9.00
Spooner, clear 30.00
Sugar bowl, cov. 43.00
Syrup pitcher, original top dated
    "June 29, '84" 110.00
Wine 40.00

BIRD & STRAWBERRY (Bluebird)

Berry set: master bowl & 5 sauce
    dishes; w/color, 6 pcs. 250.00
Berry set: master bowl & 6 sauce
    dishes; footed, clear, 7 pcs. 175.00
Bowl, 5½" d., clear 33.00
Bowl, 5½" d., w/color 35.00
Bowl, 7½" d., footed, clear 62.00
Bowl, 7½" d., footed, w/color 70.00
Bowl, 9" d., flat, w/color 75.00
Bowl, 9½" l., 6" w. oval, footed,
    clear 77.00
Bowl, 10" d., flat, clear . . . . . . 60.00 to 70.00
Bowl, 10" d., flat w/color & gold
    trim 115.00
Butter dish, cov., clear 125.00
Butter dish, cov., w/color 213.00
Celery vase, pedestal base, 7½" h. . . . 65.00
Compote, cov., jelly, 4½" d., 7½" h.,
    clear 165.00
Compote, cov., jelly, 4½" d., 7½" h.,
    w/color 250.00
Compote, cov., 6" d., low stand,
    clear 85.00
Compote, cov., 6" d., low stand,
    w/color 125.00
*Compote, cov., 6½" d., 9½" h.,
    clear 150.00
*Compote, cov., 6½" d., 9½" h.,
    w/color 200.00
Compote, open, 6" d., ruffled rim,
    clear 85.00

Compote, open, 6" d., ruffled rim,
w/color 125.00
Creamer, clear . . . . 60.00 to 70.00
Creamer, w/color 115.00
Dish, heart-shaped 65.00
Goblet, flared bowl, w/color 700.00
Pitcher, water, clear . . . . . 285.00 to 325.00
Pitcher, water, w/color 448.00
Relish, 8¼" oval, clear 22.00
Sauce dish, flat or footed, clear 22.00
Sauce dish, w/color 40.00
Spooner, clear 60.00
Spooner, w/color . . . . 100.00 to 125.00
Sugar bowl, cov., clear. 65.00
Table set: creamer, cov. sugar bowl,
cov. butter dish & spooner; clear,
4 pcs. . . . . 225.00 to 250.00
Table set: w/color,4 pcs. . . 425.00 to 450.00
Tumbler, clear 53.00
Tumbler, w/color. 95.00
Water set: pitcher & 6 tumblers;
w/color, 7 pcs. 725.00
Wine 65.00

BLOCK & FAN

Bowl, berry, 8" d., footed 28.00
Bowl, 9¾" d. 32.00
Butter dish, cov. 65.00
Cake stand 9" to 10" d. 47.00
Celery tray 25.00

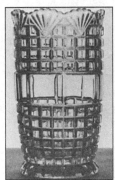

Block & Fan Celery Vase

Celery vase (ILLUS.) . . . . 35.00 to 40.00
Compote, open, 8" d., high
stand 45.00
Cracker jar, cov. 77.00
Creamer 34.00
Cruet w/original stopper, small,
6" h. 25.00
Cruet w/original stopper,
medium . . . . 40.00 to 45.00
Goblet, clear 49.00
Goblet, ruby-stained 110.00

Ice bucket 60.00
Pitcher, water, clear 48.00
Pitcher, water, ruby-stained 325.00
Plate, 6" d. 22.00
Plate, 10" d. 30.00
Relish, 4¼ x 6½" oval 9.00
Relish, 11½" l. 45.00
Rose bowl 35.00
**Salt & pepper shakers w/original
tops,** pr. 43.00
Sauce dish, flat or footed, clear 10.00
Sauce dish, flat or footed, ruby-
stained. 28.00
Spooner, clear 33.00
Sugar bowl, cov. . . . . 40.00 to 50.00
Sugar shaker w/original top 40.00
Syrup pitcher w/original top,
7" h. 140.00
Waste bowl. 35.00
Wine, ruby-stained 75.00

BLUEBIRD - See Bird & Strawberry Pattern

BOHEMIAN (or Floradora)

Berry bowl, boat-shaped, green. 48.00
Berry set: boat-shaped master bowl
& 6 sauce dishes; rose-stained
w/gold trim, 7 pcs. 185.00
Bowl, 11½" d., green w/gold trim 323.00
Butter dish, cov., green w/gold
trim 110.00
Cologne bottle w/original stopper,
clear w/gold trim 100.00
Cologne bottle w/original stopper,
green w/gold trim . . . . . . 225.00 to 275.00
Creamer, clear w/rose & gold trim 75.00
Creamer, individual size, green 30.00
Mug, clear w/rose-stained leaves &
gold trim. 70.00
Spooner, clear w/rose-stained
flowers & gold trim . . . . 70.00 to 80.00
Spooner, green. 87.00
Sugar bowl, cov., green w/gold
trim 125.00
Toothpick holder, green w/gold
trim 225.00
Tumbler, clear w/rose-stained
flowers. 45.00
Wine, clear 15.00

BOW TIE

Bowl, 6" d. . . . . 20.00 to 25.00
Bowl, 6¾" d., flat. 35.00
Bowl, berry, 8" d. 32.00
Bowl, 10" d., 5" h. 60.00
Butter dish, cov. 80.00

Compote, cov., 7" d. 165.00
Compote, open, 6½" d., low stand 40.00
Compote, open, 8" d., low stand 45.00
Compote, open, 8½" d., high
   stand 53.00
Creamer 35.00
Goblet. 68.00
Marmalade jar, cov. 55.00
Pitcher, milk 58.00
Pitcher, water. . . . . 85.00 to 90.00
Punch bowl, 1 pc. 125.00
Relish, rectangular 28.00
Salt dip, individual size. 23.00
Salt dip, master size. 95.00
Salt shaker w/original top. 45.00
Sauce dish, flat. 18.00
Spooner 35.00
Sugar bowl, cov. . . . . 55.00 to 65.00
Tumbler 55.00

BUCKLE

Bowl, 10" d., rolled edge. 70.00
Butter dish, cov. 78.00
Champagne, flint 75.00
Compote, open, 8" d., low stand,
   flint. 39.00
Creamer, applied handle, flint. 95.00
Creamer, applied handle, non-flint 50.00
Egg cup, flint. 37.00
Egg cup, non-flint. . . . . 20.00 to 30.00

Buckle Goblet

Goblet, flint (ILLUS.). . . . . 45.00 to 50.00
Goblet, non-flint 34.00
Honey dish. 20.00
Lamp, kerosene-type, brass & iron
   base. 138.00
Lamp, kerosene-type, clear flint font,
   clambroth base . . . . 250.00 to 300.00
Lamp, kerosene-type, clear font,
   brass & iron base . . . . . . 150.00 to 165.00
Lamp, whale oil, etched flint font,
   opalescent base w/gold trim 175.00
Marmalade jar, cov. 125.00
Pitcher, water, bulbous, applied
   handle, flint . . . . 625.00 to 675.00

Salt dip, master size, flat, oval,
   flint . . . . 40.00 to 55.00
Salt dip, master size, footed, flint 35.00
Sauce dish, flint . . . . 10.00 to 15.00
Sauce dish, non-flint. 7.00
Spooner, flint 60.00
Spooner, non-flint 30.00
Sugar bowl, cov., w/acorn finial,
   flint. 95.00
Sugar bowl, cov., w/acorn finial,
   flint. 95.00
Sugar bowl, cov., w/acorn finial,
   non-flint 45.00
Sugar bowl, open, non-flint . . 20.00 to 25.00
Syrup jug w/spring lid, flint 125.00
Tumbler, bar, flint. . . . . 70.00 to 80.00
Wine, flint . . . . 100.00 to 125.00
Wine, non-flint. 35.00

BULL'S EYE

Ale glass. 65.00
Bitters bottle 100.00
Bowl, 8" d. 45.00
Carafe, flint, qt. 123.00
Celery vase, flint. 85.00
Claret, flint. 75.00
Creamer 155.00
Creamer, applied handle, flint. 155.00
Decanter, w/original stopper, pt. 238.00
Decanter, w/original stopper, qt. 288.00
Decanter w/bar lip, flint, qt. 190.00
Decanter w/bar lip, flint, qt. 190.00
Decanter w/bar lip, pt. 168.00
Decanter w/original stopper, pt. 238.00
Egg cup, opalescent milk glass 500.00
Egg cup, clear, flint, 3 3/4" h. 58.00
Goblet. 98.00
Goblet, flint 80.00
Lamp, miniature, flint 60.00
Lamp, whale oil, complete 138.00
Pitcher, water, non-flint. 85.00
Salt dip, individual size, rectangular. . . 35.00
Salt dip, master size, footed, flint 63.00
Sugar bowl, cov., flint. 135.00
Tumbler, bar, flint 100.00
Tumbler, footed, flint. 95.00
Tumbler, footed, non-flint 65.00
Wine, knob stem, flint 50.00

BULL'S EYE VARIANT - See Texas Bull's Eye Pattern

BULL'S EYE WITH FLEUR DE LIS

Butter dish, cov. . . . . 130.00 to 160.00
Celery vase, 11" h. . . . . 110.00 to 130.00
Compote, open, 8¼" d., low stand . . . 125.00

Creamer 155.00
Decanter w/bar lip, pt. . . . . 135.00 to 150.00
Decanter w/bar lip, qt. . . . . 175.00 to 200.00
Decanter w/original stopper,
  pt. . . . . 225.00 to 250.00
Decanter w/original stopper,
  qt. . . . . 275.00 to 300.00
Lamp, kerosene-type, pear-shaped
  font w/brass standard on marble
  base . . . . 160.00 to 170.00
Lamp, whale oil w/glass base 213.00

Bull's Eye With Fleur De Lis Pitcher

Pitcher, water, 9½" h. (ILLUS.) 550.00
Sugar bowl, cov. 130.00
Sugar bowl, open 58.00
Vase, 8½" h., flared rim 145.00

BUTTON ARCHES

Banana dish, clear 20.00
Banana dish, green 35.00
Bowl, 8" d., ruby-stained, souvenir 60.00

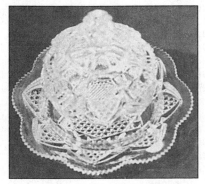

Button Arches Butter Dish

Butter dish, cov., clear (ILLUS.) 52.00
*Butter dish, cov., ruby-stained 95.00

Celery vase, ruby-stained,
  souvenir . . . . 75.00 to 85.00
Compote, open, jelly, 4½" h.,
  ruby-stained. 40.00
*Creamer, ruby-stained. 38.00
Creamer, ruby-stained, souvenir,
  2¾" h. 15.00
Creamer, ruby-stained, souvenir,
  3½" h. 30.00
Creamer, individual size, clambroth . . . 35.00
*Creamer, individual size,
  ruby-stained. 28.00
Cruet w/original stopper, ruby-
  stained . . . . 180.00 to 185.00
Goblet, clambroth, souvenir 20.00
Goblet, clear 24.00
*Goblet, ruby-stained 50.00
Match holder, clambroth, souvenir. . . . 35.00
Mug, child's, ruby-stained, souvenir . . . 23.00
Mug, clear 25.00
Mug, ruby-stained. . . . . 30.00 to 35.00
Pitcher, water, tankard, ruby-stained,
  souvenir of Pan American
  Exposition 150.00
Pitcher, tankard, 8¾" h., clear 117.00
Pitcher, water, tankard, 12" h.,
  ruby-stained. 130.00
Punch cup, clear 9.00
Punch cup, ruby-stained 19.00
Salt dip 19.00
Salt shaker w/original top, clear. 18.00
Salt shaker w/original top, ruby-
  stained. 27.00
Sauce dish, clear 17.00
Sauce dish., ruby-stained. 30.00
*Spooner, ruby-stained. 43.00
Spooner, ruby-stained w/clear
  band 63.00
Sugar bowl, cov., clear. 45.00
*Sugar bowl, cov., ruby-stained 85.00
Syrup pitcher w/original top,
  clear. 133.00
Syrup pitcher w/original top,
  ruby-stained. 175.00
Toothpick holder, clear 15.00
Toothpick holder, ruby-stained 28.00
Toothpick holder, ruby-stained,
  souvenir. 33.00
Tumbler, clambroth, souvenir. 23.00
Tumbler, clear 16.00
Tumbler, clear w/frosted band 25.00
Tumbler, ruby-stained 44.00
Wine, clear 31.00
Wine, ruby-stained 38.00

CHANDELIER (Crown Jewel)

Butter dish, cov. 92.00
Cake stand, 10" d. . . . . 70.00 to 75.00

Chandelier Celery Vase

Celery vase (ILLUS.) **55.00**
Compote, open, 6½" d. . . . . . **40.00 to 45.00**
Creamer . . . . **40.00 to 50.00**
Goblet **55.00**

Chandelier Engraved Goblet

Goblet engraved (ILLUS.). **68.00**
Inkwell . . . . **80.00 to 90.00**
Pitcher, water, tankard,
  ½ pt. . . . . **50.00 to 60.00**
Pitcher, water, tankard, 2 qt. **118.00**
Sauce dish, flat, clear. **16.00**
Spooner . . . . **40.00 to 45.00**
Sugar bowl, cov. . . . . **55.00 to 65.00**
Tumbler **43.00**
Waste bowl. **25.00**

CLASSIC

Berry set, master bowl & 8 sauce
  dishes, 9 pcs. **475.00**
Bowl, open, 8" hexagon, open log
  feet . . . . **100.00 to 125.00**
Butter dish, cov., open log
  feet . . . . **200.00 to 225.00**
Celery vase, collared base. **140.00**
Celery vase, open log feet **185.00**
Compote, cov., 6½" d., collared
  base . . . . **175.00 to 200.00**
Compote, cov., 7½" d., 8" h., open
  log feet . . . . **250.00 to 275.00**

Compote, cov., 9" d., open log feet . . **350.00**
Creamer, collared base **125.00**
Creamer, open log feet. . . . **140.00 to 150.00**

Classic Goblet

Goblet (ILLUS.) . . . . **250.00 to 275.00**
Marmalade jar, cov., open log
  feet . . . . **550.00 to 650.00**
Pitcher, milk, 8½" h., open log
  feet . . . . **400.00 to 500.00**
Pitcher, water, 9½" h., collared
  base . . . . **250.00 to 275.00**
Pitcher, water, 9½" h., open log
  feet . . . . **395.00 to 450.00**
Plate, 10" d., "Blaine" or "Hendricks,"
  signed Jacobus, each **215.00**
Plate, 10" d., "Logan" **195.00**
Plate, 10" d., "Warrior" . . . . **160.00 to 170.00**
Sauce dish, open log feet. **40.00**
Spooner, collared base **95.00**
Spooner, open log feet. . . . **125.00 to 150.00**
Sugar bowl, cov., open log
  feet . . . . **200.00 to 225.00**
Sugar bowl, open, collared base **95.00**

CUPID & VENUS (Guardian Angel)

Berry set, master bowl & 4 sauce
  dishes, 5 pcs. **90.00**
Bowl, cov., 8" d., footed **125.00**
Bowl, 6½" d., open **30.00**
Bowl, 8" d., open, footed **38.00**
Bread plate, amber, 10½" d. **139.00**
Bread plate, canary, 10½" d. **170.00**
Bread plate, clear, 10½" d. **65.00**
Butter dish, cov. **110.00**
Cake plate, 11" d., blue **125.00**
Cake plate, 11" d., canary **155.00**
Cake plate, 11" d., clear **65.00**
Celery vase **60.00**
Champagne . . . . **100.00 to 125.00**
Compote, cov., 7" d., low stand **65.00**
Compote, cov., 8" d., high stand **110.00**
Compote, cov., 9" d., high stand **128.00**

Compote, cov., 9" d., low stand 85.00
Compote, cov., 10" d., high stand . . . 125.00
Compote, open, 7" d., low stand 60.00
Compote, open, 8½" d., low stand,
   scalloped rim 60.00
Compote, open, 9" d., low stand 75.00
Cordial 80.00
Creamer 55.00
Cruet w/original stopper 175.00
Goblet. . . . . 65.00 to 70.00
Marmalade jar. cov. 85.00
Mug, 2" h. 35.00

Small Cupid & Venus Mug

Mug, 2½" h. (ILLUS.) 55.00
Mug, 3½" h. 60.00
Pickle castor insert, cov. 75.00
Pickle castor w/resilvered frame,
   cover & tongs 185.00
Pitcher, milk, amber 175.00
Pitcher, milk, clear 95.00
Pitcher, water. . . . . 125.00 to 135.00
Relish, oval, 4½ x 7". 30.00
Relish, 9" oval. 20.00
Sauce dish, footed, 3½" to 4½" d. 15.00
Spooner 40.00
Sugar bowl, cov. 90.00
Table set, creamer, cov. sugar bowl
   & creamer, 3 pcs. 165.00
Wine . . . . 85.00 to 100.00

DAHLIA

Bowl, 6 x 9" oval, clear 25.00
Bread platter, 8 x 12". 40.00
Butter dish, cov., apple green 100.00
Butter dish, cov., canary 65.00
Butter dish, cov., clear. 54.00
Cake stand, amber, 9½" d. 73.00
Cake stand, blue, 9½" d. 53.00
Cake stand, canary, 9½" d. 75.00
Cake stand, clear, 9½" d. . . . . 30.00 to 35.00
Cake stand, blue, 10" d. 95.00
Cake stand, clear, 10" d. 25.00
Champagne, amber 75.00
Champagne, clear 35.00
Compote, cov., 8" d., high stand,
   clear. 50.00
Compote, open, 8" d., high stand 40.00

Cordial, clear 40.00
Creamer, amber 70.00
Creamer, blue. 40.00
Creamer, clear 25.00
Creamer, green. 40.00
Cruet w/original stopper, clear 45.00
Egg cup, double, clear . . . . . 45.00 to 50.00
Egg cup, single, clear. 25.00
Goblet, blue 55.00
Goblet, clear 35.00
Mug, child's, apple green 45.00
Mug, child's, blue 40.00
Mug, child's, clear. 30.00
Mug, amber. 45.00
Mug, blue 55.00
Mug, canary 55.00
Mug, clear. 35.00
Pickle dish, amber 40.00
Pickle dish, clear 20.00
Pickle dish, shell handles, clear. 55.00
Pitcher, milk, canary 70.00
Pitcher, milk, clear, applied handle. . . . 51.00
Pitcher, water, amber 105.00
Pitcher, water, apple green 100.00
Pitcher, water, blue. 100.00
Pitcher, water, canary. 100.00
Pitcher, water, clear 50.00
Plate, 9" d., w/handles, apple
   green 38.00
Plate, 9" d., w/handles, canary 38.00
Plate, 9" d., w/handles, clear. 18.00
Relish, apple green, 5 x 9½". 25.00
Relish, blue, 5 x 9½". 25.00
Sauce dish, flat, amber 22.00
Sauce dish, flat, canary 35.00
Sauce dish, flat, clear. 15.00
Sauce dish, footed, clear 7.00
Spooner, amber 48.00
Spooner, apple green. 65.00
Spooner, canary 55.00
Spooner, clear 35.00
Sugar bowl, cov., canary 75.00
Sugar bowl, cov., clear . . . . . 45.00 to 55.00
Wine, amber 70.00
Wine, apple green. 60.00
Wine, canary. 70.00
Wine, clear 45.00

DAISY & BUTTON WITH NARCISSUS

Berry set, master bowl & 6 sauce
   dishes, 7 pcs. 100.00
*Bowl, 6 x 9½" oval, footed. 46.00
Decanter w/original stopper 52.00
Goblet. 20.00
Pitcher, water 60.00

D&B with Narcissus Decorated Pitcher

Pitcher, water, cranberry-stained
  (ILLUS.). . . . . **75.00 to 100.00**
Punch cup **11.00**
Sauce dish, flat or three-footed **18.00**
Sugar bowl, cov. **35.00**
Tray, 10½" d. . . . . **40.00 to 50.00**
Tumbler **17.00**
*****Wine,** clear. **22.00**

DAISY & BUTTON WITH "V" ORNAMENT (Vandyke)

Berry set: 9" d. master bowl & six
  4¼" d. sauce dishes; canary,
  7 pcs.. . . . . **175.00**
Bowl, 9" d., blue . . . . **40.00 to 50.00**
Butter chip, canary. **12.00**
Butter chip, clear **8.00**
Butter dish, cov., amber. **80.00**
Butter dish, cov., blue **75.00**
Butter dish, cov., canary **95.00**
Butter dish, cov., clear. **55.00**
Celery vase, amber **38.00**
Celery vase, blue **50.00**
Celery vase, canary **60.00**
Celery vase, clear. **32.00**
Creamer, clear **30.00**
Finger bowl, amber **25.00**
Finger bowl, blue **30.00**
Mug, amber. **28.00**
Mug, blue **35.00**
Mug, canary **38.00**
Mug, clear. . . . . **20.00 to 25.00**
Mug, miniature, canary **31.00**
Pitcher, milk . . . . **55.00 to 80.00**
Pitcher, water, amber. **75.00**
Pitcher, water, canary. **65.00**
Pitcher, water, clear. . . . . **40.00 to 50.00**
Salt & pepper shakers w/original
  tops, amber, pr. **55.00**
Sauce dish, amber. **14.00**
Sauce dish, blue. **15.00**
Sauce dish, canary. **20.00**

Sauce dish, clear **10.00**
Spooner, amber **35.00**
Spooner, blue. **40.00**
Spooner, clear. **30.00**
Toothpick holder, amber. **35.00**
Toothpick holder, blue **45.00**
Toothpick holder, canary **35.00**
Toothpick holder, clear **25.00**
Tray, water, canoe shape. . . . **50.00 to 75.00**
Tray, water, square w/rounded
  corners, amber, 8 x 11". **59.00**
Tumbler, amber **24.00**
Tumbler, blue **20.00**
Waste bowl, canary . . . . **50.00 to 60.00**
Waste bowl, clear. **23.00**
Water set: pitcher & 4 tumblers; blue,
  5 pcs.. . . . . **175.00**
Wine, amber **35.00**

DAISY IN PANEL - See Two Panel Pattern

DARBY - See Pleat & Panel Pattern

DEWDROP

Bread Tray **25.00**
Goblet, amber. **24.00**
Goblet, canary **29.00**
Tumbler, canary **14.00**

DEWDROP WITH STAR

Bread tray, "Sheaf of Wheat"
  center **43.00**
Butter dish, cov.. . . . . **55.00**
Cake stand, 11" d. **45.00**
Cheese dish, cov.. . . . . **128.00**
Compote, cov., 7⅛" d., 9½" h. **83.00**
Goblet. . . . . **25.00 to 30.00**
Lamp, all-glass, patented "Aug. 29,
  1876," footed w/finger grip, 8½" h. . **145.00**
*****Plate,** 7" d.. **15.00**
Sauce dish, flat. **9.00**
*****Sauce dish,** footed **6.00**
Sugar bowl, cov. . . . . **35.00 to 45.00**

DIAGONAL BAND

Butter dish, cov.. . . . . **35.00**
Cake stand **30.00**
Celery vase . . . . **20.00 to 30.00**
Compote, cov., 7½" d., low stand. **30.00**
Compote, cov., 7½" d., 9¼" h. **45.00**
Compote, cov., 8" d., low stand **45.00**
Compote, open, 7½" d., high stand . . . **18.00**
Creamer **30.00**

Diagonal Band Goblet

Goblet (ILLUS.) . . . . 20.00 to 30.00
Marmalade jar w/original lid 50.00
Pickle castor w/amber insert 165.00
Pitcher, water 40.00
Plate, 6" d. 10.00
Plate, 7" d. 10.00
Salt dip, footed 25.00
Sauce dish, flat or footed . . . . . 7.00 to 10.00
Spooner 20.00
Tray, handled, 7¼ x 13" 20.00
Wine 22.00

DIAMOND & BULL'S EYE BAND - See Reverse Torpedo Pattern

DIAMOND MEDALLION - See Grand Pattern

DIAMOND POINT

Bowl, 7" d., blue, flint 110.00
Bowl, 8½" d., clear, flint 95.00
Butter dish, cov., clear, flint 83.00
Cake stand, clear, non-flint, 9" d. 75.00
Cake stand, clear, flint, 10" d.
   to 12" d. . . . . 175.00 to 275.00
Candlesticks, clear, flint,
   pr. . . . . 145.00 to 175.00
Castor set, 4-bottle, clear, flint, in
   silver plate frame 350.00
Castor set, 6-bottle, clear, non-flint,
   in silver plate frame 165.00
Celery vase, pedestal base w/knob
   stem, clear, flint . . . . 80.00 to 90.00
Champagne, clear, flint . . . 125.00 to 150.00
Claret, clear, flint 105.00
Compote, open, 6" d., high stand,
   clear, flint 75.00
Compote, open, 7" d., high stand,
   milk white, flint 175.00
Compote, open, 7" d., low stand,
   clear, flint . . . . 70.00 to 75.00

Compote, open, 7½" d., high stand,
   clear, flint . . . . 125.00 to 150.00
Compote, open, 8" d., shallow bowl,
   high stand, clear, non-flint 100.00
Compote, open, 10¼" d., high stand,
   milk white, flint 350.00
Cordial, clear, flint. 195.00
Creamer, applied handle, clear, flint. . 165.00
Cup plate, clear, flint. 60.00
Decanter, w/bar lip, clear, flint, pt. . . . 150.00
Decanter, w/bar lip, clear, flint, qt. . . . 130.00
Decanter w/original stopper, clear,
   flint, pt. 150.00
Decanter w/original stopper, clear,
   flint, qt. 175.00
Egg cup, canary, flint . . . . 300.00 to 350.00
Egg cup, clambroth, flint. 133.00
Egg cup, clear, flint . . . . 45.00 to 50.00
Egg cup, translucent sea green 650.00

Diamond Point Egg Cup

Egg cup, cov., powder blue opaque,
   flint (ILLUS.) . . . . 550.00 to 750.00

Diamond Point Goblet

Goblet, clear, flint
   (ILLUS.). . . . . 50.00 to 65.00
Goblet, clear, non-flint 38.00
Honey dish, clear, flint 18.00
Honey dish, coarse points, non-flint. . . 12.00
Honey dish, milk white, flint 60.00

Lamp, whale oil, w/wafer connector,
clear, flint, 10⅛" h. **295.00**
Pickle castor, blue non-flint insert,
original silver plate frame & lid **160.00**
Pitcher, milk, applied handle, clear,
flint . . . . **140.00 to 150.00**
Pitcher, milk, applied handle, milk
white, flint **550.00**
Pitcher, water, bulbous, clear,
flint. **350.00**
Plate, 8" d., milk white, flint **125.00**
Sauce dish, clear, flint, 4¼" d. **13.00**
Sauce dish, clear, non-flint, 3½" to
5½" d. **10.00**
Spillholder, clear, flint . . . . . **35.00 to 45.00**
Spillholder, clear w/gold rim, flint. . . . **165.00**
Spooner, clear, non-flint. . . . . **20.00 to 30.00**
Sugar bowl, cov., clear, non-flint **45.00**
Sugar bowl, cov., flat base, clear,
flint . . . . **95.00 to 125.00**
Sugar bowl, cov., footed, clear,
flint . . . . **175.00 to 200.00**
Sugar shaker w/original top,
bulbous, clear, non-flint. . **200.00 to 250.00**
Syrup pitcher w/original top, clear,
non-flint **75.00**
Tumbler, bar, clear, flint **95.00**
Tumbler, clear, flint, ½ pt. **45.00**
Tumbler, whiskey, clear, flint **125.00**
Tumbler, whiskey, handled, clear,
flint, 3" h. **150.00**
Wine, canary, non-flint **35.00**
Wine, clear, flint **95.00**
Wine, clear, non-flint **30.00**

DOUBLE LEAF & DART - See
Leaf & Dart Pattern

DOUBLE WEDDING RING
(Wedding Ring)

Butter dish, cov. . . . . **100.00 to 125.00**
Champagne . . . . **100.00 to 125.00**
Decanter w/original stopper **125.00**

Double Wedding Ring Goblet

***Goblet** (ILLUS.) **82.00**
Lamp, kerosene, hand-type w/flat
base, applied handle. . . . **150.00 to 180.00**
Lamp, kerosene, patterned font,
brass standard, marble
base . . . . **200.00 to 250.00**
Pitcher, water . . . . **175.00 to 200.00**
Spooner **70.00**
***Sugar bowl,** cov. . . . . **125.00 to 150.00**
Syrup pitcher w/original top,
6" h. . . . . **155.00 to 165.00**
Tumbler, bar. . . . . **85.00 to 100.00**
Tumbler, footed . . . . **100.00 to 110.00**
Wine . . . . **75.00 to 90.00**

DRAGON

Butter dish, cov. **450.00**
Compote cov., 8¼" d., 8" h. **825.00**
Compote cov., 8¼" d., 9¾" h. **825.00**
Goblet **1,900.00**
Spooner **300.00**
Sugar bowl, open **325.00**

DRAPERY

Butter dish, cov. **60.00**
Cake plate, square, footed . . . **40.00 to 45.00**
Celery vase **40.00**
Creamer, applied handle . . . . **35.00 to 40.00**
Egg cup **28.00**
Goblet **40.00**
Pitcher, water, applied handle **75.00**
Plate, 6" d. **35.00**
Sauce dish, flat. **17.00**

Drapery Spooner

Spooner (ILLUS.) **40.00**
Sugar bowl, cov. . . . . **40.00 to 45.00**
Tumbler **35.00**
Water set, pitcher & 6 tumblers,
7 pcs. . . . . **275.00 to 325.00**

EARLY OREGON - See Skilton
Pattern

EGG IN SAND

Bread tray, handled,
  clear . . . . 30.00 to 35.00
Butter dish, cov. 48.00
Creamer, amber 40.00
Creamer, blue 65.00
Creamer, clear 32.00
Dish, flat, swan center, 7" d. 75.00
Goblet, amber. 45.00
Goblet, blue 60.00
Goblet, clear. 28.00

Egg In Sand Milk Pitcher

Pitcher, milk (ILLUS.) 45.00
Pitcher, water, blue. 98.00
Pitcher, water, clear 45.00
Platter, 12½" oblong 42.00
Spooner, amber 45.00
Spooner, blue. 60.00
Spooner, clear. 35.00
Sugar bowl, cov., amber 65.00
Sugar bowl, cov., blue . . . . . . 85.00 to 95.00
Sugar bowl, cov., clear. 35.00
Tray, water, flat 45.00
Tumbler, amber 35.00
Tumbler, blue 65.00
Tumbler, clear 30.00
Water set, pitcher & 4 goblets, clear,
  5 pcs. 165.00
Water set, pitcher, tray & 5 goblets,
  amber, 7 pcs. 350.00
Water set, pitcher, tray & 5 goblets,
  blue, 7 pcs. 400.00

EMPRESS

Bowl, master berry, 8½" d., clear 40.00
Bowl, master berry, 8½" d., emerald
  green w/gold 95.00
Butter dish, cov., emerald green 130.00
Celery vase, clear. 60.00
Celery vase, emerald green 85.00
Compote, open, 6" d., high standard,
  clear. 45.00

Compote, open, 6" d., high standard,
  emerald green 125.00
Creamer, table size, clear, 5¼" h. 40.00
Creamer, table size, emerald green,
  5¼" h. 75.00
Creamer, individual, clear. 30.00
Creamer, individual, emerald green . . . 60.00
Cruet w/original stopper, emerald
  green. . . . . 195.00 to 225.00
Lamp, kerosene, hand-type w/finger
  grip, original burner & chimney,
  clear. 65.00
Lamp, kerosene, hand-type w/finger
  grip, original burner & chimney,
  emerald green 165.00
Lamp, kerosene, table model, original
  burner & chimney, clear 75.00
Lamp, kerosene, table model, original
  burner & chimney, emerald green. . 190.00
Pitcher, water, clear, ½ gal. 75.00
Pitcher, water, emerald green,
  ½ gal. 225.00
**Salt & pepper shakers w/original
  tops,** clear, pr. 60.00
**Salt & pepper shakers w/original
  tops,** emerald green, pr. 135.00
Salt shaker w/original top, clear
  w/gold 35.00
Sauce dish, clear, 4½" d. 15.00
Sauce dish, emerald green w/gold,
  4½" d. 45.00
Spoonholder clear 30.00
Spoonholder emerald green 45.00
Spoonholder rose w/gold. 65.00
Sugar bowl, cov., clear. 65.00
Sugar bowl, cov., emerald green 125.00
Sugar bowl, cov., emerald green
  w/gold 140.00
Sugar shaker w/original top,
  clear. 60.00
Sugar shaker w/original top,
  emerald green 125.00
Syrup pitcher w/original top,
  clear. 110.00
Syrup pitcher w/original top,
  emerald green 250.00
Toothpick holder, clear . . . . . 55.00 to 60.00
Toothpick holder, emerald green . . . 175.00
Tumbler, water, clear 40.00
Tumbler, water, emerald green 70.00

FESTOON

Bowl, berry, 5½ x 9"
  rectangle . . . . 20.00 to 25.00
Bowl, 7" d. 25.00
Cake stand, high pedestal,
  9" d. 45.00

Compote, open, 9" d., high
stand **56.00**
Creamer . . . . **25.00 to 30.00**
Mug, handled **58.00**
Pitcher, water **58.00**
Plate, 7" d.. . . . . **36.00**
Plate, 8" d.. . . . . **42.00**
Plate, 9" d.. . . . . **46.00**
Relish, 5½ x 9" **30.00**
Sauce dish **10.00**
Spooner **35.00**
Tray, water, 10" d.. . . . . **34.00**
Tumbler **26.00**
Waste bowl. **53.00**
Water set, pitcher, tray & 4 tumblers,
6 pcs.. . . . . **215.00**

FINECUT

Bread tray, handled, canary,
7½ x 14½" **53.00**
Cake stand, amber, 10" d.,7¼" h. **45.00**
Cake stand, clear, 10" d., 7¼" h. **35.00**
Creamer, clear **28.00**
Cruet w/matching stopper,
canary **130.00**
Finger bowl, canary **35.00**
Goblet, canary **43.00**
Goblet, clear. **25.00**
Pickle castor, canary, w/Reed &
Barton silver plate frame & fork. . . . **275.00**
Pitcher, water, canary. **100.00**
Pitcher, water, clear **53.00**
Plate, 6" d., clear. **8.00**
Plate, 7" d., clear. **14.00**
Plate, 10" d., amber **40.00**
Plate, 10" d., canary **55.00**
Plate, 10" d., clear. **25.00**
Relish, boat-shaped, apple green. **35.00**
Salt & pepper shakers w/original
tops, clear, pr.. . . . . **35.00**
Spooner, amber **33.00**
Toothpick holder, hat shape on
plate, blue **25.00**
Tray, water, canary, 9¼" d.. . . . . **47.00**
Wine, clear **15.00**

FINECUT & PANEL (Paneled Finecut)

Bread tray, amber, 9 x 13" **48.00**
Bread tray, canary, 9 x 13". **25.00**
Bread tray, clear, 9 x 13" **29.00**
Celery vase **25.00**
Compote, open, high stand, amber . . . **45.00**
Compote, open, high stand, clear **34.00**
Creamer, amber **43.00**
Goblet, amber. **33.00**
Goblet, canary **24.00**

Goblet, clear. **20.00**
Pitcher, milk, amber **85.00**
Pitcher, water, amber **120.00**

Finecut & Panel Plate

Plate, 6" d., amber (ILLUS.) **25.00**
Plate, 6" d., blue **27.00**
Plate, 6" d., canary **23.00**
Plate, 6" d., clear. **10.00**
Plate, 7" d., clear. **11.00**
Relish, blue, 3½ x 7". **23.00**
Relish, canary, 3½ x 7". **22.00**
Salt shaker w/original top, amber. . . . **38.00**
Sauce dish, canary. **14.00**
Sauce dish, clear. **8.00**
Sugar bowl, cov., canary **60.00**
Tray, water, canary, 12" w.. . . . . **95.00**
Tumbler, amber **18.00**
Waste bowl, canary **30.00**
Wine, amber. . . . . 30.00 to **40.00**
Wine, blue. . . . . 30.00 to **35.00**
Wine, canary. . . . . 35.00 to **40.00**
Wine, clear **15.00**

FLORADORA - See Bohemian Pattern

FLUTE

Bar bottle, clear, flint, pt. **75.00**
Claret **22.00**
Compote, open, 8¼" d., 3" h. **35.00**
Egg cup, single. **27.00**
Egg cup, single, handled **50.00**
Goblet. **26.00**
Mug, applied handle **135.00**
Tumbler, whiskey, handled, clear. **43.00**
Wine **33.00**

FROSTED LEAF

Celery vase **125.00**
Champagne . . . . 200.00 to **225.00**
Egg cup . . . . 95.00 to **100.00**

Goblet 135.00
Salt dip 50.00
Salt dip master size 125.00
Sauce dish 25.00
Sugar bowl, cov. 175.00
Wine 170.00

GARFIELD DRAPE

Bowl, 6" d.. . . . . 43.00

Garfield Drape Bread Plate

Bread plate, "We Mourn Our Nation's
  Loss," 11½" d. (ILLUS.) . . . 45.00 to 50.00
Butter dish, cov. . . . . 75.00 to 80.00
Cake stand, 9½" d. 85.00
Celery vase, pedestal base 50.00
Compote, cov., 7" d., 9½" h. 155.00
Compote, cov., 8" d., 12½" h. 185.00
Creamer 54.00

Garfield Drape Goblet

Goblet (ILLUS.). 50.00
Pitcher, milk . . . . 145.00 to 155.00
Pitcher, water 114.00
Plate, 10" d., star center 70.00
Sauce dish, flat or footed, each 12.00
Spooner 35.00
Sugar bowl, cov. 80.00

GOOSEBERRY

Cake stand 52.00
Creamer 40.00

Gooseberry Goblet

*Goblet (ILLUS.) 35.00
*Mug . . . . 35.00 to 45.00
Mug, child's, blue opaque 45.00
Spooner, milk white 28.00
Sugar bowl, cov., milk white. 50.00
Tumbler, bar. 38.00
Tumbler, water 32.00

GRAND (Diamond Medallion)

Bowl, 6¼ x 9" oval 25.00
Bread plate, 10" d. . . . . 20.00 to 25.00
Butter dish, cov. . . . . 35.00 to 45.00
Cake stand, 8" d. . . . . 30.00 to 35.00
Cake stand, 10" d. . . . . 35.00 to 40.00
Celery vase 25.00
Compote, cov., 6" d., 9" h. 65.00
Compote, cov., 8" d., low stand 80.00
Cordial 50.00

Grand Creamer

Creamer, footed (ILLUS.) 25.00
Goblet . . . . 25.00 to 35.00
Pitcher, water 39.00
Relish, 7½" oval 9.00
Salt shaker w/original top. 33.00
Spooner 23.00
Sugar bowl, cov. 32.00
Wine . . . . 25.00 to 30.00

GRAPE & FESTOON

Butter dish, cov., stippled leaf **41.00**
Celery vase, stippled leaf **42.00**
Creamer, stippled leaf. **43.00**
Egg cup, stippled leaf. **20.00**
Goblet, stippled leaf . . . . **20.00 to 25.00**
Goblet, veined leaf **25.00**
Pitcher, water, stippled leaf **90.00**
Plate, 6" d., stippled leaf **18.00**
Relish, stippled leaf **10.00**
Salt dip, footed, stippled leaf **22.00**
Sauce dish, flat, veined leaf, 4" d. **13.00**
Sauce dish, flat, stippled leaf, 4" d. **8.00**

Grape & Festoon Spooner

Spooner, stippled leaf (ILLUS.) **33.00**
Spooner, veined leaf **25.00**
Sugar bowl, cov., stippled
   leaf . . . . **55.00 to 60.00**
Wine, stippled leaf. **50.00**

GUARDIAN ANGEL - See Cupid & Venus Pattern

HAMILTON

Butter dish, cov. **75.00**
Compote, open, 7" d., low stand **46.00**

Hamilton Compote

Compote, open, 8" d., 5½" h.
   (ILLUS.). . . . . **60.00 to 70.00**
Compote, open, 8" d.,
   8" h. . . . . **250.00 to 300.00**
Creamer **55.00**
Egg cup **48.00**
Goblet. . . . . **50.00 to 55.00**
Honey dish, 3½" d. **20.00**

Sauce dish **14.00**
Spooner **44.00**
Sugar bowl, cov. . . . . **100.00 to 125.00**
Tumbler, bar. . . . . **100.00 to 125.00**
Tumbler, whiskey, applied handle **95.00**

HARP

Bowl, 6" d. **45.00**
Goblet, flared sides **1,300.00**
Lamp, kerosene, hand-type w/applied
   finger grip **199.00**
Lamp, kerosene, hexagonal font,
   shaped base, brass collar, flint,
   9½" h. . . . . **350.00 to 400.00**
Salt dip, master size **55.00**

Harp Spooner

Spooner (ILLUS.) **80.00**

HICKMAN (Le Clede)

Bowl, 6" d., green **25.00**
Bowl, 8" d. **25.00**
Butter dish, cov. **35.00**
Cake stand, 8½" to 9½" d. **65.00**
Compote, open, jelly, green **15.00**
Compote, cov., 5" d. . . . . **35.00 to 40.00**
Compote, open, 7½" d., 5½" h. **20.00**
Condiment set, miniature: salt &
   pepper shakers & cruet w/original
   stopper on cloverleaf-shaped tray;
   clear, 4 pcs. **90.00**
Cracker jar, cov., clear **150.00**

Hickman Creamer

Creamer, green (ILLUS.) **23.00**
Goblet, clear. . . . . **35.00 to 40.00**
Goblet, green **75.00**
Ice tub, clear. **80.00**
Pitcher, water **45.00**
Plate, 6" d. **25.00**

Punch cup, clear 8.00
Punch cup, green. 19.00
Relish, green 23.00
Rose bowl 26.00
Salt dip 23.00
Sauce dish, green 13.00
Sauce dish, ruby-stained 19.00
Sugar bowl, cov., clear. 65.00
Syrup pitcher w/original top. 110.00
Toothpick holder, clear. . . . . 35.00 to 40.00
Vase, 8" h., trumpet-shaped, green . . . 18.00
Vase, 10" h., green 38.00
Wine, clear 30.00
Wine, green . . . . 35.00 to 40.00

HORN OF PLENTY (McKee's Comet)

Bar bottle w/original stopper,
 qt. . . . . 135.00 to 145.00
Bowl, 7½" d. 70.00
Bowl, 8" oval. 110.00
Butter dish, cov. 118.00
Butter pat 16.00
Celery vase . . . . 160.00 to 165.00
Champagne 175.00
Compote, open, 6" d. 100.00
Compote, open, 6¾" d.,
 3½" h. . . . . 75.00 to 85.00
Compote, open, 7" d., 3" h. 123.00
Compote, open, 7" d., 5½" h. 225.00
Compote, open, 7" d., 7½" h., waffle
 base. 105.00
Compote, open, 8" d., low stand 125.00
Compote, open, 8" d.,
 6" h. . . . . 135.00 to 140.00

Horn of Plenty Compote

Compote, open, 8" d., 8" h.
 (ILLUS.). 130.00
Compote, open, 9" d., low stand 105.00
Compote, open, 9" d., 8½" h. 200.00
Compote, open, 10½" d., 9¾" h. 350.00
Cordial 140.00
Creamer, applied handle,
 7" h. . . . . 175.00 to 200.00
Decanter, bar lip, pt. 110.00

Decanter w/original stopper,
 pt. . . . . 200.00 to 225.00
Decanter w/original stopper, qt. 175.00
Dish, low foot, 7¼" d. 55.00
Egg cup, 3¾" h. 43.00
*Goblet 78.00
Honey dish. 18.00
*Lamp, w/whale oil burner, all-glass,
 11" h. . . . . 225.00 to 250.00
Peppersauce bottle w/stopper 162.00
Pitcher, water, 9" h. 1,100.00
Plate, 6" d., canary 248.00
Plate, 6" d., clear. 102.00
Relish, 5 x 7" oval
Salt dip, master size, oval 80.00
Sauce dish, 3½" to 5" d. 14.00
Spooner, 4½" h., clear 82.00
Sugar bowl, cov. 145.00
Tumbler, bar. . . . . 100.00 to 125.00
*Tumbler, water, 3 5/8" h. 60.00
Tumbler, whiskey, 3" h. 141.00
Tumbler, whiskey, handled. 220.00
Wine 147.00

ILLINOIS

Bowl, 6" sq. 26.00

Illinois Butter Dish

*Butter dish, cov., 7" sq.
 (ILLUS.). . . . . 70.00 to 75.00
*Celery vase. 38.00
Creamer, large 40.00
Creamer, small 29.00
Cruet w/original stopper 108.00
Doughnut stand, 7½" sq., 4¼" h. 65.00
Marmalade jar in silver plate frame
 w/spoon, 3 pcs. 170.00
Pitcher, water, squatty, silver plate
 rim, clear 115.00
Pitcher, water, tankard 75.00
Plate, 7" sq. 22.00
Salt dip, individual size. . . . . . 15.00 to 20.00
Sauce dish 14.00
Soda fountain (straw-holder) jar,
 cov., clear, 12½" h. 309.00
Spooner 40.00
Toothpick holder. . . . . 40.00 to 45.00
Tumbler 52.00
Vase, 9" h., 4" d. 41.00

IVY IN SNOW

Bowl, 7" d.. . . . . 22.00
*Cake stand, 8" to 10" d. 42.00
*Celery vase, 8" h. 30.00
Compote, open, jelly. 19.00
Coridal, ruby-stained ivy sprigs 100.00
*Creamer, clear. 25.00
*Goblet, clear 50.00
Goblet, green & red ivy sprigs & gold
  band at top & base 175.00
Goblet, ruby-stained 90.00
Honey dish, cov., amber-stained ivy
  sprigs . . . . 125.00 to 150.00
Plate, 7" d.. . . . . 18.00
*Spooner, clear. 25.00
Sugar bowl, cov., clear . . . . . 30.00 to 35.00
Sugar bowl, cov., ruby-stained. 135.00
Tumbler, clear 20.00
Tumbler, ruby-stained 40.00

Ivy In Snow Wine

Wine, clear (ILLUS.) 38.00

JEWEL BAND - See Scalloped Tape Pattern

JEWEL & CRESCENT - See Tennessee Pattern

JEWELED DIAMOND & FAN - See Tacoma

JEWELED MOON & STAR (Moon & Star with Waffle)

*Banana boat, w/amber & blue
  staining . . . . 275.00 TO 325.00
*Bowl, 6¾" d., flat 14.00
Butter dish, cov., w/amber & blue
  staining . . . . 130.00 to 140.00
Carafe, clear 39.00
Celery vase, frosted w/amber & blue
  staining 83.00
*Goblet, clear 29.00

Goblet, frosted moons w/red jewels,
  amber & blue staining 90.00
Salt shaker w/original top, w/amber
  & blue staining. 125.00
Spooner, w/amber & blue
  staining . . . . 60.00 to 65.00
Tumbler, w/amber & blue staining 60.00
*Wine 33.00

KING'S 500

Butter dish, cov., clear 275.00
Butter dish, cov., cobalt
  blue . . . . 350.00 to 375.00
Creamer, bulbous, clear 35.00
Cruet w/original swirled stopper,
  clear, 4 oz 30.00
Cruet w/original swirled stopper,
  cobalt blue w/gold trim, 8 oz. 350.00
Sauce dish, 4" d., frosted 18.00
Shot glass, souvenir, Midwinter Fair,
  1894, San Francisco, clear,
  ruby-stained. 35.00
Spooner, scalloped rim, cobalt blue . . . 55.00
Tumbler, clear 13.00

LE CLEDE - See Hickman Pattern

LEAF & DART (Double Leaf & Dart)

Celery vase, pedestal base 38.00
Creamer, applied handle 40.00
Egg cup 21.00
Goblet 24.00
Pitcher, water, applied handle 110.00
Salt dip, open, master size 27.00
Spooner . . . . 30.00 to 35.00
Sugar bowl, cov. . . . . 45.00 to 55.00

Leaf & Dart Tumbler

Tumbler, footed (ILLUS.) . . . . 25.00 to 30.00
Wine 37.00

LILY-OF-THE-VALLEY

Butter dish, cov................ **100.00**
Celery vase **66.00**
Champagne **175.00**
Compote, cov., 8" d., low stand **127.00**
Compote, cov., 8½" d., high stand ... **138.00**
Compote, open, 7" d., low stand **56.00**
Compote, open, 8½" d., 5" h......... **54.00**
Creamer, plain base, applied
   handle **62.00**
Creamer, three-footed, molded
   handle................ **60.00 to 65.00**
Cruet w/original stopper. . **150.00 to 200.00**
Goblet, plain **81.00**
Pitcher, milk, applied
   handle............... **200.00 to 225.00**

Lily-of-the-Valley Pitcher

Pitcher, water, bulbous, applied
   handle (ILLUS.)............... **120.00**
Relish, 4½ x 7" **23.00**
Relish, 5½ x 8" **28.00**
Salt dip, open, master size, three-
   footed **60.00**
Spooner, plain base........ **40.00 to 45.00**
Spooner, three-footed **50.00**
Sugar bowl, open, three-footed **55.00**
Tumbler, flat **10.00**
Wine **155.00**

LOOP (Seneca Loop)

Butter dish, cov., flint............. **195.00**
Celery vase, flint................. **65.00**
Celery vase, non-flint **28.00**
Champagne, non-flint.............. **30.00**
Compote, open, 8" d., 6" h.,
   non-flint **75.00**
Compote, open, lobed rim, 8" d.,
   6" h., canary, flint **1,760.00**
Compote, open, 8" d., 8" h., flint...... **85.00**

Compote, open, 9½" d., 7" h., flint ... **275.00**
Compote, open, 10" d., 8" h.,
   flint .... **275.00 to 300.00**
Compote, open, 12¼" d., 9½" h.,
   flint......................... **400.00**
Creamer, clear, flint **73.00**
Egg cup, flint .... **30.00 to 35.00**

Loop Goblet

Goblet, flint (ILLUS.).............. **25.00**
Pitcher, water, applied handle,
   flint......................... **195.00**
Pitcher, water, non-flint............ **65.00**
Salt dip, master size, flint **25.00**
Spooner, clear, non-flint........... **19.00**
Spooner, flint **32.00**
Sugar bowl, cov., flint ..... **75.00 to 100.00**
Vase, 9 5/8" h., flint............... **75.00**
Wine, flint **28.00**

LOOP WITH DEWDROP

Celery vase **30.00**
Compote, cov., 9" d............... **55.00**
Creamer **38.00**
Goblet........................ **35.00**
Spooner **30.00**
Sugar bowl, cov. .... **30.00 to 35.00**
Tumbler **30.00**

LOOPS & DROPS - See New Jersey Pattern

MAGNET & GRAPE

Champagne, frosted leaf, flint **176.00**
Champagne, stippled leaf, non-flint ... **45.00**
Cordial, frosted leaf, flint, 4" h....... **125.00**
Creamer, stippled leaf, non-flint **35.00**
***Egg cup,** clear leaf, non-flint........ **32.00**
Egg cup, stippled leaf, non-flint **18.00**
Goblet, clear leaf, non-flint **22.00**
Goblet, frosted leaf & American
   Shield, flint .... **400.00 to 600.00**

Magnet & Grape Goblet

*Goblet, frosted leaf, flint (ILLUS.) . . . **103.00**
Goblet, stippled leaf, non-flint **31.00**
Sauce dish, clear leaf, non-flint **5.00**
Sauce dish, frosted leaf, flint **20.00**
Sauce dish, stippled leaf, non-flint **6.00**
Spooner, frosted leaf, flint **85.00**
Spooner, stippled leaf, non-flint **28.00**
*Wine, frosted leaf, flint. . . . **175.00 to 200.00**

MANHATTAN

Bowl, 8½" d., master berry,
    pink-stained **40.00**
*Bowl, 8½" d., master berry, clear **25.00**
Cake stand, clear . . . . **35.00 to 40.00**
Celery tray **26.00**
Cracker jar, cov., pink
    stained . . . . **100.00 to 125.00**
Creamer **28.00**
Creamer, individual size **19.00**
Cruet w/original stopper . . . . **55.00 to 60.00**
Dish, flat, 6 x 7" oval **22.00**
*Goblet, clear **25.00**
Ice bucket, pink-stained **50.00**
Marmalade jar, cov. **38.00**
Pitcher, water, pink-stained **125.00**
Pitcher, water, w/silver rim **90.00**
*Punch cup, clear **20.00**
Sauce dish, flat, amber or pink-stained,
    each **13.00**
*Sauce dish, flat, clear **12.00**
Spooner **20.00**
Sugar bowl, open **16.00**
Toothpick holder, clear **29.00**
*Tumbler, clear **13.00**
Tumbler, clear w/gold trim **25.00**
Tumbler, pink-stained **16.00**
Vase, 6" h. **20.00**
*Wine **18.00**

MC KEE'S COMET - See Horn of Plenty Pattern

MINERVA

Bread tray, 13" l **55.00**
Butter dish, cov. **80.00**
Cake stand, 8" d. . . . . **55.00 to 75.00**
Cake stand, 9" d. **110.00**
Cake stand, 10½" d. . . . . . . **110.00 to 115.00**
Champagne **350.00**
Compote, cov., 7" d., low stand **125.00**
Compote, cov., 8" d., high
    stand . . . . **140.00 to 150.00**
Compote, cov., 8" d., low stand **175.00**
Creamer **51.00**
Goblet. . . . . **85.00 to 95.00**
Pitcher, water **219.00**
Plate, 8" d., Bates (J.C.) portrait
    center, scalloped rim **75.00**

Minerva "Mars" Plate

Plate, 10" d., Mars center
    (ILLUS.) **50.00**
Platter, 13" oval **60.00**
Relish, 5 x 8" oblong **34.00**
Sauce dish, footed, 4" d. **17.00**
Sauce dish, flat, 5" d. **20.00**
Spooner **40.00**
Sugar bowl, cov. . . . . **90.00 to 95.00**
Wine **50.00**

MINNESOTA

Banana bowl, flat . . . . **50.00 to 55.00**
Bowl, 6" sq. **32.00**
Bowl, 8" sq. **32.00**
Bowl, 6 x 8¼" **38.00**
Bowl, 8½" d., clear **40.00**
Bowl, 7½ x 10½" **38.00**
Bowl, 7½ x 10½", ruby-stained **375.00**
Carafe **48.00**
Celery tray, 13" l. **42.00**
Cheese dish, cov. **58.00**
Compote, open, 7" **40.00**
Cracker jar, cov. . . . . **85.00 to 100.00**

Creamer, individual size, w/gold
trim 18.00
Creamer, 3½" h. 36.00
Cruet w/original stopper 50.00
Goblet, clear 30.00
Goblet clear w/gold. 35.00
Mug. 25.00
Nappy, 4½" d. 12.00
Pitcher, water, tankard . . . . . . 50.00 to 75.00
Plate, 7⅜" d., turned-up rim 17.00

Minnesota Relish

Relish, 6½ x 8¾" oblong
(ILLUS.). 21.00
Sauce dish 10.00
Sugar bowl, cov. 37.00
Syrup pitcher w/original top 65.00
Toothpick holder, three-handled,
clear. 28.00
Toothpick holder, three-handled,
green 130.00
Tumbler 18.00
Wine . . . . 15.00 to 20.00

NAIL

Bowl, berry, master, ruby-stained. 90.00
Butter dish, cov. 74.00
Celery tray, flat, 5 x 11" 75.00
Celery vase, ruby-stained. 65.00
Claret 55.00
Compote, 8" d., clear, engraved. 85.00
Creamer, clear, plain 40.00
Creamer, ruby-stained, 4½" h. 95.00
Goblet, clear, engraved . . . . . 45.00 to 55.00
Goblet, clear, plain . . . . 40.00 to 45.00
Goblet, ruby-stained. . . . . 70.00 to 80.00
Pitcher, water, engraved 120.00
Pitcher, water, plain 83.00
Pitcher, water, ruby-
stained . . . . 200.00 to 225.00
Salt shaker w/original top, ruby-
stained w/engraving 75.00
Sauce dish, flat or footed, each 20.00
Sauce dish, flat or footed, ruby-
stained, each. 50.00
Spooner, ruby-stained 78.00
Sugar bowl, cov., clear. 45.00

Sugar bowl, cov., clear w/engraved
cover 46.00
Sugar bowl, cov., ruby-stained. 125.00
Syrup jug w/original top, ruby-
stained. 230.00
Tumbler, clear . . . . 20.00 to 25.00

NEW JERSEY (Loops & Drops)

Berry set, master bowl & 6 sauce
dishes, 7 pcs. 175.00
Bowl, 7½" d. 75.00
Bowl, 9" d.. . . . . 29.00
Butter dish, cov., ruby-
stained . . . . 150.00 to 200.00
Butter dish, cov., w/gold trim 75.00
Celery tray, flat. 35.00
Compote, open, jelly. 32.00
Compote, open, 7" d., high stand. 60.00
Compote, open, 7" d., low stand 32.00
Compote, open, 8" d., low stand 24.00
Creamer, clear 36.00
Creamer, ruby-stained 65.00
Cruet w/original stopper 50.00
Goblet, clear. 42.00
Goblet, ruby-stained. 195.00
Pitcher, water, bulbous . . . 150.00 to 175.00
Plate, 8" d.
Plate, 10½" d. 36.00
Salt shaker w/original top 35.00
Sauce dish, flat. 11.00
Spooner, clear 34.00
Spooner, ruby-stained 65.00
Sugar bowl, cov. 46.00
Toothpick holder, clear 49.00
Toothpick holder, w/gold trim 65.00
Tumbler, clear 26.00
Vase, 10" h., green . . . . 40.00 to 50.00
Wine 40.00

OPEN ROSE

Butter dish, cov. 65.00
Creamer 41.00
Egg cup 23.00

Open Rose Goblet

*Goblet (ILLUS.) 28.00

Salt dip, master size 24.00
Sauce dish 8.00
*Spooner 32.00
Sugar bowl, cov. 54.00
Tumbler 43.00

PANELED DAISY

Bowl, 5 x 7" oval 16.00
Bowl, master berry, 5¾ x 8¼"
   oval 17.00
Bowl, 9" sq.. 18.00
Bowl, 7 x 9½" oval 17.00
Butter dish, cov.. . . . . 45.00
Cake stand, 8" to 11" d., high
   stand 44.00
Celery vase 30.00
*Compote, cov., 7" d., high stand 60.00
Compote, cov., 8" d., 12½" h. 110.00
Compote, open, 6" d., 6¾" h. 22.00
*Goblet 27.00
Mug. 35.00
Plate, 9" sq.. 23.00
Plate, 10" sq.. . . . . 42.00
Relish, 5 x 7" oval. 18.00
Sauce dish, flat or footed, each 9.00

PAVONIA (Pineapple Stem)

Butter dish, cov., clear, engraved 90.00
Butter dish, cov., clear, plain 72.00
Butter dish, cov., ruby-stained. 108.00
Cake stand, 10" d. . . . . 70.00 to 75.00
Celery vase, engraved 45.00
Celery vase, plain. 35.00
Compote, cov., 6" d., high stand 55.00
Compote, cov, 7" d., engraved. 100.00
Creamer, engraved. 41.00
Goblet, engraved 43.00
Goblet, plainz 25.00
Pitcher, water, tall tankard, clear,
   engraved. . . . . 110.00 to 125.00
Pitcher, water, tall tankard, clear,
   plain . . . . 65.00 to 70.00
Pitcher, water, tall tankard, ruby-
   stained . . . . 135.00 to 140.00
Pitcher, water, tall tankard, ruby-
   stained, engraved 275.00
Salt dip, master size. 17.00
Sauce dish, flat or footed, each 15.00
Spooner, clear 41.00
Sugar bowl, cov., clear. 50.00
Sugar bowl, cov., ruby-stained. 85.00
Tray, water 73.00
Tumbler, clear 25.00

Pavonia Etched Tumbler

Tumbler, clear, acid-etched
   (ILLUS.). . . . . 20.00 to 30.00
Tumbler, ruby-stained 35.00
Tumbler, ruby-stained, engraved 45.00
Waste bowl, clear, engraved 48.00
Water set: tankard pitcher &
   4 tumblers; clear, 5 pcs. 168.00
Water set: tankard pitcher &
   5 tumblers; clear, 6 pcs. 200.00
Water set: tankard pitcher &
   6 tumblers; ruby-stained, 7 pcs. . . . 375.00
Wine, clear, engraved. 30.00
Wine, clear, plain 25.00
Wine, ruby-stained 39.00

PINEAPPLE STEM - See Pavonia Pattern

PLEAT & PANEL (Darby)

Bowl, 6" sq., flat 28.00
Bowl, 8" rectangle, footed. 35.00
Bowl, 8" sq., flat 45.00
Bowl, cov., 8" rectangle, flat 90.00
Bread tray, pierced handles. . 25.00 to 30.00
Bread tray, closed handles,
   8½ x 13" . . . . 40.00 to 45.00
Cake stand, 8" sq. 40.00
Cake stand, 9" to 10" sq. 75.00
Celery vase, footed 48.00
Compote, cov., 8" d., high
   stand . . . . 135.00 to 145.00
Compote, open, 7" d., high stand. 31.00
Compote, open, 8" d., high stand. 35.00
Creamer 25.00
*Goblet, clear 32.00
Marmalade jar, cov. 100.00
Pitcher, milk . . . . 175.00 to 180.00
Pitcher, water. . . . . 100.00 to 125.00
Plate, 6" sq. . . . . 20.00 to 25.00
Plate, 7" sq., clear. 19.00
Relish, open, handled, 5 x 8½". 24.00
Sauce dish, flat, handled 18.00
Sauce dish, footed 23.00
Tray, water, 9¼ x 14" 45.00

POPCORN

Popcorn Cake Stand

Cake stand, 11" d. (ILLUS.) **43.00**
Creamer **23.00**
Creamer w/raised ears
   of corn . . . . **55.00 to 65.00**
Goblet **33.00**
Goblet w/raised ears of corn **45.00**
Wine **38.00**
Wine w/raised ears of corn **50.00**

POST (Square Panes)

Bowl, 8" sq., engraved **65.00**
Butter dish, cov. **68.00**
Celery vase **32.00**
Compote, cov., 5" sq.,
   10" h. . . . . **85.00 to 90.00**
Goblet, engraved **51.00**
Goblet, plain **39.00**
Lamp, kerosene-type, collared,
   engraved, 5" h. **125.00**
Lamp, kerosene-type, 8½" h. **125.00**
Pitcher, milk **75.00**
Pitcher, water **108.00**
Spooner **30.00**

PRESSED LEAF

Champagne **48.00**
Compote, cov., acorn finial, low
   stand **45.00**
Compote, open, 8" d., low
   stand . . . . **65.00 to 70.00**
Compote, open, 7" d. . . . . **55.00 to 60.00**
Creamer, applied handle **75.00**
Egg cup **30.00**
Goblet . . . . **50.00 to 60.00**
Pitcher, water, applied
   handle . . . . **85.00 to 100.00**
Relish, 5 x 7". **25.00**
Salt dip, master size **31.00**

Pressed Leaf Spooner

Spooner (ILLUS.) . . . . **30.00 to 35.00**
Sugar bowl, cov. **74.00**
Wine **47.00**

PSYCHE & CUPID

Celery vase **51.00**
Compote, cov., 6½" d., 8" h. **100.00**
Creamer . . . . **35.00 to 45.00**

Psyche & Cupid Goblet

Goblet (ILLUS.) . . . . **50.00 to 55.00**
Pitcher, water . . . . **65.00 to 70.00**
Spooner . . . . **45.00 to 50.00**
Sugar bowl, cov. **60.00**

REVERSE TORPEDO (Diamond & Bull's Eye Band)

Banana stand **130.00**
Basket, high stand **160.00**
Bowl, 7½" d., ruffled rim **48.00**
Bowl, 9" d., piecrust rim **75.00**
Butter dish, cov. **75.00**
Cake stand . . . . **75.00 to 85.00**
Celery vase **70.00**
Compote, open, jelly. **40.00**
Compote, cov., 6" d., high stand **85.00**
Compote, open, 6" d., piecrust rim **40.00**
Compote, open, 8" d., piecrust rim,
   high stand **105.00**

Goblet. . . . . 55.00 to 60.00
Goblet, w/engraved flower . . 75.00 to 100.00
Pitcher, water, tankard. . . . 125.00 to 150.00
Pitcher, water, tankard w/engraved
   flowers. 225.00
Sauce dish 19.00
Syrup pitcher w/original top. 215.00
Tumbler 51.00

RIBBED FORGET-ME-NOT

Bread plate, 10¾". 30.00
Creamer . . . . 30.00 to 35.00
Creamer, individual size 33.00
Mug. 40.00
Mustard pot, cov. 45.00
Sugar bowl, cov. 38.00

RIBBED IVY

Butter dish, cov. 120.00
Champagne . . . . 150.00 to 200.00
Compote, open, 8" d., 5" h. 75.00
Compote, open, 8½" d., 7½" h., high
   stand. . . . . 85.00 to 95.00
Creamer, applied handle 145.00
Egg cup 36.00

Ribbed Ivy Goblet

Goblet (ILLUS.). 56.00
Salt dip, open, master size, beaded
   rim. 30.00
Spooner 50.00
Sugar bowl, cov. 100.00 to125.00
Tumbler, water. . . . . 85.00 to 95.00
Tumbler, whiskey. . . . . 125.00 to 150.00
Wine 65.00

ROMAN KEY (Roman Key with Flutes or Ribs)

Celery vase 78.00
Champagne . . . . 95.00 to 100.00
Compote, cov., 7" d. 65.00

Roman Key Creamer

Creamer, applied handle (ILLUS.) 45.00
Decanter w/stopper, qt. 252.00
Egg cup 45.00
Goblet. 46.00
Salt dip, master size 35.00
Spooner 36.00
*Sugar bowl, cov. 125.00
Tumbler, bar. 65.00
Wine 72.00

ROMAN KEY WITH FLUTES OR RIBS - See Roman Key Pattern

ROMAN ROSETTE, EARLY

Honey dish, clear, 4⅛" d., flint 20.00
Honey dish, opalescent, flint,
   4⅛" d. 65.00
Plate, 6" d., medium golden amber. . . 413.00
Plate, 9½" d., clear, flint 248.00
Sauce dish, reddish amber,
   5⅜" d. . . . . 100.00 to 150.00

ROSETTE

Butter dish, cov. 35.00
Cake stand, 8½" to 11" d. 28.00
Celery vase 26.00

Rosette Jelly Compote

Compote, open, jelly, 4½" d., 5" h.
   (ILLUS.). 16.00
Creamer, clear 25.00
Goblet. 29.00
Pitcher, water, tankard. . . . . . 55.00 to 60.00
Plate, 7" d.. 16.00

Plate, 9" d., two-handled 21.00
Salt shaker w/original top, tall 23.00
Spooner 24.00
Wine 25.00

ROYAL CRYSTAL

Bowl, round, flat, 8" d., flared sides,
  clear 12.00
Bread plate, clear 25.00
Cake stand, high standard, clear,
  9" d. 25.00
Cologne bottle w/original stopper,
  ruby-stained, 4 oz. 50.00
Creamer, 5¼" h., ruby-stained 59.00
Cruet w/original stopper, ruby-
  stained, small 395.00
Cruet w/original stopper, 5 oz.,
  clear . . . . 30.00 to 35.00
Pitcher, bulbous, water,½ gal., clear . 115.00
Pitcher, bulbous, milk, 1 qt., ruby-
  stained 250.00
Pitcher, tankard, water, 9½" h.,
  ½ gal., ruby-stained 95.00
Salt shaker w/original top, ruby-
  stained 65.00
Sauce dish, flat, 4" d., ruby-stained . . . 25.00
Spoonholder, ruby-stained 56.00
Sugar bowl, cov., ruby-stained 89.00
Syrup pitcher w/original metal top,
  6" h., ruby-stained 275.00
Tumbler, water, 4" h., 1/3 pt., ruby-
  stained 32.00
Wine, 4" h., clear 35.00
Wine, 4" h., ruby-stained . . . . 60.00 to 65.00

ROYAL IVY (Northwood)

Berry set: master bowl & 3 sauce
  dishes; craquelle, (cranberry &
  vaseline spatter), 4 pcs. 175.00
Bowl, 8" d., craquelle (cranberry &
  vaseline spatter) . . . . 150.00 to 175.00
Bowl, 8" d., frosted rubina crystal 150.00
Bowl, fruit, 9" d., craquelle (cranberry
  & vaseline spatter) 235.00
Bowl, fruit, 9" d., frosted rubina
  crystal 115.00
Butter dish, cov., clear & frosted 120.00
Butter dish, cov., frosted rubina
  crystal 375.00
Creamer, clear & frosted 81.00
Creamer, craquelle (cranberry &
  vaseline spatter) 220.00
Creamer, frosted rubina crystal 210.00
Cruet w/original stopper, craquelle
  (cranberry & vaseline spatter) 703.00
Cruet w/original stopper, frosted
  rubina crystal 410.00

Cruet w/original stopper, rubina
  crystal 310.00
Pickle castor, clear & frosted insert,
  complete w/silver plate frame . . . 125.00
  150.00
Pickle castor, frosted rubina crystal
  insert, complete w/silver plate
  frame 363.00
Pitcher, water, cased spatter
  (cranberry & vaseline w/white
  lining) 338.00
Pitcher, water, craquelle (cranberry &
  vaseline spatter) 375.00
Pitcher, water, frosted rubina crystal . 378.00
Rose bowl, cased spatter (cranberry
  & vaseline w/white
  lining) . . . . 250.00 to 300.00
Rose bowl, frosted rubina crystal 130.00
Rose bowl, rubina crystal 79.00
Salt shaker w/original top, clear &
  frosted 60.00
Salt shaker w/original top, frosted
  rubina crystal 78.00
Sauce dish, craquelle (cranberry &
  vaseline spatter) 58.00
Sauce dish, rubina crystal 35.00
Spooner, clear & frosted 36.00
Spooner, craquelle (cranberry &
  vaseline spatter) 140.00
Sugar bowl, cov., frosted rubina
  crystal 220.00
Sugar bowl, cov., rubina crystal 124.00
Sugar shaker w/original top, frosted
  rubina crystal . . . . 350.00 to 375.00
Syrup pitcher w/original top, cased
  spatter (cranberry & vaseline
  w/white lining) 895.00
Syrup pitcher w/original top, frosted
  rubina crystal 513.00
Toothpick holder, cased spatter
  (cranberry & vaseline w/white
  lining) . . . . 250.00 to 300.00
Toothpick holder, clear & frosted 48.00
Toothpick holder, frosted rubina
  crystal 105.00
Toothpick holder, rubina crystal 83.00
Tumbler, clear & frosted 36.00
Tumbler, frosted rubina crystal 70.00
Water set: pitcher & 5 tumblers;
  cased spatter (cranberry & vaseline
  w/white lining), 6 pcs. 800.00

SCALLOPED TAPE (Jewel Band)

Bread platter 38.00
Cake stand, 9½" d. 32.00
Celery vase, 8" h. 32.00
Compote, cov., 8¼" d., 12" h. 55.00

Scalloped Tape Creamer

Creamer (ILLUS.) 25.00
Egg cup 25.00
Pitcher, water, 9¼" h. 55.00
Wine, blue 55.00
Wine, clear 15.00

SHERATON

Bread platter, amber, 8 x 10". 40.00
Bread platter, clear, 8 x 10". . 25.00 to 30.00
Cake stand, clear, 10½" d. 42.00
Celery vase 25.00

Sheraton Compote

Compote, open, 8" d., high stand ,
   clear (ILLUS.) 33.00
Creamer, amber 35.00
Creamer, blue 42.00
Goblet, amber. 40.00
Goblet, clear 26.00
Pitcher, milk, clear 39.00
Plate, 7" sq., amber. 20.00
Plate, 8½" sq., clear 20.00
Relish, handled, blue 23.00
Relish, handled, clear. 16.00
Spooner, amber 33.00
Wine, amber 45.00
Wine, clear 26.00

SHOSHONE

Bowl, master berry, ruby-stained 110.00
Bowl, 8" d., ruffled, green 23.00
Butter dish, cov., clear w/gold trim. . . . 70.00
Cake stand, clear 45.00
Cake stand, green 48.00

Celery vase, ruby-stained. 107.00
Compote, jelly. 30.00
Compote, open, 7 x 9", scalloped
   rim 38.00
Cruet w/original stopper, clear 57.00
Cruet w/original stopper, green 135.00
Goblet, clear w/gold trim . . . . 80.00 to 85.00
Plate, 7½" d., green 19.00
Relish, 7½" l. 30.00
Toothpick holder, clear w/gold trim . . . 30.00
Tumblers, clear w/gold, set of 4 . . . . . . 80.00
Wine, ruby-stained 48.00

SKILTON (Early Oregon)

Bowl, 7¾" d., 2½" h. 13.00
Butter dish, cov., ruby-stained. 90.00
Compote, open, 8½" d., low stand,
   clear. 24.00
Decanter, whiskey 29.00
Goblet. 32.00
Goblet, ruby-stained 75.00
Pitcher, milk, ruby-stained 110.00
Pitcher, water, tankard, ruby-
   stained. 115.00
Spooner, ruby-stained 45.00
Sugar bowl, cov., ruby-stained. 83.00
Tumbler, ruby-stained 42.00
Wine 34.00

SPIREA BAND

Bowl, 8" oval, flat, amber 18.00
Bowl, 8" oval, flat, blue 36.00
Butter dish, cov., clear. 45.00
Cake stand, amber, 8½" d. 45.00
Cake stand, blue, 10½" d. 80.00
Celery vase, blue 60.00
Celery vase, clear. 25.00
Creamer, amber 29.00
Creamer, clear 26.00
Goblet, amber . . . . 35.00 to 45.00
Goblet, blue . . . . 40.00 to 45.00
Goblet, canary 40.00
Pitcher, water, clear 45.00
Platter, 8½ x 10½", blue 26.00
Relish, amber, 5½ x 9" 17.00
Relish, blue, 4½ x 7". 33.00
Relish, blue, 5½ x 8". 15.00
Sauce dish, flat or footed,
   amber . . . . 6.00 to 12.00
Sauce dish, flat or footed, blue. 12.00
Spooner, amber 30.00
Spooner, canary. 30.00
Sugar bowl, cov., clear. 28.00
Wine, amber 30.00
Wine, blue. . . . . 30.00 to 35.00
Wine, clear . . . . 15.00 to 20.00

SQUARE PANES - See Post Pattern

STEDMAN

Champagne 80.00
Creamer . . . . 80.00 to 90.00
Egg cup 20.00
Goblet. 65.00
Sauce dish, flat. 14.00
Wine 43.00

STIPPLED CHERRY

Bread platter 26.00
Butter dish, cov. . . . . 60.00 to 65.00
Pitcher, water 35.00
Plate, 6" d.. 17.00

STIPPLED FORGET-ME-NOT

Cake stand, 8" to 9" d. 73.00
Compote, cov., 6" d., high stand 80.00
Compote, cov., 7" d., high stand 85.00
Cup & saucer 27.00
Goblet. . . . . 40.00 to 45.00
Mug. 25.00
Pitcher, water. . . . . 50.00 to 75.00
Plate, 7" d., w/baby in tub reaching
    for ball on floor center . . . . . 60.00 to 65.00
Plate, 9" d., w/kitten center, handled. . . 65.00
Plate, 9" d., w/star center, handled. . . . 55.00
Plate, 11" d., w/stork center 92.00
Relish 13.00

Stippled Forget-Me-Not Wine

Wine (ILLUS.) 35.00

STIPPLED GRAPE & FESTOON

Butter dish, cov., w/clear leaf. 65.00
Celery vase 44.00
Compote, 8" d., low stand 29.00
Compote, 8" d., low stand, w/clear
    leaf. 110.00
Creamer, clear 34.00
Goblet. . . . . 20.00 to 25.00

Pitcher, water 95.00
Spooner 30.00
Spooner, w/clear leaf 28.00
Sugar bowl, cov., w/clear leaf 70.00

SWAN

Celery vase, etched 38.00
Compote, cov., w/swan finial, 8" d.. . . 365.00
Compote, open, 8½" h. 85.00
Compote, open, 10" d., 7½" h. 165.00

Swan Creamer

Creamer, clear (ILLUS.) . . . . . 50.00 to 60.00
*Creamer, milk white. 33.00
Cup, handled. 35.00
Marmalade jar, cov. 130.00
Pitcher, water. . . . . 185.00 to 200.00
Sauce dish, flat or footed, clear 21.00
Spooner, clear 55.00

TACOMA (Jeweled Diamond & Fan)

Banana dish, flat 35.00
Bowl, 8½" d., 5" h., ruby-stained 48.00
Butter dish, cov., amber-stained 130.00
Celery vase 23.00
Creamer 60.00
Pitcher, water, ruby-stained 120.00
Punch cup 22.00
Sauce dish, ruby-stained 24.00
Toothpick holder. . . . . 30.00 to 35.00
Toothpick holder ruby-stained 95.00
Wine 18.00

TENNESSEE (Jewel & Crescent)

Bread plate. 50.00
Butter dish, cov.. . . . . 85.00
Cake stand, 8½" d., high stand 32.00
Cake stand, 10½" d., high
    stand . . . . 60.00 to 70.00
Celery vase 70.00
Compote, open, 8" d., flared rim,
    shallow round bowl, high stand 48.00
Creamer 60.00
Mug. 60.00
Pitcher, milk, 1 qt.. . . . . 100.00
Relish tray 20.00

Salt shaker w/original top 95.00
Sauce dish, flat, round 12.00
Toothpick holder 75.00
Wine . . . . 100.00 to 125.00

TEXAS BULL'S EYE (Bull's Eye Variant)

Champagne 35.00
Cordial 28.00
Goblet 37.00
Pitcher, water, ½ gal. 55.00
Tumbler 25.00
Wine 23.00

THREE FACE

*Butter dish, cov.,
  engraved . . . . 200.00 to 225.00
*Butter dish, cov., plain 190.00
*Cake stand, 8" to 10½" d. . 175.00 to 250.00
Claret, engraved 265.00
*Compote, cov., 6" d., high
  stand . . . . 150.00 to 175.00
Compote, cov., 7" d., high stand 285.00
Compote, cov., 8" d., high stand 295.00
Compote, open, 6" d., high stand 80.00
Compote, open, 8½" d., high
  stand . . . . 90.00 to 100.00
Compote, open, 9½" d., high stand,
  engraved 375.00
Compote, open, 9½" d., high stand,
  plain 168.00
Creamer 93.00

Three Face Creamer

*Creamer w/mask spout (ILLUS.) . . . 150.00
*Goblet, engraved 150.00
*Goblet, plain . . . . 40.00 to 45.00
*Lamp, kerosene-type, pedestal
  base, 8" h. . . . . 200.00 to 250.00
Marmalade jar, cov. 325.00
Pitcher, milk 750.00
Pitcher, water 575.00
*Salt dip, individual 43.00
*Salt shaker w/original top 65.00
*Sauce dish, 4" d. 35.00
*Spooner, engraved . . . . . . 120.00 to 125.00

*Spooner, plain 70.00
*Sugar bowl, cov. . . . . . . 125.00 to 150.00
*Sugar shaker, w/original top 155.00
*Wine 225.00

THREE PANEL

Bowl, 7" d., footed, blue 30.00
Bowl, 7" d., footed, canary 32.00
Bowl, 9" d., footed, canary 45.00
Bowl, 9" d., footed, clear 23.00
Bowl, 10" d., blue 65.00
Bowl, 10" d., canary 40.00
Butter dish, cov., canary 50.00
Celery vase, canary 55.00
Celery vase, clear 35.00
Compote, open, 7" d., low stand,
  amber 32.00
Compote, open, 7" d., low stand,
  canary 28.00
Compote, open, 8½" d., low stand,
  blue 40.00
Compote, open, 9" d., canary 43.00
Compote, open, 9" d., 4¼" h.,
  amber 40.00
Compote, open, 10" d., low stand,
  blue 65.00
Creamer, amber 33.00
Creamer, blue 43.00
Creamer, canary 30.00
Creamer, clear 20.00
Cruet w/original stopper 155.00
*Goblet, amber 43.00
*Goblet, blue 33.00
*Goblet, canary 36.00
*Goblet, clear 22.00

Three Panel Mug

Mug, blue, small (ILLUS.) 40.00
Mug, clear, small 30.00
Sauce dish, footed, amber 17.00
Sauce dish, footed, blue 20.00
Sauce dish, footed, canary 18.00
Sauce dish, footed, clear 12.00
Spooner, amber 30.00
Spooner, blue 38.00
Spooner, canary 35.00
Spooner, clear 12.00
Sugar bowl, cov., blue 75.00

Sugar bowl, cov., canary 55.00
Table set, clear, 4 pcs. 175.00
Tumbler, blue 40.00

THUMBPRINT, EARLY (Bakewell, Pears & Co.'s "Argus")

Bitters bottle 150.00
*Butter dish, cov. 115.00
*Cake stand, 8" to 9½" d. 275.00
*Celery vase, plain base. 110.00

Early Thumbprint Celery Vase

Celery vase, scalloped rim, pattern in
  base (ILLUS.) 135.00
Champagne 145.00
Compote, open, 5" d., low stand,
  scalloped rim 72.00
Compote, open, 7½" d., low stand 55.00
*Compote, open, 8" d., high stand . . . 100.00
Compote, open, 8½" d., high stand,
  scalloped rim 275.00
*Creamer 100.00
*Goblet, baluster stem 67.00
Goblet, plain stem. 21.00
Pitcher, milk 90.00

Early Thumbprint Pitcher

*Pitcher, water, 8¼" h. (ILLUS.) 350.00
*Sauce dish, clear 15.00
Sauce dish, milk white 75.00
Spooner, non-flint. 45.00
*Sugar bowl, cov. 55.00
*Tumbler, footed. 38.00
*Wine, baluster stem. 60.00

TRIPLE TRIANGLE

Butter dish, cov., handled, ruby-
  stained. 85.00
*Goblet, ruby-stained 57.00
Mug, clear. 30.00
Mug, ruby-stained 35.00
Pitcher, water, 8" h.,½ gal., ruby-
  stained. 125.00
Spoonholder, handled, clear 25.00
Spoonholder, handled, ruby-stained . . 33.00
Sugar bowl, cov., clear. 40.00
Sugar bowl, cov., ruby-stained. 50.00
Tumbler, water, ruby-stained 35.00
*Wine, clear. 40.00
*Wine, ruby-stained. 50.00

TULIP WITH SAWTOOTH

Celery vase, flint. 85.00
Celery vase, non-flint 45.00
Champagne, flint 165.00
Champagne, non-flint. 75.00
Compote, cov., 6" d., low stand, flint . . 75.00

Tulip With Sawtooth Compote

Compote, cov., 7" d., 12½" h.
  (ILLUS.) 248.00
Compote, open, 7" d., low stand,
  non-flint 67.00
Compote, open, 8" d., low stand,
  flint. 75.00
Compote, open, 9" d., 7⅜" h., flint 78.00
Compote, open, 9" d., 10" h., flint. . . . 130.00
Cruet w/original stopper, flint,
  8⅝" h. 165.00
Decanter w/bar lip, flint, pt. 123.00
Egg cup, flint. 35.00

*Goblet, flint 50.00
Goblet, non-flint 26.00
Pitcher, 9¾" h., flint 250.00
Salt dip, master size, scalloped rim,
   flint. 32.00
Salt dip, open, non-flint. 15.00
Salt dip, cov., flint, 5½" h. 285.00
Tumbler, bar, flint 80.00
Tumbler, flint. 45.00
Tumbler, footed, flint. 61.00
Wine, flint 45.00
*Wine, non-flint 23.00

TWO PANEL (Daisy in Panel)

Bowl, cov., 7" oval, canary 75.00
Bowl, 6 x 8" oval, blue 39.00
Bowl, 7½ x 9" oval, apple green 36.00
Butter dish, cov., canary 50.00
Celery vase, canary 48.00
Celery vase, clear. 30.00
Compote, cov., high stand, apple
   green. 135.00
Compote, cov., high stand, blue. 85.00
Compote, open, 9" oval, 4" h., apple
   green. 60.00
Compote, open, 9" oval, 4" h.,
   canary 45.00
Creamer, amber 36.00
Creamer, apple green. 45.00
Creamer, blue. 45.00
Creamer, clear 23.00

Two Panel Goblet

*Goblet, amber (ILLUS.). 34.00
*Goblet, apple green. 32.00
*Goblet, blue. 41.00
*Goblet, canary. 40.00
*Goblet, clear 20.00
Pitcher, water, blue. 90.00
Relish, amber 17.00
Relish, blue. 30.00

Salt dip, individual size, amber. 14.00
Salt dip, individual size, apple green . . 24.00
Salt dip, individual size, canary 9.00
Salt dip, master size, apple
   green. 28.00
Sauce dish, flat or footed,
   amber 10.00
Sauce dish, flat or footed, apple
   green. 12.00
Sauce dish, flat or footed, canary. . . . 17.00
Sauce dish, flat or footed, clear 10.00
Spooner, amber 36.00
Spooner, blue. 43.00
Spooner, canary. 33.00
Sugar bowl, cov., apple green 55.00
Tray, water, apple green, 10 x 15"
   oval 68.00
Tray, water, blue, 10 x 15" oval. 60.00
Tumbler, canary 40.00
Waste bowl, amber 36.00
*Wine, amber 35.00
*Wine, apple green 38.00
*Wine, blue 40.00
*Wine, canary 35.00
*Wine, clear. 29.00

VANDYKE - See Daisy & Button with "V" Ornament Pattern

WAFFLE

Celery vase 85.00
Champagne . . . . 120.00 to 140.00
Creamer, applied handle 125.00
Goblet. 95.00
Sugar bowl, cov. 125.00
Tumbler, bar. 95.00
Waste bowl, ruffled top. 45.00
Wine 120.00

WAFFLE AND THUMBPRINT

Bowl, 6 x 8½", flint 45.00
Celery vase, flint. 138.00
Champagne, flint 130.00
Claret, flint. 110.00
Compote, open, 6" d., 6" h., flint. . . . 163.00
Decanter w/bar lip, flint, pt. 120.00
Decanter w/bar lip, qt. 95.00
Decanter w/matching stopper,
   pt. 325.00
Egg cup, flint. 53.00
Goblet, flint 78.00
Lamp, w/original two-tube burner,
   hand-type w/applied handle, flint,
   3" h. 135.00

Waffle and Thumbprint Spooner

Spooner, flint (ILLUS.) 83.00
Sugar bowl, cov., flint. 195.00
Sweetmeat dish, cov.. . . . . 113.00
Tray, 8¼" l. 66.00
Tumbler, bar, flint 110.00
Wine, flint 82.00

WASHINGTON, EARLY

Butter dish, cov., flint. 55.00

Early Washington Celery Vase

Celery vase, flint (ILLUS.) 139.00
Decanter w/original stopper, flint,
  qt. 210.00
Egg cup, flint. 58.00
Goblet, flint 70.00
Salt dip, individual size, flint 20.00
Salt dip, master size, flat, round, flint . . 40.00

WEDDING RING - See Double Wedding Ring Pattern

WESTMORELAND (Gillinder's)

Celery tray 38.00
Celery vase 38.00
Cologne bottles, original stoppers,
  pr. 85.00

Compote, cov., low (footed) 28.00
Compote, open, straight rim, 7-9" d.,
  high stand 85.00
Creamer, ... 25.00
Cruet w/original stopper, 5" h. 35.00
Egg cup 35.00
Goblet 50.00
Lamp, finger, one-handle, 3½" h.
  (no shade) 115.00
Lamp, 8½" h.. . . . . 125.00
Pitcher, tall, scalloped rim 65.00
Water bottle, 8¼" h. 45.00

WHEAT & BARLEY

Bowl, open, 7" d., clear. 17.00
Bread plate, amber. 30.00
Bread plate, clear. 33.00
Cake stand, blue, 8" d. 55.00
Cake stand, amber, 8" to 10" d. 44.00
Cake stand, clear, 8" to 10" d. 38.00
Compote, cov., 8½" d., high
  stand 48.00
Compote, open, jelly, amber 30.00
Compote, open, jelly, blue 33.00
Compote, open, jelly, clear. 25.00
Compote, open, 8¼" d., amber 65.00
Creamer, amber 45.00
Creamer, blue. 55.00
Creamer, clear 21.00
***Goblet,** amber 41.00
***Goblet,** blue. 65.00
***Goblet,** clear 43.00
Mug, amber. 33.00
Mug, clear. 22.00
Pitcher, milk, amber 58.00
Pitcher, milk, clear 45.00
Pitcher, water, amber. 93.00
Plate, 6" d., clear. 30.00
Plate, 9" d., closed handles, amber . . . 43.00
Salt shaker w/original top, blue 38.00
Sauce dish, flat, handled, amber 12.00
Sauce dish, footed, amber 12.00
Spooner, amber 40.00
Spooner, clear 28.00
Sugar bowl, cov., blue 65.00
Sugar bowl, cov., clear. 38.00
Tumbler, amber 30.00
Tumbler canary 28.00
Tumbler, clear 20.00

WILLOW OAK

Bowl, cov., 7" d., flat. 49.00
Bowl, open, 7" d., amber 14.00

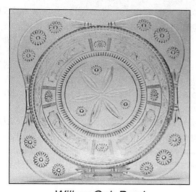

Willow Oak Bowl

Bowl, open, 7" d., clear (ILLUS.) 32.00
Bread plate, amber, 9" d. 40.00
Bread plate, clear, 9" d. 35.00
Bread plate, amber, 11" d. 40.00
Bread plate, clear, 11" d. 32.00
Butter dish, cov., amber. 65.00
Butter dish, cov., clear. 50.00
Cake stand, amber, 8" to 10" d. 61.00
Cake stand, blue, 8" to 10" d. 65.00
Cake stand, clear, 8" to 10" d. 35.00
Celery vase, amber 45.00
Celery vase, blue 125.00
Celery vase, clear. 48.00
Compote, cov., 6" h. 75.00
Compote, cov., 8" d. 65.00
Compote, open, 6" d., scalloped top . . 40.00
Compote, open, 7" d., high stand,
 clear. 26.00
Compote, open, 8" d., low stand,
 amber 53.00
Creamer, blue. 65.00
Creamer, canary. 45.00
Creamer, clear 35.00
Goblet, amber. 43.00
Goblet, blue 48.00
Goblet, clear 33.00
Pitcher, milk, amber 85.00
Pitcher, milk, clear 35.00
Pitcher, water, amber 70.00
Plate, 9" d. handled, amber. 41.00
Plate, 9" d. handled, blue 45.00
Plate, 9" d. handled, clear. 28.00
Salt shaker w/original top, amber. . . . 40.00
Sauce dish, clear, flat or footed, each . 10.00
Spooner, blue. 50.00
Spooner, clear 40.00
Sugar bowl, cov., clear. 53.00
Tray, water, amber, 10½" d. 125.00
Tray, water, blue, 10½" d. 58.00
Tray, water, clear, 10½" d. 38.00
Tumbler, blue 65.00

Tumbler, clear 42.00
Water set: pitcher, tray & 5 goblets;
 clear, 7 pcs. 285.00

X-RAY

Berry set: 8" d., master bowl & 6
 sauce dishes; emerald green,
 7 pcs. 155.00
Bowl, berry, 8" d., beaded edge,
 clear. 85.00
Butter dish, cov., amethyst w/gold. . . 250.00
Butter dish, cov., emerald green
 w/gold 125.00
Celery vase, clear w/gold 89.00
Celery vase, emerald green 100.00
Compote, cov., high stand, emerald
 green. 65.00
Compote, jelly, clear. 42.00
Creamer, breakfast size, emerald
 green w/gold 60.00
Cruet w/original stopper, emerald
 green w/gold 115.00

X-Ray Pitcher

Pitcher, water, 9½" h., clear,
 w/gold, ½ gal. (ILLUS.). 50.00
Salt shaker w/original top,
 amethyst 50.00
Salt shaker w/original top, clear. . . . 19.00
Salt shaker w/original top, emerald
 green. 75.00
Sauce dish, clear, 4½" d. 12.00
Sauce dish, emerald green, 4½" d. . . . 23.00
Spooner, emerald green w/gold 45.00
Sugar bowl, cov., amethyst w/gold . . 150.00
Sugar bowl, cov., breakfast size,
 emerald green w/gold 60.00
Sugar bowl, cov., emerald green
 w/gold 55.00
Syrup pitcher, clear w/gold 225.00
Toothpick holder, clear 30.00
Toothpick holder, emerald green 53.00
Tumbler, emerald green. 25.00

PEACH BLOW

Several types of glass lumped together by collectors as Peach Blow were produced by half a dozen glasshouses. Hobbs, Brockunier & Co., Wheeling, West Virginia, made Peach Blow as a plated ware that shaded from red at the top to yellow at the bottom and is referred to as Wheeling Peach Blow. Mt. Washington Glass Works produced an homogeneous Peach Blow shading from a rose color at the top to pale blue in the lower portion. The New England Glass Works' Peach Blow, called Wild Rose, shaded from rose at the top to white. Gunderson-Pairpoint Co. also reproduced some of the Mt. Washington Peach Blow in the early 1950s and some glass of a somewhat similar type was made by Steuben Glass Works, Thomas Webb & Sons and Stevens & Williams of England. New England Peach Blow is one-layered glass and the English is two-layered.

Another single layered shaded art glass was produced early in this century by the New Martinsville Glass Mfg. Co. Originally called "Muranese," collectors today refer to it as "New Martinsville Peach Blow."

MT. WASHINGTON

Tumbler, cylindrical, soft pink shading to soft blue, glossy finish, 3¾" h. $2,530.00

NEW ENGLAND

Creamer, squatty bulbous lightly ribbed body tapering slightly to a wide flat rim w/pinched spout, applied handle, decorated w/leafy branches of asters, 2½" h. 495.00

Finger bowls, round w/upright crimped & ruffled sides, satin finish, 5¼" d., 2½" h., pr. 385.00

Tumbler, cylindrical, satin finish, 3¾" h. 193.00

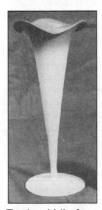

New England Lily-form Vase

Vase, 9½" h., lily-form w/a round foot & tricorner rolled rim, attributed to New England Glass Co. (ILLUS.) . . **374.00**

Whiskey tumbler, cylindrical, satin finish, 3½" h. **330.00**

SANDWICH

Cruet w/facet-cut amber ball stopper, ovoid body tapering to a cylindrical neck w/scissor-cut spouted rim, shading from pale pink below to soft white above, applied amber branch handle, 6" h. **770.00**

WEBB

Cologne bottle w/silver screw cap, spherical body decorated w/delicate gold enameled prunus blossoms & a flying butterfly, cased in white, hallmarked cap, Thomas Webb, England, 5" h. **748.00**

Webb Peach Blow Vase

Vase, 3½" h., 2⅝" d., wide bulbous ovoid body tapering to a cushion foot & w/a short, widely flaring neck, deep rose shaded to pale pink & decorated w/heavy gilt daisy-like flowers, leaves & vines, one dragonfly, glossy finish (ILLUS.) **295.00**

Vase, 6" h., baluster-form w/a short neck w/deeply ruffled rolled rim pulled into four points, deep pink shaded to pale pink & decorated overall w/gold florals w/butterflies, white lining. **220.00**

Vase, bottle-form, 10" h., footed squatty bulbous body w/the rounded shoulder centered by a tall slender slightly flaring 'stick' neck, the sides finely enamel-decorated w/a purple & rust butterfly & insect above clusters of white flowers & green leafy branches **1,650.00**

Vase, 12½" h., bottle-form, ring-footed bulbous body w/a wide shoulder tapering to a slender, slightly flaring 'stick' neck **176.00**

WHEELING

Carafe, pyramidal body tapering to a slightly flaring cylindrical neck w/a molded ring around the base, 8" h. . **935.00**

Wheeling Peach Blow Cruet

Cruet w/original facet-cut amber ball stopper, bulbous ovoid body tapering to a short neck w/high arched spout, dark reddish amber applied reeded handle, 7" h. (ILLUS.). **880.00**
Pitcher, 7½" h., bulbous ovoid body tapering to a squared, rolled neck, applied amber handle, glossy finish **825.00**
Syrup pitcher w/original hinged metal lid, footed tapering cylindrical body, applied amber handle, fine even coloring **3,520.00**
Tumbler, cylindrical, good even color, 3¾" h. **275.00**

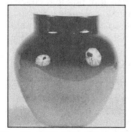

Wheeling Peach Blow Vase

Vase, 6¼" h., bulbous ovoid body w/a wide rounded shoulder centered by a wide, short cylindrical neck, glossy finish (ILLUS.) **1,100.00**
Vase, 7" h., double-gourd form, a large & smaller spherical section below a small cylindrical neck w/flared rim, glossy finish **3,300.00**
Vase, 7½" h., double-gourd form, a large & smaller spherical section below a small flaring neck, satin finish **1,265.00**

Peach Blow "Morgan Vase"

Vase, 7¾" h., "Morgan Vase," slender ovoid shouldered body w/slender cylindrical ringed neck w/flared rim, glossy finish, set in original glossy amber gargoyle base, 2 pcs. (ILLUS.) **1,705.00**
Vase, 8¼" h., bottle-form, footrim below the bulbous body tapering to a very slender tall 'stick' neck, glossy finish. **495.00**

PELOTON

Made in Bohemia, Germany and England in the late 19th century, this glassware is characterized by threads or filaments of glass rolled into the glass body of the objects in random patterns. Some of these wares were then further decorated.

Bowl, 6" w., 4¾" h., deep rounded clear rib-molded body pulled into a squared rim w/four points, cased in white, applied w/pink, yellow & blue strands, applied clear petal feet & applied band of rigaree around the rim **$440.00**
Celery vase, scalloped rim & exquisite enameled decoration, clear w/raspberry strings of glass applied to the surface, enameled w/green foliage & white & yellow flower w/a bumble bee flying above. **335.00**
Cracker jar, cov., bulbous spherical rib-molded body, blue exterior w/multicolored strands, satin finish, white interior, silver plate rim, cover & bail handle, 7¾" h. **1,070.00**

Peloton Cracker Jar

Cracker jar, cov., bulbous spherical
rib-molded body, deep pink exterior
w/multicolored strands of white,
rose & yellow, satin finish, white
interior, resilvered rim, bail handle
& cover, overall 7¾" h. (ILLUS.).. **1,070.00**

Cruet w/clear facet-cut stopper,
ovoid melon-lobed swirled blue
body tapering to a short cylindrical
neck w/tricorner rim, applied clear
handle, overall pink, white, yellow
& blue threading, 7" h............ **550.00**

Peloton Pitcher

Pitcher, 6¼" h., 4" w., squared
bulbous body tapering to a
cylindrical neck w/pinched spout,
multicolored strands embedded in
overshot crystal, applied clear
handle (ILLUS.)............... **200.00**

Vase, 6½" h., lavender pink bulbous
ovoid body tapering to a cylindrical
neck w/a widely flaring rolled &
crimped tricorner rim, clear ribbed
cased surface w/scattered yellow,
pink & blue strands **275.00**

PHOENIX

*This ware was made by the Phoenix Glass
Co. of Beaver County, Pennsylvania, which
produced various types of glass from the 1880s.
One special type that attracts collectors now is a
molded ware with a vague resemblance to cameo
in its "sculptured" decoration. Similar pieces
with relief-molded designs were produced by the
Consolidated Lamp & Glass Co. (which see) and
care must be taken to differentiate between the
two companies' wares. Some Consolidated molds
were moved to the Phoenix plant in the mid-
1930s but later returned and used again at
Consolidated. These pieces we will list under
"Consolidated."*

Phoenix "Wild Geese" Vase

Vase, 9½" h., 11½" w., pillow-type,
Wild Geese patt., white birds
against a dusty rose-colored
ground (ILLUS.) ...... **$225.00 to 250.00**

Vase, 10" h., Madonna patt., relief-
molded pearlized bust on a cream
ground...................... **100.00**

Vase, 11½" h., Dancing Girl patt.,
relief-molded white dancing girls,
background in Wedgwood blue.... **390.00**

PIGEON BLOOD

*This name refers to the color of this glass, a
deep blood-red. It was popular in the late 19th
century and was featured in a number of mold-
blown patterns.*

Cracker jar, cov., Florette patt., silver
plate rim, cover & bail handle **$275.00**

Pitcher, water, Bulging Loops patt.... **325.00**

**Salt & pepper shakers w/original
lids,** Bulging Loops patt., pr....... **133.00**

**Salt & pepper shakers w/original
tops,** Globule patt., pr. **160.00**

Spooner, Torquay patt.............. **150.00**

Sweetmeat dish, cov., Satin Heart
patt., enameled decoration, original
silver plate collar, cover &
overhead bail handle............ **235.00**

Decorated Pigeon Blood Vase

Vase, 4¾" h., 4⅛" d., blown bulbous
nearly spherical body w/a squared
& deeply fluted rim, heavy gold
vining blossoms & leaves around
the body & a gold rim band
(ILLUS.)..................... **165.00**
Water set: pitcher & five tumblers;
Bulging Loops patt., the set....... **500.00**

PILLAR-MOLDED

*This heavily ribbed glassware was produced
by blowing glass into full-sized ribbed molds
and then finishing it by hand. The technique
evolved from earlier "pattern moulding" used on
glass since ancient times, but in pillar-molded
glass the ribs are very heavy and prominent.
Most examples found in this country were
produced in the Pittsburgh, Pennsylvania, area
from around 1850 to 1870, but similar English-
made wares made before and after this period
are also available. Most American items were
made from clear flint glass and colored examples
or pieces with colored strands in the ribs are rare
and highly prized. Some collectors refer to this
as "steamboat" glass believing that it was made
to be used on American riverboats, but most
likely it was used anywhere that a sturdy,
relatively inexpensive glassware was needed,
such as taverns and hotels.*

Bar bottle, eight-rib, tapering
pyramidal form w/a heavy neck ring
& bar lip, probably Pittsburgh,
cobalt blue, 10⅛" h.......... **$2,090.00**
Bar bottle, clear w/cobalt edging
along the ribs, Pittsburgh, mid-
19th c., 11⅝" h. (minor chips)..... **489.00**
Candlesticks, eight-rib, bulbous
tapering ribbed standard fitted at
the top w/silver plated socket
liners, the standard resting on an
applied thick solid ball attached to
a round pressed, stepped ring foot
w/a design of narrow diamonds on
the underside, the socket fitted w/a
tall tulip-form frosted & engraved
shade decorated w/outlining of

large flowers & leaves between
narrow upper & lower blossom-
engraved bands, some light flaking
along edges of bases, shallow
slightly disfiguring chip on rim
of one shade, clear, overall
20½" h., pr................. **1,100.00**
Celery vase, twelve-rib, the tall bell-
form bowl swirled & widely flaring
at the rim, raised on an applied
knobbed stem on a thick disc foot,
clear, 8⅛" h. **275.00**

Rare Pillar-Molded Pieces

Celery vase, eight-rib, tall tulip-form
bowl w/heavy ribbing & flared,
scalloped rim, on compressed
baluster stem & disc foot, blue
opalescent w/presentation gilding
between the ribs, polished pontil,
9½" h. (ILLUS. left)........... **10,230.00**
Celery vase, eight-rib, tall waisted
tulip-form bowl w/a widely flaring &
flattened scalloped rim, raised on
an applied cylindrical pedestal on
an applied disc foot w/a polished
pontil, Pittsburgh, ca. 1845-70,
deep fiery opalescent, 9¾" h..... **4,290.00**
Celery vase, eight-rib, tall cylindrical
tulip-form bowl w/a deeply ruffled
rim above the ribs alternating
w/vertical molded swag bands, on
an applied waisted hollow stem &
thick applied foot, clear, 10¼" h.... **209.00**
Celery vase, eight-rib, tall tulip-form
bowl w/a flared rim, attached by
two large wafers to a pressed
hexagonal base, clear, 10½" h.
(two chips on points of base)..... **209.00**
Compote, open, 10⅛" d., 9" h., eight-
rib, deep bowl w/a widely flaring
flattened rim w/three tooled bands,
raised on an applied solid baluster-
form pedestal on an applied heavy
disc foot w/a polished pontil,
Pittsburgh, ca. 1840, clear........ **715.00**
Decanter w/bar lip, eight-rib,
tapering triangular form w/neck
ring, medium cornflower blue,
10½" h...................... **2,200.00**

Decanter w/bar lip, eight-rib,
tapering triangular form w/neck
ring, sapphire blue, 10½" h. **2,475.00**
Decanter w/bar lip, eight-rib,
tapering triangular form w/neck ring
& flattened applied flaring mouth,
flattened ribbing, deep amethyst,
10⅝" h. **3,300.00**
Decanter w/bar lip, eight-rib,
tapering triangular form w/double-
ring neck, flared mouth above a
thin ring, probably Pittsburgh, steel
blue, 10¾" h. **2,090.00**
Decanter w/bar lip, eight-rib,
cylindrical body w/a rounded
shoulder to the tall, slender twisted
neck topped by a thick bar lip,
probably Pittsburgh, canary yellow,
12" h. **1,650.00**
Decanter w/handle, eight-rib,
tapering triangular form w/a thick
applied neck ring flanked by thinner
applied rings below the short
cylindrical neck, an applied hollow
strap handle w/curled end,
amethystine tint, 9⅛" h. (trace of
haze on interior bottom) **770.00**
Decanter w/original stopper, eight-
rib, pronounced waisted cylindrical
body w/each rib applied w/a blue
band ending at the shoulder, thick
applied clear shoulder ring below
the cylindrical neck w/a flattened
flaring rim, fitted w/a period
pressed umbrella stopper,
overall 12¼" h. **825.00**
Pitcher, 5¾" h., eight-rib, opaque white
cased in clear, bulbous tapering body
w/an in-body twist tapering to the
broad spout, applied strap handle
w/curled end, check at handle
(ILLUS. right previous page) **4,510.00**
Pitcher, 9½" h., eight-rib, gently
tapering cylindrical body w/a wide,
high arched spout, applied solid
strap handle w/"pulled feather" &
end curl, clear **330.00**
Sugar bowl, cov., eight-rib, bulbous
ovoid body tapering to a galleried
rim, applied solid foot, swirled
tapering ribbed steeple cover w/ball
finial, clear, 4½" d., 7½" h. **1,540.00**
Sugar bowl, cov., eight-rib, ovoid
body w/a wide galleried rim raised
on an applied waisted pedestal w/a
round foot, pyramidal ribbed cover
w/a large knob finial, clear, overall
10" h. (minute nick on rim) **2,040.00**
**Syrup jug w/original metal collar &
hinged lid,** eight-rib, footed ovoid
body tapering to a ringed collar,
applied strap handle w/end curl,
polished pontil, clear, 8" h. **468.00**

Syrup pitcher w/hinged metal lid,
twelve-rib, tapering pear-shaped
body on an applied smooth foot,
applied strap handle w/end curl,
clear, 6¾" h. **440.00**

POMONA

*First produced by the New England Glass
Company under a patent received by Joseph
Locke in 1885, Pomona has a frosted ground on
clear glass decorated with mineral stains, most
frequently amber-yellow, sometimes pale blue.
Some pieces bore smooth etched floral
decorations highlighted with staining. Two types
of Pomona were made. The first Locke patent
covered a technique whereby the piece was first
covered with an acid resistant coating which was
then needle-carved with thousands of minute
criss-crossing lines. The piece was then dipped
into acid which cut into the etched lines giving
the finished piece a notable "brilliance."*

*A cheaper method, covered by a second Locke
patent on June 15, 1886, was accomplished by
rolling the glass piece in particles of acid-
resistant material which were picked up by it.
The glass was then etched by acid which
attacked areas not protected by the resistant
particles. A favorite design on Pomona was the
cornflower.*

Cracker jar, cov., bulbous ovoid body
w/fitted domed cover w/clear ball
finial, amber-stained etched
acanthus leaf border trim, raised on
applied amber wishbone feet & w/a
band of amber wishbones around
the cover finial, 1st patent, 10" h.
(chip on base & finial trim) **$385.00**
Pitcher, tankard, 9" h., tall slender
slightly tapering body w/a pinched
rim spout & applied handle,
Diamond Quilted patt. w/plain rim
band etched w/acanthus leaves,
1st patent **358.00**

Pomona Punch Cup

Punch cup, rounded body w/amber-
stained rim & applied handle, blue
cornflower decoration, 1st patent,
2⅝" d., 2¾" h. (ILLUS.) **150.00**

Vase, 3¾" h., ovoid body w/ruffled top, on applied amber wishbone feet, 1st patent **138.00**

Vase, 4½" h., shouldered body w/applied rigaree collar below ruffled rim, Inverted Thumbprint patt., 1st patent **77.00**

QUEZAL

In 1901, Martin Bach and Thomas Johnson , who had worked for Louis Tiffany, opened a competing glassworks in Brooklyn, New York. The Quezal Art Glass and Decorating Co. produced wares closely resembling those of Tiffany until the plant's closing in 1925.

Quezal

Quezal Mark

Bowl, 8" d., 4½" h., deep rounded flat-rimmed bowl raised on a trumpet foot, orangish gold iridescent ground decorated on the exterior w/iridescent royal blue pulled swirls, signed (internal heat line in bottom above base) **$550.00**

Decorative Quezal Compote

Compote, open, 5½" h., wide squatty bulbous body tapering to a short flaring crimped & ruffled neck, raised on a tall widely flaring funnel foot, opal white decorated w/three broad green leaves interspersed w/gold tracery, iridescent gold interior, signed on base (ILLUS.) **2,415.00**

Finger bowl, wide bulbous ovoid tapering body w/a flat mouth, the exterior decorated w/pulled green leaves w/iridescent gold tips on an almond brown ground, iridescent gold interior, signed, 4¾" d., 2¾" h. (internal line encircles base) **440.00**

Finger bowl, wide bulbous ovoid tapering body w/a flat mouth, the exterior decorated w/pulled green leaves w/iridescent gold tips on an almond brown ground, iridescent gold interior, signed, 4¾" d., 2¾" h. (internal line encircles base) **440.00**

Lamps, mantel-type, ten-ribbed tulip-form gold iridescent shade inverted on the gilt-metal ringed & knob short pedestal w/domed round foot w/electric switch, shades signed on rims, overall 9" h., pr. **575.00**

Vase, 4½" h., wide squatty ovoid body w/the wide shoulder centered by a short, wide flaring neck, translucent amber w/delicate green & gold feathers on a thin opal surface, gold iridescent interior, signed on base (surface bubbles in feather area) **920.00**

Vase, 4⅝" h., footed squatty bulbous baluster-form w/flaring rim, cased double-decorated opal body w/hooked & pulled gold feathers below green hooked elements w/medial gold band, gold iridescent surface above & within flared rim, signed "Quezal 490" **2,070.00**

Vase, 4¾" h., cased slender cylindrical body on a flat disc foot, decorated w/five pointed gold iridescent feathers on an opal white body, flaring gold foot inscribed "Quezal". **575.00**

Vase, 5" h., lily-form, a thin round cushion foot tapering to a tall slender waisted body w/a widely flaring quatraform rim, golden iridescent ground w/five subtle green spiked feathers, large partial label cover pontil reading "Art Quezal - Brooklyn" **1,035.00**

Vase, 6" h., cushion-footed baluster-form w/a short neck & widely rolled three-lobed mouth, delicate gold & green iridescent vertically lined leaf decoration on exterior, gold iridescent interior, signed "Quezal T 918" **1,610.00**

Vase, 8½" h., simple ovoid body tapering to a short trumpet neck, amber w/gold iridescence decorated w/overall white pulled & hooked tracery design, base signed (interior in-the-making annealing line). **690.00**

Vase, 12" h., slender baluster-form body w/a cushion foot & closed rim, rich opalescent cased over amber decorated w/pulled green leafage

Fine Tall Quezal Vase

reserved against gold, applied
w/six large iridescent drips in white,
amber & blue, signed (ILLUS.). . . **6,325.00**
Vase, 9¾" h., baluster-shaped w/a
trumpet neck & cushion foot,
iridescent gold neck above the
shoulder decorated w/pulled &
swirled emerald green & opal white
design above iridescent gold pulled
leaves continuing down over the
foot, #C268, signed **3,850.00**
Vase, 10½" h., tall slender baluster-
form w/short trumpet neck, overall
blue iridescent finish, signed **1,375.00**

Quezal Pulled Feather Tall Vase

Vase, 14" h., footed tall slender
waisted form w/bulbous base &
gently flaring sides to a flat rim,
cased, elaborate green & gold
pulled feathers on opaque white on
the exterior, gold iridescent interior,
base signed, crack across the
pontil (ILLUS.) **1,150.00**

ROSE BOWLS

*These decorative small bowls were widely
popular in the late 19th and early 20th
centuries. Produced in various types of glass,
they are most common in satin glass or spatter
glass. They are generally a spherical shape with
an incurved crimped rim, but ovoid or egg-
shaped examples were also popular.*

*Their name derives from their reported use,
to hold dried rose petal potpourri or small fresh-
cut roses.*

Cased glass, shaded dark blue to
white, spherical w/eight-crimp rim,
decorated around the body w/gold
enameled floral branches, white
interior, 4½" d. **$330.00**

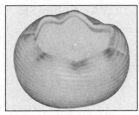

Rainbow Mother-of-Pearl Rose Bowl

Cased satin, shaded rainbow
mother-of-pearl Concentric Circles
patt., wide squatty form w/a six-
crimp rim, shaded pink, blue &
yellow, signed "Patent," creamy
white lining, 4⅜" d., 2½" h.
(ILLUS.). **665.00**
Cased satin, shaded pink mother-of-
pearl Herringbone patt., crimped
rim, 3½" h. **154.00**
Cased satin, shaded rainbow
mother-of-pearl Diamond Quilted
patt., wide bands of pink alternating
w/narrow bands of yellow around
the top half, marked "Patent," six-
crimp rim, 4" h. **495.00**

Herringbone Satin Rose Bowl

Cased satin, shaded blue mother-of-
pearl Herringbone patt., tall egg-
shaped body w/a six-crimp rim,
white interior, 3⅜" d., 4" h. (ILLUS.). . **185.00**

Cased satin, blue decorated
w/delicate purple floral enameling,
white lining, spherical w/six-crimp
rim, 4" d., 4" h.. . . . . **138.00**

Cased satin, shaded blue exterior
enameled w/bands & swags in
gold & black, spherical w/large
molded shells around the bottom
& an eight-crimp rim,
5" h. **165.00**

Shaded rose pink opalescent,
exterior w/swirled amber stripes &
the body completely wrapped
w/applied amber banding, widely
rolled four-lobe rim pulled into
points, attributed to Stevens &
Williams. **358.00**

ROYAL FLEMISH

*This ware, made by Mt. Washington Glass
Co., is characterized by very heavy enameled
gold lines dividing the surface into separate
areas or sections. The body, with a matte finish,
is variously decorated.*

Cracker jar, cov., barrel-shaped,
decorated overall w/assorted
bubble medallions in pastel
hues outlined in raised gold upon
a maroon ground, raised gold
mum blossoms w/autumn color
leaves cascading from the rim,
decorative silver plate flared &
fluted rim w/inset floral-embossed
domed cover & bail handle,
6" h. **$1,375.00**

Lamp, kerosene table model,
the bulbous cylindrical glass
font decorated w/round gold
portrait medallions separated by
heavy gold banding from random
pale colored panels, a scroll-
embossed wide brass collar
& domed foot w/four scroll
feet, converted to
electricity **358.00**

Vase, 5½" h., footed wide squatty
bulbous body tapering sharply to
a small flaring neck flanked by
small applied leaf loop handles,
decorated w/scattered bouquets
of colorful pastel pansies trimmed
w/raised gold sun rays & a
gilt network of berried
vines. **2,200.00**

Vase, 10¼" h., 6¼" d., footed bulbous
body w/short wide cylindrical neck
w/leaf decoration & flared rim,
heavy gold enamel lines separating
areas in shades of green, yellow &

Fine Royal Flemish Vase

w/large six-point stars, ring of
applied glass separating the neck
from the base (ILLUS.). **5,385.00**

Vase, 12" h., footed wide squatty
bulbous base centered by a tall,
slender swelled "stick" neck w/flat
rim, the body decorated w/raised
gold sections w/subtle earthtones,
three decorative medallions, the
main one w/a griffin head, the other
w/flowers, raised gold leafy vine
w/wild berries & florals meander
across the shoulder, the neck
w/frosty leafy scrolls trimmed in
raised gold on a wine red ground . . **3,575.00**

RUBINA

*This glass, sometimes spelled "Rubena" is a
flashed ware, shading from ruby to clear. Some
pieces are decorated.*

Castor set, four tall square glass
containers, two w/stoppers & two
w/metal tops, all fitted in a silver
plate square rack frame w/upright
squared bar center handle,
the set **$743.00**

Celery vase, tall slightly flaring
cylindrical glass insert w/scalloped
rim in the Inverted Thumbprint patt.,
enameled decoration of a bird &
flowers, fitted in a Tufts silver plate
stand w/high loop side handles,
cupped holder raised on a slender
stem w/a squared foot, 8" h. **851.00**

Fine Rubina Creamer

Creamer, Inverted Thumbprint patt.,
bulbous body w/a flaring squared
neck wrapped w/a rope band
continuing to the applied twisted
rope handle w/two prunt
attachments, engraved under the
spout "Mt. McGregor," 3¾" h.
(ILLUS. previous page) **220.00**

Rubina Ice Bucket

Ice bucket, tapering cylindrical form
w/an overall mold-blown swirled
leaf & blossom design shading
cranberry to clear, silver plate rim
band & bail handle, 4½" d., 5½" h.
(ILLUS.) **165.00**
Pitcher, 7½" h., Hobnail patt.,
bulbous body tapering to a squared
flaring neck, applied clear handle
(minor stains, small chips) **182.00**

RUBINA VERDE

*This decorative glass, popular in the late
19th and early 20th centuries, shades from ruby
or deep cranberry to green or greenish-yellow.*

**Cruet w/original greenish amber
facet-cut ball stopper,** wide
sharply tapering body w/a
slender cylindrical neck & tricorner
rim, Inverted Thumbprint patt.,
applied greenish amber handle,
7" h. **$248.00**
Cruet w/original stopper, Inverted
Thumbprint patt., petticoat
mold. **450.00**
Pitcher, water, enameled decoration,
polished pontil **125.00**

Rare Rubina Verde Punch Bowl

Punch bowl, cov., tall ovoid body
w/two applied greenish loop
handles & raised on pale green
applied scroll feet, the domed
cover w/ladle cut-out & an applied
pale green bubble knop w/berry
prunt, the cover & sides of the body
ornately enameled w/white flowers
w/yellow centers on brown
branches, gold trim on body, feet
& cover, overall 7¼" w., 9¾" h.
(ILLUS.) **550.00**

RUBY-STAINED

*This name derives from the color of the glass,
a deep red. The red staining was thinly painted
on clear pressed glass patterns and refired at a
low temperature. Many pieces were further
engraved as souvenir items and were very
popular from the 1890s into the 1920s. This
technique should not be confused with "flashed"
glass where a clear glass piece is actually dipped
in molten glass of a contrasting color. Also see
PATTERN GLASS.*

Berry set: master bowl & four sauce
dishes, Thumbnail patt., the set . . **$165.00**
Bowl, Scalloped Swirl patt., in silver
plated frame **375.00**
Butter dish, cov., Duncan's
Thumbprint patt. **225.00**
Butter dish, cov., Prize patt. **185.00**
Celery vase, Beaded Swirl & Lens patt. . . **65.00**
Celery vase, Hexagon Block patt. **127.00**
Celery vase, Prize patt. **159.00**
Creamer, Diamonds & Double Fans
patt. **79.00**
Creamer, miniature, Box in Box patt. . . **59.00**
Creamer & open sugar bowl, Triple
Triangle patt., pr. **46.00**
Cup, Sterling patt. **39.00**
Decanter w/original stopper,
Model's Gem patt. **135.00**

Decanter w/original stopper,
  Pentagon patt., engraved **75.00**
Goblet, Beaded Dart Band patt. **59.00**
Goblet, Majestic patt. **50.00**
Pitcher, water, Alden patt. **225.00**
Pitcher, water, Majestic patt. **295.00**
Salt & pepper shakers w/original
  tops, Big Buttress patt., pr. **110.00**
Sauce dish, Box in Box patt. **15.00**
Tray, Box in Box patt. **49.00**
Tumbler, Roanoke patt. **30.00**
Tumbler, whiskey, Sunbeam patt. **65.00**

Blocked Thumbprint Water Set

Water set: pitcher & four tumblers;
  Blocked Thumbprint patt., ruby &
  clear frosted band, the set (ILLUS.) . . **395.00**
Water set: tankard pitcher & four
  tumblers; Beaded Lobe patt.,
  the set. **250.00**
Wine, Prize patt. **175.00**
Wine, Sterling patt. **79.00**
Wine set: decanter w/stopper & six
  wine glasses; Loop & Block patt.,
  the set (stopper damaged) **325.00**

SANDWICH

Numerous types of glass were produced at The Boston & Sandwich Glass Works in Sandwich, Massachusetts, on Cape Cod, from 1826 to 1888. Those listed here represent a sampling. Also see PATTERN GLASS and LACY in the "Glass" section.

All pieces are pressed glass unless otherwise noted. Numbers after salt dips refer to listings in Pressed Glass Salt Dishes of the Lacy Period, 1825-1850, *by Logan W. and Dorothy B. Neal.*

Candlestick, hexagonal tulip-form
  socket attached w/a wafer to a
  ringed hexagonal pedestal w/a
  flaring base, sapphire blue, 7¾" h.
  (several tiny flakes on socket &
  base) **$660.00**
Candlestick, hexagonal tulip-form
  socket attached w/a wafer to the
  ringed hexagonal pedestal on a
  hexagonal base, amethyst, 8⅜" h. . . **660.00**

Candlesticks, hexagonal tulip-form
  socket attached w/a wafer to a
  ringed flaring hexagonal pedestal
  base, canary, 7¾" h., pr. (tiny crack
  on one socket, shallow spall on
  other). **275.00**
Candlesticks, dolphin-type, the
  petal-form socket attached w/a
  wafer to the figural dolphin shaft on
  a double-stepped square base,
  clambroth, 10" h., pr. **1,210.00**

Ring & Oval Whale Oil Lamp

Lamp, whale oil, table model, bulb-
  shaped Ring & Oval patt. font,
  attached w/wafer to flaring
  hexagonal pedestal base, original
  pewter collar & double burner,
  amethyst, slightly disfiguring corner
  base chip, 8⅜" h. (ILLUS.) **1,760.00**
Lamp, whale oil, table model, Loop
  patt. font, attached w/a wafer to an
  octagonal baluster-form pedestal
  on a square foot, original pewter
  collar somewhat bent, deep
  amethyst, 10½" h. (two tiny flakes
  on sides of a loop, five bruises or
  flakes on corners of base) **2,200.00**

Cavalier Pomade Jar in Rare Color

Pomade jar, cov., figural, a Cavalier
  sitting w/arms crossed, bearded,
  wearing a large plumed hat,
  embossed on base "E.T.S. & Co
  NY," opaque powder blue, ca.
  1850-70, 3¾" h. (ILLUS.) **4,840.00**

Vase, 9⁷⁄₁₆" h., tulip-form, flaring octagonal bowl attached w/a wafer to a conforming flaring pedestal base, amethyst **825.00**

Vase, 10¼" h., tulip-form w/eight-panel top w/scalloped rim, attached w/a wafer to a matching pedestal base, bright violet (few nicks on the ribs, some light mold roughness on base) **3,630.00**

Vase, 10⁵⁄₁₆" h., tulip-form w/eight-panel top w/flaring scalloped rim, attached w/a wafer to a matching pedestal base, steel blue (light mold roughness on base, shallow unseen base chip) **3,310.00**

Vases, 9¾" h., tulip-form w/eight panels & flaring scalloped rim, attached w/wafer to matching pedestal base, bright emerald green, pr. **9,075.00**

SATIN

Satin glass was a popular decorative glass developed in the late 19th century. Most pieces were composed of two layers of glass with the exterior layer usually in a shaded pastel color. The name derives from the soft matte finish, caused by exposure to acid fumes, which gave the surface a "satiny" feel. Mother-of-pearl satin glass was a specialized variety wherein air trapped between the layers of glass provided subtle surface patterns such as Herringbone and Diamond Quilted. A majority of satin glass was produced in England, Bohemia and America, but collectors should be aware that reproductions have been produced for many years.

Bowl, 4" h., tapering sides, pink exterior decorated w/yellowish brown spur & floral branches w/a window decorated w/a bird & fan in landscape, glossy white interior, attributed to Webb **$385.00**

Bowl-vase, wide squatty bulbous body w/a dimpled shoulder tapering to a waisted neck below the deep cupped tricorner rim, lavender blue & amethyst mother-of-pearl Flower & Acorn patt., enameled around the body w/three clusters of maroon & white floral bouquets & golden leaves, 5" h. . . **1,210.00**

Cameo vase, 7¾" h., wide squatty bulbous base tapering to a tall tapering cylindrical neck w/flared rim, rose red mother-of-pearl Diamond Quilted patt., overlaid & acid-etched w/a white band around the body of scrolling leaves

enclosing petalled blossoms, upright scrolls & blossoms around the neck, England **2,200.00**

Cracker jar, cov., ovoid shaded pink satin molded in the Shell patt., cased in white, some yellow enamel decoration, silver plate rim, cover & bail handle **358.00**

Raindrop Pattern Satin Creamer

Creamer, bulbous body w/a wide cylindrical neck & pinched spout, applied blue satin reeded handle, heavenly blue mother-of-pearl Raindrop patt., white lining, 3⅛" d., 4½" h. (ILLUS.) **165.00**

Cruet w/frosted clear thorn stopper, ovoid body tapering to a short cylindrical neck w/small rolled spout, shaded blue mother-of-pearl Diamond Quilted patt., enameled w/a branch of yellow & white flowers around the sides, 7½" h. **798.00**

Cruet w/original facet-cut frosted clear ball stopper, flaring cylindrical bottom half below the wide angled shoulder tapering to a cylindrical ringed neck w/a tricorner rim, rainbow mother-of-pearl Herringbone patt. w/alternating stripes of pink, blue & yellow, applied clear frosted handle, 8" h. . . **1,485.00**

Ewer, footed wide bulbous, nearly spherical body centered by a slender cylindrical neck w/a tri-corner rim, shaded yellow mother-of-pearl Herringbone patt., applied frosted clear handle, 7" h. **330.00**

Ewer, pedestaled cushion foot supporting the wide squatty bulbous body tapering to a tall slender ringed cylindrical neck w/a rolled tricorner rim, applied frosted clear angled handle, rainbow mother-of-pearl Herringbone patt., alternating stripes of yellow, pink & blue, 10" h. **825.00**

Juice tumbler, cylindrical, rainbow mother-of-pearl Diamond Quilted patt., pale pink, yellow & blue, marked "Patent," 3½" h. **193.00**

Pitcher, 5½" h., spherical body w/four large indentations, a three-lobed cylindrical neck w/a flat rim, high arched applied frosted clear handle, shaded deep pink mother-of-pearl Coin Spot patt. **330.00**

Tumbler, rainbow mother-of-pearl Coin Spot patt., alternating stripes of pale pink & blue, 3¾" h. **220.00**

Tumbler, cylindrical, pink mother-of-pearl Diamond Quilted patt., enameled w/a brown & white bird on a branch w/blue berries, 4" h. . . . **165.00**

Small Gold-Decorated Satin Vase

Vase, 4⅛" h., 3¼" d., bulbous nearly spherical body w/a short cylindrical neck w/a flaring, lightly ruffled rim, chartreuse mother-of-pearl Ribbon patt., white lining, heavy gold decoration of prunus branches & blossoms around the body (ILLUS.). **325.00**

Vase, 6" h., bulbous ovoid body tapering sharply to a slender ringed cylindrical neck w/a flattened tricorner rim, rainbow mother-of-pearl Diamond Quilted patt., stripes of alternating yellow, blue & pink. . . **715.00**

Vase, 6¾" h., mother-of-pearl "Federzeichnung" patt., pearl trailings trimmed w/gold tracery on a chocolate brown ground, ovoid body tapering to a short flaring four-lobed & ribbed neck, gilt neck interior, marked "Pat. #9156" **2,310.00**

Vase, 7½" h., tall ovoid body w/a six-crimped rim, mother-of-pearl Swirled Stripe patt., green shaded to rose w/yellow swirls, lined in white, attributed to Stevens & Williams. **805.00**

Vase, 8¼" h., bulbous ovoid body tapering to a cylindrical neck w/a widely flaring tricorner rolled & crimped rim, shaded blue mother-of-pearl Coin Spot patt. **193.00**

Vase, 8¼" h., footed ovoid body tapering to a waisted short neck w/a wide deeply cupped rim, shaded pink decorated w/white enameled florals & gold leaves, white lining. **220.00**

Vase, 8½" h., bulbous ovoid body tapering to a short slightly flaring cylindrical neck, blue mother-of-pearl Diamond Quilted patt., decorated overall w/a gilt design of vining foliage & dragonflies, white lining **413.00**

Diamond Quilted Tall Satin Vase

Vase, 10⅛" h., 4⅛" d., a bulbous spherical base tapering to a slender tall waisted neck swelled near the top, shaded blue mother-of-pearl Diamond Quilted patt., white lining (ILLUS.) **135.00**

Vase, 12" h., bottle-form, bulbous spherical body tapering to a tall slender "stick" neck, shaded pink mother-of-pearl Coin Spot patt., decorated w/raised gold florals & leafy vine down the sides w/a single butterfly **495.00**

SCHNEIDER

This ware is made in France at Cristallerie Schneider, established in 1913 near Paris by Ernest and Charles Schneider. Some pieces of cameo were marked "Le Verre Francais" (which see) and others were signed "Charder."

Schneider Mark

Lamp, hanging-type, a half-round light bowl of creamy white enameled in speckled yellow & red, inscribed "Schneider" at edge, suspended from a ceiling mount by twisted & knotted cord & wire chain decorated by three matching glass beads, bowl 15½" d **$1,380.00**

Vase, 7½" h., ribbed compressed spherical body, clear internally decorated w/a profusion of bubbles, on a circular aubergine foot, engraved "Schneider - France," w/partial paper label **978.00**

Internally-decorated Schneider Vase

Vase, 8" h., bulbous nearly spherical body w/a short cylindrical neck, thick sides in clear over burnt orange, internally decorated w/a band of asymmetrical discs in mottled white & orange shading to grey & green marbleizing, acid-etched "SCHNEIDER," acid-stamped "FRANCE," ca. 1925 (ILLUS.) **1,265.00**

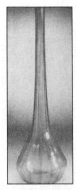

Ribbed Schneider Vase

Vase, 20" h., bottle-form, a bulbous optic-ribbed base tapering to a very tall slender ribbed "stick" neck, clear accented w/orangish amber, candy cane mark on base, some interior stain (ILLUS.) **230.00**

Vase, 25" h., cushion-footed baluster-form, clear internally decorated w/splotches & swirls of orange, yellow, amber & honey brown shaded to a blue foot, engraved on the side "Schneider France" **900.00**

SILVER DEPOSIT - SILVER OVERLAY

Silver Deposit and Silver Overlay have been made commercially since the last quarter of the 19th century. Silver is deposited on the glass by various means, most commonly by utilizing an electric current. The glass was very popular during the first three decades of this century, and some pieces are still being produced. During the late 1970s, silver commanded exceptionally high prices and this was reflected in a surge of interest in silver overlay glass, especially in pieces marked "Sterling" or "925" on the heavy silver overlay.

Silver Deposit Cocktail Set

Cocktail set: decanter w/stopper & two martini glasses; decanter w/ovoid black body tapering to a silver-mounted shoulder & double-spout rim w/knobbed stopper above the sides decorated w/large triangular panels of delicate silver deposit florals, each glass w/a plain black stem w/silver footrim & Flambo red flaring bowl w/triangular silver deposit floral panels, shields on bases marked "Rockwell," Czechoslovakia, ca. 1920s, each glass 5¼" h., decanter 11" h., the set (ILLUS.) **$690.00**

Cologne bottle w/ball stopper, squatty compressed round cranberry body centered by a short cylindrical neck w/a flattened, flared rim, overall tightly looped lattice design w/shoulder cartouche, matching design on stopper, 5" d., 4½" h **716.00**

Cologne bottle w/ball stopper, cranberry spherical body tapering to a tall slender cylindrical neck w/a tricorner rim, overlaid overall in tight lacy vines w/a cartouche on the front, matching design on the stopper, 6½" h. **660.00**

Silver Overlay Cologne & Decanters

Cologne bottle w/pointed ribbed stopper, the squatty bulbous melon-lobed body in clear tapering to a short cylindrical neck w/flattened rim, decorated overall w/delicate silver scrolling, American-made, ca. 1900, 7¼" h. (ILLUS. center). **546.00**

Decanter w/original stopper, molded & pinched ovoid bottle-form w/overall surface decoration of bamboo, base disc impressed "Yuan Shun - Sterling," faceted crystal hollow stopper, 11½" h. **374.00**

Decanters w/tall knopped stoppers, footed bulbous nearly spherical base w/a tall lady's lead neck fitted w/stopper w/solid silver overlay, the clear body covered w/an overall openwork foliate design, monogrammed, retailed by Black, Star & Frost, ca. 1900, 12" h., pr. (ILLUS. left & right). **2,070.00**

Vase, 4¼" h., simple ovoid body tapering to a short flaring neck, burgundy red cased to opal white, the exterior overlaid overall w/swirling stylized large blossoms & leaves on stems w/two silver bands around the lower half, silver marked "Sterling". **431.00**

Vase, 4½" h., simple ovoid body w/four dimples around the shoulder below the four-lobed rolled short neck, gold iridescent surface overlaid in scrolling silver foliate vines & blossoms, polished pontil, Austria, early 20th c. **546.00**

Vase, bud, 6¼" h., slender waisted cylindrical body w/a swelled shoulder & wide flat mouth, cranberry overlaid around the sides w/vining silver leaves **440.00**

Vase, 6½" h., bulbous base below a tall waisted neck, dark amethyst overlaid w/large silver upright palmette leaves joined by scrolling bands, unmarked. **83.00**

Vase, 6¾" h., gently flaring cylindrical body w/a swelled rounded shoulder tapering to a short neck, faintly ribbed bright blue lined w/silvery green & overlaid in sterling silver around the neck & shoulder w/swirling large blossoms & leafy vines, silver impressed "Sterling" Austria, early 20th c. (slight silver damage at rim) **374.00**

Vase, 10" h., slender baluster-form body in emerald green w/relief-blown oval sections through the ornate pierced sterling silver lattice design of lilies, leaves & vines, silver marked "G3223 - 925 fine". . . **825.00**

Vase, 10½" h., black amethyst ovoid body w/short flaring neck, a hammered silver border, the body decorated w/silver overlay Art Deco foliate designs, base stamped "Rockwell" in a shield (base edge ground) **374.00**

Vase, 12" h., tall slightly tapering cylindrical body w/a narrow rounded shoulder to the short, wide cylindrical neck, bright rose red cased in white, the exterior overlaid in an elaborate silver floral design w/scrolls & swirling stems around the body & centering a medallion crest **1,380.00**

Fine Tall Silver Overlay Vase

Vase, 16" h., baluster-form body w/a widely flaring trumpet neck & a slender ringed stem on a domed disc foot, emerald green overlaid w/long upward scrolling silver vines around the lower portion centered by shield devices below a wide central band of repeating scrolls w/further swag designs around the neck, American-made, ca. 1900, chip on pontil (ILLUS.) **1,093.00**

SMITH BROTHERS

Originally established as a decorating department of the Mt. Washington Glass Company in the 1870s, the firm later was an independent business in New Bedford, Massachusetts. Beautifully decorated opal white glass was their hallmark but they also did glass cutting. Some examples carry their lion-in-the-shield mark.

Smith Brothers Mark

Bowl, 4" d., 2½" h., squatty bulbous melon-lobed body w/a wide flat mouth, creamy beige ground enameled w/large blue pansies & green leaves, blue beaded rim band, white opal lining, lion trademark (minor rim bead damage) **$127.00**

Cracker jar, cov., raised footring supported a wide bulbous squared body in white opaque decorated around the shoulder w/bouquets of blue forget-me-nots w/some enhanced w/pale enamel, scattered yellowish brown coiled designs, embossed silver plate rim band w/low scalloped rim, domed & swirled cover w/knop finial & reeded bail handle, signed, 4½" h. **633.00**

Smith Brothers Cracker Jar

Cracker jar, cov., bulbous melon-lobed body in creamy white decorated w/enameled pink roses & raised gold leaves outlined in gold, ornate silver plate rim, cover & bail handle w/looped lattice trim,

bottom w/lion trade mark, 7" h. (ILLUS.) **1,045.00**

Cracker jar, cov., square w/swirled mold, decorated w/blue pansies on a cream ground, resilvered cover, rim & bail handle, 4¾" w., 8¾" h. to top of handle **715.00**

Creamer & cov. sugar bowl, creamer w/ovoid body below the silver plate rim & low wide spout & loop rim handle, the squatty bulbous sugar bowl w/a matching silver plate rim, domed cover & flat bail handle, each body w/a satin ivory ground decorated w/gilt floral branches outlined w/raised gold, sugar 2¾" h., creamer 3½" h., pr. . . **495.00**

Creamer & open sugar, each w/a white opal cylindrical body decorated w/a rim band of blue, purple, yellow & white blossoms & leaves on a pink ground, each fitted in an openwork silver plate pedestal-based stand, fixed loop handle on creamer frame, swing bail handle on sugar frame, frames marked "Middletown Quadruple Plate" late 19th c., 4¾" h., pr. **303.00**

Sugar shaker w/original silver-gilt lid, ovoid melon-lobed body, satin ivory ground decorated w/gilt floral branches & raised gold outlines, 4¾" h. **468.00**

Vase, 4" h., spherical body w/a short cylindrical neck, beige ground decorated w/large orchid & yellow pansies & green leaves, beading around the neck, lion trademark . . . **138.00**

Vase, 4½" h., bulbous cylindrical body w/three wide side dimples, the rounded shoulder centered by a short cylindrical neck w/flared rim, ivory ground decorated around the shoulder & down the corners w/long graceful leafy stems of daisies w/enameled highlights, enamel beaded rim, one side enameled in script "World's Fair 1893," marked **440.00**

Vase, 4½" h., bulbous upright body w/four pinched-in sides tapering to a tiny flared neck, decorated around the shoulder w/lavender & pink carnations & green stems on a biscuit colored ground, gilt beaded rim, marked **385.00**

Vase, 5½" h., 2½" d., melon-ribbed body, enameled daisies front & back, red rampant lion trademark on base **150.00**

Vase, 8½" h., large tapering ovoid melon-lobed body w/a rounded shoulder centered by a domed ivory-tinted neck molded w/repeated stylized flowers & ribbing & a gilt-trimmed flat rim, the body w/a white ground decorated w/fall & shadow grey leaves on thorny branches lavished w/raised gold scroll, marked **605.00**

Vase, 8½" h., wide bulbous melon-lobed body w/the rounded shoulder centered by a short swelled neck molded w/stylized flowers tinted w/leaf color & gilt trim at the flat mouth, the body painted w/large lavender blue wisteria blossoms cascading from a greyish green leafy vine, gold outlining, original paper label. **853.00**

Vase, 8¾" h., decorated w/clusters of naturalistically colored wisteria blossoms clinging to the raised gold vine encircling the shoulder like a necklace. **750.00**

SPANGLED

Spangled glass incorporated particles of mica or metallic flakes and variegated colored glass particles embedded in the transparent glass. Usually made of two layers, it might have either an opaque or transparent casing. The Vasa Murrhina Glass Company of Sandwich, Massachusetts, first patented the process for producing Spangled glass in 1884 and this factory is known to have produced great quantities of this ware. It was, however, also produced by numerous other American and English glasshouses. This type, along with Spatter, is often erroneously called "End of the Day."

A related decorative glass, Aventurine, features a fine speckled pattern resembling gold dust on a solid color ground. Also, see ART GLASS BASKETS and ROSE BOWLS under Glass.

Bowl-vase, footed bulbous nearly spherical body w/a closed rim, four small applied prunts around the shoulder, dark green w/overall gold mica Aventurine, possibly Union Glass Co., ca. 1880, 4¾" w., 4½" h. **$138.00**

Cruet w/original facet-cut amber ball stopper, spherical body of amber cased over white enclosing large mica flecks, tall cylindrical neck w/tricorner rim, applied arched amber handle, 7" h. **220.00**

Rose bowl, deeply ribbed spherical body w/inwardly crimped rim, raised on clear applied petal feet,

Pink Spangled Rose Bowl

white spatter w/mica flecks cased in deep pink, 3½" d., 3¾" h. (ILLUS.). **110.00**

Blue Spangled Vases

Vases, 7⅜" h., 3" d., footed swelled cylindrical body in a blue ground streaked w/silver mica flecks in a coral-like design & cased in white, mounted w/a gilt-metal crown-form rim band & raised on a gilt-metal ring w/scrolled feet, pr. (ILLUS.) . . . **265.00**

SPATTER

This variegated color ware is similar to Spangled glass but does not contain metallic flakes. The various colors are applied on a clear, opaque white or colored body. Much of it was made in Europe and England. It is sometimes called "End Of Day."

Pitcher, 7⅜" h., spherical body w/a swirled rib design below the wide, short cylindrical neck w/pinched spout, cased two-tone blue spatter body w/applied black lip, applied black ribbed handle **$116.00**

Pitcher, 8" h., bulbous ovoid body tapering to a wide squared mouth, cased rainbow spatter in brownish amber, yellow, pink & blue, swirled clear exterior casing & smooth white interior casing, applied clear reeded handle, late 19th c. **275.00**

Enameled Spatter Vase

Vase, 7" h., 4½" d., footed bulbous spherical body tapering to a wide trumpet neck flanked by applied clear angled handle, white streaked spatter cased in yellow, decorated w/elaborate enamel decoration of a bird on flowering leafy branches (ILLUS.)...................... **145.00**

Satin Spatter Vase

Vase, 7½" h., 3⅜" d., squatty bulbous base below a swelled knob at the base of the tall slightly flaring cylindrical "stick" neck, swirled rainbow spatter in yellow, pink, blue & white w/a white lining & satin finish (ILLUS.).............. **95.00**

STEUBEN

Most of the Steuben glass listed below was made at the Steuben Glass Works, now a division of Corning Glass, between 1903 and about 1933. The factory was organized by T.G. Hawkes, noted glass designer, Frederick Carder, and others. Mr. Carder devised many types of glass and revived many old techniques.

Steuben Marks

Acid Cut-Back

Lamp base, rectangular upright form in Jade Yellow cut w/an overall design of floral buds & frilly leaves on each side, mounted upon a gilt-metal base w/beading & Greek Key design, a shoulder mount w/acanthus leaf trim, body 5¾" h., overall 20" h. **$1,540.00**

Vase, 4¾" h., ovoid body tapering to a short wide cylindrical neck, Roseline overlaid on Alabaster & cut-back w/a wide central band of Oriental designs w/lappet bands around the shoulder & base, shape No. 1500 variant............. **1,265.00**

Vase, 7" h., wide bulbous nearly spherical body w/a closed rim, Jade green cut to Alabaster w/an overall stylized floral design w/large flowers on slender leafy branches, shape No. 6078 .... **1,595.00**

Vase, 11¾" h., footed slender ovoid body tapering to a flaring rim, pink Rosaline cut to Alabaster in the "Mayfair" patt., tall upright flowering leafy branches against the textured ground, glossy applied Alabaster foot, shape No. 7442 .... **2,090.00**

Alabaster

Ornate Alabaster & Aurene Lamp

Lamp, table model, baluster-form glass standard in opaque white Alabaster w/gold Aurene heart & vine decoration, mounted to an elaborate gilt-metal base & electrified cap w/three Art Nouveau ladies as fittings, shape No. 429, overall 12" h. **1,725.00**

Steuben Alabaster Lamp Base

Lamp base, the tall slender waisted neck above a squatty bulbous base, overall deeply acid-etched w/a grapevine design w/spiraled leaves & vines around the neck, mounted on an unsigned scrolling footed gilt-metal base & two-socket electric shaft, shape No. 8006, glass 14" h., overall 26" h........ **920.00**

Urn, tall classical form w/flaring rim trimmed w/a black band, raised on a ringed flaring pedestal on a stepped square foot, upright applied black loop side handles flanking the bulbous body, 11¾" h. (chips on two corners of the base) . **990.00**

Aurene

Bonbon, round w/a six-lobed flattened ruffled narrow rim, overall silvery blue iridescence, base signed "Aurene 138," 4½" d., 1¼" h. **546.00**

Bowl, 5¼" d., round w/ten prominent ribs molded into the scalloped rim, gold iridescence, signed "Aurene 565"........................ **374.00**

Bowl, 6" d., 3" h., squatty bulbous body tapering toward the base & w/a wide incurved rim, overall gold iridescence, shape No. 2687, signed **460.00**

Bulb bowl, wide shallow flat-bottomed form w/incurved sides, silvery transparent blue iridescence, shape No. 2586, 9¾" d., 1¾" h. (base scratches) ... **259.00**

Candlesticks, the elongated tulip-form socket applied to a tall stem w/a swelled & twisted top segment continuing to a slender smooth section applied to the disc foot,

Steuben Aurene Candlestick

overall blue iridescence, signed "Aurene 686," one w/partial label, 10" h., pr. (ILLUS. of one) **1,840.00**

Center bowl, wide squatty bulbous lower body below the pulled upright pinched & crimped sides forming eight small apertures, overall gold Aurene finish, 8" d., 4" h.......... **546.00**

Center bowl, flared form w/eight spaced rim crimps, blue iridescence shades from deep purple to golden & silvery cobalt, shape No. 7423, 12" d., 4¾" h. .. **2,300.00**

Champagne, saucer-type, wide shallow rounded bowl raised on a slender swelled stem on a flaring round foot, overall gold iridescence, shape No. 2642, 5¾" h. **460.00**

Cologne bottle w/matching mushroom stopper, squatty bulbous melon-lobed body raised on three reeded scroll feet, a short flaring neck fitted w/a lobed stopper, overall blue iridescence, 5" h. **2,640.00**

Cologne bottle w/original pointed stopper, tall slender tapering cylindrical body on a round foot, the narrow shoulder tapering to a short cylindrical neck w/flattened, flared rim, overall gold iridescence w/reddish blush on the foot, signed "Aurene #1414," overall 7¾" h. **880.00**

Cologne bottle w/pointed stopper, squatty bulbous eight-lobed body tapering to a short cylindrical neck w/flared rim, matching pointed & ribbed stopper, overall gold iridescence, signed "Aurene 1455," 5" h. **805.00**

Cologne bottle w/pointed stopper, squatty bulbous eight-lobed body tapering to a short cylindrical neck w/a flared rim, matching ribbed & pointed stopper, overall gold iridescence, signed "Aurene 1455," 6½" h. (very minor stopper rim chips) **805.00**

Compote, open, 10" h., 7½" d., shallow rounded & widely flaring bowl w/rim pulled into six points, applied to a slender stem swelled & twisted at the top & ending on a disc foot, overall blue iridescence, signed "Steuben Aurene 367" . . . **1,265.00**

Darner, spherical top attached w/a knop to the long teardrop-form handle, overall blue iridescence, 6½" l. **468.00**

Goblet, inverted bell-form bowl raised on a tapering knopped & twisted stem on a round foot, overall gold iridescence, marked "Aurene Haviland & Co.," shape No. 705, 6" h. **550.00**

Nut dish, individual, half-round bowl raised on three small wishbone feet, overall gold iridescence, signed "Steuben Aurene #255" **550.00**

Nut dish, squatty bulbous round body below the six-lobed flattened flaring rim, overall gold iridescence, signed "Aurene #138," 3½" d., 1¼" h. **193.00**

Perfume atomizer, thin round foot below the slender flaring cylindrical body w/gilt-metal atomizer fittings & mesh-covered bulb, for Devilbiss, overall strong blue iridescence on the body, shape No. 6136, 7½" h. **1,093.00**

Fine Steuben Aurene Perfume Bottle

Perfume bottle w/blossom-form stopper, baluster-form body w/a tall flaring neck fitted w/the original Mirror Black stopper w/peach to

alabaster blossom-form finial & full-length dauber, overall strong blue iridescence, base signed "Steuben Aurene 3425," 7" h. (ILLUS.) **1,840.00**

Salt dip, round foot supporting a deep widely flaring inverted bell-form bowl, overall blue iridescence, signed "Aurene #3067," 2½" d., 1½" h. **550.00**

Sherbet & underplate, the sherbet w/a wide deep flaring inverted bell-form bowl raised on a twisted stem & round foot, fitted into a deep underplate w/a wide flattened rim, both w/overall reddish gold iridescence, each signed "Aurene #2361," underplate 6¼" d., 4½" h., 2 pcs. **440.00**

Tumbler, cylindrical w/a flaring rim, overall gold iridescence, silver mark "Aurene - Haviland & Co.," 3¾" h. **330.00**

Vase, miniature, 3⅛" h., footed swelled cylindrical body w/flared mouth above two pinched-in sides, overall gold iridescence, signed "Aurene 2768" **413.00**

Vase, 4¼" h., the bulbous base w/four dimples around the sides below a narrow rounded shoulder centering a short cylindrical neck w/a widely flaring upright quatraform rim, overall platinum gold iridescence, base inscribed "Aurene 131" **546.00**

Small Aurene Vase

Vase, 4½" h., widely flaring pointed quatrefoil rim above a bulbous dimpled body, platinum gold iridized surface decorated w/subtle green swirls, base signed "Aurene 131B" (ILLUS.) **1,265.00**

Vase, 6" h., a short cylindrical base below a stack of two bulbous compressed sections below the tall, widely flaring neck, ribbed body w/an overall bright iridescent blue finish, signed by Steuben w/shape No. 7447 . . . . **1,210.00**

Vase, 6" h., flared body w/ruffled rim, overall blue iridescence, signed "Aurene #723" **523.00**

Vase, 6" h., short cylindrical base below a stack of two bulbous compressed sections below the tall, widely flaring neck, ribbed body w/an overall reddish gold iridescence, signed **633.00**

Vase, 6" h., wide flat slightly rolled mouth above a broad bulbous shoulder tapering sharply to a cylindrical base, overall dark iridescent blue finish, signed "Aurene - 2413" **990.00**

Unusual Gold Aurene Vase

Vase, 7¼" h., a cushion disc foot tapering to a slender tall stem supporting a bulbous body w/four pinched-in dimples below the small flaring & ruffled neck, overall platinum gold iridescence, signed "Aurene 136" (ILLUS.) **920.00**

Vase, 8" h., wide slightly ovoid body tapering to a short, wide flaring neck, overall blue iridescence, shape No. 2114, some surface bumps, signed **863.00**

Vase, stick-type, 8" h., round foot centered by a tall very slender cylindrical "stick" body, overall iridescent blue, signed "Steuben Aurene #2556". **358.00**

Vase, 8¼" h., bulbous ovoid body w/the wide shoulder tapering to a short neck w/rolled, flattened rim, overall reddish gold iridescence, the shoulder wrapped w/ivory & green entwined vines w/scattered leaves, shape No. 3426, signed. . **3,795.00**

Vase, 8¼" h., wide ovoid body tapering to a short rolled neck, overall gold iridescence, shape No. 2683, signed **1,380.00**

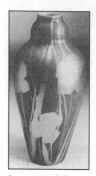

Floral-decorated Aurene Vase

Vase, 9" h., ovoid body w/a bulbed neck & flat rim, green cased in iridized opal & decorated by gold Aurene blossoms & vertical stems, signed "Aurene 260" (ILLUS.) **863.00**

Vase, 12½" h., footed tall slender trumpet-form body, overall gold iridescence w/a reddish gold round foot, signed "Steuben Aurene #2909" **1,045.00**

Rare Decorated Aurene Vase

Vase, 12½" h., slender baluster-form body w/a short flaring deeply ruffled neck, Alabaster ground decorated w/four green eyed peacock feathers in gold Aurene, signed "Aurene 273" (ILLUS.) **4,600.00**

Bristol Yellow

Plates, bread & butter, 6" d., signed, set of 8. . . . . **160.00**

Plates, luncheon, 8½" d., signed, set of 4. . . . . **100.00**

Vase, 8½" h., ribbed fan shape, partial company mark **330.00**

Vase, 8½" h., widely flaring flattened fan-shaped bowl raised on a double-knop stem & round foot, signed **330.00**

Vase, 10" h., flared ovoid optic-ribbed body w/a strong twist to the right, bulbed foot, fleur-de-lis mark on foot, shape No. 6030 (small sand grain bubble at side) **201.00**

Calcite

Bonbon, round ribbed exterior, white Calcite exterior & gold iridescent Aurene interior, 6¼" d. **193.00**

Bowl, 10½" d., 2½" h., low widely flaring form w/a white Calcite exterior & gold Aurene interior, shape No. 5061 . . . . **209.00**

Center bowl, low wide form w/flattened flaring rim, white Calcite exterior & gold Aurene interior, shape No. 5029, 14" d., 1¾" h. **127.00**

Compote, open, 7" h., 8½" d., a shallow rounded bowl w/a wide flattened rim raised on a slender ovoid spiral ribbed stem & round foot, the bowl interior in gold Aurene. **920.00**

Compote, open, 2¾" h., 10" d., widely flaring shallow bowl w/a flattened rim set on a low disc foot, the bowl interior w/gold Aurene **460.00**

Compote, open, 10" d., 3½" h., Calcite exterior & foot, gold iridescent Aurene interior, shape No. 5065 . . . . **275.00**

Finger bowl & underplate, the deep rounded bowl w/flared rim molded w/twelve slender ribs, matching underplate w/wide flattened rim, each w/white Calcite exterior & gold Aurene interior, undertray 6" d., bowl 4¾" d., 2¼" h., 2 pcs.. . . **345.00**

Nut dish, squatty round body below the six-lobed flaring rim, white exterior & gold Aurene interior, 3½" d., 1¼" h. **220.00**

Sherbet & underplate, bell-shaped bowl on a slender stem & round foot, dished flattened & flaring underplate, each w/a white Calcite exterior & gold Aurene interior, shape No. 2960, signed "F. Carder Aurene," underplate 6" d., overall 3¾" h., 2 pcs. **288.00**

Sherbet & underplate, sherbet w/wide bell-formed bowl on a slender stem & round foot, white Calcite exterior & gold Aurene interior, on a matching underplate w/a wide flattened rim, white Calcite exterior & gold Aurene interior, underplate 5¼" d., sherbet 4" h., 2 pcs. **193.00**

Sherbet & underplate, rounded bowl w/flattened flaring rim raised on a slender stem & round foot, deep dished underplate w/flattened angled sides, each w/a white Calcite exterior & gold Aurene interior, underplate 6" d., sherbet 3¾" h., 2 pcs. **209.00**

Vase, 7" h., 6¾" d., tall slender waisted form w/a widely flaring six-ruffled rim, Calcite white exterior & gold Aurene interior, fine gold veining on the exterior, shape No. 1952 . . . . **374.00**

Vase, 8" h., trumpet-form, a round foot supporting a slender stem & widely flaring body w/a ruffled rim, white Calcite exterior, gold iridescent Aurene interior **468.00**

Vase, 10" h., tall slender trumpet-form body w/widely flaring crimped rim, raised on a short disc pedestal & round foot, white Calcite exterior & blue iridescent Aurene interior **1,540.00**

Celeste Blue

Center bowl, a wide low optic ribbed & bulbed Celeste Blue bowl w/incurved sides raised on a funnel-form transparent topaz amber pedestal base, shape No. 6044, 12" d., 5¼" h. **288.00**

Vase, 6" h., fan-type, flattened optic-ribbed bowl on a triple wafer pedestal base & round foot, stamped fleur-de-lis mark, shape No. 6287 . . . . **316.00**

Vase, 8¾" h., footed wide cylindrical body w/a rounded bottom & narrow rounded shoulder to the short, wide rolled neck, fleur-de-lis mark on foot **288.00**

Cintra

Plate, 6½" d., wide flanged rim, the center top w/a green, pale blue & almond brown duck flying above dark green grasses, the textured background in greyish green w/a hobnail-like border. **330.00**

Cluthra

Goblet, sharply tapering hexagonal bowl on a flaring round foot, mottled blue & clear top band shading to a mottled white & clear bottom, shape No. 6909, signed, 6½" h. **605.00**

Angular Cluthra Vase

Vase, 8¼" h., flaring base w/an angular shoulder to the tapering conical sides, two-color w/rose at rim shading to white below, elongated bubbles throughout, shape No. 6882 (ILLUS.)........ **575.00**

Vase, double-lily, 10" h., tall & slightly shorter upright flaring triangular angled lilies in Pomona Green shading to mottled white, set on a clear oval base w/an applied pulled pod, stamped, shape No. 6874.................... **1,430.00**

Vase, 10½" h., tall gently rounded & tapering triangular body w/a molded rim, creamy white swirled Cluthra w/applied clear polished rim & foot wrap, shape No. 7273, marked on base............... **748.00**

Vase, 12½" h., ovoid body, bi-colored w/yellow at the top shading to bright rose pink below, overlaid in Rosaline & etched in Carder's Art Deco "Cliffwood" patt., shape No. 8494................... **3,738.00**

Flemish Blue

Bowl, 8" l., 4½" h., narrow rectangular gently arched form raised on short canted peg feet, optic ridges swirled to right, fleur-de-lis mark, shape No. 6380 .... **489.00**

Bowl, 14" d., 4" h., widely flaring ribbed body & foot, block company mark **193.00**

Perfume jars w/original stoppers, square form w/a flattened shoulder centering a cylindrical neck w/flattened rim & fitted mushroom stopper, swirled optic-ribbed design in base & threading on stopper, fleur-de-lis marks on back, shape No. 6887 variant, 3¾" h., pr. **460.00**

Grotesque

Bowl, 7¼" h., 12" w., upright flaring ruffled & four-pillar oblong body in light topaz, signed "Steuben" on the base, shape No. 7535........ **403.00**

Center bowl, widely flaring oblong deeply ruffled eight-ribbed crystal form, engraved "Steuben" on the base, shape No.7534, 13" l., 7" h... **345.00**

Ivrene

Candleholders, wide flattened disc foot connected by a thin wafer to the widely flaring ruffled "jack-in-the-pulpit-form" socket, shape No. 7564, 3" h., pr. **431.00**

Night light, a low domed Ivrene shade etched w/laurel leaf swags & bows, resting on a metal footed base w/white opaque glass insert, shade 4½" d., 1¼" h............. **165.00**

Vase, 6¼" h., 8" w., Ivrene fan-shaped four-pillar Grotesque bowl raised on a domed Mirror Black foot, shape No. 7564............ **460.00**

Vase, 8¼" h., wide ovoid body tapering to a short widely rolled neck, shape No. 2683 .... **518.00**

Etched Ivrene Steuben Vase

Vase, 10¾" h., wide ovoid body tapering to a short neck w/a widely rolled rim, the body etched overall w/the "Stanford" Art Deco design of leaping stag & doe gazelles, matte finish, integrated "Steuben" fleur-de-lis mark on lower edge, shape No. 2683 (ILLUS.) **2,300.00**

Vase, 8½" h., 11" w., fan-type, Grotesque design w/a widely flaring ribbed body w/randomly ruffled rim, raised on a ribbed domed foot **385.00**

Vases, 5" h., 5" d., footed squatty bulbous base below the trumpet-form ten-ribbed sides, shape No. 2533, pr.................. **460.00**

Jade

Bowl, 12" d., 3¼" h., widely flaring flattened Jade Green bowl w/an upright wide rim band of applied gold Aurene threading, interior & exterior iridescence, shape No. 6774 . . . . **863.00**

Center bowl, a compressed bulbed integral foot below the shallow widely flaring bowl, Jade Yellow, shape No. 3200, 16" d., 5½" h. (two small sand grain spots on the interior) **230.00**

Compote, open, 7" d., 3" h., shallow widely flaring translucent Jade Blue bowl raised on a slender white Alabaster stem & round flaring foot, shape No. 3234 . . . . **575.00**

Vase, 6¼" h., Jade Green modified four-pillar Grotesque design w/unusual vertical shading, shape No. 7311 . . . . **403.00**

Vase, 7" h., 7½" d., wide bulbous ovoid form w/a wide closed rim, Jade Green acid-etched overall w/a fir cone decoration, etched fleur-de-lis mark on lower edge, shape No. 6078. . . . . **1,035.00**

Vase, 9½" h., 5¾" l., 3¼" w., tall upright narrow rectangular form w/a swirled rib design around the sides, Jade Green, polished top rim, shape No. 6199 (some interior stain) **288.00**

Vase, 10¼" h., wide baluster-form body in Green Jade w/applied M-form Alabaster shoulder handles, shape No. 2939, stamped script mark on base. **748.00**

Vase, 10½" h., triple-prong, three Jade Green triangular graduated cones applied atop a round Alabaster foot, signed, shape No. 7128 . . . . **863.00**

Mirror Black

Bowl, 8" d., 3¼" h., flared sides, shape No. 5022, fleur-de-lis mark on the foot (minor scratches) **431.00**

Vase, 12¼" h., simple ovoid body w/a low, wide rolled rim, shape No. 6989 - 7008, gold foil triangular label on the base reads "Steuben Made in Corning, N.Y." **633.00**

Vases, 10½" h., three-prong style, three triangular slender vases issuing from a round foot, the two side ones tilted at a slight angle, one marked, pr. **920.00**

Moss Agate

Fine Moss Agate Lamp

Lamp, table model, angular shouldered ovoid glass shaft of purple & lavender w/mica flecks & occasional swirls of green Aventurine, amber, red & blue, mounted on an elegant gilt-metal leaf band- and bead-cast base & a single socket electric fitting, purple finial, glass 11" h., overall 30" h. (ILLUS.) **1,725.00**

Mantel torchere, a flared glass shade w/eight-scalloped rim in mottled amber, green, yellow, rust & red swirled w/Cluthra bubbles & crackling, mounted on a black-painted cast-iron lamp base, overall 15" h. **1,610.00**

Pomona Green

Candlestick, tall crystal optic ribbed stem, socket & foot, the sides applied w/four Pomona Green prunts & matching rim edging, shape No.3374, block mark, 10" h. **193.00**

Candlesticks, a tulip-shaped socket w/deeply rolled rim above a disc wafer stem applied w/small raspberry prunts above the slightly domed round foot, similar to shape No. 6384, signed, 3¾" h., pr. **385.00**

Center bowl, a compressed cushion base issuing a central waisted neck flanked by four slender hollow "legs" below the widely flaring compressed bowl w/wide incurved rim, shape No. 3080, 10" d., 5¼" h. . . . **345.00**

Ice teas, shape No. 5192, 6½" h., set of 4. . . . . **160.00**

Pitcher, 8½" h., ovoid optic-ribbed body w/a narrow angled shoulder to the slightly flaring short cylindrical neck w/a pinched spout, applied amber handle, shape No. 6232 . . . . **230.00**

Vase, 11" h., 9" d., wide urn-form body on a disc foot, a narrow angled shoulder to the wide rolled mouth, engraved w/five repeating foliate designs centering wheel-cut vertical designs **345.00**

Vase, 12" h., optic-ribbed trumpet-form body w/a wide engraved grapevine border, set on an applied topaz funnel foot, fleur-de-lis mark on foot **460.00**

Rosaline

Vase, miniature, 2½" h., classical form **242.00**

Vase, 6¼" h., flattened fan-shaped Rosaline bowl raised on a double-knop stem & round Alabaster foot . . **550.00**

Rose Quartz

Steuben Rose Quartz Lamp

Lamp, table model, Pompeian type, tall slender baluster-form body of lightly crackled variegated rose extensively etched overall w/classical scene of three draped ladies in various poses under tall trees in a garden setting, drilled & mounted on gilt-metal Crest lamp fittings, shape No. 6467, glass 15" h., overall 29" h. (ILLUS.) **2,530.00**

Silverina

Candlesticks, slender tall ovoid stem supporting an inverted bell-form candle socket w/a cupped rim in clear internally decorated by diamond patterned air-trap mica flecks, shaft raised on a domed Mirror Black round foot, No. 3328, bases stamped "Steuben," 12" h., pr. **978.00**

Vase, 11" h., 10" d., flaring funnel foot below the tall rounded flaring trumpet-form body, Pomona Green, the body decorated overall w/a Silverina mica fleck diamond design, shape No. 6914 variant, stamped "Steuben" **489.00**

Vase, bud, 12" h., round foot & swelled short stem below the bulbed body tapering to a tall slender "stick" neck w/flared rim, topaz w/decorative overall mica flecks, applied Pomona Green disc foot. **403.00**

Spanish Green

Candlestick, optic-ribbed baluster-form w/a double ball below the ovoid candle socket w/a flattened rim, on a stepped, domed wide round foot, fleur-de-lis base mark, plus a matching damaged stick, 12" h., 2 pcs. **230.00**

Champagne goblets, floriform w/deep flaring bubbled bowls above five applied ribbed leaves raised on a slender, straight "nubby" stem w/a folded rim slightly domed round foot, stamped mark on bases, 6¼" h., set of 10. . . . . . **1,380.00**

Topaz

Bowl, 10" d., shape No. 3200 . . . . **125.00**

Verre de Soie

Center bowl, wide low rounded incurved sides w/the rim pinched into eight rounded apertures for flower arrangement, shape No. 2775, 8" d., 3" h. **288.00**

Cologne bottle w/ball stopper, spherical body tapering to a short small cylindrical neck w/flattened rim, the body completely wrapped w/random iridescent green threading, Pomona green stopper, similar to shape No.500A, 3½" h. . . . **385.00**

Urn, cov., goblet-form body raised on a double-knopped stem & flaring round foot, fitted w/a domed & stepped cover w/a pear & ribbed leaf finial, iridescent aquamarine, shape No. 2968, 14½" h. **978.00**

Vase, 12¾" h., early baluster candlestick-form of iridized clear frosted, triangular gold foil label on the base, shape No. 334 . . . . **431.00**

Miscellaneous Wares

Bowl, 9½" h., exhibition-type, crystal, wide deep rounded bowl w/a flat rim, heavy applied short pointed handles at the base above the applied smaller funnel foot, engraved w/a wood sprite playing a stringed instrument among blossoms & bees below inscription "Sounds and Sweet Airs That Give Delight," shape No. X1924A, designed by George Thompson, engraving by Donald Wier, signed on base. **1,495.00**

Bowls, 5¼" d., 3¾" h., crystal, each w/a thick flaring bell-shaped bowl raised on an integrated small cylindrical foot, designed by Donald Pollard, signed "Steuben," set of 6. . . **690.00**

Figure of an angel, "Guardian Angel," stylized crystal figure w/wings outspread, the round head wreathed in an 18k gold halo, base signed, shape No. 1027, 6" h. **1,955.00**

Goblet, cov., "American Ballard Series," crystal, "The Arts," a tall gently swelled cylindrical cup engraved w/patriotic wartime scenes, inset domed cover w/pointed ribbed finial, compressed ribbed knop above the disc foot, designed by George Thompson, engraving designed by Sydney Waugh, signed on base, 11¾" h. **1,840.00**

Goblets, water, crystal, plain trumpet-form bowl above a wide teardrop knop in the stem above a smaller knop above the disc foot, designed by Sidney Waugh, each signed, 7¼" h., set of 6 . . . . **345.00**

Model of a dolphin, leaping position, crystal, on a pillar base, script signature, 9" h. **523.00**

Model of a frog, crystal, stylized crouching animal w/applied eyes & feet, designed by Lloyd Atkins, signed "Steuben," 4¾" l. **403.00**

Model of a koala bear, crystal, the stylized animal seated w/large round disc ears & applied legs, designed by Lloyd Atkins, shape No. 8268, signed on the base, 5¼" h. **920.00**

Model of a pear, "Partridge in a Pear Tree," large crystal pear enclosing an 18k gold fruit-laden tree w/central bird, designed by Lloyd Atkins, shape No. 1014, Christmas item, signed, 5¼" h. **1,840.00**

Steuben Porpoise Sculpture

Model of a porpoise, crystal, blown as a leaping bottle-nose porpoise resting on its snout & tail flukes, designed by Lloyd Atkins, 12" l. (ILLUS.). **863.00**

Model of an owl, stylized oblong crystal bird w/large frosted eyes, facing right & perched on a small domed crystal foot, designed by Donald Pollard, signed "Steuben," 5½" h. **230.00**

Model of an owl on a column, a small cast 18k gold figural owl atop a crystal reeded pedestal-form base w/square foot, designed by James Houston, shape No. 1005, 7¾" h. **1,840.00**

Paperweight, crystal, squatty rounded form w/an internal spiraled design centered by a teardrop, designed by George Tompson, signed "Steuben," 3½" d. **345.00**

Pendant, crystal, modeled as a strawberry, bubbled berry w/18k gold hull leafage suspended from a 14k mesh braided 24" l. chain, w/red leather velvet-lined presentation case, shape No. 1055, designed by Donald Pollard **690.00**

Two Steuben Audubon Plates

Plates, 10" d., "Audubon" series, crystal, each round piece w/a wide flanged rim & central frosted design of a different bird including a great blue heron, white pelican, flamingo, barred owl, horned grebe & swallow-tailed kite, four engraved "Steuben," two "S," set of 6 (ILLUS. of part). **2,990.00**

Steuben Thistle Rock Sculpture

Sculpture, "Thistle Rock," crystal & vermeil, a cut & polished craggy crystal rock supporting a golden upright branching thistle, designed by James Houston, signed "Steuben" on the base, w/velvet-lined red leather case, 7" h. (ILLUS.) **2,185.00**

Steuben Commemorative Sculpture

Sculpture, commemorative, an upright flattened pedestal w/faceted edges, from the historical series of four great Presidents showing Theodore Roosevelt presenting "True American Ideals," signed "Steuben" on the base, designed by Donald Pollard, engraved by Bruce Moore, w/original red leather velvet lined case & binder, 15½" h. (ILLUS.). . **2,530.00**

Vase, 6" h., bulbous ovoid body w/a wide flat rim, on a thick disc foot, the sides wheel-cut in stepped blocks of parallel lines around the body, designed by Sidney Waugh, signed on the base **230.00**

Vase, 7¼" h., crystal, cylindrical body w/a rounded bottom set on a round disc foot, engraved "Angus Dei" design, designed by Sidney

Waugh, shape No. 8607, signed on base **345.00**

Vase, 7¼" h., "Gazelle," tall crystal cylindrical bowl w/a rounded base set on an applied disc foot, the side engraved w/a stylized Art Deco gazelle, designed by Sidney Waugh, shape No. 8608, signed . . . **403.00**

Wines, crystal, plain trumpet-form bowl above a wide teardrop knop in the stem above a smaller knop above the disc foot, designed by Sidney Waugh, each signed, 6" h., set of 10. **345.00**

STEVENS & WILLIAMS

This long-established English glasshouse has turned out a wide variety of artistic glasswares through the years. Fine satin glass pieces and items with applied decoration (sometimes referred to as "Matsu-No-Ke") are especially sought after today. The following represents a cross-section of its wares.

Appliqued Stevens & Williams Vase

Bowl-vase, spherical body in creamy opaque cased in deep rose pink, applied around the sides w/long ruffled swirling amber, green & cranberry leaves ending in loop feet, an applied amber ruffled rim band, 5½" d., 6½" h. (ILLUS.) **$245.00**

Cameo vase, 4½" h., wide ovoid body tapering to a small round mouth, bright blue overlaid in white & etched & cut overall w/clusters of cherries on leafy boughs, circular base mark "Stevens & Williams Art Glass Stourbridge" **1,265.00**

Candlestick, a pink jade gently flaring cylindrical socket above a base ring raised on a tapering columnar alabaster standard above the flaring ringed pink jade round base, 9" h. **193.00**

Rose bowl, miniature, rib-molded
ruby spherical form w/a crimped
rim, applied threading & zippered
sides, "Jewel" line, marked on
pontil "Rd55693," ca. 1886, 2" h.. . . **220.00**

Rose bowl, nearly spherical body
tapering toward the base,
cranberry w/trapped air bubbles
forming overall bands of bumps,
12-crimp rim, polished pontil
marked "Rd. 81051," ca. 1880s,
5¼" d., 4½" h. **143.00**

Rose bowl, spherical w/six-crimp rim,
pale pink opalescent "Rose du
Barry" w/a clear applied vine & leaf
wrapped around the sides, late
19th c., 5½" h. **110.00**

Cut-overlay Stevens & Williams Vase

Vase, 4¼" h., 2⅛" d., cut-overlay,
white interior cased in deep pink
cut w/bands of dots & stylized
florettes between leaf sprigs,
applied clear opalescent wafer
foot (ILLUS.) **195.00**

Vase, 10" h., bright yellow ovoid body
tapering to a square upright ruffled
mouth w/applied green rim, the
sides applied w/a band of large
poppies, leaves & stem, raised on
an applied green wishbone-footed
base, late 19th c. **193.00**

TIFFANY

*This glassware, covering a wide diversity of
types, was produced in glasshouses operated by
Louis Comfort Tiffany, America's outstanding
glass designer of the Art Nouveau period, from
the last quarter of the 19th century until the
early 1930s. Tiffany revived early techniques
and devised many new ones.*

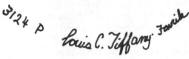

Tiffany Marks

Basket, domed disc foot below a
short ringed stem supporting the
waisted cylindrical body w/a widely
flaring & ruffled rim w/two sides
pulled up & joined by a high arched
applied handle, overall gold
iridescence w/an applied
transparent ambergris handle,
base signed "L.C.T. Favrile 1849,"
10" h. **$1,955.00**

Bonbon, shallow dished form w/a low
widely flaring rim w/wide scallops,
cased w/a marigold iridescent
interior & the exterior w/ribbed
opalescent rays, signed "L.C.T.
Favrile #3359C," 6" d. **715.00**

Bowl, 6" d., 3½" h., a squatty bulbous
slightly ribbed body below a widely
flaring upturned & scalloped rim,
raised on four tiny pulled peg feet,
overall gold iridescence, signed
"L.C. Tiffany Favrile - #1951C". . . **1,100.00**

Bowl, 6¾" d., 2" h., footed, shallow
widely flaring sides w/a flattened
rim, shaded pink pastel "stretch"
border on clear Diamond Quilted
patt. body, signed "L.C.T. Favrile
#1855," original paper label. **770.00**

Bowl, flower-type, 7¼" d., 2¾" h.,
wide shallow form w/low incurved
sides, bright cornflower blue
graduating to white opal, internally
decorated in Tiffany's molded
herringbone leaf design, apparently
unsigned **920.00**

Bowl, 7¾" d., 3½" h., deep rounded
sides w/widely flaring flattened rim,
ribbed laurel leaf patt., overall
iridescent bluish gold w/"stretch"
border, signed "L.C. Tiffany Favrile
#1925". **660.00**

Bowls, 4¼" d., 2½" h., aquamarine
squared squatty bulbous dimpled
sides raised on an applied foot,
wide flared rolled rim, foot inscribed
"L.C. Tiffany Favrile," one
numbered "V493," pr. **500.00**

Butter pat, round ribbed slightly dished form w/a scalloped rim, overall bluish gold iridescence, opalescent underside, signed "L.C.T. Favrile," small **187.00**

Candle lamp, 7¼" d. umbrella-form iridescent bluish gold shade w/a stretched ruffled rim, raised on an opal cylindrical stem w/green pulled leaves inserted within a cupped socket on the iridescent gold swirled & flaring base, shade & base signed "L.C.T.," overall 12" h. **1,430.00**

Centerpiece, widely flaring shallow bowl w/a cylindrical center opening, clear iridescent ground decorated w/gold leafy vines shading to iridescent blue, ca. 1916, 9¾" d. **550.00**

Cologne bottle w/acorn-form stopper, the double-bulbed tapering bottle w/eight applied prunts trailing threads down to the base, overall iridescent gold, signed "L.C.T. Q4736," 7¼" h. (some interior stain) **2,415.00**

Compote, open, a small optic ribbed rounded bowl w/a widely flaring flattened & slightly scalloped rim above the slender stem on a round foot, overall gold iridescence, small, signed "L.C.Tiffany Favrile #1701" **1,375.00**

Compote, open, 7" h., a delicately ribbed round foot centered by a slender baluster-form stem supporting a ringed knob below the wide shallow ribbed bowl w/a wide flattened rim, pale green w/aqua highlights, signed "L.C.T. - Favrile - P18" **660.00**

Cordial, squatty wide round bowl w/widely flaring rim, the bowl w/an iridescent pastel green interior & pale opalescent exterior, raised on a yellow opalescent stem & round foot, the bowl exterior etched w/leafy branches w/cherries, signed "L.C.T. Favrile," 4¼" h. **440.00**

Flower bowl, wide shallow rounded bowl centered by an inserted two-tier slightly tapering cylindrical flower arranger, stretched golden iridescence w/five green lily pads around the interior, two pieces each marked "LC Tiffany Favrile" & numbered, 10½" d. **1,840.00**

Tiffany Iridescent Goblets

Goblets, wide lightly ribbed tulip-form bowl w/a ruffled rim raised on a slender swelled stem on a disc foot, transparent amber w/gold iridescence, signed "L.C.T." & numbered either "N8639," "N8623," "8630" or "8642," 3½" d., 5" h., set of 6 (ILLUS.) **1,200.00**

Decorative Tiffany Loving Cup

Loving cup, swelled cylindrical body w/flared rim w/three applied reeded loop handles down the sides, ambergris w/three green leaf forms between the handles amid trailing vines, overall gold iridescent ground, top rim out of round, light blemish on inside rim in-the-making, signed "L.C. Tiffany 2024D," 8" h. (ILLUS.) **2,600.00**

Parfait glass, tall morning glory-form bowl w/flaring rim, clear w/white opal stripes & a pale aqua rim band, on a short clear stem & round foot, signed "L.C.T. Favrile #1872" **248.00**

Place setting: 9" d. scalloped plate, 2¼" h. footed sherbet & three sizes of goblets, 7¼", 7½" & 8½" h.; all in aqua pastel & signed "L.C.T. Favrile," the set. **1,210.00**

Punch bowl, footed, the large twelve-paneled wide bowl in iridescent gold decorated on the exterior w/emerald green feathers connected w/iridescent gold pulled veins, applied stem numbered "7228C," on a slender pedestal base w/domed foot in iridescent bluish gold, base signed "L.C. Tiffany - Favrile - #4223C," bowl 14" w., overall 10½" h. **4,400.00**

Salt dip, bulbous tapering body on four tiny feet, w/an indented band around the neck below the widely flaring low rim, overall gold iridescence, signed, 1¾" h. **193.00**

Vase, miniature, 2½" h., 3" d., a squatty spherical body on four tiny pulled legs, the neck pulled, crimped & ruffled into a floral form, overall iridescent gold, signed "L.C.T. W8686" **575.00**

Vase, miniature, 3½" h., small cushion foot supporting a wide squatty bulbous ribbed body centered by a ribbed cylindrical neck, overall gold iridescence w/orange & blue highlights, signed "L.C. Tiffany - Favrile - 1447" **605.00**

Vase, 4¾" h., padded & engraved, slightly flaring crystal cylindrical body w/a heavy rounded shoulder centered by a small cylindrical neck, applied purple blossoms & green leaf pads, intaglio-cut & carved w/blossom-laden scrolls & swags, base inscribed "L.C.T. L342" **2,530.00**

Vase, 5" h., ovoid body w/a sharply angled wide shoulder tapering to a short, small cylindrical neck, lustrous gold ground decorated w/green heart-shaped leaves on amber vines, further decorated w/subtle white millefiore canes in blossom-form, inscribed on the base "L.C. Tiffany Favrile 4927G" **1,150.00**

Fine Tiffany "Paperweight" Vase

Vase, 7" h., "paperweight" type, thick-walled baluster form in aquamarine Favrile cased to bright iridescent reddish orange decorated internally w/six red-centered white blossoms & green leaves, base signed "L.C. Tiffany Favrile 5779C," chips on button pontil (ILLUS.) **5,463.00**

Vase, 5¼" h., 7¼" d., floral-form, a short ribbed stem in green spreading to leaves around the rounded opal lower body of the bowl w/a widely flaring & gently ruffled gold iridescent rim, signed "L.C. Tiffany - Favrile #6443D" . . . **1,375.00**

Vase, 7½" h., floral-form, an optic ribbed flaring cylindrical body w/a wide squatty bulbous closed rim, the slender stem on a round foot, overall bluish gold iridescence, signed "L.C.T. X287" **1,210.00**

Vase, 8" h., "paperweight" type, slender ovoid body w/a tapering bulbed neck, amber w/interior gold lustre internally decorated by vertical stripes composed of golden amber dots in a "zipper" pattern, inscribed "L.C.T. Favrile" **1,495.00**

Vase, 8" h., widely flaring conical base tapering sharply to a tall, slender slightly flaring "stick" neck, wide iridescent leaftips around the base shading to overall gold iridescence, signed "L.C. Tiffany Favrile #1557K" **770.00**

Vase, 9" h., "Cypriote," tapered cylinder w/metallic inclusions & rough-textured surface w/golden purple iridescence, inscribed "L.C. Tiffany Favrile 8500 B" **1,610.00**

Vase, 12" h., floral-form, the bulbous ovoid upper body w/a short, flared flat mouth, body tapering sharply to a tall slender knopped stem on a round foot, reddish gold iridescence decorated w/strewn green leaf pods dangling from entangled threaded vines, signed "L.C. Tiffany, Inc., Favrile - #1517" **2,750.00**

Vase, 13¾" h., swelled compressed base tapering to tall cylindrical sides decorated w/iridescent blue w/silver flowers & leafage up & around the sides, inscribed "Louis C. Tiffany - Favrile - 07496" **8,625.00**

Vase, 15" h., glass & bronze, a domed & ribbed gilt-bronze foot w/a swelled short stem fitted w/a tall trumpet-form glass vase in overall golden iridescence, vase

signed "L.C.T.," base impressed
"Louis C. Tiffany Furnaces Inc.
160"........................ **863.00**

Vase, 15" h., tall slender trumpet-form
body above a knopped stem &
round domed foot, overall golden
iridescence, signed "L.C. Tiffany
Favrile" & numbered "1536 3
129K," ca. 1916 .... **2,090.00**

Rare Tiffany "Paperweight" Vase

Vase, 16" h., tall elongated ovoid
form w/swelled shoulder & flaring
cushion foot, "paperweight" style,
clear internally decorated w/ten
paperwhite Narcissus blossoms
w/red & yellow millefiore cane
centers, perched on naturalized
brown stems w/green spike leaves
extending from the base, signed
"L.C. Tiffany Favrile 2731G"
(ILLUS.) **17,250.00**

TIFFIN

*A wide variety of fine glasswares was
produced by the Tiffin Glass Company of Tiffin,
Ohio. Beginning as a part of the large U.S. Glass
Company early in this century, the Tiffin factory
continued making a wide range of wares until its
final closing in 1984. One popular line is now
called "Black Satin" and included various vases
with raised floral designs. Many other acid-
etched and hand-cut patterns were also
produced over the years and are very collectible
today. The three "Tiffin Glassmasters" books by
Fred Bickenheuser, are the standard references
for Tiffin collectors.*

Tiffin Mark

Basket, Twilight cutting, clear,
5½" w., 9" h. **$295.00**

Bonbon, two-handled, etched
Flanders patt., yellow **24.00**

Bowl, 9¼" d., four-footed, oblong
w/square corners, Twilight cutting. . **195.00**

Bowl, oval, 8 x 14", Cascade patt.,
clear........................ **35.00**

Champagne, etched Cherokee Rose
patt., No. 17403, clear.......... **18.00**

Champagne, etched Cordelia patt.,
No. 15047, yellow **16.00**

Champagne, No. 17507-1, Twilight
cutting **48.00**

Champagne, etched Cherokee Rose
patt., No. 17399 stem, clear, 4 oz. . . **38.00**

Cocktail, etched Persian Pheasant
patt., No. 15083, clear........... **23.00**

Cocktail, liquor, cut Athlone patt.,
clear........................ **8.00**

Compote, open, 5" d., 3¾" h., a short
pedestal base below the bowl w/a
fluted rim, canary yellow, original
paper label................... **28.00**

Cordial, etched Fuchsia patt.,
No. 15083, clear **45.00**

Goblet, etched Persian Pheasant
patt., No. 17358, clear........... **26.00**

Goblet, gold-encrusted Minton patt.,
clear........................ **38.00**

Goblet, Laurel Wreath patt.,
No.17361, clear................ **10.00**

Goblet, Spikes patt., clear **10.00**

Goblet, water, etched Cadena patt.,
yellow bowl w/crystal stem **50.00**

Goblet, water, etched Cerise patt.,
No. 15072, clear **22.00**

Goblet, water, etched Persian
Pheasant patt., clear **30.00**

Goblet, water, etched La Fleure patt.,
yellow bowl w/crystal stem, 8¼" h. . . . **35.00**

Oyster cocktail, etched Byzantine
patt., clear **11.00**

Oyster cocktail, etched Flanders
patt., clear **20.00**

Pitcher, etched Cadena patt., clear . . **150.00**

Pitcher, footed ball stem w/teardrop
bubble, Era line, No. 5961, clear,
24 oz....................... **55.00**

Plate, 6" d., etched Flanders patt.,
clear........................ **9.00**

Plate, 6" d., etched La Fleure patt.,
yellow **8.00**
Plate, 7½" d., etched La Fleure patt.,
yellow **15.00**
Plate, 8" d., etched Flanders patt.,
yellow **14.00**
Plate, 8½" d., etched La Fleure patt.,
yellow **14.00**
Plate, 9¼" d., etched Cadena patt.,
yellow **40.00**
Plate, lily, 13" d., etched Cerise patt.,
clear. **45.00**
Sherbet, Laurel Wreath patt.,
No. 17361, clear **8.00**
Sundae, tall stem, cut Mt. Vernon
patt., clear **12.00**
Sundae, tall stem, etched Fuchsia
patt., clear **14.00**
Tumbler, iced tea, etched Cherokee
Rose patt., No. 17403, clear **30.00**
Tumbler, iced tea, Spikes patt., clear. . **10.00**
Tumbler, juice, footed, cut Mt.
Vernon patt., clear. **12.00**
Tumbler, juice, footed, cut Mystic
patt., clear **12.00**
Tumbler, juice, footed, etched June
Night patt., No. 17403, clear **25.00**
Tumbler, juice, footed, etched
Cadena patt., clear, 4¼" h. **27.00**
Tumbler, footed, etched Arcadian
patt., No. 185, pink & crystal,
5 oz.. . . . . **45.00**
Tumbler, iced tea, footed, etched
Psyche patt., clear w/green trim,
No. 194, 12 oz. **60.00**
Tumbler, seltzer, footed, etched
Classic patt., clear, 14 oz. **30.00**
Vase, bud, 8" h., etched Cherokee
Rose patt., clear **45.00**
Vase, 8⅛" h., tall gently flaring
trumpet-form body on a round foot,
shaded deep orangish red to
yellow Flame color. **88.00**
Vase, bud, 10" h., etched Cherokee
Rose patt., clear **45.00**
Vase, bud, 10" h., etched Fuchsia
patt., No. 14185, clear. **43.00**
Wine, etched Byzantine patt.,
clear. **18.00**
Wine, etched Cerise patt., No. 15072,
clear. **17.00**
Wine, etched Flanders patt.,
pink **75.00**
Wine, No. 17501, Wisteria (light
pink). **36.00**
Wine, Twilight, No. 17507, clear **38.00**
Wine, etched June Night patt., 3 oz.,
clear, 5½" h. **34.00**

VAL ST. LAMBERT

*This Belgian glassworks was founded in
1790. Items listed here represent a sampling of
its numerous and varied lines.*

Val St. Lambert Mark

Berry bowls, round w/diamond &
panel cutting, signed, ca. 1900,
5" d., set of 6 . . . . **$193.00**
Cameo vase, 6¼" h., ovoid body
w/everted rim, pale yellow ground
overlaid in aquamarine & etched to
depict a sailboat on a wooded lake,
cameo signature **368.00**
Cameo vase, 8" h., ovoid body
tapering to a slightly flaring
cylindrical neck w/a serpentine rim,
clear overlaid w/light green & cut
w/a design of large poppy
blossoms & leaves, wavy bands
cut around the neck, signed "Made
in Belgium - Val St. Lambert,"
ca. 1920s. **825.00**
Cameo vase, 10" h., textured frosted
clear ground overlaid in ruby red &
cut w/a single iris blossom, bud
& spiked leaves **440.00**
Candlestick, tall six-paneled
standard w/a knop below the
candle socket, hexagonal foot,
clear, signed "MVSL," 9½" h. **66.00**
Tumbler, cylindrical, 1½" acid-cut
band of women in gold against a
stippled ground w/cranberry bands
above & below, cut crystal panels
on bottom, 3⅛" d., 5¼" h. **195.00**

Teardrop-form Val St. Lambert Vase

Vase, 5¼" h., 6¾" l., elliptical thick-
walled inverted teardrop form in
line green transparent glass, acid-
stamped on the base "Val St.
Lambert" (ILLUS.) **345.00**

VASELINE

This glass takes its name from its color which is akin to that of petroleum jelly used for medicinal purposes. Originally manufacturers usually referred to the color as "canary." We list miscellaneous pieces below. Also see OPALESCENT GLASS and PATTERN GLASS.

Butter dish, cov., Ransom patt.,
   gold trim. **$250.00**
Celery dish, Panel patt. **48.00**
Cruet w/original stopper, Ransom
   patt. **250.00**
Egg cup, double, Inverted
   Thumbprint patt. **45.00**
Goblet, Panel patt. **40.00**
Pitcher, water, applied handle,
   Swirl Optic patt. **110.00**
Serving dish, oval, two-part, in silver
   holder, 9" d. **28.00**
Spooner, Panel patt. **28.00**
Vase, 7½" h., opalescent, central
   thorny stem w/two attached bud
   vases & applied feet, England,
   late 19th c. **255.00**

VENETIAN

Venetian glass has been made for six centuries on the island of Murano, where it continues to be produced. The skilled glass artisans developed numerous techniques, subsequently imitated elsewhere.

Block aquarium, two thick green &
   clear rectangular blocks encasing a
   silver fish w/red-striped fins & tail
   among green water grasses,
   attributed to Gino Cenedese,
   6¼" l., 4¾" h. **$575.00**
Block aquarium, two thick clear
   rectangular tablets encasing four
   colorful exotic fish swimming
   among green & red aquatic plants,
   attributed to Cenedese, 8¾" l.,
   5½" h. (some base chips) **403.00**
Bowl, 4½" h., cased yellow jardiniere-
   form w/applied black
   handles, prunts & body wraps. **230.00**
Bowl, 6¼" w., 2½" h., "Aureliano
   Toso Oriente," a thick-walled
   round-bottomed tricorner form in
   clear w/enclosed white, red, yellow,
   blue, black & green squares & gold
   Aventurine sections, by Dino
   Martens **460.00**
Candleholder, clear w/silver mica
   flecks, a skirted base w/applied
   leaves & apple green flower buds,
   20th c., 4½" h. **39.00**

Collectible Venetian Clown

Figure of a clown, bottle-type, multicolored costume & applied facial
   features, head form stopper, round
   foil Murano label, 14" h.
   (ILLUS.) **55.00**
Lamps, table model, emerald green
   w/applied clear rigaree & colored
   enameling, 15" h., pr. **375.00**
Model of a dog, body w/red
   controlled bubbles & heavy gold
   speckling, applied amber ears &
   tail, solid red nose, eyes, mouth
   & neck ribbon, 8" h. **295.00**
Model of a hat, man's cowboy-style
   hat w/upturned sides, mottled dark
   navy blue decorated w/a white hat
   band & symmetrical red threading
   on the brim, 13" l., 5" h. **345.00**
Model of a pheasant, raised tail,
   multicolored body w/overall gold
   flecks,16" l. **125.00**
Model of a walrus, the recumbent
   animal w/head up, applied tusks,
   eyes & ears, solid lattimo white in
   topaz shaded to clear, attributed to
   Salviati, 10½" l., 5¾" h. **173.00**

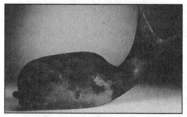

Venetian Model of a Whale

Model of a whale, "Vetreria
   Cenedese Corroso," stylized
   humpback whale executed in
   heavy aquamarine w/turquoise
   blue lips & eyes, etched overall &
   splotched w/mettalic oxides to
   produce a corroded effect, base

inscribed "Cenedese Murano 97V" & "Talberto," 15" l. (ILLUS. on previous page) **1,380.00**

Plate of fruits, 11" d., the round dished black aubergine plate w/oro antico aventurine accompanied by six matching blown glass pieces of fruit, designed by Ercole Barovier for 1934 Biennale, the set **316.00**

Vase, 5½" h., 7" d., "sommerso"-style, a wide squatty bulbous body w/a wide rounded shoulder to the short cylindrical neck w/a flattened, flaring mouth, heavy clear body cased over red & purple graduating toward the rim, designed by Flavio Poli, Seguso Vetri d'Arte, ca. 1950 . . . . **1,100.00**

Vase, 7¼" h., flaring quatreform body composed of orange-centered red window squares framed in white & fused, attributed to Archimedes Seguso **920.00**

Vase, 8" h., 3" d., "bullicante"-style, designed by Archimede Seguso, black appliqué on grey & white **295.00**

Fine Venetian "Intarsio" Vase

Vase, 8½" h., 5¾" d., thick-walled cylindrical form w/a rounded base, "Intarsio" type, composed of fused transparent red & green squares checkered w/colorless segments w/symmetrically controlled bubbles, designed by Ercole Barovier, Barovier & Toso, mid-20th c. (ILLUS.) **4,600.00**

Vase, 6" h., 9" d., "fazzoletto"-style, handkerchief-type, deep flaring cylindrical sides randomly crimped & ruffled, composed of alternating canes of deep translucent red & white zanfirico, attributed to Fratelli Toso, ca. 1950s **231.00**

Vase, 9¼" h., "Bianca Nero," simple baluster-form body decorated w/parallel groups of spiraled white & black filagrana separated by d'oro aventurine threads in a clear ground, by Dino Martens **374.00**

Vase, 10" h., "Zanfirico," bulbous ovoid elliptical body flaring slightly at the indented rim, clear internally decorated by spiraled polychrome rods & glass canes, possibly A.VE.M. **201.00**

Vase, 10" h., 5¾" d., "Ferro Lazzarini," red, black & blue striped exterior **330.00**

Vase, 11" h., "saterneo"-style, flat-bottomed ovoid bottle-form w/a flared mouth, clear w/gold aventurine inclusions decorated w/rows of white stripes alternating w/stripes of blue concentric circles, original Barovier & Toso paper label, designed by Ercole Barovier, ca. 1951 . . . . **2,587.00**

Vase, 11" h., tall slender tapering ovoid body w/a thick rolled neck band, in the style of Fratelli Toso, heavy walled fiery amber embedded w/polychrome murrine glass canes in blossom arrangements **374.00**

Vase, 11" h., tall slightly tapering cylindrical body, "Graffito" style w/a design executed on a clear ground w/combed lattimo white outlines on airtrap windows accented by gold aventurine inclusions, designed by Ercole Barovier, Barovier & Toso, 1969 . . . . **1,380.00**

Fine Venetian Bottle-form Vase

Vase, 11½" h., "Saturneo," free-blown ovoid bottle form w/a small cylindrical neck, clear internally decorated by five double rows of teal greenish aqua bull's-eye murrine separated by lattimo white filligrana vertical rods highlighted by aventurine accents throughout, Ercole Barovier, 1951, Barovier & Toso (ILLUS.) **9,200.00**

Vase, 13½" h., swirled twelve-rib molded baluster-form in lavender amethyst internally decorated by controlled trapped bubbles connected by purple powders **460.00**

Venetian "Vaso a Canne" Vase

Vase, 15¼" h., "Vaso a Canne," flattened oval cylinder composed of fused blue, green, blackish aubergine & aventurine stripes swirled to the right w/optical illusory effect, engraved three-line mark on base "Barovier - & Toso - Murano," Barovier & Toso, mid-20th c. (ILLUS.) **2,300.00**

Vase, 15½" h., footed gently waisted & flaring cylindrical form, clear w/prominent vertical cords cased to aqua blue w/controlled bubble & gold fleck decoration fused between, Barovier & Toso, 20th c. **920.00**

VENINI

Founded by former lawyer Paolo Venini in 1925, this Venetian glasshouse soon developed a reputation for its fine quality decorative glass and tablewares. Several noted designers have worked for the firm over the years and their unique pieces in the modern spirit, made using traditional techniques, are increasingly popular with collectors today. The factory continues in operation.

Bottle set: a 15" h. bottle & five matching 2" h. bowls; the bottle w/a cylindrical lower body tapering to a flaring trumpet-form flattened shoulder centered by a small, tall cylindrical neck fitted w/a tall ovoid stopper, teal green fused to deep blue waist fused to a green neck w/a blue stopper, matching deep

half-round bowls, circular stamp mark "venini ITALY murano," designed by Gio Ponti, ca. 1950s, the set **$1,870.00**

Bowl-vase, "Fazzoletto," deep rounded form w/upright crimped & pleated sides, "camichato" slumped handkerchief form in lattimo white cased to cornflower blue, stamped on base "Venini - Murano - Italia," 4½" h. **316.00**

Bowl-vase, deep rounded sides pulled upright w/a folded handkerchief form, striped clear design w/alternating zanfirico ribbons of turquoise & lattimo white, base stamped "Venini Murano Italia," 10" d., 6¼" h. (some minor sand blemishes) **575.00**

Ceiling lamp, tall slender swelled cylindrical form, lattimo white glass fused to transparent horizontal fasce of blue, green, red, blue, aubergine & clear stripes, mounted to socket fixture, by Massimo Vignelli, 1954, 19½" h. **1,035.00**

Center bowl, rectangular dished form w/rounded corners & slightly upturned sides, heavy walled colorless form w/symmetrically arranged internal bolla bubbles, applied ring foot stamped "Venini Murano," pre-war design, 11½ x 14½", 4¼" h. **230.00**

Cologne bottle w/original stopper, ovoid body w/a short cylindrical neck, teardrop stopper, pastel green w/tiny bubbles throughout, clear smooth exterior w/trapped gold foil inclusions, base stamped "Venini Murano Made in Italy," 5¾" h. **173.00**

Cordial set: a carafe-form decanter & three cordials; the carafe w/a tapering cylindrical body & widely flaring neck composed of multicolored canes, the slender waisted cylindrical cordials in deep blue, one cordial w/a paper label, designed by Paolo Venini, ca. 1950s, cordials 5½" h., carafe 10½" h., the set **1,870.00**

Hourglass, "clessidre"-style, composed of two tapering ovoid segments of light plum & ocean blue joined "incalmo" at a tiny neck, filled w/sand, designed by Paolo Venini, acid-stamped "venini murano italia," ca. 1950s **1,210.00**

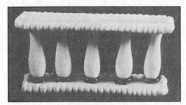

Venini Glass Balustrade

Model of a balustrade, composed of
five baluster-form spindles of
lattimo white glass trimmed in black
& attached top & bottom to glass
railing w/white rigaree, stamped
"Venini Murano Italia," designed by
Fulvio Bianconi for the series
inspired by Giovan Battista Tieplo,
8¼" l., 4¼" h. (ILLUS.). **690.00**

Model of a chicken, stylized bird w/a
lattimo white swirled tilted conical
body of lattimo white swirled design
w/an applied yellow beak & feet,
red comb, black eyes, wings & disc
foot, Fulvio Bianconi design
Gallina, 1950, 6½" h. **1,380.00**

Model of an obelisk, "Obelischi a
canne de zanfirico," solid clear
swelled cylindrical form w/a core of
spiraled multi-colored glass
threads, designed by Paolo Venini,
exhibited at Biennale, 1954, base
stamped "Venini Murano Italia,"
6" h. **380.00**

Shade, hanging-type, "fasce"-style,
opaque white w/applied bands of
brilliant red, deep amethyst, blue &
green, designed by Massimo
Vignelli, ca. 1950, 9" d., 9½" h. **550.00**

Vase, 3½" h., "fazzoletto"-style,
handkerchief-form, an upright flora-
form w/deep ruffled sides, light blue
cased over lattimo, circular acid-
stamped mark "venini - ITALY -
murano," designed by Fulvio
Bianconi, ca. 1950s **165.00**

Vase, 4¾" h., simple ovoid form
flaring to a wide, flat mouth,
"Merletto," a netted design in clear
w/a complex pattern of white
lattimo & filligrana webs
interspersed w/controlled seed
bubbles, stamped mark on
base. **920.00**

Vase, 8" h., "fazzoletto"-style,
handkerchief-form, upright rounded
randomly ruffled sides pulled into
random points, opaque white
interior cased clear, designed by
Paolo Venini, acid-stamped "venini
murano - ITALIA," ca. 1950s **660.00**

Vase, 8" h., squared upright form
w/rounded corners & a wide
shoulder centering a squared neck,
"Tessuto," composed of red
alternating w/white glass threads
on one half, black & red on the
other, marked on the base w/an
early stamp "Venini Murano Italia,"
designed by Carlo Scarpa,
exhibited Biennial 1940 . . . . **2,530.00**

Venini Spherical Vase

Vase, 8¼" h., 9½" d., slightly squatty
spherical body w/a wide rounded
shoulder centered by a short, small
flaring neck flanked by long angled
shoulder handles, transparent teal
bluish green, stamped on the base
"Venini Murano Italia," design
attributed to Napoleone Martinuzzi
(ILLUS.). **978.00**

Vase, 8¾" h., large spherical form,
"Fasce Orizzontale," clear body
enclosing a lattimo white ribbon of
glass, attributed to Gio Ponte, base
stamped "Venini Murano Made in
Italy" (some interior stain) **489.00**

Fine Free-blown Venini Vase

Vase, 10½" h., free-blown widely
flaring elliptical form tapering
sharply to a gently flared base,
fused stripes of alternating red,
blue & green transparent glass,
designed by Fulvio Bianconi, 1952,
Studio Fasce Verticali, unsigned
(ILLUS.) **4,140.00**

VICTORIAN COLORED GLASS

There are, of course, many types of colored glassware of the Victorian era and we cover a great variety of these in our various glass categories. However, there are some pieces of pressed, mold-blown and free-blown Victorian colored glass which don't fit well into other specific listings, so we have chosen to include a selection of them here.

Animal covered dish, Dog on Steamer Rug, blue opaque, flower-molded base, Vallerysthal, France **$250.00**

Animal covered dish, Fish, blue opaque, Vallerysthal, France. **425.00**

Animal covered dish, Pig on Drum, blue opaque, marked "PV," Vallerysthal, France, 3" h. **120.00**

Animal covered dish, Hen on nest, blue w/white head, 5" l. **40.00**

Animal covered dish, Squirrel on fancy dish, blue opaque, Vallerysthal, France, 5" l., 5" h. **83.00**

Animal covered dish, Frog, black, 5¾" l. **300.00**

Bowl, master berry, Torquay patt., cobalt blue **200.00**

Amber Glass & Pewter Claret Jug

Claret jug, footed spherical amber glass body w/delicate swirled ribbing, topped by a tall ring & embossed French pewter collar w/mask spout, hinged domed cover w/thumbrest & loop & scroll handle, 5" d., 8⅝" h. (ILLUS.) **225.00**

Cracker jar, cov., Torquay patt., cobalt blue, silver plate rim, cover & bail handle **595.00**

Cruet set, Forget-me-not patt., blue opaque, 4 pcs. **250.00**

Blown Cased Glass Candlestick

Candlestick, rose pink overlay lined in white forming the cylindrical candle socket & conical base, applied clear rigaree around the socket rim & base, top & base joined by a ring of thorny branches, 4½" d., 8⅜" h. (ILLUS.) **195.00**

Apple Green Glass Ring Tree

Ring tree, slender pedestal base on a disc foot supports a shallow flaring ruffled dish centered by a tall tapering ring spike, apple green opaque trimmed w/gilt, 3¼" d., 5⅛" h. (ILLUS.) **110.00**

Shaker w/original top, Forget-me-not patt., blue opaque . . **165.00**

Sugar shaker w/original lid, Acorn patt., black amethyst w/gold flecks . . **395.00**

Blue Inverted Thumbprint Vase

Vase, 4⅞" h., 4¾" d., footed broad
shouldered ovoid body w/a short,
wide cylindrical neck, sapphire blue
Inverted Thumbprint patt. w/white
enamel Roman key band around
the neck & lacy heart band around
the shoulder, applied angled amber
shoulder handles (ILLUS.). **145.00**

Water carafe, Torquay patt., cobalt
blue **395.00**

WAVE CREST

*Now much sought after, Wave Crest was
produced by the C.F. Monroe Co., Meriden,
Connecticut, in the late 19th and early 20th
centuries from opaque white glass blown into
molds.*

*It was then hand-decorated in enamels and
metal trim was often added. Boudoir accessories
such as jewel boxes, hair receivers, etc., were
predominant.*

WAVE CREST WARE

Wave Crest Mark

Box w/hinged cover, Baroque Shell
mold, blackened base & cover
border centering a faintly outlined
bust portrait of a Victorian lady
wearing a large fancy hat, body
highlighted w/sponged gold, wide
gilt-metal fittings, 5½" d., 3" h.. . . . . **$550.00**

Ornate Wave Crest Squared Box

Box w/hinged cover, squared body
& cover w/overall C-scroll molded
borders, the top decorated
w/delicate pink flowers, the side
panels.w/similar flowers or scrolls,
marked, front panel "Collar" writing
removed, scratches, 6" h.
(ILLUS.). **489.00**

Box w/hinged lid, Egg Crate mold,
Rococo base w/footed appearance,
h.p pink & white flowers, 6½" w.,
3¾" h. **450.00**

Carafe, squatty bulbous round body
centered by a tall reverse-swirl
molded cylindrical neck in glossy
white, the body w/a pale satin pink
ground decorated in sepia brown
monotone w/a scene of lakeside
building & a distant bridge, the
reverse side w/a lighthouse
scene, 8¼" h. **1,073.00**

Card holder, light blue ground w/pink
tea roses, original metal lining,
1¼ x 2¾", 4" h. **410.00**

Cracker jar, cov., Egg Crate mold,
decorated w/large pink & yellow
roses & yellow foliage on a creamy
white ground, paper label intact . . . **851.00**

Cracker jar, cov., Egg Crate mold,
pink floral decoration, silver plate
rim, cover & bail handle, paper
label mostly intact on the base. . . . **1,210.00**

Cracker jar, cov., raised florals &
beading decoration, silver plate
cover, rim & bail handle,
unsigned **285.00**

Cracker jar, cov., scroll-molded
square form, floral decorated side
panels w/soft blue highlights,
signed, silver plate rim, cover & bail
handle **440.00**

Cracker jar, cov., scroll-molded
square form, decorated w/floral
panels & pink trim, original label on
the base, silver plate rim, cover &
bail handle. **418.00**

Cracker jar, cov., simple barrel-
shaped milk white body h.p. w/a
large red rose on a leafy green
stem, shaded ground, signed,
simple silver plate rim & low
domed cover **83.00**

Cracker jar, cov.,smooth barrel
shape, h.p. blue & rose large florals
in soft tan scrolls, shades of lemon
to peach background, silver plate
cover, rim & twisted bail handle. . . . **250.00**

Cracker jar, cov., Helmschmied Swirl
mold, decorated w/a pink floral
bough & delicate grasses,
alternating pale blue ground,

embossed silver plate rim w/plain low domed cover w/knob finial & scrolled bail handle, 6½" h. **633.00**

Creamer & cov. sugar bowl, squatty bulbous form decorated w/white flowers & green & brown leaves on a creamy white ground, ornate silver plate rim spout w/handle on creamer, silver plate rim & cover w/handle & loop finial, pr. **450.00**

Dresser box w/hinged cover, round, the cover molded in bold-relief w/a large single zinnia blossom in pink & white w/a yellow center & dark green border, squatty bulbous dark green base w/four molded blossoms, marked, 4½" d., 2½" h. **990.00**

Dresser box w/hinged cover, Baroque Shell mold, round, the flattened cover & body w/a satin almond ground, the cover center decorated w/a mauve & pink daisy bouqet, pale enamel-dotted ground bordered w/enameled plum scrolls, 7" d., 4" h. **770.00**

Dresser box w/hinged cover, Helmschmied Swirl mold, decorated on base & cover w/unusual brown leafy thistle stalk w/amethyst blossoms, 7" d., 4" h. . . **440.00**

Dresser box w/hinged cover, Petal mold, pale blue ground the flattened cover decorated in the center w/a spreading pink floral bouquet, the squatty bulbous base w/matching floral bouquet, 7¾" d., 3½" h., signed **660.00**

Jewelry box w/hinged lid, piecrust edge around top, relief-molded florals on sides, h.p. flowers on top, back & front **525.00**

Key box w/original key, Petticoat & Mushroom mold, nicely decorated, 7½" d. **900.00**

Letter receiver, Egg Crate mold, ormolu trim, floral decoration. **425.00**

Match holder, low plain cylindrical form w/a gilt-metal rim, floral decoration, originally part of a cigar set, unmarked. **165.00**

Match holder, bulbous ovoid milk white holder tapering slightly to a wide, short cylindrical neck, decorated w/a blue daisy bouquet against a pale pink & blue ground, set upon an ornate gilt-metal footed base, marked, 2¾" h. **605.00**

Photo receiver, Egg Crate mold, upright rectangular form, floral decoration on a creamy white ground w/gilt-metal rim **475.00**

Salt & pepper shakers w/original metal lids, cylindrical base below a bulbous shoulder, house decoration, pr. **250.00**

Salt shaker w/original lid, jug-shaped, blue shading to white w/a transfer of a pointer dog in foliage, 2" h. **95.00**

Tobacco box w/hinged cover, Egg Crate mold, white ground decorated w/green clover, unmarked, 5" w. **66.00**

Toothbrush jar, cov., tall cylindrical body w/original silver plate cover, floral decoration. **525.00**

Vase, short cylindrical neck above an ovoid body w/scrolled trim, reverse decoration w/blue florals, pale yellow ground, fitted w/a gilt-metal rim w/small scroll handles & floral flower holder, set into a gilt-metal scrolling branch-form pedestal base, small **375.00**

Vase, bud, 5" h., cylindrical, tapering at base, beaded metal rim & footed metal base, decorated w/blue flowers on a creamy ground **320.00**

Rare Wave Crest Whisk Broom Holder

Whisk broom holder, cylindrical body w/pointed ribbing decorated w/a large gilt scroll-trimmed cartouche of pink & purple rose buds & green leafy stems & white dotting, very pale blue ground, mounted w/a brass base & rim ring & ornate pierced & scrolling backplate (ILLUS.) **1,600.00**

WEBB

This glass is made by Thomas Webb & Sons of Stourbridge, one of England's most prolific glasshouses. Numerous types of glass, including cameo, have been produced by this firm through the years. The company also produced various types of novelty and "art" glass during the late Victorian period. Also see "Glass" BURMESE, ROSE BOWLS, and SATIN & MOTHER-OF-PEARL.

Striped & Appliqued Webb Bowl

Bowl, 5¾" d., 4½" h., rounded bottom below the rolled tricorner rim w/applied dripping clear icicles, the body w/slightly embossed ribbing in alternating stripes of avocado green & sapphire blue w/mica flecks, on three applied clear peg feet & a berry pontil (ILLUS.). **$235.00**

Cameo cologne bottle w/hinged silver cap, spherical body in yellow layered in white & etched overall as decumbent fuchsia w/elaborate borders above & below, butterfly at center, sterling silver rim & hinged cap w/English hallmarks, 4¾" h. (tiny glass chip on butterfly antenna) **978.00**

Cameo scent bottle w/gilt-metal hinged cap, flattened teardrop form in sapphire blue overlaid in white & cut w/white ferns & grasses w/a butterfly at the side, 4" l. **920.00**

Cameo vase, 4¼" h., footed bulbous ovoid body tapering to a cylindrical slightly waisted neck, tri-color, w/white cut to red bellflower & bud on a leafy stem w/a butterfly on the reverse side all against a citron yellow ground, decorative cut rim **2,915.00**

Cameo vase, 4½" h., simple ovoid form w/a small closed rim, pale raisin-colored ground overlaid in white & etched around the shoulder w/a leafy bough bearing delicate blossom clusters, linear border at the rim **575.00**

Cameo vase, 5" h., footed spherical body below a tall slender "stick" neck w/a ruffled, flared rim, deep pink cased on white & cut w/a design of fern fronds & grass blades, glossy finish **193.00**

Cameo vase, 5¼" h., pilgrim flask-form, a domed foot w/flattened rim supporting a wide flattened round body tapering to a short cylindrical neck w/flared rim, applied pink handles from rim to shoulder, the body in duBarry pink cut to white w/a solitary dragonfly above meadow grasses, white beaded enamel decoration on the rim & foot, glossy finish **743.00**

Cameo vase, 5½" h., squatty bulbous body tapering to a trumpet neck, red layered in white & cameo-etched w/five detailed seashells on various seaweed clusters, base marked "Thomas Webb & Sons - Cameo," 19th c. **2,645.00**

Cameo vase, 7" h., bottle-form w/a spherical base centered by a tall cylindrical neck, simulated ivory ground etched w/ivy above berries on leafy vines enhanced by sepia coloration, semicircular base mark "Thos. Webb & Sons" **805.00**

Cameo vase, 9" h., simple ovoid body w/a small closed mouth, Peach Blow ground overlaid in white & cut w/a solitary butterfly by exotic passion flower blossoms dangling from a meandering leafy vine cascading from the rim, further cameo-cut ornate daisy blossoms, all on a ground etched w/scrolled tendrils **3,300.00**

Cracker jar, cov., simple barrel shape in opaque pink cased over white, the exterior decorated w/ornate gilt floral decoration, silver plate rim, domed cover & bail handle, rim inscribed "From Mother and Jay, Dec. 25, 1889," paper label mostly intact on base **440.00**

Gilt-decorated Webb Vase

Vase, 4" h., 2⅜" d., ovoid body w/a short flaring neck, ivory opaque w/heavy gilt floral decoration around the sides including a butterfly on the back, unsigned (ILLUS.). **165.00**

Vase, 5½" h., 5¼" d., a small round foot supporting a squatty bulbous body w/a short cylindrical neck, shaded brown satin decorated w/heavy gold pine needles & prunus blossoms & a gold butterfly on the back, gilt rim & foot bands . . **495.00**

Vase, 8" h., footed slender optic-ribbed flora-form body w/flaring rim w/an overall orangish gold iridescent finish similar to Steuben Aurene, base inscribed "Webb Iris Glass" **173.00**

Vase, 8½" h., a gently tapering cylindrical body raised on three gold knob feet, cased pink exterior enameled w/a gold rim band w/white beading & delicate enameled florals around the sides, white interior, script signature, early 20th c. **248.00**

WESTMORELAND

Westmoreland Specialty Company was founded in East Liverpool, Ohio in 1889 and relocated in 1890 to Grapeville, Pennsylvania where it remained until its closing in 1985.

During its early years Westmoreland specialized in glass food containers and novelties but by the turn of the century they had a large line of milk white items and clear tableware patterns. In 1925 the company name was shortened to The Westmoreland Glass Company and it was during that decade that more colored glasswares entered their line-up. When Victorian-style milk glass again became popular in the 1940s and 1950s, Westmoreland produced extensive amounts in several patterns which closely resemble late-19th-century wares. These and their figural animal dishes in milk white and colors are widely collected today but buyers should not confuse them with the antique originals. Watch for Westmoreland's "WG" mark on some pieces. A majority of our listings are products from the 1940s through the 1970s. Earlier pieces will be indicated.

Westmoreland Marks

Animal covered dish, Pintail duck on diamond basketweave base, milk white, 5½" l. **$40.00**

Basket, 6½" oval, Paneled Grape patt., milk white **30.00**

Bowl, pickle, oval, Paneled Grape patt. milk white. **18.00**

Bowl, cov., 4" sq., Beaded Grape patt., milk white **30.00**

Bowl, cov., 5" sq., footed w/flared rim, Beaded Grape patt., milk white **25.00**

Bowl, cov., 7" sq., high-footed, Beaded Grape patt., milk white **40.00**

Bowl, 8" d., round, two-handled, footed, English Hobnail patt., milk white **25.00**

Bowl, 9" d., footed w/flared rim, Beaded Grape patt., milk white **45.00**

Bowl, cov., 9" h., square, high-footed, Beaded Grape patt., milk white **45.00**

Bowl, fruit, 9" d., footed w/crimped edge, Old Quilt patt., No. 43, milk white **45.00**

Bowl, 9" d., 6" h., skirted rim, footed, Paneled Grape patt., milk white **55.00**

Bowl, 9½" d., scalloped, Paneled Grape patt., milk white. **125.00**

Bowl, 11" oval, footed, Paneled Grape patt., milk white. **100.00**

Bowl, 11½" oval, scalloped foot, Paneled Grape patt., milk white . . . **100.00**

Box, cov., square, flat, Beaded Grape patt., milk white **35.00**

Box, cov., square, Beaded Grape patt., milk white, 4" d. **35.00**

Cake salver, Waterford patt., clear w/ruby stain **85.00**

Cake salver, skirted square, footed, Beaded Grape patt., milk white, 11" d. **100.00**

Cake stand, flat squared top w/scalloped ring & petal border raised on a ringed pedestal & domed base w/a flat squared foot, Blue Moonstone, 11" d. **99.00**

Cake stand, skirted, Paneled Grape patt., milk white, 11" d. **70.00**

Candlesticks, ball-shape, Thousand Eye patt., clear, pr. **35.00**

Candlesticks, Beaded Grape patt., milk white, pr. **23.00**

Candlesticks, Paneled Grape patt., milk white, 4" pr. **28.00**

Candlesticks, Thousand Eye patt., clear w/ruby stain, 5" h., pr. **60.00**

Candlesticks, dolphin-form standard w/a petal-form socket, round scalloped foot, Blue Moonstone, 1930-31, 9½" h., pr. **358.00**

Candy dish, cov., No. 26, Paneled Grape patt., milk white, ... **30.00**

Candy dish, three-footed, Paneled Grape patt., milk white, crimped and ruffled, 8" **35.00**

Celery vase, Paneled Grape patt.,
milk white. **35.00**
Celery vase, footed, Paneled Grape
patt., milk white, 6" h. **42.00**
Cheese dish, cov., Paneled Grape
patt., milk white **60.00**
Chocolate box, cov., Paneled Grape
patt., milk white **35.00**
Compote, cov., 7" h., footed, Paneled
Grape patt., milk white. **22.00**
Compote, open, 8½" d., crimped &
ruffled rim, stem-footed, Paneled
Grape patt., milk white. **45.00**
Creamer & open sugar, Paneled
Grape patt., milk white, pr. **20.00**
Creamer & open sugar bowl, Della
Robbia patt., milk white, pr. **25.00**
Creamer & open sugar bowl,
footed, English Hobnail patt., milk
white, pr. **29.00**
Creamer & open sugar bowl, Maple
Leaf (Bramble) patt., milk
white, pr. **30.00**
Creamer & open sugar bowl, Old
Quilt patt., milk white, large, pr. **28.00**
Cruet w/original stopper, oil, Old
Quilt patt., milk white **20.00**
Cruet w/original stopper, Paneled
Grape patt., milk white. **23.00**
Cup & saucer, Paneled Grape patt.,
milk white. **18.00**
Dish, heart-shaped, handled, Della
Robbia patt., 8" **45.00**
Dresser tray, Paneled Grape patt.,
milk white. **60.00**
Epergne, Paneled Grape patt., milk
white, 12" lip bowl & 8½" vase, ... **185.00**
Goblet, water, Della Robbia patt.,
clear w/colored staining, 8 oz. **28.00**
Goblet, water Della Robbia patt., milk
white w/red stain, 8 oz. **19.00**
Goblet, water, Della Robbia patt.,
milk white, 8 oz. **17.00**
Goblet, water, round, footed, English
Hobnail patt., milk white, 8 oz. **9.00**
Goblet, water, Waterford patt., clear
w/ruby stain **10.00**
Goblet, wine, round footed, English
Hobnail patt., light blue, 2 oz.,
4½" h. **65.00**
Gravyboat & undertray, Paneled
Grape patt., milk white, 2 pcs. **69.00**
Honey, cov., Beaded Grape patt.,
milk white, 5" d. **35.00**
Honey, cov., Beaded Grape patt.,
milk white w/gold grapes, 5" d. **50.00**
Honey, cov., Beaded Grape patt.,
Roses & Bows decoration, milk
white, 5" d. **45.00**
Ice tub, Rocker patt., pink. **95.00**

Mayonnaise dish & underplate,
Paneled Grape patt., milk white,
3½" d., 2 pcs. **23.00**
Mayonnaise dish, underplate &
ladle, Paneled Grape patt., milk
white, 3½" d., 3 pcs. **35.00**
Nappy, round, handled, Paneled
Grape patt., milk white, 5" d. **30.00**
Pitcher, No. 13, Paneled Grape patt.,
milk white. **40.00**
Pitcher, water, Old Quilt patt., milk
white **40.00**
Planter, square, Paneled Grape patt.,
milk white, 4½" w **40.00**
Planter, window-type, oblong,
Paneled Grape patt., milk white,
3 x 8½" **35.00**
Planter, rectangular, Paneled Grape
patt., milk white, 4¾" x 8¾" **45.00**
Plate, salad, 8½" d., Paneled Grape
patt., milk white **22.00**
Plate, dinner 10½ d., Paneled Grape
patt., milk white **43.00**
Plate, torte,14" d., Thousand Eye
patt., clear w/ruby stain **75.00**
Puff box, cov., Paneled Grape patt.,
milk white, 4½" d. **20.00**
Punch cup, Paneled Grape patt.,
milk white. **10.00**
Salt & pepper shakers, flat bottom,
Old Quilt patt., milk glass, pr. **25.00**
Salt & pepper shakers, flat bottom,
Paneled Grape patt., milk white, pr. . **48.00**
Sugar bowl, Beaded Grape patt.,
milk white. **15.00**
Sugar bowl, footed, Thousand Eye
patt., clear w/ruby stain **20.00**
Sweetmeat, cov.,high-footed, Old
Quilt patt., milk white, 6½" h. **12.00**
Tidbit, two-tier, Paneled Grape patt.,
milk white. **50.00**
Tumbler, Beaded Edge patt., No. 64-
2 fruit decoration, milk white **17.00**
Tumbler, iced tea, Paneled Grape
patt., milk white **25.00**
Tumbler, juice, Paneled Grape patt.,
milk white. **22.00**
Urn, cov., Waterford patt., clear
w/ruby stain, 12½" h. **95.00**
Vase, 9" h., bell-rimmed, footed, Old
Quilt patt., milk white **55.00**
Vase, 11½" h., bell-rimmed, footed,
Paneled Grape patt., milk white **80.00**
Vase, bud, 16" h., swung-type, flat,
Paneled Grape patt., milk white **90.00**
Vase, bud, 18" h., footed, Paneled
Grape patt., milk white. **55.00**

GLOBE MAPS

Celestial globe, table model, a 6" d. globe fitted in a cherry stand w/vertical & horizontal medial rings & raised on three baluster- and ring-turned legs joined by swelled stretchers joined at the center, by Gilman Joslin, United States, ca. 1840 (minor abrasions) **$4,025.00**

Celestial & terrestrial globes, table models, each globe raised on a foliate-molded cast-iron base, issued by Merriam & Moore, Troy, New York, 1852, 8¾" d., 9" h., pr. **9,775.00**

Celestial & Terrestrial Globes

Celestrial & terrestrial globes, table models, the terrestrial globe embroidered w/gold silk threads & inscribed w/black ink, the celestial globe similarly decorated w/the addition of watercolor highlights, both on cream silk grounds, & mounted on a wooden baluster-turned stem & circular molded foot, probably Westtown School, Chester County, Pennsylvania, 5" d., 12¼" h., pr. (ILLUS.) **8,625.00**

Terrestrial globe, mounted in half round ring on ebonized turned wooden stand w/round foot, Strand Publications, England, ca. 1920, 6" d., 11" h. **633.00**

Bardin's Terrestial Table Globe

Terrestrial globe, table model, 12" d. globe mounted within a round ring supported on ebonized baluster- and knob-turned legs joined by stretchers, by W. & T. M. Bardin, England, corrected to 1817, 16" h. to meridian (ILLUS.) **1,380.00**

Terrestrial globe, floor model, 18" d. globe mounted on a partial gilt Art Nouveau-style metal stand, Geo. F. Cram, United States, ca. 1900 .... **2,990.00**

Terrestrial globe, floor model, mahogany, raised on a baluster standard continuing to sabre legs ending in brass casters, J. W. Carey, Strand, London, early 19th c., 44" h. **14,950.00**

GRANITEWARE

This is a name given to metal (customarily iron) kitchenware covered with an enamel coating. Featured at the 1876 Philadelphia Centennial Exposition, it became quite popular for it was lightweight, attractive, and easy to clean. Although it was made in huge quantities and is still produced, it has caught the attention of a younger generation of collectors and prices have steadily risen over the past few years. There continues to be a constant demand for the wide variety of these utilitarian articles turned out earlier in this century and rare forms now command high prices.

BLUE AND WHITE SWIRL

Berry bucket, tin cover w/wire handle, 4¼" d., 5¾" h. **$225.00**

Butter churn, wooden cover, 10" d., 18" h. **1,800.00**

Chamber pail, cov., 10" d., 11½" h. ... **225.00**

Chamber pot, 10" d., 4¾" h. **125.00**

Coffee boiler, cov., Columbian Ware, 9" d., 10½" h. **425.00**

Coffeepot, tin cover, goose neck spout, 4½" d., 7¾" h. **265.00**

Cream can, tin cover, Columbian Ware, 4" d., 7¾" h. **800.00**

Creamer, Columbian Ware, 4" d., 5" h. **700.00**

Cup, Columbian Ware, 4" d., 3" h. **120.00**

Cuspidor, 9½" d., 4½" h., 2 pcs. **225.00**

Dish pan, oval, 12¼ x 17", 5" h. **250.00**

Jelly roll pan, 8¾" d., ¾" h. **65.00**

Kettle, straight sided, cooking, Columbian Ware, 14" d., 13" h. **425.00**

Loaf pan, 6½ x 11¾", 3½" h. **300.00**

Lunch bucket, cov., oval w/wire &
   wood handle, 8¼ x 9", 7" h.,
   3 pcs.. . . . . **600.00**
Muffin pan, 6 cup **1,350.00**
Mug, miner's, 6" d., 5" h. **140.00**
Roaster, cov., oval w/flat top,
   9½ x 14, 7½" h.. . . . . **175.00**
Sauce pan w/long black handle,
   10" d., 5¼" h.. . . . . **125.00**
Spoon, 2½" d., 12" l.. . . . . **225.00**

BLUE DIAMOND WARE
(Iris Blue & White Swirl)

Baking pan, 7¾ x 10", 2" h. **225.00**
Chamber pot, cov., 10¼" d., 8" h. . . . **275.00**
Coffeepot, cov., 5½" d., 9¾" h. **350.00**

Diamond Ware Creamer & Sugar Bowl

Creamer, 3½" d., 5" h. (ILLUS.
   right) **325.00**
Cuspidor, 8¾" d., 5" h.. . . . . **275.00**
Measuring cup, 3" d., 4½" h. **600.00**

Molasses Pitcher

Molasses pitcher, cov., 3½" d., 6" h.
   (ILLUS.). **900.00**
Mug, 3" d., 3" h. **100.00**
Pitcher, water, 10½" h., 6" d. **575.00**
Sugar bowl, cov., 4¼" d., 6¼" h.
   (ILLUS. left). **450.00**
Wash basin, 14½" d., 4" h.. . . . . **200.00**

BROWN & WHITE SWIRL

Brown Swirl Chamber Pail

Chamber pail, cov., 10½" d., 11½" h.
   (ILLUS.). **300.00**
Coffee boiler, cov., 8½" d.,
   11½" h. **325.00**
Creamer, 3½" d., 5" h. **825.00**
Dipper, 4½" d., 12" l. handle. **145.00**
Jelly roll pan, 10" d., 1¼" h.. . . . . **120.00**
Mug, miner's, 6" d., 4½" h. **225.00**
Pitcher, water, 8¾" h., 6¼" d.. . . . . . . **450.00**
Teakettle, cov., coiled iron handle,
   7¼" d., 7" h.. . . . . **750.00**
Tumbler, 3¼" d., 3½" h. **325.00**

CHRYSOLITE & WHITE SWIRL
(Dark Green & White Swirl)

Baking pan, 8 x 9½", 2" h. **225.00**
Coffee boiler, cov., 9¼" d., 11¾" h. . . . **350.00**
Coffeepot, cov., gooseneck spout,
   5¼" d., 8½" h. **450.00**

Chrysolite Pitcher

Pitcher, water, 9" h., 5½" d., (ILLUS.). . **350.00**
Plate, 9" d.,¾" h.. . . . . **125.00**

COBALT BLUE & WHITE SWIRL

Baking dish, 8 x 14", 2¼" h.. . . . . **225.00**
Coffeepot, cov., belle-shape, 4½" d.,
   8¼" h. **650.00**
Funnel, tapered, 4¼" d., 4¾" h. **180.00**
Measuring cup, 3" d., 3½" h. **550.00**
Milk pan, 10½" d., 2½" h. **75.00**
Mold, fluted, 4¾" d., 2¼" h.. . . . . **400.00**

Mug, 4" d., 3¼" h. **90.00**
Roaster, cov., 12" d., 8½" h. **325.00**
Spooner, 4" d., 5¼" h. **1,100.00**

Cobalt Blue Swirl Teakettle

Teakettle, cov., coiled iron handle,
7¼" d., 7¼" h. (ILLUS.) **750.00**

EMERALD WARE
(Green & White Swirl)

Baking pan, 8½ x 14¼", 2⅛" h. **325.00**
Berry bucket, cov., 5¾" d., 6½" h. **400.00**
Coffeepot, cov., gooseneck spout,
5¾" d., 10" h. **500.00**
Funnel, bulbous, 5¾" d., 4" h. **375.00**

Emerald Ware Measuring Cup

Measuring cup, 4¼" d., 6½" h.
(ILLUS.) **675.00**
Pitcher, water, 8¾" h., 6¼" d. **500.00**
Skimmer, 5" d., handle, 11" l. **225.00**

RED & WHITE SWIRL

Red Swirl Berry Bucket

Berry bucket, tin cover, 6¼" d.,
6½" h. (ILLUS.) **2,000.00**
Coffee boiler, cov., 9¼" d., 12" h. . . . **1,800.00**
Kettle, cov., swirled inside & out, light
weight, ca. 1950s, 8¼" d., 4" h. **40.00**
Mug **40.00**
Pitcher, water, 9¼" h., 6" d. **2,000.00**
Plate, 10¼" d., 1" h., swirled inside &
out, light weight, ca. 1950s to
1960s. **30.00**

GRAY (Mottled)

Berry bucket, cov., 6½" d., 5¾" h. **80.00**
Butter churn, cov., floor model,
wooden frame, 13 x 19", 30" h. . . **1,100.00**
Coffee boiler, cov., 8¾" d., 11" h. . . . **100.00**
Coffeepot, tin cover, 1 cup size,
3" d., 4" h. **225.00**

Comb Case

Comb case, marked "The Jewel,"
3 x 7¼", 5½" h. (ILLUS.) **550.00**
Funnel, canning, 4" d., 3" h. **25.00**
Ladle, 3¼" d., handle 10" l. **35.00**
Measuring cup, 2¼" d., 2¾" h. **300.00**
Measuring cup, embossed "1 quart
liquid," labeled "Royal
Graniteware," 4½" d., 6¼" h. **200.00**
Pitcher, 10½" h., 7" d. **150.00**
Scoop, spice, 2" w., 5" l. **250.00**
Strainer, screen bottom, labeled
"Sterling Enameled Ware," 7¼" d.,
2½" h. **140.00**

SOLID COLORS

Baking pan, white w/red trim, 8 x 13",
2" h. **25.00**
Coffee boiler, cov., solid blue,
8¾" d., 11" h. **125.00**
Coffee flask, round, solid blue,
3½" d., 4½" h. **400.00**
Cream can, cov., cream w/green
trim, 4¾" d., 9" h. **120.00**
Cuspidor, solid blue inside & out
w/black trim, 7½" d., 4¼" h. **75.00**

Blue Grater

Grater, solid blue, 3¾" d., 10" h.
(ILLUS.). **75.00**
Measuring cup, solid cobalt blue,
3½" d., 4¾" h. **70.00**
Molasses pitcher, cov., white w/navy
trim, 3½" d., 5½" h. **120.00**
Mug, miner's, cream w/green trim,
5" d., 4" h. **50.00**
Pitcher, water, 9" h., 6" d., solid
blue **75.00**
Scoop, spice, solid blue, 2¼" d.,
5¼" h. **100.00**
Soap dish, hanging, solid blue,
3 x 5¼", 5" h., ... **65.00**
Spoon, white w/red handle, 2½" d.,
12" l. **25.00**
Sugar bowl, cov., bulbous body,
white w/cobalt blue trim, 4½" d.,
5" h. **100.00**
Teapot, cov., bulbous body, solid
blue, 4½" d., 5¼" h. **80.00**

CHILDREN'S ITEMS, MINIATURES & SALESMAN'S SAMPLES

Bowl, child's, feeding, cream w/green
trim, "Hickory Dickory Dock," 8" d. . . . **40.00**
Colander, salesman's sample,
footed, grey, 3¾" d., 1¾" h. **600.00**
Cuspidor, advertising, salesman's
sample, blue & white swirl, inside
marked "United States Stamping
Co., Moundsville, W. Va.," 3½" d.,
2" h. **700.00**

Miniature Fish Molds

Fish mold, miniature, blue w/white
specks, 3" l., 2½" h. (ILLUS. left). . . **250.00**

Fish mold, miniature, solid light blue,
3" l., 2½" h. (ILLUS. right) **250.00**
Grater, miniature, solid blue, 1¼" d.,
3¾" h. **175.00**
Mug, salesman's sample, brown &
white swirl, 1¼" d., 1" h. **675.00**
Potty, salesman's sample, blue &
white swirl, 2¾" d., 1¾" h. **550.00**
Roaster, salesman's sample, oval,
cobalt & white swirl, w/insert,
3½ x 6¼", 3¼" h., 3 pcs. **1,800.00**

Salesman's Sample Stove

Stove, wood burning, salesman's
sample, blue w/white specks, Karr
Range Co., Bellville, Ill.,
10 x 13, 21" h. (ILLUS.) **4,000.00**
Strainer, miniature, blue w/white
specks, w/handle & hook, 2 x 5,
1¼" h. **100.00**
Tea set: miniature, cov. teapot, four
cups, four saucers, creamer, open
sugar; blue, teapot 3¼" h., the set . **450.00**
Wash basin, salesman's sample,
cobalt & white swirl, 3¾" h. **175.00**

MISCELLANEOUS GRANITEWARE & RELATED ITEMS

Emerald Swirl Coaster

Coaster, Emerald Swirl, 4" d.
(ILLUS.). **250.00**

Coaster, Iris Swirl, advertising "Norvell-Shapleigh Hdw., St. Louis, Distributors Blue Diamond Ware," 4" d.......................... **250.00**

Coffeepot, cov., Shamrock Ware, dark green shading to lighter green back to dark green, gooseneck spout, 5¼" d., 9" h. **250.00**

Custard cup, Bluebell Ware, blue shading to a lighter blue back to blue, 4" d., 2½" h. **50.00**

Double boiler, cov., Stewart Ware, shaded blue w/yellow & pink flowers, 7" d., 8" h., 3 pcs......... **150.00**

Kettle, preserving, blue & white mottled, 17" d., 8½" h........... **100.00**

Muffin pan, aqua & white swirl, 6 cup **575.00**

Mug, miner's, Duchess Ware, large blue dots w/white & brown veins, 5" d., 4½" h................... **225.00**

Platter, 8½ x 13¾", oval, End of Day, multicolored w/red, yellow, green, cobalt blue & white large swirl..... **775.00**

Skillet, Onyx Ware, dark brown & white mottled, 8" d., 1¾" h. **75.00**

Sugar bowl, cov., Shamrock Ware, dark green shading to a lighter green back to a dark green, 3¾" d., 6" h.................... **250.00**

Washboard, "Soap Saver," solid cobalt blue w/wooden frame, 12½" w., 24" h. **140.00**

HATPINS & HATPIN HOLDERS

HATPINS

Amethyst & gold (14k), Art Nouveau style, pierced chased openwork design w/collet-set amethyst **$288.00**

Citrine, Arts & Crafts style, oval citrine in openwork sterling mount, signed "Kalo".................. **575.00**

Citrine & gold (14k), Art Nouveau style, faceted citrine terminal in scrolled gold openwork mount accented by small pearls, steel pin stem, hallmark for Krementz **546.00**

Cloisonné enamel, polychrome, accented by red stone, silver mount w/steel stem **201.00**

Diamond & enamel, Art Nouveau style, spherical stylized floral & scroll motif in polychrome enamel accented w/diamonds, 14k yellow gold mount, hallmark (slight enamel loss) **748.00**

Diamond & enamel, Art Nouveau style, sword w/eagle motifs & white enamel on handle, hilt accented w/channel-set diamonds (some enamel loss) **575.00**

Gold (14k), Art Nouveau style depicting face of lady, gold-filled stem....................... **230.00**

Gold (14k), Art Nouveau style, griffin set w/red stone eye & wing accents holding pearl in mouth, swivel top, hallmark for Rickers............. **805.00**

Gold (14k), Art Nouveau style, open scrollwork accented by blue & white enamel top, gold-filled stem .. **144.00**

Gold (14k) & enamel, Art Nouveau style, red guilloche enamel ball w/black vine decoration, surmounted by green dragonfly, hallmark for Hedges **1,495.00**

Gold (14k) & enamel, light blue guilloche enamel top w/overlay & pearl terminal in fluted base, gold-filled stem, Edwardian **1,265.00**

Opal & gold (14k), decorated in wire-twist w/blue glass terminal, hallmark, Victorian.............. **230.00**

Opal & gold (14k), opal terminal accented w/four freshwater pearls, wire-twist accent, gold-filled stem, Victorian..................... **374.00**

Pearl & diamond, a Baroque pearl framed in old mine-cut diamonds, 18k yellow gold mounting, set en tremblant, gold-filled double pin stem (pearl drilled, not tested for natural) **259.00**

Pearl & enamel, Art Nouveau enamel leaves in shades of green & pink accented by freshwater pearls, hallmark for Carrington & Co..... **1,610.00**

Pearl & gold (14k), splayed pearl terminals in bouquet-form, Victorian **518.00**

Pearl & gold (14k), star-shaped, pave-set w/half pearls, swivel top .. **259.00**

Sapphire & enamel, Art Nouveau style, collet-set sapphires in enameled flowerheads, screw top, gold-filled stem............... **2,990.00**

HATPIN HOLDERS

Nippon porcelain, h.p. tiny pink florals w/heavy raised gold design & colored "jewel" beading, signed "Nippon" **135.00**

Ornate Noritake Hatpin Holder

Noritake porcelain, tapering cylindrical form, gold rim & base bands w/burnt orange & gold h.p. bands & panels around the top & gold & white clusters of stylized blossoms on the lower sides, marked, 2⅞" d., 4⅞" h. (ILLUS.) **65.00**

Torquay pottery, redware, Motto ware, waisted cylindrical form w/domed pierced top, Scandy patt., motto "Keep me on the dressing table," impressed mark "Long Park," England, early 20th c., 5" h. ... **61.00**

HEINTZ ART METAL SHOP WARES

Otto Heintz (Buffalo, NY, 1877-1918) changed the name of his Art Crafts Shop to Heintz Art Metal Shop in 1906 as he shifted his focus from copper to machine formed bronze bodies and from colored enamels to sterling silver overlays as decoration. A patent for the solderless application of the overlays was awarded in 1912 and the diamond mark enclosing the conjoined letters "HAMS" came into use. A series of sophisticated chemical patinas and plated finishes was developed for a line of vases, bowls and book ends. Otto died suddenly in 1918, but the company struggled through the Depression until the end came on Feb. 11, 1930. Values are a function of form, rarity, overlay and originality of patina.

Ashtray, cigar-type, No. 2652, green patina, silver design of two dogs fighting, single cigar rest, glass insert, 4¼" d. **$110.00**

Ashtray, cigar-type, No. 2643, green patina, silver Arts & Crafts geometric design, two cigar rests, 6" d. **190.00**

Book ends, No. 7090, brown patina, silver Venetian gondolier scene, 3 x 5", pr. **300.00**

Heintz Art Metal Book Ends

Book ends, No. 7148, green patina, silver pine cone & pine needles, 5½ x 6", pr. (ILLUS.) **375.00**

Bowl, No. 3706, brown patina, silver pine needles, 9" d., 1½" h. **425.00**

Heintz Art Metal Bowl

Bowl, No. 3665, brown patina, silver stylized florals, 9½" d., 3" h. (ILLUS.). **300.00**

Candlesticks, No. 3126, brown patina, half-inch diameter shaft, silver stylized scarab, 3" d. saucer base, 8" h., pr. **500.00**

Cigar box w/hinged cover, No. 4090, acid-etched silver design of dogs & mountain lion, cedar-lined, perforated screen in the cover, 8 x 10", 3" h. **775.00**

Cigar humidor, cov., No. 2647, green patina, silver Egyptian Revival water lily design, glass liner, 5" d., overall 7" h. **525.00**

Cigarette box, cov., No.4081, brown patina, silver Art Deco geometric design, cedar-lined, 3 x 4", 1" h. **250.00**

Console set: pair No. 3128 candlesticks w/brown patina & inverted trumpet-form base & trumpet socket w/removable bobeches, silver stylized florals, together w/a No. 3655 bowl, the set **850.00**

Desk set: letter holder w/perpetual calendar, rounded blotter, cov. inkwell, letter opener & pen tray; each piece w/sterling silver overlay in a lily-of-the-valley design, original dark patina, impressed marks, the set **330.00**

Desk set, No. 1182, brown patina,
silver pine needles design,
including blotter pad, 6 pcs........ **550.00**

Desk set, No. 1203, green patina,
silver cardinal on branch design,
including blotter pad, 5 pcs........ **450.00**

Humidor, cov., wide slightly tapering
cylindrical body w/a low domed
cover w/an angular handle & green
patina, the body w/sterling silver
overlay of a fox hunting scene,
impressed mark, 6" d., 6¾" h...... **715.00**

Lamp, boudoir-type, conical shade
w/cut-out design supported on a
three-arm spider atop a spherical
base, green patina, silver poppies
& leaves, 8½" d. shade, overall
10" h..................... **1,000.00**

Heintz Art Metal Table Lamp

Lamp, table model, helmet-shaped
metal shade mounted in a curved
harp above a trumpet-form base,
brown patina, silver Arts & Crafts
geometric design, 9½" h. (ILLUS.).. **880.00**

Lamp, table model, domed 8" d.
"helmet" shade in bronze overlaid
w/silver flowers each w/a coral
cabochon center, slender flaring
pedestal base, original silvered
finish, 9¾" h. (small dent on shade
back)...................... **770.00**

Lamp, table model, 9½" d. sharply
conical sterling silver on bronze
shade w/verdigris patina decorated
w/a repeated cut-out scrolling vine
design w/silk lining, the squatty
domed foot overlaid w/a stylized
flower, original silk lining, original
foil label, 14½" h. (small chip to
finish on shade)............. **2,420.00**

Lamp, table, a domical mushroom-
shaped bronze shade w/stylized
floral silver inlay suspended
between angular arm brackets
above a slender cylindrical bronze
base w/a widely flaring foot &
stylized floral overlay, unsigned,
9½" d. shade, 14½" h. (cleaned)... **920.00**

Picture frame, No. 2124, green
patina, flat edges w/silver American
eagle at the top & a military shield
w/"US" at the bottom, opening
5 x 7", overall 7½ x 9½"......... **400.00**

Plate, copper, advertising-type, round
w/low flaring sides, acid-etched
around the wide rim w/ornate
scrolling, the center embossed w/a
business card-size plaque reading
"Heintz Bros. - Makers of Rings,"
7" d. (some patina loss)......... **165.00**

Heintz Art Metal Trophy

Trophy, No. 6621, urn-form w/high
inwardly-curled handles, brown
patina, silver golfing scene, no
engraving, 3½" d., 8" h. (ILLUS.)... **450.00**

Trophy, tall slender trumpet-form
fluted body on a flaring foot, long
angular handles from near the rim
to the edge of the foot, applied
silver band decoration down the
sides, engraved "Young Men's
Division Club Trophy," followed by
winners' names from 1918 to 1935,
original patina, marked, 9½" w.,
15" h........................ **187.00**

Vase, No. 3817, wide bulbous ovoid
body tapering to a wide flaring
neck, green patina, silver single
rose design, 5" h., 5" d.......... **400.00**

Vase, cylindrical body w/a swelled
bulbous shoulder & closed rim, the
bronze ground inlaid w/a silver
foliate design, good patina,
impressed mark, 8" h., 5" d....... **288.00**

Vase, slender ovoid body w/a short
cylindrical neck, inlaid silver foliate
design, 8½" h. (cleaned)........ **403.00**

Vase, slender baluster-form w/a wide
flaring foot & a wide, flat closed
rim, sterling silver overlay of
slender twigs w/long leaves & small
blossom hanging down from the
rim, original patina, marked, 9¾" h.,
4½" d....................... **468.00**

Vase, gently tapering cylindrical body w/a flaring closed rim, sterling silver overlay of slender undulating leaves & stem w/blossom cluster up the sides, w/a commemorative message, 1922, impressed mark, 10¾" h., 4¾" d. (couple of shallow dents) **330.00**

Heintz Vase with Narcissus

Vase, No. 3708, tall slender waisted cylindrical form, brown patina, silver paperwhite narcissus design, 11" h., 4" d. (ILLUS.) **620.00**

Vase, No. 3623, cylindrical w/a rim, green patina, silver fuchsia design, 12" h., 3" d. **685.00**

Vase, very tall slender waisted form w/a widely flared mouth & foot, bronze overlaid w/sterling silver in the form of a long-stemmed blossom cluster w/looping scrolls at the base, monogrammed "K," impressed marks, 17½" h., 4⅞" d. (patina loss). **575.00**

HOLIDAY COLLECTIBLES

For collectors, Christmas offers the widest selection of desirable collectibles; however, other national and religious holidays were also noted with the production of various items which are now gaining popularity. Halloween-related pieces such as candy containers, lanterns, decorations and costumes are the most sought-after category after Christmas. Other holidays such as Thanksgiving, Easter and the 4th of July have relatively few collectibles common for collectors. Also see: CHRISTMAS COLLECTIBLES.

HALLOWEEN

Book, "Bogie Book," color cover w/spooky tree catching pumpkin poacher, 1924, Dennison, excellent. . **$300.00**

Book, "Spooky Tavern," 1923, soft cover edition of Halloween play, published by Dennison, good. . . . **2,800.00**

Candleholder & nodder, bisque skull on book, molded face, wired chin that chatters, ca. 1920, Germany, excellent, 4" l. **1,010.00**

Candles, witches w/jack-o'-lanterns (JOLs), ca. 1950s, Gurley, unused, 7" h., pr. **800.00**

Candy bag, goblin draw string, cardboard face & feet, cotton body, mesh bag, ca. 1920s, Germany, excellent, 8" h. **950.00**

Candy container, figure of a witch w/h.p. molded composition face, hands & legs, original clothes & broom, ca. 1910, stamped "Germany" on the base, near mint, 14" h. **2,500.00**

Candy container, composition, figure of a witch on flocked black cat w/glass eyes, head pulls off, ca. 1920, Germany, near mint, 3" w., 4" h. . . . **2,600.00**

Candy container, plastic acrobat witch, ca. 1960s, Rosen Bros., excellent, 15". **425.00**

Candy container & candleholder, bisque skull nodder & book, skull w/wired jaw that opens & closes, ceramic teeth, cover lifts off hollow book for candy, hole in skull for candle, ca.1930s, Japanese, near mint, 5" h.. . **700.00**

Carriage, plastic, features black cat, witch & JOL pumpkin, made to hold nine lollipops, black pumpkin wheels, ca. 1950s, Kokomo Candy Co., near mint, 9" l. **900.00**

Centerpiece, black cat cardboard & honeycomb, ca. late 1930s-1940s, unused, 10" h. **800.00**

Centerpiece, prowling black cat, cardboard & honeycomb, ca. 1940s, H.E. Luhrs, excellent, 6" w., 11" h. . . . **375.00**

Clicker, metal, devil w/pitchfork, large **35.00**

Decoration, dancing cat, ca. 1920s, Luhra, excellent, 18" l. **500.00**

Die-cut, cat & quarter moon, ca.1920s, Germany, near mint, 5" d. **1,900.00**

Die-cut, JOL playing drums, ca.1920s, Germany, excellent, 7½" h. **650.00**

Die-cut, JOL standup, ca. 1920s, Beistle, very fine, 16" h. **1,650.00**

Die-cut, owl & quarter moon, ca. 1920s, excellent, giant size, 18" d. **1,000.00**

Die-cut, witch & quarter moon, ca. 1920s, Germany, near mint, 5" d. . . **900.00**

Figure of a girl, celluloid, in pumpkin patch, Halloween party favor, cushion made of crepe & paper, ca. 1930s, excellent , 5" h. **310.00**

Figure of a JOL constable, heavy composition, blue, orange & yellow, ca. 1920, Germany, excellent, 4½" h. **1,450.00**

Game, "Stunt Halloween Quiz," ca. 1920s, H.E. Luhrs, excellent, 8½" w., 9½" l., ... **350.00**

Game, "Old Witch Brewsome Stunts," ca. 1920s, unused, 7½" w., 10" h. . . **500.00**

Hat & mask, paper, black cat, ca. 1930s, excellent, 11 x 11". **360.00**

Lantern, cardboard, black cat w/original insert & ears, replaced base, ca. 1930s, Germany, excellent, 5" h. **800.00**

Lantern, cat face, orange, original insert, American Pulp, mint, 6" h. . . **360.00**

Lantern, black cat on fence, original insert, ca. 1940s, American, excellent, 8" h. **950.00**

Lantern & candy container, JOL lantern head, compo body, pull-off head to get candy, replaced insert, stamped "Germany," very nice, 6" h. . **425.00**

Light bulbs, milk glass, figural JOL screw-in type, hand-painted pink, yellow & orange, ca. 1930s, excellent, 2½" h., lot of 3 . . . . **3,000.00**

"Lollypop Holder," Halloween little girl, lithographed face, crepe cloth, near mint, 5" h. **950.00**

"Lollypop Holder," Halloween devil, lithographed face, crepe cloth, ca. 1930s, excellent, 6" h. **725.00**

Magazine, "Mickey Mouse Magazine," November 1937, w/article on Halloween party tips, features young wolf on cover marching w/JOL on a stick, w/ad for Noma Lights, near mint. **4,200.00**

Model of a black cat, celluloid, w/bat face, spring tail, ca. 1930s, near mint, 4½" l. **2,400.00**

Model of a donkey, black & orange plastic, w/JOL on wheels, ca. 1950s, near mint, 5" l. **2,100.00**

Model of an owl, celluloid, on spooky stump, black & orange w/squirrel in stump, ca.1930s, excellent, 5½" h. . . **800.00**

Noisemaker, JOL head rachet, cloth JOL head (1" d.), wooden ratchet, ca. 1930s, very fine, 6" w., 7" h. . . . **655.00**

Ornament, composition veggie guy, full bodied w/JOL head & pickel jointed arms & legs, hook at top of head, Germany, excellent, 3½" h. . . **505.00**

Panknocker, paper & tin, giant size, decorated w/apple dunking party scene, double sided, lithographed knocker w/tin housing & handle, ca. 1910, Chein, excellent, 10" h. . . **425.00**

Photo, shows students in a Halloween float, marked 1909 on reverse, excellent, 5" w., 3" h. **700.00**

Playing cards, Gypsy witch, full deck that doubles as fortune -telling cards, ca.1960s, U.S Playing Card Co., near mint **500.00**

Postcard, "A Halloween Wish," written on but not posted, shows veggie people trying to ride a balloon, embossed, 1914 copyright by John Winsch, excellent. **550.00**

Postcard, "The Witch's Dance," embossed, not written on, 1911, excellent **500.00**

Postcard, "To Miss Hallowe'en," embossed, not written on, features beautiful woman in witch costume, ca. 1910, excellent **800.00**

Rattle parade stick, plastic devil w/molded head, ca. 1950s-60s, excellent, head 7" d., 34" overall l. **450.00**

Records, 78 rpm, called "Halloween," written & narrated by Lionel Barrymore, features Barrymore's face on record cover, released in 1945, MGM Records, excellent, set of 3 . . . . **2,800.00**

Salt & pepper shakers, composition, figural red devil, ca. 1950s, excellent, 3½" h., pr. **1,200.00**

Scrap stickers, 80 witches, unused, one sheet, 14" w., 9" h. **450.00**

Sparkler, tin, decorated w/Halloween JOL & black cat, ca. 1920s, Chein, very good w/box, 4½" h. **4,900.00**

Squeaker toy, JOL clown, hand-painted cardboard, JOL face, composition JOL parade lantern, w/attached leaves, wooden arms & legs, original clothes, press stomach & figure tips his hat, ca. 1910, excellent **400.00**

Standup figure, "Pete The Party Puss" holding JOL, ca. 1930, excellent,10" h. **2,800.00**

Tambourine, witch, ca. 1950s, excellent, 6" d. **2,650.00**

Toy, JOL windup clown, cardboard JOL head, metal legs & feet, original felt clothes, dances when wound up, ca. 1920, stamped "Germany" on bottom of feet, near mint, 10" h. **450.00**

ICONS

Icon is the Greek word meaning likeness or image and is applied to small pictures meant to be hung on the iconostasis, a screen dividing the sanctuary from the main body of Eastern Orthodox churches. Examples may be found all over Europe. The Greek, Russian and other Orthodox churches developed their own styles, but the Russian contribution to this form of art is considered outstanding.

All-Seeing Eye of God (The), Russia, 19th c., 10½ x 12" **$770.00**

Annunciation (The), Archangel Gabriel delivers the news to Mary, probably Mestera School, Russia, 19th c., 12 x 14" **880.00**

Archangel Michael, Michael seen in an Apocalyptic version riding a red-winged horse, holding a censor in one hand, the Gospels in the other, design appears to have been an early 19th c. Lubok folk print, custom-fitted in a period kiot, Russia, 19th c., 11 x 12½" **1,320.00**

The Dormition

Dormition (The), central scene of Mary being laid to rest, surrounded by saints & angels, buildings in the background, Russia, ca. 1600, 11 x 12" (ILLUS.) **4,675.00**

Extended Diesis (The), Christ enthroned at center flanked by Archangels Mary, John & various saints, Russia, 19th c., 10¼ x 12¼" . . **715.00**

Holy Trinity (The), appearing as three angels to the Patriarch Abraham at the Oak of Mamre, painted in the old style, Russia, 19th c., 4¼ x 7½" **2,420.00**

Joy of All Who Suffer Mother of God, double kovcheg, 19th c., 10½ x 12¼" **385.00**

Kazan Mother of God, egg tempera on wood panel, traditional style, overlaid w/fine repoussé & chased

silver-gilt riza w/attached brilliant halo, hallmarked, Moscow workshop of Sergiy Gupkin, in custom-fitted period kiot w/gilt frame, 15 x 17" **3,080.00**

Life of Christ, four-part folding traveling-type, each end panel w/crucifixion designs & seraphs, the interior w/four scenes from the life of Christ, each w/silver-gilt oklad & a host of saints, inscribed, Greece, 1753, each panel 3¾" sq. **1,265.00**

The Lord Almighty Icon

Lord Almighty (The), Christ raising one hand in blessing & holding open the Gospels w/the other, enamel & silver-gilt riza, Russia, late 19th c., 10 x 12" (ILLUS.) . . . **4,950.00**

Mary & John the Baptist, two large finely painted images probably from the Deisis tier of an iconostasis in a small chapel, Russia, 19th c. in the 16th c. style, pr. **2,090.00**

Icon of St. Nicholas

St. Nicholas, the half-length portrait of the saint in the center framed around the borders from scenes from his life, Russia, 19th c. (ILLUS.) **5,500.00**

St. Paraskeva, her right hand blessing in the manner favored by Old Believers, Russia, 19th c., 10½ x 12½" (some losses & lifting) . . **550.00**

Weep Not For Me, Mother Icon

Weep Not For Me, Mother, Mary supports her crucified son holding him upright in an open sarcophagus, overlaid w/fine silver repoussé & chased riza w/multi-colored enamel halves & plaques, the borders w/Saints Barbara, Evdokia, Elizabeth & the Guardian Angel, Moscow hallmark, workshop of the Brothers Zaharov, ca. 1896-1905, 11¼ x 13¾" (ILLUS.) **3,300.00**

INDIAN ARTIFACTS & JEWELRY

Basket, Pima, coiled construction w/a flat base, flaring sides & a rosette center, design of whirling meanders **$3,450.00**

Basket, Eastern Woodland Indian, woven double wall-type, painted w/red & blue swab decoration, 19th c., 17" h. (minor breaks) **863.00**

Apache Figural Basket

Basket, Apache, woven coiled construction, 17 female, male & horse figures w/zigzag bands, 18½" d. (ILLUS.) **4,600.00**

Maria & Popovi Pottery Bowl

Bowl, San Ildefonso, pottery, wide squatty rounded black-on-black design of feathers & geometric devices, signed by Maria & Popovi, 8½" d. (ILLUS.) **7,475.00**

Dress, child's, Sioux, beaded & fringed hide, 19th c. **12,360.00**

Gauntlets, plateau, Yakima or Nez Perce, floral design in colorful spot stitch beading w/opaque, translucent & some white-heart red beads, worn red & black polka dot calico lining, 13" l., pr. (some bead loss & worn & torn palms from use) **413.00**

Jacket, Sioux, pictorial beaded & fringed hide adult-size, 19th c. . . **10,925.00**

Jar, Acoma, wide squatty bulbous pottery form tapering to a wide, flat mouth, finely painted overall w/upper & lower wide bands of heart and loop-form geometric designs w/a band of checked blocks around the center, 11" h. . . **5,400.00**

Jar, San Ildefonso, pottery, flat base, flaring sides, matte water serpent design on glossy black ground, signed by Maria, 5 x 6" **3,565.00**

Olla, Acoma, pottery, painted in black, orange & red over a cream slip ground, 11 x 12½" **4,025.00**

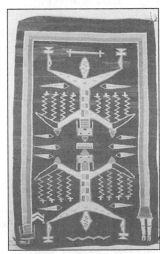

Pictorial Navajo Rug

Rug, Navajo, woven wool, color
pictorial w/black ground decorated
w/two yei figures w/arms
outstretched & zigzag lines
extending , feathers flanking,
border of elongated yei figure, red,
green & natural (ILLUS.) **7,475.00**

Rug, Navajo, central trading post,
central band of linked diamonds in
maroon red, dark brown/black, tan
& natural w/terraced bands ending
in maroon crosses, carded tan
ground w/natural & dark
brown/black borders, 29 x 48"
(minor wear, stains & warp breaks) . . **385.00**

Rug, Navajo, Ganado area, central
diamond & stepped mountain
design in double-dye red, dark
brown & natural on a carded tan
ground, 31 x 59" (several minute
warp breaks) **495.00**

Rug, Navajo, pictorial Ganado, central
diamond design w/triple band
border all in soft red, dark brown &
natural hand-carded wool on a tan
ground, crosses & feathers in dark
blue, early 20th c., 40 x 64" (edge
repair & one end rebound)....... **660.00**

Shirt, Blackfoot war-type, beaded,
quilled & fringed hide, 19th c. . . **16,960.00**

Fine Delaware Man's Shoulder Bag

Shoulder bag, man's, Delaware,
ornately beaded colorful geometric
& stylized floral designs, cloth
ground (ILLUS.) **42,550.00**

Tomahawk, Plains, bronze pipe-form,
19th c. **2,990.00**

War club, Plains, (skull-cracker),
polished stone head encircled
w/band of translucent red, green &
opaque yellow beads which is also
wrapped around handle above
leather end, 27" l. (wear to leather
& stone, bead loss) **600.00**

IVORY

Bowls, a round footring supporting a
wide deep-sided bowl finely carved
around the sides w/four vivacious
dragons in pursuit of a flaming pearl
above foaming waves, a band of
flowerheads around the rim,
w/silvered copper lining, China,
Qianlong Period, 4¾" d., pr. **$7,475.00**

Early Ivory Candlescreen

Candlescreen, surmounted by an
oval cartouche & two reclining
female terms, rectangular panel
framed by finely detailed pierce-
carved border, the panel w/a
detailed low- to high-relief carving
of four Bacchic putti in revelry in a
landscape w/mountains, trees & a
classical temple in the distance,
raised on a slender carved
adjustable baluster standard on a
domed round foot, Europe, early
19th c., 17½" h. (ILLUS.) **4,510.00**

Cup, swelled flaring cylindrical form
w/a thick flattened rim, a
countersunk base carved to
simulate basketweaving, carved
around the sides in relief w/a
procession of the Eight Immortals
bearing their attributes, the angled
side handle carved w/two addorsed
Immortals surrounding a seal, lined
w/pewter, yu ci (Imperial estowed),
China, 18th c., 2½" h........... **5,175.00**

Cup, cov., the tall cylindrical bowl
carved around the lower rim w/a
wide band of frolicking putti, raised
on a reeded columnar pedestal
wrapped w/a grape cluster w/a

band of scrolled leaves above & raised on a domed round foot w/acanthus leaf carving, the low domed cover fitted w/a large figural putto seated on a cask, Europe, possibly Dieppe, 19th c., 9½" h. . . **1,092.00**

Carved Ivory Minstrel Group

Figure group, a band of minstrels each mounted on a narrow black-painted rectangular base w/a crossroad sign at one end, each wearing a hat & coat or cloak, probably Europe, 19th c., some paint wear on base (ILLUS.). **3,300.00**

Figure of a basket seller, standing slightly stooped elderly man w/a yoke across one shoulder laden w/various types of baskets, etched w/geometric designs & geometric designs & foliage, Japan, late 19th – early 20th c., 5½" h. **805.00**

Ivory Figure of Christ

Figure of Christ, realistic carving of a crucified Christ, Europe, 18th c., 7" h. (ILLUS.) **1,760.00**

Figure of Elizabeth I of England, standing, the wide skirt hinged to reveal a triptych of the queen & Sir Walter Raleigh, Europe, 19th c., 5¼" h. (hairlines) **546.00**

Figure of "Our Madonna of the Milk," standing in long draped robes suckling the Baby Jesus, on a cloudwork base, both figures w/black hair, Portuguese, possibly colonial, 18th c., 11¼" h. (lines) . . **1,840.00**

Magnifying glass handle, slightly tapering cylindrical form carved w/a scene depicting a hunter pursuing a tiger, round glass in a metal frame, handle Oriental, overall 10¾" l. **220.00**

Carved Ivory Page Cutter - Turner

Page cutter - turner, a long flat round-tipped blade w/a tapering rounded handle coming to a point & set w/a silver fox w/stone eyes, one eye missing, silver marked for London, England, 1891-92, 19½" l. (ILLUS.) **1,725.00**

Tankard, cov., ivory & bone, the cylindrical body carved w/a scene of a bacchanalia w/maenads, satyrs & youth harvesting from trees behind them, some holding baskets, others dancing & making music, raised on a band of small arches alternating w/short feet headed by carved leopard masks, the flattened cover w/a finial carved in the form of a seated maenad & child w/a sleeping leopard, the handle carved in the form of a maenad raising a basket of fruit over her head, Europe, late 19th c., cracks, 14" h. **8,625.00**

JEWELRY

ANTIQUE (1800-1920)

Bar pin, diamond, centered by an openwork circle w/bead-set & collet-set diamonds flanked by diamond-set tapering sides w/foliate motifs, millegrain accents, platinum-topped 14k yellow gold mount, Edwardian. . . **$920.00**

Bar pin, diamond & pearl, w/collet-set diamonds & button pearls in a platinum & 14k yellow gold mount, boxed, Edwardian. **1,610.00**

Arts & Crafts Bar Pin

Bar pin, moonstone & diamond, Arts
& Crafts style, set w/moonstone
cabochons, collet-set diamond
accents, 14k gold bead &
scrollwork mount (ILLUS.) **1,380.00**

Bar pin, pearl & rose-cut diamond
fringe, rose-cut diamond spacers,
suspended from a 14k yellow gold
bar, pearl cluster terminals. **1,035.00**

Belt buckle, gold (14k), Art Nouveau
style depicting the profile of a wolf
within a scrolling frame, signed
"T.B. Starr". **805.00**

Bracelet, bangle-type, gold (14k),
designed as a hinged bangle
w/applied wiretwist, bead &
arrowhead motif decorations,
Victorian (minor scratches) **432.00**

Bracelet, carved coral & 14k yellow
gold, designed as two flowers in a
ribbon-like frame w/applied beads,
wiretwist & foliate accents on a
heavy mesh bracelet, Victorian
(small chip to coral) **805.00**

Arts & Crafts Bracelet

Bracelet, gold (14k), Arts & Crafts
style plaques depicting naturalistic
designs of fish, birds & flora
alternating w/smaller plaques,
signed "Oakes," 7½" (ILLUS. of
part) **4,830.00**

Brooch, 18k yellow gold, Art
Nouveau style, circular form
designed as a bird in flight framed
by a tree branch w/a diamond
accent set in a platinum collet,
marked "G.G." **863.00**

Brooch, 18k yellow gold, Art
Nouveau style w/a center
medallion portraying a classical
figure set in a scroll & naturalistic
motif frame, French hallmark. **920.00**

Brooch, citrine, diamond & platinum,
a center square citrine within a
platinum filigree mount, accented

Edwardian Citrine Brooch

by diamonds, 14k yellow gold back,
Edwardian (ILLUS.). **633.00**

Brooch, crescent-shaped, set w/old
mine-cut diamonds in 14k yellow
gold mount, Edwardian. **1,093.00**

Brooch, pietra dura, gold (18k), a
bouquet of delicate white flowers,
glass compartment on reverse, in a
simple domed frame w/applied
bead & wiretwist decoration,
Victorian (minor dents) **489.00**

Brooch/pendant, porcelain, pearl &
diamond, a center plaque depicting
a mother & child in a shaped 18k
gold frame accented by four pearls
& rose-cut diamonds **575.00**

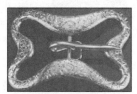

Edwardian Buckle

Buckle, 14k yellow gold, decorated
w/floral & foliate engraving,
Edwardian (ILLUS.). **489.00**

Cameo, tortoiseshell, depicting a
young woman w/silver inlaid hair
ornament & necklace, applied
engraved silver frame **403.00**

Cameo Brooch

Cameo brooch, hardstone, depicting
three-quarter profile of a Victorian
gentleman in high relief, in an 18k

yellow gold openwork frame w/gold bead & wiretwist decoration, minor dents in frame (ILLUS.) **805.00**

Chain, gold (18k), fancy link chain suspending a tassel pendant, Victorian, 16" **690.00**

Chain, platinum & diamond, comprised of diamond-set openwork navette-shaped links, Edwardian, 20" **2,530.00**

Chain, sterling silver, Arts & Crafts style, paper clip links w/four plaques accented w/lapis lazuli, 57" . . **374.00**

Chatelaine, silver, simple hook suspending an oval mirror w/floral repoussé frame, signed "Tiffany & Co.," Victorian **259.00**

Cuff links, gold (14k), Art Nouveau style, hollow double buttons depicting a goat & a lamb in wooded scene, ca. 1900, pr. **345.00**

Cuff links, hardstone cameo, rectangular w/profile of a classical male, 14k yellow gold mount, pr. . . . **460.00**

Etruscan Revival Earrings

Earrings, 18k yellow gold, Etruscan Revival style, oval form pendants w/applied gold bead, rosette & wiretwist decoration, Victorian, pr. (ILLUS.). **1,128.00**

Earrings, inlaid, designed w/three concentric pique crescent hoops suspended from oval bead tops w/silver & gold inlay, ca. 1865, pr. . . **920.00**

Lavaliere, diamond, platinum & gold, designed as an openwork pendant w/diamond drops, platinum-topped 14k yellow gold mount, Edwardian . . **1,610.00**

Locket, centered by a shakudo disc depicting a naturalistic scene within an 18k yellow gold Etruscan Revival style frame w/applied bead & wiretwist decoration, compartment w/a lock of hair on the reverse, Victorian (small scratch on top of disc) **1,323.00**

Locket, pearl & diamond, centered by an old mine-cut diamond, rose-cut diamond set scalloped center

Antique Pearl & Diamond Locket

surrounded by pearls, classical style cascading foliate frame, suspending a pearl drop, 18k yellow gold mount, pin stem replaced (ILLUS.) **1,725.00**

Memorial clasp, a sepia tone mourning scene depicting a woman in the wilderness, ivory w/14k yellow gold mount (scratches to crystal) **460.00**

Mourning ring, pearl, diamond & black enamel, a center cluster of seed pearls & a small rose-cut diamond, overall black enamel decoration, shank reads "in memory of," size 4¾ **431.00**

Necklace, pearl & 14k yellow gold, Art Nouveau style designed as a festoon w/three pink pearls suspended from three plume motif devices & fancy link chain, accented w/button pearls, hallmarked (w/certificate stating the cultured pearls are of natural color) **1,840.00**

Pendant, bone & glass, Art Nouveau style, pendant of carved dyed bone designed as leaves w/berries suspended from a brown cord w/bone & glass beads, signed "Bonte" **230.00**

Pendant, garnet & silver, designed as a rosette suspending a conformingly shaped bar further suspending five drops, garnet-set bail, glass compartment on reverse, silver mount, Victorian **575.00**

Pendant, large oval memorial type w/double-sided compartments displaying braided hair in a pinchback frame, Victorian **316.00**

Pin, diamond, sapphire & platinum, Art Deco style bow w/bead & collet-set diamonds, highlighted by a row of channel-set synthetic sapphires, millegrain accented platinum mount, hallmarks, maker's mark (one blue stone missing, pin stem replaced) **863.00**

Pin, diamond, silver & 18k yellow gold, modeled as a bird & set w/rose-cut diamonds accented by a rose-cut ruby eye in a silver & 18k yellow gold mount, French import mark **1,265.00**

Victorian Heart Locket

Pin/pendant, gold (18k), designed w/a bow top suspending a heart locket, overall turquoise blue enamel w/an applied diamond-set butterfly & flower, minor enamel repair, w/fitted box, Victorian (ILLUS.) **805.00**

Ring, cluster-type, 14k yellow gold, centered by a collet-set colorless quartz framed in half-pearls flanked by colorless quartz set in splayed shoulders, ca. 1840 . . . . **230.00**

Ring, diamond & turquoise, navette shape centered by three oval turquoise accented by bead-set diamonds, engraved pierced platinum mount, Edwardian **633.00**

Ring, garnet & 14k yellow gold, Arts & Crafts style, designed as an open flower centered by a garnet w/two collet-set diamond accents, stamped hallmark for Edward Oakes (garnet slightly abraded) . . . **748.00**

Ring, pearl, tourmaline, rhodolite & garnet, Arts & Crafts style w/center 6½ mm. pearl, flanked by collet-set green tourmalines, rhodolite & hessonite garnets within a 14k gold openwork mount, attributed to Oakes **978.00**

Star Sapphire Ring

Ring, star sapphire & 18k yellow gold, Arts & Crafts style, set w/three star sapphires, center flanked by collet-set seed pearls & diamonds, foliate & applied bead (ILLUS.) **1,093.00**

Watch chain, gold (14k), open flat links, Victorian, 24" **978.00**

Watch chain, gold (14k), wide circular links, completed by caps w/foliate tracery enamel, swivel hook, Victorian, 18" **518.00**

SETS

Brooch & earrings: 14k yellow gold & agate, the earrings w/a tapering agate drop in a pierced open foliate frame suspended from a framed agate top, the agate brooch in a similar frame, Victorian, the set (slightly tarnished) **403.00**

Brooch & earrings, coral, set comprised of a brooch centered by a carved coral rose within a wiretwist & beaded fringe frame & matching earrings, all in 14k gold mount, Victorian, the set **748.00**

Cameo Brooch & Earrings

Cameo & earrings, hardstone & 14k gold, the brooch depicting the profile of a lady within a beaded & wiretwist frame & matching ear pendants, the set (ILLUS.) **661.00**

Necklace, bracelets & ring: 14k yellow gold, emerald & seed pearls, the necklace & bracelets w/a central knot motif highlighted by seed pearls & emeralds & applied wiretwists w/similar hinged bangle bracelet & ring, Victorian, the set **920.00**

Necklace & brooch, silver & citrine quartz, Arts & Crafts style, the 15" necklace set w/five oval faceted citrines in floral & foliate frames suspending three tapering citrine drops & matching brooch, the set . . **345.00**

MODERN (1920-1960s)

Bar pin, star sapphire, diamond, pearl & platinum, a center round sapphire, flanked by a row of graduated pearls within a diamond frame **863.00**

Bar pin, platinum, onyx & diamond, Art Deco style, designed w/three round brilliant-cut diamonds & channel-set onyx, millegrain accents **920.00**

Bracelet, Bakelite, carved twist design, butterscotch **95.00**

Bracelet, bangle-type, Bakelite, carved blue & black **90.00**

Bracelet, sterling silver & rosewood, the wide band fitted w/flat-topped pyramidal small blocks of silver alternating w/rosewood, impressed early mark of William Spratling, Mexico, 1931-45, 2½" d. **1,495.00**

Bracelet, sterling silver, composed of stylized floral links w/oval moonstone cabochons, impressed "HANDWROUGHT STERLING KALO," 7" l. (small nicks to stones) **660.00**

Brooch, amethyst, diamond & pearl, starburst design w/large center amethyst surrounded by diamonds & cultured pearls, set in 14k yellow gold **863.00**

Brooch, diamond, Art Deco style, diamond-set initial within a pierced platinum frame & 18k yellow gold back over a jasper ground **575.00**

Brooch, gold (18k), modeled as an owl perched on a branch, marked "Tiffany" **863.00**

Floral Silver Brooch

Brooch, silver, an open circle set w/a naturalistic design of flowers & butterflies, hallmark for Georg Jensen, #283 (ILLUS.) **403.00**

Brooch, sterling silver, designed as a bird on a curled leaf, signed "Georg Jensen, no. 309" **173.00**

Brooch, sterling silver, a stylized perched bird centered by a leafy oval wreath, designed by Georg Jensen, Denmark, stamped mark & engraved "Marion Cocks," 1¾" d. . . . **193.00**

Cross, gold (22k), peridot, amethyst & pearl, Byzantine-style cross set w/amethyst arms centered by a peridot, ornate link chain accented w/amethyst beads & small pearls, signed "Kulicke - Reist, '72," 20" . . . **518.00**

Cuff links, 14k yellow gold, double sided w/a hound in profile & a fox's head w/red stone eyes, pr **431.00**

Cuff links, gold (14k), freeform plaques w/applied textured fish, signed "Tiffany & Co.", pr **345.00**

Cuff links, gold (18k bi-color), modeled as a white gold golf ball & yellow gold tee & curb link chain, pr **748.00**

Cuff links, onyx, diamond & platinum, Art Deco style double-sided onyx, one side decorated w/box-set green stone & diamonds, together w/one diamond-set stud **460.00**

Dress clips, diamond & platinum, Art Deco style set w/baguette, marquise & round diamonds (missing one diamond) **2,645.00**

Earrings, coral, onyx & diamond, Art Deco style, circles of graduated onyx & coral beads suspended from diamond-set pierced platinum open tops, French hallmarks, pr . . . **2,070.00**

Earrings, gold (18k bi-color) & tourmaline, modeled as stylized snails set w/pink & green cabochon tourmalines, pr **690.00**

Art Deco Lavaliere

Lavaliere, diamond & platinum, Art Deco style, designed as a pierced diamond-set plaque centered by a larger diamond edged in calibre-cut onyx, suspending from collet-set diamond drop on a platinum fetter-link chain, 15" (ILLUS. bottom of previous page) **3,450.00**

Necklace, amethyst, graduating faceted beads w/a 14k yellow gold clasp **431.00**

Necklace, jade & onyx, double strands of graduated jade beads separated by onyx & gold discs & three carved jade interlocking links, completed by a bi-color 18k yellow gold clasp marked "KYL" for Kai Yin Lo, Hong Kong **690.00**

Necklace, jade & 14k yellow gold, Art Deco style w/a carved jade plaque suspended from an overlapping open rectangular link chain accented w/a diamond, stamped hallmark for Allsopp & Allsopp, 16". . **690.00**

Pendant, diamond, Art Deco style w/a kite-shaped diamond suspended within a geometric shaped diamond-set frame, platinum mounting & fetter chain, 16" **8,912.00**

Pin, Bakelite, carved green wreath w/pine cones **85.00**

Pin, sterling silver, cut-out jumping marlin w/palm trees, 2 x 2" **250.00**

Pin, two tiger claws in a bypass design, 22k yellow gold mount w/chased foliate motif **201.00**

Ring, 14k yellow gold, Retro-style designed as a buckle w/hinged closure, sapphire & diamond accent **431.00**

Ring, diamond, Art Deco style w/center diamond flanked by blue stones in a diamond-set pierced & engraved platinum mount (one diamond missing, blue stones missing) **690.00**

Ring, gold (14k), flexible link band w/stylized buckle closure **316.00**

Ring, moonstone & diamond, Art Deco style, set w/a moonstone surrounded by diamonds, diamond-set shoulders, pierced platinum mount **920.00**

Ring, sapphire, diamond & 14k yellow gold, an oval yellow sapphire framed in diamonds **460.00**

SETS

Bracelet & earrings: silver, bracelet w/cabochon-cut white discs in floral & foliate openwork frames, matching earrings, signed "N.E. From," Denmark, the set **173.00**

Necklace, bracelet & brooch: sterling silver, bracelet & necklace composed of three-leaf cluster links alternating w/small ring links, the brooch w/addorsed three-leaf clusters within an oval framework, marked "Kalo Sterling," 3 pcs. **770.00**

COSTUME JEWELRY

The term Costume Jewelry refers to jewelry designs made of inexpensive, non-precious material. Originally made to complement designers' dress collections, it is today recognized as a combination of art, design and craftsmanship, and representative of the fashions and history of its time. Although it was meant to be discarded when the fashions for which it was made became passé, a great deal of costume jewelry has survived and is being avidly sought by collectors.

Instead of imitating precious jewelry designs, costume jewelry designs were original. Glass beads, plastic bracelets and gold-plated pins were all affordable in their time, and still are for the collector. No matter if costume jewelry has little or no intrinsic value, the enjoyment of its fine design and craftsmanship is the secret of its appeal.

Bracelet, Bakelite, bangle-type, butterscotch, randomly set w/rhinestones, ½" w. **150.00**

Bracelet, Bakelite, bangle-type, carved flowers design, burnt orange, ½" w. **75.00**

Bracelet, Bakelite, bangle-type, carved w/leaves, maroon, ¾" w. **85.00**

Bracelet, Bakelite, bangle-type, hinged, plain red, ⅞" w. **65.00**

Bracelet, Bakelite, bangle-type, marbleized amber, octagonal, large silvertone metal balls on each side, ⅞" w. **75.00**

Bracelet, rhinestone, two rows of large hand-set stones, large emerald-cut front stones, overlaid w/two oval pave-set loops, signed "Eisenberg," ¾" w. **150.00**

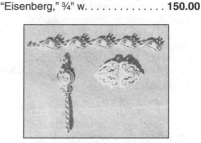

Bracelet, Pin and Clips

Bracelet, rhinestones in goldtone, clear & fanned red baguette stones in a twisted metal link chain, Retro-style, signed "Trifari" (ILLUS. top w/pin & clips) **125.00**

Bracelet, rhinestones on links, large clear marquise center stone in each link, small rhinestones trim, ⅝" w. **45.00**

Two Cameo Pins

Cameo pendant, shell cameo carved w/a seascape w/a sailing boat, set in a scalloped openwork copper frame (ILLUS. right) **75.00**

Cameo pin, shell cameo carved w/a bust profile portrait of a pretty woman w/curly hair w/scroll-carved edges, set in an ornate sterling silver frame, 2" l. (ILLUS. left) **150.00**

Clip, fur-type, Art Deco shield over bar design in pink & yellow gold on sterling silver, signed "Monet," 1¾" h. **65.00**

Clip, fur-type, enameled red & black beetle on goldplated leaves, signed "Monet," 3" l. **30.00**

Clips, duette, rhinestones set in an openwork Art Deco design, signed "Trifari," separated into two dress clips (ILLUS. right w/bracelet, previous page) **125.00**

Clips, pewter-finished metal, Art Nouveau design of openwork flowers & long leaves, 2½" h., pr. . . **40.00**

Collar necklace, hinged bangle bracelet & clip earrings, enameled metal, red w/gold designs, signed "YSL" (Yves St. Laurent), the set . . . **75.00**

Earrings, Aurora Borealis crystal bead drops, grey w/bronze enamel overlay, clip-ons, 2" l., pr. **35.00**

Earrings, button-style, red art glass in swirled shades of red, screw-on, ¾" d., pr. **25.00**

Earrings, sterling silver w/marcasite-set drops, heart design, signed "KD," 1¼" l., pr. **45.00**

Necklace, art glass beads in green & white Art Deco elephants design, ca. 1925, 28" l. **65.00**

Necklace, art glass beads, large & small oval & round shapes in fuchsia, cobalt blue & purple, knotted spacers, 38" l. **45.00**

Early Collar-style Beaded Necklace

Necklace, beaded collar-style, all-black beaded openwork designs w/triple bead drops between each design, beaded button fastener, ca. 1900, 13½" l. (ILLUS.) **150.00**

Necklace, art glass beads, pink alternating w/white-metal chains, large pink drop, original "Y" necklace, ca. 1930, 23" l. **65.00**

Necklace, beaded, large white, gold & white abstract pendant, signed "Erwin Pearl," 26" l. **80.00**

Necklace, black beads, medallion w/four long bead drops, ca. 1920, 20" l. w/a 9" l. drop. **90.00**

Necklace, plastic beads, triple-strand alternating three grey, three black & three gold beads, 24" l. . . . **35.00**

Necklace, rhinestone, clear w/emerald-cut & pear-shaped drop & matching green round accents, signed "Kramer of N.Y.," 17" l. **295.00**

Necklace, rhinestone, festoon-style w/a triple strand w/large clear stone accents & a large clear drop, 26" l. . . **250.00**

Necklace, rhinestone, large blue marquise-cut stone & round stones which turn lavender under incandescent light, signed "Kramer". **125.00**

Necklace, sterling silver, a lima bean design on a long chain, signed "Peretti - Tiffany & Co.," chain 30" l. **125.00**

Faux Pearl & Chain Pin

Pin, antiqued gold metal large ornate hanging chain w/an iridescent top pearl & drop & rhinestone trim, 4¾" l. (ILLUS.) **45.00**

Pin, Art Deco style w/beads forming white & bright multicolored flowers w/a central bugle bead arrangement, signed "Czechoslovakia," 1½ x 2" **35.00**

Pin, Bakelite, openwork carved flowers, marbleized coral & white in a frame of goldplated cylindrical bars, 1¼ x 2" **95.00**

Pin, enamel & rhinestone, model of a black-enameled leopard w/pave-set rhinestone trim, Carolee Limited Edition, 1992, 3¼" l. (ILLUS. bottom w/tiger) **55.00**

Pin, enameled metal, a pink flower w/green leaves & rhinestone trim, ca. 1935, 2" l. **35.00**

Pin, enameled metal, model of a carriage lantern w/Christmas trim including a red enameled bow & green holly, signed "Hollycraft," 2¼" l. (ILLUS. top w/Christmas tree pins, next page) **35.00**

Pin, enameled metal, model of a full-relief Christmas tree in green w/hanging red bead "ornaments," signed "Original by Robert," 2½" l. . . **90.00**

Tiger and Leopard Pins

Pin, goldplate w/black enamel & rhinestones, model of a tiger, signed "Hattie Carnegie," 3" l. (ILLUS. top) **65.00**

Pin, goldplated model of a Christmas tree w/red & green iridescent enameld balls, signed "Gerys," 2" h. (ILLUS. left w/lantern & tree, next page) **25.00**

Pin, goldtone & glass, model of a stylized cat w/a white glass body trimmed w/colored "coralene" accents, rhinestone eyes & collar, signed "Francoise". **75.00**

Pin, model of a hooded cobra, goldtone pave-set w/rhinestone & cabochon multicolored stones on the body & eyes. **85.00**

Pin, niello-decorated sterling silver filigree, blue flowers w/filigree & green enameled leaves, goldwashed, signed "Vanlon Germany," 1½" d. **75.00**

Pin, rhinestone, a scepter design in goldtone metal trimmed w/multicolored stones, dated "1955" & signed "Trifari" (ILLUS. bottom left w/bracelet & clips) **95.00**

Two Pins with Purple Stones

Pin, rhinestone, cabochon-set large oval glass stones in purple, faux agates, faux pink, red & purple gemstones, signed "Robert Original," 2½ x 3" (ILLUS. left) . . . **125.00**

Pin, rhinestone, cabochon-set w/large purple oval stones, the center w/large emerald-cut green, fuchsia, blue & clear stones, signed "Schreiner," 2½" l. **155.00**

Pin, rhinestone, large hand-set emerald-cut triangular, pear-shaped & marquise-cut multicolored stones, smaller multicolored rhinestones in the background, 2½" **75.00**

Christmas Tree & Lantern Pins

Pin, rhinestone, model of a Christmas tree, ice blue stones on white metal, signed "Weiss," 2¼" h. (ILLUS. right) **65.00**

Pin, rhinestone, model of a Christmas tree, large red, blue, gold & clear stones, baguette-cut "candles," small dark green, red, gold & clear trim, signed "Weiss," 2½" h. **85.00**

Pin, rhinestone, rhinestone flowers over a blue glass floral center, wide border of hand-set blue & green leaves, signed "Schreiner," 2¾" l. . . **135.00**

Pin, rhinestones, grape purple border of leaves around marquise-cut & custom made leaf-shaped dark purple & pale blue stones Aurora Borealis rhinestone centers, 2¾" l. (ILLUS. right, previous page) **55.00**

Pin, sterling silver, model of a peacock atop a flower w/two birds at the sides, five hanging charms, signed "Heki," 3½" h. **185.00**

Pin-pendant, rhinestone, a large green center stone in a gold filigree frame w/small green rhinestones, a filigree drop w/green stones, signed "Original by Robert," 2¾" l. . . **65.00**

Sets

Royal Blue Rhinestone Set

Necklace, bracelet & drop earrings: rhinestone, hand-set royal blue rhinestones w/clear rhinestone trim, necklace w/central large stones & drops, the bracelet w/double row of stones & a center design, matching clip-on earrings, signed "Eisenberg," earrings 1¾" l., necklace adjusts to 16", the set (ILLUS.) **$500.00**

Necklace, bracelet & earrings: a long chain necklace w/hanging plastic red, white & blue poker chips & yellow die, matching bracelet & clip-on earrings, necklace 28" l., the set **45.00**

Necklace & earrings: goldplated, the necklace w/ornate links, each alternating w/multicolored faux gemstone links, matching earrings, tagged "Alice Caviness," earrings 1¾" l., necklace 16" l., the set **75.00**

Pin & earrings: goldplated metal, a design of openwork branches, the center w/a design of blue & grey pearls w/rhinestone trim, signed "Gasty Paris," manufactured by Grosse, dated "1969," earrings 1" w., pin 2" d., the set **75.00**

KEWPIE COLLECTIBLES

Doll, bisque, jointed arms, w/costumes, signed on base of feet "O'Neill," probably made by Borgfeldt, ca. 1913, Germany, 5½" h. **$175.00**

Kewpie & Doodledog Figure

Figure, bisque, Kewpie lying on his stomach w/Doodledog seated on his back, early 20th c. (ILLUS.) . . **3,400.00**

Rare Kewpie on Goat Figure

Figure, bisque, Kewpie mounted on a
flat hinged goat figure raised on a
grassy mound w/oblong base
(ILLUS.) **5,300.00**

Figure, bisque, Kewpie riding on a
wooden rocking horse on a grass-
molded oblong base **5,500.00**

Figure, bisque, Kewpie seated on a
rearing jointed Dachshund dog
figure, grassy mound base **5,100.00**

Kewpie on Stork Figure

Figure, bisque, Kewpie seated on a
walking stork w/outstretched wings
(ILLUS.) **5,000.00**

Figure, bisque, Kewpie standing
sucking its thumb, 3" h. **125.00**

Figure, bisque, black "Hottentot,"
partial Rose O'Neill sticker on
back, 5" h. **500.00**

Figure, bisque, "Traveler,"
w/suitcase, marked, 5" h. **295.00**

Sugar bowl, cov., child's, porcelain,
decorated in color w/action
Kewpies, marked "Bavaria" **125.00**

KITCHENWARES

EGG TIMERS

Black Chef Egg Timer

Black chef, standing w/large fish,
timer in fish's mouth, ceramic,
Japan, 4¾" h. (ILLUS.) **$145.00**

Boy, skiing, ceramic, Germany, 3" **75.00**

Boy, w/red cap, stands & holds
different glass tubes in each hand,
wooden, unmarked, 4½" h. **35.00**

Cat, standing by base of grandfather
clock, ceramic, Germany, 4½" h. . . . **75.00**

Chef, w/cake, composition, Germany . . **95.00**

Chef, winking, white clothes, timer
built in back, turns upside down to
tip sand, ceramic, 4" **50.00**

Josef Originals Egg Timer

Chick with cap, Josef Originals,
ceramic (ILLUS.) **50.00**

Chimney sweep carrying ladder,
ceramic, Germany, 3¼" h. **85.00**

Clown on phone, standing, yellow
suit, ceramic, Japan, 3¾" h. **65.00**

Colonial lady w/bonnet, variety of
dresses & colors, ceramic,
Germany, 3¾" h. **75.00**

Dutch Girl & Boy Egg Timer

Dutch girl & boy, ceramic, Goebel
(ILLUS.) **100.00**

Dutch girl w/flowers, walking,
chalkware, unmarked, 4½" h. **55.00**

Elf Egg Timer

Elf by well, ceramic, Manorware,
England (ILLUS.). **45.00**

Golliwog, bisque, England, 4½" h.,
minimum value **200.00**

Lighthouse, blue, cream & orange
lustreware, ceramic, Germany,
4½" h. **85.00**

Little boy, standing wearing black
shorts & shoes & red tie, ceramic,
Germany **90.00**

Little girl on phone, ceramic,
Germany **95.00**

Goebel Egg Timer

Little girl with chick, ceramic,
Goebel, Germany (ILLUS.) **100.00**

Mammy, tin, lighographed picture of
her cooking, pot holder hooks,
unmarked, 7¾" h. **125.00**

Mammy, with potholders, painted
wood **85.00**

Parlor maid w/cat, ceramic, Japan . . . **65.00**

Penguin, chalkware, England, 3¾" h. . . . **65.00**

Rooster, cut-out painted wood
w/sequins **25.00**

Sailboat, ceramic, Manorware,
England. **45.00**

Sailor, ceramic, blue, Germany **85.00**

Scotsman w/bagpipes, plastic,
England, 4½" h. **65.00**

Swami Egg Timer

Swami, standing wearing turban,
ceramic, Germany (ILLUS.). **110.00**

Welsh woman, ceramic, Germany,
4½" h. **85.00**

Windmill, w/dog or pigs on base,
ceramic, Japan, 3¾" h. **95.00**

HOLT HOWARD WARES

Canister, cov., Pixieware, "Instant
Coffee," Holt Howard. **285.00**

Condiment jar, cov., ceramic, figural
"Pixieware," "Olives," Holt Howard . . . **135.00**

Jam & jelly container, Pixieware,
Holt Howard. **69.00**

Ketchup container, cov., Pixieware,
Holt Howard. **60.00**

Napkin holder, ceramic, figural
Santa Claus, Holt Howard. **48.00**

Olive container, cov., Pixieware,
Holt Howard. **140.00**

Salt & pepper shakers, Bride &
Groom, pr. **32.00**

Salt & pepper shakers, figural
"Pixieware," Holt Howard, pr. **625.00**

Salt & pepper shakers, mouse, pr. . . . **28.00**

Salt & pepper shakers, mule, pr.. . . . . **25.00**

Salt & pepper shakers, rabbit,
miniature, pr. **30.00**

Salt & pepper shakers, Raggedy
Ann & Andy, pr. **125.00**

Salt & pepper shakers, rooster,
brown, yellow & red, inkstamp
mark "Japan," 4¾" h., pr.. . . . . **33.00**

KITCHEN UTENSILS

Apple Corer - Segmentor

Apple correr - segmentor, cast iron
& steel, a circle w/12 segmentors,
cores & segments when apple is
pushed through it, marked "Apple
Cutter, Rollman Mfg. Co., Mt. Joy,"
4½" d. (ILLUS.) **45.00**

Apple parer, cast iron, clamp-on
type, a turntable w/push-off,
marked "D.H. Whittemore," known
as the "Union" **250.00**

Apple parer, cast iron, commerical-
size, marked "The Dandy". **400.00**

Apple parer, cast iron, turn-table-
type, occasionally galvanized,
marked "Granite State," 13" h. **250.00**

Apple parer, wooden, table mount-
style w/attached paring arm, slides
onto board, occasionally w/a paper
label. **185.00**

Bake board, tin, curved bottom to
hold rolling pin, approximately
19" w., 22" h. **325.00**

Baking pan, tin, square, advertises
"Snowking Baking Powder," 7½" w. . . **25.00**

Beater crock, stoneware w/blue
band decoration, rounded bottom
inside, marked "Beat It To Gettle &
Rusie, Groceries & Hardware,
Green Mountain, Iowa," 5" d.,
4½" h. **150.00**

Bundt pan, tin, hand-made, 10" d. **18.00**

Butter mold, wood, carved cow
design on plunger **285.00**

Can opener, cast iron & steel,
marked "World's Best,
Pittsburgh, PA" **45.00**

Can opener, cast iron, three-way,
punctures & opens can, no
markings **85.00**

Can opener, steel w/wooden handle,
marked "Sure Cut," patent-dated
"7-19-94" **15.00**

Cherry pitter, cast iron, clamp-on
style, push action pits two cherries
at one time, marked "New
Standard Cherry Stoner, Duplex
No. 35 Mt. Joy PA U.S.A.". **85.00**

Cherry pitter, tin, spring-action, pits
eight cherries at once, marked
"Marshall Mfg. Co. Cherry Pitter,
Omaha, Neb. Pat. Jan. 4 1916" . . . **275.00**

Coffee grinder, wooden, lap type
w/drawer, pewter hopper & cast-
iron crank handle, marked "Adams" . . **155.00**

Coffee roaster, cast iron, hinged
"cannon ball" shape sits in a three-
legged rim, wire bail handle,
marked "Wood's Patent, Roys and
Wilcox Co., Harrington's Import,
Berlin Ct. Pat'd 5 17 1859," two
sizes **550.00**

Collander, tin, round, footed w/two
handles, nice star design pierced
on sides. **75.00**

Cookie or cake cutter, tin, hand-
made design of a reindeer, tin cut
closely to edge of design, no
handle, 5 x 6" (ILLUS.) **125.00**

Cookie or cake cutter, tin, hand-
made in the shape of a hand,
medium weight w/back & top
handle, 4¼" l. **85.00**

Cookie or cake cutter, tin, lightweight stylized design of a lion,
manufactured, also found as a
rabbit, doll-like girl, etc., on a
rectangular background, handled,
each. **15.00**

Dough scraper, brass & tin, tubular
tin handle, stamped "P.D." for
Peter Derr **550.00**

Egg beater, cast iron, "D-O-V-E-R"
spelled out on the rotary wheel **225.00**

Cast-iron & Glass Egg Beater

Egg beater, cast-iron mechanism on
a footed glass bowl base, marked
"S &S Hutchson, New York, Pat.
Appl. For" (ILLUS.) **375.00**

Egg beater, cast-iron top, wires,
glass jar w/measurements, marked
on bottom of jar "Silvers - Brooklyn"
w/bridge outline as trademark **275.00**

Egg beater, tin, child's, marked
"Beats Anything in a Cup or Bowl,"
blue & white wooden handle, 7½" l. . . . **18.00**

Egg beater, wall mount-type, wire
looped beater w/original wall
bracket, marked "Licensed To Be
Sold Only According To
Established Price List of Maker,
Keystone, Pat. Dec. 5,85" on each
of rotary wheel. **475.00**

Reindeer Cookie Cutter

Wire Egg Carrier

Egg carrier, wire, round w/loops of wire forming bottom below six rings to hold eggs, looped wire center handle, ca. 1890 (ILLUS. bottom of previous page). **125.00**

Egg lifter, wire, two concave wire shapes at end of squeeze-action wire handle **35.00**

Egg separator, tin, circular w/edge slots, stamped "Rumford Egg Separator". **65.00**

Early Wooden Flour Sifter

Flour sifter, wooden, elevated frame w/revolving brush inside, stamped "W. Foyes Flour Sifter, Patented Sept 12, 1865" (ILLUS.) **275.00**

Fruit & lard press, cast iron, "Griswold No. 3" **275.00**

Grater, tin, central pivot displays several grating surfaces or circular base, heavy wire handle **15.00**

Grater, tin, punched half-cylinder on wire frame w/black wooden handle, 11" h. **20.00**

Griddle, cast iron, "Griswold No. 108" . . **32.00**

Griddle greaser, wire, separates on one end to hold wrapped cloth used to grease griddles, called "The Fairy," patent-dated December 29, 1903. . . . . **35.00**

Sectional Pancake Griddle

Griddle - pancake iron, cast iron, divided into three or more round areas each w/a lift-lid, marked "Pat. Jan 25 1881, S Mfg. Co., New York" (ILLUS.) **175.00**

Jar opener, cast iron, wrench-style, marked "C.A. Powell, Cleve'd. O" . . . **24.00**

Jar opener, steel, two sections rotate on a pivot to loosen jar lid, patent-dated "1 7 08" **25.00**

Knife & fork carrier, walnut, rectangular dovetailed case, divided into two sections by a raised & shaped divider used as a handle **175.00**

Lemon squeezer, wood & tin, two folded tin pieces fit into a nicely shaped handle w/center groove to catch juice, sometimes one tin section is serrated, scarce, 6¼" l. . . . **150.00**

Lemon squeezer, wooden, footed base for table-top use, hinged lever action. **175.00**

Handi-hands Lifter

Lifter, handi-hands-style, wire, two hinged hand-like sections used to lift items from kettles, etc. (ILLUS.) . . **55.00**

Lunch pail, tin, w/insert & cup on top, oval **85.00**

Tin Collapsible Lunch Pail

Lunch pail, tin & wire, collapsible-type, four sections, marked "Pat. Feb. 26 1884" (ILLUS.) **60.00**

Measuring cup, tin, one-cup w/measuring lines, marked "Rumford" **25.00**

Measuring spoons, metal, advertising Swans Down Cake Flour, graduated set of 4 . . . . **25.00**

Nutmeg grater, cast iron & tin, wire handle connected to a circular tin dish w/cast-iron nutmeg grater holder, marked on the back "Pat'd Mar 9 1886". **300.00**

Nutmeg grater, tin, elongated rectangle w/sliding box above grater, marked "The Boye" **110.00**

Nutmeg grater, tin, small grater attached to colorful box marked "Stickney & Poors," six whole nutmegs. **65.00**

Nutmeg grater, wooden, nicely turned base handle below squared grater box w/side crank handle & cylindrical top fitted w/a brass cap marked "Patent Apr. 2, 1867," paper label reads "Champion Grater Co. Boston" **475.00**

Pastry blender, wires w/wooden handle, marked "Androx, Pat. Jan. 12, 29" **8.00**

Pie crimper, brass & tin, a brass serrated wheel w/a long slender cylindrical tin handle w/end loop, 6½" l. **85.00**

Pie crimper, wood, tin & steel, green handle w/tin crimped wheel. **12.00**

Pie lifter, cast iron & heavy wire, two prongs w/center cast-iron slide, patent-dated "Jan. 30, 83". **55.00**

Pie pan, tin & wire, a tin rim w/wire screen for bottom, tiny feet, sits under a pie pan to allow for cooling. . **18.00**

Wire & Tin Popcorn Popper

Popcorn popper, tin & wire mesh, archimedian-style, round wire cylindrical cage w/a long wire handle & turned wood handle, marked "Pat. Apr. 16, 1897," rare (ILLUS.). **375.00**

Popcorn popper, wire, rectangular cage w/lift lid, wooden handle, common. **20.00**

Pot & pan scraper, tin, lithographed, advertising give-aways, various shapes, each. **400.00**

Pot & pan scraper, tin, triangular w/inverted thumbprint in center, advertising for various products, each. **85.00**

Pot scraper, wire, a series of attached wire rings form a pocket to hold soap, unusual w/the pocket. . **65.00**

Clamp-on Raisin Seeder

Raisin seeder, cast iron, clamp-on style, a frame w/seven wires below a hinged cast-iron top, clamp below, marked "Pat. June 9, 1881" (ILLUS.). **500.00**

Rolling pin, wooden, barrel roller w/T-frame handle **200.00**

Rolling pin, wooden, corrugated barrel & wooden handles, 11¼" l. . . . **45.00**

Rolling pin, turned curly maple, 18" l. . . **116.00**

Scale, brass & cast iron, spring balance-type, marked "PS&W Co.," 7". **23.00**

Scale scoop, tin, footed, center pierced for use on home scales **20.00**

Sink brush, tin & wire, scoop on one end, other end w/brush **45.00**

Cast-iron Six-in-One Tool

Six-in-one tool, cast iron, multi-purpose tool used as a trivet, dish carrier, pie lifter, stove top lifter, a tenderizer & a pouring aid, marked "Thayer Pat May 24,81" (ILLUS.) . . . **75.00**

Skillet, cast iron, "Griswold No 4". **26.00**

Spatula, tin, heart design in blade, stamped "Rumford - The Wholesome Baking Powder". **28.00**

Spice set, wood, a circular box & cover opening to reveal seven spice containers, cover stamped "Spices," check to see that all the spice containers are different, the set **325.00**

Spoon, metal w/apron center, wooden handle **35.00**

Strainer, tin, perforated bottom, wooden handle & hanger ring **25.00**

Toaster, wire w/wooden handle, bread placed between two decorative wires held together w/a sliding ring, simple circular design. . . **30.00**

Trivet, forged iron, heart-shaped w/graceful handle **225.00**

Wire Trivet

Trivet, wire, rounded starburst design of stamped wire w/double-loop ends & triangles, used as a coffeepot or teapot stand (ILLUS.) . . **45.00**

Whisk, tin & wire, spiral wire under a flat circular disc , the whole attached to a wooden handle, made in England, 9½" l. **75.00**

MISCELLANEOUS GLASSWARE

Baking dishes, crab-shaped, Glasbake by McKee, manufactured in the 1920s, boxed set of six . . **20.00-24.00**

Baking pan, Flamex Glass Bake Ware from Sears, characteristic yellow tinge of pre-1934 ovenware from the arsenic in the formula, molded pattern of flowers & leaves on the outside of the dish **6.00-10.00**

Batter bowl, decorated post-production w/green, gold & brown leaves, Federal Glass Company, perhaps a grocery or department store promotion, batter bowl (ILLUS. far right w/Mixing bowls) **15.00-25.00**

Butter dish cover, lid for one-pound butter dish, green Block Optic pattern, by Hocking Glass Co., cover alone **20.00-25.00**

Canister & lid, "Blue Circle" patt., Cereal, manufactured by the Hocking Glass Company, unusual (ILLUS. right) **32.00-38.00**

Hocking Glass Canisters & Lids

Canisters & lids, "Blue Circle" patt., Flour & Sugar, manufactured by the Hocking Glass Company, each (ILLUS. left & center) **27.00-30.00**

Canning funnel, glass, unknown production dates or manufacturer, 4⅜" across the top & 2" across the bottom, 3" h. **5.00-12.00**

Early PYREX Covered Casserole

Casserole, cov., early PYREX made by Corning Glass Works, by trademark from 1915-1925, yellow coloring at the rims caused by arsenic in the glass formula (ILLUS.). **8.00-10.00**

Casserole, cov., part of an embossed set from Glasbake, by McKee Glass Company, two-cup capacity, 6" d. across the top, not counting the tab handles **4.00-6.00**

Chevron Cream Pitcher

Cream pitcher, Chevron decorated crystal, more commonly seen in cobalt, rectangular top 2½ x 4½", to the tip of the spout, 3⅞" h. (ILLUS.). **5.00-10.00**

Anchor Hocking Glassware

Dessert sets, Fire King Leaf & Blossom, Jadeite on the left, Crystal on the right, manufactured 1951-1952 by Anchor Hocking, leaf plates 8½" d. & blossom bowls 4¾" d., depending upon color & condition, each set (ILLUS.) . . **18.00-25.00**

Drippings jar, cov., part of five-part set made by Hazel Atlas Glass Company in the 1920s, 3⅞" across the lid & 3" h. (ILLUS. center w/range sets). **18.00-25.00**

Evenflo Formula Measuring Pitcher

Formula measuring pitcher, Evenflo-made baby feeding accessories, similar shaped & poorly pictured pitchers are advertised in most catalogs of the 1940s, the measurements on the other side are in ounces, up to 32 ounces (ILLUS.) **5.00-10.00**

Grease jar, w/"Tulip" lid, Ivory, Fire King by Anchor Hocking (ILLUS. w/Fire King Ivory range set, center) **25.00-30.00**

Grease jar, w/"Tulip" lid, part of range set, Jadeite, Fire King by Anchor Hocking, 4¼" h. (ILLUS. w/Jadeite range set, center) **48.00-60.00**

Leftover jar, cov., crystal Fire King by Anchor Hocking, not documented in K&W's book on Fire King, small size **3.00-6.00**

Leftover jar, cov., crystal Fire King by Anchor Hocking, not documented in K&W's book on Fire King, large size **5.00-10.00**

Leftover jar, without clear lid, decorated post-production w/green, gold & brown leaves, Fire King by Anchor Hocking, perhaps a grocery or department store promotion (ILLUS. center front w/Mixing bowls) **5.00-8.00**

Leftover jar, cov., Jadeite, Jeannette Glass Company, unknown production dates, probably 1920s, large one 4¼ x 8½", 3⅜" h. (ILLUS. bottom). **30.00-50.00**

Leftover jar, cov., Jadeite, Fire King, by Anchor Hocking, ca. 1950s, newer jars are thinner w/plain sides & crystal lids, large 4" x 8" (ILLUS. bottom). **18.00-24.00**

Jeannette Jadeite Leftover Jars

Leftover jars, cov., Jadeite, Jeannette Glass Company, unknown production dates, probably 1920s, small ones 4¼ x 4¼", 2½" h., each (ILLUS. top) . . **25.00-40.00**

White and Jadeite Fire King Leftover Jars

Leftover jars, cov., white & Jadeite, Fire King, by Anchor Hocking, ca. 1950s, newer, thinner jars w/plain sides & crystal lids, small jars 4 x 4", each (ILLUS. top) **12.00-16.00**

Loaf pan, Glasbake by McKee, clear, red-handled, 5" x 9" **6.00-10.00**

McKee "Ships" Pieces

McKee "Ships" pieces, made by the McKee Glass Company, as part of their Deluxe Kitchen Line, from the early 1930s-1940s, white glass w/red decals, also found w/black decals; the bottom piece is a refrigerator jar, 5" x 8" w/white lid, preferred by collectors over the clear glass lids; center piece is a canister w/white lid, 24-ounce capacity, 5" across the top & 3½" h., the salt shaker is missing its lid, which was black or red plastic; refrigerator jar 22.00 to 24.00; canister 22.00 to 25.00; shaker w/lid 12.00 to 15.00 (ILLUS.). **12.00-25.00**

Jadeite Measuring Cup Set

Measuring cup set, Jadeite, Jeannette Glass Company, pictured in a company brochure from 1938, ¼ cup, 18.00 to 20.00; ⅓ cup, 20.00 to 24.00; ½ cup, 20.00 to 25.00; 1 cup, 22.00 to 28.00 (ILLUS.). **18.00-20.00**

Milk pitcher, "Beads & Bars" patt., crystal, Fire King, by Anchor Hocking. **15.00-20.00**

Jadeite "Beads & Bars" Pitcher

Milk pitcher, "Beads & Bars" patt., Fire King by Anchor Hocking, Jadeite, 20 oz., 4¼" h. (ILLUS.). . . . . **45.00 to 80.00**

Mixing Bowls, Batter Bowl, Leftover Jar and Lids

Mixing bowls, decorated post-production w/green, gold & brown leaves, Federal Glass Company, depending on size, each (ILLUS. back left & center) **8.00-18.00**

Mixing bowls, boxed set, Fire King by Anchor Hocking, W-400 Line, 1968-1978, this set is called "Sunny Side," slightly tapered w/a squared-off bottom, bowls are 5" d., Lime; 6" d, Orange; 7¼" d.,

Fire King Boxed Mixing Bowl Set

Green; 8⅜" d., Yellow; prices, 5" d. 4.00 to 6.00; 6" d. 6.00 to 8.00; 7¼" d. 8.00 to 10.00; 8⅜" d. 10.00 to 12.00 (ILLUS.) **10.00 to12.00**

Mixmaster With Jadeite Bowls

Mixmaster w/Jadeite bowls, early, wooden-handled electric mixer, from the Chicago Flexible Shaft Company, which became Sunbeam, exact dates of manufacture unknown, probably the late 1920s to 1930s, juicer bowl fit on top when the handle was turned to the side, the mixers, without the bowls 45.00-70.00; big bowl, in Jadeite, 10.00 to 12.00; spouted smaller bowl (not shown) 10.00 to 15.00; juicer bowl (ILLUS.). . . . . **5.00 to 20.00**

Fire King Mugs

Mugs, Sapphire blue Fire King by Anchor Hocking, w/Philbe design, 1942-1948, the "heavy" one is reportedly the shaving mug, the "thin" one, the coffee mug, one unmarked & w/a pronounced rim on the base, the other doesn't have the rim, each (ILLUS.) **30.00-50.00**

Fire King Ivory Range Set

Range set, Ivory, w/"Tulip" lids, Fire King by Anchor Hocking, note corrosion of Salt lid (difficult to find good condition), Ivory Beaded Rim bowls are available to complete the set, shakers each (ILLUS. left & right) **15.00-22.00**

Jadeite Range Set

Range set: salt & pepper shakers & grease or drippings jar; w/"Tulip" lids, Jadeite, Fire King by Anchor Hocking, shakers 4¼" h. , each (ILLUS. left & right) **20.00-25.00**

Five-Part Range Set

Range set, five-part set made by Hazel Atlas Glass Company in the 1920s, shakers w/"High Hat" tops 4½" h., shakers each (ILLUS.left & right) **15.00-25.00**

Refrigerator jar, cov., Crosley Shelvador, distributed w/new Crosley Shelvador refrigerators, dates unknown, probably 1930s, unknown manufacturer, 3" x 4⅜", 2½ h., without cover **5.00-8.00**

Refrigerator jar lids, Sapphire blue, Fire King by Anchor Hocking, 1942-1948, separate lids, each . . **4.00-10.00**

Gay Fad Refrigerator Jars

Refrigerator jar, cov., Gay Fad hand-painted patt., Fire King by Anchor Hocking, bought by Gay Fad Studios of Lancaster, Ohio, & hand-painted for resale, late 1950s & 1960s, large size (ILLUS. bottom) **18.00-24.00**

Refrigerator jars, cov., Gay Fad hand-painted patt., Fire King by Anchor Hocking, bought by Gay Fad Studios of Lancaster, Ohio & hand-painted for resale, late 1950s & 1960s, small size, each (ILLUS. top) **12.00-16.00**

Three-Piece Sapphire Refrigerator Set

Refrigerator jar, cov., part of three-piece set in Sapphire blue, Philbe design on the bottom, without lids these are the 4" x 4" baker and the loaf pan, Fire King by Anchor Hocking, 1942-1948, large one w/cover (ILLUS. bottom) **25.00-35.00**

Refrigerator jars, cov., three-piece set in Sapphire blue, Philbe design on the bottom, without lids these are the 4" x 4" baker and the loaf pan, Fire King by Anchor Hocking, 1942-1948, small size w/cover, each (ILLUS. top) **18.00-22.00**

Refrigerator Water Container

Refrigerator water container, one-gallon crystal water jar w/pull-down spout for dispensing cool drinks, lid missing, manufacturer unknown (ILLUS.). **18.00-25.00**

Jadeite Single-Spout Skillet

Skillet, Jadeite, single spout, not for stove top use, Fire King by Anchor Hocking, 6¼" d. at top, not counting the spout or handle (ILLUS.). **50.00-70.00**

Spice Set

Spice set, identified by Gene Florence as a product of the Jeannette Glass Co., w/a gold colored paper label on the front, a red label on the back, they contained "Bit Hit" spices from the Euclid Coffee Company, Cleveland, Ohio, 4½" h. to the top of the domed metal lid, each (ILLUS.). **28.00-35.00**

Water bottle, Criss Cross patt. by Hazel Atlas, clear, one-quart capacity. **22.00-26.00**

NAPKIN DOLLS

Ceramic, figure of a colonial lady wearing a yellow dress & holding a blue umbrella, w/a bell clapper, 9" h. **90.00**

White Ceramic Napkin Doll

Ceramic, figure of a woman in a white dress w/yellow trim, holding a toothpick basket over her head, foil label "California Originals USA," 13¾" h. (ILLUS.) **80.00**

Pink, Yellow and Green Ceramic Napkin Dolls

Ceramic, figure of a woman wearing a colonial cap, pink, yellow & green dress, foil Betsons label, 8¾" h., each (ILLUS.) **85.00**

Ceramic, figure of angel, blue & white, Japan paper label, 5⅜" h **85.00**

Ceramic, figure of bartender w/tray holding candle, black & white 8¾" h. **100.00**

Ceramic, figure of colonial lady in a green dress holding a pink umbrella, w/a bell clapper, 9" h. **90.00**

Ceramic, figure of Oriental woman holding a yellow fan, pink dress, 9¼" h. **90.00**

Ceramic, figure of peasant woman, pink w/floral design, holding toothpick tray on head, jeweled eyes, 9¼" h. **65.00**

Ceramic, figure of Spanish dancer holding tambourine, blue & white dress, marked "#460 California Originals USA," 15" h. **150.00**

Ceramic, figure of woman holding a green toothpick tray, yellow dress, 9¼" h. **90.00**

Ceramic, figure of woman in a yellow dress, fan masks candleholder, jewel-decorated, marked "Kreiss & Co.," 10½" h. **90.00**

Ceramic Candleholder Napkin Doll

Ceramic, figure of woman in pink dress, hat masks candleholder, jewel-decorated, marked "Kreiss & Co.," 10½" h. (ILLUS.) **65.00**

Ceramic, figure of woman w/candleholder in hat, green dress, 9¾" h. **75.00**

Handmade Ceramic Napkin Doll

Ceramic, figure of woman w/white dress w/pink applied roses, handmade, 9" h. (ILLUS.) **85.00**

Ceramic, figure of woman with 4¾" shakers, toothpick tray held in front, blue dress, marked "Japan," 9¾" h. **135.00**

Ceramic & wood, half-figure of German woman w/wood base & wires to hold napkins, marked "Goebel, W. Germany," ca. 1950-57, 9" h. **185.00**

Chalkware, figure of woman w/beige lace skirt & fitted jacket, candleholder in hat, 13" h. **115.00**

Chalkware & metal, figure of an Art Deco woman, black & gold, 8⅞" h. **125.00**

Wood, figure of woman on marble base, green dress, "Servy-Etta," marked "U.S.D. Patent No. 159,005," 11½" h. **40.00**

Wood Napkin Doll with Blue Hat

Wood, figure of woman w/blue hat, white dress w/pink-dotted stripes, 7" h. (ILLUS.) **65.00**

PIE BIRDS

Bird, black on white base, yellow feet & beak, Nutbrown, England. **45.00**

Bird, black, perched on log, England . . **95.00**

Bird, two-headed, Barn Pottery, Devon, England. **95.00**

Black Bird Pie Bird

Black bird, fat, yellow beak, ceramic (ILLUS.) **50.00**

Black chef, full-figure, yellow smock w/white hat, USA **95.00**

Chick, yellow w/pink lips, Josef Originals **55.00**

Chick w/dust cap, "Pie Baker," by Josef Originals, ceramic **85.00**

Duck, yellow beak, white w/black detail, England. **100.00**

Duck's head, beige w/black detail, England **125.00**

Elephant, dark gray w/yellow glaze inside, England **100.00**

Howling bear, seated, brown & white, ceramic, USA **95.00**

Mammy, outstretched arms, USA. **95.00**

"Patches" pie bird, Morton Pottery, USA. **35.00**

"Pie Baker," figure of a lady holding
a bowl, by Josef Originals,
ceramic **95.00**

"Pie Chef" Pie Bird

"Pie Chef," by Josef Originals,
ceramic (ILLUS.) **95.00**
"Pillsbury" bird, USA **45.00**
Rooster, Pearl China, USA **95.00**
Seal, black, ceramic, Japan **125.00**
Songbirds, beige, blue, and pink
ceramic, USA, each **35.00**
Songbirds, gold beaks and feet,
Lapiere (Ohio), USA **100.00**

REAMERS

Flowered Reamer with Gold Trim

Ceramic, white w/multi-colored
flowers & gold trim, tab handle
(ILLUS.) **185.00**
Ceramic, white w/multi-colored
flowers & gold trim, two-piece,
marked "Nippon" **160.00**
Ceramic, luster w/red & yellow
flowers, two-piece, marked "Made
in Japan," 2" h. **125.00**
Ceramic, saucer-type, cream & tan
with maroon & blue trim, marked "A
Present From Framington, Made in
England," 3¼" d. **125.00**
Ceramic, white w/dark blue & gold
trim, marked "Germany," 3½" h. **150.00**
Ceramic, sauce-boat shaped, blue
chintz/multicolored flowers, marked
"Crown Ducal, Made in England,"
8" l., 3½" h. **375.00**

Salt & Pepper Ceramic Reamer

Ceramic, figure clowns, reamer, salt
& pepper shakers, 2½" - 3¾",
marked "Japan," each (ILLUS.) . . **20.00-35.00**
Ceramic, yellow w/baby sleeping on
moon, blue and orange cone, two-
piece, marked "Made in Japan," 4" h. . . . **65.00**
Ceramic, clown head in saucer,
marked "Sourpuss," 4¾" d. **100.00**
Ceramic, figure of clown & lemon,
yellow, two-piece, marked "Made
In Japan," 5" h. **150.00**

Ceramic Boy Reamer

Ceramic, lavender figure of boy
sitting cross-legged, black trim,
two-piece, 5" h. (ILLUS.) **400.00**
Ceramic, model of a pear, white
w/black & gold trim, three-piece,
5" h. **55.00**
Ceramic, figure of clown, two-piece,
maroon & white w/maroon & green
cone, marked "Made in Japan,"
5½" h. **75.00**
Ceramic, figure of clown, two-piece,
green cone & floral bottom, 6" h. **65.00**

Green Hall Reamer with Cream Lining

Ceramic, green w/cream lining,
tab/loop handle, "Medallion" shape,
Hall China Co., marked "Hall,"
6" d. (ILLUS.) **400.00**

Flowered Ceramic Reamer

Ceramic, cream w/yellow & purple flowers & green leaves, two-piece, marked "Universal Cambridge, Ovenproof, Made in USA," 9½" h. (ILLUS.) **185.00**

Ceramic and wood, blue & white cone, 8¾" wooden handle, Germany **275.00**

Ceramic model of house, tan w/green & red trees, green trim & blue windows, two-piece, marked "Made in Japan" w/ six 3¼" matching cups, 5½" h. **185.00**

Glass, blue Fry w/white opal trim, tab handle, 4" d. **185.00**

Glass, blue delphite, Jeanette Glass Co., 5⅛" d. **75.00**

Glass, green opaque glass, McKee Glass Co., marked "McK," 5¼" d. **25.00**

Ultramarine Glass Reamer

Glass, ultramarine, Jeannette Glass Co., 5¼" d. (ILLUS.) **120.00**

Glass, green, two-cup pitcher & reamer set, Hazel Atlas Glass Co., 5¾" **30.00**

Glass, black, embossed "SUNKIST," marked "Pat. No. 18764 Made in USA," McKee Glass Co., 6" d. **850.00**

Glass, cobalt blue criss-cross, Hazel Atlas Glass Co., 6⅛" d. **285.00**

Glass, opalescent, tab/loop handle, Fry Glass Co., 6¼" d. **40.00**

Glass, white milk glass, embossed Valencia, 6¼" d. **100.00**

French Blue Reamer

Glass, French blue, two-piece, Fenton Glass, 6⅜" h. (ILLUS.) . . . **3,500.00**

Glass, off-green Tufglass, slick handle, 6½" d. **95.00**

Glass, pink "Party Line Measuring Set," two-piece, Paden City Glass Co., 8¾" h. **175.00**

Metal, one piece w/levered handle, marked "Super Juicer," 6" h. **30.00**

Metal, hand-held, marked "Lemon Squeezer," 6¾" l. **8.00**

Metal, "Seald Sweet Juice Extractor," tilt model, w/clamp-on base, 13" h. . . **65.00**

Metal and glass, green w/white milk glass bowl, ceramic cone, marked "Sunkist Jucit Refined", electric, 8¾" h. **50.00**

Metal and glass, green bowl & cone, "Mount Joy," green metal base w/clamp, 11" h. **175.00**

Silver plate, loop handle, 4" d. **135.00**

Silver plate, model of bird, marked "Muss Bach," 4½" l. **22.00**

Silver Plate "Meriden" Reamer

Silver plate, marked "Meriden S.P. Co. International Silver Co." 4⅝" d. (ILLUS.) **100.00**

Wood, hand-held, 6¼" l. **35.00**

Wood, hinged, hand-held, 10" l. **45.00**

SALT & PEPPER SHAKERS

NOVELTY FIGURALS

Arab sitting on camel, 4¾" h. **140.00**

Avocado half & pit, 2½" h. **24.00**

Barber shaving the pig, 3" h. **33.00**

Bartender Condiment Set

Bartender condiment, 4¼" h.
(ILLUS.)..................... **365.00**
Baseball players condiment, bat
forms mustard spoon, 3½" h. **95.00**
**Betty Boop & Bimbo in wooden
boat,** 3½" h. **38.00**
Black cat mother & baby, nodder-
type, 3¾" h.................... **235.00**
Black chef holding trays,
watermelon slices form the
shakers, 4¼" h................. **115.00**
Blackpool Tower condiment,
England, 5" h. **80.00**
Bride & groom sitting on bench,
4½" h. **11.00**
Camel Joe & Ray, plastic, 3½" h..... **28.00**
Campbell's Soup Kids, plastic, F&F
Mold & Die Co., 4" h............. **43.00**
Cat w/fireplace condiment, cat
divides in two, 5" h. **48.00**
Cat witch & pumpkin cauldron,
Omnibus, 4" h.................. **16.00**
Christmas tree condiment stacker,
6" h........................... **73.00**
Cinderella & her coach, 2½" h....... **70.00**
Clown lying on drum, 3½" h......... **17.00**

Clowns on Circus Balls

Clowns on circus balls, nodder-
type, 4" h. (ILLUS.) **390.00**
Colonel Sanders, plastic, 4" h....... **38.00**
Colorful parakeets on branch, bone
china, 3½" h................... **23.00**
Couple doing pushups, 2½" h....... **38.00**
Cowboy & gun, nodder-type, 3¾" h. . **265.00**
Ducks in common white base,
nodder-type, 3" h. **27.00**
Ferdinand the Bull, black w/flowers,
2½" h. **43.00**

Flamingos in common white base,
nodder-type, 3¼" h.............. **43.00**
Granny, Sylvester & Tweety, 6½" h... **38.00**
Happy to sad couple, turnabout-
type, 4" h. **14.00**
**Horse heads in base w/saddle in
center,** three-piece, 3½" h........ **14.00**
Horseshoe & four-leaf clover, 1" h. .. **18.00**
Howdy Doody in car, 4¼" h........ **80.00**

Katzenjammer Kids Shakers

Katzenjammer Kids, one-piece, by
Goebel, 3" h. (ILLUS.)........... **500.00**
Kitchen Prayer ladies, 4" h......... **14.00**
Lawnmower & grass catcher,
3½" h. **34.00**
**Lemon-head man w/derby hat
stacker,** 4" h. **43.00**
Leprechaun kissing Blarney Stone,
Enesco, 3" h................... **17.00**
Little Boy Blue under the haystack,
2½" h. **68.00**
Loch Ness monster condiment,
England, 3½" h................. **95.00**
Magnet & bar, 1" h. **24.00**
Millie & Willie penguins, Kool
cigarettes advertising items, 3" h. ... **14.00**
**Miniature coal bucket &
bellows,** 1" h. **17.00**
Miniature guitar & accordian, 1" h.... **33.00**
Miniature padlock & keys, ½" h...... **48.00**
Miniature pipe & slippers, ½" h...... **17.00**
**Miniature spool of thread &
thimble,** 1" h. **17.00**
**New York 1939 World's Fair Trylon
& Perisphere,** Bakelite
plastic, 3" h.................... **22.00**
**Night Before Christmas mice in
shoe,** Fitz and Floyd, 3½" h....... **38.00**
Old King Cole in his chair, 3½" h. ... **28.00**
**One-piece bellhop carrying two
suitcases,** older set, 4" h......... **34.00**
One-piece fish on tails, C. Miller,
Regal China, 4" h............... **28.00**
Orange tree napkin holder, shakers
are baskets of oranges,
plastic, 6" h.................... **20.00**
**Owl graduates w/rhinestone
eyes,** 3" h..................... **11.00**

Padlock & key, 2½" h. 12.00
Pillsbury flour sack, 4" h. 20.00
Praying pajama children, 3½" h. 14.00
Raggedy Ann & Andy, 4" h. 23.00
Reclining banana people, 2" h. 19.00
Red hearts in arrow base, three-
    piece, 2½" h. 17.00
Red schoolhouse & old-fashioned
    desk, 2" h. 17.00
Robin Hood kneeling on rock, 4" h. . . 23.00
Stacking black chef condiment,
    5½" h. 135.00
Standing zebras, 3" h. 11.00
Tomato condiment on leaf tray,
    marked "Occupied Japan," 2½" h. . . . 19.00
Tomato & Strawberry couple, 4" h. . . 80.00
Train condiment, smokestack
    salt & peppers, 3" h. 28.00
Various animals talking on the
    telephone, 4½" h., each set 14.00
Washington Monument & Capitol
    Building, white, 3" h. 7.00
Wrestlers, 4" h. 23.00

Yosemite Sam Shakers

Yosemite Sam, 4" h. (ILLUS.) 130.00

STRING HOLDERS

Apple and berries, chalkware 35.00
Apple w/face, PY, ceramic. 125.00
Babies, one happy, one crying,
    Lefton, ceramic, pair 250.00
Balloon, ceramic. 55.00

Chalkware Bird String Holder

Bird, chalkware, peeking out of
    birdhouse (ILLUS.) 150.00

Bird in birdcage, chalkware . 125.00
Bird in birdcage, chalkware. 125.00
Bird on branch, scissors in head,
    ceramic 85.00
Bird "String Nest Pull," ceramic 40.00
Black cat's face w/green eyes,
    ceramic 90.00
Bonzo (dog) with bee on chest,
    ceramic 165.00

Bonzo Ceramic String Holder

Bonzo the dog, ceramic, Japan
    (ILLUS.). 175.00
Boy, top hat and pipe, eyes to side,
    chalkware 65.00
Butler, black man w/white lips &
    eyebrows, ceramic 300.00
Cat, ceramic, w/string coming out
    extended paw, pearlized white
    glaze 148.00
Cat, climbing ball of string, Holt
    Howard, ceramic 150.00
Cat w/flowers, scissors in head,
    ceramic 45.00
Chef, black, ceramic 350.00

Ceramic String Holder

Chef, ceramic (ILLUS.) 125.00
Chef, chalkware 65.00
Chef, Japan, ceramic 125.00
Chef w/red bowtie, The Norwood
    Co., Cincinnati, Ohio, chalkware . . 100.00
Christmas chipmunk, ceramic 85.00
Clown, w/string around tooth,
    chalkware 175.00

Deco woman's face, Japan, ceramic . . **150.00**
Dutch boy, chalkware. **135.00**
Dutch Girl's head w/red hat,
    chalkware **45.00**
Green pepper, ceramic **65.00**
Heart, puffed, Cleminson's, ceramic. . . **75.00**

Indian Head String Holder

Indian w/headdress, chalkware
    (ILLUS.). **250.00**
Lady in bonnet w/bow, chalkware . . . **95.00**
Latchstring house, Cleminson's
    ceramic (ILLUS.) **150.00**
Little Red Riding Hood, chalkware . . **250.00**

"Ty-Me" Mammy String Holder

Mammy, "Ty-Me," chalkware
    (ILLUS.). **350.00**
Mammy, w/arms up & scissors in
    pocket (ILLUS.) **250.00**
Mammy face, bisque **350.00**
Mammy face, many variations,
    chalkware **200.00**
Mammy w/flowers, MAPCO,
    chalkware **250.00**
Mexican woman in sombrero,
    chalkware **175.00**
Owl, Josef Originals, ceramic **65.00**
Pear, chalkware **45.00**

Penguin, scissors in nose. **75.00**
Prayer lady, by Enesco, ceramic **300.00**
Pumpkin Cottage, Manorware,
    England, ceramic. **75.00**
Rooster head, Royal Bayreuth,
    porcelain **350.00**
Rosie the Riveter, chalkware. **150.00**
Sailor boy **125.00**
Solider head, chalkware. **75.00**
Southern belle lady, w/full skirt,
    ceramic **65.00**
Southern gentleman w/two ladies,
    ceramic **85.00**
Spanish ladies, chalkware, each **150.00**

Tomato String Holder

Tomato, ceramic (ILLUS.) **55.00**

WHISTLE CUPS

"Count Down, Blast Off" Whistle Mug

"Count Down, Blast Off," space
    mug, rocket ship on handle is
    whistle, bottom says "Personal
    Property of (space for child's
    name)" (ILLUS.) **20.00-30.00**
"Drink Milk and Whistle," three
    small bears play on front while little
    bear sits on handle, ceramic
    whistle is separate piece
    (ILLUS.). **35.00-45.00**

Florida Souvenir Whistle Cup

"Sip 'N Whistle Milk Mug For A Little Dear," similar to other Sip & Whistle Mug, but is a Florida souvenir, same poem on the back (ILLUS.)................. **45.00-55.00**

Bluebird "Whistle For Milk" Whistle Cup

"Whistle For Milk," two bluebirds face each other on handle, tail is whistle, "Grantcrest Hand Painted - Japan," smaller bird 3" h. (ILLUS.)................ **20.00-30.00**

"Whistle For Your Milk," clown w/balloon, Spencer Gifts, 1976 .... **15.00-25.00**

"Whistle For Your Milk," elephant head, trunk is whistle & ears are handles **25.00-35.00**

Owl "Whistle For Your Milk" Whistle Cup

"Whistle For Your Milk," owl w/plastic roly-poly eyes, ceramic whistle is separate piece (ILLUS.)................ **40.00-50.00**

LAUNDRY ROOM ITEMS

CLOTHES SPRINKLER BOTTLES

Bottle, plastic, "Laundry Sprinkler" . . . **$25.00**

Black Cat Sprinkler Bottle

Cat, black, homemade, ceramic (ILLUS.)..................... **150.00**

Cat, marble eyes, ceramic, American Bisque...................... **250.00**

Cat, Siamese, tan, ceramic........ **165.00**

Cat, variety of colors & designs, homemade, ceramic **75.00**

Chinese man, Sprinkle Plenty, white, green, & brown, holding iron **150.00**

Chinese man, Sprinkle Plenty, yellow & green, ceramic, Cardinal China Company...................... **30.00**

Chinese man, white & aqua, ceramic, Cleminson's **40.00**

Chinese man, white & aqua with paper shirt tag, ceramic, Cleminson's.................... **85.00**

Chinese man, with removeable head . . **200.00**

Clothespin, aqua, yellow, pink, with smiling face, ceramic............ **175.00**

Dearie is Weary, ceramic, Enesco... **275.00**

Dutch girl, plastic **35.00**

Elephant, American Bisque **300.00**

Elephant, pink & gray ceramic **65.00**

Elephant, white & pink with shamrock on tummy, ceramic **95.00**

Emperor, variety of colors & designs, homemade, ceramic **125.00**

Emperors, green or white ceramic, Holland Mold, each **145.00**

Iron, blue flowers, ceramic **150.00**

Iron, farm couple, ceramic **200.00**

Iron, green ivy, ceramic **50.00**

Iron, souvenir of Aquerena Springs, San Marcos, Texas, ceramic...... **200.00**

Iron, souvenir of Florida, pink
  flamingo, ceramic **250.00**
Iron, souvenir of Wonder Cave,
  ceramic **250.00**
Iron with rooster, ceramic **145.00**
Mammy, unmarked, ceramic **300.00**

Mammy Sprinkler Bottle Set

Mammy, w/matching clothespin
  holder, 2 pcs. (ILLUS.) **600.00**
Mary Poppins, ceramic, Cleminson's . . **250.00**
Myrtle, ceramic, Pfaltzgraff **275.00**
Poodle, gray, pink, or white, ceramic . . **200.00**
Prayer Lady, by Enesco, ceramic . . . **350.00**
Rooster, ceramic, Sierra Vista **135.00**
Rooster, red & green, ceramic **150.00**

IRONS

Acme Charcoal Iron

Charcoal iron, box, convex top,
  round damper, marked "The Acme
  Carbon Iron, Pat. Mar. 15, 1910,"
  6⅜" l. (ILLUS.) **110.00**
Charcoal iron, box, side dampers &
  lift-off top, marked "The Marvel,
  Patented Dec 30, 1924," 6⅝" l. **130.00**
Charcoal iron, cast iron, dragon
  head chimney, hinged top,
  Germany, late 1800s, 6⅝" l. **750.00**
Charcoal iron, tall chimney, vulcan-
  face damper, marked "E. Bless, R.
  Drake, Pat'd 1852," 6¾" l. **125.00**
Charcoal iron, double chimney, lift
  top, marked "Ne Plus Ultra, Pat'd
  July 29, 1902," 7½" l. **175.00**

Charcoal iron, box, all brass, latch-
  up front, cut-out sides, Dutch, mid
  1800s, 8" l. **250.00**
Charcoal iron, Pan, bronze
  w/decorative sides, ivory-carved
  handle, Oriental, late 1800s, 10" l. . . . **160.00**
Electric iron, "K&M, Flat Work
  Ironer," round, Knapp Monarch Co,
  St. Louis, ca. 1935, 5⅞" d **180.00**
Electric iron, "Universal," travel
  w/removable handle, ca. 1950, 7" l. . . . **45.00**
Electric iron, "Silver streak," Pyrex,
  light blue, mid 1900s, 7½" l. **800.00**
Flat iron, "PW Weida's," cold handle,
  pat. 1870, Phila. PA. **250.00**
Flat iron, "Ober No. 6," cast iron, pat.
  Mar 19, 1912, 6" l. **45.00**
Flat iron, "Le Gaulois No. 5"
  w/warrior motif, cast iron, France,
  ca. 1900, 6¼" l. **80.00**
Flat iron, "Sensible Artisan Co, No.
  8," 2-pc. cold handle, pat. June 18,
  1888, 6⅜" l. **65.00**
Flat iron, "Griswald," cold handle,
  late 1800s, 6⅝" l. **185.00**
Flat iron, "Hood's Patent," soapstone
  base insulator, pat. Jan. 15, 1867,
  6⅝" l. **180.00**
Flat iron, "No. 7," cast iron, double
  pointed, Keystone, late 1800s,
  8½" l. **180.00**

Ingram's Machine Fluter

Fluter, machine, box base w/brass
  plate stamped "G.W. Ingram,
  Birmingham" & motifs of crown &
  lions, England, after 1850, 4⅜" roll
  (ILLUS.). **300.00**
Fluter, "The Eric Fluter," rocker-type
  w/clip-on handle, about 1875,
  5½" l. **190.00**
Fluter, "Geneva," rocker-type, brass
  top & base plates, pat. August 21,
  1866, 5¾" l. **70.00**
Fluter, "Crown," machine, crank-type
  w/stenciling, late 1800s, 5⅞" roll . . . **150.00**
Fluter, "Clarks," roller-type, black
  painted base & handle, ca. 1875,
  6¼" l. **200.00**

Fluter, "Pat'd Aug 2, 70,"
combination, cast iron w/front latch,
6⅝" l. **160.00**

Fluter, "Magic No. 1," combination,
slug w/accessory 2-pc. fluter, pat.
Sept. 19, 1876, 7½" l. **400.00**

Gasoline iron, "Coleman" model 4A,
blue enamel. **85.00**

Gasoline iron, "Diamond," Akron
Lamp Co., early 1900s, 7⅜" l. . . . **60.00**

Goffering iron, clamp-on style, brass
barrel w/iron clamp, Europe, mid
1800s, 3½" barrel length. **500.00**

Goffering iron, single, "S" wire
standard, brass barrel w/heater,
round base, late 1800s, 7⅜" h. **100.00**

Goffering iron, single, iron w/center
brass bulbous turning, Queen Anne
tripod base, England, mid 1800s,
9½" h. **275.00**

Iron heater, pyramid, stove-top style,
holds 3 irons, late 1800s, 6" h. left,
7" h. right. **150.00**

Laundry Stove, "Walker & Pratt Mfg.
Co., Boston, No. 1," holds 8 irons
on ledge, oval top w/2 stove lids,
late 1800s, 28½" h. **300.00**

Natural gas iron, "Vulcan Gas Iron
764," early 1900s, 6¼" l. **115.00**

Slug iron, box w/high sides & lift
gate, all iron, England, late 1800s,
4" l. **100.00**

Slug Iron, box w/6-point stars on
corners, lift-off top, marked "Brown-
Foster, Mt. Morris NY," late 1800s,
6¼" l. **275.00**

Small iron, wire handle, England,
late 1800s, 2¼" l. **35.00**

Small iron, rope handle, ca. 1900,
3⅜" l. **40.00**

Small iron, "Our Pet," wood grip, by
Stevens, 3½" l. **80.00**

Small iron, "Enterprise MFG Co," No.
115, cold handle, all iron, 3⅞" l. . . . **125.00**

Small iron, "The Pearl," make-do,
ca. 1900, repaired handle, 3⅞" l. . . . **60.00**

Smoothing board, carved geometric
decoration w/horse handle,
Europe, mid 1800s, 23" l. **650.00**

Smoothing Stone, black, brown
glass w/no handle, Europe,
ca.1800, 3" d. **150.00**

Special purpose iron, polisher,
"MAB COOKS," rounded edges,
pat. Dec. 5, 1848. . . . . **140.00**

Special purpose iron, polisher,
"Mahony," diamond grid bottom,
pat. Nov 23, 1876, 4½" l. **40.00**

Special purpose iron, hat, "McCoys
Pat Pd," cast iron w/arched bottom
cutout, late 1800s, 4¾" l. **140.00**

LIGHTING DEVICES

FAIRY LAMPS

**Blue & white satin Swirl patt. glass
shade,** cupped matching base
w/crimped rim & clear candle cup,
6½" h. **$635.00**

Burmese glass shade, on a clear
marked "Clarke" base, 3⅞" d.,
4¾" h. **295.00**

Burmese glass shade, pink shading
to lavender on a matching ruffled
turn-down base, Webb, 6" h. **835.00**

Rose Teinte Swirl patt. shade, the
squatty bulbous shade tapering to
a flared, rolled open top, set on a
cylindrical cup on a
cupped round base w/scalloped
rim, signed "Baccarat - Deposé,"
4½" h. **220.00**

Spatter glass shade, white &
chartreuse green cased in crystal
w/a swirl-molded design, clear
blown glass base w/applied feet &
trim, crystal inside candle cup,
5½" h. **580.00**

Verre Moiré (Nailsea) glass shade,
satin chartreuse yellow w/white
opaque loopings, clear pressed
glass marked "Clarke" base,
4¼" h. **220.00**

World Globe Fairy Lamp

World globe shade, white ball shade
w/colored countries of the world &
blue oceans, marked around the
base "Made in Austria," raised on a
cupped brass base w/a slender
stem & domed foot w/air holes to
supply air to the burning candle,
3¾" d., 9½" h. (ILLUS.) **395.00**

HANDEL LAMPS

Boudoir lamp, 7" d., domical reverse-painted shade decorated w/a scene of pond lilies & cattails against a blue ground, marked "Handel 6554," raised on a slender baluster-form metal base w/dished rounded foot, 13½" h. (two rim chips on shade, corroded base finish, finial missing) **1,840.00**

Handel Boudoir Lamp with Meadow

Boudoir lamp, 7" d. bell-form reverse-painted shade decorated w/a meadow landscape in a natural palette, rim signed "Handel 6231," raised on a slender bronzed-metal standard w/a ribbed, flaring round foot impressed "Handel," 14" h. (ILLUS.) **2,645.00**

Boudoir lamp, 7" d. domical arched panel-molded reverse-painted shade signed "Handel #6562A," decorated w/a black foreground Mt. Fuji landscape w/trees, lakeside pagoda & the distant grey mountain against a bluish grey sky, raised on a slender bronzed metal reeded standard & round stepped foot embossed "Handel," overall 14" h. **3,300.00**

Boudoir lamp, 7" d. domical reverse-painted shade molded w/four sets of four vertical ribs, the interior painted w/tall sailing ships in port w/windmills on the far shore, pastel sea & sky ground, signed "Handel 6356" on edge, raised on a slender ribbed cast-metal base w/round foot also labeled "Handel," 14½" h. **2,415.00**

Desk lamp, a 5½ x 8" domed leaded glass shell-form shade composed of a geometric design of alternating narrow & wide segments of mottled white, amber & pale blue glass, raised on a bronzed metal base w/a curved ribbed standard above a round domed foot, original patina, 4½" h., base 7" d. **1,430.00**

Desk lamp, an open-bottomed 8" d. cylindrical adjustable shade of moss green chipped ice-design glass fitted in a forked bracket & raised on a high curved bronzed metal standard adjusting on an oblong foot, shade numbered, base signed, overall 12" h. **880.00**

Desk lamp, a cylindrical horizontal shade w/flat oblong opening, decorated w/green on the textured exterior & cased in white, marked "Mosserine Handel 6010," mounted between curved brackets joined at the top of a tall curved adjustable shaft above an oblong weighted base w/a threaded "Handel" label on the felt liner, 8" l., 15" h. **1,380.00**

Desk lamp, 7" d. domical reverse-painted shade decorated w/a peachy pink sky, dark leafy trees along a waterway & distant red roof tops hidden behind a bluish grey meadow, suspended in a bronze bell-form harp joining a slender standard on a widely flaring lobed foot, adjustable, shade signed "Handel #6578A," base incised "Handel," overall 19" h. **3,575.00**

Handel Lead Glass Desk Lamp

Desk lamp, 7½" d. curved conical six-panel leaded glass shade composed of amber slag glass panels w/six green decorative glass diamonds around the rim, the shade suspended & swiveling from an adjustable bronzed metal harp joined to a slender four-ribbed pedestal on a flaring four-lobed foot, 19" h. (ILLUS.) **1,495.00**

Floor lamp, torchere-style, inverted flaring trumpet-form shade acid-etched & enameled w/a shield & coat-of-arms, on a tall slender ring-turned metal standard w/a round, domed foot, 67" h. (three significant shade rim chips) **403.00**

Table lamp, 10½" d., domical shaded w/chipped ice finish painted w/stylized Arts & Crafts blossom clusters alternating w/leaf clusters around the rim w/slender lines radiating down from the top center, a yellow ground w/orange & red flowers & green leaves, raised on a slender bronzed-metal reeded standard on a domed & pierced base w/four scrolled feet, shade & base both marked, overall 19" h. (two flat chips to shade edge, hidden by shade ring) **880.00**

'Tam-o'-Shanter' Handel Lamp

Table lamp, 12" d. domical open-topped 'Tam-o'-Shanter' form shade reverse-painted w/a green scrolling stylized leaf design, sanded exterior, signed on the rim "Handel Co. 2642," mounted on a three-arm spider w/pierced swastika border above a paneled flaring cast-metal base, converted from a fluid lamp, corrosion, socket repair, 19" h. (ILLUS.) **546.00**

Table lamp, 15" d. domical reverse-painted "Basketweave" shade, molded w/vertical ribs & horizontal ridges, painted w/a profusion of pastel rose blossoms in shades of pink, rose & yellow w/green leaves interspersed, impressed "Handel"

on top rim, mounted on a slender cast metal squared shaft w/a flaring squared foot, base w/"Handel" threaded label, small interior shade rim chip, 22" h. **2,185.00**

Table lamp, 16" d. domical six-panel shade composed of bent amber slag glass panels within a pierced metal framework w/a wide band of oak leaves w/applied color around the scalloped lower rim, raised on a slender swelled cylindrical bronzed metal base w/flaring foot, 21" h. (worn, finial missing, rim repair) . . . **920.00**

Table lamp, 16" d. domical reverse-painted shade decorated w/a shaded green & amber interior & decorated on the outside w/a continuous riverside landscape in muted naturalistic earthtones, pierced metal cap stamped "Handel," raised on a bronzed metal slender swelled cylindrical ribbed shaft on a round flattened ribbed foot, 22" h. **4,140.00**

Table lamp, 18" d. domical reverse-painted shade decorated w/clusters of mauve & iron-red flower blooms beneath three fall foliaged trees, lavender distant hillside silhouetted against an ivory sky, signed "Handel #7106" & artist-initlals, raised on an unmarked Handel textured bronze base w/a slender inverted baluster-form standard on domed round foot, overall 24" h. **4,620.00**

Bird of Paradise Handel Lamp

Table lamp, 18" d. domical reverse-painted shade of textured glass, reverse-painted w/two pairs of long-tailed brightly colored Birds of Paradise perched in brilliant yellowish green blossoming foliage against a black ground, signed at edge "Handel 7026 Palme," mounted on a three-socket Handel gilt-metal base w/a compressed urn raised on three slender legs on a round lappet-bordered base, amber glass teardrop prisms suspended below the urn between the legs, overall 24½" h. (ILLUS. previous page) **11,500.00**

PAIRPOINT LAMPS

Boudoir lamp, 4" d. "Puffy" domical "Tivoli" shade in the Dragonfly patt. w/shaded dark green ground, raised on gilt-metal slender hexagonal urn-form pedestal & stepped hexagonal foot **9,350.00**

Pairpiont 'Puffy' Rose Bonnet Lamp

Boudoir lamp, 6⅝" d. "Puffy" domical 'Rose Bonnet' shade, grey ground molded in low-relief w/roses, reverse-painted in red, pink & yellow w/green leaves, raised on a small baluster-form base w/green patina, base impressed "Pairpoint Mfg. Co. - C3025," 10⅝" h. (ILLUS.) **11,500.00**

Boudoir lamp, 8¾" d. "Puffy" umbrella-form shade w/flattened top, relief-molded colorful rim bouquets of flowers on a frosted clear ribbed ground highlighted by overall white enamel scrolls, raised brass-colored metal standard on a flattened squared foot w/cut corners marked "Pairpoint," overall 16" h. **4,180.00**

Mantel lamp, bulbous chimney-form shade enamel-decorated w/stylized green trees against a reddish orange background, mounted on a silvered metal candlestick-form electrolier base w/flared foot, base

Pairpoint Mantel & Table Lamps

impressed w/Pairpoint trademark & "E3072," some glass rim chips, silver finish worn, 14" h. (ILLUS. right) **230.00**

Table lamp, 11½" d. closed mushroom-form domical 'Vienna' reverse-painted shade decorated w/coralene yellow interior w/stylized olive green heart-shaped leaves & red berries, gold outine on exterior, mounted on a ball-trimmed ring support by four arms on a quatreform flaring base molded w/pointed foliate designs, impressed "Pairpoint Mfg. Co. 3052," 20½" h. (ILLUS. left) **2,070.00**

Table lamp, 12" d. "Puffy" domical 'Papillion' shade w/a rare pale yellow ground, raised on a slender silvered metal shaft w/a round foot **12,650.00**

Table lamp, 15¾" d. tapering drum-shaped reverse-painted 'Seville' shade in textured grey decorated w/a silhouetted tranquil riverscape w/leafing trees, in shades of green, brownish pink & grey, raised on a bronzed metal base w/three angular S-scroll supports w/scroll feet resting on a tripartite foot, greenish brown patina, base impressed "Pairpoint 4084½," 21¼" h. **5,700.00**

Table lamp, 16" d. domical reverse-painted 'Berkeley' shade, decorated w/a Hawaiian seascape w/birds & distant ships beyond tropical foliage, artist-signed "H. Fisher" & stamped "The Pairpoint Corp'n," raised on a bronzed-metal two-socket base w/bulbous paneled shaft & squared foot w/angled corners, impressed w/Pairpoint trademark, 22" h. **4,600.00**

Nautical Theme Pairpoint Lamp

Table lamp, 20" d. domical reverse-painted 'Copley' shade, decorated w/a scene of two ships & six birds on swirling ocean waves, artist-signed "H. Fisher" on rim, raised on a matching glass baluster-form base w/interior light, stamped "Pairpoint D3000," rewired, new sockets, 24" h. (ILLUS.) **8,625.00**

Table lamp, 13½" d. "Puffy" flat-topped 'Hummingbird and Roses' shade w/gently flaring cylindrical sides, colorful hummingbirds flutter above a multicolored wreath, a ribbed mottled plum ground, frosty clear crown w/white-painted ribs, raised on a slender ring-, baluster- and knob-turned brass base w/dished round foot marked "Pairpoint #E3032," overall 20" h. **7,590.00**

Table lamp, 17½" d. waisted cylindrical dome-topped "Exeter" shade reverse-painted on frosted glass w/a continuous landscape scene w/tall trees in earthtones, brown, gold & blue, raised on a brass-plated white metal baluster-form base w/an octagonal foot, shade marked "The Pairpoint Corp'n," base marked "Pairpoint," 22½" h. (base plating worn) **3,465.00**

Table lamp, 15" d. reverse-painted 'Chesterfield' patt. shade, drum-shaped w/undulating sides, decorated w/a multicolored "Persian Carpet" patt., brick red ground w/green stylized flowers alternating w/white framed yellow & aqua stylized leaves, mounted on a four-arm brass spider support above the squared baluster-form standard & stepped, squared foot w/rounded corners, marked "Pairpoint Mfg. Co. #3088," overall 23" h. **8,800.00**

Table lamp, 17" d. hexagonal tapering "Directoire" shade reverse-painted w/a continuous colorful expansive landscaped ground including a columned waterfront building, iridescent background coloring, paneled borders above & below & marked "The Pairpoint Corp'n" on the border, raised on a candelabrum-style base w/three electric candle sockets on short gilt-metal arms w/pointed drops centered by a knob above a cut glass knop on a gilt-metal tapering pedestal & octagonal dark onyx foot, impressed "Pairpoint Mfg. Co. E3001," 27½" h. **2,645.00**

TIFFANY LAMPS

Bridge lamp, a 10" d. domical glass shade w/waisted rim in ivory cased over white decorated w/green pulled feathers reserved against amber, pivoting within a loop ring raised on a tall slender standard w/five slender splayed legs w/pointed pad feet w/a brownish green patina, shade signed "L.C.T.," base impressed "Tiffany Studios - New York - 423," 4' 10" h. **12,650.00**

Ceiling light, rectangular, w/hinged leaded glass panel in mottled amber glass centering a gold iridescent turtleback tile surrounded by iridescent cabochon "jewels," the bronze sides w/a pierced design backed by amber glass, 9 x 11", 2¼" h. **6,325.00**

Desk lamp, Farvile glass & bronze, 7" d. domical iridescent orange glass shade w/iridescent gold scalloped & scrolled decoration, supported by harp-arm bronze base, shade engraved "L.C.T." & base stamped "TIFFANY STUDIOS NEW YORK 418," 12" h. **4,370.00**

Desk lamp, "Turtleback tile," the domical bronze shade frame w/studded & wire-filigree & inset w/two green-tinted amber opalescent turtleback tiles backed w/mottled opalescent glass diffusion sheets, adjusting above a bronze harp above the domed foot w/ribbed leaves, knobs & small knob feet, base impressed "Tiffany Studios - New York - 28682" w/decorating company monogram, 14⅜" h. **5,175.00**

Tiffany Linenfold Desk Lamp

Desk lamp, "Linenfold," 10" d. domical shaded in the Abalone patt., the shade composed of 12 panels of amber linenfold glass between ruffled glass borders, raised on a gilded bronze slender four-sided shaft on an octagonal foot, shade impressed "Tiffany Studios - NY - 1928," base impressed "Tiffany Studios - New York - 604," ca. 1928, 16" h. (ILLUS.) **6,900.00**

Floor lamp, counter-balance-type, 10⅛" d. domical iridescent gold glass shade, the gilt bronze rippled base ascending to a gooseneck arm w/weighted ball supporting shade, shade engraved w/"L.C.T. Favrille (sic)" signature, base stamped "TIFFANY STUDIOS NEW YORK 681," 4' 4½" h. **5,570.00**

Floor lamp, bridge-type, a 9½" d. twelve-sided Linenfold etched bronze shade No.1936 w/panels of golden amber Favrile glass, mounted upon a swing-socket harp base on tripod legs w/spade feet, shade & base impressed "Tiffany Studios New York," bronze base numbered "423," overall 4' 7" h. (seven large & four small shade panels cracked) **1,380.00**

Lily lamp, twelve-light, Favrile glass & bronze, consisting of gold glass shades supported by twelve intertwined bronze stems on layered lily pad base w/rich greenish brown patina, eight shades engraved "L.C.T. Favrile," the base stamped "TIFFANY STUDIOS NEW YORK 685," 56½" h.................... **29,900.00**

Student lamp, a pair of domical leaded glass shades w/opalescent greenish yellow tapering tile design raised on rings above cylindrical

Tiffany Double Student Lamp

fonts on slender curved arms each adjusting on a slender shaft centering a large cylindrical font, arched crossarm at top, raised on a ringed round base, early 20th c. (ILLUS.) **10,450.00**

Table lamp, "Colonial," 16" d. domical leaded glass shade composed of variegated green slag oval panels, marked "Tiffany Studios, New York," raised on a bronze base w/a slender ovoid font raised on three wishbone legs joining at a pointed domed pedestal on the flattened square foot, base signed "Tiffany -Studios - New York - #444" **9,570.00**

Fine Tiffany Cyclamen Lamp

Table lamp, "Cyclamen," 16" d. conical leaded glass shade w/an overall pattern of cyclamen blossoms & leaves in pale pink & white striated opalescent glass against a ground of striated & textured lavender, the leaves in various shades of green & white striated glass w/some section in drapery glass, above three rows of brickwork in teal blue, flecked w/lavender, cream & cobalt blue, slender-waisted reeded bronze standard above the domed reeded base on ball feet, deep brown patina, shade unsigned, base impressed "Tiffany Studios - New York - D795," 22¼" h. (ILLUS.) . . **27,600.00**

Table lamp, "Dragonfly," 17" d. conical leaded glass shade composed of seven dragonflies w/outstretched wings in striated shades of green, salmon & white, overlaid in bronze filigree, mottled opalescent white bodies & pale yellow cabochon glass eyes, all reserved against a ground of amber glass striated w/green & white, slender bronze pedestal on a flaring paneled base foot, shade impressed "Tiffany Studios - New York -1468," base impressed "Tiffany Studios 0 New York - 333," 19½" h. **26,450.00**

Table lamp, "Geranium," 16⅛" d. conical leaded glass shade decorated w/mottled red geranium blossoms above, against a mottled pale blue & green ground, among a profusion of varied colored green leaves below, interspersed w/rippled glass leaves, against a mottled & striated pale pink & green ground, bordered by three bands in mottled pale pink, blue & green, the standard cast w/scrolling tendrils & pods, in rich greenish red patina, tag stamped "TIFFANY STUDIOS NEW YORK," 23" h. . . . **32,200.00**

Table lamp, "Linenfold," the 14½" w. twelve-sided slightly tapering shade w/an arrangement of large square amber linenfold panels between smaller amber linenfold borders between amber smooth borders, intaglio finish, shade impressed "TIFFANY STUDIOS - NEW YORK - 1950 - PAT. APPLIED FOR," the base impressed "TIFFANY STUDIOS - 442," 24½" h. **5,000.00**

Table lamp, "Pansy," 16" d. domical leaded glass shaded w/an overall pattern of rectangular tiles in mottled grey & blue opalescent glass streaked w/pale yellow, the pansy border w/blossoms in brilliant shades of deep cobalt blue, striated mauve, mottled yellow & tangerine, the leafage in various shades of green, raised on a three-armed support above a cushion-form base cast w/a raised looping design, further raised on four petal-form feet, greenish brown patina,

shaded impressed "TIFFANY STUDIOS - NEW YORK," base impressed "TIFFANY STUDIOS - NEW YORK - 6842," overall 41" h. **46,000.00**

LAMPS, MISCELLANEOUS

Alabaster floor lamp, Neoclassical-Style, the tall standard w/leaf-carved & reeded detail, domed shade, Italy, 19th c., 5' 2" h. **2,875.00**

Argand lamps, bronze & glass, each w/a caryatid-form standard supporting an urn-form oil font w/a classical head & drape border continuing to a scroll arm w/socket surmounted by a ball & trumpet-form floral-etched glass shade & a glass scalloped bobeche hung w/long triangular prisms, the whole raised on a square stepped base, J. & I. Cox, New York City, ca. 1840, electrified, 22¾" h., pr. (bobeches possibly later, one repaired) **4,830.00**

Arts & Crafts floor lamp, oak & leaded glass, the four-sided 24½" w. square leaded glass shade composed of curved & oblong glass in red, green, yellow & white, raised on four angled oak arm supports above the original kerosene metal burner fitted atop the tall slightly tapering four-sided base w/an arched opening above three tiered open shelves, the bottom shelf flanked on each side by double oval cut-outs, rounded cut-out feet, original dark finish, paper label of the Shop of the Crafters, Model No. 153, early 20th c., 6' h. **4,600.00**

Arts & Crafts table lamp, a low pyramidal upper shade frame in brass & copper enclosing triangular panels of olive green, amber & white & overhanging a vertical pierced metal apron w/pierced overlay designs of landscapes over slag glass in pink, blue & white w/ruby red glass in corner panels, raised on a slender plain square metal pedestal on a square flaring foot, early 20th c., overall 21¼" h. . . **440.00**

Astral lamp, brass base w/inverted pear-shaped font supporting a round collar hung w/long triangular prisms above a floriform tapped fluted column standard raised on a molded spreading base on a square marble foot, the spherical frosted, molded & etched glass shade w/Gothic arch windows alternating w/arching columns, mid-19th c., electrified, 24" h. (one prism missing, one incomplete). . . . **431.00**

Banquet lamp, figural, a hand-painted white ball shade decorated w/scrolls framing a transfer-printed color scene of cupids, clear glass chimney, brass shade ring & burner on a brass collar above the bulbous bronzed metal ornately scroll-embossed font tapering to a lower knop held aloft by a large full-figure cupid above an ornately embossed metal flaring & stepped base w/four scroll feet, late 19th c., 30" h. **385.00**

Bradley & Hubbard desk lamp, a flaring rectangular metal shade frame w/solid ends & front & back rectangular glass panels in narrow ribbed glass reverse-painted w/green, blue & brown stylized Arts & Crafts design bands, raised on forked brass supports joining a knop above the flaring, ringed pedestal base, shade 8½" l., 13" h. **460.00**

Bradley & Hubbard table lamp, Prairie School-style, 16" sq. pyramidal leaded glass shade w/tapering narrow geometric glass panels in a gilt-metal frame w/pierced overlay, glass in shades of purple, blue & yellow slag, raised on a curved wire spider above the slender square pedestal on a low sloping square foot, early 20th c., 21" h. **1,380.00**

Chicago Mosaic Co. table lamp, 18" d. domical leaded glass shade composed of segments forming nine full-blown pink lotus blossoms amid variegated green leaves around the uneven border & below a wide panel of chartreuse slag glass honeycomb pattern w/a bronzed metal cap, raised on a slender square flaring bronzed-metal base molded w/acanthus leaves, overall 26" h. **2,310.00**

Classique table lamp, 18" d. domed bell-form reverse-painted shade decorated w/a continuous yellowish brown meadow w/boulder banks, emerald green foliaged trees along a reflective waterway, distant green hills, chartreuse & orange sky, numbered "8271," raised on a bronzed metal hexagonal baluster-

form heavy base marked "Classique Lamps" on stem & on cloth label on foot, early 20th c. . . . **1,815.00**

Cranberry glass table lamp, Kerosene-type, a mold-blown ringed baluster-form pedestal base w/round cushion foot tapers to a stepped ringed font below a brass collar & burner supporting a Rubina Inverted Thumbprint patt. ribbed tulip-form shade w/a flaring crimped & ruffled rim, enameled white flowers on the pedestal, 6½" d., overall 17" h. **595.00**

Desk lamp, a domical oblong glass shade w/a chocolate brown exterior acid-cut to frosted clear w/an overall design of tightly scrolling flowers, leaves & scrolls, the interior rim painted w/a band of orange blossoms framed by brown scrolls bordered w/green, stamped "Bellova Czech," suspended on a bronze arching arm w/electric socket continuing to a tri-lobed foot cast w/acorns & leaves decorated in natural colors above a beaded border band, base marked "Bellova H.C. McFaddin & Co., N.Y.," 8" h. . . **990.00**

Fine Duffner & Kimberly Lamp

Duffner & Kimberly table lamp, 21" d. conical leaded glass shade composed of amber slag background panels centering three repeating intricate heraldic designs of lavender glass superimposed on a crimson red medial band, the lower border in a chevron design w/amber granite & mauve ripple accent colors, raised on a three-socket slender bronzed-metal shaft on a slightly domed scalloped round foot cast w/foliate designs, overal 24" h. (ILLUS.) **4,600.00**

Rare Cut Velvet Hanging Lamp

Kerosene hanging parlor lamp, 14" d. domical blue Cut Velvet glass shade mounted in a pierced brass & button-stamped ring & topped w/a pierced brass crown, the ring suspending facet-cut prisms, pierced leafy scrollwork side brackets w/large reddish jewels joining shade to brass font frame w/squatty bulbous blue Cut Velvet font w/brass drop, suspended on forked brass chains adjusting below pierced ceiling cap & smoke bell, ca. 1890 (ILLUS.) **1,760.00**

Kerosene table lamp, pressed glass, a kerosene burner & brass collar on the squatty ringed onion-form blue opaline glass font above a turned brass connector & flaring ringed pedestal on a square white marble foot, ca. 1860, 9" h. **61.00**

Kerosene table lamp, "Ripley Marriage lamp," two bulbous translucent blue fonts flanking a central match holder & joined on a tapering flange to a threaded brass connector on an opaque milk glass stepped, square pedestal foot, connector dated "1868," lamp marked "D.C. Ripley, Patent Pending," brass font collars w/kerosene burners, 11½" h. **880.00**

Kerosene table lamp, pressed Triple Swag & Diamond clear pear-shaped font w/brass collar & connector to the milk white pedestal on a stepped square base, 12¼" h. **77.00**

Kerosene table lamp, cut-overlay, the inverted pear-shaped glass font cut from cobalt blue to white to clear, brass collar w/burner supporting a tall white cut to clear

tulip-shaped shade, the font raised on a brass connector to the black opaque glass pedestal stem on a stepped square foot, ca. 1860, chips & edge grinding on shade, overall 21¼" h. **1,650.00**

Leaded glass table lamp, wide umbrella-shaped domical leaded glass shade w/uneven rim, composed of an overall design of small blossoms & leaves in greens, reds & ambers w/ruby jewels, raised in a slender baluster-form dark brown enameled metal base, 23" h. **550.00**

Two Fine Peg Lamps

Peg lamp, cased shaded pink satin glass mother-of-pearl Swirl patt. shade & font, the inverted tulip-form shade w/a wide flaring & crimped rim fitted on a kerosene burner w/clear chimney above the squatty bulbous matching font fitted on a reeded columnar gilt-metal base, shade 5¾" d., overal 12⅝" h. (ILLUS. left) **695.00**

Peg lamp, frosted lime green glass shade & font, the tall slender inverted tulip-form shade w/a flaring ruffled rim decorated w/a gilt rim band & gilt mistletoe sprigs w/white berries, on a kerosene burner w/clear glass chimney above the squatty bulbous optic ribbed matching font raised on an ornate brass reeded columnar candlestick w/scrolled capital & stepped square embossed base, shade 4½" d., overall 15¾" h. **395.00**

Peg lamp, dark cranberry glass shade & font, the tall optic-ribbed inverted tulip shade w/a flaring & crimped rim resting on a kerosene burner w/clear chimney above the squatty bulbous tapering optic-patterned matching font trimmed w/gilt scrolls, raised on a tall ornate reeded columnar brass candlestick base w/scrolled capital & stepped embossed foot, shade 5" d., overall 16¼" h. (ILLUS. right) **450.00**

Pittsburgh table lamp, 17" d. domical reverse-painted shade decorated on each side w/a scene of two galleons sailing on stormy seas of teal & blue, cloudy yellow sky, raised on a gilt-metal ribbed gourd-form base tapering to two small loop handles at the top, molded floral pods & leaves around the bottom, early 20th c. **2,200.00**

Filigree-decorated Slag Lamp

Slag glass table lamp, a pyramidal eight-paneled shade w/caramel slag panels in a bronzed metal framework above a conforming vertical border band of matching glass panels faced w/leafy scroll & swag filigree, raised on a slender bronze metal shaft on an embossed stepped, domed foot, early 20th c., 21" h. (ILLUS.) **286.00**

Student lamp, a domed open-topped cased-green glass shade above a burner & acorn-form brass font issuing from the mouth of a scrolling griffin-form cross-arm w/a longer acorn-form font w/raised torch design at opposite end of the adjustable arm, on a tall slender standard w/a scrolled loop top & centered on a squared base w/notched corners & embossed bands on four paw feet, by Edward Miller, late 19th c. **9,250.00**

Student lamp, single-arm, brass, a domical open-topped green overlay shade in a ring above a cylindrical column at the end of a curved arm

opposite the cylindrical font adjusting on a slender metal standard w/a ring top & flaring round foot, late 19th - early 20th c., minor chip on top shade flange, dent in base, electrified, 21¼" h. . . **330.00**

U.S. Glass Novelty Lamp

U.S. Glass Company novelty lamp, the figural glass shade molded as a colorful bouquet of large flowers overflowing a tall waisted black basketweave container resting on a silver plate base w/a decorative chased base band & three ribbed paw feet, electric, small, ca. 1926-35 (ILLUS.) **660.00**

Whale oil table lamps, pressed sapphire blue flint glass, the tapering ovoid fonts w/the Arch patt. fitted w/original pewter collar & double burner, fonts joined w/a wafer to an ornate flaring tiered octagonal pedestal base, Pittsburgh, ca. 1830-50, 10⅜" h., pr. **7,425.00**

White metal figural lamp, the base cast as a cylindrical rockwork well w/a scantily clad Art Nouveau maiden seated on the edge holding a water jug w/one hand, the other hand reaching into the tall ornate arching trelliswork of leafy grapevines suspending at the top a glass cluster of grapes enclosing the light fixture, electrified, early 20th c., overall 4' 6" h. **3,540.00**

Wilkinson table lamp, 20" d. scalloped conical leaded glass shade w/yellow-centered pink & peach blossoms & green leaves border amber & green slag segments arranged in ladderwork progression, mount w/locking mechanism on a three-socket metal shaft w/bulbed turnings on a stepped platform base impressed "Wilkinson Co. - Brooklyn, N.Y.," overall 27½" h. **3,220.00**

Williamson (R.) & Co. floor lamp, 22" d. domical leaded glass shade composed of shield-shaped opalescent yellowish white granite segments spaced by green & framed by tannish amber panels centering four green slag shell-form designs at the irregular border, raised on a three-socket bronzed metal slender standard on a flaring paneled base w/three paw feet, early 20th c., overall 5' 2" h. **13,225.00**

MINIATURE LAMPS

Amber, ribbed low cylindrical font w/an attached cylindrical basketweave pattern match holder w/ring handle to the side, ribbed conical matching shade, clear chimney, Hornet burner, 8" h., No. 52 . . . . **200.00**

Amethyst "Little Buttercup" finger-type, applied handle, embossed name on side, clear chimney, Hornet burner, 6⅞" h., No. 36 . . . . . **100.00**

Cased yellow glass, Cosmos patt., base & umbrella shade w/pink-stained band & colored florals, Nutmeg burner, 7½" h., No. 286 . . . **475.00**

Clear "Little Beauty" finger-type, applied handle, embossed name on side, clear glass chimney, Nutmeg burner, 6¼" h., No. 16 (slight chip on chimney base) **95.00**

Clear "waffle" bulbous tapering font raised on a slender brass pedestal base w/a flaring foot, cranberry chimney, Acorn burner, 8¼" h., No. 117 . . . . **90.00**

Milk glass w/embossed beads & scrolling, fired-on painted flowers in red & green & green beads, Nutmeg burner, 8¼" h., No. 283 . . . **400.00**

Milk white glass, square base w/embossed overlapping leaves design & square ribbed shade w/draped swag border highlighted in gold, clear glass chimney, Nutmeg burner, 8" h., No.255 . . . . . **220.00**

Milk white glass, plain & embossed beaded panels on base & globe-chimney, Hornet burner, 8½" h., No. 183 . . . . **72.00**

Vaseline glass "Cathedral lamp," pedestal lamp w/embossed base & shade, Nutmeg burner, 8¾" h., No. 480 . . . . **775.00**

OTHER LIGHTING DEVICES

CHANDELIERS

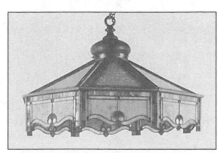

Arts & Crafts Leaded Glass Chandelier

Arts & Crafts, leaded glass w/six upper angled triangular panels of caramel slag glass above a vertical deep paneled border w/scalloped rim composed of bands & panels of yellow, caramel & green slag glass, some damage, early 20th c., 27" d., 18" h. (ILLUS.) **1,380.00**

Bradley & Hubbard, hand-hammered brass & glass, a wide low domical shade w/a hand-beaten metal frame w/curved straps enclosing six panels of curved caramel slag glass, high domed crown below the heavy brass hanging chain & mounting, attributed to Bradley & Hubbard, early 20th c., 25" d. **978.00**

Dutch Baroque-Style, brass, eight-light, a wrought-iron chain suspending a ring-turned slender standard, the medial collar issuing eight spurred scrolling candlearms centering star designs & terminating in drip pans & cylindrical candle sockets, a large ball-shaped lower drop w/a pendent finial, late 19th - early 20th c., 24" d., 18" h. **1,035.00**

Neo-classical style, gilt-bronze & cut glass, 18-light, the corona w/etched branches suspending a bead link above a circular tier supporting scrolling candlearms cresting in sockets, all hung w/faceted cut glass drops & pendants, Russia, early 19th c. **21,850.00**

Painted tin & turned wood, eight-light, a slender baluster- and ring-turned upper post w/a domed tin cap ring above a thick round central disk issuing eight S-scroll scroll-trimmed candlearms, a long

European Tin & Wood Chandelier

ring-turned drop pendant at the
bottom, probably northern Europe,
first half 19th c., very minor losses,
minor paint loss, 31" h. (ILLUS.) . . **1,495.00**

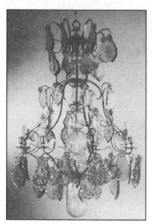

Rococo-Style Ornate Chandelier

Rococo-Style, gilt-bronze, amber &
clear glass, eight-light, of cage
form w/C-scroll metal bands
around the top suspending large
teardrop prisms above a central
ring centering long slender scroll
bands w/large teardrop prisms &
ending in eight candle sockets, the
central shaft composed of several
clear bulbs of glass w/facet-cutting,
Europe, 19th c., 44" h. (ILLUS.) . . **2,300.00**
Tiffany-signed, bronze & glass
"Moorish" style, an arched bronze
ceiling mount supports elaborate
twisted wire double ring
suspending bronze beading,
decorative balls & six sockets
w/gold iridescent ribbed bell-form

Fine Tiffany "Moorish" Chandelier

Favrile glass shades w/a large
triple-bulbed matching central
shade, marked "L.C. Tiffany
Favrile" at rim, adjustable, 30" h.
(ILLUS.) **18,400.00**

Ornate Victorian Cast-Iron Chandelier

Victorian, cast iron, four-light, a tall
central bar shaft flanked by four
long tapering scroll-pierced flanges
tapering down to upturned flat arms
ending in pierced cup sockets for
supporting clear pressed glass
kerosene lamp fonts, complete
w/fonts, burners & chimneys,
ca. 1875-85 (ILLUS.) **1,100.00**

LANTERNS

Barn lantern, painted pine & glass, a
pine frame w/old greenish paint
enclosing a wooden door & three
panes of glass, reputtied glazer's
bevel w/brownish red paint,
14½" h. **303.00**
Bicycle lantern, carbide-type, brass
w/worn nickel plate, large round
clear front lens on square form
w/covered top vent opening,
marked "Lucas, Silver King,
Birmingham," England, late 19th -
early 20th c., 5" h. **94.00**

Candle lantern, tin & glass, a semi-circular tin frame w/a flat glass front & tin back door, a pyramidal top w/punched circle designs, small loop handle, cylindrical tin candle socket, 19th c., 12¼" h. plus handle (light rust) **380.00**

Candle lantern, tin & glass, triangular form w/two glass sides w/wire guards, conical pierced cap w/ring handle, 19th c., 12½" h. plus handle **358.00**

Floor lantern, Gothic Revival, enameled green metal, hexagonal, w/openwork panels of Gothic arches & foliage, flared feet, 20th c., 34" h. **374.00**

Fine Glass & Brass Hall Lantern

Hall lantern, glass & pressed gilt brass, hexagonal form w/each glass panel wheel-cut & acid-etched w/alternating Gothic arches & large diamond & dot designs, an ornate stamped crown crest band w/six leafy scroll hanging hooks, a round stamped base cap w/drop finial, very minor chips, missing smoke bell, mid-19th c., 15¼" h. (ILLUS.) **2,530.00**

Hall lanterns, brass, four-light, Georgian-Style, round w/glazed panels between the brass uprights, one panel a hinged door, the upper rim w/beaded swags suspended from ribbons, undulating braces from the top rim to the center shaft which drops down into the center & curves up to end in candle sockets, England, 12½" d., 14¾" h., pr. (electrified) **4,025.00**

Signal lantern, tin & glass, a short cylindrical base w/font & tall pierced cylindrical top w/conical cap & large loop handle, fitted w/a blown cranberry glass globe engraved "C.R.R., first half 19th c., 12½" h. plus handle (replaced brass font w/burner) **1,100.00**

Tin & Glass Skater's Lanterns

Skater's lantern, tin & glass, a pierced domed tin cap w/bail handle & tin font base support a light green globe, 6⅝" h. (ILLUS. center) **275.00**

Skater's lantern, tin & glass, a pierced domed tin cap w/bail handle & tin font base support a cornflower blue glass globe, 7⅛" h. (ILLUS. right) **303.00**

Skater's lantern, tin & glass, a pierced domed tin cap w/bail handle & tin font base support an electric blue glass globe, tin w/black & gold designs, 7" h. (ILLUS. left) **330.00**

Skater's lantern, tin & glass, a pierced domed tin cap w/bail handle & tin font base support an emerald green glass globe, 6½" h. . . **440.00**

Skater's lantern, tin & glass, a pierced domed tin cap w/bail handle & tin font base support an amethyst glass globe, 7" h. **523.00**

Skater's lantern, tin & glass, pierced domed cap & domed font base, wire bail handle, peacock green glass globe, traces of red paint on tin, 7⅜" h. (bail handle replaced) . . . **358.00**

Whale oil lantern, glass & tin, a cylindrical pierced tin top w/a conical cap & wide hanging ring, a clear blown ball globe above a low pierced cylindrical tin base, worn black paint, rust on base, no font or burner, 8½" h. plus ring handle **182.00**

Whale oil lantern, glass & tin, the cylindrical top w/pierced star & diamond designs below the conical cap & wire loop handle, paneled glass tapering sides above a removable tin font w/whale oil burner, probably by the New England Glass Co., traces of black paint, 11" h. plus handle (wire handle a replacement, short glass crack under tin, base dented & damaged) **154.00**

SHADES

Art glass, slender hexagonal bell-form, mottled & streaked iridescent green & amber glass, 5¾" h., set of 4 (chips) **198.00**

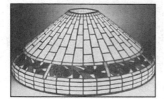

Bigelow Kennard Leaded Shade

Bigelow Kennard-signed, large conical leaded glass shade w/white opalescent brickwork segments above & below a border belt of repeating reddish amber ripple glass pine cones & shaded green needles w/yellow border glass, rim tag signed "Bigelow Kennard Boston Studios," four border glass segments broken out, early 20th c., 22" d., 9½" h. (ILLUS.) **2,760.00**

Bohemian, blown trumpet-form w/a gold iridescent papillion surface w/green & red raised spots & vertical stripes, attributed to Loetz, 6" h. **431.00**

Handel Ball Shade

Handel-signed, ball-form shade w/iridescent orange interior, the exterior h.p. w/a scenic landscape w/two birds in flight, rim signed "Handel 7004," base hole drilled, some rim chips under edge, 3⅛" d., 6" h. (ILLUS.) **1,495.00**

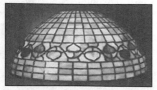

Acorn Design Leaded Shade

Leaded glass, 16" d. domical shade composed of rose pink slag glass blocks w/a lower band of vining green acorn-shaped leaves, attributed to Bigelow & Kennard, areas of restoration, early 20th c. (ILLUS.) **1,150.00**

Lustre Art-signed, elongated blossom-form w/angled shoulder, sixteen lighted molded ribs, plain opal exterior, iridescent gold interior, rims marked "Lustre Art," 2¼" d., 5¼" h., set of 3 (ILLUS. of part, right below) **230.00**

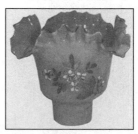

Pink Opalescent Decorated Shade

Pink opalescent, tulip-form blown shade in Inverted Thumbprint patt. w/crimped & ruffled rim & long collar, enameled w/gold & silver leaves & blue & white blossoms, late 19th c., 4⅞" d., 5" h. (ILLUS.). . **165.00**

Quezal-signed, ribbed morning glory shape, iridescent white exterior w/a golden rick-rack band, iridescent gold interior, 5" h. **248.00**

Quezal and Lustre Art Shades

Quezal-signed, elongated tulip-form, the exterior w/five green pulled feathers on a white ground, the interior w/gold iridescence, signed on rims, 2¼" d., 5" h., set of 3 (ILLUS. of part, left) **460.00**

Quezal-signed, bulbous baluster-form w/a flaring slightly ruffled rim, wide stripes of iridescent gold in a scale-like pattern alternating w/thin opal white stripes, iridescent gold interior, 5¼" h., pr. **550.00**

Quezal-signed, bell-form w/a paneled Calcite white exterior & a gold iridescent interior, signed, 5¾" h. **121.00**

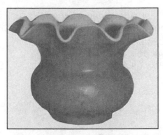

Lovely Satin Glass Shade

Satin glass, squatty bulbous tulip-form w/widely flaring ruffled rim, deep rose mother-of-pearl Diamond Quilted patt., white lining, 5¼" d., 3½" h. (ILLUS.) **250.00**

Steuben-signed, Intarsia pattern w/Aurene border, brown **675.00**

Steuben-signed, tall trumpet flower-form w/ten lightly molded ribs, overall gold Aurene iridescence, marked on the rims, 6½" h., set of 4 . . . . **748.00**

Verre Moiré, shaded blue w/panels of white swags, flaring deeply ruffled & crimped rim, peg lamp-type, 5½" d., 4⅛" h., pr. **265.00**

LUNCH BOXES

Addams Family, metal, Aladdin Industries, 1974. . . . . **$45.00**

Beatles Lunch Box

Beatles (The), metal, marked "Aladdin Industeries Incoporated, Nashville, Tenn. Copyright 1965

NEMS Enterprises, Ltd.," scratches & soiling, no thermos, 8" w., 3¾" h. deep, 7" h. (ILLUS.). **259.00**

Black Hole, metal, Aladdin Industries, 1979. . . . . **35.00**

Bonanza, metal, black rim, Aladdin Industries,1968 . . . . **110.00**

Gene Autry Lunch Box

Gene Autry, metal w/thermos, marked "Universal Landers, Frary & Clark, New Britain, Conn.," 1954, scratches, 8½" w., 3½" deep, 7" h. (ILLUS.). **275.00**

Globe Trotter, metal, dome-type, Ohio Art, 1959 . . . . **140.00**

Gunsmoke, metal, stagecoach scene, Aladdin Industries, 1973 . . . . **90.00**

Junior Miss, metal, w/matching plastic thermos, Aladdin Industries, 1978 . . . . **35.00**

Lone Ranger, metal, red border, ADCO Liberty, 1954 . . . . **250.00**

Movie Monsters, metal, Aladdin Industries, 1979. . . . . **45.00**

The Munsters Lunch Box

Munsters (The), metal w/thermos, made by Thermos Division, King-Seeley Thermos Co.,1965, some scratches & soiling, 8¾" w., 7" h. (ILLUS.). **187.00**

Planet of the Apes, metal, w/matching steel thermos, Aladdin Industries, 1974. . . . . **45.00**

Rainbo Bread truck, metal, in the shape of Rainbo Bread delivery truck, w/matching plastic thermos, 1984 . . . . **75.00**

Roy Rogers, metal, leather handle,
blue band,Thermos, 1954 . . **100.00 to 150.00**
Space 1999, metal, King Seeley
Thermos, 1976 . . . . **35.00**
Wild Bill Hickock, metal, red border,
Aladdin Industries, 1956 . . . . **130.00**
Yankee Doodle, metal, w/matching
plastic thermos, King Seeley
Thermos, 1975 . . . . **45.00**

MARBLES

Glass, Lutz-type, clear w/yellow
band, ½" d. **$200.00**
Glass, Lutz-type, "onionskin," ¹¹⁄₁₆" d. . . **275.00**
Glass, Lutz-type, green, ¾" d. **400.00**
Glass, Indian swirl, black w/two red,
white, blue & yellow outer bands,
¹⁵⁄₁₆" d. **303.00**
Glass, Lutz-type, black opaque
w/blue bands, ¹⁵⁄₁₆" d. **500.00**
Glass, "onionskin," blue & white
w/mica, ¹⁵⁄₁₆" d. **225.00**
Glass, Lutz-type, aqua w/two
goldstone & four mint green bands,
1⅛" d. **468.00**
Glass, ribbon-core type, tight red,
white & blue core, 1¼" d. (overall
haziness). **154.00**
Glass, Lutz-type, clear w/two
goldstone & four yellow bands,
1⅜" d. **468.00**
Glass, sulphide, clear w/figural
running horse, 1⅜" d. **93.00**
Glass, sulphide, clear w/figural
standing razorback boar, 1⅜" d. . . . **88.00**

Ribbon Swirl Marble

Glass, clear w/red, white, yellow &
green ribbon swirl core, 1⁷⁄₁₆" d.
(ILLUS.). **468.00**
Glass, end-of-day-type, red, white,
yellow & orange w/heavy layer of
mica chips surrounding core, one
pontil, 1½" d. **440.00**
Glass, end-of-day-type, red, white,
green & yellow w/flakes of mica,
1⁹⁄₁₆" d. **253.00**

Sulphide Marble with "1"

Glass, sulphide, clear w/figural
numeral one, 1⁹⁄₁₆" d. (ILLUS.) **288.00**
Glass, sulphide, clear w/standing
figural pelican, 1¹¹⁄₁₆" d. (two
shallow chips to right of figure) **93.00**

*From left: Porcelain Hand-painted Marble
Spatter Design Marble*

Glass, porcelain, white w/h.p. black,
green & lavender floral decoration
on both sides, 1¾" d. (ILLUS.) **777.00**
Glass, sulphide, clear w/figural lizard
on a rock, 1¾" d. (minor chip
beneath figure) **138.00**
Glass, end-of-day spatter design,
blue & white w/trace of red &
yellow in core, mica flakes, minor
overall wear, 1⅞" d. (ILLUS.) **275.00**

Clambroth Swirl Marble

Glass, opalescent clambroth w/red,
green & blue alternating outer-
swirled bands, some minor
"moons" in pontil area, 1⅞" d.
(ILLUS.) **2,209.00**
Glass, sulphide, clear w/figural boy
sitting on a stump, 1⅞" d. **160.00**
Glass, sulphide, clear w/standing
figural horse, 2" d. (three tiny
bruises, surface wear) **143.00**
Glass, sulphide, clear w/figural
standing sheep, 2⅛" d. (three
moon bruises) **44.00**
Glass, sulphide, smoky clear
w/detailed figural spread-winged
angel, 2⅛" d. (several chips
overall). **176.00**

Courtesy of Skinner, Inc.

Classical Style Coin Tea Set

METALS

ALUMINUM

Tea kettle, cov., cast, bail handle,
Wagner **$125.00**
Waffle iron, cast, hinged, Wagner . . . **175.00**

BRASS

Coal scuttle, tapered form w/two
hinged lids, bail handle, decorated
w/repoussé work w/masks &
scrolled foliage, 19th c., 20" h. **259.00**
Doorknocker, figural, model of a
grotesque sea creature, late
19th c., 12" h. **863.00**
Kettle, round spun-type w/iron bail
handle, 14" d. (dents) **61.00**
Vase, hand-hammered Arts & Crafts
style, shell casing-type w/a slightly
tapering cylindrical lower section
w/a widely flaring upper section w/a
deeply ruffled rim, Dirk Van Erp,
early 20th c., impressed "U.M.C.
Co.," 6" d., 9¾" h. (light wear to
patina) **1,430.00**
Wall sconces, each w/oval reflector
plate decorated w/pair of winged
putti flanked by stylized foliage &
fruit, centers a convex reserve
w/C-scroll embossed surrounds
two removable serpentine

projecting candlearms below,
cylindrical candle cups w/dished
drip plates, 12½" w., 16" h., pr. . . **13,800.00**

Wick Trimmer & Stand

Wick trimmer & stand, a ringed &
slightly flaring cylindrical cup atop a
knopped stem on a stepped,
squared foot, ring handle w/thumb
rest at side of rim, holds scissor-
form trimmer, handle soldered,
England, probably 19th c., 1" h.
(ILLUS.). **330.00**

BRONZE

Tiffany Floor Model Ashtray

Ashtray, floor model, an elaborate platform base w/ribbed tripartite shaft w/knob ends flaring to support a shallow dished tray & bowl-form holder w/mesh ash receiver, impressed "Tiffany Studios New York 1658," 24½" h. (ILLUS.) **1,265.00**

Ashtray, floor model, bright gold patina w/etched surface on an elaborate artichoke pattern on a platform base & shaft, supporting a hinged conforming gilt-metal ash receiver, base impressed "Tiffany Studios New York 1651," 25½" h. **1,035.00**

Rare Victorian Bronze Doorknob

Doorknob, round w/a boldly cast Victorian Aesthetic design of an Oriental style flying crane among flowering branches w/stylized borders, marked on reverse "Russel & Erwin Mfg. Co. New Britain Ct. USA," made as part of a series, early 1880s (ILLUS.) **660.00**

Humidor, cov., Renaissance-style, the cover & sides w/panels of figures & foliage, E. F. Caldwell & Co., New York, early 20th c., 6" l. . . **431.00**

Bronze Satyr Lamp Base

Lamp base, figural, a kneeling naked leering satyr holding out in each hand an urn-form torch w/pedestal & knob w/three-light electric socket, black marble base, probably American, patinated, early 20th c., abrasions, 29" h. (ILLUS.) **1,725.00**

Mortar & pestle, the cylindrical mortar cast w/masks & shaped dividers, Europe, late 19th c., 6" d., 2 pcs. **144.00**

Sun dial, cast, round, mounted on a clay chimney pot, 33" h. **220.00**

Vase, ovoid body tapering to a squared base on pointed tab feet, the rounded shoulder tapering to a short rolled neck issuing whiplash scrolls down the sides w/arching foliate designs around the rim & upper portion & incised w/ground cover about the lower half, brown patina, by Hector Guimard, inscribed "HG," impressed "R C" twice & "309," France, ca. 1900, 5½" h. **17,250.00**

Vase, figural, wide bulbous body tapering to a wide cylindrical short neck w/molded rim, the lower body cast in bold relief w/the large faces of various Art Nouveau women peering out from among leafy clusters which continue up the shoulder & neck, Antonin Larroux, France, brown patination, ca. 1900, 11½" h. **4,312.00**

Vase, the baluster-form body w/oversized faceted rim, modeled w/section of paneling resembling a swollen bamboo stalk, brownish

red patina, inscribed "Lucian
bonvallet - Paris" w/monogram, ca.
1900, 15⅜" h. **8,050.00**

Japanese Bronze Vase

Vase, baluster-form, cast w/a petal-
form mouth & short neck, the sides
w/high-relief designs of eagles,
fleeing plovers, rockwork &
crashing waves, Japan, Meiji
Period, 19th c., 29" h. (ILLUS.) . . **3,162.00**

Neoclassical Bronze Vases

Vases, Barbedienne-style, tall
slender ovoid body tapering to a
flaring mouth, raised on four hoof
feet resting on a quatrefoil base,
Neoclassical relief designs of
bacchantes picking grapes & a
classical bust, late 19th c.,
17½" h., pr. (ILLUS.) **3,105.00**

COPPER

Arts & Crafts Copper Bowl

Bowl, Arts & Crafts style, deep
rounded & tapering sides w/a rolled
rim, decorated w/chased &
repoussé waves highlighted
w/silver beads of spray & a silver
rim, rich patina, impressed mark of
Arthur J. Stone, ca. 1901-12,
5¾" d., 2¾" h. (ILLUS.) **6,325.00**
Bowl, hand-hammered, Arts & Crafts
style, deep rounded & gently
tapering form w/incurved wide rim,
original brown patina, script
signature, Jarvie, early 20th c.,
6½" d., 3" h. **523.00**
Bowl, hand-hammered, Arts & Crafts
style, wide deep rounded form
w/tapering sides & a wide closed
rim, applied initial "E" on the side,
original dark brown patina,
impressed mark of the Kalo Shop,
Chicago, Illinois, early 20th c.,
9" d., 3½" h. **468.00**
Bowl, hand-hammered, squat-warty
camelia form w/heavily-raised
hammer marks, fine medium-dark
brown original patina w/traces of
red, Dirk Van Erp closed-box
marked "D'arcy Gaw," 9¼" d.,
3¼" h. **3,630.00**
Bowl, hand-hammered, Arts & Crafts
style, footed w/wide rounded sides
& a flat rim, medium bronze patina,
impressed mark of Karl F.
Leinonen, Boston, Massachusetts,
early 20th c., 9⅞" d., 3¼" h. **173.00**
Candlesticks, hand-hammered
copper, Arts & Crafts-style, tall
slender three-sided shaft w/swelled
bulbs at the top & base, each side
w/a round-edged flat pierced fin at
the top & case, the top bulb
enameled w/stylized red, blue &
green blossoms, a triangular drip
pan centered by a cylindrical flaring
candle socket, Buffalo Art Crafts
Shop, early 20th c., unmarked,
12" h., pr. (loss of patina) **705.00**

Candy kettle, deep rounded dovetailed bottom w/riveted steel side loop handles, 21½" d. **248.00**

Cartridge box, cov., flattened half-round shape, marked "B. Kittredge & Co., Cin. Ohio" w/patent dates, 3¾ x 4½" **660.00**

Coal skuttle, cov., Art Nouveau style, flaring rectangular base supporting a swelled rectangular deep compartment w/embossed stylized swirling flowers around the sides, loop end rim handles w/turned wood grips, a flat roof-form hinged top w/an opening at each end for a small brass shovel w/turned wood handle, England, early 20th c., unmarked, 13 x 22", 18" h. (break to two hinges) **275.00**

Jardiniere, hand-hammered, rolled rim w/original dark brown patina, unmarked, probably Dirk Van Erp, 8½" d., 11" h. **440.00**

Jardiniere, hand-hammered, large bulbous ovoid form w/a closed rim, decorated w/a scalloped band of nubby repoussé, fine original dark patina, possibly San Francisco, early 20th c., 14" d., 11" h. **2,200.00**

Jardiniere, hand-hammered, Arts & Crafts-style, a wide squatty bulbous body raised on three short, angled knob legs, a short widely flaring neck, side knobs holding slender loose ring handles, original patina, 18" d., 12" h. **220.00**

Kettle, hand-hammered w/flared rim, wrought-copper handles, 14" d., 6¼" h. **72.00**

Lamp, boudoir model, hand-hammered copper & mica, Arts & Crafts-style, squat bulbous base w/four-panel flaring shade, original dark patina & mica, open box stamp & "Dirk Van Erp - San Francisco," shade 11" d., 14¾" h. **6,320.00**

Teakettle, cov., bulbous slightly tapering dovetailed body w/a wide rounded shoulder to a fitted low domed cover w/brass finial, high arched swing strap handle stamped "5," swan's-neck spout, 7½" h. plus handle (soldered repair on bottom, minor dents) **83.00**

Teakettle, cov., wide bulbous shouldered body w/an angled swan's-neck spout, a low domed cover w/knob finial & swing strap

Rare Harbeson Teakettle

top handle stamped "HARBESON," Joseph Harbeson, Philadelphia, ca. 1800, 11" h. (ILLUS.) **3,737.00**

Tray, riveted & hand-hammered, rectangular, Arts & Crafts style w/low upright sides & arched ends w/pierced oblong hand holes, oak bottom, fine dark patina, impressed "ONS" for Onondaga Metal Shops, 7¾ x 15¾", 3¼" h. **1,100.00**

Tray, hand-hammered, Arts & Crafts style, rectangular w/low beveled edge, decorated w/a scene of a windmill backed by low water & distant land w/stylized trees, tiny windmill & swirling clouds in original nut brown patina, attributed to Carence Crafters, early 20th c., 3 x 6½" **132.00**

Tray, hand-hammered, Arts & Crafts style, oval, a dished center w/a wide flanged rim pierced w/oblong hand holds at the ends, original nut brown patina, impressed mark "Hand Wrought by Lyman P. Clark," early 20th c., 6½ x 9½" **138.00**

Tray, hand-hammered, Arts & Crafts style, round, a broad flattened rim w/rolled edge & decorated w/six raised bumps corresponding w/six swirled lobes on the dished interior also decorated w/linear outlining, lightly cleaned patina, 16" d. **358.00**

Tray, hand-hammered, Arts & Crafts style, irregular rectangular form w/rolled & crimped sides, tooled design of circles & lines atop four brass ball feet w/two applied pointed loop brass end handles, original brown & green patina, early 20th c., 7 x 16" **143.00**

Tray, Arts & Crafts style, twisted brass handles, cleaned patina, impressed Gustav Stickley mark, 12 x 17½" (some scratching) **374.00**

Dirk Van Erp Copper Tray

Tray, hand-hammered, Arts & Crafts style, oval w/low incurved flattened sides, the interior w/a tooled & painted picture of a rooster covered in glass, arched riveted end handles, original light brown patina, leather signed "G.M. Lee," copper w/windmill mark of Dirk Van Erp, 1912, 16 x 24" (ILLUS.) **1,980.00**

Vase, cylindrical, hand-hammered Arts & Crafts style, embossed around the rim w/stylized quatrefoils, fine original dark patina, die-stamped mark of Karl Kipp, early 20th c., 1¾" d., 4" h. .. **2,310.00**

Vase, hand-hammered, Arts & Crafts style, gently flaring cylindrical body w/a rolled rim & three heavy gauge applied strap handles, original brown patina, Stickley Brothers, early 20th c., 6" d., 6" h. **193.00**

Vase, hand-hammered, Arts & Crafts style, a short broad flaring foot supports a squatty bulbous base gently tapering to a flat mouth w/rolled rim, original dark brown patina, impressed "98," Stickley Brothers, early 20th c., 7" h. (dent in bottom) **253.00**

Vase, hand-hammered, Arts & Crafts style, bulbous bottom & flaring neck, deeply textured w/red warty & "curtained" surface, recent cordovan patina, Dirk Van Erp, open box mark, 5¼" d., 7" h. **1,980.00**

Vase, hand-hammered, Arts & Crafts style, a broad ovoid body on a molded foot & tapering to a wide rolled mouth, three applied brass strap handles w/delicate stylized decoration extend from the rim to the waist, rich original patina, attributed to the Stickley Brothers, early 20th c., 8" h. **110.00**

Vase, hand-hammered, Arts & Crafts style, bulbous form w/tapered rim, excellent dark brown original patina, Dirk Van Erp, open box mark, 6½" d., 8¼" h............ **1,430.00**

Vase, hand-hammered copper, tapering swelled foot below the tall cylindrical body w/a tooled string of bellflowers down one side, a three-lobed rolled rim, dark brown patina, impressed mark, 3¾" d., 9½" h...................... **1,100.00**

Wall sconces, candle-type, hand-hammered, Arts & Crafts style, rectangular backplate w/tooled linear edge decoration & a domed panel above the flattened scroll bracket supporting the tall cylindrical candle socket w/a wide dished drip pan, lightly cleaned patina, Karl Kipp, early 20th c., 3" w., 10" h., pr................ **468.00**

IRON

Boot scraper, hand-wrought, scrolled posts w/crossbar fitted into a stone base,15½" h. **303.00**

Bridge lamp, hand-wrought, the floor lamp w/a tripod base w/flat, arched legs centered by a tall thin bar fitted w/a scrolled bracket arm ending in the electric socket, first half 20th c., 55" h. **94.00**

Figural Advertising Card Tray

Card tray, cast, figural, a standing figure of a blackamoor holding shallow basket-cast tray, atop a

stepped rectangular base, base
w/advertising for "The Hoefinchoff
& Lane Foundry Co., Cin.,O.,"
1875-1903, old black, gold, silver &
red paint, 9" h. (ILLUS.). **550.00**

Fire marker, cast, raised decoration
& clasped handles, salmon-painted
surface, for Baltimore Equitable
Society, Baltimore, Maryland,
second quarter 19th c., dated
"1794," 9⅜ x 10" (weathered
surface) **748.00**

Fireplace trammel, hand-wrought,
sawtooth rim, 29" l. **138.00**

Hitching post, cast, figure of a black
jockey holding out a ring, standing
on a square stone block, old
polychrome repaint, 33" h. (back
edge of hat damaged, ring
replaced, base repaired) **660.00**

Model of a snake, hand-wrought,
coiled position w/elaborate
impressed decoration, delineated
eyes & projecting tongue, signed
"UT," American, 19th c., 3¾ x 7¼",
3½" h. **3,335.00**

Nutcracker, cast, model of a parrot,
hinged beak to crack nuts, old
green paint w/red & gold, 5¾" h. . . . **248.00**

Nutcracker, cast, stylized model of
an elephant, flattened body & head
w/curved trunk forming handle,
large oval ears w/hinge bolt
forming the eye, worn red paint
w/black & white, 9¾" l. **138.00**

Nutcracker, cast, figural alligator,
13" l. **165.00**

Shooting gallery target, rooster,
long arched & serrated tail, detailed
head w/comb, old black paint, 8" h.
(some rust) **275.00**

Shooting gallery target, cast,
double-type w/a stylized bird on a
shaft above a stylized duck, old
yellow & orange paint, 9" l. **149.00**

Stove finial, cast, a footed
rectangular flaring base supporting
a rectangular reticulated top cast
w/a large spread-winged eagle
above rockwork, mid-19th c.,
10½" l. **99.00**

Toaster, hand-wrought, a long
narrow three-bar rack w/a long
central twisted iron handle w/wood
grip, rack on four peg feet, 26" l. . . . **110.00**

Trivet, hand-wrought, openwork
spearpoint frame enclosing an
open heart design, oblong pointed
end handle, on three small legs,
12" l. (old breaks at seams in top). . **358.00**

Rare Sailor Umbrella Stand

Umbrella stand, cast, figural, a figure
of a standing sailor holding a
coiling rope support & resting atop
crossed oars, anchor & various
other nautical items, oblong low
shallow drip pan base w/acanthus
leaf cast border, removable pan,
marked "1927 Marcy Foundry Co.,"
repainted, 27½" h. (ILLUS.) **2,760.00**

Rare Cast-Iron Washboard

Washboard, cast, rectangular
flattened form w/narrow molded
edges & flat bracket legs w/round
cut-outs below the corrugated
washing surface below a smooth
top band pierced w/a heart, original
surface, Pennsylvania, 19th c.,
12½ x 22½" (ILLUS.) **2,415.00**

Cast-Iron Watch Hutch

Watch hutch, cast, an upright leafy scroll-cast frame w/a round opening resting on a base cast w/further leafy scrolling surrounding a spread-winged eagle, traces of black paint, light rust, 19th c., 10¼" h. (ILLUS.). **83.00**

Watering troughs, cast, oblong w/rectangular base, one painted green, one signed "J.L. Mott Ironworks, New York," 19th c., 24½ x 45", 21" h., pr. (corrosion, paint loss) **2,990.00**

PEWTER

Basin, deep rounded sides w/molded rim, unmarked, American-made, 19th c., 8" d., 2" h. (dents). **193.00**

Pewter Bowl & Tall Teapot

Bowl, shallow wide form w/flanged rim, Thomas Danforth III, Philadelphia, 1807-13, minor wear & scratches, 11⅝" d. (ILLUS. left). . **385.00**

Candlesticks, a domed reeded foot below a slender trumpet-form standard w/two swelled reeded sections near the base & top, a flaring reeded section at the base of the cylindrical candle socket w/a flared rim, unmarked, 19th c., 10⅝" h., pr. **385.00**

Charger, wide round form w/flanged rim, Samuel Pierce, Greenfield, Massachusetts, 1807-31, 11¼" d. (minor wear, pitting). **358.00**

Charger, round, Gershom Jones, Providence, Rhode Island, 1774-1809, 13½" d. (worn & pitted) **446.00**

Charger, round w/wide flanged rim, eagle touch of Nathaniel Austion, Charlestown, Massachusetts, ca. 1800, engraved on the back "T.E.," 13½" d. (wear, dents & knife scratches) **550.00**

Charger, round, Frederick Bassett, New York, New York, 1761-80, 14¾" d. (very minor dents & pitting) **1,265.00**

Thomas Badger Pewter Charger

Charger, wide round dished form w/wide flanged rim, Thomas Badger, Boston, Massachusetts, 1787-1815, wear, scratches, pitting, 15" d. (ILLUS.). **523.00**

Communion service: a cov. flagon, a pair of chalices & a 13½" d. basin; the flagon of tapering cylindrical form w/a flattened, domed, hinged cover & scroll thumbpiece & scroll handle w/bud terminal, a curved rim spout, each chalice w/a bell-form bowl above a baluster-turned stem on a domed, ringed foot, the round basin w/a wide flanged rim w/a single reed brim, attributed to Timothy Brigden, Albany, New York, 1816-19, flagon, 10¼" h., the set **18,400.00**

Dishes, deep, round, Thomas D. Boardman, Hartford, Connecticut, 1805-20, 9⅜" d., pr.. . . . . **805.00**

Figures of Westerners, standing man wearing a top hat, frock coat & kneebreeches, raised on a waisted

Chinese Pewter Figures

rectangular pedestal base w/scroll-cast trim, overall polychrome decoration, China, late 18th - early 19th c., imperfections, 7½" h., pr. (ILLUS.) **2,990.00**

Hot water platter, oblong w/a flattened flanged rim above the deep molded sides raised on small ball feet, scrolled loop end rim handles, marked "Compton, London," wooden hand grips, 20" l. (wear, scratches) **193.00**

Lamp, fluid-type, a bulbous acorn-form font raised on a short pedestal & round domed foot, w/early camphene burner w/snuffer caps, Roswell Gleason, Dorchester, Massachusetts, 1821-71, 5½" h. plus burner **385.00**

Lamp, early burning fluid-type, a cylindrical font raised on a ringed & flaring cylindrical shaft on a flaring dished foot, w/camphene burner w/snuffer caps, Capen & Molineux, New York, New York, 1848-54, 7⅛" h. plus burner **275.00**

Pitcher, cov., water, wide baluster-form body w/a curved rim spout & C-scroll handle, hinged domed cover w/finial w/disk, lion touch of Thomas D. Boardman, ca. 1830-50, 8¼" h. (somewhat battered) . . . **248.00**

Plate, flanged rim, Harbeson, Philadelphia, ca. 1800, 7⅞" d. (wear, scratches). **275.00**

Plate, flanged rim, Frederick Bassket, New York, New York, 1761-80 & 1785-99, 8½" d. (wear, pitting & knife scratches) **165.00**

Plate, wide flat flanged rim, Gershom Jones, Providence, Rhode Island, 1774-1809, 9⅛" d. (wear, knife scratches, 1" crack along edge of bouge) **358.00**

Plate, Boardman & Hart, Hartford, Connecticut, 1830-50, 9⅜" d. **633.00**

Plate, Europe, partial touch mark, 19th c., 9⅝" d. (wear, pitting) **94.00**

Plates, Continental w/various touch marks, set of 4 (some damage). . . . **220.00**

Plates, William Danforth, Middletown, Connecticut, 1792-1820, 8¾" d., set of 6 (pitting) **1,035.00**

Platter, meat, oval w/pierced insert, Townsend & Compton, London, England, 1801-11, 21⅞ x 28¾" (dents) **2,415.00**

Sundial, round, sill-type, late 18th c., 4½" d. (nail holes, minor losses) . . . **288.00**

Sundial, sill-type, Josiah Miller, New England, 18th c., 4½" d. (very minor loss) **690.00**

Syrup pitcher w/hinged lid, cylindrical body w/flaring base, pointed domed cover, rim spout & S-curved handle, Hall & Cotton, Middlefield, Connecticut, ca. 1840-45, 6⅛" h. **660.00**

Tankard, cov., communion-type, tapering cylindrical body w/a screw-top opening to a fitted pewter bowl, the body w/a spurred scroll handle, on a molded base, Roswell Gleason, Dorchester, Massachusetts, 1822-71 . . . . **1,380.00**

Teapot, cov., individual-size, pear-shaped body tapering to a flared rim & hinged domed cover, slender swan's-neck spout & black C-scroll handle, Bailey & Putnam, Walden, Massachusetts, 1830-35, 6½" h. (repairs). **413.00**

Teapot, cov., flaring foot below a squatty bulbous body w/a wide shoulder to a short waisted flaring neck w/a hinged pyramidal cover, wooden finial knob missing, swan's-neck spout, ornate C-scroll handle, Thomas D. Boardman, Hartford, Connecticut, 1830s, 7⅛" h. (bottom repair, some wear). . . **210.00**

Teapot, cov., footed bulbous body w/short waisted flaring neck, swan's-neck spout & C-scroll handle, domed hinged cover w/finial, mark of Sellew & Co., Cincinnati, Ohio, mid-19th c., 7⅜" h. (some battering & repair some surface pitting). **116.00**

Teapot, cov., squatty bulbous body raised on a flaring base & tapering to a low flaring neck w/a hinged, domed lid w/finial, swan's-neck spout & angled S-scroll handle,

eagle touch of Thomas Danforth
Boardman, ca. 1830, 7⅜" h. (minor
damage & dents, old hinge repair) . . **303.00**

Teapot, cov., footed spherical body
tapering to a short, flared neck,
inset domed cover, swan's-neck
spout, C-scroll handle, George
Richardson, Boston & Cranstone,
Rhode Island, 1818-45, 7½" h.
(repairs, particularly to handle) **204.00**

Teapot, cov., footed squatty bulbous
body tapering to a short flaring
neck, hinged pagoda cover
w/round finial, swan's-neck spout &
C-scroll handle, James Putnam,
Malden, Massachusetts, 1830-55,
8¾" h. (several small holes in
handle) **248.00**

Teapot, cov., pedestal foot on ringed
pear-form body w/flared rim &
hinged domed cover, paneled
swan's-neck spout & C-scroll
handle, William McQuilkin,
Philadelphia, 1839-53, 8⅞" h.
(dents) **220.00**

Teapot, cov., footed slightly flaring
short cylindrical body w/a tall flaring
neck, swan's-neck spout, S-scroll
handle, domed cover w/finial,
Roswell Gleason, Dorchester,
Massachusetts, 1822-71, 9" h.
(battered). **110.00**

Teapot, cov., lighthouse-shape, tall
tapering ringed cylindrical sides
w/a flared foot, hinged domed
cover w/wooden finial button
missing, swan's-neck spout,
angular C-scroll black-painted
metal handle, William Savaage,
Middletown, Connecticut, late
1830s, 9¼" h. (some wear) **250.00**

Teapot, cov., tall slightly tapering
body w/central ring band & flaring
rim, hinged domed cover w/round
finial, ribbed swan's-neck spout,
long C-scroll handle, retailer's mark
of John Whitlock, Troy, New York,
1847-56, 10¾" h. (some wear &
pitting) **242.00**

Teapot, cov., tall tapering
"lighthouse" shape w/flared base &
domed cover, swan's-neck spout &
C-scroll handle, Freeman Porter,
Westbrook, Maine, 1835-60, finial
wafer missing, minor cover dents,
10¾" h.(ILLUS. right with bowl). . . . **248.00**

Teapot, cov., tall urn-form body
w/gadrooned bottom & knobbed
pedestal base, curved spring
spout, domed cover & C-form

handle, mark of Dixon & Son,
England, mid-19th c., 12½" h.
(damage to wooden finial disk) **220.00**

Teapot, cov., short pedestal base
below the nearly spherical line-
incised body w/a short waisted
neck & hinged domed cover
w/finial, angled loop handle, Ashbil
Griswold, Meriden, Connecticut,
first half 19th c., 8⅛" h. (some
battering & repair, splits in bottom) . . **193.00**

Teapot, cov., tall baluster-form body
w/a tapering conical hinged cover
w/disc knob, swan's-neck spout,
ornate C-scroll repainted black
handle, John Munson, Yalesville,
Connecticut, 1846-52, 11⅜" h.
(minor dents, small nick on bottom
edge) **220.00**

Tureen, cover & ladle, a wide
tapering pedestal base supporting
a deep rounded bowl w/a domed
cover topped by a figural fish finial,
figural fish handles at the side rims,
the ladle w/a rounded shell-shaped
bowl & a cut-out fish handle tip, Old
Newbury Pewter, 12" d., 12½" h.,
the set **460.00**

SHEFFIELD PLATE

Candlesticks, telescoping-type,
baluster-form, flute & rib
decoration, early 19th c., 7¾" h.,
set of 4 (rosing) **575.00**

Candlesticks, flat-rimmed urn-form
socket above a ringed neck &
slightly tapering cylindrical
standard on a ringed, stepped
round foot, gadrooned borders, two
w/scrolling double-arm - three-
socket inserts, Matthew Bolton,
England, early 19th c. w/arms
overall 20" h., set of 4
(light rosing) **2,875.00**

Sheffield Silver Dish Cover

Dish cover, high oval domed form
w/a wide gadrooned central section
around the reeded loop handle a
beaded medial band, engraved
armorial whippet, early 19th c.,
22" l., 11" h. (ILLUS.). **575.00**

Hot water urn, cov., classical-style, caryatid accents, wooden handles, early 19th c., 17½" h. (damaged) . . **345.00**

Serving dish, cov., gadroon borders, acanthus leaf & shell details, lion head handles, paw feet, engraved crests, early 19th c., 9⁹⁄₁₆ x 16¾", 10⅜" h. **1,610.00**

SILVER

AMERICAN (STERLING & COIN)

Bowl, hand-hammered, Arts & Crafts style, a low flaring oval foot supporting deep oval four-lobed sides w/a flattened flanged rim, marked "Sterling - Hand Wrought at the Kalo Shops," Chicago, Illinois, early 20th c., 6½ x 10", 2½" h. **605.00**

Bowl, shaped body w/applied acanthus leaf & scroll rim, shell & scroll feet, monogrammed, ca. 1875, Gorham Mfg. Co., Providence, Rhode Island, 8¾ x 12½", 3¾" h. **288.00**

Bowl, Arts & Crafts style, rounded form w/a shaped hand-hammered rim & foot, engraved "S," Shreve & Co., early 20th c., 9" d., 4¾" h. **633.00**

Bowl, flaring body w/hammered surface, lobed foot , monogrammed, marked "Tiffany & Co.," ca. 1907-47, 8¼" l. **920.00**

Bowl, hammer-textured lotus blossom-form, engraved name & date, Whiting, ca. 1886, 8⅜" w. . . . **345.00**

Bowl, sterling, footed, repoussé decoration on the body & foot of flowers, leaves & ferns, Samuel Kirk & Son, Baltimore, ca. 1900, 9" d. **747.00**

Kirk & Son Sterling Bowl

Bowl, round deep center w/a wide flanged rim hand-decorated w/an ornate repoussé floral border in the Chrysanthemum patt., footed base, marked "Hand Decorated S. Kirk & Son Sterling 179A," late 19th - early 20th c., 11" d. (ILLUS.) **688.00**

Bowl, seven-lobed flanged rim w/delicate embossed scrolls in each surrounding a boldly swirled center w/a monogram, dated 1899, Gorham Mfg. Co., Providence, Rhode Island, 11" d. (minor pitting, surface scratches) **431.00**

Bowl, oval w/chased floral border, monogrammed, Unger Bros., early 20th c., 7⅛ x 12½" **316.00**

Bowl, sterling, footed oval, w/a fretwork rim & upraised palmette handles, Tiffany & Co., New York, New York, ca. 1860, 13¾" l. **977.00**

Bowl & plate set, child's, sterling, the shallow round plate w/a wide flanged rim acid-etched w/scenes of Noah's Ark & animals, the waisted cylindrical bowl decorated w/a matching body band, Tiffany & Co., New York, 1907-38, bowl 4" d., plate 6³⁄₁₆" d., the set **748.00**

Bowls, rounded form w/wide rolled rim boldly cast & pierced w/the scrolling "Clover" patt., plain center, Tiffany & Co., New York, late 19th c., 9" d., pr. (pittings & dings) **1,035.00**

Cake plate, round w/chased poppy border, Black, Starr & Frost sterling, ca. 1900, 11¹⁄₁₆" d. **633.00**

Candle snuffer, profile of a covered wagon attached to top of handle, marked, 20th c., 7¾" l. **115.00**

Cann, coin, footed baluster-form w/slightly flared mouth & double-scroll handle, engraved on base "PPP," marked "P.A.," possibly American, last quarter 18th c., 4½" h. **3,220.00**

Cann, coin, tapering cylindrical form w/ringed rim & base, doulbe C-scroll handle w/foliate thumb rest, monogrammed within an ellipse, Col. Standish Barry, Baltimore, Maryland, late 18th c., 4½" h. **8,500.00**

Cann, coin, footed baluster-form w/ornate S-scroll handle, engraved on bottom "FG to RG," marked

Early American Silver Cann

under rim "J. Coburn" in rectangle,
John Coburn, Boston, ca. 1775,
5⅜" h. (ILLUS.). **2,070.00**

Centerpiece, circular foot pierced
w/laurel branches alternating
w/rectangular cartouches cast
w/swags, flaring body applied
w/wide, everted rim, pierced &
chased w/foliate & cartouche band,
fitted w/silver-plated foliate grill,
Layfayette patt., Dominick & Hagg,
ca. 20th c., 8½" h. **2,645.00**

Cocktail set: cov. cocktail shaker
w/finely cut-out strainer & twelve
9¼" h. goblets; Art Deco style, tall
ovoid shaker w/raised shoulder
band & domed cap, each goblet
w/a flaring rounded bowl on a
gently tapering stem & round disk
foot, each marked "Tiffany & Co.
1885 - 1512," w/eleven goblet bags
& strainer bag, goblets 4" h.,
the set **1,265.00**

Coffee service: cov. coffeepot, cov.
sugar bowl & creamer; Classical
style w/each having a partially
lobed & stepped flattened ovoid
body w/egg-and-dart borders & C-
scroll handles & a stepped
shoulder, short pedestal & stepped
round foot w/beaded bands, the
stepped & domed covers
w/blossom finials, S. Reed, New
York, New York, ca. 1810-34, each
monogrammed, sugar bowl 9¼" h.,
3 pcs. **1,955.00**

Coffeepot, cov., coin, tall footed
baluster-form body w/a stepped
domed cover w/pointed knop finial,
ornate C-scroll handle, the handle
& spout w/applied & chased
naturalistic leaves & berries, the
cover, neck & foot w/chased

acanthus leaf borders,
monogrammed & w/an inscription
dated "1859," Tiffany & Co., New
York, New York, 11¾" h. **1,495.00**

Compotes, open, chased floral rim &
base, Tiffany & Co., late 19th c.,
10" d., 4" h., pr. **3,450.00**

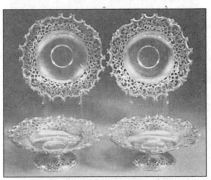

Ornately Pierced Compotes

Compotes, open, plain dished center
w/a wide pierced scrolling border
w/cast rim scrolls, raised on a low
pierced & domed foot, Howard &
Co., late 19th – early 20th c.,
8¾" d., set of 4 (ILLUS.). **1,265.00**

Creamer, Arts & Crafts style, simple
oviform w/rolled rim,
monogrammed w/initial "G" for
Herman Glendenning, marked
w/Arthur Stone logo, 1920-36,
4½" d., 3¼" h. **288.00**

Creamer & cov. sugar bowl, coin,
each w/a bulbous-form body
w/applied foliate banding, molded
circular base, sugar cover w/flower
bud finial, ca. 1830, 6¾" h., pr.
(minor dents) **403.00**

Cup, child's, cylindrical w/angular
loop handle, the side w/an
embossed rabbit & inscription
"Betty - Christmas - 1916," Kalo
mark, 3¾" d., 2" h. **550.00**

Curling iron, traveling-type, a floral
repoussé rectangular box
w/engraved monogram & date
"1894" on the cover, the gold-
washed interior fitted w/an alcohol
burner & folding iron holder, folding
iron w/repoussé handles, Gorham
Mfg. Co., Providence, Rhode
Island, box 2⅜ x 6¼", 2⁵⁄₁₆" h.,
the set **805.00**

Demitasse set: cov. pot, open sugar,
creamer & octagonal tray, each of
paneled tapered Neo-Greek style,
Greek key & urn borders,
monogrammed, inscription on tray

reverse, 1917, Gorham Mfg. Co.,
Providence, Rhode Island, pot
9" h., tray 16⅞" l., 4 pcs. **978.00**

Dishes, figural, model of a peacock,
the bird w/a cast body & wide
fanned ribbed & dished tail chased
w/feathers, Gorham Mfg. Co.,
Providence, Rhode Island,
20th c., pr. **2,300.00**

Dresser set: hand mirror, two cov.
jars, pin tray, nail file & five
assorted brushes; Art Nouveau
design of morning glory & poppy,
engraved script monograms,
Gorham Mfg. Company,
Providence, Rhode Island, the set . . **518.00**

Egg-cutter cups, flat round disc foot
supporting a short waisted pedestal
supporting the egg-form hinged
body, the domed lid hinged w/two
swing-out cutting arms, applied
side clawfoot handles, gold-
washed interior, monogrammed,
ca. 1910, pr. **690.00**

Fruit basket, wide round shallow
basket w/a pierced latticework
band below the reeded rim, raised
on a plain flaring pedestal foot,
high arched strap swing handle,
Tiffany & Co., early 20th c., 8⅞" d. . . **230.00**

Fruit basket, squared tapering
basket w/rounded bottom & wide
flattened round flanged rim, raised
on four curved & pointed tab feet,
the rim & sides w/a pierced scroll
design, pierced arched swing
handle, Towle, early 20th c.,
10⅜" d. **403.00**

Fruit bowl, shaped rectangular form,
repoussé & chased poppy design
border, ca. 1900, Gorham Mfg.
Co., Providence, Rhode Island,
11¾" d. **230.00**

Hot water kettle, cov., Classical urn-
form w/a partially lobed & stepped
flattened ovoid body w/grape
cluster & leafy vine borders w/a
central foliate decorated spout
w/fan-form control spigot on one
side, applied foliate & cross-hatch-
capped large C-scroll side handles
surmounted by a domed cover w/a
figural dolphin finial, raised on a
waisted openwork pedestal above
a rectangular stepped & molded
base w/rounded corners ending on
ball feet, Shreve & Co., San
Francisco, ca. 1860, 11½" h. **1,955.00**

Hot water kettle, cover & stand,
coin, chased decoration, on a silver
plated burner stand, Ball, Tomkins
& Black, New York, New York,
ca. 1850, overall 15¼" h., the set . . **1,092.00**

Hot water kettle on stand, kettle in
paneled Colonial Revival style,
engraved floral swag decoration,
ivory heat stops on handle,
monogrammed, Gorham Mfg. Co.,
Providence, Rhode Island, 1919,
13½" h. (burner dented) **633.00**

Ice cream knife, gold-washed &
bright-cut blade, Medici patt.,
Gorham Mfg. Company,
Providence, Rhode Island, late
19th c., 12¼" l. **149.00**

Mug, coin, cylindrical w/applied star
in circle banding on base & shaped
foliate banding handle,
monogrammed "AGR - AMT,"
inscribed on base "Redman 1817,"
early 19th c., 3½" h. (minor dents) . . **518.00**

Nutmeg grater, covered
compartment & exposed grating
surface, monogrammed, Jacobi &
Jenkins, Baltimore, Maryland,
ca. 1900, 4⅜" h. **863.00**

Pepper grinder, cylindrical, overall
chased floral decoration,
monogrammed, Gorham Mfg. Co.,
Providence, Rhode Island, 1898,
3½" h. **115.00**

Pitcher, water, baluster-form
w/ribbed details, retailed by C.
Hartdegen & Co., Whiting Mfg. co.,
Providence, Rhode Island, 9" h. **489.00**

Pitcher, water, jug-form, plain barrel-
shaped body w/a short pointed rim
spout rising from three diminishing
beads, partly faceted slender
hollow scroll handle w/strut
support, marked twice on base
"PITTMAN," Saunders Pittman,
Providence, Rhode Island,
ca. 1800, 9⅛" h. **6,900.00**

Pitcher, water, baluster-form
w/gadroon borders & acanthus leaf
detail on the spout & handle,
engraved monogram, Gorham Mfg.
Co., Providence, Rhode Island,
1928, 9⅝" h. **748.00**

Pitcher, hot milk, vasiform shape
w/beaded edge, on molded circular
base, w/a later monogram,
probably Loring Bailey, Hingham,
Massachusetts, 1780-1814, 9⅞" h.
(very minor dents) **863.00**

Pitcher, water, urn-form body w/egg-
and-dart borders & applied floral
garland beneath a tapering neck
w/a molded edge & an applied
peaked scroll handle, raised on a
spreading round base, Whiting
Mfg. Co., Providence, Rhode
Island, 1908, 10⅛" h. **748.00**

Pitcher, a bulbous tapering body, the lower section decorated w/a flattened lobe & diamond design beneath a floral banded neck, scrolling rim & high arched spout, the peaked S-scroll handle w/acanthus caps & floral terminations, raised on a short pedestal on the stepped flaring round foot w/floral-banded edge, inscribed w/a name, dated 1831, William Thomson, New York, New York, 10⅝" h. (minor body dents) . . **1,725.00**

Floral-decorated Coin Silver Pitcher

Pitcher, coin, wide ovoid body tapering to a cylindrical neck w/a wide, high arched spout, angled leaf-cast handle, the sides chased w/naturalistic floral sprigs, handle w/bearded face at the corner, Ball, Black & Co., mid-19th c., 11" h. (ILLUS.) **1,093.00**

Pitcher, water, bulbous tapering paneled baluster form w/chased Colonial & Renaissance Revival designs, monogrammed, Graf, Washburne & Dunn, 1909, 11⅛" h. **2,300.00**

Porringer, double-arched keyhole handle engraved w/early initials "A" over "IA," marked "SV" above mullet in heart in bowl & back of handle, Samuel Vernon, Newport, Rhode Island, ca. 1730, 5⅛" d. . . . **4,312.00**

Porringer, round w/slightly flared straight rim & pierced keyhole handle, engraved on base "IHJ," marked under rim & on handle "ID" within an oval, possibly John Dixwell, ca. 1725, 5¼" d. **920.00**

Porringer, round shallow bowl w/pierced "keyhole" handle, handle engraved "DFS," base engraved "Dorothy Farnham Smith 1753-

Early Coin Silver Porringer

1801," marked twice "T. Edwards" in rectangle, Thomas Edwards, Boston, ca. 1740, 5½" d. (ILLUS.) **2,070.00**

Porringer, Arts & Crafts style, finely pierced & chased handle, bowl engraved "Mary Louise Lawser - Christmas 1909 - from Auntie Mary," initialed "B" for William Blair, Arthur Stone logo, 6¼" d., 1¾" h. . . . **460.00**

Punch ladle, Olympian patt., Tiffany & Co., monogrammed on reverse . . **862.00**

Punch pot, cov., coin, oval shaped, the domed cover w/an urn finial, wooden scroll handle, decorated w/a repoussé & leaf-engraved band at the shoulder, engraved w/an oval open cartouche within cornucopia, probably American, early 19th c., 10¼" h. **1,610.00**

Dominick & Haff Punch Set

Punch set: footed bowl w/reticulated rim, 12 handled cups & a ladle w/reticulated handle end; the deep bowl w/a widely flaring base, monogrammed on the side of bowl & cups, Dominick & Haff, early 20th c., retailed by Smith Patterson & Co., bowl 11¾" d., 8⅞" h., the set (ILLUS.) **2,645.00**

Salt dips & spoons, round form w/shell feet, chased w/chinoiserie decoration, worn engraved crest, shell design spoons, Kirk & Son, ca. 1828, 3¼", four sets **460.00**

Soup ladle, coin, oval bowl w/pierced & engraved attached strainer, beaded edge pattern, engraved initials, marked "S.T. Crosby & Co., Boston," ca. 1850 . . . . **173.00**

Spectacle case, oblong flattened shape w/side hinge, engraved floral & scroll decoration, monogrammed, ca. 1900 . . . . **173.00**

Sugar basket, coin, shaped oval foot supporting the tapering pedestal below the deep, flaring conforming basket w/a high arched swing strap handle from side to side, chased foliate banding & shield-form cartouches, marked twice on base "HW," American, ca. 1790, 5¾" h. (minor dents) **1,610.00**

Sugar bowl, cov., coin, ovoid boat-form w/swing handle, scrolled border detail, chased floral decoration on the body, monogrammed, J.E. Standwood, Boston, 1850s, 5¾" l., 4⅜" h. **288.00**

Sugar bowl, cov., coin, baluster-form w/a chased athemion band on the body & cover, bud finial, marked by Bigelow Bros. & Kennard, Boston, ca. 1845, 5" h. **288.00**

Sugar caster, domed pierced top w/pointed knob finial, the tapered cylindrical body w/a flaring base & medial band & further decorated w/scrolling flower & swag designs, Black, Starr & Frost, ca. 1876, 7⅛" h. **633.00**

Tankard, cov., tapering cylindrical body w/a molded domed cover, base & mid-band, engraved "EBA" on handle, marked on neck & cover, William Cowell, Boston, ca. 1730, 7¼" h. **5,175.00**

Paul Revere Silver Tankard

Tankard, cov., flaring ringed foot below the tapering cylindrical ringed body w/a hinged stepped & domed cover w/pineapple finial, corkscrew thumbpiece, C-form handle, engraved initials "JLH" in oval & under swag on the front, marked under rim "REVERE" in rectangle, Paul Revere, Boston, ca. 1765, 10" h. (ILLUS. bottom of previous column) **8,050.00**

Tea caddy, cov., ovoid body w/a fitted high domed cap, the body decorated around the shoulder w/a repoussé floral design above plain lancets up from the base, a shell-banded neck, matching design on cap, opening to reveal a removable foliate decorated lid & a gold-washed interior, base engraved "J.H. & J. B.B. - Sept. 8th - 1859-1884," Tiffany & Co., 6¼" h. **920.00**

Tea & coffee service: cov. teapot, cov. coffeepot, cov. sugar bowl, creamer & waste bowl; each in Colonial Revival style, engraved w/scrolling foliage, monogrammed, International Silver, 20th c., the set . . **920.00**

Tea & coffee set: cov. coffeepot, cov. teapot, creamer, cov. sugar; chased in flowers & scrollwork, monogrammed, Dunkirk Silversmiths, mid-20th c., the set (dented creamer). **920.00**

Classical-form Coin Tea Set

Tea & coffee set: cov. teapot, cov. coffeepot, cov. sugar bowl & creamer; coin, classical design w/oblong bulbous lobed body on a stepped oval base, domed cover w/sheaf of wheat finial, applied fruit & foliate banding, paneled serpent-form spouts on pots & C-scroll handles, William B. North & Co., New York, New York, 1822-29, minor dents, repairs to coffeepot base, coffeepot 10" h., the set (ILLUS.) **3,220.00**

Tea set: cov. teapot, creamer, cov. sugar; each of squatty footed round form decorated w/a medial band of relief-cast leafy scrolls, C-scroll handles, acanthus leaf details under the spouts, domed covers w/floral ball finials, monogrammed, Tiffany & Co., New York, 1891-1902, 3 pcs. (pin missing on teapot handle) **1,840.00**

Tea set: cov. teapot, cov. sugar bowl, creamer & waste bowl; coin, each w/a faceted body & engine-turned borders, floriform knops, monogrammed, Ball, Black & Co., New York, New York, ca. 1855, teapot 10" h., the set **1,840.00**

Tray, coin, oval, dished top w/gadrooned rim band, raised on tapering scroll feet, the center engraved w/entwined initials, the base w/a presentation inscription dated 1863, Gorham Mfg. Co., Providence, Rhode Island, retailed by Crosby, Hunnewell & Mores, 9" l. **460.00**

Tray, coin, round, dished top w/gadrooned rim band, on three scroll feet, engraved initials in the center, marked twice on base, Robert & William Wilson, Philadelphia, ca. 1830, 10" d. (scratches) **1,840.00**

Tray, Arts & Crafts style, sterling, rectangular w/openwork handles, engraved initial "C," Arthur Stone logo, early 20th c., 9 x 12" (minor scratches) **863.00**

Tray, Arts & Crafts style, oval, hand-hammered flattened upright low sides w/arched pierced end handles, quarter-sawn oak bottom, Shreve, stamped & hallmarked, early 20th c., 17 x 23½" **770.00**

Durgin Sterling Covered Urn

Urn, cov., tall elongated classical-form w/ringed upper body below the flared rim w/a ringed domed cover w/pointed finial, double-C-scroll long handles, raised on a knobbed pedestal & ringed, domed foot, heraldic crest engraved on each side, Durgin Silver Co., ca. 1900, 18½" h. (ILLUS. bottom of previous column) **1,150.00**

Vase, tall slender trumpet-form, softly hammered surface, the lightly lobed flaring round foot supports the slender flaring body w/a band of lappets around its base, marked in the underside, stamped "Special Hand Work," Tiffany & Co., New York, numbered "22082" & "313," ca. 1915, 17" h. **4,025.00**

Vase, trumpet-form, pierced acanthus leaf rim, weighted base, Frank Smith Co., early 20th c., 20" h. **518.00**

Ornate Coin Silver Waste Bowl

Waste bowl, coin, footed deep bulbous bowl tapering to a flaring crimped rim, the body w/a continuous Chinese landscape scene w/people, trees, flowers, etc., J.E. Caldwell & Co., Philadelphia, mid-19th c., 4⅝" h. (ILLUS.) **518.00**

Wine coaster, flat round footed base w/undulating & gently flaring low reticulated sides, monogrammed, dated 1897, Gorham Mfg. Co., Providence, Rhode Island, 4¾" d. .. **230.00**

Wine jug, coin, decorated in the Rococo style w/repoussé flowers & a cartouche, dated "1858," John L. Westervelt, Newburgh, New York, 12" h. **1,035.00**

ENGLISH & OTHERS

Apple corer, tapering cylindrical silver handle & half-round long blade, "H&T" maker's mark, Birmingham, England, 1870, 5⅞" l. ... **460.00**

Basket, round flaring body cast w/bands centering a cartouche w/engraved monogram, continuing to a twisted hinged handle, raised on a shaped circular foot, Richard Sawyer, Dublin, Ireland, 1855-56, w/handle 6¾" h. **316.00**

Basket, oblong boat-shaped body w/upswept flattened & flaring pierced border band, rounded bottom raised on a low pedestal on a stepped & banded rounded rectangular foot, high arched tapering strap swing handle, engraved leaf design under the rim, Holland, 19th c., 11½" l. **805.00**

Bowl, rounded form on a raised foot, chased w/chrysanthemums on a stippled ground, China, 19th c., 6" d. **345.00**

Bowls, footed, round w/reticulated foliate & lattice rim w/a gadrooned border, raised on scrolled feet, retailed by Mappin & Webb, produced in Sheffield, 1910-11, 6⅛" d., 2½" h., pr. **288.00**

English Sterling Cake Basket

Cake basket, rectangular dished form w/steep lobed sides & leaf-cast end-to-end swing handle, raised on a rectangular foot, handle & rim w/engraved armorial crest, Philip Rundell, London, 1821-22, 14" l. (ILLUS.). **1,725.00**

Cake basket, rectangular w/lobed & gilt-decorated interior continuing to a leaf-cast border & bail handle, raised on a rectangular pedestal base, Moscow, Russia, early 19th c., 10½" h. **1,092.00**

Candlesticks, baluster-form w/twisted neck, raised on three scroll-form feet, chased overall w/classical scenes amid a foliate background, matching Dutch bobeches, Denmark, 19th c., 13" h., pr. **2,185.00**

Russian Silver Chalice

Chalice, bell-form bowl w/engraved scrolls & oval reserves of religious figures, a Cyrallic inscription around the rim, a palmette-engraved baluster-form stem on a flaring domed foot further chased w/scrolls & figural panels, Russia, dated 1860 (ILLUS.). **1,650.00**

Chalice, cov., tapered cylindrical form w/a domed cover mounted w/a figural finial, decorated w/chased cherub faces & fruit amid chased & engraved scrolling, gilt interior, above sterling standard, London, 1901-02, 12" h. **805.00**

Coffee & tea set: cov. coffeepot, cov. teapot, creamer & sugar; all melon-fluted w/melon finials, Edward Barnard & Sons, London, England, 1833, coffeepot 10¼" h., the set . . **4,025.00**

Coffee & tea set: cov. coffeepot, cov. teapot, creamer & tripod sugar bowl; each partly lobed & w/a cast classical frieze of figures & horses, the handles parting from theatrical masks, Frederick Elkington, Birmingham, England, 1896, coffeepot 12½" h., the set **3,162.00**

Coffeepot, cov., plain pyriform, the front centering an engraved armorial crest continuing to a shell-cast scroll spout & wooden scroll handle, surmounted by a guilloché edged domed hinged cover, on a similarly decorated pedestal foot, Frasier Crump, London, England, 1768-69, 11¼" h. **2,530.00**

Coffeepot, cov., gold-washed baluster-form on a pedestal base, beaded detail, wooden handle, engraved decoration, Hester Bateman, England, 1789, 12⅞" h. (restored) **1,380.00**

Communion cup, beaker-shaped bowl engraved w/a collar of arabesques within strapwork, knopped reel-shaped stem & domed foot w/egg & dart rim, maker's mark a pr. of bellows, London, England, 1570, 6¼" h. **4,312.00**

Compote, open, deep widely flaring stepped bell-form bowl raised on a domed, stepped thick pedestal base, hammered surface, w/a clear cut glass insert, Georg Jensen, Denmark, 1925-32, impressed marks, 9" d., 5¼" h. **575.00**

Compote, open, a deep wide round bowl w/alternating round & fanned slat-pierced openings around the sides, raised on a ring-incised foot atop four slender cylindrical columns resting on a flaring flat-topped cylindrical base w/matching pierced openings, impressed marks, Austria, early 20th c., 8" d., 9¾" h. **805.00**

Dish, oval form, castle embossed in center w/beaded interior rim, side chased w/scrolling foliage w/lobed rim, mounted w/scrolling handles, marked "Vienna, 1694," Austria, 6⅛" l. **1,495.00**

English Silver Covered Ewer

Ewer, cov., classical urn-form w/a tall flaring neck w/long spout & hinged domed cover w/knob finial, raised on a ringed pedestal base w/domed & beaded round feet, the angled handle of carved ivory, chased floral & scroll decoration

around the body, Abraham Peterson & Peter Podie, England, ca. 1783, dents, 12⅜" h. (ILLUS.) . . **1,093.00**

Ewer, Empire-style, applied w/figures & masks & w/female caryatid handle, engraved w/arms, France, late 19th c., 13¼" h. **2,185.00**

Fish server, the blade w/a heraldic device surrounded by open wrigglework, John Emes, London, England, 1800 . . . . **575.00**

Fish set, service for five w/ivory handles, floral-engraved blades, Birmingham, England, 1876, maker "FE," in fitted case, the set **201.00**

English Victorian Fish Slice

Fish slice, half-round dished blade bright-cut w/florals & scrolls, twist-carved long ivory handle, Atkin Brothers, Sheffield, 1891, 13⅞" l. (ILLUS.). **345.00**

Fruit bowl, presentation-type, footed rectangular form, engraved w/inscription around rim, maker's mark "F.M.," China, early 19th c., 13¹³⁄₁₆" l., 5" h. **2,645.00**

Inkstand, footed oval tray w/two polished cut bottles, acanthus leaf & Greek key decoration, London, ca. 1874, 11⅝" l., 3⅞" h., 3 pcs. **748.00**

Knife tray, oblong w/gadrooned rim, engraved on both sides w/crest & at one end w/a baron's coronet, John Houle, London, England, 1817, 15¾" h. **5,750.00**

Ladle, chased scrolling floral bowl, handle w/chased floral detail, turned wood handles, maker "A.T.," Glasgow, Scotland, 1837-38, 18" h. . . . **115.00**

Mirror, table model, heart-shaped beveled mirror plate within a cartouche-form repoussé velvet-backed frame, cast w/putti & winged female figures amid scrolling foliate leafage & rocaille decoration, the top w/a monogrammed cartouche, William Comyns & Sons, London, England, 1889-90, 17" h. **1,035.00**

Napkin rings, each decorated w/a floral repoussé design, individually numbered, maker "JR," London, England, 1861, in a fitted case, set of 6 . . . . **805.00**

Plates, round w/gadroon & shell rim, engraved crest on rim, gold-washed, R. Garrard, London, 1836, 10³⁄₁₆" d., set of 6 . . . . **4,313.00**

Platter, oval w/shaped, beaded rim, engraved crest in center, Germany, 19th c., 18½" l. **489.00**

Punch bowl, deep round sides chased w/leaf & acanthus leaf bands, Hunt & Roskell, London, ca. 1889, 10" d., 6¾" h. **978.00**

Punch bowl, the domed base applied w/two winged hippocamps, the lower body chased w/husks in strapwork panels, one side embossed w/Queen Elizabeth giving Leicester the keys of Kenilworth, foliate scroll handles mounted w/seated putto musicians, gilt interior, Elkington & Co., London, England, 1873, 21" w.. . . **18,400.00**

Ring tree, chased base w/fluted rim, Sheffield, England, 1900, maker's mark **115.00**

Salt dips, rounded body raised on hooved feet, chased w/floral decoration, cobalt blue glass liner, England, 1759-60, unknown maker, w/Gorham sterling salt spoons, salts 1⅝" h., pr. **201.00**

Salver, round w/a piercrust border cast w/shells centering a plain surface engraved w/triple armorial crest, raised on hoof feet, Ebenezer Coker, London, England, 1768-69, 11¼" d. **862.00**

Salver, square, molded rim w/intervals of shellwork, four shaped bracket feet, maker's mark of Cornelis Kuypers, Schhoonhoven, 1779, Holland, 11⅜" w. **2,070.00**

Sauce boats, cov., boat-shaped body on ribbed base, monogrammed, John Emes, London, 1798-99, pr. (one cover bent) **1,955.00**

Sauceboat, rounded boat-shape w/a scroll handle & hooved feet, engraved crest, Benjamin Cartwright, London, 1747-48, 6⁵⁄₁₆" l., 3¹³⁄₁₆" h. **345.00**

Sugar basket, beaded shaped edge over a reticulated wave pattern, repeated on the foot, w/blue glass liner, A. Calame, London, 1777-78, 5½" h. **920.00**

Sugar shaker, cov., baluster-form w/shaped, pierced lid w/swirled finial, monogrammed, John Delmester, London, 1761-62, 7½" h. **920.00**

Sweetmeat dish, oval form, embossed center w/nosegay tied w/bow, embossed sides w/four beaded ovals connected by a foliate swag w/beaded rim, Breslau, Germany, circa 1780, 6¾" l. **1,380.00**

Tankard, cov., tapered cylindrical body w/a flat hinged cover & corkscrew thumbpiece, the front engraved w/contemporary arms, fully marked w/"RL" in a dotted circle, London, England, 1685, 6¾" h. **7,187.00**

Tea set: cov. teapot, creamer, cov. sugar bowl, sweetmeat basket & sugar tongs; each chased w/chrysanthemum design on a stippled ground, sugar w/silver plated matched cover, applied monogram, Japan, late 19th - early 20th c., the set **2,128.00**

German Tea & Coffee Set

Tea & coffee set: cov. teapot, cov. coffeepot, cov. kettle on stand, cov. sugar bowl & creamer; each of squatty bulbous melon-lobed form w/cast mythological sea figures on the necks & shoulders, Germany, 800 fine, late 19th c., the set (ILLUS.) **6,900.00**

Teakettle on lampstand, globular form kettle engraved w/band of pendant foliage at shoulder, mounted w/stationary scroll handle w/shell terminals, tripod base engraved w/conforming band of decoration, pierced scrolls centering shaped cartouches on three scroll supports, lamp w/cartouche-form feet, maker's mark of RH, London, 1853, 14½" h. **1,265.00**

Tea urn, cov., classical-form, the tall tapering body w/an undulating bead-trimmed shoulder w/upturned scroll handles, flaring tall neck w/domed cover & urn finial, a spigot w/carved ivory handle on the

English Sterling Tea Urn

lower front above the beaded-ring
pedestal & squared undulating
base raised on four small paw feet,
Charles Wright or Chas.
Woodward, London, 1775-76,
minor dents, 20½" h. (ILLUS.) . . . **2,415.00**

Teapot, cov., paneled ovoid form,
engraved floral & swag decoration,
ivory finial & handle, Langlands &
Robertson, Newcastle, England,
1806-07, 5⅝" h. (patched to
remove monogram) **575.00**

Teapot, cov., inverted pear-shape,
engraved w/sprays of foliage &
scrolls around rim, marked on
base, Thomas Whipham, London,
England, 1750, 5¾" h. **1,840.00**

Teapot on lampstand, inverted pear-
shape, cast & chased w/Teniers
scenes, the eagle head spout rising
from a grotesque head mask, rustic
caryatid handle capped by reclining
reveling youths, the stand
decorated w/bacchic masks & rich
rococo ornament above ball & claw
feet, fully marked & stamped "Hunt
& Roskell Late Storr & Mortimer
6396," John S. Hunt, London,
England, 1853, 17¼" h., 2 pcs. . . **5,750.00**

Wedding cup, formed as two cups
joined at the center, each
pineapple-shaped, cast w/flowers &
scrolling leafage, raised on a lobed
circular foot, Germany, 19th c.,
overall 11" h. **1,840.00**

SILVER PLATE (Hollowware)

Basket, footed fluted form w/a
gadrooned edge & twisted
openwork bail handle, Pairpoint
Quadruple Plate, signed, 9¼"
w., 8" h. **83.00**

Cake stand, two-tiered, acanthus leaf
& scroll details on the column, cast
horse heads at base, graduated
scalloped dished, 23" h. **633.00**

Candelabra, three-light, three-arm
insert on pedestal base, egg-and-
dart border designs, Reed &
Barton, early 20th c., 13⁷⁄₁₆" h., pr. . . **230.00**

Card holder, a pedestal-based
compote form w/full-figural
parakeets around the standard,
scrolled handles mounted on sides
of rim, applied leaves on the sides,
good original plating, Webster &
Son, New York **375.00**

Chafing dish, cov., Arts & Crafts
style, round low cylindrical sides
above the deep rounded bottom &
a long tapering square riveted
ebony side handle, the low domed
cover w/an angular loop handle,
raised on a frame w/four flat
buttress-style legs w/block feet &
joined by slender cross braces
centered by a ring to hold the
cylindrical handled burner, cover
marked "Als ik Kan," Gustav
Stickley, from Stickley's Craftsman
restaurant in New York, all parts
marked "THE CRAFTSMAN -
INTERNATIOINAL SILVER CO.,"
17" l., 10½" h. **2,970.00**

Cocktail set: shaker & 12 matching
stemmed cocktails; the footed
swelled cylindrical shaker w/a
hammered finish tapering to a fitted
cover, short angled rim spout &
angled loop handle, matching
conical cocktails w/tall slender
stems & round feet, marked
"Homan plate on nickel silver W.M.
Mounts. Made in U.S.A.," & patent
number, wines by the Meridan
Silver Plate Co., early 20th c.,
the set **77.00**

Creamer & cov. sugar bowl, each
w/shoulders embossed w/stylized
flowers, the bodies etched w/floral
swags, each w/the Pairpoint mark,
3" h., pr. **165.00**

Hair receiver, cov., round, the cover
w/an Art Nouveau design w/
repoussé florals, marked by the
Pairpoint Mfg. Co., No. 7403,
quadruple plate, 3¼" h. **77.00**

English Hot Water Kettle on Stand

English Silver Plated Toast Rack

Hot water kettle on stand, the squatty bulbous melon-lobed kettle w/high arched reeded swing handle & swan's-neck spout tilting in an ornate shell- and scroll-cast four-footed stand, w/burner, England, late 19th c., 14½" h. (ILLUS.) **460.00**

Ice water set: cov. pitcher, goblet, footed bowl & tray; decorated w/scenes of people drawing water at a well, Reed & Barton, ca. 1880, pitcher 14¾" h., the set **403.00**

Pitcher, character-type w/grotesque face, Reed & Barton, late 19th c., 6¾" h. **86.00**

Pitcher, chased acorn branch design below an acorn leaf border, lobed foot w/acorn leaf design, grotesque face under spout, American-made, ca. 1855, 11½" h. **489.00**

Tea & coffee service: 18" h. cov. hot water urn w/double handles, cov. 10" h. coffeepot, cov. 11" h. teapot, 8½" h. cov. sugar bowl & 6" h. creamer; all w/acanthus leaf legs, the bodies etched w/meadow flowers, leaves & grasses, the urn w/a spout w/ivory handle marked "Patent Jan. 1869," Meriden Silver Plate Company, the set **688.00**

Tea & coffee set: cov. teapot, cov. coffeepot, kettle on stand, open sugar & creamer w/a similar pair of sugar tongs; each w/a tapering ovoid body, ivory kettle handle, horn heat stops & wooden finials, G. & S., London, England, 19th c., the set **288.00**

Toast rack, golf-motif, a rectangular tray base w/scalloped edge mounted w/five pairs of crossed golf clubs to form the rack, a ring handle at the top, on small feet, resilvered, England, late 19th - early 20th c., 3½ x 5¼", 5¼" h. (ILLUS.) **295.00**

Vase, Arts & Crafts style, bulbous form, hand-hammered surface, rim decorated w/four riveted mounts, Derby Silver Co., Derby, Connecticut, 11" d., 7" h. **316.00**

Vegetable dish, cov., oblong w/scalloped, domed sides & rope edging on the base, ornate domed cover, electroplating on copper, early 20th c., 12" l. **28.00**

Warming tureen, cov., round w/a domed cover, beaded detail, engraved decoration & crest, inner 1-quart bowl, 19th c., 9" d., 12" h. . . **316.00**

SILVER PLATE (Flatware)

CHARTER OAK (1847 ROGERS)

Baby spoon, bent-handled **35.00**
Butter spreader, individual **20.00**
Fruit spoons, gold-washed bowl, set of 6 . . . . **110.00**
Orange knife, hollow-handled **20.00**
Sugar spoon **20.00**
Tomato server **158.00**

LA VIGNE (1881 ROGERS)

Berry fork **98.00**
Butter spreader, master **30.00**
Iced tea spoon **85.00**
Pastry fork **45.00**
Punch ladle **425.00**
Salad fork **40.00**
Sugar spoon **30.00**

MOSELLE (AMERICAN SILVER CO.)

Baby spoon, curved handle **60.00**
Berry spoon **165.00**

Casserole spoon 150.00
Cold meat fork 50.00
Demitasse spoon. 25.00
Jelly spoon. 95.00
Oyster ladle 350.00
Punch ladle 750.00
Soup spoon, oval bowl. 25.00
Sugar spoon 55.00
Tablespoon 30.00
Teaspoon 20.00

ORANGE BLOSSOM (1910 ROGERS BROS.)

Butter spreader, individual. 12.00
Butter spreader, master. 15.00
Fruit spoons, set of 6. . . . . 45.00
Ice Cream fork 25.00

VINTAGE (ROGERS)

Baby spoon, bent-handled. 52.00
Butter spreader 20.00
Carving set, large, 3 pcs. 138.00
Cheese scoop, hollow handle 125.00
Chocolate muddler 170.00
Demitasse spoon. 18.00
Dinner fork 14.00
Food pusher. 48.00
Fruit spoon. 25.00
Gravy ladel 25.00
Ice cream fork 65.00
Iced tea spoon 75.00
Jelly knife. 75.00
Meat fork 35.00
Olive spoon, open bowl 44.00
Pastry fork 55.00
Salad fork 32.00
Seafood fork 16.00
Tablespoon 15.00
Youth set, 3 pcs. 65.00

STERLING SILVER (Flatware)

ALHAMBRA (WHITING MFG. CO.)

Berry spoon, 8¾" l. 100.00
Egg spoons, set of 10 . . . . 250.00
Grapefruit spoon 6.00
Mustard ladle 35.00
Teaspoon 13.00

ANTIQUE LILY ENGRAVED (WHITING MFG. CO.)

Berry spoon, 9" l. 130.00
Butter serving knife. 55.00
Cake saw 195.00

Dinner fork 26.00
Fish knife 45.00
Luncheon fork 30.00
Luncheon knife 20.00
Oyster ladle, 11½" l. 235.00
Serving spoon 48.00
Soup spoon, oval 30.00
Stuffing spoon 175.00
Tablespoon 50.00
Teaspoon 18.00

ARABESQUE (WHITING MFG. CO.)

Berry spoon 150.00
Berry spoon, oval, large, bright cut, matte finish, fluted bowl. 195.00
Cheese scoop, bright-cut, gold washed 350.00
Cracker scoop 225.00
Cream ladle 225.00
Demitasse spoon. 20.00
Dessert spoon 25.00
Dinner fork 45.00
Gravy ladle. 125.00
Luncheon fork 29.00
Pastry fork 85.00
Serving spoon w/gold-washed bowl . . 95.00
Soup spoon, oval 35.00
Sugar shell 58.00
Tablespoon 50.00
Teaspoon 18.00
Youth set, 2 pcs. 135.00

BEEKMAN (TIFFANY & CO.)

Butter 47.00
Butter, master size 84.00
Dessert spoon 38.00
Fish knife 165.00
Ice cream fork 32.00
Ice cream spoon 48.00
Salad spoon. 150.00
Salt spoon, master size 45.00
Tablespoon 60.00

BERRY (WHITING MFG. CO.)

Berry spoon 185.00
Demitasse spoon. 25.00
Dinner fork 45.00
Gravy ladle, gold-washed. 125.00
Olive fork 60.00
Tea caddy spoon 75.00

CANTERBURY (TOWLE MFG. CO.)

Almond scoop 85.00
Almond scoop, gold-washed 185.00

Citrus spoon 14.00
Confection server 125.00
Cream ladle 45.00
Dessert spoon 19.00
Ice tongs. 395.00
Luncheon fork, 7" l. 21.00
Olive fork 55.00
Punch ladle 375.00
Sardine fork 85.00
Serving spoon 37.00
Soup ladle 250.00
Strawberry fork 35.00
Teaspoon 8.00

CHARLES II (DOMINICK & HAFF)

Cocktail 20.00
Cold meat fork 100.00
Cream ladle 72.00
Demitasse spoon. 18.00
Dessert spoon 30.00
Gravy ladle. 129.00
Jelly knife. 189.00
Luncheon fork 23.00
Salt spoon, master. 27.00
Soup ladle, gold-washed bowl 250.00
Strawberry fork 35.00
Sugar shell. 35.00
Tablespoon 38.00
Teaspoon 20.00

DRESDEN (WHITING MFG. CO.)

Berry spoon. 118.00
Berry spoon, enameled 650.00
Cheese scoop, 8⅜" 155.00
Cucumber server . . . . 150.00 to 175.00
Dinner service: six each luncheon
  forks, tablespoons, salad forks,
  teaspoons, twelve demitasse
  spoons, one sugar spoon, two
  dinner spoons, 39 pcs. 1,010.00
Fish set . . . . 325.00 to 350.00
Lettuce fork 85.00
Meat fork (beef) 95.00
Nut spoon. 45.00
Salad fork. 65.00
Salad serving set, long handles 650.00
Soup ladle 350.00
Sugar shell. 43.00
Sugar sifter, gold-washed 95.00
Sugar tongs 40.00

ETON (R. WALLACE & SONS)

Bonbon spoon. 95.00
Carving fork, roast, 5" l. 32.00
Citrus spoon 22.00

Cocktail fork. 18.00
Cream ladle 50.00
Fish fork 50.00
Fish knife, 7⅛" l. 75.00
Fork, 7" l. 14.00
Fruit knife, 3¼" l. 30.00
Gravy ladle. 150.00
Gumbo spoon, 7" l. 47.00
Luncheon fork 46.00
Luncheon knife 36.00
Seafood fork 20.00
Serving spoon, pierced 59.00
Sugar tongs, small. 38.00

HERALDIC (WHITING MFG. CO.)

Asparagus fork . . . . 325.00 to 350.00
Dessert spoon 28.00
Dinner fork. 55.00
Dinner knife 45.00
Fish fork 150.00
Fish server. 195.00
Fruit spoon. 35.00
Ice cream server 240.00
Ice cream spoon 40.00
Jelly spoon. 40.00
Lettuce fork 55.00
Luncheon fork 32.00
Olive fork 73.00
Pastry fork, 3-tine. 45.00
Pickle fork, 3-tine 42.00
Preserve spoon 120.00
Sugar shell. 40.00
Sugar sifter 110.00
Teaspoon 18.00

HYPERION (WHITING MFG. CO.)

Berry spoon. 130.00
Cheese scoop 175.00
Demitasse spoon. 20.00
Ice cream server 135.00
Mustard ladle 85.00
Salad set, large 325.00
Sauce ladle, 6" l. 75.00
Strawberry fork 35.00
Sugar sifter 75.00
Sugar spoon 35.00
Sugar tongs 55.00
Teaspoon 31.00

IMPERIAL (WHITING MFG. CO.)

Beef fork. 68.00
Bonbon spoon. 47.00
Butter spreader 20.00
Cheese scoop . . . . 200.00 to 225.00
Cold meat fork. 90.00
Crumb knife 205.00

Demitasse spoon. 20.00
Dinner fork. 41.00
Fish serving set. 425.00
Fish slice 195.00
Gravy ladle. . . . . 150.00 to 200.00
Gumbo spoon 65.00
Ice cream spoon 195.00
Lettuce fork 150.00
Melon spoon 48.00
Olive fork, long handle. 35.00
Pastry fork, 6½" l.. . . . . 65.00
Pickle fork 58.00
Pie server, silver blade. 225.00
Punch ladle 450.00
Salad serving fork, long handled. . . . 285.00
Salad serving set. 295.00
Salad serving set, long handled 650.00
Salad spoon. 135.00
Salt spoon, individual size 25.00
Sardine fork. . . . . 100.00 to 125.00
Sauce ladle. 72.00
Soup ladle 325.00
Strawberry fork 45.00
Sugar shell. 75.00
Sugar sifter 155.00
Sugar tongs 65.00
Tablespoon . . . . 50.00 to 75.00

IRIAN (R. WALLACE & SONS)

Berry spoon. 200.00
Bonbon spoon. 95.00
Bouillon spoon 95.00
Butter serving knife. 85.00
Butter spreader 110.00
Cold meat fork. 150.00
Cream ladle 110.00
Dinner fork. 54.00
Fish fork. 75.00
Fish serving fork. . . . . 250.00 to 275.00
Gravy ladle. 200.00
Jelly cake server 395.00
Luncheon fork 42.00
Pancake server 250.00
Sugar spoon 95.00
Tablespoon 72.00
Teaspoon 30.00

JAPANESE (AUDUBON)

Coffee spoon. 55.00
Demitasse spoon. 50.00
Luncheon fork 95.00
Tablespoon 135.00

KING ALBERT (WHITING MFG. CO.)

Berry spoon. 55.00

Berry spoon, large. 120.00
Bonbon spoon. 31.00
Bouillon spoon 12.00
Butter spreader, flat handle. 15.00
Citrus spoon 18.00
Cocktail fork. 18.00
Cold meat fork. 51.00
Cream ladle 31.00
Dinner fork. 16.00
Gravy ladle. 43.00
Lemon fork. 20.00
Luncheon fork 16.00
Olive spoon 30.00
Pie fork. 35.00
Salad fork. 26.00
Sauce ladle. 20.00
Sugar spoon 21.00
Sugar tongs 28.00
Tablespoon 41.00
Teaspoon 13.00

LA REINE (REED & BARTON)

Berry spoon, large. 100.00
Butter spreader, master. 65.00
Crumber 125.00
Gravy ladle. 50.00
Ice cream fork 15.00
Jelly server. 140.00
Luncheon forks, set of 6 . . . . 150.00
Salad fork. 20.00
Salad set. 325.00
Serving spoon, pierced. . . . 75.00 to 100.00
Tablespoon 48.00
Teaspoon 23.00

MAZARIN (DOMINICK & HAFF)

Asparagus fork 235.00
Asparagus server 350.00
Berry spoon, gold-washed bowl 269.00
Bouillon spoon 17.00
Cold meat fork. 91.00
Dessert spoon 36.00
Dinner fork. 34.00
Gravy ladle. 90.00
Ice cream spoon 29.00
Lettuce fork 73.00
Luncheon fork 30.00
Luncheon knife 20.00
Mustard ladle. 95.00
Seafood fork 20.00
Soup ladle 350.00
Soup spoon, oval. 25.00
Sugar spoon 39.00
Sugar tongs 85.00
Tablespoon 63.00
Teaspoon 15.00

NO. 10 (DOMINICK & HAFF)

Berry spoon 100.00
Berry spoon, gold-washed bowl 125.00
Berry spoon, large 185.00
Butter serving knife. 55.00
Butter spreader, flat handle. 45.00
Butter spreader, master, gold-
  washed 55.00
Chocolate spoon, 9" l. 38.00
Claret spoon, 15½" l. 175.00
Fish set, gold-washed 395.00
Fried egg server 375.00
Fruit spoon. 45.00
Gravy ladle, gold-washed. 120.00
Gumbo spoon 29.00
Ice cream spoon 30.00
Lettuce fork 75.00
Luncheon fork 30.00
Pie server, pierced 375.00
Preserve spoon, gold-washed. 80.00
Salad fork. 58.00
Salad serving set. 240.00
Seafood fork 27.00
Soup ladle, large 400.00
Sugar sifter 80.00
Sugar tongs 50.00
Tablespoon 53.00
Tomato server 95.00

PERSIAN (TIFFANY & CO.)

Berry serving spoon 225.00
Butter spreader 65.00
Crumb knife, large 650.00
Demitasse spoon. 30.00
Dinner fork. 60.00
Fish serving knife 495.00
Fish slice 425.00
Gravy ladle. 183.00
Ice cream fork 50.00
Ice cream spoon 58.00
Jelly spoon. 130.00
Luncheon fork 45.00
Luncheon knife 50.00
Olive spoon, long handle 195.00
Pate knife 95.00
Pie server, silver blade. 495.00
Serving spoon 118.00
Soup ladle 550.00
Sugar shell. 110.00
Sugar tongs 120.00
Tablespoon 83.00
Teaspoon 34.00

PLYMOUTH (GORHAM MFG.)

Asparagus fork 230.00
Berry spoon, small. 70.00

Bouillon spoon 8.00
Butter serving knife. 30.00
Cocktail fork. 11.00
Dinner fork 15.00
Dinner knife 23.00
Ice spoon, pierced 25.00
Iced tea spoon 20.00
Lettuce fork 28.00
Mustard ladle 45.00
Olive spoon, pierced 24.00
Pie server 185.00
Salad serving fork 95.00
Soup ladle 200.00
Soup spoon, oval bowl. 16.00
Sugar tongs 30.00

POMPADOUR (WHITING MFG. CO.)

Berry fork. 43.00
Berry spoon, large 150.00
Bouillon ladle. 80.00
Cheese scoop, small 85.00
Chocolate set: muddler & 12 spoons
  in fitted box, 13 pcs. 425.00
Citrus spoons, set of 12 . . . . 423.00
Cocktail fork. 22.00
Cold meat fork 100.00
Cream soup spoon 35.00
Dessert spoon 22.00
Dinner fork. 40.00
Gravy ladle. 95.00
Jelly spoon. 18.00
Luncheon fork 30.00
Olive spoon, long handle, filigree
  work, gold-washed bowl 30.00
Salad fork. 36.00
Sardine tongs 125.00
Sauce ladle. 45.00
Serving fork, gold-washed tines, 9" l. . . 130.00
Soup ladle 225.00
Soup spoon 30.00
Stuffing spoon. 325.00
Sugar shell 25.00
Sugar tongs 40.00
Teaspoon 15.00

ROCOCO (DOMINICK & HAFF)

Bouillon spoon 25.00
Chocolate spoon. 45.00
Fish serving knife 225.00
Fish set. 450.00
Grapefruit spoon 26.00
Ice cream spoon 35.00
Luncheon fork 25.00
Macaroni server. 425.00
Orange knife 45.00

Parfait spoon 25.00
Pie server, silver blade 150.00
Salt spoon, master size 30.00
Sardine fork 90.00
Seafood fork 22.00
Serving spoon 35.00
Stuffing spoon, 14" l 350.00

VERSAILLES (GORHAM MFG. CO.)

Asparagus 634.00
Berry fork, 2-tine 55.00
Berry spoon, small 110.00
Bonbon spoon 87.00
Bonbon spoon, gold-washed bowl . . 225.00
Bouillon spoon 33.00
Butter, master 100.00
Butter spreader 36.00
Cake knife . . . . 350.00 to 400.00
Cheese scoop, large 210.00
Cheese scoop, small 95.00
Cocktail fork 31.00
Coffee spoon 18.00
Cold meat fork 115.00
Cream ladle 85.00
Cream soup 65.00
Crumb knife 350.00
Demitasse spoon 27.00
Dessert fork 56.00
Dinner fork 55.00

Versailles Pattern

Dinner service: 12 each dinner
  knives, lunch knives, salad forks,
  bouillon spoons, dessert spoons,

dinner forks, lunch forks, butter
spreaders, demitasse spoons, 24
teaspoons, 6 tablespoons, pair of
salad servers & 1 each butter knife,
jelly spoon, serving fork, sauce
ladle & berry spoon; in fitted
wooden chest, 145 pcs. (ILLUS.
bottom of prev. column) 10,350.00
Fish serving set, 2 pcs. 475.00
Fish slice, gold-washed 335.00
Food pusher 110.00
Fruit knife 35.00
Fruit spoon 32.00
Iced tea spoon 45.00
Jelly spoon, gold-washed bowl 50.00
Meat fork 145.00
Orange knife 60.00
Pickle fork 65.00
Pie server, silver blade 295.00
Preserve spoon 85.00
Salad fork 56.00
Salad serving set, gold-washed
  bowls 350.00
Salt spoon, master 66.00
Sardine fork 130.00
Sugar spoon 63.00
Sugar spoon, gold-washed 55.00
Sugar tongs 84.00
Tablespoon 62.00
Teaspoon 23.00

WAVE EDGE (TIFFANY & CO.)

Berry spoon, kidney shaped bowl . . . 350.00
Breakfast knife 55.00
Butter knife, flat handle 40.00
Cheese knife w/picks 150.00
Cheese scoop 250.00
Citrus spoon 60.00
Coffee spoon, gold-washed bowl 35.00
Dinner fork 83.00
Dinner knife 80.00
Fish knife 70.00
Grapefruit spoon, gold-washed bowl . 55.00
Ice cream spoon, ruffled edge 60.00
Luncheon fork 59.00
Pate knife 65.00
Pickle fork 75.00
Salad fork 45.00
Sauce ladle, double pour 135.00
Sorbet spoon, ruffled 48.00
Sugar shell 65.00
Sugar sifter 195.00
Tablespoon 87.00
Teaspoon 46.00

WAVERLY (R. WALLACE & SONS)

Berry spoon 60.00
Butter knife, master size 35.00
Butter pick 69.00
Butter serving knife, flat handle 22.00
Butter spreader, flat handle 19.00
Cake saw 75.00
Cold meat fork, 8¼" l. 67.00
Demitasse spoon. 15.00
Dinner fork 20.00
Dinner knife 26.00
Fish fork 45.00
Honey spoon 75.00
Lettuce fork 85.00
Mustard ladle 45.00
Sardine fork 50.00
Sherbet spoon 15.00
Spoon, oval bowl 18.00
Strawberry fork 25.00
Sugar spoon 32.00
Tablespoon 26.00
Teaspoon 13.00

TIN & TOLE

Cache pots, tole, gently flaring cylindrical body w/a raised top band below the deeply scalloped upright rim, the body & rim decorated w/neoclassical decoration in black & gilt on a red ground, Europe, 19th c., 8¼" d., 6¾" h., pr. 1,725.00

Candle box, cov., tin, hanging-type, horizontal cylinder w/long hinged top cover below the long pointed backplate w/hanging hole, worn brown japanning, 10¼" l. (some battering & damage, one crest support missing) 116.00

Candle mold, tin, eight-tube, rectangular flanged top w/loop end handle, base of tubes joined by arched feet, 19th c., 11¼" h. 303.00

Candle sconce, tin, hanging-type, the high backplate w/a rounded scalloped knobby border above a panel w/a raised vine above the half-round ring-molded socket holder, light rust, 14" h. 495.00

Cheese sieve, tin, heart-shaped w/overall punched holes w/a starburst central design, hanging ring resoldered, 19th c., 6" h. 358.00

Coffee urn, tole, worn black paint w/gold striping & floral decoration w/city scene, 19¾" h. 358.00

Coffeepot, cov., tole, tall tapering cylindrical body w/a hinged domed cover w/curled tin finial, angled stick spout & C-form ribbon handle, japanned ground, the cover decorated w/a yellow petaled flower, the sides w/a wide yellow band below the rim w/a red & black berry design, the sides decorated w/a large round reserve w/a cream ground & a large red, green, yellow & black floral pinwheel design, the reserve outlined in a yellow feather-like design, mid-19th c., 6⅛" d., 8⅞" h. (minor wear). 900.00

Coffeepot, cov., tole, tall slender tapering cylindrical body w/hinged domed cover, angled spout & C-form strap handle, original dark brown japanning w/stylized floral bands around top & base in yellow, white, red, blue & black, 10½" h. (wear, old paint touchup). 605.00

Deed box, tole, domed w/very worn original japanning w/white band & stylized floral decoration in red, green, yellow & black, 8⅞" l. (small hole in one flower in front band) . . . 204.00

Document box, cov., tole, rectangular w/deep sides & a hinged domed cover w/a cast brass bail handle, japanned ground, the cover w/yellow band striping forming a rectangular reserve, the sides & lid w/yellow feather designs, the front decorated w/a wide band w/a scalloped bottom edge smoke-decorated on a white ground w/red, yellow, green & black floral designs, simple yellow scalloped line design across the bottom of the box on the front, the sides w/yellow feather-like designs, tin hinged hasp on cover, mid-19th c., 4½ x 8⅞", 5¾" h. (some wear) . . 575.00

Tole Document Box

Document box, cov., tole, rectangular w/low domed hinged cover w/wire bail, hasp at front, original dark brown japanning decorated w/stylized florals in red, yellow, white & faded green, minor wear, 10" l. (ILLUS. bottom of previous column) **935.00**

Swiss Tole Figure of a Man

Figures of a man & woman, tole, each in traditional peasant dress & carrying a cylindrical kindling basket on their back, polychrome decoration, stepped round base, Switzerland, 19th c., 14" h., pr. (ILLUS. of one) **2,530.00**

Jardinieres, tole, each of oval three-tiered deep-sided graduated form w/each tier decorated in the chinoiserie style in tones of cream, brown & gilt on a teal blue ground, Europe, 19th c., 7" l., 13" h., pr. . . . **920.00**

Monteiths, tole, oval w/deep sides w/deeply undulating rim, painted w/neoclassical decoration in black & gilding on a dark green ground, Europe, 19th c., 12¾" l., 4½" h., pr. **1,495.00**

Flower-decorated Tole Mug

Mug, tole, tall slightly tapering cylindrical body w/a strap rim handle, worn original dark brown japanning w/a large single stylized blossom on the front in red, yellow & white, 5¾" h. (ILLUS.) **963.00**

Plate warmer, tin, two open tiers & a loop lifting handle, painted red w/gilt stenciled decoration, 19th c., 27½" h. **259.00**

Tea caddies, tole, worn original black paint w/gilded decoration, larger w/two compartments, 4⅜" d., 5¾" h., pr. **143.00**

Tray, tole, rectangular w/cut corners, flanged rim & pierced end rim handles, the center decorated w/a scene of a ship in ice flying the American flag, titled "Ship Red Jacket in the ice 1854," red & green rim, 19th c., 16½" l. (several rim seams loose, hanger added) . . **330.00**

Early European Tole Tray

Tray, tole, rectangular w/rounded corners, angled edges w/end hand holes, the center decorated w/a garden landscape w/classical ruins & figures, Europe, early 19th c., paint loss, 30" l. (ILLUS.) **1,955.00**

Tray, tole, oval, decorated en grisaille w/historical vignettes centering an oval mythological scene, continuing to a slanted border band w/scrolling & fruiting grapevines, raised on a later conforming stand, England, early 19th c., 19 x 30" . . **1,092.00**

Urns, tole, cov., Chinese Export-style decoration on a black-painted ground, shaped rectangular form, leaf-scrolled side handles, comforming cover, raised on tapering pedestal base, England, late 19th c., 10" h., pr. **2,300.00**

Urns, tole, Empire-style, rectangular flared body painted w/allegorical scenes & musical trophies, raised on stylized winged paw feet on faux marble plinth, painted on black ground & highlighted w/gilding, 11" h., pr. **1,955.00**

MILITARIA & WARTIME MEMORABILIA

CIVIL WAR

Medal, metal, reunion of Union & Confederate soldiers at Gettysburg, Union soldier missing hand but shaking hands w/a Confederate veteran missing a leg, reverse shows inscribed "Eternal Light Peace Memorial," early 20th c. **$75.00**

Pinback button, celluloid, Grand Army of the Republic reunion, illustration of a graveside scene, early 1900s, 1¾" d. **100.00**

Pinback button, celluloid w/fabric ribbon, "Confederate Veteran Reunion - 1917 - Washington. D.C.," photo of the United States Capitol, reads "27th United Confederate Veterans - 32 Sons of Veterans Reunion - Washington, D.C. 1917," 1½" d. **50.00**

Early G.A.R. Pinback Button

Pinback button, round celluloid printed in color w/a Grand Army of the Republic eagle, flag & star logo printed w/"Grand Army of the Republic - Veteran - 1861-1865," an attached red, white & blue short ribbon, late 19th - early 20th c., some staining on bottom, 1½" d. (ILLUS.). **25.00**

Reunion medal, "Confederate Veterans Reunion - Macon Georgia - Oct. 26, 1887," w/portrait of Jefferson Davis & "Confederate States of America," red, white & blue fabric attachment, 1½" d. **125.00**

SPANISH-AMERICAN WAR

Program, souvenir of the three-day celebration of Admiral Dewey's arrival in New York City, dated September 28-30, 1899, cover w/American eagle w/flag, includes various events, parade route & story of Dewey's life, 16 pp. **125.00**

Stickpin, replica of a small bullet, brass & lead, on original small cardboard card reading "Sample of bullet that will Free Cuba" **125.00**

WORLD WAR I

Book, "History and Rhymes of the Lost Battalion," by "Buck Private" McCollumn, 1919, self-published, leatherette cover w/gold & black printing. **50.00**

"In Flanders Fields" Book

Book, "In Flanders Fields," by Colonel John McCrae, 1919, Knickerbocker Press, New York, New York, dark blue covers w/gold printing (ILLUS.) **100.00**

Book, "The United States in the Great War," by Willis J. Abbot, 1919, Doubleday and Company, colorful battlefield scene against a brown ground **100.00**

World War I Certificate

Certificate, paper, printed in red & black w/a figure of Britannia & soldiers, given to a disabled veteran, Private Edward Willis of the 15th Canadian Infantry Battalion, honorably discharged in 1919 (ILLUS.) **20.00**

Edith Cavell Commemorative Plaque

Plaque, shield-shaped, hanging-type, molded plaster of Paris, molded w/the bust portrait of Nurse Edith Cavell, shot by the Germans as a spy, scroll reads "1914 - 1918 - Remember" above her name, white w/gold & red trim, England, 3¼ x 5¼" (ILLUS.). **15.00**

Plaque, shield-shaped, hanging-type, molded plaster of Paris, the indented front w/an inscription on a banner above a kneeling soldier flanked by two pink & green poppies above the dates "1914 - 1918" flanking a short poem titled "The Extra," marked on the back "Sale of this article is benefiting a returned soldier. Price 25¢," also printed in French, British **15.00**

Two World War I Postcards

Postcards, printed in color, one German showing two German military men enclosed in a leafy

wreath w/ribbon, the British one showing a battlefield scene, part of a series about the Royal Medical Corp., each (ILLUS.) **20.00**

Stereo Card from World War I

Stereoptican card, photograph on cardboard, scene showing the return of the American World War I Unknown Soldier, by the Keystone View Company, New York (ILLUS.) . . **40.00**

WORLD WAR II

World War II Baby Ruth Ad

Advertisement, "Baby Ruth" candy bar, color-printed ad on the back of a World War II era comic book, promotes "energy" obtained from the candy w/a battle scene at the top, also promotes buying War Bonds & Stamps (ILLUS.) **25.00**

Blackout kit, contains a new material that would glow in the dark, includes a booklet, rolls of blackout material, card & Civil Defense insignias, by Vernon Company of Newton, Iowa, complete kit **200.00**

World War II Series Book

Book, "Dave Dawson with the Air
Corps -The War Adventure Series,"
by Robert Bowen, numerous other
titles in the series, green cloth
cover w/black printing (ILLUS.) **10.00**

Book, "Fighters for Freedom," one of
a series published by Whitman
Publishing Co., Racine, Wisconsin,
various titles including "Kitty Carter
of the Canteen Corps," "Nancy
Dale - Army Nurse," "March Anson
and Scoot Bailey of the United
States Navy," etc., green covers,
5½ x 8", each **25.00**

Booklet, Coca-Cola premium, "Know
Your War Planes," 1943 .... **100.00**

Booklet, "Let's Consider Jobs -
Newspaper Work and Freelance
Writing," one of a series of booklets
published to assist returning war
veterans looking for a new career,
yellow paper printed in black,
Canadian Legion Educational
Services **5.00**

War Bond Shares Booklet

Booklet, War Bond shares, titled
"Victory Shares For A 'Miracle
Home' of Our Own," printed in red,
white & dark blue w/a black & white
vignette of a modernistic new home
to save for (ILLUS.) **10.00**

Books, "Combat Scientists - Science
in World War II," by Lincoln
Thiesmeyer & John Burchard, a
series commemorating various
World War II scientists & weapons
experts, Little, Brown & Company,
September 1947, each volume **25.00**

1944 Canadian Calendar

Calendar, 1944, stiff paper printed in
red, white & blue w/a tinted blue
battle scene on a small complete
calendar pad, printed in English &
French, Canada (ILLUS.) **50.00**

Rare "Superman #24" Comic Book

Comic Book, "Superman #24,"
September - October 1943, color
cover featuring Superman holding
a large American flag (ILLUS.)... **1,100.00**

Cookbook, "Daughters of the
American Revolution Cookbook,"
1943 .... **20.00**

Cookbook, "Stove Pilot - Favorite
Recipes from Maxwell," recipes
from wives of personnel at Maxwell

Air Force Base, Alabama, pale blue printed in black spiral-bound covers 20.00

Cookbook, "Your Share" Betty Crocker cookbook w/recipes geared to ingredient shortages, dust jacket printed in red, white & blue 15.00

Doll, Air Force woman, cloth body w/composition arms & head, dressed in appropriate Canadian uniform, 1942, Reliable Toy Company of Toronto, 18" h. 250.00

Doll, Army soldier, cloth body & composition arms & head, dressed in a Canadian uniform, Reliable Toy Company of Toronto, 13" h. . . 115.00

Doll, Army soldier, cloth body & composition arms & head, dressed in a Canadian uniform, Reliable Toy Company of Toronto, 18" h. . . 225.00

Doll, Canadian Army woman, dressed in appropriate uniform, part of a series which includes an Air Force woman & a nurse, composition, Reliable Toy Company of Toronto, 8" h., each . . . 50.00

Doll, Navy sailor, cloth body & composition arms & head, dressed in a Canadian blue navy uniform w/hat, Reliable Toy Company of Toronto, 16" h. 175.00

Doll, nurse, cloth body w/composition arms & head, wearing nurse hat & a Red Cross on the uniform, Reliable Toy Company of Toronto, 1942, 18" h. 150.00

World War II Movie Promotion Hat

Hat, movie promotional piece for "A Yank in The R.A.F." starring Tyrone Power & Betty Grable, 1941, give-away item at showings of the movie, blue cloth w/gold printing, regular hat size (ILLUS.) . . . 75.00

Junior Air Raid Warden Kit, shown advertised in color on the back of a World War II vintage child's comic book, the coupon shown was sent to the Kay Novelty Company of New York, New York, the original

Junior Air Raid Warden Kit Ad

kit cost $1.69 & included a helmet, note pad, gas mask & other items, rare, complete kit (ILLUS. of advertisement only) 2,000.00

Magazine, "Life," issue published shortly after the war ended w/the whole issue devoted to war wounds & surgery performed on veterans 75.00

Magazine, "Look," March 11, 1941, article titled "Hitler's Plan to Invade England and how Churchill expects to stop him" 20.00

Magazine, "Model Airplane News," November 1943, ads for Modelcraft's B-17 Bomber, Catalina Flying Boat or Japanese Zero, complete 15.00

Model airplane kits, wooden, Cleveland Models of Cleveland, Ohio model airplanes including a P-40, Lockheed Hudson Bomber, P-51 Mustang, Stuka, etc., each kit starting at 40.00

Movie lobby card, black & white printed cardboard, for "Range Busters" by Monogram, starring "Crash" Corrigan, front w/scenes from the movie, both front & back w/ads promoting the purchase of War Bonds & Stamps, 8 x 10" 40.00

Pillow, commemorative, satin, decorated w/"United States Coast Guard, Cape May, New Jersey," red rose border, light yellow w/yellow fringe, motto "Sweetheart" & action scene of PT boats firing on airplanes w/a blimp overhead, 16 x 19" 25.00

"V" for Victory Pin

Pin, metal, figural, a "V" for Victory framing a small British Bulldog figure, English (ILLUS.) **25.00**

Postcard, color printed scenic front, back postdated 1942 & carrying a green stamp, one of a series of wartime stamps, top condition. **1.00**

Poster, propaganda-type, "Buy War Bonds," paratroopers on the ground firing machine gun w/others floating to the ground, 16 x 20" **200.00**

Poster, propaganda-type, "Defend American Freedom," scene of Uncle Sam w/factories in the background, 16 x 20" **100.00**

Cracker Jack Premium Cards

Premium cards, set of 50 aircraft cards used as Cracker Jack premiums during the war, each shows a different Allied warplane, complete set in top condition (ILLUS. of part) **350.00**

Atomic Bomb Skill Puzzle

Puzzle, skill-type, "Drop the Atomic Bomb on Japan," metal frame w/clear cover, printed in black & yellow w/a bomb & a map of Japan, three small metal "bombs" to fit into little holes by Hiroshima, Nagasaki & Tokyo, A.C. Gilbert Company, 1946 (ILLUS.). **400.00**

Ring, Lone Ranger premium, brass, "Marine Corps," photo of the Lone Ranger & Tonto inside, 1942 . . . . . **850.00**

Stamp album, General Mills premium, "War Album of Victory Battles," spaces for stamps inside, 1942 . . . . **150.00**

Toy planes, Wheaties premiums, cut-out cardboard set of toy planes, 1944, set of 7 . . . . **100.00**

Reliable Toy Soldiers

Toy soldiers, plastic figure on a metal base, various poses, produced by Reliable Toy Company of Toronto, Canada, brown & black on green base, 2½" h., each (ILLUS. of group) **5.00**

KOREAN WAR

1951 Li'l Abner Comic Book

Comic book, "Al Capp's Li'l Abner Joins the Navy," color cover picture of Abner in uniform w/Daisy Mae & Mammy, Toby Press, 1951 (ILLUS.). **125.00**

Card set, "Freedom's War," set showing scenes from World War II & the Korean War, Topps, 1950s,

COLD WAR

"Freedom's War" Card

printed in color, each 2¹⁄₁₆ x 2⅝",
complete set of 203 (ILLUS. of
one) **450.00**
Card set, "Power for Peace," set
picturing various uses for atomic
power, Topps, 1950s, 2½ x 3¼",
complete set of 96 . . . . **300.00**

Oak Ridge Postcard Booklet

Postcard folder, "Oak Ridge,
Tennessee - 'Home of The Atomic
Bomb,'" printed in color, 1950s
(ILLUS.). **100.00**

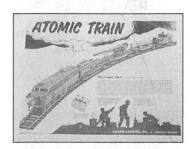

Atomic Train Advertisement

Toy train set, the "Atomic Train,"
produced by Kusan-Auburn
Company in the 1950s, includes an
engine & three cars, including an
"atomic cannon" w/a caboose,
complete set in top condition
(ILLUS. of advertisement) **500.00**

VIETNAM WAR

"Design For Survival" Comic Book

Comic book, "Design for Survival,"
by General Thomas S. Power,
colorful cover w/various warplanes,
American Security Press, 1968
(ILLUS.) **25.00**
Training manual, "Officer
Candidates School - Marine Corps
Schools - Quantico, Virginia - U.S.
Rifle 7.62MM M 14 - Student
Handout," 1967 . . . . **15.00**

WARTIME ANNIVERSARY
COMMEMORATIVES

Cigarette lighter set, limited edition
set to commemorate the 50th
Anniversary of D-Day, decorated
w/an antique brass medallion & a
black crackle finish duplicating the
World War II version, set of four in
a tin holder, each w/a different
portrait including Eisenhower,
Montgomery, DeGaulle & Lt.
General Bradley, Zippo, 1994,
the set **300.00**
Painting, oil on canvas, "Against All
Odds," by Robert Taylor, shows
U-Boat & PBY **295.00**
Painting, oil on canvas, "Scaling the
Alps," by Robert Bailey, shows
B-17s flying **125.00**
Sub-machine gun, Thompson
model, commemorates the 50th
Anniversary of D-Day, reads
"In Honor of the D-Day Invasion -
Operation Overlord - Sixth of June
1944," limited edition **2,000.00**
Tee shirt, 1962, commemorating the
25th anniversary of the United
States Air Force, reads "Pride in
the Past - Faith in the Future," front
w/Air Force pilot w/jet & rocket in
background, wording printed in red,
white & blue **50.00**

MINIATURES (REPLICAS)

Blanket chest, painted wood, six-board construction, the hinged rectangular top inscribed on the underside "Sam'l Hamblin made this for Grandma Forber Margarets Great Grandmother," dated 1816, 2¾ x 4¾", 4" h. (losses to leather hinge, lid loose, very minor paint wear) **$1,840.00**

Chippendale Blanket Chest

Blanket chest, Chippendale style, inlaid cherry, hinged rectangular top w/molded edge opening to a well & case w/a false drawer over a long drawer w/a divided interior, resting on scroll-cut bracket feet, Mid-Atlantic States, 19th c., 9 x 13¾", 14" h. (ILLUS.) **2,875.00**

Candlesticks, pressed flint glass, paneled baluster-form shaft w/a tulip-form socket & round foot, probably Boston & Sandwich Glass Co., 19th c., electric blue, 2" h., pr. **358.00**

Chamberstick, pressed lacy glass, a round dished base centered by a short columnar stem w/flaring socket, loop handle at one side of base, probably European, amethyst, 19th c., 2" h. **132.00**

Chest of drawers, Federal, mahogany, rectangular top above a case w/four long drawers above a scalloped apron continuing to splayed bracket feet, 19th c., 9 x 14½", 12½" h. **575.00**

Federal Miniature Chest of Drawers

Chest of drawers, Federal country-style, painted & decorated, a rectangular top above four long drawers, serpentine apron continuing to bracket feet, overall grain painting, early 19th c., 10¾ x 20", 18¾" h. (ILLUS.) **5,175.00**

Desk, Chippendale style slant-front, mahogany, a narrow top over a hinged slant front opening to an interior w/two small drawers, the case w/three long graduated drawers, molded base & bracket feet, 19th c., 7 x 12¾", 11¾" h. . . **1,265.00**

Sideboard, Classical, mahogany, a rectangular top above two frieze drawers over a shaped & paneled deep drawer flanked by columns, resting on scroll feet, second quarter 19th c., 8¾ x 13", 12" h. **1,092.00**

MOVIE MEMORABILIA

COSTUMES

Baseball costume, woman's, "A League of Their Own," 1990s, comprising a yellow cotton tunic dress w/embroidered label to the front "City of Racine Belles," a pair of brown leggings & a baseball hat w/an "R" on the front, together w/a letter of authenticity, the group . . . **$690.00**

Ben Hur Slave Loin Cloth

Charlton Heston, "Ben Hur," MGM, 1959, loin cloth, used in scene w/Ben Hur as a slave rower, raw silk, w/a vintage color movie still of Heston in the loin cloth & other photos, the group (ILLUS. of loin cloth) **10,350.00**

Clark Gable, "Key to The City," 1949, double-breasted suit, navy beaded striped wool comprising jacket & trousers, striped shirt w/monogram tag, together w/navy polka dot tie, designed by Irene, jacket w/Metro-

Goldwyn-Mayer label marked "C.L. Gable 1463640l," pants also labeled, the group **2,415.00**

Dorothy Lamour, "Her Jungle Love," 1938, sarong, rose red tie-dyed one-piece style gathered at the waist, w/two photos of Lamour wearing it, the group **4,600.00**

Early Elizabeth Taylor Child's Dress

Elizabeth Taylor, "National Velvet," 1944, child's dress, red figured shantung decorated in stylized florals w/short sleeves, Peter Pan collar & pocketed skirt, designed by Irene, w/bias tag marked "Elizabeth Taylor 1315" & MGM paper tag (ILLUS.) **4,025.00**

Errol Flynn, "The Adventures of Robin Hood," Warner's, 1938, shirt of green cotton, long sleeves w/collar designed by Milo Anderson, costumer's tag marked "5905" attached inside collar, framed together w/a movie still & 12 other stills **5,175.00**

Gene Kelly, "An American in Paris," 1951, soft black leather "loafer" style shoes worn by Kelly in the film, mounted & framed w/a signed letter from Kelly, frame 15 x 26" . . **3,220.00**

Grace Kelly, "Mogambo," MGM, 1953, a two-piece coffee-colored suit possibly from this production, a gaucho/skirt w/a cloth tag at waist reading "1616-2614 Grace Kelly" in black ink, tailored top fitted at the waist w/a self-belt, designed w/large lapels & deep V-neck front w/cloth tag in right arm reading "Grace Kelly 1616-2613" **1,265.00**

Judy Garland, "The Good Old Summertime," MGM, 1949, Edwardian-style blouse & skirt of ecru cotton, trimmed w/black & cream striped taffeta sash detailing, the petticoat & blouse stamped "MGM Wardrobe," the blouse marked "1440 Judy Garland," w/two additional tags, the group **2,760.00**

"Gigi" Bathing Ensemble

Leslie Caron, "Gigi," 1958, bathing ensemble designed by Cecil Beaton, blue bather dress w/short sleeves & sailor collar, trimmed w/bands of white piping, Kartinska of Paris tag marked "L. Caron," matching pantalettes w/bias label marked "L. Caron," mob cap & belt, the group (ILLUS. of part) **2,760.00**

Marlon Brando, "Mutiny on the Bounty," 1962, worn by Brando as Fletcher Christian, includes an 18th c. style wool cutaway coat trimmed w/brass anchor buttons, cream piping at collar, cuffs & front panels, w/lace cuffs, cream-colored vest, white linen breeches, linen V-neck shirt & silk hose, the coat, pants & vest w/MGM Studio labels marked "M. Brando 1769," shirt monogrammed "MB," the group **11,500.00**

Natalie Wood, "West Side Story," 1961, Chinese Red cotton jersey dress w/scoop neck & short sleeves, the seams run down the length of the front & meet two pleats at the hem, w/letter of authenticity **3,450.00**

Sam Neil "Jurassic Park" Outfit

Sam Neil, "Jurassic Park," 1993, outfit of Dr. Alan Grant, includes blue denim shirt & khaki pants studio airbrushed to appear mud-soaked, both garments marked inside "Sam," w/four photos of Neil in the role & an original press kit, the group (ILLUS. of outfit)...... **4,600.00**

LOBBY CARDS

"Alien," title card,1979, near mint **25.00**
"Bad Sister," starring Humphrey Bogart, 1931................ **1,200.00**
"It - The Terror from Beyond Space," 1958 .... **295.00**
"Queen of Outer Space," 1958..... **250.00**
"Return of Dr. X," starring Humphrey Bogart, 1939 .... **875.00**
"She," science fiction, 1948 .... **95.00**
"The Colossus of New York," science fiction, 1958 .... **295.00**
"The Time Machine," 1960 .... **295.00**
"The Two Mrs. Carrolls," starring Humphrey Bogart, 1947 .... **95.00**

MISCELLANEOUS

Address book, personal book of Dorothy Lamour, binder-style w/monogrammed needlepoint cover, dozens of famous Hollywood stars............... **517.00**

Armchair from Shirley Temple Movie

Armchair, from "The Little Princess" starring Shirley Temple, 1939, Victorian-style w/original green velvet check fabric on the ornately carved ebonized frame, Gothic details & gold-painted scroll & floral designs, marked on the inside frame "20th C-Fox - A-433 - 11-5-35" & "A18," w/a video of the movie & two shots of Temple w/the chair, the group (ILLUS. of chair)...... **3,737.00**
Army I.D. card, Dorothy Lamour's "War Department U.S. Army Air Forces," issued "11/9/44," laminated photo I.D. w/her picture on the front & right index finger print on the back **632.00**
Attaché case, James Bond toy model, complete, MPC, 1964, very fine.................... **550.00**

Book, "Gone With The Wind," by Margaret Mitchell, autographed presentation copy for Governor James H. Price of Virginia, over 100 signatures including Clark Gable, Vivien Leigh, Leslie Howard & Olivia de Havilland, w/a custom-fitted leather slipcase **5,175.00**
Candy box, "Butterfinger," showing Natalie Wood in "Gypsy," 1950s, very fine..................... **220.00**
Cigar, George Burns used for his imprint at Mann's Chinese Theater, November 26, 1979, cigar encased in glass, exhibits some of the residue from the cement, cigar inscribed w/the date, w/letter of authenticity & two signed photos of Burns, the group............. **1,380.00**
Close Encounters of the Third Kind game, board-type, Parker Bros., 1978, sealed, near mint........... **25.00**
Clothing outfit, owned by Marilyn Monroe, a black silk crepe dress w/front drape panel, a pair of black high-heeled 'alligator' pumps from Saks Fifth Avenue, a 'gold' bracelet engraved "Marilyn Love Joe," & a black & white photograph of Monroe, the group **5,175.00**
Draft script, Three Stooges feature "Shot in the Frontier," Columbia, dated "October 13, 1953," the script w/the character Shemp **575.00**
Game, board-type, "Sons of Hercules," Milton Bradley, 1966, very fine...................... **75.00**
Game, "Gracie Allen Murder Case," board-type, Milton Bradley, 1939, very good.................... **150.00**
Handkerchief, white cotton, owned by Marilyn Monroe, embroidered w/the initial "M," together w/a letter of authenticity, 2 pcs............. **920.00**
Jigsaw puzzle, James Bond "Goldfinger," Milton Bradley, 1965, very good. **15.00**
Letter, handwritten in pencil, from Greta Garbo to Gilbert Roland while he was in the service, the envelope w/postal stamp dated 1943, 2 pcs. **3,220.00**

John Candy "Spaceballs" Life Mask

Life mask, made for John Candy for "Spaceballs," 1987, plaster mask of Candy in character, orangish brown paint w/dark nose (ILLUS.).. **172.00**

Magazine, "Official James Dean Anniversary Scrapbook," Dell, 1956, very good. **25.00**

Money clip, silver & 'gold,' No. 21 horseshoe-shaped, owned by Joan Crawford, together w/a letter of authenticity from I. Magnin & Co., 2 pcs. **1,035.00**

Medusa Bust from "Citizen Kane"

Movie prop, bust of Medusa from "Citizen Kane," RKO, 1941, plaster bust of the mythological Medusa w/serpent hair, mounted on a rough base encased in a three-sided original crate w/rope braces, 68" h. (ILLUS.) **4,600.00**

Cowardly Lion "Courage" Medal

Movie prop, Cowardly Lion 'Courage' medal from "The Wizard of Oz," 1939, presented to Mal Caplan in the 1950s, polychromed metal w/a lion in profile above a crown & a knight's helmet, a blue scroll w/"Courage" in raised gold letters (ILLUS.) **33,350.00**

Movie prop, gold brick from "Goldfinger," James Bond 1964 classic, painted plaster. **1,265.00**

Movie prop, knife, used by Johnny Weissmuller in the original Tarzan movies of the 1930s (ILLUS.). . . . **9,500.00**

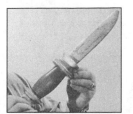

Weissmuller 'Tarzan' Knife

Movie prop, license plate from "Ghostbusters," one of several painted plastic prop "Ecto-1, New York" plates used **920.00**

Movie props, collection of spears from "King Kong," 1933, eight spears & swords of various styles, each approximately 6 to 8' long, the group **3,737.00**

Photograph, signed & inscribed by Marlene Dietrich, full-length pose in her famous 'naked' dress, inscribed in blue ink on both sides of the image, matted & framed, 15 x 18".. **287.00**

Picnic basket set, owned by Rudolph Valentino, wicker basket w/two loop closures w/attached wicker peg for locking, fitted w/leather straps & contains five 8" d. enamelware plates, one 7" d. plate, five cups, a metal box w/clips, a green tin stamped "Hotakold," inside cover stamped "Made In England for Ville de Paris B. H. Dyas Co. Los Angeles," the set. **1,495.00**

Pillowcase, James Bond, PFI, 1965, mint in package. **143.00**

Play set, "Raiders of the Lost Ark - Well of the Souls," 1981, unused, very fine. **83.00**

"Gremlin" Stop-Action Puppet

Puppet, stop-action Gremlin from "Gremlins," 1984, the demonic creature in menacing stance w/bright red eyes, evil grin, extended arms & gnarled claws, marked on back of head "1B," fitted w/armature for posing, mounted in lucite custom case, 7" h. (ILLUS.) **3,737.00**

Record, "The Ballad of James Dean,"
45 r.p.m., Coral, 1956, by Dick
Jacobs, very fine **25.00**

Marilyn Monroe Sweater Set

Sweater set, owned by Marilyn
Monroe, hand-knitted Mohair, a
sweater & a matching vest, given
to Marilyn on her 36th birthday,
w/letter of authenticity, the group
(ILLUS.) **2,990.00**

"Funny Face" Harold Lloyd Toy

Toy, windup tin, called "Funny Face,"
represents early comedian Harold
Lloyd, walker-type, Marx, ca.
1930s, w/original box (ILLUS.) . . . **1,150.00**

MUSIC BOXES

Paillard cylinder music box, table
model, inlaid walnut case, single
comb & zither attachment, 2" d.,
10½" l., cylinder playing tunes, late
19th c., 20" l. **$1,035.00**

Polyphon Table Top Music Box

**Polyphon (Polyphon Musikwerke,
Leipzig, Germany) disc music
box,** table model, walnut case
w/raised banded panels of burl trim
above a flaring leaf-carved base,
monochrome print inside the lid,
twin-comb movement, side handle,
plays 15½" d. discs, Russian
retailer's label, w/106 discs, leads
corroded, base molding detached,
22½" w. (ILLUS.) **4,025.00**

Rare Regina Disc Floor Model

Regina disc music box, floor model,
automatic disc changing model,
rare walnut case w/spool-
decorated gallery top above a pair
of glass panels flanked by columns
above a large glass panel w/gilt
trim & "Regina Corona," plays
27" d. discs (ILLUS.) **23,000.00**

Regina disc music box, table model,
carved oak case, double-comb
mechanism, plays 15¾" d. discs,
w/24 discs. **2,875.00**

Regina disc music box, table model,
upright oak case w/coin slider &
glazed door flanked by pilasters,
twin-comb movement, plays 11" d.
discs, w/15 discs, lacks coin
mechanism, back panel &
sounding boards, 19" h. **2,530.00**

Stella disc music box, inlaid walnut
case, double comb, six discs,
11¼" h. **1,265.00**

Swiss cylinder music box,
marquetry-inlaid rosewood-grained
case, single comb playing eight
tunes, cylinder 13" l., ca. 1900,
8¼ x 22½", 6¼" h. **1,725.00**

Swiss cylinder music box, burl
walnut case on matching four-
legged stand w/burl & ebonized
trim, plays 13" cylinders, w/three
additional cylinders, ca. 1900,
overall 22 x 43", 34" h. (ILLUS.) . . **6,613.00**

Swiss Cylinder Music Box on Stand

Swiss disc music box, walnut case, keywind mechanism, plays 4½" d. discs, w/ten extra discs, early 20th c., 6½ x 10½", 4" h. **550.00**

MUSICAL INSTRUMENTS

Drum, snare-type, painted w/American eagle on the side, labeled "Russell & Patee successors to Gilmore & Russell, 61 Court Street, Boston, Mass....," w/ink inscription "sold 1849," mid-19th c., imperfections, 15" d., 12" h. **$345.00**

Large Labeled Snare Drum

Drum, snare-type, paint-decorated w/a reserve of musical instruments on the side & the name "H.W. Maynard," labeled "William Sempf Manufacturer of Bass & Snare Drums, 209 & 211 Grand Steet, New York....," mid-19th c., minor losses, 17" d., 13⅝" h. (ILLUS.) . . . **460.00**

Drum, cylindrical, worn original varnish & transfer decorations around the sides including an eagle & shield, old heads, side ropes & leather replaced, labeled "Carl Fischer, New York," w/two drumsticks, 16½" d. (one head split). **330.00**

Fiddle, hand-made, the back of the body profusely inlaid w/stars, hearts, birds, cups & geometric designs, the center w/an inlaid profile bust of a woman wearing a hat & smoking a pipe, at the top an inlay of four male acrobats, the sides of the body constructed w/multicolored inlaid wood, the top grained & stenciled w/apples, horse hair bow, probably Midwest, late 19th c., fiddle 24" l., 2 pcs. . . **1,876.00**

Unusual Carved Fiddle

Fiddle, hand-carved, the carved body w/f-shaped resonance holes, a solid carved & polychromed tailpiece in the form of a reclining dog, a one-piece carved neck surmounted w/a pegbox carved in the form of an African-American male head wearing a kepi, bill inscribed "SAMBO," inlaid eyes & teeth, w/casket-shaped case of walnut w/heart & star inlays, horsehair bow, probably Southeastern U.S., ca. 1860-80, fiddle 28" l., the group (ILLUS.) . . **2,090.00**

Guitar, "Les Paul Gold Top," 1952, hardly used, w/case **4,500.00**

Early Austrian Harpsichord

Harpsichord, mahogany, penwork, ivory & ebonized wood, rectangular hinged top opening to a keyboard & a lower frieze drawer fitted w/inkwells & various other wells, raised on octagonal tapering slender legs, the whole decorated

w/Neo-classical penwork, signed
"Ant. Mart Thymvienne, No. 99,"
Austria, first quarter 19th c.,
19¼ x 34¼", 33½" h. (ILLUS.) . . . **4,887.00**
Piano, baby grand, walnut case of
simple form w/square tapered legs,
William Knabe & Co., Serial No.
107742, together w/companion
stool, 2 pcs. **750.00**

Early Classical Piano

Piano, mahogany & mahogany
veneer Classical-style case,
rectangular w/rounded front
corners, lift-lid above short
keyboard, raised on six heavy ring-
and baluster-turned legs ending in
peg feet on casters, lyre-form
pedal, w/paper label & brand "John
Osborn No. 122," Boston, ca. 1820,
26 x 66½", 33" h. (ILLUS.) **1,840.00**
Pitchpipe, walnut, in the form of a
book, the interior w/a paper label
"WN," American, 19th c.,
6" l. (crack) **201.00**

MUSICAL
INSTRUMENTS,
MECHANICAL

Peerless Style 44 Cabinet Piano

Cabinet piano, "Peerless Style 44,"
coin-operated, hardwood upright
case w/scalloped beveled glass top
window, 44-note, uses endless
music roll, early 20th c. (ILLUS.) . . **$4,750.00**
Carousel organ, "Wurlitzer No. 153,"
plays 150 rolls, w/orchestra bells,
duplex spool box, snare & bass
drum & cymbals, operating. **26,000.00**
Cremona Orchestral K, w/violin,
piccolo & flute pipes, tambourine,
castanets & triangle, Marquette Co.
of Chicago **40,000.00**
Double Violano, Mills, four-string
violin, mahogany case,
unrestored **53,000.00**
Military band organ, "Wurlitzer No.
125," restored, 6' 2" h. **28,000.00**
Orchestrion, Mortier, 84-key book-
operated, made in Belgium,
w/books **51,000.00**
Orchestrion, "Seeburg G,"
w/mandolin, violin, flute pipes,
tympani, snare drum, cymbal &
unusual bird whistle
(unrestored) **46,000.00**
Orchestrion, "Seeburg KT Special,"
ca. 1925-27 working. **20,000.00**
Orchestrion, "Wurlitzer Model LX,"
w/bass & snare drums, triangle,
violin pipes, doppel flute pipes
& wonder light (unrestored) **36,000.00**
Pipe organ, "Reproduco," duplex
spool box (unrestored) **36,000.00**
Street organ, 72-key, Dutch,
w/books, 8' h. (unrestored). **22,000.00**
Violano Virtuoso, Mills, four-string
violin, mahogany cabinet
(unrestored) **22,000.00**

NAPKIN RINGS

**Bird w/long tail on stem of large
leaf,** Meridan Britannia Co.,
No.202. . . . . **$325.00**
Eagles (2) on base, Middletown
Silver Co., No. 94 . . . . **400.00**
Foxes (2) reach for bird,
Philadelphia Plate Co., No. 01534 . **325.00**
**Native Americans (2) in feathered
headdresses support the ring,**
lacy rectangular base **165.00**
**Owl w/long ears on violin base &
sheet music,** Rogers, No. 4394 . . . **350.00**
Parrot & ring, Toronto Silver Plate
Co., No. 1108 . . . . **450.00**

Squirrel & Acorns Bone Napkin Ring

Squirrel w/acorns, carved in low-
relief on a bone ring
(ILLUS.). . . . . **20.00 to 30.00**
Tulip & ring, Meriden Britannia Co.,
No. 168 . . . . **300.00**

NAUTICAL ITEMS

Account book, for the whaling ship
"Constitution" of Nantucket,
Massachusetts, together
w/geometry & arithmetic less
books, 1839-52, the group (varying
sizes & condition) **$748.00**

Early English Ship's Chronometer

Chronometer, gimbal-mounted in
brass fitted rosewood case, brass
bezel w/silver washed dial, marked
"Morris Tobias, London, Maker to
the Admiralty 31 Minories London,"
second quarter 19th c., ca. 1845,
Serial No. 1430, 6¾" sq.,
7½" h. (ILLUS.). **1,495.00**
Compass, brass, gimballed & lighted,
a domed brass cover w/round side
opening & flaring base w/a box
compartment w/cap to one side,
ring handle on top, 19th c.,
9 x 11", 9" h. **440.00**
Model of a schooner, painted wood,
"Gaele Trader," three-masted,
w/rigging, painted hull, identified
"E. Lecleare," 20th c., 46" l. **288.00**

Painting, oil on canvas, portrait of the
American three-masted schooner
"Mary E. Morse," a lighthouse in
the distance, signed "W.P. Stubbs,"
19th c., framed, retouched, lined,
craquelure, 22 x 36" **7,475.00**

Ship Model of "Sevo" in a Frame

Ship model, carved & painted ,
depicting the cutter "Sevo" under
full sail, mounted in a shadowbox
frame, American, 19th c., very
minor imperfections, 21¼ x 28 14"
(ILLUS.) **2,185.00**
Ship model, carved & painted wood
& canvas, model of a schooner
yacht, two-masted w/three canvas
sails, mounted on a platform base,
early 20th c., overall 44" l. **1,955.00**
Yacht tender, cedar & oak, the
rowboat-style craft of cedar carved
planked oak ribbed, bright finish
w/mahogany trim, two rowing
stations, bronze fastenings & oar
locks, equipped w/two falls, built by
Geo. Lawley & Son Corp.,
Neponset, Massachusetts, No.
1615 or 1618, 49" w., 11' 3" l.
(crack in the false keel) **4,600.00**

NUTTING (WALLACE) COLLECTIBLES

FURNITURE

Armchair, mahogany,
Chippendale-style. **$1,265.00**
Armchair, Windsor sack-back **825.00**
Beds, maple, pair **908.00**
Candlestand, whirling-type. **495.00**
Candlestand, Windsor **462.00**
Chair, mahogany, bedroom **440.00**
Chair, side, mahogany,
Chippendale-style. **1,155.00**

Chair, side, Windsor-
   Style . . . . **578.00 to 605.00**
Chair, slipper. **715.00**
Costumer (coat rack) **413.00**
Desk, child's **770.00**
Hutch table, pine **825.00**

Maple Rushed Stool

Stool, four-legged maple rushed
   (ILLUS.) **231.00**
Table, crane bracket-type **715.00**
Table, mahogany,
   Pembroke-style **1,430.00**
Table, maple, trestle-type **605.00**
Table, trestle-type **495.00**

PRINTS (ARRANGED BY TOPIC)

CAT PRINTS

All the Comforts of Home, 13 x 15" . **209.00**
Ancestral Cradle (The), 14 x 20" **264.00**
Comfort and the Cat, 14 x 17" **440.00**
Home Charm, 15 x 22" **303.00**
Old Home (The), 12 x 20" **286.00**
Three Chums, 14 x 17" **413.00**

EXTERIOR SCENES

Accommodating Curves, 13 x 16" . . **319.00**
Among October Birches, 13 x 16" . . . **99.00**
Among the Ferns, 14 x 17" **165.00**
An Alstead Drive, 13 x 17" **154.00**
An Auspicious Entrance, 13 x 16" . . . **77.00**
An Elaborate Dinner, 14 x 17" **198.00**
An Overflowing Cup, 13 x 16" **61.00**
Apple Blossom Lane, 7 x 11" **28.00**
Blossoms at the Bend, 10 x 12" **50.00**
Blossoms at the Bend, 13 x 15" **39.00**
Blossoms that Meet, 12 x 15" **50.00**
Bonnie May, 16 x 20" **39.00**
Bridge and the Elm (The), 9 x 14" . . . **72.00**
Brook and Blossoms, 14 x 17" **22.00**
Brook's Mirror (The), 16 x 20" **105.00**
California Hilltops, 11 x 14" **165.00**
Call of the Road (The), 11 x 14" **66.00**
Canopied Road (A), 13 x 16" **94.00**

Cathedral Brook, 9 x 11" **83.00**
Catskill Summit Blooms, 11 x 14" . . **165.00**
Concord Banks, 16 x 20" **187.00**
Honeymoon Drive, 13 x 16" **83.00**
Honeymoon Shore, 13 x 16" **160.00**
Honeymoon Stroll, 11 x 14" **149.00**
Honeymoon Windings, 12 x 20" **182.00**
Housatonic Blossoms, 11 x 17" **138.00**
Hurrying Brook (A), 10 x 12" **61.00**
In Tenderleaf, 13 x 20" **88.00**
Into the Birchwood, 13 x 16" **165.00**
Into the West, 10 x 16" **44.00**
Keene Road (A), 13 x 17" **165.00**
LaMoille Twilight (A), 13 x 15" **187.00**
Lane in Norwich Town (A), 11 x 14" . **198.00**
Laughing Water, 13 x 16" **94.00**
Lingering Water, 16 x 20" **99.00**

A Little River

Little River (A), 10 x 16" (ILLUS.) . . . **165.00**
Little River (A), 13 x 22" **182.00**
Meeting of the Waters (The),
   16 x 20" **429.00**
Meeting of the Ways (The), 11 x 14" . . **99.00**
Mellow Birches, 13 x 16" **94.00**
Middlesex Glen, 13 x 15" **121.00**
Newton October (A), 12 x 14" **39.00**
November Sunset (A), 10 x 16" **11.00**
October Splendors, 12 x 16" **66.00**
October Vista, 8 x 10" **66.00**
On Worcester Hills, 13 x 15" **110.00**
Orchard Heights, 16 x 20" **83.00**
Pennsylvania Arches, 14 x 17" **297.00**
Pennsylvania Stream (A), 13 x 16" . . **374.00**
   14 x 17" **66.00**
Water Gambols, 13 x 16" **132.00**
Water Maples, 14 x 17" **110.00**
Waterside Convention (A), 13 x 16" . . **28.00**
Way Through the Orchard (The),
   13 x 16" **121.00**
Wilton Waters, 13 x 16" **154.00**
Windsor Blossoms, 14 x 20" **72.00**

FLORAL PRINTS

Cluster of Zinnias (A), 13 x 16" **330.00**
Fleur-de-lis and Spirea, 13 x 16" **682.00**
Miniature floral, 3 x 4" **198.00**

Miniature floral, 4 x 5" 242.00
Sheffield Basket (A), 13 x 16" 578.00
Spring Basket, 8 x 10" 413.00
Trumpets, 8 x 10" 578.00
Two Lilies, 9 x 11" 578.00
Zinnias, 13 x 16" 495.00

FOREIGN SCENES

Amalfi, 14 x 17" 633.00
Among Saffron Sails, 11 x 14" 264.00
An Airing at the Haven, 14 x 17" 330.00
An English Door, 11 x 14" 132.00
Arches & Domes, 9 x 15" 468.00
At the Well, Sorrento, 14 x 17" 385.00
Bonnie Dale, 10 x 12" 149.00
Footbridge by the Ford (The),
   16 x 20" 440.00
Garden of Larkspur (A), 9 x 12" 94.00
Garden of Larkspur (A), 10 x 12" 94.00
Italian Cypress Lane, 10 x 12" 132.00
Joy Path, 13 x 16" 209.00
Lane in Sorrento (A), 10 x 16" 506.00
Lane or Highway, 13 x 16" 572.00
Old Venice, 13 x 17" 688.00
On the Heights, 10 x 16" 99.00
Orta in Blossom Time, 11 x 14" 110.00
Ovaca's Colleens, 12 x 16" 209.00
Path of Roses (A), 10 x 12" 297.00
Peak in Donegal (A), 13 x 16" 396.00
Peasant's Palace (A), 14 x 17" 462.00
Pergola, Amalfi (The), 14 x 17" 165.00
Spanning the Glen, 10 x 12" 132.00
Stepping Stones to Bolton Abbey,
   11 x 14" 330.00
Venice's Chief Glory, 14 x 17" 578.00
Vico Equisne, 13 x 17" 187.00
Water Garden in Venice (A),
   10 x 12" 358.00
Water Path (A), 14 x 17" 154.00
Westport Garden (A), 13 x 16" 308.00
Windings in Holland, 13 x 15" 187.00

INTERIOR SCENES

Affectionately Yours, 14 x 17" 231.00
Affectionately Yours, 22 x 25" 121.00
Afternoon Tea, 13 x 16" 154.00
All the News, 15 x 18" 72.00
Almost Ready, 9 x 12" 66.00
An Afternoon Tea, 10 x 14" 105.00
An Elaborate Dinner, 13 x 17" 77.00
An Informal Call, 11 x 15" 121.00
An Inspiration, 11 x 15" 99.00
Corner Cupboard (The), 11 x 17" . . . 165.00
Feminine Finery, 11 x 14" 143.00
Final Touch (The), 14 x 17) 341.00
Fine Effect (A), 13 x 17" 132.00
Fireside Fancy Work, 16 x 20" 154.00

Fleck of Sunshine (A), 13 x 17" 154.00
From a Friend, 11 x 15" 187.00
Fruit Luncheon (A), 9 x 12" 187.00
Grandmother's China, 13 x 22" 110.00
Great Grandma's Sewing, 10 x 12" . . 198.00
Hallway Glimpse (A), 10 x 15" 176.00
His Rose, 12 x16" 275.00
Home Hearth (The), 10 x 16" 105.00
Home Room (The), 14 x 17" 231.00
Lost in Admiration, 12 x 15" 88.00
Maple Sugar Cupboard (The),
   13 x 16" 220.00
Pilgrim Daughter (A), 14 x 16" 110.00
Pilgrim Fireside (A), 11 x 14" 132.00
Preparing an "At Home," 13 x 22" . . 264.00
Reeling the Yarn, 14 x 17" 143.00
Returning from a Walk, 11 x 17" 132.00
Settle Nook (The), 11 x 14" 77.00
Southern Colonial Room (A),
   13 x 17" 242.00
Spinet Corner, 10 x 12" 132.00
Spinet Corner (The), 13 x 16" 220.00
Stitch in Time (A), 10 x 12" 187.00
Sunshine and Music, 13 x 16" 231.00
Tea for Two, 14 x 17" 143.00
Tea Maid (The), 13 x 16" 77.00
Touching Tale (A), 11 x 14" 165.00
What a Beauty!, 14 x 16" 308.00
Winding an Old Tall Clock, 14 x 17" . 165.00
Winding Stair (A), 7 x 14" 39.00
Work Basket (The), 11 x 14" 154.00

SCENES WITH CHILDREN

Call for More (A), 10 x 13" 330.00
Coming Out of Rosa (The),
   11 x 14" 138.00

The Coming Out of Rosa

Coming Out of Rosa (The),
   14 x 17" (ILLUS.) 325.00
Coming Out of Rosa (The),
   16 x 20" 358.00
Difficult Lesson (A), 11 x 14" 286.00
First Lesson (The), 12 x 14" 495.00
Guardian Mother (The), 11 x 17" . . 2,970.00
Helping Mother, 14 x 17" 407.00
Toward Slumberland, 13 x 17" 770.00

Untitled "Children on Settee,"
8 x 12" **575.00**
Untitled "Rosa Sitting on Porch,"
7 x 9" **83.00**
Watching for Papa, 13 x 16" **413.00**
Whirling Candlestand (The),
11 x 14" **132.00**

SCENES WITH COWS

Four O'Clock, 14 x 17" **853.00**
Genial Stream (The), 10 x 16" **248.00**

The Meeting Place

Meeting Place (The), 18 x 22"
(ILLUS.) **1,750.00**
Untitled, cows in a field, 9 x 15" **83.00**

SCENES WITH DOGS

Dog-On-It, 7 x 11" **1,265.00**

SCENES WITH MEN

A Heart Chord, 13 x 16" **440.00**
An Ambush for a Redcoat, 13 x 15". **770.00**
An Old Parlor Idyl, 13 x 16" **330.00**
An Old Tune Revived, 10 x 12" **165.00**
Better than Mowing, 16 x 20" **484.00**
Canoeing, 8 x 11" **495.00**
Capture of a Redcoat, 13 x 16" **220.00**
Drying Apples, 14 x 17" **495.00**
Old Cabinet Maker (The),
12 x 14" **4,510.00**
Parting at the Gate, 10 x 14" **550.00**
The Way It Begins, 13 x 16" **468.00**
Uncle Sam Taking Leave, 12 x 15". . **385.00**

SEASCAPES

A Maine Coast Sky, 13 x 16" **385.00**
A New England Shore, 10 x 12" **66.00**
Cypress Rocks, 16 x 20" **176.00**
La Jolla, 11 x 17" **275.00**
LaJolla, 13 x 16" **77.00**
Rocks Off Portland, 11 x 14" **231.00**
Sea Ledges, 14 x 17" **275.00**
Sea Ledges (North Shore),
13 x 15" **253.00**
The Sea Ledges of New England,

13 x 15" **220.00**
Untitled seascape, 7 x 11" **99.00**

SNOW SCENES

A Snow Road, 8 x 10" **1,733.00**
Fairbanks Homestead, 6 x 7" **231.00**
Untitled snow scene, 7 x 9" **193.00**

PAPER COLLECTIBLES

Arrest warrant, dated 1881 from
New Mexico Territory for Texas
outlaw Tom "Cat" Selman, who
was the brother of noted lawman,
outlaw & gunfighter John Selman &
lynched by a mob for his criminal
activities. **$425.00**
Billhead, dated 1887 from Wyoming
Territory & signed by Asa Mercer,
who was a noted newspaper
publisher & author of "The Johnson
County War" **192.00**

Early Calligraphic Drawing

Calligraphic drawing, pen & ink &
water-color on paper, a rectangular
reserve at the top w/an urn of
flowers & flowering trees above
large letters "IVNE" over a script
inscription & signed in a bottom
block flanked by floral urns
"George Macness, age 12, Salem,
Massachusetts, October 24, 1812,"
framed, some toning & foxing,
8½ x 14¼" (ILLUS.) **1,150.00**
Certificate of election, from Oregon
Territory, dated 1858 .... **150.00**
Certification, dated 1881, handwritten by Sheriff Pat Garrett, who
was the Sheriff who killed Billy
the Kid **2,000.00**

Certification, handwritten on paper, by William Larimer, a main founder of Denver, from "Denver City, Kansas Territory," date 1860 . . . . **1,054.00**

Court voucher, issued for serving an arrest warrant against Robert & Grat Dalton, Western outlaws, on "murder" charges while they were still serving as lawmen, dated 1888 . . . . **3,364.00**

Envelope front, franked by President Andrew Jackson & sent to South Carolinian, Hon. J.R. Poinsett **743.00**

Family record, pen & ink & watercolor on paper, "The Children of Alpheus Shumway and Lucy A. Jepson, Married 1800," within floral-entwined columns joined by a floral swag, 18 x 24½" **650.00**

Holographic letter, dated 1888 from Senator Henry Teller of Colorado . . **325.00**

Land deed, dated 1889 from Montana Territory, signed by "Copper King" millionaire Marcus Daly **170.00**

Letter dated April 20, 1865 from Sacramento, California w/content about Lincoln's assassination **212.00**

Letter, hand-written by a husband to his wife describing Indian attacks & killings in the area of "Big Turkey," Kansas, dated 1865 . . . . **397.00**

Letter, written by future Civil War General Samuel Curtis, concerning an expedition against Pawnee Indians after their attack on the new townsite of Omaha, Nebraska, dated 1859, 10 pp. **1,238.00**

Letterhead from "North Western Express, Stage & Transportation Co.," dated 1880 from Dakota Territory **150.00**

Menu, "Victoria Hotel, Chicago," Christmas, 1899 . . . . **25.00**

Military document, from Fort Sedgewick, Colorado Territory, dated 1866 . . . . **128.00**

Military voucher for soldiers on patrol at Fort McIntosh, Texas, 1853 . . . . **83.00**

Mining payroll, from Arizona Territory, signed by several Native Americans who were hired as laborers, dated 1904 . . . . **367.00**

Mining stock certificate, signed by Nevada banker & mining promoter John Cook, Bullfrog, Nevada, 1500 . . . . **185.00**

Program, Buffalo Bill Cody Wild West show, 1902 . . . . **390.00**

Railroad bond, "St. Joseph & Denver City Railroad Co.," unissued, printed in 1870, one of only four known to exist **220.00**

Stock certificate, "Lady Jameson Gold & Silver Mining Co.," Nevada Territory, dated 1864 . . . . **425.00**

Stock certificate, "Standard Oil Company," 1878, autographed by John D. Rockefeller as President **10,000.00**

Stock certificate, "Studebaker Corporation," common stock, issued in 1965, green, vignette of man holding piston, factory in background, engraved by Security-Columbian Bank Note Co. **6.00**

Rare Tombstone Stock Certificate

Stock certificate, "Tombstone Mill and Mining Co.," vignette of Native American warrior in lower left corner & vignette of Native American warrier & maiden in the upper right, Tombstone, Arizona, November 2, 1881 (ILLUS.) **1,500.00**

PAPER DOLLS

Buffy & Jody Paper Dolls

Buffy & Jody, 1970, uncut, includes magic stay-on clothing w/stands & scissors, Whitman (ILLUS.). **$20.00**

Donny & Marie Osmond, 1977,
   uncut **20.00**
Princess Diana, 1985, uncut **65.00**
Robin Hood & Maid Marian, 1940,
   uncut **65.00**
Sesame Doll Players, 1976, uncut . . . **20.00**
World of Barbie 1972, uncut,
   includes Barbie, Ken, P.J., Stacey,
   Francie, Tutti, Skipper & Christie,
   magic stay-on clothing
   w/accessories **70.00**

PAPERWEIGHTS

American "Clematis" weight, eight
alternating red & blue flowers
surrounding a central red blossom,
attributed to the Somerville Union
Glass Company, 3¼" d. **$374.00**

Baccarat "Bouquet" Weight

Baccarat "Bouquet" weight, clear
glass set w/a central blue & white
primrose w/a yellow star honeycomb
stamen encompassed by two
pansies, each formed w/two upper
purple petals, three lower white
cogwheel cane petals lined in cobalt
blue w/white stripes about a blue,
white & red composite cane stamen
surmounted by a partially bloomed
rose, growing from two entwined
green stems w/several leaves & a red
bud, star-cut base,
19th c., repolished, 3⅜" d.(ILLUS.) . **9,775.00**
Baccarat "Close Millefiori" weight,
clear glass set w/assorted brightly
colored millefiori canes including
silhouettes of approximately one
goat, one rooster, one dancing
monkey, one deer, two pelicans,
two elephants, two squirrels, two
horses, three dogs & shamrocks,
19th c., 3¹⁄₁₆" d. (internal crack in
one pelican cane) **3,335.00**
**Baccarat "Double Clematis"
weight,** clear glass set w/a flower
formed w/two overlapping rows of
ribbed & pointed lavender petals
about a white stardust stamen &
green whorl cane center, growing

from a curved green stem w/four
leaves & a red bud & four further
leaves about the flower, star-cut
base, 19th c., 2¹³⁄₁₆" d.
(repolished) **2,875.00**
**Baccarat "Garlanded Primrose on
Muslin Ground" weight,** clear
glass set w/a flower formed w/six
rounded red petals w/white stripes
about a white stardust stamen &
red whorl cane center, growing
from a curved green stem w/two
leaves, a red bud & six further
leaves about the flower,
encompassed by a garland of
white, red & yellow pastry mold
composite star-arrowhead canes,
set on an upset muslin ground,
19th c., 3" d. (repolished) **6,037.00**
**Baccarat "Patterned Millefiori
Carpet Ground" weight,** clear
glass set w/a central red & white
cogwheel cane encompassed by
four rows of coral red, cobalt blue &
white composite canes & six
clusters of coral red, blue & white
star-silhouette composite canes
alternating w/red, white & blue
arrowhead canes within a border of
cobalt blue & white star-silhouette
canes, set on a pale blue
honeycomb cane ground, 19th c.,
repolished, 2⅞" d. **11,500.00**
**Baccarat "Wallflower with Garland"
weight,** green, white & red
arrowhead cane center w/six green
leaves, stem & a red bud, garland
of green, white & red canes
alternating w/red & white stardust
canes, star-cut base, 19th c.,
2¾" d. **2,420.00**
**Clichy "Barber's Pole Chequer"
weight,** clear glass set w/assorted
brightly colored millefiori canes
including two pink & white rose
canes & a central pink & green
rose cane divided by short lengths
of cobalt blue & white latticinio
tubing, set on a ground of white
parallel muslin cables, 19th c.,
2⅝" d.(repolished) **2,990.00**
Clichy "Bouquet" weight, clear
glass set w/a central cobalt blue
flower w/a red & white composite
cane stamen (one petal separated)
encompassed by a flower formed
w/shaded red ribbed & pointed
petals about a red pastry mold
cane stamen facing another flower
formed w/pink & white-striped
petals about a pink & green
composite cane stamen, growing

from three green stems w/several green leaves & three buds in shades of red, blue & white, tied at the base w/a pale blue ribbon, 19th c., 3³⁄₁₆" d. **10,350.00**

Faceted Double-Overlay Clichy Weight

Clichy "Faceted Double-Overlay Concentric Millefiori Mushroom" weight, clear glass w/the tuft formed w/a central white floral cane w/two borders of pale yellow & green stave canes encompassed by five rows of assorted millefiori canes in shades of pink, blue, white, coral & green including fourteen purple rose canes within a basket of alternating cobalt blue & white stave canes, overlaid w/a layer of turquoise blue over white glass, cut w/a window & five side printies, grid-cut base, 19th c., 3³⁄₁₆" d. (ILLUS.) **7,475.00**

Clichy "Faceted Patterned Millefiori on Muslin Ground" weight, clear glass set w/five assorted millefiori canes in circular formations in shades of pink, turquoise, green, cobalt blue & white encompassing a central pink & green rose, set on an upset muslin ground, cut w/a window & two rows of five side printies, 19th c., 2⅞" d. (later faceted, minor surface wear) **2,070.00**

Czechoslovakian "Doe & Deer Sulphide" weight, the figures of the doe & deer sitting on a multi-colored ground surrounded by a light blue marbled effect, overall faceting, 3" d. (some light scratching) **413.00**

Kaziun (Charles, Jr.) "Pompon" weight, a small white flower w/yellow center, six green leaves & stem surrounded by a white, purple & lime green twist w/a silver "K" signature cane, 20th c., 2⁵⁄₁₆" d. . . . **187.00**

Kaziun (Charles) "Spider Lily" pedestal weight, yellow blossom w/orange center, green leaves, set

on swirling latticinio on a light amethyst ground, gold "K" on back, 1⅜" d., 2³⁄₁₆" h. **550.00**

Milleville "Home Sweet Home" weight, the arched wording "Home Sweet Home" above a stylized outline of a small house suspended above a multi-colored pebble ground, New Jersey, late 19th - early 20th c., 3¹⁄₁₆" d. **143.00**

New England "Apple" weight, model of an apple in dark to light orange & yellow to lime yellow set on a thick round "cookie" base, 19th c., 3½" d. (minute open bubble) **770.00**

New England Stylized Flower Weight

New England "Stylized Flower on Latticinio Ground" weight, clear glass set w/a flower formed w/six pointed shaded blue petals & six pointed & curved upright red petals about a blue & white running hare silhouette, cane stamen growing from a curved green stem w/two leaves & a further leaf about the flower, set on a white latticinio ground, 19th c., repolished, small chips on base, 2¹⁵⁄₁₆" d. **2,415.00**

Sandwich "Floral" weight, seven-petaled cobalt blue blossoms on eight green leaves w/pastel blue centered white millefiore canes around the edge, attributed to Nicholas Lutz, 2½" d. **489.00**

St. Clair "Upright Rose" weight, a pink rose w/three green leaves centered on a red & green mottled ground, impressed mark on base, ca. 1970s, 3¹³⁄₁₆" d. **660.00**

St. Louis "Dahlia" weight, clear glass set w/numerous recessed & shaded ribbed blue pointed petals above an ochre cogwheel cane stamen & periwinkle blue floret center encompassed by five serrated green leaves, star-cut base, 19th c., 2½" d. (repolished) **4,887.00**

St. Louis "Faceted Cherries" Weight

St. Louis "Faceted Cherries" weight, clear glass set w/two red cherries on green stems pendent from two ochre branches w/three green leaves, cut w/overall geometric facets & eight side printies, grid-cut base, 19th c., 2¹³⁄₁₆" d. (ILLUS.) **2,875.00**

St. Louis "Faceted Upright Bouquet" weight, clear glass set w/a central white flower, two flowers in shades of red & blue divided by two millefiori canes in shades of ochre, cobalt blue & white within a cluster of several green leaves encompassed by a yellow spiral thread & white latticinio torsade, cut overall w/geometric facets, 19th c., 2¹¹⁄₁₆" d. **4,312.00**

St. Louis "Gilded Lizard on Faceted Gilt Opaline Base" weight, the naturalistically formed white opaline partially gilded lizard coiled above a white opaline weight base, cut w/three rows of printies encompassed by traces of gilt leaf sprigs below a gilt border, painted in red enamel w/accession number "1965.364," 19th c., 3⅜" d. (wear to gilding) **6,900.00**

Stankard (Paul) "Floral Color Ground" weight, the clear glass set w/a cattleya orchid formed w/shaded pink petals scattered w/orange spots, growing from a green stem w/clusters of leaves in varying shades of green & a forked variegated brown & beige branch, partially covered w/patches of moss, set on an opaque red ground, signed w/a single "S" cane & engraved "A363 1985," 3⅛" d. . . **1,955.00**

Unionville Glass Works weight, large central five-petal stylized blue blossom w/light blue center surrounded by a ring of dark blue small stars, late 19th c., 3¼" d. **55.00**

Ysart (Paul) "Millefiori Heart" weight, a red & green millefiori heart containing a "PY" signature cane suspended above a stave basket of canes & latticinio twists, 20th c., 3" d. (two canes in heart tipped) **605.00**

PARRISH (MAXFIELD) ARTWORK

ART PRINTS

HOUSE OF ART - REINTHAL & NEWMAN - CRANE PRINTING

Acussin Seeks Nicolette: 1905 Prince riding horse in a deep, dark valley, 11½ x 17". **$645.00**

Air Castles: 1904 Nude blowing bubbles w/castles & clouds in background, 12 x 16" **325.00**

Canyon: 1924 Blonde girl clinging to rocky cliffs edge w/raging river below, 6 x 10" **180.00**

Canyon: 1924 12 x 15". **365.00**

"Cleopatra"

Cleopatra: 1917 Cleopatra in bed of roses, riding in a barge, w/rowers & servants, 6½ x 5" (ILLUS.) **405.00**

Cleopatra: 1917 15 x 16" **825.00**

Cleopatra: 1917 24½ x 28" **2,350.00**

Daybreak: 1922 Young nude leaning over reclined blonde woman, open temple, pool, 6 x 10" **150.00**

Daybreak: 1922 10 x 18" **275.00**

Daybreak: 1922 18 x 30" **600.00**

Dreaming: 1928 Nude sitting on roots of huge tree, 6 x 10" **285.00**

Dreaming: 1928 10 x 18" **675.00**

Dreaming: 1928 18 x 30". **1,850.00**

Evening: 1922 Nude sitting on rock within a dark pool, 6 x 10" **205.00**

Evening: 1922 12 x 15" **385.00**

Garden of Allah: 1918 Three women reclining by reflecting pool,
9 x 18" (R) **225.00**
Garden of Allah: 1918 15 x 30" (R) . . **610.00**
Hilltop: 1927 Two girls upon knoll, sitting under big oak, 6 x 10" **180.00**
Hilltop: 1927 12 x 20" **450.00**
Hilltop: 1927 18 x 30" **1,125.00**
Morning: 1926 Blonde girl sitting on rocks with her arms around her legs, high on mountain peak,
6 x 10" **180.00**
Morning: 1926 12 x 15" **315.00**
Prince, The: 1928 A prince lying down in a field of flowers w/bridge in background, 10 x 12 (R) **345.00**
Romance: 1925 Knave & Maiden on pillared balcony w/castles & mountains in background,
12 x 24" **1,550.00**
Rubiayat: 1917 Man w/book on far right, woman w/book on far left, outdoors, 4 x 14" **350.00**
Rubiayat: 1917 8 x 30" **1,000.00**
Stars: 1927 Nude woman on a rock, stargazing, darkest blues, 6 x 10" . . **335.00**
Stars: 1927 12 x 20" **950.00**
Stars: 1927 18 x 30" **1,775.00**
Wild Geese: 1924 Blonde lady lying on her stomach upon rock, dark mountains, 12 x 15" **305.00**

EDISON-MAZDA CALENDAR PRINTS

1918: Night is Fled or Dawn Large, complete. **3,850.00**
1918: Night is Fled or Dawn Small, complete. **1,400.00**
1919: Spirit of Night Large, complete. **4,900.00**
1919: Spirit of Night Small, complete. **1,675.00**
1920: Prometheus Large, complete **430.00**
1920: Prometheus Small, complete. **1,525.00**
1921: Primitive Man Large, complete. **3,450.00**
1921: Primitive Man Small, complete. **1,620.00**
1922: Egypt Large, complete **4,200.00**
1922: Egypt Small, complete. **1,870.00**
1923: Lampseller of Bagdad Large, complete (ILLUS.) **3,625.00**
1923: Lampseller of Bagdad Small, complete **1,395.00**
1924: The Venetian Lamplighter Large, complete **3,000.00**

"Lampseller of Bagdad" 1923 Calendar

1924: The Venetian Lamplighter Small, complete **1,000.00**
1925: Dreamlight Large, complete. **2,800.00**
1925: Dreamlight Small, complete . **1,000.00**
1926: Enchantment Large, complete **2,950.00**
1926: Enchantment Small, complete. **1,000.00**
1927: Reveries Large, complete . . . **2,225.00**
1927: Reveries Small, complete. **650.00**
1928: Contentment Large, complete. **2,300.00**
1928: Contentment Small, complete **695.00**
1929: Golden Hours Large, complete **2,000.00**
1929: Golden Hours Small, complete **665.00**
1930: Ecstasy Large, complete. . . . **2,100.00**
1930: Ecstasy Small, complete **620.00**
1931: Waterfall Large, complete . . . **2,100.00**
1931: Waterfall Small, complete **595.00**

"Solitude" Calendar

1932: Solitude Small, complete (ILLUS.). **950.00**
1933: Sunrise Large, complete **3,000.00**
1933: Sunrise Small, complete **800.00**
1934: Moonlight Small, complete . . . **925.00**

PERFUME, SCENT & COLOGNE BOTTLES

Amber, cologne, bellows-form
w/crown & fleur-de-lis embossing,
sheared lip, pontil-scarred base,
ca. 1840-1860, 3¼" h. **$154.00**

Aqua, scent, mold-blown, flattened
round pinwheel design, rolled lip,
pontil-scarred base, ca. 1845-1855,
2⅛" h. **99.00**

Polygonal-form Cologne Bottle

Cobalt blue glass, cologne, mold-
blown polygonal-form, rolled lip,
smooth base, ca. 1865-1880,
4¾" h. (ILLUS.) **468.00**

Milk white glass, cologne, tapering
vertical rib & star-in-banner design,
long smooth neck w/rolled lip,
smooth base, ca. 1865-1885,
5¾" h. **77.00**

Opalescent turquoise glass,
cologne, mold-blown tapered
cylindrical, rolled lip, rough pontil,
8½" h. **187.00**

Pink amethyst, cologne, slightly
tapering twelve-sided cylindrical
w/flared lip, smooth base, ca.
1860-1880, 6½" h. **209.00**

Smoky ice blue, cologne, tapering
square w/herringbone corners, long
neck w/tooled lip, smooth base, ca.
1855-1875, Boston & Sandwich
Glass Co., 6¼" h. **303.00**

Starch blue glass, cologne, pressed
Acorn & Leaf patt., cylindrical body
w/rounded ribbed shoulder,
bulbous ribbed stopper, wide body
band relief-molded acorns & leaves
between beaded bands, Boston &
Sandwich Glass Co.,
mid-19th c., pr. **1,045.00**

Teal green glass, cologne, figural
monument w/brick design, partially
flared lip, smooth base, ca. 1865-
1875, 12" h. (ILLUS.) **1,705.00**

Monument Cologne Bottle

Violet cobalt blue, toilet water, blown
three-mold cylindrical w/top &
bottom rings, vertical ribbing on
base, large lower neck ring, rolled
& flared lip, pontil-scarred base,
ca. 1815-1830, 5¼" h. **715.00**

PHONOGRAPHS

EDISON CYLINDER PHONOGRAPHS

Amberola 30, w/internal horn **$400.00**

Amberola 50, inside horn table
model. **450.00**

Amberola 75, inside horn floor
model. **570.00**

Concert, w/large all-brass horn &
floor stand. **2,175.00**

Edison Amberola 50, cylinder-type
movement, mahogany-veneered
table-top case, side-crank handle,
ca. 1905. . . . . **425.00**

Edison Maroon Gem Phonograph

Edison Gem, maroon metal case
w/cylindrical movement, maroon
metal morning glory horn, ca. 1895
(ILLUS.) **1,400.00**

Fireside, w/cygnet black metal
horn 1,200.00
Fireside, w/maroon Fireside, two-
piece 19" l. horn 875.00
Fireside, without horn 475.00
Gem, black, w/black horn 495.00
Gem, maroon, w/one-piece maroon
horn 1,300.00
Gem Model #2, oak case 468.00
Home, w/"witches' hat" black horn . . . 575.00
Home, w/14" black & brass bell horn . 490.00
Home, w/colored horn w/flowers
painted inside 875.00
Home, w/cygnet (shaped like a
question mark) black horn. 915.00
Home, without horn 425.00
Opera. 5,000.00
Standard, w/"witches' hat" black horn 575.00
Standard, w/14" black & brass bell
horn 425.00
Standard, w/colored horn w/flowers
painted inside 825.00
Standard, w/cygnet black metal horn 850.00
Standard, without horn 380.00
Triumph, w/"withches' hat" black
horn. 895.00
Triumph, w/10-panel cygnet black
metal horn 1,200.00
Triumph, w/large colored horn
w/flowers painted inside 975.00
Triumph, w/oak cygnet horn, wooden
bell & metal elbow 2,750.00
Triumph, w11-panel cygnet black
metal horn 1,750.00
Triumph, without horn 825.00

EDISON DIAMOND DISK PHONOGRAPHS

Model A-100. . . . . 375.00
Model A-250. . . . . 400.00
Model A-425, very fancy Louis
XV-style case 2,000.00
Model B-80. . . . . 400.00
Model C-150. . . . . 300.00
Model C-19. . . . . 400.00
Model C-250. . . . . 500.00
Model H-19. . . . . 300.00
Model S-19. . . . . 300.00

OTHER MODELS

Brunswick, simple style floor model. . 200.00
Cameraphone 285.00
Columbia AT, cylinder player. 490.00
Columbia Grafanola, louver door
floor model. 300.00

Columbia Grafanola, louver door
table model 200.00
Columbia Q, cylinder player. 375.00
Harmony, w/inside horn 170.00
Harmony, w/outside horn 680.00
Pathé, inside horn floor model 200.00

VICTOR DISC PHONOGRAPHS

Victor E Phonograph

Victor E (Monarch Jr.), table model
w/oak case, disc player, pre-dog
logo tag, black metal & brass horn,
ca. 1910 (ILLUS.) 1,400.00
Victor IV, w/black & brass bell
horn 1,475.00
Victor IV, w/smooth mahogany wood
horn 3,400.00
Victor I (Vic. I or V-I), w/black &
brass bell-metal horn 1,175.00
Victor II, w/black & brass bell
horn 1,225.00
Victor III, w/black & brass bell
horn 1,275.00
Victor III, w/black metal morning
glory horn 1,275.00
Victor III, w/oak wood "spear tip"
horn 3,000.00
Victor M (Monarch), front mount or
rear mount w/metal horn 1,400.00
Victor M (Monarch), rear mount
w/wood horn. 3,200.00
Victor MS (Monarch Special),
w/metal horn. 1,550.00
Victor MS (Monarch Special),
w/wood horn. 4,000.00
Victor P (Premium). 1,000.00
Victor R (Royal) 1,275.00

Victor V with Black & Brass Horn

Victor V, w/black & brass bell horn
(ILLUS.) 1,525.00

Victor V, w/oak wood "spear tip"
horn 3,575.00
Victor VI, w/black & brass bell
horn 3,975.00
Victor VI, w/black morning glory
horn 3,975.00
Victor VI, w/mahogany "spear tip"
horn 5,800.00

VICTOR VICTROLAS

VV-210 . . . . 150.00
VV-50 . . . . 190.00
VV-8-30 (orthophonic). 580.00
VV-IV. 200.00
VV-IX. 325.00
VV-VI. 210.00
VV-VIII. 275.00
VV-X, floor model 340.00
VV-X, table model 280.00
VV-XIV. 350.00
VV-XI, floor model. 375.00
VV-XI, table model 280.00
VV-XII 500.00
VV-XVII. 1,000.00
VV-XVIII 2,700.00
VV-XVI. 500.00

PHOTOGRAPHIC ITEMS

Ambrotype, cased ninth-plate image
of Confederate soldier, a Virginia
Private seated & wearing a high-
collar calvary jacket & kepi,
thermoplastic case w/molded fruit
& flower design $550.00
Ambrotype, cased quarter plate image
of a Confederate soldier, seated next
to a table w/his hat covering two
books, gilt detail on buttons & watch
fob, attributed to Voegler of North
Carolina, 3¼ x 4¼". 1,100.00
Ambrotype, cased sixth plate image
of a Confederate soldier, gilt
buttons on coat & collar, pencil
inscription on back "S. Whitfield,
6-Tenn., Vols."` 798.00

Rare Civil War Ruby Ambrotype

Ambrotype, cased sixth plate image
of an Union Zouave soldier boy,
holding a rifle & knife, Civil War
era (ILLUS.) 1,725.00
Ambrotype, cased sixth plate of a
Confederate soldier, a Private
seated w/elbow on a table w/tinted
green cloth & his kepi on top (small
spots in image along liner) 413.00
Book, "The Photographic Process,"
1939, first edition. 28.00
Cabinet photo, Francis Wilson, actor
& author, inscribed & autographed . . 60.00
Cabinet photo, traveler seated next
to a Victorian table displaying an
Oriental statue & other pieces. 30.00

Leica Model M-3 Camera

Camera, Leica Model M-3, 35 mm
model (ILLUS.). 1,375.00
Carte de visite, General Braxton
Bragg, in Confederate uniform 145.00
Carte de visite, General George A.
Custer, signed. 975.00

Soujourner Truth Carte de Visite

Carte de visite, Soujouner Truth,
famous African-American
Abolistionist leader, reads "I Sell
the Shadow to Support the
Substance - Sojourner Truth"
(ILLUS.) 1,380.00
Daguerreotype, half-length portrait of
a pretty young woman w/long curls,
seated beside a table, wearing an
orange lacy pelerine, fine neck
brooch, tailored silk dress & fur
stole, by James E. McClees &

Washington L. Germon, Philadelphia, ca. 1840s, sixth plate, original leather case (case separated at spine). **1,075.00**

Daguerreotype, half-length portrait of a teenage girl seated facing right, short-cropped curled hair, wearing a slightly off-the-shoulder patterned dress w/lacy trim on half-length sleeves, crossed black ribbon w/gold button around her neck, holding a japanned mother-of-pearl case in one hand, sixth plate, leather case w/floral design (spine split) **350.00**

Daguerreotype, post-mortem, a tender portrait of a pretty baby girl laid out on a simple cloth ground wearing a homespun dress, hands together at her waist, sixth plate, resealed surface, leather case w/broken hinge **595.00**

Fred Thompson Tinted Photograph

Photograph, "Toiler of the Sea," a Fred Thompson hand-colored photograph, large clean mat, framed, early 20th c. (ILLUS.) **577.00**

Photograph, advertising-type, Karl Moon's bust portrait of a Native American w/advertising for "Stetson Hats - Made to Last a Lifetime," hand-tinted, 16 x 20" **3,300.00**

Tintype, sixth plate image of a man w/a Springfield-type musket, civilian clothes **45.00**

Tintype, sixth plate image of a man wearing a great coat w/brass buttons & cuff stripes. **50.00**

Tintype, cased sixth plate **275.00**

Tintype, sixth plate image of a Scotsman in full regalia wearing tartan kilt, belts, tam, etc. **100.00**

POLITICAL & CAMPAIGN ITEMS

CAMPAIGN

Book, 1856 campaign, John C. Fremont **$25.00**

Book, 1936 Democratic Convention, large size, many pictures. **35.00**

Hesler Cabinet Photo of Lincoln

Cabinet photo, 1860 campaign, a photographic print by Alexander Hesler of Chicago showing the famous "tossled hair" shot taken of Abraham Lincoln at the time of his 1860 campaign for the presidency, cardboard backing w/Hesler's printed name in the lower left & address, "70 State Street Chicago" in the lower right (ILLUS.). **2,588.00**

Rare Henry Clay Cigar Case

Cigar case, painted leather, flattened oblong form, the top painted w/a bust portrait of Henry Clay w/the inscription "Henry Clay - Candidate for 1844" above & a lengthy political poem below, varnished, 5½" l. (ILLUS.) **2,185.00**

1880 Garfield & Arthur Cloak

Cloak, campaign of 1880, Garfield (James) & Arthur (Chester), painted canvas, rounded shape decorated w/a flying eagle holding a banner reading "Garfield & Arthur," scattered losses & fading, 30" l. (ILLUS.). **1,093.00**

Doll, 1964 campaign, Barry Goldwater, mint in box. **75.00**

Doll, 1964 campaign, Lyndon Johnson, mint in box **75.00**

Engraving, 1868 campaign, "Grant & Colfax - Liberty and Loyalty - Justice and Public Safety," U.S. Grant & Schuyler Colfax, black & white bust portraits of the candidates below a spread-winged eagle w/banner, images flanked on one side by a soldier & on the other by a farmer, matted & framed, 18¼ x 21½" (horizontal fold line, glued between board & mat). **83.00**

Horn, painted & stenciled tin, 1892 campaign, Grover Cleveland & Adlai Stevenson, long slender form painted w/a wide band of blue w/small gold stars, a wide center section in white printed w/"Cleveland And Stevenson," & a wide red end section, 38" l. **977.00**

1840 Campaign Lantern

Lantern, campaign of 1840, tin & glass, for the campaign of William Henry Harrison, a round tin font, base & pierced cylindrical & domed vent cap w/ring handle, the clear frosted globe engraved w/an American eagle, shield, stars, a log cabin & American flag on a pole, etched banner w/"C. Chapman" (ILLUS.) **7,700.00**

Lapel pin, 1880 campaign, James Garfield, model of an armchair, metal, mechanical **195.00**

Pencil, 1928 campaign, Herbert Hoover, w/eraser top. **15.00**

Pinback button, 1908 campaign, Taft (William H.) & Sherman (James), jugate-style. **125.00**

Plate, ceramic, 1840 campaign, William Henry Harrison, "Columbian Star -- Side View" patt., wide border of stars, log cabin & man plowing in center, brown transfer, by Ridgway, 10" d. **165.00**

Postcard, 1908 campaign, Taft (William H.) & Sherman (James), double jugate-style **25.00**

Snuff box, cov., pewter, 1840 campaign, William Henry Harrison, oval w/flat base & lid, the top w/an embossed log cabin scene w/a cider barrel, two lines at cover rim, loose fit, 3⅛" l.,½" h. **495.00**

NON-CAMPAIGN

Truman White House Desk Set

Desk set, owned by Harry S Truman & used on his desk at the White House, the base made of wood removed from the White House during its renovation during his term, a central glass ashtray flanked by two pens (ILLUS.) **8,855.00**

James Polk Presidential Fan

Fan, printed paper & bone, celebrating the election of James Polk, oval color vignettes of the first ten Presidents w/Polk shown as President-elect, creamy yellow ground w/delicate printed green scrolling, in a display case, 10½ x 20" (ILLUS.). **2,500.00**

Matzos box, hinged lid, presentation plaque inside the top for President Harding, leatherette finish & metal fittings. **11,385.00**

Miniature portrait of Franklin Pierce, water-color on ivory, attributed to Elkanah Tisdale, unsigned, in a leather case frame, 2⅝ x 3⅛" (very minor staining & surface abrasions, damage to case) **748.00**

Mug, ceramic, cylindrical w/molded base & slightly rolled rim, small ring handle near the rim, white ground w/one side featuring a black transfer-printed bust portrait of "Major Gen. Ulysses S. Grant" & the reverse w/a bust portrait of "Maj. Gen. Q.A. Gillmore," 3½" h. (two short rim hairlines & unseen base chip) **550.00**

Paperweight, memorial-type, a bright multicolored ground w/a yellow eagle above the inscription "PRESIDENT MCKINLEY - SHOT SEPT. 6TH - DIED SEPT. 14TH - BUFFALO. 1901. NEW YORK," pontiled, 3¾" d. (refracting line on the ground) **165.00**

Plaque, bas-relief silver plated bust portrait of Abraham Lincoln in a circular gilt plaster shadowbox frame on a dark ground, signed "J. Powell" & marked "Patented 1865," frame 15" d. (some frame damages) **500.00**

Rare James Monroe Plate

Plate, porcelain, central round medallion w/a black stipple transfer bust portrait of James Monroe framed by the inscription "James Monroe - President of the United States" within a gold center ring, plain gold rim band, France, ca. 1817-25, slight wear, 9¼" d. (ILLUS.) **6,600.00**

Yacht "Sequoia" Kennedy Era Tumbler

Tumbler, cylindrical glass printed w/the presidential seal & the name of the presidential yacht "Sequoia" & the name "John F. Kennedy," etched in gold, used during Kennedy's term (ILLUS.) **1,035.00**

Vase, Parian ware, slender baluster-form w/applied clusters of grapes on each shoulder, the body molded in relief w/a profile bust portrait of U.S. Grant within a swag medallion, attributed to Bennington, ca. 1870-80, light damage to twisted side vines, 7¼" h. **105.00**

Watch fob, pot metal, fancy foliate design w/celluloid inset photo of Calvin Coolidge. **125.00**

President Truman's Whiskey Jigger

Whiskey jigger, sterling silver, in the shape of a thimble, personally used by President Truman, engraved w/his initials (ILLUS.) **6,930.00**

POSTCARDS

Animals, cats. $2-5.00
Animals, cows 2-5.00
Animals, frogs 10-25.00
Animals, pigs. 10-25.00
Advertising, Coca-Cola, Duster
    Girl 1,500-2,500.00
Advertising, Cracker Jack
    Bears 5-75.00
Advertising, Gold Dust
    Twins 35-55.00
Advertising, Sleepy Eye Flour
    Indians 100-200.00
Afro-American, negative
    images 5-35.00
Afro-American, pro-images 25-70.00
Artist, Phillip Boileau 15-95.00
Artist, Francis Brundage 10-25.00
Artist, Ellen Clapsaddle. 8-15.00
Artist, Ellen Clapsaddle, signed, . 75-100.00
Artist, Grace Drayton 20-45.00
Artist, Harrison Fisher 12-25.00
Artist, Alphonse Mucha 300-700.00
Expositions, St. Louis, 1904. . . . . . 10-20.00
Expositions, St. Louis, hold-to-
    light. 35-200.00
Expositions, World Columbian
    Pre-Official 100-200.00
Famous People 3-5.00
Flowers 1-2.00
Hold-to-Lights. 25-45.00
Holidays, April Fools Day 1-3.00
Holidays, Christmas, not Santa. 1-5.00
Holidays, Decoration Day 3-7.00
Holidays, Easter, no animals 1-2.00
Holidays, Easter, chicks 6-10.00
Holidays, Easter, rabbits 3-10.00
Holidays, Halloween (see Artist,
    Ellen Clapsaddle, signed) 20-100.00
Holidays, Labor Day 75-150.00
Holidays, New Years. 1-3.00
Kewpies, O'Neill 15-35.00
Kewpie, Klever Kards 50-75.00
Leather 2-4.00
Native Americans, real photo,
    signed 50-100.00
Political, 1904 . . . . 50-100.00
Roosevelt Bears, No. 17-34 . . . . . . 40-50.00
Roosevelt Bears, unnumbered. . 100-150.00
Russo-Japanese War. 55-85.00
Santa, small images 5-8.00
Santa, red suit 10-20.00
Santa, other than red suit 20-45.00
State Capitols 5-10.00
Suffrage, comic 45-95.00
Sunbonnets 12-20.00

Transportation, automobiles, photo . . 10-15.00
Transportation, steamship, Titanic . . 50-500.00
Views, small town main streets 10-35.00
Views, train depots 25-35.00
WWII-Propaganda, comic. 5-15.00
Wood 1-4.00

PURSES & BAGS

Alligator, three compartment
    w/central clasp, goldtone & cord
    chain handles, ca. 1950, Chanel
    insignia, France $1,150.00
Gold mesh, 14k yellow gold, top-set
    w/emeralds & diamonds
    suspending the mesh purse, paper
    clip chain handle, dated "1913,"
    Germany. 1,495.00
Gold mesh, 14k yellow gold w/a
    pierced & chased frame edged in
    diamonds, having a center blue
    enamel disc depicting a woman in
    cameo, the inside opens to reveal
    a mirror, hallmark for Frank T. May
    Co., N.Y. & N.J., Edwardian 4,600.00
Leather, Hermes Kelly, black
    w/Hermes padlock & keys,
    ca. 1950, France 805.00
Needlework, rectangular flattened
    pocketbook w/flame stitch design,
    American, late 18th c., 8¾" l.
    (minor losses & insect damage) . . . 633.00
Rose gold (10k), coin purse
    w/chased leaf design case,
    ca. 1898, English hallmarks 230.00

1   2   3
Three Small Silver Purses

Sterling silver, flattened rectangular
    form w/slender chain handle,
    overall low-relief scroll foliate
    engraving, monogrammed, Wm. B.
    Kerr & Co., ca. 1900, 2⅝ x 3½"
    (ILLUS. No. 3) 288.00
Sterling silver, a flattened
    rectangular form w/rounded top
    corners & a slender chain handle,
    the top half bright-cut w/floral
    foliate design, maker's mark
    "M.H.H.," Birmingham, England,
    1913, 2¾ x 4¼" (ILLUS. No. 1) 259.00
Sterling silver, serpentine form w/a
    slender chain handle & delicate acid-
    etched foliate scroll designs,

monogrammed, Wm. B. Kerr & Co.,
ca. 1900, 3 x 4½" (ILLUS. No. 2) **489.00**

RADIO & TELEVISION MEMORABILIA

Addams Family paint book set,
"Wet the Brush & Bring Out
Colors," Saalfield, 1965, w/box,
unused, very fine............. **$400.00**

**Alvin & The Chipmunks (TV) record
player,** Gabriel, 1963 ...... **80.00-100.00**

Amos & Andy game, card-type,
bridge, ca. 1930, complete in box . . . **90.00**

Batman (TV) magazine, "TV Guide,"
March 26 - April 1, 1966, cover
photo of Adam West as Batman . . . **154.00**

Batman (TV) radio, "Batman Micro-
Bat Radio," complete in original
package **2,659.00**

Beany & Cecil (TV) jack-in-the-box,
Mattel, 1961 .... **75.00-100.00**

Ben Casey Play Hospital set,
TransoGram, 1961 .... **75.00-125.00**

Beverly Hillbillies paper dolls,
Whitman, 1964, very fine......... **45.00**

Bewitched "Samantha" doll, Ideal,
1965, unused, near mint........ **4,296.00**

Bewitched "Tabatha" Doll

Bewitched "Tabatha" (TV) doll,
boxed (ILLUS.).............. **2,420.00**

Boss Hogg doll, Dukes of Hazard,
Mego, ca. 1981, never removed
from package, 8" h............. **20.00**

Bozo Lunch Box

Bozo (TV) lunch box, Aladdin, 1963
(ILLUS.)............... **100.00-150.00**

Bugs Bunny figure, ceramic,
American Pottery, 4" h........... **58.00**

Bullwinkle Moose Viewmaster reel . . **125.00**

Captain Video game, board-type,
"Capt. Video Space Game," Milton
Bradley, early 1950s, complete
contents & colorful box in fine
condition **120.00**

Charlie McCarthy doll, marked
"Edgar Bergen's Charlie McCarthy,
An Effanbee Product" on original
button, composition shoulder head,
working mouth controlled w/pull
string, painted brown eyes w/single
stroke brows, painted upper
lashes, ventriloquist mouth
w/painted lower teeth, molded &
painted hair, original black tuxedo
& top hat, 17" h................ **500.00**

Charlie McCarthy game, "Charlie
McCarthy Radio Party Game,"
unpunched, 1930s.............. **75.00**

Charlie's Angels dolls gift set,
includes three "Charlie's Angels"
dolls, Hasbro, ca.1977........... **140.00**

**Clarabell Clown (Howdy Doody)
costume,** Collegeville, 1950s,
w/metal horn, very fine **85.00**

Combat (TV) coloring book,
Artcraft, 1964, unused **25.00-45.00**

Daniel Boone "Frontier Attack" Play Set

**Daniel Boone "Frontier Attack"
(TV) Play Set,** MPC, 1964, Grant
store exclusive (ILLUS.) . . . **200.00-250.00**

Ding Dong School record player,
RCA, 1950s, near mint **134.00**

Dr. Kildare game, board-type, Ideal,
1962, unused................. **103.00**

F-Troop coloring book, Saalfield,
1967, unused.................. **50.00**

Family Affair doll, "Buffy Bendible
Doll," Mattel, w/Mrs. Beasley, 1967,
very fine..................... **165.00**

Family Affair game, board-type,
Remco, 1968, very fine **330.00**

Flintstones (TV) "Dino Stroller "
Ideal, 1963, w/box........ **200.00-250.00**

Flintstones (TV) play set, Marx,
1962 (ILLUS.) **300.00-400.00**

Flintstones Play Set

Flying Nun (TV) Doll, in original
box **1,000.00**

Get Smart game, board-type, Ideal,
1966, unused. **40.00**

Gidget game, board-type, S.T., 1965,
unused. **330.00**

Gilligan's Island writing tablet,
1965, unused. **20.00**

Groucho Marx game, "Groucho TV
Quiz Game," board-type, 1950s **35.00**

Hector Heathcote (TV) lunch box,
Aladdin, 1964 . . . . **100.00-135.00**

Hogan's Heroes lunch box, Aladdin,
1965, very good. **75.00**

Hogan's Heroes trading cards,
complete set plus wrapper, Fleer,
1965, 67 pcs. (some cards are
slightly off-center). **1,831.00**

Honey West game, board-type,
Ideal, 1965, unused. **200.00**

Honeymooners book, "Love Alice,"
written & autographed by Audrey
Meadows, 1994, mint **30.00**

Howdy Doody camera w/film &
papers, on original card. **165.00**

Howdy Doody marionette,
composition head, hands & feet,
h.p. features, in original box,
1950s, 16" h. **242.00**

Howdy Doody night light, w/original
box. **95.00**

Howdy Doody pencil, figural,
Kagran. **55.00**

Howdy Doody Uke

Howdy Doody uke, Emenee, 1954,
w/box (ILLUS.) **100.00-150.00**

Howdy Doody wristwatch,
Ingraham, 1954, very fine **75.00**

Huckleberry Hound figure, "TV
Tinykins" **15.00**

Huckleberry Hound record album,
"Huckleberry Hound for President" . . **25.00**

I Dream of Jeannie game, board-
type, Milton Bradley, 1964, unused. **100.00**

I Love Lucy cut-out doll kit, "I Love
Lucy Packaway Cut-Out Doll Kit,"
Whitman, 1953, very fine. **220.00**

I Love Lucy magazine, "T.V.
Showtime," June 19, 1964. . . . . **25.00**

I Love Lucy record, "I Love Lucy"
theme, 45 r.p.m. recorded by Desi
Arnez, 1950s, near mint **45.00**

Incredible Hulk tumbler, glass
w/printed green & red picture of a
running Hulk, Marvel, 1978 . . . . **67.00**

It's About Time game, board-type,
Ideal, 1964, unused. **250.00**

Jackie Gleason game, "Jackie
Gleason and Away We Go" game,
TransOGram, 1955, fine **126.00**

**Jerry Mahoney ventriloquist
dummy,** Juro, 1950s, very fine in
fine box **175.00**

Jetsons record album, original
soundtrack album, 1960s **152.00**

Lassie button, "I Voted For Lassie,"
1950s, very fine. **60.00**

Lassie comic book, "Forest Ranger
Handbook," 1967, near mint **45.00**

Lassie Stuffed Doll

Lassie stuffed doll, Knickerbocker,
1956, w/tag, 13" (ILLUS.) . . . **75.00-100.00**

Laugh-In pencils, Empire, 1969,
mint in package. **81.00**

*Lucille Ball, Desi Arnaz & Little Ricky
Paper Doll Packaway Kit*

Lucille Ball, Desi Arnaz & Little Ricky (TV) Paper Doll Packaway Kit, Whitman, 1952 (ILLUS.). **100.00-200.00**

M.A.S.H. toy, helicopter, Durham, 1975, unused, w/box **165.00**

M-Squad handcuffs, J.H., 1959, unused. **218.00**

Mr. Ed talking hand puppet, Mattel, 1962, w/box. **100.00-125.00**

Mr. Jinx coloring book **25.00**

My Favorite Martian Board Game

My Favorite Martian game, board-type,TransoGram, 1963 (ILLUS.). **50.00-75.00**

My Favorite Martian toy, "My Favorite Martian Trick Set," Gilbert, 1964, fine. **185.00**

Patty Duke coloring book, Whitman, 1964, very good. **10.00**

Pinkie Lee puzzle set, Gabriel, 1950s, fine. **30.00**

Princess Summerfall - Winterspring (Howdy Doody TV) push-up puppet, wood, Kohner, ca. 1950. **128.00**

Rin Tin Tin gun & holster set, 1956, very fine (minus shoulder strap) **96.00**

Rin Tin Tin record album, Columbia, 1956, very fine. **18.00**

Ripcord game, Ripcord Skydiving Game, board-type, Lowell, 1962, fine. **50.00**

Rocky & Friends Sewing Cards, Whitman, 1961 . . . . **65.00-100.00**

Romper Room Do-Bee bath container, Manon Freres, 1959, very fine. **100.00**

Sea Hunt game, board-type, Sea Hunt Underwater Game, Lowell, 1960, very fine. **111.00**

77 Sunset Strip game, "77 Sunset Strip," board-type, Lowell Toys, 1960, box 10 x 20", very good in box. **33.00**

Shari Lewis Activity Set, Saalfield, 1962, very fine. **40.00**

Shari Lewis game, "Chariland," board-type, TransOGram, 1959, very fine. **50.00**

SWAT lunch box, Thermos, 1975, near mint **25.00**

That Girl coloring book, Saalfield, 1967, very fine. **25.00**

That Girl magazine, "TV Showtime," August 4, 1967, very fine. **12.00**

That Girl paper dolls, Saalfield, 1967, unused. **50.00**

The Avengers book, paperback No. 1, 1967, fine **5.00**

The Fugitive magazine, "TV Showtime," November 19, 1965, fine. **22.00**

The Man From U.N.C.L.E. cloth banner, manufactured in Scotland, 1965, very fine. **138.00**

The Man From U.N.C.L.E. coloring book, "Crush Thrush," Watkins-Strathmore, 1965, unused. **35.00**

The Man From U.N.C.L.E. Halloween mask, Napoleon Solo, Halco, 1965, unused **20.00**

The Man From U.N.C.L.E. lunch box, Thermos, 1966, very fine **101.00**

The Munsters magazine, "TV Showtime," August 21, 1964, near mint **700.00**

Shadow (The) blotter, 1940s. **45.00**

Time Tunnel game, board-type, Ideal, 1966, unused. **431.00**

Time Tunnel game, "Spin to Win," Pressman, 1967, unused **270.00**

12 O'Clock High game, board-type, Ideal, 1965, unused, mint **150.00**

Voyage to the Bottom of the Sea 8mm movie, on original retail card, 1960s. **118.00**

Voyage to the Bottom of the Sea jigsaw puzzle, Milton Bradley, 1966, very fine. **70.00**

Voyage to the Bottom of the Sea Play Set

Voyage to the Bottom of the Sea play set, w/box (ILLUS.) **2,800.00**

Welcome Back Kotter jumprope, MSS, 1977, mint in package **20.00**

Whirlybirds coloring book, Whitman, 1959, fine **20.00**

Wile E. Coyote model kit, MPC, circa 1971 . . . . **50.00-75.00**

Yogi Bear squeeze figure, Dell,
1959, 5" h. **25.00-35.00**
You Bet Your Life game, board-
type, Lowell, 1955, unused in fine
box. **92.00**

RADIOS

*By carefully comparing the age, style and
condition of your vintage radio you can often
approximate its value:*

General Electric Deco Console Radio

A. C. Dayton XL-10, mid-1920s with
5 tubes, 5 knobs on front Bakelite
panel **$100.00**
Addison Model 5, large Catalin sets,
yellow body in unbroken
condition. **1,200.00**
Admiral 5Y22, oversized radio-
phonograph table top in brown
Bakelite **30.00**
Air King 52, classic 1933
"skyscraper" style in white Bakelite,
a few small stress cracks but
complete and unbroken **2,000.00**
Atwater Kent 20, simple wide
wooden table top from the 1920s . . . **75.00**
Atwater Kent 40 or 41, simple metal
table top from the late 1920s. **65.00**
**Atwater Kent Model 10 breadboard
(4340)** with exposed controls and
tubes, all original **850.00**
Bendix 0526C in tan and brown thin
plastic case **250.00**
Bendix, 1940s brown Bakelite, nice
lines. **50.00**
Colonial New World Globe, novelty
white Bakelite radio circa 1930s,
small crack **400.00**
Crosley 9-119, simple Bakelite table
top from the late 1940s **30.00**
Emerson AU-190, table top Catalin
radio, green case and knobs, mint
condition. **1,500.00**

Emerson AX-235, small Catalin style
table top with blue body, small
fracture or crack **2,200.00**
Emerson U-5A, white Bakelite case
and back, clean without cracks **245.00**
FADA Model 16, wide metal table top
from the late 1920s **60.00**
FADA Model 115, pre-WWII "Bullet"
Catalin table top in all yellow or
pumpkin, no breaks or burns **550.00**
General Electric, Deco console, late
1930s style (ILLUS.) **100.00**
Kadette Junior, small, tall1930s
2-tube portable in brown Bakelite . . **225.00**
Kadette Junior K10, Classic
oversized table radio, case and
trim excellent. **675.00**
Motorola 50XC1, Circle Grille Catalin
table top in turquoise with yellow
trim, no cracks or burns **4,000.00**
RCA 6T10, tall mid-1930s radio with
circular grille and tubular chrome
frame **2,500.00**
RCA 8BX5, cloth covered late 1940s
portable with handle **30.00**
Sparton 1300, mid-1950s double
door radio-phono console with
square lines. **45.00**
Zenith 5D011, mid-1940s square
wooden table top. **25.00**
Zenith 6D311, Wavemagnet late
1930s Bakelite table top **125.00**
excellent **145.00**
Zenith Stratosphere, 25-tube Deco
console from the 1930s . . . . **3,500.00+**
Zenith T-600L, tan colored
Trans-Oceanic. **175.00**

RAILROADIANA

Silhouette Pattern Railroad Ashtray

Ashtray, "Chesapeake & Ohio
Railway," china, "Silhouette" patt.
(ILLUS.). **100.00**
Booklet, "Union Pacific Railroad,"
discussing Kansas, dated 1890 . . . . **65.00**
Bouillon cup, "Union Pacific
Railroad," china, Harriman Blue
patt. **35.00**

Bowl, shallow, "Union Pacific Railroad," china, Harriman Blue patt., 6" d. **25.00**

Calendar, "Pennsylvania Railroad," 1956, colorful landscape scene of trains passing on tracks, calendar pad below, signature of agent at top corner of calendar, write-up about the "Truc Train" on the back, framed, scratches at top, overall creases, minor frame wear, 30½" sq. **275.00**

Cap badge, "Atchison, Topeka & Santa Fe Railway," metal, brakeman, ... **95.00**

Creamer, "Wabash Railroad," silver plate, by International Silver **90.00**

Cup, "Baltimore & Ohio Railroad," china, "Centenary" patt. **40.00**

Cup & Saucer, "Missouri Pacific Railroad," china, "Bismark" patt. **53.00**

Engine headlight, Illinois Central, #2545 . . . . **2,100.00**

Engine light, black metal w/red lens . . **250.00**

Glass, juice, "Chesapeake & Ohio Railway " **4.00**

Ladle, "St. Louis & San Francisco Railway," silver plate **40.00**

Lantern, "Atchison, Topeka & Santa Fe Railroad," short globe-type, red globe w/raised lettering **140.00**

Lantern, "Baltimore & Ohio Railroad," tall globe-type, clear globe w/raised wording & "Safety First" **120.00**

Lantern, "Western Maryland Railway," tall globe-type, clear matching globe **100.00**

Lock, signal-type, "Missouri Pacific Railroad" **80.00**

Lock, signal-type, "Rock Island Lines". **50.00**

Pillow, "St. Louis & San Francisco Railway" (Frisco Lines) **33.00**

Pillow case, "Union Pacific Railroad" . . **20.00**

Plate, "Denver & Rio Grande Western Railroad," bread & butter, china, "Blue Adam" patt. **20.00**

Plate, "Western Pacific Railroad," grapefruit, china, "Feather River" patt. **200.00**

Plate, "Union Pacific Railroad," china, "Circus" patt., scene of bareback rider, 8¼" d. **95.00**

Railroad map of Pennsylvania, color lithograph, one-sided, stamped "Compliments of Isaac B. Brown, Supt. Bureau of Railways," dated 1887, museum-mounted, edge wear, soiling & staining, 36¾ x 57½" **72.00**

Sauce dish, "Pennsylvania Railroad," china, "Liberty" patt. **25.00**

Sauce dish, "Southern Railway," china, "Piedmont" patt. **11.00**

Service plate, "Baltimore & Ohio Railroad," china, "Camden" patt. . . . **50.00**

ROYALTY COMMEMORATIVES

GEORGE IV (1820-30)

Soup tureen, cover, ladle & undertray, earthenware, oval deep turned on high oval foot w/heavy scroll-molded upturned loop end handles, high domed & stepped cover w/blossom finial, dark blue transfer-printed historical scene of "The Coronation of George IV," the undertray w/a central scene of "The Bishops conveyed to the Tower," Jones & Son, ca. 1826-28, undertray w/paint touch-ups on rim, tureen 14½" l., 11½" h., the set . . **3,740.00**

Plate, earthenware, finely embossed border of roses & leaves w/a black rim band, the center w/a black transfer-printed bust portrait of Queen Caroline framed by a printed rose wreath, ca. 1820, 6½" d. **770.00**

QUEEN VICTORIA (1837-1901)

Mug, pottery, 1897 Diamond Jubilee commemorative, cylindrical w/angled handle, printed in black & white w/an oval bust portrait of

Queen Victoria Jubilee Mug

Queen Victoria framed by flags & banners, marked on the bottom "Wood & Hulme, Burslem," 4" d., 4" h, (ILLUS.)   **100.00**

Pitcher, stoneware, slightly swelled cylindrical body gently tapering to a flared rim w/deep spout, angular handle w/a crown-form thumbrest, one side molded in relief w/a bust portrait of the late Prince Albert, The Prince Consort within a wreath & framed by various orders & medals, the reverse molded w/the British royal arms, ca. 1860s, 8" h. . . **303.00**

Plate, earthenware, an embossed floral flanged border surrounding blue transfer-printed bust portraits of Queen Victoria & Prince Albert framed by the inscription "Queen Victoria & Prince Albert - Married 10th February 1840," Staffordshire, England, 4½" d. **385.00**

GEORGE V (1910-36)

Pitcher, milk, china, 1911 coronation commemorative, Shelley, 5" h. **110.00**

Plate, china, 1911 coronation commemorative, by Aynsley, 6" d. . . **50.00**

Plate, china, 1911 coronation commemorative, portraits of King George & Queen Mary, Royal Doulton, 10½" d. **138.00**

ELIZABETH II (1952-)

Ashtray, china, 1953 coronation commemorative, Royal Winton **20.00**

Silver Miniature Coronation Chair

Coronation chair, sterling silver w/gold overlay miniature rendition, 1953 coronation commemorative, the Stone of Scone under the seat, chair supported on four lions, w/commemorative plaque, in fitted case, Birmingham, 4⅝" h. (ILLUS.). . **748.00**

Cup & saucer, china, commemorative of 1957 visit to Canada, Paragon **45.00**

Cup & saucer, china, commemorative of 1959 opening of the St. Lawrence Seaway, Paragon . . **45.00**

Pin tray, porcelain, 1953 Coronation commemorative, Shelley, 5½" l. **38.00**

Pub pitcher, clear glass w/white enamel picture around a crown logo, 1953 Coronation commemorative. **32.00**

ROYCROFT ITEMS

Andirons, wrought iron, Secessionist-style, slender tall S-scroll uprights w/a section of open spiral-twists below the tightly scrolled finial, delicate scrolls down the sides & at the base including the feet, square log bar, the two joined by a heavy round twist-link chain, black finish, Model No. 69, unmarked, 13¼" w., 27½" h., pr. . **$2,640.00**

Book ends, hand-hammered copper, tapering rectangular uprights w/curled-up edges & embossed in the center w/a trillium blossom, fine original patina, orb & cross mark, 3¾" w., 5½" h., pr. **220.00**

Large Roycroft Bowl

Bowl, hand-hammered copper, three-footed, wide flattened bottom below squatty rounded & tapering sides to a flat wide rolled rim, fine new dark brown patina, early mark, 10½" d., 4½" h. **850.00**

Candleholder, eight-light, hand-hammered heavy gauge brass, a long narrow flat bar w/curled-under ends supports eight bell-form candle sockets, raised on arched scroll-tipped end legs, original patina, marked, 4 x 21", 3" h. **358.00**

Plaque, carved oak, motto-type, rectangular board-form, incised words "Be Yourself," original dark finish, carved orb & cross mark, 5¼ x 19¼" **3,740.00**

Rocker w/arms, Mission-style (Arts & Crafts movement), oak, a flat crestrail & narrower lower rail flanking a slightly waisted wide splat between the square stiles, flat open arms on square supports forming the front legs, new tacked-on black leather seat, new dark finish, carved orb & cross mark, 35½" h. **825.00**

Tea bell, hand-hammered copper, w/flat brass handle, original dark patina, w/early orb & cross mark, 1¾" d., 3¼" h. **303.00**

Vase, hand-hammered copper, bulbous base below upright deeply dimpled sides w/a flaring, ruffled rim, original dark patina, orb & cross mark, 5½" d., 6" h. **605.00**

Vase, hand-hammered copper, flaring trumpet-form foot tapering to a raised band below the tall slender cylindrical body w/a molded rim, fine original patina, marked, 10½" h. **2,090.00**

RUGS - HOOKED & OTHER

HOOKED

Animal & flowers, striped border centering a reserve of a domestic animal standing beside a vase of flowers, worked in blue, purple, red, brown, taupe & grey, American, late 19th - early 20th c., framed, 34¼ X 40" (fiber wear, minor loss, fading) **122.00**

Cats, a geometric border centering a reserve of two cats, worked in yellow, red, blue, white, terra-cotta, sage & pink on a black & white field, early 20th c., 23½ X 37½" (minor losses, staining) **374.00**

Compass star, circular, the large star design in red, grey, black, blue & yellow, some wear, 55" d. **413.00**

Dog reclining on grass, primitive Frost pattern w/large dog on grass w/flowering branch at its rear, within narrow border w/scrolled corners, brilliant colors, 30 x 50" . . **3,000.00**

Horse w/saddle, the walking animal in a grassy landscape w/trees in the distance, brown horse on a variegated ground, New England, 19th c., repairs, mounted, 30½ x 51" **2,185.00**

Hunter & animals, stylized leaf band upper & lower borders enclosing a long scene of a running hunter & dogs chasing flying oversized birds among bare trees, worked in grey, black, sage, red & ecru on a cream ground, late 19th - early 20th c., minor repair, fading, staining, 28½ x 52" (ILLUS.) **863.00**

Lovebirds & flowers, large facing birds in center flanked by large stems of blossoms, light blue, red

Hunter & Animals Hooked Rug

& beige on a black ground, flowers also w/purple, yellow & orange, mounted on a stretcher, 20 x 38" (some repair, wear, edge damage) . . **616.00**

Vase of flowers, rectangular, the design worked in olive green, red, yellow, cream & blue on a black ground, dated 1921, 19½ x 33½" (backed) **460.00**

OTHER

Drugget rug, woven, Arts & Crafts style, rectangular w/an oatmeal ground decorated w/scattered dark bluish grey geometric devices composed of small triangles all within a wide border band, Gustav Stickley, early 20th c., 4' 2" x 6' 9" (light wear in one corner) **468.00**

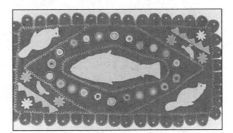

Fine Appliqued Wool Penny Rug

Penny rug, an applied scallop border on the long rectangular rung applied in wool w/a large central fish surrounded by a ring of applied colored spots w/birds & stars in two corners & beavers in the other two, all against a black ground (ILLUS.) **1,733.00**

Woven rag runner, four strips sewn together w/stripes of black, blue, red, yellow & white, Pennsylvania, 3' X 11' 2" (wear, stains, some damage) **468.00**

SCIENTIFIC INSTRUMENTS

Air flow meter, w/lacquered & oxidized brass frame, waxed & lacquered vanes, silvered dial w/subsidiary counters, original pine case, 19th c., by Davis of Darby, 12" d. **$1,380.00**

Early French Armillary Sphere

Armillary sphere, wood & paper, a 2½" d. terrestrial globe, signed & dated "A Paris chez 1. St. Fortm rue de la Harpe 1773," sun & moon discs on metal arms, Equatorial & Tropical circles, hour & zodiac rings, supported by four quadrants w/latitudes & longitudes of various cities on a turned ebonized wood stand, France, late 18th c., 40½" h. (ILLUS.). **5,520.00**

Astrolabe, cast iron, a small rotating model of the earth & moon at the end of a long rotating straight arms w/cranch mechanism, on a stepped, round metal base, ca.1890, restorations, 22" l., 16" h. **6,325.00**

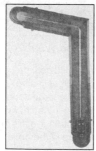

Rare "Angle" Barometer

Barometer, stick-type, mahogany "angle" style, the wooden backboard w/molded edges & a sharp angle at the upper half enclosing the long tube & bottom bulb, w/etched brass plaque, signed by John Berry, Manchester, England, third quarter 18th c., 23" w., 44" h. (ILLUS.) **5,175.00**

Barometer, wheel-type, painted & parcel-gilt wood, w/a cream-painted circular dial flanked by fruit-filled cornucopia & carved w/a flaming torch w/a pair of doves & a quiver of arrows, surmounted by a rectangular thermometer, laurel wreath & flowerheads, terminating in a pine cone finial, now painted celadon green & trimmed in gold, Louis XVI style, France, last quarter 18th c., 22" w., 4' 1" h. . . **2,587.00**

Chronometer, marine, eight-day w/lever escapement in brass-bound mahogany case w/inspection label dated 1921 in lid, Waltham, No. 22122702, 5" w. **1,380.00**

Microscope, portable, brass-cased, w/a 2½" body-tube, draw-tube & fine-screw focusing mounted to underside, the case end forming a sprung stage & sub-stage mirror, the sliding lid signed "Nachet et fils, Rue Serpentine 16, Paris," lacks part of case, France, 19th c., 2" w., 3½" h. **4,370.00**

Rare Early English Microscope

Microscope, compound model, Culpeper pattern, w/a brass eyepiece, dust slide, lignum vitae upper body-tube, velum draw-tube graduated 1-5, shagreen-covered lower body-tube, lignum nose piece & brass tage on three pillar supports to ebonized mahogany base w/accessories drawer containing shaped tweezers, multiple specimen discs & other items, England, ca. 1730, 16" h. (ILLUS.) **5,980.00**

Sundial, turned ivory, the base interior w/engraved dial for Italian time divided 10 & 23, the lid engraved "EQUINO AND TIOLOS," the outer lid & base w/turned decoration, 3¼" d. **633.00**

Surveyor's compass, brass cased model, complete w/detachable brass sight vanes & brass tripod adaptor in dovetailed mahogany box w/ paper label reading "Loring & Churchill successors to C.G. King...72 Washington St. (2d door from State St.) Boston," J.W. Loring, Boston, ca. 1850, 5½ x 14½", box 9½" h. **1,265.00**

Telescope on stand, brass, the long cylindrical telescope adjusting on a cylindrical pedestal raised on an adjustable tripod base, signed "Worthington & Allan, late M. Berge, London," England, late 19th c., extended telescope 46¾" l. . . **2,587.00**

Weather station, mahogany, long upright rectangular mahogany cased w/two round dials flanking a central cylindrical drum, one dial an aneroid barometer w/blued steel needle & silvered diald signed "Stereoscopic Company Instrument Depart 110 & 108 Regent Street, London," a Dimenum-patent minimum/maximum therometer, a lacquarted brass barograph operated by a single-train timepiece w/silvered dial, blued-steel hands & auxiliary dial, 19th c., 24¾" l. **2,300.00**

SCRIMSHAW

Scrimshaw is a folk art by-product of the 19th century American whaling industry. Intricately carved and engraved pieces of whalebone, whale's teeth and walrus tusks were produced by whalers during their spare time at sea. In recent years numerous fine grade hard plastic reproductions have appeared on the market so the novice collector must use caution to distinguish these from the rare originals.

Busk, engraved whalebone, narrow thin strip engraved & polychrome-decorated w/a central memorial monument w/a willow tree, leafy branches & urns of flowers above & below, 19th c., cracks, 11⅞" l. . **$316.00**

Busk, whalebone, decorated w/incised designs including a church, stars, bars & entwined loop designs, 19th c., 13⅜" l. (slight warpage) **316.00**

Jagging wheel, whale ivory w/the curving handle ornately pierce-carved w/small rings & loops w/flared end, serrated wheel, 19th c., minute losses, 5¾" l. **2,875.00**

Jagging wheel, the swelling, squared raised band-carved handle w/a central open-carved section, serrated wheel, 19th c., minor cracks, minute chips, 6¼" l. **920.00**

Panbone, rectangular, engraved w/a scene of the British whaling ship "Argus" towing & processing dead whales, flanked by towers flying the British flag & a vine border, polychrome highlights, England, 19th c., 8¾ x 18¾" **4,600.00**

Ornate Scrimshaw Walrus Tusk

Walrus tusks, each decorated w/various reserves of animals, courting couples, ships under sail, memorials, sailors & armaments, w/later engraved brass presentation caps reading "Presented by George M. Chase to Ike B. Dunlap Jan. 25th, 1908," 19th c., cracks, one restored, 17¾" l., pr. (ILLUS. of one) **2,530.00**

Whale's teeth, decorated w/incised whaling barks flying American flags, one depicts cutting in a sperm whale flying "MP" flag, the other shows the ship under sail flying an "M" flag, 19th c., 4½ & 4¾" h., pr. (very minor scratches) . . **978.00**

Whale's teeth, decorated w/two incised three-masted ships under sail flying the American flag, the reverse decorated w/an elegant couple, the lady being asleep in her chair, 19th c., 7½" h., pr. (cracks, chips, scratches) **3,335.00**

Whale's tooth, etched w/various ships under sail & a young lady, 19th c., 6⅞" h. (cracks) **1,380.00**

Whale's tooth, decorated w/an incised figure of Liberty holding an American flag & shield w/a spread-winged eagle holding arrows above her & on the reverse w/a cannon, anchor & flag on a barrel, flowering vine borders, 19th c., 7''' h. (cracks, very minor losses) **518.00**

SEWING ADJUNCTS

Over the last decade, sewing accessories have become one of the most popular collectibles in the United States, Canade and England. With a wide variety of sewing tools available in all price ranges, one can assemble a fine collection in nearly any budget. Be careful as the prices have risen, so has the availabilty of reproductions. Check sterling items carefully Georgian-stayle and Victorian-style needlecases and thimbleholders marked "Thailand" are seen often, and sell wholesale for less that ten dollars each. Plenty of good books on antique sewing items are available a good start would be An Illustrated History of Needlework Tools by Gay Ann Rogers. All items listed below are in excellent condition, with no missing parts.

Bodkin, brass, engraved florals, English, ca. 1860s **$38.00**

Bodkin, sterling silver, set of three in a shagreen case, decorated in a Greek Key design, ca. 1890 . . . . . . **195.00**

Darner, china, h.p. stylized figure of a girl decoration, 1940s **65.00**

Darner, glove-type, sterling silver, delicate floral design, double-ended, ca. 1880s **195.00**

Emery, cloth & sterling silver, strawberry-shaped, velvet w/a sterling top marked "Sterling," made in the U.S.A., ca. 1900, 1¾" . . **135.00**

Emery-waxer, Tunbridge stickware design, England, ca. 1870s **195.00**

Lace bobbin, bone, delicately turned design dyed green & red, 1850s, English **95.00**

Lace bobbin, bone, the name "Joseph" in a red dot design, English, 1850s . . **115.00**

Lace-making pillow, lap-style, sawdust-filled pillow on top of a wooden bobbin box w/one drawer, English, ca. 1850 . . . . **580.00**

Needlebook, folding-style, book-form w/diagonal overall design of white beads over pink silk, woven flannel leaves inside, English, 1890s **90.00**

Needlecase, ivory, plain cylinder without decoration, English, 1860s . . **85.00**

Needlecase, ivory, Stanhope-type, tiny scene of the Port of Torquay, English, ca. 1880 . . . . **170.00**

Needleholder, brass, figural butterfly, Avery, 1880s **675.00**

Pin disc, cut steel, from a sterling silver chatelaine, English, 1850s . . . **90.00**

Pin disc, embroidered velvet, rectangular, decorated w/florals, ca. 1890 . . . . **85.00**

Pin disc, Fernware, Scottish, ca. 1870s **155.00**

Figural Bisque Pincushion

Pincushion, bisque, model of a rabbit pulling a cart , cloth pincushion in the cart, ca. 1900 (ILLUS.) **95.00**

Pincushion, ivory, bellows-shaped, pierced designs, ca. 1820, rare . . . **235.00**

Pincushion, make-do type, cloth top on glass base, 1880s **145.00**

Scissors, sterling silver, Art Nouveau design of a woman w/flowing hair, ca. 1920 . . . . **165.00**

Scissors, sterling silver, ornate floral design, English, 1850s **155.00**

Scissors, steel, Sheffield, England, 1860s, 3½" l **44.00**

Sewing kit, brass, egg-shaped, engraved scrolling decoration, w/thread, needleholder & thimble, heavy, English, ca. 1900 . . . . **115.00**

Sewing kit, brass, egg-shaped w/tassel & embossed design, w/thread, needleholder & thimble, case marked "Austria," 1940s **48.00**

Sewing kit, celluloid, made for Boy Scouts of America, 1940s **38.00**

Silk winder, mother-of-pearl, round w/notches, English, 19th c. **38.00**

Silk winder, sterling silver, diamond-shaped, repousse' details, English, ca. 1880s **165.00**

Silk winder, bone, snowflake-form,
English, 1850s, 1" d. 35.00
Stiletto, bone, turned design,
English, 19th c., 2" l. 10.00
Stiletto, mother-of-pearl handle
w/carved feather design, steel
shaft, English, ca. 1900, 5" l. 45.00
Tape measure, bone, Stanhope-type,
barrel-shaped w/a turned design,
manual-wind, English, ca. 1850s-
60s 175.00
Tape measure, celluloid, model of a
sailing ship, spring-wind, 1930s
155.00
Tape measure, celluloid, model of a
Scotty dog on a tree stump, spring-
wind, 1930s 180.00
Tape measure, celluloid, model of an
English cottage, spring-wind,
1920s-30s 195.00
Tape measure, ornate copper &
brass, model of a coffee grinder,
manual-wind, European, ca. 1900 . . 300.00
Tape measure, round, souvenir of
the 1933 Chicago "Century of
Progress" exhibition, buildings
shown, spring-wind 88.00

Tape Measure with Cat's Face

Tape measure, white metal, round,
an embossed cat's face featuring
green rhinestone eyes, marked
"Germany," ca. 1900 (ILLUS.) 95.00
Tape measure, wooden, Mauchline
ware, transfer-printed scene of the
Isle of Man, Scottish, 1860s 175.00
Tatting shuttle, tortoiseshell, hard to
find, ca. 1860 . . . . 65.00
Thimble, gold, finely engraved w/a
scene of buildings & bridges, Wait
Thresher Company, late 19th c. 225.00
Thimble, Meissen porcelain, finely
hand-decorated w/chinoiserie figures
in scenes, Germany, early 18th c.,
extremely rare, sold in London at
auction, December 1997 . . . . 6,373.00
Thimble, sterling silver, Charles
Horner, England, hallmarked, plain . . 55.00

Thimble, sterling silver, decorated
w/cupids holding swags, Simons
Bros., ca. 1900 . . . . 275.00
Thimble holder, mother-of-pearl,
shell-form, sailing ship w/bisque
boy, marked "World's Columbian
Exposition 1893," sold at auction in
London, December 1997 . . . . 562.00
Thimble holder, tortoiseshell case,
thimble post inside, English,
ca. 1860s 235.00

SHAKER ITEMS

*The Shakers, a religious sect founded by Ann
Lee, first settled in this country at Watervliet,
New York, near Albany, in 1774. By 1880 there
were nine settlements in America. Workmanship
in Shaker crafts is an extension of their religious
beliefs and features plain and simple designs
reflecting a chaste elegance that is now much in
demand though relatively few early items are
common.*

Basket, woven splint, two-handled,
Sabbathday Lake, Maine, 19th c.,
16" d., 8" h. (staining, minor breaks) $173.00
Basket, laundry, ash, rectangular, the
crest joined through spindles to the
frame, old weathered surface, 19th
c., 23 x 24", 11" h. (one break in
the crest) 518.00
Bench, painted wood, rectangular top
on demi-lune cut-out ends joined
by dovetailed diagonal bracing, old
red-painted surface, ca. 1830,
9¾ x 72", 16" h. 4,888.00
Blanket chest, painted wood, six-
board construction, the hinged
molded rectangular top opens to a
cavity w/an unlidded till above a
molded base on four small turned
legs, original orange wash, black
metal end carrrying handles, a
Maine, New Hampshire or
Massachusetts community, mid-
19th c., 18¼ x 44¼", 21⅛" h.
(minor surface imperfections) . . . 1,725.00
Bonnet, palm leaf or straw, half-
round form w/steel blue silk lining &
cape, Canterbury, New Hampshire,
mid-19th c., 8½" l., 6½" h. (lacking
ties, wear, fading to silk) 978.00
Chest of drawers, butternut,
rectangular top w/half-round
molded overhanging top above the
case of five long graduated drawers
w/small turned wood pulls,

recessed end panels, canted cut-out feet, original color, Mt. Lebanon, ca. 1880, 19 x 40", 42" h. **14,950.00**

Dining table, ministry-type, cherry, a long narrow rectangular top supported on cross braces above the trestle-form base w/a high, wide stretcher & arched shoe feet, dark varnish stain, probably Enfield, New Hampshire, first half 19th c., reduced in size, 34½ x 108¼", 28½" h. **11,500.00**

Fireplace tools, wrought iron, a stove ash shovel & an ember tongs, 19th c., shovel 24" l., tongs 25¼" l., the set **201.00**

Footwarmer, painted pine, leather & tin, rectangular red-painted canvas-covered lid opens to a tin-lined interior w/a fitted cylindrical oil font, turned wood feet, painted red, 19th c., 7¼ x 8¼", 5¼" h. (wear to canvas, minor paint wear & gouging) **518.00**

Measure, round bentwood, painted chrome yellow, 1 qt., 19th c., 5⅞" d., 3⅜" h. (very minor paint wear) . . **5,463.00**

Fine Early Shaker Rocker

Rocking chair w/arms, tiger maple & cherry, the tall back w/four arched slats between turned tapering stiles w/turned finials, flat shaped arms on tapering supports continuing to form front legs, double stretchers on front & sides, replaced rush seat, old surface, New Lebanon, ca. 1840, 44¾" h. (ILLUS.). **4,313.00**

Seed box, stained pine, rectangular, 11½ x 23⅜", 3¼" h. (missing labels, minor loss to one corner) . . **115.00**

Seed sower, pine & poplar w/galvanized metal, a long, narrow wood device w/metal fittings & handle, old red paint, Enfield, New Hampshire origin, 10' l. **220.00**

Shaker Caned-Seat Side Chair

Side chair, maple, tall back w/three arched slats between turned stiles w/pointed turned finials, caned seat, double stretchers in front & sides, original surface, Harvard, Massachusetts, ca. 1860, fractured cane, 40" h. (ILLUS.) **1,093.00**

Storage box, cov., oval bentwood w/two finger lappets on base & one on the cover, copper tacks, old natural finish, 9" l. **550.00**

Swift, stained hardwood, a cup-form finial & barrel-form clamp, stained yellow, 19th c., 18¼" l. **345.00**

Table, rectangular top overhanging an apron w/a row of three flush-fitting drawers w/original small wood knobs, square tapering legs, old surface, New Lebanon, New York, ca. 1840, 22 x 47", 25" h. . . . **14,950.00**

Tape loom, maple, narrow board ends joined by numerous slender square slats, old surface, Mt. Lebanon, New York, 1820-40, 1¼ x 13", 31" h. **431.00**

Wall cupboard, stained pine, two-part construction: the upper section w/a rectangular top above a narrow coved cornice above a pair of tall 8-pane glazed doors opening to three shelves; the stepped-out lower section w/a mid-molding above two stacks of three drawers each on the molded base raised on three curved bracket feet, inscribed "Ziba Winchester 1836" w/further inscriptions, Harvard, Massachusetts Community, burnt orange stain, 18 x 51", 7' 4" h. **46,000.00**

Woodbox, butternut, rectangular hinged lid w/rounded edge above the tall dovetailed box w/a divided interior, original finish, mid-19th c., 17⅜ x 24½", 25" h. **4,600.00**

SIGNS & SIGNBOARDS

Also see: ADVERTISING ITEMS, BREWERIANA, COCA-COLA COLLECTIBLES, DRUGSTORE & PHARMACY ITEMS and TOBACCIANA.

Beer, "M.K. Goetz Brewing Co.," oval rolled self-framed tin, a half-length portrait of a poor African-American man smiling & holding a large glass of beer, titled "Jerry's Smile," advertising for the company on the wood-grained frame border, copyrighted in 1903, some frame wear, minor background chipping, 22½ x 28½" **$7,475.00**

Kis-Me Gum Sign

Chewing gum, "Kis-Me Gum," die-cut cardboard, lithographed in color w/a beautiful young woman wearing a low-cut pink gown leaning against a background of arching pink & red roses, advertising above her head, matted & framed, 9½ x 15½" (ILLUS.) . . . **2,805.00**

Cigarettes, "Mecca Cigarettes," lithographed paper, a colorful half-length portrait of a lovely lady wearing a wide-brimmed hat w/her back to the viewer & looking over her shoulder, signed "P. Earl Christy," advertising below "Mecca Cigarettes - Perfect Satisfaction," wide flat wooden frame, some staining in upper corner, 15½ x 23½" **285.00**

Cigars, "Bloomer Club Cigar," lithographed paper, unusual design of a scene in a ladies' athletic club w/two seated woman in the foreground wearing bloomer outfits and smoking cigars, other figures in the background, molded wooden frame, small chip under a lady's chair, 22 x 27" **3,163.00**

Cocoa, "Fry's Cocoa," porcelain, rectangular, large yellow can of the product w/royal crest & red & black lettering against a dark blue ground w/white lettering across the bottom "4½ D. per¼ lb Tin 4½ D.," minor edge chips & corner mounting hole, 14 x 21" **385.00**

Cream separators, "De Laval Cream Separators," framed tin, an ornate gold Victorian-style frame around the colorful sign w/black border & gold lettering at top "De Laval Cream Separators" above a colored central oval reserve of a pretty maiden w/a cow flanked by four colorful farm scene vignettes featuring the separator, "De Laval" tag also on frame bottom edge, some filigree missing on lower frame edge, 30 x 41" **1,870.00**

Fine "Sleepy Eye" Flour Sign

Flour, "Sleepy Eye Milling Co.," self-framed tin, large colorful oval central reserve w/bust portrait of Chief Sleepy Eye marked "Trade Mark - Old Sleepy Eye," the edges w/various Native American vignette scenes & symbols, banner across the bottom w/" 'Sleepy Eye' The Meritorious Flour," 20 x 24" (ILLUS.) **8,050.00**

Flour, "King Arthur Flour," porcelain, rectangular w/white lettering a blue ground, central round logo w/"King Arthur Flour - Sands, Taylor & Wood Co." above & below, chipping, ragged edges, 36 x 40". **204.00**

Guns, "Remington Guns," lithographed paper w/original metal bands at top & bottom, central rectangular scene of a flying duck w/examples of guns & shells above & below, wide flat wood frame,

Framed Remington Guns Sign

some overall creases, minor
chipping & tearing at edges,
25 x 30" (ILLUS.) **2,300.00**

Hatter's trade sign, painted iron, full-
figure model of a tall top hat w/a
cockcade at the upper rim, 19th c.,
paint wear, corrosion, 12" h. **1,150.00**

Health services, "Red Cross,"
porcelain flange-type, red, white &
blue reading "Field Director of The
American Red Cross" w/Red Cross
logo, minor scratches, some minor
edge chips, 11 x 14" **160.00**

Ice cream, "Borden's Ice Cream,"
painted metal, flange-type, nearly
square w/rounded corners, bust
portrait of Elsie the Cow w/wording
"Borden's Ice Cream - If It's
Borden's It's Got To Be Good," in
red, white, blue & yellow,
scratches, small spot of paint loss,
15 x 16" **550.00**

Rare "Majestic Range" Tin Sign

Kitchen ranges, "The Great Majestic
Range," embossed tin, a colorful
scene of a young maid working at a
large Majestic kitchen range,
wording above reads "The Great
Majestic Range," wording at bottom
reads "Charcoal Iron Bodies
Malleable Iron Frames," wide flat
oak frame, some in-painting, overall
soiling, 20½ x 25½" (ILLUS.) **3,738.00**

Oysters, "Oysters R in Season -
Shelder Island Oyster Co.,"
embossed rectangular cardboard,
green & red lettering on yellow
ground, ca. 1930s, 7 x 11" **23.00**

Radio, "Motorola Auto Radio," neon-
type, glass & metal, pink & yellow
neon lighting, 25½" w., 11½" h. . . . **715.00**

Salt, "Carey-iized Salt," die-cut
porcelain, silhouetted salt products
above a wide diamond, printed in
red w/white & blue lettering, overall
chips, fading, scratches, 49 x 50" . . **716.00**

Sewing machine, "Illinois Sewing
Machine Co.," lithographed paper,
a colorful bust portrait of a Native
American chief in a feathered
headdress which is printed w/"New
Royal is Chief," across the white
bottom edging "Illinois Sewing
Machine Co.," in molded wood
frame, minor crease in left border,
25½ x 32" **1,438.00**

Shoes, "Walk-Over Shoes,"
lithographed paper, a tall narrow
rectangular color scene of a young
cowgirl in leather outfit leaning
against a large tree w/"Walk-Over"
carved in the trunk, artist-signed,
copyright 1911, in a wide flat wood
frame, 18 x 38" **1,150.00**

Shotgun shells, "Winchester,"
lithographed cardboard, color
scene of a flock of grouse in tall
grass, reads "Winchester - Factory
Loaded Shotgun Shells - The
Hunter's Choice - We Carry A Full
Stock" **2,255.00**

Early Campbell's Soup Sign

Soup, "Campbell's Tomato Soup,"
porcelain, cut-out can shape
printed in red, white, gold & black
w/familiar label, curved, top edge
ragged, chips to edges & mounting
holes, rust on back, 12½ x 22"
(ILLUS.) **468.00**

Early New England Tavern Sign

Tavern sign, "Independence," painted & gilt wood, a black-painted frame of turned posts enclosing molded panels, both sides painted dark green w/a gilt spread-winged eagle & stars w/the word "Independence" in red, New England, ca. 1800, 31 x 41½" (ILLUS.) **17,250.00**

Tea, "Lipton's Teas," lithographed cardboard, colorful scene of a Ceylonese girl w/parasol standing before a tea harvesting scene, titled "The Belle," the reverse w/"Drink And Enjoy Lipton's Teas," some water staining, 16 x 19½" **72.00**

Fine "King Cole Tea & Coffee" Sign

Tea & Coffee, "King Cole Tea and Coffee," porcelain, one-sided, top oval reserve w/a color bust portrait of a jolly King Cole holding cup & saucer, rectangle below w/wording "King Cole Tea and Coffee," corner tip missing at bottom, scratches, minor fading, 9 x 15" (ILLUS.) ...**1,760.00**

Tobacco, "Spear Head Tobacco," lithographed cardboard, one edge w/a half-length profile portrait of a Native American chief in headdress holding a long pointed spear above

his head, large writing to the left reads "Chew Spear Head Tobacco - Save The Tags," in a wooden frame, some minor paint loss, crease in upper right corner, 15 x 21"........**285.00**

Rare "Buffalo Bill's Wild West" Sign

Traveling show, "Buffalo Bill's Wild West," lithographed poster, large colorful scene of a Native American warrior on horseback in the fore-ground, advertising above "Buffalo Bill's Wild West and Congress of Rough Riders of the World," at bottom "The Red Fox 'Red Cloud' Waiting and Watching," w/wide flat oak frame w/beaded rim, minor soiling, 28 x 34½" (ILLUS.)......**5,175.00**

Underwear, "Munsing Wear," porcelain, a black background w/white lettering & the figure of a young man opening his red robe to show his white long underwear, reads "Beyond Compare - Munsing Wear - Always Perfect Fitting - The fit won't wash out"...........**10,000.00**

Watchmaker, painted wood, model of a large pocket watch w/top stem & loop, dial w/Arabic numerals marked "J. Fiske Boston," painted in gold, white & black, 19th c., 24" h. **440.00**

Whiskey, "Fern Glen Rye," self-framed tin, a landscape scene of a standing elderly African-American man in a roadway, a chicken under one arm, a watermelon under the other & looking down at a bottle of the product which has fallen from a wagon onto the road, caption reads "I'se in a perdickermunt," large sign in book reads "Fern Glen Rye," further advertising on lower frame plaque, small scratch, minor paint loss, 23 x 33" **5,175.00**

SILHOUETTES

These cut-out paper portraits in profile were named after Etinne de Silhouette, Louis XV's unpopular minister of finance and an amateur profile cutter. As originally applied, the term was synonymous with cheapness, or anything reduced to its simplest state. These substitutes for the more expensive oil painting or miniatures were popular from about 1770 until 1850 when daguerreotype images replaced the vogue. Silhouettes may be either hollow-cut, with the head cut away leaving the white paper frame for mounting against a dark background, or the profile itself may be cut from black paper and pasted to a light background.

Bust portrait of a gentleman, hollow-cut, a young man facing left, high-collared shirt & jacket, pencil detail & illegible inscription, flat curly maple frame w/oval opening & black & gold-painted liner, paper damage, holes, first half 19th c., 3⅞ x 4¼" . . **$385.00**

Well-done Gentleman's Silhouette

Bust portrait of a gentleman, hollow-cut, a well-detailed view of a young man facing left wearing a high-collared shirt & jacket, highlighted w/red & black ink, ornate rectangular embossed brass frame w/oval opening, first-half 19th c., 4⅜ x 5⅛" (ILLUS.) **385.00**

Bust portrait of a woman, facing right, hollow-cut, her hair piled on her head, brushed ink bodice & shoulder detail on paper, old black wood frame w/gilt stenciling, 4¼ x 5¼" h. (tear, stains) **330.00**

Bust portraits of a family, hollow cut, a framed & matted grouping including the facing parents at the top w/their six daughters arranged chronologically below them, the eglomisé mat w/openings for each person painted in gilt & blue w/a leafy swag & ribbon across the top & small starflowers between each portrait, all embossed "T. P. Jones fecit," giltwood shadowbox frame,

Family Grouping of Silhouettes

first half 19th c., very minor staining, mat repainted, 9¾ x 13½" (ILLUS.) **2,875.00**

Full-length cut profiles of a man & woman, he standing holding his long clay pipe, a small dog at his feet & gold highlights, she standing holding a book, a cat at her feet, details in gold, white & red, label on back states subjects are "Mr. & Mrs. Josiah Gil Martin by J. Wood, N.Y.," mid-19th c., modern beveled wood frames, 9¾ x 10½", pr. (background paper stains, glue stains, one w/corner crease) **660.00**

Full-length profile of a lady, hollow-cut head facing right, her hair pulled up & back & held by two tall combs, on an ink & water-color out-of-proportion body rather crudely drawn w/a long dress w/mutton-leg pleated sleeves, pleated bodice & upper skirt trimmed w/two bands of ruffles, tiny feet showing below, ca. 1825-35, framed, 3½ x 7⅜" (light toning) **4,313.00**

SODA FOUNTAIN COLLECTIBLES

APPLIANCES

Ice crusher, Dazey, red plastic & metal **$60.00**

Malt machine, "Hamilton-Beach," porcelain, three-head, fountain-type **250.00**

Milk shake mixer, "Arnold," w/metal cup, electric, ca. 1920s **95.00**

Milk shake mixer, "Hamilton Beach," chrome & enamel, single-head, original green porcelain w/chrome trim, includes canister, working **165.00**

CONTAINERS & DISPENSERS

Hires Root Beer Straw Dispenser

Straw dispenser, metal, advertising Hires Root Beer, reads on front "Straws Show Where Hires goes 5¢ a glass" & "5¢ Hires for thirst" on side, metal tabs release straws, 10" l. (ILLUS.). **15,125.00**

Syrup dispenser, "Grape Crush" ceramic, wording below cluster of hanging grapes front & back, figural barrel w/pump, lavender textured glass, 10½" h. without pump **3,163.00**

Hires Syrup Dispenser

Syrup dispenser, "Drink Hires 5¢" front & back, ceramic, figural barrel, pump marked "Hires" on top, 11½" h. without pump (ILLUS.) **2,875.00**

Miniature Syrup Dispenser

Syrup dispenser, salesman's sample Hires Root Beer Munimaker in original carrying case, 12" h. (ILLUS.) **77,000.00**

Syrup dispenser, "Drink Orange Crush Ice Cold," rectangular, stainless steel w/porcelain advertising on sides, "Crushy" finial on lid, 19" h. to top of finial **748.00**

MISCELLANEOUS

Whistle Chalkboard Sign

Chalkboard sign, "Whistle," one-sided embossed tin, reads "Thirsty? Just Whistle," decorated w/an elf at each corner of chalkboard, 20" w., 17" h., ca. 1948, U.S.A., new old stock, minor scratches (ILLUS.). . . . **825.00**

Chalkboard sign, "Dad's Root Beer," one-sided embossed tin, reads "You'll love Dad's...tastes like Root Beer should!," dents to edge, 19½ w., 27½" h. **220.00**

Clock, "Chico's Ice Cream," lights up, reads "Chico's Dairy Co. - Ice Cream - Milk" in center w/"It May Be Good And Not Be Ours" in border above & "But It Can't Be Ours And Not Be Good" below, plastic body & face w/glass front, paint speckles, minor wear to face, small crack to side, working **75.00**

Glass, "Dr. Pepper - King of Beverages" **506.00**

Glass, Pepsi "Space Mouse" **55.00**

Glass, "Rahr's - Beverages -Oshkosh" . . **77.00**

Ice cream parlor set, round oak table w/bent wire legs & four bent wire "heart design" chairs, 19th c., table 30" d., the set **413.00**

National Dairy Malted Milk Can

Malted milk can, cov., "National Dairy," aluminium, large knobbed finial, painted advertising on panel reads "National Dairy - Malted Milk - Extra rich," denting, scratches & scuffs, 6" d., 8½" h. (ILLUS.) **160.00**

Stools, white wicker seat on porcelain base w/brass foot rest, 38" h., pr. **173.00**

Hires Store Sign

Store sign, die-cut tin, suspended from hanging chain, colorful figure of smiling child holding a mug marked "Hires" & sign reading "Drink - Hires - It's Pure," 5 x 8" **22,000.00**

SPACE AGE COLLECTIBLES

Captain Kirk doll, Star Trek, Mego, ca. 1979, never removed from box, 12½" h. **$45.00**

Darth Vader doll, Star Wars Collector Series, No. 27726, Kenner, ca. 1996, 12" h. **20.00**

Lost in Space magazine, "TV Showtime," October 8, 1965, near mint **586.00**

Lost in Space robot, Remco, 1966, near mint **1,210.00**

Lost in Space toy, Cyclops with Chariot model kit, No. 420, Aurora, 1966, near mint **2,000.00**

Lost in Space toy, "Lost in Space Robot," battery-operated, Remco Industries, ca. 1965, original box 8 x 10 x 14", robot 12" h., very good in box **861.00**

Lost in Space writing tablet, ca. 1965, unused. **83.00**

Luke Skywalker doll, Star Wars Collector Series, No. 27724, Kenner, ca. 1996, never removed from box, 12" h. **20.00**

Mr. Spock Mint in Box Doll

Mr. Spock doll, Star Trek, Mego, ca. 1979, never removed from box, 12½" h. (ILLUS.) **50.00**

Outer Limits Jigsaw Puzzle

Outer Limits jigsaw puzzles, Milton Bradley, 1964, series of six different puzzles, each (ILLUS. of one) **150.00-200.00**

Star Trek coloring book, Saalfield, 1968, unused. **46.00**

Star Trek letter, signed by Gene Rodenberry on Desilu Productions stationery, 1966, very fine **163.00**

Star Trek Lunch Box

Star Trek lunch box, Aladdin, 1967
(ILLUS.). **350.00-500.00**

Star Trek lunch box thermos,
Aladdin, 1967 . . . . **75.00 to 125.00**

Star Trek magazine, "TV Showtime,"
January 6, 1967, Mr. Spock cover,
near mint **30.00**

Star Trek wristwatch, 1970s, near
mint **45.00**

Star Trek writing tablet, 1960s,
unused. **30.00**

Star Wars premium card set, Burger
King, 1980, unused **25.00**

Twiki (Buck Rogers TV) doll, 25th
Century Walking Twiki, Mego,
ca. 1979, never removed from
box, 7" h. **55.00**

SPORTS MEMORABILIA

BASKETBALL

Media kit, 1968-69 Los Angeles
Lakers, official 70 page edition
w/portraits & action shots, 22
autographs of players & coaches
scattered throughout **$414.00**

Player card, 1986-87 Rookie card for
Michael Jordan, Fleer No. 57, near
mint (ILLUS.) **843.00**

Player card set, 1969-70 Topps
series, "tallboy" issue, many
notable players, 99 cards, mint,
the set. **2,105.00**

Michael Jordan Rookie Card

Store display sign, "Seamless
Athletic Balls," printed cardboard in
red, white & black w/photo of large
basketball, 3-D free-standing
display piece, 1950s, easel back,
14 x 22" **281.00**

Ticket, printed paper, first game of
Michael Jordan for the Chicago Bulls,
October 19, 1984, red, white & black,
complete & unused, near mint **1,149.00**

BOXING

Book, "Gladiators of the Prize Ring -
Heroes of All Nations," by Billy
Edwards, 1894, hardcover, over
110 portraits of legendary fighters
of the 1880s & 1890s, excellent
condition, 11 x 14¾" **460.00**

Check, personal check made out &
signed by Muhammad Ali, dated
2/2/74, made out to cash, near mint . . **542.00**

Chromolithograph, color drawing
showing match between Peter
Mahar & Robert Fitzsimmons, late
19th c., matted & framed (ILLUS.). . **850.00**

Early Mahar-Fitzsimmons Lithograph

Hat, owned by Rocky Marciano,
green beaver skin, labeled "Pure
Canadian Beaver - Made Expressly
For Rocky Marciano by Biltmore
Hats, Ltd., Canada," w/original hat
box, size 7⅜" **766.00**

Playing cards, "Jeffries vs Johnson,"
1909, photo of two boxers in
fighting pose before the match in
oval reserve on each card, 54 card
deck, w/box in poor condition,
cards near mint, the set **449.00**

Rare Louis vs Schmeling Poster

Poster, on-site type, cardboard, "Joe Louis vs Max Schmeling," advertising their first bout in June 1936 at Yankee Stadium, photos of both boxers, mounted, 22 x 28½" (ILLUS.) **3,479.00**

Program, "The World's Heavy Weight Championship Official Souvenir," September 22, 1927, famous "long count" match between Jack Dempsey & Gene Tunney, boxers shown on cover, like-new condition, 48 pp. **1,225.00**

FOOTBALL

Rare Early Football Game Sign

Advertisement, printed cardboard, "Football - California vs Olympic - Saturday, Nov. 11, 1899...," rectangular, black on white w/a blue & gold ribbon in upper right corner, photo of U.C. captain James Whipple on the left, San Francisco, few small holes at corners, 13½ x 21¾" (ILLUS.) **1,850.00**

Book, "Walter Camp's Book of College Sports," by Walter Camp, 1893, hardcover, well illustrated, autographed by Camp, 329 pp. **550.00**

Football, 1966 NCCA All-American Team autographed example, signed by 21 members of the All-American team, special gold leather Rawlins model **383.00**

Football helmet, Knute Rockne model leather helmet, Rockne's facsimile signature & Wilson manufacturer's stamping, lustrous chocolate brown leather, only limited use, late 1920s **673.00**

Pennant, felt, "Chicago Bears," w/bear head logo, sold at Wrigley Field, 1930s-40s, black & orange, near mint **767.00**

Player card, Jack Kemp, photo card, 1961 Fleer card #155, mint **713.00**

Ticket, "Super Bowl III," 1969, full ticket, January 12, 1969, Miami Florida, Baltimore Colts vs New York Jets, near mint, 2⅝ x 6½" **3,498.00**

Ticket stub, printed paper, "Football Homecoming - Saturday November 21 at 2:30 P.M. - Illinois - Ohio...," 1925, dark blue printing on patterned stock, Red Grange's last college game, excellent condition, 2⅝ x 3⅞" **127.00**

GOLF CLUBS

WOODEN SHAFTED

Abercrombie & Fitch, driver, Master model, patent face insert w/seven ivory plugs (U) **150.00**

Abercrombie & Fitch, niblick, model J1L mussel back, Monel **65.00**

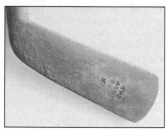

Acme Cleek

Acme, cleek, "The Acme," smooth face, Carrick cross cleek mark, B (ILLUS.) **250.00**

Aitken (Alex), driver, short splice head, fibre face insert **125.00**

Aitken (Alex), wooden mashie, pear-shaped splice head w/dished face. . **400.00**

Alexander (G.), driver, hammerhead-shaped wood w/ two hitting faces (B) **1,800.00**

Auchterlonie (D. & W.), putter, transitional shaped splice head, ca. 1900 (S) **600.00**

B. G. I. Company, niblick brassie,
No. 893, Kilgour model, splice head . . **500.00**

MacGregor, driver, model 27-H,
Samson faced **275.00**

Nicoll, George, cleek, leather face
insert, before 1898 (B) **2,000.00**

Nicolson (T.), putter, bent neck,
Edinburgh Gold Medal cleek mark. . **150.00**

O-V-B, putter, model 932, iron blade . . **60.00**

Park & Son (William), spoon, Willie
Sr., long head (L) **3,000.00-6,000.00**

Patrick & Son (A.), putter, gunmetal
blade, thick hosel, 19th C. **150.00**

Reach Company (A.J.), niblick,
Hammer brand, corrugated face (D). . **100.00**

Saunders (Fred), putter, straightline
model, large back lobe, A (ILLUS.) . . **800.00**

Stewart (Thomas), niblick, small
head, smooth face, serpent cleek
mark **400.00**

Stream-Line Company, putter,
Melhorn model 10P, rail sole, A . . . **150.00**

Winchester Arms Company, driving
iron, model 6590, Vardon series,
Monel, dash/line face **100.00**

Winton Company (W.M.), cleek,
model 86, "Bogie" groove in bottom
center at back **90.00**

Wright & Ditson, driver, model O,
ivory two-screw face insert **150.00**

Wright & Ditson, putter, A.H. Findlay
series, thick T-shaped gun metal
head **1,200.00**

HORSE RACING

Belmont Stakes glass, 1982, frosted
clear cylindrical form printed in
green, brown & yellow **150.00**

Belmont Stakes glass, 1983, frosted
clear cylindrical form printed in
green, brown, yellow & red **170.00**

English Derby glass, frosted clear
cylindrical form w/a color print
design showing the 1865 winner
'Gladiateur' **26.00**

Early Kentucky Derby Glasses

Kentucky Derby glass, 1940,
aluminum, tall tapering cylindrical
form (ILLUS. left) **421.00**

Kentucky Derby glass, 1950, frosted
clear cylindrical form w/green
printed scene **225.00**

Kentucky Derby glass, 1951, frosted
clear cylindrical glass w/green
printing. **333.00**

Kentucky Derby jigger, 1945,
tapering cylindrical clear glass
w/green printing (ILLUS.right) **609.00**

Program, "Sixty-Seventh Kentucky
Derby Official Program," May 3,
1941, picture of Gallahadion,
winner of the 1940 Derby on the
cover, black on cream paper,
winner was Whirlaway, a triple
crown winner **403.00**

STATUARY

BRONZE

Bayre "Theseus Slaying the Minotaur"

Bayre, Antoine Louis, "Theseus
Slaying the Minotaur," two figures
on a rectangular base, dark patina,
14" h. (ILLUS.) **$12,075.00**

Chapu, H., "La Jeunesse," a young
classical maiden kneeling against a
wall & holding up a laurel branch . **2,970.00**

Ferrand, Ernest Justin, "Indiscrete,"
a figure of a maid in 18th c.
costume leaning against a small
table & holding a tray w/letters
w/one hand while pinching open a
letter w/her other hand to try & read
the contents, red patina, signed,
w/foundry seal, 19th c., 26" h. . . . **3,738.00**

"The Pearl Gatherer"

Himmelstoss, K., "The Pearl
Gatherer," kneeling nude young
woman holding a large shallow
shell & picking up pearls, brown
patina, signed & dated 1903,
12½" h. (ILLUS.) **748.00**

Kelety, Alexander, model of a sea
gull in flight, raised on a stepped
block base, dark patina, inscribed
"Kelety," early 20th c., 24" h. **2,507.00**

Lanceray, Eugene, figure group,
depicts a victorious cossack leading
a captured horse & wiping his sword
on his horse's mane, w/ministry
stamp, late 19th c., 18¼" h. **4,025.00**

Millet, Aime, figure of "Anguish," a
kneeling nude woman leaning
against a rock, her hand covering
her face in grief, brown patina,
France, 19th c., 13½" h. **1,100.00**

Verschneider, Jean, "Golden
Apples," a standing nude young girl
holding a basket of apples under
one arm & holding out an apple
w/her other hand, on a round socle
marble base, patinated, inscribed
"Jean Verschneider," late 19th -
early 20th c., 22½" h. **1,955.00**

Vienna bronze, model of a recumbent
puppy, cold-painted in shades of
brown, Austria, ca. 1920, 4" l. **288.00**

Vienna bronze, figure group of a
courting black couple in turn of the
century costume, he seated on a
stool, she standing in front of him,
detailed cold painting, Austria,
4¼" h. **748.00**

Vienna Bronze Cat Band

Vienna bronzes, cold-painted
miniature models of a cat band,
ca. 1920, 1½" h., 8 pcs.
(ILLUS. of part) **1,035.00**

MARBLE

Marble Bust of a Maiden

Bacherini, A., bust of a maiden,
wearing a head scarf & coronet, a
Renaissance-style gown w/roses at
the bodice, gently smiling
w/downcast eyes, Italy, signed &
dated "Florence 1897," minor
abrasion, socle chipped, 18" w.,
24" h. (ILLUS.) **1,725.00**

Bazzanti, P., bust of Dante, on a
rectangular base w/chamfered
corners, "Dante" carved at the
front, Italy, signed & dated
"Florence 1923," minor abrasions,
19" w., 15" h. **518.00**

Bust of Augustus Caesar, raised on
a round plinth, after the Antique,
Italy, 19th c., 22" h. **2,415.00**

OTHER

Alabaster, Scheggi, C., allegorical
bust of a woman titled "Spring," her
head turned w/flowers in her long
hair & on her draped bodice, Italy,
late 19th c., minor chips &
abrasions 18½" h. (ILLUS.) **1,380.00**

Allegorical Bust of "Spring"

Alabaster, figure of young boy & dove, on a black-painted base mounted w/an etched ivory plaque, Italy, ca. 1880, 23½" h. (losses) . . . **863.00**

Alabaster, Fiaschi, P.E., standing figure of a partially-clad classical maiden, leaning against a low pedestal w/a figural griffin base, 47" h.) **9,775.00**

STEIFF TOYS & DOLLS

Bear on wheels, brown mohair, steel eyes, embroidered nose, mouth & claws, moveable head, excelsior stuffing, steel frame & wheels, ca. 1920, 21" l., 15" h. (fabric loss on head & back) **$345.00**

Clown, life-size, dressed in white polka dot shirt & suspendered pants, includes proof of authenticity, 17 x 50" **575.00**

Dog, seated, light brown mohair, button in ear, 8½" h. **110.00**

Elephant, pull toy, mohair, button eyes, on cast-iron wheels, excelsior stuffing, early 20th c., 21½" l., 11½" h. (wear & loss to stuffing) **288.00**

Fox terrier, riding-type, plush mohair, glass eyes, ear button, all on steel frame & wheels, ca. 1910, 21" l., 20¾" h. (moth & fiber loss & damage, voice not functioning) **546.00**

Lamb, pull toy, curly wool, felt face, ears & legs, glass eyes, ear button, excelsior stuffing, all on metal frame & wheels, ca. 1913, 12½" l., 11⅛" h. (some moth damage) . . . **1,610.00**

Rabbit, blonde mohair, fully jointed, pink glass eyes, excelsior stuffing, ca. 1913, 12" (slight moth damage) **805.00**

Snail, multicolored velvet, vinyl shell, rubber antennae, button & cloth tag, paper tag, 1960s, 6½" l. **316.00**

Squirrel, blonde mohair, black steel eyes w/felt backing, embroidered nose, mouth & claws, excelsior stuffing, ca. 1920, 7½" **402.00**

Weasel, marked "Wiggy," synthetic white winter fur, black plastic eyes, embroidered nose & mouth, felt pads, ear button & chest tag, ca. 1970s, 7⅝" l. **259.00**

TEDDY BEARS

Teddy bear, miniature, black mohair & glass eyes, original tags & ear button, 4" h. **165.00**

Teddy bear, cinnamon mohair, black steel eyes, embroidered nose, mouth & claws, felt pads, fully jointed, ear button, ca. 1906, 9" h. (slight fur loss on muzzle, needs more stuffing) **2,990.00**

Teddy bear, blonde mohair, fully jointed, black shoe button eyes, embroidered nose, mouth & claws, nose stitched over black felt, felt pads, excelsior stuffing, ca. 1906, 15" (moth damage, fiber loss, red felt shoes bled on lower body) **978.00**

Teddy Bear, marked w/silver button w/raised script, gold tag #0202/51, beige mohair body w/swivel head, excelsior stuffing, brown glass eyes, shaved muzzle w/dark brown floss nose & mouth, felt pads, 18" h. **350.00**

Rare Early Steiff Teddy Bear

Teddy bear, golden mohair, early center seam-type w/black steel eyes, embroidered nose, mouth & claws, fully jointed, excelsior stuffing, felt pads, button in ear, spotty moth damage on fur & pads, fiber unstable at ankles, needs stuffing, ca. 1905, 22" h. (ILLUS.) **10,063.00**

STEINS

Character, "Black Man," pottery,
marked "#737," ½ liter **$650.00**
Character, "Falstaff," pottery,
marked "M.W.G.," ½ liter **300.00**

Porcelain Frog Stein

Character, "Frog," porcelain, marked
"Musterschutz," by Schierholz,
½ liter (ILLUS.) **1,000.00**
Character, "Hops Lady," porcelain,
marked "Musterschutz," by
Schierholz, ½ liter **600.00**
Character, "Owl," stoneware, marked
"M.W.G.," ½ liter **220.00**
Character, "Sad Radish," porcelain,
marked "Musterschutz" **299.00**
Character, "Wilhelm I," porcelain,
marked "Musterschutz," by
Schierholz, ½ liter. **1,300.00**
Character, "Wrap Around Alligator,"
porcelain, by E. Bohne Sohne,
³⁄₁₀ liter **650.00**
Faience, bird, pewter lid, Thuringia,
ca. 1780, 1 liter **600.00**
Faience, man & bull, pewter lid &
footring, Erfurt, ca. 1770, 1¼ liter . . **1,200.00**

Enameled Glass Stein

Glass, blown, amber, enameled
decoration, tavern scene, pewter
lid & base, ½ liter (ILLUS.) **400.00**

Glass, blown, amber, etched leaves
& grapes, glass inlaid lid, ½ liter . . . **250.00**
Mettlach, No. 1212 (1909), PUG,
man bowling, pewter lid, ½ liter. . . . **250.00**
Mettlach, No. 1395, etched, French
card stein, inlaid lid, ½ liter **500.00**

Mettlach Etched Heidelberg

Mettlach, No. 1675, etched
Heidelberg, inlaid lid, 1386 to 1886
on rear of some steins, ½ liter
(ILLUS.). **500.00**
Mettlach, No. 1940, etched, keeper
of wine cellar, signed "Warth,"
inlaid lid, 3 liters **1,200.00**
Mettlach, No. 2002, etched 'Munich'
design, w/town scene & verse,
inlaid lid, 1 liter **450.00**
Mettlach, No. 2382, etched, Thirsty
Knight, knight drinking in cellar &
riding off into night, signed "Schlitt,"
conical inlaid lid, ½ liter **700.00**
Mettlach, No. 2726, etched,
goldsmith occupational, inlaid lid,
½ liter **2,200.00**
Mettlach, No. 2833B, etched, hunters
in forest, signed "MC," inlaid lid,
½ liter. **450.00**
Mettlach, No. 2894, etched
Heidelberg student stein, view of
Heidelberg, Perkeo & Rodenstein
on rear of stein, turret roof inlay,
inlaid lid, ½ liter. **2,300.00**
Mettlach, No. 2903, etched, Art
Nouveau, inlaid lid, ½ liter **600.00**
Mettlach, No. 727 (1909), PUG,
bowling gnomes, signed "Schlitt,"
pewter lid, ½ liter **250.00**
Mettlach, No. 732 (1909), PUG, owl
shining lantern on drunken man,
signed "Schlitt," ½ liter. **300.00**
Musterschutz, porcelain, bicycle
stein w/large high-wheeled bicycle
wheel forming flattened sides,
banderole across the front reads
"L.A.W." for "League of American
Wheelers," inset lid w/scrolled

cartouche w/"L.A.W." insignia,
bicycling scene lithophane in the
bottom, ½ liter, 6¾" h. **390.00**

Occupational, barrel maker, transfer,
lithophane, porcelain,
pewter lid, ½ liter.............. **350.00**

Occupational, butcher, transfer,
lithophane, porcelain, pewter lid,
½ liter...................... **275.00**

Porcelain, h.p. Indian, marked
"C.A.C.," Lenox, silver & copper lid,
½ liter...................... **800.00**

Capo di Monte-style Stein

Porcelain, relief, heraldic scene,
Capo di Monte-style, boy on lid,
ca.1880, 1½ liters (ILLUS.)...... **1,000.00**

Porcelain, Royal Vienna-type, h.p.,
marked w/beehive, metal lid,
1 liter...................... **1,600.00**

Pottery, etched, marked "HR, 161,"
by Hauber & Reuther, pewter lid,
½ liter...................... **275.00**

Pottery, etched, marked "HR, 433,"
by Hauber & Reuther, pewter lid,
2 liters **500.00**

Regimental Stein

Regimental, "Pionier Batl. Nr. 21
Mainz, 1905-1907," porcelain,
pewter lid, ½ liter (ILLUS.)........ **600.00**

Regimental, "S.M.S. Moltke, 1911-
1914," four side scenes, roster,
eagle thumblift, pottery, 1 liter,
14.8" h..................... **1,000.00**

Stoneware, transfer decoration,
target shooting, pewter lid, 1 liter .. **150.00**

Decorative Stoneware Stein

Stoneware, Weserwald, incised, blue
saltglaze, pewter lid, ca. 1750,
1 liter (ILLUS.)................. **700.00**

STEREOSCOPES & STEREO VIEWS

STEREO VIEWS

Civil War hospital, interior view of a
facility for Union soliders shown
sitting in a well-ordered hospital
w/flags & bunting from the rafters,
reverse identifies it as "McClellan
Hospital - Ward 13," buff ground,
by M.S. Hagaman, Philadelphia,
slight soiling.................. **$424.00**

Hawaiian Children, Underwood &
Underwood, 1899 .... **15.00**

Early "Iron Clad" Stereo View

"Iron Clad," view of the Iron Clad
moored in Charleston,
Massachusetts Navy Yard,
probably post-Civil War, yellow
mount, slight soiling, Kilburn
No.770 (ILLUS.) **63.00**

Nez Perce Woman & Child

Native American scene, Nez Perce woman & child, titled "A Belle of the Nez-Perce Indians, in Idaho," Continent Stereoscopic Co., No. 566, original issue, ca. 1880s, very light soil & foxing (ILLUS.) **97.00**

Native American scene, Tesuque Pueblo girls carrying water, Bennett & Brown, No. 64, slight soiling, edge & crease wear **79.00**

President McKinley & Cabinet, Underwood & Underwood, 1899 . . . **20.00**

STEREOSCOPES

Stereo viewer, hand-held, wood & etched aluminum, marked "Underwood & Underwood, N.Y. Patented June 11, 1901" **95.00**

Stereopticans, three drawers each containing 20 aluminum & wood turn-of-the-century viewers from a educational facility, the set **1,100.00**

TEDDY BEAR COLLECTIBLES

Tea set, porcelain, yellow lustre ground w/color scenes of little girls & their Teddy bears, early 20th c., 15 pcs. **$375.00**

Teddy bear, yellow mohair, black steel eyes, eye glasses, Schuco "yes/no," ca. early 1900s, 4¾" (minor fur loss) **432.00**

Teddy bear, cinnamon mohair body w/swivel head, excelsior stuffing, black shoe button eyes, brown cotton floss nose, oversized feet, hump back, felt pads, four floss claws, fully jointed, non-working squeeze-type growler, unmarked w/Steiff characteristics, 10" **2,700.00**

Teddy bear, white mohair, black shoe button eyes, fully jointed, rust embroidered nose, mouth & claws, includes X-ray of joints, Bing, ca. 1910, 15" **1,265.00**

Teddy bear, orange mohair, fully jointed, glass eyes, mouth opens to reveal white glass teeth, long oval body, straight short arms & legs, early 20th c., 16½" (one tooth broken, moth damage & fiber loss) **460.00**

Teddy bear, golden mohair body w/swivel head, black floss mouth & nose, shaved mohair muzzle, brown glass eyes, felt pads, small back hump, unmarked, 18" **375.00**

Teddy bear, golden mohair body w/swivel head, excelsior stuffing, black shoe button eyes, hump, beige felt pads, four rust floss claws, fully jointed, unmarked, 18" **2,500.00**

Early Ideal Teddy Bear

Teddy bear, golden mohair, black steel eyes, fully jointed, tan felt pads, black embroidered nose, mouth & claws, Ideal Toy Co., ca. 1905, 19" (ILLUS.) **5,750.00**

Teddy bear, pink mohair body w/swivel head, five-piece excelsior body, brown glass eyes, pink felt pads, three black felt claws, unmarked, 21" **575.00**

Teddy bear, light yellow mohair, black shoe button eyes, black knit fabric nose, embroidered mouth & claws, felt pads, fully jointed, ca. 1905, w/owner provenance & early photo, Ideal Toy Co., 25" (very slight pad damage & fur loss) . . **13,800.00**

Teddy bear on wheels, light brown velveteen, glass eyes, on wooden platform w/metal wheels, ca. early 1900s, 7½" l., 5¾" **202.00**

Teddy bear on wheels, brown mohair, black shoe button eyes, embroidered nose, felt pads, excelsior stuffing, unjointed, "Teddy B" leather collar, steel frame w/wooden wheels, ca. 1920, 19½" l., 12½" (fur bare in spots, some fabric loss) **288.00**

Log Cabin and Broderie Perse Quilts

Courtesy of Skinner, Inc.

TEXTILES

COVERLETS

Jacquard, single weave, two-piece, clusters of small blossoms & leaves alternating w/rows of large rounded stylized florettes, vintage borders, corner signed "Made 1868," deep red, medium blue & natural white, 68 x 85" (minor wear & damage, some fringe loss). **$440.00**

Jacquard Coverlet with Birds & Trees

Jacquard, single weave, two-piece, floral & starflower center medallions & a wide border of pairs of birds w/stylized small trees, corners labeled "Peace and Plenty 1847," navy blue & white, good fringe, top edge turned & rebound 76 x 79" (ILLUS.) **605.00**

Jacquard, single weave, two-piece, a design of rows of four-rose leafy clusters alternating w/scattered large blossomheads, wide vintage border, corners labeled "Ch. S. Meily, Wayne County, Ohio 1848," navy blue & natural white, 74 x 80" (minor fringe wear & stains, some top edge damage) **330.00**

Jacquard, single weave, two-piece, bands of four-rose clusters alternating w/large scalloped rings centered by four-arm crosses, vining vintage borders, corners labeled "Made 1858," attributed to Bucyrus, Crawford County, Ohio, royal blue, teal, red & natural white, good color, 65 x 81" (wear, stains & fringe loss, top edge frayed) **385.00**

Jacquard, double woven, a central design of rows of flower-filled urns alternating w/facing pairs of perched birds & facing pairs of birds feeding nestlings, double border in Boston Town patt., fringe on three sides, red, dark blue & natural white, mid-19th c., 78 x 81½" (wear on reverse) **403.00**

Four-Rose Medallion Coverlet

Jacquard, single weave, two-piece, rows of four-rose medallions alternating w/large snow flake-like eight-point medallions, pots of flowers & double row of buildings borders, corners labeled "J. Swank, Hancock County, Ohio 1848," navy blue, red & white, overall & fringe wear, minor stains, 72 x 82" (ILLUS. previous page) **385.00**

Jacquard, single weave, two-piece, a central design of floral medallions w/pinwheel borders & roosters in the corners, all-wool, tomato red & royal blue, 19th c., 76 x 82" **220.00**

Jacquard, single weave, two-piece, a design of tight rows of large round medallions w/a diamond center framed by leafy scrolls within a gadroon-style border, the large medallions alternating w/small double-scroll quatrefoils, vintage borders, corners labeled "W. in Mt. Vernon, Knox County, Ohio by Jacob and Michael Ardner 1860," navy blue, red & natural white, 72 x 83" (wear, damage w/repair along top edge, incomplete fringe) **385.00**

Jacquard, double woven, an overall design of alternating rows of large light & dark florette medallions within octagonal panels joined by small squares, in red, blue & natural white, mid-19th c., 73 x 83" . . **403.00**

Jacquard, single weave, two-piece, the center w/four-rose medallions, the borders w/birds & roses & birds, corners labeled "W. Shank, Shelby Co. Ohio 1842," navy blue, light blue, tomato red & bleached white, 70 x 85" **770.00**

Jacquard, single weave, two-piece, the center w/continuous bands of large starburst within octagonal panels alternating w/florettes in diamonds, stylized floral border, dated 1825, navy blue & natural white, 78 x 85" **330.00**

Jacquard, double woven, two-piece, showy bold floral grid in navy blue & natural white, 80 x 85" (wear, repair, some stains). **248.00**

Jacquard, single weave, two-piece, the center w/bands of large stylized floral medallions w/large pairs of curled leaves framing small tulip-like blossoms, rosette in medallions borders w/a rose blossom border at the bottom, corners labeled "W. Minster, Allen Co. 1848" w/rooster, navy blue, tomato red, olive green

& natural white, 62 x 86" (minor wear, stains w/small holes in top edge) **468.00**

Jacquard, single weave, one-piece, rows of oval medallions w/a standing heron in each alternating w/rows of oblong reserves w/a geometric oval reserve, red, olive green & natural white, 66 x 86" (some wear & damaged areas). . . . **468.00**

Jacquard, single weave, one-piece, two long oblong turtle-shaped center medallions enclosing leafy scrolls & bordered by floral vines within paired hearts borders on the sides & houses & trees borders at the ends w/eagles in the corners, navy blue, red, olive gold & natural, 76 x 86" (some color bleeding & wear). **248.00**

Jacquard with Oval Rose Medallions

Jacquard, single weave, one-piece, a center design of rows of four-rose clusters within oval medallions alternating w/large stars, compotes of flowers in the borders, corners labeled "Made by D. Crosley, Xenia, Ohio 1859," olive green, deep red & natural white, very minor wear & stains, 86 x 87" (ILLUS.) **1,320.00**

Jacquard, single weave, two-piece, the center design of bands of large floral medallions against a striped ground, rosebush borders, corners labeled "Manufactured by C.K. Hinkel, Shippensburg, PA. 1843, Caroline Helt," burgundy red, gold, deep blue & natural white stripes, 70 x 88" **413.00**

Jacquard, double woven, two-piece, overall design of large starbursts & small six-point stars, floral medallion & birds in branches borders, cornucopias in the corners, navy blue & tomato red, 71 x 88" (wear, repaired holes) **495.00**

Jacquard, single weave, two-piece, four-rose clusters alternating w/compass star medallions in the center, bird borders w/swags, corners labeled "Mathias Klein 1844," tomato red & natural white, Jefferson, Montgomery County, Pennsylvania, 81 x 88" (very minor stain) **825.00**

Jacquard, single weave, two-piece, bands of four-rose clusters alternating w/star medallions, bird borders, corners labeled "Austintown 1841," navy blue, royal blue, olive green, deep pink & natural white, 71 x 89" (some wear & stains w/fringe loss, top edge w/wear & small holes) **330.00**

Jacquard, single weave, two-piece, a central design of rows of starbursts within rings of small six-petal flowerheads, pairs of birds & trees alternating w/small two-story houses in the border, corners labeled "Somerset Ohio, 1847, L. Hesse Weaver," 72 x 90" (wear, fringe loss). **413.00**

Jacquard, single weave, one-piece, an overall vintage vine center design w/Christian & Heathen border on sides & bird border on end, corners labeled "Daniel Bury Cornersburgh, Ohio 1850," unusual colors of purple, gold, bluish black & natural white, 76 x 90" **853.00**

Jacquard, single weave, one-piece, rows of large oblong four-lobed floral medallions within oblong octagonal panels alternating w/narrow geometric bands & small flowerheads, corners labeled "Probst & Seip 1847," navy blue, red, green & natural white bands of color, 76 x 90" (some wear & stains) **495.00**

Jacquard, single weave, two-piece, a design of rows of four-rose clusters w/an eagle & tree border, corners signed "The Property of Ann Dobbs, D.P. Johnson Weaver, Orleans County, N.Y. 1847," salmon red & natural white, 69 x 91" (stains) **440.00**

Jacquard, single weave, two-piece, rows of oval four-rose medallions alternating w/rows of large four-leaf clusters within vining borders of birds, corners labeled "John King, Andrew Kump, Damask Coverlet Manufacturer, Hanover, York County, Pa. 1846," medium blue, tomato red & natural white, 76 x 92" (minor wear) **523.00**

Jacquard, single weave, two-piece, rows of four-rose medallions alternating w/rows of four-blossom & leaf clusters, wide undulating

floral border, signed in border & corner block "Croton 1833," navy blue & natural white, 76 x 93" (minor wear & stains, no fringe) . . . **385.00**

Jacquard, single weave, two-piece, rows of four-rose medallions alternating w/rows of starbursts within bird borders & corner blocks marked "Made by C. L. Kean," deep sage green, red & natural, 92 x 95" (minor wear, small stains). **1,210.00**

Jacquard, single weave, two-piece, a central design of large stylized floral medallions alternating w/small four-leaf medallions, tiny blossomheads & buildings borders, corners labeled "Made by J. Witmer, Manor Township for Elizabeth Pfantz 1845," navy blue, olive green, tomato red & natural white, Lancaster, Pennsylvania, good fringe, 74 x 99" **1,320.00**

Jacquard, double woven, one-piece, star center design within floral borders w/the corners labeled "Made by E. Hausman, Trexler-town, Pa. 1851," vibrant bands of red, green & blue, 79 x 99" **633.00**

Overshot, two-piece, optical pattern of large continous block crosses in navy blue & natural white, 74" sq. (minor stains, tied fringe at one end) . . **138.00**

Overshot, "summer-winter" type, overall center geometric design of rows of small oblong blocks alternating w/four-arm crosses, pine tree border, tomato red, navy blue & natural white, 19th c., 64 x 75" (wear & some damage) . . **165.00**

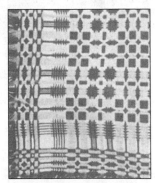

Snowball & Pine Tree Overshot

Overshot, double woven, two-piece, "summer-winter" type w/a snowball & pine tree design in navy blue, soft red & natural white, minor wear, repair, 64 x 78"(IILUS.) **138.00**

Overshot, two-piece, round snowflake bands alternating w/geometric chain-like bands, red, navy blue, green & natural white, good fringe, 71 x 82" (minor stains) **385.00**

Overshot, geometrical optical design w/bands of optic ovals, navy blue, salmon red & natural white, 19th c., 70 x 85" (light stains, incomplete fringe) **248.00**

Overshot, two-piece, optical pattern of blocks & bands in navy blue & natural white, 84 x 100" (minor stains, fringe loss) **248.00**

LINENS & NEEDLEWORK

Blanket, homespun wool, two-piece construction w/a center seam, decorated w/crewel embroidery along one edge w/an arching stylized floral design worked in red, blue & black, probably Pennsylvania, 19th c., 70 x 76" (holes, other damage) **303.00**

Mattress cover, homespun linen, overall small red, blue & white plaid design, white back, white tape ties, 19th c., 55 x 61" (minor wear repair) . . **204.00**

Mattress cover, homespun linen, blue & white overall check design in two sizes, all hand-sewn, white tape ties, American, 19th c., 64 x 68". . . . **275.00**

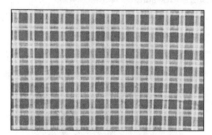

Early Linen Mattress Cover

Mattress cover, homespun linen, blue & white overall check design, self-backed, all hand-sewn, black ribbon ties, American 19th c., 67 x 68" (ILLUS. of part) **193.00**

Mattress cover, homespun linen, blue, white & tan overall check design w/a white backing, all hand-sewn, woven tape ties, American, 19th c., 61 x 73" **220.00**

Needlework embroidery on linen, a design of a large spread-winged American eagle w/long ruffled wing feathers grasping a slender pole draped w/an American flag in its talons, worked in shades of brown,

white, black & red, white & blue, 19th c., framed, 25¼" sq. (some overall wear, fading, stained background fabric) **193.00**

Table runner, Arts & Crafts style, a stylized organic design in red, yellow & gold, w/fringe on edge, 15 x 53" (some stains) **110.00**

Table runner, Arts & Crafts style, each end w/a hand-woven panel w/a row of trees w/narrow, twisting trunks in rose & black w/olive & violet leaves, the scene reflected in orange, gold & olive water, backed by a shoreline of brush & trees in olive, rose & pink, sky of orange & gold, black & brown stitched border on coarse weave oatmeal background, initialed by Newcomb College Pottery artist Anna Frances Simpson, early 20th c., some staining, 19 x 77" **3,300.00**

Tablecloth, overshot woven linen, scalloped lace borders, 60 x 65" . . . **83.00**

Wall hanging, embroidered linen, Arts & Crafts style, embroidered w/tall irises & short crocuses in yellow, white & purple on a neutral ground, early 20th c., 62 x 94" (some stains, minor edge wear) . . . **275.00**

NEEDLEWORK PICTURES

Allegorical Silkwork Picture

Allegorical scene, silkwork, a standing classical figure leaning on a post & looking straight ahead, a lighthouse & sailing ship tossed in stormy seas in the background, titled "Hope" on the black eglomisé mat w/gold-trimmed oval opening, possibly worked at the Balch School, Providence, Rhode Island, early 19th c., replaced mat, few small tears, stains to painted background, molded giltwood frame, 8½ x 10½" (ILLUS.)...... **1,265.00**

Biblical scene, depicting the story of Balaam & the Ass w/an angel about to draw his sword in front of them & two figures behind them, a castle in the background, within an oval reserve, the border composed of flowers & insects, all in muted colors of blue, green, ochre & red on an ivory silk ground, in a tortoiseshell frame, England, late 17th c., 11¼ x 14⅝"........... **2,875.00**

Classical urn, silk, a scene of a large two-handled classical urn on a rectangular plinth, overflowing w/colorful flowers, worked in shades of green, cream, brown, blue & pink silk thread on a cream silk ground, monogram on the plinth, within a rectangular reverse-painted black glass matte & giltwood shadowbox frame, 19th c., 17⅝ x 22⅞" (distress & foxing on ground)................... **201.00**

Jacob's Dream, petit point, worked in muted colors of blue, green & brown & w/silver threads, depicting Jacob asleep at the foot of a ladder w/two angels ascending, surrounded by animals & flowers in a landscape, a huntsman w/hare & hound & a large castle in the background, in a tortoiseshell frame, England, late 17th c., 7½ x 10¾" (cut from a larger picture)............... **2,875.00**

Landscape, a large landscape scene worked in chenille yarn of two men duck hunting from a small boat in a lake w/trees, houses & hills in the background, signed "Angelique L.C. Picot aged 9 Richmond 1 1819," framed, 19 x 19½" (some water staining, tears to ground) .. **7,475.00**

Romantic Landscape Needlework

Landscape scene, silkwork, a scene of two ladies walking in the foreground w/a reclining man beside a lake w/boat in the background & a distant arched bridge w/further hills & structures beyond, black eglomisé mat titled "View of Lake Lugano," signed "Clarissa Fuller 1821," probably from Miss Balch School, Providence, Rhode Island, in original molded wood frame, toning, minor staining, losses to mat, 16¼ x 20¼" (ILLUS.) **2,530.00**

Needlework Hunter Picture

Landscape scenes, one w/a hunter seated w/his rifle under a leafy tree, a landscape w/cottage & hills to the right, the other w/a similar scene of a shepherdess, silk embroidery on silk w/a water-color background, in period gilt gesso shadowbox frames, English School, early 19th c., scattered foxing, minor staining & tears, 14⅜ x 18¼", pr. (ILLUS. of one) .. **2,530.00**

Early Needlework of a Queen

Landscape w/a Queen, tent stitch, a long view w/a seated queen wearing a crown & holding a Bible, flanked on each side by oversized flowering & fruiting trees & animals, polychrome wool threads on a linen ground, England, 17th c., framed, 6¾ x 12½" (ILLUS.) **1,840.00**

Landscape w/shepherdess, silk, a scene of a young shepherdess feeding her child, in a landscape w/cows & sheep, painted highlights, England, early 19th c., 16 x 20" **1,150.00**

Mourning picture, rectangular, a row of six figures, two adults & four children, before a pointed monument flanked by arching willow trees, early 19th c., framed, 11 x 12½" **6,250.00**

Mourning picture, a scene of a young lady in a long dress standing & mourning beside a tall urn-topped monument inscribed "Sacred TO THE MEMORY OF PEREZ LINCOLN, Born Oct 24, 1816 - Died Dec. 27, 1821 - AGED 5 YEARS," a water-color & needlework landscape w/lakeside buildings in the background, silk embroidery & printed form on silk, probably executed in Boston, ca. 1800, framed, 17½ x 20¾" . . . **3,450.00**

Needlework embroidery on silk, a design of a spread-winged American eagle flying above large crossed American flags & shield w/banners, worked in silk in shades of red, greyish blue, white, beige & brown on dark navy blue, cloth stitched to paper backing, Chinese Export, 19th c., framed, 11⅝ x 15½" (minor wear) **165.00**

Parrot Needlework Picture

Parrot & cherry, the large bird perched on a short tree stump holding a large cherry, stem & leaf in its beak, small florals around tree, silk thread on paper, signed "Eliza Holman's work 1821," framed, toning, staining, very minor tears, 6⅝ x 8½" (ILLUS.) **1,955.00**

Ship in medallion, woolwork, a round central medallion showing a three-masted sailing ship, the wide outer border decorated w/leafy branches & flowers, inscribed at bottom "A Present from R. Willis," England, 19th c., framed, 17⅝ x 21⅝" (ILLUS.) **1,955.00**

Early English Ship Picture

Solomon & the Queen of Sheba, petit point & appliqué, finely worked w/Solomon seated under a tent, the Queen of Sheba standing in front of him w/two attendants, one holding a parasol, the other carrying her train, an elder standing behind the tent, the whole surrounded by birds & flowers, a leopard & a lion recumbent in front, a castle & a building in the background, England, late 17th c., in a tortoiseshell frame, 13¾" x 17¾" (some losses on the borders) **5,462.00**

Solomon & the Queen of Sheba, silk & wool, elaborately worked in muted colors w/the king seated on his throne, the queen & two noble women kneeling in front of him, numerous figures around them, buildings & a garden visible in the background through draped arches, a dog in the foreground, framed, repairs, losses, Europe, late 17th - early 18th c., 23¾" x 24½" **4,312.00**

The Finding of Moses, petit point, depicting the Pharaoh enthroned on the left & a warrior carrying an infant in swaddling clothes & women finding the infant Moses & pulling him from the river, a castle in the background, all in a landscape w/trees, flowers & animals worked in muted colors of green, yellow & blue, in a tortoiseshell frame, England, late 17th c., holes in the lower right, 11¾" x 16¼" **2,645.00**

The Story of Abraham, petit point, Hager & Ishmael, worked in muted colors of blue, green & ochre showing Abraham talking to Hagar who holds her son by the hand, at the left an angel appears to the kneeling Hagar, set in a landscape of prancing animals, a building in the distance & billowing clouds above, in a tortoiseshell frame, England, early 18th c., 10⅛" x 14" (hole in center) **1,610.00**

QUILTS

Appliqued Daffodil Wreath patt., composed of twelve medallions w/daffodil wreaths in yellow, goldenrod & two shades of green, yellow grid & binding on the scalloped edge, finely quilted in floral & feather designs, 74 x 98" (small repair) **495.00**

Appliqued Floral Medallions patt., four large four-stem radiating clusters w/fan-shaped blossoms alternating w/ large pointed sawtooth leaves, two color border bands separated by a white band, worked in blocks of red, khaki & goldenrod, well-quilted, 19th c., 83 x 85" (several dark stains, some light overall stains) **385.00**

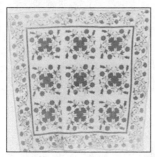

Floral Medallions Appliqued Quilt

Appliqued Floral Medallions patt., nine large blocks arranged in rows of three, each w/a central blossom w/four fluted petals surrounded by swirled leafy stems, blossoms & berries, within a narrow band & framed by a wide continuous vining floral border w/small birds & berries, worked in red & green patches on white w/puffed-out berries, well-quilted ground, minor stains & fading, edge binding frayed, 19th c., 86" sq. (ILLUS.) . . **1,320.00**

Appliqued Floral Pinwheel patt., composed of four stylized floral pinwheels & a vining border in red & green on white, 90 x 92" (some stains, overall wear & damage) . . **1,155.00**

Appliqued Floral Wreath patt., composed of nine large floral wreaths w/four blossoms alternating w/pairs of buds & small leaves, each wreath within a leafy vine-bordered block w/an outside flowering vine border band, patches in shades of red & green w/yellow, well-quilted white ground, added tag states quilt made by

Julia Howard in 1860, 86" sq. (loss to green color in several spots, wear, stains) **385.00**

Appliqued Morning Glories patt., worked in patches of purple, violet, green, etc. on a white ground, embroidered name & date "Sylvia Harris 1936," 67 x 82" (wear) **198.00**

Appliqued Pinwheel patt., a large nine-leaved pinwheel w/serrated arm edges in white centered on a deep pink ground, pairs of matching corner leaves & a wide border in white w/a thin pink binding, well quilted, 19th c., 77 x 81" **385.00**

Appliqued Pinwheel patt., composed of nine stylized floral pinwheels & a vining border in red & green on white, 83" sq. (some stains & overall wear) **935.00**

Fine Broderie Perse Quilt

Broderie perse quilt, colorful floral fabrics arranged to form a large central Tree of Life scene w/exotic birds perched on a flowering tree within a square floral band framed by a white band applied w/large & small floral clusters, a narrow floral & then white band all within a wide delicate floral & leaf outer border band, American, early 19th c., staining, 112 x 114" (ILLUS.) **4,600.00**

Crazy quilt, composed of pieced colorful irregular patches of satins, velvets, etc. decorated w/well-executed appliqued, embroidered & painted scenes of people, flowers, animals, nursery rhyme characters, etc., signed "L.M.," found in Mason County, Kentucky, late 19th c., 70 x 76" (very worn tattered) **495.00**

Pieced Baskets of Flowers patt., composed of beige & red blocks on a white ground, well-quilted w/feather wreath & meandering feather border, 82 x 85" (minor overall wear & stains) **330.00**

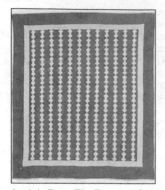

Amish Bow Tie Pattern Quilt

Pieced Bow Tie patt., composed of light green bow tie stripes on a black ground, outer border bands, Amish, early 20th c., very minor imperfections, 71½ x 82½" (ILLUS.) . . **863.00**

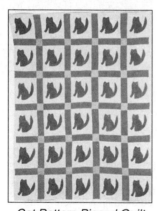

Cat Pattern Pieced Quilt

Pieced Cat patt., composed of white blocks centering stylized silhouetted sitting cats arranged in rows divided by wide colored borders. ca. 1930, 63 x 84½" (ILLUS.) **1,265.00**

Pieced Double Wedding Ring patt., worked in multicolored patches on a white ground, ca. 1930s, 80 x 81" . . . **72.00**

Pieced Dresden Plate patt., worked in multicolor patches on white, ca. 1930s, 66 x 81", pr. **143.00**

Pieced Drunkard's Path patt., worked in deep pink patches on a white ground, 80 x 92" **303.00**

Pieced Flying Geese patt., composed of navy blue print blocks w/white & ecru blocks, wreath, feather & wavy line background quilting, pencil quilt designs intact, one corner w/stitched date "Jan 13, 1899," 71 x 79" (minor age stains) . . **660.00**

Pieced Grandmother's Flower Garden patt., composed of hexagons of wheel prints & solids on a quilted white ground w/a yellow binding, 76 x 90" (overall wear) **281.00**

Pieced Irish Chain patt., worked in blocks of small navy blue star print & white on a white quilted ground, 19th c., 74" sq. (some overall wear & stains) **385.00**

Pieced Irish Chain patt., composed of multicolored print & solid orangish red patches on a white ground, 76 x 89" (minor stains) . . . **160.00**

Victorian Log Cabin Quilt

Pieced Log Cabin patt., assembly block-style w/multicolored strips of fabric, ca. 1860-80, 70½ x 71" (ILLUS.) **805.00**

Pieced Lone Star patt., worked in patches in shades of pink, blue, lavender & salmon on a blue ground, well-quilted w/horses, flowers, etc., wide border band, Mennonite, 76 x 79" (minor stains) . . **600.00**

Pieced Nine Patch with Sawtooth Border patt., composed of blocks of prints, calicos & solids in shades of red, brown, yellow, green, etc., 70 x 84" (some wear & stains) **270.00**

Pieced Pinwheels patt., rows of small four-arm pinwheels arranged to form a design of blocks & half-blocks within a sawtooth inner & outer border band, worked in red print blocks on white, finely quilted ground w/trapunto border w/baskets of flowers & meandering feather stitch, 19th c., 108 x 112" (overall wear, red slightly faded, small hanging holes in corners, stains) . . . **770.00**

Pieced Star patt., composed of white blocks containing a red & white patterned calico eight-point star forming rows alternating w/blocks of the same red & white calico material, 68 x 84" **385.00**

Trapunto quilt, white on white w/central diamond filled w/a large urn of flowers within an undulating feather band frame & a wide border band of finely stitched flowers & leaves, all in high-relief, white cotton homespun panels, 86 x 88" (stain, some wear & damage) . . . **3,520.00**

SAMPLERS

Alphabets above stylized flower clusters & a stylized small bird, worked in a variety of blue, red & brown stitches on a linen ground, signed "Mary Rutt," probably Pennsylvania, early 19th c., unframed, 13 x 13¼". **632.00**

Alphabets & numerals above inscription & landscape, the rows of letters & numbers above the large sewn inscription "Abigail Sawyer's Sampler Aged 11 years Phillipston June the 24, 1817. Massachusetts State," over a large rectangular panel w/a landscape centered by a large three-story Federal house flanked by flowering trees, a basket of fruit, animals & other foliate designs, wide flowering vine border on three sides, framed, 17⅛ x 17 ⅝" (toning, minor staining). **7,475.00**

Alphabets & numerals below stylized flowers, pots of trees, birds, a squirrel & crown over a lengthy pious verse signed "Alice Stephenson Aged 8 years, born Sept. 14, 1792," silk on homespun linen worked in shades of green, brown, blue, white & gold all within a vining floral border, framed, 19½" sq. (blue in lower border bled). . **660.00**

Signed Early Sampler

Alphabets, numerals & pious verse, rows of alphabets & numerals above a short pious verse & the name "Ruth Crandon Aged 12," stylized floral bands & a wide outer geometric block border enclosing foliate designs, toning, minor staining, minor fading, very minor fiber wear, early 19th c., 13½ x 19⅝" (ILLUS.) **1,495.00**

Alphabets, numerals & pious verse, arranged in rows within a rectangular reserve including the verse near the bottom beside a small oval inscribed "Let virtue be your guide" above the signature "Mary Pollard born July 7th 1809 and wrought this June 17th 1824," the reserve above a wide bottom band decorated w/geometric trees & baskets of flowers, a geometric floral border around the upper reserve, probably New Hampshire, framed, 17½ x 23¾" (toning, minor staining, minor losses, fading) . . . **2,415.00**

Alphabets over a landscape band over a pious verse, silk on homespun linen, the landscape band consisting of trees, birds & a house over the verse & the signature "Sally Sticklan her sampler made in the eleventh year of her age, September 8th, 1814," faded shades of blue, yellow & white, minor stains, framed, 13½ x 19" **440.00**

Alphabets & pious verse, all above a wide flowering vine above the signature "Hannah Mosher Aged 12 Hollis 8 June 98" & dated "1798," all within a stitched sawtooth rectangle framed on three sides by a wide geometric blocked floral design, New Hampshire, framed, 16⅜ x 17" (toning, minor fading) **1,380.00**

Alphabets & pious verse, the verse framed on three sides by a zigzag border above a large overflowing basket of flowers above the bottom inscription "Wrought by Eliza Ann Hayward Aged 12 April 24th 1827," vining border of large blossoms on three sides, on homespun linen, framed, toning, very minor staining, 13¾ x 17⅝" **2,875.00**

Alphabets & pious verse, the rows of alphabets above the inscription "Martha Jane Larcom Aged 1? Years AD 1835 Born Aug. 18 AD 1823," above a rectangular diamond-border reserve w/the

Sampler with Urn of Flowers & Palms

pious verse flanked by floral bouquets above a wide bottom band w/a large central urn overflowing w/flowers flanked by small palm trees, sawtooth bottom border, in period ogee wood frame, toning, fading, 17⅜ x 17½" (ILLUS.) **4,025.00**

Sampler with Multiple Alphabets

Alphabets & pious verse, arranged in rows separated by narrow needlework bands, the verse at the bottom flanked by two baskets of fruit above the bottom inscription "Wrought by Anna J. Rowell at the age of 8 years 1832," all within geometric floral borders, framed, toning, very minor staining, 15½ x 17½" (ILLUS.). **1,495.00**

Alphabets, pious verse & family record, all above a pair of flower-filled vases in each bottom corner flanking an arch over a small two-story house, meandering vine border, signed "Marian Webbster, completed Feb. 21, 1877 - Bennington, VT," worked in shades of green, red, white, blue & yellow, wool on punched paper, walnut shadowbox frame, 20½ x 21½" (minor edge damage) **605.00**

Alphabets & pious verse w/fruits & flowers, silk on homespun linen, the rows of letters above a pious verse & the signature "Mary Wing Dodge. In the 12th year of her age, Marietta, Ohio, August 26th, 1826," a large flower, a basket of fruit & a floral wreath around & below the wording, worked in green, blue, yellow, white & black, old frame w/veneer loss, 18⅝ x 19⅝" (minor stains) **4,400.00**

Building & landscape w/floral border, worked in wool yarn on cotton, a wide geometric flowering vine border enclosing the inscription "Sarah Ann Haigh, work finish Dec. 31, 1859" flanked by large floral clusters centered by a wreath w/"Jesus Wept" above a long multi-windowed turreted building above a long narrow bottom landscape w/a shepherd flanked by rows of sheep, in old colors of red, green, blue, yellow, brown & black, framed without glass, 26¾ x 27¾" (stains) **710.00**

Butterflies above an arched flower band flanked by small peacocks all above a lengthy inscription signed "Ann Goodwin, Aged 11 Years" over floral vines & two pine trees, all within zigzag floral borders, silk on homespun linen w/precise small stitches, worked in shades of green, brown, yellow & black, in a beveled rosewood frame, 16½ x 23½" (some wear, stains w/some damage & small holes). **1,265.00**

Family register, a small central section w/a family register worked in tiny letters & framed all around by a wide border worked w/vining side borders w/large blossoms & scattered urns of flowers, flower sprigs & basket of fruit above two small pious verses above the bottom landscape border w/various animals among trees, signed "Elizabeth H. Kay's work," Pennsylvania, framed, 21⅝ x 22¾" (toning, scattered staining, fading) **1,955.00**

Pious verse & building, a linen ground sewn near the top w/a pious verse titled "Extract" within a leafy oval wreath flanked by flowers & above baskets of fruit & bouquets of flowers all above a large two-storied Federal building w/a tall belltower, signed by Elizabeth Sanger, Burlington County, New Jersey, ca. 1830, framed 17 x 17¼" (scattered losses to ground) **1,725.00**

Pious verse & building on linen, the top third w/a long, two-column verse above a large full-width embroidered three-story building w/windowed towers titled "A Front View of the Temple of Solomon Wrought by Dinah Hopkin Aged 8 1846," the wide lower section w/a row of three large flower-filled baskets, framed, 22¾ x 25" (toning, fading, minor staining & losses) ... **863.00**

Pious verse & designs above a building, linen ground embroidered across the top w/a two-line verse above pairs of urns, figures & birds flanking a central flower-filled urn & other designs all above a large two-story Georgian building labeled beneath "Walter Scotts Charity School founded Dec..1786," building flanked by two standing ladies above large crowns above initials "TW" & "EW," signed across the bottom "Elizabeth Webb her Work done in the 14th year of her age 1813," probably English, 8¾" sq. (several holes, discoloration to ground) **2,185.00**

Pious verse & landscape, rectangular w/an ivy leaf top border & vining side borders w/large blossoms framing the top inscription "Henrietta Kays work wrought at Greenville school 1816" flanked by a basket of fruit & floral sprigs over the pious verse above a landscape scene w/trees, flowers & birds along the bottom edge, framed, 12¾ x 17 ⅝" (toning, fading, very minor staining) **2,185.00**

Pious verse surrounded by varied designs, silk on homespun linen, a wide band of birds, stylized trees, flowers, animals & a crown within a narrow leafy vine border, signed "Sarah Whittles Work Aged 9 Years," good colors of red, pink, green, yellow, blue & white, curly maple frame, 20¾ x 21" (stains on ground, minor thread loss) **715.00**

TAPESTRIES

Aubusson-style panel, worked in multicolors w/a narrow, tall scene of three royal ladies in a wooded landscape, leafy scroll border bands, France, early 20th c., losses, tears, 63 x 128" (ILLUS.)... **575.00**

Belgian, a stag hunt scene in a forest w/hunters to the right & their hounds bringing down a stag to the left, worked in naturalistic colors within a gold, red & black frame-style border, 72 x 92" **4,950.00**

Continental, tapestry fragment woven w/four bust-length figures near a building in a landscape, in muted blue, brown, grey & ochre, 16th c., framed, 31½ x 32½" (repairs) **4,025.00**

Continental panel, a tall rectangular center landscape w/a large tree & flowers in the foreground & wooded hills in the distance, wide entwined leafy vine border, in tones of brown, yellow & black on a coarse burlap backing, Europe, 19th c., 4' 9" x 7' 3" (minor losses) **2,300.00**

Flemish, panel showing "The Sacrifice of Isaac," woven w/Abraham about to strike the kneeling child, an angel above reaching out to stop him, all in a mountainous terrain, w/two figures & a donkey in the background, the border w/fruit & the date "1573," in a tortoiseshell frame, repairs & losses, 28 x 30" **3,737.00**

Flemish, large rectangular lush landscape scene w/hills & large trees in the foreground done in verdure tones w/wide multicolored foliate & vase borders, w/two fragmentary panels stitched on the reverse, early 18th c., 5' 3" x 7' 3" (losses) **2,990.00**

Flemish, a large central hunting scene w/a crowd of hunters in period costume w/horses & stags surrounding a wounded stag, wide foliate & fruited borders, woven in multicolors, late 17th - early 18th c., 8' 8" x 8' (restorations) **13,800.00**

Aubusson-style Tapestry Panel

Flemish "verdure," a large rectangular wooded landscape scene w/figures of men & women in 17th c. costume in a lush forest w/a stream & waterfall nearby, typical colors w/scrolling red borders, 18th c., 4' 9" x 6' 10" (restorations) **5,750.00**

Flemish "Verdure" Tapestry

Flemish "verdure" fragment, dense woodland scene w/riding figures before a riverscape w/a large palace in the distance, early 18th c., restorations, 41 x 62" (ILLUS.) . . . **2,875.00**

Flemish "verdure" panel, a lush wooded landscape scene w/a dog & guinea hen w/chicks, early 18th c., 6' 6" x 7' 10" (brittle, losses) **5,175.00**

THEOREMS

Basket of Flowers Theorem

Basket of flowers, oil on cloth, a deep oval basket overflowing w/large colorful flowers, unsigned, unframed, 19th c., scattered foxing, small puncture to background, 14 x 15" (ILLUS.) **$3,680.00**

Basket of flowers, on velvet, a rounded tan basket w/three horizontal ribs filled to overflowing w/a variety of colorful flowers & green leaves, including a number of large roses, unsigned, backing w/a paper label inscribed "Done by Lavinia Kimball about the year 1830," in early giltwood frame, 18 x 22" (toning, minor scattered foxing) . . . **1,725.00**

Basket of fruit, on paper, a yellow & black latticework basket w/loop end handles filled w/a variety of colorful fruits including grapes, peaches, apples & a watermelon, in an early giltwood frame, 11½ x 13¼" (time toning, tears, tape repaired, minor water staining) **4,025.00**

Basket of fruit, water-color on velvet, unsigned, 19th c., framed, 11 x 13½" (cut out & laid down, toning, very minor staining) **288.00**

Basket of fruit, on velvet, a very tall & wide grouping of various leafy fruits including peaches, grapes, apples & pears in a low basket w/a double herringbone design, early 19th c., 14⅛ x 16" **1,725.00**

Basket of fruit w/bird & butterfly, on velvet, a ringed oval basket filled w/a large branch of grapes & leaves & other fruits w/a large bird perched atop the branch reaching for fruit & a butterfly flying at the left side, unsigned, in early narrow wooden frame, 14 x 18½" (toning, some water staining) **2,875.00**

Basket of roses & flowers, on paper, a pair of large roses framed by leaves & stalks of other flowers in an open-ribbed basket, in red, blue, green & yellow, in an early beveled frame w/alligatored finish, 14¾ x 17¼" (minor stains) **550.00**

Lafayette commemorative, water-color on velvet & chintz, a banner w/"United We Stand - Divided We Fall" enclosing a wreath which centers a transfer-printed chintz Lafayette Commemorative trimmed in water-color w/"Lafayette the Nation's Guest," signed "Sophronia Whitney Burlington February 2nd 1826," framed, 22 x 22½" (toning, staining) **4,600.00**

Laurel wreath with silhouette, water-color & applied paper on velvet, a nearly square ground w/a large laurel wreath centering a starburst w/a small ring of stars centered by hollow cut silhouette of a young girl surrounded by letters,

Wreath Theorem with Silhouette

an inscription across the bottom edge reading "...Whitney Aug. 18, 1827," laid down, toning, staining, wear, minor losses to silhouette, framed, 16 x 16¼" (ILLUS.) **3,105.00**

Memorial scene, water-color on velvet w/applied paper inscription, scene of a large central urn-topped monument w/a lady standing to the right of it, large trees & shrubs behind & to the sides, American, early 19th c., unsigned, framed, 16 x 19" (toning, minor staining) . . . **431.00**

Peacock in tree, water-color on paper, shades of green, red, blue & yellow, presentation inscription on the back, narrow gilt frame, 5½ x 7" . . **330.00**

Vase of flowers, on paper, a small ovoid blue vase tapering to a narrow neck issuing a large bouquet of flowers framed w/large vining leaves in yellow, red & dark green, pen & ink inscription to the right side reads "Sarah Hiestand was born on 12th day of February A.D. 1821 at 5 O'Clock PM.," matted & framed, 12¾ x 16¾" (light stains w/fold lines, minor tears) **880.00**

TOBACCIANA

Prices quoted are retail prices. If you are selling to a collector or dealer, expect 40% to 75% of these prices, with higher percentages going to higher priced items. Some tobacciana markets are quite changeable at present.

ASHTRAYS

Ashtray, black poodle, ceramic, open mouth style, black with red and white bow, painted eyes and nose, approximately 4" long, valueless if chipped or cracked **$20.00-30.00**

Ashtray, fish, ceramic, open mouth style, red orange, approximately 5" long, may have no chips or cracks **10.00-15.00**

Ashtray, tiki, ceramic, open mouth style, light brown, approximately 5" tall **20.00-30.00**

Ashtray, WWII USN ship, brass or bronze, various styles, with ship depicted. **50.00-100.00**
Without ship depicted **15.00-30.00**

Ashtray, advertising, glass table top style as found in bars, casinos and hotels, 3"-5" with no cracks or chips. Only a small select handful of this type ashtray are worth more than **2.00-15.00**

Ashtray, advertising, glass table top style, round or rectangluar, 3" to 7", with advertising for Las Vegas Hotel. No cracks or chips. Nearly all sell for **5.00-15.00**

CIGARETTE LIGHTERS

Cigarette lighter, WWII fighter plane, heavy metal, made in Japan, rests on wheels, wingspan approximately 10". At least four different German, Japanese and US aircraft. Must be unbroken with wheels, propeller and lighter intact. Little value if damaged **75.00-125.00**

Cigarette lighter & cigarette case set by Evans in mother-of-pearl. Numerous styles, poodle dog lighter and case is highly prized, value drops by 75% if mother-of-pearl is chipped or cracked . . **50.00-150.00**

Cigarette lighter, Ronson Queen Anne tabletop, silver plated, 2⅝" high, Ronson made 15,000 of these a week for many years, it was sold alone and in combination with wood or metal cigarette boxes, with trays, and/or a cigarette urn, damaged or worn pieces have no value, even fine ones are difficult to sell, lighter alone (if perfect) **5.00-8.00**
Box, with tray. **15.00-20.00**
With tray and urn. **30.00-40.00**

Cigarette lighter, Ronson Capri, made in 15 designs including leather, tortoise, blue, pearl and black enamels plus black with floral design, all except the gold plated model are considered common **3.00-10.00**
Complete in original box **15.00**
Tortoise in original box **25.00**

Cigarette lighter and matching cigarette case, Ronson Adonis, sterling silver, although the sterling Adonis lighter is common, worth about **$15.00-20.00,** the lighter in combination with the cigarette case is considered rare, especially in its original plush lined, spring hinged leatherette covered metal gift box. **100.00-125.00**

Ronson Spartan Cigarette Lighter

Cigarette lighter, Ronson Spartan, chromium plated with three enamel bands, looking very Art Deco, actually made in 1950s. Felt base earlier than cork, but both common, damaged or scratched lighters have little if any value. If near mint (ILLUS.) **8.00-15.00**

CIGAR BOXES

Cigar box, Santa Fe (Patties or Panatellas size), trimmed wooden box, 1950s, popular California made cigar sold nationwide for half a century. If clean and complete with inner liner, more if before 1926. . . . . **5.00-20.00**

Corina Larks Cigar Box

Cigar box, Corina Larks, redwood with interlocked corners, hinges and clasp, collar and partial paper label. 1940s and 1950s, one of the four most common boxes of this type, the other common brands,

worth about the same, are Webster, Brooks & Company, and House of Windsor. Collectors have little interest, for people who want a nice sturdy box (ILLUS.). **3.00-5.00**

Cigar box, Magnolia, trimmed nailed wood. 1878-1885, label in style of 1870s, flower theme, cigars made by Straiton and Storm in New York City, soiled boxes or those without liners, bring half, box of 100 in excellent condition, liner and labels clean and complete, some themes a great deal more **50.00-75.00**

Dolly Dollars Cigar Jar

Cigar jar, Dolly Dollars, glass with zinc top, paper label of actress, revenue stamp, 1910-1916. 7" tall; 5¼" in diameter, no chips or cracks (ILLUS.) **25.00-40.00**

Cigar box, Merry Christmas and Happy New Year. Hundreds of variations are known: Christmas scenes, angels, cherubs, trees, domestic scenes, snow scenes, women, children, etc. Condition is particularly important for Christmas boxes. Soil, staining, etc., can substantially affect value. Most Christmas boxes, including those shaped like books, in near mint condition . . . . **35.00-75.00** More unusual themes sell for . . . . **60.00-150.00** Some very rare and desirable Christmas boxes can go to **300.00**

CIGAR LABELS

Cigar label, Sun Maid. Rip-off of Sun Maid raisins girl. 7" x 9". Second quarter of 20th century. Desirable, but not rare **15.00**

Cigar label, Socrates. Depicts Greek philosopher. 7" x 9" embossed full color lithograph, 1915-1935. . . . . **15.00**

Cigar label, Arthur Donaldson. Image of man in 18th century military uniform enjoying a cigar. Embossed and gilded, relatively common, second quarter of 20th century **10.00-15.00**

Cigar box, Lime Kiln Club. Same label on fine condition cigar box 1880s is much more rare than label alone. Demand for box is less than for the label at this time **400.00-750.00**

Cigar label, Betsy Ross. Depicts Ms. Ross, flags, her home, the Liberty Bell. 6¾" x 8¼". Second quarter of the 20th century. **15.00**

Cigar label, Blue Bird. Striking image on blue background, lots of gold. 6½" x 9" gilded and embossed **15.00-20.00**

Cigar label, Big Wolf. Snarling greenish looking wolf's head/torso. Gilded and embossed. Second quarter of 20th century. 6¼" x 9". . . . **10.00**

CIGAR MAKERS UNION MEMORABILIA

Cigar Makers Union Items

Cigar Makers Union matchbox holder. Painted tin three-sided matchbox holder 2⅜" x 1½" x ⅜". Holds standard U.S. 20th century matchbox. Depicts C.M.I.U. blue label on each side (ILLUS. right) **30.00-50.00**

Cigar Makers Union pocket mirror. Mirror 2" diameter. Promotional material for Union blue label. Emphasizes sanitary conditions. 1900-1915. Fine condition (ILLUS. left) **40.00-75.00**

Cigar Makers Union match safe. Celluloid over metal, 2¾" x 1½". Design of stamped envelope on one side, promotion for Union blue label on other **60.00-100.00**

Cigar Makers Union match safe. Celluloid over metal, 2¾ x 1½". Full color depiction of salesman behind counter on one side, promotion for Union blue label on other . . **150.00-250.00**

MISCELLANY

Two Tobacco Packages

Tobacco package, Plowboy, full, 2¾" x 4⅝" package with full color lithographed label, in original cellophane overwrap. Liggett & Myers (ILLUS. left) **30.00-40.00**

Tobacco package, Bagpipe, full, 3½" x 5" paper wrapped package of smoking tobacco. 1928 cancellation on stamp. Two color, depicts bagpiper and dancer (ILLUS right) **15.00-25.00**

Cigarette packages, paper, Cuban, assortment of six different brands from 1930s, with original revenue stamps, with or without original premium coupons. Assortment in good condition. **35.00-75.00**

Cigar bands, pasted on glass plate or shallow bowl or similar, approximately 3" to 9". May also be shallow bowl. If your bands are pink rather than red, value is reduced by 80%. Quality and uniqueness of design are part of the value. Very large and unusual items covered with bands, such as furniture, bring substantially more, but are a matter of individual negotiations, as there are too few sales to estimate value accurately. If colors are bright, **$20.00-35.00** for small plain plates to **$75.00-100.00** for well done elaborate pieces in fine condition. Urns and other more unusual small objects from 50% to 200% higher.

Late 1880s Cigarette Card Album

Cigarette card album, fish, published by Allen & Ginter tobacco, late 1880s, beautiful

12 page (including covers) 9¼" x 6" stiff card page album depicting the 50 cards in the "Fish from American Waters" insert card set. The height of quality commercial printing, including seldom seen work in silver ink (ILLUS.) . . **125.00-200.00**

Magazine advertising for cigars, cigarettes and lighters, full page, pre-1970. Although a few specialized ads may bring more, most are **3.00-7.00**

TOOLS

Ax, hand-wrought goosewing-style, various punch decorations & smith marks, Europe **$300.00**

Bevel, rosewood body & brass trim, Hold-Fast, patent dated "12-15-14," 10" l. **35.00**

Boring machine, heavy cast iron, Buckeye Mfg. Co., w/one bit **95.00**

Caliper rule, boxwood, Faukner & Son, 3" **55.00**

Door mortiser, cast iron, Champion Door Mortiser, patent-dated "Sept. 10, 1912," portable machine for installing mortise locks **375.00**

Draw knife, handled, Cantello Folding model **25.00**

Hammer, broom maker's **35.00**

Hammer, saddlemaker's, European . . . **60.00**

Hammer, tack hammer, patent-dated "Dec. 8, 1891" **40.00**

Hammer, tack puller **30.00**

Inclinometer, gold striping, L.L. Davis No. 2, 12" l. (small chip) **160.00**

Level, rosewood, Stratton Bros. 6½", marked "No. 10" on end plate **350.00**

Level, Stanley No. 96, rosewood w/brass binding **150.00**

Level, Starrett No. 98, black crackle finish, like new in box, 8" l. **75.00**

Marking gauge, rosewood & brass, English **35.00**

Miter gauge, Bleys Adjustable, patent-dated "July 30, 1912" **75.00**

Mortice gauge, boxwood, S.A. Jones **30.00**

Mortice gauge, rosewood, Philips patent model w/brass slide **145.00**

Plane, block plane, screw-type lever cap, boat-shaped, L. Bailey Victor No. 0 . . . . **195.00**

Plane, block plane, stamped steel, Stanley Defiance No. 205, offered briefly before World War II. **55.00**

Plane, cabinetmaker's edge plane, Stanley No. 97, SR & L blade **325.00**

Plane, combination, Stanley A-45, early sweetheart trademark on skate, w/aluminum cam stop, complete w/one box of blades (minor crack on rosewood handle). . **2,800.00**

Plane, combination-type, complete w/gate, gauge, & fillister bed, Stanley No. 41 Miller's Patent, pre-slitter model (tight crack in handle), the set **900.00**

Plane, complex molder, Ohio Tool Co. No. 62½ **48.00**

Plane, cornice molding plane, Hall, Case & Co. **125.00**

Plane, dado plane, ½", fruitwood, T.J. McMaster & Co.. . . . . **25.00**

Plane, dado plane, Gladwin ¼". **30.00**

Plane, jointer-type, corrugated bottom, Union X No. 8 . . . . **105.00**

Plane, plow plane, ebony-handled w/boxwood arms & nuts, A. Howland & Co. (ebony w/some minor restoration) **1,200.00**

Plane, plow plane w/ivory tips, boxwood handle, Ohio Tool Co., No. 105 (handle horn repaired) **375.00**

Plane, smoothing plane, wood bottom, Stanley No. G-35 . . . . **65.00**

Plane, Stanley No. 48, combination tongue & groove, patent-dated 1875 . . . . **175.00**

Plane, wood bottom plane, Ohio Tool Co. No. 021, Auburn, New York, smallest of this type by Ohio **195.00**

Protractor, draftsman's, K & E **45.00**

Protractor rule w/level, Lufkin No. 863 L. **55.00**

Rule, ½ bound boxwood, Stanley No. 52 . . . . **105.00**

Rule, carriage maker's, Stanley No. 94 . . . . **140.00**

Rule shrinkage-type, Stanley No. 30½ H **85.00**

Rule, Stanley No. 27, two-fold, two foot, "S R & L" mark. **80.00**

Scraper, Stanley No. 81 . . . . **35.00**

Screw driver kit, Clark's Patent, handle & two bits, original wooden box, the set (end of box & one bit missing) **45.00**

Spokeshave, brass, adjustable **45.00**

Spokeshave, wooden, Wm. Johnson. . **13.00**

Surface gauge, Starrett No. 257-A, blued, marbleized finish, new in box **75.00**

Wagon wrench & boot jack combination, decorative piping cast in boot frame, unmarked **115.00**

TOYS

Airplane, "Boeing 707," tin, friction-
type, jet plane w/correct logos, by
DAIYA, Japan, in original box,
10" l. **$109.00**

Airplane, die-cast metal, "Autogyro,"
Tootsietoy (Dowst Bros., Chicago,
Illinois), painted white w/blue prop,
ca. 1930s, wingspan 4¼" w. **150.00**

Airplane, "Pan America," tin, marked
"Pan America Air Lines" w/American
flag, Japan SHI SHI, in original box,
6" l., 7½" wingspan (minor rust) **385.00**

Arcadia Airport, wooden, Arcade
Mfg. Co. (Freeport, Illinois) **660.00**

Two Battery-Operated Toys

Battery-operated, "Arthur A Go-Go,"
long-haired fellow playing drums,
cloth & metal (ILLUS. left) **143.00**

Battery-operated, duck's popcorn
vendor **72.00**

Battery-operated, Guitar playing
Chimp, standing furry chimp at a
microphone w/guitar, one leg
raised on step, cloth & metal
(ILLUS. right) **121.00**

Battery-operated, Santa Claus
walking & playing drums & cymbals . . **35.00**

Blocks, building-type, wood,
"Crandall's Building Blocks,"
w/original box & instructions, ca.
1880, the set (no box lid, fair to
good condition) **58.00**

Blocks, wooden, light stacking type,
lithographed pictures of children
except largest w/animals, tops
w/numbers or alphabet except
largest, sized 4" x 4" x 3½" to
1½" x 1½", set of seven. **275.00**

Boat, outboard motor-type, wooden
boat w/adjustable centerboard & a
tin windup outboard motor,
ca. 1930, 23¼" l. **201.00**

Britain's (soldiers), cast metal,
"Arabs of the Desert," five mounted
& one marching soldier on slope,
Model No. 164, original box, the
set **144.00**

Bus, cast iron, painted blue w/nickel-
plated wheels, Arcade, 1920s,
4⅝" l. **144.00**

Cannon, cast iron & pressed steel,
"Big Bang Cannon," 1950s,18" l. . . . **58.00**

Cap pistol, cast iron, "Pirate,"
Hubley **125.00**

Cement mixer, painted cast iron, in
orange, light blue & nickel-plate,
four small pierced metal wheels,
embossed "Jaeger" on side of
engine hood, Kenton Hardware
(Kenton, Ohio), ca. 1930, 6⅝" l. . . . **374.00**

Circus animal, alligator, jointed
wood, painted body & eyes, leather
feet, standard size, Schoenhut &
Co. (Philadelphia, Pennsylvania),
12" l. (two feet damaged, needs
restringing) **230.00**

Circus animal, elephant, jointed
wood, painted w/painted eyes,
leather ears & tusks, hemp tail &
rubber trunk, standard size,
Schoenhut & Co., w/original color-
lithographed cardboard box,
elephant 10⅜" l. (some paint wear
on head, trunk damaged, box
w/edge wear). **633.00**

Circus animal, giraffe, jointed wood,
realistically painted body w/painted
eyes, leather ears & cotton tail,
standard size, Schoenhut & Co.,
11⅝" h. (normal paint wear, needs
restringing) **316.00**

Circus animal, lion in wooden cage,
jointed wood, Schoenhut & Co. **990.00**

Circus animal, tiger, jointed wood,
realistically painted w/painted eyes,
cloth tail, standard size, Schoenhut
& Co. (some paint wear, needs
restringing) **230.00**

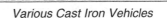

Various Cast Iron Vehicles

Circus cage wagon, cast iron,
"Overland Circus," wagon w/two
white horses w/riders & driver,
pulling a polar bear cage, Kenton
Hardware, unused w/original box,
14" l. (ILLUS. left) . . . . . . **350.00 to 450.00**

Circus set, "Humpty Dumpty Circus,"
reduced size, includes tent w/flags
& base, two clowns, donkey,
elephant, two chairs, two ladders &
center ring, Schoenhut & Co., base
9 x 18", the set (fabric wear &
staining, paint fair to good, figures
need restringing) **863.00**

Clockwork fire engine house,
complete w/bell which rang when
fire pumper rushed through the
door, Ives Corp., (Bridgeport,
Connecticut) **2,970.00**

Rare Bing Clockwork Limousine

Clockwork limousine, tinplate,
hand-painted w/beveled glass
windows, kilometer taxi meter,
nickel-plated carriage lights, rubber
wheels, original key & box built for
storage, minor flaking, missing
windshield, driver & rear luggage
rack, damage to roof luggage rack,
Bing (Germany), ca. 1910, 14¼" l.
(ILLUS.) **21,850.00**

Clockwork polar bear, off-white
mohair, glass eyes, composition
nose & open mouth w/teeth,
French clockwork mechanism,
Distler key, 12" l. (nose rubbed) . . . **978.00**

Corgi vehicle, 1012 S.P.E.C.T.R.E.
bobsled, used by head of
S.P.E.C.T.R.E. when fleeing from
James Bond, good condition **140.00**

Corgi vehicle, 1102 Crane w/orange
Fruehauf bottom dumper & red
Berliet cab, near mint toy & good
box. **65.00**

Corgi vehicle, 1106 Mack Container
truck, yellow cab & trailer w/red
containers marked "ACL," near
mint toy & good box. **65.00**

Corgi vehicle, 24-C1 Shazam
Thunderbolt race car, yellow (from
Capt. Marvel comics), near mint **35.00**

Corgi vehicle, 259 Penguinmobile,
white body w/Penguin labels, near
mint toy & good box. **55.00**

Corgi vehicle, 260 Metropolis
(Superman's city) Buick police car,
blue & white body, mint toy & box . . . **55.00**

Corgi vehicle, 267 Batmobile, black
body/silver hubs/gold tow hook,
Batman & Robin figures, mint toy &
box. **65.00**

Corgi vehicle, GS-15-B1 Corgi Pony
Club Land Rover & Horse Box,
blue & white, good. **80.00**

Corgi vehicle, GS-24 Construction
set, near mint toys & box. **230.00**

Corgi vehicle, GS-31 Buick Riviera
(blue) w/boat on red trailer & water
skier, near mint toy & box **300.00**

Covered wagon, cast iron, pulled by
two horses, cloth top sealed in
original envelope, Kenton
Hardware Co., first half 20th c.,
unused in original box, 15¼" l. **468.00**

Covered wagon, open buckboard
w/driver & two horses, cloth top
sealed in original envelope, unused
w/original box, Kenton Hardware,
15" l. (ILLUS. center w/Circus cage
wagon prev. page) . . . . . **350.00 to 450.00**

Dairy wagon, painted wood, a
silhouetted white house w/string tail
hinged to pull the closed wagon
printed on the side w/"Sheffield
Farms Company - The National
Dairy Milk...," w/six tiny glass milk
bottles in a tin carrier, Rich & Co.
(Clinton, Iowa), ca. 1930, 20½" l. . . . **633.00**

Schoenhut Dairy Wagon Set

Dairy wagon, painted wood, the
white cloth-covered horse on a
platform wheeled base pulling the
closed wooden wagon w/a sign
across the top "Hood's Grade 'A'
Milk" & a company logo on the
side, original driver, wooden crate
& seven milk bottles, Schoenhut,
early 20th c., horse missing tail,
damage to driver's head, 25" l.,
the set (ILLUS.) **3,105.00**

Dinky vehicle, 110, Aston Martin
DB3S gray body & blue interior,
racing decal, near mint body & fair
box. **80.00**

Dinky vehicle, 147, Cadillac 72, blue body & red interior, near mint body & box **90.00**

Dinky vehicle, 156, Rover 75 Saloon, maroon body & red hubcaps, near mint toy & box **140.00**

Dinky vehicle, 162, Ford Zephyr, two-tone blue, near mint body **95.00**

Dinky vehicle, 294, Police Vehicles Gift Set (boxed), good toys & box . . **130.00**

Dinky vehicle, 353, Shado 2 Mobile, olive green body & pale green base, near mint toy & box **60.00**

Dinky vehicle, 370, Dragster set, good toy & box **55.00**

Dinky vehicle, 678, Air Sea Rescue launch w/black hull & light grey deck, yellow superstructure, near mint toy & box **55.00**

Dinky vehicle, 724, Sikorsky Sea King helicopter, white & blue w/red interior, near mint toy w/box **70.00**

Dinky vehicle, 822, M-3 Half track, olive body & no machine gun, good body & box **150.00**

Dinky vehicle, 945, A.E.C. Esso fuel tanker w/white body but no rear label, near mint toy & box **85.00**

Dinky vehicle, 948, McLean Tractor trailer w/red cab & grey trailer, near mint toy & box **475.00**

Dump truck, pressed steel, hydraulic-type, dual rear wheels, rubber tires, headlight & bumper, Buddy "L" (Moline Pressed Steel Co., E. Moline, Illinois), Model #201A, ca. 1930, 24½" l. (poor condition, some overpaint) **1,093.00**

Tonka Dump Truck

Dump truck, pressed steel, large plow attachment on the front, sign on side of door "State Highway Dept.," side dump-type, Tonka Toys, 1950s, 17" l. (ILLUS.) **248.00**

Dump wagon, cast iron, contractors' horse-drawn style, two white horses pulling a deep wagon molded on the side w/"Contractors' Dump Wagon," body in black paint, large rear & smaller front yellow painted wheels, Arcade Mfg. Co. (Freeport, Illinois), ca. 1920, 14" l. . . . **173.00**

Early Wooden Express Wagon

Express wagon, painted wood, two carved horses on wheeled platform pulling a wooden flatbed wagon w/metal wheels, red wagon w/gold striping & the word "Express," black horses on red platform, some paint wear, late 19th c., 31" l. (ILLUS.) . . **920.00**

Farm wagon, cast iron, one horse & driver, worn paint, marked "Kenton Toys, Made in USA," 15" l. **275.00**

Fire engine house, wooden, Arcade **1,375.00**

Fire extension-ladder truck, lithographed tin, friction-type, automatic ladder mechanism, Cragstone (Japan), 1960s, w/original box, 14¼" l. **81.00**

Fire ladder wagon, cast iron, Kingsbury Mfg. Co. (Keen, New Hampshire). **2,090.00**

Early Cast-Iron Fire Ladder Wagon

Fire ladder wagon, cast iron, the long red wagon w/gold striping, blue ladder racks & yellow wheels pulled by a black & a white horse on wheels, two drivers & wooden ladders, early 20th c., 24½" l. (ILLUS.). **978.00**

Fire pumper wagon, horse-drawn, painted cast iron, one black horse & one nickel-plated horse, Ives & Blakeslee Company, ca. 1890, 20" l. (missing driver) **920.00**

Fire truck, pressed steel, Suburban Pumper #46, Tonka. **180.00**

G.I. Joe doll, Collector's Edition "Home for the Holidays" Soldier, No. 35946, Hasbro Mfg. Co. (Pawtucket, Rhode Island), ca. 1996, never removed from box . . **30.00**

G.I. Joe Space Capsule, w/Astronaut, the set **465.00**

Hansom cab, cast iron, w/driver & one white prancing horse, passenger inside, Kenton

Hardware, original box, passenger damaged, 15¼" l. (ILLUS. right w/Circus cage wagon prev. page). . **330.00**

Early Cast-Iron Harvester

Harvester, cast iron, John Deere model, painted silver w/green blades & yellow wheels, original standing driver, Vindex, early 20th c. (ILLUS.) **7,150.00**

Marble game, includes one light sapphire blue w/mica, six green micas & twenty-seven clear glass mica marbles, round finished hard wood board w/34 holes, marbles 1¹⁄₁₆" d. **210.00**

Mary & her lamb, painted jointed wood & cloth, Schoenhut, 2 pcs. . . **1,430.00**

Matchbox set, "Sea Fury" play set w/carrying case & three figures, near mint toy & good box **105.00**

Matchbox toy, jigsaw puzzles featuring eight different vehicle toys issued in 1969, mint, set of eight. . . **130.00**

Matchbox vehicle, Coronation Coach, small silver-plated, issued 1953 . . . . **100.00**

Matchbox vehicle, CY-104, Kenworth Superstar Transporter Sunoco Ultra Racing Team Set #94, without "Sterlin Marlin" on trailer, mint vehicle w/good box. **80.00**

Matchbox vehicle, G-14, Grand Prix Set w/near mint toys & good box. . . . **45.00**

Matchbox vehicle, G-6-B, Commercial Truck set, pristine toy & box. **150.00**

Matchbox vehicle, MB-42-2, Studebaker Lark Wagonaire w/rare dark blue roof, good **75.00**

Matchbox vehicle, MB-46-1, Morris Minor GPW in rare green color, good **135.00**

Matchbox vehicle, MB-66-2, Harley Davidson motorcycle & rider, good toy & fair box **110.00**

Matchbox vehicle, MB-66-3, Greyhound Bus w/silver body & rare clear windows, both toy & box mint **85.00**

Matchbox vehicle, PS1000, Gift Set (road construction vehicles) pristine toy & box **155.00**

Matchbox vehicle, SB-29-A SR-71, spy plane w/USAF markings, preproduction resin model, near mint w/fair box **120.00**

Milk wagon, lithographed tin & wood, tin enclosed wagon body lithographed in color & marked "Rich's 1922" & "Rich's" on sides, wooden wheels & flat printed horse on front small wheels, the saddle printed "A Rich Toy," Rich & Co., 1930s, 20" l. **288.00**

Motorcycle w/side car, cast iron, w/driver & passenger, olive green, black, silver & pink, wheels marked "Harley Davidson," 9" l. (some wear) **605.00**

Movie camera, child sized, painted wood, Schoenhut & Co.. . . . . **935.00**

Noah's Ark set, painted wood, painted wooden ark accompanied by some 183 finely carved & painted small animals, fine overall quality & condition, American-made, 19th c., the set **16,675.00**

Pedal car, pressed steel, "Austin J40" model, light blue, opening trunk & hood, electric headlights & horn, leatherette upholstery, nickel-plated grille, bumpers & hood ornament, surface rust to left front fender, England, 1950s, 61" l. **1,610.00**

Fire Chief's Pedal Car

Pedal car, pressed steel, fire chief's car, wood chassis, red w/yellow striping, Rickenbacker, American National (Toledo, Ohio), late 1920s, missing front bell, poor finish, surface rust, 42" l. (ILLUS.) . . **1,840.00**

Penny toy, lithographed tin, black dancer, hand-cranked mechanism, Distler (Germany), early 20th c., 3⅜" h. **201.00**

Child's Piano with Dancing Dolls

Piano, wooden w/ornate cast-iron legs & base, eight wooden white keys w/eleven black keys, eight tiny "dancing" Flat Top china dolls inside mirrored display area, 14" h. (ILLUS.) **2,900.00**

Play set, "Bradley's Historiscope," panoramic history of America & the United States including poster, tickets, lecture & instructions, case w/metal handle, early 20th c., case 6⁵⁄₁₆ x 11⁷⁄₁₆", 2" h. (case w/imperfections) **489.00**

Pull toy, donkey on wheels, the standing animal w/an amber velvet body, glass eyes & black mohair tail & mane raised on a thin rectangular board platform w/tiny tin wheels, late 19th - early 20th c., 13" l. **303.00**

Pull toy, horse, mohair & burlap covering, black metal eyes, leather ears, fur mane, composition muzzle w/open-closed mouth, horsehair tail, leather bridle & saddle, marked "Made in Germany" on underside of wheeled platform, 18" l., 19" h. **450.00**

Pull toy, horse on wheeled platform, wood & composition w/original dark brown mohair coat, fur, mane & tail, fairly complete saddle & harness, thin rectangular wood platform w/tiny cast-iron wheels, late 19th c., 11" l., 12" h. (legs loose). **358.00**

Pull toy, "Kiddie-Kar-Kid," composition boy doll w/molded head & painted features on a straw-filled cloth body w/composition hands, sitting astride a wooden three-wheeled kiddy car & wearing a cotton suit & hat, natural finish on car w/original

label & red wheels, H.C. White Co., North Bennington, Vermont, patented in 1924, 9¼" l., 10" h. (paint damage on doll's head & hands, clothes faded) **288.00**

Early Fisher-Price Pull Toy Set

Pull toys, lithographed paper on wood, includes a goat, pig, cow, mule & cart all in original colorfully lithographed box, Fisher-Price No. 207, minor paper separations & creasing, box edge wear & staining, ca. 1931, box 9 x 11", 2" h., the set (ILLUS.) **863.00**

Puzzle, jigsaw-type, "Hood's Double-Sided Rainy Day and Balloon Puzzle," lithographed, framed, original box, ca. 1891 (wear, staining to box) **109.00**

Rocking horse on platform, carved & painted wood, the crudely carved animal decorated w/dapple grey paint w/darkened brown varnish, glass eyes, worn original saddle & harness, raised on board cross braces & suspended from swinging iron bands above a trestle-form platform base w/old red paint, 19th c., 40" l., 34" h. **578.00**

Fine Victorian Platform Rocking Horse

Rocking horse on platform, painted wood, the rearing dapple grey horse w/painted mane & real hair long tail, leather bridle, leather saddle & stirrups, raised on a long angled spring-hinged tapering board on a slightly arched platform base, fine painted base decoration, England or America, late 19th c., minor paint loss, other minor losses, 47" l., 43¼" h. (ILLUS.) . . **3,450.00**

Rocking horse on platform, painted wood, well-carved animal w/a dapple grey coat, glass eyes, horse hair mane & tail, leather ears, red base w/yellow & black striping, remnants of leather saddle, some paint loss, late 19th - early 20th c., 38¾" l. **460.00**

Rocking horse on rockers, carved & painted wood, the full-bodied primitive horse mounted on long curved rockers w/crossbars near the tips & a wooden platform under the horse, the horse in worn old dapple grey paint w/traces of red on the rockers, worn remains of saddle, missing mane & tail, rocker platform incomplete, 19th c., 45" l., 24½" h. **495.00**

Early Rocking Horse on Rockers

Rocking horse on rockers, painted wood, well-carved animal painted off-white w/leather saddle & reins, hair mane & tail, on long curved rocker base, repairs, minor losses, old repaint, 19th c., 48½" l., 27¼" h. (ILLUS.) **920.00**

Rocking horse on stationary base, painted wood, old red & brown repaint w/black trim, mane & tail replaced, harness replaced & saddle incomplete, paint wear, 19th c., 35" l. **330.00**

Service station set, wooden, Arcade **413.00**

Sewing machine, "Kayanee" model, metal, made in U.S. Zone, Germany, 1950s **95.00**

Sewing machine, "The Little Comfort Automatic Hand Sewing Machine," metal frame, chain-drive mechanism, original wooden box w/paper label, ca. 1897, machine 6½" h., box 7¹⁄₁₆ x 7¾", 3³⁄₁₆" h. **518.00**

Sled, child's push-type, wood, painted black & red w/cherry red upholstery, late 19th c., 50" l. (some edge paint wear) **288.00**

Sled, child's size, decorated wood & iron, the board platform curved at each end & decorated w/original red & green w/yellow striping & black printed designs of looping scrolls at each end & a bird on branch in the center, raised on curved steel-tipped runners w/wooden braces, late 19th - early 20th c., 32" l. **220.00**

Sled, child's size, painted wood, long wooden platform w/rounded rear & incurved scalloped front end, on bentwood runners, the platform decorated w/a square lake & mountain landscape w/stenciled colored band, sprig bands & a starburst on the ends, 40" l. (damage, old repair) **385.00**

Unique Steam Engine Accessory

Steam engine accessory, lithographed & painted metal, a row of silhouette-cut lithographed hinged lathe workers standing in a line w/pulleys & crank shaft above supported between slender metal poles, all mounted on a thin rectangular wooden base, late 19th - early 20th c., 13" l. (ILLUS.) **2,090.00**

Steam roller, painted cast iron, early tractor-style w/driver & cab at rear above large pierced rear wheels, small front roller wheel, embossed "Huber" under driver's compartment, original driver, painted green, Hubley Mfg. Co. (Lancaster, Pennsylvania), ca. 1930, 7½" l. (some surface rust) . . **345.00**

Steamboat, side-wheeler,
lithographed paper on wood,
marked "Providence," W.S. Reed
Toy Co. (Leominster,
Massachusetts), late 19th c., 20" l.
(tears, edge wear) **690.00**

Steamboat, side-wheeler, painted
cast iron, name "Puritan" raised
across side-wheel frame, Wilkins
Toy Co. (Keene, New Hampshire),
ca. 1900, 11" l. (fair condition,
some flaking) **431.00**

Steamshovel truck, lithographed tin,
green open cab w/red & blue
stripings, red shovel cab w/green
roof, boom arm & bucket, Mack
truck marked "Hercules," J. Chein
& Co. (New York, New York),
1920s, 27½" l. **2,530.00**

Taxi cab, cast iron, Arcade, No. 2
Yellow Cab, w/driver, 7¾" l. **800.00**

Train engine, brass, B & O "Tom
Thumb" engine, non-standard
gauge, runs on coal or bench top
propane, manufactured by R.
Ebert, 7¼" l. **138.00**

Train engine, brass, electric,
Pennsylvania GG-1 locomotive, "O"
gauge, manufactured by
Samhongsa, fine, 20½" l. **825.00**

Train engine, brass, electric, Union
Pacific #9000 4-12-2 locomotive,
"O" gauge, manufactured by
Samhongsa, mint in box, 25½" l. . . . **1,210.00**

Train engine, brass & steel, Richard
Trevithick's 1804 locomotive,
wooden coal car, manufactured by
R. Ebert, 19½" l. **715.00**

Train engine, brass, three truck Shay
locomotive and tender, "O" gauge,
manufactured by Katsumi
Mokeiten, good with original box,
16½" l. **1,375.00**

Train engine, brass, Union Pacific 4-
8-8-4 "Big Boy" locomotive,
manufactured by Katsumi
Mokeiten, fine w/original box,
34" l. **2,255.00**

Train engine, brass, Virginian triplex
2-8-8-8-4 locomotive & tender, "O"
gauge, manufactured by
Samhongsa, fine, 25½" l. **1,293.00**

Train engine, electric, Southern
Pacific 4-8-8-4 cab forward
locomotive, gauge one,
manufactured by Samhongsa, mint
w/carrying case, ... **11,000.00**

Train engine, Lionel "Santa Fe"
model w/AA unit, electric, grey &
red w/gold striping (ILLUS.). **660.00**

Lionel Train Engine with AA Unit

Train engine, live steam, Union
Pacific 4-8-8-4 "Big Boy," gauge
one, manufactured by Samhongsa,
mint w/carrying case. **7,150.00**

Train set, "American Flyer S Gauge,"
tinplate, No. 290 steam locomotive,
No. 370 diesel locomotive, eight
freight cars, two transformers, ten
original boxes of track, instructions,
a Marx street light & Keystone
buildings, some original boxes, the
set (various conditions) **316.00**

Train set, lithographed paper on
wood, a locomotive, tender &
passenger car w/removable roof,
marked "Buffalo" on the sides, Bliss
Mfg. Co. (Pawtucket, Rhode
Island), ca. 1900, minor paper loss,
missing alphabet blocks, one
connecting rod & pull cord eyelet,
overall 45" l. **7,188.00**

Truck, die-cast, gasoline tanker,
"Sinclair," Tootsietoy **66.00**

Truck, die-cast metal, Mack Auto
Transport, yellow cab & trailer
w/four autos, Tootsietoy, ca.
1930s, w/original box, 10¾" l.
(missing one box flap) **230.00**

Truck, die-cast, oil tanker, "Mobil,"
Tootsietoy **45.00**

Truck, die-cast, tow truck, Tootsietoy . . **40.00**

Truck, pressed steel, livestock van-
type, No. 36, Tonka **125.00**

Truck, pressed steel, Tonka Farms
stock rack-type, No. 32 . . . . **146.00**

Velocipede, carved & painted wood,
a carved & white-painted leaping
horse w/hair mane & tail, leather
saddle, raised on three large
wooden wheels w/crank shaft for
front wheels through the horse's
head, worn paint & split in horse's
body, late 19th c. **550.00**

Velocipede, carved & painted wood,
a dapple-painted leaping horse
w/white hair mane & tail raised on
three large wooden wheels w/a
turn handle through the body,
leather saddle & reins, turned wood
hand grips, late 19th c. **1,000.00**

Water pistol, "Daisy," **65.00**

Water Tower wagon, cast iron,
horse-drawn **1,760.00**

Windup celluloid, clown figure, C.K.,
Japan, 1930s, w/original box, 8" h. . . **230.00**

Windup tin, "Bulky Mule,"
lithographed in color, Lehmann
(Germany), Model #425, early
20th c., 7¼" l. **230.00**

Windup tin, circus cage wagon
pulled by an elephant, the
articulated elephant pulled a box-
style cage on large solid metal
wheels, one side of cage w/hinged
opening doors, colorfully
lithographed, possibly Ferdinand
Strauss Corp. (New York, New
York), ca. 1930 (possibly
incomplete) **173.00**

Windup tin, "Cowboy Rider," cowboy
twirling a lasso while astride a
rearing horse, lithographed in color,
Louis Marx & Co. (New York, New
York), 1930s, w/original box, 7" h. . . **431.00**

Windup tin, "Oh-My Alabama Coon
Jigger," lithographed in color w/a
black dancer, Model 685, Lehmann
(Germany), early 20th c., 10" h.
(wear to top of base) **403.00**

Early Lehmann Windup Tin Racer

Windup tin, racer, painted yellow
a/blue & cream trim & white & red
metal wheels, marked "D-R Patent,
Patd. USA Az Dec. 1913 - Made in
Germany," Lehmann Co.
(Germany), very minor scratches,
6" l. (ILLUS.). **1,045.00**

Early Marklin Windup Racer

Windup tin, racer, red chassis
w/black & white number, white
fenders & pale green side pipe &
grill, black rubber wheels, Marklin
(Germany), missing driver,
repainted fenders (ILLUS.). **1,650.00**

Windup tin, "Rodeo Joe," crazy car
w/cowboy driver, lithographed in
color, Unique Art Mfg. Co., Inc.
(New York City also Newark, New
Jersey), 1930s, 7" l. **201.00**

Windup tin, steamroller, corrigated
metal roof, large smokestack, large
rear wheels & smaller diameter
roller at front, ca. 1930, 11½" l. . . . **230.00**

Windup tin, "Whoopie Car,"
lithographed in color, Model #150,
Marx, 1930s, w/original box, 7" l.
(box fair to good condition) **748.00**

Windup tin, zeppelin, silver-colored
body w/propeller at the tail,
Ferdinand Strauss Corp., 1930s,
9½" l. **201.00**

Winross vehicle, 1992 York Fair
Doubles w/Wind-Up Music &
Reithoffer's logo, Ford cab in
orange w/orange & white trailer &
tandem axles, issued 1992, mint
toy & box **140.00**

Winross vehicle, A.D. Frey White
7000 cab in white w/red/white
trailer, tandem axles, issued 1985,
120 made, near mint toy & box **425.00**

Winross vehicle, Branch Motor
Express, White 9000 cab in green,
grey trailer & tandem axle, issued
1982, near mint toy & box **240.00**

Winross vehicle, Hanover Shoe
Company 1st Edition, Mack cab in
green, white trailer, tandem axles,
issued 1991, near mint toy & box . . . **80.00**

Winross vehicle, Helms Express,
White 9000 cab in dark green/white
trailer, tandem axles & issued
1980, near mint toy & box **230.00**

Winross vehicle, New Penn 50
Years Of Service 931-1981, White
9000 cab in green, white trailer,
tandem axles, issued 1982, near
mint toy & box **90.00**

Winross vehicle, The Chief Freight
Lines Co., White 7000 cab in red &
white, white trailer, tandem axles,
issued 1982, near mint toy & box . . **180.00**

Winross vehicle, Ward Trucking
Corp., International 8300 cab in
green, white trailer, tandem axles,
issued 1991, near mint toy & box . . . **60.00**

Winross vehicle, York Paper Box
100th Anniversary 1894-1994,
Aeromax cab in metallic gold, pale
yellow & cream trailer, tandem
axles, issued 1994, only 600 made,
mint toy & box **40.00**

Zeppelin, cast iron, marked "Zep,"
painted silver, ca. 1930s, 4¾" l. **86.00**

TRADE CATALOGS

**Abercrombie & Fitch Sporting
Goods,** 1936 . . . . **$20.00**

Arcade Christmas Book, "Fred and
Jane with the Tiny Arcadians," 1931,
illustrations w/price list & illustrated
leaflet in mailing envelope **259.00**

Boston Hose Co., 1905, includes fire
hats, lanterns, badges, hoses, etc.,
30 pp. **65.00**

Brass founder's, probably
Birmingham, England, ca. 1780,
approximately 150 engraved plates,
a portion of them bound w/binder's
titled "Musler=Berdnugen fur Gold
Gilber und Girenarbeiter" (varying
conditions, some toning & tears) . . **5,463.00**

Granite Iron Ware, catalog &
cookbook, colorful chromolitho-
graphed covers, ca. 1880, 64 pp. . . . **85.00**

Matchbox toy catalog, 1959, near
mint condition **165.00**

Monogram Model Kits, 1964. . . . . . . **25.00**

Montgomery Ward, 1938 . . . . **38.00**

**National Enameling & Stamping
Co. (Nesco),** 1932, includes Royal
Granite, Greystone & other granite-
ware & japanned ware, 190 pp. . . . **185.00**

Old Town Canoes, 1936 . . . . **75.00**

R. Ogilvy Co., fishing tackle, 1922,
126 pp. **110.00**

Stevens Shotguns, 1929 . . . . **40.00**

United States Jeweler's Catalog,
1916, shows watches, sterling silver,
silver plate, cut glass, clocks &
jewelry, several color pages, 153 pp. . . **95.00**

Woolworths, Christmas 1940. . . . . . . **26.00**

TRAMP ART

*Tramp art flourished in the United States
from about 1875 into the 1930s. These chip-
carved woodenwares, mostly in the form of boxes
or other useful items, were made mainly from
old cigar boxes although fruit and vegetable
crates were also used. The wood is
predominately edge-carved and subsequently
layered to create a unique effect. Completed
items were given an overall stained finish which
was sometimes further enhanced with painted
highlights. Though there seems to be no written
record of the artists, many of whom were
itinerants, there is a growing interest in
collecting this ware.*

Bank, layered rosettes on sides &
front, decorative brass tacks
securing pyramids, coin deposited

in slot when drawer is pulled,
signed "A.L. 1885," 5" h., 7½" w.,
5" deep **$295.00**

Applied-carving Birdcage

Birdcage, house-shaped
w/sculptured & applied bird &
flower carvings, metal & wooden
grills, ca. 1885, 18" h., 14¼" w.,
13½" deep (ILLUS.). **600.00**

Box, five pyramids on top w/large
pyramids on sides, sits on painted
gold footed legs, ca. 1915, 6½" h.,
6" w., 3" deep **475.00**

Box, book-shaped, large heart cut-
out on front w/initials "F.S." & dated
"1914," 6" h., 6" w., 3" deep **395.00**

Box, cigar box w/applied diamond &
circular layered shapes, porcelain
button adorns each section,
ca. 1900, 6" h., 8½" w., 6" deep . . . **250.00**

Box, jewelry, decorated w/brass lion
pulls on sides, lock & key lid
w/carved wood legend, marked
"Alfons Cuns 1908 Marla Maes,"
web-footed, 6¼" h., 13" w.,
10¾" deep **950.00**

Box, round w/carved acorn finial, built
up pyramids around sides,
woman's photo under lid, ca. 1890,
7" h., 6½" w., 6½" deep. **485.00**

Ziggurat-style Stacking Box

Box, ziggurat-style stacking box
w/pineapple finial, seven drawers &
a lift-out compartment, double-

sided notching w/wave effect, signed "Miss Lizzie H. Huber, December 24," ca. 1880, 19½" h., 16½" w., 11½" deep (ILLUS.). . . . **3,200.00**

Victorian-style Table

Center hall table, Victorian-style, scalloped apron w/wood buttons, built-up pyramids on apron perimeter, serpentine legs, strong use of light & dark alternating woods, ca. 1920, 29" h., 33½" w., 33½" deep (ILLUS.) **8,500.00**

Chest of drawers, drawers w/crudely attached hearts & pyramids, metal pulls, scratch-built from crate wood, full-sized, ca. 1890, 49" h., 28" w., 14" deep **3,500.00**

Clock, serpentine outline w/light & dark woods covering plywood backing, easel stand, ca. 1940, 13¾" h., 15¾" w., 4¾" deep **475.00**

Clock, house-shaped case w/glass doors to access clock, incorporates shingle roof, windows & chimney, ca. 1890, 25" h., 14" w., 9" deep **1,800.00**

Dove & Horseshoe Comb Case

Comb case, dove & horseshoe design, two smaller heart-shaped mirrors above & one larger in center, two drawers marked with crosses, dated 1913, 27½" h., 15" w., 4½" deep. (ILLUS.) **3,400.00**

Crucifix, wood-carved figural Jesus, footed base, ca. 1920, 26" h., 12" w. . . . **550.00**

Doll furniture, chair, decorated w/brass tacks & scalloped rounds on all edges, ca. 1930, 14" h., 9" w., 12" deep **750.00**

Humidor, circular-box style, decorated sides lined w/linoleum on layered feet, ca. 1900, 11" h, 11" w., 7" deep. **1,200.00**

Inkwell, compartment for two ink bottles, includes pen & bottles, 3⅜" h., 6½" w., 4" deep **175.00**

Lamp, pyramid base supports box w/a column holding light socket, ca. 1930, 26" h., 6" w., 6" deep **750.00**

Lamp, floor model, carved slender feet w/narrow stem on three-tiered pedestal base, scratch-built w/dark stain, ca. 1930, 68" h., 18" w **2,800.00**

Match Safe

Match safe, star decoration on front, top lifts to insert stick matches held in open cup in the bottom, painted gold & silver, 7" h., 4" w., 4" deep (ILLUS.) **125.00**

Medicine cabinet, scrolling shapes around front, mirrored door, interior shelves & glass knob, ca. 1940, 27" h., 20" w., 6½" deep **750.00**

Medicine cabinet, mirrored door over shelves & drawers, towel bar at bottom, sides layered w/diamonds & rosettes, light & dark woods, ca. 1920, 30" h., 12" w., 8" deep . . . **900.00**

Music box, top crank mechanism w/porcelain knob, marked "FH," plays three different tunes, ca. 1880, 3" h., 7" w., 6" deep **600.00**

Pedestal stand, flat double-sided rows dividing areas of squares on column, painted green, black & tan, ca. 1930, 25" h., 12½" w., 12½" deep **1,700.00**

Picture frame, tabletop-style w/easel back, cross-corner style w/three layers, ca. 1940, 6½" h., 4½" w. **135.00**

Picture frame, tabletop-style, star
shape w/center photo, metal wire
support, ca. 1900, 6¼" h., 6" w. . . . **350.00**

Rare Picture Frame

Picture frame, three oval openings
surrounded by cut-out stars,
hearts, diamonds & rosettes,
ca. 1930, 13" h., 24¼" w. (ILLUS.) . . **2,800.00**

Picture frame, seventeen openings
w/lithographs of saints, adorned
w/porcelain buttons, ca. 1890,
13½" h. 15½" w. **725.00**

Shield Picture Frame

Picture frame, shield-shaped w/gilt
liner, six layers of multiple woods,
several geometric shapes topped
by a heart, ca. 1915, 14" h., 10" w.
(ILLUS.). **650.00**

Picture frame, eight multiple
openings, rectangular shape cigar
box pyramids over crate wood,
ca. 1915, 14" h., 22" w. **365.00**

Picture frame, tulip-shaped corners,
balance of frame w/many layered
designs of rectangles, rosettes &
diamonds extending beyond
perimeter edges, ca. 1920, 32" h.,
23" w. **3,900.00**

Picture frame & mirror, two-sided
tabletop-style, mirror on one side,
picture frame on reverse, finger-like
projections around frame w/heart

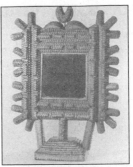

Two-sided Frame

on top, gold painted base, ca.
1930, 23" h., 17" w., 7½" deep
(ILLUS.). **950.00**

Sewing stand, lift-top compartment
lined in felt, large pyramids on
sides w/curved legs & open shelf
on bottom, ca. 1930, 26" h., 17" w.,
11" deep **1,800.00**

Shrine, open box w/cross on top,
29" h., 9" w., 10" deep **400.00**

Spice cabinet, eight drawers w/metal
pulls, fretwork decorated top, light
layering, ca. 1890, 18" h., 12" w.,
7" deep **775.00**

Vanity mirror, tabletop-style,
decorated w/hearts & circles,
curved base w/drawer, ca. 1930,
24" h., 16" w., 10" deep **400.00**

Wall cabinet, diamond pattern
decoration on door w/small
porcelain knob, layered sides,
ca. 1910, 27" h., 15" w., 8" deep. . **1,100.00**

Wall cabinet, shaped crest centering a
swivel mirror above a single door
opening to a fitted interior over a
single drawer, painted & carved,
early 20th c., 7½ x 16½", 29½" h.
(repainted, paint wear, minor losses) **288.00**

Wall pocket, mirror in center over
built-out pocket surrounded by
contrasting woods in vertical
stripes, curved top dated "1902,"
30" h., 16" w., 4" deep **675.00**

Wall pocket, "New York Times,"
deeply layered geometric forms,
scratch-built from crate woods,
named for Sunday-sized news-
paper, 39" h., 31" w., 12" deep . . **8,500.00**

Wall shelf, decorated w/chip-carved
icicle-like projections on top,
mirrored back, curved bottom,
ca. 1900, 11¼" h., 17" w.,
14" deep **1,500.00**

Watch holder, hanging-type, metal
numerals on access door, 11½" h.,
7" w., 1½" deep **800.00**

TRAYS, SERVING & CHANGE

Both serving and change trays once used in taverns, cafes and the like and usually bearing advertising for a beverage maker are now being widely collected. All trays listed are heavy tin serving trays, unless otherwise noted.

A. Gettelman Milwaukee Beer, metal, round, center lithograph of hand holding glass of beer, surrounded by "A. Gettelman - Milwaukee Beer," done in red, yellow, black, green & cream, 13" d. (minor scratches) **$28.00**

Anheuser-Busch, metal, oval, colorful lithograph of classically dressed woman holding Anheuser-Busch logo surrounded by cherubs & beer bottle, all below "Anheuser-Busch - Brewing Assn. - St. Louis, Mo. - U.S.A.," 10½ x 13" (chips & wear overall) **143.00**

Anheuser-Busch, oval, factory scene showing various trains & horse-drawn vechicles, "Anheuser Busch Brewing Ass'n.," Standard Adv. Co., 15½ x 18½" (some minor crazing & chipping)............ **2,588.00**

Clysmic King of Table Waters, rectangular, multicolored lithograph depicting woman sitting at spring w/bottle of Clysmic Water & an elk, marked "The American Art Works Co.," 14¼" x 10¾" **209.00**

D. G. Yuengling & Son Tray

D.G. Yuengling & Son, Inc., Pottsville, Pa. Beer Ale Porter, round, depicts horse's head inside letter "Y," ca. 1900-1925, 11¾" d. (ILLUS.)...................... **88.00**

Dawes Black Horse Ale & Porter, porcelain, round, logo above oval that reads "Dawes - Black Horse - Ale and Porter" all above "Dawes Brewery," done in white, yellow & green, 13" d. (minor scratches) **77.00**

Eye-Fix tip tray, tin, round w/raised rim, center colorfully painted w/portrait of classically dressed woman & a cherub holding eye dropper to her eye, blue rim marked "Eye-Fix - The Great Eye Remedy" in red, 4¼" d. (minor scratches, some wear to bottom) .. **358.00**

Fairy Soap Tip Tray

Fairy Soap tip tray, round, colorfully lithographed center has a little girl sitting on the side of a bar of soap marked "Fairy," black rim reads "Have You A Little 'Fairy' In Your Home?" across bottom, 4¼" d. (minor scratches) (ILLUS.) **33.00**

Ferro-Phos tip tray, round, tin, center of tray reads "Drink" above image of the drink in a glass, flanked by "Non-Narcotic - Non-Alcoholic," all above "Ferro-Phos - The Favorite Beverage - Five Cents," rim reads "Ferro-Phos Co. - Pottstown, PA.," done in brown, black, blue & white, 5" d. (minor scratches) **154.00**

Fort Schuyzer Ales & Lager, round, white lettering reads "Fort Schuyzer - Ales & Lager" on black ground, 11¼" d. (some scratches) .. **44.00**

Garcia Grandé Cigar tip tray, rectangular, sides read "Garcia Grandé" on long sides & "Mild Havanna" & "Cigar" on short sides, center of tray reads "don't be fooled - Ask for by FULL NAME - Garcia Grandé - Cigar - 'Finest Mild Havana Blend'" all to the left of a jester sitting on a mushroom holding a slate chalkboard that reads "2+2=7," 4¼ x 6¼" (minor paint chips & scratches) **75.00**

Gold Medal Beer tip tray, round, image of bottle of Gold Medal Beer above "The World's Standard of

Perfection," rim reads "Indianapolis Brewing Co. - Lieber's Gold Medal Beer," done in red, blue, yellow, gold & green, 5" d. (minor scratches) **83.00**

Grand Complete Horse Furnishers, tin, entitled "Good Morning," depicts stable scene w/dogs coming to visit a mare & her colt, ca. 1909, artist-signed, Henry Stoll American Art Works, 13 x 13" (some overall crazing, pitting, scratching & surface rust) **230.00**

Heptol Splits For Health's Sake tip tray, round, center image of cowboy riding a bucking bronco, rim reads "Heptol Splits - For Health's Sake," 4¼" d. (minor scratches & crazing) **314.00**

Hershey's Tray

Hershey's Milk Chocolate, depicts a child holding a bar of chocolate hatching from a cocoa shell, 8¾ x 12" (ILLUS.) **86.00**

Iroquois Beer & Ale, round, center reads "Iroquois - Indian Head" above image of Indian chief head, all above "Beer & Ale - Buffalo, N.Y.," done in red, blue, yellow & green, 12" d. **94.00**

Jenney Aero Gasoline, tin, round w/orange, black & white car decoration & lettering, 4 1/8" d. **149.00**

Labatt's Ale Beer, porcelain, round, red lettering "Ale, Lager - And Stout - Labatt's - London Canada - Established Over 100 Years" above Union tradmark, all on white ground, 13" d. (minor chips & scratches) **88.00**

Lykens Brewing Company, oval, tin, depicts beautiful woman & horse, "Lykens Brewing Company - The Home of 'Cream Top' Lager Beer," ca. 1905, Chas. Ehlen, some minor chipping & light staining, 13½ x 16½" (ILLUS.) **403.00**

Lykens Brewing Company Tray

Maltosia Beer tip tray, round, center w/image of spade w/angel astride goose, reads "Bottled At The Brewery" above "Maltosia - Pure Food Beer - Brewed According To The - World-Famed - Maltosia - Process - By The - German American Brewing Co. - Buffalo, N.Y. - U.S.A.," the rim marked "German American Brewing Co. Buffalo, N.Y. - Our Beer is Sterilized - Not Pasteurized," done in gold, white & black, 5" d. (minor scratches) **55.00**

Old Reliable Coffee tip tray, round, colorfully painted portrait of young woman in center, reads "Old Reliable Coffee" in gold top & bottom edges, black ground, 4½" d. (crazing to center, wear to edge & bottom) **176.00**

Old Scotch Whiskey tip tray, porcelain, oval, reads "The 'Antiquary' " above man dressed in 18th c. outfit & "Old Scotch Whiskey," all above "At Last I Have Found It!," 4½" w., 6" h. **50.00**

Pepsi Cola, "Drink Pepsi Cola Delicious-Healthful 5¢," oval, tin, lithograph w/multicolored scene depicting woman in fancy dress holding glass of Pepsi Cola at soda fountain, made by "Niagara - Buffalo," ca. 1909, 4⅜ x 6⅛" (several pin-size rust spots on right edge) **908.00**

Sears tip tray, oval, depicts factory scene of Sears, Roebuck & Co., 4½ x 6" **115.00**

Stegmaier Brewing Co. tip tray, round, center shows a hand holding four different types of Stegmaier, rim marked "Stegmaier Brewing Co. Wilkes-Barre, Pa.," done in green, yellow, gold, brown & blue, 4¼" d. (minor crazing) **121.00**

Terre Haute Brewing Co. tip tray,
tin, round w/upturned rim, colorfully
painted center scene of a group of
people dressed in 18th c. attire
standing around table holding their
glasses in a toast to four cherubs
holding beer bottles, all above
"That - Ever Welcome - Beer -
Terre Haute Brewing Co. - Terre
Haute, Ind.," inside rim reads
"Champagne - Velvet - Radium,"
4½" d.,½" h. (minor scratches &
crazing) **170.00**

Utica-Club Beer, round w/upturned
rim, outside of center reads "Utica-
Club - West End Brewery Co. Utica
Co.," in the center is a graphic of
the brewery below "the Famous
Utica Beer," inside of rim reads
"Pilsner Lager Beer - XXX Cream
le" painted red, yellow, blue, green
& black, 12" d. (minor scratches) . . . **18.00**

White Rock water, fairy lady on
rock **125.00**

Wieland's Beer Tray

Wieland's Beer, rectangular, tin,
depicts beautiful lady reading a
letter in a garden, American Art
Works, ca. 1909, some overall
crazing & chipping to rim,
10½ x 13½" (ILLUS.) **173.00**

VALENTINES

Fold-out type, boy in airplane,
ca. 1920s **$95.00**

Folded & cut paper, large lacy-cut
central circle w/lover's knot &
inverted hearts at four points along
the edge, laid paper, framed,
16¼" sq. (stains, damage at fold
lines) **165.00**

Pinpricked paper, water-color on
paper w/pinpricked design,
unsigned, 19th c., framed, 12¾" sq.
(fold creases, minor losses,
staining, toning) **489.00**

Sailor's Shell Valentines

Sailor's valentine, hinged octagonal
wooden case enclosing shell-
arranged designs, one half w/a
blossom-form design w/the center
enclosing "With Love," the other
half w/rings of shells surrounding a
shell "bouquet," 19th c., 8¾" w.
(ILLUS.) **2,185.00**

Sailor's valentine, folding octagonal
wood box composed of pink, green
& brown small mollusk shells, one
side w/a heart & rose, the other
inscribed "For my sister,"
9¼" d. **1,265.00**

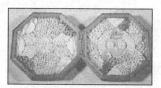

Sailor's Valentine

Sailor's valentine, wooden hinged
octagonal case, one half enclosing
a starburst & central blossom
arrangement of shells, the other
half enclosing a cross-form
arrangement of shells w/a central
shell "heart," very minor losses,
19th c., 9⅝" w.(ILLUS.) **2,530.00**

Shellwork, a hinged wooden
octagonal case enclosing two
ornate arrangements of small &
tiny seashells including rings,
flowerheads & geometric designs,
labeled "Brought From St. Helena,"
pencil inscription "Henry M. Hale
Bark Wave Capt. Briggs," age
cracks in case, 19th c., 13½" w. . . . **4,600.00**

VENDING & GAMBLING

Arcade, "Midget Baseball Game" by
Hercules Novelty Co. of Chicago,
Illinois, countertop model, wooden
cabinet w/cast-iron front, ca. 1931-
32, 1-cent play for inning w/batter,
base light ups when hit is made,
includes original paper instructions,
15½" h. **$1,035.00**

Arcade, "Little Whirl-Wind" rectangular countertop model, sheet metal construction, five shots per 1-cent play, ca. 1930s, 16½" h. (repainted) **316.00**

Arcade, "Weegee" wall-mount fortune teller machine, manufactured by Boyce Coin Machine Amusement Corp., ca. 1930s, 17½" h. **460.00**

Arcade, "Zipper Skill" by Binks Industries, Inc., wooden countertop model, gumball & five shots w/1-cent play, ca. 1950s, 18" h. **98.00**

Countertop Fortune Teller

Arcade, "Ask Me Another" fortune teller, countertop model by Exhibit Supply Company, ca. 1939-41, 15" w., 21½" h. (ILLUS.) **180.00**

Arcade, "Baby Mutoscope" by International Mutoscope Reel Co., Inc. of New York, floor model, wrought-iron stand w/rare Felix reel, 9 x 15", 4' 4" h. **11,438.00**

Arcade, "Play Football" floor model by the Chester-Pollard Amusement Co., two-player soccer game, 73" h. **2,990.00**

Arcade, "Punch-A-Bag" by International Mutoscope Reel Co., floor model punching bag, ca. 1920s, 6' 7" h. (missing back door, tin dial in poor condition) **748.00**

Candy vendor, "Penny King," countertop miniature gumball w/domed globe, ca. 1930s, 11½" h. (repainted base) **127.00**

Candy vendor, "Northwestern 39," glass globe w/blue porcelain top & base, 1-cent operation bulk model, ca. 1939, 14" h. **230.00**

Candy vendor, "Northwestern 31," glass globe w/reddish orange top & base, includes slug rejector, 1-cent operation, 16" h. **460.00**

Candy vendor, "Sweet Chocolate" countertop model, "The Model S" by National Automatic Vending Machine Company, 1-cent operation, patented Dec.18, 1917, 17" h. **550.00**

Card & gum vendor, "Victor" card vendor attached to a "Baby Grand" gumball machine, countertop model, 5-cent operation, ca.1950, 18½" to top of card vendor **258.00**

Card vendor, metal two-column countertop model, includes 25 original cards inside, 1-cent operation, ca. 1933, 12" h. **259.00**

Cigarette vendor, "Lucky Strike" countertop model, cast aluminum w/slanted top section, green painted cast-iron base marked "Lucky Strike," sold single cigarettes w/1-cent operation, ca. 1920, 11½" h. **350.00**

Collar button vendor, "Price" eight-sided cast-iron countertop model w/collar button finial, 10-cent operation, ca. 1905, 11" h. **700.00**

Cup vendor, "Puritan" tall dome wall-mount model by APG Company, ca. 1930s, 35" h. **250.00**

Baker's "Racers" Gambling Machine

Gambling, Baker's "Racers" floor model, 25-cent play, 22 x 36 x 47" (ILLUS.) **4,500.00**

Caille's "Centaur Twin" Slot Machine

Gambling, Caille's "Centaur Twin" slot machine, ca. 1910 (ILLUS.). **31,650.00**

Gambling, Caille's "Superior Jackpot" countertop slot machine, 25-cent play, ca. 1928 . . . . **1,725.00**

Gambling, Groechen's "Columbia" three-quarter size countertop slot machine, 25-cent play, ca. 1936 . . . **230.00**

Gambling, Jennings' "Duchess" countertop slot machine, 5-cent play, ca. 1934 . . . . **1,150.00**

Gambling, Jennings' "Jackpot" countertop slot machine, 5-cent play, ca. 1935 . . . . **978.00**

Gambling, Jennings' "Little Duke" countertop slot machine, 1-cent play, ca. 1932-36 . . . . **1,955.00**

Gambling, Jennings' "Mint" countertop slot machine w/side vendor, 5-cent play, ca. 1930s . . . **1,725.00**

Gambling, Mills' "Cherry" countertop slot machine, ca. 1937-41, 5-cent play. **2,013.00**

Gambling, Mills' "Horse Head" countertop slot machine, 5-cent play, ca. 1937-43 . . . . **1,697.00**

Gambling, Mills' "Liberty Bell" countertop slot machine, ca.1909-11, 5-cent play (replaced header card) **6,325.00**

Gambling, Mills' "Operator Bell" countertop slot machine, 25-cent play, ca. 1929. . . . . **1,093.00**

Gambling, Mills' "Silent Gooseneck" countertop slot machine, 5-cent play, ca. 1931 (restored) **1,380.00**

Gambling, Mills' "Silent War Eagle" countertop slot machine, 10-cent play, ca. 1931-44 . . . . . . **1,610.00**

Gambling, Watling's "Treasury" countertop slot machine, 5-cent play, ca. 1936-41 . . . . **4,025.00**

Gambling, Mills' "QT" three-quarter size countertop slot machine, 1-cent play w/double jackpot, ca. 1935, 19" h. **1,093.00**

Olympia Slot Machine

Gambling, Olympia's "Bunny XO" electric countertop slot machine, metal & plastic, 1-cent play, #0101803/039348, comes w/coins to operate, 19" w., 32" h. (ILLUS.). . **300.00**

Gum & candy vendor, Columbus' "Bi-More," double compartment bulk model on original stand, "Model 32" by Columbus Vending Company, ca. 1936, 46" h. (incorrect globes). **350.00**

Gum vendor, "Advance" countertop gumball machine w/protruding No. 4 mechanism, rolled steel body w/small round globe, patented Aug. 8, 1916, 12½" h. (repainted) . . **110.00**

Gum vendor, "Ford" gumball machine w/spout cover, ca. 1930s, 11" h. **64.00**

Atlas Gumball Machine

Gum vendor, "Atlas" countertop model, glass & metal mounted on chrome tray, by Atlas Mgf. & Sales Corporation Cleveland Ohio, 5-cent operation, includes key, 6½" w., 11" h. (ILLUS.) **90.00**

Gum vendor, Mansfield's "Auto
Clerk" two-column countertop
model, top celluloid advertising
"Peppermint" or "Blood Orange"
gum, 5-cent operation, patented
June 10, 1902, 12" h.. . . . . **650.00**

Gum vendor, "Perfection" countertop
model, sheet metal body w/cast-
iron base & collar, flange holding
globe, ca. 1915, 12" h. **450.00**

Beech-Nut Chewing Gum Vendor

Gum vendor, "Beech-Nut Chewing
Gum" countertop model, depicts
woman in hat w/piece of chewing
gum, double-column dispenser, 1-
or 5-cent operation, ca. 1947,
13½" h. (ILLUS.) **450.00**

Gum vendor, "Silver King"
countertop model w/music box, 1-
cent operation, original decal on
globe depicting musical notes,
ca. 1950, 14" h. **230.00**

Gum vendor, "Northwestern 33,"
reddish-orange porcelain lid &
base, small 3½-lb. globe, ca. 1933,
14½" h. **144.00**

Gum vendor, "Your Penny Helps
Build a Citizen at Boysville" in
bottom right-hand corner, metal &
glass countertop model,1-cent
operation, #57255, 10" w., 14¾" h.
(scratches & overall soiling) **125.00**

Gum vendor, Columbus' "Model 14"
countertop gumball model, glass
globe w/green porcelain pedestal
base, 15" h. **575.00**

Gum vendor, "National" metal &
glass countertop model, marked
"National Self-Service Machine,
Mints 5¢ Chewing Gum, Chicago
Gum And Candy Co. Chicago, Ill.,"
8" w., 15" h. (some soiling
& wear) **250.00**

Gum vendor, "Baker Boy" countertop
gumball machine, rare black man
manikin version, clockwork
mechanism, by Manikin Vendor
Co., patented August 27, 1929,
16" h. (replaced coin drawer) **1,525.00**

Gum vendor, "Master No. 2" or
"Gooseneck Masters" countertop
gumball machine, red & black
w/one penny turn & five nickel
turns, ca. 1925, 16" h. **325.00**

Gum vendor, "Improved Hilo"
countertop gumball machine, tall
globe w/cast-iron base, by Hilo
Gum Company, patented
April 7, 1908, 17" h. **1,250.00**

Gum vendor, "Hit The Target" 1-cent
play gumball machine & game,
10% chance of money return as
penny falls through a space motif
pin field, rectangular machine on
cast-iron-stand, ca. 1950, 19" h. . . . **98.00**

Gum vendor, Snacks "Gum" tab
model by Trimont Coin Machine
Company, designed to compliment
bulk vendor, patented 1939, 19" h. . . **127.00**

Gum vendor, "Pansy Gum,"
rectangular wooden countertop
model stenciled "Roth's Pansy
Gum - Your Fortune And A Love
Letter 1 Cent," ca. 1905, 20" h. . . . **1,400.00**

Gum vendor, "Pulver" red porcelain
countertop model, short-case
w/cop & robber characters, 21" h. . . . **750.00**

Pulver Gum Vendor

Gum vendor, "Pulver" rectangular
porcelain countertop model,
marked "Pulver Kola-Pepsin Gum
& Sweet Chocolate," 1-cent
operation, ca. 1910, missing lock,
some chipping, 24" h. (ILLUS.) . . **1,600.00**

Gum vendor, "Pulver" three-column
red porcelain tab vendor w/beveled
mirror on front, 31" h. (some
chipping) **202.00**

Gum vendor, "Adams' Pepsin Tutti-
Frutti," wooden L-shaped
countertop gum or chocolate
machine, by United States Slot
Machine Company, patented
Dec. 4, 1894, 31½" h. **750.00**

Gum vendor, "Teft's Pepsin Gum," two-column rectangular oak model w/rounded sides & front advertising, ornate Art Nouveau stand, by Peerless Gum Vendor Co., patented July 24, 1906, 62" h. w/stand (alligator finish to varnish) **2,000.00**

Lotion vendor, "Frostilla" wall-mount dispenser by Merchandise Dispensers Inc., 1-cent operation, "Frostilla Fragrant Lotion" on original advertising sign, ca. 1950s, 15½" h. to top of sign **240.00**

Match vendor, "Diamond Book Matches," sheet metal body w/cast-iron lid & base, 1-cent operation for two packs matches, patented 1928, 13" h. (some chipping to paint & decals). **240.00**

Match vendor, "The Number 4 Perfection" cast-iron countertop model by the Specialty Mfg. Co., depicts two fire-breathing dragons & Art Nouveau castings, includes cigar cutter, ca. 1920s, 13" h. (some rust to cast iron) **725.00**

Peanut vendor, "Northwestern 33 Peanut" countertop model, small 3-lb. globe, light brown & white porcelain base, original barrel lock, 14½" h. **288.00**

Peanut vendor, "Silver King Hot Nut" countertop model, ruby hobnail glass top, tapering glass globe & aluminum base, ca. 1947, 16" h. . . . **156.00**

Peanut vendor, "Cebco" electric countertop hot nut machine, cast aluminum w/two globes & side cup dispenser, includes original carrying case, ca. 1930, 18" h. **500.00**

Peanut vendor, Fenachen Mgf. hot nut machine, wall-mount figural aluminum radio, window in front to display nuts, pull-chain mechanism, ca. 1930s, 18" h. **104.00**

Peanut vendor, Kingery Mfg. Co., Cinncinati, Ohio, four-spoke wheeled cart w/copper dome-top peanut roaster, 41 x 27 x 39" (ILLUS.) **2,875.00**

Stamp vendor, Standard-Harvard Metal Typer, Inc. countertop model, marked "Print your own identification number," includes 1,000 unused good-luck medallions, ca. 1920s, 39" h. **546.00**

Stamp vendor, "Roover's Bros." floor model, oak casing w/cast-iron front & working mechanism, 14 x 18", 4' 9" h. **1,380.00**

"Little Midget" Trade Stimulator

Trade stimulator, Atlas' "Little Midget" countertop model, 5-cent play, ca. 1920s (ILLUS.) **760.00**

Trade stimulator, Acme's "Pepsin Gum Cash Depository," rectangular wood casing countertop model, 1-cent play for gum plus chance of cash return, 19" h. **259.00**

Trade stimulator, Mills' "New Target Practice" aluminum countertop model, ca. 1930, 19" h. **374.00**

VINAIGRETTES

These were originally tiny boxes, usually silver, with an inner perforated lid enclosing a sponge soaked in aromatic vinegar to lessen offensive odors. Later versions made of glass in this country contained perfume.

Kingery Mfg. Peanut Vendor

Pink Agate & Gold Vinaigrette

Gold, 14k rose gold, circular double
  handle-form, decorated w/applied
  texturing centered by a bi-color
  gold & platinum seascape **$748.00**
Gold & agate, rectangular, lid & base
  set w/pink agate sides of 18k gold,
  chased on base w/scrolling foliage
  on stippled ground, band around lid
  chased w/rosettes, hinged interior
  grill pierced & chased w/scrolling
  foliage surrounding basket of
  roses, France, ca. 1819, 1⅝" l.,
  1" w. (ILLUS.) **2,300.00**
Silver, modeled in repoussé design,
  angel mounted on lid, hinged,
  footed pillbox base, hallmarked,
  unascribed, Germany, mid-late
  19th c., 3½" h. **250.00**
Silver, urn-shaped w/two loose
  handles, studded w/ruby-like cut
  faceted stones, hinged, footed
  pillbox base, hallmarked "CA,"
  unascribed, mid-19th c., 3¾" h. **100.00**
Silver, urn-shaped w/two loose-ring
  handles, dome-shaped lid, footed
  base, hinged square pillbox,
  hallmarked, unascribed, engraved
  "From Wm & L July 25, 1892" on
  base, 4" h. **125.00**
Silver, urn-shaped w/hinged lid
  surmounted by crown, two handles,
  studded w/cut faceted ruby-like
  stones, diamond-shaped hinged,
  footed base, hallmarked,
  unascribed, early to mid-19th c.,
  4¼" h. **325.00**
Silver, urn-shaped, two handles on
  lid surmounted by crown, gem-
  studded w/ruby, emerald &
  sapphire-like stones & small pearls,
  engraved "T. Jensen, Maria P.
  Lassen 1842" on base, 5⅜" h. **300.00**
Silver-gilt, engraved scrolling foliate
  decoration, Thomas Willmore,
  Birmingham, England, 1814, 1¼" l. . **345.00**
Silver-gilt, urn-shaped w/two
  handles, hinged lid, faceted ruby,
  emerald & sapphire-like stones,
  diamond-shaped footed base
  w/hinged box, "PHA 1842"
  engraved on base, hallmarked,
  unascribed, 4⅝" h. **325.00**
Silver-gilt & agate, rectangular,
  hinged lid set w/amber colored
  translucent agate w/ferrous-like
  inclusion, silver case chased
  w/vermicule patt., interior hinged
  pierced silver-gilt grille in form of
  roses, 2" l., 1" w. **575.00**

WEATHERVANES

Arrow, gilt-copper, fine verdigris
  surface, late 19th c., 43¾" l. (gilt
  loss, minor dents) **$805.00**

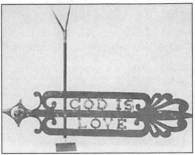

Arrow Bannerette Weathervane

Arrow bannerette, sheet metal, the
  silhouetted banner cut w/wording
  "God is Love" & scrolling design,
  two-pronged finial, America, late
  19th c., minor imperfections, 56" l.,
  38" h. (ILLUS.) **1,840.00**
Banner, scrolled gilt copper, long
  pierced design w/a quatrefoil tail &
  arrowhead tip, fine verdigris
  surface, America, late 19th c.,
  49⅝" l., 37¾" h. (bullet holes,
  dents, minor seam splits,
  scrollwork separation) **1,955.00**
Bannerette gilt-copper & zinc, fine
  verdigris surface, America, late
  19th c., 23" l. (gilt loss, crack, minor
  losses) **1,150.00**
Fish, gilt-copper, long hollow body
  w/overall detailed scale design,
  pointed snout, traces of verdigris,
  America, late 19th c., 34½" l. (gilt
  loss, repaired bullet holes, seam
  splits) **3,220.00**
Horse, cast iron, small swell-bodied
  figure w/oversized tail, attached to
  an iron base, vibrant patina of rust
  bleeding through mustard-colored
  sizing, Rochester Iron Works,
  c.1890, 18½" l., 14½" h. **31,050.00**
Horse, sheet iron, cutout figure
  w/painted mane & muzzle, original
  surface, 19th c., 20" l.,13½" h . . . **2,530.00**
Horse, molded gilt-copper,
  "Blackhawk," running position,
  areas of verdigris, American, late
  19th c., 24½" l. (repaired bullet
  holes, minor dents & seam splits). . **2,300.00**
Horse, running, molded copper,
  swell-bodied model w/flowing tail
  mounted on a rod, fine verdigris,

Copper Running Horse Weathervane

New England, last quarter 19th c.,
minor imperfections, traces of
gilting, 30" l., 15½" h., (ILLUS.) . . **2,530.00**
Horse, cast iron, large swell-bodied
figure w/oversized tail, mounted on
a rod in iron base, exceptional
surface of rust bleeding through
paint, Rochester Iron Works,
c. 1890, 34" l., 26" h. **48,300.00**

Rare Steeplechase Weathervane

Horse, patinated copper w/verdigris
surface, the fully sculpted body
w/applied ears & eyes, applied
repoussé mane & tail, figure
jumping over a gate to which it is
mounted, New England, c. 1885,
rare, 34" l., 26" h. **86,100.00**
Horse, molded copper w/cast iron
head, swell-bodied figure of trotting
horse w/flowing tail, mounted on a
rod, fine verdigris, America,
late19th c., 48¾" l., 21½" h.
(imperfections) **2,990.00**
Pig, lightning rod-style, copper, zinc &
steel, the small standing animal on
one end of a crossbar w/a pierced
scroll & pointed tip, fitted on a long
lightning rod above an opaque
white glass lightning rod ball above
the lower twisted metal rod, overall
72" h. **358.00**
Rooster, copper, rare miniature
model, swell-bodied figure w/fine
detail, mounted on a rod, yellow
sizing, verdigris & traces of gold
leaf, J.W. Fiske, New York City,
c.1890, 12" l., 10" h. **6,325.00**

Rooster, molded gilt copper, traces
of verdigris, late 19th c., 14¼" h.
(old regilding, gilt loss,minor dents. . **1,610.00**
Rooster, molded gilt copper, areas of
verdigris, America, late 19th c.,
28½" l., 28¼" h. (repaired, bullet
holes, gilt wear, minor dents) **4,600.00**

WESTERN CHARACTER COLLECTIBLES

*Annie Oakley Neckerchief & Hanky
Embroidery Set*

**Annie Oakley Neckerchief & Hanky
Embroidery Set,** ST, 1955
(ILLUS.). **$60.00-75.00**
Bat Masterson wallet, Croyder,
1950s, unused, mint in box **99.00**
Bonanza model kit, Revell, 1965,
assembled. **35.00-40.00**

Bonanza Model Kit

Bonanza model kit, Revell, 1965,
unused (ILLUS.) **75.00-125.00**
Bonanza model kit, Revell, 1966,
near mint **175.00**
Branded game, board-type, Milton
Bradley, 1966 . . . . **35.00-40.00**
Bret Maverick figure, plastic,
Hartland, 1958, w/box &
tag **350.00-450.00**

Bret Maverick Hartland Figure

Bret Maverick figure, plastic,
Hartland, 1958, without box
(ILLUS.). **150.00-200.00**
Bret Maverick Hartland Figure,
Hartland, 1958, w/box,
no tag **350.00-400.00**
Cowboy doll, marked "Effanbee,
Skippy,© P.L. Crosby" on back of
head, composition head
w/character face, large blue eyes
painted to side, single-stroke
brows, painted upper lashes,
accented nostrils, closed mouth,
molded & painted blond hair, cloth
body w/composition arms & legs,
jointed at shoulders & hips, original
cowboy outfit w/rose shirt, beige
leather vest & chaps, leather belt &
holster w/gun, socks, black shoes,
felt ten-gallon hat, 14" **1,050.00**
Gene Autry cap pistol, cast iron, 1930s,
very fine. **90.00**
Gene Autry chaps, children's, fine
graphics & Gene's name on the
front, ca. 1950 . . . . **175.00**

Rare Gene Autry Doll

Gene Autry doll, composition,
portrait-style wearing all-original
tagged cowboy outfit including
boots, belt, hat & kerchief
(ILLUS.) **3,100.00**

Gene Autry flashlight **65.00**
Gunsmoke coloring book, Whitman, 1959,
fine **36.00**
Gunsmoke game, Lowell, 1955,
unused. **125.00**
Gunsmoke lamp, figural, Hartline,
1950s, very fine (one spur broken) . . **636.00**
Have Gun Will Travel vest,
Togs, mint in packet w/cards, 1950s . . **110.00**
Hopalong Cassidy book, popup
type, "Hopalong Cassidy at the
Double X Ranch," Garden City
Publishing, 1950, fine **116.00**
Hopalong Cassidy cookie jar,
ceramic, tall barrel-shape in tan
w/brown specks **525.00**
Hopalong Cassidy dinnerware set,
ceramic, creamy white w/colored
decals, 1950s, each piece. . . . **35.00-50.00**

Hoppy Dinnerware Set

Hopalong Cassidy dinnerware set,
ceramic, creamy white w/colored
decals, 1950s, set w/box
(ILLUS.). **200.00-300.00**
Hopalong Cassidy fork & spoon,
metal, the set **50.00**
Hopalong Cassidy radio, Arvin,
1950, near mint **550.00**

Hopalong Cassidy Spurs

Hopalong Cassidy spurs, child's,
silvered & gilt-metal w/leather
straps, bust portrait of Hopalong
w/his name on side rondels,
ca. 1950s, pr. (ILLUS.) **198.00**
Hopalong Cassidy thermos,
Aladdin, 1950, near mint **61.00**
Hopalong Cassidy wristwatch, U.S.
Time, 1950, fine. **119.00**

Indian doll, marked "Effanbee - Anne-Shirley" on back, brown composition head, painted brown eyes, multi-stroke brows, painted upper & lower lashes, accented nostrils, closed mouth, original human-hair wig, reddish-brown five-piece composition body w/large hands, original grey leather Indian outfit, no underclothing, socks or shoes, includes metal heart bracelet marked "Effanbee Durable Dolls" & "Historical Doll" booklet, 14" (small crack in finish on torso bottom, missing little finger on left hand) **750.00**

Lone Ranger arcade card, photo of Lee Powell as the Lone Ranger wearing a net mask **45.00**

Lone Ranger badge, Secret Compartment-type, w/instructions & mailer **175.00**

Lone Ranger game, target-type, 1938 . . . . **240.00**

Lone Ranger guitar, child's, pressed wood, by Supertone, ca. 1940 . . . . **150.00**

Maverick coin, silver, premium for Kaiser Foil, 1950s, near mint. **25.00**

Maverick Oil Painting Set

Maverick oil painting set, "Maverick Oil Painting by Numbers," Hasbro, 1958 (ILLUS.) **60.00-75.00**

Northwest Passage coloring book, Lowe, 1959, unused **35.00**

The Rebel Game

Rebel game (The), board-type, Ideal, 1961 (ILLUS.) **75.00-125.00**

Rebel game, (The) board-type, Ideal, 1961, unused, very fine. **220.00**

The Restless Gun Game

Restless Gun Game (The), board-type, Milton Bradley, 1960 (ILLUS.). **50.00-65.00**

Rifleman rifle, Hubley, 1960, very fine. **220.00**

Roy Rogers binoculars. **90.00**

Roy Rogers cowboy hat, green felt . . **100.00**

Roy Rogers pants, boy's, heavy brown cotton w/colorful Roy Rogers patch sewn on pocket, near mint **95.00**

Shotgun Slade game, board-type, Milton Bradley, 1960, unused **85.00**

Shotgun Slade Jigsaw Puzzle

Shotgun Slade jigsaw puzzle, Milton Bradley, 1960 (ILLUS.). **25.00-30.00**

Tom Mix bird call & telescope, w/papers & mailer **175.00**

Tom Mix "bullet" telescope, Ralston premium **70.00**

Tom Mix cowboy boots, child's, in original box **375.00**

Topper (Hopalong Cassidy's horse) soap, in original cut-out gun & target box, unused **45.00**

Virginian record, Virginian - Men From Shilo 45 r.p.m. record, DJ copy, 1971, near mint **35.00**

Wagon Train Covered Wagon

Wagon Train covered wagon model, Marx, 1960, w/box (ILLUS.). **135.00-175.00**

Wagon Train Gun & Holster Set

Wagon Train gun & holster set, Hubley, 1959, w/box (ILLUS.). **175.00-250.00**

Wagon Train gun & holster set, Hubley, 1959, without box . . . **40.00-50.00**

Wanted: Dead or Alive miniature gun, Marx, 1960, very fine **26.00**

Wanted: Dead or Alive Target Game

Wanted: Dead or Alive Target Game, Marx, 1960, w/box (ILLUS.). **250.00-350.00**

Wanted: Dead or Alive Target Game, Marx, 1960, without box **100.00-125.00**

Wild Wild West (TV) game, board-type, Transogram, 1966, unused, mint **666.00**

Wyatt Earp (TV) cap gun, original box **150.00**

WIENER WERKSTATTE

The Wiener Werkstatte (Vienna Workshops) were co-founded in 1903 in Vienna, Austria by Josef Hoffmann and Koloman Moser. An offshoot of the Vienna Secession movement, closely related to the Art Nouveau and Arts and Crafts movements elsewhere, this studio was established to design and produce unique and high-quality pieces covering all aspects of the fine arts. Hoffmann and Moser were the first artistic directors and oversaw the work of up to 100 workers, including thirty-seven masters who signed their work. Bookbinding, leatherwork, gold, silver and lacquer pieces as well as enamels and furniture all originated from these shops over a period of nearly thirty years. The finest pieces from the Wiener Werkstatte are now bringing tremendous prices.

Basket, painted metal, lozenge-shaped openwork design w/an arched handle, painted white, designed by Josef Hoffmann, stamped "WIENER - WERK - STATTE," 10½" l., 6½" h. **$575.00**

Bowl, figural, ceramic, composed of an overlapping ring of walking geese in white w/black eyes & yellow beaks & feet atop a round green base, glossy glaze, artist-initialed "LCH," impressed mark "Austria 389 - 477 - 0," 8½" d., 5½" h. **1,210.00**

Bust of a woman, ceramic, stylized portrait bust w/a long neck & elongated head w/orange, green & blue facial details against an ivory ground, resting on an orange & mauve base, designed by Gudrin Baudisch, impressed "MADE IN AUSTRIA 3¾," w/the firm & artist's monograms 9¾" h. **4,025.00**

Equestrian group, ceramic, a woman riding side-saddle on a spotted horse w/three dogs leaping around below, on a thin rectangular base, painted in blue, yellow, orange & brown, impressed "WW - Made in Austria 327" & initials "KR," 4½ x 6¾", 8¼" h. **1,495.00**

Figure, ceramic, modeled as a nude maiden kneeling on a mauve & orange square base, holding two bowls at her sides, in flesh, orange & blue tones, designed by Gudrin Baudisch, impressed "MADE IN AUSTRIA 262 - 2," & w/the firm & designer's monograms, 7¼" h. . . . **2,070.00**

Model of a horse, ceramic, a stylized animal w/thick legs, carrying a cup-form basket on its back, black w/orange stars & highlights, impressed marks, 4" l., 4" h. **330.00**

Postcard in frame, the rectangular card designed by Mela Koehler shows a slender standing woman wearing a large white hat & green & grey striped dress w/two small brown dogs at her feet, in a rectangular molded Art Nouveau design frame w/rounded corners & undulating lines, early 20th c., overall 9 x10½" **231.00**

WITCH BALLS

Amber ball, large round ball on a matching tall cylindrical stand w/a widely flaring rim & foot, probably from Stoddard, New Hampshire, first half 19th c., 12½" h., 2 pcs. . . **$770.00**

Clear w/white loopings ball, large, widely spaced loops, rough pontil, probably South Jersey, 5¾" d. **413.00**

Greenish aqua w/white loopings ball, interior w/wad of cotton w/dried spices, other slight dirt inside, 5" d. **275.00**

Opaque white & spatter ball, the white ground rolled in fragments of red, blue & yellow glass to produce the spatter effect, attributed to the Boston & Sandwich Glass Co. 4½" d. **495.00**

Opaque white w/pink & lavender loopings ball, bold looping repeated design, 5¼" d. **880.00**

Opaque white w/red & blue loopings ball, repeated bold looping design, 5¼" d. **413.00**

Opaque white w/red & blue spatter ball, white ground w/red & blue fragments & overall tiny black specks, 4" d. **220.00**

Red, white & clear ball, finely looped ball resting on matching waisted cylindrical tall holder tapering to acushion foot, overall 11½" h., 2 pcs. (open bubbles on ball) **440.00**

Silvered glass ball, large ball w/open pontil on a tall urn-form pedestal-based matching stand, possibly from New England Glass Co., mid-19th c., overall 13¼" h., 2 pcs. (small shallow chip on ball pontil) . . **165.00**

WOOD SCULPTURES

Cigar store figure of a military man, "Corporal Joe," standing w/legs together, arms crossed on chest, cigar in mouth, black hair & long moustache, dark blue jacket & light blue pants, square base, foot damage, carved by Samuel Robb **$46,750.00**

Cigar store figure of an Indian Princess, the standing full-figured woman leaning forward wearing a yellow, green & red-painted feathered headdress & a green-painted tunic w/red sash & brown belt w/black, yellow & red-painted

features, yellow shoes, on a green & yellow-painted rectangular base, late 19th-early 20th c., 57¾" h. . . **7,475.00**

Cigar store figure of Columbia, carved & painted, full-bodied figure of a classical lady standing w/brown-painted Grecian helmet w/carved feathers above a red-painted face & articulated black hair over a body w/a black-painted feather-carved dress, bent arms hold cigars & tobacco leaves, red legs & feet, on a black oval base, late 19th c., 55½" h. **5,750.00**

Figural towel holder, carved & painted wood in the form of a woman w/outstretched arms holding a bar, blue dress w/applied black leather strips & foil-covered belt buckle & buttons, 20th c., 14" w., 8½" h. **9,775.00**

Rare Carved Figure

Figure of a black man, carved & painted wood, wearing carved & painted overalls & collared shirt, looking slightly to his right, resting his hands on the end of a hoe or shovel, his right leg crossed over his left, rare 19th c., minor imperfections, 31" h. **29,900.00**

Figure of a male saint, painted & gessoed, standing bearded man wearing long robes & a trimmed cloak held closed w/one hand, the other hand holding an upright stem of lilies, Spanish Colonial, 43" h. (restorations) **1,553.00**

Figure of a man, flattened full-bodied standing carved man painted on one side w/black hair, eyebrows, eyelashes & moustache, blue eyes, red lips, white teeth & a protruding triangular nose, above a body w/green-painted uniform w/black belt & sash, on two legs w/blue pants & stump feet, on a rectangular wood base, 19th c., 4 x 15", 67" h. (arms missing) . . . **4,600.00**

Figure of a Native American woman, carved & painted wood dancing toy, the finely carved figure w/articulated arms & legs, wearing an embroidered dress w/owl decoration, a necklace & bracelet, has tattoo on her lower back, mounted on square painted wooden base, mid-19th c., 13½" h.. . . . . . . **9,200.00**

Model of a Phrygian cap, carved & painted pine, the blue cap w/gold tassels & red, white & gold bottom border, now mounted on a black metal base, ca. 1870-80, 12" h. . . **10,925.00**

Carved Model of an Eagle

Model of an eagle, carved gilt wood, the long spread-winged figure perched on a rockery base w/head turned to its right & articulated feathered wings, 19th c., minor imperfections, 16¼" w., 11½" h. (ILLUS.) **1,840.00**

Model of an eagle, carved & painted pine, the spread-winged American eagle wall plaque flat-carved clasping an American shield in its talons & a banner above its head engraved w/a star & the legend "Liberty," retains traces of red, blue & white polychrome, probably New England, ca. 1910, 36" l., 17½" h.. . **3,450.00**

Models of birds, carved & painted wood, the standing birds carved in the round, on metal feet w/arched wood stands, fitted w/glass eyes, original painted surfaces, one painted orange & black, the other yellow & black, late 19th - early 20th c., 4½" h., pr. **6,325.00**

Whirligig, painted pine, a figure of an American Indian standing in a canoe, arms for the blades, early 20th c., 11½" l., 7¾" h. (very minor losses). **489.00**

Whirligig, carved & painted pine & tin, a figure of a stylized boxer w/incised eyes & mouth, the body painted red & black & fitted w/sheet metal arm baffles, mounted on a rectangular pine base, 19th c., overall 10" h. **1,955.00**

Whirligig, carved & painted pine, figure of a bathing beauty, stylized full-figured lady w/bobbed hair, wearing a blue bathing costume, the rotating arms ending in paddle baffles, now mounted on a black metal base, early 20th c., overall 13" h. **5,175.00**

Whirligig, carved & painted pine, a stylized standing soldier wearing a tricorner hat, blue swallow-tail coat & yellow vest, the rotating arms fitted w/paddle baffles, 19th c., overall 16" h. **4,025.00**

Rare Indian Woman Whirligig

Whirligig, carved & painted wood, rare figure of an Indian woman, her hair made of horse hair, depicted w/open eyes & slightly parted lips showing carved & painted teeth, dressed in leather bustier, skirt & boots, w/zinc cuff protecting her arm joints & a copper cross around her neck, wearing metal loop earrings, carved w/defined bicep & calf muscles, on square painted base, Maine, 19th c., 24" h (ILLUS.) **27,600.00**

Wood sign, carved & painted, one side showing the English foxhound "Darby", the dog carved in relief against a blue & white sky w/grass at his feet, the reverse side signed "A.B. MacGregor / Norfolk Hunt Medfield, Mass," sapling bound, 15" w., 13½" h. **4,600.00**

WOODENWARES

The patina and mellow coloring, along with the lightness and smoothness that come only with age and wear, attract collectors to old woodenwares. The earliest forms were the simplest and the shapes of items whittled out in the late 19th century varied little in form from those turned out in the American colonies two centuries earlier. A burl is a growth, or wart, on some trees in which the grain of the wood is twisted and turned in a manner which strengthens the fibers and causes a beautiful pattern to be formed. Treenware is simply a term for utilitarian items made from "treen," another word for wood. While maple was the primary wood used for these items, they are also abundant in pine, ash, oak, walnut, and other woods. "Lignum Vitae" is a species of wood from the West Indies that can always be identified by the contrasting colors of dark heartwood and light sapwood and by its heavy weight, which caused it to sink in water. Also see KITCHENWARES.

Abacus, carved maple, a rectangular frame flat on three sides & baluster-turned along the bottom, supporting twelve horizontal wires w/wooden beads, a slender turned handle at the center of the bottom edge, probably American-made, 19th c., 12½ x 17" **$460.00**

Birdhouse, painted, model of a house w/peaked roof & shaped chimney, sawtooth borders, white paint w/green banding, 19th c., 11 x 13¾", 18" h. (minor breaks & losses, paint wear) **115.00**

Birdhouse, painted, architectural-form, model of an ornate church steeple, painted light grey, late 19th - early 20th c., 68¾" h. (minor imperfections) **1,725.00**

Bowl, turned burl, American-made, 18th c., 7¾" d., 2¼" h. **374.00**

Bowl, turned burl, footed, American-made, 19th c., 6¼" d., 3" h. **690.00**

Bowl, ash burl, turned rings on flaring sides, old refinishing w/good color, well-worn interior, 15" d., 4¾" h. . . . **495.00**

Bowl, carved wood, oblong w/deeply canted sides & carved end rim handles, w/a table ring, old worn patina w/traces of grey paint on the exterior, 11¾ x 19", 5" h. **231.00**

Bowl, carved, long shallow oval form, old light blue exterior paint, scrubbed interior, 10½ x 27¾", 5" h. (one end w/small split) **220.00**

Bowl, turned burl, early, 15¾" d., 5¼" h. **633.00**

Bowl, turned poplar, wide deep rounded sides w/molded rim, gold old worn surface w/traces of white on exterior, found in Connecticut, 17¼" d., 6½" h. **330.00**

Bowl, turned ash, worn interior patina, old red & white exterior, 21" d., 7" h. **330.00**

Bowl, turned, deep wide rounded form, old scrubbed & stained finish, 23" d., 7½" h. **275.00**

Bowl, cov., turned poplar, probably originally grain-painted, now w/old dark varnish finish, 8" d. **248.00**

Bowl, carved & painted birch, oval form w/double finger hole handles, painted red, 19th c., 10½ x 27" (minor cracks & paint wear) **3,738.00**

Bucket, stave construction w/wire metal bands & wire bale w/diamond fasteners, added red stain, probably Shaker. **105.00**

Butter paddle w/burl bowl, traces of brown paint, 8½" l. (bowl has edge damage) **61.00**

Butter paddle, curly maple w/old worn finish, cut out handle w/hook finial, 9½" l. (bowl worn from use) **154.00**

Butter paddle, maple, carved hook handle, 10½" l. (very worn old finish). **220.00**

Turned Treen Canns

Canns, hand-turned, tall swelled cylindrical bodies w/incised ring bands & small angular pierced side handles, old surface, one w/lighter surface, America, late 18th c., 3¾" d., 4¾" h., pr. (ILLUS.) **1,380.00**

Canteen, stave construction, short cylindrical form w/bentwood bands, bung hole at one side, scratch-carved initials, 7" d. (bung hole damaged) **165.00**

Charger, turned maple, round dished form w/a wide flanged rim, traces of old paint in the mellow patina, American-made, 18th c., 18 x 19" d. (minor imperfections) **978.00**

Comb case, hanging-type, cigar box construction w/chip carving & old dark finish, 16¼" h. (old repair to bottom scrollwork) **187.00**

Conestoga wagon box, cov., pine, tall deep rectangular box w/hinged, slanted cover, iron band braces around top & base continuing to form mounting brackets, iron strap latch on top flanked by J-scroll strap hinges, good wear, 19th c., 12" h. **275.00**

Cranberry scoop, steel tines & root handle, old dark finish has been varnished, 16" l. **275.00**

Cutlery tray, refinished cherry, rectangular w/slightly canted dovetailed sides & arched center handle divider, 8 x 13¼" **275.00**

Cutlery tray, tiger stripe maple, rectangular w/gently flaring sides, center divider w/rectangular hand hold cut-out w/a turned grip, early 19th c., 10 x 13¾", 5½" h. (refinished) **863.00**

Dipper, curly maple w/natural-shaped bowl, refinished, rim repair, 12" **110.00**

Dough box on legs, painted pine, rectangular top w/end braces fitted on a deep rectangular box w/one-board ends w/cut-out bootjack legs, divided interior, old worn dark green repair over earlier colors, 19th c., 16½ x 37", 31" h. (wear, edge damage) **495.00**

Drying rack, painted softwood, hinged two-part style, each section w/three horizontal slats between the slender flat uprights, old blue repaint, each section 30 x 46" **61.00**

Carved Wood Pig Footrest

Footrest, carved wood, model of a pig w/long felt ears, button eyes & long snout, velvet-wrapped cylindrical body, American, 19th c., surface imperfections, velvet wear, 20" l., 9¾" h. (ILLUS.) **1,265.00**

Grain measure, painted ash bentwood, round w/nailed molded rim band, old bluish grey paint, branded "O.H. Cofrin," 19th c., 15" d., 7¼" h. **215.00**

Keg, slender cylindrical form w/a small side hole, worn red paint & scratch-carved initials & date "J.G.1809," 6¾" l. (minor age cracks) **138.00**

Mangle (smoothing) board, painted, narrow long thin board w/a crudely-carved horse-form top handle, old red repaint & two shades of green, probably from Europe, 24¾" l. **330.00**

Model of a tree, carved & painted, a slender square center shaft w/wire branches ending in ovoid turned 'fruits' w/turned projections, a wooden crossbar near the bottom supports on upturned & downturned iron bars ending in the crossed shoe feet, original surface, possibly Pennsylvania, 19th c., 30¼" h. (paint wear, minute losses, minor repair) **1,265.00**

Paddle, curly maple w/spoon-like bowl, carved "98," old soft finish, 12½" l. **149.00**

Pipe box, cherry w/dark original finish, one molded edge drawer & scrolled top edge w/hanging crest, 18" h. (minor damage & age cracks w/small old repair on front left edge at drawer) **6,600.00**

Plate rack, hanging-type, painted pine, long deeply scalloped ends joined by four narrow crossbars forming two open racks, dovetailed construction, old grey paint, 47¾" w., 22¾" h. **550.00**

Salt box, cov., hanging-type, pine, the high scalloped backboard w/hanging hole above narrow shaped sides & hinged slant lid above rectangular box, wire nail construction, good old finish, 9½" l., 11¼" h. **193.00**

Seed planter, an upright slightly tapering box base w/a tall slender turned handle extending through the top, the sides stenciled in black w/an eagle & "Norcross & Boynton, Makers, Monmouth, Me. Patent Applied For," late 19th - early 20th c., 39½" h. (age cracks) **154.00**

Spice box, cov., round low bentwood box w/tin edging holds seven small interior round spice canisters each w/tin edging & stenciled labels, stamped "New York" label, 9" d., the set (eighth canister missing) . . . **248.00**

Storage boxes, oval bentwood,
finger lappet construction, in red,
green, yellow, brown & blue,
graduated largest 11¾" d.,
set of 6 .... **1,800.00**

Sugar bucket, cov., stave
construction w/two bentwood
bands, old dark finish, 12" h....... **138.00**

Tape loom, poplar w/old dark brown
patina, 7¼ x 18¾" **385.00**

Tub, stave construction w/wire bands
& worn blue paint, two staves
extended w/cut-out handles, 23" d. ... **413.00**

Wall box, painted pine, double-
compartment, backboard w/high
arched & rounded crest w/hanging
hole above two narrow rectangular
open pocket compartments, old
brown paint, signed in pencil on
back "F.A. Brimmer made Oct.
1860," 10¾" w., 16¾" h. (paint
wear, crack, minor losses) **1,035.00**

Wood bin, painted softwood,
rectangular, the tall wide-board
back above sharply slanted sides &
a shorter wide-board front, worn
green repaint, wear, 19¾ x 30",
34" h. **248.00**

WRITING ACCESSORIES

*Early writing accessories are popular
collectibles and offer a wide variety to select
from. A collection may be formed around any one
segment pens, letter openers, lap desks or
inkwellsor the collection may revolve around
choice specimens of all types. Material, design
and age usually determine the value. Pen
collectors like the large fountain pens developed
in the 1920s but also look for pens and
mechanical pencils that are solid gold or goldplated. Also see: BOTTLES & FLASKS*

INKWELLS & STANDS

Brass well, double, a rectangular
platform w/gently angled side
bands cast w/ornate scrolling &
centered by a slightly raised
platform w/two scroll-cast domed
wells w/hinged covers & original
white porcelain liners, England,
19th c., 9¾" l. **$138.00**

Bronze & glass stand, the pierced
metal inkwell w/hinged top opening
to an iridescent Favrile amber
glass liner, raised on a leaf-form
base at one end of a long oblong
shallow pen tray, the whole cast
w/raised stylized, undulating
striated leafage, brownish red
patina, liner inscribed "L.C.T.,"
base impressed "TIFFANY
STUDIOS - NEW YORK,"
ca.1900, 11¾" l. **4,600.00**

Bronze & glass well, bulbous
spherical body raised on three tiny
scroll feet, a short ringed neck w/a
hinged top fitted w/a green
turtleback tile, the shoulder of the
body set w/six cabochon glass
jewels, metal w/a brownish green
patina, impressed "TIFFANY
STUDIOS - NEW YORK," lacks
liner, 3¾" h. **3,220.00**

Bronze stand, Art Nouveau style, a
figure of a female scribe holding a
quill & globe enclosing the well, w/a
shaped tray, early 20th c., 8¼" l. ... **633.00**

Bronze well, cast in the form of a
basket of fish, gilt trim & patinated,
Japan, ca. 1900, 2¾" w. **460.00**

Bronze Figural Dog Inkwell

Bronze well, figural, a shaggy dog
head hinged to reveal inkwell,
w/circular plate inscribed "1802.13.
Janner 1872," Europe, late 19th c.,
9" d., 6" h. (ILLUS.) **1,150.00**

Bronze well, figural, a rectangular
platform w/two setter dogs walking
along a rough ground toward a
raised lidded compartment at one
end containing the inkwell, gilt
patination, by A. Gornik, 18" l. **518.00**

Copper well, Arts & Crafts style,
hand-hammered, low conical form
w/a widely flaring curved base,
hinged flattened lid w/button finial,
impressed mark of Gustav Stickley,
5½" d., 2¼" h., (missing insert) ... **201.00**

Cut glass inkwell, polished tapering
square-cut, amber, rounded hinged
lid w/button finial & brass binding,
2 ⅜" w., 3½" h. **210.00**

Faience stand, a flat rectangular
platform raised on short tapering
legs, the raised back section
centered by a medievel-style
seated dog w/open toothy mouth
flanked on one side by an ink pot &

the other by a sander, curved upright shells at each back corner, the front flat surface panel decorated w/a scene of a wild dog in a landscape in shades of blue, green & mustard yellow, further scroll detail on the back section, Talavera, Spain, 10½" l. **880.00**

Figural Bronze Inkwell

Gilt-bronze inkwell, figural Art Nouveau design, a nude maiden seated sideways on a cloth-draped rocky outcrop, designed by Francois-Raoul Larche, France, impressed "RAOUL LARCHE," liner replaced, 12½" h. (ILLUS.). **16,100.00**

Glass inkwell, square, amber glass w/stippling & plain round center dimple on all sides, round flat-top hinged lid, brass mounts, 2⅝" d., 4⅛" h. **235.00**

Ivory & Tortoiseshell Boullework Inkstand

Ivory & tortoiseshell Boullework inkstand, double, rectangular top w/three square compartments, two fitted w/glass bottles w/metal-covered casters & center stamp compartment, long curved pen tray at front w/fine bird & scrollwork design, matching bird & scrollwork design around the sides, ornate center metal loop handle on top & metal claw foot, late 18th c., Europe, minor losses, 7¼" l. (ILLUS.). **690.00**

Painted metal well, figural, model of a howling cat, 19th c., 3⅞" h. (paint wear, minor corrosion, damage to hinge) **403.00**

Pewter well, model of a honeypot w/relief-molded bees, on a matching underplate, Kayserzinn, Germany, early 20th c., 2 pcs. **400.00**

Porcelain well, model of a book w/the metal-trimmed hinged cover opening to two porcelain wells, orange ground decorated w/brightly colored flowers & birds w/the cover interior in white w/a large pink blossom & green leaves, early, Chantilly, France, 3½ x 5¾" **165.00**

Silver plate well, figural golfer, Reed & Barton **275.00**

Sterling silver stand, round w/hinged lid, front hinged compartment w/gold washed interior for stamps, Birmingham, England, 20th c. **259.00**

Wood well, carved in the shape of a well-worn man's shoe, the lid shaped like a sock, old patina, 5½" h. **226.00**

LAP DESKS & WRITING BOXES

Brass-inlaid Coromandel, rectangular box w/lid centered by brass tablet inscribed "W.H. Cranswick, May 2nd 1889," mahogany-lined interior fitted w/a burgundy leather covered writing slope & compartments, on a short-legged conforming stand, ca. 1889, 17½" l., 16" h. **460.00**

Burl Walnut Writing Box

Burl walnut, rectangular box w/lid centered by inset brass shield, the interior lined in black leather & fitted w/a writing slope & compartments, on a matching stand w/tall, tapering square legs, ca. late 19th c., 15½" l., 21" h. (ILLUS.) **748.00**

Burl walnut w/brass mountings, rectangular box w/lid centered by brass tablet, similar brass tablet forming the keyhole escutcheon, the interior w/gilt-tooled black leather writing slope & compartments, on a later conforming stand w/heavy square legs & an H-stretcher, late 19th c., 17½" l., 21½" h. **690.00**

Curly walnut veneer, hinged rectangular box w/a fitted interior in cherry, 19th c., 8¾ x 13" **165.00**

Grain-painted wood, rectangular w/a hinged top opening to a compartmented interior painted salmon red w/graining, New England, ca. 1830, 23 x 27¾", 11" h. **173.00**

Mahogany, rectangular box hinged to open to writing surface, includes contents such as ledger books, letters, deeds, trade cards & writing instruments dating between 1841 & 1888, Danvers, Massachusetts, the group **518.00**

Mahoghany w/brass binding, rectangular hinged form w/interior writing surface & small storage compartments, probably England, 19th c., 10½ x 19⅞", 6⅜" h. (minor cracks, very minor losses) **403.00**

Oak & composition, elaborate high-relief foliate design, fitted interior, England, ca. 1855-1860, minor crackling, 13" l., 10" deep **288.00**

Inlaid Satinwood Lap Desk

Satinwood, rectangular box, the top marquetry inlaid satinwood w/"Prince of Wales" plume, trees, vines & birds, fitted interior w/satinwood fronted drawers, England, mid-19th c., 12" w., 14½" l. (ILLUS.). **633.00**

Tortoiseshell & inlaid wood, a real domed, bumpy bisected turtle shell w/a carved & inlaid wood turtle head & legs opens to a single lift-top compartment w/exotic wood inlay of stars, fans & geometric banding, atop a rectangular main case w/similar inlay & containing a slide-out jointed lap top desk w/baleen border & fitted compartments, 19th c., 9¼ x 14½", 10¼" h. (very minor losses) **4,888.00**

YARN WINDERS

Early Floor Model Yarn Reel

Floor model, stained hardwood, a four-arm reel w/double bars to central crossbar set in flat, shaped uprights on a trestle base w/shaped shoe feet, old worn reddish brown finish, mortised construction, found in Maine, 20" d., 24½" h. (ILLUS.) **$138.00**

Niddy noddy, painted hardwood, cross-form w/bars at right angles to each other at each end, old yellow paint, 18¼" l. (one end w/age crack at mortise) **110.00**

Swift, floor model, all-wood w/expandable crossarms joined to a central tall post w/a cupped top, resting on tapering cross-form shoe feet, old patina, 27½" h. **127.00**

Table model yarn "swift," whale bone, whale ivory & baleen, a ring of long expandable crossed slats raised on a slender ring-turned central standard above a quadrapartite base w/four out-scrolled & carved legs, highlighted w/stained rings, 19th c., imperfections, 17½" h. **3,450.00**

INDEX